THE
BOWKER
ANNUAL

43rd Edition • 1998

THE
BOWKER
ANNUAL

Library and
Book Trade Almanac™

Editor • Dave Bogart
Consultant • Julia C. Blixrud

R.R. Bowker®
New Providence, New Jersey

Published by R. R. Bowker,
a unit of Cahners Business Information
Copyright © 1998 by Reed Elsevier Inc.
All rights reserved
Printed and bound in the United States of America
Bowker® is a registered trademark of Reed Elsevier Inc.
The Bowker Annual Library and Book Trade Almanac™ is a trademark of Reed
Elsevier Properties Inc., used under license.

International Standard Book Number 0–8352–4052–5
International Standard Serial Number 0068–0540
Library of Congress Catalog Card Number 55–12434

ISBN 0 - 8352 - 4052 - 5

9 780835 240529

Contents

Part 1
Reports from the Field

International Reports

Special Reports

Part 2
Legislation, Funding, and Grants

Legislation

Funding Programs and Grant-Making Agencies

Part 3
Library/Information Science
Education, Placement, and Salaries

Part 4
Research and Statistics

Part 5
Reference Information

Distinguished Books

Part 6
Directory of Organizations

Directory of Library and Related Organizations

Directory of Book Trade and Related Organizations

Preface

This 43rd edition of *The Bowker Annual*, like its predecessors, presents a mix of informed analysis and practical information of interest to the library, information, and book trade communities.

It documents a time of heightening challenge as the "Information Superhighway" grows by leaps and bounds, influencing every sphere of the world of words.

The ever-increasing role of digital information is addressed in this edition's Special Reports:

- Sarah K. Wiant, director of the law library and professor of law at Washington and Lee University, analyses developments in copyright law, particularly as they affect the exchange of information in education and research.
- Clifford Lynch, executive director of the Coalition for Networked Information, examines Internet 2 and the Next Generation Internet, which he says "can be expected to deliver a high payoff . . . not only in enhancing research, teaching, and learning, but in building the U.S. networking industry."
- Two national leaders in networking, Kate Nevins of SOLINET and Bonnie Juergens of AMIGOS, look at developments in networking during 1997, a year in which there was increased adoption and effective use of the Internet and Internet-based resources.

Reports from federal agencies and libraries document a year of continuing challenge and accomplishment. The year's trends and developments are also chronicled in Part 1 in reports from *Library Journal*, *School Library Journal*, and *Publishers Weekly*.

Detailed examinations of the year's legislation and regulations affecting libraries and the publishing industry are found in Part 2; among the issues in both spheres were intellectual property protection, freedom of expression, and new technologies. Also in Part 2 are reports from funding programs and grant-making agencies.

Part 3 offers professional information for librarians: a review of placements and salaries, guides to scholarship and employment sources, and lists of library scholarship and award winners.

Research and statistics on libraries and the book trade fill Part 4, including a look at acquisition expenditures by all types of libraries and detailed indexes of the price of library materials. Other data include book title output, prices, and U.S. and world book trade statistics.

Part 5 features reference information—a list of publishers' toll-free telephone numbers, how the ISBN, SAN, and ISSN systems operate, and lists of the year's best books, bestselling books, and literary prize-winners.

Part 6 is our annual directory of library and publishing organizations in the United States and around the world, plus a calendar of information industry events.

Many people have a role in producing *The Bowker Annual*. As always, we are grateful to those who contributed articles, assembled reports, and responded to our requests for information. Particular thanks are owed Consulting Editor Julia C. Blixrud and editor/consultant Catherine Barr.

We believe you will find this edition of *The Bowker Annual* a valuable resource, and—as always—we welcome your comments and suggestions for future editions.

Dave Bogart
Editor

Part 1
Reports from the Field

News of the Year

LJ News Report:
Public Libraries Post Solid Fiscal Gains

Evan St. Lifer

Senior Editor, News, *Library Journal*

Budgeting in such a way as to strike a delicate balance between print collections and electronic materials has emerged as public library administrators' fundamental fiscal challenge.

In an effort to chronicle how libraries nationwide are faring financially, *Library Journal (LJ)* conducted its eighth annual Public Library Budget Report, sending out questionnaires to 2,000 public libraries. A total of 412 libraries—more than 20 percent—responded.

Libraries have taken a public relations hit in the national debate over their potential role as public guardian of the Internet, an issue over which they've been scrutinized, criticized, and even sued. But as this Budget Report tellingly illustrates, the Internet poses as much of a financial challenge as an ideological one. Libraries are spending anywhere from $6,500 to more than $350,000 just to implement Internet service. *LJ*'s survey also reveals that after their initial investment, maintaining their Net-based services costs the smallest libraries almost $2,500 annually, the largest more than $300,000.

Libraries are seeing their Internet-related expenditures continue to climb, as evidenced by the projected 27 percent increase for fiscal year (FY) 1998 over FY 1997. This year's increase is less pronounced than last year's 41 percent, but the difference stems from more libraries already being linked to the Net and only paying to maintain their services, not install them.

All the money to pay for new technology isn't coming from operating budgets, however. Of those libraries receiving grant assistance (62 percent), 60 percent plan to allocate the funding for technology/Internet costs. Further, of those libraries that said they hope to apply for a grant in the next two years (72 percent), almost 75 percent said they would allocate grant funds to cover the cost of integrating technology and the Net.

Still, despite assistance from external sources, many libraries are seeing their technology costs impinge on other appropriations, namely materials. Twenty percent of respondents said they had to take money allocated for materials to pay for the Internet, a troubling development until one compares the data with last year's, when 52 percent of libraries dug into their materials budgets to come up

Adapted from *Library Journal*, January 1998

with Net funding. Many more libraries (45 percent) have developed separate line items for Internet costs.

Respondents provided further evidence that they are less inclined to take their Internet costs from other parts of their budget: only 25 percent expect to cut back spending in other areas to fund Net-related services, compared with 36 percent last year.

Although public libraries (PLs) have endured a tough year, and despite recent news that the Federal Communications Commission has acquiesced to telecommunications' major corporate players and cut proposed telecommunications subsidies to libraries and schools by $625 million so far, several mitigating factors help to paint a more promising budgetary picture for PLs.

- While total budgets dipped below the five-year average annual increase of 4.8 percent (to 4.1 percent), both materials (7 percent) and salary (7.3 percent) have increased this year at a greater rate than their five-year histories, 6.4 percent and 4.6 percent, respectively.
- Average per capita funding ($24.59) continues its climb, jumping more than $1 over last year's figure ($23.54) and maintaining a five-year streak of a $1-plus increase annually.
- In the last five years, libraries have almost tripled the amount of money they garner from fund-raising, rising from an average $53,308 in 1992 to $137,476 in FY 1997. That number constitutes 4 percent of the average total budget, $3,745,100, reported to *LJ* by libraries across the board.
- Concerns about libraries' enduring commitment to books giving way to technology should be allayed by average per capita circulation figures that continue to rise: per capita circulation numbers are up from 7.97 in 1996 to 8.35 this year.

Although these aggregate budgetary gains are notable, the more revealing budget numbers can be found by breaking libraries down by size: libraries serving 10,000 or fewer are projecting an average FY 1998 budget of $164,000, a 12 percent jump over FY 1997; PLs serving 10,000 to 24,999 are projecting $454,300 in FY 1998, the same as in FY 1997; those serving 25,000 to 49,000 see a 3.5 percent increase at $1,081,900; the next largest library group, those serving populations of 50,000 to 99,999, reported an average total budget of $1,509,200, an anticipated jump of 5 percent; PLs serving 100,000 to 499,999 project 3 percent increases with an average $4,235,500 appropriated for FY 1998; libraries serving 500,000 to 999,999 reported that they will climb 4 percent in FY 1998 with average budgets of $15,631,7000, while the largest PLs, those serving more than one million people, project an average 2.5 percent increase with total budgets of $38,296,000.

No Specific Formula

A public library's financial success is not tied to any detailed formula but rather to the health of its local economy. Libraries serving emerging communities often see the biggest budgetary gains, while those situated in economically pressed areas often founder. Libraries in states that offer strong support also tend to do well, Ohio being the most striking example. According to *LJ*'s survey, 47 percent of respondents said their funding is local, with counties contributing 31 percent; 15 percent receive state funding; 3 percent derive income from fee-based services; 2 percent from grants; and 1 percent each from fund-raising and federal monies.

Public libraries continued to fare well in local elections, with voters approving additional funding 70 percent of the time, although that was down from last year's impressive 80 percent. Libraries claimed to spend capital funds on new branches, expansions, and renovations, in that order. Libraries that garnered operating funds used them to add hours and staff, enhance their collections, and pay for automation or Internet services.

America's nearly 16,000 public libraries have overcome every hurdle thrown before them, from searing budget cuts at the beginning of the decade to the latest public and widespread debate over their role as potential selectors/mediators of Internet content. Still, apart from efforts to obtain grants and devise creative financing alternatives, they continue to have solid budgetary support from the quarter that matters most: the people they serve, who supply roughly 80 percent of the money libraries receive via revenues derived from property taxes.

Table 1 / Cost of Linking to the Internet

Size (Patrons served)	Average Expenditure
Fewer than 10,000	$6,472
10,000–24,999	25,607
25,000–49,999	29,686
50,000–99,999	42,639
100,000–499,999	119,558
500,000–999,999	317,853

Table 1A / Cost of Internet Maintenance

Size (Patrons served)	Average Expenditure
Fewer than 10,000	$2,421
10,000–24,999	10,659
25,000–49,999	16,105
50,000–99,999	16,682
100,000–499,999	69,663
500,000–999,999	242,353
More than 1 million	311,666

Source: *Library Journal* Budget Report 1998

Table 2 / Public Library Snapshots
Changes in Budgets from Fiscal Year 1997 to Fiscal Year 1998

Library	Pop. Served	Total Budget FY 1997	Materials	Salaries	Total Budget
Serving Fewer Than 10,000					
Hayden PL, CO	2,400	$96,040	+9%	+4%	+3.5%
McCall PL, ID	2,500	134,105	+2.5%	+24.5%	+19%
Irene Ingle PL, Wrangell, AK	2,532	167,000	+20%	+27.5%	-5.5%
Oneida Community Lib., WI	4,500	356,627	-15%	+4.5%	+3.5%
Camden PL, ME	5,060	375,000	NC	+12%	+5%
W. R. Darmony PL, Carlstadt, NJ	5,510	450,000	+4.5%	+4%	+4.5%
Carnegie-Schuyler Lib., Pana, IL	5,796	120,000	NC	+9%	+5%
Plattsmouth PL, NE	6,642	155,346	+21%	+7%	+8.5%
Miami Memorial Lib., AZ	7,000	115,000	+25%	-8%	-9.5%
Port Townsend PL, WA	8,330	443,951	+2%	+28%	+12.5%
Serving 10,000–24,999					
Marlboro Free Lib., NY	10,613	$419,609	+4%	+4.5%	+4%
Medfield PL, MA	11,575	293,125	+17.5%	+15%	+5%
McPherson PL, KS	12,800	353,800	+2.5%	+9%	+6.5%
Peru PL, IN	13,000	347,000	+3%	+1%	-4%
Reddick Lib., Ottawa, IL	18,000	330,000	NC	+9.5%	+7%
Richmond Mem. Lib., Batavia, NY	19,145	793,526	+3%	+3.5%	+7%
New Madrid Cty. Lib., Portageville, MO	19,416	364,000	+3.5%	+3.5%	+4%
Northfield PL, MN	20,000	582,840	+8%	+5%	+9%
Wilkinsburg PL, PA	21,080	375,000	+3%	+4%	+4%
Plumas Cty. PL, Quincy, CA	23,710	350,497	+3.5%	+4.5%	+5%
Serving 25,000–49,999					
Cumberland PL, RI	30,000	$703,754	+15.5%	+3%	+7%
Prescott PL, AZ	30,606	890,000	+1.5%	+2%	+4%
Albany Cty. Lib., Laramie, WY	31,000	418,134	+9%	+9.5%	+7.5%
Culpeper Cty. Lib., VA	32,000	330,662	+4.5%	+41.5%	+24.5%
East Chicago PL, IN	33,892	3,547,717	-14.5%	+5%	-1%
DeSoto PL, TX	36,500	497,725	+40%	+3%	+9%
Douglas Cty. PL, Minden, NV	37,000	820,000	-1%	+3%	NC
Pinellas Park PL, FL	44,472	1,050,044	-4.5%	+7%	+5%
Warren-Newport PL, Gurnee, IL	48,000	2,915,000	+6.5%	+8%	+5%
Beloit PL, WI	48,215	1,559,495	+5%	+5.5%	+3.5%
Serving 50,000–99,999					
Washington-Centerville PL, OH	50,213	$4,361,280	+13%	+21%	+16.5%
Marion Cty. PL, Fairmont, WV	57,249	561,325	+1%	+18%	+16.5%
Baldwin Cty Lib. Coop., Robertsdale, AL	63,164	206,681	+39%	+21.5%	+18.5%
Calvert Cty. PL, Prince Frederick, MD	67,000	1,398,329	+3.5%	+3%	+2.5%
Newport Beach PL, CA	70,000	3,637,534	+3.5%	+.05%	-1.5%
Tompkins Cty. PL, NY	94,097	1,686,911	-3%	-2.5%	-4.5%
Davenport PL, IA	95,333	2,575,000	+3.5%	+3%	+3%
E. Albemarle Reg., Elizabeth City, NC	80,000	1,272,918	+4%	+5%	+4.5%

Source: *Library Journal* Budget Report 1998
NC—No Change

Table 2 / Public Library Snapshots
Changes in Budgets from Fiscal Year 1997 to Fiscal Year 1998 *(cont.)*

Library	Pop. Served	Total Budget FY 1997	Materials	Salaries	Total Budget
Serving 100,000–499,999					
Portsmouth PL, VA	103,000	$1,580,000	+2%	NC	+6.5%
Martin Cty. Lib. Sys., Stuart, FL	129,614	2,688,249	+12%	+11%	+21.5%
Salt Lake City PL	168,000	8,013,584	+13%	+7%	+8%
Harrison Cty. Lib. Sys., Gulfport, MS	183,400	2,849,925	+11%	+9%	+3%
Grand Rapids PL, MI	189,126	7,481,149	+2%	+.05%	+4%
Pioneer Lib. Sys., Norman, OK	256,150	3,934,958	+10%	+6.5%	+6.5%
Dakota Cty. Lib., Eagan, MN	296,017	6,486,241	+.05%	+5%	+5%
Fort Bend Cty. Lib., Richmond, TX	305,375	5,310,432	+9.5%	+15.5%	+14%
Ocean Cty. Lib., Toms River, NJ	411,114	16,585,500	+9%	+4%	+5%
Pierce Cty. Lib. Sys., Tacoma	423,457	11,049,121	+8%	+6.5%	+5.5%
Serving 500,000–999,999					
Gwinnett Cty. PL, Lawrenceville, GA	503,280	$10,521,572	+12%	+5.5%	+.04%
El Paso PL, TX	615,000	6,194,440	+2.7%	+11.5%	+2.1%
Kern Cty. Lib., Bakersfield, CA	628,200	7,507,999	-72%	+5.9%	+5.9%
Palm Beach Cty. Lib., W. Palm Beach, FL	643,187	19,781,532	+21%	+4%	+3.4%
Orange Cty. PL, FL	758,962	18,848,198	+11%	+7%	+8.5%
Atlanta-Fulton PL	766,394	27,908,250	-1.8%	+24.5%	+20%
Indianapolis-Marion Cty. PL	800,000	27,000,000	+10%	+15.4%	+5.6%
Buffalo & Erie Cty. Lib., NY	968,532	28,216,555	+11.3%	+2.8%	+3.9%
Serving More Than 1 Million*					
Detroit PL	1,027,974	$26,765,505	NC	+1%	+1%
Sacramento PL, CA	1,097,290	20,097,469	+16%	+12%	+8.5%
San Diego PL	1,218,000	21,499,833	+4.5%	+6.5%	+8.5%
San Antonio PL	1,363,600	16,151,350	+1%	-.50%	+4.5%
Miami-Dade PL Sys., FL	1,626,510	32,160,000	-9.5%	+.05%	-3%
Queens Borough PL, Jamaica, NY	1,950,000	77,275,000	+25%	+3%	+7%
Chicago PL	2,783,726	91,758,665	-7.5%	-1.5%	-.05%

Source: *Library Journal* Budget Report 1998

NC—No Change

* Only seven libraries in this category responded to the survey

SLJ News Report: I Spy— Librarians in the Public Eye

Renée Olson

News and Features Editor, *School Library Journal*

Look at me! Don't look at me! To me, those cries sum up the year in librarianship. Campaigns to capture the attention of library directors, principals, and others in charge around the country have, of late, been of epic proportions. But librarians in 1997 also baked under the glare of public scrutiny.

It's satisfying to report that many attempts to attract attention to libraries have been successful. If you made a case for a flexible schedule, more staff, or maybe a renovation project, and you got it, you know your message hit home.

But there were too many other times in this age of rampantly spreading attention-deficit disorder when, from my vantage point, getting attention seemed nearly impossible. You saw this in our news this year: the school districts that replaced librarians with assistants and the politicians who sought to cut public library funding to avoid raising taxes.

Ironically, 1997 was also the year we saw the public eyeballing librarians more closely and more frequently than in recent years. The culprit? The wars over whether to install Internet filters in libraries. Of course, some librarians relished the opportunity to espouse First Amendment principles for young people. But once the conflict hit the local press in burgs around the nation, librarians who believed in open Internet access risked being branded online porn advocates. I invite you to see how that plays when you're in the produce aisle at the grocery store.

And speaking of attention, there's that big gift from Bill Gates. He certainly noticed libraries, but some are asking whether it's a good idea.

Despite the downsides, the attention that librarians and libraries got this year is a very, very good sign and one I hope continues next year. Because without the attentive ear of administrators, politicians, and parents, librarians who work with young people can call it a day.

Filters Stole the Scene

The clash of readily available pornography on the Web and community concern over unfiltered Internet access for children created, hands down, the highest-profile library news story of the year.

If 1996 was the year that Web use exploded in school and public libraries, 1997 was the year that the public caught wind of the pornographic and violent nature of some of its offerings. Librarians got a rude awakening when the resource that was to liberate them from limited print collections also brought them protracted headaches.

At Boston Public Library, which holds the dubious distinction of being one of the country's filtering pioneers, BPL President Bernard Margolis first decried

Adapted from *School Library Journal*, December 1997

Internet filters, but then installed Cyber Patrol on computers used by children. There's a name now for this approach (unfiltered access for adults and filtered access for young people): the Boston Solution.

Until the Supreme Court struck down the Communications Decency Act in late June, most librarians cooled their heels on installing filters. But once the decision came down, it was clear it gave the filter crowd more clout. Case in point: What may be the most restrictive policy in the country recently went into effect when the board of trustees at the Loudoun County (Virginia) Public Library voted to filter Internet access for both adults and children.

Right after the Supreme Court decision, the American Library Association (ALA) released its "Statement on Library Use of Filtering Software" (www.ala. org/alaorg/oif/filt_res.html), alerting librarians to its stance on filters. The statement explains that libraries that use filters are blocking access to constitutionally protected speech.

To assuage concerned parents, the association drew up a well-received handout listing kid-friendly sites. Not surprisingly, Karen Jo Gounaud was not assuaged. Gounaud, of Family Friendly Libraries, a Virginia-based group that advocates restricting youth access to sexually oriented materials, called ALA's solution "pure hypocrisy." Her take on the list? "A nutritious lemonade stand does not make up for a fenceless crater."

Two librarians jumped into the filter fray, attracting a flurry of media attention. Filter supporter David Burt caught the attention of MSNBC columnist Brock Meeks, who first applauded Burt, information technology librarian at Lake Oswego (Oregon) Public Library, for his stand. But one week later, Meeks reversed his opinion, "smarting," he admitted, "from an intellectual belly-flop."

His change of heart came from hearing about the other librarian in this picture—Karen Schneider and her Internet Assessment Project—and looking at the project's findings (www.bluehighways.com/tifap.htm). Schneider, a librarian at the Environmental Protection Agency in New York City, started the project when she got tired of hearing librarians discuss filters without understanding them. She's told *School Library Journal* (*SLJ*) that whether or not librarians use filters, they should know how they function. Otherwise, in her view, they are abdicating responsibility to an outside vendor.

The Entrenched Internet

In October, *SLJ*'s biennial survey on school library spending and services showed that 62 percent of library media centers have access to the Internet, while nearly half—49 percent—have access to the Web. A full third of respondents saw extra funding to pay for Internet access.

Ask and You Shall Receive

A takeover by New York State of the Roosevelt Junior/Senior High School led to a library renaissance within its walls, thanks to Carol Kroll, director of the Nassau County School Library System, and Library Media Specialist Barbara

Hamill. To revive the Long Island facility, the district offered Kroll $17,000. But she turned it down and instead asked for $125,000—and got it.

Subaru Gets It, *Time* Doesn't

Support for librarians popped up this year in an unusual place—*Drive* magazine, a promotional publication put out by Subaru. Yes, the car company. But *Time* magazine's October 27 report "What Makes a Good School" failed to note the importance of librarians and libraries, despite being a more likely venue for the topic.

In *Drive*, oddly juxtaposed with an update on Subaru locks, is an article called "The Internet: Is It Replacing the Library?" (www.subaru.com/press/drive_magazine/97_03_fall/library.html). Readers learn that:

> Students need librarians and other educators to teach them the skills needed to locate and organize information in the face of a multitude of electronic sources. No matter how user-friendly interfaces and search engines appear, students must learn how to use them correctly and efficiently. They must understand how to define a research topic, how to conduct an effective search, and how to interpret and evaluate information resulting from that search. Once students attain these skills, the Internet can prove to be an excellent library resource.

On the other hand, *Time*'s treatment of libraries boiled down to a mention of a "mentally unstable teacher" who, after telling her principal that she feared that she might harm a child, was transferred to a school library "in order to reduce her contact with students."

Enough said.

Hear! Hear! for Advocacy

In an *SLJ* article in November headlined "The Invisible School Librarian," Gary N. Hartzell, a former high school principal, gently scolded library media specialists for spending too much time with other librarians and not enough time with other educators.

Would schmoozing with educators have helped in Philadelphia, a district profiled in *SLJ*'s August issue as having a schizophrenic attitude toward its elementary school libraries?

Perhaps.

While some of Philadelphia's students are in active Library Power schools, others have principals who hang on to their certified library media specialist in order to cover teacher preparation periods. A library assistant would be cheaper—and therefore preferable—but without credentials, he or she can't cover prep periods. No one can deny that the message, the reason for having a library media specialist, has been completely lost.

What's also at play in Philadelphia, as in other cities and towns, is a troubling disconnect in the minds of administrators between library media specialists and electronic information. Sure, some library media specialists skirt online resources, but the majority embrace them, albeit with healthy skepticism.

Still, the fact that these impressions are without basis hardly negates their ability to do damage. If they're not ushered straight out of town, it will be the person with the word "technology" in his or her title who stays on the payroll, not the school librarian.

What holds promise now is that Ken Haycock, president of the American Association of School Librarians (AASL), is using his office to kick off a five-year national effort to promote the profession. What's not as promising is the likelihood of getting the education community's attention. With just 10 percent of the nation's school librarian population, AASL doesn't have a large crowd to help make a racket.

The Money Maze

The prize for 1997's most unusual library fund-raiser undeniably goes to the Cornfield of Dreams Maze in Caledonia, Michigan. Volunteers, including a farmer, recruited through the local grain elevator, and a fire chief, planted a three-and-a-half acre field with sorghum in the shape of a 15th-century French maze. Once the crop reached its normal height of up to seven feet, the library charged adults $5 and children $3 for the opportunity to get lost in its two miles of trails. The maze netted $32,000 to go toward construction of a new 7,000-square-foot library. The idea came not from library staff, but from a local court reporter who got the idea after speaking with a bookstore clerk about mazes.

The Roll of the Dice

Where is the Internet going in 1998? That's not an easy question. For the sake of education, let's hope that librarians will spend more time next year focused on how to search and organize content on the Web and less on whether the content is likely to offend.

In the charmingly titled "Taking the 'Dick' Out of Moby Dick," an October Hotseat interview on HotWired (www.hotwired.com/synapse/hotseat/97/42/index2a.html), Karen Coyle, a librarian in the University of California system, succinctly explained why the state of information retrieval on the Web needs to improve.

> Go onto the Internet and do a search on Bambi. And half the sites you get are about a Disney-animated character, and the other half are about "Bambi's Nude Adventure." Now this is simply bad information retrieval, that that word, pulling up entirely different kinds of materials, just shows you that this is not an organized information space.

While Coyle works in a university setting, the need for good information retrieval for younger students is even more important because they are just learning how to do research. PICS, the Platform for Internet Content Selection, may help because it provides a way to embed cataloging information in a Web page, but to date, it's better known due to speculation as to whether it should be used to embed rating labels.

Coyle also commented on an issue that deserves more attention—that is, if librarians want students to be able to research anything other than a current event on the Internet. "I find it so ironic that as we move into the information age we're starting to treat our information more and more shoddily in terms of how we take care of it," she said. "We aren't archiving; things disappear off the Internet never to come back again."

Still, the filter debate won't evaporate, in part because filters are a fantastic money-making proposition. For the retail market, Microsoft announced in the fall that it would bundle Cyber Patrol with the newest version of its Web browser, Internet Explorer. However, librarians who are eyeing Gates Library Foundation grants should not expect Cyber Patrol as part of the deal: the foundation told *SLJ* that it does not plan to ship it to participating libraries.

The *Other* Big Headlines

Gates Opens Wallet

In December 1996, *SLJ* predicted that we'd "watch Microsoft continue to cultivate a cozy relationship with librarians in the interest of marketing its products." And look what Bill Gates did. He went and donated $400 million in funds to U.S. public libraries for technology and software through the new Gates Library Foundation. There's no doubt that libraries benefit from Gates opening his wallet, but Gates also wins big: he's secured for Microsoft a captive audience of people using computers for the first time.

Clinton Supports Education?

Secretary of Education Richard Riley told ALA Midwinter Meeting attendees in February 1997 that President Clinton had made education "his number-one priority." Meanwhile, Clinton zeroed out the only federal funding available for school library materials. Congress put that money—$350 million—back in the fiscal year (FY) 1998 budget. Another smile-producing event: funds for educational technology soared to $541 million.

Symons Beats Dowlin

Juneau (Alaska) High School Librarian Ann K. Symons neatly won ALA's 1998–1999 presidency over former San Francisco Public Library Director Ken Dowlin. The vote was decisive: 8,925 votes for Symons and 3,197 for Dowlin. Still, the total represented only a fraction of ALA's some 58,000 members.

Libraries Trim Telecom Costs

While the process of approving federal telecommunications discounts for schools and libraries and then figuring out how to administer them consumed all of 1997, the wait may be worthwhile. K. G. Ouye, who heads the federal group that will review discount applications, is also City Librarian in San Mateo, California. Back home, Ouye helped set up statewide discounts earlier this year. As a result, her library now saves $8,000 a year on telecom costs and her eight-library consortium saves approximately $1,000 a month. Federal telecom discounts were scheduled to go into effect January 1, 1998.

Library Power Funds Dry Up?

The Dewitt Wallace-Reader's Digest Fund, the sponsor of the National Library Power Program, announced in the fall that it would investigate whether to continue its support for the program on a smaller scale, now that the decade-long program has wound down. But financial problems may thwart that. Reader's Digest stock prices took a dive this year, and while the fund expects to maintain support for its charitable trusts at current levels through 1998, the more distant future is less clear, said Bruce Trachtenberg, a company spokesperson. Fifty percent of the fund's assets come from Reader's Digest stock; the other half is invested in stocks and bonds.

It's the Babies, Stupid

A gift came to librarians this year who work with very young children—a renewal of interest in infant brain research. Of major significance to librarians is that some researchers, according to the April 17, 1997, *New York Times*, believe "the number of words an infant hears each day is the single most important predictor of later intelligence, school success, and social competence." Put that in your next grant application.

Adios to Aloha State Contract

Hawaii's outsourcing contract with book wholesaler Baker & Taylor died a very public death this summer when the state library system yanked the plug on the $11.2-million, five-year book selection, acquisitions, cataloging, and processing deal. In the end, both B&T and State Librarian Bart Kane, engineer of the outsourcing-to-save-cash plan, suffered: B&T's experimental venture into large-scale outsourcing went belly up and Hawaii's board of education put Kane on a short leash by renewing his contract on July 25 for just six months.

Baker and Taylor, Part II

In the same year that B&T took a beating in Hawaii, it also got served with a federal lawsuit charging that since 1979 it has overcharged libraries by as much as $100 million by playing with discounts based on types of binding. A U.S. District Court judge threw out the case in July due to vagueness in the charges, but the federal government refiled an amended suit in August. The Chicago Public Library has also filed a similar suit on its own.

PW News Reports

Scanning the Globe for Growth

Jim Milliot

Editor, Business and Finance, *Publishers Weekly*

American publishers have been notably expanding their international operations lately, and—despite current problems in Asia—they see more opportunities ahead, particularly in professional and educational publishing areas.

"The international publishing market represents a set of opportunities and threats," observes Martin Maleska, president of the International and Business & Professional group at Simon & Schuster—a theme echoed by most industry members interviewed by *Publishers Weekly* (*PW*) on the topic of how American publishing companies view international business prospects for 1998.

Maleska says the opportunities stem from "a greater acceptance of American thought abroad," especially in such areas as business, finance, and education, as well as the continuing spread of American English as the global language. John Negroponte, executive vice-president of global markets for the McGraw-Hill Companies, holds a similar view, noting that the end of the Cold War and the spread of democracy represent a "significant opportunity for the sale of knowledge and information products" abroad.

Among American publishers, the most sophisticated global operations are usually found at professional and educational publishers. "With only a few exceptions in the college and professional ranks, few American publishers looked to international markets years ago," Scholastic Chairman Richard Robinson notes, adding that "trade and school publishers came to the market later."

Although trade publishers and professional and educational publishers approach the international market in different ways, most publishers are bullish on the long-term prospects for growth abroad, despite the economic problems in Asia. Maleska notes that S&S holds huge market shares in the various publishing segments in the United States, making further growth hard to come by, but it has a very small share of the worldwide book market, which offers a much better prospect for growth than the domestic one. S&S's international sales grew at an average rate of 20 percent between 1992 and 1996, and international revenues were expected to be up by more than 20 percent for 1997, far exceeding growth in the domestic market.

S&S is not the only company to report stronger growth in foreign markets than at home. Negroponte notes that since 1991 McGraw-Hill has grown twice as fast in the international market as domestically, and the company expects that pattern to continue. In 1996 MHC had foreign sales of $450 million, which contributed nearly 15 percent to total company sales. Within the educational and professional group, the professional publishing division operates 23 international publishing centers, either directly or through copublishing arrangements. Among its largest overseas operations are McGraw-Hill Interamericana, McGraw-Hill

Adapted from *Publishers Weekly*, January 5, 1998

Europe, Tata McGraw-Hill and McGraw-Hill Ryerson. The centers produce titles in 16 languages, and MHC considers itself one of the largest educational publishers of Spanish-language materials. Typically, international markets account for nearly two-thirds of the professional publishing group's sales.

John Wiley is another publisher that expects its international sales to grow at a faster rate than its domestic revenues. Wiley is one of the United States' most internationally oriented companies. In fiscal 1997, 48 percent of its total sales of $432 million came from overseas. It considers its June 1996 purchase of the German publisher VCH Verlag a "landmark" acquisition that positions it for additional expansion abroad. Company Chief Operating Officer Will Pesce notes that one reason Wiley has succeeded internationally is because the areas it in which it publishes—such as science, engineering, and business—travel well abroad. S&S's Maleska says his company is testing the traditional wisdom that American elhi materials don't travel well, adapting school product in math and science and meeting with success in foreign markets.

To reach the international market, the large American publishers typically adopt a multi-pronged approach. John Wiley, for example, has companies in the United Kingdom, Germany, Canada, Australia, and Singapore that it uses to maximize sales of English-language publications. Wiley also does selective indigenous publishing projects, while continuing to sell rights and do copublishing deals, to reach non-English-speaking countries. At S&S, Maleska says the company is adapting to the demands of developing countries for more local product by adopting "local, local" strategy. In this approach, S&S will tailor its core U.S. product to meet the needs of a particular customer, either through translations or by giving a book a more local perspective.

Another American publisher with substantial overseas operations is Harcourt Brace, which established Harcourt Brace Publishers International in London in 1995 under the direction of Timothy Hailstone. The company made a major addition to its operations in mid-1997 when it acquired Churchill Livingstone from Pearson. According to HB, the Churchill purchase "rounds out our international capability, particularly in medicine." Hailstone says that for the fiscal year ended October 31, 1997, the international unit had double-digit growth in both revenues and profits.

Not All Smooth Sailing

While American publishers see the international market as an avenue for growth, it is not without obstacles, and the main problems facing all publishers today are the Asian currency crisis and international protection of intellectual property. And while technology is helping to spur global growth it is also contributing to the breakdown of traditional publishing practices, particularly as it pertains to territorial rights. "The disappearance of international borders will have significant ramifications for U.S. publishing," one industry observer tells *PW*.

The Internet is a major factor in bringing down international barriers, whether through the sale of a book by an American online bookseller to a customer abroad or the delivery of information over the Internet to customers anywhere in the world. It is no surprise, then, that copyright protection is a major concern for American publishers, and that the Association of American Publishers (AAP) and its president, Pat Schroeder, have been leading the charge for Congress to approve the WIPO treaties.

While Wiley is in favor of making information as accessible as possible, Pesce warns that the "protection of intellectual property rights remains one of the critical challenges in the rapidly emerging digital world." Brian Davies, president of Random House International, says he sees no simple solution to the copyright problem. He says publishers may need to develop computer systems that can better track sales, but wonders if, in the end, such a system would be cost effective.

Territorial rights is a problem that needs to be addressed quickly, according to John Lyon, vice-president and managing director of international sales for the Time Warner trade group. Not only are online booksellers blurring the lines of rights ownership, but the expansion of American booksellers abroad raises rights issues as well. For example, the Borders store in Singapore is being served by both American and British publishers. And there is a growing sense among publishers that Australia could very well become an open market before long. News that Borders is planning to enter that country in 1998 "could be the straw that breaks the camel's back" in terms of Australia remaining an exclusively British territory, one industry observer notes. Lyon says he thinks it is important that the British publishing industry remain strong and is willing to concede exclusivity in its historic regions, but he insists that the rest of the world remain open. Lyon is critical of American editors who acquire rights and then "give away Europe."

Scholastic's Robinson says that while territorial rights may be an issue now and may create uncertainties in the near term, he thinks it will become less so as the major publishers "become world publishers and acquire world rights to most major books." A veteran international publisher offered a more extreme view, predicting that "the next couple of years will probably see the biggest change in territorial rights since the world was carved up by the Brits and Yanks after World War II. By the turn of the century, the world will be an open market for English-language publishing, with only the U.K. and the U.S. and Canada as exclusive markets."

Because of its strong distribution capabilities, Scholastic has one of the largest international operations among trade publishers. International sales grew 60 percent from fiscal 1994 to $179 million in fiscal 1997, with sales growing 20 percent in fiscal 1997 alone. Scholastic was one of the first American trade publishers to move overseas because it entered a country to set up a distribution system and "became part of the school fabric in the country where we were located," Robinson says. In the international market, Scholastic plays to its strengths, with some 90 percent of revenues generated by children's books.

Random House's Davies said 1997 was "a tough year. We got the results we wanted, but we had to fight every inch of the way." In addition to the fourth-quarter meltdown in Asia, Random saw heavy returns from Australia. "Australia is suffering at retail, so the entrance of Borders is probably a positive thing," Davies says. Borders will create an increased need for titles, something that could help U.S. publishers, he suggests. Nevertheless, he doesn't think that business "will get any easier in 1998."

An Eye on Asia

In interviews with publishers it was clear that the rocky economic situation in Asia will dominate the attention of both trade and educational/professional publishers for at least the first half of 1998. Harcourt's Hailstone says, and many of his colleagues agree, that the major focus of publishers in Asia in early 1998 "will be trying to get paid." Fortunately, many American publishers have long-established relationships with their Asian partners and are fairly confident that payment will be forthcoming. Nonetheless, most publishers see little new business coming from Asia in the first half of 1998.

"We'll have to tackle the market differently in '98," Davies says, noting that Random is hoping some signs of recovery may occur by the end of the first quarter. Even if the economies stabilize, however, it is likely that the dollar will be extremely strong against nearly all the Asian currencies. Another Davies, Alun, president and publisher of Bantam Doubleday Dell's international division, rattled off a litany of depressed currencies. Near the end of 1997 the value of Indonesia's currency against the dollar had fallen by 45 percent, South Korea's currency was off 42 percent, and Thailand was down 38 percent. Such exchange rates will make the sale of American books extremely difficult, and exports will suffer, publishers agree.

Wiley's Pesce highlighted another potential problem that the strong dollar could bring in Asia: a return to widespread book piracy as prices soar for legally copyrighted books. Pesce's remarks were echoed by an expert on the Asian market who predicts that the "prices of academic textbooks are likely to be out of the reach of the majority of Asian students, while discretionary sales of professional and trade books can also be expected to suffer as a result of the reduced purchasing power of libraries, institutions, and individuals."

Robinson was a little less concerned with the problems in Asia than some of his colleagues, although such problems have led to some Asian publishers canceling contracts that were signed at the recent Frankfurt Book Fair. The problems in Asia "won't last forever. The market will come back," Robinson says. Pesce tells PW that "although we are concerned about the recent volatility in the Asian markets, we believe this represents a short-term correction in our business. We've gained significant market share in this region during the past few years, with strong double-digit revenue increases. Although the growth rate will moderate in the short term, we remain committed to Asia."

For Maleska, the biggest problem in Asia is the "currency chaos." He says the volatility of the various currencies is the worst possible scenario because it forces a customer to make another decision on when to buy a book. A stable currency, either at a high or low exchange rate, at least lends some certainty to prices, he notes. Currently, the Asian market "is less robust than it could be," he acknowledges.

Strong demand for its medical, business, and science textbooks resulted in increased sales for McGraw-Hill in 1997, and Terry McGraw thinks the company will see some more growth in the Pacific Rim in 1998.

With the problems in Asia, as well as with a weak retail market in Canada, Bantam Doubleday Dell's Davies thinks 1998 could be "the toughest year BDD will face [in the international market] for a long time." Like some of his colleagues, Davies says that the news of Borders going international "is a silver lining in the clouds of currency problems." Davies also sees BDD's British affiliate, Transworld, having a strong year in Europe. Indeed, nearly every publisher *PW* spoke with, on both the trade and professional/education side, is expecting higher sales in Europe to help offset some of the negative effects in Asia. Hailstone says Europe will be Harcourt's largest foreign market, and that the continent has "more room for growth than the U.S."

Latin America was seen as another area that will provide growth opportunities in 1998. "Everyone will want to become a Spanish publisher," Robinson says. "Spanish is a world language." Random's Davies said his company has done well in Latin America in recent years, especially since there has been recovery in the Mexican economy. Hailstone called Latin America "a coming market."

Perhaps the country that provides the greatest intrigue for publishers is India, which to date has avoided the economic problems of Asia. Indeed, one Asia-based agent observes that "the thought that India might also be dragged in [to Asia's economic problems] is too horrible to contemplate." For the time being, however, publishers are increasing their presence in India. Robinson is excited about the possibilities there, and Scholastic has seen strong growth in its Indian book clubs and book fairs. He attributes the good response to a rising middle class in India that has a high regard for education. In looking to expand into other countries, Robinson says a key criterion the company will use is the strength of the middle class.

Brian Davies says Random is also expecting to see growth in India. He points out that the size of the Indian middle class that speaks English is roughly equivalent to the population of Australia. The lack of effective retailing, however, could hold down sales, he says. Time Warner's Lyon is also bullish on prospects in India, predicting that "I'm sure I won't be the only American publisher at the New Delhi Book Fair."

And finally, there is China. Random's Davies says he is beginning to see some positive signs coming from the Chinese government about its willingness to work with American publishers, especially on the distribution side. S&S already has eight people in a Beijing office and expects to open an office in Shanghai in August. According to Maleska, the company has received a good response to its computer and English-training books, and he adds that in only a short period of time S&S has built a profitable Chinese operation.

The economic upheaval in Asia is likely to slow down American publishers' drive into the international market, but it will not stop it. U.S. publishers own the largest amount of content in the world and are in the best position to take advantage of the technological advances that will make disseminating material abroad easier than ever. Although the international arena will always offer a series of challenges—such as copyright protection, changes in territorial rights and a region that develops unexpected economic problems—in the end, the opportunities overseas are too great for American publishers to pass up.

Publishing's Bold Apprentices

Jonathan Bing

Editor, *Publishers Weekly* Interview

They don't do back-to-back power lunches at Michael's, but prefer to meet clients over the boxed lunch at Japonica or at other restaurants off the beaten path. They have little patience for the slow proceedings of the editorial board, but will crash a book through production on a dime. They don't partake of seven-figure auctions with superagents and franchise authors, but prowl independent bookstores, the Internet, and the mass media, divining book ideas where few editors have thought to look before.

The next generation of *wunderkinder* who may one day compete to fill the shoes of a Sonny Mehta, Nan Graham, or Michael Naumann have arrived, and the new ideas they've brought to the way books are acquired and sold have begun to make waves in an industry where power and prestige have long been concentrated in the hands of editors who remember the days when hardcovers cost $10 or less.

In an effort to better gauge the situation of young editors in the business today, *PW* reporters fanned out across the industry, discovering a group of newly high-positioned editors under age 40 at small, large, and regional houses. Making no claim that those interviewed for this article are the only gifted and important young editors in the business, nor assuming that the reasons for their success can be easily summarized ("It's either in your blood or it's not," quipped Grove Press editor-in-chief Ira Silverberg), *PW* did find that many of these editors share certain qualities. Self-confessed media junkies, they tend to be well-connected and promotion-minded, idealistic about the health of book publishing but realistic about the demands of the bottom line, and harboring no nostalgia for a mythic golden age of publishing that preceded the consolidation of large publishers, the rise of chain bookstores, and skyrocketing profit expectations.

"Every editor has a dollar sign attached to their head," said Holly McGhee, executive editor and associate publisher of the Michael di Capua imprint at HarperCollins Children's Books. "This isn't true just at my house, but across the board. This is the environment in which you have to survive."

For this article, several young editors convened on an evening in December in the back room of the M&R Bar in lower Manhattan. For these would-be players who may soon find themselves counterbidding on some of the same projects, it was an occasion to kick rivalries aside, trade gossip, and dispute the widespread notion that a career in publishing no longer holds the same appeal as it did for the bright, ambitious college graduates of a few decades ago.

Book publishing has always been an apprenticeship business in which the rewards, both financial and intellectual, of publishing serious and important new books are often years away. Recently, the attrition rate for editors, whose starting salaries are distressingly lower than those in Hollywood or on Madison Avenue, has seemingly risen. Amy Einhorn, now the executive editor of trade paperbacks at Warner, began her career as an editorial assistant at Farrar, Straus & Giroux earning $13,000 and "cleaning apartments on weekends to make ends meet."

Said Simon & Schuster editor Laurie Chittenden, "I ate a lot of rice dinners. I didn't go to movies." She added that "People who stay in publishing do not do it for the money. There's a big turnover rate at the two-year mark" as aspiring editors are often asked to prove an aptitude at typing FedEx labels, booking reservations, and the like before being given the chance to act on their instincts and acquire their own titles.

Even those who do persevere and are lucky enough to develop a list of their own are required to wheedle and plead for the attention of agents, the respect of older colleagues, and the corporate resources necessary to better position the books they acquire. As FSG editor Ethan Nosowsky—who arrived at the bar with a manuscript in hand and a pencil tucked behind his ear—put it: "No matter how good an editor you are, you don't wield power. Your only power is your taste."

But even taste is not always easy to put into practice. As the pressure to produce quick results has recently led to the slashing of lists and the collapse of distinguished imprints, young editors are also acutely aware of the instability of the field in which they work. Elaine Mason, an editor at Norton who lost her job at Harcourt Brace in the "bloodbath" that also ousted her mentor, Cork Smith, worried, "This is a good job to be young in, but you can't necessarily grow old in it." She joked that she wouldn't want to be an editor who wins a Roger Klein/PEN award for creative editing: "They all seem to be out of the business." Harper-Collins senior editor Eamon Dolan, who recently watched his company cancel more than 100 contracts, added that "I had never experienced a round of cutbacks before, and would not enjoy one again. But I'm sure it will happen, as there are always cycles. I've been lucky because I've survived, and most of my books have survived. But I've lost a lot of friends because of the cutbacks. You can't underestimate the pain."

Like Dolan, today's Young Turks have learned not only to live with the pain, but to grow stronger from it, gradually mastering a system that often seems rigged against them. In an industry expanding and retracting in sometimes bewildering ways, an old-fashioned blend of hustling, diplomacy, gut instinct, and business acuity remains the chief trait of a successful young editor. "The good thing about publishing," said FSG editor Paul Elie, "is that people don't imagine they can control everything. The bad thing is that it means we often work on hearsay, finger-to-the-wind assumptions, and conjectures that don't have any basis in fact."

Others have found another ace in their hand, however, as publishers have put a premium on snaring readers under the age of 40, an elusive market to which these young editors presumably hold the key. Einhorn said Warner paperbacks publisher Mel Parker hired her specifically because he wanted a young editor for the job, "someone in touch with 20-something popular culture." Said Dolan, "There is a mania over youth these days. Everyone seems to think that a fresh eye is valuable because most of the media these days are crazy for youth."

Diversity Matters

The parochial cottage industry of decades past, of fabled gentlemen publishers with bottomless trust funds and multiple-martini lunches, couldn't seem more alien to those entering the profession today. While many of the editors we spoke with got their start in the usual ways—an Ivy League education or a stint in publishing programs like Radcliffe and Stanford—the backgrounds of others are as diverse as the books they publish. For Tracy Sherrod, who worked at *Essence* magazine and Feminist Press before "starting over" as an editorial assistant at Holt, circumventing the traditional avenues to a career in publishing has helped her build a list that she feels speaks better to "the everyday consumer." Being "a young person from a working-class background, knowing that people don't have the luxury cash to go in and buy something on a whim keeps me more in tune."

Kirsty Melville, a vice-president of the fast-growing Ten Speed Press in Berkeley and former head of Australian S&S, has parlayed her outsider status into a reputation for seeking out unconventional fare, like *The Road Kill Cookbook*, that East Coast publishers might overlook. "Editors and agents have relationships that are built over time," she said. "When I came to Ten Speed I had to start from scratch. I don't sit and wonder if someone's going to ring me."

Grove's Silverberg, in the time-honored tradition of that imprint, "grew up in the underground culture of New York," working as a VIP doorman and party promoter at the nightclub Limelight, when he took his first job as an editorial and publicity assistant at Overlook in the early 1980s. Senior editor Carolyn Carlson, the daughter of a Lutheran minister from St. Paul, Minnesota, lured Jan Karon, now a major cash cow at Viking, from Lion, a Christian press, in an effort to reach "gentle readers," whom she said are ill-served by contemporary fiction. "I wanted to do some books that had great storytelling that weren't all about angst. I thought about what people at church would want to read. And I was right."

More typical are backgrounds in academe (Riverhead senior editor Cindy Spiegel and Carlson are both former doctoral students) or journalism, which yielded Metropolitan Books senior editor Stephen Hubbell, previously at Harpers, and Random House senior editor Jonathan Karp. Karp was a reporter for the *Providence Journal* and the *Miami Herald* before answering a classified ad in the *New York Times* to be Kate Medina's assistant at Random House in 1989. "After the crunch of daily [newspaper] deadlines, I find publishing oddly relaxing," he said. Not incidentally, Karp also edits *At Random*, which serves as an invaluable showcase for his books and those of Little Random in general.

The Hustle

Assistant editors who have labored for years in the trenches understand all too well that one's livelihood hangs on the ability to assume a proactive stance, discerning book ideas below the radar of one's superiors, mounting blitzkriegs of fan letters to anonymous writers and lunches with unfamiliar agents. "You have to use energy and imagination if you're not dependent on your check-writing capacity," said Norton's Elaine Mason, who goes to writers' conferences and, in keeping with Norton tradition, visits a lot of university campuses. For these editors, simply awaiting the diamond in the rough to materialize in the slush pile is a fool's game.

Said Geoffrey Kloske of Little, Brown, "You have to make it happen yourself—you can't just cry in your cubicle." Kloske scored an enviable coup as the first editor to approach David Sedaris, the NPR radio storyteller, about a book deal. "He was listed. I asked him if he was interested in doing a book, and he brought in a stack of short stories." Kloske has just published Sedaris's third book in a print run of 250,000 copies.

In a similar maneuver, Laurie Chittenden leapt the lower ranks of editorial assistant work at S&S after discovering a *People* magazine story on Richard Paul Evans, whose self-published book *The Christmas Box* had sold 100,000 copies in Utah alone. *The Christmas Box* has sold seven million copies worldwide since Chittenden acquired the book for S&S, but she still finds herself making cold calls to agents who don't know her track record, an ordeal she finds "scary as hell. You never know what the reaction will be. It's like asking someone on a blind date."

Although Warner's Amy Einhorn is aggressive about meeting agents, and lunches on average four times a week, she pointed out that recognition from major agents doesn't come overnight: "Some of them will pat you on the head and then sell something to the editor-in-chief or publisher. They don't realize it will only get passed along to us anyway. I don't know when you get to the point where they automatically think of you first."

New Press editor Matt Weiland, who is also managing editor of the magazine of cultural criticism *The Baffler*, has effectively plied his own social circle for book ideas. Two of his former roommates and Baffler contributors, Tom Vanderbilt and Joe Sacco, are now under contract to the New Press. Weiland is presently sharing an apartment with *Newsday* editorial page editor Chris Lehmann. "The joke around here is when am I going to sign him up," he said.

Double Agentry

In a 1980 article in *PW*, Jonathan Galassi, then a Young Turk at Houghton Mifflin, wrote that literary editors at commercial publishing houses must act as "double agents," as their loyalties are inescapably divided between the limited resources of the company they work for and the needs of the books they acquire. That has proven true of most young book editors in conglomerate publishing, whose work-life is increasingly fragmented by the imperatives of corporate bureaucracy. "To mobilize an entire company behind something," said Metropolitan's Hubbell, "You have to be a diplomat, a facilitator, and a cheerleader. You have to mediate between agents and writers on the one hand and the tempestuousness and the different fiefdoms of your own house on the other."

Perhaps the biggest pitfall of such a balancing act is the threat it poses to line editing, once viewed as the ne plus ultra of the vocation, but now an increasingly compartmentalized cog in the production machine—one almost every editor would like to have more time for. "In many houses there is pressure to spend your time in the most fiscally rewarding way, which is acquiring," said HarperCollins's Dolan.

Riverhead senior editor Cindy Spiegel worries that young editors, under intense pressure to produce, can't always help see that a book reaches its full potential. "To be a viable editor, you have to go out and keep buying new things. And you get new submissions because you're publishing well," said Spiegel, who confessed that she has less and less time to line-edit.

If the launch of a new imprint, like an expansion team in professional sports, allows the talents of young editors like Spiegel or Broadway's Lauren Marino to stand in sharper relief, it also compounds the pressure to grow their list. Just two years since the Broadway launch, Marino has been "acquiring like mad," having bought something like 35 hardcover originals and paperback reprints. Though she's now much busier editing books she has acquired ("I don't understand how an editor can not edit a book; it's sometimes hard to fit in, but you have to do it"), she still keeps an eye on authors to pursue, avidly reading new magazines and watching TV.

Indeed, most young editors insist they are still prepared to nurture books through tough times if that's what it takes, and to that end acquire many of their writers in multiple-book contracts, building house authors in the traditional sense. "I'm in a unique position because I was taught the old-fashioned way— editing from the very beginning to the very end," said Holly McGhee of Michael di Capua, who recently went through 21 versions of a manuscript as it gradually evolved from a picture book to a novel. "All it takes is your weekends," offered Random's Karp, who pointed out that the tradition of standing by authors through years of difficult work still thrives at Random House. "To me this is the best part of the job, to watch a book develop over many years and see a writer rise to a new level and break through in his work," said Karp.

FSG's Elie argued that it is incumbent on editors to take a chance on authors who are willing to "follow the story," wherever it leads and for as long as it takes: "It's pathetic when nobody takes on a project until it gets published in the *New York Times Magazine*." Elie cited a book in the pipeline about a writer whose sojourn in Iceland is changed by the sudden death of his mother. "We were able to give him a good advance. He needed time. He needed to be able to come back and say, 'My story is different from the one I set out to write.' "

At independent houses, not surprisingly, young editors are less likely to feel themselves at odds with a monolithic, bureaucratic machine. "Collaborative work is so central to how we work here," said Weiland of the New Press, "it's sometimes difficult in the end to suss out whose book is whose." Although Weiland conceded that this collaborative process runs "the risk that a vary good idea can get muddied by too many editors," he prizes the "support and sense of exchange among editors" who are "all encouraged to develop and commission new ideas in the fields we're working in."

Few editors can feel quite as involved in the book-making process as former Crown editor Kathryn Belden, one of three editors on staff at Four Walls Eight Windows, who edits three books of her own each year and is responsible for every aspect of each book's production. "I'm the production manager. I'm the proofreader. I do the publicity. We have no bureaucracy. There are no P&Ls,' she said. "There's no real hierarchy for me to climb up."

High-Voltage Marketing

Given the superabundance of books against which most new titles compete, Grove's Silverberg (who also runs his own publicity firm on the side) epitomizes the high-voltage promotional efforts many of his colleagues are prepared to undertake for the right book: "My background in PR is as important as my taste, in that if you can't promote the books, it seems pointless to publish them at all." Silverberg's reissues of Jacqueline Susann novels, in the spirit of Susann herself, have been accompanied by a traveling circus of promotional activity, including Susann revival parties, symposia, mass mailings and close coordination with 20th Century Fox, which is reissuing the video of *Valley of the Dolls*.

Also hoping to better exploit a zeitgeist that often places more value on personality than intellectual content, Lauren Marino of Broadway says that in preparing for weekly editorial meetings "we like to meet the author or get a video of the author in action if possible." More radically, Weiland at the New Press also believes that the promotional process itself needs to be reinvented, with the emphasis shifted away from celebrity and toward the ideas behind the books. With the assistance of the Kellogg foundation, the New Press has set up a series of traveling panels they call "idea tours," in which authors of books on related subjects are brought together for public lectures and meetings. Weiland put this idea into practice last fall when the *Baffler* anthology *Commodify Your Dissent* appeared from Norton in the same month that *Baffler* editor Tom Frank's book *The Conquest of Cool* was published by the University of Chicago. Barnstorming across the country, Weiland and Frank hosted panels, the screening of a film on a related subject, and a controversial discussion with labor activist Elaine Bernard at Borders in Boston, which was recently beset by its own labor troubles. "We didn't want to do the usual sign, smile, and greet stuff," says Weiland. "Borders wants to sell books. That's fine, but we want to sell ideas, too."

The Changing Book

For Weiland, a town hall approach to the commissioning and distribution of ideas has led to a whole new series of books that call into question the process of consumption itself. At the New Press, Weiland oversees a labor and economics advisory committee of outside experts offering guidance on what kinds of books to pursue. One result is Bazaar Books, a series of short, illustrated paperback originals taking one commodity and exploring in great detail who makes it, how it is delivered to the marketplace, and so on. The first book, about sneakers, is called *The Sneaker Book*. If this series performs well, one might imagine it will one day be followed by *The Book Book*.

In an effort to better understand the mass culture in which he operates, Dolan has spearheaded the launch of the HarperEdge imprint, whose books explore what he calls "the nexus between culture and technology." Among the best examples of Edge books, said Dolan, is *Interface Culture* by Steven Johnson, a founding editor of the Webzine *Feed*. *Interface Culture*, Dolan said, "makes the argument that interface is the art form of the next century, as film is the art form of this century." Johnson, he added, "is perfectly poised between two worlds, which is exactly the type of author we try to find for Edge."

An interest in books poised between markets, books that slide between categories, that upset convention and pose challenging questions about the reading experience itself, is a hallmark of many of Dolan's peers. "I like books that make you think differently, that fudge genres or use varied elements, like David Foster

Wallace's footnotes in *Infinite Jest*," said Nosowsky of FSG. "That kind of innovation makes people less receptive, but gradually they come around."

But few generalizations can be made about the vast spectrum of books that captivate these editors. Some extend and expand on the world of TV and magazine journalism, such as Einhorn's book on QVC salesperson Kathy Levine for Warner or Marino's celebrity titles for Broadway, such as the Cindy Crawford makeup book; others, like Elie at FSG and Carlson at Viking, hope to publish books that assume a role the mass media has abdicated.

As is perhaps symptomatic of those who have painstakingly worked their way up through the ranks, few of the young editors we spoke with, if any, seemed to see any need to rethink the publication process from ground zero. They see their books as preserving, rather than subverting, the legacy that has already shaped the house in which they work. Sherrod at Holt, who has assembled a distinguished list of African American authors including Paul Beatty and A. J. Verdelle, resists the idea that she is breaking new ground for Holt, pointing out that well before her time Holt published Toni Morrison and John Edgar Wideman. "We have a tradition of publishing African American writers," she said, "but just too few."

The idealism that drove many of these editors into publishing remains largely undiminished. "I've always wanted to work at FSG," said Elie. "I used to walk by the building just to look at it. Once I saw Roger [Straus] walking down the street and it was like I'd seen George Washington." But for these bold, high-spirited editors who remain the enlightened proletariat of an industry in which change comes only in small increments, it is an idealism well-tempered by principles of efficiency, a keen interest in packaging and a hard-earned understanding of the satisfactions of working within the system.

On leaving the M&R Bar, it's notable that not a single editor loosened his or her tie, got drunk, and stayed late into the night to talk about books. It was simply another well-bracketed segment of a tightly regimented day of work. As Rob Weisbach senior editor Colin Dickerman put it, before donning his overcoat and heading off into the cold, "I'm really hungry, but I'm just going to ignore it. I have to go home and read."

Federal Agency and
Federal Library Reports

National Commission on Libraries and Information Science

1110 Vermont Ave. N.W., Suite 820, Washington, DC 20005-3522
202-606-9200, fax 202-606-9203
World Wide Web: http://www.nclis.gov

Jane Williams
Acting Executive Director

Highlights of the Year

Jeanne Hurley Simon continued as chairperson of the National Commission on Libraries and Information Science (NCLIS). Her nomination to a second term as a commissioner was pending in the Senate at year's end. Peter R. Young resigned at the end of May as executive director. The longest-serving NCLIS director, Mr. Young went to the Library of Congress to head its Cataloging Distribution Service. Jane Williams was named acting executive director for NCLIS. John G. Lorenz retired in September, having coordinated the Library Statistics Program for NCLIS since 1988.

Gary N. Sudduth, an NCLIS commissioner since 1992, died July 28, 1997. Mr. Sudduth, who was president and chief executive officer of the Minneapolis Urban League, was a member of the Minneapolis Public Library Board of Trustees for more than ten years. As board president, he led planning for a new $150 million facility.

The only new commissioner in 1997 was José-Marie Griffiths, a well-known and respected information scientist and presently the University of Michigan's Chief Information Officer. Dr. Griffiths replaced Shirley Adamovich.

Continuing commissioners are NCLIS Vice Chairperson Martha Gould, Abe Abramson, Walter Anderson, LeVar Burton, Joan Challinor, Mary Furlong, Frank Lucchino, Bobby Roberts, Joel Valdez, and Robert Willard. Winston Tabb represents James H. Billington, the Librarian of Congress, a permanent NCLIS member. Diane Frankel, director of the Institute of Museum and Library Services (IMLS), is an ex officio commissioner.

Efforts begun by Executive Director Young continued throughout 1997, chiefly a study for the Government Printing Office on electronic government information and cosponsorship with the American Library Association (ALA) of a third survey of public libraries and the Internet. NCLIS also embarked on its first year of advising on the new Library Services and Technology Act (LSTA).

The NCLIS budget for fiscal year (FY) 1997 was $897,000, up from $829,000 for FY 1996 and back to the level for FY 1995. The budget for FY 1998, which began October 1, 1997, is $1 million, the largest ever for NCLIS. The commission met in May and October. The search committee for a new director also met twice and at year's end the appointment of a new director was pending.

Support for Executive and Legislative Branches

In 1997 NCLIS advised on major issues of federal policy concerning libraries and information services:

- Federal support for libraries as enacted in LSTA and administered by IMLS
- Copyright and intellectual property
- Access to government information

During the year the commission focused on the general policy advice it is mandated to give IMLS on federal grant programs for libraries under LSTA, which consolidates library funds for technology and services, retains state-based programs for most of the funds, and removes federal targeting of funds for public libraries. Both the state-based and discretionary grants began with FY 1998 funding, so 1997 was the time to plan and prepare.

The NCLIS chairperson and the executive director met often with the IMLS director on the processes and priorities for advising on LSTA. The commission was represented at a March 1997 gathering called by the IMLS director so that library and museum people could acquaint her with their needs and wishes for the new agency and the new federal program. Commissioners advised on IMLS's strategic plan.

Within this new context for federal grant programs for libraries, NCLIS commissioners concentrated on advice for the National Leadership Grants, which include education and training, research and demonstration, preservation or digitization of library materials, and cooperative efforts between libraries and museums. In May NCLIS had its first joint meeting with the National Museum Services Board, to advise on the library-museum cooperative portion of the National Leadership Grants. IMLS subsequently published draft guidelines, on which NCLIS and others commented, and then published the final set, by which to judge applications and awards in 1998.

In other executive matters, NCLIS staff and consultants worked closely with the Office of Management and Budget's Office of Information and Regulatory Affairs on the study of electronic government information and also with the Department of Education's National Center for Education Statistics (NCES), operating the Library Statistics Program and assessing NCLIS's role in it. These items are covered elsewhere in this report.

The commission was involved in legislative discussions of intellectual property, with draft bills to implement the 1996 treaty of the World Intellectual

Property Organization regarding copyright, performances, and phonograms. In addition, NCLIS responded to the Office of Management and Budget's Legislative Reference Division on inquiries for views on bills, draft bills, and drafts of testimony for reforming government printing. NCLIS urged:

- Completing evaluations then under way before changing U.S. Code Title 44, Public Printing and Documents
- Attending to function, not just organization (e.g., executive vs. legislative)
- Giving whatever agency/agencies responsible for procuring, presenting, and preserving public information the resources and authority to meet its/their mandates

Library and Information Services in a Networked Environment

In 1997 negotiations continued on the study "Assessment of Standards for the Creation, Dissemination, and Permanent Accessibility of Electronic Government Information Products" to be conducted by NCLIS pursuant to a January interagency agreement with the Government Printing Office (GPO).

The Computer Science and Telecommunications Board (of the National Research Council, National Academy of Sciences) developed an overall study framework, which recommended that the overarching goal should be to evaluate the availability, reliability, and accessibility of existing or planned electronic information products of the federal government, whether disseminated to the public through the Federal Depository Library Program or directly, via agencies' electronic services such as Web sites.

In August 1997 NCLIS employed consultant Forest Woody Horton to develop a statement of work for a contractor and to collect basic data from a sample of federal agencies' electronic public information products. The purpose of collecting these data is to identify and evaluate some of the problems and trends as a result of migrating information products from paper and microform to electronic formats and mediums.

By late 1997 the Government Printing Office and the Joint Committee on Printing (U.S. Congress) had approved the statement of work and NCLIS was negotiating for a contractor to collect the data. The study will be completed in 1998. The final report will present findings, conclusions, and recommendations upon which the federal government might take further action.

With ALA as primary sponsor and coordinator, NCLIS cosponsored the 1997 survey of public libraries and the Internet. Principal investigators were John Bertot, Assistant Professor, Department of Information Systems, University of Maryland Baltimore County, and Charles McClure, Distinguished Professor, School of Information Studies, Syracuse University. Major findings are the following:

- 72.3 percent of central or headquarter public libraries are connected to the Internet, up from 44.4 percent in 1996.

- 12 percent of central or headquarter public libraries have connected some or all of their branch libraries to the Internet.
- 87 percent of central city libraries, 83.5 percent of suburban libraries, and 66 percent of rural libraries have Internet connections.
- 100 percent of libraries serving over 1 million population are connected; as are 95.5 percent of libraries serving 500,000 to 1 million; 93.1 percent of libraries serving 100,000 to 499,999; 92.5 percent of libraries serving 25,000 to 99,999; 79.2 percent of libraries serving 5,000 to 24,999; 56.3 percent of libraries serving fewer than 5,000.

Two thousand libraries were surveyed, with a 71.3 percent response rate. The sample was drawn from the universe file of public libraries, set up as part of the Library Statistics Program. In the fall ALA published a summary report for broad distribution and in early 1998 was to publish the full report. The commission contracted with the report's authors for a short, analytical report, identifying policy issues and trends from the 1997 and earlier surveys that NCLIS sponsored. This policy document will be published in 1998.

Throughout the year NCLIS stayed abreast of developments with the Federal Communications Commission (FCC) regarding universal service discounts for libraries and schools. In several sets of 1996 comments to the FCC, NCLIS stressed identifying high-cost and economically disadvantaged areas and noted the importance of discounts that facilitate access to advanced network services sufficient to individual communities' needs.

NCLIS commented on "A Framework for Global Electronic Commerce," a paper from the Interagency Working Group on Electronic Commerce and the Clinton administration's starting point for developing strategies to accelerate the growth of global commerce across the Internet. The commission recommended that needs of students and citizens be addressed by involving libraries and schools in issues addressed by the paper. NCLIS also suggested a framework principle addressing universal service.

Other activities in the area of networked services in an electronic environment included staff attendance at various meetings such as those of the Conference on Fair Use. Staff also coordinated plans for a task force on output measures for electronic library services and met with the Executive Branch Printing Study Team to discuss reinventing government printing for the 21st century.

Library Statistics

For the tenth consecutive year NCLIS and the National Center for Education Statistics (NCES) operated the Library Statistics Program (LSP) through a memorandum of agreement, under which the commission serves as liaison to the library community, helps plan the content of meetings and training workshops, monitors trends, and advises NCES on policy matters.

In the summer of 1997 NCLIS proposed and NCES agreed to fund an assessment of the Library Statistics Program, especially NCLIS's role. Consultant

Howard Harris began the assessment in August 1997. Results were to be published in early 1998 and were to address:

- Values NCLIS contributes to and derives from the LSP
- Goals NCLIS and NCES share for the program
- Directions for NCLIS's future involvement
- Long-term goals for improving the program

The survey of state library agencies continued, with data for FY 1995 published in August 1997. A steering committee recommended revisions and improvements for these annual data collections.

A national survey of library cooperatives was prepared. Cooperatives include library networks, systems, and consortiums with formal arrangements to support library and information services for the mutual benefit of participating libraries. A universe file of library cooperatives was compiled and a survey instrument drafted.

For the eighth consecutive year, data on public libraries were collected, reviewed, and distributed. The 1994 data were published in May 1997. The annual workshop for state data coordinators for public library data was held in March 1997.

Academic library data are collected biennially as part of the Integrated Postsecondary Data System. ALA's Office for Research and Statistics and a committee of academic library specialists advise NCES and NCLIS on improving the biennial survey.

On September 15 and 16, NCLIS and NCES cosponsored the fifth annual Forum on Library and Information Services Policy, "Library Services and Technology Act, State Grant Programs: Implications for Use of and Additions to National Library Data." The forums' objectives are to ensure that statistics about libraries and information services meet the needs of policymakers and to help guide development of public policy on libraries and information services.

International Activities

The commission completed its 12th year of cooperation with the Department of State to coordinate and monitor proposals for International Contributions for Scientific, Educational, and Cultural Activities (ICSECA) funds and to disburse the funds. The allocation for ICSECA, included in the State Department's International Organizations and Programs account, was formerly under International Conventions and Scientific Organizations Contributions (ICSOC). The amount for FY 1997 was $100,000, up from $35,000 for FY 1996.

NCLIS was represented at the 1997 general conference of the International Federation of Library Associations in Copenhagen and will be an International Distinguished Partner for the 2001 IFLA conference in Boston. The commission also contracted for a survey of U.S. participation in international library and archive activities and will use this baseline inventory to assess and develop its international role.

The commission continued to host or lead sessions to orient and share information with librarians and other officials visiting the United States, usually under the auspices of the U.S. Information Agency. In 1997 visitors were from Bolivia, Brazil, China, France, Japan, and Russia.

Publications

Annual Report, 1995–1996.

Reports, hearings and other publications are available on the commission's Web site, http://www.nclis.gov.

National Technical Information Service

Technology Administration
U.S. Department of Commerce, Springfield, VA 22161
703-605-6000
World Wide Web: http://www.ntis.gov

Janet E. Wooding
Writer/Editor
Marketing Communications

The National Technical Information Service (NTIS), a relatively small government organization located on the outskirts of Washington, D.C., serves as the nation's largest central resource and primary disseminator of scientific, technical, engineering, and business-related information produced by the U.S. government and worldwide, primarily governmental, sources. NTIS is thus a key participant in the world of information exchange.

The mission of NTIS is to improve the efficiency and effectiveness of the U.S. research and development enterprise, increase productivity and innovation in the United States, and increase U.S. competitiveness in the global economy.

Although categorized as a government agency by its creation and the terms of its mission, NTIS operates very much like a private business and is somewhat unusual in that it pays its own way. NTIS is a self-supporting federal agency within the Technology Administration of the U.S. Department of Commerce. All costs associated with operating NTIS are paid for by revenue generated from the sale of the products and services it offers. Therefore, costs and the continuing operation of NTIS are considered when setting prices. NTIS's goal is to set the most reasonable prices possible for its customers.

The NTIS collection of nearly three million titles contains products available in various formats. The collection includes reports describing research conducted or sponsored by federal agencies and their contractors, statistical and business information, U.S. military publications, multimedia/training products, computer software and electronic databases developed by federal agencies, and technical reports prepared by research organizations worldwide. Approximately 100,000 new titles are indexed and added to the NTIS collection annually. A permanent repository is maintained of all material available for sale to NTIS customers.

NTIS recognizes the evolution taking place in the "electronic world" and the needs of the people who reside in it. Today's rapid advances in technology allow more information to be processed at a much greater speed than previously and users may want or need to locate, access, and receive information in a nontraditional way. To accommodate the requirements of all of its customers, NTIS is a key participant in the electronic arena yet maintains a sharp focus on the needs of its traditional customers.

U.S. Government Contributors

More than 200 U.S. government agencies contribute to the NTIS collection, including the National Aeronautics and Space Administration, the Environmental

Protection Agency, the National Institute of Standards and Technology, the National Institutes of Health, and the Departments of Agriculture, Commerce, Defense, Energy, Health and Human Services, Interior, Labor, Treasury, Veterans Affairs, Housing and Urban Development, Education, and Transportation. Numerous independent agencies also contribute.

The American Technology Preeminence Act (ATPA) of 1991 (P.L. 102-245) requires all federal agencies to submit their federally funded unclassified scientific, technical, and engineering information products to NTIS within 15 days of the date the product is made publicly available. With the passage of this act, NTIS's wealth of information increased dramatically. NTIS is now able to provide its customers with timely access to a more diverse and practical range of information.

The primary purposes of ATPA are to help U.S. industries accelerate the development of new processes and products, and to help the United States maintain a leading, economically competitive position worldwide. Under ATPA, information products include technical reports, articles, papers, and books; regulations, standards, and specifications; charts, maps, and graphs; software, data collection, datafiles, and data compilations software; audio and video products; technology application assessments; training packages; and other federally owned or originated technologies.

Worldwide Source Contributors

NTIS is a leading U.S. government agency in international technical and business information exchange. It actively acquires and distributes valuable information produced by a large number of international government departments and other organizations. Approximately one-fourth of NTIS's total product offerings come from worldwide sources.

NTIS continues to negotiate agreements to improve the coverage of reports from major industrialized countries, as well as from newly industrialized countries producing advanced technologies. NTIS focuses its acquisition efforts on topics of major interest to NTIS customers.

The NTIS National Audiovisual Center

In October 1994 the National Audiovisual Center (NAC) joined NTIS to consolidate most of the U.S. government's collection of audio, visual, and multimedia products. This merger provides the opportunity to make federally sponsored or produced multimedia products available to a wider audience.

NAC's collection includes approximately 9,000 active titles covering 600 subject areas from more than 200 federal agencies. Included in the collection are language training materials, occupational safety and health training materials, fire service and law enforcement training materials, drug education programs for schools and industry, travelogues, fine arts programs, and documentaries chronicling American history.

Award-winning World War II films from many of Hollywood's most celebrated directors are included in the NAC collection. *December 7th—Long Version* is the full-length version of John Ford's *December 7th*. This film, made in collaboration with famed cinematographer Gregg Toland, explores the history and re-creates the events of the attack on Pearl Harbor in 1941. A shorter version was produced and won an Academy Award for Best Short Documentary. Another important film in NTIS's NAC collection is *The Negro Soldier*, directed by Frank Capra and Stuart Heisler, which shows the enormous contributions and sacrifices made by black Americans in the nation's armed conflicts from 1776 to 1944.

Videos on current concerns include such topics as AIDS. For example, *Nobody's Immune*, a color video by the Walter Reed Institute of Research, Department of the Army, discusses how AIDS can be contracted and the impact it has on the lives of the patient and the patient's family. *Olga's Story*, available in English and Spanish, is about one woman's personal experience with AIDS, how she contracted it, and how it is affecting her life and her family. *At Home with AIDS* was produced by a Veterans Administration medical center and provides help to caregivers of HIV patients.

The center's Web address is http://www.ntis.gov/nac.

FedWorld

In 1992 NTIS began experimenting with online information dissemination and created FedWorld to test customer reaction to this type of service. As a result of overwhelming demand, FedWorld—which provides a user-friendly, centralized electronic resource for government information—has become a central and growing component of the suite of information dissemination services NTIS offers to the public. FedWorld currently serves the information needs of thousands of customers daily.

FedWorld delivers a wide range of bibliographic services exclusively on the World Wide Web. The result has been an increase in the reach of services and a decrease in product delivery time. FedWorld recognizes the rate of Internet growth and yet understands that there still are many people without Internet access. FedWorld offers a choice of user platforms: dial-up, file transfer protocol, and the World Wide Web. Anyone with a computer and a modem can thus access valuable government information online.

As demand for government information increases, it is crucial for government entities to make their information readily available. FedWorld offers solutions for those agencies with limited funding to disseminate information electronically to the American public.

To connect to FedWorld by modem: Set modem parity to none, data bits to 8, and stop bit to 1. Set terminal emulation to ANSI. Set duplex to full. Then set your communication software to dial FedWorld at 703-321-FEDW (321-3339).

To connect to FedWorld via the Internet: Telnet to fedworld.gov. For Internet file transfer protocol services, connect to ftp.fedworld.gov. For World Wide Web services, point the Web browser to http://www.fedworld.gov.

FedWorld access is free. For more information on FedWorld, call 703-605-6585.

NTIS on the World Wide Web

In June 1997 NTIS relaunched its corporate Web site with a number of enhancements. The new version of the site contains more than 300,000 additional product listings. The site now offers information on government manuals, handbooks, computer products, audiovisual/training products, and other products added to the NTIS collection within the last ten years. These enhancements make the site a powerful tool for researching and pricing NTIS products.

The site also includes more powerful search options, expanded coverage of specialized collections, a new Help section, and quick access to the latest information. A new Guided Tour helps the user navigate this large and varied site.

New Listings

A new technical reports database contains more than 300,000 listings of products acquired by NTIS from 1988 to the present. It contains a modified NTIS database listing that does not include a product abstract or keywords.

Special Collections

The NTIS Web site offers expanded coverage of a number of collections including the National Audiovisual Center and Published Searches (bibliographies of current research data). The NAC site offers a browse feature for best-selling training collections such as foreign languages, law enforcement, occupational safety and health, and fire service. A new Science and Technology section complements existing product home pages for Business, Environment, Health and Safety, and Computer Products.

Added Search Options

With this increased information, the NTIS Web site also provides several new search options to make locating products even easier. Visitors to the site can use the Search by Keyword feature to query nearly half a million product listings across all collections. For those who prefer a more structured search, the site also provides an advanced search option. This option can be used to specify a collection and to provide more control over how search results are presented.

Help Section

The NTIS site offers a new Help section to assist users in navigating the site and in locating the government information they need. This section provides a Guided Tour, Frequently Asked Questions, and a Site Map.

Latest Information

The What's New section focuses on the latest information on the site such as recent product announcements, the NTIS exhibit schedule, news about other NTIS-managed Web sites (including the new International Trade Center Bookstore), and the Industry Standards Collection.

Online International Trade and Business Center Bookstore

In late 1997 NTIS announced the opening of the online International Trade and Business Center Bookstore (http://tradecenter.ntis.gov), operated by NTIS on behalf of the Department of Commerce. This site brings together the world's most comprehensive collection of business and international trade information from U.S. government and nonprofit organizations. The site is useful in locating international bestsellers, finding links to other trade-related sites, and searching for industry trading standards.

The physical location of the International Trade and Business Center Bookstore was scheduled to open in April 1998 in the new Ronald Reagan World Trade Center at 13th Street and Pennsylvania Avenue N.W. in Washington.

NTIS OrderNow Catalog on CD-ROM

The NTIS OrderNow CD-ROM offers quick and easy searching for novice, intermediate, and expert users. With this product, customers can quickly identify and purchase valuable government research findings added to the NTIS collection within the previous two years. The CD-ROM gives descriptions of more than 100,000 quality products and provides a built-in ordering module. Each user can electronically complete an order form and fax or e-mail it to NTIS.

Developed in cooperation with the National Information Services Corporation (NISC), the user-friendly NTIS OrderNow CD-ROM includes NISC's powerful ROMWright software (supporting novice, intermediate, and expert searchers). NTIS OrderNow CD-ROM requires a 386 (or higher) IBM-compatible computer.

NTIS OrderNow CD-ROM is affordably priced: single issue, order number SUB-5398LOS, $39 plus handling ($78 plus handling outside the United States, Canada, and Mexico); one-year subscription with quarterly updates, order number SUB-5398LOS, $124. (Prices are subject to change.) To subscribe, call the NTIS Subscriptions Department at 703-605-6060.

NTIS OrderNow Online

NTIS offers a free, convenient online service called NTIS OrderNow Online (http://www.ntis.gov/ordernow), which allows users to locate and purchase quickly the most recent products added to the NTIS collection.

Secure Online Ordering Via the Internet

NTIS understands the concerns a customer may have about Internet security when placing an order, and encourages customers to register their credit card at NTIS to avoid the need to send an account number with each order. To register, customers should call 703-605-6070 and leave their card number and expiration date; NTIS will charge their card when their e-mail order is processed. Orders may be placed through the Internet (orders@ntis.fedworld.gov) 24 hours a day.

NTIS Database Lease Program

NTIS's Database Lease Program offers several valuable research-oriented database products. For more information about accessing these databases, visit the NTIS Web site (http://www.ntis.gov/ntisdb.htm) or contact the NTIS Office of Product Management at 703-605-6515. The following is a listing of available database lease products.

The NTIS Database

The NTIS database (listing information products acquired by NTIS since 1964) offers unparalleled bibliographic coverage of U.S. government and worldwide government-sponsored research. It represents hundreds of billions of research dollars and covers a range of important topics, among them agriculture, biotechnology, business, communication, energy, engineering, the environment, health and safety, medicine, research and development, science, space, technology, and transportation.

Each year NTIS adds approximately 100,000 new entries (most including abstracts) to the database. Database summaries describe technical reports, datafiles, multimedia/training products, and software. These titles are often unique to NTIS and generally are not available from any other source. If a user is looking for information about state-of-the-art technology or practical and applied research, or if a user wants to learn more about available government-sponsored software, the NTIS database is the answer. It provides instant access to approximately two million records.

The NTIS database is available through several commercial services, and also can be leased directly from NTIS. The commercial vendors are Cambridge Scientific Abstracts (301-961-6700), Canada Institute for Scientific and Technical Information (800-668-1222), DATA-STAR (800-221-7754), DIALOG (800-334-2564), EBSCO (800-653-2726), Manning & Napier (716-325-6880), NERAC (860-872-7000), Ovid Technologies (800-950-2035), Questel-Orbit (800-456-7248), SilverPlatter Information (800-343-0064), and STN International/CAS (800-848-6533). To lease the NTIS database directly from NTIS, contact the Office of Product Management at 703-605-6515.

Federal Research in Progress Database

As the U.S. government's central technical and scientific information service, NTIS is responsible for providing access to summaries of current and ongoing projects via the Federal Research in Progress Database (FEDRIP). FEDRIP provides advance information about the more than 150,000 research projects currently under way. The U.S. government funds billions of dollars of research and development and engineering programs annually. The ongoing research announced in FEDRIP is an important component of the technology transfer process in the United States.

The FEDRIP database focus includes health, physical sciences, agriculture, engineering, and life sciences. There are many reasons to search FEDRIP, among them: to avoid research duplication, locate sources of support, identify leads in the literature, stimulate ideas for planning, identify gaps in areas of investigation, and locate individuals with expertise.

Agricultural Online Access Database

As one of the most comprehensive sources of U.S. agricultural and life sciences information, the Agricultural Online Access Database (AGRICOLA) contains bibliographic records for documents acquired by the National Agricultural Library (NAL) of the U.S. Department of Agriculture. The complete database dates from 1970 and contains more than 3.3 million citations to journal articles, monographs, theses, patents, software, audiovisual materials, and technical reports related to agriculture. AGRICOLA serves as the document locator and bibliographic control system for the NAL collection. The extensive file provides comprehensive coverage of newly acquired worldwide publications in agriculture and related fields. AGRICOLA covers the field of agriculture in the broadest sense. Subjects include: agricultural economics, agricultural education, agricultural products, animal science, aquaculture, biotechnology, botany, cytology, energy, engineering feed science, fertilizers, fibers and textiles, food and nutrition, forestry, horticulture, human ecology, human nutrition, hydrology, hydroponics, microbiology, natural resources, pesticides, physiology, plant and animal, plant sciences, public health, rural sociology, soil sciences, veterinary medicine, and water quality.

Agricultural Science and Technology Database

The international information system for the Agricultural Science and Technology Database (AGRIS) is a cooperative system (in which over 100 national and multinational centers take part) for collecting and disseminating information on the world's agricultural literature. References to U.S. publications given coverage in AGRICOLA are not included in AGRIS. A large number of citations in AGRIS are not found in any other database. References to nonconventional literature (such as documents not commercially available) contain a note saying where a copy may be obtained. Anyone needing access to information pertaining to agriculture should use AGRIS to find citations from developed and developing countries around the world.

NIOSH Certified Equipment List Database

The National Institute for Occupational Safety and Health (NIOSH) Certified Equipment List database contains comprehensive certification information on self-contained breathing apparatuses, gas masks, supplied air respirators, particulate respirators, chemical cartridges, and powered purifiers. The database is useful to such audiences as manufacturers, labor organizations, industrial hygienists, safety professionals, and emergency response personnel.

Energy Science and Technology Database

The Energy Science and Technology Database is a multidisciplinary file containing worldwide references to basic and applied scientific and technical research literature. The information is collected for use by government managers, researchers at the national laboratories, and other research efforts sponsored by the U.S. Department of Energy, and the results of this research are available to the public. Abstracts are included for records from 1976 to the present. The database also contains the Nuclear Science Abstracts, a comprehensive index of the international nuclear science and technology literature for the period 1948–1976. Included are scientific and technical reports of the U.S. Atomic Energy Commission, the U.S. Energy Research and Development Administration and its contractors, other agencies, universities, and industrial and research organizations. The database contains more than three million bibliographic records.

Immediately Dangerous to Life or Health Concentrations Database

The NIOSH Documentation for the Immediately Dangerous to Life or Health Concentrations Database (IDLHs) contains air concentration values used by NIOSH as respirator-selection criteria. This compilation is the rationale and source of information used by NIOSH during the original determination of 387 IDLHs and their review and revision in 1994. Toxicologists, persons concerned with the use of respirators, industrial hygienists, persons concerned with indoor air quality, and emergency response personnel will find this product beneficial. This database enables users to compare NIOSH limits to other limits and will be an important resource for those concerned with acute chemical exposures.

NIOSH Manual of Analytical Methods Database

The NIOSH Manual of Analytical Methods (NMAM) database is a compilation of methods for sampling and analysis of contaminants in workplace air and in the bodily fluids of workers who are occupationally exposed to that air. These methods have been developed specifically to have adequate sensitivity to detect the lowest concentrations and sufficient flexibility of range to detect concentrations exceeding safe levels of exposure, as regulated by the Occupational Safety and Health Administration (OSHA) and recommended by NIOSH. The Threshold Values and Biological Exposure Indices of the American Conference of Governmental Industrial Hygienists are also cited.

NIOSH Pocket Guide to Chemical Hazards Database

The NIOSH Pocket Guide to Chemical Hazards (NPG) database is intended as a quick and convenient source of general industrial hygiene information for workers, employers, and occupational health professionals. The NPG presents key information and data in abbreviated tabular form for chemicals or substance groupings (for example, cyanides, fluorides, manganese compounds) found in the work environment. The industrial hygiene information found in the NPG should help users recognize and control occupational chemical hazards. The information in the NPG includes chemical structures or formulas, identification codes, synonyms, exposure limits, chemical and physical properties, incompatibilities and reactivities, measurement methods, recommended respirator selections, signs and symptoms of exposure, and procedures for emergency treatment. Industrial hygienists, industrial hygiene technicians, safety professionals, occupational health physicians and nurses, and hazardous-material managers will find that the database can be a versatile and indispensable tool in their work.

NIOSHTIC Database

NIOSHTIC is a bibliographic database of literature in the field of occupational safety and health. About 160 current, English-language technical journals provide approximately 35 percent of the additions to NIOSHTIC annually. Retrospective information, some of which is from the 19th century, is also acquired and entered. NIOSH examines all aspects of adverse effects experienced by workers; thus much of the information contained in NIOSHTIC comes from sources that do not have a primary occupational safety and health orientation. NIOSHTIC is a beneficial resource for anyone needing information on the subject of occupational safety and health. Among subjects covered by NIOSHTIC are the behavioral sciences; biochemistry, physiology and metabolism; biological hazards; chemistry; control technology; education and training; epidemiological studies of disease/disorders; ergonomics; hazardous waste; health physics; occupational medicine; pathology and histology; safety; and toxicology.

Registry of Toxic Effects of Chemical Substances Database

The Registry of Toxic Effects of Chemical Substances (RTECS) is a database of toxicological information compiled, maintained, and updated by NIOSH. The program is mandated by the Occupational Safety and Health Act of 1970. The original edition, known as the "Toxic Substances List," was published in 1971 and included toxicologic data for approximately 5,000 chemicals. Since that time, the list has continuously grown and been updated, and its name changed to the current title. RTECS now contains over 133,000 chemicals as NIOSH strives to fulfill the mandate to list "all known toxic substances . . . and the concentrations at which . . . toxicity is known to occur." RTECS is a compendium of data extracted from the open scientific literature, recorded in the format developed by the RTECS staff and arranged in alphabetical order by prime chemical name. No attempt has been made to evaluate the studies cited in RTECS; the user has the responsibility of making such assessments.

World News Connection

The World News Connection (WNC) is an NTIS online news service accessible via the World Wide Web. WNC was developed as a companion news source to help individuals obtain news information they could not find elsewhere, particularly in English. WNC provides English-language translations of time-sensitive news and information from thousands of non-U.S. media sources.

Particularly effective in its coverage of local media sources, WNC enables users to identify what is really happening in a specific country or region. Compiled from thousands of non-U.S. media sources (such as speeches, television and radio broadcasts, newspaper articles, periodicals, and books), the information covers significant socioeconomic, political, scientific, technical, and environmental issues and events.

The information in WNC is provided to NTIS by the Foreign Broadcast Information Service (FBIS), a U.S. government agency. For more than 50 years, analysts from FBIS's domestic and overseas bureaus have monitored timely and pertinent open-source material, including "gray literature." Uniquely, WNC allows subscribers to take advantage of the intelligence-gathering experience of FBIS.

The information in WNC is obtained from the full text and summaries of newspaper articles, conference proceedings, television and radio broadcasts, periodicals, and nonclassified technical reports. New information is entered into WNC every business day. Generally, new information is available within 48 to 72 hours of the original publication or broadcast time.

WNC incorporates a powerful search engine designed to make it easy for subscribers to get to the information they want regardless of their online search skills. Subscribers can conduct unlimited interactive searches and can set up automated searches known as profiles. When a profile is created, a search is run against WNC's latest news feed to identify articles relevant to a subscriber's topic of interest. Once the search is completed, the results are automatically sent to the subscriber's e-mail address; users who receive profile results need not log into WNC to view the articles. Profiles can help reduce the amount of time spent on research activities and are useful for tracking the latest international news and information. Users can change their profiles at any time.

For more information on WNC individual pricing and subscription plans, connect to the WNC Web site (http://wnc.fedworld.gov) or call NTIS Fax Direct at 703-487-4140 and enter product code 8645.

Worldtec

Worldtec, a science and technology alert service found at http://worldtec. fedworld.gov, offers time-sensitive and retrospective foreign science and technology information gathered from thousands of U.S. and non-U.S. sources including political speeches, seminars and workshops, internships, meetings and visits, and abstracts of foreign government laws, regulations, plans, and studies.

Worldtec sources include U.S. Department of State science and technology information; Technologies France; the Asian Office of Aerospace R&D Science Letter; U.S. Army Material Command Monthly Reports; the Asian Technology Information Program; the Australian S&T Newsletter; European Office of Aviation R&D; European Space Agency press releases; Fraunhofer Gesellschaft Research News; NATO S&T press releases; National Science Foundation reports from Asia and Europe; NWO News: Research from the Netherlands; the Office of Naval Research, Sdeibersdorb Press Release (Austria); SWOV Newsletter; SWOV Institute for Road Safety Research; and TNO News: Netherlands Applied Science Organization.

Subscribers receive an extensive and in-depth collection of unclassified technology and scientific information briefs from Asia, Europe, and U.S. foreign missions. All materials are in English.

NTIS Alerts

More than 1,600 new titles are added to the NTIS collection every week. NTIS Alerts were developed in response to requests from customers to search this new information resource. NTIS prepares a list of search strategies that are run against all new studies and R&D reports in 16 subject areas. An NTIS Alert provides a twice-monthly information briefing service covering a wide range of technology topics, offering an efficient, economical, and timely way to stay in touch with the latest information in a given field. An NTIS Alert subscription provides numerous benefits:

- Access to the latest U.S. government technical studies
- Concise, easy-to-read summaries
- Information not readily available from any other source
- Contributions from more than 100 countries
- Subheadings within each copy designed to identify essential information quickly

For more information about NTIS Alerts, call the NTIS Subscriptions Department at 703-605-6060 or access the Web site http://www.ntis.gov/atopics.htm.

Published Searches

Published Searches are bibliographies that provide the most current research data available from both the U.S. government and worldwide sources. Each Published Search contains the 50 to 250 most recent abstracts of reports and studies on a given topic. An emphasis is placed on (but not limited to) scientific, technical, and engineering information. Materials dealing with business, law, security issues, manufacturing, mathematical sciences, and many other topics are also available.

Published Searches are jointly produced through an agreement between NTIS and NERAC, Inc. With this agreement, NTIS and NERAC can provide abstracts of completed research literature derived from one of approximately 40 specialty databases. With each Published Search order, a new database search is run and an updated bibliography is produced.

Published Search titles can be searched via the NTIS Database, NTIS OrderNow CD-ROM, NTIS OrderNow Online, or on the NTIS Web site (http://www.ntis.gov/pubsrch.htm).

NTIS Fax Direct Central

The NTIS Fax Direct service provides free information by fax on NTIS products or services, offering subject-specific listings of the most frequently requested titles, detailed product descriptions for those products, and general information on NTIS services and events. Call NTIS Fax Direct Central at 703-487-4142 and follow the voice prompts to receive requested information.

NTIS Customer Service

Automated systems at NTIS offer dramatic improvements in the service provided to customers. Electronic document storage is fully integrated with NTIS's order-taking process, which allows NTIS to provide same-day reproduction for the most recent additions to the NTIS document collection. Orders for materials in electronic storage or available from shelf stock are generally shipped within 24 hours. NTIS ships all larger domestic-order packages by express carrier with two-day delivery at no additional cost to the customer.

To provide easier order placement, NTIS has implemented a simplified flat-rate document-handling fee policy that also reduces costs for many customers. The new fee—a flat-rate handling fee of $4 per total order for delivery to any location in the United States, Canada, or Mexico—replaces the former multiple-rate shipping and handling fee structure. Orders outside North America will carry a flat-rate handling fee of $8 per order.

NTIS Catalog

Many of NTIS's most popular catalogs can be viewed, downloaded, or ordered at the Web site http://www.ntis.gov/catalogs.htm.

- *NTIS Products Catalog* (PR-827LOS)
- *Environment Highlights* (PR-868LOS)
- *Health & Safety Highlights* (PR-745LOS)
- *Law Enforcement Training Catalog* (PR-1000LOS)
- *Occupational Safety and Health Audiovisual Training Programs* (PR-996LOS)
- *Foreign Language Training Audio and Video Courses Produced by the Federal Government* (PR1002LOS)

To receive a catalog by mail, call the NTIS Sales Desk at 800-553-NTIS (553-6847) or 703-605-6000, or fax your request to 703-321-8547. Please quote the appropriate PR number.

Key NTIS Contact Numbers

Order by Phone

8:00 A.M.–8:00 P.M., Eastern time, Monday–Friday
Sales Desk: 800-553-NTIS (6847) or 703-605-6000
TDD: 703-605-6043

Order by Fax

24 hours a day, seven days a week: 703-321-8547
To verify receipt of fax: call   703-605-6090
(7:00 A.M.–5:00 P.M., Eastern time, Monday–Friday.

Order by Mail

National Technical Information Service
5285 Port Royal Road
Springfield, VA 22161
RUSH Service (available for an additional fee)   800-553-NTIS (553-6847)
                                                         or 703-605-6000

NTIS OrderNow Online

Order the most recent additions to the NTIS collection at the NTIS Web site
http://www.ntis.gov/ordernow

Order by E-Mail

Order by e-mail 24 hours a day: orders@ntis.fedworld.gov.
To register a credit card at NTIS, call   703-605-6070.

National Archives and Records Administration

Seventh and Pennsylvania Ave. N.W., Washington, DC 20408
202-501-5400
World Wide Web: http://www.nara.gov

Lori A. Lisowski
Assistant Director for Policy

The National Archives and Records Administration (NARA), an independent federal agency, ensures for the citizen, the public servant, the president, the Congress, and the courts ready access to essential evidence that documents the rights of American citizens, the actions of federal officials, and the national experience.

NARA is singular among the world's archives as a unified federal institution that accessions and preserves materials from all three branches of government. NARA assists federal agencies in documenting their activities, administering records management programs, scheduling records, and retiring noncurrent records to Federal Records Centers. The agency also manages the Presidential Libraries system; assists the National Historical Publications and Records Commission in its grant program for state and local records and edited publications of the papers of prominent Americans; publishes the laws, regulations, presidential documents, and other official notices of the federal government; and oversees classification and declassification policy in the federal government through the Information Security Oversight Office. NARA constituents include the federal government, a history-minded public, the media, the archival community, and a broad spectrum of professional associations and researchers in such fields as history, political science, law, library and information services, and genealogy.

The size and breadth of NARA's holdings are staggering. Together, NARA's facilities hold approximately 21.5 million cubic feet of original textual materials—more than four billion pieces of paper from the executive, legislative, and judicial branches of the federal government. Its multimedia collections include nearly 300,000 reels of motion picture films; more than five million maps, charts, and architectural drawings; more than 200,000 sound and video recordings; more than 15 million aerial photographs; nearly 10 million still pictures and posters; and about 11,300 computer data sets.

Strategic Plan

To fully comply with the Government Performance and Results Act, NARA revised its strategic plan in 1997 to include performance measurements and targets. The revised plan was delivered to Congress on October 3, 1997.

NARA's mission remains the same—ready access to essential evidence—but the agency's goals were strengthened and focused into the following:

- Essential evidence will be created, identified, appropriately scheduled, and managed, for as long as needed.
- Essential evidence will be easy to access regardless of where it is or where users are, for as long as needed.
- All records will be preserved in appropriate space, for as long as needed.
- NARA's capabilities for making changes necessary to realize its vision will continuously expand.

The strategic plan lays out strategies for reaching these goals, sets up milestone targets for accomplishment through the next ten years, and identifies measurements for gauging progress. A copy of the plan is available on the NARA Web site at http://www.nara.gov/nara/vision/naraplan.html or by calling the Policy and Communications staff at 301-713-7360.

Records and Access

Internet

NARA's information on the Internet is accessible via World Wide Web browsers at www.nara.gov and by gopher clients at gopher.nara.gov. NARA's Web site offers immediate access to more than 10,000 files, including the NARA Archival Information Locator, the John F. Kennedy Assassination Records Collection Reference System, publications, on-line exhibits, teaching guides, digital historical documents, links to Internet information servers maintained by the Presidential Libraries, and pointers to related Internet resources.

Electronic Access Project

The Electronic Access Project is a significant piece of NARA's electronic-access strategy as outlined in the agency's strategic plan. The project has three main goals:

- Develop an electronic catalog of NARA holdings nationwide, including the holdings of the National and Regional Archives and Presidential Libraries
- Digitize up to 200,000 items from NARA holdings nationwide
- Upgrade NARA's public-access server capabilities

The result of the project will be tangible: a comprehensive online catalog that will provide information to citizens about NARA holdings nationwide and a core collection of digital copies of selected high-interest documents that illustrate the breadth and value of NARA's holdings and bring them directly to classrooms, public libraries, and homes. The catalog, called the NARA Archival Information Locator (NAIL), contains more than 300,000 record descriptions and links to more than 20,000 digital images, which represents only a small fraction of NARA's vast holdings. Descriptions and images are being added each month.

To access NAIL or find the most current information about the project, visit http://www.nara.gov/nara/nail.html.

Fax-on-Demand

Fax-on-Demand is an interactive fax retrieval system in which a single digital copy of a document is stored on the hard drive of a computer, where it can be selected and retrieved by any customer with access to a fax machine. Each month the system receives about 2,000 calls and sends more than 5,000 documents. There is no charge for the service except for any long-distance telephone charges the user may incur. Documents are updated or added regularly and include General Information Leaflets, press releases, training bulletins, records-finding aids, regional archives and Presidential Library fact sheets, NARA library news, preservation reports, and *Federal Register* notices. The system can be reached at 301-713-6905.

Presidential Libraries

On November 6, 1997, the George Bush Presidential Library was dedicated in College Station, Texas. The library's museum exhibits opened to the public on November 7, and the library opened for research on January 20, 1998. After three-and-a-half years of renovation, the Ford Museum's new permanent exhibit opened on April 17, 1997. The exhibit's ten adjoining galleries feature the latest advances in interactive-exhibit technology.

As part of the effort to fulfill the requirements of Executive Order 12958, NARA and the interagency External Referral Working Group implemented the Remote Archives Capture Project. The project was created to optically scan the estimated 7,000,000 pages of classified materials more than 25 years old that are held by the Presidential Libraries and to make digital copies available to all of the classifying agencies for declassification review. Classified materials at the Kennedy, Eisenhower, Truman, and Johnson libraries will be scanned in 1998 for declassification review.

The Nixon Presidential Materials staff recently opened several key Watergate-related collections as a result of an agreement reached between the Archivist of the United States, the Nixon Estate, and Public Citizen in April of 1996. In 1996 approximately 201 hours of Nixon tape-recorded segments demonstrating abuse of governmental power were opened for research. In addition, approximately 150,000 pages of materials that had been contested by former President Nixon at the time of the opening of the Special Files in 1987 were opened to the public. Most recently, 154 hours of cabinet room conversations were opened in October 1997.

Both the Kennedy and Johnson libraries have released audio recordings and transcripts of presidential telephone conversations. The Kennedy Library has made more than 15 hours of audiotapes of meetings and conversations held during the Cuban Missile Crisis available for research. The Johnson Library has released recorded conversations for the period January–August 1964. These recordings offer in rich detail unique insights into a significant period of the Johnson presidency, including such topics as the Gulf of Tonkin attacks and the passage and implementation of significant civil rights legislation.

Online Federal Register

The *Federal Register* is the daily newspaper of the federal government and includes notices of meetings, proposed and final regulations, reorganizations, and presidential legal documents. The *Federal Register* is published by the Office of the Federal Register and printed and distributed by the Government Printing Office (GPO). The two agencies also cooperate to produce the annual revisions of the *Code of Federal Regulations* (*CFR*). Free access to the full text of the electronic version of the *Federal Register* and most of the volumes of the *CFR* is available through GPO's electronic delivery system, GPO ACCESS, at federal depository libraries or from PCs via the Internet. The full text of the *United States Government Manual*, another publication of the Office of the Federal Register, is also available through GPO ACCESS and through the NARA Web site. In addition to these publications, the Office of the Federal Register publishes the *Weekly Compilation of Presidential Documents* and the *Public Papers of the President*, the slip laws, and the *U.S. Statutes at Large*.

Customer Service

Customers

Few archives serve as many customers as NARA. In fiscal year (FY) 1997 there were more than 286,000 research visits made to NARA facilities nationwide, including Presidential Libraries. At the same time, customers made approximately 819,000 requests by mail and by phone. The National Personnel Records Center in St. Louis, Missouri, received two million requests for information from military and civilian government service records. In addition to providing research and reference services, NARA annually provides informative exhibits for almost one million people in the National Archives Rotunda in Washington, D.C., and 1.2 million more visit the Presidential Library museums each year. NARA also serves the executive agencies of the federal government, the courts, and the Congress by providing records storage, reference service, training, advice, and guidance on many issues relating to records management. The agency's current *Customer Service Plan* and *Customer Service Performance Reports* list the many types of customers NARA serves and describe the agency's goals for customer service standards. These publications, available free in NARA research rooms nationwide or on the Internet, may also be ordered from the Product Sales Section, Room G8, National Archives and Records Administration, 700 Pennsylvania Ave. N.W., Washington, DC 20408; by telephone at 800-234-8861; or by fax at 202-501-7170.

Customer Opinion

NARA cares about what its customers think of its services. Among the specific strategies published in *Ready Access to Essential Evidence: The Strategic Plan of the National Archives and Records Administration, 1997–2007* (September 30, 1997) is an explicit commitment to expanding the opportunities of NARA customers to inform NARA about information and services they need. In support of that strategy, a major survey of customers using the NARA research rooms in the

Washington, D.C., area was conducted in the past year. NARA continues to survey, hold focus groups, and meet with customers to evaluate and constantly improve services.

Centers Information Processing System (CIPS)

CIPS allows federal agencies to make electronic reference requests for records stored at a regional records services facility. CIPS improves customer service by reducing reference preparation time and cost, delivery delays, and turnaround times. Begun as a pilot project in October 1993, CIPS processed more than 1,180,650 electronic requests in FY 1997 and turnaround times have been reduced from 10–12 days to 2–3 days. NARA's service improvement allows other federal agencies to provide faster service to their public customers as well.

Administration

NARA employs approximately 2,850 people, of whom about 2,050 are full-time permanent staff members. For FY 1997 NARA's budget was $218 million, with $5 million to support the National Historic Publications and Records Commission (NHPRC). An annual description of the activities and finances of NARA can be found in the *Annual Report of the National Archives and Records Administration*. For a copy of the report or for further information about NARA, call the Policy and Communications staff at 301-713-7360.

United States Information Agency

Bureau of Information
Room 130, 301 Fourth St. S.W., Washington, DC 20547
202-619-4225

Cynthia Borys
Information Resource Center

The United States Information Agency (USIA), an independent organization within the executive branch, is responsible for the U.S. government's overseas information, educational exchange, and cultural programs. The work of the agency is carried out by a staff of foreign service officers assigned to U.S. missions abroad and by a professional staff of career civil servants in Washington, D.C. Known abroad as the United States Information Service (USIS), the agency has more than 200 posts in 146 countries that are grouped in six geographic areas: Africa; Western Europe; Eastern Europe and the Newly Independent States; East Asia and the Pacific; the American Republics; and North Africa, the Near East, and South Asia. Posts in these areas report to area offices in Washington, D.C.

History of USIS Library Programs

Today's worldwide system of USIS libraries evolved from a matrix of programs. First, in Latin America, came libraries associated with President Franklin Roosevelt's "Good Neighbor" program. In 1941 the coordinator of inter-American affairs, Nelson Rockefeller, contracted with the American Library Association (ALA) to establish and operate a library in Mexico City, the now-famous Biblioteca Benjamin Franklin. Under similar contracts, ALA opened and operated on behalf of the U.S. government two other libraries in Latin America: in Managua, Nicaragua (1942), and Montevideo, Uruguay (1943).

Beginning in 1942 the Office of War Information (OWI) began to establish reference libraries as part of its overseas information program. These were separate and distinct from U.S. Embassy reference libraries at the outset. Later, parts of many embassy collections were turned over to USIS libraries. The American Library in London started operations in December 1942 and officially opened in April 1943. The London library was the first overseas library directly under U.S. government control. Between 1942 and 1945 OWI established libraries in 40 more locations throughout the world. In 1945 the Department of State assumed responsibility for overseas libraries.

Shortly after World War II the U.S. Military Government began opening Information Center (Amerika Häuser) libraries and reading rooms in Germany, throughout the American Zone and in the major cities of the British and French zones. At the same time Information Center libraries were started under the auspices of the United States Forces in Austria, Japan, and Korea. The State Department assumed responsibility for these centers when civilian control was restored in each country. Nine centers came under the department's auspices in

January 1949, and ten centers in Austria were added in 1950. These centers were initially transferred to the State Department and finally, on August 1, 1953, to the newly created United States Information Agency. Since that time USIS libraries and information resource centers have been opened in virtually every country with which the United States maintains diplomatic relations.

Current Programs

Although USIS library and information centers vary significantly from country to country, all advance two mutually supportive functions:

- To provide the most current and authoritative information about official U.S. government policies
- To serve as a primary source of informed commentary on the origin, growth, and development of American social, political, economic, and cultural values and institutions

Activities of USIS libraries and information resource centers are carried out by host country staff. They provide a vital communication link between USIS posts and local audiences. A corps of 20 American information specialists periodically travels to overseas posts to provide professional guidance and to define the roles of libraries and information centers in relation to American foreign policy objectives. As greater emphasis is placed on current awareness and outreach services to foreign opinion leaders, USIS staff rely on direct, electronic access to the wealth of information sources in the United States. In places where information about the United States is extremely limited or virtually nonexistent, USIS libraries provide a balanced cross section of outstanding American contributions in the social sciences and humanities, which promote appreciation and understanding of American intellectual and cultural history, American economic and social institutions, and American political traditions. Book collections at these places usually range from 3,000 to 10,000 volumes.

USIA Washington continues to operate one of the federal government's most dynamic special libraries. Annually, the Information Resource Center (IRC) fields over 18,000 research and reference requests from USIA Washington staff and overseas posts. The IRC maintains a collection of 50,000 monographs, 800 journals, and access to 1,000 online and CD-ROM sources. USIA headquarters is also responsible for the professional development of field librarians.

Public Diplomacy Query Database

USIA also produces and maintains a family of databases called Public Diplomacy Query (PDQ), to index, store, and make available to USIS libraries most program and foreign policy materials acquired and produced by USIA. PDQ is available online and via CD-ROM.

Book Programs

USIA also supports the publication of American books abroad, both in English and in translation. The agency, through its field posts abroad, works with publishers to produce a variety of translated books in the humanities and social sciences that reflect a broad range of American thought and serve to explain American life and institutions.

Through programs of book translation and through a variety of seminars, conferences, and short-term professional publishing workshops, USIA seeks to encourage respect for and adherence to international standards of intellectual property rights protection. The agency works closely on this issue both with foreign governments and with domestic and foreign nongovernment organizations.

American publishers seeking additional information about the agency's book program should direct their inquiries to Print Publications (I/TPP), Bureau of Information, USIA, 301 Fourth St. S.W., Washington, DC 20547. Foreign publishers should turn for assistance to the Public Affairs Office of the U.S. Embassy in their country.

National Center for Education Statistics Library Statistics Cooperative Program

U.S. Department of Education, Office of Educational Research and Improvement
555 New Jersey Ave. N.W., Washington, DC 20208-5652

Adrienne Chute
Surveys and Cooperative Systems Group

The mandate of the National Center for Education Statistics (NCES) to collect library statistics is included in the Improving America's Schools Act of 1994 (P.L. 103-382) under Title IV, the National Education Statistics Act of 1994. The Library Statistics Cooperative Program is administered and funded by NCES, which regularly collects and disseminates statistical information on libraries under six surveys. These surveys include the Public Libraries Survey, the Academic Libraries Survey, the School Library Media Center Survey, the State Library Agency Survey, the Federal Libraries Survey and the Library Cooperatives Survey. The U.S. National Commission on Libraries and Information Science (NCLIS) and the U.S. Bureau of the Census work cooperatively with NCES in implementing the Library Statistics Cooperative Program.

The six library surveys provide the only current, comprehensive, national data on the status of libraries. They are used by federal, state, and local officials, professional associations, and local practitioners for planning, evaluation, and making policy, and drawing samples for special surveys. These data are also available to researchers and educators to analyze the state of the art of librarianship and to improve its practice.

Public Libraries

Descriptive statistics for nearly 9,000 public libraries are collected and disseminated annually through a voluntary census, the Public Libraries Survey. The survey is conducted by the National Center for Education Statistics (NCES) through the Federal-State Cooperative System (FSCS) for public library data. In 1997 FSCS completed its ninth data collection.

Data files on diskette that contain 1994 data on about 9,000 responding libraries and identifying information about their outlets were made available in 1997. The 1994 data were also aggregated to state and national levels in an E.D. Tabs, an NCES publication designed to present major findings with minimal statistical analyses. The 1995 FSCS data were collected in July 1996, with release scheduled for winter 1997. The 1995 data were collected in July 1996, with release scheduled for winter 1998. The 1996 data were collected in July 1997, with release scheduled for late 1998. The 1997 data will be collected in July 1998, with release scheduled for summer 1999.

Note: Carrol Kindel, Jeffrey Williams, Elaine Kroe, Rosa Fernandez, and Martha Hollins of NCES and Chris Dunn of Library Programs contributed to this article.

The 50 states and the District of Columbia participate in data collection. Beginning in 1993 the following outlying areas joined the FSCS: Guam, Northern Marianas, Palau, Puerto Rico, and the Virgin Islands. For the 1995 data collection, the respondents were the nearly 9,000 public libraries, identified by state library agencies in the 50 states and the District of Columbia, plus two of the outlying areas.

The Public Libraries Survey collects data on staffing; type of governance; type of administrative structure; service outlets; operating income and expenditures; size of collection; service measures such as reference transactions, interlibrary loans, circulation, public service hours, library visits, circulation of children's materials, children's program attendance, and interlibrary relationship; and other data items. Beginning with 1996 for the collection of 1995 data, six technology-oriented data items were added to the Public Libraries Survey. These are:

- Does the public library have access to the Internet?
- Is the Internet used by library staff only, patrons through a staff intermediary, or patrons either directly or through a staff intermediary?
- Does the library provide access to electronic services?
- The number of library materials in electronic format
- Operating expenditures for library materials in electronic format
- Operating expenditures for electronic access

Beginning with 1998 for the collection of fiscal year (FY) 1997 data, one new data element, "Web address of the outlet," has been added to the Public Libraries Survey.

In general, both unit response and response to specific items are very high. Efforts to improve FSCS data quality are ongoing. For example, beginning with FY 1995 data, most items with response rates below 100 percent include imputations for nonresponse. In prior years the data were based on responding libraries only. NCES has also sponsored a series of studies on coverage, definitions, finance data, and staffing data. These studies were conducted by the Governments Division, Bureau of the Census. Over the past several years the clarity of FSCS definitions, software, and tables has been significantly improved.

At the state level and in the outlying areas, FSCS is administered by data coordinators, appointed by each state or outlying area's chief officer of the state library agency. FSCS is a working network. State Data Coordinators collect the requested data from public libraries and submit these data to NCES. NCES aggregates the data to provide state and national totals. An annual training conference is provided for the state data coordinators and a steering committee that represents them is active in the development of the Public Libraries Survey and its data-entry software. Technical assistance to states is provided by phone and in person by state data coordinators, by NCES staff, by the Bureau of the Census, and by NCLIS. NCES also works cooperatively with NCLIS, the U.S. Department of Commerce's Bureau of the Census, the Institute of Museum and Library Services' Office of Library Programs, the Chief Officers of State Library Agencies (COSLA), the American Library Association (ALA), the U.S. Department of Education's National Institute on Postsecondary Education,

Libraries, and Lifelong Learning (PLLI), and the National Library of Education. Westat, Inc. works under contract to NCES to support cooperative activities of the NCES Library Statistics Cooperative Program.

FSCS is an example of the synergy that can result from combining federal/ state cooperation with state-of-the-art technology. FSCS was the first national NCES data collection in which the respondents supplied the data electronically. The data can also be edited and tabulated electronically at the state and national levels through NCES-developed software. All nine FSCS data collections have been collected electronically.

To enhance the Public Libraries Survey, NCES developed the first comprehensive public library universe file (PLUS) and merged it with existing software into a revised software package called DECPLUS. DECPLUS has been used to collect data since 1992. DECPLUS collects identifying information on all known public libraries and their service outlets, all state library agencies, and some library systems, federations, and cooperative services. This resource is now available for use in drawing samples for special surveys on such topics as literacy, access for the disabled, library construction, and the like. A historical change tracking mechanism has also been established beginning with DECPLUS. Closings, additions, and mergers of public libraries and public library service outlets, for example, are tracked in a historical file. DECPLUS software is cost-effective and has improved data quality.

The following are highlights from *E.D. TABS Public Libraries in the United States: 1994* released in June 1997.

Number of Public Libraries and Their Service Outlets and Governance

- 8,921 public libraries (administrative entities) were reported in the 50 states and the District of Columbia in 1994.
- About 11 percent of the public libraries serve 70 percent of the population of legally served areas in the United States (derived from tables 1A and 1B). Each of these public libraries has a legal service area population of 50,000 or more.
- 1,455 public libraries (over 16 percent) reported one or more branch library outlets, with a total of 7,025. The total number of central library outlets reported was 8,879. The total number of stationary outlets reported (central library outlets and branch library outlets) was 15,904. About 9 percent of reporting public libraries had one or more bookmobile outlets, with a total of 997.
- About 55 percent of public libraries were part of a municipal government; nearly 12 percent were part of a county/parish; nearly 6 percent had multi-jurisdictional governance under an intergovernmental agreement; over 9 percent were nonprofit association or agency libraries; about 4 percent were part of a school district; and about 8 percent were separate government units known as library districts. Less than 1 percent were combinations of academic/public libraries or school/public libraries. Just over 5 percent did not report or reported a form of governance not mentioned here.
- 80.4 percent of public libraries had a single direct service outlet.

Income, Expenditure, and Staffing

- Public libraries reported that approximately 78 percent of their total operating income of about $5.3 billion came from local sources, about 12 percent from the state, 1 percent from federal sources, and over 8 percent from other sources, such as gifts and donations, service fees and fines.
- Per capita operating income from local sources was under $3 for 13 percent of public libraries, $3 to $14.99 for approximately 51 percent, and $15 to $29.99 for 25 percent of public libraries; 10.7 percent of libraries had a per capita income from local sources of $30 or more.
- Total operating expenditures for public libraries were over $4.9 billion in 1994. Of this, about 65 percent was expended for paid staff and nearly 15 percent for the library collection (table 12). the average U.S. per capita operating expenditure was $19.93. The highest average per capita operating expenditure in the 50 states was $35.40 and the lowest was $8.45.
- About 40 percent of public libraries reported operating expenditures of less than $50,000 in 1994, about 39 percent expended between $50,000 and $399,999, and about 22 percent exceeded $400,000.

Staffing and Collections

- Public libraries reported a total of nearly 112,823 paid full-time equivalent (FTE) staff.
- Nationwide, public libraries reported nearly 672 million books and serial volumes in their collections or 2.7 volumes per capita. By state, the number of volumes per capita ranged from 1.7 to 4.9.
- Nationwide, public libraries reported collections of nearly 24 million audio materials and nearly 9.3 million video materials.

Circulation and Interlibrary Loans

- Total nationwide circulation of library materials was nearly 1.6 billion or 6.4 per capita. Highest statewide circulation per capita in the 50 states was 11.8 and lowest was 3.1.
- Nationwide, nearly 7.9 million library materials were loaned by public libraries to other libraries.

Children's Services

- Nationwide circulation of children's materials was nearly 492 million or about 31 percent of total circulation. Attendance at children's programs was over 38 million.

Per capita figures in these highlights are based on the total unduplicated population of legal service areas in the states, not on the total population of the states. Population of legal service area means the population of those areas in the state for which a public library has been established to offer services and from which (or on behalf of which) the library derives income, plus any areas served under contract for which the library is the primary service provider. It does not include the population of unserved areas.

Public library questions are also being included as parts of other NCES surveys. For example, in 1996 questions about frequency of use and the purposes for which households use public libraries were included on an expanded household screener for the NCES National Household Education Survey. More than 55,000 households nationwide were surveyed in such a way as to provide state- and national-level estimates on library items. A Statistics in Brief reporting the survey results was published in 1997. A CD-ROM and User's Manual was made available in July 1997. Additional analysis of these data, including demographic analysis, is planned for 1998.

The following are highlights from *Statistics in Brief: Use of Public Library Services by Households in the United States: 1996*, released in July 1997.

Public Library Use in the Past Month and Year

- About 44 percent of U.S. households included individuals who had used public library services in the month prior to the interview, and 65 percent of households had used public library services in the past year (including the past month). About one-third of households (35 percent) reported that no household members had used library services in the past year.
- When the entire past year is taken into account, households with children under 18 show substantially higher rates of use than households without children (82 percent versus 54 percent).

Ways of Using Public Library Services

- The most common way of using public library services in the past month was to go to a library to borrow or drop off books or tapes (36 percent).
- Eighteen percent of households reported visiting a library for other purposes, such as a lecture or story hour or to use library equipment (the second most common form of use).
- About 14 percent of households had called a library for information during the past month.
- Only very small percentages of households reported using a computer to link to a library (4 percent), having materials mailed or delivered to their homes (2 percent), or visiting a bookmobile (2 percent).

Purposes for Using Public Library Services

- The highest percentage of households reported library use for enjoyment or hobbies, including borrowing books and tapes or attending activities (32 percent).
- Two other purposes for using public libraries that were commonly acknowledged by household respondents were getting information for personal use (such as information on consumer or health issues, investments, and so on; 20 percent), and using library services or materials for a school or class assignment (19 percent).

- Fewer household respondents said that household members had used public library services for the purposes of keeping up to date at a job (8 percent), getting information to help find a job (5 percent), attending a
  program for children (4 percent), or working with a tutor or taking a class
  to learn to read (1 percent).

Additional information on FSCS may be obtained from Adrienne Chute
(202-219-1772), Surveys and Cooperatives Systems Group, National Center for
Education Statistics, Room 311A, 555 New Jersey Ave. N.W., Washington, DC
20208-5652.

Academic libraries

NCES surveyed academic libraries on a three-year cycle between 1966 and 1988.
Since 1988, the Academic Libraries Survey (ALS) has been a component of the
Integrated Postsecondary Education Data System (IPEDS) and is on a two-year
cycle. ALS provides data on about 3,500 academic libraries. In aggregate, these
data provide an overview of the status of academic libraries nationally and
statewide.

The survey collects data on the libraries in the entire universe of accredited
higher education institutions and on the libraries in nonaccredited institutions
with a program of four years or more. ALS produces descriptive statistics on academic libraries in postsecondary institutions in the 50 states, the District of
Columbia, and the outlying areas.

The first release of ALS 1996 data was in spring 1997 over the Internet.
Several data products will follow—an ED Tabs and a diskette of the data.

NCES has developed IDEALS, a software package for states to use in sub-
mitting ALS data to NCES. Its model was DECTOP, the predecessor of DEC-
PLUS, the software developed for the collection of public library data in the
FSCS program. IDEALS was used by 45 states in the collection of 1996 data.

ALS, using FSCS as a model, has established a working group comprised of
representatives of the academic library community. Its mission is to improve data
quality and the timeliness of data collection, processing, and release. This network of academic library professionals works closely with state IPEDS coordinators (representatives from each state who work with NCES to coordinate the
collection of IPEDS data from postsecondary institutions in their states). NCES
also works cooperatively with ALA, NCLIS, the Association of Research
Libraries, the Association of College and Research Libraries, and numerous academic libraries in the collection of ALS. ALS collects data on total operating
expenditures, full-time-equivalent library staff, service outlets, total volumes
held at the end of the fiscal year, circulation, interlibrary loans, public service
hours, gate count, reference transactions per typical week, and online services.
New data elements focusing on electronic access and other new technologies
were added to the survey, beginning with 1996.

The following are highlights from *E.D. TABS Academic Libraries: 1994*,
released in March 1998.

Services

- In 1993, 3,303 of the 3,639 institutions of higher education in the United States reported that they had their own academic library.
- In fiscal year 1994, general collection circulation transactions in the nation's academic libraries at institutions of high education totaled 183.1 million. Reserve collection circulation transactions totaled 48.4 million. For general and reference circulation transactions taken together, the median circulation was 16.6 per full-time equivalent (FTE) student[1]. The median total circulation ranged from 9.5 per FTE in less than four-year institutions to 31.1 in doctorate-granting institutions.
- In 1994 academic libraries provided a total of about 8.8 million interlibrary loans to other libraries (both higher education and other types of libraries) and received about 6.3 million loans.
- Overall, the largest percentage of academic libraries (43 percent) reported having 60–70 hours of service per typical week. However, 41 percent provided 80 or more public service hours per typical week. The percent of institutions providing 80 or more public service hours ranged from 6.9 percent in less than four-year institutions to 77.8 percent in doctorate-granting institutions.
- Taken together, academic libraries reported a gate count of about 17.8 million visitors per typical week (about 1.8 visits per total FTE enrollment).
- About 21 million reference transactions were reported in a typical week. Over the fiscal year 1994, about 487,000 presentations to groups serving about 6.1 million were reported.

Collections

- Taken together, the nation's 3,033 academic libraries at institutions of higher education held a total of 776.4 million volumes (books, bound serials, and government documents), representing about 422.3 million unduplicated titles at the end of FY 1994.
- The median number of volumes held per FTE student was 56.9 volumes. Median volumes held ranged from 18.4 per FTE in less than four-year institutions to 111.2 in doctorate-granting institutions.
- Of the total volumes held at the end of the year, 43.3 percent (336.6 million) were held at the 125 institutions categorized under the 1994 Carnegie classification as Research I or Research II institutions. About 54.6 percent of the volumes were at those institutions classified as either Research or Doctoral in the Carnegie classification.
- In FY 1994, the median number of volumes added to collections per FTE student was 1.6. The median number added range from .6 per FTE in less than four-year institutions to 3.1 in doctorate-granting institutions.

---

[1]FTE enrollment is calculated by adding one-third of part-time enrollment to full-time enrollment. Enrollment data are from the 1993–94 IPEDS Fall Enrollment Survey.

Staff

- There was a total of 95,843 FTE staff working in academic libraries in 1994. Of these about 26,726 (27.9 percent) were librarians or other professional staff; 40,381 (42.1 percent) were other paid staff; 326 (.3 percent) were contributed services staff; and 28,411 (29.6 percent) were student assistants.
- Excluding student assistants, the institutional median number of academic library FTE staff per 1,000 FTE students was 5.9. The median ranged from 3.6 in less than four-year institutions to 9.8 in doctorate-granting institutions.

Expenditures

- In 1994, total operating expenditures for libraries at the 3,303 institutions of higher education totaled $4.01 billion. The three largest individual expenditure items for all academic libraries were salaries and wages, $2.02 billion (50.4 percent); current serial subscription expenditures, $690.4 million (17.2 percent); and books and bound serials, $442.5 million (11.0 percent).
- The libraries of the 514 doctorate-granting institutions (15.6 percent of the total institutions) accounted for $2.496 billion, or 62.2 percent of the total operating expenditure dollars at all college and university libraries.
- In 1994, the median total operating expenditure per FTE student was $290.81 and the median for information resource expenditures was $86.15.
- The median percentage of total institutional Education & General (E&G) expenditures for academic libraries was 2.8 percent in 1994. In 1990 the media was 3.0 percent (*Academic Library Survey: 1990*, unpublished tabulation).

A descriptive report of changes in academic libraries between 1990 and 1992 was released in June 1997.

Several questions about the role of academic libraries in distance education were included as part of another survey sponsored by the National Institute on Postsecondary Education, Libraries and Lifelong Learning. The Survey on Distance Education Courses Offered by Higher Education Institutions was conducted in fall 1995 under NCES's Postsecondary Education Quick Information system (Peqis). The following is a highlight from the resulting *Statistical Analysis Report: Distance Education in Higher Education Institutions*, released October 1997.

Access to library resources varied depending on the type of library resource. Access to an electronic link with the institution's library was available for some or all courses at 56 percent of the institutions, and cooperative agreements for students to use other libraries were available at 62 percent of institutions. Institution library staff were assigned to assist distance education students at 45 percent of the institutions, while library deposit collections were available at remote sites at 39 percent of institutions.

Additional information on academic library statistics may be obtained from Jeffrey Williams, Surveys and Cooperative Systems Group, National Center for

Education Statistics, 320A, 555 New Jersey Ave. N.W., Washington, DC 20208-5652 (202-219-1362).

School Library Media Centers

In 1991 a small amount of data on school libraries was collected as embedded items from a sample of public and private elementary and secondary schools as part of the NCES 1990–1991 Schools and Staffing Survey (SASS). Data collected included number of students served, number of professional staff and aides, number of full-time equivalent librarians/media specialists, number of vacant positions, number of positions abolished, number of approved positions, and amount of librarian input in establishing curriculum. NCES released a short report on these data in November 1994.

The following are highlights from this report, titled *Survey Report School Library Media Centers in the United States 1990–91.*

Historical Overview

- In 1958 only 50 percent of public elementary and secondary schools in the United States had a library or library media center. As of 1990–1991, 96 percent of public and 87 percent of private elementary and secondary schools in the United States had a library or library media center (Table 3).
- From 1960 to 1980 the number of public school librarians/media specialists in the United States nearly tripled, from 17,363 to 48,018, outstripping increases in student enrollments. Since 1980, expansion in the number of public school librarians/media specialists substantially slowed, and in the early 1990s school library media center staffing levels did not keep pace with increases in student enrollments (Table 4).

The Availability of School Library Media Centers

- In the public sector, small schools (those with fewer than 300 students) and combined schools (those jointly offering both elementary and secondary levels) were the least likely to be equipped with library media centers in 1990–1991. Ten percent of small public schools and 15 percent of combined public schools did not have library media centers (Table 6).
- In the private sector, small schools, elementary schools, combined schools, and non-Catholic private schools, both religious and nonsectarian, were the least likely to be equipped with library media centers in 1990–1991. The percentages of schools in these groups without library media centers ranged from 14 to 23 percent (Table 6).

Staffing Levels of School Library Media Centers

- In the public sector, 8 percent of schools with library media centers did not employ some kind of library media center staff, neither a professional librarian/media specialist nor a library aide, in 1990–1991. Four percent of public school students attended such schools. Elementary schools, combined schools, and small public schools were the most likely to have employed no library staff. One third of small public schools had no librarian/media specialist, and one-fifth of those same schools had neither a librarian/media specialist nor an aide (Table 9).

- The proportion of private schools with unstaffed library media centers was far greater than for public schools in 1990–1991. Over half of smaller, elementary, and non-Catholic religious private schools employed neither a librarian/media specialist nor a library aide. Overall, a quarter of all private school students were enrolled in schools with no employed library media center staff (Table 9).

The Role of School Library Media Specialists

- Teachers in public schools were slightly more likely than teachers in private schools to strongly agree that the materials in their school library media centers were supportive of their instructional objectives (Table 15).
- Few school principals (16 percent) reported that school librarians/media specialists had a great deal of influence over decisions concerned with establishing the curriculum in their schools. Librarians/media specialists in private schools were more frequently reported to have a great deal of influence over curricular decisions than in public schools (Table 17).

A national survey on school library media centers was conducted in school year 1993–1994, the first since school year 1985–1986. NCES, with the assistance of the U.S. Bureau of the Census, conducted this survey as part of the 1994 Schools and Staffing Survey (SASS). The survey consisted of two questionnaires. The school library media specialist questionnaire data will provide a nationwide profile of the school library media specialist workforce. The school library media center questionnaire data will provide a national picture of school library collections, expenditures, technology, and services. This effort will be used to assess the status of school library media centers nationwide and to assess the federal role in their support. The report on the 1993–1994 survey was expected to be released in early 1998.

Additional information on school library media center statistics may be obtained from Jeffrey Williams, Surveys and Cooperative Systems Group, National Center for Education Statistics, 320A, 555 New Jersey Ave. N.W., Washington, DC 20208-5652 (202-219-1362).

Surveys on Children, Young Adults

In spring 1994, under the sponsorship of the U.S. Department of Education's Library Programs Office, NCES conducted two fast-response surveys—one on public library services and resources for children and another on public library services and resources for young adults. These surveys updated similar surveys from 1989 and 1988, respectively. The two surveys collected data directly from two different representative samples of public libraries.

The Survey on Library Services and Resources for Children in Public Libraries included questions regarding the availability of specialized staff and resources for children and the adults who live and work with them, use of available services, prevalence of cooperative activities between public libraries and other organizations serving children, and barriers to providing increased library services for children.

The Survey on Library Services and Resources for Young Adults in Public Libraries obtained information on services for young adults, use of available services, cooperation between libraries and other organizations, ways in which libraries interact with schools, and factors perceived as barriers to increasing young adult services and their use. The data from the two surveys were consolidated into one report.

The following are highlights from the report *Services and Resources for Children and Young Adults in Public Libraries* (1995).

- Sixty percent of the 18 million people entering public libraries during a typical week in fall 1993 were youth—children and young adults.
- The percentage of libraries with children's and young adult librarians has not changed since the late 1980s. Thirty-nine percent of libraries employ a children's librarian, 11 percent have a young adult librarian, and 24 percent have a youth services library specialist on staff.
- Librarians report that ethnic diversity of children and young adult patrons has increased in over 40 percent of U.S. public libraries over the last five years. Seventy-six percent of public libraries currently have children's materials and 64 percent have young adult materials in languages other than English.
- Although computer technologies are among the most heavily used children's and young adult resources in public libraries, they are also among the most scarce. Only 30 percent of public libraries reported the availability of personal computers for use by children and young adults. However, 75 percent of libraries having this resource report moderate to heavy use by children, and 71 percent report moderate to heavy use by young adults.
- Less than half of all public libraries (40 percent) offer group programs for infants and toddlers. These programs are more prevalent now than in 1988, when only 29 percent of libraries offered group programs for infants to two-year-olds. Eighty-six percent of libraries offer group programs, such as story times, booktalks, puppetry, and crafts, for preschool and kindergarten age children; 79 percent of libraries offer group programs for school-age children.
- Seventy-six percent of public libraries report working with schools; 66 percent work with preschools and 56 percent with day care centers.
- While almost all libraries provide reference assistance, only about 1 in 7 libraries offer homework assistance programs for children or young adults. However, fairly large percentages of libraries with homework assistance programs report moderate to heavy use by children and young adults. Sixty-four percent report moderate to heavy use by children and 58 percent report moderate to heavy use by young adults.

- Librarians report that insufficient library staff is a leading barrier to increasing services and resources for both children and young adults. Sixty-five percent of librarians consider this a moderate or major barrier to increasing services for children, and 58 percent consider lack of staff a barrier to increasing services for young adults.

Additional information on these surveys may be obtained from Edith McArthur, National Center for Education Statistics, 402K, 555 New Jersey Ave. N.W., Washington, DC 20208-5652 (202-219-1442).

Federal Libraries and Information Centers Survey

The Federal Library Survey is designed to obtain data on the mission and function, administrative and managerial components (e.g., staff size and expenditures), information resources (e.g., collection size), and services of federal libraries and information centers. The Federal Library Survey is a cooperative effort between NCES and the staff of the Federal Library and Information Center Committee (FLICC) of the Library of Congress. The survey has established a nationwide profile of federal libraries and information centers. This survey has made available the first national data on federal libraries since 1978. NCES plans to conduct the survey every five years.

The survey was pretested in 1993 and 1994 and the full-scale survey conducted in 1995. Four data products resulted from this survey: an E.D. TABS with the 1994 data (released July 1996), the survey data base (released 1996), a directory of federal libraries and information centers (released August 1997), and a *Statistical Analysis Report: The Status of Federal Libraries and Information Centers in the United States: Results from the 1994 Federal Libraries and Information Centers Survey* (released February 1998). One highlight from this report is:

About 40 percent of responding federal libraries and information centers reported the general public among their users, and about 53 percent reported having services available to the general public.

Additional information on the Federal Libraries and Information Centers Survey may be obtained from Martha Hollins, Surveys and Cooperative Systems Group, National Center for Education Statistics, 315B, 555 New Jersey Ave. N.W., Washington, DC 20208-5652 (202-219-1462).

State Library Agency Survey

NCES conducted a new survey on state library agencies in FY 1995. Two data products were released on the Internet through the NCES Website: an E.D. TABS, with 28 tables for the 50 states and the District of Columbia (also available in print), and the survey data base (also available on diskette). The state library agency survey is a cooperative effort between NCES, COSLA, and NCLIS and is planned to be conducted annually. The following are highlights from *E.D. TABS State Library Agencies, Fiscal Year 1995*, released in August 1997.

Governance

- Virtually all state library agencies (48 states and the District of Columbia) are located in the executive branch of government. Of these, over 60 percent are part of a larger agency, the most common being the state department of education. In two states, Arizona and Michigan, the agency reports to the legislature.

Allied and Other Special Operations

- A total of 19 state library agencies reported having one or more allied operations. Allied operations most frequently linked with a state library agency are the state archives (10 states), the state records management service (11 states), and the state legislative reference/research service (nine states).
- Fourteen state agencies contract with libraries in their states to serve as resource or reference/information service centers. Seventeen state agencies operate a State Center for the Book[1].

Electronic Network Development

- In all 50 states, the state library agency plans or monitors electronic network development, 42 states operate such networks, and 46 states develop network content.
- State agencies also provide significant support to library access to the Internet. Almost all of them (49 states and the District of Columbia) are involved in facilitating library access to the Internet in one or more of the following ways: training library staff or consulting in the use of the Internet; providing a subsidy for Internet participation; providing equipment needed to access the Internet; managing gophers, file servers, bulletin boards, or listservs; or mounting directors, data bases, or online catalogs.

Library Development Services

Services to Public Libraries

- Every state library agency provides these types of services to public libraries: administration of LSCA (Library Services and Construction Act) grants; collection of library statistics; continuing education; and library planning, evaluation, and research.
- Services to public libraries provided by at least three-quarters of state agencies include: administration of state aid, consulting services, interli-

---

[1]The State Center for the Book is part of the Center for the Book program sponsored by the Library of Congress, which promotes books, reading, and literacy and is hosted or funded by the state.

brary loan referral services, library legislation preparation or review, literacy program support, public relations or promotional campaigns, reference referral services, state standards or guidelines, summer reading program support, and union list development.

- Services to public libraries provided by at least half of state agencies include Online Computer Library Center (OCLC) Group Access Capability and certification of librarians.

- Less common services to public libraries include: accreditation of libraries, cooperative purchasing of library materials, preservation/conservation services, and retrospective conversion of bibliographic records.

Services to Academic Libraries

- Over two-thirds of state library agencies report the following services to the academic sector: administering LSCA Title III grants, referring interlibrary loans, offering reference referral services, and developing union lists. Three-fifths of state agencies serve academic libraries through continuing education.

- Less common services to academic libraries provided by state agencies include: literacy program support, preservation/conservation, retrospective conversion, and standards or guidelines. No state agency accredits academic libraries or certifies academic librarians.

Services to School Library Media Centers

- Over two-thirds of state library agencies provide interlibrary loan referral services to school library media centers (LMCs) (table 4c). Services to LMCs provided by over half of state agencies include: administration of LSCA Title III grants, continuing education, reference referral, and union list development.

- Less common services to LMCs include: administration of state aid and cooperative purchasing of library materials. No state agency accredits LMCs or certifies librarians.

Services to Special Libraries

- At least two-thirds of state agencies serve special libraries through administration of LSCA grants, continuing education, interlibrary loan referral, and reference referral. Over half provide union list development and consulting services.

- Less common services to special libraries include administration of state aid, cooperative purchase of library materials, or summer reading program support. No state agency accredits special libraries or certifies special librarians.

Services to Systems

- Three-fifths of state agencies serve library systems through administration of LSCA grants, consulting services, continuing education, interlibrary loan referral services, library legislation preparation or review, reference referral, and library planning, evaluation, and research.
- Accreditation of systems is provided by only six states and certification of system librarians by only seven states.

Service Outlets

- State library agencies reported a total of 159 service outlets. Main or central outlets accounted for 34 percent, other outlets (excluding bookmobiles) made up 58.5 percent (with Kentucky and Washington reporting the largest number, at 21 each) and bookmobiles represented 7.5 percent of the total.

Collections

- The number of books and serial volumes held by state library agencies totaled 20.3 million, with New York accounting for the largest collection (2.3 million). Five state agencies had book and serial volumes of over one million. In other states, these collections ranged from 500,000 to 1 million (11 states), 200,000 to 499,999 (8 states), 100,000 to 199,999 (12 states), 50,000 to 99,999 (5 states) and less than 50,000 (10 states). The state library agency in Maryland does not maintain a collection, and the District of Columbia does not maintain a collection in its function as a state library agency.
- The number of serial subscriptions held by state library agencies totaled almost 80,000, with New York holding the largest number (over 14,000). Seventeen state agencies reported serial subscriptions of over 1,000. In other states, these collections ranged from 500 to 999 (17 states), 100 to 499 (13 states), and under 100 (3 states).

Staff

- The total number of budgeted full-time equivalent (FTE) positions in state library agencies was 3,602.2. Librarians with ALA-MLS degrees accounted for 1,158.3 of these positions, or 32.2 percent of total FTE positions. Rhode Island reported the largest percentage (57.1) of ALA-MLS librarians, and West Virginia reported the lowest (16.1 percent).

Income

- State library agencies reported a total income of $752.9 million in FY 1995 (82.1 percent came from state sources, 16.3 percent from federal, and 1.6 percent from other sources).
- Of state library agency income received from state sources, nearly $420 million (67.9 percent) was designated for state aid to libraries.

Massachusetts had the largest percentage of state library agency income set aside for state aid (96.6 percent). Eight states targeted no state funds for aid to libraries. The District of Columbia, Hawaii, Iowa, Louisiana, Nevada, South Dakota, Vermont, and Washington reported state income only for operation of the state agency[2].

Expenditures

- State library agencies reported total expenditures of over $725.2 million. The largest percentage (81.6 percent) came from state funds, followed by federal funds (17.1 percent), and other funds (1.3 percent).
- Three states shared the highest percentage of expenditures from state sources (92 percent). These states were Georgia (92 percent), Illinois (91.7 percent), and New York (91.8 percent). Louisiana had the lowest percentage of expenditures from state sources (45 percent), with 54.7 percent of its expenditures coming from federal sources.
- Sixty-nine percent of total state library expenditures were for aid to libraries, with the largest percentages expended on individual public libraries (49.6 percent) and public library systems (21.1 percent).
- Sixteen state library agencies reported expenditures on allied operations totaling $18.8 million—just under 3 percent (2.6 percent) of total expenditures by state library agencies. Among the state agencies reporting such expenditures, the highest was reported by Texas ($3.2 million) and the lowest by Georgia ($6,000)[3].
- Twenty-nine state library agencies reported a total of $20.6 million in grants and contracts expenditures to assist public libraries with state education reform initiatives or the National Education Goals. Almost three-quarters of the expenditures were used to promote adult literacy and lifelong learning, and over one- quarter to promote readiness for school. Of these state agencies, four (Minnesota, Nebraska, Pennsylvania, and Wisconsin) focused their grants and contracts expenditures exclusively on readiness-for-school projects, and five (Connecticut, Illinois, New Jersey, Oklahoma, and Texas) focused their expenditures exclusively on adult literacy and lifelong learning projects.

A study evaluating the new state library survey including the comparison of data with other sources is planned for release in 1998.

Additional information on the state library agency survey may be obtained from Elaine Kroe, Surveys and Cooperative Systems Group, National Center for

---

[2] The District of Columbia Public Library functions as a state library agency and is eligible for federal LSCA (Library Services and Construction Act) in this capacity. The state library agency in Hawaii is associated with the Hawaii State Public Library System and operates all public libraries within its jurisdiction. The state funds for aid to libraries for these two agencies are reported on the NCES Public Libraries Survey, rather than on the STLA survey, because of the unique situation of these two state agencies, and in order to eliminate duplicative reporting of these data.

[3] Alaska, Kansas, and Pennsylvania have allied operations, but the expenditures are not from the state library agency budget.

Education Statistics, 315A, 555 New Jersey Ave. N.W., Washington, DC 20208-5652 (202-219-1361).

Survey of Library Cooperatives

A new Survey of Library Cooperatives is moving forward in FY 1998 with completion targeted for FY 1998. It is expected to be conducted every five years. A working committee was formed and met in December 1995 to work on definitions, a universe file, and survey design. The committee also reviewed a preliminary list of existing library cooperatives, compiled by the bureau of the Census from several sources. In September 1997 the committee redesigned the survey based on pretest findings. Survey forms requesting FY 1997 data were mailed in January 1998. A report of the project will be available in July 1998.

Additional information on the Interlibrary Cooperation Survey may be obtained from Rosa Fernandez, Surveys and Cooperative Systems Group, National Center for Education Statistics, 317, 555 New Jersey Ave. N.W., Washington, DC 20208-5652 (202-219-1358).

Library Statistics Surveys—Plans

NCES plans to continue the Public Libraries Survey. Opportunities for expanded electronic data collection from states are now being offered in the survey. For example, 12 states submitted FY 1995 data via the Internet. Beginning with 1994 data, NCES has also implemented an early-release policy. On a weekly basis, data provided by states are released over the Internet as received by NCES. These are preliminary data and subject to revision until replaced by a final fully-edited data file.

NCES is continuing to sponsor its series of studies on data quality. In 1998 the Governments Division of the Bureau of the Census will complete a report on data collection processes and technology, the sixth in the series for public libraries. Data quality reports will also be completed for the School Library Media Centers, State Library Agencies, and Federal Libraries and Information Centers surveys.

Also in 1998, American Institutes for Research has initiated a review of the content and comparability of NCES's six library surveys. The resulting report will be a first step in assessing the potential for a more integrated approach to the library surveys, including determining the prospects for sharing and comparing information across surveys to address key policy issues.

For the first time, the Public Libraries Survey has imputed data for nonresponse beginning with FY 1995 data. NCES also plans to impute three to four years of earlier Public Libraries Survey data and release it on a CD-ROM in 1998. The CD-ROM will also include trend analysis on about 15 variables and software for customizing tabulations and peer comparisons.

In 1998 NCES and PLLI plan to publish "How Does Your Library Compare?" by Keri Bassman of Westat, Inc. This Statistics in Brief will categorize the almost 9,000 public libraries in the public libraries data set into peer groups based on size of population of the legal service area and total operating expenditures. These peer groups will control for variability in library size. Once libraries are assigned to peer groups based on these two variables, comparisons of service performance will be made.

NCES has also fostered the use and analysis of FSCS data. A Data Use Subcommittee of the FSCS Steering Committee has been addressing the dissemination, use, and analysis of FSCS data.

Several analytical projects are currently under way. NCES has sponsored a project through the American Institutes for Research that has developed indices on inflation for public libraries, a cost index, and a price index. A report of the project will be available in 1998. NCES has been exploring the potential of geographic mapping for public libraries. In September 1996 NCES sponsored a two-year project through Westat, Inc. to develop the capability to link census demographic data with Public Libraries Survey data through geographic mapping software.

Work is under way to geocode public library service outlets nationwide and map and digitize the boundaries of the almost 9,000 public library legal service area jurisdictions, so that they can be matched to Census Tiger files and to Public Libraries Survey data files. The project will also produce a public use data file linking Public Libraries Survey data with key census demographic variables and a user's guide. A technical report will describe the methods of geocoding and public library mapping.

A fast-response survey on the topic of public library programming for adults, including adults at risk, is under way. Westat, Inc. is conducting the survey. NCES, PLLI, and the National Library of Education are supporting and/or working on this project.

NCES also plans to include some library-oriented questions on their new Early Childhood Longitudinal Study. Questions are being field tested in 1997. Data collection is scheduled for 1998 and 1999, with data release scheduled for 2000.

Data dissemination for the library surveys has also been broadened with electronic release of both current and back years data and E.D. TABS on the Internet. In addition an information service called the National Education Data Resource Center (NEDRC) has been set up. The NEDRC helps customers obtain reports and data files and also responds to requests for tabulations on library and other NCES studies and surveys. (See below for ways to contact the NEDRC.)

The collection of academic library data through IPEDS will also be continued. NCES plans to improve the quality of the data by promoting the use of IDEALS software for data collection.

NCES will continue school library data collection. Surveys are planned for once every five years, with the next survey planned for 1999–2000.

The Library Statistics Program also sponsors activities that cut across all types of libraries. For example, in 1993 NCES sponsored an invitational forum on policy analysis using library data from all types of libraries. The 1994 forum focused on electronic technology. The 1995 forum topic was "Changes in Library and Information Services in the Next Five Years." The fourth forum topic was "Impact of Information Technology and Special Programming on Library Services to Special Populations." The fifth forum covered national data needs for the new Library Services and Technology Act. Beginning in 1993 and 1994 NCES has also sponsored the attendance of librarians from all sectors at NCES training opportunities, including the semiannual Cooperative System Fellows Program. NCES is also considering developing an expanded cooperative that would better integrate the six library surveys and expand participation to add local practitioners, experts from allied professions such as publishing and technology, more data users, and possibly the media. The advantage of such a cooperative would be the opportunity to focus on crosscutting policy issues. There would also be opportunities to identify unnecessary duplication, gaps, and encourage participation by diverse groups and all levels of government.

Dissemination of Statistics, Reports, and Data

Under its six library surveys, NCES regularly publishes E.D. TABS, which consist of tables, usually presenting state and national totals, a survey description, and data highlights. NCES has also published separate, more in-depth studies analyzing library data. Many of these publications are available in printed format and over the Internet. Edited raw data from the library surveys are made available on data diskettes, CD-ROMs, and also over the Internet.

Publications

Public Libraries in Forty-Four States and the District of Columbia: 1988; An NCES Working Paper (November 1989). o.p.

E.D. TABS: Academic Libraries: 1988 (September 1990). o.p.

E.D. TABS: Public Libraries in Fifty States and the District of Columbia: 1989 (April 1991). o.p.

E.D. TABS: Public Libraries in the U.S.: 1990 (June 1992). o.p.

E.D. TABS: Academic Libraries: 1990 (December 1992). Government Printing Office No., 065-000-00549-2. o.p.

Survey Report: School Library Media Centers in the United States: 1990–91 (November 1994). Government Printing Office, No. 065-000-00715-1. o.p.

E.D. TABS: Public Libraries in the United States: 1991 (April 1993). Government Printing Office, No. 065-000-00561-1. o.p.

E.D. TABS: Public Libraries in the United States: 1992 (August 1994). Government Printing Office, No. 065-000-00670-7. o.p.

E.D. TABS: Academic Libraries: 1992 (November 1994). Government Printing Office, No. 065-000-00717-7. $3.75

Data Comparability and Public Policy: New Interest in Public Library Data; papers presented at Meetings of the American Statistical Association. Working Paper No. 94-07. National Center for Education Statistics, November 1994.

Report on Coverage Evaluation of the Public Library Statistics Program (June 1994). Prepared for the National Center for Education Statistics by the Governments Division, Bureau of the Census. Government Printing Office, No. 065-00-00662-6. o.p.

Finance Data in the Public Library Statistics Program: Definitions, Internal Consistency, and Comparisons to Secondary Sources (1995). Prepared for NCES by the Governments Division, Bureau of the Census. Government Printing Office, No 065-000-00794-9. o.p.

Report on Evaluation of Definitions Used in the Public Library Statistics Program (1995). Prepared for the National Center for Education Statistics by the Governments Division, Bureau of the Census. Government Printing Office, No. 065-000-00736-3. o.p.

Staffing Data in the Public Library Statistics program: Definitions, Internal Consistency, and Comparisons to Secondary Sources (1995). Prepared for NCES by the Governments Division, Bureau of the Census. Government Printing Office, No. 065-000-00795-9. o.p.

Statistical Analysis Report: Services and Resources for Children and Young Adults in Public Libraries (August 1995). Prepared for NCES by Westat, Inc. Government Printing Office, No. 065-000-00797-5. $9.

E.D. TABS: Public Libraries in the United States: 1993 (September 1995). Government Printing Office, No. 065-000-00800-9. $8.

Public Library Structure and Organization in the United States. NCES No. 96-229 (March 1996).

E.D. TABS: State Library Agencies, Fiscal Year 1994 (June 1996). Government Printing Office No. 065-000-00878-5. $12.

E.D. TABS: Federal Libraries and Information Centers in the United States: 1994 (July 1996).

Statistics in Brief: Use of Public Library Services by Households in the United States: 1996 (March 1997). Government Printing Office.

E.D. TABS: Public Libraries in the United States: FY 1994 (May 1997). Government Printing Office.

The Status of Academic Libraries in the United States; Results form the 1990 and 1992 Academic Library Surveys (June 1997). Prepared for NCES by American Institutes for Research.

E.D. TABS: State Library Agencies Fiscal Year 1995 (August 1997). Government Printing Office, No. 065-000-010510-8. $14.

Technical Report: Directory of Federal Libraries and Information Centers: 1994 (August 1997). Government Printing Office.

Statistical Analysis Report: Distance Education in Higher Education Institutions (October 1997). Prepared for NCES by Westat, Inc. Government Printing Office.

Statistical Analysis Report: The Status of Federal Libraries and Information Centers in the United States: Results from the 1994 Federal Libraries and Information Centers Survey (February 1988). Government Printing Office.

E.D. TABS: Academic Libraries: 1994 (March 1998). Government Printing Office.

Data Files Released on Computer Diskette

Public Libraries in Forty-Four States and the District of Columbia: 1988 (March 1990).

Public Libraries in Fifty States and the District of Columbia: 1989 (May 1990).

Academic Libraries: 1988 (October 1990).

Public Libraries Data, 1990 (July 1992).

Academic Libraries: 1990 (February 1993).

The NCES data files above are generally available on computer diskette through the U.S. Department of Education, Office of Educational Research and Improvement, National Library of Education, 555 New Jersey Ave. N.W., Washington, DC 20208-5725.

Public Library Data 1992 (September 1994). Government Printing Office, No. 065-000-00675-8.

Academic Libraries: 1992 (November 1994). Available through the NEDRC.

Public Library Data FY 1993 on Disk (July 1995). Government Printing Office, No. 065-000-00790-8. $17.

State Library Agencies Data, FY 1994 on Disk (May 1996).

Public Libraries Data FY 1994 (June 1997). Government Printing Office, No. 065-000-01043-7. $17.

National Household Education Survey; 1991, 1993, 1995, and 1996 Surveys Data Files and Electronic Codebook (July 1997).

State Library Agencies Data, FY 1995 on Disk (September 1997).

The NCES data files above are generally available through the Government Printing Office. Upon request, the National Education Data Resource Center (NEDRC) will provide the data files and some publications free of charge. The NEDRC also responds to requests for tabulations on NCES studies and surveys. (See below for ways to contact the NEDRC.)

Electronic Releases of Publications and Data Files

Many NCES products are also available on the Internet.

To reach the NCES Web site, where you can view or download publications and data files, type the URL address http://nces.ed.gov/pubsearch.

For more information about obtaining NCES reports and data files through the Internet, GPO or the NEDRC, or for special tabulations, contact the NEDRC, 1900 N. Beauregard Street, Suite 200, Alexandria, VA 22311-1722, telephone 703-845-3151, fax 703-820-7465, e-mail nedrc@pcci.com.

Library of Congress

Washington, DC 20540
202-707-5000, World Wide Web: http://www.loc.gov

Audrey Fischer
Writer-Editor, Library of Congress

The Library of Congress was established in 1800 to serve the research needs of the U.S. Congress. For nearly two centuries the library has grown both in the size of its collections (now totaling more than 113 million items) and in its mission. As the largest library in the world and the oldest federal cultural institution in the nation, the Library of Congress serves not only Congress but also government agencies, libraries around the world, and scholars and ordinary citizens in the United States and abroad. At the forefront of technology, the library now serves patrons on-site in its 22 reading rooms and at remote locations through its highly acclaimed World Wide Web site on the Internet.

The Thomas Jefferson Building reopened to the public on May 1, 1997, after more than a decade of renovation. A public "Festival of Cultures" was held on May 4 to showcase the building and to unveil *American Treasures of the Library of Congress*, a permanent exhibition. On November 4 the library celebrated the centennial of the Thomas Jefferson Building with a commemorative postal cancellation and the lighting of the gilded Torch of Learning (cast from the original) that crowns the Jefferson Building's dome. At year's end, plans to celebrate the library's bicentennial in the year 2000 were well under way, with the appointment of a steering committee, a legislative effort to create a commemorative coin, and the adoption of a theme—"Libraries•Creativity•Liberty"—and a goal—to inspire creativity in the century ahead by stimulating greater use of libraries everywhere.

The library developed a strategic plan (1997–2004) that identifies the mission, priorities, values, and objectives to take the library into the 21st century. A newly established Planning, Management, and Evaluation Directorate (PMED) has begun to implement the plan and synchronize the planning and budgeting processes. The development of a strategic plan and establishment of PMED fulfilled two critical tasks contained in the library's Management Improvement Plan. Management improvement efforts during recent years were rewarded with an unqualified "clean" audit opinion on the library's "Fiscal 1996 Consolidated Financial Statements" by KPMG Peat Marwick.

In fiscal year (FY) 1997 (October 1, 1996–September 30, 1997) the library operated with a budget of $361,896,000, an increase of $9,497,000, or 2.6 percent, over FY 1996, including authority to spend $30,295,000 in copyright receipts and cataloging data sales.

Service to Congress

Serving Congress is the library's highest priority. In 1997 the Congressional Research Service (CRS) delivered approximately 530,000 research responses to members and committees of Congress. A new, networked, automated Inquiry Status and Information System is used to track these requests. CRS staff supplied timely, objective analysis for Congress during a busy legislative year marked by complex reform proposals in many fields, notably welfare, health care, and education, and efforts to reach a balanced-budget agreement.

Working with the Committee on House Oversight and the Senate Committee on Rules and Administration and in consultation with the House and Senate subcommittees on legislative branch appropriations, the library developed a plan for a single integrated Legislative Information System (LIS) to serve Congress. Delivered to Congress on January 7, 1997, the first phase of the new LIS provides information to Congress on current legislation, floor action, amendments, the full text of the *Congressional Record* and the *Congressional Record Index*, committee reports on bills for recent Congresses, summaries of legislation, CRS Issue Briefs, and links to House and Senate information.

Sharing of electronic resources enhanced the comprehensiveness and timeliness of CRS support for Congress. The CRS home page on the World Wide Web, available 24 hours a day, provided members of Congress and their staff with access to legislative information; the CRS Guide to the Legislative Process, the full text of CRS online products; guides to Internet resources by topic; and the CRS Legislative Alert, a list of selected CRS products that focus on legislative issues expected to receive floor action in Congress (this is also faxed weekly to all member offices).

Other direct assistance to Congress was provided by the Law Library, which answered nearly 4,500 reference requests from congressional users. Law Library research staff produced 902 written reports for Congress, including comprehensive multinational studies on such issues as legislative ethics, human cloning, and telecommunications laws.

Service to the Nation

The library reduced the total unprocessed arrearage by more than one million items while keeping current with new receipts. This represented a cumulative reduction of about 50 percent—39.9 million to 19.9 million—since the initial arrearage census in September 1989.

Linked to the library's arrearage reduction effort was the development of a secondary storage site to house processed materials and to provide for growth of the collection through the early years of the 21st century. During the year the library worked closely with the Architect of the Capitol to ensure that the first storage module at the Fort Meade, Maryland, campus meets environmental specifications and is ready for occupancy by the end of FY 1999. On November 13, 1997, Congress passed a bill (H.R. 2979) authorizing the Architect of the Capitol, on behalf of the Library of Congress, to acquire a 140,078-square-foot building in Culpeper, Virginia, for the storage and preservation of audiovisual materials. The David and Lucile Packard Foundation agreed in principle to provide the funds for the acquisition of the property.

Powerful new PC-based terminals enabled cataloging staff to catalog more efficiently through enhanced automation capabilities. Processing of print materials continued at record-high levels as staff created cataloging records for 289,154 volumes. Building on the momentum generated in FY 1996 through the Program for Cooperative Cataloging, member libraries reached a high of 239 participants and contributed record-breaking totals in FY 1997: 57,446 bibliographic records (29,907 for monographs and 27,539 for serials); 137,494 name authorities; 9,364 series authorities; 2,088 subject authorities; and 685 classification numbers. On November 4 the library's Cataloging Directorate celebrated the 20th anniversary of the Name Authority Cooperative (NACO) Program, which has produced more than one million authority records since 1977.

The National Library Service for the Blind and Physically Handicapped (NLS/BPH) distributed more than 23 million items to some 777,000 readers in 1997. Outreach to Native Americans continued to be a priority area for NLS/BPH, along with adding more Native American literature to the collection.

Copyright

The Copyright Office received nearly 630,000 claims and made some 570,000 registrations in 1997. Through its Web site, the Copyright Office disseminated public information and provided electronic access to its registration and recordation databases. In August the Copyright Office delivered two comprehensive reports to Congress in the areas of cable and satellite compulsory licensing and intellectual-property protection for databases. In November Congress passed legislation that would give the Copyright Office greater discretion in setting fees for its services, subject to congressional approval.

Electronic Access

The library continued to provide Congress and the nation with a growing amount of information through its Internet-based systems. As a result, use of the library's public electronic systems grew exponentially. Having tripled between 1992 and 1996, the average number of monthly transactions doubled to 40 million during FY 1997. In October 1997 the library logged a record 56 million transactions.

The library's Internet-based systems were cited for excellence several times in 1997.

- A February 16, 1997, *New York Times* article recommended the Library of Congress Web site as an "Internet Hit."
- *PC Magazine* rated both the American Memory online historical collections and the THOMAS congressional database in its Top-100 list, making the cut for the fifth time since July 1996.
- American Memory was selected by Britannica as one the Top-40 Web sites.
- The library's Web site was given the Lycos Top 5 Percent of the Internet Award.
- The National Information Infrastructure (NII) Awards Program chose the library's Web site as one of the six finalists in the education category.

- Magellan Internet Guide gave American Memory a four-star review.
- American Memory was awarded five stars by the Net Guide Best of the Web.
- The History Channel On-line included American Memory among its recommended history Web sites.
- The Learning Page and the online *Handbook of Latin American Studies* received notice in the *Scout Report.*

Advancements made in 1997 to increase electronic access to the library's resources included the National Digital Library Program, THOMAS, geographic information systems, the Global Legal Information Network, and several technology projects in test status.

National Digital Library Program

During 1997 the library gained momentum toward its ambitious goal of digitizing millions of items by the year 2000, the library's 200th anniversary. To support the effort, more than $28 million in cash and pledges was raised from the private sector while Congress continued to honor its multiyear pledge to contribute $15 million in appropriated funds toward this major library initiative.

As of September 30, 1997, more than 400,000 digital files were available online or in digital archives. In addition, three million digital files from both the library's collections and other repositories are now in various stages of production as part of a national collaborative effort. This includes more than 100,000 items as a result of the LC/Ameritech National Digital Library Competition. In the first year of the multiyear competition, made possible by a $2 million gift from the Ameritech Foundation, the library awarded ten institutions more than $500,000 to digitize unique American history collections and make them available on the library's American Memory Web site.

During 1997 ten new multimedia American history collections were added to the library's Web site. Added at year's end, *Words and Deeds in American History* celebrates the Manuscript Division's first 100 years. Three new library exhibitions were made available online, including the *American Treasures of the Library of Congress* exhibition, which will be updated periodically to reflect the rotation of items through this permanent exhibition. On April 1 the *Today in History* service was added and soon became one of the more popular features on the library's Web site. For each day of the year, a notable event that took place on that day is featured with a small essay, illustrated by documents from the American Memory collections.

The National Digital Library effort continued to reach out to the education community. The pilot American Memory Fellows Program, funded by the Kellogg Foundation, enabled 25 teams of K–12 humanities teachers and school media specialists from across the country to learn about electronic primary sources and to create exemplary teaching units that can be shared online with other educators.

THOMAS

Named in honor of Thomas Jefferson, THOMAS is a public database designed to make legislative information more accessible to the public. THOMAS is available 24 hours a day, free of charge to Internet users. Use of the THOMAS increased nearly fourfold in 1997—from 2.6 million to more than 10 million monthly transactions. As of December 31, 1997, more than 136 million transactions had been processed by the THOMAS system since its inception on January 5, 1995. A redesigned home page, upgraded search engine (InQuery 4.0), and addition of such files as the Bill Digest dating back to the 93rd Congress all contributed to the system's enormous popularity.

Geographic Information Systems

The Geography and Map Division (G&M) is a leader in the cartographic and geographic communities through its work in geographic information systems (GIS). Working closely with private-sector partners, G&M put into production the capability to create large-format digital images and the ability to transmit and display these images through the Internet. In 1997 a collection of more than 450 panoramic maps (1,700 images) of 19th-century American cities was released worldwide, inaugurating a new chapter in the library's efforts to make its collections available to a broader audience.

Global Legal Information Network

The Global Legal Information Network (GLIN) is a cooperative international network in which member nations contribute the full text of statutes and regulations to a database hosted by the Law Library of Congress. The library demonstrated a new input/update system to the Fourth Annual GLIN Project Directors Meeting in August 1997 and is testing the new GLIN software release prior to the production phase. The library also began requirements analysis for conversion of existing abstract data into a new format required for production release of the system. There are 11 members currently participating via the Internet, with GLIN membership projected to increase to 15–20 nations in the near future.

Technology Projects in Test Status

Congress approved the library's FY 1998 budget request for an Integrated Library System (ILS) to improve automation support for bibliographic control and inventory management activities at the library. The ILS project will implement a single system that uses a shared bibliographic database to integrate all major Library Services functional areas, such as acquisitions, cataloging, serials management, circulation, inventory control, and reference. A project team has been assembled and is proceeding with the procurement of the system and implementation planning. A formal source selection process is under way for the procurement. Following congressional review, the selection of a commercially available system was scheduled for the spring of 1998.

The Copyright Office Electronic Registration, Recordation and Deposit System (CORDS), a major new pilot system for digital registration and deposit of copyrighted works over the Internet, uses the latest advances in networking and computer technology. It is being developed by the Copyright Office in collaboration with national high-technology research and development partners (Advanced Research Projects Agency and the Corporation for National Research Initiatives). CORDS will eventually streamline the copyright registration, recordation, and deposit processes, as well as provide the Library of Congress with copies of new copyrighted works in digital format for its National Digital Library repository. Two new external test sites were opened in 1997 at Stanford University and the Massachusetts Institute of Technology Press to continue developing, testing, and enhancing the basic CORDS production system.

The Electronic Cataloging in Publication (ECIP) project is enabling the library to obtain texts of forthcoming publications from publishers via the Internet, catalog them entirely in an electronic environment, and transmit the completed catalog records via e-mail to the publisher for inclusion on the copyright page of the printed book. Sixty-four publishers are now participating in this project. Staff cataloged 1,076 titles last year, bringing the cumulative total since the experiment's inception to 2,158 titles.

Collections

The library receives millions of pieces each year, from copyright deposits, federal agencies, purchases, exchanges, and gifts. Notable acquisitions during 1997 included:

- Supreme Court Justice Harry A. Blackmun's donation of his substantial collection of personal papers to the library, which will shed light on the evolution of modern constitutional history
- The addition of 1,200 drawings and illustrations and 15,000 items from the personal papers of cartoonist and dramatist Jules Feiffer
- Eight vintage silver gelatin prints of the end of World War II by Soviet photojournalist Yevgeny Khaldei
- A rare poster, Ben Shahn's "For Full Employment After the War"
- Eight Beaux Arts drawings and one print by Napoléon Le Brun, including those of two of the earliest American skyscrapers
- Papers and theatrical designs of Peggy Clark, one of the foremost lighting designers in the American theater
- Material additions to the Ned Rorem Collection: nearly 75,000 items— manuscript and printed music, diaries, essays, etc.—devoted to one of this generation's most celebrated musicians
- Important additions to the papers of lyric poet and biographer Muriel Rukeyser
- Approximately 1,200 radio transcription discs donated by the University of California at Los Angeles Film and Television Archive, including extremely rare radio recordings of Ed Wynn broadcasts from 1934

- A 1825–1903 collection of manuscript maps, pencil sketches, and field notes representing Gustavus Sohon's work as a cartographer and artist on the Pacific Railroad and the Mull Road surveys in the Pacific Northwest
- A splendid 1745 edition of *Horace*, owned by Thomas Jefferson, who annotated the inside cover with the meter scheme of each poem

Publications

The Publishing Office produced more than 40 books, calendars, CD-ROMs, and other products describing and illustrating the library's collections. Four new co-publishing agreements were signed with major trade and university presses, and 22 cooperative agreements were in effect with such publishers as Harry N. Abrams, Alfred A. Knopf, W. W. Norton & Co., University Press of New England, Yale University Press, Pomegranate Artbooks, and Fulcrum Publishing; several others were in various stages of development or negotiation.

Highlights of these copublishing programs were the release of *American Treasures in the Library of Congress: Memory/Reason/Imagination*, published by Harry N. Abrams; *Eyes of the Nation*, published by Alfred A. Knopf; and *The Library of Congress: The Art and Architecture of the Thomas Jefferson Building*, published by W. W. Norton & Co. *American Treasures in the Library of Congress* was a Book-of-the-Month Club alternate selection for May 1997. *Eyes of the Nation* was selected by the Book-of-the-Month Club and the History Book Club.

The Publishing Office won two Washington Book Publishers Design Effectiveness Awards for excellence in illustrated books. The two award winners were *Many Nations: A Library of Congress Resource Guide for the Study of Indian and Alaska Native Peoples of the United States* and *Heart of the Circle: Photographs by Edward S. Curtis of Native American Women. The Work of Charles and Ray Eames: A Legacy of Invention* was a main selection of the Architects and Designs Book Service and received a distinguished-achievement award from the American Institute of Architects. *Dresden: Treasures From the Saxon State Library* was chosen by the American Institute of Graphic Arts for their AIGA 50 Excellence in Design show.

Exhibitions and Literary Events

The library's collections were shared with tens of thousands of Americans through exhibitions, special events, symposia, and traveling exhibitions. The major 1997 exhibition was *American Treasures of the Library of Congress*, which opened in May as a permanent installation of library treasures relating America's past, including a rotating display of "Top Treasures."

Other exhibitions included *Hong Kong: From Fishing Village to Financial Center* (May 22–November 22, 1997); *Let There Be Light: William Tyndale and the Making of the English Bible* (June 4–September 6); and *For European Recovery: The Fiftieth Anniversary of the Marshall Plan* (June 2–August 30). *The Work of Charles and Ray Eames: A Legacy of Invention*, opened in September at the Vitra Design Museum in Weil am Rhein, Germany, its first

European venue. The *Eames* exhibition will open at the Library of Congress, its first U.S. venue, in May 1999. A special exhibition, *The Thomas Jefferson Building: Book Palace of the American People* (November 4, 1997–April 30, 1998), commemorated the centennial of the library's Thomas Jefferson Building, which first opened on November 1, 1897.

The library's traveling-exhibition program sent eight exhibitions to 23 sites in 16 states. Traveling exhibitions included *The Work of Charles and Ray Eames: A Legacy of Invention*; *From the Ends of the Earth: Judaic Treasures from the Library of Congress*; *Women Come to the Front: Journalists, Photographers, and Broadcasters During World War II*; and *The Cultural Landscape of the Plantation*.

Robert Pinsky of Boston University was appointed the library's ninth poet laureate consultant for the 1997–1998 term.

The fifth Joanna Jackson Goldman Memorial Lecture on American Civilization and Government was presented by author Richard Reeves on April 10. The title of his lecture was "Journalism: New, Old, or Dead."

Under the terms of the National Film Preservation Act, each year the Librarian of Congress names 25 "culturally, historically, or aesthetically" significant motion pictures to the National Film Registry. Each list serves to increase awareness of the richness of American cinema and the need for its preservation.

The following 25 films were named to the National Film Registry in 1997, bringing the total to 225:

Ben Hur (1926)
The Big Sleep (1946)
The Bridge on the River Kwai (1957)
Cops (1922)
Czechoslovakia 1968 (1968)
Grass (1925)
The Great Dictator (1940)
Harold and Maude (1972)
Hindenburg Disaster Newsreel Footage (1937)
How the West Was Won (1962)
The Hustler (1961)
Knute Rockne, All American (1940)
The Life and Death of 9413—A Hollywood Extra (1928)
The Little Fugitive (1953)
Mean Streets (1973)
Motion Painting No. 1 (1947)
The Music Box (1932)
The Naked Spur (1953)
Rear Window (1954)
Republic Steel Strike Riots Newsreel Footage (1937)
Return of the Secaucus 7 (1980)
The Thin Man (1934)
Tulips Shall Grow (1942)
West Side Story (1961)
Wings (1927)

Security

A centralized security office was established and the library's first Director of Security was appointed in February 1997. Several hundred of the recommendations of the comprehensive physical-security survey of the library and its collections, conducted by Computer Sciences Corporation, were implemented. Many of these involved additional key and lock controls, closed-circuit surveillance and intrusion detection systems, and access control measures for areas housing collections. The highlight of the library's security efforts during the year was the development of a comprehensive security plan that provides a framework for the physical security of the library's collections, facilities, staff, visitors, and other assets. The library also developed a computer security plan for safeguarding the library's valuable electronic resources and computer systems and a "year 2000" plan to ensure that these systems will function properly at the turn of the century.

Other security accomplishments during the year included:

- Completion of access control and internal-security measures for the reopened and renovated Jefferson Building
- Installation of extensive high-technology physical and electronic security measures for the *American Treasures of the Library of Congress* exhibition
- Completion of a vulnerability assessment of the library buildings' exterior and parking facilities
- Installation or upgrading of surveillance systems in nine reading rooms
- Expansion of the reader registration system to reading rooms in the Adams and Jefferson buildings
- Modification of the library's interim inventory control database (the Collections Control Facility) to permit retention of information on mutilated collections items
- Provision of increased physical security of collections storage areas through installation of electronic access control systems to the Main Control Room in the Jefferson Building
- Completion of an inventory of several collections in the custody of the Rare Book and Special Collections Division

Preservation

The library took action during 1997 to improve the preservation of its vast and diverse collections by

- Developing a strategy for unified preservation of audio and video collections in digital and analog formats
- Completing the mass deacidification treatment of 67,000 additional books from the general and special collections using the Bookkeeper limited-production contract and obtaining congressional approval of a plan that

will make deacidification a permanent preservation activity and enable the library to deacidify many more books in the next four years

- Implementing the emergency response plan by planning for advance contracting in the event of a disaster, initiating risk assessments in collections storage areas, training library staff, refining emergency notification and communication systems, and replenishing response and recovery supplies
- Producing protective enclosures using the computer-driven, automated box-making machine
- Increasing labeling output by using an improved automation program and transferring labeling duties to the technicians in the Cataloging Directorate
- Completing the microfilming of telephone directories from as early as 1884 through 1987
- Contributing to the National Digital Library Program by training staff and contractors in the proper handling of materials during preparation and scanning

Restoration and Renovation

The library continued to execute its multiyear plan to outfit and occupy the remaining renovated spaces of the Thomas Jefferson and Adams buildings. The library officially opened the Thomas Jefferson Building to the public on May 1, 1997, after more than a decade of renovation. The renovated spaces include the African and Middle Eastern, Asian, European, Hispanic, Main, and Rare Book and Special Collection reading rooms, a new Visitors' Center, and permanent exhibition space. The Coolidge Auditorium reopened on October 29 with a performance by the Juilliard String Quartet, now in its 35th season as the library's resident chamber music group.

Human Resources

The trend toward a reduced staff continued, with 4,070 permanent library employees on board during 1997. The library enhanced the efficiency of its merit selection system by reducing the average time required to fill positions by 35 percent—from 168 days to 110 workdays over comparable ten-month periods in calendar years 1996 and 1997. The library also implemented key provisions of the *Cook* class action settlement agreement, including back-pay awards, promotions, and reassignments. A three-day facilitative leadership training program strengthened the management skills and abilities of all library managers and supervisors, and the library established, as a part of the Office of the Librarian, an Internal University office to coordinate and enrich library-wide training and development efforts and activities. The library also continued to provide diversity awareness training to staff. In August four Hispanic Association of Colleges and Universities (HACU) interns completed the National Internship Program, now in its second year. The program provides college students an opportunity to serve as interns for a ten-week summer program at the library.

Additional Sources of Information

Library of Congress telephone numbers for public information:

Main switchboard (with menu)	202-707-5000
Reading room hours and locations	202-707-6400
General reference	202-707-5522
	202-707-4210 TTY
Visitor information	202-707-8000
	202-707-6200 TTY
Exhibition hours	202-707-4604
Research advice	202-707-6500
Sales shop	202-707-0204
Copyright information	202-707-3000
Copyright hotline (to order forms)	202-707-9100

Center for the Book

John Y. Cole
Director, The Center for the Book
Library of Congress

With its network of 34 affiliated state centers and more than 50 national and civic organizations serving as reading-promotion partners, the Center for the Book is one of the Library of Congress's most dynamic and visible educational outreach programs. Since 1977, when it was established by Librarian of Congress Daniel J. Boorstin, the center has used the prestige and resources of the Library of Congress (LC) to stimulate public interest in books, reading, libraries, and literacy and to encourage the study of books and the printed word.

The center is a successful public-private partnership. The Library of Congress supports its four full-time positions, but the center's projects, events, and publications are funded primarily through contributions from individuals, corporations, foundations, and government organizations.

Highlights of 1997

- The addition of four new states—Connecticut, Georgia, Maine, and Maryland—to the center's national network of state affiliates
- The presentation to the Florida and Nebraska state centers of the first two Boorstin Center for the Book Awards
- With help from Tara Holland, Miss America 1997, the launching of "Building a Nation of Readers," the center's national reading-promotion theme for the years 1997–2000
- Sponsorship of "Library: The Drama Within," a photography exhibit on display at the Library of Congress from March through May 1997, and the acquisition of the 26 exhibition photographs for LC collections
- The expansion of the center's home page on the LC Web site
- Publication of *Even Anchors Need Lifelines: Public Libraries in Adult Literacy,* by Gail Spangenberg; *Readers and Libraries: Toward a History of Libraries and Culture,* by Kenneth E. Carpenter; and, with Milkweed Editions of Minneapolis, *The Most Wonderful Books: Writers on Discovering the Pleasures of Reading,* edited by Michael Dorris and Emilie Buchwald
- Sponsorship of more than 30 programs and events, including lectures and symposia, that promote books, reading, and libraries

Themes

The Center for the Book establishes national reading-promotion themes to stimulate interest and support for reading and literacy projects that benefit all age groups. Used by state centers, national organizational partners, and hundreds of schools and libraries across the nation, each theme reminds Americans of the importance of books, reading, and libraries in today's world. In 1997 "Building a Nation of Readers" was inaugurated as the center's national reading-promotion theme through the year 2000. It was chosen to reinforce "Libraries-Creativity-Liberty," the theme of the Library of Congress's bicentennial commemoration in 2000. A six-page brochure was published describing how individuals, families, schools, libraries, civic and educational organizations, and businesses can participate in "Building a Nation of Readers."

Reading-Promotion Partners

The center's partnership program includes more than 50 civic, educational, and governmental organizations that work with the center to promote books, reading, libraries, and literacy. On March 21, 1997, more than 40 organizations met to discuss ideas about using the center's "Building a Nation of Readers" theme. On September 21 the center and Friends of Library U.S.A. staged a "readathon" using this theme at the New York Is Book Country book fair in New York City. The center's partnership with the American Institute of Graphic Arts continued with cosponsorship of the AIGA exhibit "50 Books/50 Covers" during the New York Is Book Country fair and with a lecture series at the Library of Congress.

State Centers

When James H. Billington became Librarian of Congress in 1987, the Center for the Book had ten affiliated state centers; at the end of 1997 there were 34. The newest state centers are in Connecticut, located at Hartford Public Library; Georgia, based at the DeKalb County Library; Maine, at the Maine Humanities Council in Portland; and Maryland, at the Howard County Library in Columbia.

Each state center works with the Library of Congress to promote books, reading, and libraries as well as the state's own literary and intellectual heritage. Each also develops and funds its own operations and projects, using LC reading-promotion themes when appropriate and occasionally hosting LC-sponsored events and traveling exhibits. When its application is approved, a state center is granted affiliate status for three years. Renewals are for three-year periods.

On May 6, 1997, representatives from 29 state centers participated in an idea-sharing session at the Library of Congress. They discussed such topics as state center staffing, advisory boards, fund-raising, Internet sites, and programming. The meeting highlight was the presentation of the first two Boorstin Center for the Book Awards by Librarian of Congress Emeritus Daniel J. Boorstin. Each of these annual awards includes a cash prize of $5,000. The National Award, won by Florida, the first state center (1984), recognizes the contribution a state center has made to the Center for the Book's overall program and objectives. The State Award, won by Nebraska, recognizes a specific project—in this instance, the Nebraska Literature Festival.

In 1997 the "Bonfire of Liberties: Censorship of the Humanities" traveling exhibit was seen in Washington, Wyoming, and Montana.

Projects

The literary, historical, and environmental heritage of U.S. rivers will be examined and celebrated in the four-year "Rivers of America" educational initiative launched in 1997. Aimed primarily at the general public, teachers, and students, the project was launched on April 9–10, 1997, when the center, in cooperation with LC's American Folklife Center, celebrated the 60th anniversary of the *Rivers of America* (1937–1974) book series.

Also in cooperation with the American Folklife Center, the Center for the Book continued to represent the Library of Congress in the "Montana Heritage" project, a community-based oral history project for high school students in small Montana towns.

In 1997 the center successfully concluded the "Library-Head Start-Museum" partnership project, funded since 1992 by Head Start to develop cooperative, community-level projects to promote reading and family literacy. It also received a three-year grant from the Viburnum Foundation to help promote library-sponsored family literacy programs in rural areas.

Outreach

The center's Web site (http://lcweb.loc.gov/loc/cfbook/) continued to expand during 1997. Established and maintained by program officer Maurvene D. Williams, the Web site includes an overview of the center's development, history, projects, and publications; a calendar of current and forthcoming events; press releases; information about state centers and organizational partners, with home page links when available; information about book arts and book-history programs and organizations; and a current calendar of book- and reading-promotion events throughout the United States.

In 1997 the center prepared 14 reading lists for the Library of Congress/CBS Television "Read More About It" project. The 30-second messages appeared during several major prime-time telecasts, including the Rose Bowl, the presidential inauguration, and the NCAA basketball championship. Since 1979 "Read More About It" messages from the Library of Congress, which send viewers to books in their local libraries and bookstores, have been broadcast on more than 400 CBS Television programs. In 1997 "Read More About It" lists were also prepared for 21 digitized collections on the Web site of LC's National Digital Library.

The center also continued its cooperation with Discovery Communication's Learning Channel in the production of its "Great Books" series of one-hour specials about classics of world literature. Each "Great Books" program carries a separate acknowledgment, "Produced in Cooperation with the Center for the Book in the Library of Congress."

Two Center for the Book projects continued on National Public Radio (NPR). "The Sound of Writing" is a program of short-story readings broadcast on more than 100 NPR affiliates. Center Director John Y. Cole continued his regular guest appearances on "The Book Guys," an NPR program about the world of books and book collecting that is broadcast on more than 20 NPR affiliates. The activities of several state centers and national reading-promotion partners were featured on "Book Guys" programs.

Five issues of the newsletter *Center for the Book News* were produced in 1997. A new edition of the state center handbook was published in May 1997. The Library of Congress issued 40 press releases about center activities, and a two-page "News from the Center for the Book" feature appeared in each issue of the Library of Congress's *Information Bulletin*. Director Cole made 18 presentations during visits to 13 states and to England, Denmark, and Egypt.

Events

Sponsorship of events, symposia, and lectures—at the Library of Congress and elsewhere—is an important center activity. Through such special events, the center brings diverse audiences together on behalf of books and reading and publicizes its activities nationally and locally. Examples of events at the Library of Congress in 1997 include eight talks by current authors in the center's "Books & Beyond" lecture series; a symposium on "Public Libraries in Adult Literacy"; a poetry reading with students from the District of Columbia public schools, cosponsored with the District Lines Poetry Project; a public "Preservation Awareness Day," cosponsored with LC's Preservation Directorate; a nationally televised "Satellite Town Meeting" about reading, cosponsored with the U.S. Department of Education; a public lecture on the history of libraries in American culture in the 19th century; three public lectures on book design; and, with the National Center on Adult Literacy, a forum on "Literacy and the Internet."

Federal Library and Information Center Committee

Library of Congress, Washington, DC 20540
202-707-4800
World Wide Web: http://lcweb.loc.gov/flicc

Susan M. Tarr

Executive Director

Highlights of the Year

During fiscal year (FY) 1997 the Federal Library and Information Center Committee (FLICC) worked to meet the changing professional and service needs of the federal library and information center community. FLICC's annual information policy forum featured expert panelists exploring how changes in policy and advances in technology and the telecommunications industry are moving federal information providers toward new devices and content and how these advances will affect the quality of information. FLICC also held its annual information technology update, this year focusing on agency intranets and how librarians can participate in their development.

During the year FLICC reconstituted two previous working groups: the Policy Working Group and the Personnel Working Group. Other FLICC working groups continued working with the National Center for Education Statistics (NCES) to complete the final publication from the 1994 nationwide survey of federal libraries and information centers; developed new educational initiatives in the areas of acquisitions, cataloging, advocacy, library technician training, and distance learning; issued surveys to members on education programming and fees and analyzed their responses; and expanded access to resources through the FLICC Web site. FLICC sponsored 31 seminars and workshops for 1,413 participants. Staff also conducted 113 Online Computer Library Center (OCLC) and Internet training classes for 820 students.

FLICC's cooperative network, FEDLINK, continued to enhance its fiscal operations, successfully passing the Library of Congress (LC) financial audit of FY 1996 and closing FY 1997 with the highest service dollars total in its history. In FY 1997 FEDLINK provided its members with $55.4 million in transfer-pay services and $72.3 million in direct-pay services, saving federal agencies more than $9 million in cost avoidance and millions more in vendor discounts.

FEDLINK Network Operations (FNO) and FLICC Publications and Education (FPE) Office revised and expanded the FLICC/FEDLINK Web site (http://lcweb.loc.gov/flicc), including lists of FLICC and FEDLINK executive and advisory boards, information about working groups, links to FEDLINK member and vendor home pages, and referrals to other sites of interest to federal librarians.

FEDLINK contracted with Abacus Technology Corporation to perform a strategic review of the program in the following areas: program cost/benefit analysis, development of a formal five-year business plan, and program cost allocation/accounting for transfer-pay and direct-pay activity. FEDLINK program managers collectively reviewed and approved the Abacus reports; staff will implement a number of the Abacus recommendations in FY 1998. FEDLINK completed the year with 96 vendors, including expanded technical-processing services and online services.

Quarterly Membership Meetings

The first FLICC Quarterly Membership Meeting featured guest speaker James Matarazzo, Dean of the Graduate School of Library and Information Science, Simmons College, on the topic of outcome measurement. This presentation concluded a series that focused on advocacy for libraries through demonstrating results to agency management.

The second FLICC Quarterly Membership Meeting was host to two guest speakers: Jane Bortnick Griffith, Specialist in Information Technology Policy, Science Policy Research Division, LC/Congressional Research Service; and Glenn Schlarman, Policy Analyst for Information Policy and Technology, Office of Management and Budget (OMB). Griffith gave a legislative update on the 105th Congress, while Schlarman reported on new OMB policy initiatives. Members also reviewed and approved the new FLICC bylaws.

The third FLICC Quarterly Membership Meeting centered on participatory/breakout discussions on the FEDLINK five-year business plan and the role of FEDLINK within the FLICC mission. The meeting highlighted standard FLICC Working Group updates and reports from LC and FLICC/FEDLINK managers. Members reviewed, discussed, and approved the FLICC FY 1998 budget.

The fourth quarterly membership meeting was held in early FY 1998.

Working Groups

Budget and Finance Working Group

The FLICC Budget and Finance Working Group began meeting in January to develop the FY 1998 FEDLINK budget and fee structure. Before the first meeting, FEDLINK had Abacus Technology review all FEDLINK cost centers and evaluate the FEDLINK methods of calculating and allotting program costs. That review concluded that more staff time was spent on technical assistance for the direct-pay interagency agreements (IAGs) than had previously been estimated and that the allocation of costs between direct-and transfer-pay accounts needed revision. Based on that study, FEDLINK modified its direct-pay service fees for FY 1998. After four years of level fees, the working group proposed that the direct-pay account fee increase from $800 to $1,200 for all accounts; the supplemental fee increased to 0.6% on accounts exceeding $100,000. Transfer-pay fees remained at FY 1997 levels.

Members of the working group called 30 of the largest direct-pay account holders to gauge their reactions to the proposed fee increases. The issue was also the topic of a Web site survey. Responses to both the phone and the Web surveys were positive; most of the respondents said they could weather the proposed direct-pay fee increase.

Working group members first presented the budget proposal to FEDLINK and FLICC memberships and then mailed the proposal to all members. The FLICC voting members unanimously supported the FY 1998 budget proposal.

Education Working Group

The FLICC Education Working Group developed or supported more than 30 programs in the areas of library advocacy and marketing, acquisitions, technician training, and federal library advocacy. The working group also developed, issued, and analyzed the results of a member survey to gain a clear perspective on the educational needs of member libraries and librarians.

In December 1996 the working group sponsored "Getting the Word Out: Marketing Your Library's Information Service," with speakers including Stephen Abrams, Director of Corporate and News Information, Micromedia Limited; Barbara Smith, Smithsonian Institution Libraries; Annette Gohlke, Library Benchmarking International; and Herb White, Indiana University. Nearly 80 federal librarians attended this program to discuss the necessity of library advocacy and to consider various techniques for marketing the services offered in their respective libraries.

During the winter FLICC continued its commitment to continuing-education initiatives for librarians and library technicians education by hosting satellite downlinks to two popular teleconference series, "Soaring to . . . Excellence" and "Dancing with . . . Change," both sponsored by the College of DuPage (Glen Ellyn, Illinois). A week-long institute at the Library of Congress in August 1997 continued to focus on educating library paraprofessionals. Federal and academic libraries joined FLICC professionals to offer "The Federal Library Paraprofessional Institute," which focused on various areas of librarianship, including acquisitions, cataloging, reference, and automation. FLICC received overwhelmingly positive evaluations from participants. The working group intends to repeat this program in summer 1998 so that more library technicians can attend. The working group also sponsored a week-long institute on federal acquisitions in July. The program included speakers from the federal, academic, and vendor communities and offered participants a chance to network and share experiences.

The working group continued to sponsor a number of tours of other federal libraries as part of the "FLICC Orientation to National Libraries" program. Featured libraries included the Library of Congress, National Agricultural Library, Government Printing Office, National Archives and Records Administration, National Library of Medicine, National Library of Education, Defense Technical Information Center, National Technical Information Service, and Smithsonian Institution Libraries.

Information Technology Working Group

The Information Technology Working Group continued to address three areas members had identified as having the greatest importance: making informed choices about new technology and automation issues, facing the challenges of constant technology change, and developing Web sites and resources. To promote information sharing on technology issues among federal librarians, the working group developed an assessment instrument to gather information about systems that the libraries are using. The results of this informative questionnaire will be accessible through the FLICC/FEDLINK Web site and will allow federal librarians to assess the level of automation in their libraries by comparing their agency's use of technology with other agencies' library profiles.

The working group also sponsored a series of guest articles in the *FLICC Newsletter* that asked former federal librarians to share their thoughts on how technology change will affect federal libraries in the future. To assist federal librarians in the use of Internet technologies in their agencies, the working group sponsored the 1997 FLICC Information Technology Update, "Spinning the Intranet Web." This day-long discussion, held in January 1997, featured a hands-on presentation of the how's and why's of intranets. A result of this program was the development of a series of Internet-focused brown-bag sessions.

In FY 1997 the working group also created two new subgroups: one to focus on maintenance contracts for integrated library systems and another on consortium purchasing of electronic products among federal agencies and how FEDLINK might play a role in facilitating those purchases.

Membership and Governance Working Group

The working group completed its revisions of the bylaws. The FLICC Executive Board voted unanimously to endorse the revised bylaws in its November 1996 meeting. The FLICC membership subsequently approved the revised bylaws, and FLICC Chair Winston Tabb signed them in February 1997. Because the major change in the bylaws affected the election process, the working group also worked closely with FLICC staff as they revised the election procedures for the Nominating Working Group.

Nominating Working Group

The Nominating Working Group oversaw the 1997 election process for FLICC rotating members, the FEDLINK Advisory Council, and the FLICC Executive Board. Librarians representing nearly 20 federal agencies agreed to place their names in nomination for these positions. The working group also presided over the review and revision of two documents: "FLICC Nominating Working Group Mission Statement" and "Annual Nomination/Election Procedures and Schedules."

Personnel Working Group

The Personnel Working Group met twice in 1997, first in June to discuss the status of the Office of Personnel and Management's (OPM) test for qualifying non-MLS personnel as librarians and to consider the influence a previous FLICC document, "Qualification Needs for Federal Librarians," may have had on OPM's consideration of the MLS as a positive education requirement for the 1410 series.

The working group's second meeting, held in September, continued to clarify issues raised during the first meeting. Steve Perloff (OPM) attended as a guest speaker to answer questions and provide suggestions for projects that will be useful in improving requirements for the 1410 series. Perloff stated that OPM does not currently consider the MLS degree to be a positive minimal education requirement for the 1410 series. He reported that at present candidates for librarian vacancies may be qualified either by possession of an MLS degree, by other degrees, by experience, or by some combination of these elements. Given this situation, OPM has advised the working group that particular effort is needed to develop knowledge, skill, and ability statements within vacancy announcements that fully reflect the professional qualifications that are required for specific vacancies. In response to this discussion, FLICC staff, with OPM's concurrence, is now preparing a notice for federal librarians that states that OPM no longer administers the qualifying test for the librarian series.

The working group continued its efforts to develop sample knowledge, skill, and ability requirements for job vacancy announcements. These samples will be adaptable for specific announcements and will help attract qualified applicants. The group will also attempt to determine how many staff members without MLS degrees are currently employed in the 1410 series in federal libraries.

Preservation and Binding Working Group

The Preservation and Binding Work Group reviewed preservation resources on the Web and selected sites for links to the FLICC Web site. Members of the group also worked with the Government Printing Office to review its library-binding contract. During the year the working group helped promote many local preservation training opportunities sponsored by the National Archives and Records Administration, the Library of Congress Preservation Directorate, and CAPNET, a local preservation organization. The latter part of the year was spent working with FEDLINK staff and others to develop vendor lists, guidelines, and possible contracts for various preservation services, such as box enclosures, preservation photocopying, collection assessment, and book repair.

Survey Working Group

Organized in FY 1991 to update 1978 federal library statistics, the FLICC Survey Working Group continued its efforts with the National Center for Education Statistics (NCES) to interpret FY 1994 census data of federal libraries and information centers. (The working group published the first product, the survey tabulations and highlights, in July 1996.) In August 1997 the working group released the *Directory of Federal Libraries and Information Centers*, a compilation of libraries identified through the survey. Arranged by branch of government, independent agency, and other categories, it lists libraries and information centers by state, offering addresses, contacts, telephone numbers, and types of libraries and information centers. The document is available from GPO and at the NCES Web site. The group also reviewed and revised the third and final product, an extended analysis of selected topics, prepared by consultants and published in December 1997.

Publications and Education Office

Publications

The FLICC Publications and Education (FPE) Office supported an ambitious publications schedule with the help of a new editor-in-chief and education coordinator and the addition of a permanent writer/editor in August. During FY 1997 FPE produced 12 issues of *FEDLINK Technical Notes* (ranging from 8 to 16 pages) and four issues of *FLICC Quarterly Newsletter* (8–16 pages). FPE also published a 48-page summary of the 1996 FLICC Forum, "The Public's Information: Striking a Balance Between Access and Control." FPE published expanded and enhanced materials to support the FEDLINK program, including the 63-page FY 1998 *FEDLINK Registration Booklet*; a 63-page update and a complete 175-page revision of the looseleaf *FEDLINK Member Handbook*, with index, tabs, and binder; FLICC Bylaws; the 130-page *Vendor Services Directory*; 13 FEDLINK Information Alerts; and a FEDLINK new-member brochure. FPE also produced the minutes of the FY 1997 FLICC Quarterly Meetings and bimonthly FEB meetings and all FLICC Education Program promotional and support materials including the FLICC Forum announcement, attendee and speaker badges, press advisories, speeches and speaker remarks, and collateral materials. In addition, the office produced 31 FLICC Meeting Announcements to promote FLICC Education Programs; FEDLINK membership, vendor, and OCLC User Meetings; and three education institutes along with badges, programs, certificates of completion, and other supporting materials.

FPE and FEDLINK Network Operations (FNO) also worked diligently throughout 1997 to revise and expand the FLICC/FEDLINK Web site. The site now contains a variety of information resources, member information, links to vendors and other members, listings of FLICC membership, access to online account management, event calendars, and an online registration system that is updated nightly. Contract and FLICC staff converted all publications, newsletters, announcements, alerts, member materials, and working group resources into HTML format, uploading current materials within days of their being printed.

Education

In conjunction with the FLICC Education Working Group, FLICC offered a total of 31 seminars, workshops, and lunchtime discussions to 1,413 members of the federal library and information center community. The FY 1997 FLICC education schedule underscored cooperative relationships as FLICC sponsored programs with other organizations in the library, education, and association community, including CAPCON Library Network, Learning Resources Center and Library Technical Assistant Program at the College of DuPage, the metro-Washington area chapters of the Special Libraries Association, the American Society for Information Science, Federal Librarians Special Interest Section of the Law Librarians Society of Washington, D.C., Potomac Valley Chapter of the American Society for Information Science, DC Library Association, and DC Online Users Group.

FLICC also provided organizational, promotional, and logistical support for FEDLINK meetings and events, including the FEDLINK Fall and Spring Membership Meetings, two FEDLINK OCLC Users Group meetings, the FEDLINK FY 1997 Vendor Briefing, and a program on "How to Use FEDLINK in FY 1998" (August 1997).

FLICC continued and expanded its videotaping of FLICC programs and, through its arrangement with the National Library of Education, made more than 30 FLICC videotapes more readily available to federal libraries through interlibrary loans.

FEDLINK

The Federal Library and Information Network (FEDLINK) gave federal agencies cost-effective access to an array of automated information retrieval services for online research, cataloging, and interlibrary loan (ILL). FEDLINK members also procured technical processing services and publications, serials, electronic journals, CD-ROMs, books, and document delivery via LC/FEDLINK contracts with major vendors.

The FEDLINK Advisory Council (FAC) met monthly during FY 1997, except in November 1996 and July and August 1997. During the year, FAC approved the FY 1998 FEDLINK budget and spent several meetings interacting with representatives of Abacus Technology to develop a mission statement and a business plan for the organization.

The Fall FEDLINK Membership Meeting (November 5, 1996) featured Erik Jul, Manager of Custom Services and Project Manager of the Internet Cataloging Project. He spoke on "Cataloging Internet Resources: Emerging Strategies." The FEDLINK Spring Membership Meeting (May 2, 1997) reviewed and discussed the proposed 1998 FLICC/FEDLINK budget. The program included a briefing on the Internet by Marie O'Mara from the Defense Technical Information Center (DTIC) and reports from working-group chairs and staff.

FEDLINK Network Operations—OCLC Network Activity

During the first quarter of the fiscal year the OCLC team briefed 55 federal librarians at the Fall OCLC Users Meeting. Staff reviewed enhancements to the online systems and cost-saving opportunities in interlibrary loan, provided the Users Council Update, and outlined OCLC's plans for upgrading its telecommunications networks. In November Susan Olson, OCLC Director of Network Relations, visited FEDLINK to conduct the annual review of joint activities. Claudette Watson—an OCLC staff member who helps federal libraries in their equipment and telecommunications orders and configuration changes—accompanied Olson during the review. Watson met with FEDLINK staff and visited key FEDLINK members.

Staff attended quarterly meetings at OCLC in December 1996, and in March, June, and September 1997 where OCLC briefed and trained them on new services and software, such as the Interlibrary Loan MicroEnhancer for Windows. Beyond shifting software to the Windows environment, OCLC began offering TCP/IP-based telecommunications options via phone lines for those libraries where Internet access is not viable or cost effective. The OCLC team learned to install and use these new options during the second quarter and continued to inform members about the changes in newsletter articles, mailings, and phone consultations. In the second and third quarters, they cooperated with OCLC in a project to help small libraries analyze their telecom usage and migrate to the most cost-effective method, which was usually the Internet. Throughout the year staff consultations and visits to libraries often involved helping members as they ordered and installed Windows-based software and more-efficient telecommunications methods. FNO developed new classes for the fourth quarter: a basic overview of Windows to complement the current Passport for Windows class and an advanced interlibrary loan class.

The Spring OCLC Users Meeting (May 2) included an overview of OCLC's new electronic journals program. Librarians from the National Agricultural Library and the Smithsonian Institution Libraries explained their experience as test libraries of the new e-journal interface. The 65 attendees also heard briefings by FNO staff on continuing enhancements to the OCLC systems and the status of software and telecommunications upgrades.

Outreach to members throughout the year supported effective use of OCLC in the changing environment. FEDLINK staff joined OCLC in site visits to FEDLINK member libraries throughout the year including the U.S. Naval Academy Library, the Pentagon Library, the Walter Reed Institute for Research, and the U.S. Geological Survey Library. FNO staff helped each site analyze its current use of OCLC and plan improvements, for example in their use of FirstSearch, ILL, and cataloging work flows. FNO also worked extensively with the U.S. Courts Library Program to extract archival OCLC records in the most effective manner for use in their new integrated library system. At the American Library Association (ALA) and Special Library Association (SLA) conferences, FEDLINK staff joined OCLC in meetings with their joint members to provide updates and assistance in planning for effective use of OCLC.

Executive Director Susan Tarr attended the quarterly meetings of the Regional OCLC Network Directors Advisory Council (RONDAC) and began a one-year term as RONDAC chair in July 1997.

Internet/Technology Program

In FY 1997 FNO and FPE focused on Internet training, worked with FPE on revising and expanding the FLICC/FEDLINK Web site, and continued to guide its members on using the Web as a tool. Staff conducted 30 Internet classes in the Washington, D.C., area and three in the field. FNO also participated in three special projects:

- In April staff provided a "FEDLINK Internet Overview and Demonstration" at the Law Librarians Seminar in Washington, D.C., for 80 law librarians and paraprofessionals from 73 U.S. Attorneys' offices throughout the United States; and in August staff conducted more in-depth Internet training for the U.S. Attorney's nonlibrary personnel in Florida.
- During November 1996 staff traveled to Moscow, Russia, with three other LC staff members to train 50 Russian librarians on legislative systems on the Internet.
- In March staff provided Internet training to visiting Eastern European librarians who were participating in the Soros program. Other FNO staff also made presentations at local conferences on various technology issues.

Staff collaborated with FPE on revisions of the FLICC/FEDLINK Web site, including implementation of online registration for training and educational programs, addition of a subject index for the *FEDLINK Services Directory*, listing of FLICC Working Group members, access to FAC minutes, creation of Web versions of FLICC program materials, and conversion of many documents to HTML language, including the *FEDLINK Member Handbook*.

Staff made significant progress on the Information Technology Working Group's technology survey. While they completed the content, staff arranged for LC's Information Technology Services Office to mount the survey on the FLICC/FEDLINK Web site. FNO staff also worked with the FLICC Information Technology Working Group to plan and execute the 1997 FLICC Information Technology Update, "Spinning the Intranet Web," on January 29, 1997.

Exhibits Program

FLICC/FEDLINK exhibited at four events in FY 1997: the Online World Conference in Washington, D.C., in October 1996; the DTIC Users' Meeting in November 1996; the ALA Midwinter Conference in Washington, D.C., in February 1997; and the SLA Conference in Seattle in June 1997.

Training Program

Staff conducted 113 OCLC, Internet, and related classes for 820 students. Of the OCLC classes held, 55 were at field sites, as part of the Air Force's continuing effort to train its librarians on the Pacific Rim. FEDLINK staff conducted training sessions in Korea, Japan, Okinawa, Guam, Alaska, and Hawaii. In addition, other network contract training provided through FEDLINK reached 255 members during FY 1997: 24 by OCLC Pacific, 205 by CAPCON, 1 by MLC, and 25 by SOLINET. FNO staff also facilitated two FLICC training programs in April by making the arrangements and preparing the purchase order requests and the relevant statements of work. The two events were a position description-writing workshop for federal librarians in the Norfolk area and a benchmarking workshop for the U.S. Army Corps of Engineers. FNO staff worked closely with working group members to sponsor the first FLICC Acquisition Institute in July 1997, the first FLICC Paraprofessional Institute in August 1997, and a four-day subject-cataloging workshop in September 1997.

Procurement Services

In FY 1997 FEDLINK wholly revised its solicitation for electronic information retrieval services to reflect the changes in the information industry. The services in this category—which include online databases, CD-ROM publications, electronic serials, gateway services, and document delivery—are used by most federal libraries and account for a large percentage of the service dollars spent through FEDLINK in FY 1997. The revised solicitation included several firsts for FEDLINK: It specifically addressed electronic serials; it identified the federal community's preferred terms for licensing of electronic publications; it allowed vendors to offer print publications associated with their electronic offerings, thereby consolidating sources for members; and it allowed vendors to make customer-specific offerings of their electronic materials and associated research services.

Another noteworthy aspect of this year's solicitation was the way it accommodated new procurement regulations and simplified procedures mandated by the Federal Acquisitions Streamlining Act (FASA) and Federal Acquisitions Reform Act (FARA). For example, FEDLINK did not issue the solicitation on paper, but made it available electronically through Internet file transfer protocol (FTP) and through the FLICC Web site. FEDLINK lessened the burden on vendors by allowing them to respond using standard commercial materials where appropriate. Finally, in the most cutting-edge contractual change for the procurement, FEDLINK allowed vendors to make oral presentations as part of their technical proposals. FEDLINK received and reviewed 57 proposals. Where appropriate, FEDLINK included members in the technical review, asking LC's Congressional Research Service, for example, for input on the proposals from the law database vendors.

In another significant development, FEDLINK has been working with LC's Office of General Counsel to develop a model licensing agreement for electronic databases and publications and to identify specific points for negotiation regarding the licenses offered by the largest FEDLINK vendors (Knight-Ridder DIALOG, LEXIS-NEXIS, Westlaw, Chemical Abstracts, et al.). The model licensing agreement provides baseline language that federal libraries can propose as an alternative to the standard commercial language vendors expect in the licenses. This will save individual agencies the effort of developing language to address the licensing concerns of the federal government and a library's concerns with user and site definition, access, and preservation issues.

In FY 1997 FNO staff worked to regularize and simplify procedures for conducting competitions for individual members among the five contractors that provide copy cataloging, original cataloging, retrospective conversion, and physical processing under FEDLINK's Technical Processing Services program. Keeping in mind those libraries that have small cataloging requirements and those federal organizations that need bibliographic control but have no professional catalogers on staff, FEDLINK developed a set of standard specifications that can be used as the basis of a request for quotation on the member's requirement. FEDLINK published these standard specifications and offered instructions for conducting lowest-price and best-value source selection and for establishing and monitoring technical processing services accounts through FEDLINK in the *FEDLINK Technical Processing Kit*. In addition, FEDLINK helped the National Library of Education contract for its $250,000 project for copy cataloging, original cataloging, and retrospective conversion.

Other FEDLINK basic ordering agreements (BOAs) for serials subscription services, bibliographic utilities, interlibrary loan fee payment, copyright clearance, and training were renewed during FY 1997. FNO staff reviewed new products and services that vendors proposed adding to their BOAs and participated in cost evaluations for renewal contracts and new products. As Contract Officer's Technical Representatives (COTRs), FNO staff followed up on the Vendor Evaluation Forms issued to customers with accounts over $100,000 to resolve any problems the customers were having.

FEDLINK Fiscal Operations

FEDLINK enjoyed its biggest year ever in terms of total service dollars spent under FEDLINK BOAs. To support this record-breaking volume, FEDLINK Fiscal Operations (FFO)

- Processed 10,140 member service transaction requests for current and prior years, representing $55.4 million in current-year transfer pay, $8.8 million in prior-year transfer pay, $72.3 million in current-year direct pay, and $100,000 in prior-year direct-pay service dollars, saving members more than $9 million in cost avoidance and millions more in vendor discounts

- Issued 54,866 invoices for payment of current-and prior-year orders
- Incurred virtually zero net interest expense for late payment of FEDLINK vendor invoices
- Completed FY 1992 member service dollar refunds to close out obligations for expired appropriations
- Successfully passed the Library of Congress financial audit of FY 1996 transactions performed by KPMG Marwick LLP
- Successfully completed work associated with FY 1996 task orders for Abacus Technology Corporation to perform strategic reviews of the FEDLINK program to enhance customer service and program planning and execution
- Ensured that administrative expenditures/obligations did not exceed program fee projections
- Implemented plans to develop requirements for the successor automated financial system (SYMIN) and improve the efficiency of FEDLINK's financial processes

Vendor Services

Total FEDLINK vendor service dollars for FY 1997 alone comprised $55.4 million for transfer-pay customers and $72.3 million for direct-pay customers. Database retrieval services represent $15.4 million and $58.2 million, respectively, for transfer-pay and direct-pay customers. Within this service category, online services comprise the largest procurement for transfer pay and direct pay customers, representing $14 million and $56.5 million, respectively. Publication acquisition services represent $33.5 million and $14.0 million, respectively, for transfer-pay and direct-pay customers. Within this service category, serials subscription services comprise the largest procurement for transfer-pay and direct-pay customers, representing $26.1 million and $14 million, respectively. Library support services represent $6.4 million and $0.1 million, respectively, for transfer-pay and direct-pay customers. Within this service category, bibliographic utilities are the largest procurement representing $5.0 million and $0.1 million, respectively, for transfer-pay and direct-pay customers.

Accounts Receivable and Member Services

FEDLINK Fiscal Operations (FFO) accounts receivable processed FY 1997 registrations from federal libraries, information centers, and other offices that resulted in 744 signed FY 1997 IAGs. In addition, FFO processed 2,932 IAG amendments (1,327 for FY 1997 and 1,605 for prior-year adjustments) for agencies that added, adjusted, or ended service funding. These IAGs and IAG amendments represented 10,140 individual service requests to begin, move, convert, or cancel service from FEDLINK vendors. FFO executed service requests by generating 9,823 delivery orders that LC Contracts and Logistics issued to vendors.

For FY 1997 alone FEDLINK processed approximately $55.4 million in service dollars for 2,836 transfer-pay accounts and approximately $72.3 million in service dollars for 219 direct-pay accounts. Included in the above member service transactions are 782 member requests to move prior-year (no-year and multi-year) funds across fiscal-year boundaries. These service request transactions represented an additional contracting volume of $3.2 million, comprising 1,280 delivery orders.

The FEDLINK Fiscal Hotline responded to a variety of member questions, ranging from routine queries about IAGs, delivery orders, and account balances to complicated questions regarding FEDLINK policies and operating procedures. In addition, FFO e-mail continued to offer FEDLINK members and vendors 24-hour access to fiscal operations. FFO continued the practice of scheduling appointments with FEDLINK member agencies and FEDLINK vendors to discuss complicated account problems and assigned senior staff to concentrate on resolving complex current and prior-year situations. FEDLINK ALIX-FS maintained 2,836 accounts in FY 1997 and continued to provide members early access to their monthly balance information throughout the fiscal year. FFO prepared monthly mailings that alerted individual members to unsigned IAG amendments, deficit accounts, rejected invoices, and delinquent accounts.

Transfer Pay Accounts Payable Services

For transfer-pay users, FFO issued 54,866 invoices for payment during FY 1997 for both current-and prior-year orders. FFO accounts payable efficiently processed vendor invoices and earned $500 in discounts in excess of interest payment penalties levied for the late payment of invoices to FEDLINK vendors. FFO continued to maintain open accounts for three prior years to pay publications service invoices ("bill laters" and "back orders") for members using books and serials services. FFO issued 91,671 statements to members (27,158 for the current year and 64,513 for prior years) and continued to generate current-fiscal-year statements for database retrieval service accounts on the 30th or the last working day of each month and publications and acquisitions account statements on the 15th of each month. FFO issued final FY 1992 statements in support of closing obligations for expired FY 1992 appropriations. FFO issued quarterly statements for prior fiscal years, including FY 1993, and supported reconciliation of FY 1993 FEDLINK vendor services accounts.

Financial Management

FFO completed all unfinished work associated with reconciling FY 1992 vendor obligations and payments and collaborated with LC Financial Services to refund member remaining-account balances. This facilitated member agency compliance with statutory requirements for retiring obligations associated with FY 1992 expired appropriations.

FEDLINK successfully passed the Library of Congress financial audit of FY 1996 transactions done by KPMG Marwick LLP. FFO completed the limited review of FEDLINK's automated financial system for the Library of Congress financial audit. FFO invested time and effort to support the audit, including

- Financial systems briefings
- Documented review and analysis of financial system
- Testing and verification of account balances in the central and subsidiary financial system
- Financial statement preparation support
- Security briefings and reviews
- Research and documented responses to followup audit questions and findings

Strategic Reviews

FEDLINK contracted Abacus Technology to conduct strategic reviews of the program in the following areas: program cost/benefit analysis, development of a formal five-year business plan, and program cost allocation/accounting for transfer-pay and direct-pay activity. FEDLINK program managers collectively reviewed and approved the Abacus reports, and some of the recommendations are scheduled for implementation in FY 1998.

Budget and Revenue

FEDLINK ensured that administrative expenditures and obligations did not exceed the program fee projections. As FY 1997 ended, FEDLINK service dollars and fees were approximately 1 percent above FY 1996 levels for the same time period. FEDLINK earned 103 percent of its FY 1997 operating budget in fee revenues from signed IAGs. The surplus was spent on high-priority automation projects that the FLICC Budget and Finance Working Group and FAC approved, on behalf of the membership.

Financial Management Systems

FEDLINK carried out plans to develop requirements for a new automated financial system that would replace the current SYMIN system and improve the efficiency of FEDLINK's financial processes; with year-end funding, FLICC executed a contract with Price Waterhouse to develop a systems requirements analysis for the replacement financial system. FLICC management and systems staff actively supported automation vision development meetings using facilitative management techniques to determine the best strategy to administer this activity. FFO staff also exploited year-end funding to contract for an AMS billing automation/improvement project and a document imaging and archiving system.

National Agricultural Library

U.S. Department of Agriculture, NAL Bldg., 10301 Baltimore Ave.,
Beltsville, MD 20705-2351
E-mail: agref@nal.usda.gov
World Wide Web: http://www.nal.usda.gov

Brian Norris
Public Affairs Officer

The National Agricultural Library (NAL) is the primary agricultural information resource for the nation and is the largest agricultural library in the world, with a collection of over 3.2 million items including nearly 2.3 million volumes in print. The collection includes journals (the library receives nearly 25,000 serial titles annually), audiovisuals, reports, theses, software, laser discs, and artifacts.

Established in 1862 under legislation signed by Abraham Lincoln, NAL is part of the Agricultural Research Service (ARS) of the U.S. Department of Agriculture (USDA). In addition to being a national library, NAL is the departmental library for USDA, serving USDA employees worldwide. NAL is a keystone of USDA's scientific and research activities.

As the nation's chief resource and service for agricultural information, NAL's mission is to increase the availability and use of agricultural information for researchers, educators, policy makers, farmers, consumers, and the public at large. NAL also serves a growing international clientele.

The NAL staff of about 200 includes librarians, computer specialists, administrators, information specialists, and clerical personnel. A number of volunteers, ranging from college students to retired persons, work on various programs at the library. NAL also has an active visiting-scholar program that allows scientists, researchers, professors, and students from universities around the world to work on projects of mutual interest.

NAL works closely with land-grant university libraries on programs to improve access to and maintenance of the nation's agricultural knowledge.

AGRICOLA (AGRICultural OnLine Access) is NAL's bibliographic database, providing quick access to the NAL collection. AGRICOLA contains more than three million citations of agricultural literature and is available online and on CD-ROM. NAL's online catalog is available over the Internet.

The NAL home page on the World Wide Web, accessible at http://www.nal.usda.gov, offers general and specific information on using NAL and its collection and links to agricultural information throughout the world. In 1997 the NAL home page was accessed more than 4.5 million times.

The library maintains specialized information centers in areas of particular interest to the agricultural community. These centers provide a wide range of customized services, from responding to reference requests and developing reference publications to coordinating outreach activities and setting up dissemination networks. Subjects covered by the information centers include alternative farming systems, animal welfare, and food and nutrition, to name a few.

Some of the major NAL activities in 1997 follow.

Agricultural Network Information Center

NAL and its land-grant university partners continued to enhance the services and resources of AgNIC (Agricultural Network Information Center), a virtual information center that provides a focal point to access agriculture-related resources on the Internet. AgNIC use continues to grow, and plans are under way to expand participation to additional universities and organizations. Three popular components of AgNIC (http://www.agnic.org) are AgDB, which describes and links to more than 750 databases, data sets, and information systems; AgCal, a calendar listing more than 1,000 agricultural conferences, meetings, and seminars; and AgNIC Online Reference Services, through which NAL, Cornell University, Iowa State University, the University of Arizona, and the University of Nebraska–Lincoln provide online reference assistance in selected subject areas.

Electronic Media Center

During the year, NAL worked to phase in its Electronic Media Center (EMC) so that library users could begin accessing information from NAL electronic resources. NAL increased the number of databases available to its customers from two to 30. Eleven networked databases also became accessible to customers at the NAL DC Reference Center in Washington, D.C. The EMC has seven customer-dedicated computers and network printers. Also, NAL upgraded five customer computer terminals near the NAL reference desk. These terminals were also integrated with EMC services. NAL customers can now access, on demand, all 30 databases, seven CD-ROM information products, general Internet-based services, electronic federal depository collections, 45 Web-based full-text electronic scientific journals, and a selection of electronic newspapers.

In addition, via an NAL server, the library provided the National Program Staff (NPS) of the Agricultural Research Service with desktop computer access to more than 30 databases on agriculture and related sciences. This enables the NPS to efficiently and effectively search databases immediately on their own without NAL assistance.

Document Delivery Demand Increasing

Demand for delivery of materials increased in 1997 as NAL users became more familiar with electronic methods for accessing information. Analysis of fiscal year (FY) 1997 statistics indicate that the NAL's Document Delivery Services Branch responded to 23 percent more requests for materials than in FY 1996 (electronic responses rose to 24 percent from 17 percent in 1996). Total requests averaged about 14,000 per month. Requests from USDA patrons were significantly higher than requests from non-USDA patrons in 1997, with a 46 percent increase over 1996. Document delivery requests received electronically at NAL increased from 46 percent to 66 percent of all requests received. There was a dramatic 314 percent increase by USDA patrons using electronic methods to request materials from the library. NAL expects this figure will continue to grow as desktop access to NAL electronic resources is expanded for off-site USDA staff.

NAL continued to encourage its patrons to send requests and receive materials electronically. Part of this effort included providing complimentary copies of Ariel software, with technical support, to more than 20 USDA regional offices and to the libraries of Historically Black Colleges and Universities (HBCUs) and Tuskegee University. The Ariel software, produced by Research Libraries Group, facilitates the scanning, transferring, and receiving of documents over the Internet, which reduces the cost and time involved in mailing or faxing documents. Through Ariel, documents can be sent directly to a user's workstation anywhere in the world in less than a minute.

Electronic Preservation Plans

The year saw NAL take the lead in developing plans to preserve USDA electronic publications.

With the growth of the Internet, many USDA agencies have begun publishing exclusively in electronic formats. Preservation of and long-term access to many of these publications has become an important issue due to the ephemeral nature of electronic formats. To meet this need, NAL brought together key stakeholders and responsible parties to develop a preservation and access plan for digital USDA publications. NAL, USDA's Economic Research Service (ERS), the Government Printing Office (GPO), Cornell University, and the Farm Foundation took the first step in a cooperative venture by convening a two-day national meeting in Washington, D.C., to identify the major elements of such a plan.

Among the issues discussed at the conference were the management framework and institutional roles and responsibilities, both within USDA and externally, for the long-term preservation of USDA digital publications; the underlying technological infrastructure and technical-document management requirements; the development of long-term retention criteria and processes for USDA digital publications; and the issues of long-term user access to and retrieval of those digital publications.

Based on the results of the meeting, a draft preservation plan was developed that identifies the USDA agencies involved, the resources required, and short-term and long-term actions. NAL will continue to work with USDA agencies, GPO, the National Archives and Records Administration, land-grant university libraries, and other agricultural institutions to move this important effort forward.

Brittle Books Preserved Digitally

NAL established initial procedures and standards for digital conversion of USDA embrittled-paper publications. During the year, collections of three USDA paper publications were converted to preservation-quality digital format. These included 19 volumes of the *Journal of Agricultural Research*. More than 24,000 pages were digitized and have become the first publications in NAL's digital archive collection. NAL is working to make these images available on the Internet.

NAL believes that the outcome of these initial efforts in digital preservation will have a long-term impact on the availability and distribution of agricultural information. Through digital conversion of significant brittle publications, NAL is making endangered materials available to researchers and the public.

Pfiesteria Web Site Established

Responding to a 1997 outbreak of *Pfiesteria piscicida* in certain East Coast waterways that resulted in large fish kills and human health concerns, NAL's Water Quality Information Center (WQIC) developed a Web site on the deadly microorganism. The site links related national information sources and includes a bibliography of *Pfiesteria* materials.

Animal Care CD-ROM

During the year, NAL made available the *Compendium of Animal CARE*, a CD-ROM containing 162 documents that relate to the care of animals in research, teaching, and testing. The CD-ROM provides researchers regulated under the Animal Welfare Act and the Public Health Service's requirements for animal care with the regulations and guidelines, in an easily retrievable format, that affect their research. The disc was funded by the National Institutes of Health, USDA's Animal and Plant Health Inspection Service, and the American Association for Accreditation of Laboratory Animal Care. NAL staff prepared the information for the disc, which was produced by the Government Printing Office. GPO reported that the CD-ROM was a "bestseller" and met the need for making critical information easily available to researchers and educators who use animals in research.

National Microfilm Archive

NAL signed a cooperative agreement with Cornell University that names NAL as the national preservation depository and manager for archival microfilm of state and local agricultural literature identified by the U.S. Agricultural Information Network (USAIN). Consequently, NAL began receiving archival microfilm for cataloging and storage in an environmentally controlled space. To ensure compliance with nationally recognized preservation guidelines, NAL uses state-of-the-art equipment to monitor the microfilm storage environment.

Library Assistance Sought by American Rivers Group

The federal Working Group of the American Heritage Rivers Initiative (AHRI) asked NAL's Rural Information Center (RIC) to assist the group in developing and maintaining a Web site. AHRI, proposed in 1997 by President Clinton, supports efforts by communities along U.S. rivers to spur economic revitalization, protect natural resources and the environment, and preserve the historic and cultural heritage of river communities. Responding to the request for assistance,

RIC provided information on AHRI to river communities applying to participate in the initiative. The working group also asked that RIC serve as the information resource to those communities (up to ten) that will ultimately be selected as American Heritage River communities. RIC has agreed to fill this role.

Site Helps Improve School Meals

NAL's "Healthy School Meals Resource System" (HSMRS) Web site was activated in 1997 to help school nutrition personnel and trainers easily locate appropriate and useful training materials on nutrition. Available on the site are full-text training documents, regulations, menu-planning resources, food safety information, links to related Web sites, and connections to professional chefs participating in school food service programs. Another part of the site is an e-mail discussion group called "Mealtalk" that links nutrition professionals working in child nutrition programs. Currently, more than 775 professionals participate in the discussion group. Mealtalk archives are listed on the Web site by date, author, and subject. The site is a component of the "Team Nutrition Initiative" of the U.S. Department of Agriculture.

U.S. Dietary Guidelines for the Year 2000

NAL is performing literature searches in support of the effort by the federal Center for Nutrition Policy and Promotion (CNPP) to develop the Dietary Guidelines for Americans that will be issued in the year 2000.

The literature identified by NAL will serve as the background to research on the new guidelines being performed by a CNPP advisory panel of nutrition experts. The Dietary Guidelines for Americans provide recommended levels of nutrition and diet for the American public and are used by government and industry to develop regulations, public policy, and nutrition education materials.

Also related to the nation's food and nutrition, NAL maintains the Web site of the Foodborne Illness Education Information Center of the U.S. Department of Agriculture and the U.S. Food and Drug Administration. The site features foodborne-illness statistics, government reports, consumer education materials, plans for controlling foodborne illnesses (Hazard Analysis Critical Control Points plans), and a Food Safety Index that provides links to other food safety sites. The site also includes Foodsafe, an electronic discussion group, that has been used by more than 900 food safety experts.

During the year, NAL continued working with the Office of Dietary Supplements of the National Institutes of Health to develop an Internet site on dietary supplements. The site will include the International Bibliographic Information on Dietary Supplements (IBIDS) database, which contains citations on dietary supplement (vitamin, mineral, phytochemical, botanical, and herbal) research published in international scientific journals. NIH believes that putting the IBIDS database on the Internet will help to improve international nutritional research on dietary supplements.

Federal Telemedicine Project

NAL staff members are serving on the federal Joint Working Group on Telemedicine (JWGT), an interagency effort to resolve issues related to the use of telemedicine in underserved areas of the nation. JWGT proposed various activities to advance the effort in a year-end report to Vice President Gore, who had proposed formation of the group. A Web site has been established to inventory federal telemedicine projects and links to related sources.

NAL Given USDA History Collection

In 1996 NAL acquired the USDA History Collection from the former Agricultural and Rural History Section of USDA's Economic Research Service (ERS). This collection was created by ERS as a practical research tool to assist historians, economists, and others interested in the history of USDA. NAL assigned a full-time archivist and three part-time graduate students to process and organize the materials so that it is more accessible.

Strawberry and Bean Research on the Internet

NAL's Plant Genome Data and Information Center (PGDIC) is working to make key information on the history and breeding of strawberries and beans available on the Internet.

For strawberries, PGDIC is collaborating with land-grant university scientists, ARS staff, and the family of noted agricultural researcher George Darrow to provide Internet access to information on breeding strawberries from ancient times to 1965. PGDIC expects that the site will connect researchers to past and current information, provide information to help farmers decide on the feasibility of growing strawberries on their land, and perhaps encourage students to pursue careers in agriculture. The site includes links to many other research sites, including the National Center for Biotechnology Information, the National Library of Medicine, and the National Institutes of Health. Also on the site are lists of resources for educators, researchers, and strawberry producers.

PGDIC, in collaboration with the Dry Bean Research Council (DBRC), the Bean Improvement Cooperative, and land-grant university scientists, is digitizing research information on beans. The Web site, which includes 5,000 pages of DBRC materials, was announced and well received at the council's biennial conference. Bean researchers expect the site to greatly facilitate access to research materials.

Visiting-Scholar Program

NAL hosted or cosponsored visiting librarians and scholars from several countries in 1997. Assignments ranged from one week to several months.

NAL and its parent agency, the Agricultural Research Service, sponsored a three-month visiting-librarian assignment to the ARS European Biological

Control Laboratory (EBCL) in Montpellier, France. The person selected from among several candidates was from New Mexico State University. During his tour in Montpellier, he worked with EBCL scientists and the Center for Biology and Management of Populations (Institut National de la Recherche Agronomique, or INRA) to integrate EBCL biological-control research materials into a documentation center that serves the international research community. The center is being located on the Baillarguet International Campus for Biological Control near Montpellier.

Visiting librarians/scholars at NAL during the year included

- An information officer with the Tropical Beef Centre, Commonwealth Scientific and Industrial Research Organization (CSIRO), Queensland, Australia, who studied NAL's efforts in remote end user education, including establishing virtual information centers and developing programs to teach NAL users (farmers, scientists, etc.) how to use electronic resources
- Two library officials from the Universidad de São Paulo, Brazil, who learned about the operations of NAL's Rural Information Center, Technology Transfer Information Center, and Alternative Farming Systems Information Center
- A scientist from the National Center for Gene Research, Chinese Academy of Sciences, in Shanghai, China, who worked with NAL plant genome staff
- A researcher from the Indian National Science Academy in New Delhi, who studied NAL's automation activities
- A scientist from the Indian Council of Forestry Research and Education, Dehra Dun, India, who studied NAL's use of information technologies
- The head of Technical Information Projects for the Jamaica Bureau of Standards, who interned with NAL's Food and Nutrition Information Center
- An agricultural engineer with the Ministry of Agriculture and Rural Affairs, Ankara, Turkey, who studied NAL's computerized library and documentation systems

Assistance Offered to Tribal Colleges

NAL participated in the USDA and Tribal Colleges Summit in Albuquerque, New Mexico. The summit was titled "A New Partnership, Current Opportunities and Future Possibilities Through Learning and Understanding." USDA and the American Indian Higher Education Consortium convened the summit to lay a foundation for partnerships between 1994 land-grant Tribal Colleges and USDA. At the summit, Tribal College presidents, deans, faculty, and students were introduced to USDA resources and programs, including NAL, that support academic programs in the food and agricultural sciences.

ENAL/NAL Meet on Cooperative Research

NAL hosted the summer meeting of the Egyptian National Agricultural Library (ENAL)/National Agricultural Library Joint Committee on Cooperation. The committee provides guidance and coordination to various USDA/Egyptian-supported activities. NAL has worked with the government of Egypt since 1989 to develop ENAL. At the summer committee meeting officials from ENAL, NAL, the Egyptian Agricultural Research Center, Cairo University, and USDA's Agricultural Research Service met for four days to discuss cooperative research activities.

Help to Students Expands

NAL expanded its participation in the USDA student employment programs that target various segments of American youth. The library hosted groups from

- The Hispanic Association of Colleges and Universities Internship Program, a ten-week paid internship for Hispanic college students
- The USDA Summer Intern Program, which provides paid summer internships for college students
- The USDA Research Apprenticeship Program for high school students interested in food and agricultural sciences
- The USDA/1890 National Scholars Program, which provides four-year scholarships to high school seniors planning to attend one of the Historically Black 1890 institutions

Water Quality Web Site Wins Award

The World Wide Web site of NAL's Water Quality Information Center (WQIC) received a Blue Ribbon Award from the American Society of Agricultural Engineers and was listed on the "Best Environmental Directories" Web page of the Centre for Economic and Social Studies for the Environment (CESSE) at the Université Libre de Bruxelles, Brussels, Belgium. The WQIC Web site serves as the focal point for customer access to information on agricultural pollution of water sources. The site has provided thousands of customers with links to water-related databases, Internet discussion lists, bibliographies, and other information. WQIC added 60 water quality information sources to the site in 1997, and bibliographies listed on the site were accessed more than 27,000 times.

NAL Hosts Program for USDA Employees

In an effort to encourage more employees of USDA to use NAL, the library in April 1997 hosted three days of exhibits and demonstrations of its electronic information systems at USDA headquarters in Washington, D.C. Hundreds of federal employees visited the exhibit site during the event. The exhibits and demonstrations focused on the wealth of agricultural information that is available from NAL and on the various methods, both traditional and electronic, by which the information can be obtained. The event officially opened with NAL Director Pamela Andre presenting to Secretary of Agriculture Dan Glickman framed copies of the NAL's Thomas Jefferson letters.

Library Hosts Elder Hostel

As part of its active community involvement program, NAL hosted an Elder Hostel for the Collington Episcopal Life Care Community campus of the Prince George's County (Maryland) Community College. The theme of the Elder Hostel, held as part of the Prince George's County Tricentennial Celebration, was "Aviation, Architecture, and Agriculture." Senior participants from throughout the United States came to NAL to discuss and learn about the history of U.S. agriculture and the role of government, including NAL, in advancing the quality of life in the United States through agricultural research.

Banner Year for Special Visitors

During 1997 NAL hosted more than 500 special visitors interested in the operations of the library. These included USDA administrators, university presidents, foreign dignitaries, visiting scholars, and library directors from throughout the world. Groups included Fulbright, Soros, and Cochrane fellows; ministries of agriculture in Albania, China, Egypt, and Russia; the United States Agricultural Information Network; the Federal Library and Information Center Committee; the Bicultural Museum of Texas, the Horticultural Promotional Council; and the Agricultural Women's Leadership Network. More than one-third of the visitors were from foreign countries.

NAL Provides Computer Training to USDA Agencies

NAL's proficiency in the use of electronic information systems is being recognized and put to good use by many USDA agencies and offices. NAL is assisting many USDA programs in improving electronic-information skills. The library provided 240 members of USDA's National Agricultural Statistics Service (NASS) with general training on using the Internet. NAL also provided training to USDA plant genome researchers in using molecular biology e-mail to access genome databases. The NAL Reference Section is putting increased emphasis on training on-site NAL users in doing their own database searches.

Biofuels Home Page Opens

NAL officially opened a Biofuels Home Page, which describes ARS ethanol and biodiesel research projects and lists publications, patents, and opportunities for technology development. The site also links to other biofuel sites on the Internet. The new home page is designed to make companies, researchers, and the public aware of ARS biofuels research and USDA energy-related programs. ARS scientists provided research content for the page, while NAL's Technology Transfer Information Center provided technical assistance in designing the page and some additional content.

Library Helps Move Technology to Private Sector

NAL began assisting scientists from ARS in identifying companies that may be interested in commercializing ARS-developed technologies. NAL staff meets with ARS researchers to discuss newly developed technologies and real or potential applications. NAL then conducts reference searches to identify potential private manufacturers and supplier companies with an interest in the new technologies. ARS and the private enterprise can then begin cooperative interaction on commercializing the technology.

New Home Page Links USDA Research Information

Under the guidance of ARS and the USDA CO-AgRA (Capitalizing on Opportunities in Agriculture for Rural America) working group, NAL developed a Web site that provides one-stop access to USDA research, development, and business opportunities. The site helps private companies and state and local economic-development agencies gain access to information on food and fiber research activities, technology development opportunities, and other aspects of initiating and promoting business (funding, marketing, etc.).

National Library of Medicine

8600 Rockville Pike, Bethesda, MD 20894
301-496-6308, fax 301-496-4450
E-mail: publicinfo@nlm.nih.gov
World Wide Web: http://www.nlm.nih.gov

Robert Mehnert

Public Information Officer

The National Library of Medicine (NLM), a part of the Department of Health and Human Services' National Institutes of Health in Bethesda, Maryland, is the world's largest library of the health sciences. The director, Donald A. B. Lindberg, is a physician with wide experience in developing systems that use computer and communications technology to improve health science research, education, and health care delivery.

NLM has two buildings containing more than 420,000 square feet. The older building (1962) houses the collection, public reading rooms, catalog area, and library staff and administrative offices. The 10-story Lister Hill Center Building (1981) contains the main computer room, auditorium, audiovisual facility, offices, and research/demonstration laboratories.

MEDLINE on the Web

On June 26, 1997, at a press conference on Capitol Hill, NLM announced that it would provide free access to MEDLINE for users of the World Wide Web. Doing the first free search in front of the assembled press was Vice President Al Gore. In demonstrating MEDLINE, Gore used a new access interface called PubMed, which not only searches the entire database, but also links users to medical publishers for the full text of articles from a growing number of medical journals. The announcement received a considerable amount of attention in the press and on television and, within a month, all MEDLINE daily usage records were broken. By the end of the year, between the Internet Grateful Med (introduced in 1996) and the new PubMed system, it was estimated that more than a quarter million searches were done each day—ten times the previous rate of searching.

MEDLINE, the world's largest collection of published medical information, is NLM's premier database. It contains some nine million records dating from the early 1960s to the present. Every day an average of 1,000 references and abstracts are added to MEDLINE. They are derived from almost 4,000 journals, and 40 languages are represented (although the majority are in English-language journals).

Late in 1996 a new database, OLDMEDLINE, joined the family of MEDLINE databases. OLDMEDLINE contains more than 307,000 citations originally printed in the 1964 and 1965 issues of *Cumulated Index Medicus*. As part of its effort to get more printed data into machine-readable form, NLM has begun to add 1962–1963 data to OLDMEDLINE. By spring 1998 nearly 276,000 additional citations will be available to the public.

In a separate project, NLM is working with a private consortium to create a *really* old MEDLINE—a machine-readable version of the *Index-Catalogue* (a publication that began in 1880 and continued in various versions through 1961). In the face of deterioration of the physical volumes and the cumbersome nature of searching this publication, the *Index-Catalogue* can be made vastly more usable in digital form. A pilot phase, funded by the Burroughs Wellcome Fund, is now under way to assess the feasibility and cost of the electronic conversion. The project will not only result in the preservation of this great achievement in medical information, but will provide a product of immeasurable value to health professionals and historians.

At a February 5, 1997, ceremony in which the Russian Minister of Health and the U.S. Secretary of Health and Human Services participated, Russia became the 21st International MEDLARS (Medical Literature Analysis and Retrieval System) Center. The center is at the State Scientific Medical Library in Moscow, which will assist health professionals in that country to access NLM databases, offer search training, and provide document delivery services.

Next Generation Internet

Today's Internet suffers from its own success. Technology designed for a network of thousands is laboring to serve millions. To ensure that the Internet will be up to handling the pressure of future usage, an interagency Next Generation Internet (NGI) initiative has been created. NGI will provide affordable, secure information delivery at rates thousands of times faster than today and it will accelerate the introduction of new networking services for businesses, schools, hospitals, and homes.

NLM plans to sponsor a variety of NGI health care applications in such areas as advanced telemedicine, digital libraries, and distance learning. Such applications often require the nearly instantaneous transfer of many gigabits of data, for example in applications involving imaging. Perhaps as important as the ability to transfer massive amounts of data is the requirement that this transfer be highly reliable and that the integrity of the data be rigorously maintained. Still other applications (such as pathology and mammography) require the prompt transfer of very detailed images. Many health care applications require the retrieval of reference multimedia data from libraries.

Telemedicine

One of the most important aspects of NGI in the health sciences is the use of computer and telecommunication technology for medical diagnosis and patient care—what has come to be called telemedicine. The concept encompasses everything from the use of standard telephone service to high-speed, wide-bandwidth transmission of digitized signals in conjunction with computers, fiber optics, satellites, and other sophisticated peripheral equipment and software. Not only does the library collect and index the literature related to telemedicine; it has also made a serious commitment to furthering telemedicine by sponsoring several dozen projects around the country, in a variety of rural and urban settings. Through these projects, NLM hopes to evaluate the impact of telemedicine on the cost and quality of and access to health care.

Digital Libraries Initiative

Also intimately related to NGI is Phase II of the Digital Libraries Initiative. The initiative is closely linked to advances in High Performance Computing and Communications (HPCC), and thus a number of HPCC agencies are involved: the National Science Foundation, the Defense Advanced Research Projects Agency, the National Aeronautics and Space Administration, and NLM. The Library of Congress has also joined the Digital Libraries Initiative. The goals of the first phase were to advance fundamental research and to build test-bed networks for developing and demonstrating new technologies. Phase II, which is just under way, seeks to look beyond the technology and test beds and to seek to apply what has been learned to library collections such as NLM's. To do this, the library is entering into an agreement with the National Science Foundation for a grant program to support such projects. NLM, for more than three decades, has successfully used computer technology to manage its collections and to distribute information to the health science community. Phase II of Digital Libraries Initiative will greatly extend this capability.

Visible Human Project

One of the most fascinating of the library's enterprises, and one that will make excellent use of enhanced NGI capabilities, is the Visible Human Project. In the late 1980s a group of advisers recommended that NLM could render great assistance to the world of medicine by creating a digital library of computerized images of the human body. They said that the rapidly developing technology of computer-based imaging would soon be capable of handling the immense datafiles resulting from such a project. This prediction was borne out when the Visible Human Male and Visible Human Female were introduced to the scientific community. Together, the two take up 55 gigabytes of computer space.

The data sets were prepared using state-of-the-art radiographic (CT, MR, and X-ray) and full-color photographic techniques on the carefully selected cadavers. NLM's relatively modest investment in the project has resulted in 1,000 licenses for use of the data sets by individual scientists and corporations in 27 countries. Thanks to the NLM's Visible Humans, doctors can practice procedures on "surgical simulators"; medical students can conduct dissection over and over using a CD-ROM called "The Recyclable Cadaver"; and noninvasive cancer-screening techniques such as "virtual colonoscopy" are being developed that may eliminate the need for costly invasive procedures. Other activities lie ahead, such as the segmentation and labeling process (to make the Visible Human data set into a Visible Human database), and the addition of other Visible Humans (of different ages, and with various health conditions) to the data sets.

Genetic Medicine

Continuing research into human DNA is one of science's great adventures. Human molecular genetics not only forms the cutting edge of biomedical research, but also has immediate application to the diagnosis of disease and great potential for treatment. To cope with this flood of information, new methods are needed to store and analyze the data and make the results easily accessible. Established by Congress in 1988, the library's National Center for Biotechnology Information (NCBI) has assumed a leadership role in developing information services for the scientific disciplines of molecular biology and genetics. NCBI stores and makes accessible the staggering amounts of data about the human genome resulting from genetic research at the National Institutes of Health and at laboratories around the world.

NCBI is responsible for maintaining GenBank, a database of DNA sequences. In 1997 a major milestone was reached when GenBank added the billionth base to the sequence database. Like MEDLINE, GenBank is accessed via the World Wide Web and is queried more than 60,000 times a day. It has grown rapidly and today contains 1.7 million sequences. In fact GenBank has outgrown the CD-ROM distribution medium and after April 15, 1998, it will be available only via NCBI Internet services. The Human Gene Map, a Web service introduced in 1996 by the National Center for Biotechnology Information, continues to be a popular site accessible from the NLM home page. It contains extensive information about human genes and genetic diseases and is used by both scientists and students.

Outreach

As the NGI initiative increases NLM's ability to deliver quality health care, the library will continue its special outreach effort to the health care community to encourage the use of these services. Much of the health care community is just discovering the advantages and efficiencies afforded through the use of advanced communications technologies, such as the Internet. Getting medical practices connected, especially in rural areas, is still a formidable problem.

NLM has a number of special outreach programs designed to acquaint the scientific community and even the general public with its services. It is assisted in its outreach efforts by the 4,500 member institutions of the National Network of Libraries of Medicine. Since the network's formation in the 1960s, its mission has been to make biomedical information readily accessible to U.S. health professionals irrespective of their geographic location. The eight Regional Medical Libraries that form the backbone of the network are supported by NLM contracts. Network institutions provide a wide range of services to American scientists, educators, practitioners, and the public based on the collections and information resources provided by NLM.

Closely connected to the National Network of Libraries of Medicine is NLM's Extramural Program for providing grant assistance. Several of these grant programs are outreach related, including support to assist medical institutions in connecting to the Internet. Other grant programs support improving library resources within the network, research and development into health science communications, and research training in medical informatics and the related subfields that deal with biotechnology and molecular biology.

An unusual outreach activity in 1997 was a major exhibit mounted in the library's rotunda, "Frankenstein: Penetrating the Secrets of Nature." The exhibit was opened at a reception on Halloween eve. Sara Karloff, the daughter of legendary actor Boris Karloff, was a special guest at the opening. NLM's Frankenstein exhibition explores the popularization of the Frankenstein myth as well as broader questions about the public's fear of science and its powers.

Perhaps the most successful outreach tool is the library's popular World Wide Web site at http://www.nlm.nih.gov. Begun in October 1993 and updated regularly, the site provides information about how to get to the library and what services are available and also provides a wealth of detailed health information for practitioners, scientists, public health professionals, students, and consumers. Fact sheets, newsletters, journal listings, reports, press releases and news items, information about job openings, grant and contract programs, and so forth, are all there.

MEDLINE is also accessible on the library's Web site (through PubMed and the Internet Grateful Med), along with extensive information files in health services research, molecular biology information (such as the Human Gene Map), patient guidelines, and image databases. These information resources, although provided over the Web, are in many cases grounded in the basic medical library services that the NLM has built up over the past 150 years.

Basic Library Services

In fiscal year (FY) 1997 NLM received and processed 172,000 modern books, serial issues, audiovisuals, and computer-based materials. Preservation microfilming was done for 6,472 volumes (2,760,000 pages). A net total of 11 journals was added to those indexed for MEDLINE (the number of journals indexed is now 3,879).

In January 1997 the *Current Bibliographies in Medicine* series became available free in electronic format from the library's Web site. Formerly available on subscription from the Government Printing Office, this is the first NLM publica-

Table 1 / Selected NLM Statistics*

Library Operation	Volume
Collection (book and nonbook)	5,260,000
Items cataloged	20,300
Serial titles received	22,760
Articles indexed for MEDLINE	519,000
Circulation requests filled	630,000
For interlibrary loan	353,000
For on-site users	277,000
Computerized searches (all databases)**	8,741,000
Budget authority	$150,376,000
Full-time staff	575

* For the year ending September 30, 1997

** This figure does not include MEDLINE searching on the Web via the new PubMed program. An estimated 200,000 such searches were being done daily by December 1997.

tion to be published without a print counterpart. At the end of the year the NLM ceased publishing the monthly *Abridged Index Medicus* (*AIM*), which was begun in 1970 as a small subset (about 120 titles) of *Index Medicus*. Even though the printed version is being discontinued, it will still be possible to search the *AIM* subset list in MEDLINE.

A new toll-free telephone service was begun in 1997 allowing users to reach a variety of NLM service areas that previously were reachable only by separate phone numbers. The new number, 888-346-3656 (1-888-FINDNLM), has several short, easy-to-use menu choices.

The library is guided in matters of policy by a board of regents consisting of 10 appointed and 11 ex officio members. Michael E. DeBakey, M.D. (Chancellor Emeritus and Distinguished Service Professor, Baylor College of Medicine, Houston, Texas) chairs the board. In 1997 the regents welcomed two new members: Michele S. Klein (Manager of Library Services at Children's Hospital of Michigan, Detroit) and Jordan J. Baruch, Sc.D. (President of Jordan Baruch Associates, Washington, D.C., a consulting firm to industry and governments on the planning, management, and integration of strategy and technology).

Educational Resources Information Center

ERIC Processing and Reference Facility
Computer Sciences Corporation
1100 West Street, Laurel, MD 20707-3598
301-497-4080, 800-799-3742, fax 301-953-0263
E-mail: ericfac@inet.ed.gov
World Wide Web: http://ericfac.piccard.csc.com

Ted Brandhorst
Director

ERIC Budget (FY 1998)

The fiscal year (FY) 1998 appropriation bill covering the Educational Resources Information Center (ERIC), signed on November 13, 1997, allocated $10,000,000 for ERIC. This represents a $1,000,000 (11 percent) increase over FY 1997 and continues an upward funding trend that started in FY 1997 after several years of a fairly flat trend line.

The 16 ERIC Clearinghouse contracts are generally being extended through 1998 in order to provide sufficient time for the next round of competition, which will in all likelihood take place during the last half of 1998.

United States Education Information Network

The National Library of Education (NLE), established by Congress in 1994 and ERIC's parent organization within the U.S. Department of Education, has been mandated to develop and implement a national network of education information providers—including libraries, archives, educational institutions and schools, and other information providers—to provide "education information in all formats, to all customers, in all education-related subjects." This national network is currently referred to as the United States Education Information Network (USEIN), and it will be developed based on the recommendations of the NLE Advisory Task Force, as contained in that group's report "Access for All: A New National Library for Tomorrow's Learners" (ED 405 007).

To brainstorm the USEIN concept, NLE sponsored a kick-off conference at Gallaudet University November 13–14, 1997. Nearly 100 organization representatives met in plenary and small-group work sessions to discuss the possible direction and goals of the USEIN and to react to a series of commissioned papers that identified and analyzed key issues for the initial stages of the network. The commissioned papers are being revised in the light of conference developments. When final versions are available later in 1998, these papers will be added to the ERIC database.

ERIC Database Size and Growth

The ERIC database consists of two files, one corresponding to the monthly abstract journal *Resources in Education* (*RIE*) and one corresponding to the

monthly *Current Index to Journals in Education (CIJE)*. *RIE* announces education-related documents and books, each with an accession number beginning
"ED" (for "educational document"). *CIJE* announces education-related journal
articles, each with an accession number beginning "EJ" (for "educational journal").

Document records include a full abstract and are approximately 1,800 characters long on average. Journal article records include a brief annotation and are
approximately 650 characters long on average.

Through 1997 the ERIC database includes 403,324 records for documents
and 548,446 records for journal articles, for a grand total of 951,770 bibliographic records. Approximately 12,500 document records and 20,000 article records
are added annually, for a total of 32,500 records per year. Overall, the ERIC
database through 1997 is approximately 1,085 million bytes (1.085 gigabytes) in
size and is growing at a rate of around 35 million bytes per year.

	Number of Records		
File	**1966–1996**	**1997**	**Total**
Resources in Education (RIE)—ED Records	391,305	12,019	403,324
Current Index to Journals in Education (CIJE)—EJ Records	528,867	19,579	548,446
Totals	920,172	31,598	951,770

ERIC Document Reproduction Service

The ERIC Document Reproduction Service (EDRS) is the document delivery
arm of ERIC and handles all subscriptions for ERIC microfiche and on-demand
requests for reproduced paper copy or microfiche. During 1997 the number of
standing order customers (SOCs) subscribing to the total ERIC microfiche collection (about 12,000 titles on 16,000 fiche cards, for approximately $2,700
annually) rose to 1,000. SOCs include more than 100 overseas addresses.

EDRS prices usually increase about 3 percent annually, due to increases in
the cost of basic materials and labor. The table below presents prices in effect for
the period January 1–December 31, 1998.

An updated order form reflecting the 1998 prices and shipping rates is now
available from EDRS. The form also shows the new flat-fee schedule for international shipping. There are no shipping charges associated with electronic delivery.

In the summer of 1997 EDRS made the online ERIC database available to
the public on its Web site. This version of the ERIC bibliographic database offers
a user-friendly search template to access all ED references from 1966 forward.
Users may order documents they find in their search from the same online session. The EDRS Web site also provides a quick-order feature for users who
already know the document number of the material they want to order.

In September 1997 EDRS added a new document delivery format to its suite
of ERIC products: digital image. Images of selected recent ERIC documents can
now be delivered online in Adobe Portable Document Format (PDF) as part of

Product	1998 Prices
Microfiche	
Annual subscription (approximate)	$2,700.00
Monthly subscription (price/fiche)	$ 0.2907 (Silver)
	$ 0.1421 (Diazo)
Back collections (1966–previous month) (price/fiche)	$ 0.1672
Clearinghouse collections (price/fiche)	$ 0.3060
On-demand Documents, per title	
Microfiche (MF) Up to 5 fiche (5 fiche = 480 pages)	$ 1.42
Each additional fiche (up to 96 pages)	$ 0.25
Reproduced Paper Copies (PC) First 1–25 pages	$ 4.21
Each additional 25-page increment (or part thereof)	$ 4.21
Electronic Page Images	
Base price per electronic document	$ 2.50
Price per page	$ 0.10
Example: A 15-page document costs $4 ($2.50 + $1.50)	
1997 Cumulative Indexes (on Microfiche)	
Subject, Author, Title, Institution, Descriptor, and Identifier indexes	$ 75.00

EDRS's on-demand delivery service. The EDRS Web site allows users to search for ERIC Documents (EDs) in the bibliographic database, order documents in the same session, and request online delivery of any copyright-cleared document (designated Level 1) that has been added to ERIC since 1993.

EDRS plans to offer electronic subscriptions to ERIC document collections in 1998. The types of collections to be offered will meet the needs of a variety of libraries, including public libraries and those at large research centers, universities and colleges, teacher research centers, and schools. Institutions will find an array of selections available, from the full ERIC collection to individual ERIC Clearinghouse collections to highly specialized topical collections. Subscriptions will be available in both online and CD-ROM formats.

For more information, the EDRS Web site can be accessed at http://edrs. com. To reach a customer service representative, contact EDRS at 703-440-1400 or 800-443-3742, or via e-mail at Service@edrs.com.

ACCESS ERIC

ACCESS ERIC is responsible for systemwide outreach, marketing, publicity, and promotion for the ERIC system. One major outreach activity is staffing exhibits and giving presentations on ERIC at education and library conferences. In 1997 ACCESS ERIC exhibited at conferences of the American Library Association (ALA), Association for Supervision and Curriculum Development (ASCD), National School Boards Association (NSBA), and International Society for Technology in Education (Tel*ED). Presentations were also given for members of the Education Writers Association, Phi Delta Kappa, and Federal Library and Information Center Committee (FLICC).

ACCESS ERIC works closely with the ERIC Clearinghouses to produce The *ERIC Review*, a free journal on current education issues. Recent issues focused on: "Inclusion," "Information Dissemination," and "The Path to College." The Clearinghouses also provide material for a series of Parent Brochures, which included these titles in 1997: *How Can I Support My Daughter in Early Adolescence? How Can I Support My Gifted Child? How Can We Prevent and Resolve Parent-Teacher Differences? Why, How, and When Should My Child Learn a Second Language?* and *Getting Online: A Friendly Guide for Parents, Students, and Teachers. Striving for Excellence (Volume 3)*, a compilation of more than 80 ERIC Digests related to the National Education Goals, was also produced in 1997.

ACCESS ERIC maintains the ERIC systemwide Web site (http://www. aspensys.com/eric), which provides links to all ERIC-sponsored sites as well as full-text copies of Parent Brochures, The *ERIC Review*, *All About ERIC*, and other systemwide materials. This site features the Online ERIC Publications Catalog, which enables users to browse, search, and place online orders for print copies of ERIC Clearinghouse publications (or to download information for traditional ordering). In 1997 the ERICNews listserv was introduced. This read-only mailing list brings more than 800 subscribers bimonthly updates on the latest ERIC systemwide initiatives, products, and services.

ACCESS ERIC continues to produce a number of information and referral databases and publications, including the *Catalog of ERIC Clearinghouse Publications*, the *ERIC Directory of Education-Related Information Centers*, the *Directory of ERIC Resource Collections*, and the *Calendar of Education-Related Conferences*.

ACCESS ERIC also maintains the database for the Education Resource Organizations Directory, available on the Department of Education's Web site (http://www.ed.gov). This directory includes information on almost 2,100 education-related national, regional, and state organizations and is constantly being updated and expanded.

AskERIC

AskERIC, a project of the ERIC Clearinghouse on Information and Technology, is an Internet-based reference and referral system providing question-answering, reference, and referral service to educators throughout the world. AskERIC first opened its electronic doors in November 1992 and in 1997 celebrated its fifth anniversary. In those five years AskERIC provided customized responses to more than 100,000 questions and is currently handling questions at a rate of approximately 1,000 per week. Responses draw on the total resources of the ERIC system, and e-mail answers to all inquiries are generated within 48 hours. Users generally receive a list of ERIC citations that deal with the topic in question and referrals to other resources for additional information. In order to handle the increasing volume of e-mail efficiently, AskERIC has implemented a new "digital triage" system based on help desk software. This software also helps AskERIC to locate resources that have been previously identified to answer frequently asked questions (FAQs) and that have been archived for possible future reference.

In addition, AskERIC has established a growing file of full-text resources (called the "AskERIC Virtual Library") on its Web site, for use by those wishing to search for materials on their own. These include lesson plans, AskERIC Info Guides, ERIC Digests, education listserv archives, and a Personal Librarian (PL Web) search interface to the entire ERIC database. The Virtual Library is currently accessed by Web users at the impressive rate of over 125,000 electronic visits per week.

AskERIC's new e-mail and Web addressees are AskERIC@askeric.org and www.askeric.org, respectively.

National Parent Information Network

The ERIC Clearinghouse on Elementary and Early Childhood Education and the ERIC Clearinghouse on Urban Education continue to jointly operate the National Parent Information Network (NPIN). This project includes an expanding Web site (http://npin.org), a question-answering service for parents (as part of the AskERIC project, parenting questions are referred to NPIN, where they are responded to by a parent educator), a discussion group on parenting, a major annual national conference on "Families, Technology, and Education" in Chicago, and many other presentations and workshops on the use of the Internet to support parents and parenting. NPIN is devoted specifically to providing high-quality, noncommercial information on child development, child care, education, and the parenting of children from birth through adolescence, to an audience including parents and those who work with parents.

During 1997 the NPIN Web site continued to expand in resources offered and in use. The site is updated bimonthly and provides links to many Internet sites on parenting and related issues. Parent News, a monthly electronic newsletter, which includes summaries of research and resources on parenting and education written specifically for parents, has become a major feature of the site.

NPIN was the recipient of three Internet awards during 1997.

ERIC on NISC DISC CD-ROM

Since April 1995 the ERIC Facility has offered for sale a CD-ROM product providing access to the entire ERIC database, including the full text of ERIC Digests. This product is prepared by the National Information Services Corporation (NISC) and is sold exclusively to ERIC for resale to users at a special low price aimed at bringing the product within the financial reach of all parts of the educational community ($100/year for quarterly updated discs).

During 1997 the ERIC data were reallocated across the two discs, in order to provide for future expansion on the Current disc. The Archival disc now contains ERIC data for 1966–1984 (19 years). The Current disc contains ERIC data for 1985 to the present. Because the Current disc contains the retrieval software, it is an essential component for accessing the database.

Beginning with the first quarterly disc for 1998, the NISC product will offer a Windows 95/98/NT version of the retrieval system as an option on the same disc as the MS-DOS version.

ERIC Database Computer System Change

The original ERIC database-building computer system was designed in 1968–1969 by North American Rockwell. This "legacy" system was operated by the ERIC Facility for 29 years. At the end of September 1997, the facility converted to the STAR system (offered by Cuadra Associates), operating on an internal Sun Sparcstation.

In connection with this major change of software and hardware, numerous backfile corrections were made to the database. Two new fields were added: International Standard Book Number (ISBN) and International Standard Serial Number (ISSN). The Personal Author field was expanded to accept as many authors as may be cited on the original document, book, or article. Any codes used have been associated with their textual translations more explicitly than before. All redundancies have been eliminated. Obsolete data fields were discontinued. All calendar dates in the Publication Date field have been entered in the form "YYYY-MM-DD" in order to eliminate the "Year 2000" problem and to make the dates more searchable than they were before.

During 1998 the ERIC distribution format will change from the old EBCDIC format to DIALOG Format B. All database recipients who can receive data via FTP will be moved to that data transmission process in lieu of the physical distribution of magnetic tapes.

National Clearinghouse on Educational Facilities

In August 1997 a contract was let by the U.S. Department of Education to Zeiders Enterprises, Inc., to operate a National Clearinghouse on Educational Facilities (NCEF), whose objective is to provide information support for the upcoming federal funding initiative directed at renovating, refurbishing, and rebuilding the aging physical infrastructure of K–12 educational buildings and facilities throughout the United States.

Although funded independently of ERIC, NCEF will be cooperating and coordinating with ERIC to avoid duplication and improve efficiency. NCEF will be contributing documents and articles to ERIC (using the existing EF prefix) that are related to educational facilities. In addition, NCEF will be developing its own database of facilities-related literature (e.g., asbestos removal, rewiring, etc.) that is not specifically related to education.

In ERIC brochures and literature, NCEF will be referred to as an "affiliate" of the ERIC system. To contact NCEF, call 888-552-0624 (toll free) or e-mail at ncefinfo@edfacilities.org.

Most Popular ERIC Documents Ordered from EDRS in 1997 (Paper Copies)

Title	ED Number	Clearinghouse
1 Employability Skills for Students with Mild Disabilities: A Sequenced Curriculum Package for Teachers	ED 357 534	Disabilities and Gifted Education
2 Teaching Mathematics to Limited English Proficient Students	ED 317 086	Languages and Linguistics
3 Storyboarding: A Brief Description of the Process	ED 384 171	Disabilities and Gifted Education
4 A Vocabulary of the Omaha Language	ED 358 698	Languages and Linguistics
5 Guide to Quality: Even Start Family Literacy Programs	ED 393 087	Reading, English, and Communication
6 The Online Classroom: Teaching with the Internet	ED 400 577	Reading, English, and Communication
7 An American Imperative: Higher Expectations for Higher Education. An Open Letter to Those Concerned about the American Future. Report of the Wingspread Group on Higher Education	ED 364 144	Higher Education
8 At-Risk Families & Schools: Becoming Partners	ED 342 055	Educational Management
9 Turning Points: Preparing American Youth for the 21st Century: The Report of the Task Force on Education of Young Adolescents	ED 312 322	Urban Education
10 Full-Day Kindergarten: A Summary of the Research	ED 345 868	Elementary and Early Childhood Education
11 Inner World, Outer World: Understanding the Struggles of Adolescence	ED 290 118	Counseling and Student Services
12 The Community College of the Future	ED 281 191	Community Colleges
13 The Principal's Role in Shaping School Culture	ED 325 914	Educational Management
14 Adolescence—A Tough Time for Indian Youth. What Can We Do?	ED 326 340	Rural Education and Small Schools
15 Pass the Word. A Resource Booklet for the Native American Community Concerning New Concepts about Alcoholism	ED 326 344	Rural Education and Small Schools
16 Healthy Children 2000: National Health Promotion and Disease Prevention Objectives Related to Mothers, Infants, Children, Adolescents, and Youth	ED 345 860	Elementary and Early Childhood Education
17 A New Generation of Evidence: The Family Is Critical to Student Achievement	ED 375 968	Elementary and Early Childhood Education
18 An Administrator's Handbook on Designing Programs for the Gifted and Talented	ED 196 179	Disabilities and Gifted Education

Most Popular ERIC Documents Ordered from EDRS in 1997 (Paper Copies) (cont.)

Title	ED Number	Clearinghouse
19 Survey of Instructional Development Models with an Annotated ERIC Bibliography	ED 335 027	Information and Technology
20 Producing a Comprehensive Academic Advising Handbook	ED 339 435	Community Colleges
21 Contexts That Matter for Teaching and Learning: Strategic Opportunities for Meeting the Nation's Educational Goals	ED 357 023	Teaching and Teacher Education
22 Evaluation of a High School Block Schedule Restructuring Program	ED 384 652	Assessment and Evaluation
23 Manual on School Uniforms	ED 387 947	Educational Management
24 Confronting Dialect Minority Issues in Special Education	ED 356 673	Languages and Linguistics
25 How Long Term Presidents Lead	ED 361 044	Community Colleges

ERIC Web Sites

ERIC Program Office

Educational Resources Information Center (ERIC):
   http://www.ed.gov

ERIC Support Contractors

ACCESS ERIC (*general information about the ERIC system and links to all other ERIC Web sites*):
   http://www.aspensys.com/eric

ERIC Document Reproduction Service (EDRS):
   http://edrs.com

ERIC Processing and Reference Facility:
   http://ericfac.piccard.csc.com

Oryx Press (publisher of *Current Index to Journals in Education*):
   http://www.oryxpress.com

ERIC Clearinghouses

ERIC Clearinghouse on Adult, Career, and Vocational Education:
   http://coe.ohio-state.edu/cete/ericacve/index.htm

ERIC Clearinghouse on Assessment and Evaluation:
   http://ericae.net

ERIC Clearinghouse for Community Colleges:
   http://www.gseis.ucla.edu/ERIC/eric.html

ERIC Clearinghouse on Counseling and Student Services:
   http://www.uncg.edu/~ericcas2

ERIC Clearinghouse on Disabilities and Gifted Education:
http://www.cec.sped.org/ericec.htm

ERIC Clearinghouse on Educational Management:
http://darkwing.uoregon.edu/~ericcem

ERIC Clearinghouse on Elementary and Early Childhood Education:
http://ericps.crc.uiuc.edu/ericeece.html

(NPIN [National Parent Information Network]:
http://npin.org)

ERIC Clearinghouse on Higher Education:
http://www.gwu.edu/~eriche/

ERIC Clearinghouse on Information & Technology:
http://ericir.syr.edu/ithome; AskERIC: http://www.askeric.org

ERIC Clearinghouse on Languages and Linguistics:
http://www.cal.org/ericcll

ERIC Clearinghouse on Reading, English, and Communication:
http://www.indiana.edu/~eric_rec

ERIC Clearinghouse on Rural Education and Small Schools:
http://aelvira.ael.org/erichp.htm

ERIC Clearinghouse for Science, Mathematics, and Environmental Education:
http://www.ericse.org

ERIC Clearinghouse for Social Studies/Social Science Education:
http://www.indiana.edu/~ssdc/eric_chess.htm

ERIC Clearinghouse on Teaching and Teacher Education:
http://www.ericsp.org

ERIC Clearinghouse on Urban Education:
http://eric-web.tc.columbia.edu

Adjunct ERIC Clearinghouses

Adjunct ERIC Clearinghouse for Child Care:
http://ericps.crc.uiuc.edu/nccic/nccichome.html

Adjunct ERIC Clearinghouse on Clinical Schools:
http://www.aacte.org/menu2.html

Adjunct ERIC Clearinghouse for Consumer Education:
http://www.emich.edu/public/coe/nice

Adjunct ERIC Clearinghouse on Entrepreneurship Education:
http://www.celcee.edu

Adjunct ERIC Clearinghouse for ESL Literacy Education:
http://www.cal.org/ncle

Adjunct ERIC Clearinghouse for International Civic Education: [None]

Adjunct ERIC Clearinghouse for Law-Related Education:
http://www.indiana.edu/~ssdc/lre.html

Adjunct ERIC Clearinghouse for Service-Learning:
http://www.nicsl.coled.umn.edu

Adjunct ERIC Clearinghouse for the Test Collection:
http://ericae.net/testcol.htm

Adjunct ERIC Clearinghouse for United States–Japan Studies:
http://www.indiana.edu/~japan

Affliliates

National Clearinghouse for Educational Facilities:
http://www.edfacilities.org

National TRIO Clearinghouse (NTC):
http://www.trioprograms.org

United States Government Printing Office

North Capitol and H Streets N.W., Washington, DC 20401
202-512-1991
E-mail: asherman@gpo.gov
World Wide Web: http://www.access.gpo.gov

Andrew M. Sherman
Director, Office of Congressional, Legislative, and Public Affairs

The United States Government Printing Office (GPO) produces or procures printed and electronic products for Congress and the agencies of the federal government. GPO also disseminates printed and electronic government information to the public through the Superintendent of Documents' sales and depository library programs. It hosts a major government World Wide Web home page, the GPO Access service, which provides free public access to major government information databases. GPO Access is located on the World Wide Web at http://www.access.gpo.gov.

GPO's primary facility is in Washington, D.C. Across the country, 14 regional printing procurement offices, six satellite procurement facilities, a field printing office, a major distribution facility in Pueblo, Colorado, a retail sales branch, and 23 bookstores complete the GPO printing and sales structure.

This report focuses on GPO's expanding role as the producer, disseminator, and coordinator of U.S. government information in electronic formats. Previous reports have detailed GPO's printing services to the federal government.

Superintendent of Documents

GPO's original job when it opened in 1860 was to handle printing. Responsibility for the sale and distribution of government documents, previously handled by other departments, was added in 1895. Today, through its documents program, overseen by the Superintendent of Documents, GPO disseminates one of the world's largest volumes of informational literature, distributing more than 65 million government publications every year in print, microform, and electronic formats.

Library Programs

Most products produced by or through GPO are available to the public for reference through nearly 1,375 depository libraries located in the United States and its possessions. Depository libraries are public, academic, or other types of libraries designated by members of Congress or by law as official depositories. The Federal Depository Library Program (FDLP) is administered by the Library Programs Service (LPS), under the Superintendent of Documents. The mission of FDLP is to provide equitable, efficient, timely, and dependable no-fee public access to print and electronic government information within the scope of the program.

Many of the day-to-day administrative functions of FDLP are now handled via the FDLP administration page on the World Wide Web (http://access.gpo. gov/su_docs/dpos/fdlp.html). Depository libraries are now able to use the Web to update their library profiles, view and download their library item selection profiles, make new selections and drop unneeded items online, and respond to the Biennial Survey of Depository Libraries. Future Web electronic projects include an e-mail response system for depository library inquiries and an automated claims system.

Federal Depository Libraries assist users in locating government information in tangible formats, such as paper, microfiche, CD-ROM, and floppy disks, as well as information that is also available on the Web and in some paid subscription services. FDLP has made arrangements for users to access STAT-USA, CenStats, and Environmental Health Information Service at no charge to the user or the library. LPS continues to look for additional cooperative opportunities to expand the public's access to federal agencies' online services.

Transition to Electronic Offerings

In August 1995 GPO, at the direction of Congress, initiated the "Study to Identify Measures Necessary for a Successful Transition to a More Electronic Federal Depository Library Program." The key findings of the study report, which was published in June 1996, addressed the following issues:

- Scope of the Federal Depository Library Program
- Notification and Compliance
- Permanent Access to Authentic Information
- Locator Services
- Timetable for Implementation
- Assessment of Standards for Creation and Dissemination of Electronic Government Information Products
- Cost of Electronic Information Dissemination
- Legislative Changes

Conclusions drawn in the study report reflect the views and advice of the library community, federal publishing agencies, and users of government information. Strong support emerged in the working-group discussions over two major issues concerning FDLP as a whole. The first issue concerned the value of having the authority for a broad-based public information program rest in the legislative branch. Nearly all of the participants felt that this model has served the public well. High value was placed on the presence of FDLP in nearly every congressional district to directly serve the public in local library settings.

There was also strong support for the value to the library community of having a single entity in the Superintendent of Documents to coordinate library-related information dissemination activities. The depository library community has consistently affirmed the utility and cost-effectiveness of a "one-stop shopping" approach to acquiring government information.

Permanent access to government information is a critical issue in the electronic environment. GPO will, through the mechanism of FDLP, ensure that electronic government information products are maintained for permanent public access, in the same spirit in which regional depositories provide permanent access to print products. This requires the development of a distributed system that comprises all of the institutional program stakeholders, including information-producing agencies, GPO, depository libraries, the Library of Congress and other national libraries, and the National Archives and Records Administration (NARA).

Federal Depository Library Program

Depository libraries receive government information products at no cost in return for providing free public access to the information. The information products are sent in a variety of formats, including paper, microfiche, and CD-ROM. An increasing number are available as online files. With the increasing use of electronic information technologies by federal publishing agencies, LPS is working to ensure that federal information content, regardless of format, is available to the public through FDLP.

In fiscal year (FY) 1997, 12,460,000 million copies of 30,300 titles in all formats were distributed to depository libraries under authority of the Superintendent of Documents. U.S. Geological Survey and National Imagery and Mapping Administration maps are distributed by those agencies under agreements negotiated with LPS.

LPS acquires government documents, determines the format (paper, microfiche, or electronic) of publications distributed to depository libraries, and assigns Superintendent of Documents (SuDocs) classification numbers. LPS also acts as the documents distribution agent to foreign libraries in the International Exchange Service Program, on behalf of the Library of Congress.

LPS administers the designation and termination of depository libraries and monitors the condition of depository libraries through periodic inspection visits, self-studies, and a biennial survey. LPS also organizes continuing-education efforts for documents librarians. In 1998 the annual Federal Depository Conference in Washington, D.C., which attracts a large audience of information professionals, will present new federal electronic information products. The popular Interagency Depository Seminar, held each spring, familiarizes new depository library staff with major federal information products and services.

LPS identifies, assesses, and implements information technology solutions as FDLP moves toward a more electronic future. LPS coordinates the LPS World Wide Web applications, including the suite of Pathway Services that facilitate access to federal information on the Web. It also coordinates efforts to establish partnerships with federal agencies, depository libraries, and other library service institutions, such as the Online Computer Library Center (OCLC).

Usage of FDLP and GPO Access

The Federal Depository Library Program continues to be a principal mechanism to meet the government information needs of the American public. Responses from the 1995 Biennial Survey of Depository Libraries yielded an estimate that 189,000 to 237,000 persons used FDLP information each week. The transactions included both on-site usage in libraries and remote electronic usage, such as reference service via e-mail. In addition, users are electronically accessing free government information available from the GPO Access service at a rapidly growing rate. Users are downloading approximately eight million documents per month from more than 70 databases.

FDLP Electronic Collection

After GPO established the GPO Access databases, it assumed practical responsibility for permanent access to those electronic government information products. This expanded mission has led to the creation of the FDLP Electronic Collection. The collection consists of remotely accessible electronic government information products, including core legislative and regulatory products, that will reside permanently on GPO servers and other products maintained either by GPO or by other institutions with which GPO has established formal agreements. This collection requires standard library collection management policies and techniques, such as selection, acquisition, bibliographic control, access, organization, maintenance, deselection, and preservation for access. GPO's Collection Management Plan provides a policy framework through which the collection of resources is developed and maintained. The plan will guide GPO in executing its permanent access responsibility for government information products, such as the online *Federal Register*, *Congressional Record*, and *Commerce Business Daily*.

Sales

The Superintendent of Documents' sales program currently offers for public sale approximately 10,000 federal information products on a wide array of subjects. These are sold principally by mail order and through GPO bookstores across the country. The program operates on a cost recovery basis without the use of tax dollars.

Publications for sale include books, forms, posters, pamphlets, and maps. Subscription services for both dated periodicals and basic-and-supplement services (involving an initial volume and supplemental issues) are also offered. A growing selection of electronic information products, including CD-ROMs, computer disks, and magnetic tapes are now available in the sales program.

U.S. Fax Watch offers U.S. and Canadian customers free access to information on a variety of sales products, electronic products and services, and depository library locations. To use the service, customers call in from a touchtone telephone, follow voice prompts to select the document they want, and then have the requested information faxed back to them in minutes. U.S. Fax Watch is available 24 hours a day, seven days a week, at 202-512-1716.

Express service, which includes priority handling and Federal Express delivery, is available for orders placed by telephone for domestic delivery. Orders placed before noon eastern time for in-stock publications and single-copy subscriptions will be delivered within two working days. Some quantity restrictions apply. Call the telephone order desk at 202-512-1800 for more information.

Consumer-oriented publications are also either sold or distributed at no charge through the Consumer Information Center, in Pueblo, Colorado, which GPO operates on behalf of the General Services Administration.

Sales Operations Modernized

GPO's Documents Sales area will have a state-of-the-art, customer-oriented business system in place in mid-1998. The Integrated Processing System (IPS) is a computer system that will replace approximately 20 different mainframe systems that were developed during the past 20 years to perform a variety of functions. IPS will integrate all these functions using one database.

IPS is being brought in to modernize Documents Sales and to improve customer service. The goal is to process all orders, inquiries, and complaints within 24 hours of receipt in the Customer Service Center. Documents Sales hopes to accomplish this with the following:

- One central database: All transactions go into one database, eliminating duplication and giving faster order processing and real-time access to all customer, inventory, warehouse, and financial information. This will streamline order processing and tracking. Scanning and imaging technology will speed work from desk to desk, eliminating the paper trail.
- Inventory management and forecasting tools: IPS includes a comprehensive set of forecasting, demand modeling, trend analysis, and seasonal indices tools to help inventory specialists better identify customer demand.
- State-of-the-art warehouse management technology: The IPS system will automatically assign put-away locations and even prioritize the picking locations to maximize warehouse efficiency and space utilization. In addition, hand-held radio frequency bar code scanners will be used to pick the stock, further reducing paperwork and speeding order-processing times.

IPS will bring significant improvements to GPO's sales program. Soon after implementation in the spring of 1998, evaluations will begin on the feasibility of extending IPS to Library Programs Service and other GPO systems. Documents Sales expects big differences in 1998 as GPO moves to provide world class customer service through a state-of-the-art system.

U.S. Government Bookstores

Publications of particular public interest are made available in government bookstores. In addition, to meet the information needs of all customers, any bookstore can order any government information product currently offered for sale and have it sent directly to the customer. Customers can order by phone, mail, or fax from any government bookstore.

Government bookstores are located in major cities throughout the United States. Their addresses, hours, and a map are available on the GPO Web site.

Catalogs

GPO publishes a variety of free catalogs that cover hundreds of information products on a vast array of subjects. The free catalogs include:

- *U.S. Government Information*: new and popular information products of interest to the general public
- *New Information*: bi-monthly listing of new titles; distributed to librarians and other information professionals
- *U.S. Government Subscriptions*: periodicals and other subscription services*
- *Subject Bibliographies (SBs)*: nearly 200 lists, each containing titles relating to a single subject or field of interest*
- *Subject Bibliography Index*: lists all *SB* subject areas
- *Catalog of Information Products for Business*: GPO's largest catalog for business audiences

Sales Product Catalog

The Superintendent of Documents issues the GPO *Sales Product Catalog (SPC)*, a guide to current U.S. government information products offered for sale through the Superintendent of Documents. The fully searchable SPC database, which is updated every working day, is available online via GPO's Web site.

The *SPC* is also available online through DIALOG (File Code 166), which offers online ordering, retrieval, and research capabilities.

Monthly Catalog of United States Government Publications

More than two million bibliographic records for government information products have been published in the *Monthly Catalog of United States Government Publications*. This catalog is the most comprehensive listing of government publications issued by more than 250 federal departments and agencies within the legislative, judicial, and executive branches.

The full cataloging records are available online through the Online Computer Library Center (OCLC) at approximately 17,000 libraries worldwide. Additional dissemination occurs through commercial vendors and online catalogs of many public and university libraries.

Catalog records are also published on the GPO Web site, as soon as one day after original production. Approximately 87,000 records are available for searching at the Web site. A locator application links the *Catalog of United States Government Publications* records with the names and locations of depositories that selected each title. Approximately 2,300 records for online titles contain links to the actual electronic texts. GPO is working to establish OCLC's Persistent Uniform Resource Locator services (PURL) to assist in maintaining hot links associated with the *Catalog of United States Government Publications* and other applications on GPO's Web site.

---

* These catalogs are also available from U.S. Fax Watch at 202-512-1716 and via the Web at http://www.access.gpo.gov/su_docs.

The CD-ROM edition of the *Monthly Catalog* features both DOS and Windows user interfaces. It cumulates complete records on a monthly basis and includes multiple years on a single disc. The CD-ROM edition is for sale at $245 per year (12 issues).

An abridged paper edition of the *Monthly Catalog*, using abbreviated records and a single-keyword title index, also is available. Each monthly issue consists of discrete monthly data sets and is intended as a ready-reference paper adjunct to the complete *Monthly Catalog* edition on CD-ROM. This edition is available for sale as a subscription service for $42 per year.

GPO Access

GPO Access is a service of GPO that provides free public access to electronic information products produced by the federal government. The information retrieved from GPO Access is the official published version and it may be used without restriction. This service was established by Public Law 103-40, the Government Printing Office Electronic Information Enhancement Act of 1993. GPO Access is one of the few information systems set up by law, and it is one of the few systems providing access to information from all three branches of the federal government.

GPO Access currently averages more than three million searches per month and approximately eight million document retrievals from more than 70 databases. The databases with the most retrievals include: Federal Register, Commerce Business Daily, United States Code, and Code of Federal Regulations.

New and Improved GPO Access Web Pages

The Superintendent of Documents has a new GPO Access home page, redesigned to provide users with easier and more efficient access to GPO's online resources. The new address is http://www.access.gpo.gov/su_docs.

GPO Access Web pages have been redesigned to be more intuitive to users, with easy-to-follow paths for locating government information products. In addition to the home page, several new second-level pages have been developed that allow users to quickly and conveniently access products and services. These pages are available as hot links from the new SuDocs page, with quick jumps to the most popular applications. These improvements are in response to feedback GPO received through focus group sessions, user surveys, and comments provided to the GPO Access User Support Team.

The free services of GPO Access fall within the following categories:

- Government information databases available for online use that provide full-text search and retrieval capabilities
- Individual federal agency files available for download from the Federal Bulletin Board
- Tools to assist users in finding government information
- Collections of government information available for free use at a nearby library
- User support

Government Information Databases

The GPO Access service currently provides access to many databases through a wide area information server (WAIS). Several databases were added in 1997, including a number of Code of Federal Regulations (CFR) titles, FY 1998 Federal Budget Publications, and the Constitution of the United States, to name a few. The majority of these databases offer results in both ASCII and Adobe Acrobat's portable document format (PDF), which offers users a nearly exact typeset copy of the government information product.

Federal Bulletin Board

Individual federal agency files are available from the Federal Bulletin Board (FBB), a free electronic bulletin board service maintained by GPO. The FBB enables federal agencies to provide to the public immediate self-service access to federal information in electronic form. Federal agencies use the FBB as a means to distribute electronic files to the public in a variety of file formats. Users can access information from the White House and executive branch agencies (including independent agencies). The FBB can be accessed as a link from GPO Access or directly at http://www.access.gpo.gov/su_docs/fedbbs.html.

Locator Tools and Access to Collections

GPO Access provides a number of useful tools for locating government information products available on GPO Access or other federal agency Internet sites:

- The *Catalog of United States Government Publications* consists of bibliographic records that describe government information products received for cataloging
- The *Sales Product Catalog* provides information on product availability and how to purchase government information products available through GPO
- The Government Information Locator Service (GILS)
- Pathway Indexer searches more than 1,350 official U.S. federal agency and military Internet sites, at http://www.access.gpo.gov/su_docs/dpos searche.html
- A variety of other search tools allow users to find government information by title, topic, or keyword

GPO Access also assists users in finding collections of government information available at federal depository libraries. GPO Access search applications help users find a depository library in their area that can provide them with tangible government information products.

Methods of Access

GPO Access recognizes the various needs and technological capabilities of the public. A wide range of information dissemination technologies are supported, from the latest client/server applications through the Internet to dial-up modem access, including methods compatible with assistive technologies. Even those without computers can use GPO Access through public access terminals located at federal depository libraries throughout the country. All depositories are expected to offer users access to workstations with a graphical user interface, CD-ROM capability, an Internet connection, and the ability to access government information via the World Wide Web.

GPO Access Training and Demonstrations

GPO will continue to provide GPO Access training classes and demonstrations during 1998 at various locations throughout the United States. Training classes involve hands-on use of GPO Access by participants at individual workstations. GPO Access demonstrations, which are not hands-on, are used by GPO to provide presentations to larger audiences. In addition, GPO has inaugurated "train the trainer" sessions to expand training opportunities to a wider audience.

Commerce Business Daily

GPO has established an alliance with the Department of Commerce to make the *Commerce Business Daily* (*CBD*) available online via GPO Access (CBDNet). This online service provides free public access to the information contained in the *CBD* in real time.

CBDNet also allows for the posting of synopses electronically through the World Wide Web, e-mail, and manuscript formats. More and more agencies are seeing the financial advantage to directly submitting notices electronically and are abandoning the traditional manuscript method. For example, in its first month CBDNet received 82 percent of notice submissions electronically. By April 1997 that number rose to more than 93 percent and by October to more than 97 percent. As more agencies gain access to the Internet and realize the cost savings available to them, the number of electronic submissions is expected to increase even more.

CBDNet is available as a link from GPO Access or directly at http://cbdnet. access.gpo.gov/.

Improvements to Government Information Locator Service

The Government Information Locator Service (GILS) is a federal government-wide initiative to direct users to information resources and includes electronic information resources. GILS records identify public information resources within the federal government, describe the information available in these resources, and assist in obtaining the information. GILS is a decentralized collection of agency-based information locators using network technology and international standards to direct users to relevant information resources within the federal government.

GPO is continuing its efforts to provide a single point of entry to access, link to, or browse all U.S. federal GILS databases. The GILS application on GPO Access now searches all known WAIS-based U.S. federal GILS sites as the default selection. This includes all GILS records maintained by GPO and those on other government GILS sites. A search using the default will return a results list of relevant records on any of these sites, and those records can be retrieved.

Recognition

GPO Access was chosen as a select site by the editors of the *Dow Jones Business Directory*. The GPO Web site has been included in the National Research Foundation (NRF) Small Business Innovative Research (SBIR) Internet Resources Catalog. The Weekly Compilation of Presidential Documents available on GPO Access was chosen as a selection for the Scout Report for Social Sciences. Also, the National Performance Review (NPR), under the leadership of Vice President Al Gore, presented GPO's CBDNet Team with a Hammer Award for its efforts in creating CBDNet.

User Support

Questions or comments regarding GPO Access can be directed to the GPO Access User Support Team by e-mail at gpoaccess@gpo.gov, by toll-free telephone at 888-293-6498, by phone locally at 202-512-1530, or by fax at 202-512-1262.

National Library of Education

555 New Jersey Ave. N.W., Washington, DC 20208-5721
202-219-1692, e-mail: library@inet.ed.gov, World Wide Web: http://www.ed.gov

The National Library of Education (NLE) is the largest federally funded library in the world devoted solely to education. An expansion of the former U.S. Department of Education Research Library, NLE houses on-site more than 200,000 books and about 750 periodical subscriptions in addition to studies, reports, Educational Resources Information Center (ERIC) microfiche, and CD-ROM databases. NLE's holdings include books on education, management, public policy, and related social sciences; dictionaries, encyclopedias, handbooks, directories, abstracts, indexes, and legal and other research sources in print and CD-ROM; current and historical journals and newsletters; and more than 450,000 microforms.

Special collections include rare books published before 1800, mostly in education; historical books, 1800–1964; early American textbooks, 1775–1900; modern American textbooks, 1900–1959; U.S. Department of Education reports, bibliographies, and studies; archived speeches, policy papers, and reports; and children's classics.

Mission

The mission of the National Library of Education is to ensure the improvement of educational achievement at all levels by becoming a principal center for the collection, preservation, and effective use of research and other information related to education. NLE will promote widespread access to its materials, expand coverage of all education issues and subjects, and maintain quality control. NLE will also participate with other major libraries, schools, and educational centers across the United States in providing a network of national education resources.

Organizational Structure

NLE reports to the Office of the Assistant Secretary for the Office of Educational Research and Improvement (OERI) and is organized into three divisions: Reference and Information Services, Collection and Technical Services, and Resource Sharing and Cooperation.

History

The U.S. Department of Education was established by an act of Congress in 1867 for the purpose of

> collecting such statistics and facts as shall show the condition and progress of education in the several states and territories, and of diffusing information as shall aid in the establishment and maintenance of efficient school systems and otherwise promote the cause of education throughout the country. (Statutes at Large 14 [1867]: 434)

The prominent educator Henry Barnard was named commissioner of education. After one year of independent operation, however, the Department of Education was transferred to the Department of the Interior, where it was known as the Bureau of Education. When Barnard, who was interested in establishing an education library, resigned as commissioner in 1870, he left his own extensive private collection of books on education with the bureau. During the 70 years of its operation in the Department of the Interior, the Bureau of Education administered an independent library serving the specialized needs of its employees.

In 1939 the Bureau of Education became one of the five constituent agencies of the new Federal Security Agency, forerunner of the Department of Health, Education, and Welfare (HEW). The Bureau of Education library then became part of the Federal Security Agency library, which eventually became the HEW library.

As a result of a 1973 management study of the HEW library, which recommended decentralization of the library, the education collection was transferred to the newly established (1972) National Institute of Education (NIE). NIE agreed to maintain an educational research library in an effort to fulfill its mandate to "provide leadership in the conduct and support of scientific inquiry in the education process." (Education Amendments of 1972, U.S. Code, vol. 20, sec. 1221 a [1972])

From 1973 to 1985 the NIE Educational Research Library was the recipient of several fine education collections, including the education and library and information science collections of the HEW library, the library of the Center for Urban Education (formerly in New York City), the National Education Association library, the Community Services Administration library, and the former Central Midwest Regional Education Laboratory (CEMREL) library.

A major reorganization of OERI, which had included NIE as a component, occurred in October 1985. The name of the library was changed to U.S. Department of Education Research Library and it operated as part of Information Services, one of the five units of OERI. More recently, it operated under OERI's Library Programs.

In March 1994 Congress authorized the establishment of the National Library of Education, with specific charges. By law, two other units in OERI—the former Education Information Branch and the former Education Information Resources Division—have joined forces with the library staff to form NLE, boosting services to department employees and other clients. The Educational Resources Information Center (ERIC) is a major U.S. Department of Education program that serves the education community, the government, and the general public with ready access to education information nationwide. [See the article on the Educational Resources Information Center—*Ed.*]

This new designation as National Library and the expansion of functions meant a broader range of services and a larger staff. NLE now has approximately 50 staff members compared to the former Education Research Library's staff of seven.

Functions

NLE provides a central location within the federal government for information about education; provides comprehensive reference services on education to employees of the U.S. Department of Education and its contractors and grantees, other federal employees, and members of the public; and promotes cooperation and resource sharing among providers and repositories of education information in the United States.

Major Themes and Goals

Among the major themes and goals of NLE are to establish and maintain a one-stop, central information and referral service to respond to telephone, mail, electronic, and other inquiries from the public on:

- Programs and activities of the U.S. Department of Education
- ERIC resources and services of the 16 clearinghouses and ERIC Support Components, including the ERIC database of more than 850,000 records of journal articles, research reports, curriculum and teaching guides, conference papers, and books
- U.S. Department of Education publications
- Research and referral services available to the public, including ERIC, the OERI Institutes, and the national education dissemination system
- Statistics from the National Center for Education Statistics
- Referrals to additional sources of information and expertise about educational issues available through educational associations and foundations, the private sector, colleges and universities, libraries, and bibliographic databases

In addition, NLE aims to:

- Provide for the delivery of a full range of reference services (including specialized subject searches; search and retrieval of electronic databases; document delivery by mail and fax; research counseling, bibliographic instruction, and other training; interlibrary loan services; and selective information dissemination) on subjects related to education
- Promote greater cooperation and resource sharing among libraries and archives with significant collections in education by establishing networks; developing a national union list of education journals held by education libraries throughout the United States; developing directories and indexes to textbook and other specialized collections held by education libraries; and cooperating to preserve, maintain, and promote access to educational items of special historical value or interest

Current Activities

During its first year, the library focused on selecting the National Library of Education Task Force and planning for its 1996 meetings, creating a budget, establishing collection assessment and collection development policies, producing a commemorative poster, designing outreach and promotion programs, setting up and monitoring a toll-free customer-service line, creating a World Wide Web home page and site, organizing a quarterly lecture series, creating and carrying out a customer service survey, and establishing near- and long-term goals and objectives.

The library also continues to provide legislative reference services through a branch library in the department's headquarters building. Further, NLE is establishing liaisons with the OERI Institutes and other offices within OERI, participating in the orientation of new department employees, and undergoing an internal management review and evaluation.

Future Plans

NLE's future plans include:

- Establishing a networking/resource-sharing program
- Developing a three-year plan to eliminate the arrearage of uncataloged books and other materials in the library's collection and to preserve and maintain their usability
- Expanding NLE's presence on the Internet through INet (the U.S. Department of Education's Internet) and ERIC
- Initiating a digitization program
- Carrying out a functional analysis of the library

Publications

NLE's primary publication is *The Open Window*, a quarterly newsletter of the library. Flyers and other informational material are available on request.

Primary Collections

NLE's primary collections include its circulating, reference, serials, and microform collections. The circulating collection largely includes books in the field of education published since 1965. The broad coverage of the collection includes not only education but such related areas as law, public policy, economics, urban affairs, sociology, history, philosophy, and library and information science. The reference collection includes current dictionaries, general and specialized encyclopedias, handbooks, directories, major abstracting services, newspapers and journals related to education and the social sciences, and indexes.

Current periodical holdings number more than 750 English-language journals and newsletters. The collection includes nearly all of the primary journals indexed by *Current Index to Journals in Education* (*CIJE*) and *Education Index*. The library subscribes to eight major national newspapers and maintains back issues in microform of four national newspapers.

The microform collection consists of more than 450,000 items, including newspapers, the *Federal Register*, the *Congressional Record*, *Newsbank*, college catalogs, the William S. Gray Collection on Reading, the Kraus Curriculum Collection, and various education and related journals. It also includes the complete microfiche collection of ERIC documents, a program funded by the U.S. Department of Education. NLE's ERIC collection contains complete sets of the ERIC indexes and recent ERIC clearinghouse publications and products. ERIC research publications are in varied formats—bibliographies, state-of-the-art papers, reviews, and information analyses in the 16 areas of education presently covered by the ERIC system.

Special Collections

The earliest volumes of NLE's special collections date to the 15th century and include early American textbooks, children's books, and books about education. Some restoration has taken place; items are housed in controlled space, and a catalog—*Early American Textbooks, 1775–1900*—has been issued. This collection began with Henry Barnard's private collection of American schoolbooks, was nurtured by Commissioner John Eaton during his tenure (1870–1886), and was further enriched by several private donors. Other special collections maintained by the library are (1) material from the former National Institute of Education, the former U.S. Office of Education, and the U.S. Department of Education, including reports, studies, manuals, and other documents; (2) archives of the former U.S. Office of Education and the former National Institute of Education, including speeches, policy papers, and other documents.

Interlibrary Loan

NLE offers an active interlibrary loan service and is a member of the Online Computer Library Center (OCLC). Through the OCLC database, library staff can tap the resources of a large number of research library collections throughout the United States and draw on their holdings, as well as offer interlibrary loan service to other libraries.

Technology Resources

NLE's Technology Resources Center offers users an opportunity to explore what is available in technology, use the equipment, and look at hundreds of programs designed for use in classrooms. The center has computer programs, CD-ROM, videotapes, and videodiscs. It offers a range of hardware and software for all levels of education and training.

The center is open to visits from all educators, researchers, administrators, curriculum specialists, teachers, librarians, and anyone else interested in the effective use of technology in education and training. Publishers of computer materials have provided over 400 programs from preschool to postgraduate levels. The collection of computer programs is strong in science, reading, mathematics, and word processing. Programs on art, music, science, biology, history, mathematics, chemistry, and employment skills are included. Many of the titles are chosen from programs listed in the Association for Supervision and Development's "Only the Best."

Equipment represents state-of-the-art computer technology available for use in schools. Included are Apple, IBM, and Compaq systems, as well as Kodak Photo CD and Philips Full-Motion CDi systems. Several models of CD-ROM units are demonstrated for both MS-DOS and Macintosh. Interactive videodiscs using computers and barcode readers are also shown; and videotape, electronic mail, online data services (including the Internet), and closed-captioned decoders are all on display.

The Technology Resources Center regularly provides programs on the use of technology in education. Special presentations and demonstrations are arranged on request. Tours of the facilities and demonstrations of materials are given for visiting educators and the public. Center staff work with school systems, software publishers, and vendors to arrange special demonstrations related to individual school system needs.

Copies of commercially published software evaluations and an index of software programs are available for use in the center. Software lists from state and local education agencies are welcomed. The center does not evaluate, recommend, or endorse hardware or software, nor does it lend software or equipment. Equipment is used solely for demonstration.

OERI Online Access

NLE maintains an electronic repository of education information and provides public access through two electronic networks:

- INet. An Internet-based service, INet makes information available through World Wide Web, gopher, and ftp servers.
- OERI Toll-Free Bulletin Board System. For educators who do not yet have access to the Internet, the bulletin board provides access to most of the same information as INet.

How to Access the U.S. Department of Education via Internet

The U.S. Department of Education maintains several types of Internet servers and tries to make all its holdings accessible to the public through channels commonly used by educators.

- *World Wide Web*. NLE's World Wide Web server can be accessed at http://www.ed.gov/.
- *Gopher*. The gopher server's address is gopher.ed.gov; or select North America—>USA—>General—>U.S. Department of Education from the All/Other Gophers menu on your system.
- *Ftp*. Ftp users can access the information by ftping to ftp.ed.gov (log on anonymous).

- *E-mail.* E-mail users can get a catalog and instructions for using the NLE mail server by sending e-mail to almanac@inet.ed.gov. In the body of the message, type: send catalog<M>. Avoid the use of signature blocks.
- *Telnet.* No public telnet access is available. Users must either have an appropriate WWW, gopher, or ftp client at their site or be able to telnet to a public access client elsewhere.

Questions and Comments

Suggestions or questions about the contents of the WWW, gopher, ftp, and mail servers should be directed to one of the following:

E-mail	webmaster@inet.ed.gov
	gopheradm@inet.ed.gov
	wwwadmin@inet.ed.gov
Telephone	202-219-2266
Fax	202-219-1817
Mail	INet Project Manager
	U.S. Department of Education
	Office of Educational Research and Improvement
	National Library of Education/RSCD
	555 New Jersey Ave. N.W., Rm. 214
	Washington, DC 20208-5725

How to Access the OERI Toll-Free Bulletin Board System

Virtually any computer with telecommunications software can be used to access the OERI Toll-Free Bulletin Board System.

For any computer, set the following parameters in the communications software before dialing the bulletin board:

- speed up to 14,400 baud
- 8 data bits
- 1 stop bit
- no parity
- full duplex

The BBS toll-free number is 800-222-4922 (within Washington, D.C., area 202-219-1511). Call 202-219-1526 with any system access problems.

How to Find Out What's New Online

The INet World Wide Web, gopher, ftp, and e-mail servers are continuously updated with new press releases, grant announcements, publication summaries, full-text documents, and statistical data sets. New material on major U.S. Department of Education initiatives such as Goal 2000, School-to-Work, Technology, and Elementary and Secondary Education Act (ESEA) Schoolwides is added frequently.

To find new items on the INet World Wide Web Server, select News near the top of the home page to display a list of recent additions.

To find new items on the gopher server, follow the path:

What's New in This Gopher/
What's New (Format: nn=#days back or mm/dd/yy=since date)<?>

and enter a search string in one of the formats indicated (e.g., "7 days" or "12/31/94"). The gopher will quickly build and present a menu of items added or changed during that time.

To find new items on the OERI Toll-Free Bulletin Board System, type G to select [G]opher from the main menu. Then follow the instructions for gopher above.

NLE Telephones

Library Administration	202-219-1884
Reference/Research/Statistics	202-219-1692
Outside Washington, D.C., area	800-424-1616
fax	202-219-1696
Circulation/Interlibrary loan	202-219-2238
Collection Development/Technical Services	202-219-1883
Legislative Reference Service	202-401-1045
fax	202-401-9023
Technology Resources Center	202-219-1699
ACCESS ERIC	800-LET-ERIC

National Association
and Organization Reports

American Library Association

50 E. Huron St., Chicago, IL 60611
312-944-6780, 800-545-2433
World Wide Web: http://www.ala.org

Barbara J. Ford
President

As the millennium approaches, members of the American Library Association (ALA) are addressing a major challenge of the next century: making sure that all Americans have the skills and resources they need to fully participate in the global information society.

Major achievements in 1997 include a historic Supreme Court victory for First Amendment rights in cyberspace, authorization of telecommunications discounts for libraries, and a new campaign to educate parents and children about the Internet. These achievements mark significant progress toward ALA Goal 2000, a five-year initiative to position the association, libraries, and librarians for the 21st century.

Founded in 1876, the American Library Association is the voice of U.S. libraries and the millions of people who depend on them. The 56,703 members of the oldest and largest library association in the world are primarily librarians, but also trustees, publishers, and other supporters.

The mission of ALA is to promote the highest quality library and information services. Diversity, education and continuous learning, equity of access, intellectual freedom, and the 21st century are key action areas for the 1997–1998 fiscal year.

The association encompasses 11 membership divisions focused on areas of special interest: the American Association of School Librarians (AASL), the American Library Trustee Association (ALTA), the Association for Library Collections and Technical Services (ALCTS), the Association for Library Service to Children (ALSC), the Association of College and Research Libraries (ACRL), the Association of Specialized and Cooperative Library Agencies (ASCLA), the Library Administration and Management Association (LAMA), the Library and Information Technology Association (LITA), the Public Library Association (PLA), the Reference and User Services Association (RUSA), and the Young Adult Library Services Association (YALSA).

ALA maintains its headquarters in Chicago as well as a legislative office and Office for Information Technology Policy in Washington, D.C., and an editorial office in Middletown, Connecticut, for *Choice*, a review journal for academic libraries.

Washington Report

The Library Services and Technology Act (LSTA) marked its first full year of funding in 1997 with an appropriation of $146 million, a $10 million increase over predecessor programs. The act was developed by ALA in cooperation with other library groups to replace the Library Services and Construction Act in 1996. With an emphasis on technological innovation and outreach services, LSTA also transferred library programs administered by the U.S. Department of Education to the new Institute of Museum and Library Services (formerly the Institute of Museum Services).

School and public libraries are scheduled to receive $2.5 billion in discounts on telecommunications services effective January 1, 1998. The discounts were announced in May 1997 by the Federal Communications Commission (FCC) as part of rules to implement discounts for libraries and schools authorized in the Telecommunications Act of 1996. The discounts, ranging from 20 to 90 percent, are expected to make Internet connections affordable for many more school and public libraries. Libraries in low-income and high-cost communities will receive deeper discounts.

These discounts resulted from extensive work by the ALA Washington Office and Office for Information Technology Policy (OITP) with the library community, the FCC, the Education and Libraries Network Coalition (EdLINC), and federal agencies. ALA also secured media support and mailed two "Special Reports" on library telecom discounts to public and school libraries, state library agencies, and others.

The Washington Office staff has provided leadership in helping to ensure that principles of fair use are preserved and applied in cyberspace. These activities included a key role in blocking digital copyright policies endorsed by the Clinton administration and many private-industry groups that would sharply curtail information now available free or at low cost to students, researchers, and library users. Through the Digital Future Coalition—which ALA helped to found—ALA continues to work to educate the press and policy makers on intellectual-property issues as they relate to libraries and the public interest.

ALA worked with the U.S. Department of Education to ensure that libraries and library materials were included in the Clinton administration's America Reads Challenge legislation. The challenge calls on all Americans to support teachers and help ensure that every American child can read well and independently by the end of third grade. ALA also secured key library amendments in a pending House version of the legislation.

The association organized and staffed an Inter-Association Working Group on Government Information Policy, which developed and submitted to Congress a legislative proposal to amend the Federal Depository Library Program. The proposal was designed to improve public access to government information, especially as much more government information becomes available to the public only in electronic format.

Intellectual Freedom

"The legal birth certificate of the Internet"—that was how Bruce Ennis, attorney for the American Library Association and the Freedom to Read Foundation, described the June 26, 1997, Supreme Court decision declaring the Communications Decency Act (CDA) unconstitutional. In its ruling, the court agreed with the association and other plaintiffs that communications over the Internet should not be limited to what is suitable for minors. The case was the first to establish that First Amendment rights apply in cyberspace.

"The Supreme Court ruling means that Americans will enjoy the same access to information online that we have on library and bookstores shelves. It means parents can decide for their own children what they do—and don't—want them to read," said 1996–1997 ALA President Mary R. Somerville in welcoming the news.

"Banned Books Week: Celebrating the Freedom to Read" (September 20–27, 1997) focused attention on the dangers of censorship with displays of challenged books in libraries and bookstores and news reports in the media. The annual event is sponsored by ALA, the American Booksellers Association, the American Booksellers Foundation for Free Expression, the Association of American Publishers, the American Society of Journalists and Authors, and the National Association of College Stores. The 1998 observance will be September 26–October 3.

The ALA Office for Intellectual Freedom received a $40,000 grant from the Nathan Cummings Foundation to provide ten regional institutes on the topic "Libraries, the Internet and the First Amendment: Strategies for the Future." The training was introduced at the 1998 ALA Midwinter Meeting with funding from a $5,000 ALA/World Book Goal Award.

Children's Book and Media Awards

E. L. (Elaine) Konigsburg, author of *The View from Saturday*, won the 1997 Newbery Medal for the most distinguished contribution to American literature for children. The Caldecott Medal for the most distinguished American picture book went to David Wisniewski, author and illustrator of *Golem*. The awards are presented annually by the Association for Library Service to Children, a division of ALA.

The 1997 Coretta Scott King Awards for outstanding children's books by African American authors and illustrators went to author Walter Dean Myers for *Slam!* and to Jerry Pinkney for his illustrations for *Minty: A Story of Young Harriet Tubman*.

The Andrew Carnegie Medal for Excellence in Children's Video went to Tacy Mangan for *NotesAlive! On the Day You Were Born*.

Farrar Straus Giroux, publisher of *The Friends* by Kazumi Yumoto, received the 1997 Mildred L. Batchelder Award for the most outstanding children's book published first in another language and then in English in the United States.

Gary Paulsen—author of *Hatchet, Woodsong, Winter Room, The Crossing, Canyons,* and other books for teenagers, received the Margaret A. Edwards Award for his lifetime contribution to literature for young adults. The award is sponsored by *School Library Journal* and administered by the Young Adult Library Services Association, an ALA division.

Technology Initiatives

The association's technology initiatives focus on services to the public, as well as the needs of the profession. Special concerns include ensuring that all people have access to electronic information through school and public libraries.

In a major boon for libraries in 1997, Microsoft founder Bill Gates and his wife, Melinda French Gates, announced formation of the Gates Library Foundation, a philanthropic act that parallels Andrew Carnegie's commitment to libraries in the 19th century. The new foundation pledges to develop and extend the work of Libraries Online, a pilot project launched by Microsoft and ALA in 1995. The new foundation will provide some $400 million in cash and software to extend Internet access at public libraries serving low-income communities.

Helping children find the answers they need is the goal of KidsConnect, a technology initiative sponsored by the American Association of School Librarians division of ALA, in partnership with the Information Institute of Syracuse and underwritten by Microsoft. Answers to some 3,841 questions were provided during the project's first year. These ranged from "Why is the sky blue?" to "How do astronauts eat in space?" and "What are the words for the Alaska state song?"

The KidsConnect team includes more than 200 volunteer school library media specialists from 41 states and nine countries. Questions are sent by e-mail with answers promised within two school days.

Ten libraries were selected to receive grants in the third year of MCI Library LINK, a national community service initiative to help bring the Information Superhighway closer to Main Street, U.S.A. A total of 27 public libraries have received grants totaling $1 million to extend Internet services in their communities. The project is administered by the Reference and User Services Association, a division of ALA.

The ALA Office for Information Technology conducted a survey on U.S. public library involvement with the Internet in cooperation with the National Commission on Libraries and Information Science (NCLIS). The survey, released in fall 1997, found that about 60 percent of public library systems offer some type of Internet access to the public at one or more branches.

Public Awareness

Like radio, movies, and television before it, the Internet has raised concerns about possible negative impact on children. To help provide guidance, ALA launched a special Web site and brochure, "The Librarian's Guide to Cyberspace for Parents and Kids" (www.ala.org/parentspage/greatsites) and a "cybercollection" of more than 700 "Amazing, Spectacular, Mysterious, Wonderful Web

Sites for Kids and the Adults Who Care About Them," developed by the Association for Library Service to Children.

The association's initiatives were featured at the national "Online/Internet Summit: Focus on Children," held in December 1997 by a coalition of industry, education, parent, and other groups.

President Clinton praised ALA's efforts at a White House meeting attended by 1997–1998 ALA President Barbara Ford and representatives of parent groups, the computer industry, and other organizations. ALA's Web site and leadership role in educating parents was featured in media from coast to coast, including the "Today Show," "CNN News," *Sunday Parade* magazine, the *Washington Post* and *USA Today*.

National Library Week 1997, April 13–19, focused on library services to youth with the theme "Kids Connect @ the Library." National events included thousands of Americans participating in the second annual "Log-on @ the Library Day," sponsored by ALA and libraries across the country as an introduction to the Internet. Activities ranged from the launching of a "Cyber-buddies" volunteer program in Green Bay, Wisconsin, to the opening of a Kids Connection computer center in Ann Arbor, Michigan. At Butler University Libraries in Indianapolis, astronomer Thomas Bopp, codiscoverer of Comet Hale-Bopp, joined in a demonstration of the Internet.

"Kids can't wait . . ." was the theme for youth advocacy efforts led by 1996–1997 President Somerville. A videotape and brochure for policymakers focused on the need for library services to children. The theme was also the focus of a meeting attended by representatives of national youth agencies at the ALA Midwinter Meeting with Secretary of Education Richard W. Riley as guest of honor. Somerville declared Riley a Library Champion for his efforts to promote youth literacy and library use.

ALA Special Projects

The association sponsors a variety of projects that promote learning, literacy, and cultural education at libraries, as well as professional-development opportunities for librarians around the world. Many initiatives are grant supported and provide program models and materials, training, and technical assistance, as well as evaluation and dissemination of results.

"I wish I had this information when my son was in elementary school," wrote a listserv participant to "Roads to Learning," a national initiative to increase understanding about learning disabilities and improve library access for all. The project—administered by the Association of Specialized and Cooperative Library Agencies with funding from the Emily Hall Tremaine Foundation—provides a Web site, education, and support materials for librarians.

Thirteen libraries in four states received grants to expand and improve literacy training for adults as part of "Literacy in Libraries Across America" (LILAA), a three-year, $6.3 million initiative funded by the Lila Wallace-Reader's Digest Fund. With training and support provided by ALA, the sites are improving their curriculum and instructional practices, expanding their use of computer technology, and developing better methods to measure and document student learning gains. The program is administered by the Office for Literacy and Outreach Services.

Another ALA literacy initiative, "Born to Read," was cited by First Lady Hillary Clinton as a model for helping low-literacy parents raise readers. The project, administered by the Association for Library Service to Children, promotes partnerships between librarians and health care providers to reach out to expectant and new parents. The program received a 1997 Award of Excellence from the American Society of Association Executives. More than 35,000 parents and children have participated since the project was established in 1994.

Libraries in more than 700 schools in 19 communities were transformed into state-of-the-art educational centers as a result of the National Library Power Program, a $40 million initiative funded by the DeWitt Wallace-Reader's Digest Fund. Administrative and technical support were provided by the American Association of School Librarians in cooperation with the Public Education Network in Washington, D.C. Preliminary results of a national evaluation are scheduled to be presented in fall 1998.

ALA's Office of Public Programs supports cultural and literary programming at libraries across the country. More than four million people viewed exhibits and participated in programs developed by ALA and hosted by some 300 public and academic libraries. These included the popular "Beyond Category: The Musical Genius of Duke Ellington" and "The Frontier in American Culture" exhibits and "The Nation That Works" reading and discussion series, all funded by the National Endowment for the Humanities.

"StoryLines America," a series of radio programs that offer listeners a chance to participate in discussions of regional literature with scholars and authors, went "live" in late 1997 on more than 100 radio stations in the Northwest and Southwest. The project, funded by the National Endowment for the Humanities and produced by ALA, makes series books available to participating local libraries.

Europe's early jazz movement and the impact of American artists, writers, and musicians who lived in Paris will be the focus of "The Jazz Age in Paris: 1914–1940," a new traveling exhibition funded with a $250,545 grant from the National Endowment for the Humanities that will tour 40 libraries starting in November 1998.

Other Highlights

To increase the number of minority librarians and better serve library users in the 21st century, the association launched Spectrum, a $1.3 million, three-year initiative that will award 50 annual scholarships of $5,000 each to library and information science students representing the four largest minority populations: African American, Asian/Pacific Islander, Latino/Hispanic, and Native American. In addition to providing scholarships, the initiative will provide leadership training and other support. The first round of scholarships will be awarded in spring 1998.

"Diversity by Design," a program proposed by 1997–1998 ALA President Ford to provide interactive Web-based diversity training for librarians, library works, trustees, and others, received a $5,000 World Book/ALA Goal Award.

Twenty-five librarians representing diverse backgrounds and types of librarianship attended the first Emerging Leaders Institute hosted by 1996–1997

President Somerville. The institute was a preconference to the 1997 ALA Annual Conference, and its participants received training and coaching in such areas as conflict resolution, decision making, coalition building, communication, and professional image.

ALA President Ford's theme of "Libraries: Global Reach, Local Touch" was reflected in a wide range of association activities. The first Regional Institute, sponsored by ALA with funding from the U.S. Information Agency, was held March 9–13, 1997, in Cairo, Egypt. The institute involved ALA leaders and librarians from nine Middle Eastern and North African nations in discussions on serving diverse populations, intellectual freedom, literacy, the role of the Internet, and other issues. Ford led the first delegation of American librarians to attend the Zimbabwe Book Fair, August 2–9, 1997, and an ALA-sponsored delegation attended the Guadalajara Book Fair, November 29–December 7, 1997.

"Local Libraries: Global Awareness," a new partnership between ALA and Global Learning, Inc., was established to involve school and public libraries in creative international programming. The project, funded by the U.S. Agency for International Development, will be coordinated by the ALA International Relations Office in cooperation with the American Association of School Librarians and the Public Library Association. The program and support materials will be presented at the 1998 ALA Annual Conference.

The Library Fellows program, sponsored in cooperation with the U.S. Information Agency, sent ten U.S. librarians in its tenth year to projects in Brazil, the Czech Republic, Egypt, Ethiopia, Ghana, Israel, Jordan, Kazakstan, and the Ukraine. Five librarians from Argentina, Bolivia, Mexico, Portugal, and Thailand were brought to the United States as part of the international exchange program.

The Fund for America's Libraries, in its second year of operation to support the work of the American Library Association, provided $4.3 million from grants and contributions to association priority programs.

More than 200 individuals and libraries received awards and scholarships from the American Library Association in 1996–1997.

The association awarded its highest honor—Honorary Membership—to Oprah Winfrey and Henriette Avram. Winfrey was cited for doing "more to revitalize and promote the importance of reading than any other public figure in recent time." Avram, now retired after a distinguished career at the Library of Congress (1955–1991), was instrumental in the development of a standard vehicle for the communication of bibliographic data, the structure now known as the Machine Readable Cataloging (MARC) format.

Richard Dougherty, professor at the University of Michigan's School of Information in Ann Arbor, received the Joseph W. Lippincott Award honoring distinguished service to the profession. As president of ALA in 1990–1991, he led a "Rally for America's Libraries" campaign to protest funding cuts to libraries.

Conferences and Institutes

National conferences and regional institutes sponsored by ALA and its member units provide opportunities for professional growth and renewal throughout the year. The ALA Annual Conference is the largest gathering of librarians in the world. The 1997 Annual Conference, held June 27–July 2 in San Francisco, drew 23,201 librarians, exhibitors, and other guests. Keynote speaker Walter Anderson, literacy advocate and editor of *Sunday Parade* magazine, addressed the conference theme "Kids Can't Wait for Libraries." The Midwinter business meeting, held February 14–18, drew 14,069 to the nation's capital.

Division and affiliate conferences included the eighth national conference of the American Association of School Librarians, held April 2–6, 1997, in Portland, Oregon (3,444 attendance) and the eighth national conference of the Association of College and Research Libraries, held April 11–14, 1997, in Nashville (2,973 attendance).

The Black Caucus sponsored the third National Conference of African American Librarians, July 31–August 3, 1997, in Winston Salem, North Carolina, with the theme "Culture Keepers III: Making Global Connections" (1,102 attendance).

Regional programs included "The Electronic Library: Administrative and Management Issues," sponsored by the Association for Library Collections and Technical Services, and "Staffing Issues for the Year 2000," sponsored by the Library Administration and Management Association.

Publishing Highlights

Several ALA Editions titles won prestigious awards in 1997. Wayne Wiegand's biography of Melvil Dewey, *Irrepressible Reformer*, received the G. K. Hall Award for library literature, the third time an ALA Editions title has won this award in the last four years. *Black Heritage Sites* by Nancy Curtis received the Denali Press Award for the outstanding multicultural reference work of the past two years. *Future Libraries* by Walt Crawford and Michael Gorman won the Blackwell/North America Award for outstanding monograph.

Booklist, the popular review magazine for public and school libraries, announced a partnership with NoveList, an electronic reader's advisory product that will make reviews, articles, and reader's advisory features available to assist librarians in answering queries about related fiction offerings.

Leadership

Barbara Ford, executive director of library services at Virginia Commonwealth University in Richmond, assumed the 1997–1998 presidency of ALA in July 1997. Ann Symons, librarian at Juneau-Douglas High School in Alaska, was elected vice-president/president-elect. Bruce Daniels, director of the Onondaga County Public Library in Syracuse, New York, continues as treasurer.

Mary Ghikas, associate executive director for ALA Member Programs and Services, was named acting executive director following the resignation of Elizabeth Martinez in August. William R. Gordon, director of the Prince George's County (Maryland) Memorial Library System, was named to assume the duties of executive director on March 1, 1998.

Association of American Publishers

71 Fifth Ave., New York, NY 10003-3004
212-255-0200
1718 Connecticut Ave. N.W., Washington, DC 20009
202-232-3335
World Wide Web: http://www.publishers.org

Judith Platt
Director of Communications and Public Affairs

The Association of American Publishers (AAP) is the national trade association of the U.S. book publishing industry. AAP was created in 1970 through the merger of the American Book Publishers Council, a trade publishing group, and the American Textbook Publishers Institute, a group of educational publishers. AAP's approximately 200 members include most of the major commercial book publishers in the United States, as well as smaller and nonprofit publishers, university presses, and scholarly societies. AAP members publish hardcover and paperback books in every field and a range of educational materials for the elementary, secondary, postsecondary, and professional markets. Members of the association also produce computer software and electronic products and services, such as online databases and CD-ROMs. AAP's primary concerns are the protection of intellectual property rights in all media, the defense of free expression and freedom to publish at home and abroad, the management of new technologies, development of education markets and funding for instructional materials, and the development of national and global markets for its members' products.

AAP is formally affiliated with four regional publishing groups: the Publishers Association of the South, the Rocky Mountain Book Publishers Association, the Florida Publishers Association, and the Small Publishers Association of North America.

Additional information on AAP can be found on the World Wide Web at http://www.publishers.org.

Highlights of 1997

- The year-long search for a new AAP president ended successfully in February with announcement that former Colorado Congresswoman Pat Schroeder would become president and chief executive officer on June 1.
- AAP became a cosponsor of BookExpo America (the former American Booksellers Association Convention and Trade Exhibit), giving publishers, for the first time, a role in policy-making and planning decisions for the event.
- AAP continued to lead the search for electronic-commerce solutions for the industry, unveiling the Digital Object Identifier (DOI) system and opening it to public participation.
- A unanimous Supreme Court decision overturned the Communications Decency Act (CDA) as an unacceptable infringement of constitutionally

protected speech. AAP was one of the plaintiffs in this highly publicized free-speech case.

- AAP was also a plaintiff in the successful court challenge to New York State's "Little CDA."
- Pubnet, LLC, a new corporate entity, was established under the joint ownership of AAP, the American Booksellers Association (ABA), the National Association of College Stores (NACS), and R. R. Bowker.
- Overturning a lower court ruling, the Fourth Circuit Court of Appeals refused to dismiss a civil suit brought by the families of victims of a triple murder against the publisher of *Hit Man*; AAP had joined an *amicus* brief arguing for dismissal of the suit on First Amendment grounds.
- U.S. book sales totaled $20.75 billion in 1996, according to figures released by AAP in February.
- The AAP Annual Meeting in Washington, D.C., was both a farewell for Nick Veliotes and a welcome to Pat Schroeder.
- Tom McCormack of St. Martin's Press received the Curtis Benjamin Award.
- The U.S. Supreme Court refused to review the Michigan Document Services (MDS) case and left standing a Sixth Circuit ruling affirming the need for permission to use copyrighted materials in college course packs. Under a settlement announced in June, MDS was permanently enjoined from unauthorized use of copyrighted material belonging to *any* AAP member.
- Despite early concerns over the absence of many large publishers, BookExpo '97 was a decidedly upbeat show, and Pat Schroeder was given a warm welcome by booksellers, publishers, and the press.
- AAP was a major player in the Conference on Fair Use, which ended the first phase of its work in May.
- AAP lobbied hard for speedy ratification and implementation of the new international World Intellectual Property Organization (WIPO) copyright treaties, but it saw its best efforts frustrated by political jockeying by the telephone companies and others.
- AAP was one of a prestigious group of national organizations protesting the seizure of the Academy Award-winning film *The Tin Drum* by Oklahoma City police.
- The International Freedom to Publish Committee cosponsored an event to support Chinese prisoner of conscience Wei Jingsheng.
- A new School Division survey revealed a serious shortage of textbooks in New York State.
- AAP and the Copyright Clearance Center established a joint program to promote copyright compliance on American college campuses.
- AAP again cosponsored the International Rights Directors Meeting at Frankfurt Book Fair.

- AAP's education program continued its popular "Introduction to Publishing" course.
- AAP took the lead in organizing a new broad-based initiative to encourage adults to read to young children.
- The Small Publishers Association of North America (SPAN) became the fourth regional publishers organization to establish formal ties with AAP.

Government Affairs

AAP's Washington Office is the industry's front line on matters of federal legislation and government policy. The Washington Office keeps AAP members informed about developments on Capitol Hill and in the executive branch, to enable the membership to develop consensus positions on national policy issues. AAP serves as the industry's voice, communicating these positions to Congress, government officials, and the media.

An AAP Government Affairs Council was established in 1997 to strengthen communications between the Washington Office and the AAP leadership. The council comprises individuals specially designated by AAP Board members to speak on behalf of their publishing houses in formulating positions on legislative issues that require a rapid response. [For a full report on legislative and regulatory issues, see the article "Legislation and Regulations Affecting Publishing" in Part 2.—Ed.]

BookExpo America

Early in 1997 AAP became a cosponsor of BookExpo America (BEA, formerly the ABA Convention and Trade Exhibit), with the goal of making BEA the premier book event of the English-speaking world. For the first time under the new arrangement, publishers have a formal role to play in strategic planning and policymaking for BookExpo America. Among its contributions, AAP will sponsor a range of educational programs at the event.

Despite some initial misgivings about the show's viability in the absence of a number of large publishers, BookExpo '97 was a success. AAP's new president, Pat Schroeder—whose official term of office began on June 1—received an enthusiastic welcome from booksellers, exhibitors, and show management. The decidedly upbeat Chicago event picked up momentum as booksellers and publishers (AAP members and nonmembers) sought Schroeder out to extend a personal welcome and express their pleasure at her becoming "one of us."

Schroeder delighted an audience of children's booksellers, authors, and publishers with a reading of *Goodnight Moon* at a dinner celebrating the book's 50th anniversary, and she joined filmmaker Oliver Stone in fielding questions on free expression at a program cosponsored by ABA, AAP, and the American Library Association (ALA). A Sunday evening reception for Schroeder, cohosted by ABA and Association Exposition & Services, also served to kick off the book industry's campaign supporting President Clinton's America Reads Challenge.

Copyright

The Copyright Committee coordinates AAP efforts to protect and strengthen intellectual property rights and to enhance public awareness of the importance of copyright as an incentive to creativity. The Copyright Committee works closely with the AAP Washington staff to develop and disseminate industry positions on legislation involving intellectual property rights and, through its Rights and Permissions Advisory Committee, coordinates AAP's work in the area of rights and permissions education. Peter Jovanovich (Addison-Wesley Longman) chaired the committee in 1997.

The committee coordinated AAP's support for the publisher plaintiffs in their copyright infringement suit against Michigan Document Services (MDS). On March 31, 1997, the U.S. Supreme Court refused to review the case, leaving in place an *en banc* ruling by the Sixth Circuit that MDS's activities were *not* fair use and that permission is needed to use copyrighted materials in college course anthologies. The case was successfully concluded with a settlement announced in June under which MDS was enjoined from unauthorized use of copyrighted materials belonging to any AAP member.

One of the committee's major concerns over the past several years has been the administration-sponsored Conference on Fair Use (CONFU). Mandated in the NII White Paper, CONFU established an ongoing dialogue among publishers and other producers of copyrighted works and representatives of the library and academic communities, in an attempt to clarify the application of the fair-use doctrine to the digital environment. CONFU participants, including representatives of AAP and a number of member houses, met regularly for almost three years in an attempt to create guidelines for a variety of digital uses of copyrighted materials, including the creation of educational multimedia, image archiving, and distance learning.

The first phase of the CONFU process ended on May 19, 1997. The guidelines developed for educational multimedia received the endorsement of a wide range of producer and user organizations, including AAP; and although they are voluntary, the guidelines provide a frame of reference for faculty and students and are expected to be used widely. (The multimedia guidelines were issued in a nonlegislative congressional report).

AAP viewed the first phase of CONFU as a success, both as a vehicle for bringing producers and users of copyrighted material together and as a model for future discussions.

The Copyright Committee coordinates AAP efforts to encourage and improve compliance with the copyright law on college and university campuses. AAP and the Software Publishers Association developed a new video, "A Shared Set of Values: Copyright and Intellectual Property in the Academic Community," aimed at increasing copyright awareness and respect for intellectual-property rights in the higher education community. AAP joined with the Copyright Clearance Center, the National Association of College Stores, the American Association of University Presses (AAUP), and the Software Publishers Association in publishing a new edition of *Questions and Answers on Copyright for the Campus Community*.

At its September meeting the AAP board gave final approval to a new joint campus copyright education program that AAP will undertake with the Copyright Clearance Center. The program combines AAP's advocacy role in promoting campus compliance with effective licensing solutions developed by the CCC's Academic Licensing Service.

AAP joined other copyright industry groups in filing an *amicus* brief in the U.S. Supreme Court in *Quality King* v. *L'anza*, a case involving parallel imports. Although the case does not pertain directly to publishing, it is significant because an adverse decision could undermine the principle of territorial exclusivity, a cornerstone of copyright protection.

The Copyright Committee also coordinates AAP's antipiracy activities. The association works through the International Intellectual Property Alliance to enlist the help of the U.S. government in raising the level of copyright protection among our trading partners. The seriousness of the problem was underscored by the alliance's "Special 301" filing to the U.S. Trade Representative in February 1997, which estimated that the U.S. copyright industries lost in excess of $10.6 billion in 1996 as a result of piracy in 52 countries.

AAP also is waging its own antipiracy campaign by going after pirates in their own countries and taking them to court. In August AAP reached a long-awaited settlement with a photocopy shop in Taiwan under which the pirates paid almost $22,000 in damages for infringing AAP members' copyrights, issued a public apology, and agreed to refrain from infringement of AAP members' titles in the future.

AAP views as essential weapons in the fight against international piracy two international copyright treaties adopted by the World Intellectual Property Organization and awaiting ratification by member nations. AAP lobbied hard for passage of bipartisan legislation to implement the treaties, introduced last summer in both houses of Congress. Its efforts have been frustrated by the politically powerful telephone companies, which are attempting to use the legislation as a vehicle to obtain special immunity from copyright infringement liability.

In addition to sponsoring a number of seminars during the year, the Rights and Permissions Advisory Committee published *The Copyright Primer: A Survival Guide to the Copyrights and Permissions Process*.

Communications and Public Affairs

The Communications and Public Affairs program is AAP's voice. Through regular publications, press releases and advisories, op-ed pieces, and other means, AAP expresses the views of the industry and provides up-to-the-minute information on subjects of concern to its members. Senior AAP staff addressed a host of audiences in 1997, taking AAP's message to groups throughout the United States and overseas.

AAP's public affairs activities include outreach and cooperative programs with such organizations as the Center for the Book in the Library of Congress, the Arts Advocacy Alliance (supporting the National Endowment for the Arts and other federal arts programs), PEN American Center and its International Freedom to Write Program (AAP was a founding member of the U.S. Rushdie

Defense Committee), and a multitude of literacy and reading promotion efforts, including an early-childhood literacy initiative, Reach Out and Read, President Clinton's America Reads Challenge, and the White House Prescription for Reading. AAP continues to work closely with affiliated regional publishing groups and gained a fourth affiliate in 1997—SPAN, the Small Publishers Association of North America.

The association has a home page on the World Wide Web at http://www. publishers.org, and the AAP newsletter, *AAP Monthly Report*, can also be found online, in addition to its traditional print distribution.

Education Program

Several years ago AAP inaugurated a program to provide educational opportunities for publishing industry personnel. The first course offered was an intensive "Introduction to Publishing," designed to give entry-level employees an overview of the industry and a better understanding of the publishing process. The course has been given several times each year since its inauguration and continues to draw enthusiastic registrants.

Enabling Technologies

The Enabling Technologies Committee focuses on publishing in the electronic networked environment and serves as a steering committee directing AAP's efforts to promote the development of workable systems for managing copyright in the digital environment. Craig Van Dyck (John Wiley & Sons) chairs the committee.

Early in its work, the committee recognized a fundamental need for a unique, unambiguous way to identify digital materials traveling the Information Superhighway. This was the genesis of AAP's project, undertaken in collaboration with the Corporation for National Research Initiatives (CNRI), to develop a Digital Object Identifier (DOI) system. The project focused on developing a system for publishers to use in identifying digital objects and developing a network-based directory to link these digital object identifiers to the publisher, using open standards that would allow publishers and other companies to build their own products and services based around DOIs.

Local and national media got their first look at the DOI system at a briefing at the National Press Club in Washington, D.C., in September. The press event attracted much attention from the media, including a comprehensive story on page 1 of the Business Section of the *New York Times*.

The National Press Club event was a prelude to presenting the DOI system to the international publishing community at Frankfurt Book Fair in October and inaugurating the second phase of the system's development by opening it to public participation. A standing-room-only crowd of international publishing executives attended the October 15 presentation, which was organized by the Information Identifier Committee (IIC), a joint committee of the International Publishers Association and International STM. As an international standard, the DOI will promote interoperability on the global Information Superhighway.

The DOI presentation was accompanied by announcement of a newly established International DOI Foundation with overall responsibility for administering the system. With offices in Geneva and Washington, the foundation will be guided by a board chaired by IIC Chairman Charles Ellis (John Wiley & Sons).

Freedom to Read

Protecting intellectual freedom is a fundamental concern for both AAP members and the industry as a whole. The Freedom to Read Committee continues to serve as AAP's front line in identifying and responding to free-speech issues that affect the business of book publishing. The Freedom to Read Committee performs three basic functions: early warning, intervention, and education. Serving as the association's watchdog in the area of free speech, the committee alerts the AAP membership to developments in such areas as libel, privacy, school censorship, attacks on public libraries, reporters' privilege (confidentiality of source materials), the Internet and filtering technology, sexually explicit materials, third-party liability, and efforts to punish speech that "causes harm." The Freedom to Read Committee coordinates AAP's participation (as plaintiff or friend of the court) in important First Amendment court cases and provides guidance in developing AAP's posture on legislative issues with free-speech ramifications. Through its publications, educational programs, and other activities, the committee carries the message to the industry and beyond, stressing the need for constant vigilance to protect rights guaranteed by the First Amendment. Lisa Drew (Lisa Drew Books/Scribner) chairs the committee.

The Freedom to Read Committee works closely with allied organizations, especially ALA's Office for Intellectual Freedom and the American Booksellers Foundation for Free Expression (ABFFE), and coordinates AAP participation as a member of the Media Coalition, a group of trade associations formed to fight censorship.

The committee had a full agenda over the past year. Among the highlights:

- The committee coordinated AAP's participation as a plaintiff in one of the most highly publicized free-speech cases in recent memory, the challenge to the Communications Decency Act (CDA). The case was argued before the U.S. Supreme Court in March 1997, and on June 26, in one of the strongest defenses of the First Amendment in recent memory, the court overturned the CDA as an unacceptable infringement of constitutionally protected speech. The opinion emphasized the Internet's unique status as a means of communication deserving the highest constitutional protection.
- In January 1997 AAP became a plaintiff in a second lawsuit challenging government censorship of the Internet when it joined other Media Coalition members, the ACLU, and the New York Library Association as a plaintiff in *ALA* v. *Pataki*. The lawsuit asked the courts to strike down New York State's "Little CDA," which attempted to criminalize computer transmission of "harmful-to-minors" materials. On June 20, shortly before the Supreme Court ruled in the CDA case, a federal judge in New York struck down the New York law. Leaving First Amendment considerations

to the Supreme Court, the judge overturned the New York law as a violation of the Commerce Clause and ruled that the Internet is an area of commerce requiring regulation on a national rather than a local basis.

- AAP, ALA, and ABFFE were among the prestigious group of organizations that issued a statement denouncing the seizure of the Academy Award-winning film *The Tin Drum* by police in Oklahoma City (who claimed the film violates the state's child pornography laws). AAP and other members of the Media Coalition filed an *amicus* brief in a lawsuit subsequently brought by the Video Software Dealers Association, arguing that removal of the film from the Oklahoma County Library, two video stores, and the home of a private individual was illegal. On December 24 a federal judge in Oklahoma City ruled that removal of the film without a prior adversarial hearing was unconstitutional. He ordered copies of the film returned to public access pending the outcome of a lawsuit to determine whether the film, taken as a whole, constitutes the kind of criminal material targeted by the state statute.

- Alerted to a potentially serious move in the Massachusetts legislature to give individuals proprietary rights in their life stories, the committee arranged to have a strong letter sent to the governor of Massachusetts arguing that the bill could be used to cripple the ability of publishers to create a wide range of First Amendment-protected materials. The bill was derailed for at least the current legislative session.

- Several years ago AAP joined media and civil liberties organizations in asking for dismissal of a civil lawsuit against the publisher of *Hit Man* brought by the families of three murder victims. The suit accused the publisher of being an accessory to murder because information in the book was used in committing the crime. The case was dismissed on First Amendment grounds by a federal judge in Maryland in August 1996, but this ruling was overturned in November 1997 by the Fourth Circuit Court of Appeals, which held that families of the victims could proceed with a civil suit under Maryland law.

- AAP and other members of the Media Coalition filed an *amicus* brief protesting the order of the California Superior Court enjoining the sale of an issue of *Playgirl* magazine and recalling all copies already in circulation in a lawsuit filed by actor Brad Pitt over publication of nude photographs that had been previously published on the Internet. The Media Coalition *amicus* brief does not address the actor's underlying claim of injury but focuses on "the breadth and nature of the prior restraint," arguing that while the First Amendment does permit subsequent punishment of the media for violations of rights protected by state laws, the First Amendment's free-press guarantees preclude the use of state tort law to impose a prior restraint on publication.

- The committee testified at hearings before the California State Senate, expressing the publishing industry's opposition to proposed legislation that would dangerously broaden the state's defamation law.

- AAP joined a narrowly tailored Media Coalition brief to the Ninth Circuit, arguing that a new law aimed at further protecting children from the effects of child pornography fails to achieve its objective while threatening legitimate expression.
- In November 1997 the U.S. Supreme Court agreed to hear *NEA* v. *Finley*, a case dealing with the legality of requiring the National Endowment for the Arts (NEA) to take into account "general standards of decency" in awarding grants. The "decency" language, which was added to NEA-authorizing legislation several years ago, has been declared unconstitutional by a federal district court and by the U.S. Court of Appeals for the Ninth Circuit. (AAP had joined a friend-of-the-court brief asking the Ninth Circuit to strike down the provision.)

In carrying out its educational function, the committee worked with ABFFE in presenting a First Amendment program at BookExpo America and with the ALA Office for Intellectual Freedom in sponsoring a program at the ALA Annual Conference in San Francisco. The committee organized a panel on Internet censorship at the AAP Annual Meeting in Washington, D.C., in March.

The committee coordinates the publishing industry's participation in "Banned Books Week: A Celebration of the Freedom to Read," which focuses media attention on the serious issue of book banning.

Higher Education

AAP's Higher Education Committee continues to serve the needs and interests of AAP members who publish for the postsecondary educational market. The Higher Education Committee is chaired by June Smith (Houghton Mifflin).

The committee again coordinated AAP's participation at the NACS Annual Meeting and Campus Exposition in Baltimore in April.

Committee members met in Washington, D.C., with AAP's Government Affairs staff to develop strategies to get AAP college publishers a more active role in dealing with legislative issues affecting postsecondary education.

The committee published its annual *AAP College Textbook Publishers Greenbook*, a resource for college store buyers that provides a wealth of information on the college publishing industry.

International

The International Committee represents a broad cross-section of the AAP membership. Deborah Wiley (John Wiley & Sons) chairs the committee.

The committee operated an expanded International Rights and Sales Center at BookExpo '97, providing AAP members exhibiting at the show with excellent facilities for meeting their international customers.

The committee sponsored its fifth Frankfurt Intern Program, in cooperation with the Frankfurt Book Fair. The program—which gives young publishers from

Central and Eastern Europe an opportunity to attend the fair and work at a U.S. publisher's stand—brought eight interns from six countries to Frankfurt this year.

The International Committee again cosponsored the International Rights Directors Meeting at Frankfurt. This gathering—which AAP inaugurated at the 1987 fair as a modest forum for exchanging information on the buying and selling of foreign rights—has grown over the past decade into one of the most popular events at the fair. The 1997 program looked at books that transcended language and cultural barriers to become international bestsellers.

International Freedom to Publish

AAP's International Freedom to Publish (IFTP) Committee defends and promotes freedom of written communication worldwide. The IFTP Committee monitors human rights issues and provides moral support and practical assistance to publishers and authors outside the United States who are denied basic freedoms. The committee carries on its work in close cooperation with other human rights groups, including Human Rights Watch and PEN American Center. William Schwalbe (Hyperion) is the IFTP Committee chair.

AAP was a founding member of the U.S. Committee to Defend Salman Rushdie. February 14, 1997, marked the eighth anniversary of Rushdie's death sentence; and not only has it has never been rescinded, but the bounty on Rushdie has been increased to $2.5 million. The U.S. Defense Committee wrote to Secretary of State Madeleine Albright reasserting the publishing community's determination to see the *fatwa* officially ended. The letter pointed out that presidential elections scheduled to be held in Iran this year presented an opportunity for the secretary to consider "fresh and concrete means" of influencing the government of Iran and bolstering "forces of moderation and tolerance that still exist within the country."

The committee joined PEN American Center, Human Rights Watch, Amnesty International, and several other organizations in sponsoring an event to support Chinese prisoner of conscience Wei Jingsheng. Released only briefly in 1995, Wei had been imprisoned since 1979 for the crime of urging respect for human rights and advocating democratic government in China. The event was held in May at the New York Public Library to mark publication of *The Courage to Stand Alone* (Viking), a collection of Wei's writings and letters from prison and featured readings and tributes from a host of authors, journalists, and human rights activists, including playwright Arthur Miller, Human Rights Watch Chairman Robert Bernstein, authors E. L. Doctorow and David Henry Hwang, and New York Mayor Rudolph Giuliani. Though unable to attend, President Vaclav Havel of the Czech Republic sent a message noting that he had nominated Wei for the Nobel Peace Prize. Wei was subsequently released by the Chinese government and sent into exile, arriving in the United States in November.

Among the ways in which the committee aids foreign writers and publishers is by issuing invitations to visit the United States. The committee has sent two letters of invitation to Vietnamese novelist Duong Thu Huong. It was hoped that she could visit the United States in the fall of 1997, but she has still not been permitted to travel. The invitation remains open. In early 1997 AAP sent a letter of invitation and provided a small grant for dissident Chinese poet Huang Xiang and his wife, Zhang Ling, to visit the United States. The couple arrived in the United States in September.

In the fall of 1997 committee chairman Will Schwalbe and Rose Styron went to Turkey to participate in a program at the Istanbul Book Fair commemorating the 21 Turkish writers who have received Hellman-Hammett Awards in recent years for their political courage. They met with Turkish journalists and publishers—including publisher Aysenur Zarakolu, recently released from prison and still facing dozens of charges by the government—and with the head of the Turkish Publishers Association to discuss free-expression issues. During the visit Schwalbe spoke out against the imprisonment of Esber Yagamurdereli, a blind lawyer who was jailed for a speech he had given. Yagamurdereli was subsequently released.

The IFTP Committee continued to voice protests on behalf of writers, journalists, and publishers who are denied basic rights of free expression. In 1997 letters were sent to the prime minister of Turkey regarding the detention of human rights activist and writer Sanar Yurdatapan, and to the president of Iran concerning the fate of Iranian editor Faraj Sarkuhi. The committee also issued a strong statement protesting the imprisonment of Andi Syahputra, the printer of an underground magazine in Indonesia.

Literacy

AAP is concerned with the promotion of reading and literacy in the United States. Over the years AAP has lent its support to a wide variety of reading promotion and literacy programs, working with partners such as the International Reading Association, Reading Is Fundamental, the Barbara Bush Foundation for Family Literacy, and the Center for the Book in the Library of Congress.

Several years ago AAP became involved in supporting an innovative program, Reach Out and Read, which uses pediatrics clinics and medical personnel to promote early-childhood literacy. The program is now operating at clinics and hospitals nationwide.

AAP is involved in promoting President Clinton's America Reads Challenge, and was among the organizations represented at a White House conference in April 1997 at which First Lady Hillary Rodham Clinton launched the Prescription for Reading partnership. The partnership is a new national reading-promotion effort aimed at having pediatricians "prescribe" reading to infants and young children as part of their standard well-child care. The First Lady cited AAP's early and continuing support for Reach Out and Read.

AAP is working with the Department of Housing and Urban Development to get books directly into the hands of the more than 165,000 children in the country who are homeless. The program got under way on December 22 with a press conference at HUD at which Vice President Al Gore and HUD Secretary Andrew Cuomo, with the help of AAP and several of its members, presented the first books to a group of children from shelters around the Washington, D.C., area. At the event, Secretary Cuomo announced that more than 200,000 books had been donated by AAP members and will be distributed in the next few months to children in shelters across the nation. HUD hopes to eventually have more than 500,000 new children's books to give to kids in shelters.

AAP, working with the Institute for Civil Society, is exploring a new broad-based initiative to get more adults involved in regularly reading to children. Plans call for rolling out the new program in the spring of 1998.

Postal Committee

AAP's Postal Committee coordinates activities in the area of postal rates and regulations, monitors developments at the U.S. Postal Service (USPS) and the independent Postal Rate Commission, and intervenes on the industry's behalf in formal proceedings before the commission. The committee also directs AAP lobbying activities on postal issues. Stephen Bair (Time Life Books) continued to serve as chair.

In addition to focusing its attention on a new postal-rate case, AAP has been concerned with new postal-reform legislation reintroduced in the 105th Congress and a highly controversial bill introduced by Sen. Thad Cochran (R-Miss.) that would redefine USPS's financial structure and permit it to buy into businesses that provide similar services. A more comprehensive discussion of these issues can be found in the legislative section of this report.

Concerned that a prolonged strike by the United Parcel Service (UPS) in the summer of 1997 could prevent large shipments of textbooks from reaching schools and bookstores just weeks before the beginning of the new school year, AAP President Pat Schroeder asked President Clinton and the postmaster general for help in seeing that the timely delivery of educational materials was given top priority by USPS for the duration of the UPS strike.

Professional and Scholarly Publishing

The Professional and Scholarly Publishing (PSP) Division comprises AAP members who publish technical, scientific, medical, and scholarly materials, including books, journals, computer software, databases, and CD-ROM products. Professional societies and university presses play an important role in the division. Eric Swanson (John Wiley & Sons) is division chair.

PSP's 1997 annual meeting was held in Washington, D.C., in February. The division sponsors a prestigious awards program, open only to AAP/PSP members, to acknowledge outstanding achievements in professional, scholarly, and reference publishing. At the 21st Annual PSP Awards banquet in Washington, D.C., the R. R. Hawkins Award for the outstanding professional/scholarly work of the year went to Oxford University Press for its *Oxford History of the Reformation*. In addition, book awards were presented in 28 subject categories, in design and production, and in journal and electronic publishing.

The PSP Electronic Information Committee published its second Internet White Paper. Covering the traditional and changing role of the publisher, trends and tools in Internet publishing, and such key issues as archiving and copyright, *White Paper II* was written and edited entirely online on a secure Web site.

The division sponsors a journals-publishing course so intensive that it has come to be known as "journals boot camp." The course targets not only personnel new to journals publishing but journals professionals who want a broader understanding of the entire publishing process. It was held this year in Washington, D.C., in September.

Pubnet

Pubnet—which began as an electronic book-ordering service developed by AAP using electronic data interchange (EDI) to serve the higher-education community and grew into an industry-wide commercial network—continued its extraordinary growth and evolution. Early in 1997 a new corporate entity, Pubnet LLC, was established to invest in and develop an expanded suite of electronic services that will provide the publishing/bookselling community with one-stop access to all their electronic-commerce partners. Pubnet LLC is now operated as an industry partnership with the American Booksellers Association, the National Association of College Stores, and R. R. Bowker joining AAP as principals in the venture. In March 1997 Pubnet LLC entered into a new agreement with its longtime network provider GEIS and is now a reseller of services for the publishing/bookselling communities.

Among the first initiatives undertaken by Pubnet LLC was to be the release in early 1998 of a major revision to the Pubnet service system, with advanced features, Internet connectivity, and online access to the industry's leading reference database, Books in Print.

The 1997 Pubnet Annual Meeting, held in New York in October, featured discussions of the new advanced features and Internet connectivity to be offered early in 1998, recent changes in customer service, and the first online Books in Print product to be linked with the Pubnet Title File.

In 1997 Pubnet LLC moved out of the AAP New York office and relocated to Virginia.

School Division

The School Division is concerned with publishing for the elementary and secondary school (K–12) market. The division works to enhance the role of instructional materials in the education process, to maintain categorical funding for instructional materials and increase the funds available for the purchase of these materials, and to simplify and rationalize the process of state adoptions for instructional materials. It serves as a bridge between the publishing industry and the educational community, promoting the cause of education at the national and state levels, and works closely with the AAP Washington Office and an effective lobbying network in key adoption states. Buzz Ellis (Glencoe/McGraw-Hill) chairs the division.

AAP school publishers served on a task force convened by the Florida State Education Commissioner to study the instructional-materials funding process and the issue of categorical funding. The task force was instrumental in developing the commissioner's legislative recommendations that, among other things, retained categorical funding. Passage by the Florida legislature of instructional-materials legislation incorporating important modifications negotiated by AAP was seen as a significant win for publishers. AAP's legislative advocate and member publishers played a key role in efforts to increase instructional-materials funding in Florida, and these efforts were reflected in the $183 million allocation for instructional materials recommended by the commissioner in his 1998–1999 budget (a $24 million increase over last year).

The effects of the 1996 School Division instructional-materials survey that revealed severe nationwide shortages of up-to-date textbooks continued to reverberate throughout 1997. The division produced a video and brochure titled *Crisis in the Classroom*, highlighting the survey's results and demonstrating the pressing need for a basic educational reform: putting textbooks and other instructional materials in the hands of children in the classroom. The materials were sent to school boards, education officials, lawmakers, and PTAs across the country.

School Division members went to Washington, D.C., for meetings with the AAP Government Affairs staff to explore ways of increasing the publishers' involvement in educational issues of concern to the industry.

A new AAP School Division study conducted in New York State revealed a serious shortage of textbooks in the state. Nearly one-fourth of the more than 500 New York public school teachers surveyed said that their students do not have a copy of the textbooks needed for class, and one-third said their students don't have textbooks to take home. Results of the New York survey were announced at a June press conference in Albany. Among the survey's other findings: 35 percent of New York teachers have to borrow textbooks from their colleagues; 56 percent say they have had to purchase materials with their own money; and 20 percent of New York teachers say that their newest textbooks are more than five years old.

Trade Publishing

AAP's Trade Publishing group comprises publishers of fiction, general nonfiction, poetry, children's literature, religious texts, and reference publications in hardcover, paperback, and electronic formats. The newly restructured Trade Executive Committee, chaired by Mel Parker (Warner Books), met in May to adopt a mission statement identifying the group's two primary goals: "to further the interests of trade publishers by finding ways to increase the sales of hardcover and paperback books in all outlets, and to advocate the development of literacy programs for young readers as well as the promotion of reading for society." Noting that "Unlike the milk industry or the cotton growers—to cite two examples—the book industry does not yet seem to have an effective voice in promoting books to the general public," the mission statement advocates "working in a shared effort with the entire book selling community [in order to] find appropriate solutions to common problems in trade publishing—from changes in the retail landscape to the challenges of new technologies—and to achieve the broad goal of helping to make reading, both for information and entertainment, the number-one activity in America."

Several years ago, AAP's trade publishers became involved in supporting an innovative early childhood literacy program called Reach Out and Read, which uses pediatrics clinics and personnel to make reading promotion a component of "well-baby" programs in inner-city and rural clinics that serve economically disadvantaged populations.

Under Mel Parker's chairmanship, a new Publicity Task Force began meeting to brainstorm an industry-wide campaign to promote books and reading.

In the hope that computerized sales-tracking systems can help alleviate the returns problem by giving publishers specific sales data and allowing them to bring inventories into line with market realities, AAP sponsored a forum in September that brought publishers and systems developers together.

Administrative Committees

Two administrative committees direct and coordinate AAP member services.

Compensation Survey

This committee coordinates and supervises preparation of the *AAP Survey of Compensation and Personnel Practices in the Publishing Industry*. Published every two years, the report is available only to AAP members and is designed to provide current and accurate information on prevailing compensation levels for representative management and professional positions in the book-publishing industry. A report was published in 1997.

Lawyers Committee

The Lawyers Committee is composed of both in-house and outside counsel of AAP member companies. It meets quarterly to discuss legal issues under review in the committees and divisions.

Annual Meeting

The three-day Annual Meeting in Washington, D.C., served as both a formal farewell to Nicholas Veliotes, retiring after 11 years as AAP president, and an official welcome for former Colorado Congresswoman Patricia Schroeder, AAP's new president and CEO as of June 1.

Speaking to the AAP membership for the first time, Schroeder echoed a theme that Senate Judiciary Committee Chair Orrin Hatch had sounded earlier at the meeting: the need for publishers to engage directly with members of Congress and to bring home to them the economic importance of intellectual-property issues for their constituents.

The rarely seen Diplomatic Reception Rooms at the State Department were an elegant background for a reception and dinner honoring Ambassador Veliotes. Former AAP Chair Charles Ellis (John Wiley & Sons) delivered a moving tribute to Veliotes's leadership at AAP.

Richard Robinson (Scholastic) began his second year as chair of the AAP Board of Directors.

The board voted unanimously to confer the honorary title of President Emeritus on Ambassador Veliotes upon his retirement from AAP on June 1, in recognition of his leadership during a period of rapid and dramatic change in the industry and within the association. The board's action marked the first time such an honor has been granted.

Thomas J. McCormack, who headed St. Martin's Press for 26 years, received the Curtis Benjamin Award for Creative Publishing. The award was presented by Lawrence Hughes (Hearst Book Group), a former AAP chair and a member of the Award Committee.

American Booksellers Association

828 S. Broadway, Tarrytown, NY 10591
914-591-2665
World Wide Web: http://www.bookweb.org
E-mail: aba-info@bookweb.org

Carol Miles
Director of Research

The calendar year 1997 was defined for the American Booksellers Association (ABA) by three significant events, the first of which was a change in staff leadership. Having initiated a strategic planning process in late 1996, Bernie Rath, ABA executive director since 1984, announced his resignation (to be effective March 1) early in the year. He was succeeded on an interim basis by Avin Mark Domnitz, immediate past president of the association. Following an exhaustive search by a board-appointed committee, Domnitz was officially selected by the board of directors for the top staff position, effective January 1, 1998.

Under the leadership of Domnitz, ABA President Barbara Bonds Thomas, and ABA Vice President and Strategic Planning Committee Chair Richard Howorth, the association plunged head first into the strategic planning process in February 1997. Extensive input was sought from members of the association in determining its future direction and emphasis. In particular, multiple sets of focus groups were held with ABA members and the leadership of the regional booksellers associations, and all bookstore members were surveyed by means of an extensive mailed questionnaire.

Concern emanating from the realities of independent bookselling in the late 1990s—as reflected in many of the statistics developed, analyzed, and released by ABA during 1997—was repeatedly voiced during the "front-loading" phase of the strategic planning process. Among the trends cited is the continuing decline in market share of bookstores and of independent bookstores in particular. A primary source of information on this trend during the past several years has been the *Consumer Research Study on Book Purchasing*, based on research sponsored jointly by ABA and the Book Industry Study Group (BISG) and published by BISG. Although the 1996 edition of the report showed a slight improvement in the growth rate of purchases of adult books (a return to the 1994 growth rate of 3 percent, up from 1 percent in 1995), unpublished data collected for the study and analyzed by the ABA Research Department showed that independent bookstores did not share in even that minimal growth in size of the adult book market. The analysis showed that, as a whole, the size of the bookstore market for bookstores shrank. In particular, the independents' market size declined by nearly 2 percent, although the large chains showed a small unit increase of about 1 percent.

Looking at market share, bookstores continued their decline, from 57.3 percent of all adult books purchased in 1991 to 47.9 percent in 1996, down nearly 2 percentage points from the 1995 figure of 49.7 percent. Independents, which had commanded a dominant 32.5 percent share of the market as recently as 1991, dropped another percentage point between 1995 and 1996, from 19.5 percent to 18.6 percent. Chains, on the other hand, held steady at about 26 percent of the total adult book market in 1996. Aside from mail order, growth occurred in all other book outlet sectors, most notably in the mass market sector, where discount stores, including mass merchandisers, showed a year-to-year increase in the number of unit purchases of approximately 22 percent. Their market share, on the other hand, was 8.7 percent in 1996, up from 7.4 percent.

Corroborating evidence of the continuing erosion of independent bookstore market share came from an analysis of data from the *Current Retail Census*— based on dollar sales of bookstores selling predominantly new books and periodicals—and financial reports of the four largest bookstore chains (Barnes & Noble, the Borders Group, Crown Books, and Books-a-Million). Published in *Bookselling This Week* in April of 1997, the data showed that dollar growth of the bookstore market between 1995 and 1996 was 4.4 percent, rising to an estimated $10.7 billion in 1996. This growth rate was just above the inflation rate of 3.0 percent for the year and just under the growth rate for the entire retail sector, measured at 5.3 percent.

In order to assess relative dollar market share of the four largest chains compared to all other new-book bookstores, total bookstore sales figures were compiled for the period corresponding to the fiscal years of the four leading chains (approximately February 1 through January 31). Although the results showed that bookstore sales for the fiscal year ending January 31, 1997, had increased 5.4 percent, sales for the four largest chains had increased a substantial 17.3 percent. All other bookstores, in contrast, suffered declining sales of 3 percent. Similarly, concentration among the largest four bookstore chains intensified as they increased their market share from 41.1 percent during fiscal year 1995 to 46.0 percent of all bookstore sales in fiscal 1996. Conversely, the share of all other bookstores dropped from 58.6 percent to 54.0 percent.

Concurrent with the development of its new strategic plan (the second defining event of the year), ABA unexpectedly found itself involved in the third: a new legal action arising from the revelation by Pearson plc that "unauthorized practices" at its Penguin USA division might result in as much as $163 million being charged against the parent company's 1996 profits. Following Pearson's announcement that improper discounting and accounting practices had been discovered, concerns arose that the discounts may have constituted a violation of the consent order signed when ABA's earlier antitrust lawsuit against Penguin, settled in 1995, assured nondiscrimination in pricing policies. Subsequently, ABA and Penguin USA asked a U.S. District Court to proceed with an investigation into special discounts that were given to certain Penguin customers.

In early October, in what turned out to be a watershed month for ABA, a special issue of *Bookselling This Week* announced the terms of an unprecedented settlement between Penguin Putnam Inc. and the American Booksellers Association. The settlement, heralded as by far the largest in the history of U.S. antitrust discrimination law, included Penguin's agreement to pay ABA and its independent bookstore members a total of $25 million. Arrangements were made for an independent third party to disburse half of the settlement proportionally to ABA members based on their purchases of Penguin books, either directly or indirectly, in 1996. The claims submission process was under way as the year drew to a close.

Later in October, at its fall meeting at national headquarters, the ABA Board of Directors not only ratified the Domnitz appointment but also approved the new strategic plan. Designed to take the association beyond the year 2000, the document contains management goals intended to institutionalize strategic thinking and management. The new plan defines ABA's core member, to which primary focus will be directed, as "the independent bookstore with a store front location which is operated by professional independent booksellers according to sound business principles," while also noting that "ABA will provide programs and services to others in the bookselling industry." The strategic plan's three program goals are as follows:

- Goal I: Serve as the voice of professional independent booksellers and advocate on their behalf
- Goal II: Provide independent professional booksellers with access to the information and competencies they need to succeed in a changing world
- Goal III: Foster development of business systems, services, and new business models

By the end of 1997 the association stood poised to begin implementation of the plan.

Membership

Consistent with the declining market share of independent bookstores, membership in ABA at the end of 1997 dropped to somewhat over 6,000. Closings, consolidations, and conversion to other types of retail operations—such as gift shops, card shops, and office supply stores—continued to make a negative impact on the main store membership category, albeit not as severely as during the previous year.

As in the past, most of ABA's specialty membership segments (Scientific/Technical/Professional, Science Fiction, Travel, African American, and Gay/Lesbian) held roundtable discussion sessions at the 1997 ABA Convention (an integral part of BookExpo America), and members of each segment also continued to receive a tabloid-sized specialty newsletter published quarterly by ABA's Periodicals Publishing Division. In addition, the African American booksellers segment held a full-day conference in conjunction with BookExpo America and the ABA Convention.

ABA added a captive health insurance plan to its portfolio of Group Service Programs in 1997. Other services developed in previous years in response to member requests include a low-cost, small-package shipping program, a credit card processing program, and a business insurance program. These services are available not only to main store members (bookstores) but also to the associate category of members (publishers, wholesalers, distributors, and all who provide goods or services that might be of interest to booksellers).

BookWeb, ABA's consumer site on the World Wide Web inaugurated in 1995, continued to be popular in 1997. Current traffic is in excess of 220,000 page impressions monthly. Among other things, the site, which is fully searchable by keyword, contains articles from *Bookselling This Week* and *American*

Bookseller magazine, a monthly contest entitling the winner to a gift certificate redeemable at the member bookstore of their choice, and other news and information of interest to consumers. Designed to promote member booksellers to consumers, BookWeb contains a fully searchable database of member bookstores featuring business descriptions. It also provides hyperlinks to any member bookstore's Web page, as well as hosting low cost Web pages for bookstore members. The current BookWeb bookstore directory provides links to almost 600 bookstore Web sites, with the number continually growing. A members-only Web site was in the planning stages at year's end. Anticipated features included forum areas, up-to-date member services information, and prepublication release of articles to be printed in ABA publications.

ABA also increased its use of other electronic media to communicate instantaneously with its members during 1997. E-mail newsletters were transmitted on an irregular schedule, including *BookFlash* for breaking news and *ABA Update* for association news. Both fax broadcast and e-mail were used to contact members quickly about critical issues, such as strategic planning, and for polling members on topics appropriate to those data-collection methods. Free fax-on-demand service, expanded in 1996, continued to offer current bookselling statistics and business-related information about an array of ABA services.

1997 Convention and Trade Exhibit

For the third year in succession, the annual gathering of the book industry in the United States was held in Chicago, from May 31 through June 2. For the first time, the ABA Convention was held in conjunction with BookExpo America, owned and managed by Reed Exhibition Companies' Association Expositions and Services since ABA's sale of its remaining 51 percent interest in the former ABA Trade Exhibit to Reed in the latter half of 1996. ABA and the Association of American Publishers (AAP) joined forces as cosponsors of BookExpo America (BEA), serving as advisors on policy decisions regarding the future direction of the trade show. In another first, the show settled into the newly completed South Hall of McCormick Place, and the new facilities were widely lauded by those in attendance.

Overall trade exhibit attendance in 1997 dropped to 25,732, largely because of lower numbers of exhibiting personnel, reflecting the absence of many of the largest publishing houses from the ranks of those displaying their wares. The decline in book buyer attendance was proportionately much less, with 7,402 recorded in a category that includes booksellers, other retailers, wholesalers, and librarians. Bookseller attendance was augmented by a $50,000 grant from ABA proportionally to the ten regional booksellers associations. The grant was earmarked for subsidizing attendance of booksellers who would not otherwise be able to attend. In addition to supporting the show, this was intended to ensure the broadest possible bookstore participation in ABA's strategic planning sessions conducted during BEA. The absence of major publishers notwithstanding, the show was deemed a huge success by those present. Exhibitors expressed particular satisfaction with what they termed the "quality of the book buyers attending."

Among the undisputed highlights of the 1997 show was Saturday evening's spirited Celebration of Bookselling, a wine and cheese event that offered the opportunity for peers to engage in quality conversation. The highlight of this first-ever event was the presentation of the adult ABBY award to author Frank McCourt for *Angela's Ashes* (Scribner). This was ABA's seventh annual American Booksellers Book of the Year award for the adult trade book that ABA member booksellers most enjoyed hand-selling during 1996. The fifth annual children's ABBY award, for the children's book that ABA member booksellers most enjoyed hand-selling during 1996, was presented during Saturday morning's Wake-up with Children's Writers. The winner of the award was Kevin Hawkes for *Lilly's Purple Plastic Purse* (Greenwillow).

Also presented at the Saturday morning event, which was sponsored by the Children's Book Council, were the Lucile Micheels Pannell Awards, given to one bookseller specializing in children's books and one general-interest bookseller who also sells children's books. The recipient of the award for bookstores specializing in children's books was Jennifer Anglin, owner of Enchanted Forest Books for Children in Dallas, Texas, and the winner in the general bookstore category was Roxanne Coady, owner of R. J. Julia Booksellers in Madison, Connecticut. Speakers at the Wake-Up with Children's Writers event were ABBY winner Henkes; Nancy Farmer, author of *A Girl Named Disaster* (Orchard Books); and Vera Williams, author of *Lucky Song* (Greenwillow).

Sunday morning's "Live with Charlie Rose Breakfast" was extremely popular, drawing approximately 1,000 attendees. Utilizing a TV talk show format, Rose maintained lively interaction with best-selling authors Howard Fast, *Independent Woman* (Harcourt) and James Patterson, *Cat and Mouse* (Little, Brown); Olympic track star Jackie Joyner-Kersee, *A Kind of Grace: The Autobiography of the World's Greatest Female Athlete* (Warner); and Pulitzer Prize and 1997 Adult ABBY winner Frank McCourt.

The Sunday luncheon, "Authors, Books, and Booksellers Make History," was moderated by publisher and former ABA President Gail See of Hungry Mind Press. Panelists included Larry Brown, *Father and Son* (Henry Holt); Robert Olen Butler, *Tabloid Dreams* (Henry Holt); James Galvin, *Resurrection Update: Collected Poems, 1975–1997* (Copper Canyon Press); and Sandra Benitz, *A Place Where the Sea Remembers* (Coffee House Press). Several awards were also presented at the event. The winner of the Charley Haslam International Scholarship Award was David Tweet of Wexter Bookshop in Columbus, Ohio. The prize entitled him to attend the International Convention of Young Booksellers in Barcelona. The Charles S. Haslam Award for Excellence in Bookselling was presented to Tom Campbell of the Regulator Bookshop in Durham, North Carolina. The 1997 Blackboard African-American Bestsellers Inc. Awards were also bestowed during the Saturday luncheon. The awards recognize the accomplishments of African American writers and an African American bookseller. Brother Simba of Karibu Books in Hyattsville, Maryland, won the Blackboard Bookseller of the Year award, and Blackboard Books of the Year were named in three categories. The year's fiction award was claimed by Connie Briscoe, *Big Girls Don't Cry* (HarperCollins); the nonfiction award was accepted by Iyanla Vanzant, *Faith in the Valley: Lessons for Women on the Journey Toward Peace* (Fireside); and the children's award, accepted on her behalf by her publisher, was won by Rosa Parks, *Dear Mrs. Parks: A Dialogue with Today's Youth* (Lee & Low).

On Sunday evening ABA and BEA jointly hosted a cocktail reception honoring Pat Schroeder, the new president of AAP. Following the reception large numbers of convention attendees headed to the Navy Pier for the Third Annual Great Chili Cookoff & Party sponsored by Ingram Book Company. The Great Chili Cookoff was one of several events held at the 1997 BEA to benefit the Book Industry Foundation (BIF). Launched earlier in the year by Ingram Book Company, BEA, AAP, and the American Booksellers Foundation for Free Expression (ABFFE), BIF is a joint book industry endeavor supporting literacy, free expression, and other book-related causes.

As always, popular features of the annual event included reading rooms and a full roster of authors autographing their works, among them Charlton Heston, Naomi Judd, Richard Simmons, and Roger Ebert. The ABA Convention featured, as in past years, a full plate of educational offerings developed by the association's Education Committee and implemented by its Department of Education and Professional Development. Programs garnering particularly high attendance and enthusiastic response included three very practical sessions in the area of financial management: "Managing Your Cash Flow," "Understanding and Using Financial Documents to Make Management Decisions," and "Determining the Proper Level of Inventory and Using a System to Control the Dollar Volume of Purchases." An overflow audience of wannabes attended the session "So You Want to Open a Bookstore: Financial Considerations."

Several sessions with guest authors as panelists focused on book content and were particularly well received. These included "Trends in Travel Bookselling," "Current Trends in Religious Books," and "Hot Topics and Products in the New Age Market." Among other highlights was a baker's dozen of roundtable discussions for large and small bookstores, as well as for bookstore/cafes and specialists in specific bookselling areas, including African American, feminist, gay/lesbian, travel, romance, mystery, new age, science fiction, recovery, and used books. In addition to the full-day conference held by African American booksellers, there was also a full-day seminar for large-store owners and managers and a session titled "Playing to Win: Keeping Your Children's Bookstore Alive and Exciting," the latter sponsored by the ABA-Children's Book Council (CBC) joint committee. In total, there were more than 6,000 participants in the 1997 Convention's educational programs.

American Booksellers Foundation for Free Expression

The American Booksellers Foundation for Free Expression (ABFFE) continued to be a leading force against censorship on behalf of booksellers and others throughout 1997. When ABFFE joined the Citizens Internet Empowerment Coalition (CIEC) to contest the communications decency provisions of the Telecommunications Act of 1996, it was known that the Supreme Court would be hearing its arguments in 1997, even after a victory before a three-judge panel. Bruce Ennis, ABFFE board member and one of the nation's preeminent First

Amendment attorneys, successfully convinced the court that the Communications Decency Act (CDA) was unconstitutional.

Also during 1997 ABFFE, in cooperation with Barnes & Noble Booksellers and Borders Books & Music, issued a formal protest on behalf of all booksellers against the physical destruction of books containing the works of the photographer Jock Sturges instigated by special interest groups, including Randall Terry's Loyal Opposition. In addition, ABFFE's efforts to encourage booksellers in Illinois to push for the defeat of Senate Bill 1036, which would have given the power to define obscenity to each of the state's 102 counties, contributed largely to that bill's defeat. The foundation also joined other Media Coalition members in a lawsuit filed in July by the Video Software Dealers Association protesting Oklahoma City police actions in seizing videos of the 1979 Academy Award-winning film *The Tin Drum* from libraries, video stores, and private homes.

At past ABA conventions ABFFE has sponsored a special event, and 1997 was no exception. "A Conversation with Oliver Stone" was jointly presented by ABFFE, the Freedom-to-Read Committee of AAP, and the Freedom-to-Read Foundation of the American Library Association (ALA). ABFFE President Oren Teicher and AAP President Pat Schroeder joined Stone in a discussion of free expression and film, including references to his autobiographical novel *A Child's Night Dream* (St. Martin's Press). ABFFE, as a founding member of the Book Industry Foundation, also shared responsibility with AAP, BEA, and Ingram for a reception honoring Stone, the annual silent auction, and the Good Foundations retail store, all to benefit BIF.

Other ABFFE activities during 1997 included publication of its quarterly newsletter *Free Expression*, participation in New York Is Book Country and the Hudson Valley Book Fair, and cosponsorship of the annual Banned Books Week. To enhance and encourage special activities during that week, ABFFE provided special Banned Books Week educational and promotional materials to 800 booksellers.

Education and Professional Development

A continuing high priority of the Education Department throughout 1997 was the development of more convenient and economical educational opportunities for professional booksellers. One such approach, the night-school format of the professional bookselling curriculum—an enthusiastically received innovation of 1996—was repeated with much success in 1997. During the second year of the program, schools were held one night a week for five consecutive weeks in each of three cities: Berkeley, California; Portland, Oregon; and Seattle, Washington—with a total of more than 350 booksellers participating. In addition, four traditional four-day schools for prospective booksellers were held in various locations around the country, with attendance once again on the increase, and a two-day school for professional booksellers was held in Chicago immediately preceding BEA and the ABA Convention.

ABA's most significant educational milestone of 1997 was the development of its open-learning self-paced study series titled "The Fundamentals of Bookselling." The series was introduced in a special convention educational session conducted by ABA's director of education at which the first volume, *Customers and Service*, was unveiled. It was anticipated that one new volume per month would be completed starting in January 1998.

Among other initiatives of the Education Department in 1997 were planning for the establishment of an Internet users group to help bookstore trainers share effective ways they have used "Fundamentals of Bookselling" in training front-line staff. In addition, many requests of the Education Department for information were answered by electronic mail, rather than by more traditional methods. Furthermore, the curriculum outline of the booksellers schools, featured on ABA's Web site, drew numerous responses, and rental of ABA's training videos continued to provide in-house training for many member bookstores.

Publications

Throughout 1997, as in past years, the ABA Publications Department continued its efforts to provide booksellers with a wide range of informational and practical books and periodicals. Resources such as *Manual on Bookselling: Practical Advice for the Bookstore Professional, Display & Visual Merchandising*, and *Operating a Bookstore: Practical Details for Improving Profit* were widely consulted by book industry professionals for information about competing successfully in today's competitive retail environment.

The association published a new edition of the *Book Buyer's Handbook* that was more comprehensive than ever before, providing information from more than 2,000 publishers. During the past few years ABA has increased the number of companies included by more than 20 percent, while at the same time expanding the amount of data provided. In addition to information on ordering, returns, discounts, freight, and co-op advertising policies, the 1997 edition contained fields housing e-mail addresses and electronic ordering information. In 1997 ABA also offered an electronic version of the *ABA Book Buyer's Handbook*. The "infobase" version allows users to conduct searches through the material by selecting a keyword, name, or field, and listings can be printed from the program. In addition, for the first time an interim update to the *Book Buyer's Handbook* was compiled and offered to ABA member bookstores. This interim update for the *1997 ABA Book Buyer's Handbook*, covering more than 130 vendors, included terms and conditions that had changed or become effective since the *Handbook* was published.

Booksellers Publishing, Inc. (BPI), the book publishing subsidiary of ABA, expanded its list of professional titles available for people in the book community. BPI's Booksellers House imprint, which is dedicated to publishing titles that hold special significance for those interested in the history and business of bookselling, published its first original title in 1997. *Off in Zora* by Alan Armstrong is the true story of a Philadelphia lawyer who sets out in an old Volkswagen bus (named Zora) that serves as his bookshop. This book tells the story of Armstrong's bookselling odyssey, as he takes the reader on the road to share his first year's adventures. In addition to this new original book, Booksellers House has reprinted seven other titles that tell the stories of booksellers and bookstores across the country.

BPI also published a new edition of *ABACUS Expanded*, which reports the results of ABA's annual financial survey of member bookstores. As in the past the study was compiled by the ABA Research Department. The 1997 edition, based on 1995 operations, contains data supplied by 182 ABA-member independent booksellers operating in 242 locations and offers a range of newly derived ratios, as well as income statement and balance sheet results. Improvements and enhancements include a new analytic variable, used-book sales groupings; revised sales volume categories that better reflect the latest statistics; a new measure, rent expense per square foot, for booksellers who do not own their own buildings; the inclusion of median sales per organization (in addition to average sales); and a combined product mix table that incorporates new books, used books, textbooks, audio and electronic books, magazines, and other sidelines.

Entering its fourth year of publication, *Bookselling This Week (BTW)* focused on providing timely information to ABA member booksellers and others in the book industry. In expanded editions published before and after BookExpo America, ABA's weekly covered the book industry's annual trade show in detail. In October a special edition of *BTW* was published to bring readers up to date on details of ABA's antitrust discrimination settlement with Penguin Putnam, including the payment of funds to be dispersed to ABA's independent bookstore members. *BTW* also offered thorough coverage of controversial panel discussions on book "megastores," online bookselling, and the challenges facing booksellers and publishers. Additionally, *BTW* continued to publish its listings of authors on tour, its guide to books featured in other media, and its announcements of changing terms, special offers, and book-related events. ABA's publications department also continued to publish quarterly specialty newsletters for members of ABA's five specialty membership segments as well as *Free Expression*, ABFFE's four-page quarterly newsletter covering the First Amendment and other free-speech issues.

As it began its third decade, *American Bookseller* magazine tailored its editorial program to better assist booksellers and others in the publishing community to meet the business challenges of rapidly changing times. A major component of the year's efforts was expanded coverage of small presses and their offerings. In the magazine's "Omnibus" department, readers got an advance notice of titles like Walter Mosley's *Gone Fishin'* and *The Kennedy Tapes*, from Harvard University Press—both of which received extensive media attention on and off the book review page. Further, timely profiles of such influential independent houses as David R. Godine Publisher and Sasquatch Books deepened readers' understanding of the challenges and opportunities facing independent and regional presses.

In addition, recognizing that booksellers were continually being challenged to retool their business strategies, the magazine worked to assist readers in their professional development, with a special focus on marketing and the intelligent uses of technology. Best-selling authors Bob Nelson and Jay Conrad Levinson both wrote exclusive *American Bookseller* pieces on marketing business books and becoming an expert "techno-guerrilla marketer," respectively. And each month, the magazine's "BiblioTech" and "Web Watch" departments showed how technological developments could be harnessed to sell more books in the digital age. Further, working to keep booksellers current, the magazine ran pieces from

J. Walker Smith of Yankelovich Partners on selling books to baby boomers and to Generation Xers, profiled a number of promising young booksellers, and showed how online life on college campuses was changing the face of reading.

The magazine also continued many of its well-known features, with an expanded children's "Pick of the Lists" (a selection by children's bookselling experts of the best titles of the selling season); in-depth coverage of the national BookExpo America trade show and the association's national convention; a comprehensive excerpt from BPI's *ABACUS Expanded*; the booksellers' annual merchandising calendar; and the *Bookstore Source Guide*, a directory of sources for everything the bookstore needs except books.

Research

Once again during 1997 the ABA Research Department produced and disseminated to booksellers and others in the book industry a substantial amount of research information of both the benchmark and trend variety. Among the findings reported in *Bookselling This Week* and on BookWeb were those referenced earlier in this article, and others, from the *1996 Consumer Research Study on Book Purchasing* and the *Current Retail Census*. As it has done for a number of years, the research department analyzed, compiled, and made available on a custom basis to its various constituencies (ABA members, regional booksellers associations, other industry members, the public, and the media) detailed information from the consumer study's proprietary database on such topics as retail outlet market share by region and household demographics of purchasers of books in specified subject categories. The research department also continued its regular preparation of material for several standard *BTW* features, including the monthly report on sales in bookstores, personal consumption expenditures (PCEs) on books and maps, and "In Fact. . . ," in addition to analyzing results of various ABA studies for press releases, speeches, and articles.

The declining growth and market share of independent booksellers discussed above was further confirmed by *1997 ABACUS Expanded*, which reported the results of ABA's most recent financial survey of member independent booksellers. The findings, based on 1995 operations of the participating 165 businesses, showed average income before taxes amounting to 1 percent of sales, with a slightly lower median figure of 0.7 percent. Trended results were also not encouraging for the 78 responding booksellers who participated in all three of the most recent studies. Declining net income for this group in 1993, 1994, and 1995 was, respectively, 3.6 percent of sales, 2.8 percent, and 1.9 percent, although constant participants' average 1995 results were decidedly better than those of all participants (1.9 percent versus 1.0 percent). The high-profitability grouping (the top 25 percent of participants based on total return on assets) did considerably better, however, at 9.7 percent of sales, on average. As in past financial studies, this high-profitability group shared four major characteristics: much lower average operating expenses, higher average inventory productivity (including a higher gross margin, higher gross margin return on inventory investment, and a lower rate of returned products to vendors), higher average sales and gross margin per full-time-equivalent employee, and more-favorable balance sheets. Survey participants reported a modest average book returns rate to vendors of 9.7 percent of purchases.

In an effort to stimulate and facilitate participation in the annual ABACUS financial survey, a standardized chart of accounts for booksellers was developed by ABA's Industry Standardization Committee working closely with the research department, which then assumed responsibility for its introduction to the membership in early 1997. Following the research department's development of a comprehensive marketing plan, the new ABA Standard Chart of Accounts was formally unveiled at BookExpo America. Designed to be adaptable to the needs of booksellers of various sizes and complexity, the chart of accounts facilitates the use of a single set of numbers for tax preparation, use of ABACUS results, and participation in a variety of government and industry surveys, including ABACUS. Made available by phone, fax, and mail, in hard copy or electronically, it had been widely disseminated by the end of 1997. Six months after its introduction, nearly 1,300 booksellers had requested hard copies of the chart of accounts, and 1,100 Internet surfers had viewed it on BookWeb, for a total exposure of more than 2,400.

Findings of the 1996 ABA Book Buying Study were also released in 1997. This annual tracking study, conducted for ABA by the Gallup Organization, is based on the combined results of four quarterly telephone surveys, each covering book-buying activity during the previous three months. Results for 1996 indicated that about the same proportion of adults as in 1995 reported purchasing a book during the previous three months (63 percent). Among other findings of interest, the majority of books purchased at a discounted price were not purchased in bookstores (chain stores, including their superstores, 27 percent; independent bookstores, 11 percent). On the other hand, the bulk of the books bought at regular price by consumers in 1996 were acquired at a bookstore (chains, including superstores, 38 percent; independent bookstores, 16 percent).

Further to its responsibilities in disseminating research findings and other information, the research department also continued to operate ABA's extensive bookselling and publishing library and to respond to a large volume of requests for reference information and research statistics, aided by the staff of ABA's Information Service Center. The department also updated its four information modules, which contain excerpts from various ABA research studies and other materials and are available for sale. The modules are titled *Opening a Bookstore*, *Statistical Overview of Retail Bookselling*, *Children's Bookselling*, and *Audio, Video, and Multimedia*. Finally, the director of research participated in a panel held during the ABA Convention/BookExpo America titled "The Need to Know: Current and Future State of Book Industry Information and Trends."

Bookstore Promotion

ABA undertook several projects intended to promote its member bookstores to the book-buying public. One of these, the fourth annual National Independent Bookstore Week (NIBW), was observed during the week of July 19–26. The NIBW Advisory Council conceived the concept of a book to celebrate independent bookselling and approached several authors, poets, illustrators, and journalists and requested from them materials for the project. The resulting 195-page book, *Out of the Mold: Independent Voices Breaking Out of the Mold*, was published by ABA in less than eight months from conception. The collection of pieces and illustrations speaks to the importance of independence, personal strength, and diversity. The book received regional media attention in addition to a mention in *USA Today*. ABA provided participating member stores with an information kit complete with promotional ideas and supporting materials, in addition to five complimentary copies of *Out of the Mold*, T-shirts, bookmarks, and posters were available for in-store promotions. NIBW 1998 will be held July 18–25, although materials will be ready prior to BEA to allow more-flexible options for participating in the campaign.

Another undertaking marked the first annual National Black Bookstore Week (NBBW), held June 14–21, 1997. The theme, "Keeping Us Connected," was intended to remind the public about the important contributions African American bookstores make by sustaining the culture of African Americans through books. NBBW was celebrated in conjunction with "Juneteenth"—the day in 1865 that the slaves in Texas learned of their freedom. Participating bookstores and publishers collected and donated books to the Soweto Book Project; more than seven tons of books were given to the children of South Africa. Poet Maya Angelou, spokesperson for NBBW, said, "Thoughts by African American thinkers have helped us to survive. Poetry by African American poets has helped us to thrive. Bookstores owned by African American merchants have helped us to survive and to thrive with some passion, some compassion, some humor and some style."

In response to President Clinton's America Reads Challenge, the American Booksellers Association, in partnership with Scholastic, Inc., the Association of Booksellers for Children (ABC), and Ingram Book Company, distributed more than 200,000 free copies of a special paperback edition of *Read to Your Bunny* by Rosemary Wells. The books were given out at participating bookstores to parents and guardians of young children through the Prescription for Reading Partnership. An integral component of the America Reads Challenge, the Prescription for Reading Partnership was launched in April 1997 by First Lady Hillary Rodham Clinton on the eve of the White House Conference on Early Childhood and Brain Development. The partnership encourages businesses, community organizations, and others to work with health care providers to "prescribe" reading during "well-baby" checkups. This program is based on the successful work of a Boston-based organization, Reach Out and Read, which corroborates that reading to very young children enhances the child's overall intellectual, emotional, and physical development. The goal of the America Reads Challenge, to be met by the year 2000, is to ensure that all children learn to read well and independently by the time they enter third grade. An accompanying information kit sent to booksellers contained "prescription" coupons for *Read to Your Bunny*, in addition to promotional suggestions, a list of Reach Out and Read centers, and a suggested reading list for babies, toddlers, and pre-schoolers. Booksellers were asked to provide the prescription coupons to pediatricians, well-baby clinics, etc., where the coupons would be given to parents and guardians to be redeemed at the sponsoring bookstore.

In yet another initiative to promote bookstores during 1997, ABA created a plastic counter-card to help raise public awareness of the dwindling number of independent bookstores by reprinting with permission the *New York Times* editorial "The Endangered Bookshop" (June 19, 1997). The commentary laments the passing of New York City's Doubleday Book Shop on Fifth Avenue and points out that "more than a physical" void is left on many U.S. Main Streets in the wake of closing independent bookstores.

Finally, ABA once again joined forces with the Department of Culture of Barcelona, Spain, in celebrating World Book Day. Fresh-cut roses were once again supplied by ABA to participating booksellers, who in turn presented them to anyone buying a book on April 23.

Booksellers Order Service

Booksellers Order Service (BOS), a wholly owned subsidiary of ABA, provides members with a group-buying program. Throughout 1997 BOS continued to offer advantageously priced products (most shipped freight-free) that could be used or sold by booksellers in their day-to-day operations. BOS continues to stock a wide range of products, including book-related T-shirts that can be imprinted with the bookstore's logo, heavyweight canvas tote bags (plain or imprinted with a store logo), 3M security strips, four types of gift-wrapping paper for adults and children, plastic and paper bags in three sizes imprinted with BOS's definition of a book on one side and a bookstore on the other. Also available are many types of booklights, reprint editions of fine-art books, and recycled-paper shopping bags. All these items, as well as new products, are features in the full-color *ABA Quarterly Merchandising Catalog*. This quarterly catalog provides booksellers with a continually updated list of products from BOS, ABA, BPI, and ABFFE and simplifies ordering through the inclusion of an order form.

Association of Research Libraries

21 Dupont Circle N.W., Washington, DC 20036
202-286-2296; e-mail arlhq@cni.org
World Wide Web: http://www.arl.org

Duane E. Webster
Executive Director

The Association of Research Libraries (ARL) represents the 121 principal research libraries that serve major research institutions in the United States and Canada. ARL's mission is to shape and influence forces affecting the future of research libraries in the process of scholarly communication. ARL programs and services promote equitable access to and effective use of recorded knowledge in support of teaching, research, scholarship, and community service. The association articulates the concerns of research libraries and their institutions, forges coalitions, influences information policy development, and supports innovation and improvement in research library operations.

ARL fulfills it mission and builds its programs through a set of strategic objectives.

1 *Scholarly Communication and Information Policies*: To understand, contribute to, and improve the system of scholarly communication and the information policies that affect the availability and usefulness of research resources

2 *Access to Research Resources*: To make access to research resources more efficient and effective

3 *Collection Development*: To support member libraries' efforts to develop and maintain research collections, both individually and in the aggregate

4 *Preservation*: To support member libraries' efforts to preserve research collections, both individually and in the aggregate

5 *Technology*: To assist member libraries to exploit technology in fulfillment of their mission and assess the impact of educational technologies on scholarly communication and on the role of research libraries

6 *Staffing*: To identify on an ongoing basis the capabilities and characteristics required for research library personnel to best serve their constituencies, and to assist member libraries and educational programs in the recruitment, development, and effective use of staff

7 *Management*: To assist member libraries in augmenting their management capabilities

8 *Performance Measures*: To describe and measure the performance of research libraries and their contributions to teaching, research, scholarship, and community service

To meet these objectives, ARL resources are organized into a framework of programs and capabilities. Annually the ARL Board of Directors identifies priorities for the year. ARL program staff and the association's standing committees address these priorities in the coming year. The 1998 priority activities as outlined in the ARL Program Plan are to

- Accelerate and broaden copyright advocacy and education within the research and educational communities and to the general public
- Create cost-effective models and strategies for managing global scholarly communication in partnership with other organizations
- Help research libraries, and the communities of which they are a part, move into a transformed and increasingly diverse environment through the development of programs and products
- Ensure that research and learning will flourish through the development of advanced networking applications and Internet 2 (I2).

Scholarly Communication

The Office of Scholarly Communication (OSC) undertakes activities to understand and influence the forces affecting the production, dissemination, and use of scholarly and scientific information. These activities include promoting innovative, creative, and alternative ways of sharing scholarly findings, particularly through championing evolving electronic techniques for recording and disseminating academic and research scholarship. The OSC also collaborates with others in the scholarly community to build common understanding of the challenges presented by electronic scholarly communication and to generate options for concerted action. OSC was initially created as the Office of Scientific and Academic Publishing and the capability was renamed in spring 1996.

As a result of discussions with the associate director of the Pew Higher Education Roundtable, ARL was invited, along with the Association of American Universities (AAU), to cosponsor a national roundtable on the management of intellectual property in higher education. The purpose of the roundtable was to examine how the academy, in cooperation with not-for-profit publishers and scholarly societies, can take steps to manage its own intellectual property in more cost-effective ways while assuring sustained access to scholarly research. The group agreed to five strategies that need to be undertaken to ensure future access to scholarly communication: (1) a de-emphasis on volume as a measure of quality in the review of faculty work; (2) a continued effort by libraries to shape a more coherent marketplace; (3) a well-organized campaign to teach the faculty the economics of scholarly publishing and the options they have for assigning their copyrights; (4) an investment in electronic forms of scholarly communication; and (5) the decoupling of publication and peer review for the purposes of promotion and tenure.

The ARL membership has banded together to create an electronic-publishing fund and to identify partners willing to publish scientific, technical, and medical journals in order to develop a more cost-effective market for these products. The project, now designated as the Scholarly Publishing & Academic Resources Coalition (SPARC), has been formalized as a project of the ARL Office of

Scholarly Communication. SPARC is an ARL partnership project with a mission to be a catalyst to promote competition in the marketplace for research information, to promote the academic values of access to and ethical use of information for research and teaching, and to encourage the innovative use of technology to improve scholarly communication. The first steps for the group are to develop a business plan and an action agenda to support the establishment of at least five alternative publishing ventures during the next year.

A set of principles for licensing electronic resources was developed by a working group representing six library associations. The principles are intended to guide libraries in negotiating license agreements for access to electronic resources and provide licensors with a sense of the issues important to libraries and their communities. The principles can be found on the ARL Web site at http://www.arl.org/scomm/licensing/principles.html. ARL also developed a booklet titled *Licensing Electronic Resources: Strategic and Practical Considerations for Signing Electronic Information Delivery Agreements*. It is available in print and in electronic form at http://www.arl.org/scomm/licensing/licbooklet.html.

The office published the seventh annual edition of the *Directory of Electronic Journals, Newsletters, & Academic Discussion Lists*. This directory documents the advances in electronic/Internet publishing and has become the standard reference book in this area. An electronic version of the publication is mounted on the ARL Web site. Quick surveys on trends in serials and monograph purchasing also are conducted by the OSC, and results are made available on the ARL Web site.

Federal Relations and Information Policy

The Federal Relations and Information Policy Program is designed to monitor activities resulting from legislative, regulatory, or operating practices of international and domestic government agencies and other relevant bodies on matters of concern to research libraries; prepare analysis of and response to federal information policies; influence federal action on issues related to research libraries; examine issues of importance to the development of research libraries; and develop ARL positions on issues that reflect the needs and interests of members.

Copyright and intellectual property issues continue to be a major focus for this and other ARL programs in 1998. ARL actively participated in information policy debates by responding to and shaping national and international legislative initiatives that impact research libraries, including numerous Government Printing Office proposals, such as the GPO Transition Plan and proposed changes to Title 44, including the InterAssociation Working Group on Government Information (IAWG).

ARL actively opposed provisions included in Title V (the Communications Decency Act [CDA]) of the Telecommunications Act that sought to prohibit access to indecent or patently offensive materials via the Internet. These provisions would impose fines and criminal penalties for transmitting and/or providing access to these resources. In 1997 the Supreme Court struck down the Communications Decency Act, a move seen by many in the public-interest and civil-liberties communities as a step toward establishing a "Bill of Rights for the 21st century" and a clear victory for the First Amendment.

ARL staff worked with several government agencies in designing and proposing network applications programs, such as the NASA Information Infrastructure Technology and Applications Program, the NSF/ARPA/NASA Digital Library Initiative (DLI), and the NTIA TIIAP program. Staff participated in Project Alexandria, an NSF/ARPA/NASA Digital Library Initiative; meetings of the High Performance Computing Coalition (HPCC) regarding continued support for HPCC programs and Next Generation Internet (NGI); and in NSF network-related efforts.

ARL staff participated in the Internet 2 initiative, in addition to working with executive branch agencies involved in the related effort Next Generation Internet. A number of ARL directors have been nominated to work with the members of I2 on applications issues. ARL also joined with NASULGC, AAU, and others in presenting testimony on NGI and I2 initiatives.

The ARL Geographic Information System (GIS) Literacy Project continues to expand and evolve. The project seeks to educate librarians and users about GIS as well as to develop GIS capabilities in research libraries. Background materials related to this project, including a database of all project participants, are available on the Web at http://www.arl.org/info/gis/index.html. ARL also participates in numerous discussions and conferences related to the development of a national spatial-data standard and issues relating to access to GIS resources. The increasing reliance upon GIS by multiple communities, including government agencies and members of the academic and research communities, indicates the need for research librarians to be well situated to provide access to the growing array of digital cartographic and spatial information. Under the auspices of ARL, a new effort to address GIS literacy for library and information science professionals will be undertaken during the next year. With additional funding from the Environmental Systems Research Institute (ESRI) and the American Library Association (ALA), ARL, with librarians and geographers from the University of Texas–Austin, ESRI, the University of Dalhousie Library, and the University of Maryland, will develop a Web-based introduction to GIS for library and information science schools throughout North America.

Intellectual Property and Copyright Issues

The ARL Board of Directors identified intellectual property and copyright as a defining set of issues for the future of scholarly communications. As part of the association's interest in raising library and scholarly community awareness of issues associated with copyright and intellectual property management, several activities were undertaken to advance the ARL agenda in these critical areas.

ARL is collaborating very closely with four other library associations on copyright and National Information Infrastructure (NII) issues through the formation of the Shared Legal Capability (SLC). During fall 1997 SLC met with members of the Clinton administration and congressional staff to discuss many proposed changes to the Copyright Act; submitted statements to the House and Senate regarding copyright legislation; drafted alternative legislative proposals with others in the Digital Future Coalition (DFC); participated in congressional negotiations with online service providers and content owners on online service provider liability issues; sent a joint statement to members in support of the Ashcroft and Boucher-Campbell bills; worked with members of the House on the No Electronic Theft Act to design language to address concerns with liability issues; agreed to explore the development of "best practices" issue briefs (in lieu of "fair use guidelines") in selected areas, such as e-reserves, interlibrary loan, and licensing; and joined other interested associations in the issuance of a press release that pledged a renewed effort to explore fair use in the digital environment in the aftermath of the last meeting of the Conference on Fair Use (CONFU). The signatories noted that no agreement was reached on proposals for fair-use guidelines, and their shared goal is to encourage the development, use, and sharing of fair-use policies and practices that provide for the special needs and concerns of education and scholarship, while also providing as much clarity as possible about the boundaries of fair use as experience and good faith permit.

To help provide guidance in the evolving environment of licensing electronic resources, the American Association of Law Libraries (AALL), ALA, the Association of Academic Health Science Libraries (AAHSL), ARL, the Medical Library Association (MLA), and the Special Libraries Association (SLA) have combined to develop a statement of principles. The six associations represent an international membership of libraries of all types and sizes. The intent of the statement is twofold: to guide libraries in negotiating license agreements for access to electronic resources and to provide licensors with a sense of the issues of importance to libraries and their user communities in such negotiations. The principles are available on the Web at http://www.arl.org/scomm/licensing/principles.html.

With others in the public and private sectors, ARL formed the Digital Future Coalition (DFC), comprised of a diverse constituency of library, education, legal, scholarly, consumer, and public-interest associations; hardware and software manufacturers; and telecommunications providers that share concerns with pending legislation and that share the belief that any copyright legislation must strike a balance between owners, users, and creators of copyrighted works.

In 1997 DFC submitted testimony to both the House and Senate on copyright-related bills; conducted numerous visits to meet with members of Congress, their staff, and senior members of the administration on copyright issues; launched a campaign focused on the international dimensions of copyright legislation; and began a public-awareness campaign regarding the critical importance of this legislation. DFC developed new legislative language that addresses a host of issues, such as fair use, preservation, distance education, online service provider liability, and more.

ARL is collaborating with a number of constituencies to address issues relating to the database proposal "Collections of Information Antipiracy Act," pending in the House. ARL also participated in numerous database forums, including presentations to the National and International Data Center Directors. Staff also conducted numerous visits to House and Senate offices to discuss pending legislation on copyright-related bills, legislation seeking to extend copyright terms, and legislation seeking to extend new intellectual-property protections to databases.

CONFU participants met in May 1997 to determine whether the "proposals" for educational fair use for distance education, digital images, and multimedia have received sufficient endorsement to be included in a final report of CONFU. ARL did not endorse any of the proposed guidelines. It was anticipated that another meeting of CONFU participants would occur in spring 1998. Three themes emerged from ARL member library comments on all of the draft guidelines concerning electronic reserves, digital images, distance learning, interlibrary loan, and multimedia:

- The quantitative limitations and restrictions included in the proposals unduly narrow the interpretation of fair use by moving away from the four-factor analysis that is specified in Section 107 of the Copyright Act of 1976.
- Guidelines as rigid and specific as those proposed were premature, given the rapid evolution of new technologies and the lack of experience in these five areas.
- The proposals are technically and administratively burdensome to libraries and their institutions because they add new responsibilities and raise new liability issues.

The June 1997 issue of the *ARL Newsletter* was a special issue devoted to copyright and fair use in digital environments. It included reports about the fallout from the Conference on Fair Use; ARL's specific concerns with the proposed fair-use guidelines; ways the educational community can work toward consensus on copyright in the digital environment; a showcase of Northwestern University's e-reserve policies; the NHA Basic Principles for Managing Intellectual Property; reports on the World Intellectual Property Organization (WIPO) process, including the controversial proposal for database protection; and U.S. and Canadian legislation updates. The newsletter is available on the Web (http://www.arl.org/newsletter/192/192toc.html) or via the ARL Publications Department.

Access and Technology

A centerpiece of the ARL Access capability is the North American Interlibrary Loan and Document Delivery (NAILDD) Project. Established in 1993, the NAILDD Project promotes developments to maximize access to research resources while minimizing the costs associated with such activities. The operating philosophy is to seek practical technical developments that enable libraries to redesign their interlibrary loan/document delivery (ILL/DD) services for a networked environment. The strategy is to seek actions on the part of private-sector developers that will respond to the priority needs of the library community.

The NAILDD Project convenes three groups to facilitate technical developments and sharing of information. The Developers/Implementors Group (DIG) seeks to accelerate collaboration between libraries and the more than 70 private-sector players to advance the project's three technical goals. The ILL Protocol Implementors Group (IPIG) supports the implementation of the international standard for ILL communication by more than 40 organizations.

The Directors Forum provides an occasion for interaction between library directors and senior staff and representatives from members of the DIG and IPIG. Reports describing the 1997 NAILDD Project meetings are on the ARL Access Web page (http://www.arl.org/access/index.shtml).

In addition to the work of the NAILDD Project to promote implementation of the International Standards Organization (ISO) ILL Protocol, ARL Senior Program Officer Julia Blixrud agreed to chair a National Information Standards Organization (NISO) committee to develop a proposal for a new identifier: BICI (Book Item and Contribution Identifier). Like its predecessor for serials, the SICI code, the BICI will be an identifier of specific items, such as a specific volume in a multivolume work or chapters within a book. Both ARL and the Coalition for Networked Information (CNI) are heavily involved in SICI and BICI work. In October 1997 CNI's Clifford Lynch prepared a well-received article for the *ARL Newsletter*, "Identifiers and Their Role in Networked Information Applications."

Funded by the Andrew W. Mellon Foundation, the ILL/DD Performance Measures Study collected data on 119 ILL/DD operations in North American research and college libraries. Analysis of the findings of research libraries reveals an average borrowing unit cost of $18.35, a lending unit cost of $9.48, borrowing turnaround time of 15.6 calendar days, a borrowing fill rate of 85 percent, and a lending fill rate of 58 percent. Users are very satisfied with the performance of ILL operations. ILL operations in college libraries filled requests at a lower unit cost, with faster turnaround time, and higher fill rates. The performance of the best research libraries is comparable to the average performance of college libraries.

Six research libraries were identified as top borrowers and two as top lenders—that is, libraries with performance in the top 10 percent in two or more performance categories. A detailed description of the characteristics of the top-performing borrowing and lending operations will be included in the final report of the study, which will conclude with the publication in 1998 of the final report and the announcement of a series of workshops designed to improve ILL operations by highlighting best practices.

Collections and Preservation

At the end of December 1997 ARL completed the first year of a three-year grant from the Andrew W. Mellon Foundation in support of the AAU/ARL Global Resources Program. This initiative emerged from a set of earlier activities focused on the state of foreign acquisitions, which culminated in 1996 with the publication of *Scholarship, Research Libraries, and Global Publishing*. The principal goal of the Global Resources Program is broad: to improve access to international research resources, regardless of format or location. The program is sponsoring four ongoing projects (in Germany, Japan, Latin America, and South Asia) and developing two new projects (in Africa and Southeast Asia). Other Global Resources Program activities include a clearinghouse of Web-based international resources, an inventory of linkages and agreements that North American research libraries maintain with libraries and research institutes abroad, participation in efforts to recruit and train future area librarians, and plans for symposia that bring together faculty and librarians to identify future resource needs of particular fields and to develop cooperative strategies to meet those needs. The Global Resources Program Web site provides background information on projects under way as well as updated information on new activities related to this initiative at http://www.arl.org/collect/grp/index.html.

Three demonstration projects were originally suggested in 1994 in the final report of the AAU/ARL Task Force on the Acquisition and Distribution of Foreign Language and Area Studies Materials, one of three task forces that formed the AAU Research Libraries Project. The three projects—on Germany, Japan, and Latin America—were intended to examine different models for a distributed approach to the provision of resources. In 1997, with the experience of several years, it was possible to derive lessons from the projects and to identify common characteristics for success. A new two-year project, "The Digital South Asia Library: A Pilot Project," was launched in 1997 and is coordinated by the libraries of the University of Chicago and Columbia University. Two other projects are under development.

The Latin American Research Resources Project has several components: the digitization and indexing of presidential messages from Argentina and Mexico; a cooperative table-of-contents database maintained by the University of Texas Network Information Center (UT-LANIC) into which participating libraries contribute contents information from more than 300 Argentine, Brazilian, and Mexican journals via a template; a pilot interlibrary loan service, designed by UT-LANIC and OCLC, that facilitates requests for articles from the database; a monographic component, in which participating libraries reallocate a percentage of their Latin American monographic budget to deepen coverage of an area of strength; and a study, "Is Cooperation Cost-Effective?" conducted by an economist at the University of Florida and focused on resource sharing involving the extensive Caribbean collection at the University of Florida.

The Japanese Journals Access Project originally began with a focus on scientific and technical literature from Japan, but it has developed a broader approach with two sets of objectives: to improve access to Japanese journals available in North America and to improve access to Japanese journals and journal articles in Japan. Project activities have included efforts to facilitate interlibrary loan from Japan, working with a Japanese library committee; the addition to the project's Web page of useful sites for locating serials and enabling document delivery (http://pears.lib.ohio-state.edu); the exploration of the feasibility of loading records from participants' local systems into a Web-based union list of serials; the training of North American librarians at NACSIS in Tokyo in the use of electronic resources (with funding from the Center for Global Partnership), expertise that can now be shared via workshops for other librarians and end users in the United States; and an agreement with NACSIS under which it makes available indefinitely and at no cost its Webcat, containing both the Union List of Books and the Union List of Serials for all Japanese libraries (more than 400) that catalog on the NACSIS system.

The German Demonstration Project's primary goals have been to ensure effective and timely access to German-language research materials through electronic resource sharing and improved interlibrary document delivery services, and to test linking between North American and German libraries to expand access to specialized research resources. Efforts to secure start-up funding have caused a delay in fully undertaking the project's activities. Early in 1998 the project secured funding from the Andrew W. Mellon Foundation to strengthen trinational ties (United States, Canada, Germany) to advance the goals of electronic resources sharing.

The Digital South Asia Library is the newest Global Resources Program project. It encompasses a two-year effort to develop the infrastructure for intercontinental electronic document delivery to and from selected South Asian libraries and to create new electronic reference sources. Project results will include electronic indexing for approximately 38,000 articles in Tamil journals, 38,000 articles in Urdu journals, and 4,750 English journal articles, published during the 19th and 20th centuries; delivery on demand via the Internet of page images of the Tamil and Urdu journal articles indexed, either directly to scholars or through libraries; electronic full-text versions of three classic 19th-century South Asian reference works; and full-text versions of five titles from the Official Publications of India, one of which will be a statistical source structured as an electronic database.

ARL joined the Center for Research Libraries, the Council on Library and Information Resources, and the Library of Congress in sponsoring the Symposium on Access to and Preservation of Global Newspapers, held May 27–28, 1997, at the Library of Congress. The event included an assessment of the state of acquisition and collection management of foreign newspapers and featured presentations by faculty and librarians concerning the importance of newspapers as research tools and the need to develop better means of preserving them. Elements of a preliminary action agenda were identified and will be developed further by the International Coalition on Newspapers (ICON) Working Group, to be named by the Center for Research Libraries early in 1998.

A milestone was reached at the end of 1997 with the completion of the National Register of Microform Masters (NRMM) RECON project, funded by the National Endowment for the Humanities. This multiyear effort has completed the conversion of more than 22,000 serials and 500,000 monographic reports of preservation microfilm masters into machine-readable records. The availability of these records in OCLC and RLIN increases accessibility for scholars and eliminates redundancy in preservation microfilming efforts in libraries. Details of the project will be published on the ARL Web site.

Diversity

The charge of the Diversity Program is twofold: defining and addressing diversity issues in ARL libraries and supporting activities that encourage broad participation in the field. To this end, the program focuses on issues surrounding work relationships in libraries, while considering the impact of diversity on library services, interactions with library users, and the development of collections. The primary concern is the development of workplace climates that embrace diversity. The program also seeks to encourage exploration of the rich gifts and talents diverse individuals bring to the library. Program staff work closely with a broad range of libraries, graduate library education programs, and other library associations to promote awareness of career opportunities in research libraries and support the academic success of students from groups currently under-represented in the profession.

To meet the program's goals, ARL provides staff development seminars, presentations, and on-site, e-mail, and telephone consultation; facilitates staff discussions; conducts research via reviews of the literature and site visits to institutions; prepares articles and publications to share the findings from the program; seeks to identify strategies for adoption by libraries and library schools; and identifies issues and strategies and promotes them within ARL, as well as other national library-affiliated groups; and fosters partnerships on behalf of ARL with natural allies in the profession. During 1997 dozens of site visits were conducted across the United States and Canada.

The Diversity Program was awarded funding through an HEA Title IIB grant to support the creation of the ARL Leadership and Career Development (LCD) Program. The LCD Program prepares racial-minority librarians to pursue leadership roles in academic and research libraries. The program consists of two components. The first is an institute to provide advanced leadership skills to experienced and promising minority librarians; the second component is a support program, during which time a mentoring relationship is put in place and a practical project pursued. Evaluation and strengthening of the LCD Program will begin upon its completion in July 1998. The program will then be available to be replicated for all experienced and promising librarians. Its strength will draw from its initial emphasis on diversity issues in leadership and from the experience in conducting the program with a diverse mix of individuals from minority groups comparable to the work force that is the goal of the late-20th-century research library.

ARL Partnerships Program: Breaking Down Walls and Building Bridges was published in June and is available through the ARL Publications Department. It provides a vehicle for institutions participating in the ARL Partnership Program to tell their stories and relate their experiences with diversity. "Leading Ideas" is an ongoing publication series that synthesizes current issues and trends in diversity, leadership, and career development. The first edition, focusing on promotion and tenure and the minority academic librarian, was slated for distribution in March 1998.

Office of Management Services

Established to help research and academic libraries develop better ways of managing their human and material resources, the Office of Management Services (OMS) has assisted library leaders in finding more-efficient and more-effective ways of meeting user needs for more than 25 years. OMS staff stay abreast of current organizational and management theory and practice, seeking concepts and techniques that are applicable to, and have the potential for contributing to, the improved effectiveness of academic and research libraries. In recognition of the importa nce of leadership in libraries, the office has been renamed the Office of Leadership and Management Services (OLMS), effective January 1, 1998.

Three programs make up OLMS: the Organizational Development and Consulting Program, the Information Services Program, and the Training and Leadership Development Program.

To assist libraries in making the transition from an archival role to that of an information gateway in a period of limited resources and digital transformation, the OLMS Consulting and Organizational Development Program provides a wide range of consulting services, incorporating new research on service delivery and marketing as well as on organizational effectiveness. Using an assisted self-study approach, the program provides academic and research libraries with programs to develop workable plans for improvement in such areas as public and technical services, planning, team building, and organizational review and design. The OLMS provides on-site and telephone consultation, staff training, manuals, and other materials to aid participants in gathering information and in situation analysis. OLMS staff conduct projects in organizational redesign and review, leadership development, strategic planning, collection management, technical services process improvement, facilitation, resources sharing, and team building.

The OLMS Information Services Program maintains an active publications program, with the principal components including the Systems and Procedures Exchange Center (SPEC) and the OLMS Occasional Paper Series. Through the OLMS Collaborative Research Writing Program, librarians work with OLMS staff in joint research and writing projects that are published by OLMS. Participants and staff work together in all aspects of the publication process, from survey design, writing, and editing to seeking management perspectives on current academic concerns.

SPEC Kits organize and collect selected library documents concerning a specific area of library management. Kits are designed to illustrate alternatives and innovations used in dealing with particular issues. Documents describing both the administrative and operational aspects of the topic are included. Although this program was established to exchange useful information for strengthening library operations and programs among ARL members, a number of academic, public, and special libraries subscribe. Topics covered in 1997 include Internet training, electronic resource sharing, approval plans, staff training and development, and diversity.

"Transforming Libraries" is an OLMS publication series that focuses on how libraries are using tools and technology to transform library services and operations. Each issue addresses how institutions and individuals are pioneering in a particular area, and each includes a Web-based resource center for continued learning and updating. Issues released to date focused on geographic information systems, electronic scholarly publication, user surveys, and preservation of digital information.

The OLMS Training and Leadership Development Program provides support for libraries by delivering unique and dynamic learning events that actively and positively assist academic and research libraries to recognize, develop, optimize, and refine staff talents and skills. Program staff stay abreast of innovations in library services, library technologies, and library methods while maintaining current in the latest research findings in the areas of organizational structure, productivity, learning, and development.

In 1997 the Training and Leadership Development Program was invited to contribute curricula for two important grant proposals to support the leadership development of individuals from underrepresented groups. Both the ARL Diversity Program Leadership and Career Development Program and the University of Minnesota Training Institute for Library Science Interns and Residents were funded by the Department of Education, and the Training and Leadership Development Program staff is taking an active design and training role in both programs, which will take place in 1998.

In addition, approximately 900 library staff participated in OLMS Training and Leadership Development Program events in 1997. The program continues to experience a high demand for on-site delivery of learning events—already designed events and events tailored to meet organization-specific needs.

Statistics and Measurement

The ARL Statistics and Measurement Program collects, analyzes, and publishes quantifiable information about library collections, personnel, and expenditures, as well as expenditures and indicators of the nature of research institutions. The program and its oversight committee are also developing new ways to describe and measure traditional and networked information resources and services. The program sponsors workshops to give library staff and others opportunities to develop skills for developing survey instruments and for handling and managing statistical data. Customized, confidential analyses can be provided from the program's data.

Five statistical compilations were produced during 1997: *ARL Statistics 1995–96, ARL Academic Law and Medical Libraries Statistics 1995–96, Developing Indicators for Academic Library Performance Ratios 1995–96, ARL Annual Salary Survey 1996–97,* and *ARL Preservation Statistics 1995–96.*

The Council on Library and Information Resources awarded a grant to ARL to study the "Character and Nature of Research Library Investment in Electronic Resources." The project goal is to develop new definitions that support collection of information about the transformation of research library collections. A revised set of questions regarding research library investments in electronic resources will be distributed to ARL members as part of the 1996–1997 Supplementary Statistics questionnaire. The questions focus on expenditures because that is of primary interest to both library directors and campus administrators. Institutions are being asked to supply expenditures from both library and external (e.g., campus) budgets. The intent is to determine the total institutional investment in electronic resources that are managed by research libraries.

Successful workshops on User Surveys in Academic Libraries and on Electronic Publishing of Datasets on the World Wide Web were held across the country throughout 1997. Plans are under way to hold more workshops in 1998.

Office of Research and Development

The ARL Office of Research and Development consolidates the administration of grants and grant-supported projects administered by ARL. The major goal within this capability is to identify and match ARL projects that support the research library community's mission with sources of external funding. Among the projects not previously mentioned and under way in 1997 were the following.

Copyright Education Initiative

The H. W. Wilson Foundation awarded ARL funding to develop an educational initiative on copyright compliance. The initiative includes development of training resources to assist library managers and supports the design of workshops for librarians who have a training or spokesperson role in copyright compliance. Four workshops for U.S. librarians have already been held. In addition, in collaboration with CARL and the Association of Universities and Colleges of Canada, ARL developed a workshop for Canadian educational institutions. To date, two publications have resulted: a notebook used in the workshops and a booklet on licensing agreements.

Streamlining Network ILL/DD Requests for Users and Libraries

In November 1995 OCLC agreed to collaborate with the NAILDD Project to build a standards-based linkage between the AAU/ARL Table of Contents Database located at UT-LANIC and the OCLC ILL messaging system. The linkage allows network users to initiate an ILL/DD request for an article cited in the database and have it forwarded into the online system of the holding library and, if desired, into the system of the user's home library for user authentication. Lessons from this application will be applied to other databases, other ILL messaging systems, and sets of libraries.

Another initiative is the ARL Visiting Program Officer (VPO) program, which provides an opportunity for a staff member in a member library to assume responsibility for carrying out part or all of a project for ARL. It provides a very visible staff development opportunity for an outstanding staff member and serves the membership as a whole by extending the capacity of ARL to undertake additional activities.

Typically, the member library supports the salary of the staff person, and ARL supports or seeks grant funding for travel or other project-related expenses. Depending on the nature of the project and the circumstances of the individual, a VPO may spend extended periods of time in Washington, D.C., or may conduct most of his or her project from his or her home library. Currently, VPOs are addressing the development of a Web resource on digital library activities in ARL libraries; researching and writing on diversity issues in academic libraries; designing a licensing workshop and producing supporting written materials; studying the character and nature of research library investments in electronic resources; and developing the AAU/ARL Global Resources Program, coordinating the work of the ongoing pilot projects (Latin America, Japan, Germany, South Asia) and promoting projects for other world areas (Africa and Southeast Asia).

Two VPO assignments were under discussion and expected to be formalized in early 1998. These include the analysis of copyright and other intellectual-property issues, and contributing to the design and delivery of OLMS training and leadership development events. The ARL Web site (http://www.arl.org) reflects the scope of ARL's current agenda and suggests the range of issues where a Visiting Program Officer project could make a contribution.

Communication and External Relations

The capability for Communication and External Relations is designed to

- Acquaint ARL members with current important developments of interest to research libraries
- Inform the library profession of ARL's position on these issues
- Influence policy and decision makers within higher education and other areas related to research and scholarship
- Educate academic communities about issues related to research libraries

Through print and electronic publications and direct outreach, members of the library, higher education, and scholarly communication communities are informed of important developments and ARL positions on issues that affect the research library community. External relations with relevant constituencies are also carried on through all ARL programs.

Many of ARL's statements and publications are available on the ARL Web server, and the ARL-Announce service provides timely information about ARL and news items about ARL member library activities. ARL sponsors more than 50 electronic discussion groups, including such private lists as the ARL directors and ARL committee lists and such public lists as ARL-E-RESERVES and ARL-E-JOURNAL. Archives for the lists are updated monthly and made available on the ARL server.

Six issues of ARL's newsletter were published in 1997, including a special issue on copyright. Other topics covered include fair use and intellectual property rights, global resources, age demographics of academic libraries, diversity, statistics on library expenditures, keynote addresses from university leaders, and updates on the progress of ARL. Newsletters are available online at http://www.arl.org/newsltr/newsltr.html.

ARL collaborated with the Andrew W. Mellon Foundation to make papers from the Conference on Scholarly Communication and Technology available via the ARL Web site (http://www.arl.org/scomm/scat/index.html).

Association Governance and Membership Activities

The spring 1997 meeting was held in Albuquerque, New Mexico, hosted by the University of New Mexico. The program theme was "Consortial Leadership: Cooperation in a Competitive Environment." The fall Membership Meeting sessions were held in Washington, D.C. The program was developed by the Preservation Committee around the theme "Preservation of Digital Information."

The site of the May 12–15, 1998, meeting is Eugene, Oregon, hosted by the University of Oregon. The program theme is "The Future Network: Transforming Learning and Scholarship."

At the conclusion of the ARL Business Meeting in October, ARL President Gloria Werner (University of California at Los Angeles) handed over the gavel to James G. Neal (Johns Hopkins University). During the business meeting, Betty L. Bengtson (University of Washington) was elected Vice President/President-elect. Scott Bennett (Yale University), Paula Kaufman (University of Tennessee), and Carla Stoffle (University of Arizona) were elected to three-year terms on the ARL Board of Directors.

Council on Library and Information Resources

1755 Massachusetts Avenue N.W., Suite 500, Washington, DC 20036
202-939-4750, fax 202-939-4765
World Wide Web: http://clir.stanford.edu

James M. Morris
Vice President

The Council on Library and Information Resources (CLIR) is the outcome of the merger of the Council on Library Resources (CLR) and the Commission on Preservation and Access (CPA). CLIR officially came into being on May 30, 1997, when the board ratified its articles of incorporation and its bylaws. The merger marked the end of a two-and-a-half-year process of examining the missions, programs, and aspirations of CLR and CPA.

The separate boards of CLR and CPA, whose members had every reason to take pride in past accomplishments, dropped their respective claims on programs and projects and found substantial common ground. With high regard for one another's history and achievements, they took the opportunity to create an organization better adapted to meet the future needs of libraries, archives, and their many constituencies.

The period of analysis and reflection that led to the merger was a valuable exercise in assessing the established programs of CLR and CPA. There were long discussions about the challenges faced by libraries and archives as they acquire, store, preserve, and provide access to information resources. The institutional missions of these repositories are fundamentally unchanged, but the demands on them have increased dramatically as the dollars to support them have remained largely constant.

CLIR's statement of mission calls on the organization to identify the critical issues that affect the welfare and prospects of libraries and archives, to convene individuals and organizations in the best position to engage these issues, and to encourage institutions to work collaboratively to achieve and manage change. CLIR bases its mission on the conviction that information is a public good and of great social, intellectual, and cultural utility. It has set its sights on a few targeted programs: the Commission on Preservation and Access will retain its identity as a program of CLIR, along with programs for Digital Libraries, the Economics of Information, and Leadership. Much of 1997 was spent working out agendas for these programs and recruiting the appropriate individuals to oversee them.

The agenda for work in these program areas is extensive and CLIR can address only a portion of it now. To do so effectively requires a fundamental change in what had been the practice of one of the predecessor organizations, the Council on Library Resources, which was an operating foundation. CLIR will not maintain the kinds of grant programs that were a feature of CLR, nor will it be open to unsolicited requests for project support. It will adopt instead what has been the mode of operation of the Commission on Preservation and Access. That is to say, after consultation with knowledgeable advisers, it will identify the individuals and organizations best suited to undertake particular components of the overall agenda in each program area and seek their participation. From time to time, CLIR may issue a broad invitation for research proposals on specific topics, but that procedure will be exceptional.

During 1997 CLIR (and its predecessor organizations) organized and hosted dozens of program-based meetings. Staff members and individuals serving on various task forces and committees spoke about the programs at scores of professional and scholarly meetings. In all these activities, CLIR has sought to raise the level of awareness about important issues, to solicit help from appropriate groups, and to coordinate efforts toward a constructive purpose.

Underlying all the programmatic activity of CLIR is an abiding concern for the well-being of libraries and archives. Many recent articles in the popular press have called into question the nature of the library. There is no doubt about the importance of technology for increasing access to information, but what is the proper balance between the traditional functions of libraries and the new opportunities opened up by the technology? Technology may be, as many believe, a tool of empowerment and of democracy. But technology alone will not serve the needs of scholars or students.

CLIR will work with many different associations, scholarly societies, networks, and institutions of higher education, both national and international. It aims to be a forum for discussing candidly the changes—welcome and unwelcome, anticipated and unforeseen—that will inevitably accompany the efforts of libraries, archives, and information organizations to integrate digital resources and services into their well-established print-based environments.

The following pages will look principally to the future of CLIR's programs rather than to the accomplishments of 1997 because it seems more important to communicate the nature of the new agenda than to dwell on past activity that no longer reflects the organization's current practice.

As noted earlier, CLIR will initially maintain four major programs: the Commission on Preservation and Access, Digital Libraries, the Economics of Information, and Leadership. In each of these programs, it will consider libraries and archives not as isolated organizations but as components of a larger information structure that also includes colleges and universities, computer centers, and publishers.

Commission on Preservation and Access

As a fundamental principle of all its programs, CLIR will encourage institutions to achieve and manage change through collaboration, and nowhere is collaborative action more possible than within the preservation community. The most striking evidence of this is the success of the ongoing effort to rescue through microfilm large portions of the deteriorating print-based collections in libraries in the United States and elsewhere. Since its inception, CPA has worked to assure that knowledge produced by the scholarly communities of the world is saved and kept accessible. CLIR will continue that role.

With advice from its standing committees and task forces, CPA will publish materials that inform and instruct the preservation community, document the economic implications of establishing sound preservation environments for collections, frame the next set of issues to be considered within the changing definition of "preservation and access," and develop new strategies to sharpen the professional skills of individuals with preservation responsibilities.

The International Program

Because few of the critical issues of preservation and access today can be addressed outside an international context, CPA maintains an International Program to promote preservation awareness throughout the world. The program has helped to establish many collaborative projects, and through training seminars, workshops, translation projects, publications, and a policy of generous response to requests for counsel and advice from colleagues abroad, it continues to promote the long-term preservation and accessibility of information.

The International Program has focused its efforts to date on Eastern and Western Europe, the former Soviet Union, China, and Latin America. Thanks to new support from the Andrew W. Mellon Foundation, the work in Latin America will be extended, and CLIR will initiate new activity in southern Europe and South Africa. The program also hopes to expand in Asia and is seeking funds to develop new projects there. Examples of activities that will be undertaken in the next several years include the provision of U.S. expertise for preservation-needs assessments at libraries abroad, the development of cooperative filming and digitizing projects for specific collections, and the design of strategies to increase the production and use of permanent paper.

The following projects of the International Program are especially noteworthy.

International Register of Microform Masters. An international register of microform masters is essential if scholars and librarians are to know what has been filmed at locations throughout the world. The program encourages national libraries to contribute records to regional nodes for the collection, organization, and distribution of information about reformatted collections. It supports efforts to link these records to an emerging international register and to reach international consensus on the elements and the record structure for listings of digitized materials.

Translations. Most preservation literature is written in English, and there is little state-of-the-art information available to non-English-speakers. The program supports the translation and broad dissemination of key works on preservation. For example, preservation activity in Brazil has been given a great boost thanks to the completion in 1997 of a project the commission undertook in partnership with Brazilian institutions. The project accomplished the translation into Portuguese of 52 English-language publications dealing with all aspects of preservation activity. For the first time, large numbers of Brazilian institutions and preservation staff members have easy access to the best current thinking about numerous important technical and practical preservation matters. There are plans to distribute the translations in Portugal and in the Portuguese-speaking countries of Africa. A similar translation effort—to make preservation literature available in Spanish—is now under way at the National Library of Venezuela, and, farther afield, the European Commission on Preservation and Access is planning a translation program for other languages in Central and Eastern European countries.

Advisory Councils of the Commission

Preservation Science Council. Because the cost of environmental systems for storing all types of library collections—paper, magnetic media, and film—is substantial, establishing a sound preservation environment has become a major economic issue for academic institutions. Additionally, the storage environment for collections affects human comfort, and changes may disrupt established ways of working with materials. The commission's 20-member Preservation Science Council, composed of 16 preservation administrators and four scientists, has recommended an investigation of the extent to which scientifically regulated environmental conditions can increase the life expectancy of materials, even as operating costs remain the same or decrease.

Preservation Managers Council. This council, a longstanding committee of preservation administrators from research libraries, will develop ideas for projects that support essential traditional preservation activities, explore preservation issues around "non-book" materials (audio, video, film), and integrate preservation concerns into the design of digital library projects.

Digital Libraries

CLIR is committed to helping libraries of all types and sizes understand the far-reaching implications of digitization. To that end, CLIR supports pilot projects and experiments whose purpose is to build confidence in the digital component that libraries are now adding to their traditional print holdings.

Digital Library Federation

The Digital Library Federation (DLF), which was begun as the National Digital Library Federation by a group of 15 research libraries in 1996 and changed its name in September 1997, has become an official project of CLIR.

The primary mission of DLF is to establish the necessary conditions for creating, maintaining, expanding, and preserving a distributed collection of digital materials accessible to scholars and a wider public. Participants in the federation are committed to a shared investment in developing the infrastructure needed for libraries of digital works. The infrastructure is intended to enable digital libraries to bring together, or "federate," the works they manage for their readers.

DLF has now opened its membership, and libraries and archives generally are invited to participate on the same terms as charter members: they must meet the financial obligations for capital and operating expenses and demonstrate a serious commitment to the development of digital libraries. At the end of 1997 DLF included 17 research-library participants; in addition, the Research Libraries Group (RLG) and the Online Computer Library Center (OCLC) sit on the federation's Advisory Committee "with voice, but without vote."

The initial focus of DLF is on establishing best practices for discovery and retrieval, rights management and economic modeling, and the preservation and archiving of digital information. To advance these areas of program development, DLF has endorsed four testbed projects at participating institutions: the Making of America, Part II (MoAII); the Advanced Papyrological Information

System (APIS); the Social Sciences Digital Library Consortium (SSDLC); and the Berkeley/Columbia Digital Scriptorium.

The committee that acts as a general technical advisory body for DLF has taken as its agenda the following: to articulate the overall architecture for federating distributed digital libraries for the participating institutions; to identify areas in which DLF projects are needed to clarify, define, or establish prototype elements of the architecture; to consult on and review the architectural and technical components of specific DLF projects; to review the results of DLF projects for possible adoption as DLF practice; and to communicate the technical directions and accomplishments of DLF to a wide audience.

Nearly all the work of DLF to date has focused on creating digital libraries out of materials digitized from other formats. Conversion to digital formats is valuable, particularly for the education it provides to libraries and readers about the digital environment. However, for many purposes, conversion is prohibitively expensive, even with substantial philanthropic support. The federation must turn the attention of libraries to the numerous—and difficult—issues associated with works born in, rather than converted to, digital form.

Digital Archiving

Much has been written about the need to document digital information in order for it to serve the role of "record" in an archival sense, as well as about the need to "migrate" digital information to new media in order to prevent loss from media decay and obsolescence. However, relatively little effort has gone toward answering the more fundamental question of how to ensure that digital documents will remain readable and understandable in the future. The documents depend on computer software, and the software depends in turn on computer environments and hardware platforms, which become obsolete even faster than storage media. While it is important to develop metadata description standards, records-management procedures, and migration strategies to prevent the loss of records, these concerns will be moot if digital records cannot be read in the future. It is therefore crucial to perform a serious investigation of the underlying technological issues surrounding software dependence.

New electronic systems of scholarly communication will work only when there is a thoroughly dependable process for archiving digital information. Without such a process, libraries will continue to meet their preservation responsibilities by buying and storing paper versions. CLIR will work with relevant groups of scholars, university administrators, librarians, and computer-center personnel to develop a plan for digital archiving that builds confidence in new modes of scholarly communication and peer evaluation. The plan will consider the economics of digital archiving and set the systems and governance requirements for assured preservation and access and the safe migration of data.

The first phase of the effort to develop a firm technological basis for preserving digital records will identify and analyze existing models of digital archiving and describe and evaluate the technological alternatives they propose for providing true digital preservation. A subsequent phase may then pursue and make recommendations about the most promising of these strategies.

The Economics of Information

In 1997 CLIR made the last of a series of small grants for research on the economics of information in a program funded by the Andrew W. Mellon Foundation. These grants went to the following projects:

- The University of Minnesota. "The Theory of Cost Allocation for Information Resources." Principal Investigator: Beth Allen, Professor of Economics
- Northwestern University. "America On and Off Line: Access to Commercial Internet Service Providers." Principal Investigator: Shane Greenstein, Professor of Economics, Kellogg School of Management

The two new awards brought to 12 the number of projects funded by the program, and it was halted at that point in favor of a more ambitious and precisely defined research effort on the economics of information linked to the concerns of the other three programs of CLIR.

Questions about the economics of information will be asked within large institutional frameworks. A major study of how universities invest in information resources will describe, comprehensively, what it means at the end of the 20th century for a university to provide information resources to all its constituent elements. It is no longer appropriate, or even possible, to regard library budgets as the sole investment by universities in providing the information that serves as a basis for research and scholarship. The study will develop a model that can be used, first, to identify the full scope of "information resources" on a university campus and, second, to assess the real costs of the university's investment in them. The developed model will be distributed widely to institutions that stand to benefit from its findings.

Leadership

The much-talked-about transformation of both public and academic libraries will be accomplished only if talented and creative individuals are available to manage them and to define library services in the 21st century. CLIR's Leadership Program will sponsor projects that promise to build a new cadre of skilled leaders. The hybrid research library—with its massive print-based collections and ever-growing digital resources—calls for a kind of leadership that accepts responsibility not just for managing the staff and resources of the library building but for managing, in partnership with others, information resources not bounded by buildings or physical environments. Although some schools of information studies now offer curricula that prepare graduates to work effectively in the environment of print and digital media, the nation's libraries are largely staffed by individuals who have not had an opportunity for formal training in the contemporary demands of the profession.

Digital Leadership Institute

CLIR intends to establish a university-based institute, with a formal curriculum of several weeks' duration and a subsequent practicum experience, the purpose of which will be to train individuals who can effect fundamental change in the way universities manage their information resources in the digital era. This cadre of professionals drawn from library and computer-center personnel, academic administrators, and faculty members will preside over a transformation on the nation's campuses with far-reaching consequences for the way universities allocate their financial resources and fulfill their educational mission.

Innovative Uses of Technology by Colleges

Developments in digital technology and the growth of electronic information are changing the way information is provided on college campuses. Yet the reasons for making information available remain much the same as ever. CLIR is exploring how libraries have used technology to strengthen their role on college campuses, enhance their services, and improve instruction and research.

W. K. Kellogg Foundation Project

In 1996 the Council on Library Resources published case studies of 12 public libraries that have made innovative use of technology to improve library services. The studies, which were supported by the W. K. Kellogg Foundation, were well received by the library community. As a result, the foundation asked CLIR in 1997 to work with participants in the Kellogg Human Resources in Information Systems Management (HRISM) program to develop educational and training resources that can be used by many public libraries. CLIR will assess materials that have been developed within the HRISM program and build a coherent package that can be shared widely. At the same time, CLIR will adapt the public-library case studies for distribution to city managers and other local government officials and to information-policy experts.

In 1997 the Commission on Preservation and Access concluded a joint publication and distribution agreement with the European Commission on Preservation and Access (ECPA). ECPA's offer to act as CPA's distribution agent in Europe will save considerable time and expense in disseminating reports to that region. And the joint development of selected reports will provide CPA with broader perspectives and a larger talent pool from which to draw authors and reviewers.

CPA will complete a joint publication project with the International Federation of Library Associations and Institutions' Core Programmer for Preservation and Conservation (IFLA-PAC) that will result in a revised and expanded version of IFLA-PAC's "Preservation Principles for Library Materials." CPA agreed to help distribute the report and to mount it on the World Wide Web.

Early in 1998 CLIR will introduce an expanded publications agenda that reflects the work being done within each of its four programs. Some aspects of the publications agenda are familiar and some are new. Beginning in January 1998, the monthly CPA newsletter was replaced by a bimonthly CLIR newsletter, with information on the organization's full range of activities and interests. In the spring of 1998 CLIR will launch a second newsletter, to be issued on a quarterly basis, that will inform audiences outside the United States about preservation-related developments.

In addition, CLIR will issue up to half a dozen substantive reports annually, similar in content to previous CPA reports, on a variety of technical and managerial topics—for example, an overview of reformatting and its role in preserving and making accessible the print record that exists on brittle paper; a position paper on both the advantages and limitations of digitizing library materials; and the first in a series on preservation-and-management factors that influence or guide the selection for digitization of existing collections. CLIR will maintain the Research Briefs series begun in 1997 to describe the outcome or the current status of projects it has supported. The CLIR Web site, redesigned and enlarged in 1998, will be an essential adjunct to the print publications program.

Publications

In 1997 CLIR (and its two predecessor organizations) published the following:

Commission on Preservation and Access Newsletter: nos. 95–104 (January 1997–November/December 1997).

Commission on Preservation and Access Newsletter inserts:

"Task Force on Hispanic Resources Issues Recommendations" (March 1997).
"On the Fiscal Year 1998 Appropriations for the National Endowment for the Humanities." Written Statement from the Association of Research Libraries, the Commission on Preservation and Access, and the National Humanities Alliance (April 1997).

Reports

Coleman, James, and Don Willis. *SGML as a Framework for Preservation and Access.*
Weber, Hartmut, and Marianne Dorr. *Digitization as a Method of Preservation?* (translated from the German and co published with the European Commission on Preservation and Access).

Research Briefs

"How Users, Publishers, and Librarians Are Responding to E-Journal Publication" (July 1997).
"Relationships Between Libraries and Computer Centers at Liberal Arts Colleges" (November 1997).
"Comprehensive Access to Off-Site Print Materials at Johns Hopkins University" (November 1997).
"Cost Centers and Measures in the Networked-Information Value Chain" (December 1997).

Council on Library and Information Resources. Annual Report 1996–1997.

Scholarships and Awards

CLIR administers the A. R. Zipf Fellowship in Information Management. The fellowship is awarded annually to a student currently enrolled in graduate school, in the early stages of study, who shows exceptional promise for leadership and technical achievement in information management. Applicants for the fellowship must be citizens or permanent residents of the United States. For additional information, write or call the council.

The winner of the Zipf Fellowship in 1997 was John Chung-I Chuang of Carnegie Mellon University.

International Reports

International Federation of Library Associations and Institutions

Box 95312, 2509 CH, The Hague, Netherlands
31-70-3-14-08-84; fax 31-70-3-83-48-27
E-mail: ifla.hq@ifla.nl
World Wide Web: http://www.nlc-bnc.ca/ifla

Edward J. Valauskas
Member, IFLA Professional Board

As it approaches the 21st century, the International Federation of Library Associations and Institutions (IFLA) is moving forward enthusiastically in handling critical issues for librarians and information professionals on a global stage.

Information access, intellectual property, technology, literacy, and professional development are just a few of the crucial topics that IFLA is addressing, with its conferences, workshops, committees, offices, and programs and by the efforts of its member institutions and organizations. Much of IFLA's flourishing involvement in these sensitive and complex issues took form at the 63rd Council and General Conference in Copenhagen in 1997. The conference was both a climax to activities that had been evolving since the last Council and General Conference in 1995 in Istanbul, and a catalyst for activities well into the next century.

63rd Council and General Conference

Called the "most successful conference in the history of IFLA" by outgoing President Robert Wedgeworth, the Copenhagen conference set a number of records and standards that will test the mettle of future conference organizers and planners. Thanks to the remarkable efforts of the Danish Organizing Committee, 2,976 delegates from 141 countries attended the conference (August 31–September 5), taking advantage of a program that featured 170 papers (the papers can be found at http://www.nlc-bnc.ca/ifla/IV/ifla6/63cp.htm) in conjunction with 20 workshops and poster sessions, 35 visits to libraries in Denmark, 185 booths in the exhibition area, and an Internet cafe. The Danish Foreign Ministry (DANIDA) and the Danish Organizing Committee, led by Morten Laursen Vig and Hellen Niegaard, were able

Note: Edward J. Valauskas is Principal, Internet Mechanics, Chicago, and Chief and Managing Editor, *First Monday*, a peer-reviewed journal on the Internet about the Internet (http://www. firstmonday.dk).

to dramatically increase the participation in the conference by librarians from the developing world with the creation of the Danida Grant; 141 librarians from 81 countries were able to participate in the Copenhagen conference thanks to this remarkable and exciting program. In addition, 42 librarians from developing countries attended a preconference seminar in Aarhus, Denmark, designed especially for them. In addition to the conference papers, workshops, and exhibits, three guest lectures highlighted critical issues at the conference. Ursula Owen, editor of the Index on Censorship, discussed the ambiguities of censorship.

Esther Sibanyoni, Librarian at the State Library of Pretoria, South Africa, and the 1997 South African Woman of the Year, treated delegates to a personal description of her efforts in many South African community projects. Sir Roger Elliott, chairman of the International Council of Scientific Unions (ICSU) Press, analyzed the impact of electronic publishing on scientific information.

Copenhagen also represented a turning point for IFLA with a series of elections for a new president, members of the executive and professional boards, and chairs and secretaries of IFLA's 45 sections and roundtables. Robert Wedgeworth, president of IFLA since his election at the 57th Council and General Conference in 1991 in Moscow, was elected overwhelmingly as honorary president. Marianne Scott, director of the National Library of Canada, and Christine Deschamps, director of the Bibliothèque de l'Université Paris V, were candidates for IFLA president for the term 1997–2001. In addition, six positions on the IFLA Executive Board were contested. Christine Deschamps was elected its president and joins on the executive board newly elected members Klaus-Dieter Lehmann (Germany), Kay Raseroka (Botswana), Nancy John (United States), and Derek Law (United Kingdom). Ekaterina Genieva (Russian Federation) and Sun Beixin (China) were reelected to the executive board for a two-year term. Børge Sørensen (Denmark) continues as a member of the executive board; Sissel Nilsen (Norway) becomes an ex officio member of the executive board because of her election as chair of the IFLA Professional Board. The professional board consists of new members Winston Tabb (United States), Ilona Glashoff (Germany), Lis Byberg (Norway), and Stan Made (Zimbabwe); reelected to the board were Ralph Manning (Canada), Marjorie Bloss (United States), and Edward Valauskas (United States).

In addition to the elections, the IFLA Council examined four resolutions. The first resolution proposed that Chinese would be added to English, French, German, Spanish, and Russian as an official working language for IFLA. Chinese is already one of the working languages of the United Nations, and it is used by some 600,000 librarians and library staff in China. The council decided to refer the matter to an executive board working group for analysis.

A second resolution asked the French government and French municipalities to support the principles of the UNESCO Public Library Manifesto. Librarians working in four French public libraries have been subjected to enormous pressure by members of their communities over the nature of the collections in the libraries. The UNESCO Public Library Manifesto states, in part, that "collections and services should not be subject to any form of ideological, political or religious censorship, nor commercial pressures." The IFLA Council supported this resolution, which urged the French government to take steps to protect librarians to work in their institutions in accordance to the manifesto.

Two critically important resolutions were also considered by the IFLA Council, relative to censorship and intellectual property. IFLA's Committee on Access to Information and Freedom of Expression (CAIFE) recommended that the executive board establish a Committee on Freedom of Access to Information and Freedom of Expression to advise IFLA on international matters related to censorship and pressures to limit access to information in libraries. The council voted to establish this formal committee, which will be made up of members from the IFLA community. A second resolution called for the executive board to create a Committee on Copyright and Other Legal Matters; the council accepted this proposal as well.

A number of other activities made the Copenhagen conference professionally intriguing, such as the completion by IFLA sections, roundtables, and core programs of documents related to the overall IFLA 1998–2001 Medium-Term Programme; and the development of several new IFLA discussion groups dedicated to corporate libraries, friends and advocates of libraries, reference work, and social responsibilities. These groups hope to enjoy the success of the IFLA Internet Discussion Group, which drew 170 delegates from 31 countries to its meeting at the Copenhagen conference. In the exhibits, the *IFLANET Unplugged* CD-ROM—a snapshot of the contents of the IFLA Web site—was distributed free to delegates, thanks to the support of SilverPlatter Information and the National Library of Canada.

Thirty representatives of national library associations in 22 countries met with IFLA's executive board and Secretary General Leo Voogt to discuss a number of topics of mutual interest, including changes in IFLA publications and procedures for formally hosting future IFLA conferences.

A number of social programs were also a major element of the conference, including a gala reception at Øksnehallen, where delegates were greeted by Ebbe Lundgaard, Danish Minister of Culture. One measure of the success of the conference certainly comes in the growth of IFLA in Copenhagen; IFLA recorded 50 new members and two new sponsors during the conference and added two new sponsors shortly after the conference concluded. In collaboration with the Royal School of Library and Information Science (Copenhagen), the IFLA Professional Board evaluated the conference by several different avenues with the delegates; preliminary results from the survey have indicated that participants rated the conference as "excellent" or "very excellent."

IFLA's Finances

Outgoing IFLA Treasurer Warren Horton (Australia) provided an overview of IFLA finances at the Copenhagen conference. In the late 1980s and early 1990s IFLA's financial picture was cloudy, with declining reserves and membership. Thanks to the work of a special working group under the leadership of Marcelle Beaudiquez (France), the executive board, President Wedgeworth, and IFLA Secretary General Voogt, financial matters were successfully addressed with a number of innovations and conservative policies. As a result, in 1995 total income for IFLA was 1,457,251 Dutch guilders (NLG); expenditures in 1995 were 1,380,828 NLG. In 1996 total income equaled 1,543,988 NLG, with expenditures of 1,459,510 NLG. Over the course of the two years, 160,901 NLG were added to IFLA reserves (for a 1997 total of 425,843 NLG). Income was derived in 1996 in large part from membership fees (1,227,570 NLG), corporate sponsors (82,981 NLG), and publications (57,233 NLG). The 1997 budget conservatively was set at 1,465,000 NLG, with increased expenditures for activities in the developing world; IFLANET, IFLA's successful presence on the Internet; and professional activities as determined by the IFLA Professional Board. IFLA plans to continue to build reserves and to fund further development of programs for libraries and librarians in developing countries, as well as other professional activities.

Future Conferences

The recent success of the IFLA conferences has made the conference itself an attractive event for tourist authorities and convention organizers. In response to this welcome development, IFLA has created a new process to evaluate future sites. The federation is already committed to future conferences in Amsterdam in 1998, Bangkok in 1999, Jerusalem in 2000, Boston in 2001, and the United Kingdom in 2002. The new procedure will first collect statements of interest from national associations with completion of a standard form. After an initial review, potential hosts will be asked to organize a bid book that will describe specific features in a given host city and nation that will lead to a successful conference. These bid books will be analyzed by the executive board, and a decision on a future site for a conference will be made as a result.

Evaluations are currently in process for selecting a site for the IFLA Council and General Conference in 2003.

Publications

A number of significant reports, guidelines, and conference proceedings were issued by IFLA headquarters and its supporting publisher, K. G. Saur (Munich). Members receive the *IFLA Journal*, *IFLA Directory*, and the *IFLA Council Report* as benefits. In addition to the now bimonthly issues of the *IFLA Journal*, the up-to-the-minute reports of sections, divisions, roundtables, core programs, and offices on IFLA's Web site and the CD-ROM *IFLANET Unplugged*, several sections and divisions released directories and other guides over the course of 1997, supported by IFLA's publications program. Not all of these publications can be cited here, but a few of the titles include *Parliamentary Libraries in Asia and the Pacific*; the *International Directory of Art Libraries*; *Guidelines for Young Adult Library Services*; *Resource Book for School Libraries*; and the *Concise UNIMARC*. IFLA discontinued publication of its *IFLA Annual* and replaced it with the new *IFLA Council Report 1995–1997*. The *Council Report* was distributed to the membership in advance of the Copenhagen conference as well as at the conference itself. The 67-page publication provides a summary of IFLA's activities, beginning at the 61st Council and General Conference in Istanbul and culminating with the 63rd Council and General Conference in Copenhagen.

Grants and Prizes

Several awards and prizes have been established within IFLA to encourage professional development and stimulate participation in IFLA events from librarians in the developing countries. These programs include:

- Guust van Wesemael Literacy Prize. Awarded every two years, this prize recognizes efforts to increase adult literacy. Carmen Checa de Silva of the Piura Public Library Service in Peru was awarded the prize for her efforts in developing and executing a literacy and postliteracy program in Tangarara in the Piura region.
- Gustav Hofmann Grant. This grant permits a young library professional in the developing world to take advantage of training in the Library School in the Hague and to visit libraries and other organizations in Western Europe. Wala Hasan Musnad, a librarian at the National Documentation Center in Sudan was awarded the Hofmann Grant in 1997.
- Hans-Peter Geh Grant for Conference Participation. Sponsored by former IFLA President Hans-Peter Geh, this grant increases IFLA participation among librarians in Eastern Europe and the former Soviet Union. Sirje Virkus of Tallinn Pedagogical University in Estonia was awarded the grant in 1997 to permit her to attend IFLA's Copenhagen conference and to present papers at the open session of the IFLA Section on Education and Training and the Third Conference on Continuing Professional Education.
- Shawky Salem Training Grant for Arab Specialists. Encouraging professional development among Arab specialists, this grant was given to Mohammed Elyass, information officer at the Islamic Development Bank (Jeddah, Saudi Arabia). Elyass attended the Copenhagen conference and participated in a study program at the Royal School of Library and Information Science in Copenhagen.
- Scholarships and Attachments of the IFLA ALP Core Programme. With funding from the Swedish and Finnish library associations, the Swedish International Development Cooperation Agency, and other organizations, these scholarships and attachments allow librarians in developing countries to undertake training courses and other programs. In 1997 awards were made to librarians from Fiji, Ghana, Indonesia, Malaysia, Nepal, Pakistan, the Philippines, Senegal, Sri Lanka, and Vietnam for further educational opportunities.
- Presidents' Fund for IFLA Participation from the Developing World. In response to an initiative by American members of IFLA to pay tribute to the IFLA presidency of Robert Wedgeworth, a new fund has been established to increase participation in IFLA events by librarians from the developing world. Fund-raising efforts have begun in the United States and will continue through 1998. The fund will be managed by IFLA headquarters, with a jury composed of members of the IFLA boards and staff.

Other Activities

IFLA representatives develop programs and workshops around the world and participate in a number of other events sponsored by other organizations. In just the first six months of 1997 IFLA representatives attended more than 20 events in Africa, the Americas, Asia, and Europe. These included the following:

- Fifth IFLA ALP Core Programme/Africa Section Microcomputer Workshop. Twenty-seven participants from six of the nine South African provincial legislatures attended this six-day workshop at the University of the Western Cape (South Africa). Designed for librarians with a limited knowledge of computers and computer programs, the workshop examined library databases, networking, information literacy, SABINET (South African Bibliographic and Information Network), and the Internet. Financial support for the workshop was provided by the Swedish International Development Cooperation Agency, with logistic support arranged by the Centre for Adult and Continuing Education at the University of the Western Cape. Proceedings will be available from the IFLA ALP (Advancement of Librarianship in the Third World) Core Programme Headquarters at the Library of Uppsala University in Sweden.
- Standards for the Evaluation of the Information Provision to Rural Libraries in Developing Countries. Thanks to the efforts of the IFLA ALP Core Programme over the past three years, standards for assessing the performance of rural information centers are being developed that can be applied to libraries throughout the developing world. Funded by UNESCO and the Swedish International Development Cooperation Agency, the working group creating these standards met in Dakar, Senegal, June 2–6, 1997, to organize the final draft for comments by UNESCO. The standard includes a basic definition of rural information centers, their utility within their communities, indicators to assess performance, and guidelines to assist in the interpretation of centers' performance.
- Information Technology and Library Services for Visually Impaired People, Expert Meeting of the IFLA Section of Libraries for the Blind. Attracting 160 participants, this session in Koge, Denmark, in advance of the Copenhagen conference, analyzed advances in technology that are assisting the blind in accessing information. Lively discussions analyzed potential developments in a global standard for digital talking books and access to bibliographic information embedded in online public-access catalogs. Additional papers addressed copyright issues that restrict access to current information and examined options for resolving these problems. Recommendations were made to the Standing Committee of the Section of Libraries for the Blind for further work in the near future.

Conclusion

Stimulated by recent successful conferences, an increasingly diverse and active membership, and financial stability, IFLA is taking a strong lead in attacking serious problems faced by the global library community. The establishment in 1997 of two new committees to address problems related to censorship and intellectual property will lead IFLA to the center of some complex and highly political controversies. The strength of the federation will be revealed in how well it meets these challenges at the end of this century and the beginning of a new one.

With additional efforts to enhance membership by increased participation from developing countries, IFLA will be in a much stronger position to address some of the fundamental disparities among libraries around the world. Given its rapid progress in the past five years, IFLA's momentum will continue to grow as it continues to develop into the premier international library organization.

Special Libraries Association

1700 18th St. N.W., Washington, DC 20009-2514
202-234-4700, fax 202-265-9317
World Wide Web: http://www.sla.org

Jennifer L. Stowe
Director, Public Relations

Headquartered in Washington, D.C., the Special Libraries Association (SLA) is an international association representing the interests of nearly 15,000 information professionals in 60 countries. Special librarians are information resource experts who collect, analyze, evaluate, package, and disseminate information to facilitate accurate decision-making in corporate, academic, and government settings.

As of June 1997 the association had 56 regional chapters in the United States, Canada, Europe, and the Middle East; 25 divisions representing a variety of industries; and 12 special-interest caucuses.

SLA offers myriad programs and services designed to help its members serve their customers more effectively and succeed in an increasingly challenging environment of information management and technology. Association activities are developed with specific direction toward achieving SLA's strategic priorities: to ensure that SLA members have opportunities to develop professional competencies and skills; to narrow the gap between the value of the information professional and the perceived value of special librarians and information professionals among decision-makers; and to ensure the ongoing relevance of SLA to its members in the next century by managing the transition to SLA's vision of a virtual association, whereby all members will be able to access SLA services globally, equitably, and continuously.

Computer Services and Technology

Computer Services and Technology's continued commitment to merging new and existing technologies with the association's existing computer system and management techniques to achieve the business goals of the association was displayed this year with the creation of a "virtual association."

At the 1996 Annual Conference in Boston, a Web Committee was formed by the president and charged with creating a three-year Web development plan. The Computer Services and Technology staff assisted the committee with the creation of this plan, "Virtual Association: Year 2000," which was presented to the SLA Board of Directors for review at its October meeting and to leadership at the 1997 Winter Meeting. As one of the board's goals for 1996–1997, Computer Services began development of a virtual association, where the association's products and services will be available globally, seven days a week, 365 days a year. With the board's objectives, Computer Services developed an online purchasing-system prototype, the Virtual Bookstore, where members and nonmembers can purchase SLA publications via the Web; an electronic tracking system for the exchange of membership information between the association and its officers; the hosting of an electronic discussion list for units; and the hosting of Web sites for units.

In addition, Computer Services assisted in the development and presentation of the association's electronic-information policy and draft guidelines presented to leadership at the 1997 Winter Meeting in Fort Lauderdale, Florida. The electronic-information policy and guidelines is a cutting-edge policy and set of procedural statements aimed at providing electronic commerce and a virtual association, while protecting the intellectual property rights of the association.

The migration of all but one of the association's DOS applications to the Windows platform to improve office productivity was a major accomplishment this year. The new environment provided the capability to use multiple applications at one time and easily exchange information between them, further streamlining association operations. However, the Association Management System (AMS), which houses the association's membership and financial information, will remain in DOS until a complete, stable Windows version is released in 1998.

The association's output capability was expanded by integrating a new color laser printer and new digital copiers with the network. The color printer provides the ability to produce color pamphlets, presentations, and *Information Outlook* proofs before sending them to press. The new digital copiers improved office productivity by providing the ability to submit requests for electronic documents to the copiers from their desktops.

Through the generous three-year Web site sponsorship of Disclosure, Inc., and the generous donation of software from Microsoft, the department was able to expand the capabilities of the association's Web site into the arena of electronic commerce. SLA's Web site now has the infrastructure in place to enable members and nonmembers to securely submit credit card transactions for SLA products and services.

Computer Services implemented its listserv and Web site hosting service for association units. In November unit listservs began to be hosted on SLA's Internet server. This new service is sponsored by Moody's and the West Group for a three-year period. In January the association began hosting unit Web sites on the SLA Web server. This new service minimized unit expenditures for implementing a Web site.

The association's Web site, www.sla.org, was revised in January 1997 to incorporate the association's new logo. The revised site features a new side-navigation menu bar that includes a search tool for the site, new graphics, and two new main menu selections for the "Information Resources Center" and "What's New" sections. By April the association's Web site had received over one million visits. With the addition of the searchable preliminary and final conference programs, traffic to the site increased dramatically. The site won the World Class Web Site award in July from the American Society of Association Executives, which is the premier professional organization for associations.

A fund-raising module was integrated with AMS to support the "Fund Development" section with managing contributions. This new module provides the capability of producing various contribution reports, labels, and mail merges.

New services currently under development include forms software for the association's Internet and intranet sites, providing the ability to electronically capture and analyze data entered via these sites; label printers to minimize the use of typewriters to produce address labels for odd-size mailing pieces; and audio enhancements for Windows applications, allowing staff to explore new methods of delivering and receiving information.

Conferences and Meetings

Commitment to their professional association and to advancing their careers was apparent when information professionals from around the world went to Seattle, Washington, to participate in the 88th Annual Conference, "Information Professionals at the Crossroads: Change as Opportunity," held June 7–12, 1997. Approximately 6,935 special librarians and other interested people attended this successful conference.

The second annual exhibit hall ribbon-cutting ceremony opened the doors to an exciting exhibit show. One of the most diverse shows ever, it included 445 booths sponsored by 330 companies. The hall was filled with the newest technologies, products, and services to help special librarians be more effective and proficient in their jobs.

The general-session address was given by Bill Gates, cofounder and CEO of Microsoft Corporation, headquartered in Seattle. Gates spoke on developments in information technology and the important role of special librarians in these developments. Advancements in technology will increase the importance of information professionals in corporations as companies work to translate information into knowledge. "It's no exaggeration to say that in most industries the basis of competition will be on how a company deals with information," Gates said. His address was also broadcast live on the Internet. The Microsoft Library, in association with Microsoft NetShow and UMI, was the sponsor of this historic event.

Eugenie Prime, corporate library manager at Hewlett Packard, delivered the Practitioners' Perspective, "The Fault Dear Brutus," on Tuesday, June 10, to an enthralled audience. Prime challenged information professionals to stop blaming others, carve their own future in the Information Age, and take charge of their own fate.

Under the guidance of Corinne Campbell, 1997 Conference Program Committee Chair, SLA division program planners were responsible for implementing many of the program sessions. Conference attendees had the opportunity to choose from more than 500 programs, special events, continuing-education courses, meetings, and field trips to plan their personal conference itineraries. As in past years the most popular sessions at the conference dealt with the Internet and information technology.

Finally, more than 1,300 information professionals took part in this year's preconference and postconference professional-development programs, which featured courses on topics ranging from strategic planning to the World Wide Web. The courses were geared toward professionals at all levels.

Special highlights at the Seattle conference featured sessions hosted by the Japan Special Libraries Association ("Japanese Information Sources in the

Electronic Era") and the Western Council of State Libraries ("Service to State Government").

Finance and Administration

Organizational governance, structure, and staff competencies continue to be a focus of the senior management and leadership in maintaining the direction set forth in the association's Strategic Plan and Vision Statement.

This focus has enabled the staff to develop and implement program philosophies and financial assumptions, the association program plan, and the association budget. In addition, the staff job descriptions and performance appraisal process have been reviewed and revised, where necessary, to incorporate the above.

Each spring the staff provides a report to the Office Operations Committee regarding the competencies required of staff to fulfill the goals and objectives of the association. During the past few years, there has been a significant shift in the competencies required as changes in technology place different demands on both employers and employees. From SLA's position as the employer, the strategies and activities relating to recruitment, training, compensation, and program development and delivery have certainly changed in response to new technologies. Employees also share in the change process; they are expected to continually revise the means by which they organize their work and perform their job.

In the recruitment process, a desk audit and needs analysis is routinely performed when a position is being recruited. However, SLA must also be able to forecast the specific staffing requirements needed several years in the future. In addition, it needs to know how future technologies will impact the organization, staff positions, and the delivery of products and services.

In the past SLA assessed an individual's experience as one of the major determinants of his or her qualifications. This is no longer a sufficient means of evaluation. In addition to assessing specific skills, SLA will also assess an individual's familiarity with technological advances (which is often difficult, especially at higher-level positions), responsiveness to change, adaptation to globalization, and so forth. The recruitment process has become much more complicated and time consuming and the skills required of recruiting personnel have become much more extensive.

With regard to the training and development of staff, SLA is challenged by both technology and diversity in the workplace. Having a membership that is educated, technologically advanced, and savvy poses challenges in meeting members' expectations. SLA must focus on bridging the gap between issues relating to both associations and the profession. As new technologies are employed, SLA must train the staff to master these technologies, which affect both routine operations and advanced program development. SLA requires each staff member to maintain a working knowledge of operating in a totally automated office, and each person is expected to keep abreast of emerging technologies to develop and deliver products and services to the membership. It seems that just as one technology is fully understood and implemented, another one comes along that is bigger and better. Training has become a full-time, ongoing process, and often staff is working in more than one mode to accommodate technological changes.

Although SLA's 39.5 staffing positions have commonalities, each is also driven by a diverse set of skills specific to the position or function. Each person is expected to develop and retain myriad skills. Designing a training and development program to enhance and advance a diverse staff poses many challenges. Although SLA implements an extensive annual staff development program, the resources of staff time and operational dollars are limited. SLA must carefully design and execute a training and development program that advances the organization and the staff and that also is adaptive to change. The assistant executive directors are responsible for creating, implementing, and monitoring the staff development program. The current program has been designed to address the needs of the staff as a whole, as well as support the team structure and the individual staff positions.

In addition, the Finance and Administration staff has implemented a customer service education series for the entire staff, with a focus on increasing operational efficiency and providing exceptional service to the membership. The program staff has also maintained its interdepartmental cross-training program to ensure maximum use of staffing resources. Another means of maximizing resources is the implementation of a bank lock box service for the collection of dues and fees. This service expedites the deposit of funds and the processing of member records.

In the planning phases of the organizational objectives, staff must determine the best means by which to administer, develop, and deliver products and services to the membership. Outsourcing is one such means that can add to an organization's or department's efficiency and effectiveness. According to the Association Information Management Service (AIMS), associations with external professional services that are a higher percentage of total expenses usually have a higher level of productivity. Utilizing external professional services is a good way to stretch the capabilities of staff and to meet the special and/or episodic needs of the association without a long-term staffing commitment. For example, SLA may not have on staff someone with the precise skills or time needed to accomplish a specific task, or a third party may be able to do something faster, more easily, and/or with less expense. Outsourcing can be brief or long term, depending on the nature of the task and the resources of the organization.

SLA currently utilizes outsourcing on a limited basis to fulfill functions related to insurance services, legal services, nonprofit postal monitoring, payroll, public relations, editing, graphic design, program planning, archiving, exhibit management, audit and financial advice and analysis, travel services, tabulation, mail services, printing, computer system analysis, training, and building maintenance. The average proportion of a typical association's outsourcing to total expenses is nearly 9 percent, whereas SLA's proportion is 6 percent. AIMS suggests an increase in specialized outsourcing as a means to enhance the competencies of staff.

A major focus of the Financial Services section this year has been the monitoring and implementation of the various new laws and regulations affecting nonprofit organizations. The collection, recording, and dissemination of financial information has changed significantly in the past few years under rulings issued by the Internal Revenue Service and the Financial Accounting Standards Board. In addition, the association continued its work with the Internal Revenue Service on the examination of the association's books and records. The examination was completed in the spring of 1997. Staff is communicating the compliance issues of the Internal Revenue Code as it applies to tax-exempt organizations to the association's units.

The Administrative Services staff has also monitored the various laws and regulations affecting the general operations of SLA, including personnel management, salary administration, benefits compliance, and occupancy/building code compliance. Other administrative projects completed include the revision of SLA's emergency procedures, an analysis of internal equipment needs, an update to the 15-year building plan and schedule of capital improvements, and an office technology plan to link general office services to computer technology for enhanced processing. As approved by the board of directors, the association completed its first major building renovation since 1985 in the fall of 1996.

Fund Development

Members were supportive of the Third Annual President's Reception, held in conjunction with the 1997 Annual Conference in Seattle. The event, sponsored by Microsoft Corporation and hosted at its headquarters, was attended by more than 250 individuals. Thanks to Microsoft's generosity, the event provided more than $20,000 in support of leadership enhancement and development activities.

Members were also supportive of the association's established affinity programs, which provide member discounts on various products and services.

The MBNA Visa program, the AT&T communication services program, the Airborne Express overnight delivery program, and the Hertz car rental program all continued to be valued member services. In addition, members encouraged and supported expansion of the list of available programs. As a result, SLA added two new affinity programs, providing discounts to members on professional products and services: the *Information Today* professional publications program and the Knight-Ridder information-professional online services program.

Finally, SLA enjoyed continued growth of the SLA Legacy Club, the association's long-term giving program, supporting the association through wills, insurance, property, stocks, bonds, and other instruments. New members of the Legacy Club this year include Margaret Downey, Judith J. Field, Dorothy McGarry, Doris Lee Schild, and Guy St. Clair. Many others have expressed interest in the program.

SLA's corporate supporters also got into the act of giving. Corporate supporters requested a method to assist the association both above the existing Patron level ($1,000) and below the Sponsor level ($500). In November 1995 SLA introduced its new investment categories: President's Circle ($10,000), Benefactor ($5,000), Contributor ($250), and Donor ($100), in addition to the Patron and Sponsor categories. This year there were three members of the President's Circle (The H. W. Wilson Company Foundation, Knight-Ridder Information, and LEXIS-NEXIS), one member of the Benefactor category

(Readmore/Blackwell's, Inc.), and several new Patrons, Sponsors, Contributors, and Donors.

In addition, corporate supporters took advantage of the improved conferences and meetings program. SLA's Technology Fair had 34 booths, and the Annual Conference exhibit hall housed an astounding 448 booths and 25 tabletop displays. For the first time ever, the exhibit hall offered new-product demonstration sessions, as well as "expocards" for attendees. The introduction of *Information Outlook* provided an exciting magazine for members and corporate supporters. Advertising sales were at or above projected levels in *Information Outlook, Who's Who in Special Libraries*, the 1996–1997 *Buyer's Guide*, and the preliminary and final conference programs. This year corporate supporters expressed their greatest interest in customized partnerships, including Dun and Bradstreet's sponsorship of SLA's SpeciaLine online employment listing service, Moody's Investors Service and West Group's cosponsorship of SLA's unit listservs, Dow Jones and Company's sponsorship of SLA's exhibit booth, and Economist Intelligence Unit's sponsorship of SLA's Nonserial Publications program. In addition, Microsoft Corporation made the largest single gift to the association in its history by sponsoring SLA's Virtual Bookstore, its electronic commerce site, and committing to the future completion and implementation of SLA's virtual association. The Freedom Forum continued its generous support of the International Library Program, sending members to Europe and Asia to perform targeted training programs. Dow Jones and Company allowed the association to introduce the Competencies Award Program, introducing The Dow Jones Leadership Award: 21st Century Competencies in Action, which recognizes members for personal and professional excellence.

In order to facilitate information exchange, SLA continues to publish *Exhibit News, Development Update*, and *Legacy* for members and corporate supporters, in an effort to provide more-detailed information on these and other projects. In addition, SLA continues to update and improve its booth display for use at SLA conferences and many other meetings for information professionals and other targeted audiences, providing opportunities for promoting the association.

In 1996–1997, SLA's Fund Development Program achieved many goals through the establishment of several new initiatives and the realignment of existing ones. At the heart of the success was the cooperation and support of members and corporate supporters in introducing the initiatives and following them through.

Government Relations

The Government Relations Program seeks to inform and educate government officials on issues that affect information professionals worldwide. The program focuses on improving members' awareness of and involvement in such policy-making activities. Staff is focused on formulating and influencing government policies in these primary areas of concern:

- Copyright and intellectual property
- Access to information

- Telecommunications
- Development of the global information infrastructure
- Competitiveness for information professionals

During 1996–1997 SLA was involved in a number of activities related to the reform of international copyright law. SLA and other library organizations, educational groups, and corporations succeeded in altering key provisions of proposed international treaties on copyright in the digital age. These treaties must be ratified by the world's governments in order to have the effect of law. As the ratification process continues, SLA will monitor any changes to laws around the world to ensure balance in the outcome.

Prior to the negotiations on the treaties, SLA and the U.S. library community were also successful in defeating domestic legislation that would have codified the same provisions that made the proposed treaties so objectionable. SLA was also very active in the development of the most recent amendments to the copyright laws in Canada. Led by Susan Merry, an SLA member in Toronto, SLA worked hard to have the voices of Canada's private-sector libraries heard during the debate in Parliament. This in itself was a victory, but the result was a new copyright law that leaves out the concerns of most SLA members. The law will be reviewed three years after its enactment.

SLA also made a financial commitment to ensuring that free-speech rights are protected in the United States. A donation of $10,000 was made to the Citizen's Internet Empowerment Coalition during its fight to overturn the Communications Decency Act. This law would have had a seriously negative impact on the rights of Americans to freely express their thoughts and ideas on the Internet. SLA's contribution met with success, as the U.S. Supreme Court rejected the onerous portions of the law in June 1997.

Through the first half of 1997 SLA worked with the five major U.S. library organizations to develop legislation for reforming the federal government's printing and publishing policies. At this writing, Congress is close to introducing a bill that would incorporate the priorities of the Clinton administration and the users of government information.

During late 1996 and early 1997 SLA staff worked in conjunction with InVentures International, a private consulting group, to develop a report on enhancing competitiveness in the information age. Based on a survey of selected members, the report assesses the changes that are required of information professionals in today's ever-changing organizational environment. It was completed in the fall of 1997.

During 1996–1997 the Government Relations Section focused on accomplishing three internal goals:

- Improving the membership's awareness of and involvement with information policy-making activities. With nearly 15,000 members, SLA has the potential energy to influence public policy around the world. Grassroots communications can have a major impact on the decisions made by government officials. Staff has begun the process of disseminating targeted alerts for grassroots advocacy by the membership. Initially, this includes the use of the Internet and listservs, with direct-mail efforts to come in 1998.

- Expanding SLA's influence on information policy to all areas of the world. Historically, SLA has focused its government relations activities on North America. But the association's demographics have shifted to a more global membership, and there is a growing perception of the world as existing without borders. In response to these changes, SLA has embarked on an unprecedented campaign to educate members about global information policies that may impact the profession, particularly through interaction with organizations in other nations.

- Improving coordination with staff to further improve services for the membership. Like any other organization, SLA must continue to ensure that its staff works together to meet challenges and take advantage of opportunities. This means avoidance of redundant activities by teaming up to reach common goals. It also means improved information sharing so that work completed by one department can be used by other departments, thereby reducing workloads for many staff members. The Government Relations Program has made strides to accomplish this goal by maintaining internal lines of communication on relevant policy matters. The program has focused on teaming with the Public Relations Section, Research staff, the Information Resources Center, and the Executive Office in order to achieve common objectives and confront new challenges as they develop.

Information Resources Center

SLA's Information Resources Center (IRC) continues to respond to a high number of requests for information from staff, members, and nonmembers on a variety of aspects of special librarianship and association management. The number of requests made via the Internet and the SLA Web site have increased significantly, as have the IRC Web site hits. The majority of inquiries continue to relate to careers, salaries, and library management. However, many more requests now regard professional development and marketing the library/information center. Nearly 40 percent of the IRC Web site hits are to our lists of library, federal, and miscellaneous Internet joblines. The Consultation Service remains a popular service and often leads to referrals from the CONSULT database.

New bibliographies on such topics as knowledge management and intranets have been developed and posted to the IRC Web site. All the bibliographies—including starting and managing a special library, library automation software, copyright, the value of the information center, outsourcing library services, and space planning—have been updated and often include hypertext links to other relevant Web pages.

The Management Document Collections (MDC) continues to be a popular resource for members and nonmembers. Loans from the MDC of user surveys significantly outnumbered those of mission statements, collection development policies, library brochures, and strategic plans. The IRC staff has sought to enhance the collection by soliciting additional model materials from members.

The ongoing goal of the IRC is to create a "virtual IRC" and to become a more proactive service for members and staff, which already includes staff Internet training, new-staff orientation, a monthly *IRC Update* of information and resources transferred to the IRC Web site, and an IRC Fair planned for the fall. With the LEXIS-NEXIS sponsorship now in place, more information is becoming readily available for dissemination.

Membership Development

By working in partnership with all other program areas, the Membership Development Section continues to pursue member recruitment and retention as well as support the activities of chapters, divisions, caucuses, and student groups. In addition, the section maintains the membership database, including adding new and prospective members, processing renewals and address changes, and updating officer information. Further, the Membership Development Section administers and promotes the SLA Scholarship Program and Student Group activities.

In 1996–1997 specific section projects included increasing the overall accuracy and timeliness of the renewal notice mailings, sending membership information to prospects within 24 hours, disseminating an informative new-member packet within 10 days of a member's join date, providing a membership application and a section for updating member records on SLA's Web site, instituting a telemarketing program to encourage former association members to reinstate membership, and providing assistance to association leaders through monthly mailings and leadership training sessions.

The Membership Development Section's retention efforts are fortified at the grassroots level. The section provides unit membership chairs with monthly member notification reports, bimonthly new-member reports, and deactivated-member reports. In addition, the membership chairs receive monthly mailings containing membership information and tips about recruitment and retention.

In an effort to attract students into the field of special librarianship, SLA offers a scholarship program and supports the activities of student members. The Membership Development Section produces and mails *The Student Union*, the semiannual Student Group newsletter. The section works closely with the Student and Academic Relations Committee to build a partnership with association leaders and the student members in order to increase retention.

Activities of the scholarship program included the disbursement of $30,000 in financial aid to five students. In addition, a Certificate of Merit Program was begun this year to honor student groups, chapters, and divisions demonstrating outstanding activity and/or continued commitment to promoting professional development for students within their organizations.

Nonserial Publications

The philosophy of the Nonserial Publications Program (NSP) is to provide the information community, specifically SLA membership, with products that continue to meet their changing needs. In addition, the program endeavors to make a significant contribution to the literature of the information profession and to increase the influence of the professional and of the field itself. The program produces 10 to 15 publications each year and remains committed to providing them at a savings to the membership. The "member pricing" policy offers to SLA members publications at a substantial reduction in price, a significant benefit.

The NSP program strives to anticipate member needs by keeping abreast of what's happening in the world of information and producing quality titles that meet those needs. SLA released 11 titles in the 1996–1997 year, including books on Internet resources, results from the outsourcing study, the competencies publication, and alternative careers in librarianship. Future acquisitions are focused on evolving trends in the industry as well as advances in information technology.

The growth of the program in recent years prompted the creation of an identity within the SLA umbrella: SLA Publishing. This new logo will be used to promote SLA's publications and provide easy identification with the program's resources.

Professional Development

The Professional Development Program encompasses cutting-edge continuing-education activities and career services for SLA members. The program strives to help information professionals meet their potential by providing continuing-education opportunities based on the professional and personal competencies outlined in SLA's report *Competencies for Special Librarians of the 21st Century*. During the year a wide variety of continuing-education programs were offered in the areas of technology, library management, strategic planning, budgeting, marketing and public relations, and general management.

In October 1996 SLA produced its third videoconference. Cosponsored by Knight-Ridder Information, the program, "Getting Out of the Box: The Knowledge Management Opportunity," provided concrete ways members can expand their roles beyond the library. The videoconference reached almost 500 librarians at 15 sites.

The 1996 State-of-the-Art Institute, "The Virtual Workplace: One Size Does Not Fit All," attracted almost 100 attendees. Speakers from a variety of disciplines addressed the topic of the virtual workplace and its impact on the nature of work.

The 1997 Winter Education Conference, "Riding the Technology Tidal Wave," focused on the latest developments in information technology. In addition to the nine continuing-education courses, more than 35 vendors participated in the technology fair, demonstrating some of the newest information products. The "Technology and Applications" unit of the Middle Management Institute (MMI) was also offered during the conference.

In March 1997 SLA presented its first joint videoconference with the American Association of Law Libraries, the Medical Library Association, and LEXIS-NEXIS. "The Future for Librarians: Positioning Yourself for Success" reached approximately 4,000 librarians at 155 sites throughout the United States and Canada.

SLA's 88th Annual Conference featured 33 continuing-education courses for more than 1,300 attendees. In addition, SLA piloted the Knowledge Executive Institute, sponsored by Knight-Ridder Information and Teltech Technical Knowledge Service, as a preconference activity. This intensive institute was developed to prepare members for advancing to knowledge executive roles within their organizations. Two MMI units, "Marketing and Public Relations" and "Management Skills," were also offered.

A variety of career services were provided to members at the Annual Conference. SLA and Advanced Information Management offered six free job-search miniworkshops on such topics as résumé writing and interviewing skills. Additional career services included the Employment Clearinghouse, with over 130 job openings posted, and the Career Advisory Service, in which 30 people received career counseling from experienced members.

Some continuing-education courses were cosponsored by various SLA chapters and other organizations throughout the year. Such courses are arranged through headquarters and can be offered at any location.

The self-study program currently has 14 titles from which SLA members can choose to learn in a self-paced environment. The latest workbook, *Analyzing Costs for Decision-Making and Cost Recovery*, is the third book in the financial-management series. In addition, the *ABC's of Cataloging* workbook is available in a revised edition.

Public Relations

The primary goal of the Public Relations Program is to increase awareness and appreciation of the important role special librarians play in their organizations and in society. Another goal is to aid the association unit in creating ways in which the association and the profession can be represented positively in the public eye.

The department made strides in enhancing the image of the special librarian and the association through the creation and implementation of a new association logo, thus positioning it as the leading association for information professionals and adding credibility to the profession at large. The logo has been developed with a detailed style guide containing rules for its use.

Under the direction of the department, Strategic Communications Group (SCG) of Silver Spring, Maryland, has been instructed to increase media coverage of the association. The focus of the campaign is to get coverage of special librarians in metropolitan newspapers, major trade press, and association and business publications. Articles about the Web site have appeared in *Southeastern Association Executive*, and many solid contacts have been made with *Webmaster*, *Hemispheres* (United Airlines' in-flight magazine), and the *Chronicle of Higher Education*. A series of personal profiles about several 1997 awards and honors recipients are being compiled to use as references for the professional-value campaign.

The "Public Relations Outlook" column in *Information Outlook* is compiled and written with more emphasis on positive articles about the profession and association members. The program relies on SLA members to submit items to be included, and unit public relations chairs are encouraged to canvas fellow members for stories and testimonials regarding professional successes.

Public relations materials have been updated, and attempts were made to improve navigation within the Web site. An emphasis has been put on including the Web address in all printed materials, so that those unfamiliar with the profession can be directed to the site. The front page is designed to guide visitors to a definition of a special librarian, which is linked to a page giving seven reasons why one would use a special library.

An annual public relations highlight is International Special Librarians Day (ISLD), the Thursday of National Library Week (an American Library Association program). This is a time to gain recognition for the contributions of the profession in the global sharing of information. This year's theme was "Special Librarians: Putting Knowledge to Work." To help members celebrate International Special Librarians Day, a marketing kit was made available on the Web site and was mailed to those without Internet access. The cosponsoring company, LEXIS-NEXIS, incorporated ISLD announcements into its advertising airtime on National Public Radio during the weeks prior National Library Week.

The SLA Awards and Honors Program is a part of the SLA Public Relations Program. To stimulate member interest, the awards program is getting increased publicity through coverage in information industry publications and on the Web site. The program administers its own awards program to members who excel in promoting the profession to the general public.

SLA's Research Section goals are to provide methodologies, data, and analyses that address significant elements of the profession. SLA supports research through a variety of activities. The association independently conducts research, works in collaboration with other organizations in conducting and sponsoring research, and funds research through the Steven I. Goldspiel Memorial Research Grant.

At its June 1997 meeting the SLA Board of Directors approved the Research Committee's nomination of Claire R. McInerney as recipient of the 1997 Steven I. Goldspiel Memorial Research Grant for her proposal "Using Information in the Virtual Office: How Special Libraries Are Serving Telecommuters." The primary objective of the project is to appraise the progress of special libraries and special librarians in serving their organizations, through managing the information needs of telecommuters. McInerney plans to comprehensively review the literature in all relevant disciplines, identify applications in both library and nonlibrary environments that are relevant to special library operations and services, determine the success or failure of relevant applications, and document the determinants of success or failure. Results will be presented at the 1998 Annual Conference in Indianapolis. The findings will also be published by SLA in the fall of 1998, with highlights reported in *Information Outlook* and on SLA's Web site.

The demographic highlights and the final reports from the Third Membership Needs Assessment Survey ("Super Survey") and Nonmember Needs Assessment Survey were presented to the board of directors at its October 1996 meeting. Highlights were also featured in *Information Outlook* and on SLA's Web site. Data from both surveys continue to be interpreted and used by all SLA programs to refine existing services and to develop new ones. Working in partnership with Association Research, SLA research staff revised, administered, and analyzed the *1997 Salary Survey*, the first such survey to be conducted on an annual basis. The survey instrument was revised to capture additional relevant data and to enable more-extensive analysis of the data. Results of the survey were published by SLA in October 1997.

SLA sponsored a new study on the value of information services, in response to its identification at SLA's 1995 Research Forum as the number-one research priority. The objectives of the project were to identify and organize the dimensions of value of specific library services, to identify and test procedures for measuring the value of those services, and to develop a manual that demonstrates how to apply the research procedures at other organizations. The manual contains samples of the research instruments used in the study and an explanation of how to modify the instruments for application in other libraries. The project director is Paul B. Kantor, Director, Alexandria Project Laboratory, and Professor, School of Communication, Information and Library Studies, Rutgers University. The coinvestigator is Tefko Saracevic, also a Professor, School of Communication, Information and Library Studies, Rutgers University. The study was completed in late 1997. Results are being provided in the form of a monograph, and an executive summary of the project will be provided on SLA's Web site.

The pilot study on corporate library outsourcing, conducted by Cabtech, an independent consulting firm, has been completed, and the key findings were published in an executive summary and distributed to the membership. Examining the reasons behind senior management's decision to outsource library services and its impact on information delivery, results of the study expose some of the myths and downsides of outsourcing while highlighting the essential role the corporate library plays in providing strategic information. The full report has been published by the Nonserial Publications Program.

Research and Professional Development staff completed a Library School Curriculum Project, surveying survey deans at accredited library schools in order to determine the compatibility of curriculae in library schools and position descriptions in special libraries. The survey took place in summer 1997 and the results were tabulated and reported in the fall.

Serial Publications

Special Libraries and *SpeciaList* completed their final year of publication in 1996. The interest expressed by the membership to receive more-timely information management coverage coupled with increased advertiser interest prompted the board of directors to discontinue the two serial publications and create a new monthly magazine to take their place. The last issue of *Special Libraries* (Fall 1996) was a special retrospective edition featuring articles and advertisements that were printed in the publication since its birth in 1910.

In January 1997 *Special Libraries* and *SpeciaList* were officially retired, welcoming a new four-color monthly magazine: *Information Outlook*. The new publication provides even more timely, cutting-edge, and in-depth coverage of issues pertinent to information professionals working in a global environment.

Each month *Information Outlook* includes approximately five feature articles that focus on such topics as technological advances within the profession, management trends, marketing tactics for the information center, strategic positioning, benchmarking, and salary survey information. Interviews with the "movers and shakers" of the information industry, such as Bill Gates and Eugenie Prime, have also been included in 1997's editorial content.

Association news has also found its place on the pages of *Information Outlook*. Program updates are highlighted each month in regular columns, such as "Professional Development Outlook," "Government Relations Outlook," "Money Matters," "Conference Countdown," and "Public Relations Outlook."

Previews of the magazine are also found on SLA's Web site. The cover illustration, table of contents, advertiser index, and full texts of "On the Net," "Executive Outlook," and "In Summary" (abstracts of the feature articles in English, French, and Spanish) are available for perusal each month.

The debut year of *Information Outlook* has been a success, and plans are under way to make the publication an even more valuable tool for the membership in the years to come.

Who's Who in Special Libraries, the association's annual membership directory, contains more than 385 pages and continues to serve as a valuable networking tool and information resource for the membership. The 1996–1997 *Who's Who* included an expanded "Buyer's Guide," containing information on vendors of products and services of value to special librarians.

The publication also includes chapter and division leadership and member information; member statistics; historical highlights; SLA's Bylaws, Strategic Plan, and Vision Statement; awards and honors winners; past presidents; and a schedule of future meetings and conferences.

Trends and Issues in Library and Information Services in Canada, 1997

Ken Haycock

Frances Dodd

School of Library, Archival and Information Studies
The University of British Columbia
Vancouver, British Columbia

The key trends and issues in Canadian library and information services are consistent with previous reports: challenges and opportunities presented by information technology; information access and rights; increased demands during periods of budget restraint; partnerships with other libraries, corporations and government; lobbying for tax and copyright exemptions for libraries; the need for improved marketing and advocacy—with an increasing emphasis on interdependence and a focus on the Internet and other information technology applications to manage collections and services. Although 95 percent of Canada's information resources are in print format, their management is increasingly electronic and automated.

Information Technology

National Standards and Statistical Reports

The need for a standard protocol to exchange records and negotiate interlibrary loan requests continues to generate research. A milestone was reached in February at the National Library of Canada (NLC), when complete alignment of CanMarc and USMarc machine-readable cataloging formats was achieved. Future developments will take into consideration international standards, such as UniMarc.

NLC's Core Library Statistics Program, begun in 1994 in order to assess the economic impact of libraries, now replaces data gathered by Statistics Canada. National in scope, the program collects data from all types of libraries, except schools; the school library sector and information on electronic resources will be added. Other NLC reports included a needs survey of teacher-librarians (Canada's term for school librarians) and a survey of regional libraries.

NLC held an information session on the future of the Virtual Union Catalogue (vCuc), the participation of federal libraries, and planning for an eventual Z39.50 gateway. Results included a realigned focus on using technology rather than manual processing at NLC and on establishing consistent standards for communications. Libraries are now reporting their holdings to the NLC AMI-CUS database via the Machine Readable Accessions (MARA) program, with an increase of a third since last January. MARA reporting involves a three-way partnership among NLC, the system vendor, and the reporting library. Vendors, as partners to vCuc, will promote Z39.50 and run interoperability tests between servers. The National Library's new *Directory of Z39.50 Targets in Canada* supplements the recent launching of SIRSI's *Z39.50 Resource Directory* to provide online direction for Canadian library cooperation.

The Metro Toronto Reference Library and other public libraries in Toronto conducted a Mix and Match Searching pilot project using Z39.50 at service desks during the summer. MultiCat combined results from a variety of databases using a common search interface. The final report recommends a coordinated if costly approach to provision of Z39.50 access. Similar projects for providing a transition to a shared environment were carried out across the country, as libraries work toward "universal access" of Canada's collections.

Canadian Library Association Position Statements

The Canadian Library Association (CLA) adopted four position statements this year on copyright; services to the disabled (see CLA's newly revised *Accessible Canadian Library II*); corporate sponsorship and Internet access, building on two earlier statements on intellectual freedom; and information and telecommunication access principles. CLA also expressed reservations about the new federal copyright law and its burdensome regulations and parallel importation clause, which inhibits the direct importation of books from the United States.

Automated Services

Libraries continue to take advantage of technological developments to improve services, with a trend to introducing client-centered services.

Popular innovations include the use of "smart cards" (a single card that functions as a student, library, and debit card), self-check-out service, self-service windows at public libraries, and automated security gates.

Technical-services changes include the automation of serials records on the new Dynix system at NLC, which has made holdings information universally accessible within the library. Once a serial is checked in and barcoded, the system predicts the date of the next issue and date of arrival and generates an automatic claim notice to publishers. Services to blind and visually handicapped people are improved with new products, such as the Reading Edge Machine at the Red Deer (Alberta) Public Library.

Access to Information and Rights

Partnerships and Cooperation for Internet Access

One year after the announced partnership between Microsoft and CLA, the new Bill and Melinda Gates Library Foundation announced its donation of $400 million in cash and software to support Internet access and training in low-income communities throughout North America. This gift will expand on the Libraries Online! initiative of the Microsoft Canada KidReach program, which started in the Toronto and Ottawa Public Libraries last June.

The federal government increasingly focused on the role of libraries as "business incubators" and access points to the Information Superhighway. SchoolNet's summer program involved 420 students in digitization projects at NLC. Industry Canada's companion project, LibraryNet, is funding projects at the Calgary Public Library, Western County (Nova Scotia) Regional Library, and the University of Waterloo (Ontario). Industry Canada also introduced technology internships through the Community Access Project and the Computers for Schools and Libraries Program. CLA collaborated with the federal Department of Canadian Heritage to deliver Young Canada Works, a student summer job program in libraries that involved 130 career-oriented jobs in 91 libraries.

Following the precedent-setting 1996 agreement with the Conference des Recteurs et des Principaux des Universités du Québec, the Canadian Institute for Scientific and Technical Information (CISTI) signed two-year agreements with the Council of Prairie and Pacific University Libraries (COPPUL) and the Association of Atlantic Universities Librarian's Council for preferred access and fees for information services.

In March NLC formed the Canadian Initiative on Digital Libraries to ensure both access and quality. A survey to assess digital collections identified several issues: selection criteria, long-term access, duplication of effort, standards, copyright and licensing, equitable network access, funding, technology and management, and staff and user training.

Internet Sites and Digital Collections

Libraries and library associations increased the Canadian presence on the Internet through new and improved sites—for example: CISTI's new catalog (with online article delivery), CLA's home page, the Manitoba Library Consortium, North York Public Library's new CATNYP Web, and the Canada-Wide Health and Medical Archives Information Network. The NLC's Canadian Subject Guide in May had 1,700 links. NLC also released a subset of its catalog with a Web-based interface (ResAnet) and increased its digital collections and resource guides. The electronically accessible collections and guides reflect the new direction in publishing, with "print on demand" as a second option. Publication of the final issue on microfiche of the NLC's union serials lists is yet another indication of the trend toward electronic publishing.

Censorship and Taxation

In late April libraries across the country celebrated Information Rights Week, and Manitoba highlighted the dual Information Superhighway themes of privacy and access to government information. Concern over appropriate Internet content and viewing in public libraries, especially by children, has sparked much controversy, however. While appropriate use is sought mainly through access policies, many libraries are dealing with filtering-software issues and the implications of the latest release of Microsoft Internet Explorer, which comes with a built-in filter.

Several cases of book-banning were reported. A police order to remove Nancy Friday's *Women on Top* from the shelves of the Winnipeg Public Library was overturned. Three children's books portraying gay and lesbian families were banned from classrooms by the Surrey (British Columbia) School Board in a meeting that featured shouting, shoving, and the removal of two people by security personnel. This book-banning has been challenged by both the Ministry of Education and the British Columbia Teachers' Federation, and further action is pending. Two more titles on their way to Little Sister's bookstore in Vancouver were stopped at the Canadian border, and at this writing the case awaited trial.

The CLA and Don't Tax Reading Coalition were triumphant in removing the goods and services tax (GST) from books purchased by libraries. Libraries responded with support for the book trade by raising funds toward removing the tax from books sold in bookstores and elsewhere.

Intellectual Property and Copyright

In spite of strenuous lobbying and following bitter exchanges between library supporters and the Writer's Union of Canada, Phase II of the Canadian Copyright Act became law. Meetings and listserv discussions were held across the country to clarify the ramifications of its more restrictive language. Most libraries will be purchasing a reprography license from Cancopy, in accordance with the new Copyright Act.

Phase III of copyright reform will deal with the digital environment. Issues related to both domestic and international laws, technological neutrality, and the balance of rights of users and creators are complicated by problems of authentication and integrity of electronic material. Industry Canada hosted a series of roundtables to review liability for content circulating on the Internet and the protection of databases under Canadian law. These forums suggest that the electronic-broadcasting and filtering debates are only just beginning.

Internet Access Issues

Related to copyright in accessing electronic information is the need for affordable Internet connection rates. The national Information Highway Advisory Council released its final report, *Preparing Canada for a Digital World*, specifying the need for (1) monitoring telephone penetration rates and affordability indicators and intervening if universality is threatened and (2) for resources for public libraries to support sustainable access and a Canadian presence on the Internet. Nonetheless, the Canadian Radio and Telecommunications Commission (CRTC) announced two decisions that adversely affect Internet access in libraries: price cap pricing and competition in the local phone market, except in Saskatchewan. The decisions limit subsidies and encourage competitive pricing in local telephone rates. CLA announced a partnership with Clearnet that allows the installation of antennas on library rooftops in return for either bandwidth or cash payments.

Marketing Information Services

Training workshops were held for the national Library Advocacy Now! project in Ontario and Alberta, and the call for grass-roots advocacy was heard throughout the country. Librarians are also increasingly encouraged to market themselves and their services. The first Friend's Day was held at the CLA annual conference to share expertise and learn about innovative fund-raising and advocacy programs and to plan for a new and challenging economic and political landscape.

Provincial Outlook

Atlantic Canada

In Prince Edward Island (PEI), plans for an integrated network of libraries are under way at the Provincial Library. Three libraries achieved Internet access through the Community Access Program (CAP). Students engaged in a summer reading program in a cooperative venture with New Brunswick. The PEI Teacher-Librarian's Association based local advocacy on a provincial study highlighting the value and role of the school library. A committee of educators and board members studied the establishment and operation of school-housed public libraries.

The Nova Scotia Public Libraries Act is being rewritten, and universal municipal participation is anticipated. The provincial Public Library Board continues consolidation of services and joint initiatives with school libraries. Nova Scotia was the first province to offer Internet access to the public in all of its branches, and many regional libraries are involved in the formation of community access programs, funded by Industry Canada.

The public electronic information system, NcompasS, provides direct access to library databases throughout the province via Ednet, the Department of Education, and Culture's Wide Area Network, and provincial site licenses have been signed for commercial database access by regional libraries. The development of standards for Nova Scotia public libraries is being used to generate funds to reach minimum levels for library operations. A similar project is being undertaken for school libraries.

In Newfoundland, stable funding enabled better planning and coordination as well as an increase in joint services. For example, the New Bay Roberts Public Library consolidated the collections of three branches, and three other branches have been merged with school libraries. However, funding was reduced to academic libraries, and the 20-year joint project between the Memorial University Library and Provincial Resource Library ceased, so that newspapers are no longer microfilmed. Memorial University did introduce a one-card system and waived fees for registered alumni, however.

The New Brunswick Provincial Foundation Act and amendments to the Library Act brought the dissolution of five regional boards, with senior staff becoming civil servants rather than employees of boards; the term "librarian" was deleted from the definition of these positions; fund-raising was included in the role of local boards; and a foundation was formed to augment collections and province-wide access to online databases, planned for 1999. The University of New Brunswick's Electronic Text Centre received the 1997 Canadian Association of College and University Libraries (CACUL) Innovation Achievement Award for pioneering work in electronic access and publishing. Historical and literary texts were converted to SGML, including Chadwyck-Healey's English Poetry database and others from the archives and special collections, newspapers, and journals.

Central Canada

In Ontario, introduction of the Local Control of Public Libraries Act, giving local governments the legislated authority and responsibility to manage their own library services, was withdrawn in response to province-wide lobbying, and the government will maintain its $18 million provincial grants for libraries. Nonetheless, the Public Libraries Act and a regulation regarding possible user fees remains in effect. The amalgamation of local governments in the Toronto area resulted in the merger of the city's six public library boards and the Metro Toronto Reference Library, creating one of the largest library systems in North America. The Network 2000 virtual-library initiative will pool the databases of Ontario's public libraries through high-speed links into a virtual megalibrary; a pilot is scheduled for operation in January.

The government also introduced Ontario Library Week with four Public Library Service Awards: The Peterborough and Counties Library Automation Network allows users to identify and borrow materials from both public and school libraries; the Pickering Public Library, with the Canadian National Institute for the Blind, allows blind and visually impaired customers better access to services and collections; the Etobicoke Public Libraries' Humberwood Centre Joint Development Project integrates two elementary schools, a day care center, a community library, park space, and recreation and community facilities; and North Bay Public Library's BabyTALK, a parent-child early-education program, targets parents of newborns.

In Quebec, l'Association pour l'Avancement des Sciences et des Techniques de la Documentation (ASTED) reported a new Web site and proposed a Grande Bibliothèque Québécoise to house the separate collections of the Bibliothèque Nationale du Québec and the Bibliothèque Centrale de Montréal. ASTED published a French translation of *Dewey Decimal Classification 21*, and is working with other French-speaking library organizations in Quebec, Ontario, and the maritime provinces.

Prairie and Western Provinces

The Red River floods reached Manitoba school and public libraries last summer, causing untold damage. Winnipeg Public Library opened a new branch, its first in eight years, that features a drive-up window for requested materials pickup. The Manitoba Library Consortium sponsored several new college and public library members.

The Saskatchewan Libraries Cooperation Act created new positions that resulted in the appointment of one provincial and 17 local resource-based learning consultants. A jointly funded project through the Province-wide Library Electronic Information System (PLEIS) will research ways of providing seamless access to all catalogs and information resources. Currently, the Saskatchewan Union Catalogue and SUNCAT, which combines the records of 43 libraries across the province, are available through PLEIS.

The Provincial Library is continuing with its pilot project to have province-wide licensing for access to commercial databases. The Saskatchewan credit unions have entered into a one-year partnership with the Saskatchewan Library

Association and the Saskatchewan Literacy Network, with a substantial donation to three literacy programs.

This year marked the 19th anniversary of Alberta's first Public Libraries Act. In April Albertans celebrated Public Library Week at 308 locations across the province, and government committed $4.8 million over four years to implement an electronic library network. Although public libraries in Alberta have retained their provincial grants, they face uncertainties in how service will be delivered with new push and pull technologies, restructuring of school districts, and uncertainty about changes to municipal boundaries and allocations. Recommendations arising from an intensive public library review process urged that library operating grants be based on populations being served rather than dated census figures and that the government provide enough funding to allow all municipalities to join regional library systems. A new public library was opened in Abbotsfield, and a new Calgary Public Library branch marks its first in nine years. At the University of Alberta, the first campus to introduce smart-card technology, the library is moving to a one-campus-card environment for photocopiers and microform printing. Toward the "Alberta Library," Red Deer College will be used as a test site for a one-card system among public and college libraries in central Alberta.

British Columbia public libraries secured support for the Library Act to ensure autonomous governing boards and free access to core services. While provincial grants were maintained, some libraries felt the impact of reduced grants to municipalities. The Library Services Branch developed Youth and the Internet, a program to hire youth to train users in search skills, and distributed grants for the development of Internet sites through the Communities Connect Program. Provincial budget adjustments caused reduced support for some centralized collection-based services (e.g., large-print and multilingual), but the basic public library grant per capita was protected. The $2 million Internet Access for Public Libraries program is well under way with the automation of small public libraries; other plans focus on efforts to manage resource sharing, implementation of new technologies, and literacy-for-children programs. The Electronic Library Network (ELN) received a CACUL Innovative Achievements Award for its Online Access to Journals Project. Technological activity in the province included UBC's purchase of the DRA system, Trinity Western University and Emily Carr Institute of Art and Design's acquisition of Dynix Horizon, and the formation of a British Columbia confederation (eight partners) that purchased SIRSI's Unicorn system. Innovative services include a new multimedia research tutorial program at Capilano College and a multimedia information kiosk with a technology section for special needs, in three languages (English, Cantonese, and Mandarin) at Richmond Public Library.

Yukon and Northwest Territories

In the Northwest Territories, the provincial Library Services is preparing for the creation of a new territory. All library service representatives are working together for information resource sharing and preparing for Cancopy agreements in public libraries. Three library Web sites are online, with plans for eventual online catalogs at Inuvik Centennial Library, Nunavut Arctic College Library, and Yellowknife Public Library.

In the Yukon, government advanced the state of school libraries with increased support staff and teacher-librarian time and stable acquisition budgets. A project to pool the resources of all 28 schools is under way in the developing Resource Services Website, which provides access to collections through online catalogs and services, including the Teacher's Professional Library and media resources. Within the next two years, every student and teacher will have online access to the full range of Yukon's educational resources. Other progressive Web sites include those of Dawson City Community Library and Yukon College.

Libraries by Type: Public, School, Academic, Special

Public Libraries

A public library survey in Nova Scotia found that 98 percent of users see the library as an essential or very important service; confirmed a strong link between schools and public libraries; and discovered support for a range of funding alternatives, including user fees, but only for "nonessential" products (audio and video materials, Internet access, interlibrary lending). However, the overall outlook includes temporary closures due to financial constraints (for example, the Metro Toronto Reference Library laid off staff and closed for ten days), reduced staffing, reduced hours of service, reduced book and journal budgets, outsourcing of services, citizen boards changing to direct political governance, and challenges to free access, with increased dependence on user revenue. At best, funding and service levels are stable, with institutions demonstrating innovation and leadership in serving their diverse communities. A newer trend involves increased partnerships with local free-nets and "telecommunity" networks.

School Library Resource Centers

School libraries are facing budget reductions. In April the Vancouver School Board laid off 200 support staff, including all library assistants; and in Howe Sound (British Columbia), 50 percent of elementary teacher-librarian time was cut. The New Brunswick Teacher-Librarians' Association was dissolved due to declining membership, and school boards were amalgamated in Nova Scotia and Ontario, increasing uncertainty. Teacher-librarians are facing pressures to define their roles more clearly and to find ways to assess resource-based learning outcomes, in an environment that values accountability and the testing of measurable skills. The Association for Teacher-Librarianship in Canada and the Canadian School Library Association cooperated to produce *Students' Information Literacy Needs: Competencies for Teacher-Librarians in the 21st Century*. The two associations also organized a Symposium on Information and Literacy, hosted by NLC and the Canadian Education Association, with a broad agenda, including movement toward a set of national standards and a national policy on information literacy and school libraries.

Academic Libraries

Academic libraries also struggle for funding, and many enter into alliances to pool resources. A study of scholarly communication found that academic librarians are under pressure to make the transition to an electronic world and to keep pace with a continually expanding body of knowledge, all in a time of decreasing resources. There are several projects to digitize the special collections of university libraries. The third Canadian Title Count was undertaken by CARL in conjunction with NLC. Data from 36 participating academic libraries was collected to produce a listing of the number of titles contained in the various LC classification schedules, which can be used for collections appraisal.

Special Libraries

The Canadian Association for Special Libraries and Information Services (CASLIS) set up a listserv to discuss emerging and continuing issues: fee-based information services, new push technologies, competitive intelligence, and new methods of fast access to the Internet. Several workshops were held on methods for running a corporate-wide intranet, knowledge management, and the delivery of services in an increasingly electronic environment.

Education

Noted trends in the job market include increased contract employment, particularly in Ontario; substantial growth in employment in nontraditional settings; less use of the term "librarian"; and an increased societal need for information management skills. The seven graduate schools of library and information studies are exploring alternative ways of preparing students for the changing job market, such as through distance courses and continuing education. The Ecole de Bibliothéconomie et des Sciences de l'Information of the Université de Montréal announced a new Ph.D. in information science, offering two areas of specialization: information transfer and information systems and resources. It is the only French-language Ph.D. in information science. A study of urban public library directors examined the state of library leadership in Canada and questioned whether schools are attracting students with the attributes essential for leading libraries.

The University of Alberta placement and salary survey of 1995 graduates shows that 80 percent found positions within six months of graduation but only half of those working full-time were employed in permanent positions; earning power increased; women earned more than men; and two-thirds of the graduating class found employment in post-secondary or public libraries while the others were working in government, business, or the information industry. Fewer found placements within Alberta than previous years.

Phase II of the summary report from the Alliance of Libraries Archives and Records Management (ALARM), *Human Resources Development in the Information Resources Management Sector*, confirmed initial findings that "soft skills" are the most important training need (skills that relate to communications and management, not subject matter expertise). Parallel findings include a general concern with the worth of available training and ongoing preoccupations with the evolution of technology and its impact across all aspects of the sector's work. A strategy was developed outlining key issues: communications and management skills; technology impacts; image and identity; dialogue; identification of required skills, knowledge, and attributes; and the role for a cross-sectoral human resources committee.

Emerging Trends

As reported in previous years, the trend continues for libraries to enter into partnerships with other institutions to share resources, with business and industry to support and exploit those resources, with government to make libraries the primary information access point for citizens, and with colleagues and citizens to advocate for libraries and librarians. The challenge to achieve equitable and universal access is a major recurring issue. Advances in information technology present new issues concerning the management of electronic resources, Internet access, and adequate Canadian content. Libraries are increasingly businesslike in the sense that they are having to market and fund themselves in a competitive information and knowledge-based environment.

Special Reports

Developments in Copyright Law, 1997

Sarah K. Wiant

Director, Law Library, and Professor of Law,
Washington and Lee University

With the advent of the National Information Infrastructure Task Force on Intellectual Property and the Conference on Fair Use, it was apparent that big changes in copyright law were on Congress's agenda. During 1997 several pieces of legislation were introduced, many of them slated to be on the fast track. When user groups focused on the proposed legislation, they realized that it would severely restrict current widely adopted practices and they organized themselves to raise their concerns before Congress.

With more than 80,000 members, the Digital Future Coalition (DFC), a collaboration of 39 of the nation's leading nonprofit educational, scholarly, library, and consumer groups, is recognized as an important voice. Working on several projects, DFC has had an impact on several key issues. Most particularly, DFC organizations have worked to slow down ratification of the World Intellectual Property Organization (WIPO) treaties implementing legislation.

The White Paper[1] was endorsed by the NII Copyright Protection Act of 1995, but bills in both houses of Congress failed to pass[2]. The fight over the internet continued with the passage of the Communications Decency Act, which later was found to be unconstitutional. With the exception of the No Electronic Theft Act, little legislation was passed because there is little agreement in the industry or within Congress. Nonetheless, it was an active year as other proposals were set forth by various constituencies and courts continued to rule on copyright issues that affect information users.

WIPO Implementing Legislation

In July, at President Clinton's request, legislation to implement the WIPO treaties was introduced. On July 29, 1997, H.R. 2281[3] was introduced by Representatives Coble (R-N.C.), Hyde (R-Ill.), Conyers (D-Mich.) and Frank (D-Mass.). A companion bill, S. 1121[4], was introduced on July 31, 1997 by Senators Hatch (R-Utah), Leaky (D-Vt.), Thompson (R-Tenn.) and Kohl (D-Wis.) and was sent to the Senate Committee on the Judiciary. The DFC is concerned that H.R. 2281 goes beyond the WIPO treaties and threatens to upset the existing balance of the copyright system. Issues such as fair use, the first-sale doctrine, library preservation, distance education, and non-negotiated licenses are issues that should be discussed in a national debate and that can be resolved in a manner consistent with the WIPO treaties.

Ashcroft Bill

Senator John Ashcroft (R-Mo.) introduced the Digital Copyright Clarification and Technology Education Act (S. 1146)[5] on September 3, 1997. The Digital Future Coalition played an active role in the drafting of this legislation, which is pro-user, pro-library legislation. The bill would amend the Copyright Act to limit the liability of internet service providers (ISPs). The Ashcroft Bill would shield an ISP from liability for copyright infringements by third parties using the ISP unless the ISP receives notice of the infringement and fails to take measures to remove the offending material. Additionally, the Ashcroft bill would bring distance learning within the fair-use exceptions to copyright infringement actions. The bill has been referred to the Senate Committee on the Judiciary.

Representatives Rick Boucher (D-Va.) and Tom Campbell (R-Calif.) introduced a similar bill, H.R. 3048, the Digital Era Copyright Enhancement Act of 1997.[6] The DFC and other educators, librarians, and researchers support this legislation because it preserves fundamental rights in the digital age. The law maintains a delicate balance between law and public policy and protects copyright holders by allowing appropriate limited public access.

The legislation would amend Section 107 of the Copyright Act to reaffirm that fair use is as applicable in the electronic environment as it is in the print world. The legislation would also allow libraries to use technology to make three copies of endangered materials for archival purposes. The proposal would establish the digital equivalent of the first-sale doctrine. An application of the doctrine would permit an individual to transmit a legally acquired digital copy of a protected work so long as the sender erases the digital copy on his or her equipment at the time of the transfer.

The legislation proposes amendments to Sections 110(2) and 112(b) to permit educators to use new technology for distance learning in the way they now use television. Section 117 of the act would be amended to make explicit that temporary copies stored in RAM may not serve as the sole basis for copyright liability. A section of the proposal would prohibit non-negotiable licenses, such as the proposed changes to the Uniform Commercial Code, to preempt fair use. Finally, the legislation would implement the anticircumvention and copyright management provisions of the WIPO copyright treaties.

No Electronic Theft Act

Public Law 105-47 was signed on December 16, 1997, by President Clinton enacting the No Electronic Theft (NET) Act, which allows prosecution of willful infringement.[7] A person can be found guilty of a felony for making ten or more copies with a total retail value of $2,500 and can be sentenced to prison for up to five years and fined up to $250,000. If an individual makes one or more copies of copyrighted information with a value of $1,000 or less, the charge is a misdemeanor, carrying up to a one-year prison sentence or a $1,000 fine, or both.

The legislation was enacted to close a loophole because in 1994 a Massachusetts Institute of Technology student was accused of copying and distributing commercial software valued at millions of dollars. The case was dismissed because under copyright law there was no proof that he had infringed for "commercial advantage" or private financial gain.

Because scholarly and educational uses do not constitute infringement and are often allowed under fair use, libraries and educators are not protesting this legislation.

Database Protection

With respect to electronic compilations of information, often the real value is not the data itself (much of which is or could be unprotected) but the software and creative tools developed to manipulate and use the data.

Experts in the United States and abroad are discussing models for protecting information. One model is the new *sui generis* database right adopted by the European Union (EU) giving database owners a limited property right in the compilation of information. A majority of the delegates at the WIPO treaty meeting expressed opposition to the proposal of the EU countries, and the language was removed from the treaty. In contrast, the United States is discussing a misappropriation right grounded in an unfair-competition law. H.R. 2652[8] is currently before the House Judiciary Subcommittee on Courts and Intellectual Property Committee.

The library community believes that there is no compelling need for the proposed protections, which would go well beyond the traditional misappropriation doctrine. Many believe that through copyright, contracts, and technology adequate protection exists. In August 1997 the U.S. Copyright Office issued its *Report on the Legal Protection for Databases*, noting that "all agreed that the proponents of a new form of statutory protection have the burden of establishing the need for such protection."[9]

Misappropriation has traditionally dealt with injuries resulting from unfair competition among commercial competitors. The user community is concerned that the proposed legislation would penalize any "substantial" use of data affecting the actual or potential market. Such key terms as "substantial part" and "substantial monetary" require clarification to fully appreciate the extent of the legislation.

The misappropriation doctrine has been confined to "hot" or "time-sensitive" information. This proposal would apply to all compiled information, including archival and historical information. The impact of such a proposal on library budgets could be significant, particularly when such legislation might have the effect of requiring libraries to purchase information that otherwise would be in the public domain. The copyright on compilations—unlike the copyright on other materials with a term of life plus 50 years—would be in perpetuity. The scientific community is equally concerned about these proposed restrictions on the use of information.

The proposed legislation, unlike the Copyright Act, does not provide for exemptions for educators or libraries. A narrow provision would permit a user to extract information for "not for profit, educational, scientific or research purposes, which does not harm the actual or potential market." It is difficult to ascertain how this is a meaningful limitation.

The compiler of information has no absolute right to prevent the copying of the entire database. In order to succeed on a claim, the owner must show that its product was harmed. This is an attempt to balance interests, but—although it is a weaker form of protection than a property right, from the user's perspective—the language appears to be overly broad.

CONFU

In September 1997 the final report of the United States Conference on Fair Use (CONFU) was issued.[10] CONFU began in 1994 with a threefold mission: to bring together copyright owners and users, to discuss fair-use issues, and to develop guidelines for fair use of copyrighted works by librarians and educators. Although the guidelines produced by CONFU failed to receive sufficient endorsements by organizations to warrant official action, proposed guidelines in several areas were issued in an interim report to the Commissioner of the U.S. Patents and Trademarks Office. Additionally, some subgroups of CONFU continue to work informally toward developing more broadly accepted fair-use guidelines with the hope that more organizations would agree to endorse them.

CONFU consisted of six topical working groups: digital images, distance learning, educational multimedia, library use of computer software, electronic reserve systems, and interlibrary loan/document delivery.

The goal of the digital images working group was to establish guidelines for digital archive creation, digital images used for educational purposes, and digitizing of pre-existing analog images as well as newly acquired images. The guidelines are currently being used for a one-year trial period in hope that broader endorsement will come at the end of that trial period.

The guidelines proposed by the distance-learning subgroup extend the face-to-face teaching exemptions in Section 110 of the Copyright Act. However, the guidelines apply only to real-time performance and display of copyrighted works, not to asynchronous delivery of distance learning via computer networks. During the fall of 1997 the distance-learning working group met to work toward more broadly accepted guidelines, but the members were unable to reach consensus.

The educational-multimedia group proposed guidelines that apply to copyrighted works used in multimedia projects by students and educators as part of systematic learning activities at nonprofit educational institutions. Nonprofit educational institutions are defined as nonprofit institutions with the primary focus of supporting research and instructional activities of teachers and students. The educational-multimedia guidelines met with significant endorsement by those CONFU members actively involved with multimedia; however, most members—including most library organizations—opposed the guidelines. The library community raised strong opposition to a recent proposal to reissue the multimedia guidelines in a U.S. Copyright Office circular, despite the lack of support among a majority of CONFU participants.

Electronic reserve systems allow for the storage, access, display, and downloading of electronic versions of materials to support the instructional requirements of a specific course at a nonprofit educational institution. Guidelines in this area were viewed by many as an extension of existing library reserve guidelines. Unfortunately, the guidelines proposed by the working group met with significant opposition within CONFU, and no electronic reserve guidelines were included in either the interim or final CONFU report. Many proprietors believe that electronic reserves are a form of course pack publishing and are not fair use, while some library organizations viewed the proposed guidelines as too restrictive to endorse. In the meantime, however, some library associations and major universities feel that the guidelines are sufficiently restrictive to warrant their implementation.

The interlibrary loan/document delivery working group decided unanimously that it is not possible to draft widely acceptable guidelines at this time. In evaluating library use of computer software, the subgroup developed different scenarios to illustrate library use of computer software. CONFU participants decided that the scenarios were sufficient to provide guidance in this area and therefore did not draft guidelines. A final session of CONFU was planned for May 1998.

Judicial Decisions

Princeton University Press v. *Michigan Document Services, Inc.*

In November 1996 the Sixth Circuit Court of Appeals held that the fair-use doctrine does not protect a commercial copy shop engaged in reproducing copyrighted works and selling them in course packs to university students.[11] Although the decision of the U.S. Court of Appeals for the Sixth Circuit clarified certain aspects of fair use as it applies to educational copying for course packs, it raised serious issues causing a significant number of concerned law professors to file an *amicus curiae* brief before the Supreme Court urging it to take the case and provide guidance on the issue.[12] On March 31, 1997, the U.S. Supreme Court declined to hear the appeal, letting stand the lower-court decision denying fair use.[13]

Michigan Document Services (MDS) had copied portions of various works selected by University of Michigan professors, added a cover and table of contents, and sold the bound course packs to the professors' students. MDS did not seek permission from the copyright owners. Professors stated that they would not have assigned the entire copyrighted work if they could not include photocopied excerpts in the course packs.[14]

The Sixth Circuit Court rejected MDS's defense of fair use, relying on two previous cases. In *Basic Books, Inc.* v. *Kinko's Graphics Corp*,[15] the U.S. District Court for the Southern District of New York held that a Kinko's copy shop violated copyright law by photocopying and selling in course packs copyrighted works without the publishers' permission. In *American Geophysical Union* v. *Texaco*,[16] the Second Circuit Court found that fair use did not protect even single photocopies made by researchers working at Texaco, a for-profit oil company.

The fair-use doctrine, codified at 17 U.S.C. Section 107, permits the reproduction of a copyrighted work for teaching purposes, among other things. To determine whether the use in a given situation is fair, the statute lists four factors to consider: "(1) the purpose and character of the use. . . ; (2) the nature of the copyrighted work; (3) the amount and substantiality of the portion used. . . ; and (4) the effect of the use upon the potential market for or value of the copyrighted work."[17] The Sixth Circuit Court evaluated each factor in reaching its conclusion that MDS's use was not fair within the meaning of Section 107.

The court noted that there were two uses in this case—use by the students and use by MDS—but focused on the commercial use by MDS rather than the secondary use by the students. Because MDS duplicated the copyrighted works and sold them for a profit, the court characterized MDS's use as commercial and therefore presumably unfair. The court noted further that MDS did not transform the underlying works. Therefore, this statutory factor weighed against fair use.

The defendants acknowledged that the nature of the work, the second statutory factor, cut against fair use because the excerpts copied were creative rather than factual.[18]

With respect to the third factor, the amount and substantiality of the portion used in relation to the whole, the issue was whether so much of the original works was copied that the copies superseded the originals. In general, the court stated, the more material copied, the less likely that the use will qualify as fair. MDS copied between 5 and 30 percent of each work in question, a quantity that the court found substantial.[19] Additionally, the fact that professors selected the works for copying indicated the value of the works copied.[20]

The court analyzed this factor in conjunction with the first statutory factor, the purpose and character of the use. The court found that even if MDS's use was not commercial, the publishers proved the potential market value of the works was diminished by showing a loss of permission fee revenue.[21]

The multiple dissenting opinions in *MDS* illustrate the many unresolved issues regarding the applicability of the fair-use doctrine. Whether or not the reasoning is flawed, *MDS* remains the law in the Sixth Circuit. The result reinforces the *Kinko's* case and extends *Texaco*'s narrowing of the fair-use exception for photocopying.

West Publishing and Compilation Copyrights

The scope of copyright protection in West Publishing Company's legal reporters was the subject of great debate in 1997. The West reporters contain judicial opinions from both state and federal courts. Although the opinions themselves are in the public domain and therefore not subject to copyright, West claims copyright protection in its reporters as compilations because West organizes and modifies the opinions in a number of ways. The dispute began in 1986 when the United States Court of Appeals for the Eighth Circuit held that West could protect its page numbers against copying by competing publishers.[22]

In 1997 two cases of note further tested the bounds of West's copyright in its reporters. Oasis Publishing Company published Florida court cases on CD-ROM, including page-number references to West's Florida reporters. West objected to the use of its page-numbering system, and the parties went to federal district court in Minnesota. In May 1996 the court relied on the ruling in the *Mead Data*

Central case and upheld West's copyright in its page-numbering system, prohibiting the use of West page numbers in the Oasis CD-ROM.[23] Oasis appealed to the Eighth Circuit. Before a decision was reached, the parties announced in July 1997 that they had reached a settlement agreement. The agreement licensed Oasis to continue using West's page-numbering system in its CD-ROM product. By the terms of the settlement agreement, West expressly did not waive any of its copyright claims.

While the *Oasis* case was unfolding, a second case was under way in New York. Matthew Bender & Company published a CD-ROM product that included pages scanned from West's reporters. In May 1997 a federal district court in New York ruled that West's copyright did not include its page numbers or other elements that West sought to protect.[24] Elements excluded from copyright protection by the court included case docket numbers, parallel citations to other reporters, attorneys' and judges' names, and a case's subsequent history. West has appealed the decision to the Court of Appeals for the Second Circuit.

The American Association of Law Libraries (AALL) filed an *amicus curiae* brief with the Second Circuit in November 1997. In the brief, AALL argued that West's changes to the cases it publishes are not creative enough to warrant copyright protection.[25]

The issue of West's copyright also came up in connection with the acquisition of West by Thompson Corporation. The newly created West Group will be allowed to license the use of West reporter page numbers pursuant to a decision by the federal district court in the District of Columbia. The license fees, however, must be deferred until 2001 or until the Supreme Court settles the question of West's copyright claims.

Principles for Licensing Electronic Resources

In July 1997 the American Association of Law Libraries, American Library Association, Association of Academic Health Sciences Libraries, Association of Research Libraries, Medical Library Association, and Special Libraries Association released the final draft of *Principles for Licensing Electronic Resources*. The principles, available on the Web at http://arl.cni.org/scomm/licensing/principles.html, are intended "to guide libraries in negotiating license agreements for access to electronic resources" and to provide licensors guidance on issues of importance to libraries and users. A license, as a legal contract, represents a mutually agreed upon set of commitments arrived at through discussion and negotiation. Generally, the licensor prepares the original documents and the buyer, or licensee, reviews the documents, highlights clauses of concern, and negotiates acceptable terms. In many institutions, an individual will be designated with authority to sign contracts; however, the library staff is generally responsible for the initial review.

Licenses such as those for shrink-wrap found on packaging and software or "click-on" licenses buried in the Web often raise serious issues because there are no formal negotiations between the buyer and the seller. Principles were developed to provide guidance to library staff working within their parent organization and with licensors to create mutually acceptable agreements for the use of copyrighted information in the electronic environment.

Uniform Commercial Code Article 2B

With advances in technology, companies selling information and users buying the information will have to change business practices to accommodate new models. Because of the ease with which a user can make a single copy equal in quality to the original or with a single keystroke make multiple copies and distribute them, the relationship between intellectual property and new technology must be examined.

In order to protect the value they have added to information, businesses seek maximum protection whenever they can, often through licenses and more recently through legislation. Businesses need licenses that can be enforced worldwide. These are legitimate business concerns, but no less important are the legitimate user concerns that as a matter of public policy are already expressly exempted in the copyright act: library uses, archive uses, and fair use.

Software shrink-wrap licenses are so called because they usually consist of a sheet of paper enclosed in shrink-wrap plastic with computer discs containing a software program. Shrink-wrap licenses can also be printed on the product box or in the user's manual. One type of shrink-wrap license is referred to as a "click-on" license because the user is prompted to "click here" to agree to license terms once the software is installed on the user's computer.

The legitimacy and terms of shrink-wrap and other software licenses have produced continuing debate in the intellectual-property field. Shrink-wrap license terms frequently conflict with settled contract law as well as the Copyright Act. For instance, shrink-wrap licenses often lack one or more of the elements required under contract law—offer, acceptance, and consideration. Clauses that prevent the resale of the user's copy of the software expressly conflict with the first-sale provision of the Copyright Act.[26]

In response to these and other concerns, an amendment to the Uniform Commercial Code (UCC) is being developed by the two groups responsible for it: the American Law Institute (ALI) and the National Conference of Commissioners on Uniform State Laws (NCCUSL). Because the UCC traditionally reflects the state of contract law, proposed Article 2B will focus on that aspect of shrink-wrap licenses. The drafters intend to stay neutral toward interaction with federal intellectual-property law, but no explanation has been given as to how that goal will be achieved.

The groups anticipated the completion of Article 2B in early 1998, with a vote on the final draft scheduled to take place at the annual meetings of the ALI and NCCUSL in May and July, respectively. Once the new provision is approved by both groups, it must be adopted by a state's legislature before it becomes law in that state.

Other Developments of Note

Communications Decency Act

In 1996 President Clinton signed into law the Telecommunications Act of 1996.[27] Part of the Telecommunications Act was the Communications Decency Act (CDA)[28], which prohibited the transmission of indecent communications via telecommunications devices, including interactive computer services, to minors. The act made such actions criminal. The stated purpose of the CDA was to protect persons under 18 from obscenity over the Internet.

The CDA was ruled unconstitutional by the United States Supreme Court in 1997.[29] The court held that the CDA was overly broad and therefore violated the First Amendment of the U.S. Constitution. By limiting transmissions to minors, the Supreme Court found that the CDA also limited speech between adults, which is constitutionally protected. Proponents of the CDA failed to demonstrate that no less-restrictive alternative would achieve the act's legitimate purpose of protecting minors from obscenity.

The court's opinion noted the difficulty in ascertaining the age of Internet users as well as the vast and growing nature of cyberspace. The court also stated that the restrictions imposed by the CDA would require judging the content of transmissions, something the court has been reluctant to do. Although the court extended full First Amendment protection for the Internet, it did not completely foreclose the possibility of future Internet regulation.

Encryption

Encryption is an extremely controversial area and nothing close to a consensus or workable compromise is likely to appear soon.

European Copyright Directive

Like legislation introduced in the United States that proposed a ban on technologies used to circumvent copyright protection, a directive was issued by the European Union to its member nations concerning an amendment of copyright law to comply with the 1996 WIPO treaty. Library associations are monitoring the further development of this directive.[30]

Proposed Copyright Term Extension

A bill that would extend the term of copyright protection, H.R. 2589[31], was introduced by Representative Howard Coble (R-N.C.) on October 1, 1997. The bill would extend most copyright protection by 20 years, from the life of the author plus 50 years to life of the author plus 70 years. H.R. 2589 is one of several bills introduced that propose to amend sections 301–304 of the Copyright Act in order to extend the term of protection of most works. Proponents argue that many European countries have already adopted an extended term. Opponents are concerned that materials are kept out of the public domain for an additional 20 years.

The Coble bill adds language directed at the motion picture industry, recommending that terms should be negotiated between motion picture copyright holders and the screenwriters, directors, and actors to ensure that those who do not retain an interest in the motion picture are not unduly injured by the extended term.

Western Governor's University

In January of 1998 the Western Governor's University (WGU) opened its doors in 16 states and Guam, offering a general associate degree and emphasizing semiconductor manufacturing technology.[32] Classes will be taught through distance education. The university has none of its own professors, and all of its courses will come from other colleges.

Western Governor's University, the "Virtual University," intends to draw most of its enrollment from part-time and nontraditional students. The catalog/advisor developed with IBM is the center of WGU. A student can tell whether a course is interactive, delivered via television; tutorial, delivered over the Internet; or provided by some other technology. The catalog can connect a student to the registrar, the library, or the bookstore. The extent to which copyrighted materials may be used for distance learning is unresolved. All of the owners' exclusive rights may be at issue. Prior to distance-learning classes, there had been little need to obtain the right to perform or display publicly. Among the issues facing WGU are the issues of use of intellectual property.

Conclusion

Print and digitized information are critical to the American economy. Equally important is an informed public who can be educated and conduct research within the privileges accorded them. The development of a balanced information infrastructure relies on both protected and public-domain information.

Notes

1. Intellectual Property and the National Information Infrastructure, the Report of the Working Group on Intellectual Property Rights, Washington, D.C., Information Infrastructure Task Force, September 1995.
2. National Information Infrastructure Protection Act, H.R. 2441, 104th Cong. (1995); National Information Infrastructure Protection Act, S. 1284, 104th Cong. (1995).
3. WIPO Copyright Treaties Implementation Act, H.R. 2281, 105th Cong. (1997).
4. S. 1121, 105th Cong. (1997).
5. Digital Copyright Clarification and Technology Act, S. 1146, 105th Cong. (1997).
6. Digital ERA Copyright Enhancement Act, H.R. 3048, 105th Cong. (1997).
7. No Electronic Theft Act, P.L. 105-47, 111 STAT. 2678 (1997).
8. H.R. 2652, 105th Cong. (1997).
9. U.S. Copyright Office, Report on the Legal Protection for Databases (1997).
10. Conference on Fair Use, Report to the Commissioner on the Conclusion of the First Phase of the Conference on Fair Use (1997).
11. Princeton University Press v. Michigan Document Services, 74 F.3d 1528 (6th Cir. 1996), rev'd en banc, 99 F.3d 1381 (6th Cir. 1996) (hereinafter MDS).
12. Brief of *Amici Curiae* Concerned Law Professors, *Princeton University Press* v. *Michigan Document Services*, 99 F. 3d 1381 (6th Cir. 1996) (No. 96-1219).
13. *Princeton University Press* v. *Michigan Document Services*, 99 F. 3d 1381 (6th Cir. 1996), *cert. denied*, 65 U.S.L.W. 3665 (U.S. Mar. 31, 1997) (No. 96-1219).
14. *MDS*, 99 F. 3d at 1384.
15. 758 F. Supp. 1522 (S.D.N.Y. 1991).
16. 60 F.3d 914 (2d Cir. 1994).

17. 17 U.S.C. Section 107 (1994).

18. *Ibid.* at 1389.

19. *Ibid.* at 1384–85.

20. *Ibid.*

21. *MDS*, 99 F. 3d at 1388.

22. *West Publishing Co.* v. *Mead Data Central Inc.*, 799 F2d 1219 (8th Cir. 1986).

23. *Oasis Publishing Co. Inc.* v. *West Publishing Co.*, 924 F. Supp 918 (DC Minn 1996).

24. *Bender & Co. Inc.* v. *West Publishing Co.*, 1997 WL 266972 (S.D.N.Y. May 19, 1997), 54 PTCJ66.

25. The full text of AALL's *amicus* brief is available by contacting the Customer Services Coordinator at AALL headquarters, 312-939-4764.

26. The first sale provision permits "the owner of a particular copy . . . without the authority of the copyright owner, to sell or otherwise dispose of the possession of that copy . . . ." 17 U.S.C. Section 109(a) (1994).

27. P.L. 104-104, 110 Stat. 56 (Feb. 8 1996).

28. P.L. 104-104, tit. V, 110 Stat. 56, 133-43 (Feb. 8 1996).

29. *Reno* v. *American Civil Liberties Union*, ___ U.S. ___, 117 S.Ct. 2329, 138 L.Ed.2d 874 (1997).

30. Directive 96/9/EC of the European Parliament, Mar. 11, 1996, *Official Journal of the European Communities*, No. L77/20.

31. Copyright Term Extension Act, H.R. 2589, 105th Cong. (1997).

32. The Chronicle of Higher Education, Feb. 9, 1998, A21–22, col. 4.

Internet 2 and the Next Generation Internet: Windows to Advanced Networking Applications

Clifford Lynch

Executive Director, Coalition for Networked Information

The Context of the New Experimental Networks

In the early 1990s the U.S. government made a policy decision to privatize the U.S. part of the Internet by phasing out the NSFNET, the high-speed backbone that served the research and education communities and that was governed by an increasingly cumbersome acceptable-use policy. By 1996 the government's role in the Internet was limited to underwriting a certain amount of research in high-performance networking and applications (a traditional research role) through the National Science Foundation (NSF), the Advanced Research Projects Agency (ARPA), and other agencies under the High Performance Computing and Communications Program (HPCC) and continuing to finance a certain amount of specialized infrastructure. This support included some of the operation of the Internet Engineering Task Force and such administrative functions as the Internet Assigned Numbers Authority (IANA), as well as the management of the assignment of network numbers and part of the operation of the Domain Name System through its subcontract to Network Solutions, Inc. In 1997–1998 there have been active policy discussions to determine how best to eliminate even these vestigial government roles. (See http://www.ntia.doc.gov for a recent policy paper.)

By the mid 1990s the primary operational components of the Internet—the major Internet service provider (ISP) backbones—were entirely private, commercial operations run by such corporations as UUNET (recently acquired by Worldcom), BBN (recently acquired by GTE), Sprint, and MCI (in the process of being acquired by Worldcom). Given the explosive growth both in the number of sites and individuals connecting to the Internet and in bandwidth capacity demand from this ever growing array of users, these corporations and a vast number of second- and third-tier network service providers that purchase backbone connectivity from one of the very large backbone providers are investing vast amounts of money and effort in two areas: capacity and reliability.

Backbones are moving from DS3 (45 million bits/second) to OC3 (155 million bits/second) to OC12 (622 million bits/second) and beyond. Those ISPs offering consumer connectivity are installing and upgrading dial-up modems at a rapid rate and are trying to extend their services to include higher-speed offerings based on technologies that include ISDN, various forms of Digital Subscriber Loop (DSL), cable TV plant-based connectivity, and wireless approaches. At the same time, the Internet—which has grown ever more critical to the daily operations of many organizations, to the support of electronic commerce, and to the provision of access to a wide variety of information resources—has shown itself to be somewhat fragile and prone to congestion and disruptions as a result of physical disasters (e.g., fiber cuts), configuration errors, overloading, and malicious attacks.

Thus, the ISPs are investing heavily in developing redundancy and are upgrading both technical infrastructure and operating procedures to meet growing demands and expectations for reliable, consistent service. Their focus is on meeting commercial needs for the business and consumer communities, rather than on advancing the state of the art for the high-end research and education applications that historically drove much of the development of the Internet. It's not that the ISPs are not interested in these advanced applications and services. Rather, in relative terms, there is little short-term revenue to be earned from them when compared to the commercial demand for expanding and improving basic network services. Further, getting the current commercial Internet under control and keeping up with demand is extraordinarily challenging given current growth rates. Adding support for poorly understood experimental advanced services may be risky and disruptive at a time when risk and disruption must be minimized wherever possible.

Commercial imperatives have left the research and education communities in a difficult position. They have continued to envision and study a wide range of new advanced network applications that cannot be supported today by the commercial Internet. Many applications are in mission-critical areas for science, scholarship, and education (such as the collaborative remote control of experimental apparatus, the deployment of sophisticated instructional technology, and distance education delivery systems), and for access to enormous scientific and scholarly multimedia digital libraries and data repositories.

During the last two years plans have cohered to revitalize the development of advanced networking infrastructure to support experimentation with these sorts of applications, primarily through two major initiatives: Internet 2 and the Next Generation Internet (NGI) program. These initiatives are distinct but interdependent and interlinked in complex ways. This article provides a brief snapshot of these programs, including the technologies on which they are focused and some of the key applications they are intended to enable.

Both NGI and Internet 2 are dynamic, evolving activities. The reader should recognize that while material here about technologies and applications is relatively stable, implementation strategies are changing rapidly. Some information in this article may be overtaken by events prior to publication. There are three primary Web sites—http://www.ucaid.edu, http://www.internet2.edu, and http://www.ngi.gov—that can be consulted for the most up-to-date information.

There is a long history of experimental networks, or groups of networks, being established within the broad framework of the Internet. Indeed, a strong argument can be made that the entire design of the Internet protocol and the architecture of the Internet was developed specifically to permit the continual incorporation of new, experimental networks and networking technologies. Over the years technologies have included packet radio networks, wide-band packet satellite networks, and the experimental gigabit test beds that were developed in the early 1990s. Sites were connected to multiple networks—both production networks such as the ARPANET or, later, the NSFNET—and experimental networks. At one level, the plans for Internet 2 and the NGI should be regarded in much the same spirit. Sites, primarily within the research and education communities, will gain connectivity to new, high-performance experimental networks alongside their existing connections to the commercial (commodity) Internet.

There are no plans to disconnect sites within the research and education communities from the existing Internet, leaving them reachable in the future only by other peer sites that are fortunate enough to have connections to the new experimental networks. In this sense, terms like Internet 2 are somewhat misleading. Internet 2 and the NGI are not intended to replace the commodity Internet; rather, they are intended to supplement it with experimental networks that can provide a context for exploring advanced applications that the current commercial Internet cannot support and is unlikely to be able to support for the next few years. All existing network applications will continue to work across those sites that are connected to both the new experimental networks and the commodity Internet, as well as across sites having only commercial Internet connections, although some of the latter may work more reliably or better when used among sites sharing connectivity to the new experimental networks. To be sure, the research and education sites that will be connected to the new experimental networks already rely on connectivity through the commercial networks to a vast array of sites for mission-critical operational activities. They simply cannot function without continued, uninterrupted participation in the commercial Internet.

But, in another sense, the goals of Internet 2 and NGI are more ambitious than the incorporation of new, faster networks as protected test beds within the fabric of the existing Internet. These programs will expand the repertoire of basic network services available to hosts that are connected by the new experimental networks beyond the unreliable "best-effort" datagram services that characterize the current Internet. New services will include quality-of-service (QoS) guarantees and multicasting (both of which will be discussed in detail later). For the new breed of advanced applications that will rely on these new services, Internet 2 will actually define a more circumscribed research and education Internet within which they can operate.

Internet 2

The Internet 2 program has its roots in efforts that were developed under the auspices of EDUCOM's Networking and Telecommunications Task Force (NTTF) around 1995–1996 to explore the next generation of advanced networking applications for the higher education community and the underlying network services and performance levels that would be needed to support these applications. These discussions culminated in late 1997 with the formation of the University Consortium for Advanced Internet Development (UCAID), a not-for-profit corporation. The board of UCAID is heavily populated with university presidents, underscoring the strategic importance with which the higher education community views this effort. Higher education institutions can join UCAID by paying rather substantial fees that underwrite development of Internet 2 and related infrastructure; and it appears that roughly 100 institutions of higher education will form the initial membership. UCAID is also heavily supported by a group of corporate technology partners in the computing and networking industries, such as IBM, Cisco, and MCI.

Basically, the participants in Internet 2 envision the following set of developments over the next few years:

- Each participant will be connected to Internet 2 via a high-speed connection, ideally at a minimum bandwidth of OC3 (155 million bits/second), in addition to retaining connectivity to the commodity Internet. In a few cases, due to the unavailability of appropriate fiber optic trunking facilities, initial connections may be at the DS3 (45 Mbit/second) rate.

- Connection will be accomplished through a set of regional structures called gigapops (gigabit points of presence) that will link clusters of Internet 2 sites to the Internet 2 backbones and also, in some cases, to the commercial Internet. The role of the gigapops is still evolving and varies considerably from region to region.

- Participants will also make commitments to upgrade on-campus networking facilities as appropriate (to ATM, 100 Mbits/second Ethernet, Gigabit Ethernet, or other technologies) in order to permit relevant campus hosts to interact with hosts at other Internet 2 sites at high data rates. Funding for this expensive undertaking will be in addition to membership dues paid to UCAID.

- The Internet 2 sites will be linked by one or more very high speed—hopefully OC12 (622 Mbits/second or better)—backbones. The NSF-funded vBNS (very high speed backbone, now primarily OC12, is discussed in more detail later) will be one of the key initial backbones.

- Within Internet 2 campuses and throughout the Internet 2 backbones, new network services such as QoS and multicasting will be deployed as early as possible. Some higher-level "middleware" services, such as common authentication technologies, may also be deployed ubiquitously throughout the Internet 2 sites. There is also discussion of using Internet 2 as an early large-scale deployment environment for the new Internet protocol, IPV6.

- Under the broad leadership of UCAID, Internet 2 sites will also encourage the development and broad deployment of advanced network applications, including the sharing of experiences and the creation of demonstration applications. Joint development and sharing of applications software may also be involved.

Over time, capacity on the commodity Internet will grow to support the performance requirements of these advanced networking applications. As new network services are tested and refined in the Internet 2 environment, support for these applications will hopefully migrate to the commodity Internet as well. The heavy involvement of key technology suppliers in Internet 2 provides a logical technology migration path into the commercial Internet, although it is important to recognize that many of the deployment issues in the commercial Internet involve more than technology migration. They also call for new business and economic arrangements to make it possible for services such as QoS guarantees to operate in a commercial, multisupplier environment.

NGI Program

The Next Generation Internet is a federal funding program that was proposed during the 1996 presidential campaign. Originally, it proposed roughly $100 million per year of new federal funding for three years to support the following activities:

- Development of a network of roughly 100 sites connected at speeds about 100 times faster than the then-current commercial Internet and the exploration of advanced applications that are possible in this environment
- Development of a second, more experimental network of roughly 10 sites connected at speeds about 1,000 times faster than existing commercial networks (much of the focus would be on networking technologies themselves; yet the exploration of new applications would be enabled by these higher-performance networks)
- Research and development in new network services (e.g., quality of service, multicasting) and applications support environments (e.g., middleware, distributed object environments, and multimedia support)
- Research and development on other broad networking issues, such as security and reliability, that would presumably yield payoffs for both the existing commercial networks and new experimental networks

In the current federal fiscal cycle, Congress allocated roughly $85 million for the NGI program, but only after considerable review and discussion and some restructuring of the NGI proposal, which included the removal of the Department of Energy from the program. It is somewhat difficult to understand fully the implications of this program. First, the money is spread across a number of agencies—NSF, DOD/ARPA, National Institutes of Health/National Library of Medicine (NIH/NLM), etc.—and each agency will apply the funds in different ways, partly to expand existing programs and partly to initiate new programs. It is difficult to define how much of the NGI is simply a systematic cross-agency view of activities that to some extent might have gone forward anyway (much like the broader HPCC program) and how much it is a truly new activity. Second, there are a number of other new programs—such as the multiagency Digital Libraries Phase 2 program or the NSF Knowledge and Distributed Intelligence (KDI) program—that are receiving new money (separate from the NGI program), yet have very strong synergistic links to NGI. Finally, it's not yet clear how the next few years of the NGI program will be shaped, although it appears that it will be funded at about $100 million/year.

NGI-Internet 2 Interdependencies

Internet 2 and NGI are closely linked at several levels. As with much else in this area, these linkages are still evolving. At the most abstract level, these two programs and the people leading them share a very strong commitment to advanced networking and to the important, novel applications that advanced networks can make possible; and they thus share a common goal of advancing the state of the art. At a more technical level, there is a great deal of convergence between the two efforts on a small number of critical new network services—particularly multicasting and quality-of-service guarantees—that will serve as key building blocks for the support of the new generation of applications.

It is clear that NSF and ARPA (as well as other agencies)—both as part of their existing programs and as part of new or expanded initiatives under the NGI funding—will be providing funds to support researchers who want to explore new applications that can be supported within the context of Internet 2 and NGI. Although the Internet 2 program is largely focused on enabling infrastructure, federal agencies will play an essential role in allowing researchers to explore the applications for science, scholarship, and learning that Internet 2 will enable. Federal agencies will also be funding some of the basic networking technology work that will support the implementation and validation of some of the new network services on Internet 2, many of which are only now making the transition from pure research to experimental deployment.

At a more operational level, NSF has been funding a high-speed research network called the vBNS for some years (see http://www.vbns.net). Its initial purpose was primarily to interconnect the NSF-funded supercomputing centers, but in recent years it has become a broader test bed for advanced network applications. The vBNS will be made available as one of the initial backbones to interconnect the Internet 2 sites. It is currently provisioned to operate at OC12 (622 Mbits/second) speed and is run by MCI under contract to NSF. Additionally, NSF has for several years operated the New Connections Program, which helps higher educational institutions underwrite the cost of connecting to the vBNS or other high-speed backbone networks. Grants under this program will help underwrite the establishment of gigapops and the connection of Internet 2 sites to the Internet 2 backbone networks. NGI funding will permit the expansion of the New Connections Program.

New Networking Services

Central to both Internet 2 and NGI is the enrichment of the basic networking services offered by the Internet, beyond today's point-to-point unreliable datagram delivery, to support a broader set of applications. Oversimplifying slightly: A host connected to the Internet today can transmit packets to another network host. If the network is congested, it can discard these packets. Packets may arrive at a target host after arbitrary and variable delays; they may be duplicated or arrive in a different order than that in which they were transmitted. This is the essence of unreliable best-efforts datagram service.

The first key extension to the current set of basic network services that is being proposed for Internet 2 is quality-of-service (QoS) guarantees. This service is essential for supporting interactive multimedia, real-time video, interactive simulations, and the capture of telemetry or the real-time control of experimental equipment. Basically, a source host should be able to tell the network that it needs to transmit packets at a given data rate to a destination host and that packets must arrive at that host with a bounded delay and a guaranteed maximum loss rate. (There are substantial technical complexities in specifying the precise performance parameters that characterize acceptable network performance for a packet flow from one host to another, but this scenario should give a sense of the problem.)

The approach currently being proposed for QoS guarantees is resource reservation: A protocol such as RSVP is employed to request the parameters—from all of the routers on the path between source and destination—that need to be guaranteed and either to obtain a commitment from the network that these requirements can be met or an assertion that they cannot. An application with specific data rate and other performance requirements would issue a set of RSVP requests to the other hosts with which it needs to interact prior to sending any data, and then it would determine its behavior based on the response to these requests.

Technically, RSVP and QoS are stunningly complex and research problems abound. It is not clear how to characterize performance requirements. And it's not certain what resources to reserve in response to an RSVP request or what policies routers need to use in conjunction with resource reservations to ensure that the QoS guarantees are actually met. Further, QoS-based paths will be used in conjunction with new transport protocols that, in many cases, are better attuned to the needs of multimedia, rather than with the transmission control protocol (TCP). For example, when sending digitized video streams, if a few packets are lost, it is likely to be better to interpolate their values rather than hold up additional packets in the stream while the lost packets are retransmitted. When transferring QoS to the commercial Internet, it's clear that the propagation of guarantees from one ISP to another will require a very different business model than those used today. Finally, one must recognize that QoS is going to be a "premium" service, and not every application or every host is going to be permitted to ask for it. It's easy to believe that institutions connected to a network offering QoS will want to use these guarantees to make interactive distance education possible, but not necessarily to permit a student in a dormitory to transmit a video of his or her fish tank at high quality in real time. Somehow, reservation requests will need to be authenticated by a management authority at each participating Internet 2 site, introducing an unprecedented coupling between high-level concepts like organizational delegation of authority and low-level network service requests.

The second essential new network service is multicasting: the ability to deliver parsimoniously an information flow to a number of destinations. This process is perhaps most easily illustrated by an example. Suppose we have the following network configuration:

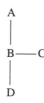

Assume that host A is sending a video broadcast (many packets per second) to hosts C and D. One way to do that would be to set up two connections, one to C and one to D. Each packet emitted by A would then be sent twice, once from A to B to C and then again from A to B to D. Another approach would be to make C and D a multicast group and to have B recognize this entity. Then A could send one copy of the packet to B; and B could duplicate it, sending one copy to C and another copy to D. This process would halve the number of packets that need to be sent from A to B.

Basically, multicasting implements the support of a protocol (IGMP, the Internet group membership protocol) that allows hosts such as C and D to join or leave a multicast group (which has a multicast group address) and support in the basic IP protocol that allows A to send packets not just to individual hosts but to all members of a multicast group. Supporting this process are some very complex routing algorithms that permit intermediate systems along the way—such as B in this very simple example—to recognize that they are branch points in a multicast tree and that they need to duplicate packets and send them out in several directions.

Note that one way to think of multicasting is as a sort of directed broadcast. In this example, A is broadcasting to a group of receivers that includes C and D. But the more general case is really characterized by group membership: C and D might also be transmitting to the rest of the group as well.

Further, multicasting and QoS may well need to be used together. For example, A, C, and D as members of a multicast group may need to exchange interactive multimedia data subject to QoS constraints. This gets very complex very quickly: Each time a host joins or leaves a multicast group, this may change the characterization of the QoS levels that are possible within the multicast group.

Again, there are many research problems related to multicasting. Not only are there the interactions with quality of service, but there are questions of scale. Suppose that multicasting is supporting a very large scale simulation, with membership in multicasting groups correlated to geographic locale. There may be hundreds of thousands of hosts involved, and one question is how quickly the network can respond to group join and leave requests. Another problem is reliable multicasting. End-to-end protocols to permit the reliable distribution of content via multicast groups is also a research problem, and solutions that work well in the unicast (TCP) case, such as time-outs and acknowledgments, do not scale gracefully to large, dynamic multicasting groups.

It should be clear that multicasting is a cornerstone technology for the distribution of multimedia across the Internet in advanced applications, as well as for collaborative applications involving simulation or shared capture and processing of telemetry.

Advanced Applications

Obviously, we don't know the full range of advanced applications that the new networking test beds will enable. It will be defined by the ingenuity of researchers in many fields. And it may well be that the most important emerging applications are in areas as yet unconsidered, much as the emergence of the graphical Web browsers through the National Center for Supercomputing

Applications' development of Mosaic, as the Internet moved to DS3 speed, surprised almost everyone. But some general comments can be made about applications already under development or in the planning stages.

It is clear that Internet 2 and similar test bed networks will support the delivery of multimedia content more readily than can the commodity Internet, due to the greatly increased bandwidth. This means that digital libraries containing video, images, and audio materials will be practical resources. The transmission of video for lectures, seminars, and similar events should be relatively routine, as should the delivery of distance education. This is a very direct extrapolation of what is possible now on the current Internet, where it is possible to deliver streamed video or audio at moderate resolution by buffering ahead to compensate for network delays. However, the much greater responsiveness that should be possible in the new networks will lend a very different and more casual character to the use of audio and video materials.

But the availability of QoS and multicasting services means that not only can this type of content be transmitted, but, more importantly, it can be used in a truly interactive mode for teaching, conferencing, and collaboration. Unpredictable delays have made this service virtually impossible on the current Internet. These services will be the foundation for highly interactive distance education applications or for the construction of collaborative environments that weave together audio and video conferencing, shared interactive whiteboards, data visualization, and other techniques. Highly interactive graphical user interfaces will also be commonplace and will include more routine use of data visualization and visual navigation systems for such applications as statistical analysis and information retrieval. Extreme examples of these graphical interfaces will be systems involving immersive virtual reality or immersive graphics, such as the linked cave visualization environments currently under development.

Multiparty simulations and interactive games should be feasible, as should multisite control of experimental equipment and capture and analysis of data from scientific apparatus, such as telescopes, particle accelerators, and earth-observing satellites. I believe that very large scale, distributed simulations and educational or recreational games are an underestimated source of novel applications.

I believe that we will see an exploration of the various roles that multicasting can play in data distribution to widely scattered communities for such applications as updating software or databases or for driving the activities of communities of software agents. We can look forward to more-extensive experiments in systems built upon large-scale, distributed, agent-based economies and ecologies.

Finally, Internet 2 should offer a hospitable context for new experiments in large-scale, distributed database searching and federation and in high-performance applications involving such techniques as data mining. These applications need to move large amounts of data rapidly from one site to another in response to user queries. Although they are possible on the existing commercial Internet, the greater speed offered by Internet 2 should make such approaches practical for a much larger range of interactive applications.

Conclusion

Internet 2 and the NGI program will have several important effects. Most fundamentally, they will reinvigorate the development of advanced applications within the research and education communities by providing a test bed offering sophisticated network services and high bandwidth to support the creation and experimental deployment of these applications. They will give the research and education communities a renewed control over the design and engineering priorities for networking in order to advance the development of this new generation of applications. This community will continue to meet the needs of science, scholarship, research, and education, rather than trying to develop applications within networks shaped primarily by the demands of commercial and consumer-oriented networking.

Over a somewhat longer time frame, these programs will ensure that a portfolio of new applications is available for the consumer and commercial worlds to motivate the continued evolution of the commodity Internet. And they will guarantee a base of technology and engineering knowledge for new network services needed by the new applications, ready to be applied when these services are moved into the commodity Internet. Internet 2 and NGI are both investments in tomorrow's research and education applications and in next year's new generation of commercial and consumer applications. In this sense, they can be expected to deliver a high payoff over time, not only in enhancing research, teaching, and learning, but in building the U.S. networking industry and the many industries involved in networked information and network applications and in enhancing the use of networking technology and applications across all sectors of our industrial base and our society at large.

Library Networking and Cooperation in 1997

Kate Nevins
Executive Director
Southeastern Library Network (SOLINET)

Bonnie Juergens
Executive Director
AMIGOS Bibliographic Council

Networking in 1997 continued to be dominated by the increasing role of the Internet in the provision of library services. Earlier authors of this annual review have noted this dominance.[1] Following this trend, networks spent 1997 focused on the adoption and effective use of the Internet and Internet-based resources. Perhaps most significant during the last year has been the widespread efforts of networks to expand the electronic Web-based resources available to patrons over the Internet. This review will analyze this trend in depth. An overview of other networking trends follows this analysis.

Regional Networks Provide Electronic Information Access

Access to electronic information has long been a staple of library programs. The advent of widespread Internet access has provided the necessary infrastructure for libraries to increase their utilization of electronic resources. There were several key developments in 1997.

First, many of the regional networks have greatly expanded their service offerings to include licensing of electronic data. These 16 large state or multistate networks provide a variety of services, including OCLC access, training and continuing education, and group purchasing. Group purchasing programs have typically focused on discounted purchase of such services as hardware, library supplies, and CD-ROM services. The last year saw many of these networks expand their group purchasing programs to include licensing of electronic data files. In some cases, the networks mounted licensed files on servers at their offices and provided access to their member libraries. More typically, the networks licensed databases for remote access using the information vendors' facilities. The regional networks bring a number of benefits to this activity:

- *Volume discounts and favorable terms through shared buying power.* Consolidating the purchasing power of many libraries provides networks with the economic power necessary to obtain discounted pricing and favorable licensing terms. Group licensing is an extension of libraries' long-standing commitment to working together through networks to realize results not possible by individual libraries.

- *Ease of contracting.* Negotiating terms and completing the contracting process is time consuming and labor intensive. Regional networks relieve individual libraries of the need to invest significant staff resources in these activities.

- *Availability of infrastructure.* Networks offer their libraries a variety of services in support of group database licenses. These services include billing and prepayment options, usage analysis, and database training.[2]

Regional network licensing provided a wide variety of databases during 1997. OCLC's suite of databases as provided through FirstSearch is the centerpiece of many networks' licensing programs; $17 million in FirstSearch usage was licensed through regional networks in FY 1996–1997.[3] Additional regional network licensing programs are active. Both state-based networks, such as INCOLSA[4] and the Michigan Library Consortium (MLC)[5], and multistate networks, such as AMIGOS[6] and SOLINET[7], offer a variety of database files, including Cambridge Scientific Abstracts, LEXIS/NEXIS, and Encyclopedia Britannica.

Electronic Library Projects

In addition to the licensing by the regional networks, 1997 saw a continued explosion of consortial and state-based electronic library projects. First described in these pages in 1996, these electronic library projects have a variety of goals, including

- Utilization of the Internet to provide access to information sources
- Provision of electronic holdings for participating libraries
- Information access by librarians and end users
- Implementation and support programs[8]

During 1997 established electronic library programs continued to grow and diversify their offerings. This diversification saw several variations:

- Some groups expanded the types of electronic information content made available to their communities. One of the earliest programs, OhioLINK, made a bold step toward full-text access through a statewide license for electronic access to 1,150 Elsevier Science journals. The license provides more than 500,000 students and faculty in Ohio with electronic access to titles that often have not been available in paper form in their institutions' libraries.[9] However, this model was not received with enthusiasm by some librarians and faculty, whose concerns centered on the price of full-text electronic information.[10]
- Some groups expanded the numbers and types of libraries participating in their electronic library programs. For example, TexShare, in operation since 1994, used increases in funding to expand from its original 52 publicly funded four-year colleges and universities in Texas to include the state's 75 two-year colleges and 57 private institutions of higher learning. TexShare will use $500,000 per year for the licensing of commercial databases.[11] Georgia Libraries Learning Online (GALILEO) expanded beyond its original membership of publicly funded institutions to include private

institutions of higher learning under a grant from the Atlanta-based Woodruff Foundation. Current efforts will expand usage to technical schools and public libraries.[12]

- Some groups pursued shared-system projects to facilitate sharing of information and other cooperative ventures. For example, the Pennsylvania Academic Library Connection Initiative (PALCI) announced plans to install the URSA system to increase the resource-sharing capabilities of its 37 academic-library members. The goal is to mount a virtual union catalog and circulation system.[13] The Committee on Institutional Cooperation (CIC) has a similar project geared to connect the diverse local systems installed in its member libraries.[14]

- Some groups have sought diversification of funding sources to support establishment or expansion of services. A notable example of this creative funding is the work of Indiana libraries to procure funding to provide EBSCO full-text file access by the 5.8 million residents of the state. A total of $1.65 million was obtained by combining state legislative appropriation, LSTA funds, and a grant from the Lilly Foundation.[15]

As established projects grew and diversified, additional networking groups of libraries were formed, largely for the purpose of providing electronic information access to their constituencies. In many cases, these emerging coalitions were modeled on established services.[16] Although they have much in common with established programs—in terms of access to shared electronic resources, provision of a technical infrastructure for the delivery of services, and resource sharing—some of these emerging groups have articulated additional outcomes for their projects. For example, the North Carolina project NC LIVE will also expand electronic access to state government information and provide "a comprehensive, systematic, ongoing program of training for staff in participating libraries."[17] The Big 12 Plus Library Consortium, based at the Linda Hall Library in Kansas City, Missouri, undertakes support for distance education and cooperative collection development, as well as information access.[18] The California Digital Library, undertaken by the University of California, will "license, acquire, develop, and manage all kinds of digital materials, including books, journals, monographs and photographs." This program will also commit to archiving its holdings and training for electronic publishing.[19]

Additional statewide projects started in 1997 include DISCUS (South Carolina), Magnolia (Mississippi), the Florida Distance Learning Initiative, and in Oklahoma, where a three-way coalition of the State Board of Education, the State Regents for Higher Education, and the Oklahoma Department of Libraries will purchase statewide electronic-database access. The advantages of consortial licensing, particularly on a state level, include

- *Procurement of funding.* Groups of libraries can develop and advocate comprehensive proposals for legislative or foundation funding. This type of consolidated funding is often available where funding for individual libraries for the same purpose is not forthcoming.

- *Infrastructure for decision making.* States often bring well-established organizations to the decision-making process, thereby facilitating the practical and political work of starting up projects. For example, NC LIVE was organized by four "communities of interest": public universities, private colleges and universities, community colleges, and public libraries. Each community of interest designated its representatives to the NC LIVE planning process through action by its appropriate association or governance board.[20]
- *High visibility for libraries and their programs among politicians, businesses, and the general public.* For example, the start-up of the Florida Distance Education Program and the GALILEO project in Georgia were supported by extensive coverage in the local press.[21]

Discussions are under way in additional states for the establishment of additional statewide electronic library projects. This trend will undoubtedly continue.

Licensing: The New Tool Kit

As the work of consortia has focused on the licensing of electronic access to a wide variety of information sources, librarians are working to develop licensing skills, facilitate their work with vendors, and decrease the time-consuming and labor-intensive nature of the activity. There were two major developments in this area in 1997: the creation of the working draft "Principles for Licensing Electronic Resources" and the rise of the International Coalition of Library Consortia (ICLC).

The "Principles for Licensing Electronic Resources" were developed jointly by the American Association of Law Libraries (AALL), the American Library Association (ALA), the Association of Academic Health Science Libraries (AAHSL), the Association of Research Libraries (ARL), the Medical Library Association (MLA), and the Special Library Association (SLA). The extremely wide representation of types of libraries in the drafting and reviewing of this document illustrates the wide-reaching importance of licensing for today's libraries and networks. The statement "is intended to guide libraries in negotiating license agreements as well as provide licensors with a sense of the issues of importance to libraries and their user communities in negotiations."[22] The principles provide a legal context for the function of licenses. Fifteen principles are outlined, providing guidance on such topics as intellectual property rights, the role of usage restrictions, appropriate authentication, and archival issues.[23] These principles establish a common understanding among those involved in licensing and provide a tool for librarians to develop the skills necessary to undertake this increasingly critical activity.

Early in 1997 a group of library consortia leaders met in St. Louis to interview senior-level managers from several electronic service providers and convey their collective opinion about the needs and limitations of library consortia as consumers of these services. Originally calling itself the Consortium of Consortia (CoC), this group grew throughout the year to comprise representatives from about 60 library consortia in North America, the United Kingdom, Germany, the

Netherlands, and Australia. Because of its international membership and because the group appears to be evolving into a strong public voice whose message may be better understood and heeded if its name reflects its membership, the CoC formalized itself as the International Coalition of Library Consortia (ICLC) at its February 1998 meeting. The purpose of the ICLC is "keeping its members informed about new electronic information resources, pricing practices of electronic providers and vendors, and other issues of importance to directors and governing boards of consortia."[24]

The ICLC provides a forum for consortia leaders to share information about successes and failures in negotiating with the information provider community. It is growing into a platform from which a now international voice of concern about library access to electronic information may be heard by those providers. By posting information to its Web site, the ICLC is becoming an information resource about licensing issues that can be tapped by library professionals beyond its membership. "Guidelines" and "preferred practices" on a variety of licensing topics will be made available via this Web site, as well as ready access to information about ICLC's more than 60 member consortial groups.

The fact that a couple of informal gatherings at ALA conferences during 1996 resulted in semiannual meetings drawing more than 150 attendees from more than 60 organizations internationally during 1997 attests to the value that the ICLC represents to its members. ICLC consortial groups are committing both time and money to this effort because they believe it lends strength to the library side of licensing for electronic resources.

Access, Access Everywhere

Both the expansion of the role of existing networks into electronic information services and the growth of new networks have done much to expand the availability of information. However, it is increasingly ironic that these networks overlap and sometimes compete for the electronic activity of their members. It is not uncommon for a library to be served by its local consortium, its state-based network, and its regional network. For example, an academic library in the greater Washington, D.C., area might be a member of the Washington Regional Library Consortium (WRLC), the Virtual Library of Virginia (VIVA), and the Association of Southeastern Research Libraries (ASERL), each of which offers it access to the same or similar databases.

This example is repeated by individual libraries across the country. Increasingly, individual libraries will balance financial benefits, available terms and conditions, and loyalty or commitment to various networks when making decisions about acceptance of database offerings. Already such networks as AMIGOS and SOLINET, as well as database aggregators and publishers, are seeing examples of libraries "shopping the options" among consortial group license offerings. While seeking to ensure that the individual library obtains the best cost/feature deal available, this can actually add to the ultimate cost of doing business as middleman networks and vendors commit exponentially more staff and management time to working through the details with many individual members of the consortial groups as well as multiple consortial groups operating on behalf of the same individual libraries. It will be interesting to follow this during the next several years to see if a consolidation of networks, increased collaboration among overlapping networks, or some other rationalization of database procurement occurs.

In one region, efforts at rationalization have begun. Early in 1997 the AMIGOS Board of Trustees created a Consortial Relations Working Group comprised of directors from eight member libraries and network staff who specialize in building coalitions. The working group's purpose is to advise AMIGOS staff on ways that the regional network can assist and work more closely with a wide variety of networks within its boundaries—the "network of networks" model that is evolving in a variety of ways across the United States. The working group's first effort was to identify the many library consortial groups in the Southwest. As a result, AMIGOS will be publishing a directory of approximately 100 consortial groups within its boundaries. Surveys among AMIGOS member libraries indicate that each library belongs to a minimum of three consortial groups (including AMIGOS), and more and more libraries report ten or more "primary" consortial relationships, with the associated commitments and benefits that those relationships engender.

Other Major Networking Developments

Although network and consortial efforts have had a large database-licensing component in 1997, other important activities were also under way. They include:

Continued Deployment of the Internet in Libraries

Studies show that the Internet is being increasingly used in public libraries. A survey sponsored by ALA and the National Commission on Libraries and Information Science (NCLIS) in 1997 showed that more than 60 percent of public libraries offer public access to the Internet, a dramatic increase over the 28-percent level in 1996. However, results varied between rural libraries (44 percent) and metropolitan libraries (64 percent). Moreover, only 13 percent of library systems offer Web access at their branches. ALA President Barbara Ford, "The increase in Internet connections is exciting, but there is still more to be done."[25]

Internet-connected libraries have started innovative programs to extend the reach and increase the utility of the Internet among the communities they serve. These include such ground-breaking projects as

- The University of Illinois, in conjunction with the Lincoln Trails Libraries System, is utilizing a $1.3 million grant from the W. K. Kellogg Foundation and the U.S. Department of Commerce Telecommunications and Information Infrastructure Assistance Program to link low-income households in Urbana and Champaign, Illinois, to the Internet. These households receive free computer equipment and support and low-cost or free access to Prairienet.[26]

- Queens Borough (New York) Public Library provides multilingual access to the Internet through the library's home page. Users can access Internet sites in Chinese, Korean, and Spanish, the major non-English-language groups in Queens. This service brings library services to one-quarter of the borough's population.[27]
- Tacoma (Washington) Public Library has begun a service providing 24-hour Internet access enabling patrons to reserve books and check their library card activity from home. In addition, patrons at all library branches have access to resources previously available only at the main branch.[28]
- The New York State Electronic Doorway Library Network is a joint project of the nine Reference and Research Councils (3R's) in New York. It provides a single online access point to the resources of academic, public, school, and special libraries across the state.[29]
- The Resource Directory of Illinois is available through the ILLINET Web site. The directory provides access to foreign-language and special collections from more than 3,900 libraries in the state.[30]
- The Nashville (Tennessee) Area Library Alliance provides simultaneous searching across the 13 academic and public libraries in the Nashville area. Located items can be requested online under a reciprocal borrowing arrangement to facilitate patron access to materials.[31]

These and the myriad other Internet-based networking projects under way throughout the United States have accomplished three major results: reaching communities previously not served effectively, providing information not previously available, and expanding the availability of existing information through enhanced resource sharing.

Filtering: In with the Good, Out with the Bad?

As libraries and the networks that serve them are increasing the information available to their users, the implications of the broad range of Internet-based resources are becoming clear. One major challenge facing libraries is the availability of materials that could be deemed as inappropriate for some segments of the user community. Networks and individual libraries are grappling with ways to balance the concerns of some parent groups and legislators with the tradition of intellectual freedom and access to information. Brenda Branch, library director of the Austin (Texas) Public Library, spoke for many librarians when she said, "I feel caught, because I am totally supportive of the American Library Association, intellectual freedom, and the First Amendment, but I also have a legal responsibility."[32]

Various courses have been pursued, from designating certain workstations in sheltered locations for unfettered Internet access, to requiring parental permission for Internet access in a library, to the use of filtering software. A logical outgrowth of increased public access to the Web is increased public awareness about the availability of materials that they may find questionable. The issues of filtering and access are certain to continue to loom large.

Interoperability: Out of Many Systems, One

The proliferation of a wide variety of library technology systems and servers in the current highly networked library world results in the challenge of achieving interoperability—that is, how can these systems be made to work together for the access and exchange of information online? Various solutions to this challenge are in operation or under development. Libraries have long utilized Z39.50 to perform searches among Z39.50-compliant systems, and this has become a critical component of much networking. Additional work is under way. The concept of "metadata," data about data, has emerged as a concept for assisting with the searching of widely diverse information sources in differing formats. Within the metadata context is the development of the Dublin Core, a set of data elements designed to be used to describe a wide variety of data objects. When implemented, it allows single searching across more than one database.[33] This and other efforts to streamline access and to bring together information from widely distributed databases will continue as one of the important innovations in networking

There are many examples of projects designed for interoperability of systems. One of the most impressive is the Virtual Library Project of the Committee on Institutional Cooperative (CIC). In conjunction with OCLC, the CIC is providing seamless electronic access to resources located in all 12 participating institutions. A single search is used to search local, consortial, and external resources, mounted on a variety of hardware platforms and running a variety of software. It is transparent to the user what hardware and software are being invoked.[34] Another example is the Monticello Electronic Library Project of SOLINET. This project uses the Dublin Core data elements to create a metadata database to provide access to special collections and state and local government information from around the southeast.[35]

Conclusion

Large-scale networked access to electronic information resources became a central component of much of the networking in 1997. Libraries are adapting their existing networks or establishing new networks to facilitate negotiating and implementation. As this activity continues, libraries are developing the necessary framework and skills for effective adoption of these electronic materials. At the same time, the advent of this type of Internet-based networking is creating challenges in the management and interoperability of electronic information resources. The year saw some important innovations and some trends that bear watching in 1998.

Notes

1. David Brunell, "Library Networking and Cooperation in 1996," *The Bowker Annual Library and Book Trade Almanac*, 42nd ed. (New Providence, N.J.: R. R. Bowker, 1997), p. 243.
2. http://www.solinet.net

3. OCLC, *Annual Report 1996/97: Furthering Access to the World's Information* (Dublin, Onio: OCLC, 1997), p. 3.

4. http://www.palni.edu/incolsa.

5. http://www.mlc.lib.mi.us/services/reference.htm.

6. http://www.amigos.org/aplus.html.

7. http://www.solinet.net.

8. Kate Nevins and Steve Baughman, "Library Networking and Cooperation in 1995," *The Bowker Annual Library and Book Trade Almanac*, 41st ed. (New Providence, N.J.: R. R. Bowker, 1996), pp. 235–246.

9. "Ohio Universities, Elsevier Deal a First in Electronic Journals," *Library Hotline*, vol. 26, no. 21 (May 26, 1997), p. 1.

10. Kenneth N. Gilpin, "Concerns about Aggressive Publishing Giant," *New York Times* (Dec. 29, 1997), p. C2.

11. "Briefly Noted," *Library Hotline*, vol. 26, no. 32, (Aug. 11, 1997), p. 4.

12. http://www.peachnet.edu/galileo/about.html.

13. "Resource Sharing in PA and MD Aided by CPS Systems Solutions," *Library Hotline*, vol. 26, no. 34, (Aug. 25, 1997), p. 6.

14. http://www.cic.net/cic.

15. "Indiana's Virtual Library Plan Begins with EBSCO Contract," *Library Hotline*, vol. 26, no. 8 (March 2, 1998), p. 6.

16. Ralph Lee Scott, "Wired to the World: A Bold Plan for North Carolina," *North Carolina Librarian*, vol. 55, no. 4, (Winter 1997), p. 172.

17. *Ibid.*, p. 4.

18. "People," *Library Hotline*, vol. 27, no. 8, (March 2, 1998), p. 6.

19. "UC's California Digital Library Distributes Holdings Statewide," *Library Hotline*, vol. 26, no. 45, (Nov. 10, 1997), p. 1.

20. Ralph Lee Scott, *op. cit.*, p. 172.

21. "Online Library Link Equal Access: Georgia Schools Team Up to Offer an Information Database Through the Internet," *Atlanta Journal-Constitution* (Sept. 6, 1997), p. C1., and "Students Have Access to Online Library Resources," *Tallahassee Democrat* (Oct. 31, 1997), p. 8B.

22. "Principles for Electronic Licensing Endorsed," *American Libraries,* vol. 29, no. 1 (Jan. 1998), p. 15.

23. http://www.arl.org/scomm/licensing/principles/html.

24. http://Isounix1.library.yale.edu/consortia.

25. "Sharp Increase in Internet Use at Public Libraries," *American Libraries*, vol. 29, no. 1 (Jan. 1998), p. 11.

26. "$1.3 Million Grant to University of IL Links Internet, Low Income Area," *Library Hotline*, vol. 26, no. 43 (Oct. 27, 1997), p. 2.

27. "Briefly Noted," *Library Hotline*, vol. 26, no. 11 (March 17, 1998), p. 8.

28. "Tacoma Public Internet Access Expanded by $189,000 Grant," *Library Hotline*, vol. 26, no. 4 (Oct. 27, 1998), p. 4.

29. "Electronic Doorway Net Link Offers Single Point Access in NY," *Library Hotline*, vol. 26, no. 16 (April 21, 1997), p. 5.

30. "Briefly Noted," *Library Hotline*, vol. 26, no. 39 (Sept. 29, 1997), p. 6.

31. "Simultaneous Catalog Searches Offered by 13 Tenn. Libraries," vol. 26, no. 45 (Nov. 10, 1997), p. 7.

32. Norman Oder, "Krug's Toughest Fight?" *Library Journal*, vol. 28, no. 5, (May 1, 1997), pp. 38–41

33. Clifford Lynch, "The Dublin Core Descriptive Metadata Program: Strategic Implications for Libraries and Networked Information Access," *ARL Newsletter*, no. 196 (Feb. 1998), pp. 5–10.

34. Barbara Allen McFadden, "The CIC Virtual Electronic Library Integrates Resources and Services," *OCLC Newsletter*, (Nov./Dec. 1997), pp. 28–29.

35. http://www.solinet.net.

Part 2
Legislation, Funding, and Grants

Legislation

Legislation and Regulations Affecting Libraries in 1997

Carol C. Henderson
Executive Director, Washington Office, American Library Association

Anne A. Heanue
Associate Director, Washington Office, American Library Association

Significant legislative and regulatory issues in Washington, D.C., made 1997 another busy and important year for libraries. Major legislative achievements for the library community included funding at $146,340,000 for the Library Services and Technology Act in fiscal year (FY) 1998—a $10 million increase over predecessor programs in FY 1997—and a unanimous decision from the Federal Communications Commission to provide discounts beginning in 1998 on a wide range of telecommunications services for the nation's libraries and schools.

In the second session of the 105th Congress, the debate will intensify over whether and how to update copyright law to reflect and encourage the development of digital networks. A legislative proposal to revise Title 44 of the United States Code, the statute governing printing and dissemination of government information, is expected early in the session. Legislation is pending for a reading initiative intended to help ensure that children can read well and independently not later than the third grade. Authorization for the Higher Education Act has been extended until September 1998 in order to complete the reauthorization process.

Library Services and Technology Act

The Library Services and Technology Act (LSTA), the major federal grant program designed specifically for libraries, revised the Library Services and Construction Act and the library sections of the Higher Education Act. LSTA, along with existing museum grant programs, is administered by the Institute of Museum and Library Services (IMLS). The institute is an independent agency created by the Museum and Library Services Act of 1996 (P.L. 104-208). The act moved federal library programs from the Department of Education and combined them with the museum programs of the former Institute of Museum Services.

LSTA is authorized for six years at $150 million (the ceiling for actual funding) for FY 1997 and "such sums" for each year through 2002. Most of the funds are allocated to state library agencies for statewide services or subgrants for technological innovation or electronic-linkage purposes, or for outreach services. Any activity funded through the state-based program can involve public, school, academic, research, or, in some cases, special libraries.

The law provides that 3.75 percent of LSTA funding will be used for a national leadership program, including library education and training, research and demonstration projects, preservation and digitization, and joint museum-library projects. The grant guidelines for this new program were developed and published (see the IMLS Web site, http://www.imls.fed.us/guidelines/natlead.pdf). The deadline for applications for FY 1998 was April 17, 1998.

Technical Amendments

Several technical and conforming amendments to the Library Services and Technology Act requested by IMLS were given final congressional approval and signed into law (P.L. 105-128, Museum and Library Services Technical and Conforming Amendments of 1997) by President Clinton on December 1, 1997. The amendments include adjustments to the appointment authority of the IMLS director, a clarification that special libraries are included in the definition of *library*, a clarification of the maintenance-of-effort requirement, a clarification that national leadership awards could include cooperative agreements, adjustments to the provisions for Native American library services, and the correction of a typographical error.

Appropriations for Fiscal Year 1998

The end of the first session of the 105th Congress was marked by avowals of bipartisan agreement but shadowed by partisan wrangling. The FY 1998 Labor, Health and Human Services and Education Appropriations bill was signed into law (P.L. 105-78) by the president on November 13. This is the second consecutive year that Congress has approved major increases for education. This year's increase is $3.2 billion over the funding level for education programs in FY 1997.

The Library Services and Technology Act is funded at $146,340,000 for FY 1998, a $10 million increase over predecessor programs in FY 1997.

ESEA Title VI, Innovative Education Program Strategies, which some schools use for school library materials, was funded at $350 million, as passed by the House, rather than $310 million, the FY 1997 level and the amount passed by the Senate.

For new reading programs, conferees provided $210 million for a child literacy initiative, with funding becoming available on October 1, 1998, only if authorizing legislation passes by July 1, 1998.

On November 14, 1997, President Clinton signed H.R. 2107, the Interior Appropriations bill, which included funding for the National Endowment for the Arts (NEA) and the National Endowment for the Humanities (NEH) (P.L. 105-83). At the bill signing, the president released a statement expressing concern about the low level of funding for these agencies, which "provide important cultural, educational, and artistic programs for communities across America." Funding for NEA was set at $98 million, $1.5 million below FY 1997. Funding for NEH was $110.7 million. This bill also included $23.3 million for museum grants administered by the Institute of Museum and Library Services.

The legislation funding the Departments of Commerce, Justice, and State, H.R. 2267, was signed on November 13 (P.L. 105-119). Included is funding for the Telecommunications and Information Infrastructure Assistance Program (TIIAP) at $20 million.

The Legislative Branch Appropriations bill, H.R. 2016, was signed by the president on September 9 (P.L. 105-45). The Government Printing Office (GPO) FY 1998 appropriation for the Superintendent of Documents (SuDocs) is $29,077,000. The GPO SuDocs operation includes the Federal Depository Library System. The Library of Congress will have available appropriations of $376,719,000, which includes the authority to spend receipts of $30,295,000. This amounts to an overall increase of 4.4 percent over FY 1997 funding.

Higher Education Act Reauthorization

Reauthorization of the Higher Education Act, begun early in 1997, had not been completed by Congress at year's end. The current law was extended for one year to September 1998 in order to complete the reauthorization process. The various approaches to HEA reauthorization by Congress, the administration, and the higher education community are subtly different but can all be characterized as a "streamlining" approach to the act.

In the last few months before adjournment, congressional activities conducted on HEA reauthorization targeted discussions on reorganization and consolidation of different student loan, financial aid, and related tax programs in order to make higher education more affordable for all.

Title VI, International Education, an area of some concern to academic libraries, previously included the international periodicals program (section 607) and the learning resource center program. Debate continued at year's end about how this title, especially section 607, would be addressed as reauthorization discussions move forward in the second session.

Government Information Programs

Depository Library Program

As Congress began considering various options to revise the law governing government printing, information dissemination, and depository libraries, the American Library Association (ALA) organized an interassociation working group to develop a legislative proposal to amend the Depository Library Act (also known as Title 44 of the United States Code, the statute that governs printing and public dissemination of government information). Seven library organizations—American Association of Law Libraries, American Library Association and representatives of several of its divisions and round tables, Association of

Research Libraries, Chief Officers of State Library Agencies, Medical Library Association, Special Libraries Association, and Urban Libraries Council—joined in the effort to develop a legislative proposal intended to improve public access to government information. The proposal, initially delivered to Congress in June and refined in December, included a draft bill, the Federal Information Access Act of 1997. The goals, principles, and legislative proposal the working group has developed can be found on the Web at http://www.lib.berkeley.edu/ GODORT.

During 1997, as staff of the Joint Committee on Printing worked on a draft bill to revise the printing and publication statute, ALA and other library groups participated actively in the policy debates. A bill was expected to be ready for introduction when the 105th Congress reconvened in January 1998, with hearings expected.

Electronic Records

On October 22 U.S. District Judge Paul L. Friedman declared null and void a regulation issued by Archivist of the United States John W. Carlin. The decision came in *Public Citizen* v. *Carlin*. On December 19 the government gave notice that it would appeal the decision. The case involved a challenge to a regulation issued by Archivist Carlin in 1995 that gave all federal agencies blanket approval to destroy all types of electronic mail and word-processing records if paper copies exist, without any review of the value of the electronic records. The ALA Washington Office coordinated ALA's participation as a coplaintiff in *Public Citizen* v. *Carlin* with the American Historical Association, Organization of American Historians, and others. Plaintiffs were represented by Public Citizen.

Intellectual Freedom Issues

In a landmark decision on June 26 the Supreme Court ruled the Communications Decency Act (CDA) unconstitutional by unanimous vote. The CDA, Title V of the Telecommunications Act of 1996, was intended to protect minors from exposure to indecent material on the Internet. If enforced, the law would have limited communication on the Internet to only what is suitable for minors. In its ruling, the court agreed with ALA and the other plaintiffs that the law was so broad and poorly defined that it violated the free-speech rights of adults.

ALA was the lead plaintiff in a suit filed by the Citizens Internet Empowerment Coalition, which included journalists, publishers, parents, online providers, and other groups. The association's involvement was spearheaded by the ALA Office for Intellectual Freedom. The suit challenged the act on the grounds that it was overly broad and so vaguely worded that it could subject librarians and other members of the public to criminal prosecution for posting materials online that are legal in other media.

The ALA case was consolidated with a similar suit filed by the American Civil Liberties Union (ACLU) known as *Reno* v. *ACLU*. On June 12, 1996, a three-judge federal court panel in Philadelphia unanimously ruled that the

Communications Decency Act would unconstitutionally restrict free speech on the Internet. That decision was affirmed by the U.S. Supreme Court.

A number of bills or amendments aimed at protecting children or addressing pornography on the Internet were proposed or introduced. The bill that attracted the most attention was introduced at the very end of the first session. S. 1482, introduced by Senator Dan Coats (R-Ind.), would prohibit commercial distribution on the Web of material that is "harmful to minors." According to Coats, S. 1482 is intended to reflect the parameters laid out by the Supreme Court in its decision on the CDA. The bill was carried over to 1998, and hearings were expected early in the session.

Intellectual Property Issues

Copyright Update for Electronic Networks

In November Representatives Rick Boucher (D-Va.) and Tom Campbell (R-Calif.) introduced the Digital Era Copyright Enhancement Act of 1997, H.R. 3048. The legislation, designed to update the U.S. Copyright Act for the electronic networked environment, would make clear that the needs of both information proprietors and consumers must be protected. In September Senator John Ashcroft (R-Mo.) introduced a similar bill, the Digital Copyright Clarification and Technology Act, S. 1146. ALA—together with other library associations, education groups, and other partners—helped develop these bills, which would update several key copyright provisions for the digital environment. These bills are likely to be considered in the second session of the 105th Congress along with other proposals related to U.S. implementation of the international copyright treaties adopted in December 1996 under the auspices of the World Intellectual Property Organization (WIPO). For more information, visit the Web sites of WIPO (www.wipo.org) and the Digital Future Coalition (www.dfc.org), of which ALA is a member.

Database Protection

The Collection of Information Antipiracy Act, H.R. 2652, was introduced in October by Representative Howard Coble (R-N.C.), chair of the Courts and Intellectual Property Subcommittee. The bill is intended to supplement current copyright law—which already protects databases that meet the low threshold of "originality" established in the Supreme Court's Feist decision—by allowing database proprietors to seek damages from any party who "misappropriates" all or part of such material without authorization. ALA and other library groups expressed serious concerns about the bill at an October hearing by Coble's subcommittee.

Specifically, the Coble bill has no limit on the duration of protection, includes nothing comparable to fair-use provisions, would apply not to "time-sensitive" portions but to the entire contents of a database, and has an extremely broad definition of what is protected. Further developments are expected in the second session of the 105th Congress.

International Book Fellows Program

After ALA was informed in early 1997 that the United States Information Agency (USIA) planned to eliminate funding for the Library Book Fellows Program beginning in FY 1998, several ALA members and staff met with USIA officials to ask them to reverse their decision. Director Joseph Duffey responded by offering to share the cost of the program with ALA on a 50-50 basis ($225,000 from USIA, $225,000 from ALA and private resources). ALA President Barbara Ford wrote to USIA indicating ALA's commitment to working to find support for the Library Fellows Program. During the remainder of 1997 ALA pursued private-sector funding possibilities, but without success.

The ALA Washington Office monitored the progress of the legislation that would have restructured the U.S. foreign-policy agencies, including USIA. Legislation merging USIA with the State Department failed to pass in the final days of the first session of the 105th Congress.

House and Senate negotiators will try to break a stalemate and clear the legislation in the early part of the second session.

Juvenile Justice Crime Bill

A juvenile justice crime bill, S.10, was introduced by Senator Orrin G. Hatch (R-Utah). The bill focuses primarily on judicial remedies, sentencing and detention. It was approved by the Senate Judiciary Committee on October 9, but no floor action was taken before the end of the session.

H.R. 1818, introduced by Representative Frank Riggs (R-Calif.), includes a juvenile delinquency prevention block grant program. This bill was approved by the House, but no action has been taken yet by the Senate. Because the two bills are different, but related, it is possible they may be merged into one bill. Some libraries have been successful in the past in obtaining grants for juvenile programs from Juvenile Delinquency Prevention funds. The ALA Washington Office monitored various juvenile justice legislation to determine the possibility for including libraries in block grant proposals.

Next Generation Internet

Of the $100 million proposed by the Clinton administration for a Next Generation Internet (NGI) initiative, involving research and development programs across federal agencies, Congress approved $95 million for FY 1998. The agencies involved are the Defense Advanced Research Projects Agency ($42 million), National Science Foundation ($23 million), National Aeronautics and Space Administration ($10 million), the National Institute of Standards and Technology ($5 million), the Department of Energy ($10 million), and the National Institutes of Health ($5 million).

However, approximately $33 million of the appropriation was not new. The Department of Energy's funds represent an agency reallocation, and the National Science Foundation (NSF) funding, although increased significantly from the $10 million in the budget request, must be taken from a fund held by Network

Solutions, Inc. (NSI). That fund came from user fees charged for domain name registration. NSI was operating under an NSF contract that specified that excess income be held aside and put in a fund to be used for improving the Internet.

At the end of 1997 both the fund and the issue of domain name registration had become controversial, with lawsuits pending. In June, Carol Henderson, on behalf of the ALA Washington Office, accepted an invitation to do a presentation on the NGI to the Presidential Advisory Committee on High Performance Computing and Communications, Information Technology, and Next Generation Internet. Additionally, ALA staff met with administration officials on NGI and related issues and participated in the High Performance Computing and Communications (HPCC) Coalition, a group of industry, education, and other groups interested in HPCC and NGI issues.

Postal Rate Case

The U.S. Postal Service (USPS) proposed a 28.57 percent increase for the first pound in the library rate as part of its July 10 request to the Postal Rate Commission (PRC) to change postal rates, fees, and classifications. This would mean a 26.53 percent increase in a typical three-pound library rate package. If the USPS proposal is implemented, the library rate for the three-pound package would be $2.48, a 117.5 percent increase in a little more than three years. The proposed increases for the library rate are much higher than the adjustments USPS says average 4.5 percent across the board for all types of domestic mail. USPS anticipated that the new rates would be effective in April or May 1998.

On August 6, 1997, ALA joined as an intervenor in USPS's rate case. ALA and the Alliance of Nonprofit Mailers requested a delay until USPS submitted a rate request that complies with the PRC's rules for rate-setting requests, and interested parties receive an adequate opportunity to review the material and submit questions based on the USPS refiled case. On November 4 the PRC denied the joint motion of ALA and the Alliance of Nonprofit Mailers requesting a stay of the pending postal rate case. Although the PRC plans to permit additional time to allow participants the opportunity for further inquiries, it intends to complete the remainder of the proceeding within its designated ten-month work period.

Reading Excellence Act

On October 22 the Reading Excellence Act, H.R. 2614, was approved in amended form by the House Committee on Education and the Workforce. Committee Chair William Goodling (R-Pa.) introduced the bill on October 6 as an alternative to H.R. 1516, the administration's America Reads Challenge initiative. No action was taken on the reading legislation by the Senate, but the House approved the bill by voice vote on November 8. The Senate is likely to consider the bill in the second session of the 105th Congress.

Two library amendments offered by Representative Dale Kildee (D-Mich.) were adopted by voice vote of the House committee. One would add a school or public library that offers reading or literacy programs for children or families to the list of optional members of a state's Reading and Literacy Partnership. The other would give a funding priority to applicants that demonstrate they have a contractual association with one or more public libraries providing reading or literacy services to preschool children or to preschool children and their families. Because these two amendments established library eligibility, they were the most important of a package of six amendments developed by the ALA Washington Office, proposed by Representative Kildee, and supported in a letter to chairman Goodling by Representative Randy "Duke" Cunningham (R-Calif.).

Telecommunications

Universal Service and Discounted Telecommunications Rates for Libraries and Schools

On May 7, 1997, the Federal Communications Commission (FCC) unanimously voted in favor of up to $2.25 billion annually in discounts on telecommunications services for libraries and schools. The new rules mandate discounts ranging from 20 to 90 percent, with deeper discounts for libraries and schools in rural, high-cost, and low-income communities. The discounts are expected to provide up to $2.25 billion annually, beginning January 1, 1998.

The new FCC rules are intended to ensure that schools and libraries will be able to afford telecommunications services for students and library users and give the flexibility to choose from the most basic to the most advanced commercially available services. The discounted rates address one of the most critical factors affecting library access: ongoing communications costs.

The ruling represented the culmination of an 18-month public FCC proceeding to implement Section 254, the universal service section, of the Telecommunications Act of 1996. ALA worked with a diverse range of groups, including the Education and Library Networks Coalition (EdLiNC), government agencies, and industry on the ruling and the subsequent implementation of the FCC order.

Despite the continued legal efforts of several major telephone companies to delay the January 1, 1998, start date, the libraries and schools program moved forward. On July 18, 1997, the FCC directed the establishment of the Schools and Libraries Corporation (SLC) and the Universal Service Administration Corporation (USAC). The SLC administers the process for libraries and schools applying for universal-service discounts and the USAC administers collections for and disbursements from the new universal-service fund.

In September 1997 the respective boards of the SLC and the USAC were named and met for the first time. Kathleen (K. G.) Ouye, city librarian at the San Mateo, California, Public Library and library representative to the new SLC board, was elected the SLC's first chairperson. In December 1997 the application forms for libraries and schools were released and mailed out to all library and school systems. Completed applications will be posted on the SLC Web site beginning in January 1998 for competitive bidding by service providers that want to do business with eligible libraries and schools.

Table 1 / Funding for Federal Library and Related Programs, FY 1998
(figures in thousands)

	FY 1997 Appropriation	FY 1998 Appropriation
Library Programs		
GPO Superintendent of Documents	29,077	29,077
Library of Congress	361,896 [1]	376,719 [2]
Library Services and Technology Act (or predecessor)	136,369 [3]	146,340
National Agricultural Library	19,000	19,000
National Commission on Libraries and Information Science	897	1,000
National Library of Medicine (includes MLAA)	151,103	161,185
Library-Related Programs		
Adult Education and Literacy	354,562	360,551
ESEA Title I: Education for Disadvantaged	7,689,000	8,012,112
Part B, Even Start	101,997	124,000
ESEA Title II: Eisenhower Professional Development		
Part A, Federal activities	13,342	23,300
Part B, State grants	310,000	335,000
ESEA Title III: Educational Technology	305,000	584,035
Part A, (includes Technology Literacy Challenge Fund)	266,965	541,000
Part B, Star Schools	30,000	34,000
ESEA Title VI: Innovative Education Program Strategies (State grants)	310,000	350,000
Education of Handicapped Children (State grants)	3,783,685	4,531,695
Educational Research (OERI)	72,785	72,567
Educational Statistics	50,000	59,000
Educational Assessment	32,623	35,471
Goal 2000	491,000	491,000
HEA Title III: Institutional Development	194,846	210,945
HEA Title IV-C: College Work-Study	830,000	830,000
HEA Title VI: International Education	59,751	60,351
HEA Title X-A: Postsecondary Education Improvement Fund	18,000	25,200
Inexpensive Book Distribution (RIF)	10,265	12,000
Literacy Initiative (proposed legislation such as America Reads)	—	210,000
Museum Grants	22,000	23,280 [4]
NTIA Information Infrastructure Grants (TIIAP)	21,490	20,000
National Archives and Records Administration	196,963	205,167
National Endowment for the Arts	99,494	98,000
National Endowment for the Humanities	110,000	110,700
National Historical Publications and Records Commission	5,000	5,500
Next Generation Internet (NGI)	—	95,000 [5]

[1] Includes authority to obligate $30.138 million in receipts

[2] Includes authority to obligate $30.3 million in receipts

[3] Includes appropriations for LSCA and HEA Title II

[4] Includes $1 million for joint library/museum projects under LSTA National Leadership Projects grants.

[5] Includes funding for NGI divided among Department of Defense, National Science Foundation, NASA, Department of Commerce, Department of Energy, and the National Institutes of Health.

Legislation and Regulations Affecting Publishing in 1997

Allan R. Adler

Vice President, Legal and Governmental Affairs
Association of American Publishers

In the first session of the 105th Congress, the interests of book and journal publishers were caught up in a number of legislative initiatives in the areas of intellectual property protection, freedom of expression, new technologies, educational funding, and postal matters. The following is a brief summary.

Intellectual Property

No Electronic Theft (NET) Act

The No Electronic Theft legislation (H.R. 2265) was signed into law by President Clinton in November 1997 (P.L. 105-147). Popularly known as "the *LaMacchia* bill," it closed a loophole in the criminal infringement provisions of the Copyright Act that was exposed when a federal court ruled that, regardless of the economic harm caused to the copyright holder, willful infringement of copyrighted works could not be criminally prosecuted if there were no personal financial gain on the part of the infringer.

To remedy the problem, the NET Act expands the statutory definition of "financial gain" in the Copyright Act to cover "receipt, or expectation of receipt, of anything of value, including the receipt of other copyrighted works," thus embracing bartering and other unconventional arrangements that facilitate the operations of pirate bulletin boards and Web sites. It also amends the criminal infringement standard in the Copyright Act to criminalize willful infringement, including infringement by electronic means, which causes more than $1,000 in damages during any 180-day period, regardless of whether the infringer committed the acts for commercial advantage or for private financial gain. In addition, the act clarifies the "willfulness" element of criminal infringement by stating that "evidence of reproduction or distribution of a copyrighted work, by itself, shall not be sufficient to establish willful infringement."

The Association of American Publishers (AAP) participated in the crucial House Judiciary Committee negotiations that readied the bill for House and Senate passage.

Copyright Clarification Act

Noncontroversial "technical corrections" copyright clarification legislation (H.R. 672) was also signed into law by President Clinton in November (P.L. 105-80). Among other things, it corrected certain errors in the Copyright Restoration Act, enacted as part of the 1994 legislation to implement the "Uruguay Round" accord under the General Agreement on Tariffs and Trade (GATT), which restored copyright protection in the United States for certain foreign works that had fallen into the public domain. From AAP's perspective, the most significant error corrected would have precluded U.S. creators of derivative works from continuing to exploit them when copyright protection in the underlying foreign works was restored under GATT. In addition, the legislation clarified the authority of the Copyright Office to raise its fees once within any five-year period to cover reasonable costs incurred plus a reasonable inflation adjustment.

Copyright Term Extension

Legislation (H.R. 2589/S. 505) to extend the basic terms of copyright protection under U.S. law by 20 years in order to match the duration of protection provided in member countries of the European Union was approved by the House Intellectual Property Subcommittee in October. It was expected to be reported by the full House Judiciary Committee early in 1998 assuming that it was not once again caught up as a hostage in the fight over statutory changes on music licensing for the benefit of restaurant owners.

AAP worked with House and Senate staff to ensure that provisions on "termination rights" were narrowly crafted. At the request of the bill's sponsors, AAP also worked with the Register of Copyrights and representatives of the library, educational, and archival communities in an effort to reach consensus on an exemption provision that would, under certain conditions, permit these communities to make specified uses of copyrighted works during the extension period without having to obtain permission from the rights holders. Although these negotiations abruptly broke off on the eve of a Senate Judiciary Committee markup, the pending House and Senate versions of the legislation contained an exemption provision based on the Register of Copyrights' version of the near-negotiated provision and was acceptable to AAP.

WIPO Copyright Treaties Implementing Legislation

For the first six months of 1997 AAP worked with other copyright industries and then with the Clinton administration to draft implementing legislation for the two copyright treaties adopted by the United States and nearly 100 other nations under the auspices of the World Intellectual Property Organization (WIPO) in December 1996.

The legislation (H.R. 2281/S. 1121), which was introduced in August and was the subject of House and Senate hearings in September, would change U.S. law only as necessary to comply with the treaties' requirements that signatory nations must provide (1) "adequate legal protection and effective legal remedies" against the circumvention of effective technological measures used by copyright holders to protect their rights in copyrighted works and (2) "adequate and effective legal remedies" against the knowing removal or alteration of electronic rights management information. AAP supports the legislation as introduced.

The circumvention provisions of the legislation are hotly contested by consumer equipment manufacturers, "home recording rights" advocates, and the library and educational communities' Digital Future Coalition. These groups oppose the legislation's prohibition on trafficking in devices and components that facilitate circumvention, claiming that such a proscription will interfere with the design and production of multi-use computers and other legitimate equipment while permitting copyright holders to prevent fair use of protected works. They want to limit the legislation's prohibition to circumvention conduct, while explicitly exempting circumvention that facilitates fair use.

In September AAP testified before the House Intellectual Property Subcommittee in support of the administration's implementing legislation. AAP continues to work with congressional members and staff to advance the legislation toward enactment.

Online Service Provider (OSP) Liability

The liability of online service providers (OSPs) for online copyright infringement committed by third-party users of their services and networks is not an issue that needs to be addressed in the WIPO implementing legislation to ensure U.S. compliance as a party to the treaties. Nevertheless, as a result of the political clout of the telephone companies that are rapidly becoming leading providers of Internet access and other online services, key House and Senate leaders have told the copyright community that implementing legislation cannot move forward unless the community works with them to develop separate legislation addressing the OSPs' concerns regarding the scope of their potential liability.

In the House, negotiations begun in December under the guidance of Rep. Bob Goodlatte (R-Va.) focused on revising a bill (H.R. 2180) by Subcommittee Chairman Howard Coble (R-N.C.), but failed to produce anything approaching a consensus. It was expected that Goodlatte and/or Coble might introduce a different bill in an effort to facilitate a subcommittee markup early in 1998. In the Senate, separate but so far equally unsuccessful negotiations have focused on drafts produced by the staff of Sen. Orrin G. Hatch (R-Utah).

AAP, in concert with other copyright industry representatives, has urged that OSP liability legislation should provide OSPs with limited relief from liability for monetary damages while preserving the availability of injunctive relief for copyright holders as an incentive for OSP cooperation in detecting and preventing infringing activities online. Although the copyright community has been willing to try to devise an exemption from liability for OSPs when they are acting as "mere conduits," it has rejected the contention that OSPs should have no obligations regarding third-party infringements except where they have "actual knowledge" of infringing activity.

Digital Copyright "Wish List"

The proposed Digital Copyright Clarification and Technology Education Act (S. 1146) introduced by Sen. John Ashcroft (R-Mo.) and the similar proposed Digital Era Copyright Enhancement Act (H.R. 3048) introduced by Reps. Rick Boucher (D-Va.) and Tom Campbell (R-Calif.) pose significant challenges for advocates of strong copyright protection and, particularly, for supporters of pending legislation to implement the WIPO copyright treaties (H.R. 2281/S. 1121).

Both bills contain "wish list" proposals by the library and educational communities' Digital Future Coalition, including amendments to expand provisions of the Copyright Act concerning fair use, library/archive exemptions, and distance learning. Both bills also contain weak, objectionable language offered as an alternative to the key "anticircumvention" provisions of the WIPO legislation. In addition, S. 1146 contains an objectionable proposal to provide extraordinary relief from copyright infringement liability for online service providers (OSPs), which does not appear in H.R. 3048. The House bill, however, contains two provisions that do not appear in Sen. Ashcroft's bill but raise substantial concerns within the copyright community. The first represents a kind of "honor-system" attempt to maintain the first-sale doctrine in the digital environment by depending on the willingness of the online transmitter of a copy of a copyrighted work to destroy his or her own copy of the work immediately upon transmission. The second provision, familiar to AAP representatives involved in the drafting of a proposed new Article 2B for the Uniform Commercial Code, would provide that non-negotiable license terms associated with the distribution of a work to the public would be unenforceable under state and common law to the extent that they limit the use of uncopyrightable materials or would restrict the limitations on the exclusive rights of copyright holders under the Copyright Act.

Letters have been sent by AAP and six other copyright industry trade associations urging the leaders and members of the House and Senate Judiciary Committees, respectively, to oppose H.R. 3048 and S. 1146.

Freedom of Expression

AAP is monitoring efforts to enact two pieces of legislation that do not directly address books and journals but raise serious First Amendment questions regarding content-based restrictions on the dissemination of materials through the Internet and other electronic media.

Online Pornography

In the wake of the Supreme Court's ruling holding the "indecent materials" provisions of the Communications Decency Act (CDA) to be unconstitutional restrictions on First Amendment speech, Sen. Dan Coats (R-Ind.) introduced a bill (S. 1482) that he believes would avoid the constitutional flaws of the CDA while achieving its basic purpose of limiting the availability of unacceptably sexually-explicit materials to children on the Internet.

S. 1482, which was expected to be considered by the Senate Commerce Committee in March, would amend the Communications Decency Act to require persons engaged in the commercial distribution, through the World Wide Web or otherwise in interstate or foreign commerce, of material that is "harmful to minors" to restrict access to such materials by persons under 17 years old. Enforceable by civil and criminal penalties, the bill would also require the Department of Justice and the Federal Communications Commission to make a definition of such material available on their respective Web sites.

Children's Protection from Violent Programming Act

In September the Senate Commerce Committee approved legislation (S. 363) that would make it unlawful for anyone to distribute to the public any violent video programming not blockable by electronic means on the basis of its violent content, during hours when children are reasonably likely to compose a substantial portion of the audience. The bill, which is expected to come before the full

Senate late in 1998, requires the Federal Communications Commission to implement this prohibition through regulations that would exempt premium and pay-per-view cable TV programming as well as programming (including news and sporting events) whose distribution does not conflict with the bill's objective of protecting children from the negative influences of violent video programming.

New Technologies

Encryption

Encryption—the use of complex numerical sequences to "scramble" electronic transmissions in order to preserve the confidentiality, integrity, or authenticity of communications—is generally viewed as a key tool for providing the privacy, security, and intellectual property protection necessary to achieve the promise of the Internet as a thriving medium for commerce, education, and entertainment. However, the government's fear that unbreakable encryption will be used to further terrorist or other criminal enterprises has caused it to place export restrictions on the most advanced and secure forms of encryption, despite strenuous objections from American industry that such restrictions hamper their ability to compete in a global marketplace where strong encryption remains available to foreign competitors.

U.S. software and hardware companies have been locked in a dispute with the Clinton administration over the latter's proposals to ease the export restrictions if makers of encryption technology (and, therefore, users) agree to a "key escrow" system requiring them to give a government-approved agent a copy of the key needed to unscramble encrypted communications. U.S. industry opposes the plan as unworkable in the face of foreign availability of strong encryption and the risk of compromise and abuse of escrow authority.

Over a four-month period in 1997, five separate House committees (National Security, Commerce, Judiciary, Intelligence, and International Relations) approved different versions of the proposed Security and Freedom Through Encryption (SAFE) Act (H.R. 695). While two of these would relax export controls and prohibit restrictions on the domestic use, sale, or import of encryption technologies (including the use of mandatory key escrow systems), the others take the opposite tack of establishing tighter controls on both domestic use and export of encryption technologies.

In the Senate, a similarly schizophrenic debate on the subject led the Commerce Committee to approve the proposed Secure Public Networks Act (S. 909) with amendments that made the bill much more restrictive than U.S. computer and software industries desire.

It is unclear whether a compromise can be brokered among the various Administration, House, and Senate approaches, but the importance of resolving the debate will undoubtedly lead to further action before Congress adjourns.

Online Privacy

Apart from its meaning with respect to the content of digital communications, "privacy on the Internet" is a growing legislative concern in connection with the collection, dissemination, and use of personally identifiable information from and about Internet users by commercial enterprises. Prodded by alarming reports in the press and from various public interest groups, the Federal Trade Commission and a number of individual legislators are focusing critical attention on several different aspects of the problem that are reflected in current online practices by many Internet entrepreneurs.

The sharpest focus of governmental concern appears to be directed to privacy issues in the context of online marketing efforts that target particular consumers, especially children. Online technology, such as the "cookies" associated with several popular browsing programs, facilitates tagging and tracking of a user's travels and activities in visiting different online sites. The use of such information for marketing purposes, without the knowledge or consent of the consumer, has raised increasing levels of protest. Tracking technologies that make it possible to monitor the online interactions between children and advertisements, with the goal of creating personalized interactive ads to "microtarget" individual children, have brought even louder outcries.

Another sensitive issue involves the proliferation of databases that compile extensive personal information about individuals, including their Social Security numbers. Periodic news stories regarding database services that include SSNs among the personally identifiable data that could be accessed for a fee have fueled concerns about the potential for abuse by persons seeking to misappropriate the identities of other individuals for wrongful purposes.

Finally, a number of legislative proposals have focused on consumer complaints regarding the proliferating use of unsolicited commercial e-mail, commonly known as "spamming."

A variety of businesses that are counting on an online future are scrambling to head off a regulatory approach to these privacy issues by devising self-enforced industry guidelines and fair information practices. Book publishers, like other Web site owners and online entrepreneurs, should be concerned about these issues, especially since their ability to maintain copyright protection for their products may depend upon technological measures and online practices that could raise additional privacy-related questions about the possible tracking and monitoring of their works and their customers.

Internet Tax Freedom Act

Bills were introduced in both the Senate and House (S. 442 and H.R. 1054) to impose a moratorium on state or local taxation of Internet commerce, as part of a national policy against state and local interference with such commerce. Although the legislation, which was approved by the Senate Commerce Committee in November, would preserve state and local taxing authority with respect to income, license, and sales taxes, its progress toward enactment has been slowed by opposition from state and local government officials who are concerned about losing a significant potential revenue source and what some perceive to be the creation of an unlevel playing field between businesses competing on- and off-line.

Education Funding

Last year, the Clinton administration and the Republican-led Congress were able to overcome their policy differences to support record-high levels of federal educational funding that emphasized the need for advanced technology in the classroom and the importance of lifelong access to job training opportunities. Although ideological disagreements continued to fuel debates over block grants, program consolidation, and the degree of federal involvement in the distribution and administration of federal education funding, a combination of major tax, appropriations, and budget legislation provided students and their parents with an array of education tax credits and deductions as well as increased funding for grants and loans.

While higher education welcomed the unprecedented outpouring of financial support and looked forward to consolidating and building on its gains through this year's process for reauthorizing the Higher Education Act and its Title IV funding mechanisms, the elementary and secondary education communities watched as the administration and Congress battled over policy disputes regarding reading improvement programs and the value of national testing.

While the administration's proposed "America Reads" legislation sought to assure the reading skills of young children through the massive funding of volunteer tutoring programs, House Republican leaders believed that upgrading teachers' skills was a better way to spend money toward that goal. As a result, some $260 million included in a bipartisan budget agreement for fiscal years 1998–2000 for reading improvement in March 1998 still awaited authorizing legislation to provide for its distribution and expenditure. In November 1997 the House passed the proposed Reading Excellence Act (H.R. 2614), which would prescribe that the money be spent to train teachers in the best methods for teaching students to read.

At the same time, a vigorous dispute over the administration's proposal to establish voluntary national reading tests for fourth graders and math tests for eighth graders led to a compromise that prohibits the development of these tests by the Department of Education. Instead, the National Academy of Sciences will be responsible for the development of the tests while placing the overall responsibility for testing within the authority of the National Assessment Governing Board, an existing independent entity established by statute. The academy is to report to Congress in September 1998 on whether commercially available tests and state tests could be substituted for the proposed new national tests.

Postal Matters

Postal Rate Case

In July 1997, in a non-legislative postal matter of significance to many AAP members, the U.S. Postal Service (USPS) filed a rate case seeking an average 4.5 percent rate increase to be effective this year, despite the fact that it has run annual surpluses of more than $1 billion for the last three years (total $4.7 billion in surplus). Based on fiscal year (FY) 1996 pre-reclassification data, USPS was then predicting a $2.4 billion loss in FY 1998. By law, the Postal Rate

Commission's decision on the request is due May 10 (i.e., ten months after the filing), and increased rates could go into effect as soon as July. Members of the mailing community have urged the PRC to delay any recommended increases in light of these surpluses, which appear likely to continue through this year.

It does not appear that the Bound Printed Matter and Standard Mail (A) subclasses, which are those typically used by book and journal publishers, respectively, would take an unreasonable hit under the USPS proposal for overall rate increases. (In an unrelated proceeding, the Postal Rate Commission last fall reached a settlement agreement with AAP and other elements of the mailing community to increase the upper weight limit in the BPM subclass from 10 pounds to 15 pounds.)

Pending Postal Legislation

Time is running out on efforts to enact comprehensive postal reform legislation. The proposed Postal Reform Act (H.R. 22), introduced early in 1997 by Rep. John McHugh (R-N.Y.), chairman of the House Subcommittee on the Postal Service, was the subject of numerous hearings but no committee action over the course of the year. In December, after the first session of the 105th Congress adjourned, Rep. McHugh circulated among members of the mailing community a white paper containing proposed revisions to H.R. 22 based on testimony from earlier hearings. Rep. McHugh has warned the mailing community that the need for postal reform is inescapable and that its failure to come together around his vehicle would simply leave the field open to other proposals that might be less attractive. It was expected that he would seek comments on his proposed revisions sometime in early 1998.

In the previous Congress, the chairman of AAP's Postal Committee had testified in general support of an earlier version of H.R. 22. His testimony focused on proposed changes to the rate-making process, praising those that would provide for negotiated rate agreements, market tests for experimental new products, the institution of price caps, and a five-year cycle for rate adjustments. However, the AAP witness expressed concerns about proposals to downgrade the significance of "content" as a criterion, to distinguish between competitive and noncompetitive product categories, and to provide an "exigent circumstances" exception to the five-year rate-making cycle for non-competitive products.

Another major postal bill, S. 1296, the proposed Postal Financing Reform Act, was introduced in October by Sen. Thad Cochran (R-Miss.), chairman of the Senate subcommittee that oversees the Postal Service. It was later withdrawn over concerns that a provision allowing USPS broad discretion to invest in equity ventures could permit USPS to buy out competitors such as UPS or Federal Express. Early in the second session, Sen. Cochran was expected to circulate proposed amendments that would alleviate these concerns by requiring Treasury Department approval of such investments. The bill, which would also remove current statutory restrictions on USPS authority to borrow and deposit funds, could receive the subcommittee's approval before the April recess.

Two other pending postal bills cut against the grain of Rep. McHugh's efforts to loosen government restrictions on the activities of USPS and represent an entirely different approach to the future of that entity.

S. 1107, the proposed Double Postage Rule Elimination Act—introduced by Sen. Paul Coverdell (R-Ga.), would amend the Private Express Statutes to allow private companies to compete more evenly with USPS in providing two-day delivery services.

H.R. 198, the proposed Postal Service Core Business Act—introduced by Rep. Duncan Hunter (R-Calif.), would more broadly establish rules for competition between USPS and private sector companies. In particular, the bill would prevent the USPS from competing with private businesses in areas that have not traditionally been served by the Postal Service, such as new packaging and photocopying services.

Funding Programs and Grant-Making Agencies

National Endowment for the Humanities

1100 Pennsylvania Ave. N.W., Washington, DC 20506
202-606-8400, 800-634-1121
E-mail: info@neh.fed.us
World Wide Web: http://www.neh.fed.us

Thomas C. Phelps

> Democracy demands wisdom and vision in its citizens.
> —National Foundation on the Arts and Humanities Act of 1965

In order to "promote progress and scholarship in the humanities and the arts in the United States," Congress enacted the National Foundation on the Arts and the Humanities Act of 1965. This act established the National Endowment for the Humanities (NEH) as an independent grant-making agency of the federal government to support research, education, and public programs in the humanities. In the act, the term *humanities* includes, but is not limited to, the study of the following: language, both modern and classical; linguistics; literature; history; jurisprudence; philosophy; archaeology; comparative religion; ethics; the history, criticism, and theory of the arts; those aspects of the social sciences that have humanistic content and employ humanistic methods; and the study and application of the humanities to the human environment, with particular attention to reflecting our diverse heritage, traditions, and history and to the relevance of the humanities to the current conditions of national life.

In the words of William R. Ferris, the recently confirmed chair of the National Endowment for the Humanities, "There has never been a more crucial time for the presence of the humanities in civic life. We must open the doors and windows of academe and reach out to the public through teaching, preservation, research, and public programming. NEH grants and partnerships with state councils, corporations, and foundations promise to lead the way. The 1998 granting cycles offer an opportunity for individuals and institutions to accomplish their best work in the humanities fields, work that will extend far into the 21st century. The Challenge Grants initiative for public libraries will help those facilities plan long-term programming. Another initiative, planning grants for schools and libraries for the new millennium, foresees a future where entire schools are networked into the finest examples of humanities through technology. Our schools and libraries are where young minds are cultivated; our goal is to leave no one behind. These efforts, and other works of the National Endowment for the Humanities, will help the humanities endure and flourish in the future and provide all Americans with the wisdom and vision to be the best citizens of this country."

To assist with this goal of providing Americans with the means and resources for effective citizenship, NEH supports projects in three divisions: Preservation and Access, Public Programs, and Research and Education Programs. Through its Challenge Grant program, it supports institutions that in some way enhance the humanities in American life to raise needed resources. Through its Office of Enterprise, NEH works with other agencies, foundations, and corporations to bring a full complement of programs to the American people in new and dynamic ways. And through its newly organized office of Federal/ State Partnerships, the endowment fosters public understanding of the humanities throughout the nation, primarily through locally developed programs aimed at general audiences. To reach this goal, NEH provides support for state humanities councils every state, the district of Columbia, Puerto Rico, the U.S. Virgin Islands, the Northern Mariana Islands, American Samoa, and Guam. (See state council addresses and telephone numbers at the end of this article, or visit the NEH home page at http://www.neh.fed.us.)

What the Endowment Supports

NEH supports exemplary work to disseminate and advance knowledge in all disciplines of the humanities. Endowment support is intended to assist cultural and educational institutions and complement private and local efforts. In the most general terms, NEH-supported projects aid scholarship and research in the humanities, help improve humanities education, and foster a greater curiosity about and understanding of the humanities.

Whom the Endowment Supports

NEH welcomes applications from nonprofit associations, institutions, and organizations. Applicants are encouraged to consult with NEH staff before submitting a formal proposal.

Applying for a Grant

Grant applicants are encouraged to consult with NEH staff by phone, letter, or e-mail before submitting a formal proposal. Given enough lead time, staff will try to comment on draft proposals and work with the applicant to submit a competitive application. Those planning to apply for NEH assistance should write to the appropriate division or office, briefly describing the proposed project and requesting guidelines and application forms. Applications and forms are available from the Public Information Office or the NEH Web site at http://www.neh. gov/. The endowment does not maintain a general mailing list; instead, it responds to specific requests for publications by mail, phone, or e-mail.

How Applications are Evaluated

Each application is assessed first by knowledgeable persons outside the agency who are asked for their judgments about the quality and significance of the proposed project. In fiscal year (FY) 1995 about 1,200 scholars, professionals in the humanities, and other experts—such as librarians, curators, and filmmakers—served on approximately 225 panels. Panelists represent a diversity of disciplinary, institutional, regional, and cultural backgrounds. In some programs the judgment of panelists is supplemented by reviews from specialists who have extensive knowledge of the specific subject or technical aspects of the application.

The advice of evaluators is assembled by the staff of the endowment, who comment on matters of fact or on significant issues that would otherwise be missing from the review. These materials are forwarded to the National Council on the Humanities, a board of 26 citizens nominated by the president of the United States and confirmed by the Senate. The National Council meets three times a year to advise the NEH chair about matters of policy and about applications. The chair, who is appointed for a four-year term by the president of the United States with consent of the Senate, takes into account the advice provided by panelists, reviewers, NEH staff, and members of the National Council, and, by law, makes the final decision about funding.

Grantmaking Programs

Public Programs

The division fosters public understanding and appreciation of the humanities by supporting projects that bring significant insights of the disciplines of the humanities to general audiences of all ages through interpretive exhibitions, radio and television programs, lectures, symposia, conferences, multimedia projects, printed materials, and reading and discussion groups.

Grants support projects that lead to the study of books, new technologies, and other resources found in collections housed in libraries and archives. Projects can be in many formats, including reading and discussion programs, lectures, symposia, and interpretive exhibitions of books, manuscripts, and other library resources. Useful supplementary materials—such as publications, media components, educational programming material, and curriculum guides—also receive support through grants from this division. The division also makes grants for the planning, scripting, and production of television and radio programs as well as for exhibitions of cultural artifacts and other resources found in the collections of museums and historical sites.

Eligible applicants:	Nonprofit institutions and organizations, including public television and radio stations and state humanities councils
Application deadlines:	January 12, 1998
	November 2, 1998 (planning only)
	February 1, 1999
Information:	202-606-8267
	E-mail: publicpgms@neh.fed.us

Preservation and Access

In this division, grants are made for projects that will create, preserve, or increase the availability of resources important for research, education, and public programming in the humanities. Projects may encompass books, journals, newspapers, manuscript and archival materials, maps, still and moving images, sound recordings, and objects of material culture held by repositories.

Support may be sought to preserve the intellectual content and aid bibliographic control of collections; to compile bibliographies, descriptive catalogs, and guides to cultural holdings; to create dictionaries, encyclopedias, databases, and other types of research tools and reference works; and to stabilize material-culture collections through the appropriate housing and storing of objects, improved environmental control, and the installation of security, lighting, and fire prevention systems. Applications may also be submitted for national and regional education and training projects, regional preservation field service programs, and research and demonstration projects that are intended to enhance institutional practice and the use of technology for preservation and access.

Eligible applicants:	Individuals, nonprofit institutions and cultural organizations, associations, state agencies, and institutional consortia
Application deadline:	July 1, 1998
Information:	202-606-8570
	E-mail: preservation@neh.fed.us

Research and Education

Through grants to educational institutions, fellowships to scholars and teachers, and the support of significant research, this division's programs are designed to strengthen sustained, thoughtful study of the humanities at all levels of education.

Education Development and Demonstration

Grants, including "next semester" Humanities Focus Grants, support curriculum and materials development efforts, faculty study programs within and among educational institutions, and conferences and networks of institutions. The endowment is interested in projects that help teachers use the new technologies to enhance students' understanding of the humanities.

Eligible applicants:	Public and private elementary and secondary schools, school systems, colleges and universities, nonprofit academic associations, and cultural institutions, such as libraries and museums
Application deadlines:	Schools for the New Millennium, April 1, 1998; Education Development and Demonstration, October 15, 1998; Humanities Focus Grants, April 17, 1998
Information:	202-606-8380
	E-mail: research@neh.fed.us

Fellowships and Stipends

Grants provide support for scholars to undertake full-time independent research and writing in the humanities. Grants are available for a maximum of one year and a minimum of six weeks of summer study.

    Eligible applicants: Individuals
    Application deadlines: Fellowships, May 1, 1998;
        Summer Stipends October 1, 1998
    Information: 202-606-8467
        E-mail: research@neh.fed.us

Seminars and Institutes

Grants support summer seminars and national institutes in the humanities for college and school teachers. These faculty development activities are conducted at colleges and universities across the country. Those wishing to participate in seminars submit their applications to the seminar director. Lists of pending seminars and institutes are available from the program.

    Eligible applicants: Individuals and institutions of higher learning
    Application deadlines: Participants, 1998 seminars, March 1, 1998;
        Directors, 1999 seminars, March 1, 1998
    Information: 202-606-8463
        E-mail: sem-inst@neh.fed.us

Challenge Grants

Regular Challenge

Nonprofit institutions interested in developing new sources of long-term support for educational, scholarly, and preservation activities and public programs in the humanities may be assisted in these efforts by an NEH Challenge Grant. Grantees are required to raise three or four dollars in new or increased donations for every federal dollar offered. Both federal and nonfederal funds may be used to establish or increase institutional endowments and thus guarantee long-term support for a variety of humanities needs. Funds may also be used for limited direct capital expenditures where such needs are compelling and clearly related to improvements in the humanities endeavors undertaken by the institution.

    Eligible applicants: Nonprofit postsecondary, educational, research, or cultural institutions and organizations, such as libraries, working within the realm of the humanities

Special Initiative

A special initiative to assist public libraries in creating endowments to support humanities programming is available to libraries that have not previously held an NEH Challenge Grant. Awards made through this initiative have a maximum of

$150,000 in federal dollars, and the recipient is required to raise two (rather than three) times the amount of federal funds offered. Applications will be accepted at the regular Challenge Grant deadline.

>   Application deadline: May 1, 1998
>   Information: 202-606-8309
>   E-mail: challenge@neh.fed.us

Enterprise

The Enterprise office implements endowment-wide special initiatives, creates partnerships with other federal agencies and private organizations, engages in raising funds for humanities activities, and explores other leadership opportunities for the agency.

Federal/State Partnership

The Federal/State Partnership fosters public understanding of the humanities throughout the nation through state humanities councils in every state, the District of Columbia, Puerto Rico, the U.S. Virgin Islands, the Northern Mariana Islands, American Samoa, and Guam.

Each state council establishes its own grant guidelines and sets its own application deadlines. State humanities councils support a wide variety of projects in the humanities, including library reading programs, lectures, conferences, seminars and institutes for teachers and school administrators, media presentations, and museum and library traveling exhibitions. A list of state councils follows:

Alabama Humanities Foundation
2217 Tenth Ct. S.
Birmingham, AL 35205
205-930-0540

Alaska Humanities Forum
421 W. First Ave., No. 210
Anchorage, AK 99501
907-272-5341

Arizona Humanities Council
The Ellis-Shackelford House
1242 N. Central Ave.
Phoenix, AZ 85004-1887
602-257-0335

Arkansas Humanities Council
10816 Executive Center Dr., No. 310
Little Rock, AR 72211-4383
501-221-0091

California Council for the Humanities
312 Sutter St., No. 601
San Francisco, CA 94108
415-391-1474

Colorado Endowment for the Humanities
1623 Blake St., No. 200
Denver, CO 80202
303-573-7733

Connecticut Humanities Council
955 S. Main St., Suite E
Middletown CT 06547
860-685-2260

Delaware Humanities Forum
1812 Newport Gap Pike
Wilmington, DE 19808-6179
302-633-2400

Humanities Council of Washington, D.C.
1331 H Street N.W., No. 902
Washington, DC 20005
202-347-1732

Florida Humanities Council
1514 ½ E. Eighth Ave.
Tampa, FL 33605-3708
813-272-3473

Georgia Humanities Council
50 Hurt Plaza S.E., No. 440
Atlanta, GA 30303-2915
404-523-6220

Hawaii Committee for the Humanities
First Hawaiian Bank Bldg.
3599 Wai'alae Ave., Rm. 23
Honolulu, HI 96816
808-732-5402

Idaho Humanities Council
217 W. State St.
Boise, ID 83702
208-345-5346

Illinois Humanities Council
203 Wabash Ave., No.#2020
Chicago, IL 60601-2417
312-422-5580

Indiana Humanities Council
1500 N. Delaware St.
Indianapolis, IN 46202
317-638-1500

Iowa Humanities Board
Oakdale Campus Northlawn
University of Iowa
Iowa City, IA 52242
319-335-4153

Kansas Humanities Council
112 S.W. Sixth Ave., No. 210
Topeka, KS 66603
913-357-0359

Kentucky Humanities Council
206 Maxwell St.
Lexington, KY 40508
606-257-5932

Louisiana Endowment for the Humanities
225 Baronne St., Suite 1414
New Orleans, LA 70112-1709
504-523-4352

Maine Humanities Council
371 Cumberland Ave.
Box 7202
Portland, ME 04112
207-773-5051

Maryland Humanities Council
601 N. Howard St.
Baltimore, MD 21201
410-625-4830

Massachusetts Foundation for the Humanities
One Woodbridge St.
South Hadley, MA 01075
413-536-1385

Michigan Humanities Council
119 Pere Marquette Dr., No. 3B
Lansing, MI 48912-1231
517-372-7770

Minnesota Humanities Commission
26 E. Ivy St.
Lower Level South
St. Paul, MN 55106-2046
612-774-0105

Mississippi Humanities Council
3825 Ridgewood Rd., Room 311
Jackson, MS 39211
601-982-6752

Missouri Humanities Council
911 Washington Ave., No. 215
St. Louis, MO 63101-1208
314-621-7705

Montana Committee for the Humanities
Box 8036, Hellgate Sta.
Missoula, MT 59807
406-243-6022

Nebraska Humanities Council
Lincoln Center Bldg., No. 225
215 Centennial Mall South
Lincoln, NE 68508
402-474-2131

Nevada Humanities Committee
1034 N. Sierra St.
Reno, NV 89507
702-784-6527

New Hampshire Humanities Council
19 Pillsbury St.
Box 2228
Concord, NH 03302-2228
603-224-4071

New Jersey Council for the Humanities
28 W. State St., Sixth fl.
Trenton, NJ 08608
609-695-4838

New Mexico Endowment for the Humanities
209 Onate Hall
University of New Mexico
Albuquerque, NM 87131
505-277-3705

New York Council for the Humanities
198 Broadway, Tenth fl.
New York, NY 10038
212-233-1131

North Carolina Humanities Council
425 Spring Garden St.
Greensboro, NC 27401
919-334-5325

North Dakota Humanities Council
2900 Broadway E., No. 3
Box 2191
Bismarck, ND 58502
701-255-3360

Ohio Humanities Council
695 Bryden Rd.
Box 06354
Columbus, OH 43206-0354
614-461-7802

Oklahoma Foundation for the Humanities
Festival Plaza
428 W. California, No. 270
Oklahoma City, OK 73102
405-235-0280

Oregon Council for the Humanities
812 S.W. Washington St., No. 225
Portland, OR 97205
503-241-0543

Pennsylvania Humanities Council
320 Walnut St., No. 305
Philadelphia, PA 19106
215-925-1005

Rhode Island Committee for the Humanities
60 Ship St.
Providence, RI 02903
401-273-2250

South Carolina Humanities Council
1308 Columbia College Dr.
Box 5287
Columbia, SC 29250
803-691-4100

South Dakota Humanities Council
Box 7050, University Sta.
Brookings, SD 57007
605-688-6113

Tennessee Humanities Council
1003 18th Ave. S.
Nashville, TN 37212
615-320-7001

Texas Council for the Humanities
Banister Place A
3809 S. Second St.
Austin, TX 78704
512-440-1991

Utah Humanities Council
350 S. 400 E., No. 110
Salt Lake City, UT 84111
801-359-9670

Vermont Council on the Humanities
17 Park St., R.R. 1, Box 7285
Morrisville, VT 05561
802-888-3183

Virginia Foundation for the Humanities
145 Ednam Dr.
Charlottesville, VA 22903-4629
804-924-3296

Washington Commission for the Humanities
615 Second Ave., No. 300
Seattle, WA 98104
206-682-1770

West Virginia Humanities Council
723 Kanawha Blvd. E., No. 800
Charleston, WV 25301
304-346-8500

Wisconsin Humanities Council
802 Regent St.
Madison, WI 53715
608-262-0706

Wyoming Council for the Humanities
Box 3643, University Sta.
Laramie, WY 82071-3643
307-766-3142

American Samoa Humanities Council
Box 5800
Pago Pago, AS 96799
684-633-4870

Guam Humanities Council
272 W. Rte. 8, No. 2A
Barrigada, Guam 96913
671-734-1713

**Commonwealth of the Northern Mariana
    Islands Council for the Humanities**
AAA-3394, Box 10001
Saipan, MP 96950
670-235-4785

**Fundación Puertorriqueña de las
    Humanidades**
109 San Jose St., Third fl.
Box 9023920
Old San Juan, PR 00902-3920
809-721-2087

Virgin Islands Humanities Council
5-6 Kongens Gade, Corbiere Complex,
    Suite 200B
St. Thomas, VI 00802
809-776-4044

Applications

Guidelines and application forms are available from the program or from the Public Information Office, National Endowment for the Humanities, 1100 Pennsylvania Ave. N.W., Washington, DC 20506, telephone 202-606-8400 or 800-634-1121, e-mail info@neh.fed.us; or from the NEH home page at http://www.neh.fed.us. For the hearing impaired, the TDD is 202-606-8282.

The Public Information Office does not maintain a general mailing list. Instead, NEH responds to specific requests for publications and guidelines.

Institute of Museum and Library Services Library Programs

1100 Pennsylvania Ave. N.W., Washington, DC 20506
202-606-5527, fax 202-606-1077
World Wide Web: http://www.imls.fed.us

Diane Frankel
Director
Institute of Museum and Library Services

The Museum and Library Services Act of 1996, which created the Institute of Museum and Library Services (IMLS) and the Library Services and Technology Act (LSTA), brought into operation a new consolidated federal library grants program. Library grants programs were moved to IMLS from the U.S. Department of Education and museum programs from the former Institute of Museum Services.

LSTA begins a new era in federal funding for library services after 40 years of operation in the Department of Education under the Library Services Act, the Library Services and Construction Act (LSCA), and Title II of the Higher Education Act (HEA). [See the following article, "U.S. Department of Education Discretionary Library Programs, Fiscal Year 1997"—*Ed.*]

State-Administered Programs

State library administrative agencies set new LSTA priorities for library services that will guide them over the next five years, submitted these plans to IMLS on August 1, 1997, and on October 1 efforts were officially launched to put the new state program into place.

In December 1997 Congress appropriated $134,201,300 for fiscal year (FY) 1998 for the state program. The formula on which each state's allocation is based is tied to its population, supplemented by a state minimum of $340,000. The Pacific region "state" entities base amount is $40,000 (Table 1). The states will be using their allocations to provide grants to libraries for

- Establishing or enhancing electronic linkages among or between libraries
- Electronically linking libraries with educational, social, or information services
- Assisting libraries in accessing information through electronic networks
- Encouraging libraries in different areas, and encouraging different types of libraries to establish consortia and share resources
- Paying costs for libraries to acquire or share computer systems and telecommunications technologies

Note: Robert Klassen, program director in the Office of Library Services at IMLS, contributed to this article.

- Targeting library and information services to persons having difficulty using a library and to underserved urban and rural communities, including children

IMLS is working with the Chief Officers of State Library Agencies (COSLA) organization to design a meaningful reporting system that will present a relatively complete picture of library services at the national level and help in defining the ultimate impact of LSTA.

IMLS also has been working with COSLA on developing an outline for "best practices," and COSLA is identifying the additional performance data that might be needed through the National Center for Education Statistics (NCES) Library Statistics Cooperative Program to enhance such reporting.

In addition to LSTA, the state program office at IMLS continues to administer the remaining funds in the Public Library Construction and Technology Enhancement Program account funded by the Library Services and Construction Act (Title II). More than $12 million remains to be released to the states for these purposes. The first awards under the aegis of IMLS, totaling $12.6 million, were made to 27 states.

With the congressional appropriation for FY 1998 in place, Discretionary Programs begins its first year of operation under LSTA at these levels:

- National Leadership Program: $5,487,750 (3.75 percent of the LSTA appropriation). An additional $1 million was appropriated for joint library museum projects under the Museum program.
- Native American Library Services Program: $2,560,950 (1.75 percent of the LSTA appropriation). The Museum and Library Services Technical and Conforming Amendments of 1997, P.L. 105-128, December 1, 1997, reserves $365,850 for Native Hawaiians.

National Leadership Program

In June and October 1997 IMLS made available for comment the draft guidelines for the National Leadership Program. The final guidelines were published in January 1998. These efforts led the Washington Office of the American Library Association (ALA) to comment that the guidelines, while not incorporating all the library community's concerns, were a model of accommodation and balance, taking into account the advice and recommendations received from its two advisory bodies, the National Museum Services Board and the National Commission on Libraries and Information Science, as well as from an IMLS forum and from the public comment process. The deadline for the first year of competition was April 17, 1998.

The FY 1998 priorities of the National Leadership Grants are

- Education and training in library and information science, including graduate fellowships, traineeships, institutes, and other programs

- Applied research and demonstration efforts that emphasize access to improved library and information sources
- Projects that preserve unique library resources useful for the broader research community or that address the challenges of preserving and archiving digital materials
- Model programs of cooperation between libraries and museums with emphasis on how the community is served, how technology is used, and how education is enhanced

IMLS expects that one-fourth of the total FY 1998 appropriation will support projects demonstrating cooperation between libraries and museums. As noted above, the FY 1998 appropriation includes $1 million within the Office of Museum Services for the National Leadership Grants. IMLS anticipates that all of this appropriation will support projects for coordination between libraries and museums.

The congressional intent in the FY 1998 appropriation language also specifies that IMLS consider funding four projects: a project to digitize a card catalog, a project regarding a historic medical library collection, a one-of-a-kind historical library in Pennsylvania, and a demonstration of interactive Internet connections.

Native American Library Services Program

The Native American Library Services Program provides some new opportunities for the improvement of library services to Indian tribes and Alaska native villages, the latter coming under the definition of eligible Indian tribes as recognized by the secretary of the interior. These grants will be made directly to Indian tribes as a result of the Technical Amendments signed by President Clinton on December 1, 1997.

IMLS guidelines outline three types of support:

Basic Library Services Grants—These small grant awards will support core library operations on a noncompetitive basis for all eligible Indian tribes and Alaska native villages that apply for such support.

Technical Assistance Grants—These technical assistance grants will be designed to heighten the level of professional proficiency of Indian tribal library staff through small noncompetitive grants to support assessments of Indian library service and provide advice for improvement.

Enhancement Grants—These grants will support new levels of Indian library service for activities specifically identified under the basic LSTA purposes.

The draft guidelines were made available for public comment. This program and the Native Hawaiian Library Service Program are successors to similar programs funded since 1985 under the Library Services and Construction Act, Title IV, at the U.S. Department of Education. The deadline for this initial competition under LSTA is June 5, 1998.

Program Staff

The leadership post for Discretionary Library Programs in the Office of Library Services was filled with the recruitment of Joyce Ray. Dr. Ray comes to IMLS from the National Historical Publications and Records Commission where she was assistant program director for technological evaluation. She joins Jane Heiser, the state program director, and Robert Klassen, Office of Library Services program director. They will serve as the library management team that will be working with the IMLS deputy director for the Office of Library Services, Elizabeth Sywetz.

Table 1 / Funding for LSTA State Program, FY 1998

	Federal Allocation
Alabama	$2,184,787
Alaska	$602,059
Arizona	$2,251,697
Arkansas	$1,423,534
California	$14,102,552
Colorado	$1,990,335
Connecticut	$1,753,562
Delaware	$652,931
District of Columbia	$574,517
Florida	$6,556,798
Georgia	$3,514,553
Hawaii	$851,040
Idaho	$853,426
Illinois	$5,454,420
Indiana	$2,861,487
Iowa	$1,571,183
Kansas	$1,450,455
Kentucky	$2,016,691
Louisiana	$2,218,243
Maine	$876,767
Maryland	$2,529,526
Massachusetts	$2,970,206
Michigan	$4,482,097
Minnesota	$2,350,859
Mississippi	$1,512,608
Missouri	$2,653,468
Montana	$719,645
Nebraska	$1,053,246
Nevada	$1,032,122
New Hampshire	$841,869
New Jersey	$3,788,571

**Table 1 / Funding for LSTA State Program,
FY 1998** *(cont.)*

	Federal Allocation
New Mexico	$1,079,716
New York	$8,190,777
North Carolina	$3,501,448
North Dakota	$617,830
Ohio	$5,163,542
Oklahoma	$1,765,074
Oregon	$1,723,125
Pennsylvania	$5,544,895
Rhode Island	$767,502
South Carolina	$1,936,832
South Dakota	$656,196
Tennessee	$2,636,614
Texas	$8,598,101
Utah	$1,203,658
Vermont	$594,135
Virginia	$3,221,943
Washington	$2,728,694
West Virginia	$1,128,219
Wisconsin	$2,567,600
Wyoming	$547,831
Puerto Rico	$1,860,543
American Samoa	$60,193
Northern Marianas	$58,713
Guam	$97,485
Virgin Islands	$83,953
Marshall Islands	$53,340
Micronesia	$71,559
Palau	$46,528
Total	$134,201,300

U.S. Department of Education Discretionary Library Programs, Fiscal Year 1997

Christina Dunn

Former Director, Discretionary Programs
Library Programs Office
Office of Educational Research and Improvement
U.S. Department of Education

Fiscal Year (FY) 1997 marked the last year of funding under the Library Services and Construction Act and Title II of the Higher Education Act. In 1996 Congress passed the Museum and Library Services Act, creating the Library Services and Technology Act as well as a new federal agency—the Institute of Museum and Library Services—to administer this program. [See the preceding article, "Institute of Museum and Library Services Library Programs"—*Ed.*]

The following report describes the FY 1997 discretionary grant programs administered by the U.S. Department of Education's Office of Library Programs.

Higher Education Act (HEA, P.L. 99-498)

For more than two decades, Title II of the Higher Education Act served as the backbone of federal financial assistance to colleges and universities. With the continuing expansion of information resources and the increasing demands on higher education libraries, Title II was an important factor in helping these libraries to preserve, acquire, and share resources, and to use new technologies to improve services. In addition, it assisted institutions of higher education in training and retraining personnel and conducting research and demonstrations in library and information science.

In FY 1997, the last year of funding under the program, only those programs under HEA II-B continued to be funded. They are Library Education and Training—Fellowships and Institutes, with an appropriation of $2,500,000, and Research and Demonstration, with an appropriation of $5,000,000.

Library Education and Human Resource Development Program (HEA II-B)

The Library Education and Human Resource Development Program (Title II-B of the Higher Education Act) authorizes a program of federal financial assistance to institutions of higher education and other library organizations and agencies to assist in training persons in library and information science and to establish, develop, and expand programs of library and information science. Grants are made for fellowships at the master's and doctoral levels, and for traineeships. Grants may also be used to assist in covering the costs of institutes, or courses, to upgrade the competencies of persons serving in all types of libraries, information centers, or instructional materials centers offering library and information services, and of those serving as educators.

Table 1 / Library Education and Human Resource Development Program Funding History:

Fiscal Year	Appropriation
1966*	$1,000,000
1970	4,000,000
1975	2,000,000
1980	667,000
1985	640,000
1990	570,000
1991	651,000
1992	5,000,000
1993	4,960,000
1994	4,960,000
1995	4,916,000
1996	2,500,000
1997	2,500,000

* Initial year

Fellowships

In FY 1997 Congress appropriated $2,500,000 for the HEA II-B, Library Education and Human Resource Development Program (see Table 1 for the program's funding history). The U.S. Department of Education awarded $1,586,273 to 20 institutions of higher education to provide new and continuing fellowships in library and information science for academic year 1997–1998; 11 grants were awarded to support 41 master's fellowships and 12 to support 29 continuing doctoral fellowships. Between 1966 and 1997, institutions of higher education received a total of $53,154,993 to support 1,503 doctoral, 282 post-master's, 3,406 master's, 16 bachelor's, 53 associate's fellowships, and 77 traineeships.

Each grant provides funding to the school to cover the cost of training ($8,000 for master's-level and $10,000 for doctoral-level studies), allowing the school to waive all tuition fees. In addition, each grant provides fellowship recipients with a stipend of up to $14,000 a year, based on demonstrated need. The stipend amount is the same for master's and doctoral students. The institution receiving the grant has the sole responsibility for selecting fellowship recipients.

Areas of study reflect the secretary of education's priorities:

- To recruit, educate, train, retrain, and retain minorities in library and information science
- To educate, train, or retrain library personnel in areas of library specialization where there are currently shortages such as school media, children's services, young adult services, science reference, and cataloging
- To educate, train, or retrain library personnel in new techniques of information acquisition, transfer, and communication technology

In FY 1997 all fellowship awards focused on recruiting and educating minorities and on training personnel in areas of library specialization where there are currently shortages, primarily school and public librarians serving youth; seven supported training personnel in new techniques of information management. Table 2 describes the grants for master's-level study.

Institutions receiving continuing doctoral grants were: Rutgers University, one fellowship; Syracuse University, three fellowships; State University of New York at Albany, one fellowship; Texas Woman's University, two fellowships; University of Alabama, one fellowship; University of California at Los Angeles, three fellowships; University of Indiana, one fellowship; University of Maryland, four fellowships; University of Michigan, five fellowships; University of Pittsburgh, three fellowships; University of North Texas, three fellowships; and University of Texas at Austin, two fellowships.

Table 2 / HEA Title II-B, Library Education and Human Resource Development Program, FY 1997 Fellowship Awards

California

University of California	Grant Number: R036B70032
Graduate School of Education and Information Studies	Award Amount: $88,000
Department of Library Information Science, Los Angeles	Project Director: Clara Chu

The Educating Librarians for Common Goals: Addressing Current Shortages fellowships will support students from under-represented groups in library and information science to work in school media, children's services, young adult services, science reference, cataloging, or library service evaluation. They will study new techniques of information acquisition, transfer, and management of communication technology.

Florida

Florida State University	Grant Number: R036B70011
School of Information Studies,	Award Amount: $88,000
Tallahassee	Project Co-directors: Pamela Barron, Thomas L. Hart, Eliza Dresang, Kathleen Burnett, Jane Robbins

The Library Training Program for Master's Fellows will emphasize services to children and young adults in both school and public libraries, focusing on evaluation techniques for library programs and services. Preference will be given to Asian, Native American, Hispanic, and Black minorities.

Kentucky

University of Kentucky	Grant Number: R036B70001
School of Library and Information Science,	Award Amount: $88,000
Lexington	Project Director: Kay Bishop

The Meeting Library Personnel Shortages fellowships will address the continuing shortages of personnel in Kentucky school libraries by recruiting and training four students in school librarianship, including training in new techniques of information acquisition, transfer, and management of communication technology. Ethnic minorities will be recruited.

Michigan

University of Michigan	Grant Number: R036B70014
School of Information and Library Studies,	Award Amount: $88,000
Ann Arbor	Project Director: Carolyn Frost

The Library Education and Human Resource Development fellowships will educate, train, or retrain personnel in areas of library specialization where there are shortages, recruiting minorities and providing training in new techniques of information acquisition, transfer, and communication technology. The fellowships will provide opportunities to specialize in the emerging area of community networking, as well as in school library media/children's services or science and engineering information.

Table 2 / HEA Title II-B, Library Education and Human Resource Development Program, FY 1997 Fellowship Awards (cont.)

Wayne State University
Library and Information Science Program,
Detroit

Grant Number: R036B70003
Award Amount: $88,000
Project Co-directors: Robert Holley, Nancy Becker Johnson

The Master's Level Fellowships for Library Education will educate students demonstrating a commitment to academic, public, and school libraries in urban communities. Ethnic minorities traditionally under-represented in the library profession will be recruited, giving preference to applicants wishing to specialize in school media, children's services, young adult services, science reference, cataloging, or library service evaluation, as well as to applicants interested in the new techniques of information acquisition, transfer, and management of communication technology.

Mississippi

University of Southern Mississippi
School of Library and Information Science,
Hattiesburg

Grant Number: R036B70028
Award Amount: $88,000
Project Director: Melanie Norton

The Addressing Critical Shortages in Mississippi Libraries fellowships will support students oriented to one of three career paths: services to children and youth in school library media centers, cataloging and electronic databases, and information technology and management of electronic technology. Minority candidates who can serve the library and information needs of the state of Mississippi will be recruited.

New York

Queens College, City University of New York
Graduate School of Library and Information Studies,
Flushing

Grant Number: R036B70030
Award Amount: $32,273
Project Director: Karen Patricia Smith

Fellowships will address the shortage of certified school media specialists and children's and young adult librarians in the New York City area and especially the shortage of minority librarians in these service areas, which is particularly acute.

North Carolina

University of North Carolina
School of Information and Library Science,
Chapel Hill

Grant Number: R036B70022
Award Amount: $88,000
Project Director: Evelyn Daniel

Fellowships for Library Services to Youth will support individuals seeking careers in school library media or children's and young adult services in public libraries. Academically superior and talented individuals who have both a demonstrated aptitude for and interest in preparing for a library career in one of these areas will be recruited. Efforts will be made to aggressively seek out minority and economically disadvantaged applicants.

Oklahoma

University of Oklahoma
School of Library and Information Studies,
Norman

Grant Number: R036B70020
Award Amount: $88,000
Project Director: June Lester

Education for Minorities in Targeted Areas of Library and Information Science fellowships will prepare qualified minority students in three areas of current shortage: cataloging, school media, and science reference. Fellows will learn new techniques of information acquisition, transfer, and communication technology.

Texas

Texas Woman's University
School of Library and Information Studies,
Denton

Grant Number: R036B70031
Award Amount: $88,000
Project Director: Keith Swigger

Educating Librarians to Serve Young People fellowships will support specialization in library services for children or young adults. Recruitment will focus on addressing the need for diversity in the profession of librarianship, with selected fellows corresponding to the demographics of the population.

Table 2 / HEA Title II-B, Library Education and Human Resource Development Program, FY 1997 Fellowship Awards *(cont.)*

Wisconsin

University of Wisconsin–Milwaukee
School of Library and Information Science

Grant Number: R036B70017
Award Amount: $66,000
Project Director: Judith Senkevitch

Multicultural Children's and Young Adult Librarianship fellowships will train highly qualified minority or other students in library service to children and young adults, with an emphasis on services to racially and ethnically diverse populations. Criteria for selecting fellows include a commitment to serving children and/or young adults in culturally and racially diverse communities, and a need for financial assistance in pursuing the master's degree.

Institutes

In FY 1997 the U.S. Department of Education awarded $888,727 to support 12 institutes or training workshops, primarily for school and public librarians, at 11 institutions—eight institutions of higher education, one public library, and two library organizations. Table 3 identifies these grantee institutions, describes the project, and gives the amount of each award. However, this amount does not necessarily reflect all of the resources devoted to an institute because the grantee institution may provide additional support.

The institutes represent a variety of subject matter and approaches. However, all address at least one of the secretary of education's priorities:

- To recruit, educate, train, retrain, and retain minorities in library and information science
- To educate, train, or retrain library personnel in areas of library specialization where there are currently shortages such as school media, children's services, young adult services, science reference, and cataloging
- To educate, train, or retrain library personnel in new techniques of information acquisition, transfer, and communication technology
- To educate, train, or retrain library personnel to serve the information needs of the elderly, the illiterate, the disadvantaged, or residents of rural America, including Native Americans

Of the 12 institutes funded in FY 1997, 10 support training library personnel in information management, eight support training in areas of library specialization where there are currently shortages, three support training to serve the information needs of special populations, and three support training and retaining minorities. In addition, one institute addresses an invitational priority, focusing on library collaboration, especially with other educationally centered organizations. Most of the institutes focus on school and public librarians working with youth.

Table 3 / HEA II-B, Library Education and Human Resource Development Program, FY 1997 Institute Awards

District of Columbia

Association of Research Libraries, Washington, D.C.

Grant Number: R036A70012
Award Amount: $99,760
Project Director: DeEtta Jones

The Association of Research Libraries Leadership and Career Development Program will identify talented minority librarians and encourage and prepare them to assume leadership roles in managing the academic and research libraries of the future. Designed to open discussion about how racial identity group membership can inform and influence both a librarian's experience and an organization's behavior, the program will encourage minority librarians to make explicit use of the cultural experience and knowledge gained outside the organization to enhance their career and leadership development.

Florida

Florida State University
School of Information Studies, Tallahassee

Grant Number: R036A70032
Award Amount: $99,910
Project Co-directors: Eliza Dresang (contact person), Pamela Barron, Kathleen Burnett

Fifty school and public librarians from five urban centers in Florida and 10 graduate students from Florida State University's School of Information Studies working with or preparing to work with minority and disadvantaged youth will participate in the Information Professionals Engage Radical Change: Connecting Youth, Books, and the Electronic World institute. Participants will gain knowledge, as well as strategies and skills, about how print and electronic resources are changing radically in the electronic world and how these changing resources are particularly relevant to minority and disadvantaged youth. School/public library teams will develop a collaborative plan of action to use resources with youth and to disseminate information from the institute to colleagues.

University of South Florida
School of Library and Information Science, Tampa

Grant Number: R036A70030
Award Amount: $46,003
Project Director: Marilyn Karrenbrock Stauffer

As a result of the Institute on Library Services to Migrant and Seasonal Farm Workers in Florida, librarians and educational media specialists will develop methods and skills for providing better services to migrant farm workers and their families. Topics to be covered include cultural, linguistic, and ethnic backgrounds of migrant and seasonal workers; communication skills; information needs and their assessment; collection development; model programs; and marketing library services to migrant and seasonal farm workers.

Iowa

University of Iowa
School of Library and Information Science, Iowa City

Grant Number: R036A70002
Award Amount: $76,489
Project Director: Jean Donham van Deusen

An Information Literacy Program with Curriculum and Student Assessment Components institute will address information literacy, assisting school librarians to develop curricula for teaching necessary skills for accessing, evaluating, using, and communicating information. The program will include instruction on information literacy models, strategies for curriculum development, methods for integrating information literacy across the curriculum, and methods for assessing students' information literacy. An electronic bulletin board will offer opportunities for ongoing communication, sharing expertise, exchanging ideas and lessons, and generating discussion about applying the concepts of the institute.

Louisiana

Louisiana State University
School of Library and Information Science, Baton Rouge

Grant Number: R036A70023
Award Amount: $45,717
Project Director: Carol Barry

The Institute on Networked Access in Libraries will allow 45 librarians from school, public, special, and small academic libraries in Louisiana to acquire basic competencies in providing networked access to information resources. Participants will prepare instructional modules for training other library staff in some aspect of networked access in libraries, and will share experiences with each other using the distance learning classrooms across the state.

Table 3 / HEA II-B, Library Education and Human Resource Development Program, FY 1997 Institute Awards (cont.)

Minnesota

University of Minnesota Libraries,
Minneapolis

Grant Number: R036A70008
Award Amount: $75,373
Project Director: Peggy Johnson

The week-long Training Institute: Affirmative Action for Library Science Interns is designed for participants in affirmative action library science internship programs. The program will focus on new telecommunication and multimedia technologies and on leadership skills. The institute will allow participants to gain a community of peers, developing a support network that will continue through their professional careers.

New York

New York Public Library
The Branch Libraries

Grant Number: R036A70007
Award Amount: $110,230
Project Director: Jane Kunstler

This five-day technology training institute is designed to improve service delivery by teaching technological skills to a core group of New York Public Library (NYPL) staff, plus an additional 226 library personnel. Participants will learn how the technology is set up, how it can be used, and how it can be repaired. The program will focus on the basic technology available in each branch library, from the nuts and bolts of hardware to the ins and outs of Microsoft Office software, and from a basic understanding of NYPL's network and integrated catalog system to HTML coding and how to use it to create documents on the World Wide Web and on NYPL's Intranet. The training will help the branch libraries to design a rapid response system within each of the regions of the NYPL system, carried out by the core group of institute participants, so that branch staff within each region can assist one another in troubleshooting technical problems and can instruct one another in the use of library technology.

North Carolina

University of North Carolina
School of Information and Library Science,
Chapel Hill

Grant Number: R036A70043
Award Amount: $81,987
Project Director: Evelyn Daniel

The Internet Training for School Librarians and School Technologists Institute is designed to promote telecommunications and networking to 30 school librarians and school technologists whose schools have recently been connected to the Internet. The program will provide instruction in basic telecommunications, networking, Internet-based information resources, network retrieval tools, network management, and network policy issues; introduce participants to new capabilities on the Internet, including exploration of multimedia technologies, especially streaming audio and video; develop a model training program that a school librarian and technologist could use in training teachers how to use the Internet for education purposes; develop model lesson plans using the Internet that could be used in collaboration with classroom teachers in teaching the Internet to children; and discuss issues surrounding Internet use in the public schools.

Ohio

Kent State University
School of Library and Information Science,
Kent

Grant Number: R036A70035
Award Amount: $100,053
Project Director: Danny Wallace

Designed for public librarians, the Ohio Library Evaluation Institute is a one-week intensive seminar on the nature, benefits, and application of techniques and tools for library service evaluation. The development of new statewide standards for and standardized measures of public library performance will provide a recurring theme for the seminar. Working from the base created by Ohio standards and measures, the seminar will educate public librarians in more complex and sophisticated evaluation methods and techniques, with the goal of instilling and sustaining an expanded culture of evaluation. Each participant will be required to complete an evaluation plan for his or her library.

Kent State University
School of Library and Information Science

Grant Number: R036A70028
Award Amount: $79,695
Project Co-directors: Greg Byerly, Carolyn Brodie

The New Partners and New Technologies: Networking Ohio's Libraries, Schools, Museums,

**Table 3 / HEA II-B, Library Education and Human Resource
Development Program, FY 1997 Institute Awards** *(cont.)*

and Agencies institute is designed to educate school librarians and youth services librarians in the role that external community-based organizations can play in programming and instruction, and in the use of new technologies to access these resources electronically. Training will focus on creating an awareness of and an appreciation for the value of establishing true collaboration between public libraries and school libraries and between libraries and educationally-centered organizations, and providing opportunities for participants to identify and establish real interagency cooperative efforts and activities. Participants will develop an awareness and understanding of how various external agencies or networks can impact instruction in schools, and how new technologies can be used to initiate and foster cooperative educational efforts.

Oklahoma

University of Oklahoma
School of Library and Information Studies,
Norman

Grant Number: R036A70037
Award Amount: $28,601
Project Co-directors: Lotsee Patterson,
Rhonda Harris Taylor, Robert Swisher

The Summer Institute for Tribal Librarians: Training for Internet-Based Resources will train 16 tribal library personnel, recruited from reservations and Indian country throughout the nation, to serve the information needs of Native Americans who live in rural America and who are elderly, illiterate, or disadvantaged, by effectively using Internet-based resources to meet the information needs of these and other tribal library patrons. By providing an opportunity for hands-on instruction, the institute will teach participants to access, evaluate, and effectively use information resources available on the Internet; assess the quality of electronically networked resources; and plan and implement electronic selective dissemination of information to patrons and tribal agencies.

Virgin Islands

Virgin Islands Library Association,
Christiansted

Grant Number: R036A70009
Award Amount: $44,909
Project Director: Laurie Cole

The goal of the Virgin Islands Library Training Institute is to retrain and educate geographically isolated library professionals in the U.S. Virgin Islands, bringing librarians from all three islands together for a shared educational experience. The program will address three critical areas: technology, children's and youth services, and management and evaluation of resources.

Library Research and Demonstration Program (HEA II-B)

The Library Research and Demonstration program (Title II-B of the Higher Education Act) authorizes grants and contracts for research and demonstration projects relating to the improvement of libraries, including the promotion of economical and efficient information delivery, cooperative efforts, training in librarianship, developmental projects, and the dissemination of information derived from these projects.

Title II, Part B, of the Higher Education Act was amended by the Higher Education Amendments of 1986. In 1987, by statutory mandate, "information technology" was deleted from the list of authorized research and demonstration purposes. This amendment precludes research on or about information technology, but allows use of technology to accomplish the goals of a research or demonstration project.

In FY 1997 Congress appropriated $5 million for the HEA II-B Research and Demonstration Program (see Table 4 for the program's funding history). The appropriations act directed that $1 million be used to continue a statewide multitype library network and database grant with a retrospective conversion component (Louisiana State University, originally funded in FY 1993); $1.5 million be

Table 4 / Library Research and Demonstration Program Funding History

Fiscal Year	Appropriation
1967*	$3,550,000
1970	2,171,000
1975	1,000,000
1980	1,000,000
1985	1,000,000
1990	285,000
1991	325,000
1992	325,000
1993	2,802,000
1994	2,802,000
1995	6,500,000
1996	3,000,000
1997	5,000,000

* Initial year

awarded to Portland State University to continue the PORTALS project, which was originally funded in FY 1995; and $1 million be competed to support a social tolerance resource center. The remaining funds—$1.5 million—were not earmarked. Of this amount, $1 million was used for an invitational competition supporting the Department of Education's America Reads Challenge, and $500,000 funded an unsolicited application from Portland State University for its Columbia River Basin Project. (Table 5 describes new grants.)

One grant for $1 million was made under the directed Social Tolerance Resource Center competition. Under the invitational competition supporting the America Reads Challenge, applicants were invited to address one or more of three invitational priorities:

- Projects that demonstrate new and promising library reading programs to raise the reading skills of young children
- Projects that develop and implement cooperative efforts among libraries, schools, and community-based organizations to recruit and train volunteers for after-school, weekend, and summer library reading programs
- Projects that demonstrate model partnerships among libraries, local business, and community groups to stimulate young children's interest in reading

Of the six grants made under this competition, five address the invitational priorities, with all developing projects that demonstrate new and promising library reading programs, four implementing cooperative efforts with other organizations, and one demonstrating model partnerships.

Until FY 1993, projects under the Library Research and Demonstration Program were small, usually under $60,000, and field-initiated, although more substantial projects—such as work leading to the establishment of the Online

(text continues on page 318)

Table 5 / HEA II-B, Library Research and Demonstration Program, FY 1997 Awards
Invitational Priorities Competition

Alaska

Ilisagvik College Corporation,
Barrow

Grant Number: R039D70042
Award Amount: $179,500
Project Director: Katherine Itta Ahgeak

The Tumikut: Pathways to Literacy project, a cooperative effort between Ilisagvik College, the North Slope Borough School District, North Slope Borough Cultural Center, and the Tuzzy Consortium Library, will develop and expand Tuzzy Consortium Library's core collection of Inupiat children's literature, contributing to the ongoing process of developing books for Inupiat children in their own language. Stories will be collected and made available in video and book formats, and the library will conduct story hours and summer reading programs in the Inupiaq language in each village. Through the analysis of these stories, Inupiaq teachers-in-training will produce curricular materials based on Inupiaq literature, providing a reading intervention program that takes into consideration the bilingual background of the students. This project will reinforce the community-wide commitment to Inupiaq language preservation by focusing on children.

Missouri

St. Louis Public Library

Grant Number: R039D70032
Award Amount: $199,551
Project Director: Leslie Edmonds Holt

Project REAL (REading And Learning), a library-based project that will improve reading performance in at-risk children ages 3 to 8, will create a library-based, reading-improvement program directed at at-risk children, their caregivers, teachers, and families in three low-income St. Louis neighborhoods; train and organize adult and teenage volunteers to provide vastly increased, cost-effective reading experiences in school and branch library settings; utilize effective evaluation mechanisms that will demonstrate REAL's qualitative and quantitative benefits; demonstrate how one library can develop private-sector support that adds value to public investment in a reading-improvement program; and develop project protocols and materials so that REAL can serve as a model for other urban public libraries.

New York

Middle Country Public Library,
Centereach

Grant Number: R039D70023
Award Amount: $208,845
Project Director: Mary Schumacher

The Creating Readers: Collaboration for Reading and Educational Success through Libraries project is based on new research in brain development and early childhood education that strongly suggests that building literacy and reading skills begins long before children enter school, and that parents can play a key role in developing emergent literacy skills in young children. The Middle Country Public Library and its partner, Libraries for the Future, will link four libraries in diverse geographic and ethnic communities—Hartford, Connecticut; Providence, Rhode Island; and Suffolk County, New York—in a collaborative partnership to build community coalitions that include businesses, schools, and community groups and to develop a unique set of programs and strategies to promote emergent literacy for families with young children (ages 3 to 5). Activities will include training for librarians in the conceptual framework and implementation of the project design, parent training workshops and support for parents as their child's first teachers, promoting reading readiness in children and providing an atmosphere for development of pre-reading skills, and participating in the America Reads Challenge initiative.

Ohio

Bowling Green State University

Grant Number: R039D70018
Award Amount: $80,865
Project Director: Linda Dobb. Contacts: Rebecca Hill
and Barbara Paff, Hayes Presidential Library

Automating the Nation's First Presidential Library—A Partnership between Bowling Green State University and the Hayes Presidential Center will automate the catalog records of the book, serial, and pamphlet collections of the Hayes Presidential Library, which contains 55,000 book, serial, and pamphlet items, many of which are unique within Ohio and 10 to 15 percent of which are unique within the United States. By partnering with Bowling Green State University,

Table 5 / HEA II-B, Library Research and Demonstration Program, FY 1997 Awards (cont.)
Invitational Priorities Competition

these holdings can be loaded cost-effectively into the statewide OhioLINK catalog, making them readily accessible to students and scholars around the world. Additionally, the project will provide internship opportunities in a unique special library for students from the Kent State library and information science program.

Utah
Utah Valley State College, Orem

Grant Number: R039D70022
Award Amount: $131,530
Project Director: Gary Phelps

The Children's Reading/Internet Training and Support Model (CRTM) project will establish CRTM phonics reading and literacy hubs in the most negatively impacted schools within each of Utah's nine geographic regions, as well as introduce a new technology—Web-based learning—for showing, training, and nurturing librarians to become reading support community magnets. Further, it will demonstrate a new and promising library reading program, the McOmber Phonics Storybook Program, which has a proven history of enabling most first graders to read at a third-grade level within one year; link teachers, parents, and principals to libraries and tutors; enhance volunteerism; and promote corporate sponsorships.

Vermont
Vermont Center for the Book, Chester

Grant Number: R039D70006
Award Amount: $189,709
Project Director: Sally Anderson

A Literature-Based Program to Link and Augment Public Library, Classroom, and Structured Support Reading Programs and Volunteer Assistance for K–1 Students proposes to strengthen the efforts of agents who provide reading experiences for children in grades K to 1 in a variety of settings—public libraries through community programming, schools through classroom and structured support programming, and at home through parental encouragement and reading activities. The project will seek to answer three key questions: (1) What would a program look like that best supports reading skills programs in schools and weaves in literature and whole language? (2) What would a program look like that creates common understanding of current strategies used by the key constituent groups: librarians, teachers, reading specialists, and parents? (3) What would a program look like that would enlarge the pool of trained resources, including parents, available to provide sustained support for children's reading efforts? The project will develop a model for establishing a team that can design and deliver literature-based programs that build on and enhance the particular mission of each constituent.

Social Tolerance Resource Center Competition
Simon Wiesenthal Center, Los Angeles

Grant Number: R039D70004
Award Amount: $997,563
Project Director: Liebe Geft

The "Teaching Steps to Tolerance" project is designed to assist fifth- and sixth-grade teachers and school librarians in becoming more effective teachers of tolerance and prejudice reduction through a program of in-service training, workshops, and the dissemination of curricular materials. Participating teachers and librarians will be able to use the teaching techniques and instructional materials developed and promoted by the project as part of their ongoing programs in American history, world history, social studies, English, and other core subjects in the school curriculum. The project, which is based on current educational research and state-of-the-art technology, will assist educators and their students in dealing more thoughtfully and constructively with the challenges of tolerance and prejudice. The project will serve as a model for widely disseminating multimedia curricular materials for use by school systems nationwide.

Unsolicited Grant
Portland State University, Portland, Oregon

Grant Number: R039U70001
Award Amount: $499,700
Project Director: William Lang

The Columbia River Basin Project is a multi-phase, integrated dissemination and curriculum development project being conducted by the Center for Columbia River History, which includes Portland State University, Washington State University–Vancouver, and the

**Table 5 / HEA II-B, Library Research and
Demonstration Program, FY 1997 Awards** *(cont.)*
Invitational Priorities Competition

Washington State Historical Society. The project includes three components that will use the Internet as the primary means of dissemination:

- The Oral History and Bibliography Program will acquire, collate and disseminate new library materials on the Columbia River Basin and publish this information on the Internet.
- The Columbia River Curriculum Program will create and test an integrated Columbia River curriculum for high school instruction and publish the final products on the Internet.
- The Community History Exhibits Program will create local history exhibits in four small Columbia River Basin towns, as well as present exhibits on the Internet.

Computer Library Center (OCLC), a major national bibliographic referral center—were undertaken. Beginning in FY 1993 and continuing through FY 1997, projects were for larger sums ($1 million to $2.5 million) and, for the most part, were specified by Congress for library networking and to make federal and other information available for public use.

Library Services for Indian Tribes and Hawaiian Natives Program (LSCA Title IV)

LSCA Title IV basic grants awarded in FY 1997 will improve public library services to 231 Indian tribes and Alaska native villages and to approximately 170,000 Hawaiian natives. Funds, totaling $2,577,381, are being used in 29 states to support a variety of activities, including outreach programs to the community, salaries and training of library staff, purchase of library materials, and the renovation of library facilities.

Since FY 1985, 2 percent of the appropriations for LSCA Titles I, II, and III has been set aside as the available funding for LSCA Title IV (1.5 percent for Indian tribes and 0.5 percent for Hawaiian natives). Only Indian tribes and Alaska native villages that are federally recognized and organizations serving Hawaiian natives that are recognized by the governor of Hawaii are eligible to participate in the program. For the past 13 years, Alu Like, Inc. has been the only organization recognized to apply for the Hawaiian native set-aside.

Two types of awards are made: basic grants and special projects grants. The basic grant is noncompetitive, and if an Indian tribe or Alaska native village is eligible and pursues authorized activities, funding is guaranteed. In FY 1997 the established basic grant for Indian tribes and Alaska native villages was $4,217, while Alu Like, Inc. received the entire Hawaiian native set-aside of $644,345. These funds continue to be used to support projects emphasizing outreach, collection development, and training of Hawaiian natives for librarianship.

Of the 547 Indian tribes and Alaska native villages eligible to compete, 221 applied for and received basic grants. Of these, two were joint funding requests, involving 10 additional tribes. Approximately $974,127 was awarded under the basic grant program (see Table 7 for basic grant awards); the remaining $950,663 was used for special projects grants.

In FY 1997 the U.S. Department of Education supported competitively awarded special projects grants to Indian tribes for the improvement of public library services. Twelve tribes in seven states received grants ranging from $49,923 to $99,499.

All recipients are required to have a librarian, a three- to five-year long-range plan for public library development, and to contribute at least 20 percent of the total project costs. Grant funds are provided for assessment of community library needs, salaries and training of library staff, costs for transportation of community members without access to libraries, purchase of needed resource materials, and support of special programs offered to young and old. (See Table 6 for special projects grant Awards.)

Table 6A / Library Services for Indian Tribes and Hawaiian Natives Program Funding History

Fiscal Year	Appropriation
1985*	$2,360,000
1990	2,419,120
1991	2,460,448
1992	2,410,480
1993	2,391,196
1994	2,415,360
1995	2,494,380
1996	2,540,000
1997	2,577,380

* Initial year

Table 6 / LSCA Title IV, Library Services for Indian Tribes and Hawaiian Natives Program, FY 1997 Special Projects Awards

Alaska

Arctic Slope Regional Corporation,
Barrow

Grant Number: R163B70067
Award Amount: $87,981

The principal goal of the Village-Based Library Management project is to increase the use of library resources by the Inupiat natives in the eight villages composing the North Slope Borough. With its first special projects grant, the Arctic Slope Regional Corporation will establish advisory committees in each village; survey the communities; assess their technological and building needs; identify, train, and hire local employees as village library technicians; and provide stability to summer reading programs in the outlying villages. The project is a cooperative effort between Arctic Slope, Naqsragmiut Tribal Council, Native Village of Barrow, Kaktovik Village of Barter Island, Native Village of Nuiqsut, Native Village of Point Hope, Native Village of Point Lay, Wainwright Traditional Council, Tuzzy Consortium Library, Ilsagvik College, and the North Slope Borough School District.

Central Council of Tlingit/Haida,
Juneau

Grant Number: R163B70049
Award Amount: $93,000

The Central Council of Tlingit and Haida Indian Tribes will use its first library services grant to complete initial staffing and library services development activities for a tribal library to be located in the tribe's new Southeast Alaska Native Employment and Training Center. The tribe will recruit professional library staff, purchase resource materials, catalog library materials, initiate programming for various age and interest groups within the community, and develop a

Table 6 / LSCA Title IV, Library Services for Indian Tribes and Hawaiian Natives Program, FY 1997 Special Projects Awards (cont.)

learning skills center that includes Internet access as well as access to online library catalogs. Villages throughout Southeast Alaska that currently lack access to library services will be linked electronically to the Central Council library.

California

Pala Band of Mission Indians,
Pala

Grant Number: R163B70061
Award Amount: $49,923

As a first-time recipient of a special projects grant, the Pala Band will use funds to support salaries of library personnel, purchase an array of library materials, and conduct special programs that include literacy and computer literacy programs for adults and children. Funds will also allow purchase of furniture and equipment for a new library being built with HUD and tribal funds.

Washoe Tribe of Nevada and California,
Alpine

Grant Number: R163B70060
Award Amount: $94,067

The Washoe Tribe will use its first special projects grant to carry out an expansion of the Woodfords Indian Education Center and Library facility to improve handicapped accessibility to library materials and services and to provide additional space for the facility. Services will be expanded to provide adult computer classes for community residents, a summer reading program based on the Mother-Daughter Book Club, and a new CD-ROM storage/retrieval system for Washoe-related resource materials. A Native American community resident will receive training to facilitate these and other programs.

Montana

Fort Peck Assiniboine and Sioux Tribes,
Poplar

Grant Number: R163B70076
Award Amount: $78,612

The Fort Peck Assiniboine and Sioux Tribes—together with other members of the Montana Indian Tribal Libraries Group—will focus on strengthening collections in the area of Native American studies. The project will provide a comprehensive bibliography concerning North American tribes to the research community through the Internet, provide libraries across the country with a comprehensive bibliography with a defined core of Native American titles for collection development, enhance the participating tribal libraries' collections, and assure interlibrary access to the collection.

New Mexico

Pueblo of Jemez

Grant Number: R163B70035
Award Amount: $99,930

The Jemez Pueblo Community Library will upgrade computer and library services to community members by providing educational programs for children and teenagers, as well as computer classes for artists seeking to market their work online. The library will also go online with an Internet home page that lists the pueblo's artists and craftspeople, and the facility will undergo an extensive renovation to create dedicated space for a computer center.

Pueblo of Santa Clara,
Espanola

Grant Number: R163B70064
Award Amount: $68,095

The Pueblo of Santa Clara will continue to train tribal members in the library sciences and to improve its needs assessment capabilities. Materials will be purchased for a variety of special programs that will encompass prevention/awareness programming for adults, a youth/teen library multicultural program, and a senior outreach program that will include a special senior remembrance project for youth, adults, and seniors.

Pueblo of Zuni

Grant Number: R163B70016
Award Amount: $99,499

The Pueblo of Zuni will expand its library facility by providing a meeting room for tribal program and community groups as well as for training and educational functions and by adding a children's theater that features storytelling, puppet shows, and other activities designed to expose children to reading at an early age. Funds will also be used to acquire computers, equipment, and software; to conduct specialized programs; and to upgrade library furnishings and other equipment.

Table 6 / LSCA Title IV, Library Services for Indian Tribes and Hawaiian Natives Program, FY 1997 Special Projects Awards *(cont.)*

Oklahoma

Iowa Tribe of Oklahoma,
Perkins

Grant Number: R163B70054
Award Amount: $60,573

With its first special projects grant, the Iowa Tribe will hire a professional librarian to organize its library materials and to develop a computer lab that utilizes new information technologies and provides training.

Miami Tribe of Oklahoma,
Miami

Grant Number: R163B70039
Award Amount: $79,363

The Miami Tribe will continue its expansion of the CHARLIE (Connecting Help and Resources Linking Indians Effectively) network, which unites the Miamis and six of the other Northeast Eight Oklahoma Tribes, permitting them to share an online library catalog. This award will support employment of added professional staff to assist each tribe on site, extend the network, and provide Internet access for all sites as well as specialized training in computer/Internet use for tribal personnel and library patrons.

South Dakota

Lower Brule Sioux Tribe,
Lower Brule

Grant Number: R163B70038
Award Amount: $62,068

The Lower Brule Community Library Project will reach 1,800 largely underserved tribal members. Funds will be used to provide continued public library management training for a library assistant, to organize volunteers for an adult literacy program, and to arrange for Native American storytelling that will encourage the strong oral tradition of the Lakota Sioux people. The tribe will also update its long-range plan for library services and identify funding sources for continued development of its library.

Wisconsin

Lac Courte Oreilles Tribal Governing Board,
Hayward

Grant Number: R163B70030
Award Amount: $77,552

The major emphasis of this project will be ensuring the reading readiness of the preschool youngsters on the Lac Courte Oreilles Ojibwa Indian Reservation in Northwest Wisconsin. Parent participation in the early education of their children will be stressed, and outreach services to area Head Start centers, as well as to senior centers and the reservation's K–12 school, will be continued and expanded. Funding will also allow for development of a system of electronic archives for preserving the text of community records.

Table 7 / LSCA Title IV, Library Services for Indian Tribes and Hawaiian Natives Program, FY 1997 Basic Grant Awards

Grantee	Award Number	Award Amount
Alabama		
Poarch Band of Creek Indians	R163A70097	$ 4,217
Alaska		
Akutan Traditional Council	R163A70167	$ 4,217
Alaska Native Village of Toksook Bay	R163A70148	$ 4,217
Algaacik Native Village	R163A70153	$ 4,217
Allakaket Tribal Council	R163A70144	$ 4,217
Anvik Traditional Council	R163A70234	$ 4,217
Artic Slope Regional Corporation	R163A70129	$ 33,736
Bill Moore's Slough	R163A70162	$ 4,217
Cantwell Village Council	R163A70018	$ 4,217
Central Council Tlingit & Haida	R163A70108	$ 4,217

Table 7 / LSCA Title IV, Library Services for Indian Tribes and Hawaiian Natives Program, FY 1997 Basic Grant Awards *(cont.)*

Grantee	Award Number	Award Amount
Chefornak Native Village	R163A70152	$ 4,217
Chevak Traditional Council	R163A70161	$ 4,217
Chugach Alaska Corporation	R163A70181	$ 4,217
City of Hydaburg	R163A70202	$ 4,217
Deering Native Village	R163A70208	$ 4,217
Egegik Village Council	R163A70225	$ 4,217
Elim Native Village	R163A70025	$ 4,217
False Pass Tribal Council	R163A70209	$ 4,217
Kenaitze Indian Tribe	R163A70103	$ 4,217
Koyukuk Tribal Council	R163A70177	$ 4,217
Kwigillingok Native Village	R163A70150	$ 4,217
Lime Village Traditional Council	R163A70184	$ 4,217
Louden Tribal Council	R163A70048	$ 4,217
McGrath Native Village Council	R163A70073	$ 4,217
Metlakatla Indian Community	R163A70052	$ 4,217
Nanwalek IRA Council	R163A70169	$ 4,217
Native Village of Atka	R163A70057	$ 4,217
Native Village of Crooked Creek	R163A70155	$ 4,217
Native Village of Eagle	R163A70071	$ 4,217
Native Village of Eyak	R163A70084	$ 4,217
Native Village of Kivalina	R163A70045	$ 4,217
Native Village of Kotzebue	R163A70138	$ 4,217
Native Village of Sheldon's Point	R163A70164	$ 4,217
Nenana Native Council	R163A70021	$ 4,217
Ninilchik Traditional Council	R163A70032	$ 4,217
Northway Village	R163A70224	$ 4,217
Ounalshka Corporation	R163A70222	$ 4,217
Ouzinkie Tribal Council	R163A70009	$ 4,217
Pedro Bay Village Council	R163A70197	$ 4,217
Pilot Station Traditional Village	R163A70159	$ 4,217
Port Graham Village Council	R163A70173	$ 4,217
Selawik IRA Council	R163A70029	$ 4,217
Shageluk IRA Council	R163A70228	$ 4,217
Tanana Chiefs Conference, Inc.	R163A70140	$ 4,217
Tatitlek Village IRA Council	R163A70221	$ 4,217
Yakutat Tlingit Tribe	R163A70127	$ 4,217

Arizona

Cocopah Indian Tribe	R163A70010	$ 4,217
Colorado River Indian Tribes	R163A70067	$ 4,217
Fort McDowell Indian Community	R163A70092	$ 4,217
Hopi Tribe	R163A70063	$ 4,217
Hualapai Nation	R163A70069	$ 4,217
Navajo Nation	R163A70226	$ 4,217
Pascua Yaqui Tribe of Arizona	R163A70196	$ 4,217
Salt River Pima-Maricopa Indian Community	R163A70060	$ 4,217
San Juan Southern Paiute Tribe	R163A70122	$ 4,217
Tohono O'odham Nation	R163A70193	$ 4,217

Table 7 / LSCA Title IV, Library Services for Indian Tribes and Hawaiian Natives Program, FY 1997 Basic Grant Awards (cont.)

Grantee	Award Number	Award Amount
Tonto Apache Tribe of Arizona	R163A70087	$ 4,217
Yavapai-Apache Nation	R163A70126	$ 4,217
California		
Agua Caliente Band of Cahuilla Indians	R163A70207	$ 4,217
Barona Band of Mission Indians	R163A70065	$ 4,217
Bear River Band of Rohnerville Rancheria	R163A70206	$ 4,217
Big Lagoon Rancheria	R163A70214	$ 4,217
Big Pine Tribe	R163A70089	$ 4,217
Big Valley Rancheria	R163A70220	$ 4,217
Blue Lake Rancheria	R163A70013	$ 4,217
Bridgeport Indian Reservation	R163A70149	$ 4,217
Cahuilla Band of Indians	R163A70156	$ 4,217
Campo Band of Mission indians	R163A70075	$ 4,217
Cher-Ae Heights Indian Community	R163A70014	$ 4,217
Coyote Valley Tribal Council	R163A70204	$ 16,868
Cuyapaipe Reservation	R163A70121	$ 4,217
Elk Valley Rancheria	R163A70082	$ 4,217
Fort Mojave Indian Tribe	R163A70165	$ 4,217
Guidiville Indian Rancheria	R163A70106	$ 4,217
Hoopa Valley Tribal Council	R163A70194	$ 4,217
Ione Band of Miwok Indians	R163A70217	$ 4,217
Jamul Band of Mission Indians	R163A70046	$ 4,217
LaPosta Band of Mission Indians	R163A70174	$ 4,217
Lytton Rancheria	R163A70124	$ 4,217
Manzanita Band of Mission Indians	R163A70047	$ 4,217
Mesa Grande Band of Mission Indians	R163A70136	$ 4,217
Mooretown Rancheria	R163A70112	$ 4,217
Pala Band of Mission Indians	R163A70098	$ 4,217
Picayune Rancheria of the Chuckchausi Indians	R163A70143	$ 4,217
Pinoleville Band of Pomo Indians	R163A70016	$ 4,217
Redding Rancheria Tribal Council	R163A70027	$ 4,217
Redwood Valley Reservation	R163A70023	$ 4,217
Robinson Rancheria	R163A70114	$ 4,217
Round Valley Indian Tribes	R163A70223	$ 4,217
Sherwood Valley Band of Pomo Indians	R163A70080	$ 4,217
Shingle Springs Rancheria	R163A70116	$ 4,217
Smith River Rancheria	R163A70038	$ 4,217
Soboba Band of Mission Indians	R163A70058	$ 4,217
Table Bluff Rancheria-Wiyot Tribe	R163A70095	$ 4,217
Table Mountain Rancheria	R163A70074	$ 4,217
Torres-Martinez Desert Cahuilla Tribe	R163A70004	$ 4,217
Tule River Tribal Council	R163A70005	$ 4,217
Tuolumne Band of Me-Wuk Indians	R163A70179	$ 4,217
Yurok Tribe	R163A70213	$ 4,217
Connecticut		
Mohegan Tribe	R163A70061	$ 4,217

Table 7 / LSCA Title IV, Library Services for Indian Tribes and Hawaiian Natives Program, FY 1997 Basic Grant Awards (cont.)

Grantee	Award Number	Award Amount
Florida		
Miccosukee Corporation	R163A70055	$ 4,217
Seminole Tribe of Florida	R163A70151	$ 4,217
Hawaii		
Alu Like, Inc.	R163A70166	$644,345
Idaho		
Shoshone-Bannock Tribes	R163A70051	$ 4,217
Louisiana		
Chitimacha Tribe of Louisiana	R163A70056	$ 4,217
Coushatta Tribe of Louisiana	R163A70078	$ 4,217
Tunica-Biloxi Indians of Louisiana	R163A70006	$ 4,217
Maine		
Aroostook Band of Micmacs	R163A70044	$ 4,217
Penobscot Indian Nation	R163A70076	$ 4,217
Massachusetts		
Wampanoag Tribe of Gay Head	R163A70088	$ 4,217
Michigan		
Grand Traverse Band/Ottawa & Chippewa Indians	R163A70043	$ 4,217
Hannahville Tribal Council	R163A70003	$ 4,217
Keweenaw Bay Indian Community	R163A70085	$ 4,217
Lac Vieux Desert Band of Lake Superior Chippewa	R163A70028	$ 4,217
Nottawaseppi Huron Band of Potawatomi	R163A70133	$ 4,217
Pokagon Band of Potawatomi Indians	R163A70081	$ 4,217
Saginaw Chippewa Indian Tribe of Michigan	R163A70192	$ 4,217
Sault Ste. Marie Tribe of Chippewa	R163A70034	$ 4,217
Minnesota		
Minnesota Chippewa Tribe	R163A70200	$ 4,217
Red Lake Band of Chippewa Indians	R163A70185	$ 4,217
Shakopee Mdewakanton Sioux Community	R163A70024	$ 4,217
Missouri		
Eastern Shawnee Tribe of Oklahoma	R163A70017	$ 4,217
Montana		
Blackfeet Tribe	R163A70158	$ 4,217
Chippewa Cree Tribe	R163A70104	$ 4,217
Confederated Salish & Kootenai Tribes	R163A70216	$ 4,217
Crow Indian Tribe	R163A70102	$ 4,217
Fort Belknap/Assiniboine/Gros Ventre Tribes	R163A70022	$ 4,217
Fort Peck Assiniboine-Sioux Tribe	R163A70093	$ 4,217
Northern Cheyenne Tribe	R163A70233	$ 4,217
Nebraska		
Ponca Tribe of Nebraska	R163A70012	$ 4,217

Table 7 / LSCA Title IV, Library Services for Indian Tribes and Hawaiian Natives Program, FY 1997 Basic Grant Awards (cont.)

Grantee	Award Number	Award Amount
Santee Sioux Tribe of Nebraska	R163A70083	$ 4,217
Winnebago Tribe of Nebraska	R163A70007	$ 4,217
Nevada		
Duckwater Shoshone Tribe	R163A70062	$ 4,217
Ely Shoshone Tribe	R163A70130	$ 4,217
Reno Sparks Indian Colony	R163A70110	$ 4,217
Washoe Tribe of Nevada & California	R163A70105	$ 4,217
New Mexico		
Jicarilla Apache Tribe	R163A70059	$ 4,217
Pueblo of Cochiti	R163A70203	$ 4,217
Pueblo of Isleta	R163A70188	$ 4,217
Pueblo of Jemez	R163A70205	$ 4,217
Pueblo of Laguna	R163A70117	$ 4,217
Pueblo of Picuris	R163A70189	$ 4,217
Pueblo of Pojoaque	R163A70041	$ 4,217
Pueblo of San Felipe	R163A70037	$ 4,217
Pueblo of San Juan	R163A70190	$ 4,217
Pueblo of Santa Clara	R163A70100	$ 4,217
Pueblo of Tesuque	R163A70198	$ 4,217
Pueblo of Zuni	R163A70139	$ 4,217
Sky City Community School	R163A70199	$ 4,217
New York		
Oneida Indian Nation	R163A70118	$ 4,217
Seneca Nation of Indians	R163A70168	$ 4,217
St. Regis Band of Mohawks	R163A70094	$ 4,217
North Carolina		
Eastern Band of Cherokee Indians	R163A70050	$ 4,217
North Dakota		
Spirit Lake Nation	R163A70172	$ 4,217
Standing Rock Sioux Tribe	R163A70210	$ 4,217
Three Affiliated Tribes	R163A70101	$ 4,217
Turtle Mountain Band of Chippewa	R163A70201	$ 4,217
Oklahoma		
Absentee Shawnee Tribe of Oklahoma	R163A70086	$ 4,217
Caddo Indian Tribe	R163A70070	$ 4,217
Cherokee Nation	R163A70099	$ 4,217
Cheyenne-Arapaho Tribe of Oklahoma	R163A70131	$ 4,217
Chickasaw Nation	R163A70020	$ 4,217
Choctaw Nation	R163A70171	$ 4,217
Citizen Potawatomi Nation	R163A70066	$ 4,217
Comanche Indian Tribe	R163A70033	$ 4,217
Fort Sill Apache Tribe of Oklahoma	R163A70090	$ 4,217
Iowa Tribe of Oklahoma	R163A70008	$ 4,217
Kaw Nation of Oklahoma	R163A70187	$ 4,217

Table 7 / LSCA Title IV, Library Services for Indian Tribes and Hawaiian Natives Program, FY 1997 Basic Grant Awards (cont.)

Grantee	Award Number	Award Amount
Kialegee Tribal Town of Oklahoma	R163A70175	$ 4,217
Kiowa Tribe of Oklahoma	R163A70180	$ 4,217
Miami Tribe of Oklahoma	R163A70120	$ 4,217
Modoc Tribe of Oklahoma	R163A70128	$ 4,217
Muscogee (Creek) Nation	R163A70212	$ 4,217
Osage Nation	R163A70176	$ 4,217
Ottawa Tribe of Oklahoma	R163A70182	$ 4,217
Pawnee Tribe of Oklahoma	R163A70030	$ 4,217
Ponca Tribe of Oklahoma	R163A70154	$ 4,217
Quapaw Tribe of Oklahoma	R163A70134	$ 4,217
Sac and Fox Nation	R163A70183	$ 4,217
Seneca-Cayuga Tribe of Oklahoma	R163A70036	$ 4,217
Wichita and Affiliated Tribes of Oklahoma	R163A70178	$ 4,217
Wyandotte Tribe of Oklahoma	R163A70072	$ 4,217
Oregon		
Confederated Tribes of Coos, et al.	R163A70113	$ 4,217
Confederated Tribes of Siletz	R163A70141	$ 4,217
Confederated Tribes of Warm Springs Reservation	R163A70191	$ 4,217
Coquille Indian Tribe	R163A70227	$ 4,217
Cow Creek Band of Umpqua Tribe of Indians	R163A70115	$ 4,217
The Klamath Tribes	R163A70039	$ 4,217
South Carolina		
Catawba Indian Nation	R163A70064	$ 4,217
South Dakota		
Flandreau Santee Sioux Tribe	R163A70026	$ 4,217
Loneman School Corporation	R163A70135	$ 4,217
Lower Brule Sioux Tribe	R163A70218	$ 4,217
Oglala Sioux Tribe	R163A70160	$ 4,217
Rosebud Sioux Tribe	R163A70042	$ 4,217
Sisseton-Wahpeton Sioux Tribe	R163A70123	$ 4,217
Yankton Sioux Indian Tribe	R163A70119	$ 4,217
Texas		
Alabama-Coushatta Tribe of Texas	R163A70053	$ 4,217
Ysleta del Sur Pueblo	R163A70054	$ 4,217
Utah		
Paiute Indian Tribe of Utah	R163A70195	$ 4,217
Washington		
Chehalis Indian Tribe	R163A70137	$ 4,217
Colville Confederated Tribes	R163A70040	$ 4,217
Jamestown S'Klallam Tribe	R163A70068	$ 4,217
Lower Elwha Klallam Tribe	R163A70079	$ 4,217
Lummi Indian Nation	R163A70170	$ 4,217
Makah Indian Tribe	R163A70146	$ 4,217
Muckleshoot Indian Tribe	R163A70031	$ 4,217

Table 7 / LSCA Title IV, Library Services for Indian Tribes and Hawaiian Natives Program, FY 1997 Basic Grant Awards *(cont.)*

Grantee	Award Number	Award Amount
Nisqually Indian Tribe	R163A70109	$ 4,217
Puyallup Indian Tribe	R163A70219	$ 4,217
Quileute Tribal School	R163A70091	$ 4,217
Samish Indian Nation	R163A70186	$ 4,217
Shoalwater Bay Indian Tribe	R163A70147	$ 4,217
Squaxin Island Tribe	R163A70163	$ 4,217
Stillaguamish Tribe of Indians	R163A70019	$ 4,217
Swinomish Indian Tribal Community	R163A70015	$ 4,217
Upper Skagit Indian Tribe	R163A70145	$ 4,217
Yakima Indian Nation	R163A70111	$ 4,217
Wisconsin		
Bad River Band of Chippewa Indians	R163A70132	$ 4,217
Forest County Potawatomi Community	R163A70125	$ 4,217
Lac Courte Oreilles Tribal Board	R163A70049	$ 4,217
Lac du Flambeau Band of Lake Superior Chippewa	R163A70215	$ 4,217
Menominee Indian Tribe of Wisconsin	R163A70211	$ 4,217
Oneida Tribe of Indians of Wisconsin	R163A70107	$ 4,217

Part 3
Library/Information Science Education, Placement, and Salaries

Guide to Employment Sources in the Library and Information Professions

Maxine Moore

Office for Library Personnel Resources, American Library Association

This guide updates the listing in the 1997 *Bowker Annual* with information on new services and changes in contacts and groups listed previously. The sources listed primarily give assistance in obtaining professional positions, although a few indicate assistance with paraprofessionals. The latter, however, tend to be recruited through local sources.

General Sources of Library and Information Jobs

Library Literature

Classified ads of library vacancies and positions wanted are carried in many of the national, regional, and state library journals and newsletters. Members of associations can sometimes list "position wanted" ads free of charge in their membership publications. Listings of positions available are regularly found in *American Libraries, Chronicle of Higher Education, College & Research Libraries News, Library Journal*, and *Library Hotline*. State and regional library association newsletters, state library journals, foreign library periodicals, and other types of periodicals carrying such ads are listed in later sections.

Newspapers

The *New York Times* Sunday "Week in Review" section carries a special section of ads for librarian jobs in addition to the regular classifieds. Local newspapers, particularly the larger city Sunday editions, such as the *Washington Post, Los Angeles Times*, and *Chicago Tribune* often carry job vacancy listings in libraries, both professional and paraprofessional.

Internet

The many library-related electronic listservs on the Internet often post library job vacancies interspersed with other news and discussion items. A growing number of general online jobsearch bulletin boards exist; these may include information-related job notices along with other types of jobs. This guide includes information on electronic access where available through the individual organizations listed below. Three useful resources are: "Making Short Work of the Job Search" by Marilyn Rosenthal, *Library Journal*, September 1, 1997, "Job Opportunities

Glitter for Librarians Who Surf the Net" by A. Paula Azar, *American Libraries*, September 1996, and a Web site created by Jeffery C. Lee, "The Librarian's Job Search Source," http://www.zoots.com/libjob/libjob.htm.

"Winning Résumé," by Scott Grusky in *Internet World*, February 1996, and "Riley's Guided Tour: Job Searching on the Net" by Margaret Riley, et al, *Library Journal*, September 15, 1996, pp. 24–27 offer guidance on databases that might lead to library and information-related position listings.

A guide to other types of employment information on the Internet is available on the same gopher clearinghouse: "Job Searching & Employment; P. Ray, B. Taylor." Several articles in the Fall 1994 *Journal of Career Planning & Employment* discuss "Career Counseling in Cyberspace" and "The Job Search Goes Computer."

Library Joblines

Library joblines or job "hotlines" give recorded telephone messages of job openings in a specific geographical area. Most tapes are changed once a week, although individual listings may sometimes be carried for several weeks. Although the information is fairly brief and the cost of calling is borne by the individual job seeker, a jobline provides a quick and up-to-date listing of vacancies that is not usually possible with printed listings or journal ads.

Most joblines carry listings for their state or region only, although some will occasionally accept out-of-state positions if there is room on the tape. While a few will list technician and other paraprofessional positions, the majority are for professional jobs only. When calling the joblines, one might occasionally find a time when the telephone keeps ringing without any answer; this will usually mean that the tape is being changed or there are no new jobs for that period. The classified section of *American Libraries* carries jobline numbers periodically as space permits.

The following joblines are in operation:

Jobline Sponsor	Job Seekers (To Hear Job Listings)	Employers (To Place Job Listings)
American Association of Law Libraries	312-939-7877	53 W. Jackson Blvd., Suite 940, Chicago, IL 60604. 312-939-4764; fax 312-431-1097
Arizona Department of Library, Archives and Public Records (Arizona libraries only)	602-275-2325	1700 W. Washington, Phoenix, AZ 85008
British Columbia Library Association (B.C. listings only)	604-430-6411	Jobline, 110-6545 Bonsor Ave., Burnaby, BC V51 1H3, Canada. 604-430-9633
California Library Association	916-447-5627	717 K St., Suite 300, Sacramento, CA 95814-3477. 916-447-8541

Jobline Sponsor	Job Seekers (To Hear Job Listings)	Employers (To Place Job Listings)
California School Library Association Educators Association	650-697-8832	1499 Old Bayshore Hwy., Suite 142, Burlingame, CA 94010. 650-692-2350
Cleveland (OH) Area Metropolitan Library System Job Listing Service	216-921-4702	CAMLS, 20600 Chagrin Blvd., Suite 500, Shaker Heights, OH 44122.
Colorado State Library[1] (includes paraprofessionals)	303-866-6741	Jobline, 201 E. Colfax, Rm. 309, Denver, CO 80203-1704. 303-866-6900; fax 303-866-6940; also via Libnet/listserv
Connecticut Library Association	860-889-1200	Box 1046, Norwich, CT 06360-1046
Delaware Division of Libraries (Del., N.J., and Pa. listings)	800-282-8696 (in-state) 302-739-4748 ext. 165 (out-of-state)	43 S. Dupont Hwy., Dover, DE 19901
Drexel University College of Info. Sci. & Tech.	215-895-1672 215-895-1048	College of Info. Sci. & Tech., Philadelphia, PA 19104. 215-895-2478; fax 215-895-2494
State Library of Florida	904-488-5232 (in-state)	R. A. Gray Bldg., Tallahassee, FL 32399-0250. 904-487-2651
Library Jobline of Illinois[2]	312-828-0930 (professional) 312-828-9198 (support staff)	Illinois Library Assn., 33 W. Grand, Suite 301, Chicago, IL 60610. 312-644-1896 ($40/2 weeks)
State Library of Iowa (professional jobs in Iowa; only during regular business hours)	515-281-7574	East 12 & Grand, Des Moines, IA 50319. 515-281-7574
Kansas State Library Jobline (also includes paraprofessional and out-of-state)	913-296-3296	State Capitol, 300 S.W. Tenth Ave. Topeka, KS 66612-1593, fax 785-296-6650
Kentucky Job Hotline	502-564-3008 (24 hours)	Dept. for Libs. and Archives, Box 537, Frankfort, KY 40602. 502-564-8300
Long Island (NY) Library Resources Council Jobline	516-632-6658	516-632-6650; fax 516-632-6662
Maryland Library Association	410-685-5760	400 Cathedral St., 3rd flr., Baltimore, MD 21201. 410-727-7422 (Mon.–Fri., 9:00 A.M.–4:30 P.M.)
Medical Library Association Jobline	312-553-4636 (24 hours)	6 N. Michigan Ave., Suite 300, Chicago, IL 60602. 312-419-9094

Jobline Sponsor	Job Seekers (To Hear Job Listings)	Employers (To Place Job Listings)
Metropolitan Washington (D.C.) Council of Governments Library Council	202-962-3712	777 N. Capitol St. N.E., Suite 300, Washington, DC 20002. 202-962-3254
Michigan Library Association	517-694-7440	6810 S. Cedar, #6, Lansing, MI 48911. 517-694-6615; fax 517-694-4330 ($40/week)
Missouri Library Association Jobline	573-442-6590	1306 Business 63 S., Suite B, Columbia, MO 65201-8404. 573-449-4627
Mountain Plains Library Association[3]	605-677-5757	c/o I. D. Weeks Library, University of South Dakota, Vermillion, SD 57069. 605-677-6082; fax 605-677-5488
Nebraska Job Hotline (in-state and other openings during regular business hours)	402-471-4019 800-307-2665 (in-state)	Nebraska Library Commission, 1200 N St. 120, Lincoln, NE 68508-2023.
New England Library Jobline (New England jobs only)	617-521-2815 (24 hours)	GSLIS, Simmons College, 300 The Fenway, Boston, MA 02115. Fax 617-521-3192
New Jersey Library Association	609-695-2121	Box 1534, Trenton, NJ 08607; 609-394-8032; fax 609-394-8164 (nonmembers $25/4 weeks)
New York Library Association	518-432-6952 800-232-6952 (in-state)	252 Hudson Ave., Albany, NY 12210-1802. 518-432-6952 (members $15/3 months, nonmembers $25/3 months)
North Carolina State Library (professional jobs in N.C. only)	919-733-6410	Division of State Library, 109 E. Jones St., Raleigh, NC 27601-2807. 919-733-2570
Ohio Library Council	614-225-6999 (24 hours)	35 E. Gay St., Suite 305, Columbus, OH 43215. 614-221-9057; fax 614-221-6234
Oklahoma Department of Libraries Jobline (5:00 P.M.–8:00 A.M., Monday–Friday and all weekend)	405-521-4202	200 N.E. 18 St., Oklahoma City, OK 73105. 405-521-2502
Oregon Library Association (Northwest listings only)	503-585-2232	Oregon State Library, State Library Bldg., Salem, OR 97310. 503-378-4243 ext. 221
Pennsylvania Cooperative Job Hotline[5]	717-234-4646 800-622-3308 (in-state)	Pennsylvania Library Assn., 1919 N. Front St., Harrisburg, PA 17102. 717-233-3113 (weekly fee for nonmembers); fax 717-233-3121

Jobline Sponsor	Job Seekers (To Hear Job Listings)	Employers (To Place Job Listings)
Pratt Institute SILS Job Hotline	718-636-3742	SILS, Brooklyn, NY 11205. 718-636-3702; fax 718-636-3733
University of South Carolina College of Library and Information Science (no geographic restrictions)	803-777-8443	University of South Carolina, Columbia, SC 29208. 803-777-3887
Special Libraries Association	202-234-3632	1700 18th St. N.W., Washington, DC 20009. 202-234-4700
Special Libraries Association, New York Chapter	212-439-7290	Fax 512-328-8852
Special Libraries Association, San Andreas-San Francisco Bay Chapter	415-528-7766	415-604-3140
Special Libraries Association, Southern California Chapter	818-795-2145	818-302-8966; fax 818-302-8983
Texas Library Association Job Hotline (24 hours; Texas listings only)	512-328-0651	3355 Bee Cave Rd., Suite 401, Austin, TX 78746. 512-328-1518; fax 512-328-8852
Texas State Library Jobline (Texas listings only)	512-463-5470	Texas State Library, Box 12927, Austin, TX 78711. 512-463-5465; fax 512-463-5447
University of Toronto Faculty of Information Studies	416-978-7073	416-978-3035; fax 416-978-5762
University of Western Ontario Faculty of Communications and Open Learning	519-661-3542	519-661-2111 ext. 8494; fax 519-661-3506
Virginia Library Association Jobline (Virginia libraries only)	703-519-8027	VLA Job Hotline, Box 8277, Norfolk, VA 23503. 757-583-0041; fax 757-583-5041

1. Weekly printed listing sent on receipt of stamps and mailing labels.
2. Cosponsored by the Special Libraries Association Illinois Chapter and the Illinois Library Association.
3. 800-356-7820 available from all MPLA states (includes listings for the states of Arizona, Colorado, Kansas, Montana, Nebraska, Nevada, North Dakota, Oklahoma, South Dakota, Utah, and Wyoming, and paid listings from out-of-region institutions—$10/week).
4. Alaska, Alberta, British Columbia, Idaho, Montana, Oregon, and Washington; includes both professional and paraprofessional jobs.
5. Sponsored by the Pennsylvania Library Association; also accepts paraprofessional out-of-state listings.

Specialized Library Associations and Groups

ACCESS, 1001 Connecticut Ave. N.W., Suite 838, Washington, DC 20036, 202-785-4233, fax 202-785-4212, e-mail commjobs@aol.com, World Wide Web http://www.essential.org/access: Comprehensive national resource on employment, voluntary service, and career development in the nonprofit sector. Promotes involvement in public issues by providing specialized employment publications and services for job seekers and serves as a resource to nonprofit organizations on recruitment, diversity, and staff development.

Advanced Information Management, 444 Castro St., Suite 320, Mountain View, CA 94041, 415-965-7799 e-mail aimno.aimusa@jun.com, World Wide Web http://www.aimusa.com: Placement agency that specializes in library and information personnel. They offer work on a temporary, permanent, and contract basis for both professional librarians and paraprofessionals in the special, public, and academic library marketplace. They supply consultants who can work with special projects in libraries or manage library development projects. They maintain offices in Southern California (900 Wilshire Blvd, Suite 1424, Los Angeles, CA 90017, 213-243-9236) as well as in the San Francisco Bay Area. There is no fee to applicants.

American Association of Law Libraries Career Hotline, 53 W. Jackson Blvd., Suite 940, Chicago, IL 60604, 312-939-4764: The Hotline (312-939-7877) is a 24-hour-a-day recording, updated each Friday at noon. Any interested person may receive the complete Job Data Base free, by request. Ads may also be viewed on AALLNET, an Internet bulletin board (http://www.lawlib.wuacc.edu/aallnet/aall-net.html). To list a position contact AALL, Placement Assistant; fax 312-431-1097.

American Libraries, "Career LEADS," c/o *American Libraries*, 50 E. Huron St., Chicago, IL 60611: Classified job listings published in each monthly issue of *American Libraries* magazine, listing some 100 job openings grouped by type, plus "Late Job Notices" added near press time as space and time permits. Contains subsections: Positions Wanted, Librarians' Classified, joblines, and regional salary scales. Also contains ConsultantBase (see below) four times annually.

American Libraries, "Career LEADS EXPRESS," c/o Georgia Okotete, 50 E. Huron St., Chicago, IL 60611: Advance galleys (3-4 weeks) of classified job listings to be published in next issue of *American Libraries*. Early notice of approximately 100 "Positions Open" sent about the 17th of each month; does not include editorial corrections and late changes as they appear in the regular *AL* LEADS section, but does include some "Late Job Notices." For each month, send $1 check made out to AL EXPRESS, self-addressed, standard business-size envelope (4x9), with 55¢ postage on envelope.

American Libraries, ConsultantBase (CBase): An *AL* service that helps match professionals offering library/information expertise with institutions seeking it. Published quarterly, CBase appears in the Career LEADS section of the January, April, June, and October issues of *AL*. Rates: $5.50/line—classified; $55/inch—display. Inquiries should be made to Jon Kartman, LEADS Editor, *American Libraries*, 50 E. Huron St., Chicago, IL 60611, 312-280-4211, e-mail careerleads@ALA.org.

American Library Association, ASCLA/SLAS State Library Consultants to Institutional Libraries Discussion Group, Institutional Library Mailed Jobline: Compilation of job openings in institutional libraries throughout the United States and territories. Send self-addressed, stamped envelope(s) to Institutional Library Jobline, c/o Gloria Spooner, State Library of Louisiana, Box 131, Baton Rouge, LA 70821-0131. Send job postings to same or call 504-342-4931; or fax 504-342-3547. Listings will appear for one month unless resubmitted.

American Library Association, Association of College and Research Libraries, 50 E. Huron St., Chicago, IL 60611-2795, 312-280-2513: Classified advertising appears each month in *College & Research Libraries News*. Ads appearing in the print *C&RL News* are also posted to *C&RL NewsNet*, an abridged electronic edition of *C&RL News* that is accessible on the Web (http://www.ala.org/acrl/c&rlnew2.html).

American Library Association, Office for Library Personnel Resources, 50 E. Huron St., Chicago, IL 60611, 312-280-4281: A placement service is provided at each Annual Conference (June or July) and Midwinter Meeting (January or February). Request job seeker or employer registration forms prior to each conference. Persons not able to attend can register with the service and can also purchase job and job seeker listings sent directly from the conference site. Information included when requesting registration forms. Handouts on interviewing, preparing a résumé, and other job search information are available from the ALA Office for Library Personnel Resources.

In addition to the ALA conference placement center, ALA division national conferences usually include a placement service. See *American Libraries* "Datebook" for dates of upcoming divisional conferences, since these are not held every year. ALA provides Web site job postings from *American Libraries*, *C&RL NewsNet*, and its conference placement services (http://www.ala.org) located in the library education and employment menu page.

American Society for Information Science, 8720 Georgia Ave., #501, Silver Spring, MD 20910-3602, 301-495-0900, fax 301-495-0810: There is an active placement service operated at ASIS Annual Meetings (usually October, locales change). All conference attendees (both ASIS members and non-members), as well as ASIS members who cannot attend the conference, are eligible to use the service to list or find jobs. Job listings are also accepted from employers who cannot attend the conference, interviews are arranged, and special seminars are given. Throughout the year, current job openings are listed in *ASIS JOBLINE*, a monthly publication sent to all members and available to non-members on request. Please check ASIS for ad rates.

Art Libraries Society/North America (ARLIS/NA), c/o Executive Director, 4101 Lake Boone Trail, Suite 201, Raleigh, NC 27607, 919-787-5181, fax 919-787-4916, e-mail 74517.3400@compuserve.com: Art information and visual resources curator jobs are listed in the *ARLIS/NA UPDATE* (6 times a year) and a job registry is maintained at society headquarters. (Any employer may list a job with the registry, but only members may request job information.) Listings also available on ARLIS-L listserv and Web site. Call headquarters for registration and/or published information.

Asian/Pacific American Libraries Newsletter, c/o Fenghua Wang-Schaefer, Reference Dept., Library, University of Illinois (M/C234), 801 S. Morgan, Box

8198, Chicago, IL 60680, 312-996-2728, fax 312-413-0424: Quarterly. Includes some job ads. Free to members of Asian/Pacific American Librarians Association. **Association for Library and Information Science Education,** Box 7640, Arlington, VA 22207, 703-243-8040, fax 703-243-4551, World Wide Web http://www.alise.org: Provides placement service at annual conference (January or February) for library and information studies faculty and administrative positions. **Association for Educational Communications and Technology,** 1025 Vermont Ave. N.W., Suite 820, Washington, DC 20005, 202-347-7834, fax 202-347-7839, e-mail aect@aect.org: AECT maintains a placement listing on the AECT Web site (www.aect.org) and provides a placement service at the annual convention, free to all registrants.

Black Caucus Newsletter, c/o George C. Grant, Editor, Rollins College, 1000 Holt Ave. #2654, Winter Park, FL 32789, 407-646-2676, fax 407-646-1515, e-mail bcnews@rollins.edu: Lists paid advertisements for vacancies. Free to members, $10/year to others. Published bimonthly by Four-G Publishers, Inc. News accepted continuously. Biographies, essays, books, and reviews of interest to members are invited.

C. Berger And Company, 327 E. Gundersen Dr., Carol Stream, IL 60188, 630-653-1115, 800-382-4222, fax 630-653-1691, e-mail c-berg@dupagels.lib.ilus, World Wide Web http://www.cberger.com: CBC conducts nationwide executive searches to fill permanent positions in libraries, information centers, and related businesses at the management, supervisory, and director level. Professionals and clerks are also available from CBC as temporary workers or contract personnel for short- and long-term assignments in special, academic, and public libraries in Illinois, Indiana, Georgia, Pennsylvania, Texas, and Wisconsin. CBC also provides library and records management consulting services and direction and staff to manage projects for clients.

Canadian Association of Special Libraries and Information Services/Ottawa Chapter Job Bank, c/o CASLIS Job Bank Coordinator, 266 Sherwood Dr., Ottawa, Ontario, K1Y 3W4, Canada: Those looking for a job should send résumé; employers with a job to list should call 613-728-9982.

Canadian Library Association, 200 Elgin St., Suite 602, Ottawa, Ontario, Canada K2P 1L5, 613-232-9625: Publishes career ads in *Feliciter* magazine. CASLIS division offers job bank service in several cities. Operates "Jobmart" at the annual conference in June.

Catholic Library Association, 9009 Carter St., Allen Park, MI 48101: Personal and institutional members of CLA are given free space (35 words) to advertise for jobs or to list job openings in *Catholic Library World* (4/year). Others may advertise. Contact advertising coordinator for rates.

Chinese-American Librarians Association Newsletter, c/o Lan Yang, Sterling C. Evans Library, Texas A&M University, College Station, TX 77843-5000: Job listings in newsletter issued in February, June, October. Free to members.

Council on Library/Media Technicians, Inc., c/o Membership Chair Julia Ree, Box 52057, Riverside, CA 92517-3057: *COLT Newsletter* appears bimonthly in *Library Mosaics*. Personal dues/U.S. $35; Foreign, $60; Students $30; Institutions/U.S. $60; Foreign $85.

Gossage Regan Associates, Inc., 25 W. 43rd St., New York, NY 10036, 212-869-3348, fax 212-997-1127: An executive search firm specializing in the recruitment of library directors and other library/information-handling organization top management. About 50 nationwide searches have been conducted since 1983 for public, academic, and large specialized libraries in all regions. Salary limitation: $60,000 up. Library Executive Recruiters: Wayne Gossage, Joan Neumann. And **Wontawk Gossage, Associates**, 25 W. 43rd St., New York, NY 10036, 212-869-3348, fax 212-997-1127, 304 Newbury St., No. 314, Boston, MA 02115, 617-867-9209, fax 617-437-9317: Temporary/long term/temporary-to-permanent assignments in the NY/NJ/CT and the Boston metropolitan areas in all types of libraries/information management, professional and support, all levels of responsibility, all skills. The original library temporaries firm, since 1980, as Gossage Regan. In charge: Nancy Melin Nelson, MLS; Gordon Gossage.

Independent Educational Services, 1101 King St., Suite 305, Alexandria, VA 22314, 800-257-5102, 703-548-9700, fax 703-548-7171, World Wide Web http://www.ies-search.org: IES is a nonprofit faculty and administrative placement agency for independent elementary and secondary schools across the country. Qualified candidates must possess an MLS degree and some experience in a school setting working with students. Jobs range from assistant librarians and interns to head librarians and rebuilding entire libraries/multimedia centers. Regional offices in Boston and San Francisco.

Labat-Anderson, Inc., 8000 Westpark Dr., No. 400, McLean, VA 22102, 703-506-9600, fax 703-506-4646: One of the largest providers of library and records management services to the federal government. Supports various federal agencies in 27 states, with many positions located in the Washington, D.C., area. Résumés and cover letters will gladly be accepted from librarians with an ALA-accredited MLS and records managers for part-time and regular full-time employment.

The Library Co-Op, Inc., 3840 Park Ave., Suite 107, Edison, NJ 08820, 908-906-1777 or 800-654-6275, fax 908-906-3562, e-mail 71334-3036@compuserve.com: The company is licensed as both a temporary and permanent employment agency and supplies consultants to work in a wide variety of information settings and functions from library moving to database management, catalog maintenance, reference, retrospective conversion, and more. Recent developments include the forming of a new division, ABCD Filing Services, and the hiring of two specialists in space planning. Another new division, LAIRD Consulting, provides a full range of automation expertise for hardware, software, LANS, and WANS.

Library Management Systems, Corporate Pointe, Suite 755, Culver City, CA 90230, 310-216-6436, 800-567-4669, fax 310-649-6388, e-mail lms@ix.netcom.com; and Three Bethesda Metro Center, Suite 700, Bethesda, MD 20814, 301-961-1984, fax 301-652-6240, e-mail lmsdc@ix.netcom.com: LMS has been providing library staffing, recruitment, and consulting to public and special libraries and businesses since 1983. LMS organizes and manages special libraries; designs and implements major projects (including retrospective conversions, automation studies, and records management); performs high-quality cataloging outsourcing; and furnishes contract staffing to all categories of information centers. LMS has a large database of librarians and library assistants on call for long- and short-term projects and provides permanent placement at all levels.

Library Mosaics, Box 5171, Culver City, CA 90231, 310-645-4998: Magazine appears bimonthly and will accept listings for library/media support staff positions. However, correspondence relating to jobs cannot be handled.

Medical Library Association, 6 N. Michigan Ave., Suite 300, Chicago, IL 60602-4805, 312-419-9094, World Wide Web http://www.mlanet.org: *MLA News* (10 issues a year, June/July and November/December combined issues) lists positions wanted and positions available in its "Employment Opportunities" column. The position available rate is $2.80 per word for non-members and for any advertisements received through an employment agency, advertising agency, or any other third party. Up to 50 free words for MLA members plus $2.45 per word over 50 words. Members and non-members may rerun ads once in the next consecutive issue for $25. All positions available advertisements must list a minimum salary; a salary range is preferred. Positions wanted rates $1.50 per word for non-members; $1.25 per word for members with 100 free words; $1.25 will be charged for each word exceeding 100. MLA also offers a placement service at annual conference each spring. Job advertisements received for *MLA News* publication are posted to the MLANET Jobline the week of receipt.

Music Library Association, c/o Elisabeth H. Rebman, MLA Placement Officer, Music Library, 240 Morrison Hall, University of California–Berkeley, Berkeley, CA 94720-6000, 510-643-5198, fax 510-642-8237, World Wide Web http://www.music.indiana.edu/tech_s/mla/index.htm: Monthly job list $15/year (individuals); $20 (organizations) to MLA Business Office, Box 487, Canton, MA 02021, 781-828-8450, fax 781-828-8915, e-mail acadsvc@aol.com.

Pro Libra Associates, Inc., 6 Inwood Pl., Maplewood, NJ 07040, 201-762-0070, 800-262-0070, e-mail prolibra-2@mail.idt.net. A multi-service agency, Pro Libra specializes in consulting, personnel, and project support for libraries and information centers.

REFORMA, National Association to Promote Library Service to the Spanish-Speaking, Box 832, Anaheim, CA 92815-0832: Employers wishing to do direct mailings to the REFORMA membership (900+) may obtain mailing labels arranged by zip code for $100. Contact Al Milo, 714-738-6383. Job ads are also published quarterly in the REFORMA newsletter. For rate information, contact Denise Adkins, 702-368-4411, fax 702-251-4903.

Search Associates, Box 922, Jackson, MI 49204-0922, 517-768-9250, fax 517-768-9252, e-mail JimAmbrose@compuserve.com, World Wide Web http://www.search-associates.com: A private organization comprised of former overseas school directors who organize about ten recruitment fairs (most occur in February) to place teachers, librarians, and administrators in about 400 independent K–12 American/international schools of various sizes around the world. These accredited schools, based on the American model, annually offer highly attractive personal and professional opportunities for experienced librarians.

Society of American Archivists, 600 S. Federal, Suite 504, Chicago, IL 60605, 312-922-0140, fax 312-347-1452, World Wide Web http://www.archivists.org, e-mail info@archivists.org: The *Archival Outlook* is sent (to members only) six times annually and contains features about the archival profession and other timely pieces on courses in archival administration, meetings, and professional opportunities (job listings). The *SAA Employment Bulletin* is a bimonthly listing of job opportunities available to members by subscription for $24 a year, and to non-members for $10 per issue. Prepayment is required.

Special Libraries Association, 1700 18th St. N.W., Washington, DC 20009-2508, 202-234-4700, fax 202-265-9317, World Wide Web http://www.sla.org, e-mail sla@sla.org: SLA maintains a telephone jobline, SpeciaLine, which is in operation 24 hours a day, seven days a week, 202-234-4700, ext. 1. Most SLA chapters have employment chairpersons who act as referral persons for employers and job seekers. Several SLA chapters have joblines. The association's monthly magazine, *Information Outlook*, carries classified advertising. SLA offers an employment clearinghouse and career advisory service during the annual conference held in June. SLA also provides a discount to members using the résumé evaluation service offered through Advanced Information Management. A "Guide to Career Opportunities" is a resource kit for $20 (SLA members, $15); "Getting a Job: Tips and Techniques" is free to unemployed SLA members. The SLA Job Bulletin Board, a computer listserv, is organized by Indiana University staff. Subscribe by sending message—subscribe SLAJOB first name, last name—to listserv@iubvm.ucs.indiana.edu.

TeleSecCorestaff, Information Management Division, 1160 Veirs Mill Rd., Suite 414, Wheaton, MD 20902, 301-949-4097, fax 301-949-7808, e-mail telesec@clark.net: Offers many opportunities to get started in the metropolitan Washington, D.C., library market through short- and long-term assignments in federal agencies, law firms, corporations, associations, and academic institutions. Founded in 1948, TeleSec Corestaff has been performing library technical projects including cataloging, interlibrary loans, database design, and acquisitions since the late 1960s.

Tuft & Associates, Inc., 1209 Astor St., Chicago, IL 60610, 312-642-8889, fax 312-642-8883: Specialists in nationwide executive searches for administrative posts in libraries and information centers.

State Library Agencies

In addition to the joblines mentioned previously, some of the state library agencies issue lists of job openings within their areas. These include: Colorado (weekly, sent on receipt of stamps and mailing labels; also available via Access Colorado Library and Information Network—ACLIN; send SASE for access); Indiana (monthly on request) 317-232-3697, 800-451-6028 (Indiana area), e-mail ehubbard@statelib.lib.in.us or Iowa (*Joblist*, monthly on request) e-mail awette@mail.lib.state.ia.us; Mississippi (*Library Job Opportunities*, monthly); and Ohio (*Library Opportunities in Ohio*, monthly, sent to accredited library education programs and interested individuals upon request).

State libraries in several states have electronic bulletin board services that list job openings. Web addresses are: Colorado http://www.aclin org; District of Columbia (Metropolitan Washington Council of Government Libraries Council) www.mwcog.org/ic/jobline.html; Florida, www.dos.state.fl.us/dlis/jobs.html; Georgia, www.gpls.public.lib.ga.us/pls/job-bank; Idaho, www.lili.org/staff/jobs.htm; Indiana, www.statelib.lib.in.us/www/ldo/posopl6.html; Iowa, www.silo.lib.ia.us; Kentucky www.kdla.state.ky.us/libserv/jobline.htm; Louisiana www.smt.state.lib.la.us/statelib.htm; Massachusetts www.mlin.lib.ma.us; Nebraska www.nlc.state.ne.us/libjob; North Carolina www.statelibrary.dcr. state.nc.us/jobs/jobs.htm (both professional and paraprofessional library positions); Texas, www.tsl.state.tx.us; Oklahoma (via modem) 405-524-4089; South Carolina, www.state.sc.us/scs/lion.html. In Pennsylvania, the listserv is maintained by Commonwealth Libraries.

On occasion, the following state library newsletters or journals will list vacancy postings: Alabama (*Cottonboll*, quarterly); Alaska (*Newspoke*, bimonthly); Arizona (*Arizona Libraries NewsWeek*); Indiana (*Focus on Indiana Libraries*, 11 times/year; Iowa (*Joblist*); Kansas (*Kansas Libraries*, monthly); Louisiana (*Library Communique*, monthly); Minnesota (*Minnesota Libraries News*, monthly); Nebraska (*Overtones*, quarterly); New Hampshire (*Granite State Libraries*, bimonthly); New Mexico (*Hitchhiker*, weekly); Tennessee (*TLA Newsletter*, bimonthly); Utah (*Directions for Utah Libraries*, monthly); and Wyoming (*Outrider*, monthly).

Many state library agencies will refer applicants informally when vacancies are known to exist, but do not have formal placement services. The following states primarily make referrals to public libraries only: Alabama, Alaska, Arizona, Arkansas, California, Louisiana, Pennsylvania, South Carolina (institutional also), Tennessee, Utah, Vermont, and Virginia. Those that refer applicants to all types of libraries are: Alaska, Delaware, Florida, Georgia, Hawaii, Idaho, Illinois, Kansas, Kentucky, Maine, Maryland, Mississippi, Montana, Nebraska, Nevada (largely public and academic), New Hampshire, New Mexico, North Carolina, North Dakota, Ohio, Pennsylvania, Rhode Island, South Dakota, Vermont, West Virginia (on Pennsylvania Jobline, public, academic, special), and Wyoming.

The following state libraries post library vacancy notices for all types of libraries on a bulletin board: California, Connecticut, Florida, Georgia, Hawaii, Illinois, Indiana, Iowa, Kentucky, Michigan, Montana, Nevada, New Jersey, New York, North Carolina, Ohio, Oklahoma, Pennsylvania, South Carolina, South Dakota, Utah, and Washington. [Addresses of the state agencies are found in Part 6 of the *Bowker Annual* and in *American Library Directory—Ed.*]

State and Regional Library Associations

State and regional library associations will often make referrals, run ads in association newsletters, or operate a placement service at annual conferences, in addition to the joblines sponsored by some groups. Referral of applicants when jobs are known is done by the following associations: Arkansas, Delaware, Hawaii, Louisiana, Michigan, Minnesota, Nevada, Pennsylvania, South Dakota, Tennessee, and Wisconsin. Although listings are infrequent, job vacancies are placed in the following association newsletters or journals when available: Alabama (*Alabama Librarian*, 7 times/year); Alaska (*Newspoke*, bimonthly); Arizona (*Newsletter*, 10 times/year); Arkansas (*Arkansas Libraries*, 6 times/year); Connecticut (*Connecticut Libraries*, 11 times/year); Delaware (*Delaware Library Association Bulletin*, 3 times/year); District of Columbia (*Intercom*, 11 times/year); Florida (*Florida Libraries*, 6 times/year); Indiana

(*Focus on Indiana Libraries*, 11 times/year); Iowa (*Catalyst*, 6 times/year); Kansas (*KLA Newsletter*, 6 issues/bimonthly); Minnesota (*MLA Newsletter*, 6 issues/bimonthly); Missouri (bimonthly); Mountain Plains (*MPLA Newsletter*, bimonthly, lists vacancies and position wanted ads for individuals and institutions); Nebraska (*NLAQ*); Nevada (*Highroller*, 4 times/year); New Hampshire (*NHLA Newsletter*, 6 times/year); New Jersey (*NJLA Newsletter*, 10 times/year); New Mexico (shares notices via State Library's *Hitchhiker*, weekly); New York (*NYLA Bulletin*, 10 times/year; free for institutional members; $25/1 week, $40/2 weeks, others); Ohio (*ACCESS*, monthly); Oklahoma (*Oklahoma Librarian*, 6 issues/year); Rhode Island (*RILA Bulletin*, 6 times/year); South Carolina (*News and Views*); South Dakota (*Book Marks*, bimonthly); Tennessee (*TLA Newsletter*); Vermont (*VLA News*, Box 803, Burlington, VT 05402, 10 issues/year); Virginia (*Virginia Librarian*, quarterly); and West Virginia (*West Virginia Libraries*, 6 times/year).

At their annual conference the following associations have indicated some type of placement service although it may only consist of bulletin board postings: Alabama, California, Connecticut, Georgia, Idaho, Illinois, Indiana, Kansas, Louisiana, Maryland, Massachusetts, Mountain Plains, New England, New Hampshire, New Jersey, New York, North Carolina (biennial), Ohio, Oregon, Pacific Northwest, Pennsylvania, South Dakota, Southeastern, Tennessee, Texas, Vermont, and Wyoming.

The following have indicated they have an electronic source for job postings in addition to voice joblines: Kansas, http://www.skyways.lib.ks.us/kansas/KLA/helpwanted (no charge to list job openings); Missouri, www.mlnc.com/~mla; Nebraska, www.nlc.state.ne.us/libjob/libjob.html; New Jersey Library Association, www.burlco.lib.in.us/NJLA; Oklahoma, www.state.ok.us/~odl/fyi/jobline.htm (e-mail bpetrie@oltn.odl.state.ok.us); Pacific Northwest Library Association, e-mail listserv@wln.com or listserv@ldbsu.idbsu.edu; Texas, www.txla.org/jobline/jobline.txt; Virginia, www.vla.org.

The following associations have indicated they have no placement service at this time: Colorado, Kentucky, Middle Atlantic Regional Library Federation, Midwest Federation, Minnesota, Mississippi, Montana, Nebraska, Nevada, New Mexico, North Dakota, Oklahoma, Utah, West Virginia, and Wisconsin. [State and regional association addresses are listed in Part 6 of the *Bowker Annual.*— Ed.]

Library and Information Studies Programs

Library and information studies programs offer some type of service for their current students as well as alumni. Most schools provide job-hunting and résumé-writing seminars. Many have outside speakers representing different types of libraries or recent graduates relating career experiences. Faculty or a designated placement officer offer individual advising services or critiquing of résumés.

Of the ALA-accredited library and information studies programs, the following handle placement activities through the program: Alabama, Albany, Alberta, Buffalo (compiles annual graduate biographical listings), British Columbia, Dalhousie, Drexel, Hawaii, Illinois, Kent State, Kentucky, Louisiana, McGill,

Missouri (College of Education), Pittsburgh (Department of Library and Information Science only), Pratt, Puerto Rico, Queens, Rhode Island, Rutgers, Saint John's, South Carolina, Syracuse, Tennessee, Texas–Austin, Toronto, UCLA, Western Ontario, Wisconsin–Madison, and Wisconsin–Milwaukee.

The central university placement center handles activities for the following schools: California–Berkeley (alumni) and Emporia. However, in most cases, faculty in the library school will still do informal counseling regarding job seeking.

In some schools, the placement services are handled in a cooperative manner; in most cases the university placement center sends out credentials while the library school posts or compiles the job listings. Schools utilizing one or both sources include: Alabama, Arizona, Buffalo, Catholic, Clarion, Dominican, Florida State, Indiana, Iowa, Kent State, Long Island, Maryland, Michigan, Montreal, North Carolina–Chapel Hill, North Carolina–Greensboro, North Carolina Central, North Texas, Oklahoma, Pittsburgh, Queens, Saint John's, San Jose, Simmons, South Florida, Southern Connecticut, Southern Mississippi, Syracuse, Tennessee, Texas Woman's, Washington, Wayne State, and Wisconsin–Milwaukee. In sending out placement credentials, schools vary as to whether they distribute these free, charge a general registration fee, or request a fee for each file or credentials sent out.

Those schools that have indicated they post job vacancy notices for review but do not issue printed lists are: Alabama, Alberta, Arizona, British Columbia, Buffalo, Catholic, Clark Atlanta, Dalhousie, Drexel, Florida State, Hawaii, Illinois, Kent State, Kentucky, Louisiana, Maryland, McGill, Montreal, North Carolina–Chapel Hill, North Carolina–Greensboro, North Carolina Central, Oklahoma, Pittsburgh, Puerto Rico, Queens, Rutgers, Saint John's, San Jose, Simmons, South Carolina, Southern Mississippi, Syracuse (general postings), Tennessee, Texas Woman's, Toronto, UCLA, Washington, Wayne State, Western Ontario, and Wisconsin–Madison.

In addition to job vacancy postings, some schools issue printed listings, operate joblines, have electronic access, or provide database services:

- Albany (Job Placement Bulletin free to SISP students; listserv@cnsibm. albany.edu to subscribe)
- British Columbia (uses BCLA Jobline, 604-430-6411)
- Buffalo (listserv for entry-level N.Y. state positions; to subscribe, send message saying SUBSCRIBE LIBJOB-L first name last name to listserv.acsu.buffalo.edu)
- California–Berkeley (weekly out-of-state job list and jobline free to all students and graduates for six months after graduation; $55 annual fee for alumni of any University of California campus; call 510-642-3283)
- Clarion (free with SASE)
- Dalhousie (listserv for Atlantic Canada jobs, send message saying sub list-joblist to mailserv@ac.dal.ca)
- Dominican (*Placement News* every 2 weeks, free for 6 months following graduation, $15/year for students and alumni; $25 to others)
- Drexel (http://www.cis.drexel.edu/placement/placement.html)

- Emporia (weekly bulletin for school, university, public jobs; separate bulletin for special; $42/6 months; Emporia graduates, $21/6 months)
- Florida State
- Hawaii
- Illinois (free online placement JOBSearch database available on campus and via access through telnet alexia.lis.uiuc.edu, login: jobs, password: Urbaign or http://www.carousel.lis.uiuc.edu/~jobs/)
- Indiana (free for one year after graduation; alumni and others may send self-addressed stamped envelopes or access http://www-slis.lib.indiana.edu/Profession/JobPlacementBulletin/jobpage.htm)
- Iowa ($15/year for registered students and alumni)
- Michigan (http://www.si.umich.edu/jobfinder; free for one year following graduation, all other grads, $15/year for 24 issues; $20 to others)
- Missouri (http://www.tiger.coe.missouri.edu/placement.html; Library Vacancy Roster, mailed weekly, $15 per quarter)
- North Carolina–Chapel Hill (listserv@ils.unc.edu to subscribe, or http://www.ils.unc.edu/ils/careers/resources)
- North Texas (free 24-hour job hotline listing for current students; $20 for former students)
- Oklahoma
- Pratt (free to students and alumni for full-time/part-time professional positions only)
- Rhode Island (monthly, $7.50/year)
- Rutgers (access http://www.scils.rutgers.edu or listserv@scils.rutgers.edu and subscribe)
- Simmons (operates the New England Jobline, which announces professional vacancies in the region, call 617-521-2815)
- South Carolina (http://www.libsci.sc.edu/career/job.htm)
- Southern Connecticut (http://www.scsu.ctstateu.edu/~jobline; printed listing twice a month, mailed to students/ alumni free, also on gopher at scsu.ctstateu.edu)
- South Florida (in cooperation with ALIS; $10/year to subscribers)
- St. John's (listserv@maelstrom.stjohns.edu)
- Syracuse (lists selected jobs online through electronic mail to students)
- Texas–Austin (free to students and alumni for one year following graduation, *Weekly Placement Bulletin*, including *Classifacts*, $26/6 months or $48/year; *Texas Job Weekly*, $16/6 months or $28/year, some jobs available on new school-only listserv; http://www.gslis.utexas.edu/~placemnt/index.html)
- Texas Woman's (electronic bulletin board for students)
- Toronto (jobline or access http://www.fis.utoronto.ca)
- Wisconsin–Madison (now sends listings from Wisconsin and Minnesota to Illinois for JOBSearch)

- Wisconsin–Milwaukee (listserv@slis.uwm.edu to subscribe; sends selected jobs online through electronic mail to students)
- Western Ontario (http://www.uwo.ca/gslis/information) resources; to list positions call 519-661-2111 ext. 8495)

Employers will often list jobs with schools only in their particular geographical area; some library schools will give information to non-alumni regarding their specific locales, but are not staffed to handle mail requests and advice is usually given in person. Schools that have indicated they will allow librarians in their areas to view listings are: Alabama, Albany, Alberta, Arizona, British Columbia, Buffalo, California–Berkeley, Catholic, Clarion, Clark Atlanta, Dalhousie, Dominican, Drexel, Emporia, Florida State, Hawaii, Illinois, Indiana, Iowa, Kent State, Kentucky, Louisiana, Maryland, McGill, Michigan, Missouri, Montreal, North Carolina–Chapel Hill, North Carolina Central, North Carolina–Greensboro, University of North Texas, Oklahoma, Pittsburgh, Pratt, Puerto Rico, Queens, Rhode Island, Rutgers, Simmons, Saint John's, San Jose, South Carolina, South Florida, Southern Connecticut, Southern Mississippi, Syracuse, Tennessee, Texas–Austin, Texas Woman's, Toronto, UCLA, Washington, Wayne State, Western Ontario, Wisconsin–Madison, and Wisconsin–Milwaukee.

A list of accredited program addresses and phones can be requested from ALA or found in the *Bowker Annual*. Individuals interested in placement services of other library education programs should contact the schools directly.

Federal Employment Information Sources

Consideration for employment in many federal libraries requires establishing civil service eligibility. Although the actual job search is your responsibility, the Office of Personnel Management (OPM) has developed the "Federal Employment Information Highway" to assist you along the way. The address for OPM's World Wide Web site is http://www.usajobs.opm.gov.

OPM's Career America Connection at 912-757-3000, TDD Service at 912-744-2299, is a telephone-based system that provides current worldwide federal job opportunities, salary and employee benefits information, special recruitment messages, and more. You can also record your request to have application packages, forms, and other employment-related literature mailed to you. This service is available 24 hours a day, seven days a week. Request Federal Employment Information Line factsheet EI-42, "Federal Employment Information Sources," for a complete listing of local telephone numbers to this nationwide network.

OPM's Federal Job Opportunities "Bulletin" Board (FJOB) at 912-757-3100, is a computer-based bulletin board system that provides current worldwide federal job opportunities, salaries and pay rates, general and specific employment information, and more. You must have a personal computer with a modem to access this system. You may also contact OPM on the Internet via Telnet at FJOB.MAIL.OPM.GOV and file transfer protocol at FTP.FJOB.MAIL.OPM.GOV. Information about obtaining federal job announcement files via Internet mail should be directed to INFO@FJOB.MAIL.OPM.GOV.

Federal Job Information "Touch Screen" Computer, is a computer-based system utilizing touch-screen technology. These kiosks, found throughout the nation in OPM offices, Federal Office Buildings, and other locations, allow you to access current worldwide federal job opportunities, online information, and more.

Once you have found an opportunity that interests you, you may obtain a copy of the vacancy announcement and a complete application package by leaving your name and address in one of the automated systems or, when available, by downloading the actual announcement and any supplementary materials from the FJOB. Although the federal government does not require a standard application form for most jobs, certain information is needed to evaluate your qualifications if you decide to submit any other format other than the OF-612 form.

Eligibility can be established in the Washington, D.C., metropolitan area by meeting specific education and/or experience requirements and submitting appropriate forms directly to federal agencies during designated "open" periods. Interested applicants should contact their local Federal Job Information/Testing Center (FJI/TC) periodically to find out which agencies are currently accepting applications. The FJI/TC will give contact numbers to request vacancy announcements and forms and to obtain the proper forms for filing. The FJI/TC is listed under "U.S. Government" in major metropolitan telephone directories. Current job openings in libraries in the Washington, D.C., area are on a recorded message with other federal jobs on 202-606-2700 (press 1 or 3). You may obtain information on jobs nationwide by visiting the Job Information Center in your area and by using the touch screen computers located in the FJI/TC.

The Federal Library and Information Center Committee operates a federal library electronic bulletin board listing professional and paraprofessional positions (telnet alix.loc.gov3000). Federal jobs are posted on the Dartmouth College FEDJOBSlist. Send a message to listserv@dartcms1 with command INDEX FED-JOBS; to get the librarian and government documents openings use command SEND LIBRARY TXT. *Washington Online: How to Access the Government's Electronic Bulletin Boards*, by Bruce Maxwell (Washington, D.C., Congressional Quarterly, 1995), can lead to other services that may list library jobs among other government positions.

Applications are evaluated for the grade(s) for which applicants are qualified and will accept. Information on beginning salary levels can be obtained from the systems noted above. To qualify for librarian positions, applicants must possess: 1) a master's degree in library science; 2) a fifth-year bachelor's degree in library science; or 3) 30 semester hours of graduate study in library science. Note: If you have a combination of qualifying education and/or experience, you may qualify to take the written subject-matter test. This test is administered in the Washington, D.C., metropolitan area. To receive consideration for librarian positions and testing outside the D.C. metropolitan area, contact your local Federal Job Information/Testing Center.

Applicants should attempt to make personal contact directly with federal agencies in which they are interested. This is essential in the Washington, D.C., area where more than half the vacancies occur. Most librarian positions are in three agencies—Army, Navy, and Veterans Administration.

There are some "excepted" agencies that are not required to hire through the usual OPM channels. While these agencies may require the standard forms, they maintain their own employee selection policies and procedures. Government establishments with positions outside the competitive civil service include: Board of Governors of the Federal Reserve System; Central Intelligence Agency; Defense Intelligence Agency; Department of Medicine and Surgery; Federal Bureau of Investigation; Foreign Service of the United States; General Accounting Office; Library of Congress; National Science Foundation; National Security Agency; Tennessee Valley Authority; U.S. Nuclear Regulatory Commission; U.S. Postal Service; Judicial Branch of the Government; Legislative Branch of the Government; U.S. Mission to the United Nations; World Bank and IFC; International Monetary Fund; Organization of American States; Pan American Health Organization; and United Nations Secretariat.

The Library of Congress, the world's largest and most comprehensive library, is an excepted service agency in the Legislative Branch and administers its own independent merit selection system. Job classifications, pay, and benefits are the same as in other federal agencies, and qualifications requirements generally correspond to those used by the U.S. Office of Personnel Management. The library does not use registers, but announces vacancies as they become available. A separate application must be submitted for each vacancy announcement. For most professional positions, announcements are widely distributed and open for a minimum period of 30 days. Qualifications requirements and ranking criteria are stated on the vacancy announcement. The Library of Congress Human Resources Operations Office is located in the James Madison Memorial Building, 101 Independence Avenue S.E., Washington, DC 20540, 202-707-5620.

Additional General and Specialized Job Sources

Affirmative Action Register, 8356 Olive Blvd., St. Louis, MO 63132: The goal is to "provide female, minority, handicapped and veteran candidates with an opportunity to learn of professional and managerial positions throughout the nation and to assist employers in implementing their Equal Opportunity Employment programs." Free distribution of a monthly bulletin is made to leading businesses, industrial and academic institutions, and over 4,000 agencies that recruit qualified minorities and women, as well as to all known female, minority, and handicapped professional organizations, placement offices, newspapers, magazines, rehabilitation facilities, and over 8,000 federal, state, and local governmental employment units with a total readership in excess of 3.5 million (audited). Individual mail subscriptions are available for $15 per year. Librarian listings are in most issues. Sent free to libraries on request.
The Chronicle of Higher Education (published weekly with breaks in August and December), 1255 23rd St. N.W., Suite 700, Washington, DC 20037, 202-466-1055; fax 202-296-2691: Publishes a variety of library positions each week, including administrative and faculty jobs. Job listings are searchable by specific categories, keywords, or geographic locations on the Internet (gopher at Chronicle.merit.edu or World Wide Web at http://www.chronicle.merit.edu).
Academic Resource Network On-Line Database (ARNOLD), 4656 W. Jefferson, Suite 140, Fort Wayne, IN 46804: This World Wide Web interactive database helps faculty, staff, and librarians to identify partners for exchange or collaborative research (http://www.arnold.snybuf.edu).

School Libraries: School librarians often find that the channels for locating positions in education are of more value than the usual library ones, e.g., contacting county or city school superintendent offices. Other sources include university placement offices that carry listings for a variety of school system jobs. A list of commercial teacher agencies may be obtained from the National Association of Teachers' Agencies, Dr. Eugene Alexander, CPC, CTC, Treas., c/o G. A. Agency, 524 South Ave., E., Cranford, NJ 07016-3209, 908-272-2080, fax 908-272-2080, World Wide Web http://www.jobsforteachers.com.

Overseas

Opportunities for employment in foreign countries are limited and immigration policies of individual countries should be investigated. Employment for Americans is virtually limited to U.S. government libraries, libraries of U.S. firms doing worldwide business, and American schools abroad. Library journals from other countries will sometimes list vacancy notices. Some persons have obtained jobs by contacting foreign publishers or vendors directly. Non-U.S. government jobs usually call for foreign language fluency. "Job-Hunting in the UK" by Diane Brooks, *Canadian Library Journal* 45:374-378 (December 1988), offers advice for those interested in the United Kingdom. *Career Opportunities for Bilinguals and Multilinguals: A Directory of Resources in Education, Employment and Business* by Vladimir F. Wertsman (Scarecrow Press, 1991, ISBN 0-8108-2439-6, $35), gives general contact names for foreign employment and business resources. "International Jobs" by Wertsman (*RQ*, Fall 1992, pp. 14–19) provides a listing of library resources for finding jobs abroad.
Council for International Exchange of Scholars (CIES), 3007 Tilden St. N.W., Suite 5M, Washington, DC 20008-3009, 202-686-7877, e-mail cies1@ciesnet.cies.org, World Wide Web http://www.cies.org/: Administers U.S. government Fulbright awards for university lecturing and advanced research abroad; usually 10–15 awards per year are made to U.S. citizens who are specialists in library or information sciences. In addition, many countries offer awards in any specialization of research or lecturing. Lecturing awards usually require university or college teaching experience. Several opportunities exist for professional librarians as well. Applications and information may be obtained, beginning in March each year, directly from CIES. Worldwide application deadline is August 1.
Department of Defense, Dependents Schools, 4040 N. Fairfax Dr., Arlington, VA 22203, 703-696-3068, fax 703-696-2697, e-mail recruitment@odeddodea.edu: Overall management and operational responsibilities for the education of dependent children of active duty U.S. military personnel and DOD civilians who are stationed in foreign areas. Also responsible for teacher recruitment. For complete application brochure, write to above address. The latest copy of *Overseas Opportunities for Educators* is available and provides information on educator employment opportunities in over 160 schools worldwide. The schools are operated for the children of U.S. military and civilian personnel stationed overseas.
International Schools Services, Box 5910, Princeton, NJ 08543, 609-452-0990: Private, not-for-profit organization founded in 1955 to serve American schools overseas other than Department of Defense schools. These are American, international elementary and secondary schools enrolling children of business and diplo-

matic families living abroad. ISS services to overseas schools include recruitment and recommendation of personnel, curricular and administrative guidance, purchasing, facility planning, and more. ISS also publishes a comprehensive directory of overseas schools and a bimonthly newsletter, *NewsLinks*, for those interested in the intercultural educational community. Information regarding these publications and other services may be obtained by writing to the above address.

Peace Corps, 1990 K St. N.W., #9300, Washington, DC 20526: Volunteer opportunities exist for those holding MA/MS or BA/BS degrees in library science with one year of related work experience. Two-year tour of duty. U.S. citizens only. Living allowance, health care, transportation, and other benefits provided. Write for additional information and application or call 800-424-8580.

U.S. Information Agency (USIA), called U.S. Information Service (USIS) overseas, employs Information Resource Officers (librarians) on an as-needed basis. Candidates must have a master's degree in librarianship from an ALA-accredited graduate program and a minimum of four years of progressively responsible experience in adult library services, with in-depth functional experience in reference services or information resources management. A subject background in the social sciences is highly desirable, as are strong written and oral communication skills. Applicants must submit a current SF-171 (Application for Federal Employment) or OF-612 (Optional Application for Federal Employment, and the OF-306 (Declaration for Federal Employment), plus a 1,000-word autobiographical statement that should include a description of qualifications and reasons for seeking employment with USIA. U.S. citizenship is required. Benefits include overseas allowances and differentials where applicable, vacation and sick leave, health and life insurance, and a 20-year retirement program. Send application to USIA, Foreign Service Recruitment Officer for IROs, M/HRFP, Rm. 508, 401 Fourth St. S.W., Washington, DC 20547. Call 202-619-4702 for more information.

Overseas Exchange Programs

International Exchanges, Most exchanges are handled by direct negotiation between interested parties. A few libraries have established exchange programs for their own staff. In order to facilitate exchange arrangements, the *IFLA Journal* (issued January, May, August, and October/November) lists persons wishing to exchange positions *outside* their own country. All listings must include the following information: full name, address, present position, qualifications (with year of obtaining), language, abilities, preferred country/city/library, and type of position. Send to International Federation of Library Associations and Institutions (IFLA) Secretariat, c/o Koninklijkebibliotheek, Box 95312, 2509 CH The Hague, Netherlands, fax 31-70-3834827, e-mail ifla@nlc-bnc.ca, World Wide Web http://www.n.c-bnc.ca/ifla/.

ALA International Relations Committee/International Relations Round Table Joint Committee on International Exchanges, c/o Lucinda Covert-Vail, New York University Libraries, 70 Washington Square S., New York, NY 10012: A database of U.S. and international libraries interested in international study visits or exchanges has been developed. The committee welcomes requests for information and inclusion in the database for and from all countries.

LIBEX Bureau for International Staff Exchange, c/o A. J. Clark, Thomas Parry Library, University of Wales, Aberystwyth, Llanbadarn Fawr, Ceredigion SY23 3AS, Wales, 011-44-1970-62247, fax 011-44-1970-622190, e-mail parrylib@ aber.ac.uk, World Wide Web http://www.aber.ac.uk/tplwww/parry.html. Assists in two-way exchanges for British librarians wishing to work abroad and for librarians from the United States, Canada, EC countries, and Commonwealth and other countries who wish to undertake exchanges.

Using Information Skills in Nonlibrary Settings

A great deal of interest has been shown in using information skills in a variety of ways in nonlibrary settings. These jobs are not usually found through the regular library placement sources, although many library and information studies programs are trying to generate such listings for their students and alumni. Job listings that do exist may not call specifically for "librarians" by that title so that ingenuity may be needed to search out jobs where information management skills are needed. Some librarians are working on a freelance basis, offering services to businesses, alternative schools, community agencies, legislators, etc.; these opportunities are usually not found in advertisements but created by developing contacts and publicity over a period of time. A number of information brokering businesses have developed from individual freelance experiences. Small companies or other organizations often need "one-time" service for organizing files or collections, bibliographic research for special projects, indexing or abstracting, compilation of directories, and consulting services. Bibliographic networks and online database companies are using librarians as information managers, trainers, researchers, systems and database analysts, online services managers, etc. Jobs in this area are sometimes found in library network newsletters or data processing journals. Librarians can also be found working in law firms as litigation case supervisors (organizing and analyzing records needed for specific legal cases); with publishers as sales representatives, marketing directors, editors, and computer services experts; with community agencies as adult education coordinators, volunteer administrators, grants writers, etc.

Classifieds in *Publishers Weekly* and The *National Business Employment Weekly* may lead to information-related positions. One might also consider reading the Sunday classified ad sections in metropolitan newspapers in their entirety to locate descriptions calling for information skills but under a variety of job titles.

The *Burwell World Directory of Information Brokers, 1995–96* ($99.50 + $5.50 s/h) is an annual publication that lists information brokers, freelance librarians, independent information specialists, and institutions that provide services for a fee. There is a minimal charge for an annual listing. The Burwell Directory Online is searchable free on the Internet at http://www.burwell.com, and a CD-ROM version is available. Burwell can be reached at Burwell Enterprises, 3724 FM 1960 West, Suite 214, Houston, TX 77068, 713-537-9051, fax 713-537-8332. Also published is a bimonthly newsletter, *Information Broker* ($40, foreign postage, $15), that includes articles by, for, and about individuals and companies in the fee-based information field, book reviews, a calendar of upcoming events, and issue-oriented articles. A bibliography and other publications on the field of information brokering are also available.

The Independent Librarians Exchange Round Table is a unit within the American Library Association that serves as a networking source for persons who own their own information businesses, are consultants, or work for companies providing support services to libraries or providing other information services outside traditional library settings. Dues are $8.00 in addition to ALA dues and include a newsletter, *ILERT Alert*. At the 1993 ALA Annual Conference, ILERT sponsored a program on "Jobs for Indexers," which is available on cassette #ALA332 for $24 from Teach'em Inc., 160 E. Illinois St., Chicago, IL 60611, 800-224-3775.

The Association of Independent Information Professionals was formed in 1987 for individuals who own and operate for-profit information companies. Contact AIIP Headquarters at 212-779-1855.

A growing number of publications are addressing opportunities for librarians in the broader information arena. "You Can Take Your MLS Out of the Library," by Wilda W. Williams (*Library Journal*, Nov. 1994, pp. 43–46); "Information Entrepreneurship: Sources for Reference Librarians," by Donna L. Gilton (*RQ*, Spring 1992, pp. 346–355); "Information Brokering: The State of Art" by Alice Sizer Warner (*Wilson Library Bulletin*, April 1989, pp. 55–57), and "The Information Broker: A Modern Profile" by Mick O'Leary (*Online*, November 1987, pp. 24–30), provide overviews on the practice of information brokerage. *The Information Broker's Handbook* by Sue Rugge and Alfred Glossbrenner (Blue Ridge Summit, Pa.: Windcrest/McGraw-Hill, 1992, 379p. ISBN 0-8306-3798-2) covers the market for information, getting started, pricing and billing, and more. *Mind Your Own Business: A Guide for the Information Entrepreneur* by Alice Sizer Warner (New York: Neal-Schuman, 1987, 165p., ISBN 1-55570-014-4) describes planning for and managing an information business, including marketing, sales, and record-keeping. *Opening New Doors: Alternative Careers for Librarians*, edited by Ellis Mount (Washington, D.C.: Special Libraries Association, 1993) provides profiles of librarians who are working outside libraries. *Extending the Librarian's Domain: A Survey of Emerging Occupation Opportunities for Librarians and Information Professionals* by Forest Woody Horton, Jr. (Washington, D.C.: Special Libraries Association, 1994) explores information job components in a variety of sectors.

Careers in Electronic Information by Wendy Wicks (1997, 184p.) and *Guide to Careers in Abstracting and Indexing* by Wendy Wicks and Ann Marie Cunningham (1992, 126p.), are available for $39 and $35, respectively, from the National Federation of Abstracting & Information Services, 1518 Walnut St., Philadelphia, PA 19102, 215-893-1561, e-mail nfais@nfais.org. The American Society of Indexers, Box 48267, Seattle, WA 98148-0267, 206-241-9196, has a number of publications that would be useful for individuals who are interested in indexing careers. Check the Web page, http://www.well.com/user/asi, for membership and publication information.

Temporary/Part-Time Positions

Working as a substitute librarian or in temporary positions may be considered to be an alternative career path as well as an interim step while looking for a regular job. This type of work can provide valuable contacts and experience. Organizations that hire library workers for part-time or temporary jobs include Advanced Information Management, 444 Castro St., Suite 320, Mountain View, CA 94041 (415-965-7799), or 900 Wilshire Blvd., Suite 1424, Los Angeles, CA 90017 (213-243-9236); C. Berger and Company, 327 E. Gundersen Dr., Carol Stream, IL 60188 (630-653-1115 or 800-382-4222); Gossage Regan Associates, Inc., 25 W. 43 St., New York, NY 10036 (212-869-3348) and Wontawk Gossage Associates, 304 Newbury St., Suite 304, Boston, MA 02115 (617-867-9209); Information Management Division, 1160 Veirs Mill Rd., Suite 414, Wheaton, MD 20902 (301-949-4097); The Library Co-Op, Inc., 3840 Park Ave., Suite 107, Edison, NJ 08820 (908-906-1777 or 800-654-6275); Library Management Systems, Corporate Pointe, Suite 755, Culver City, CA 90230 (310-216-6436; 800-567-4669) and Three Bethesda Metro Center, Suite 700, Bethesda, MD 20814 (301-961-1984); and Pro Libra Associates, Inc., 6 Inwood Place, Maplewood, NJ 07040 (201-762-0070).

Part-time jobs are not always advertised, but often found by canvasing local libraries and leaving applications.

Job Hunting in General

Wherever information needs to be organized and presented to patrons in an effective, efficient, and service-oriented fashion, the skills of librarians can be applied, whether or not they are in traditional library settings. However, it will take considerable investment of time, energy, imagination, and money on the part of an individual before a satisfying position is created or obtained, in a conventional library or another type of information service. Usually, no one method or source of job-hunting can be used alone. *Library Services for Career Planning, Job Searching, and Employment Opportunities*, edited by Byron Anderson, Haworth Press, New York (1992, 183p.) is a timely source and includes bibliographical references.

Public and school library certification requirements often vary from state to state; contact the state library agency for such information in a particular state. Certification requirements are summarized in *Certification of Public Librarians in the United States*, 4th ed., 1991, from the ALA Office for Library Personnel Resources. A summary of school library/media certification requirements by state is found in *Requirements for Certification of Teachers, Counselors, Librarians and Administrators for Elementary and Secondary Schools*, published annually by the University of Chicago Press. "School Library Media Certification Requirements: 1994 Update" by Patsy H. Perritt also provides a compilation in *School Library Journal*, June 1994, pp. 32–49. State supervisors of school library media services may also be contacted for information on specific states.

Civil service requirements either on a local, county, or state level often add another layer of procedures to the job search. Some civil service jurisdictions require written and/or oral examinations; others assign a ranking based on a review of credentials. Jobs are usually filled from the top candidates on a qualified list of applicants. Since the exams are held only at certain time periods and a variety of jobs can be filled from a single list of applicants (e.g., all Librarian I positions regardless of type of function), it is important to check whether a library in which one is interested falls under civil service procedures.

If one wishes a position in a specific subject area or in a particular geographical location, remember those reference skills to ferret information from directories and other tools regarding local industries, schools, subject collections, etc. Directories such as the *American Library Directory*, *Subject Collections*, *Directory of Special Libraries and Information Centers*, and *Directory of Federal Libraries*, as well as state directories or directories of other special subject areas can provide a wealth of information for job seekers. "The Job Hunter's Search for Company Information" by Robert Favini (*RQ*, Winter 1991, pp. 155–161) lists general reference business sources that might be useful for librarians seeking employment in companies. Some state employment offices will include library listings as part of their Job Services department. In some cases, students have pooled resources to hire a clipping service for a specific time period in order to get classified librarian ads for a particular geographical area. Other Internet access not mentioned elsewhere: Association of Research Libraries (http://arl.cni.org/careers/vacancy.html) and LibJobs (http://www.nic-nbc.ca/cgi-bin/ifla-lwgate/LIBJOBS/archives/).

For information on other job-hunting and personnel matters, request a checklist of personnel materials available from the ALA Office for Library Personnel Resources, 50 E. Huron St., Chicago, IL 60611.

Placements and Salaries, 1996:
Counting on Technology

C. Herbert Carson

Associate Professor, Graduate School of Library and Information Studies,
University of Rhode Island, Kingston

Despite evidence that incoming librarians are integrating technology into their first jobs more than ever before, and even with data pointing to technology translating into higher salaries, salaries for the class of 1996 library school graduates nonetheless grew by just 1.7 percent, the second lowest rate in a decade, according to *Library Journal*'s 46th annual Placements and Salaries survey. Not only are new graduates moving into nontraditional positions related to technology in the information industry and on the Internet, but traditional positions (including acquisitions, cataloging, and reference) involve increasingly more nontraditional tasks.

This year's sluggish salary numbers notwithstanding, there is some proof that technology is having a positive effect on pay: Those whose salaries began at under $20,000 use technology 20.68 hours per week, whereas those with starting salaries over $40,000 spend more than 25 hours per week with technology.

Slightly more than half (2,166) of the total 1996 library and information science graduates polled (4,136) responded to the survey. Their responses revealed that over half their working hours (22 hours of a 40-hour week) are spent performing technology-related tasks in their new professional positions. For the first time, the survey asked respondents how many hours a week they devote to various technologically related tasks, thus providing an up-to-date snapshot of the facets of the librarian's job.

Looking at the Week

About four hours of the average librarian/information specialist's time each week is spent on Internet searching. Three hours are used for instructing and training patrons and staff in the use of technology and for online searching.

Recent graduates in Western states tend to use technology in their new jobs to a greater extent than in any of the other regions. Those graduates who work for vendors are the heaviest users of technology (32 hrs./wk.). Graduates in the more traditional library positions (academic, public, school, special, government) tend to work less with technology on average (about 23 hrs./wk.) than those in the nontraditional areas (over 30 hrs./wk.). School library media specialists use technology least (19 hrs./wk.).

This survey is based on data submitted by 44 of the 50 library and information science programs in the United States. Complete or partial information was received from all programs except Clark Atlanta, UC–Berkeley, University of North Carolina at Greensboro, Puerto Rico, Rutgers, and St. John's. Michigan provided only summary data based on phone interviews.

Adapted from *Library Journal*, October 15, 1997   (text continues on page 359)

Table 1 / Status of 1996 U.S. Graduates, Spring 1997

Region	Number of Schools Reporting	Number of Graduates Total	Not in Lib. Positions			Employment Unknown			Perm. Prof. Positions*			Temp. Prof. Positions**			Nonprof. Lib. Positions***			Total in Lib. Positions		
			Women	Men	Total	Women	Men	Total	Women	Men	Total	Women	Men	Total	Women	Men	Total	Women	Men	Total
Northeast	14	1,329	58	17	76	529	171	700	341	88	432	46	20	67	23	6	29	410	114	524
Southeast	10	738	31	11	42	280	81	361	243	56	300	13	7	20	14	2	17	270	65	335
Midwest	11	1,271	66	8	74	476	162	659	312	78	391	25	9	34	34	6	41	371	93	464
Southwest	5	441	28	13	41	59	28	87	192	44	236	22	5	27	13	2	15	227	51	278
West	4	357	16	3	19	142	30	172	105	23	129	35	6	41	16	2	18	156	31	187
All schools	44	4,136	199	52	252	1,486	472	1,979	1,239	302	1,549	146	48	1,95	108	19	129	1,528	388	1,924

Note: Tables do not always add up, individually or collectively, because schools omitted data in some cases.

* 10 positions filled in foreign jurisdictions and 50 did not report job location.

** 1 position filled in foreign jurisdiction and 4 did not report job location.

*** 1 position filled in foreign jurisdictions and 8 did not report job location.

Table 2 / Placements and Full-Time Salaries of 1996 U.S. Graduates: Summary by Region

Region	Total Placements	Number of Reported Salaries			Low Salary		High Salary		Average Salary			Median Salary		
		Women	Men	Total	Women	Men	Women	Men	Women	Men	Total	Women	Men	Total
Northeast	544	299	85	388	$13,000	$13,650	$85,000	$70,000	$31,067	$30,993	$31,026	$30,000	$29,000	$29,611
Southeast	344	233	55	289	15,000	20,000	55,000	70,000	27,588	30,272	28,135	26,700	29,000	27,000
Midwest	477	280	75	357	15,000	11,700	106,000	65,000	28,681	29,638	28,873	27,073	28,000	27,500
Southwest	282	174	41	215	10,000	19,000	70,000	60,000	27,506	29,237	27,836	27,000	28,000	27,500
West	194	93	24	117	17,500	18,000	55,000	54,000	32,151	33,525	32,433	32,000	32,500	32,000
Combined	1,924*	1,105	295	1,407	10,000	11,700	106,000	70,000	29,226	30,428	29,480	28,500	28,500	28,000

* Includes 15 placements in foreign jurisdictions and 68 placements with unknown job location.

Table 3 / Full-Time Salaries of Traditional vs. Nontraditional Graduates

Region	Number of Placements	Number of Reported Salaries			Low		High		Average			Median		
		Women	Men	Total	Women	Men	Women	Men	Women	Men	Total	Women	Men	Total
Traditional	1,342	865	182	1,047	$10,000	$11,700	$106 000	$56,000	$28,929	$29,588	$29,044	$28,000	$28,000	$28,162
Non-Traditional	562	241	115	360	13,000	12,000	85,000	70,000	30,226	31,833	30,721	29,000	29,000	29,000
Combined	1,924	1,105	295	1,407	10,000	11,700	106,000	70,000	29,226	30,428	29,480	28,000	28,500	28,000

Table 4 / Placements by Type of Organization

Schools	Public			Elementary & Secondary			College & University			Special			Other			Total		
	Women	Men	Total	Women	Men	Total	Women	Men	Total	Women	Men	Total	Women	Men	Total	Women	Men	Total
Alabama	6	2	8	10	1	11	7	3	10	2	1	3	4	1	5	29	9	38
Arizona	6	3	9	15	0	15	6	2	8	6	1	7	6	2	8	39	8	47
California (L.A.)	1	0	1	1	0	1	2	0	2	5	1	6	1	1	2	10	2	12
Catholic	5	2	7	4	1	5	9	1	10	8	4	12	8	4	12	34	14	48
Clarion	6	1	7	9	0	9	3	2	5	3	0	3	4	0	4	24	3	27
Dominican	19	4	23	3	0	3	10	1	11	7	2	9	4	1	5	43	8	51
Drexel	7	1	8	7	1	8	7	3	10	12	3	15	2	1	3	34	9	43
Emporia	19	3	22	18	3	21	6	1	7	3	1	4	4	3	7	50	11	61
Florida State	15	2	17	25	0	25	4	2	6	4	0	4	1	5	6	49	9	58
Hawaii	2	0	2	10	1	11	6	1	7	2	0	2	7	1	8	27	3	30
Illinois	22	4	26	1	0	1	14	10	24	6	4	10	4	2	6	44	19	63
Indiana	19	3	22	21	4	25	12	4	16	5	0	5	1	1	2	57	12	69
Iowa	5	0	5	8	2	10	6	3	9	4	0	4	5	2	7	27	7	34
Kent State	25	6	32	11	0	11	7	6	13	7	3	10	7	0	7	57	15	72
Kentucky	2	0	2	2	0	2	1	1	2	2	0	2	1	0	1	8	1	9
Long Island	13	5	18	9	0	9	2	3	5	6	0	6	1	2	3	31	10	41

Table 4 / Placements by Type of Organization (cont.)

Schools	Public			Elementary & Secondary			College & University			Special			Other			Total		
	Women	Men	Total	Women	Men	Total	Women	Men	Total	Women	Men	Total	Women	Men	Total	Women	Men	Total
Louisiana State	8	2	10	4	0	4	9	0	9	2	0	2	2	0	2	25	2	27
Maryland	5	1	6	8	0	8	6	4	10	8	1	9	13	4	17	40	10	50
Michigan	—	—	4	—	—	4	—	—	8	—	—	—	—	—	4	—	—	26
Missouri	13	1	14	4	0	4	13	5	18	6	0	6	4	1	5	40	7	47
N. C. Central	3	0	3	10	2	12	2	1	3	2	2	4	1	0	1	18	5	23
N. C. Chapel Hill	5	0	5	1	0	1	9	5	14	3	0	3	1	0	1	19	5	24
North Texas	13	11	24	14	1	15	14	5	19	9	1	10	5	3	8	55	21	76
Oklahoma	2	0	2	13	0	13	5	2	7	1	0	1	1	0	1	22	2	24
Pittsburgh	13	3	16	9	0	9	6	3	9	1	0	1	5	1	6	34	7	41
Pratt	18	4	22	3	0	3	6	3	9	3	4	7	2	1	3	32	12	44
Queens	12	4	16	4	0	4	1	1	2	2	0	2	1	2	3	20	7	27
Rhode Island	15	0	15	12	0	12	6	0	6	3	0	3	0	0	0	36	0	36
San Jose	19	5	24	7	1	8	15	1	16	8	3	11	13	5	18	62	14	76
Simmons	12	6	18	9	1	10	14	1	15	0	4	4	0	3	3	35	15	50
South Carolina	12	4	16	22	2	25	3	3	10	4	0	4	1	2	3	42	15	57
South Florida	13	1	14	13	1	14	6	3	9	4	0	4	6	0	6	39	6	45
S. Connecticut	9	1	10	12	1	13	3	1	4	1	0	1	3	0	3	28	3	31
Southern Mississippi	4	0	4	9	1	10	8	4	12	0	0	0	0	0	0	21	5	26
SUNY-Albany	8	1	9	6	3	9	8	5	13	2	1	3	6	1	7	30	11	41
SUNY-Buffalo	8	3	11	16	1	17	15	2	17	5	2	7	8	3	11	51	11	62
Syracuse	6	4	6	6	0	6	3	0	3	1	1	7	1	4	5	13	9	22
Tennessee	20	1	7	0	0	0	7	0	7	1	1	2	5	2	7	19	4	23
Texas (Austin)	10	1	21	14	2	16	22	7	29	21	0	21	22	13	35	99	23	122
Texas Woman's	11	2	12	15	0	15	9	2	11	2	0	2	4	0	4	40	4	44
Washington	15	1	12	1	1	2	11	6	17	6	3	9	4	1	5	33	12	45
Wayne State	8	2	18	13	1	14	4	5	9	6	0	7	3	2	5	41	10	51
Wisconsin (Madison)	6	1	9	5	1	6	4	3	7	2	2	4	7	1	8	26	8	34
Wisconsin (Milwaukee)	6	2	8	13	0	13	7	3	10	5	1	6	1	5	6	32	11	43
Total	442	96	545	397	31	434	318	126	456	187	47	239	179	80	263	1,515	379	1,924

(continued from page 355)

Thirty-six programs that submitted data for the survey included the results of that portion of the survey dealing with the technological aspects of graduates' positions. Drexel, Illinois, Long Island, Simmons, SUNY-Buffalo, NC–Chapel Hill, and Wayne State did not collect those items with their surveys.

Number of Graduates Declines, Salaries Inch Up—Barely

The total number of graduates has fallen despite more institutions contributing data to this year's survey. Last year, 42 schools reported 4,222 graduates; this year, 44 schools reported 4,136 graduates. Still, the numbers are stronger than a decade ago, when 53 schools reported 3,538 graduates. Women (3,233) accounted for 78.2 percent of this year's pool, and men (902) represented 21.8 percent. Of those responding, 83 percent (1,798) are in professional positions, compared to 78.3 percent last year.

The average professional salary for starting library positions went up by $483 over the 1995 beginner's salary. This 1.7 percent increase is the second-lowest increase in ten years (see Table 8).

Although the average salaries for both men and women have risen in the United States as a whole, the median salaries for female graduates in full-time professional positions have remained the same, and the men's median has fallen by $50. Men continue to be placed with higher starting salaries than women in all areas except the Northeast, where the women's starting mean and median salaries are higher than the men's, by $74- and $1,000-margins, respectively.

The average salary for women rose 2.1 percent, from $28,616 in 1995 to $29,226 in 1996. The men's salary went up 1.1 percent, from $30,029 to $30,428—substantially less than the 7.8 percent increase of last year (see Table 2). The permanent full-time placements average increased from $28,997 to $29,480, roughly half of last year's 3.2 percent increase.

Salaries for minority graduates rose by only $113 (0.3 percent), from $28,894 to $29,161 (see Table 7). Last year the rise was 1 percent.

More Nontraditional Jobs

Of the 1,924 graduates in full- and part-time library positions, 562 (27.6 percent) are in nontraditional positions and 1,342 (71.2 percent) are in traditional positions. (This may in part be due to the changes made in the survey instrument to better identify the functions performed by the respondents in their new jobs.) Last year 21.9 percent reported they had taken nontraditional positions, as opposed to 78 percent traditional jobs. Of 1994 graduates, 42 percent were in traditional jobs; for 1993, the figure was 53 percent.

Those entering nontraditional fields tend to do better financially than those in the traditional areas (see Table 3). The average starting salary for women in nontraditional fields ($30,226) is 4.5 percent greater than that of women in traditional fields ($28,929); for men, $31,833, or 7.6 percent more for nontraditional jobs than for traditional ones ($29,588). For both men and women, salaries for nontraditional jobs ($30,721) are 5.8 percent greater than for traditional ($29,044) ones. Men accounted for 31.9 percent of those in nontraditional fields, but only 17.4 percent of those in traditional jobs.

Part-time and Placement Trends

The total number of graduates working in full-time permanent professional positions is 1,383 (89.3 percent). The total number of part-time permanent professional positions is 155 (10 percent), which is dramatically less than the 16.5 percent reported last year. So although the overall number of part-time or temporary positions seems steady, the use of permanent part-time professionals may be diminishing.

Twelve institutions reported an increase in the number of positions listed in their placement services. Ten saw a decrease in their listings, and eight institutions had about the same number of positions—no significant shift. The average number of listings per institution was 1,650. Fourteen institutions did not provide this information.

Only one school reported having difficulty placing its graduates. Four stated that they had even less difficulty placing their graduates during 1996, and the rest stated that it was about the same as the previous year.

Regional trends remained steady. Some 67 percent of graduates found jobs in the same state as their library school (vs. 64 percent in the previous year) and 14 percent found jobs in the same region (vs. 16 percent in the previous year) (see Table 9).

As has been true for many years, graduates with backgrounds in mathematics, the sciences, and computers are still in short supply. Several institutions also recognize the need for graduates to have coursework in advanced cataloging and information technology-related areas such as networking, systems administration, and automation.

Graduates Who Are Plugged In

Although graduates of library and information science programs still tend to find jobs in the traditional areas, these positions require technological skills and knowledge. Graduates entering the nontraditional areas appear to use technology to an even greater extent than do those in traditional positions. Those in nontraditional areas continue to have higher starting salaries. Technical competencies seem more crucial than ever to starting a library career.

Table 5 / Special Placements

	Women	Men	Total
Non-Library Settings in a For-Profit Organization			
Aerospace corporation	0	1	1
College/university	3	4	7
Computer company	2	2	4
Corporate setting	3	2	5
Database publishing and services	3	0	3
Document delivery service	3	0	3
Hospital	1	0	1
Information consulting	3	0	3
Information technology company	4	0	4
Internet indexing	2	0	2
Internet news producer	1	0	1
Internet provider	1	0	1
Internet publishing company	1	0	1
Law libraries (incl. academic, bar association, etc.)	3	0	3
Online bookstore	1	0	1
Pharmaceutical	1	0	1
Publisher	1	1	2
Non-Library Settings in a Nonprofit Organization			
Academic computer center	1	0	1
College/university	4	2	6
Government office (federal, state, county, etc.)	1	3	4
Development office	1	0	1
Educational service center	1	1	2
Educational research project	1	2	3
Foundation	2	1	3
Hospital	1	0	1
Information specialist	1	0	1
Museum	2	0	2
Professional association	2	0	2
Social services agency	0	1	1
Other Organizations			
Audiovisual and media center	1	0	1
Church library	1	0	1
Correctional institutions (federal, state, county, etc.)	0	1	1
Freelance consultants and information broker	1	1	2
Joint public/academic library	1	0	1
Law library	4	1	5
News library	1	0	1
Private library	1	0	1
Total Special Placements	60	23	83

Table 6 / Placements and Full-Time Salaries of 1996 Graduates

Schools	Total Placements	Salaries Reported			Low Salary		High Salary		Average Salary			Median Salary		
		Women	Men	Total	Women	Men	Women	Men	Women	Men	Total	Women	Men	Total
Alabama	38	19	5	24	$10,000	$21,000	$38,000	$32,000	$27,040	$27,040	$27,040	$28,000	$27,581	$28,000
Arizona	43	30	8	38	10,000	19,000	50,000	32,500	27,591	27,345	27,539	26,000	27,800	26,000
California (L.A.)	11	7	2	9	25,000	32,000	36,000	45,000	32,088	38,500	33,513	32,000	38,500	32,000
Catholic	48	34	13	47	17,000	17,000	52,000	42,000	31,430	31,062	31,326	30,000	32,317	30,250
Clarion	28	18	2	20	13,600	27,500	36,000	35,000	26,274	31,250	26,772	26,400	31,250	26,548
Dominican	51	30	8	38	23,000	26,000	106,000	33,000	33,731	28,500	32,630	27,900	27,750	27,900
Drexel	42	28	7	35	23,500	28,000	57,000	50,000	32,239	34,357	32,663	30,000	30,000	30,000
Emporia	62	43	10	53	15,000	11,700	54,000	40,000	29,294	28,570	29,157	27,700	29,000	28,000
Florida State	58	41	8	49	10,000	20,000	50,000	70,000	28,490	33,511	29,310	27,700	29,500	28,000
Hawaii	31	17	1	18	15,600	30,000	38,000	30,000	28,613	30,000	28,690	30,000	30,000	30,000
Illinois	55	31	16	47	17,500	27,000	36,115	43,000	27,399	30,032	28,295	27,400	28,500	28,500
Indiana	68	44	10	54	15,700	22,000	52,000	60,000	29,022	32,025	29,578	27,750	26,375	27,400
Iowa	34	19	7	26	21,000	25,000	39,000	36,430	27,984	30,116	28,558	27,600	31,000	28,100
Kent State	73	41	14	55	11,100	20,500	37,000	42,000	26,565	27,843	26,824	26,700	27,250	26,850
Kentucky	10	9	1	10	15,000	27,000	35,000	27,000	23,949	27,000	24,255	23,045	27,000	23,523
Long Island	42	22	6	28	25,000	23,000	46,800	50,000	33,603	31,712	33,198	32,206	29,887	32,206
Louisiana State	27	18	2	20	17,500	22,500	36,240	25,000	25,257	23,750	25,106	26,250	23,750	25,250
Maryland	50	28	8	36	20,000	23,000	65,411	44,000	31,399	31,331	31,384	30,000	29,956	30,000
Michigan	26	—	—	—	—	—	—	—	—	—	—	—	—	—
Missouri	52	32	11	43	12,417	25,000	45,000	42,000	26,121	30,800	27,235	25,000	29,000	26,750

N. C. Central	24	15	5	20	17,388	27,396	30,976	70,000	25,652	38,179	28,784	26,770	31,000	27,319
N. C. Chapel Hill	24	17	5	22	20,050	24,444	45,000	36,000	28,516	29,889	28,828	26,000	29,000	27,000
North Texas	76	43	20	63	13,200	9,840	47,000	35,000	27,217	27,037	27,159	27,000	27,500	27,500
Oklahoma	24	17	2	19	21,000	23,000	32,500	25,000	25,553	24,000	25,553	25,000	24,000	25,000
Pittsburgh	39	28	6	34	16,000	13,650	36,000	28,800	28,316	23,742	27,509	26,450	25,500	26,450
Pratt	44	30	11	41	24,000	24,000	45,000	58,000	30,243	36,468	31,913	28,800	32,500	29,000
Queens	27	14	6	20	22,549	23,000	49,000	37,000	30,974	33,333	31,682	29,750	36,000	31,000
Rhode Island	35	22	0	22	20,000	—	41,800	—	30,481	—	30,481	29,200	—	29,200
San Jose	77	41	8	49	22,000	18,000	55,000	54,000	33,551	30,975	33,130	32,000	28,000	32,000
Simmons	49	23	10	33	21,500	25,700	40,000	42,000	30,223	31,120	30,292	30,000	28,000	30,000
South Carolina	58	40	14	54	13,132	17,600	40,000	52,000	26,990	31,769	28,406	25,900	28,081	26,700
South Florida	46	35	7	42	16,000	22,760	53,500	37,000	27,970	28,117	27,994	27,000	27,300	27,106
S. Connecticut	30	23	2	25	17,940	25,000	41,200	28,000	31,446	26,500	31,034	32,900	26,500	31,900
S. Mississippi	26	21	5	26	13,200	26,000	32,500	51,500	23,576	33,300	25,446	23,743	28,000	24,000
SUNY-Albany	43	24	11	35	13,000	23,000	35,000	35,000	25,172	29,925	26,666	25,500	30,000	28,000
SUNY-Buffalo	47	34	6	40	13,000	26,500	36,919	30,000	28,562	27,945	28,469	29,150	28,000	28,180
Syracuse	22	10	6	16	15,000	22,000	50,000	37,000	30,655	28,685	29,916	28,275	28,096	28,096
Tennessee	23	16	4	20	21,350	25,000	55,000	32,000	30,737	29,475	30,485	27,750	30,450	28,000
Texas Austin	122	76	17	93	20,100	21,000	70,000	58,000	29,671	31,251	29,951	28,000	28,000	28,000
Texas Woman's	44	33	3	36	15,000	12,000	40,500	27,000	26,529	19,667	25,957	28,000	20,000	28,000
Washington	45	28	9	37	22,000	28,000	42,000	41,000	29,481	33,667	30,499	29,000	32,000	30,000
Wayne State	52	21	4	25	10,000	26,000	55,000	41,000	29,150	31,000	29,446	27,000	28,500	27,000
WI. (Madison)	34	17	6	23	20,000	19,000	42,016	28,600	30,221	25,719	29,046	30,000	26,856	28,162
WI. (Milwaukee)	43	26	7	33	18,000	13,200	50,000	65,000	28,295	31,886	29,057	26,450	28,000	26,900

Table 7 / Salaries of Minority Placements by Type of Organization

Library Type	Number	Salaries Reported	Percent of Total	Low Salary	High Salary	Average Salary	Median Salary
Academic	44	34	28.57	$15,000	$45,000	$28,387	$28,000
Public	53	18	15.13	20,300	50,000	30,271	30,549
School	24	43	36.13	18,949	36,936	26,599	27,050
Special	16	10	8.40	23,000	45,000	32,520	32,500
Government	7	5	4.20	24,000	38,600	32,920	34,000
Lib. coop/network	1	0	0.00	—	—	—	
Vendor	0	0	0.00	—	—	—	
For-Profit org.	7	4	3.36	30,000	58,000	42,500	41,000
Nonprofit org.	3	3	2.52	19,000	21,000	20,000	20,000
Other org.	3	2	1.68	30,000	43,000	36,500	36,500
Total	159	119	100.00	15,000	58,000	29,007	28,000

Table 8 / Average Salary Index
Starting Library Positions, 1985–1996

Year	Library Schools	Average Beginning Salary	Dollar Increase in Average Salary	Salary Index	BLS-CPI
1985	58	$19,753	$962	111.64	109.3
1986	54	20,874	1,121	117.98	110.5
1987	55	22,247	1,373	125.74	115.4
1988	51	23,491	1,244	132.77	120.5
1989	43	24,581	1,090	138.93	124.0
1990	38	25,306	725	143.03	130.7
1991	46	25,583	277	144.59	136.2
1992	41	26,666	1,083	150.71	140.5
1993	50	27,116	450	153.26	144.4
1994	43	28,086	970	158.74	148.4
1995	41	28,997	911	163.89	152.5
1996	44	29,480	483	166.62	159.1

* The U.S. Bureau of Labor Statistics' present Consumer Price Index is based on the average price data from 1982–1984 as equaling 100. The average beginning professional salary from the period was $17,693 and is used as the equivalent base of 100 for salary data.

Table 9 / 1996 Graduates, Placement by Location

Library School Location	Number of Graduates Placed	Placed in Same State (as library school)	Placed in Same Region (as library school)	Placed in Other Regions — Northeast	Southeast	Midwest	Southwest	West	Foreign Jurisdiction
Alabama	39	24	8	1	—	1	1	1	0
Arizona	48	28	5	1	1	1	—	7	0
California	89	79	1	0	1	1	4	—	0
Connecticut	31	29	0	—	1	0	1	0	1
District of Columbia	48	19	6	—	19	0	0	2	0
Florida	104	80	5	10	—	3	4	0	1
Hawaii	31	25	3	0	1	0	1	—	1
Illinois	114	61	24	5	2	—	8	6	2
Indiana	69	51	6	1	2	—	2	1	3
Iowa	34	18	14	0	2	—	0	0	0
Kansas	61	31	20	1	1	—	3	5	0
Kentucky	10	4	1	1	—	3	1	0	0
Louisiana	25	20	1	0	—	1	0	3	0
Maryland	50	20	19	—	9	0	0	2	0
Massachusetts	55	35	9	—	3	0	0	1	0
Michigan	52	49	2	1	0	—	1	0	0
Mississippi	26	16	5	2	—	2	—	0	0
Missouri	50	25	10	1	3	—	4	3	2
New York	251	203	26	—	6	4	6	2	1
North Carolina	47	23	9	4	—	6	3	2	0
Ohio	67	49	3	2	3	—	4	3	0
Oklahoma	24	16	3	0	1	3	—	0	0
Pennsylvania	113	74	15	—	8	8	3	3	0
Rhode Island	35	13	22	—	—	—	—	—	—
South Carolina	58	34	12	9	—	2	0	0	0
Tennessee	23	10	10	2	—	0	0	1	0
Texas	240	177	8	5	13	14	—	7	0
Washington	45	31	6	2	3	2	1	—	0
Wisconsin	75	46	16	7	2	—	0	2	1
Totals	1,914	1,290	269	65	81	51	46	51	11
Percentages	—	67%	14%	3%	4%	3%	2%	3%	1%

Table 10 / Comparison of Salaries by Type of Organization

	Total Placements	Salaries Women	Salaries Men	Salaries Total	Low Salary Women	Low Salary Men	High Salary Women	High Salary Men	Average Salary Women	Average Salary Men	Average Salary Total	Median Salary Women	Median Salary Men	Median Salary Total
Public Libraries														
Northeast	162	81	26	107	$13,832	$21,000	$38,500	$36,000	$27,175	$27,982	$27,371	$28,000	$28,156	$28,000
Southeast	89	63	10	73	17,388	22,500	53,500	35,000	24,946	28,137	25,383	24,700	26,750	25,000
Midwest	160	89	21	109	17,000	22,000	106,000	30,000	26,761	26,238	26,661	26,000	27,000	26,000
Southwest	68	44	13	57	22,464	20,000	36,000	32,000	26,053	27,362	26,351	25,900	27,500	26,000
West	43	14	2	16	17,500	32,000	55,000	35,000	31,867	33,500	32,071	32,500	33,500	32,500
All public	544	297	73	370	13,832	20,000	106,000	36,000	26,647	27,487	26,813	26,000	27,900	26,500
School Libraries														
Northeast	105	75	5	80	16,000	23,000	66,000	42,000	32,845	31,600	32,767	32,000	30,000	32,000
Southeast	113	87	6	93	17,000	26,000	52,000	40,000	29,319	32,667	29,535	28,000	32,750	28,000
Midwest	102	82	8	90	15,000	11,700	55,000	41,000	30,453	27,587	30,199	30,000	27,500	29,850
Southwest	71	57	3	60	10,000	25,000	42,000	34,000	27,580	29,000	27,651	28,000	28,000	28,000
West	24	13	1	14	24,000	41,000	55,000	41,000	35,692	41,000	36,071	32,000	41,000	32,500
All school	430	323	24	348	10,000	11,700	66,000	42,000	30,429	30,820	30,477	29,700	30,500	30,000
College/University Libraries														
Northeast	125	42	18	60	23,000	23,000	85,000	42,000	33,979	30,178	32,839	31,250	29,000	30,000
Southeast	79	30	20	50	17,085	21,000	47,000	70,000	26,798	30,532	28,291	27,000	27,198	27,000
Midwest	112	41	23	64	16,000	13,200	45,000	50,000	28,171	30,776	29,107	27,500	28,000	27,900
Southwest	65	29	10	39	15,000	19,000	33,000	35,000	26,388	28,050	26,814	26,500	28,000	27,000
West	53	12	2	14	23,000	21,500	35,916	29,000	30,499	25,250	29,749	30,600	25,250	30,000
All academic	451	157	58	237	15,000	13,200	85,000	70,000	29,305	30,633	29,468	28,000	28,000	28,000
Special Libraries														
Northeast	67	33	11	44	21,000	22,000	50,000	70,000	32,381	35,947	33,272	30,000	32,000	30,000
Southeast	23	16	5	21	19,000	22,000	37,000	37,000	28,425	30,300	28,871	30,000	30,000	30,000
Midwest	53	31	9	40	21,000	25,000	45,000	43,000	29,465	30,911	29,790	30,000	29,000	30,000
Southwest	31	19	1	20	18,000	32,000	36,000	32,000	28,237	32,000	28,425	25,000	32,000	25,000
West	38	21	5	26	23,000	31,000	45,000	38,000	33,218	34,300	33,426	32,000	33,500	32,500
All special	225	124	35	159	18,000	22,000	50,000	70,000	30,676	33,946	31,396	30,000	32,000	30,000

Government Libraries														
Northeast	24	8	4	12	27,600	31,200	35,000	37,000	30,913	33,975	31,933	30,550	33,850	31,400
Southeast	11	8	1	9	15,000	31,000	35,500	31,000	27,522	31,000	27,909	29,218	31,000	29,436
Midwest	10	7	0	7	21,000	—	54,000	—	33,393	—	33,393	30,000	—	30,000
Southwest	15	4	2	6	23,532	21,000	42,500	32,178	31,418	26,589	29,808	29,820	26,589	28,659
West	8	3	1	4	32,400	38,600	35,000	38,600	33,800	38,600	35,000	34,000	38,600	34,500
All government	70	31	9	40	15,000	21,000	54,000	38,600	31,106	31,764	31,254	30,000	32,178	31,000
Library Cooperatives/Networks														
Northeast	1	1	0	1	$33,500	—	33,500	—	33,500	—	33,500	33,500	—	33,500
Southeast	3	2	0	2	25,500	—	34,000	—	29,750	—	29,750	29,750	—	29,750
Midwest	2	1	1	2	34,000	40,000	34,000	40,000	34,000	40,000	37,000	34,000	40,000	37,000
Southwest	1	0	0	0	—	—	—	—	—	—	—	—	—	—
West	0	0	0	0	—	—	—	—	—	—	—	—	—	—
All coop./net.	7	4	1	5	25,500	40,000	34,000	40,000	31,750	40,000	33,400	33,750	40,000	34,000
Vendors														
Northeast	15	4	4	8	25,000	26,500	51,000	31,000	35,400	28,375	31,888	32,800	28,000	29,500
Southeast	4	3	1	4	28,000	27,000	35,000	27,000	30,333	27,000	29,500	28,000	27,000	28,000
Midwest	4	2	2	4	24,000	25,000	27,000	65,000	25,500	45,000	35,250	25,500	45,000	26,000
Southwest	4	1	2	3	28,000	24,000	28,000	32,000	28,000	28,000	28,000	28,000	28,000	28,000
West	4	0	3	3	—	30,000	—	35,000	—	32,667	32,667	—	33,000	33,000
All vendors	31	10	12	22	24,000	24,000	51,000	65,000	31,160	32,042	31,641	28,000	29,000	28,000
Other Organizations														
Northeast	38	20	7	27	20,000	28,000	57,000	50,000	32,725	34,929	33,296	32,000	30,000	31,000
Southeast	19	9	6	15	23,000	20,000	55,000	52,000	31,022	33,933	32,187	26,700	32,000	30,900
Midwest	31	14	4	18	21,000	26,000	50,000	58,000	29,529	35,750	30,912	30,000	29,500	30,000
Southwest	27	10	6	16	26,000	26,000	70,000	43,000	34,600	32,626	33,860	30,000	31,878	30,800
West	27	13	5	18	21,000	18,000	45,000	54,000	32,335	38,400	$34,020	30,000	39,000	34,138
All other	146	67	29	96	20,000	18,000	70,000	58,000	32,021	34,409	32,743	30,000	32,000	30,000

1,924 total placements were reported; only 1,284 professionals in permanent, full-time positions, type of library and salary.

Accredited Master's Programs in Library and Information Studies

This list of graduate programs accredited by the American Library Association was issued in January 1998. The list of accredited programs is issued annually at the start of each calendar year and is available from the ALA Office for Accreditation. A list of more than 200 institutions offering both accredited and nonaccredited programs in librarianship appears in the 50th edition of the *American Library Directory* (R. R. Bowker, 1997).

Northeast: Conn., D.C., Md., Mass., N.J., N.Y., Pa., R.I.

Catholic University of America, School of Lib. and Info. Science, Washington, DC 20064. Elizabeth S. Aversa, Dean. 202-319-5085, fax 202-219-5574, e-mail cua-slis@cua.edu. World Wide Web http://www.cua.edu/www/lsc. Admissions contact: Kevin Woods.

Clarion University of Pennsylvania, Dept. of Lib. Science, 166 Carlson, Clarion, PA 16214-1232. James T. Maccaferri, Chair. 814-226-2271, fax 814-226-2150, e-mail mccafer@mail.clarion.edu.

Drexel University, College of Info. Science and Technology, 3141 Chestnut St., Philadelphia, PA 19104-2875. Richard H. Lytle, Dean. 215-895-2474, fax 215-895-2494. World Wide Web http://www.cis.drexel.edu. Admissions contact: Anne B. Tanner. 215-895-2485, e-mail tannerab@duvm.ocs.drexel.edu

Long Island University, Palmer School of Lib. and Info. Science, C. W. Post Campus, 720 Northern Blvd., Brookville, NY 11548-1300. Anne Woodsworth, Dean. 516-299-2866, fax 516-299-4168, e-mail palmer@titan.liunet.edu. World Wide Web http://www.cwpost.liunet.edu/cwis/cwp/palmer/main.html. Admissions contact: Rosemary Chu. 516-299-2487, fax 516-299-4168.

Pratt Institute, School of Info. and Lib. Science, Info. Science Center, 200 Willoughby Ave., Brooklyn, NY 11205. S. M. Matta, Dean. 718-636-3702, fax 718-636-3733, e-mail matta@sils.pratt.edu. World Wide Web http://sils.pratt.edu.

Queens College, City University of New York, Grad. School of Lib. and Info. Studies, 65-30 Kissena Blvd., Flushing, NY 11367. Marianne Cooper, Dir. 718-997-3797, fax 718-997-3797. Admissions contact: Karen P. Smith.

Rutgers University, School of Communication, Info., and Lib. Studies, 4 Huntington St., New Brunswick, NJ 08903-1071. Todd Hunt, Acting Dean. 732-932-7917, fax 732-932-2644, e-mail scilsmls@scils.rutgers.edu. World Wide Web http://scils.rutgers.edu. Admissions contact: David Carr. 732-932-8315, e-mail dcarr@scils.rutgers.edu.

Saint John's University, Div. of Lib. and Info. Science, 8000 Utopia Pkwy., Jamaica, NY 11439. James A. Benson, Dir. 718-990-6200, fax 718-990-2071, e-mail libis@sjumusic.stjohns.edu. Admissions contact: Jeanne M. Umland. 718-990-6776, fax 718-960-1677.

Simmons College, Grad. School of Lib. and Info. Science, 300 The Fenway, Boston, MA 02115-5898. James M. Matarazzo, Dean. 617-521-2800, fax 617-521-3192, e-mail gslis@simmons.edu. Admissions contact: Judith Beals. 617-521-2801, e-mail jbeals@simmons.edu.

Southern Connecticut State University, School of Communication, Info., and Lib. Science, 501 Crescent St., New Haven, CT 06515. Edward C. Harris, Dean. 203-392-5781, fax 203-392-5780, e-mail libscienceit@scsu.ctstateu.edu. Admissions contact: Nancy Disbrow.

State University of New York at Albany, School of Info. Science and Policy, 135 Western Ave., Albany, NY 12222. Philip

B. Eppard, Dean. 518-442-5110, fax 518-442-5367, e-mail infosci@cnsvax.albany.edu. Admissions contact: Virginia Papandrea. E-mail papand@cnsvax.albany.edu.

State University of New York at Buffalo, School of Info. and Lib. Studies, 534 Baldy Hall, Buffalo, NY 14260. George S. Bobinski, Dean. 716-645-2412, fax 716-645-3775, e-mail sils@acsu.bufalo.edu. World Wide Web http://www.sils.buffalo.edu. Admissions contact: A. Neil Yerkey. 716-645-6478.

Syracuse University, School of Info. Studies, 4-206 Center for Science and Technology, Syracuse, NY 13244-4100. Raymond F. von Dran, Dean. 315-443-2911, fax 315-443-5806, e-mail vondran@syr.edu. World Wide Web http://istweb.svr.edu.

University of Maryland, College of Lib. and Info. Services, College Park, MD 20742-4345. Ann E. Prentice, Dean. 301-405-2033, fax 301-314-9145, e-mail ap57@umail.umd.edu. Admissions contact: Diane L. Barlow. 301-405-2039, e-mail dbarow@deans.umd.edu.

University of Pittsburgh, School of Info. Sciences, 505 IS Bldg., Pittsburgh, PA 15260. Toni Carbo, Dean. 412-624-5230, fax 412-624-5231. World Wide Web http://www.sis.pitt.edu. Admissions contact: Ninette Kay. 412-624-5146, e-mail nk@sis.pitt.edu.

University of Rhode Island, Grad. School of Lib. and Info. Studies, Rodman Hall, Kingston, RI 02881. Jonathan S. Tryon, Dir. 401-874-2947, fax 401-874-4395. Admissions contact: C. Herbert Carson. 401-874-4646, e-mail chcarson@uriacc.uri.edu.

Southeast: Ala., Fla., Ga., Ky., La., Miss., N.C., S.C., Tenn., P.R.

Clark Atlanta University, School of Lib. and Info. Studies, 300 Trevor Arnett Hall, 223 James P. Brawley Dr., Atlanta, GA 30314. Arthur C. Gunn, Dean. 404-880-8697, fax 404-880-8977, e-mail agunn@cau.edu. Admissions contact: Doris Callahan.

Florida State University, School of Lib. and Info. Studies, Tallahassee, FL 32306-2048. Jane B. Robbins, Dean. 850-644-5775, fax 850-644-9763. World Wide Web http://www.fsu.edu/~lis. Admissions contact: Elisabeth Logan. 850-644-8106, e-mail logan@lis.fsu.edu.

Louisiana State University, School of Lib. and Info. Science, 267 Coates Hall, Baton Rouge, LA 70803. Bert R. Boyce, Dean. 504-388-3158, fax 504-388-4581, e-mail lsslis@lsuvm.sncc.lsu.edu. World Wide Web http://adam.slis.lsu.edu. Admissions contact: Nicole Rozas.

North Carolina Central University, School of Lib. and Info. Sciences, Box 19586, Durham, NC 27707. Benjamin F. Speller, Jr., Dean. 919-560-6485, fax 919-560-6402, e-mail speller@ga.unc.edu. World Wide Web http://www.nccu.edu/slis/index.html. Admissions contact: Duane Bogenschneider, 919-560-55211, e-mail duaneb@nccu.edu.

University of Alabama, School of Lib. and Info. Studies, Box 870252, Tuscaloosa, AL 35487-0252. Joan L. Atkinson, Director. 205-348-1522, fax 205-348-3746. World Wide Web http://www.slis.ua.edu.

University of Kentucky, School of Lib. and Info. Science, 502 King Library, Building S, Lexington, KY 40506-0039. Timothy W. Sineath, Dir. 606-257-8876, fax 606-257-4205, e-mail tsineath@pop.uky.edu. World Wide Web http://www.uky.edu/CommInfoStudies/SLIS. Admissions contact: Gloria McCowan. 606-257-3317, e-mail gmccowa@pop.uky.edu.

University of North Carolina at Chapel Hill, School of Info. and Lib. Science, 100 Manning Hall, Chapel Hill, NC 27599-3360. Barbara B. Moran, Dean. 919-962-8366, fax 919-962-8071, e-mail info@ils.unc.edu. World Wide Web http://www.ils.unc.edu. Admissions contact: Betty J. Kompst. E-mail kompst@ils.unc.edu.

University of North Carolina at Greensboro, Dept. of Lib. and Info. Studies, 349 Curry Bldg., Greensboro, NC 27412-5001. Keith Wright, Chair. 910-334-3477, fax 910-334-5060, e-mail trhughes@dewey.uncg.edu. World Wide Web http://www.uncg.edu/lis/. Admissions contact: Beatrice Kovacs. 910-334-3479, e-mail kovacsb@iris.uncg.edu.

University of Puerto Rico, Graduate School of Lib. and Info. Science (Escuela Graduada de Bibliotecologia y Ciencia de la Información), Box 21906, San Juan, PR 00931-1906. Mariano A. Maura, Dir. 809-763-6199, fax 787-764-2311, e-mail mmaura@upracd.upr.clu.edu. Admissions contact: Migdalia Dávila. 809-764-0000, ext. 3530, e-mail m_davila@rrpad.upr.clu.edu.

University of South Carolina, College of Lib. and Info. Science, Davis College, Columbia, SC 29208. Fred W. Roper, Dean. 803-777-3858, fax 803-777-7938. World Wide Web http://www.libsci.sc.edu. Admissions contact: Nancy C. Beitz. 803-777-5067, fax 803-777-0457, e-mail nbeitz@sc.edu.

University of South Florida, School of Lib. and Info. Science, 4202 E. Fowler Ave., CIS 1040, Tampa, FL 33620-7800. Kathleen de la Peña McCook, Dir. 813-974-3520, fax 813-974-6840, e-mail pate@luna.cas.usf.edu. World Wide Web http://www.cas.usf.edu/lis. Admissions contact: Sonia Ra hlmuth. E-mail swohlmut@chuma.cas.usf.edu.ml.

University of Southern Mississippi, School of Lib. and Info. Science, Box 5146, Hattiesburg, MS 39406-5146. Joy M. Greiner, Dir. 601-266-4228, fax 601-266-5774.

University of Tennessee, School of Info. Sciences, 804 Volunteer Blvd., Knoxville, TN 37996-4330. W. David Penniman, Interim Dir. 423-974-2148, fax 423-974-4967. World Wide Web http://www.sis.utk.edu. Admissions contact: George Hoemann. 423-974-5917, e-mail hoemann@utk.edu.

Midwest: Ill., Ind., Iowa, Kan., Mich., Mo., Ohio, Wis.

Emporia State University, School of Lib. and Info. Management, Box 4025, Emporia, KS 66801. Faye Vowell, Dean. 316-341-5203, fax 316-341-5233. World Wide Web http://www.emporia.edu/slim/slim.htm. Admissions contact: Jean Redeker. 316-341-5734, e-mail redekerj@esumail.emporia.edu.

Indiana University, School of Lib. and Info. Science, 10th St. and Jordan Ave., Bloom-ington, IN 47405-1801. Blaise Cronin, Dean. 812-855-2018, fax 812-855-6166, e-mail iuslis@indiana.edu. World Wide Web http://www.slis.indiana.edu. Admissions contact: Mary Krutulis. E-mail krutulis@indiana.edu.

Kent State University, School of Lib. and Info. Science, Box 5190, Kent, OH 44242-0001. Danny P. Wallace, Dir. 330-672-2782, fax 330-672-7965. World Wide Web http://web.slis.kent.edu. Admissions contact: Marge Hayden. E-mail mhayden@slis.kent.edu.

Dominican University, Grad. School of Lib. and Info. Science, 7900 W. Division St., River Forest, IL 60305. Prudence W. Dalrymple, Dean. 708-524-6845, fax 708-524-6657, e-mail gslis@email.dom.edu. World Wide Web http://dom.edu/academic/gslishome.

University of Illinois at Urbana-Champaign, Grad. School of Lib. and Info. Science, 501 E. Daniel St., Champaign, IL 61820. Leigh S. Estabrook, Dean. 217-333-3280, fax 217-244-3302. World Wide Web http://alexia.lis.uiuc.edu. Admissions contact: Carol DeVoss. 217-333-7197, e-mail devoss@alexia.lis.uiuc.edu.

University of Iowa, School of Lib. and Info. Science, Iowa City, IA 52242-1420. Padmini Srinivasan, Dir. 319-335-5707, fax 319-335-5374, e-mail padmini-srinivasan@uiowa.edu. World Wide Web http://www.uiowa.edu/~libsci. Admissions contact: Ethel Bloesch. E-mail ethel-bloesch@uiowa.edu.

University of Michigan, School of Info., 550 E. University Ave., Ann Arbor, MI 48109-1092. Daniel E. Atkins, Dean. 313-763-2285, fax 313-764-2475, e-mail si.admissions@umich.edu. World Wide Web http://www.si.umich.edu. Admissions contact: Robin Jenkins.

University of Missouri–Columbia, School of Info. Science and Learning Technologies, 217 Townsend Hall, Columbia, MO 65211. John Wedman, Dir. 573-882-4546, fax 573-884-4944. World Wide Web http://tiger.coe/missouri.edu/~sislt. Admissions contact: Carol Hendrickson. 573-882-4546, e-mail carolhen@coe.missouri.edu.

University of Wisconsin–Madison, School of Lib. and Info. Studies, 600 N. Park St., Madison, WI 53706. Louise S. Robbins, Dir. 608-263-2900, fax 608-263-4849, e-mail uw_slis@doit.wisc.edu. Admissions contact: Barbara Arnold. E-mail bjarnold@facstaff.wisc.edu.

University of Wisconsin–Milwaukee, School of Lib. and Info. Science, 2400 E. Hartford Ave., Milwaukee, WI 53211. Mohammed M. Aman, Dean. 414-229-4707, fax 414-229-4848, e-mail info@slis.uwm.edu. World Wide Web http://www.slis.uwm.edu. Admissions contact: Wilfred Fong. 414-229-5421, e-mail fong@slis.uwm.edu.

Wayne State University, Lib. and Info. Science Program, 106 Kresge Library, Detroit, MI 48202. Robert P. Holley, Dir. 313-577-1825, fax 313-577-7563, e-mail rholley@lisp.purdy.wayne.edu. World Wide Web http://www.lisp.wayne.edu.

Southwest: Ariz., Okla., Tex.

Texas Woman's University, School of Lib. and Info. Studies, Box 425438, Denton, TX 76204-5438. Keith Swigger, Dean. 817-898-2602, fax 940-898-2611, e-mail a_swigger@twu.edu. World Wide Web http://www.twu.edu/slis.

University of Arizona, School of Info. Resources and Lib. Science, 1515 E. First St., Tucson, AZ 85719. Charlie D. Hurt, Dir. 520-621-3565, fax 520-621-3279, e-mail sirls@u.arizona.edu. World Wide Web http://www.sir/arizona.edu.

University of North Texas, School of Lib. and Info. Sciences, Box 311068, NT Station, Denton, TX 76203. Philip M. Turner, Dean. 817-565-2445, fax 940-565-3101, e-mail slis@unt.edu. World Wide Web http://www.unt.edu.slis. Admissions contact: Herman L. Totten. E-mail totten@lis.unt.edu.

University of Oklahoma, School of Lib. and Info. Studies, 401 W. Brooks, Norman, OK 73019-0528. June Lester, Dir. 405-325-3921, 405-325-7648, e-mail slisinfo@ou.edu. World Wide Web http://www.uoknor.edu/cas/slis. Admissions contact: Maggie Ryan.

University of Texas at Austin, Grad. School of Lib. and Info. Science, Austin, TX 78712-1276. Glynn Harmon, Interim Dean. 512-471-3821, fax 512-471-3971, e-mail gslis@uts.cc.utexas.edu. World Wide Web http://www.gslis.utexas.edu. Admissions contact: Ronald Wyllys. 512-471-8969, e-mail wyllys@uts.cc.utexas.edu.

West: Calif., Hawaii, Wash.

San Jose State University, School of Lib. and Info. Science, 1 Washington Sq., San Jose, CA 95192-0029. Blanche Woolls, Dir. 408-924-2490, 408-924-2492, e-mail office@wahoo.sjsu.edu.

University of California at Los Angeles, Grad. School of Education and Info. Studies, Mailbox 951521, Los Angeles, CA 90095-1521. Michele V. Cloonan, Chair. 310-825-8799, fax 310-206-3076, e-mail mcloonan@ucla.edu. World Wide Web http://dlis.gseis.ucla.edu. Admissions contact: Susan Abler. 310-825-5269, fax 310-206-6293, e-mail abler@gseis.ucla.edu.

University of Hawaii, Lib. and Info. Science Program, 2550 The Mall, Honolulu, HI 96822. Larry N. Osborne, Interim Dean. 808-956-7321, fax 808-956-5835, e-mail osborne@hawaii.edu. Admissions contact: Lani Teshima-Miller. 808-956-5807, e-mail teshima@hawaii.edu.

University of Washington, Grad. School of Lib. and Info. Science, Box 352930, Seattle, WA 98195-2930. Betty G. Bengtson, Acting Dir. 206-543-1794, fax 206-616-3152. World Wide Web http://weber.u.washington.edu/~gslis. Admissions contact: Dolores Potter. E-mail potterd@u.washington.edu.

Canada

Dalhousie University, School of Lib. and Info. Studies, Halifax, NS B3H 3J5. Bertrum H. MacDonald, Dir. 902-494-3656, fax 902-494-2451, e-mail slis@is.dal.ca. World Wide Web http://www.mgmt.dal.ca/slis. Admissions contact: Shanna Balogh. 902-494-2453, e-mail shanna@is.dal.ca.

McGill University, Grad. School of Lib. and Info. Studies, 3459 McTavish St., Montreal, PQ H3A 1Y1. J. Andrew Large, Dir. 514-398-4204, fax 514-398-7193, e-mail ad27@musica.mcgill.ca. World Wide Web http://www.gslis.mcgill.ca. Admissions contact: Dorothy Carruthers.

Université de Montréal, Ecole de Bibliothéconomie et des Sciences de l'Information, C.P. 6128, Succursale Centre-Ville, Montreal, PQ H3C 3J7. Gilles Deschâtelets, Dir. 514-343-6044, fax 514-343-5753, e-mail deschatg@ere.umontreal.ca. World Wide Web http://tornado.ere.umontreal.ca/~carmellu/ebsi. Admissions contact: Diane Mayer. E-mail mayerdi@daa.umontreal.ca.

University of Alberta, School of Lib. and Info. Studies, 3-20 Rutherford S., Edmonton, AB T6G 2J4. Alvin Schrader, Dir. 403-492-4578, fax 403-492-2430, e-mail office@slis.ualberta.ca.

University of British Columbia, School of Lib., Archival, and Info. Studies, 1956 Main Mall, Vancouver, BC V6T 1Z1. Ken Haycock, Dir. 604-822-2404, fax 604-822-6006, e-mail slais@unixg.ubc.ca. World Wide Web http://www.slais.ubc.ca. Admissions contact: Lynne Lighthall. 604-822-2404, e-mail admit@slais.ubc.ca.

University of Toronto, Faculty of Info. Studies, 140 George St., Toronto, ON M5S 3G6. Lynne C. Howarth, Dean. 416-978-8589, fax 416-978-5762. World Wide Web http://www.fis.utoronto.ca. Admissions contact: Rachele Muia. E-mail muia@fis.utoronto.ca.

University of Western Ontario, Grad. Programs in Lib. and Info. Science, Elborn College, London, ON N6G 1H1. Greg Moran, Acting Dean. 519-661-3542, fax 519-661-3506, e-mail slbgam@uwoadmin.uwo.ca. Admissions contact: Cindy Morrison. 519-661-2111, ext. 8484, e-mail morrison@julian.uwo.ca.

Library Scholarship Sources

For a more complete list of scholarships, fellowships, and assistantships offered for library study, see *Financial Assistance for Library and Information Studies*, published annually by the American Library Association.

American Association of Law Libraries. (1) A varying number of scholarships of a minimum of $1,000 for graduates of an accredited law school who are degree candidates in an ALA-accredited library school; (2) a varying number of scholarships of varying amounts for library school graduates working on a law degree, non-law graduates enrolled in an ALA-accredited library school, and law librarians taking a course related to law librarianship; (3) the George A. Strait Minority Stipend of $3,500 for an experienced minority librarian working toward an advanced degree to further a law library career. For information, write to: Scholarship Committee, AALL, 53 W. Jackson Blvd., Suite 940, Chicago, IL 60604.

American Library Association. (1) The Marshall Cavendish Scholarship of $3,000 for a varying number of students who have been admitted to an ALA-accredited library school. For information, write to Staff Liaison, Cavendish Scholarship Jury, ALA, 50 E. Huron St., Chicago, IL 60611; (2) The David H. Clift Scholarship of $3,000 for a varying number of students who have been admitted to an ALA-accredited library school. For information, write to: Staff Liaison, Clift Scholarship Jury, ALA, 50 E. Huron St., Chicago, IL 60611; (3) the Shirley Crawford Minority Scholarship of $3,000 for a varying number of minority students who have been admitted to an ALA-accredited library school. For information, write to: Staff Liaison, Crawford Scholarship Jury, ALA, 50 E. Huron St., Chicago, IL 60611; (4) the Tom and Roberta Drewes Scholarship of $3,000 for a varying number of library support staff. For information, write to: Staff Liaison, Drewes Scholarship Jury, ALA, 50 E. Huron St., Chicago, IL 60611; (5) the Mary V. Gaver Scholarship of $3,000 to a varying number of individuals specializing in youth services. For infor-

mation, write to: Staff Liaison, Gaver Scholarship Jury, ALA, 50 E. Huron St., Chicago, IL 60611; (6) the Miriam L. Hornback Scholarship of $3,000 for a varying number of ALA or library support staff. For information, write to: Staff Liaison, Hornback Scholarship Jury, ALA, 50 E. Huron St., Chicago, IL 60611; (7) the Christopher J. Hoy/ERT Scholarship of $3,000 for a varying number of students who have been admitted to an ALA-accredited library school. For information, write to: Staff Liaison, Hoy/ERT Scholarship Jury, ALA, 50 E. Huron St., Chicago, IL 60611; (8) the Tony B. Leisner Scholarship of $3,000 for a varying number of library support staff. For information, write to: Staff Liaison, Leisner Scholarship Jury, ALA, 50 E. Huron St., Chicago, IL 60611; (9) Spectrum Initiative Scholarships of $5,000 for 50 minority students admitted to an ALA-accredited library school. For information, write to: Staff Liaison, Spectrum Initiative Scholarship, ALA, 50 E. Huron St., Chicago, IL 60611.

ALA/American Association of School Librarians. The AASL School Librarians Workshop Scholarship of $2,500 for a candidate admitted to a full-time ALA-accredited MLS or school library media program. For information, write to: AASL/ALA, 50 E. Huron St., Chicago, IL 60611.

ALA/Association of College and Research Libraries and the Institute for Scientific Information. (1) The ACRL Doctoral Dissertation Fellowship of $1,000 for a student who has completed all coursework and submitted a dissertation proposal that has been accepted, in the area of academic librarianship; (2) the Samuel Lazerow Fellowship of $1,000 for research in acquisitions or technical services in an academic or research library; (3) the ACRL and Martinus Nijhoff International West European Specialist Study Grant, which pays travel expenses, room, and board for a ten-day trip to the Netherlands and two other European countries for an ALA member (selection is based on proposal outlining purpose of trip). For information, write to: Althea Jenkins, ACRL/ALA, 50 E. Huron St., Chicago, IL 60611.

ALA/Association for Library Service to Children. (1) The Bound to Stay Bound Books Scholarship of $6,000 each for two students who are U.S. or Canadian citizens, who have been admitted to an ALA-accredited program, and who will work with children in a library for one year after graduation; (2) the Frederic G. Melcher Scholarship of $6,000 each for two U.S. or Canadian citizens admitted to an ALA-accredited library school who will work with children in school or public libraries for one year after graduation. For information, write to: Executive Director, ALSC/ALA, 50 E. Huron St., Chicago, IL 60611.

ALA/International Relations Committee. The Bogle International Library Travel Fund grant of $1,000 for a varying number of ALA members to attend a first international conference. For information, write to: Carol Erickson, ALA, 50 E. Huron St., Chicago, IL 60611.

ALA/Library and Information Technology Association. Three LITA Scholarships in library and information technology of $2,500 each for students (two of whom are minority students) who have been admitted to an ALA-accredited program in library automation and information science. For information, write to: LITA/ALA, 50 E. Huron St., Chicago, IL 60611.

ALA/New Members Round Table. EBSCO/NMRT Scholarship of $1,000 for a U.S. or Canadian citizen who is a member of the ALA New Members Round Table. Based on financial need, professional goals, and admission to an ALA-accredited program. For information, write to: Pamela Padley, Mail Code 1-32, California Technical Library System, California Institute of Technical Libraries, Pasadena, CA 91125.

ALA/Public Library Association. The New Leaders Travel Grant Study Award of up to $1,500 for a varying number of PLA members with five years or less experi-

ence. For information, write to: PLA/ALA, 50 E. Huron St., Chicago, IL 60611.

American-Scandinavian Foundation. Fellowships and grants for 25 to 30 students, in amounts from $3,000 to $15,000, for advanced study in Denmark, Finland, Iceland, Norway, or Sweden. For information, write to: Exchange Division, American-Scandinavian Foundation, 725 Park Ave., New York, NY 10021.

Association of Jewish Libraries. The May K. Simon Memorial Scholarship Fund offers a varying number of scholarships of at least $500 each for MLS students who plan to work as Judaica librarians. For information, write to: Sharona R. Wachs, Association of Jewish Libraries, 1000 Washington Ave., Albany, NY 12203.

Association for Library and Information Science Education. A varying number of research grants of up to $2,500 each for members of ALISE. For information, write to: Association for Library and Information Science Education, Box 7640, Arlington, VA 22207.

Association of Seventh-Day Adventist Librarians. The D. Glenn Hilts Scholarship of $1,000 to a member of the Seventh-Day Adventist Church in a graduate library program. For information, write to: Ms. Wisel, Association of Seventh-Day Adventist Librarians, Columbia Union College, 7600 Flower Ave., Takoma Park, MD 20912.

Beta Phi Mu. (1) The Sarah Rebecca Reed Scholarship of $1,500 for a person accepted in an ALA-accredited library program; (2) the Frank B. Sessa Scholarship of $750 for a Beta Phi Mu member for continuing education; (3) the Harold Lancour Scholarship of $1,000 for study in a foreign country related to the applicant's work or schooling; (4) the Blanche E. Woolls Scholarship for School Library Media Service of $1,000 for a person accepted in an ALA-accredited library program; the Doctoral Dissertation Scholarship of $1,500 for a person who has completed course work toward a doctorate. For information, write to: F. William Summers, Executive Secretary, Beta Phi Mu, Florida State University, SIS, Tallahassee, FL 32306-2100.

Canadian Association of Law Libraries. The Diana M. Priestly Scholarship of $2,000 for a student with previous law library experience or for entry to an approved Canadian law school or accredited Canadian library school. For information, write to: John Eaton, Prof., Law Library, University of Western Ontario, London, ON N6A 3K7, Canada.

Canadian Federation of University Women. The Alice E. Wilson Award of $1,000 for three Canadian citizens or permanent residents with a BA degree or equivalent accepted into a program of graduate study. For information, write to: Canadian Federation of University Women, 251 Bank St., Suite 600, Ottawa, ON K2P 1X3, Canada.

Canadian Health Libraries Association. The Student Paper Prize, a scholarship of $300 to a student or recent MLIS graduate or library technician; topic of paper must be in health or information science. For information, write to: Student Paper Prize, Canadian Health Libraries Association/ABSC, Box 94038, 3332 Yonge St., Toronto, ON M4N 3R1, Canada.

Canadian Library Association. (1) The Howard V. Phalin World Book Graduate Scholarship in Library Science of $2,500; (2) the CLA Dafoe Scholarship of $1,750; and (3) the H. W. Wilson Scholarship of $2,000. Each scholarship is given to a Canadian citizen or landed immigrant to attend an accredited Canadian library school; the Phalin scholarship can also be used for an ALA-accredited U.S. school; (4) the Library Research and Development Grant of $1,000 for a member of the Canadian Library Association, in support of theoretical and applied research in library and information science. For information, write to: CLA Membership Services Department, Scholarships and Awards Committee, 200 Elgin St., Suite 602, Ottawa, ON K2P 1L5, Canada.

Catholic Library Association. The World Book, Inc., Grant of $1,500 is divided among no more than three CLA members for workshops, institutes, etc. For information, write to: Jean R. Bostley, SSJ, Scholarship Committee, St. Joseph Central High School Library, 22 Maplewood Ave., Pittsfield, MA 01201-4780.

Chinese American Librarians Association. (1) The Sheila Suen Lai Scholarship; (2) the CALA Scholarship; (3) the C. C. Seetoo/CALA Conference Travel Scholarship. Each scholarship offers $500 to a Chinese descendant who has been accepted in an ALA-accredited program. For information, write to: Yan Ma, Graduate School of Library and Information Studies, University of Rhode Island, 94 W. Alumni Ave., Kingston, RI 02881.

Church and Synagogue Library Association. The Muriel Fuller Memorial Scholarship of $115 plus cost of texts for a correspondence course offered by the University of Utah Continuing Education Division. Open to CSLA members only. For information, write to: CSLA, Box 19357, Portland, OR 97280-0357.

Council on Library and Information Resources. The A. R. Zipf Fellowship in Information Management, awarded annually to a student enrolled in graduate school who shows exceptional promise for leadership and technical achievement. For information, write to: Council on Library and Information Resources, 1755 Massachusetts Ave. N.W., Suite 500, Washington, DC 20036.

Sandra Garvie Memorial Fund. A scholarship of $1,000 for a student pursuing a course of study in library and information science. For information, write to: Sandra Garvie Memorial Fund, c/o Director, Legal Resources Centre, Faculty of Extension, University of Alberta, 8303 112th St., Edmonton, AB T6G 2T4, Canada.

Massachusetts Black Librarians' Network. Two scholarships of at least $500 and $1,000 for a minority student entering an ALA-accredited master's program in library science, with no more than 12 semester hours toward a degree. For information, write to: Pearl Mosley, Chair, Massachusetts Black Librarians' Network, 27 Beech Glen St., Roxbury, MA 02119.

Medical Library Association. (1) A scholarship of $2,000 for a person entering an ALA-accredited library program, with no more than one-half of the program yet to be completed; (2) a scholarship of $2,000 for a minority student for graduate study; (3) a varying number of Research, Development and Demonstration Project Grants of $100 to $1,000 for U.S. or Canadian citizens who are MLA members; (4) Continuing Education Grants of $100 to $500 for U.S. or Canadian citizens who are MLA members; (5) the Cunningham Memorial International Fellowship of $4,000 plus travel expenses for a foreign student for postgraduate study in the United States; (6) the MLA Doctoral Fellowship of $2,000 for doctoral work in medical librarianship or information science. For information, write to: Development Department, Medical Library Association, 6 N. Michigan Ave., Suite 300, Chicago, IL 60602.

Mountain Plains Library Association. (1) A varying number of grants of up to $600 each and (2) a varying number of grants of up to $150 each for MPLA members with at least two years of membership for continuing education. For information, write to: Joseph R. Edelen, Jr., MPLA Executive Secretary, I. D. Weeks Library, University of South Dakota, Vermillion, SD 57069.

REFORMA, the National Association to Promote Library Services to the Spanish-Speaking. A varying number of scholarships of $1,000 each for minority students interested in serving the Spanish-speaking community to attend an ALA-accredited school. For information, write to: Luis Chaparro, El Paso Community College, Box 20500, El Paso, TX 7998-0500.

Society of American Archivists. The Colonial Dames Awards, two grants of $1,200 each for specific types of repositories and collections. For information, write to: Debra Mills, Society of American Archivists, 600 S. Federal St., Suite 504, Chicago, IL 60605.

Southern Regional Education Board. For residents of Alabama, Florida, Kentucky, Louisiana, Maryland, Mississippi, Oklahoma, South Carolina, Tennessee, and Texas, a varying number of grants of varying amounts to cover in-state tuition for graduate or postgraduate study in an ALA-accredited library school. For information, write to: Academic Common Market, c/o Southern Regional Education Board, 592 Tenth St. N.W., Atlanta, GA 30318-5790.

Special Libraries Association. (1) Three $6,000 scholarships for students interested in special-library work; (2) the Plenum Scholarship of $1,000, and (3) the ISI Scholarship of $1,000, each also for students interested in special-library work; (4) the Affirmative Action Scholarship of $6,000 for minority students interested in special-library work; and (5) the Pharmaceutical Division Stipend Award of $1,200 for a student with an undergraduate degree in chemistry, life sciences, or pharmacy entering or enrolled in an ALA-accredited program. For information on the first four scholarships, write to: Scholarship Committee, Special Libraries Association, 1700 18th St. N.W., Washington, DC 20009-2508; for information on the Pharmaceutical Stipend, write to: Susan E. Katz, Awards Chair, Knoll Pharmaceuticals Science Information Center, 30 N. Jefferson St., Whippany, NJ 07981.

Library Scholarship and Award Recipients, 1997

Library awards are listed by organization. An index listing awards alphabetically by title follows this section.

American Association of Law Libraries (AALL)

AALL Scholarships. Offered by: AALL; Matthew Bender & Company; LEXIS-NEXIS; West Group. *Winners:* (Library Degree for Law School Graduates) Victoria Esposito-Smea, Steven Anderson, Carol Parker; (Library School Graduates Attending Law School) Shannon Brett; (Library Degree for Non-Law School Graduates) Holly Jo Moore, Marie-Elise Waltz; (Library School Graduates Seeking a Non-Law Degree) Mitch Counts; (George A. Strait Minority Stipend) Sandra Cox-McCarthy, David Mao, Pauline Alfuso, Lan Choi, Kristin Nelson.

American Library Association (ALA)

ALA Honorary Membership. Oprah Winfrey, Henriette Avram.

ALA/Information Today Library of the Future Award ($1,500). For a library, consortium, group of librarians, or support organization for innovative planning for, applications of, or development of patron training programs about information technology in a library setting. *Donor:* Information Today, Inc. *Winner:* Canton (Michigan) Public Library.

Hugh C. Atkinson Memorial Award ($2,000). For outstanding achievement (including risk-taking) by academic librarians that has contributed significantly to improvements in library automation, management, and/or development or research. Offered by: ACRL, ALCTS, LAMA, and LITA divisions. *Winner:* William Gray Potter.

Carroll Preston Baber Research Grant (up to $7,500). For innovative research that could lead to an improvement in library services to any specified group(s) of people. *Donor:* Eric R. Baber. *Winner:* Lynn Westbrook.

Beta Phi Mu Award ($500). For distinguished service in library education. *Donor:* Beta Phi Mu International Library Science Honorary Society. *Winner:* Charles Bunge.

Bogle International Library Travel Fund Award ($1,000). To ALA member(s) to attend their first international conference. *Donor:* Bogle Memorial Fund. *Winner:* Melissa Lamont.

William Boyd Military Novel Award ($10,000). To an author for a military novel that honors the service of American veterans. *Donor:* William Young Boyd. *Winner:* Jeff Shaara for *Gods and Generals: A Novel of the Civil War.*

Marshall Cavendish Scholarship ($3,000). To a worthy U.S. or Canadian citizen to begin an MLS degree in an ALA-accredited program. *Winner:* Steven Anderson.

David H. Clift Scholarship ($3,000). To a worthy U.S. or Canadian citizen to begin an MLS degree in an ALA-accredited program. *Winner:* Noelle Cook.

Shirley Crawford Scholarship ($3,000). To a worthy U.S. or Canadian minority student working toward an MLS degree in an ALA-accredited program. *Donor:* R. R. Bowker. *Winner:* Nicole Cooke.

Melvil Dewey Award. To an individual or group for recent creative professional achievement in library management, training, cataloging and classification, and the tools and techniques of librarianship. *Donor:* OCLC/Forest Press. *Winner:* Robert Wedgeworth.

Tom C. Drewes Scholarship ($3,000). To a library support staff person pursuing a master's degree. *Winner:* Patricia Breno.

EBSCO ALA Conference Sponsorships (up to $1,000). To allow librarians to attend ALA's Annual Conferences. *Donor:* EBSCO Subscription Services. *Winners:* Susan Benjamin, Craig Bunch, Laurie Leigh Cole, Jerome Upchurch Conley,

Denise Keller, Louise Meyers, Ronda Nisen, Amy Beach Parrish, Diana N. Skousen, Mara Warner.

Equality Award ($500). To an individual or group for an outstanding contribution that promotes equality of women and men in the library profession. *Donor:* Scarecrow Press. *Winner:* Sarah Pritchard.

Freedom to Read Foundation Roll of Honor Award. *Winner:* Bruce Ennis.

Elizabeth Futas Catalyst for Change Award ($1,000). To recognize and honor a librarian who invests time and talent to make positive change in the profession of librarianship. *Donor:* Elizabeth Futas Memorial Fund. *Winner:* Camila Alire.

Loleta D. Fyan Public Library Research Grant (up to $10,000). For projects in public library development. *Winner:* Kansas Library Network Board.

Gale Research Financial Development Award ($2,500). To a library organization for a financial development project to secure new funding resources for a public or academic library. *Donor:* Gale Research Company. *Winner:* Decorah (Iowa) Public Library.

Mary V. Gaver Scholarship ($3,000). To a library support staff specializing in youth services. *Winner:* Debra DeFouw.

Louise Giles Minority Scholarship ($3,000). To a worthy U.S. or Canadian minority student to begin an MLS degree in an ALA-accredited program. *Winner:* Juan Tomas Lee.

Grolier Foundation Award ($1,000). For stimulation and guidance of reading by children and young people. *Donor:* Grolier Education Corporation, Inc. *Winner:* Patricia R. Scales.

Grolier National Library Week Grant ($4,000). To libraries or library associations of all types for a public awareness campaign in connection with National Library Week in the year the grant is awarded. *Donor:* Grolier Educational Corporation. *Winner:* Kanawha County (West Virginia) Public Library.

G. K. Hall Award for Library Literature ($500). For outstanding contribution to library literature issued during the three years preceding presentation. *Donor:* G.

K. Hall & Company. *Winner:* Wayne A. Wiegand for *Irrepressible Reformer: A Biography of Melvil Dewey.*

Mirian L. Hornback Scholarship ($3,000). To an ALA or library support staff person pursuing a master's degree in library science. *Winner:* Elizabeth Gourley.

Paul Howard Award for Courage ($1,000). To a librarian, library board, library group, or an individual who has exhibited unusual courage for the benefit of library programs or services. *Donor:* Paul Howard. *Winner:* Not awarded in 1997.

John Ames Humphry/OCLC/Forest Press Award ($1,000). To an individual for significant contributions to international librarianship. *Donor:* OCLC/Forest Press. *Winner:* Ravindra N. Sharma.

Tony B. Leisner Scholarship ($3,000). To a library support staff member pursuing a master's degree program. *Winner:* Gregory C. Cook.

Joseph W. Lippincott Award ($1,000). To a librarian for distinguished service to the profession. *Donor:* Joseph W. Lippincott, Jr. *Winner:* Richard Dougherty.

Bessie Boehm Moore Award ($1,000). Presented to a public library that has developed an outstanding and creative program for public library services to the aging. *Donor:* Bessie Boehm Moore. *Winner:* Chavis Lifelong Learning Branch Library, Greensboro, North Carolina.

H. W. Wilson Library Staff Development Grant ($3,500). To a library organization for a program to further its staff development goals and objectives. *Donor:* The H. W. Wilson Company. *Winner:* Washoe County (Nevada) Library.

World Book–ALA Goal Grant (up to $10,000). To ALA units for the advancement of public, academic, or school library service and librarianship through support of programs that implement the goals and priorities of ALA. *Donor:* World Book, Inc. *Winners:* ALA Office for Intellectual Freedom, Presidential Advisory Committee, and the Subcommittee on Diversity Project.

American Association of School Librarians (AASL)

AASL ABC/CLIO Leadership Grant (up to $1,750). For planning and implementing leadership programs at state, regional, or local levels to be given to school library associations that are affiliates of AASL. *Donor:* ABC/CLIO. *Winner:* New England Educational Media Association.

AASL/Frances Henne Award ($1,250). To a school library media specialist with five or fewer years in the profession to attend an AASL regional conference or ALA Annual Conference for the first time. *Donor:* R. R. Bowker. *Winner:* Roxanna K. Morse.

AASL/Highsmith Research Grant (up to $5,000). To conduct innovative research aimed at measuring and evaluating the impact of school library media programs on learning and education. *Donor:* The Highsmith Company. *Winner:* Ruth Villency Small.

AASL Information Plus Continuing Education Scholarship ($500). To a school library media specialist, supervisor, or educator to attend an ALA or AASL continuing education event. *Donor:* Information Plus. *Winner:* Gail Formanack.

AASL President's Crystal Apple Award. *Winner:* Not awarded in 1997.

AASL School Librarian's Workshop Scholarship ($2,500). To a full-time student preparing to become a school library media specialist at the preschool, elementary, or secondary level. *Donor:* Jay W. Toor, President, Library Learning Resources. *Winner:* Mary Katherine Logan.

Distinguished School Administrators Award ($2,000). For expanding the role of the library in elementary and/or secondary school education. *Donor:* Social Issues Resources Series, Inc. *Winner:* David V. DeLong.

Distinguished Service Award, AASL/Baker & Taylor ($3,000). For outstanding contributions to librarianship and school library development. *Donor:* Baker & Taylor Books. *Winner:* E. Blanche Woolls.

Intellectual Freedom Award ($2,000, and $1,000 to media center of recipient's choice). To a school library media specialist who has upheld the principles of intellectual freedom. *Donor:* Social Issues Resources Series, Inc. *Winner:* Ginny Moore Kruse.

Microcomputer in the Media Center Award ($1,000 to the specialist and $500 to the library). To library media specialists for innovative approaches to microcomputer applications in the school library media center. *Donor:* Follett Software Company. *Winners:* Secondary, Lynzie Boudreaux; Elementary, not awarded in 1997.

National School Library Media Program of the Year Award ($3,000). To school districts and a single school for excellence and innovation in outstanding library media programs. *Donor:* AASL and Encyclopaedia Britannica Companies. *Winners:* Single, Timothy Dwight Elementary School, Fairfield (Connecticut) Public Schools; Small, Iowa City Community School District; Large, Gwinnett County (Georgia) Public Schools.

American Library Trustee Association (ALTA)

ALTA/Gale Outstanding Trustee Conference Grant Award ($750). *Donor:* Gale Research Company. *Winner:* Matt Wenthold.

ALTA Literacy Award (citation). To a library trustee or an individual who, in a volunteer capacity, has made a significant contribution to addressing the illiteracy problem in the United States. *Winner:* Barbara Fellows.

ALTA Major Benefactors Honor Award (citation). To individual(s), families, or corporate bodies that have made major benefactions to public libraries. *Winner:* Olive and Anthony Borgatti.

Trustee Citations. To recognize public library trustees for individual service to library development on the local, state, regional, or national level. *Winners:* Irene Hairston, Jack Short.

Armed Forces Libraries Round Table

Armed Forces Library Certificate of Merit. To librarians or "friends" who are members of AFLRT who provide an exemplary program to an Armed Forces library. *Winner:* Patricia McGill.

Armed Forces Library Round Table Achievement Citation. For contributions toward development of interest in libraries and reading in armed forces library service and organizations. Candidates must be members of the Armed Forces Libraries Round Table. *Winner:* Barbara D. Wrinkle.

Armed Forces Library Round Table News-Bank Scholarship ($1,000 to the school of the recipient's choice). To members of the Armed Forces Libraries Round Table who have given exemplary service in the area of library support for off-duty education programs in the armed forces. *Donor:* NewsBank, Inc. *Winner:* Lorna Dodt.

Association for Library Collections and Technical Services (ALCTS)

Hugh C. Atkinson Memorial Award. *See under* American Library Association.

Best of LRTS Award (citation). To the author(s) of the best paper published each year in the division's official journal. *Winner:* Michael Kaplan.

Blackwell North America Scholarship Award ($2,000 scholarship to the U.S. or Canadian library school of the recipient's choice). To honor the author(s) of the year's outstanding monograph, article, or original paper in the field of acquisitions, collection development, and related areas of resource development in libraries. *Donor:* Blackwell/North America: *Winners:* Walt Crawford, Michael Gorman, for *Future Libraries: Dreams, Madness, and Reality.*

Bowker/Ulrich's Serials Librarianship Award ($1,500). For demonstrated leadership in serials-related activities through participation in professional associations and/or library education programs, contributions to the body of serials literature, research in the area of serials, or development of tools or methods to enhance access to or management of serials. *Donor:* R. R. Bowker/Ulrich's. *Winner:* Cynthia K. Hepfer.

First Step Award (Wiley Professional Development Grant) ($1,500). For librarians new to the serials field to attend ALA's Annual Conference. *Donor:* John Wiley & Sons. *Winner:* Linda M. Pitts.

Leadership in Library Acquisitions Award ($1,500). For significant contributions by an outstanding leader in the field of library acquisitions. *Donor:* Harrassowitz. *Winner:* Katrina P. Strauch.

Margaret Mann Citation. To a cataloger or classifier for achievement in the areas of cataloging or classification. *Winner:* Sheila Intner.

Esther J. Piercy Award ($1,500). To a librarian with fewer than ten years experience for contributions and leadership in the field of library collections and technical services. *Donor:* Yankee Book Peddler. *Winner:* Birdie MacLennan.

Association for Library Service to Children (ALSC)

ALSC/Book Wholesalers Summer Reading Program Grant ($3,000). To an ALSC member for implementation of an outstanding public library summer reading program for children. *Donor:* Book Wholesalers, Inc. *Winner:* Hurst (Texas) Public Library.

ALSC/Econo-Clad Literature Program Award ($1,000). To an ALSC member who has developed and implemented an outstanding library program for children involving reading and the use of literature, to attend an ALA conference. *Donor:* Econo-Clad Books. *Winner:* Rebecca Kornman.

ALSC/REFORMA Pura Belpre Award. *Winner:* Not awarded in 1997.

May Hill Arbuthnot Honor Lecturer 1998. To invite an individual of distinction to prepare and present a paper that will be a significant contribution to the field of children's literature and that will subsequently be published in *Journal of Youth Services in Libraries.* *Winner:* Susan Hirschman.

Mildred L. Batchelder Award (citation). To an American publisher of an English-language translation of a children's book originally published in a foreign language in a foreign country. *Winner:* Farrar, Straus & Giroux for *The Friends* by Kazumi Yumoto.

Batchelder Honor Books. *Winners:* Not awarded in 1997.

Louise Seaman Bechtel Fellowship ($3,750). For librarians with 12 or more years of professional level work in children's library collections, to read and study at the Baldwin Library/George Smathers Libraries, University of Florida (must be an ALSC member with an MLS from an ALA-accredited program). *Donor:* Bechtel Fund. *Winner:* Kathy East.

Bound to Stay Bound Books Scholarship ($6,000). Two awards for study in the field of library service to children toward the MLS or beyond in an ALA-accredited program. *Donor:* Bound to Stay Bound Books. *Winners:* David Black, Kathleen McDowell.

Caldecott Medal. *See* "Literary Prizes, 1997" by Gary Ink.

Andrew Carnegie Medal. To U.S. producer of the most distinguished video for children in the previous year. *Donor:* Carnegie Corporation of New York. *Winner:* Minnesota Orchestra Visual Entertainment (MOVE) for *On the Day You Were Born,* part of MOVE's series NotesAlive!

Distinguished Service to ALSC Award ($1,000). To recognize significant contributions to, and an impact on, library services to children and/or ALSC. *Winner:* Zena Sutherland.

Frederic G. Melcher Scholarship ($5,000). To students entering the field of library service to children for graduate work in an ALA-accredited program. *Winners:* Erin O'Toole, Kristine Springer.

John Newbery Medal. *See* "Literary Prizes, 1997" by Gary Ink.

Putnam and Grosset Group Awards ($600). To children's librarians in school or public libraries with ten or fewer years of experience to attend ALA Annual Conference for the first time. Must be a member of ALSC. *Donor:* Putnam and Grosset Book Group. *Winners:* Kate Carter, Urla C. Morgan, Melinda Mullican, Donna L. Scanlon.

Laura Ingalls Wilder Medal. To an author or illustrator whose works have made a lasting contribution to children's literature. *Winner:* Not awarded in 1997.

Association of College and Research Libraries (ACRL)

ACRL Academic or Research Librarian of the Year Award ($3,000). For outstanding contribution to academic and research librarianship and library development. *Donor:* Baker & Taylor. *Winner:* James G. Neal.

ACRL EBSS Distinguished Education and Behavioral Sciences Librarian Award (citation). To an academic librarian who has made an outstanding contribution as an education and/or behavioral sciences librarian through accomplishments and service to the profession. *Winner:* Nancy P. O'Brien.

ACRL Doctoral Dissertation Fellowship ($1,500). To a doctoral student in the field of academic librarianship whose research has potential significance in the field. *Winner:* Diane Worrell.

Hugh C. Atkinson Memorial Award. *See under* American Library Association.

Miriam Dudley Bibliographic Instruction Librarian Award ($1,000). For contribution to the advancement of bibliographic instruction in a college or research institution. *Donor:* Mountainside Publishing. *Winner:* Patricia Senn Breivik.

EBSCO Community College Leadership Award ($500). *Donor:* EBSCO Subscription Services. *Winner:* Gretchen H. Neill.

EBSCO Community College Learning Resources Award ($500). *Donor:* EBSCO Subscription Services. *Winner:* Not awarded in 1997.

Instruction Section Innovation in Instruction Award (citation). Recognizes and honors librarians who have developed and implemented innovative approaches to instruction within their institution in the preceding two years. *Winners:* Debra L. Gilchrist, Kyzyl Fenno-Smith.

Instruction Section Publication of the Year Award (citation). Recognizes an outstanding publication related to instruction in a library environment published in the preceding two years. *Winner:* Gloria J. Leckie.

Marta Lange/CQ Award ($1,000). Recognizes an academic or law librarian for contributions to bibliography and information service in law or political science. *Donor:* Congressional Quarterly. *Winner:* Grace W. "Betty" Taylor.

Samuel Lazerow Fellowship for Research in Acquisitions or Technical Services

($1,000). To foster advances in acquisitions or technical services by providing librarians a fellowship for travel or writing in those fields. Sponsor: Institute for Scientific Information (ISI). *Winner:* Linda Marie Golian.

Katharine Kyes Leab and Daniel J. Leab American Book Prices Current Exhibition Catalog Awards (citations). For the three best catalogs published by American or Canadian institutions in conjunction with exhibitions of books and/or manuscripts. *Winners:* (Category One) *From Jackson to Lincoln: Democracy and Dissent,* Pierpont Morgan Library, New York; (Category Two) Not awarded in 1997; (Category Three) *The Ardent Image: Book Illustration for Adults in America, 1920–1942,* William S. Carlson Library, University of Toledo (Ohio).

Martinus Nijhoff International West European Specialist Study Grant (travel funding for up to 14 days research in Europe). Supports research pertaining to West European studies, librarianship, or the book trade. Sponsor: Martinus Nijhoff International. *Winner:* Sem C. Sutter.

Oberly Award for Bibliography in the Agricultural Sciences. Biennially, for the best English-language bibliography in the field of agriculture or a related science in the preceding two-year period. *Donor:* Eunice R. Oberly Fund. *Winner:* Wallace C. Olsen.

Rare Books & Manuscripts Librarianship Award ($1,000). For articles of superior quality published in the ACRL journal *Rare Books & Manuscripts Librarianship.* *Donor:* Christie, Manson & Woods. *Winners:* Henry F. Raine, Laura Stalker.

K. G. Saur Award for Best *College and Research Libraries* Article ($500). To author(s) to recognize the most outstanding article published in *College and Research Libraries* during the preceding year. *Donor:* K. G. Saur. *Winners:* Stephen P. Harter, Hak Joon Kim.

Association of Specialized and Cooperative Library Agencies (ASCLA)

ASCLA Exceptional Service Award. *Winner:* Stewart L. Wells.

ASCLA Leadership Achievement Award. To recognize leadership and achievement in the areas of consulting, multitype library cooperation, and state library development. *Winner:* Barbara Will.

ASCLA/National Organization on Disability Award for Library Service to People with Disabilities ($1,000). To institutions or organizations that have made the library's total service more accessible through changing physical and/or additional barriers. *Donor:* National Organization on Disability, funded by J. C. Penney. *Winner:* Lee County Library System, Fort Meyers, Florida.

ASCLA Professional Achievement Award (citation). For professional achievement within the areas of consulting, networking, statewide services, and programs. *Winner:* James A. Nelson.

ASCLA Research Grant ($500). To stimulate researchers to look at state library services, interlibrary cooperation, networking, and services to special populations as valid areas of research interest. *Donor:* Auto-Graphics, Inc. *Winner:* Nancy Everhart.

ASCLA Service Award (citation). For outstanding service and leadership to the division. *Winner:* Donna O. Dziedzic.

Francis Joseph Campbell Citation. For a contribution of recognized importance to library service for the blind and physically handicapped. *Winner:* U.S. Senator John Chafee.

Ethnic Material and Information Exchange Round Table

EMIERT Third Multicultural Award: Berkeley (California) Public Library.

Exhibits Round Table

Accessibility for Attendees with Disabilities Award (citation). *Winner:* Not awarded in 1997.

Friendly Booth Award (citation). Cosponsor: New Members Round Table. *Winners:* First place, Channel One Network; second place, Culturgrams; third place, IDG Books Worldwide.

Christopher J. Hoy/ERT Scholarship ($3,000). To an individual who will work toward an

MLS degree in an ALA accredited program. *Donor:* Family of Christopher Hoy. *Winner:* Marianne Buehler.

Kohlstedt Exhibit Award (citation). To companies or organizations for the best single, multiple, and island booth displays at the ALA Annual Conference. Citation. *Winners:* Watson Label Products, Pleasant Company Publications, Checkpoint Systems.

Federal Librarians Round Table (FLRT)

Adelaide del Frate Conference Sponsor Award. To encourage library school students to become familiar with federal librarianship and ultimately seek work in federal libraries; for attendance at ALA Annual Conference and activities of the Federal Librarians Round Table. *Winner:* Not awarded in 1997.

Distinguished Service Award (citation). To honor a FLRT member for outstanding and sustained contributions to the association and to federal librarianship. *Winner:* Laurie Stackpole.

Government Documents Round Table (GODORT)

James Bennett Childs Award. To a librarian or other individual for distinguished lifetime contributions to documents librarianship. *Winner:* Peter I. Hajnal.

CIS/GODORT/ALA Documents to the People Award ($2,000). To an individual, library, organization, or noncommercial group that most effectively encourages or enhances the use of government documents in library services. *Donor:* Congressional Information Service, Inc. (CIS). *Winner:* Prudence Adler.

Bernadine Abbott Hoduski Founders Award (plaque). To recognize documents librarians who may not be known at the national level but who have made significant contributions to the field of state, international, local, or federal documents. *Winner:* John A. Peters, Margaret T. Lane.

Readex/GODORT/ALA Catharine J. Reynolds Award ($2,000). Grants to documents librarians for travel and/or study in the field of documents librarianship or area of study benefitting performance as documents librarians. *Donor:* Readex Corporation. *Winners:* Melissa Lamont.

David Rozkuszka Scholarship ($3,000). To provide financial assistance to an individual who is currently working with government documents in a library while completing a master's program in library science. *Winner:* Thomas Reed Caswell.

Intellectual Freedom Round Table (IFRT)

John Phillip Immroth Memorial Award for Intellectual Freedom ($500). For notable contribution to intellectual freedom fueled by personal courage. *Winner:* Ronald F. Sigler.

Eli M. Oboler Memorial Award ($1,500). Biennially, to an author of a published work in English or in English translation dealing with issues, events, questions, or controversies in the area of intellectual freedom. *Donor:* Providence Associates, Inc. *Winner:* Not awarded in 1997.

State and Regional Achievement Award ($1,000). To the intellectual freedom committee of a state library state library media association, or a state/regional coalition for the most successful and creative project during the calendar year. *Donor:* Social Issues Resource Series, Inc. (SIRS). *Winner:* Georgia First Amendment Foundation.

Library Administration and Management Association (LAMA)

AIA/ALA-LAMA Library Buildings Award (citation). A biannual award given to all types of libraries for excellence in architectural design and planning by an American architect. *Donor:* American Institute of Architects and LAMA. *Winners:* Great Northwest Branch Library, San Antonio, Texas (Lake Flato Architects, San Antonio); Tottenville Branch, New York Public library (Stephen D. Weinstein/John Ellis & Associates Joint Venture Architects, New York); Paul Cummins Library, Crossroads School, Santa Monica, California (Steven Ehrlich Architect, Santa Monica); Phoenix (Arizona) Central Library (William P. Bruder–Architect, Ltd., New River, Arizona, and DWL Architects, Phoenix); Powell Library, University of California/Los Angeles (Moore Ruble Yudell, Santa Monica).

Hugh C. Atkinson Memorial Award. *See under* American Library Association.

Certificate of Appreciation: *Winner:* Robert F. Moran.

John Cotton Dana Library Public Relations Awards. To libraries or library organizations of all types for public relations programs or special projects ended during the preceding year. *Donor:* H. W. Wilson Company. *Winners:* Allen Parish Libraries, Oberlin, Louisiana; East Brunswick (New Jersey) Public Library; Kansas City (Missouri) Public Library; King County Library System, Seattle; Oklahoma State University, Stillwater; Pueblo (Colorado) Library District; Queens Borough Public Library, Jamaica, New York; San Antonio (Texas) Public Library; Timberland Regional Library, Olympia, Washington; Friends of the Waterloo (Iowa) Public Library.

Library and Information Technology Association (LITA)

Hugh C. Atkinson Memorial Award. *See under* American Library Association.

LITA/Gaylord Award for Achievement in Library and Information Technology ($1,000). *Donor:* Gaylord Bros., Inc. *Winner:* Paul Evan Peters (posthumously).

LITA/GEAC-CLSI Scholarship in Library and Information Technology ($3,000). For work toward an MLS in an ALA-accredited program with emphasis on library automation. *Donor:* CLSI, Inc. *Winner:* Gale Heimer.

LITA/Library Hi Tech Award ($1,000). To an individual or institution for a work that shows outstanding communication for continuing education in library and information technology. *Donor:* Pierian Press. *Winner:* Larry L. Learn.

LITA/LSSI Minority Scholarship in Library and Information Science ($2,500). To encourage a qualified member of a principal minority group to work toward an MLS degree in an ALA-accredited pro-

gram with emphasis on library automation. *Donor:* Library Systems & Services, Inc. *Winner:* Rosemarie Leon.

LITA/OCLC Minority Scholarship in Library and Information Technology ($2,500). To encourage a qualified member of a principal minority group to work toward an MLS degree in an ALA-accredited program with emphasis on library automation. *Donor:* OCLC. *Winner:* Julia Leggett.

Library History Round Table (LHRT)

Phyllis Dain Library History Dissertation Award ($500). To the author of a dissertation treating the history of books, libraries, librarianship, or information science. *Winner:* Not awarded in 1997.

Justin Winsor Prize Essay ($500). To an author of an outstanding essay embodying original historical research on a significant subject of library history. *Winner:* Cheryl Knott Malone for "Houston's Colored Carnegie Library, 1907–1922."

Library Research Round Table (LRRT)

Jesse H. Shera Award for Research ($1,000). For an outstanding and original paper reporting the results of research related to libraries. *Winner:* Not awarded in 1997.

Map and Geography Round Table (MAGERT)

MAGERT Honors Award (citation and cash award). To recognize outstanding contributions by a MAGERT personal member to map librarianship, MAGERT, and/or a specific MAGERT project. *Winner:* Not awarded in 1997.

New Members Round Table (NMRT)

NMRT/EBSCO Scholarship ($1,000). To a U.S. or Canadian citizen to begin an MLS degree in an ALA-accredited program. Candidates must be members of NMRT. *Donor:* EBSCO Subscription Services. *Winner:* Dixie L. Gurdak.

Shirley Olofson Memorial Award. Cash award for individuals to attend their second ALA Annual Conference. *Winner:* Jimmie Lundgren.

3M/NMRT Professional Development Grant. To NMRT members to encourage professional development and participation in national ALA and NMRT activities. *Donor:* 3M. *Winners:* Dora Ho, Carol Ritzen Kem, Billie Walker.

Public Library Association (PLA)

Advancement of Literacy Award (plaque). To a publisher, bookseller, hardware and/or software dealer, foundation or similar group that has made a significant contribution to the advancement of adult literacy. *Donor: Library Journal. Winner:* Signal Hill Publications, Syracuse, New York.

Demco Creative Merchandising Grant ($1,000 and $2,000 worth of display furniture or supplies). To a public library proposing a project for the creative display and merchandising of materials either in the library or in the community. *Donor:* Demco, Inc. *Winner:* LaCrosse County Libraries, Holomen, Wisconsin.

Excellence in Small and/or Rural Public Service Award ($1,000). Honors a library serving a population of 10,000 or less that demonstrates excellence of service to its community as exemplified by an overall service program or a special program of significant accomplishment. *Donor:* EBSCO Subscription Services. *Winner:* Waialua (Hawaii) Public Library.

Highsmith Library Innovation Award ($2,000). To recognize a public library's innovative achievement in planning and implementation of a creative program or service using technology. *Donor:* Highsmith, Inc. *Winner:* Queens Borough Public Library, Jamaica, New York.

Allie Beth Martin Award ($3,000). Honors a librarian who, in a public library setting, has demonstrated extraordinary range and depth of knowledge about books or other library materials and has distinguished ability to share that knowledge. *Donor:* Baker & Taylor Books. *Winner:* Mary Kierans.

New Leaders Travel Grant (up to $1,500 each). To enhance the professional development and improve the expertise of public librarians by making their attendance at major professional development activities

possible. *Donor:* GEAC, Inc. *Winners:* Cindy Eubank, Karen Kasacavage, Wendy Miller, Barbara O'Hara, Jean A Wipf.

NTC Career Materials Resource Grant ($500 and $2,000 worth of materials from NTC Publishing Group). To a library proposing a project for the development of a career resources collection and program for a target audience either in the library or in the community. *Donor:* NTC Publishing Group. *Winner:* Bensenville (Illinois) Community Public Library.

Leonard Wertheimer Award ($1,000). To a person, group, or organization for work that enhances and promotes multilingual public library service. *Donor:* NTC Publishing Group. *Winner:* REFORMA, the National Association to Promote Library Services to the Spanish Speaking.

Publishing Committee

Carnegie Reading List Awards (amount varies). To ALA units for preparation and publication of reading lists, indexes, and other bibliographical and library aids useful in U.S. circulating libraries. *Donor:* Andrew Carnegie Fund. *Winner:* Not awarded in 1997.

Whitney-Carnegie Awards ($5,000 maximum). For the preparation of bibliographic aids for research, with scholarly intent and general applicability. *Donor:* James Lyman Whitney and Andrew Carnegie Funds. *Winners:* Andy O. Alali, for *Health Communication: An Annotated Sourcebook*; M. Elaine Hughes, Akilash S. Nosakhere, Anne Page Mosby, and Kimberly B. Parker for *The African American Studies Core List Project*; Anthony D. Apostolides for *A Proposal for Preparation of A Guide to Research Resources on Alternative Treatments In Health Care*; George Calhoun, Jr., for *The Special Education and Interdisciplinary Internet Dictionary*.

Reference and User Services Association (RUSA)

Dartmouth Medal. For creating current reference works of outstanding quality and significance. *Donor:* Dartmouth College, Hanover, New Hampshire. *Winner:* Grove's

Dictionaries, Inc. for *The Dictionary of Art*, edited by Jane Shoaf Turner.

Denali Press Award ($500). For creating reference works of outstanding quality and significance that provide information specifically about ethnic and minority groups in the United States. *Donor:* Denali Press. *Winner:* Nancy C. Curtis for *Black Heritage Sites: An African American Odyssey and Finder's Guide.*

Disclosure Student Travel Award (BRASS) ($1,000). To enable a student in an ALA-accredited master's program interested in a career as a business librarian to attend an ALA Annual Conference. *Donor:* Disclosure, Inc. *Winner:* Heidi E. G. Senior.

Facts on File Grant ($2,000). To a library for imaginative programming that would make current affairs more meaningful to an adult audience. *Donor:* Facts on File, Inc. *Winner:* Logan Helm Woodford County Library, Versailles, Kentucky.

Gale Research Award for Excellence in Business Librarianship (BRASS) ($1,000). To an individual for distinguished activities in the field of business librarianship. *Donor:* Gale Research Co. *Winner:* Paul Wasserman.

Gale Research Award for Excellence in Reference and Adult Services. To a library or library system for developing an imaginative and unique library resource to meet patrons' reference needs ($1,000). *Donor:* Gale Research Co. *Winner:* Bay Area (California) Library and Information System.

Genealogical Publishing Company/History Section Award ($1,000). To encourage and commend professional achievement in historical reference and research librarianship. *Donor:* The Genealogical Publishing Company. *Winner:* Raymond S. Wright III.

Margaret E. Monroe Library Adult Services Award (citation). To a librarian for impact on library service to adults. *Winner:* Duncan Smith.

Isadore Gilbert Mudge—R. R. Bowker Award ($1,500). For distinguished contributions to reference librarianship. *Winner:* Joan C. Durrance.

Reference Service Press Award ($1,000). To the author of the most outstanding article published in *RQ* during the preceding two

volume years. *Donor:* Reference Service Press, Inc. *Winner:* Craig Gibson.

John Sessions Memorial Award (plaque). To a library or library system in recognition of work with the labor community. *Donor:* AFL/CIO. *Winner:* Englewood (New Jersey) Public Library.

Louis Shores Oryx Press Award ($1,000). To an individual, team, or organization to recognize excellence in reviewing of books and other materials for libraries. *Donor:* Oryx Press. *Winner:* Gail A. Schlachter.

Social Responsibilities Round Table (SRRT)

Jackie Eubanks Memorial Award ($500). To honor outstanding achievement in promoting the acquisition and use of alternative media in libraries. *Donor:* AIP Task Force. *Winner:* Mev Miller.

Genesis Award. For an outstanding book designed to bring visibility to a black writer or artist at the beginning of his or her career. *Donor:* Gay Book Award Committee. *Winner:* Martha Southgate for *Another Way to Dance.*

Coretta Scott King Awards. *See* "Literary Prizes, 1997" by Gary Ink.

SRRT Gay, Lesbian, and Bisexual Book Awards. To authors of fiction and non-fiction books of exceptional merit relating to the gay/lesbian experience. *Donor:* SRRT Gay Book Award Committee. *Winners:* Emma Donoghue for *Hood* (fiction), Fenton Johnson for *Geography of the Heart* (nonfiction).

Young Adult Library Services Association (YALSA)

Baker & Taylor Conference Grants ($1,000). To young adult librarians in public or school libraries to attend an ALA Annual Conference for the first time. Candidates must be members of YALSA and have one to ten years of library experience. *Donor:* Baker & Taylor Books. *Winners:* Rebecca Smith, Sheila Anderson.

Book Wholesalers, Inc./YALSA Collection Development Grant ($1,000). To YALSA members who represent a public library and work directly with young adults, for collection development materials for young adults. *Winners:* Marion Veld, Jean Dilger-Hill.

Econo-Clad/YALSA Literature Program Award ($1,000). To a YALSA member for development and implementation of an outstanding program for young adults, ages 12–18, involving reading and the use of literature. *Donor:* Econo-Clad Books. *Winner:* Susan Farber.

Margaret A. Edwards Award ($1,000). To an author whose book or books have provided young adults with a window through which they can view their world and which will help them to grow and to understand themselves and their role in society. *Donor: School Library Journal. Winner:* Gary Paulsen.

Frances Henne/YALSA/VOYA Research Grant ($500 minimum). To provide seed money to an individual, institution, or group for a project to encourage research on library service to young adults. *Donor: Voice of Youth Advocates. Winners:* Not awarded in 1997.

American Society for Information Science (ASIS)

ASIS Award of Merit. For an outstanding contribution to the field of information science. *Winner:* Dagobert Soergel.

ASIS Best Information Science Book. *Winner:* Bryce Allen for *Information Tasks: Toward a User-Centered Approach to Information Systems.*

ASIS Outstanding Information Science Teacher Award ($500). *Winner:* Not awarded in 1997.

ASIS Research Award. For a systematic program of research in a single area at a level beyond the single study, recognizing contributions in the field of information science. *Winner:* Nicholas Belkin.

ASIS Special Award. To recognize long-term contributions to the advancement of information science and technology and enhancement of public access to information and discovery of mechanisms for improved transfer and utilization of knowledge. *Winner:* Not awarded in 1997.

James Cretsos Leadership Award. *Winner:* Geoffrey McKim.

Watson Davis Award. *Winner:* Karla Petersen.

ISI I.S. Doctoral Dissertation Scholarship ($1,000). *Winner:* R. David Lankes for *Building and Maintaining Internet Information Services.*

JASIS Paper Award. *Winner:* Stephen P. Harter for *Variations in Relevance Assessments and the Measurement of Retrieval Effectiveness.*

Pratt Severn Student Research Award. *Winner:* Melinda Axel for *Data Warehouse Design for Pharmaceutical Drug Discovery Research.*

UMI Doctoral Dissertation Award. *Winner:* Harry Bruce for *A User-Oriented View of Internet as Information Infrastructure.*

Art Libraries Society of North America (ARLIS/NA)

Jim and Anna Emmett Travel Award ($600). To assist information professionals who are handicapped to participate in the ARLIS/NA annual conference. *Winner:* Margaret Cunningham.

G. K. Hall Conference Attendance Award ($400). To encourage attendance at the annual conference by ARLIS/NA committee members, chapter officers, and moderators. *Winner:* Iris Snyder.

Howard and Beverly Joy Karno Award ($1,000). To provide financial assistance to a professional art librarian in Latin America through interaction with ARLIS/NA members and conference participation. Cosponsor: Howard Karno Books. *Winner:* Carmen Block Iturriaga.

David Mirvish Books/Books on Art Travel Award ($500 Canadian). To encourage art librarianship in Canada. *Winner:* Cheryl Siegel.

Puvill Libros Award. To encourage professional development of European art librarians through interaction with ARLIS/NA colleagues and conference participation. *Winner:* Katja Apih.

Research Libraries Group Award. To promote participation in ARLIS/NA by supporting conference travel for an individual who has not attended an annual conference. *Winner:* Thomas Riedel.

Association for Library and Information Science Education (ALISE)

ALISE Doctoral Student Dissertation Awards ($400). To promote the exchange of research ideas between doctoral students and established researchers. *Winners:* Anne L. O'Neill, Lynne E. F. McKechnie.

ALISE Methodology Paper Competition ($250). To stimulate the communication of research methodology. *Winner:* Matthew L. Saxton.

ALISE Research Paper Competition ($500). For a research paper concerning any aspect of librarianship or information studies by a member of ALISE. *Winner:* Ingrid Hsieh-Yee.

Jane Anne Hannigan Research Award ($500). *Winner:* Not awarded in 1997.

Association of Jewish Libraries (AJL)

AJL Bibliography Book Award. *Winner:* Norman Drachler for *A Bibliography of Jewish Education in the United States.*

AJL Reference Book Award. *Winner:* Alexander Beider, for *A Dictionary of Jewish Surnames from the Kingdom of Poland.*

Special Body of Work Citation. *Winner:* Not awarded in 1997.

Sydney Taylor Children's Book Award. *Winner:* Barbara Sofer for *Shalom Haver: Goodbye, Friend.*

Sydney Taylor Manuscript Award. *Winner:* Tovah S. Yavin for *All Star Brothers.*

Sydney Taylor Older Children's Book Award. *Winner:* Maxine Rose Schur, Brian Pinkney (illus.) for *When I Left My Village.*

Beta Phi Mu

Beta Phi Mu Award. *See under* American Library Association.

Harold Lancour Scholarship for Foreign Study ($1,000). For graduate study in a foreign country related to the applicant's work or schooling. *Winner:* Mengxiong Liu.

Sarah Rebecca Reed Scholarship ($1,500). For study at an ALA-accredited library school. *Winner:* Sarah E. Reisinger.

Frank B. Sessa Scholarship for Continuing Professional Education ($750). For continuing education for a Beta Phi Mu member. *Winner:* Not awarded in 1997.

Canadian Library Association (CLA)

CLA Award for Achievement in Technical Services. *Winner:* Halifax Regional Library.

CLA Award for the Advancement of Intellectual Freedom in Canada. *Winner:* Alvin Schrader.

CLA/Information Today Award for Innovative Technology. *Donor:* Information Today Inc. *Winner:* University of Alberta, Edmonton, AB.

CLA Outstanding Service to Librarianship Award. *Donor:* R. R. Bowker. *Winner:* Alan MacDonald.

CLA Research and Development Grant ($1,000). *Winners:* Lori Van Rooijen, Alvin Schrader.

CLA Student Article Award. *Winner:* Julie Lucas.

CLA/Faxon Marketing Award. *Winner:* Fraser Valley Regional Library, Abbotsford, British Columbia.

Canadian Association of College and University Libraries (CACUL)

CACUL Award for Outstanding Academic Librarian. *Winner:* Vivienne Monty.

CACUL Innovation Achievement Award ($1,500). *Winner:* University of New Brunswick Libraries, Fredericton, New Brunswick.

CACUL/CTCL Award of Merit. *Winner:* Alice McNair.

Canadian Association of Public Libraries (CAPL)

CAPL Outstanding Public Library Service Award. *Winner:* Brian Campbell.

Canadian Association of Special Libraries and Information Services (CASLIS)

CASLIS Award for Special Librarianship in Canada. *Winner:* Carol Smale.

Canadian Library Trustees Association (CLTA)

CLTA Achievement in Literacy Award. For an innovative literacy program by a public library board. *Donor:* ABC Canada. *Winner:* North York Public Library, North York, Ontario.

CLTA Merit Award for Distinguished Service as a Public Library Trustee. For outstanding leadership in the advancement of public library trusteeship and public library service in Canada. *Winner:* Lori Isinger.

Canadian School Library Association (CSLA)

National Book Service Teacher-Librarian of the Year Award. *Winner:* Donna Des Roches, North Battleford, Saskatchewan.

Margaret B. Scott Award of Merit. For the development of school libraries in Canada. *Winner:* Pat Taylor, Saskatoon, Saskatchewan.

Chinese-American Librarians Association (CALA)

CALA Scholarship. *Winner:* Hsianghui Liu-Spencer.

Sheila Suen Lai Scholarship ($500). To a student of Chinese nationality or descent pursuing full-time graduate studies for a master's degree or Ph.D. degree in an ALA-accredited library school. *Winner:* Anthony Y. Tse.

C. C. Seetoo/CALA Conference Travel Scholarship ($500). For a student to attend

the ALA Annual Conference and CALKA program. *Winner:* Hsin-liang Chen.

Church and Synagogue Library Association (CSLA)

CSLA Award for Outstanding Congregational Librarian. For distinguished service to the congregation and/or community through devotion to the congregational library. *Winner:* Kaethe Karabinue.

CSLA Award for Outstanding Congregational Library. For responding in creative and innovative ways to the library's mission of reaching and serving the congregation and/or the wider community. *Winner:* The Greenhoe and Rainbow Libraries, Memorial Presbyterian Church, Midland, Texas.

CSLA Award for Outstanding Contribution to Congregational Libraries. For providing inspiration, guidance, leadership, or resources to enrich the field of church or synagogue librarianship. *Winner:* Dean DeBolt.

Helen Keating Ott Award for Outstanding Contribution to Congregational Libraries. *Winner:* Eve Bunting.

Pat Tabler Memorial Scholarship Award. *Winner:* Ruth Langford.

Muriel Fuller Scholarship Award. *Winner:* Penny Judd.

Council on Library and Information Resources

A. R. Zipf Fellowship in Information Management. Awarded annually to a student enrolled in graduate school who shows exceptional promise for leadership and technical achievement. *Winner:* John Chung-I Chuang.

Gale Research Company

ALTA/Gale Outstanding Trustee Conference Grant Award. *See under* American Library Association, American Library Trustee Association.

Gale Research Award for Excellence in Business Librarianship; and Gale Research

Award for Excellence in Reference and Adult Services. *See under* American Library Association, Reference and Adult Services Division.

Gale Research Financial Development Award. *See under* American Library Association.

Medical Library Association (MLA)

Estelle Brodman Award for the Academic Medical Librarian of the Year. To honor significant achievement, potential for leadership, and continuing excellence at mid-career in the area of academic health sciences librarianship. *Winner:* M. J. Tooey.

Cunningham Memorial International Fellowship ($3,000). A six-month grant and travel expenses in the United States and Canada for a foreign librarian. *Winner:* Ioana Robu.

Louise Darling Medal. For distinguished achievement in collection development in the health sciences. *Winner:* Alfred N. Brandon (posthumously).

Janet Doe Lectureship ($250). *Winner:* T. Mark Hodges.

EBSCO/MLA Annual Meeting Grant ($1,000). *Winners:* Lori Cusimano Steib, Lily W. Liu.

Ida and George Eliot Prize ($200). For an essay published in any journal in the preceding calendar year that has been judged most effective in furthering medical librarianship. *Donor:* Login Brothers Books. *Winners:* Robert M. Braude, Valerie Florance, Mark E. Frisse, Sherrilynne S. Fuller.

Murray Gottlieb Prize ($100). For the best unpublished essay submitted by a medical librarian on the history of some aspect of health sciences or a detailed description of a library exhibit. *Donor:* Ralph and Jo Grimes. *Winner:* Not awarded in 1997.

Joseph Leiter NLM/MLA Lectureship. *Winner:* William W. Stead.

MLA Award for Distinguished Public Service. *Winner:* Not awarded in 1997.

MLA Award for Excellence and Achievement in Hospital Librarianship ($500). To a member of the MLA who has made significant contributions to the profession in the area of overall distinction or leadership in hospital librarianship. *Winner:* Cheryl R. Dee.

MLA Doctoral Fellowship ($1,000). *Donor:* Institute for Scientific Information (ISI). *Winner:* Not awarded in 1997.

MLA Scholarship ($2,000). For graduate study in medical librarianship at an ALA-accredited library school. *Winner:* Joan Marie Kearns.

MLA Scholarship for Minority Students ($2,000). *Winner:* Yan Hong Li.

John P. McGovern Award Lectureships ($500). *Winner:* Kenneth I. Shine.

Marcia C. Noyes Award. For an outstanding contribution to medical librarianship. The award is the highest professional distinction of MLA. *Winner:* Erich Meyerhoff.

Rittenhouse Award ($500). For the best unpublished paper on medical librarianship submitted by a student enrolled in, or having been enrolled in, a course for credit in an ALA-accredited library school or a trainee in an internship program in medical librarianship. *Donor:* Rittenhouse Medical Bookstore. *Winner:* Not awarded in 1997.

Frank Bradway Rogers Information Advancement Award ($500). For an outstanding contribution to knowledge of health science information delivery. *Donor:* Institute for Scientific Information (ISI). *Winner:* Roger Guard.

K. G. Saur (Munich, Germany)

Hans-Peter Geh Grant. To enable a librarian from the former Soviet Union to attend a conference in Germany or elsewhere. *Winner:* Sirje Virkus, Tallinn Pedagogical University, Tallinn, Estonia.

Gustav Hofmann Study Grant. To allow a librarian in a country where librarianship is a newly developing profession to study an issue in one or more countries of Western Europe. *Winner:* Wala Hasan Musnad (Sudan).

K. G. Saur Award for Best College and Research Libraries Article. *See under* American Library Association, Association of College and Research Libraries.

Society of American Archivists (SAA)

C. F. W. Coker Prize for finding aids. *Winner:* Robert B. Matchette, compiler, for *Guide to the Federal Records in the National Archives of the United States. Honorable Mention:* Mary Lynn McCree Bryan for *The Jane Addams Papers: A Comprehensive Guide.*

Fellows Posner Prize. For an outstanding essay dealing with a facet of archival administration, history, theory, or methodology, published in the latest volume of the *American Archivist. Winner:* Fynnette Eaton, ed., et al for *Special Issue on Case Studies of the Committee on Automated Records and Techniques* (vol. 58, no. 2).

Philip M. Hamer–Elizabeth Hamer Kegan Award. For individuals and/or institutions that have increased public awareness of a specific body of documents. *Winner:* Minnesota Historical Society for the videotape *Welcome to the Research Center or Pigs Eye Parrant Discovers Minnesota History.*

Oliver Wendell Holmes Award. To enable overseas archivists already in the United States or Canada for training to attend the SAA annual meeting. *Winner:* Liu Yunming.

J. Franklin Jameson Award. For an institution not directly involved in archival work that promotes greater public awareness, appreciation, and support of archival activities and programs. *Winner:* Kraft Foods.

Sister M. Claude Lane Award. For a significant contribution to the field of religious archives. *Winner:* Not awarded in 1997.

Waldo Gifford Leland Prize. For writing of superior excellence and usefulness in the field of archival history, theory, or practice. *Winners:* Anne R. Kenney and Stephan Chapman for *Digital Imaging for Libraries and Archives.*

Minority Student Award. Encourages minority students to consider careers in the archival profession and promotes minority participation in the Society of American Archivists with complimentary registration to the annual meeting. *Winner:* Not awarded in 1997.

Theodore Calvin Pease Award. For the best student paper. *Winner:* Karen Collins for *Providing Subject Access to Images: A Study of User Queries.*

Preservation Publication Award. Recognizes an outstanding work published in North America that advances the theory or the practice of preservation in archival institutions. *Winner: Preserving Digital Information, Report of the Task Force on Archiving of Digital Information* (Research Libraries Group and Commission on Preservation and Access, May 1996).

SAA Fellows. Highest individual distinction awarded to a limited number of members for their outstanding contribution to the archival profession. *Honored:* Frank Boles, Susan Davis, Paul Conway, Megan Desnoyers, Michael J. Fox, Ellen Garrison, Waverly Lowell, Archie Motley.

Special Libraries Association (SLA)

Mary Adeline Connor Professional Development Scholarship ($6,000). *Winner:* Mary Nelson.

John Cotton Dana Award. For exceptional support and encouragement of special librarianship. *Winners:* Sarah K. Wiant, Charles F. Finnerty.

Steven I. Goldspiel Research Grant. Sponsor: Disclosure, Inc. *Winner:* Claire R. McInerney for "Using Information in the Virtual Office: How Special Libraries Are Serving Telecommuters."

Hall of Fame Award. To a member of the association at or near the end of an active professional career for an extended and sustained period of distinguished service to the association. *Winner:* Catherine A. Jones.

International Special Librarians Day Award. *Winner:* Highsmith Company, Inc.

SLA Affirmative Action Scholarship ($6,000). *Winner:* Julia Leggett.

SLA Fellows. *Winners:* Joan E. Gervino, Wilda B. Newman, Marydee Ojala, Jean M. Scanlan.

SLA Information Today Award for Innovations in Technology. *Winner:* Laurie E. Stackpole.

SLA Media Award. *Winners:* Bonnie A. Nardi, Vicki O'Day, Edward Valauskas.

SLA President's Award. *Winners:* John W. Marcus, Mary E. Beall.

SLA Professional Award. *Winner:* Not awarded in 1997.

SLA Public Relations Members Achievement Award. *Winners:* Mary E. Beall, John W. Marcus.

SLA Student Scholarships ($6,000). For students with financial need who show potential for special librarianship. *Winners:* Carolyn Edds, Janette Lawrence, Morgan Tucker.

H. W. Wilson Company Award. For the most outstanding article in the past year's *Special Libraries. Donor:* H. W. Wilson Company. *Winners:* Gwen Harris, Joanne G. Marshall.

Alphabetical List of Award Names

Individual award names are followed by a colon and the name of the awarding body; e.g., the Bound to Stay Bound Books Scholarship is given by ALA/Association for Library Service to Children. Consult the preceding list of Library Scholarship and Award Recipients, 1997, which is alphabetically arranged by organization, to locate recipients and further information. Awards named for individuals are listed by surname.

AALL Scholarships: American Association of Law Libraries

AASL ABC/CLIO Leadership Grant: ALA/American Association of School Librarians

AASL/Highsmith Research Grant: ALA/American Association of School Librarians

AASL Information Plus Continuing Education Scholarship: ALA/American Association of School Librarians

AASL President's Crystal Apple Award: ALA/American Association of School Librarians

AASL School Librarians Workshop Scholarship: ALA/American Association of School Librarians

ACRL Academic or Research Librarian of the Year Award: ALA/Association of College and Research Libraries

ACRL/EBSS Distinguished Education and Behavioral Sciences Librarian Award: ALA/Association of College and Research Libraries

ACRL Doctoral Dissertation Fellowship: ALA/Association of College and Research Libraries

AJL Bibliography Book Award: Association of Jewish Libraries

AJL Reference Book Award: Association of Jewish Libraries

ALA Honorary Membership: ALA

ALA/Information Today Library of the Future Award: ALA

ALISE Doctoral Student Dissertation Awards: Association for Library and Information Science Education

ALISE Methodology Paper Competition: Association for Library and Information Science Education

ALISE Research Award: Association for Library and Information Science Education

ALISE Research Paper Competition: Association for Library and Information Science Education

ALSC/Book Wholesalers Summer Reading Program Grant: ALA/Association for Library Service to Children

ALSC/Econo-Clad Literature Program Award: ALA/Association for Library Service to Children

ALSC/REFORMA Pura Belpre Award: ALA/Association for Library Service to Children

ALTA/Gale Outstanding Trustee Conference Grant Award: ALA/American Library Trustee Association

ALTA Literacy Award: ALA/American Library Trustee Association

ALTA Major Benefactors Honor Awards: ALA/American Library Trustee Association

ASCLA Leadership Achievement Award: ALA/Association of Specialized and Cooperative Library Agencies

ASCLA/National Organization on Disability Award: ALA/Association of Specialized and Cooperative Library Agencies

ASCLA Professional Achievement Award: ALA/Association of Specialized and Cooperative Library Agencies

ASCLA Research Award: ALA/Association of Specialized and Cooperative Library Agencies

ASCLA Service Award: ALA/Association of Specialized and Cooperative Library Agencies

ASIS Award of Merit: American Society for Information Science

ASIS Best Information Science Book: American Society for Information Science

ASIS Doctoral Dissertation Scholarship: American Society for Information Science

ASIS Outstanding Information Science Teacher Award: American Society for Information Science

ASIS Research Award: American Society for Information Science

ASIS Special AWard: American Society for Information Science

Accessibility for Attendees with Disabilities Award: ALA/Exhibits Round Table

Advancement of Literacy Award: ALA/Public Library Association

May Hill Arbuthnot Honor Lecturer: ALA/Association for Library Service to Children

Armed Forces Library Certificate of Merit: ALA/Armed Forces Libraries Round Table

Armed Forces Library Newsbank Scholarship Award: ALA/Armed Forces Libraries Round Table

Armed Forces Library Round Table Achievement Citation: ALA/Armed Forces Libraries Round Table

Hugh C. Atkinson Memorial Award: ALA

Award for the Advancement of Intellectual Freedom in Canada: Canadian Library Association

Carroll Preston Baber Research Grant: ALA

Baker & Taylor Conference Grants: ALA/Young Adult Library Services Association

Mildred L. Batchelder Award: ALA/Association for Library Service to Children

Batchelder Honor Books: ALA/Association for Library Service to Children

Louise Seaman Bechtel Fellowship: ALA/Association for Library Service to Children

Best of LRTS Award: ALA/Association for Library Collections and Technical Services

Beta Phi Mu Award: ALA

Blackwell/North America Scholarship Award: ALA/Association for Library Collections and Technical Services

Bogle International Travel Fund Award: ALA

Book Wholesalers, Inc. Collection Development Grant: ALA/Young Adult Library Services Association

Bound to Stay Bound Books Scholarship: ALA/Association for Library Service to Children

Bowker/Ulrich's Serials Librarianship Award: ALA/Association for Library Collections and Technical Services, Serials Section

William Boyd Military Novel Award: ALA

Estelle Brodman Award for the Academic Medical Librarian of the Year: Medical Library Association

CACUL Award for Outstanding Academic Librarian: Canadian Association of College and University Libraries

CACUL Innovation Achievement Award: Canadian Association of College and University Libraries

CACUL/CTCL Award of Merit: Canadian Association of College and University Libraries

CAPL Outstanding Public Library Service Award: Canadian Association of Public Libraries

CASLIS Award for Special Librarianship in Canada: Canadian Association of Special Libraries and Information Services

CIS/GODORT/ALA Documents to the People Award: ALA/Government Documents Round Table

CLA Award for Achievement in Technical Services: Canadian Library Association

CLA Award for the Advancement of Intellectual Freedom in Canada: Canadian Library Association

CLA/Faxon Marketing Award: Canadian Library Association

CLA/Information Today Award for Innovative Technology: Canadian Library Association

CLA Outstanding Service to Librarianship Award: Canadian Library Association

CLA Research and Development Grants: Canadian Library Association

CLA Student Article Award: Canadian Library Association

CLTA Achievement in Literacy Award: Canadian Library Trustees Association

CLTA Merit Award for Distinguished Service as a Public Library Trustee: Canadian Library Trustees Association

CSLA Award for Outstanding Congregational Librarian: Church and Synagogue Library Association

CSLA Award for Outstanding Congregational Library: Church and Synagogue Library Association

CSLA Award for Outstanding Contribution to Congregational Libraries: Church and Synagogue Library Association

Francis Joseph Campbell Citation: ALA/Association of Specialized and Cooperative Library Agencies

Andrew Carnegie Medal: ALA/Association for Library Service to Children

Carnegie Reading List Awards: ALA/Publishing Committee

Marshall Cavendish Scholarship: ALA

Certificate of Appreciation: ALA/Library Administration and Management Association

James Bennett Childs Award: ALA/Government Documents Round Table

David H. Clift Scholarship: ALA

C. F. W. Coker Prize: Society of American Archivists

Mary Adeline Connor Professional Development Scholarship: Special Libraries Association

Shirley Crawford Scholarship: ALA

James Cretsos Leadership Award: American Society for Information Science

Cunningham Memorial International Fellowship: Medical Library Association

Phyllis Dain Library History Dissertation Award: ALA/Library History Round Table

John Cotton Dana Award: Special Libraries Association

John Cotton Dana Library Public Relations Award: ALA/Library Administration and Management Association

Louise Darling Medal: Medical Library Association

Dartmouth Medal: ALA/Reference and Adult Services Division

Watson Davis Award: American Society for Information Science

Adelaide del Frate Conference Sponsor Award: ALA/Federal Librarians Round Table

Demco Creative Merchandising Grant: ALA/Public Library Association

Denali Press Award: ALA/Reference and Adult Services Division

Melvil Dewey Award: ALA

Disclosure Student Travel Award (BRASS): ALA/Reference and Adult Services Division

Distinguished School Administrators Award: ALA/American Association of School Librarians

Distinguished Service Award: ALA/Federal Librarians Round Table

Distinguished Service Award, AASL/Baker & Taylor: ALA/American Association of School Librarians

Distinguished Service to ALSC Award: ALA/Association for Library Service to Children

Janet Doe Lectureship: Medical Library Association

Tom C. Drewes Scholarship: ALA

Miriam Dudley Bibliographic Instruction Librarian of the Year: ALA/Association of College and Research Libraries

EBSCO ALA Conference Sponsorships: ALA

EBSCO Community College Leadership Resources Achievement Awards: ALA/Association of College and Research Libraries

EBSCO Community College Learning Resources Award: ALA/Association of College and Research Libraries

EBSCO/MLA Annual Meeting Grant: Medical Library Association

Econo-Clad/YALSA Literature Program Award: ALA/Young Adult Library Services Association

Margaret A. Edwards Award: ALA/Young Adult Library Services Association

Education Behavioral Sciences Section Library Award: ALA/Association of College and Research Libraries

Ida and George Eliot Prize: Medical Library Association

Jim and Anna Emmett Travel Award: Art Libraries Society of North America

Equality Award: ALA

Jackie Eubanks Memorial Award: ALA/Social Responsibilities Round Table

Excellence in Small and/or Rural Public Service Award: ALA/Public Library Association

Facts on File Grant: ALA/Reference and Adult Services Division

Federal Librarians Achievement Award: ALA/Federal Librarians Round Table

Fellows Posner Prize: Society of American Archivists

First Step Award, Serials Section/Wiley Professional Development Grant: ALA/Association for Library Collections and Technical Services

Freedom to Read Foundation Roll of Honor Awards: ALA

Friendly Booth Award: ALA/Exhibits Round Table

Elizabeth Futas Catalyst for Change Award: ALA

Loleta D. Fyan Award: ALA

Gale Research Award for Excellence in Business Librarianship (BRASS): ALA/Reference and Adult Services Division

Gale Research Award for Excellence in Reference and Adult Services: ALA/Reference and Adult Services Division

Gale Research Financial Development Award: ALA

Mary V. Gaver Scholarship: ALA

Hans-Peter Geh Grant: K. G. Saur

Genealogical Publishing Company/History Section Award: ALA/Reference and Adult Services Division

Genesis Award: ALA/Social Responsibilities Round Table

Louise Giles Minority Scholarship: ALA

Steven I. Goldspiel Research Grant: Special Libraries Association

Murray Gottlieb Prize: Medical Library Association

Grolier Foundation Award: ALA

Grolier National Library Week Grant: ALA

G. K. Hall Award for Library Literature: ALA

G. K. Hall Conference Attendance Award: Art Libraries Society of North America

Hall of Fame Award: Special Libraries Association

Philip M. Hamer–Elizabeth Hamer Kegan Award: Society of American Archivists

Jane Anne Hannigan Research Award: Association for Library and Information Science Education

Frances Henne Award: ALA/American Association of School Librarians

Frances Henne/YALSA/VOYA Research Grant: ALA/Young Adult Library Services Association

Highsmith Library Innovation Award: ALA/Public Library Association

Bernadine Abbott Hoduski Founders Award: ALA/Government Documents Round Table

Gustav Hofmann Study Grant: K. G. Saur

Oliver Wendell Holmes Award: Society of American Archivists

Miriam L. Hornback Scholarship: ALA

Paul Howard Award for Courage: ALA

Christopher J. Hoy/ERT Scholarship: ALA/Exhibits Round Table

John Ames Humphry/OCLC/Forest Press Award: ALA

John Phillip Immroth Memorial Award for Intellectual Freedom: ALA/Intellectual Freedom Round Table

Instruction Section Innovation in Instruction Award: ALA/Association of College and Research Libraries

Instruction Section Publication of the Year Award: ALA/Association of College and Research Libraries

International Special Librarians Day Award: Special Libraries Association.

ISI I.S. Doctoral Dissertation Scholarship: American Society for Information Science

J. Franklin Jameson Award for Archival Advocacy: Society of American Archivists

JASIS Paper Award: American Society for Information Science

Howard and Beverly Joy Karno Award: Art Libraries Society of North America

Kohlstedt Exhibit Award: ALA/Exhibits Round Table

LITA/GEAC-CLSI Scholarship in Library and Information Technology: ALA/Library and Information Technology Association

LITA/Library Hi Tech Award: ALA/Library and Information Technology Association

LITA/LSSI Minority Scholarship in Library and Information Science: ALA/Library and Information Technology Association

LITA/OCLC Minority Scholarship in Library and Information Technology: ALA/Library and Information Technology Association

Sheila Suen Lai Scholarship: Chinese-American Librarians Association

Harold Lancour Scholarship for Foreign Study: Beta Phi Mu

Marta Lange/*CQ* Award: ALA/Association of College and Research Libraries

Sister M. Claude Lane Award: Society of American Archivists

Samuel Lazerow Fellowship for Research in Acquisitions or Technical Services: ALA/Association of College and Research Libraries

Katharine Kyes Leab and Daniel J. Leab American Book Prices Current Exhibition Catalogue Awards: ALA/Association of College and Research Libraries

Leadership in Library Acquisitions Award: ALA/Association for Library Collections and Technical Services

Tony B. Leisner Scholarship: ALA

Joseph Leiter NLM/MLA Lectureship: Medical Library Association

Waldo Gifford Leland Prize: Society of American Archivists

Library Buildings Award: ALA/Library Administration and Management Association

Joseph W. Lippincott Award: ALA

MAGERT Honors Award: ALA/Map and Geography Round Table

MLA Award for Distinguished Public Service: Medical Library Association

MLA Award for Excellence and Achievement in Hospital Librarianship: Medical Library Association

MLA Doctoral Fellowship: Medical Library Association

MLA Scholarship: Medical Library Association

MLA Scholarship for Minority Students: Medical Library Association

John P. McGovern Award Lecturships: Medical Library Association

Margaret Mann Citation: ALA/Association for Library Collections and Technical Services

Marshall Cavendish Scholarship: ALA

Allie Beth Martin Award: ALA/Public Library Association

Frederic G. Melcher Scholarship: ALA/Association for Library Service to Children

Microcomputer in the Media Center Award: ALA/American Association of School Librarians

Minority Student Award: Society of American Archivists

David Mirvish Books/Books on Art Travel Award: Art Libraries Society of North America

Margaret E. Monroe Library Adult Services Award: ALA/Reference and Adult Services Division

Bessie Boehm Moore Award: ALA

Isadore Gilbert Mudge—R. R. Bowker Award: ALA/Reference and Adult Services Division

NMRT/EBSCO Scholarship: ALA/New Members Round Table

NMRT/3M Professional Development Grant: ALA/New Members Round Table

National Book Service Teacher-Librarian of the Year Award: Canadian School Library Association

National School Library Media Program of the Year Award: ALA/American Association of School Librarians

New Leaders Travel Grant: ALA/Public Library Association

Martinus Nijhoff International West European Specialist Study Grant: ALA/ Association of College and Research Libraries

Marcia C. Noyes Award: Medical Library Association

NTC Career Materials Resource Grant: ALA/Public Library Association

Oberly Award for Bibliography in the Agricultural Sciences: ALA/Association of College and Research Libraries

Eli M. Oboler Memorial Award: ALA/Intellectual Freedom Round Table

Shirley Olofson Memorial Award: ALA/New Members Round Table

Helen Keating Ott Award for Outstanding Contribution to Congregational Libraries: Church and Synagogue Library Association

Theodore Calvin Pease Award: Society of American Archivists

Esther J. Piercy Award: ALA/Association for Library Collections and Technical Services

Preservation Publication Award: Society of American Archivists

Pratt Severn Student Research Award: American Society for Information Science

Putnam and Grosset Book Group Awards: ALA/Association for Library Service to Children

Puvill Libros Award: Art Libraries Society of North America

Rare Books & Manuscripts Librarianship Award: ALA/Association of College and Research Libraries

Readex/GODORT/ALA Catharine J. Reynolds Award: ALA/Government Documents Round Table

Sarah Rebecca Reed Scholarship: Beta Phi Mu

Reference Service Press Award: ALA/Reference and Adult Services Division

Research Libraries Group Award: Art Libraries Society of North America

Rittenhouse Award: Medical Library Association

Frank Bradway Rogers Information Advancement Award: Medical Library Association

David Rozkuszka Scholarship: ALA/Government Documents Round Table

SAA Fellows: Society of American Archivists

SLA Affirmative Action Scholarship: Special Libraries Association

SLA Fellows: Special Libraries Association

SLA Information Today Award for Innovations in Technology: Special Libraries Association

SLA Media Award: Special Libraries Association

SLA President's Award: Special Libraries Association

SLA Professional Award: Special Libraries Association

SLA Public Relations Members Achievement Award: Special Libraries Association

SLA Student Scholarships: Special Libraries Association

SRRT/Gay and Lesbian Task Force, Gay, Lesbian, and Bisexual Book Awards: ALA/Social Responsibilities Round Table

K. G. Saur Award for Best College and Research Libraries Article: ALA/Association of College and Research Libraries

Margaret B. Scott Award of Merit: Canadian School Library Association

C. C. Seetoo/CALA Conference Travel Scholarship: Chinese-American Librarians Association

Frank B. Sessa Scholarship for Continuing Professional Education: Beta Phi Mu

John Sessions Memorial Award: ALA/Reference and Adult Services Division

Jesse H. Shera Award for Research: ALA/Library Research Round Table

Louis Shores Oryx Press Award: ALA/Reference and Adult Services Division

Special Body of Work Citation: Association of Jewish Libraries

State and Regional Achievement Award—Freedom to Read Foundation: ALA/Intellectual Freedom Round Table

Pat Tabler Memorial Scholarship: Church and Synagogue Library Association

Sydney Taylor Children's Book Award: Association of Jewish Libraries

Sydney Taylor Manuscript Award: Association of Jewish Libraries

Sydney Taylor Older Children's Book Award: Association of Jewish Libraries

Trustee Citations: ALA/American Library Trustee Association

UMI Doctoral Dissertation Award: American Society for Information Science

Leonard Wertheimer Award: ALA/Public Library Association

Whitney-Carnegie Awards: ALA/Publishing Committee

Laura Ingalls Wilder Award: ALA/Association for Library Service to Children

H. W. Wilson Award: Special Libraries Association

H. W. Wilson Library Staff Development Grant: ALA

Justin Winsor Prize Essay: ALA/Library History Round Table

World Book ALA Goal Grants: ALA

A. R. Zipf Fellowship in Information Management: Council on Library and Information Resources.

Part 4
Research and Statistics

Library Research and Statistics

Research on Libraries and Librarianship in 1997

Mary Jo Lynch

Director, Office for Research and Statistics, American Library Association

The year 1997 was a quiet one for research in the library field. There were no grants or meetings or publications of national significance to report on in this review. Instead, this article begins by describing a new program that may fund noteworthy research in the future, the LSTA National Leadership Grants.

As noted elsewhere in this volume [See the article "Legislation and Regulations Affecting Libraries in 1997"—*Ed.*], the Library Service and Technology Act (LSTA) is the legislation that combines previously separate library-funding legislation (Library Services and Construction Act [LSCA] and Higher Education Act, Title II-B [HEAII-B]) into one and moves the management of the funding to the newly reorganized Institute for Museum and Library Service (IMLS). Over 90 percent of the funding under LSTA goes directly to the states, but 4 percent of the total (more than $148 million in 1997–1998) is set aside for National Leadership Grants. The grants are to be given for four types of proposals: Education and Training, Research and Demonstration, Preservation or Digitalization, and Model Programs of Cooperation between Libraries and Museums.

For Fiscal Year 1998 priorities for Research and Demonstrations proposals are as follows:

- Projects that enhance library services through the effective and efficient use of appropriate and emerging technologies
- Projects that examine economic models for educational use of digital images
- Projects that create methods to evaluate the contributions to a community made by institutions providing access to information services

The application guidelines are found on the Web at http://www.imls.fed.us/guidelines/natlead.html.

Public Libraries

Five grants were made in 1997 under the soon-to-be-phased-out Higher Education Act, Title II-B Library Research and Demonstration Program. The grant with the strongest research component went to the St. Louis Public Library (SLPL), which was awarded nearly $200,000 to implement its Project REAL (REading And Learning) program, a library-based community outreach program designed to improve reading skills among children ages 3–8. The grant provides funds that will help the library build on an existing framework of community partnerships and volunteer efforts to create a reading instruction program and evaluation system that will serve as a model for other libraries throughout the country.

One of the five goals of the project is to develop measurement and evaluative techniques that measure the impact of library services on the reading and learning of at-risk children and their families. SLPL staff will work with project evaluators to develop measurements, select testing instruments, and develop survey instruments to measure baseline skills and attitudes of the target audience. SLPL staff will conduct ongoing evaluation of the project after one year and as appropriate throughout the project. Summative evaluation will be conducted by SLPL staff and project evaluators, and the project manual will include detailed information on measurement and evaluation of Project REAL programs.

Last year this article described public-opinion research contained in a report prepared by the Benton Foundation for the Kellogg Foundation titled *Buildings, Books and Bytes: Libraries and Communities in the Digital Age*. The summer 1997 issue of *Library Trends* contained 13 articles about that report, including an introduction by Herbert Goldhor and a concluding "Response" by Leigh Estabrook. Several of the other articles are quite critical of the methodologies and conclusions of the Benton report. The entire issue is a rich source of ideas about research and about the future of public libraries.

Last year's article in The *Bowker Annual* also described the 1996 National Survey of Public Libraries and the Internet, conducted by John Bertot and Charles McClure, which updated a 1994 survey on the same topic, both sponsored by the U.S. National Commission on Libraries and Information Science. In 1997 Bertot and McClure conducted the 1997 National Survey of Public Libraries and the Internet, this time for the ALA's Office for Information Technology Policy.

The 1997 study expands upon areas of public library Internet-related data as reported in the 1994 and 1996 studies. It provides information on U.S. public library infrastructure and costs associated with Internet-related services and technology.

Summary results from the 1997 study were reported in an eight-page broadside released in November 1997. Key findings include the following:

- The percentage of public libraries connected to the Internet increased from 44 percent in 1996 to 72 percent in 1997.
- The percentage of public libraries offering Internet access to the public increased from over 27 percent in 1996 to over 60 percent in 1997.
- Nearly 900 public libraries have their own Web pages.

- Public libraries spent an estimated $20 million on Internet access in 1997, with nearly 25 percent coming from sources other than the library's operating budget.

This document is available online at http://www.ala.org/oitp/research/plcon97sum/ or on request from the ALA Office for Information Technology Policy. A full technical report on the 1997 survey will be available in 1998.

ALA conducted a national survey of public library trustees in 1997, and results will be available in 1998. The survey, prepared for the American Library Trustees Association (ALTA) by the Office for Research and Statistics (ORS), featured a two-page questionnaire sent to a sample of 1,200 trustees. The sample was selected from a universe file created by merging machine-readable lists of public library trustees provided by 39 state library agencies. The resulting file was organized by the size of population served by the library of each trustee so that results would adequately represent libraries of all sizes.

Another ALA survey project involving public libraries began in September 1997. The DeWitt Wallace–Reader's Digest Fund asked ALA to develop a proposal for a survey of public libraries that would provide the fund with information needed to support a new initiative: the expansion and improvement of educational and career development programming for school-age youth in public libraries, especially in low-income communities. The ALA survey, managed by ORS, will gather data about many aspects of what is happening in public libraries for school-age youth.

At the same time, another unit of ALA, Public Programs, submitted a proposal to the Lila Wallace–Reader's Digest Fund titled "America's Libraries as Cultural Community Centers." One component of the proposal was a survey of public libraries regarding cultural programming for adults. It seemed appropriate to the staffs of the two Wallace funds and to ALA that these two surveys be combined. It was decided that two questionnaires will be mailed in one envelope and analyzed by the same contractor. The sampling methodology is the same for both surveys. Results will provide much-needed data on aspects of public library service that have not been studied in this way before.

Academic Libraries

For many years the National Center for Education Statistics (NCES) has conducted a biennial Academic Libraries Survey (ALS) as part of the Integrated Postsecondary Education Data Survey (IPEDS). Data tables were published, but no comparative reports were prepared. That situation changed in 1997 with the publication of *The Status of Academic Libraries in the United States: Results from the 1990 and 1992 Academic Library Surveys* (NCES 97-413). This 28-page report, prepared under contract by the American Institutes for Research (AIR), compares ALS data over time (1990–1992) and displays data using the Carnegie classification.

The report focuses on the following seven indicators:

- Library staff/student ratios

- Library staff/instructional faculty ratios
- Total volumes held
- Total volumes held per full-time-equivalent (FTE) student
- Total library expenditures
- Library share of institutional budgets
- Expenditures per FTE student

Work is already under way on another report, this time prepared by Mathematica, that will update the seven indicators using data from the 1994 ALS. The report will also perform additional analysis of 1994 data.

Interlibrary loan (ILL) was not one of the variables examined in the NCES/AIR report. But it is the central focus of ARL's Interlibrary Loan and Document Delivery (ILL/DD) Performance Measures Study, a two-year effort to measure 1995–1996 performance of ILL departments in North American research and college libraries. Preliminary findings from that study were released in December 1997 in ARL's Newsletter No. 195. The 119 participants in the ILL/DD Performance Measures Study included 97 research libraries, largely members of ARL, and 22 members of the Oberlin Group, an informal affiliation of highly competitive liberal arts colleges in the United States. The study examined four performance measures: cost, fill rate, turnaround time, and user satisfaction. The study also examined the differences among libraries and identified characteristics of low-cost, high-performing ILL operations to suggest strategies for other research and college libraries to improve local performance.

The findings indicate that there is a wide range of performance among ILL operations in research libraries. However, on average, a research library spends $18.35 to obtain an item for a local patron. College library ILL performance was better overall, comparable only to the performance of the top-performing research libraries. A college library spends on average $12.08 to obtain an item for a local patron. Additional information about the study, the status of the final report, and the planned workshops can be found on the ARL Web site at http://www.arl.org/access/.

School Libraries

Researchers interested in school libraries were given three new sources of statistics in 1997.

Complete results are not yet available for the surveys conducted in 1993–1994 by the National Center for Education Statistics on school library media centers (LMCs) and school library media specialists (LMSs), but results for a few variables appeared in *The Condition of Education, 1997* (NCES 97-388), and results for personnel variables appeared in a Schools and Staffing Survey, *SASS by State* (NCES 96-312).

Results of the eighth biennial survey of *School Library Journal* (*SLJ*) subscribers by Marilyn Miller and Marilyn Shontz was published in the October 1997 issue of *SLJ* as "Small Change: Expenditures for Resources in School

Library Media Centers, FY 1995–96." [An adaptation of the article appears later in Part 4—*Ed.*] In addition to topics covered in earlier surveys, this one

- Examines LMC services in schools with site-based management
- Looks at what 141 high-service school library programs offer
- Describes the type and extent of communication between LMSs and school principals

Special Libraries

Late in 1997 the Special Libraries Association (SLA) published *Exploring Outsourcing: Case Studies of Corporate Libraries* by Frank Portugal. The book reports results of a pilot study commissioned by SLA consisting of in-depth interviews with senior managers, librarians, and library users at seven U.S. corporations that have partially or fully outsourced their libraries. Topics addressed include the impact of corporate trends on libraries, the changing structure of corporate libraries, reasons for and approaches to outsourcing, and the effect of outsourcing on the quality of service. Three models are discussed: total outsourcing of all library services, outsourcing of some services, and the use of electronic databases to supplant some services. The focus of the pilot study was on corporate libraries.

Sites were carefully selected using the following criteria:

- Total or partial outsourcing
- Adequate geographic distribution
- Range of library staff size, from small to large
- Broad industry representation

Efforts were made to interview three individuals at each of the corporations selected. Included were the corporate librarian, a member of senior management with responsibility for the library or outsourcing contract, and a frequent end user of library services.

Awards that Support Research

American Library Association

Lynn Westbrook, assistant professor in the School of Library and Information Studies at the Texas Woman's University, was the winner of the 1997 American Library Association (ALA) Carroll Preston Baber Research Grant. The $7,500 grant supports innovative research that could lead to an improvement in library services to any specific group of people.

The 1997 grant funds the project "The Information Seeking Strategies of Interdisciplinary Faculty: Implications for Reference Service," whose purpose is to develop an understanding of providing reference service to an interdisciplinary population.

Building on Westbrook's earlier work on information seeking by scholars of women's studies (WS), this project will examine the user's perspective through a national survey of WS faculty and the librarian's perspective through in-depth interviews with librarians who provide long-term, customized reference service for WS scholars in a special liaison program at Texas Woman's University. Data analysis will focus on identifying possible intervention strategies in reference, instruction, or access service.

Association of College and Research Libraries

The $1,000 Samuel Lazerow Fellowship for Research in Acquisitions or Technical Service was donated to the association by the Institute for Scientific Information (ISI) to foster advances in acquisitions or technical services. The 1997 winner was Linda M. Golian, Serials Department Head at Florida Atlantic University, for her project "Thinking Style Differences Among Academic Librarians." Golian will analyze the thinking style preferences of higher-level administrative librarians by surveying librarians working in ARL institutions. The project's focus is to determine whether technical and public-service librarians think differently.

Diane Worrell, a student in library and information studies at Texas Woman's University, is the 1997 recipient of the ACRL/ISI Doctoral Dissertation Fellowship for her dissertation "Patricia B. Knapp: Pioneer in Library Use Instruction." This study investigates the evolution of user education and its role in academic librarianship as influenced by Patricia Knapp. The fellowship, $1,000, and a plaque donated by ISI, are given to assist a doctoral student in academic librarianship whose research has potential significance in the field.

Stephen P. Harter and Hak Joon Kim, from the School of Library and Information Science at Indiana University, have been selected to receive the 1997 K. G. Saur Award for best article in *College and Research Libraries* for "Accessing Electronic Journals and Other E-Publications: An Empirical Study." Caroline Coughlin, chair of the award committee, said, "The authors' documentation of the fragility of the electronic record, particularly in a medium. . . where one would expect high levels of accessibility is both methodologically strong and provocative. The policy implications of the research are significant and have implications for scholars, publishers, and the library community."

Sem C. Sutter, bibliographer for modern literatures at the University of Chicago Library, has been awarded the Martinus Nijhoff West European Specialists Study Grant for 1997. The grant of 10,000 Dutch guilders covers air travel to and from Europe, transportation in Europe, and lodging and board in selected sites for a period not to exceed 14 consecutive days. Sutter will use the grant to travel to France and Germany to do research for *Books in German-Occupied Europe: The Rosenberg Files*.

American Association of School Librarians/Highsmith Research Grant

Ruth Villency Small of the School of Information Studies at Syracuse University is the recipient of the 1997 American Association of School Librarians (AASL)/Highsmith Research Grant for her project "Motivational Aspects of Library and Information Skills Instruction." The $5,000 grant—sponsored by

AASL, a division of ALA, and the Highsmith Company, Inc.—is given to one or more school library media specialists, library educators, or library information science or education professors to conduct innovative research aimed at measuring and evaluating the impact of school library media programs on learning and education. The proposed research seeks to identify instructional motivators that stimulate task engagement and enjoyment of the information search process.

Association of Specialized and Cooperative Library Agencies

The association's 1997 Research Award, funded by Auto-Graphics, was presented to Nancy Everhart—Assistant Professor, St. John's University, Division of Libraries and Information Science, Jamaica, New York—for her research project "Characteristics of Information Provided to School Library Media Specialists by State Library Agencies." Everhart will receive $1,000 because the $500 award was not given in 1996.

Special Libraries Association

The Special Libraries Association's Stephen I. Goldspiel Memorial Research Grant for 1996 (up to $20,000) was awarded to Claire R. McInerney—Associate Professor of Information Management, College of St. Catherine, St. Paul, Minnesota—for her proposal, "Using Information in the Virtual Office: How Special Libraries Are Serving Telecommuters." The primary object of the project is to appraise the progress of special libraries and special librarians in serving their organizations through managing the information needs of telecommuters.

Documentation Abstracts, Inc.

The 1997 Information Science Abstracts (ISA) Research Grant was given to Marilyn Domas White—Associate Professor, College of Library and Information Services, University of Maryland—for her project "The Literature of Information Ethics: An Assessment of Access." The ISA Research Grant of $1,500 is awarded annually to one or more information professionals to conduct a research project oriented toward the study of the primary or secondary literature of information science.

American Association of Law Libraries

The association made two announcements in 1997 regarding projects funded by the AALL/Aspen Law and Business Grant Program. The program was designed to annually fund one or more projects of practical value to a large segment of those professions that create, disseminate, or use legal and law-related information. It was described in this article last year as the gift of Little, Brown, but that company is now owned by Aspen.

In June the association announced a grant of $12,000 for a comprehensive survey on the economics and management of legal information. The survey will focus on the improvement of data collection and analysis by ascertaining the current status of old and new information systems. It will also propose a new statistical database that will allow for interpretive analyses and make recommendations to AALL, the American Bar Association, and the American Association of Law

Schools for the improvement of data collection and analysis. This survey was proposed by AALL members Betty W. Taylor (Professor of Law and Director of the Legal Information Center, University of Florida) and Robert J. Munro (Law Librarian, College of Law, University of Florida).

In September AALL announced that the Aspen Program would fund the first phase of a study to examine the impact law libraries have on legal decision-making. This $9,700 grant was awarded to Joanne Marshall (Professor, University of Toronto), who proposed the study. The research builds on earlier impact studies for libraries in the hospital and corporate environments. It will identify potential areas of value and impact in the legal environment and use a prospective study design to determine the extent to which law libraries and librarians make a difference in decisions that are being made in their organizations.

The research will take place in two phases over the course of two years. Phase one will be a planning and development phase in which key informants in the law library community will be asked to participate in modifying the study design and instrumentation. The result will be a "Study Design Manual" that will guide individual law librarians or groups of law librarians in the use of the methodology. Phase two will implement the research using the design instrumentation and study sites that have been identified in the first phase. The result will be a final report of the study results and papers suitable for publication in law and library science journals. Funding has been provided for phase one only; funding for the second phase is subject to the satisfactory conclusion of phase one.

The following awards that support research were not given in 1997.

- MLA doctoral fellowship ($1,000)
- MLA Research, Development, and Demonstration Project Grant
- Francis Henne/YALSA/VOYA Research Grant ($500)

Awards that Recognize Research

Association for Library and Information Science Education

The first 1997 awards for research well done were made at the January 1997 ALISE conference in Washington, D.C. There were two winners in the ALISE Doctoral Dissertation Competition. Each received $400 to defray travel expenses, plus 1997 conference registration and personal membership in ALISE for 1996–1997. The winners were Anne L. O'Neill, University of South Carolina, for "Information Transfer in Professions: A Citation Analysis of Nursing Literature"; and Lynne E. F. McKechnie, University of Western Ontario, for "Opening the Preschoolers Door to Learning: An Ethnographic Study of the Use of Public Libraries by Preschool Girls."

The 1997 ALISE Research Paper Competition ($500) went to Ingrid Hsieh-Yee, Associate Professor, Catholic University of America, for "Search Tactics of Web Users: A Search Simulation Study." The 1997 ALISE Methodology Paper Award ($250) went to Matthew L. Saxton, a doctoral student at UCLA, for "Reference Service Evaluation and Meta-Analysis: Methodological Issues in Summarizing Data from Multiple Studies."

American Library Association

ALA usually announces winners of two awards during the Joint Research Awards program at its Annual Conference: the Library Research Round Table (LRRT) Jesse H. Shera Award for Research and the Library History Round Table (LHRT) Justin Winsor Prize. The Shera Award was not given this year. The 1997 Justin Winsor Prize ($500) was given to Cheryl Knott Malone, Assistant Professor, University of Illinois Graduate School of Library and Information Science, for her essay "Houston's Colored Carnegie Library, 1907–1922." In this study Malone critically analyzes original sources in the context of contemporary events and relevant historiography to tell the story of a particular library scratching out a meager existence in separate, unequal, and even hostile circumstances, yet also offering a model that held national implications for African American library leadership.

American Society for Information Science

In November 1997, at its annual meeting in Washington, D.C., the society announced awards to several researchers. The ASIS Research Award, which honors a systematic program of research in a single area at a level beyond the single study and recognizes outstanding research contributions in the field of information science, was presented to Nicholas J. Belkin, Professor, Rutgers University, for his research on the role of human factors in retrieval systems and for his efforts to engage students in the research process and to mentor new researchers.

The 1997 UMI Doctoral Dissertation Award went to Harry Bruce, University of New South Wales, for his dissertation titled "A User-Oriented View of Internet as Information Infrastructure." The 1997 Information Science Doctoral Dissertation Scholarship, sponsored by the Institute for Scientific Information (ISI), went to R. David Lenkes for his dissertation proposal "Building and Maintaining Internet Information Services." The annual Pratt-Severn Best Student Research Award in Information Science ($500) went to Melinda Axel, Drexel University, for her paper "Datawarehouse Design for Pharmaceutical Drug Discovery Research."

OCLC/LITA

A new recognition award, to be given for the first time in 1998, was announced in late 1997. The OCLC/LITA Frederick G. Kilgour Award for Research in Library and Information Technology will be presented at the ALA Annual Conference by OCLC's director of research, the chair of the LITA Research Committee, and the LITA president. The purpose of this award is to bring attention to research that is relevant to the development of information technologies—especially work that shows promise of having a positive and significant impact on any aspect of the publication, storage, retrieval, and dissemination of information. The award will consist of $2,000 cash and an expense-paid trip to the 1998 ALA Annual Conference in Washington, D.C.

Major Funding Agencies

Council on Library and Information Resources

For many years the Council on Library Resources (CLR) was mentioned in this article as a funder of research. In 1997 CLR merged with the Commission on Preservation and Access (CPA) to form the Council on Library and Information Resources (CLIR). This new organization "embraces the entire range of information resources and services, from traditional library and archival materials to emerging digital formats, and the entire network of organizations that gather, catalog, store, preserve, distribute, and provide access to information." [See the article "Council on Library and Information Resources" in Part 1—*Ed.*]

Before the change, CLR announced the following five grants for studies in the field of economics of information:

- University of Michigan, "Pricing Electronic Scholarly Information: A Research Collaboration" ($25,000). This project will study the design of pricing systems and their influence on usage of an electronic journal access system. Through a partnership with Elsevier, a commercial information provider, the University of Michigan will implement a large-scale field experiment on innovative pricing schemes and customer usage of electronic distribution of traditional print-on-paper scholarly journals. Economists, professional librarians, and a computer systems professional will collaborate on the study.

- Iowa State University, "A Decision Model for Serial Access Choices" ($18,650). This project is aimed toward building an economic model that will assist librarians in making purchases to maximize user access to serial information. The model will enable librarians to avoid making purchase decisions on the basis of rough estimates of demand or time-consuming usage studies of particular titles. The purpose of the study will be to demonstrate that the application of usage data to a decision model will allow the library to expend its funds more efficiently.

- Rutgers University, "Exploration of Variable Pricing for Online Services at Research Libraries" ($24,954). The project will address the question of whether pricing can adapt in real time to variations in demand for different publications so that revenue to publishers and providers is increased. This is an important question in the context of Internet access because the excess of such revenues over costs provides the most reliable source for fair and equal access to the digital library of the future. The goal of the study is to determine, by simulation, whether prices can adapt to variations in consumer demand in such a way as to generate an excess of income over costs. The study will lay the foundation for potential real experiments using Web sites.

- Rutgers University, "The Efficiency of Research Libraries: A new Analytical Tool and Pilot Study Using 1995 ARL Data" ($24,973). This study will assess the applicability of certain new techniques for the analysis of multiproduct firms, not unlike the "products" that libraries routinely offer their patrons. In developing a cost model, statistics collected by the

Association of Research Libraries will be used, and, by means of a technique called data envelopment analysis (DEA), the project will attempt to "score" the performance of various library operations.

- Virginia Commonwealth University, "Using the Contingent Valuation Method to Measure Patron Benefits of Reference Desk Service in an Academic Library" ($20,003). This project will apply a survey technique called contingent valuation (CV) to estimate economic value that patrons attach to reference desk service in an academic library. The contingent valuation (CV) method has been used in environmental economics for the past 30 years to determine values of environmental amenities, such as pollution abatement and recreational areas, where no explicit market transactions take place. The study will provide the basis for a cost-benefit analysis of reference desk services.

In spring 1997 two additional grants were announced in the Mellon Small Grants Economics of Information program:

- University of Minnesota, "The Theory of Cost Allocation for Information Resources"
- Northwestern University, "America On and Off Line: Access to Commercial Internet Service"

This grant program was suspended temporarily in fall 1997, but was scheduled to begin again in 1998.

Also in fall 1997 CLIR began issuing a series of Research Briefs that summarize the results of CLIR projects in a concise format. There is no plan to publish a fixed number of these briefs each year, but they will be issued as there are findings worth reporting from projects CLIR has funded.

OCLC

For many years OCLC has supported the largest research operation in the library community. A comprehensive view of OCLC's Office of Research was provided in the January/February 1997 issue (pp.14–26) of the *OCLC Newsletter*, which included 11 short items on various aspects of the office. The last item, an interview with Terry Noreault, Director of the OCLC Research and Special Projects Division, ends with a concise summary of what the OCLC Office of Research is about:

> The OCLC Office of Research is dedicated to research that explores the place of the library in the changing technology environment and to developing tools that enhance the productivity of librarians and their patrons.

The centerpiece of this special section of the January/February 1997 *OCLC Newsletter* is a two-page spread featuring brief descriptions of 12 separate projects, ranging from work on the automation of traditional library topics—Dewey, Cutter, interlibrary loan—to developmental work on managing Internet resources. Shorter articles describe the Research Advisory Committee, collaborative research projects with other organizations, metadata workshops, the distinguished Seminar Series, and the Library and Information Science Research Grant Programs (LISRG).

Winners of two $10,000 grants made under the LISRG were announced in November:

- Francis Miksa, Professor, University of Texas at Austin, received a grant for "Examining the Attributes of Information Resources on the World Wide Web and Testing for Their Usefulness as Metadata." Miksa's study will identify, compile, and test for usefulness as metadata the attributes found in information resources at two diverse kinds of Web sites: information resources in the Latin American Network Information Center (LANIC), the Web site of the Institute for Latin American Studies at the University of Texas at Austin, and information resources found in a sample of Web sites that feature software for acquisition.

- Jian Qin, Assistant Professor, University of Southern Mississippi, received a grant for "Computation Representation of Web Objects in an Interdisciplinary Digital Library: A Survey and an Experiment in Polymer Science." Qin intends to investigate the current use of metadata elements on the Web and experiment with one of the schemes, the Dublin Core, in a subject domain—polymer science. On the basis of this investigation and experiment, a framework for implementing the Dublin Core in domain-specific digital libraries will be developed. This study will enhance understanding of current metadata use and implementation in subject-specific domain digital libraries and enrich the methodology for further studies of metadata.

The Changing Face of Library Education

David J. Brier

Systems Librarian, University of Hawaii at Manoa

Vickery K. Lebbin

Reference Librarian, University of Hawaii at Manoa

An indicator of the rapid evolution of the library profession is the way related graduate programs change their names to reflect the content and focus of their courses.

This list of programs demonstrates the evolution from the traditional view of the librarian as custodian of a collection of books to the contemporary view of the librarian as an information manager who is expert in emerging technologies.

All 56 of the library programs accredited by the American Library Association (ALA) have changed their titles within the past 20 years to incorporate the word *information*. For some graduate programs, distancing themselves from past associations can be a driving force behind a name change and an emerging trend is the disappearance of the word *library* from the program title.

**Table 1 / ALA-Accredited
Graduate Program Title Changes**

Institution	Date	Program Title
Catholic University of America	1956	Department of Library Science
	1978	Department of Library & Information Science
	1982	School of Library & Information Science
Clarion University of Pennsylvania	1977	School of Library Media & Information Science
	1980	School of Library Science
	1984	College of Library Science
	1991	College of Communication, Computer Information Science, & Library Science
	1997	Department of Library Science
Clark Atlanta University	1956	School of Library Service
	1980	School of Library & Information Studies
Dalhousie University	1974	School of Library Service
	1988	School of Library & Information Studies
Drexel University	1956	School of Library Science
	1979	School of Library & Information Science
	1985	College of Information Studies
	1996	College of Information Science & Technology
Emporia State University	1956	Department of Library Science
	1967	Division of Librarianship
	1968	Department of Librarianship
	1976	School of Library Science
	1987	School of Library & Information Management
Florida State University	1956	Library School
	1971	School of Library Science
	1983	School of Library & Information Studies
	1998	School of Information Studies

Table 1 / ALA-Accredited
Graduate Program Title Changes *(cont.)*

Institution	Date	Program Title
Indiana University	1956	Division of Library Science
	1967	Library School
	1982	School of Library & Information Science
Kent State University	1964	Department of Library Science
	1967	School of Library Science
	1993	School of Library & Information Science
Long Island University	1971	Library School
	1983	School of Library & Information Science
Louisiana State University	1956	Library School
	1973	School of Library Science
	1985	School of Library & Information Science
McGill University	1956	Library School
	1967	School of Library Science
	1986	School of Library & Information Studies
North Carolina Central University	1976	School of Library Science
	1986	School of Library & Information Science
Pratt Institute	1956	Library School
	1971	School of Library and Information Science
	1988	School of Computer, Information, & Library Science
	1990	Library & Information Science Program
	1992	School of Information & Library Science
Queens College	1971	Department of Library Science
	1980	School of Library & Information Studies
Rosary College	1963	Department of Library Science
	1971	School of Library Science
	1983	School of Library & Information Science
Rutgers University	1957	School of Library Service
	1979	School of Library & Information Studies
	1983	School of Communication, Information, & Library Studies
Saint John's University	1977	Division of Library & Information Science
San Jose State University	1970	Department of Librarianship
	1980	Division of Library Science
	1986	Division of Library & Information Science
	1993	School of Library & Information Science
Simmons College	1956	School of Library Science
	1982	School of Library & Information Science
Southern Connecticut State University	1973	Division of Library Science
	1978	Division of Library Science & Instructional Technology
	1983	School of Library Science & Instructional Technology
	1996	School of Communication, Information & Library Science
State University of New York at Albany	1967	School of Library Science
	1972	School of Library & Information Science
	1987	School of Information Science & Policy

**Table 1 / ALA-Accredited
Graduate Program Title Changes** *(cont.)*

Institution	Date	Program Title
State University of New York at Buffalo	1973	School of Information & Library Studies
Syracuse University	1956	School of Library Science
	1977	School of Information Studies
Texas Woman's University	1963	School of Library Science
	1986	School of Library & Information Studies
University of Alabama	1975	School of Library Service
	1991	School of Library & Information Studies
University of Alberta	1971	School of Library Science
	1980	Faculty of Library Science
	1989	Faculty of Library & Information Studies
	1992	School of Library & Information Studies
University of Arizona	1975	Library School
	1993	School of Library Science
	1998	School of Information Resources & Library Science
University of British Columbia	1964	School of Librarianship
	1985	School of Library, Archival, & Information Studies
University of California Los Angeles	1963	School of Library Service
	1975	School of Library & Information Science
	1995	School of Education & Information Studies
University of Hawaii	1968	School of Library Studies
	1988	School of Library & Information Studies
	1998	Library & Information Science Program
University of Illinois	1956	Library School
	1960	School of Library Science
	1982	School of Library & Information Science
University of Iowa	1972	School of Library Science
	1985	School of Library & Information Science
University of Kentucky	1956	Department of Library Science
	1971	School of Library Science
	1972	College of Library Science
	1983	College of Library & Information Science
	1994	School of Library & Information Science
University of Maryland	1968	School of Library & Information Services
	1975	College of Library & Information Service
University of Michigan	1956	Department of Library Science
	1971	School of Library Science
	1988	School of Information & Library Studies
	1997	School of Information
University of Missouri–Columbia	1975	School of Library & Informational Science
	1998	School of Information Science & Learning Technology
University of Montreal	1970	School of Library Studies
	1986	School of Library Studies & Information Science
University of North Carolina at Chapel Hill	1956	School of Library Science
	1988	School of Information & Library Science

**Table 1 / ALA-Accredited
Graduate Program Title Changes** *(cont.)*

Institution	Date	Program Title
University of North Carolina at Greensboro	1983	Department of Library Science/ Educational Technology
	1989	Department of Library & Information Studies
University of North Texas	1969	Department of Library Science
	1972	School of Library & Information Sciences
University of Oklahoma	1956	School of Library Science
	1986	School of Library & Information Studies
University of Pittsburgh	1965	School of Library & Information Science
University of Puerto Rico	1991	School of Library & Information Science
University of Rhode Island	1972	Library School
	1985	School of Library & Information Studies
University of South Carolina	1975	College of Librarianship
	1984	College of Library & Information Science
University of South Florida	1976	Program of Library Science/Audiovisual
	1978	Department of Library, Media & Information Studies
	1986	School of Library & Information Science
	1993	Division of Library & Information Science
	1995	School of Library & Information Science
University of Southern Mississippi	1981	School of Library Service
	1989	School of Library Science
	1994	School of Library & Information Science
University of Tennessee	1975	School of Library & Information Science
University of Texas at Austin	1956	School of Library Science
	1982	School of Library & Information Science
University of Toronto	1956	Library School
	1967	School of Library Science
	1976	Faculty of Library Science
	1983	Faculty of Library & Information Science
	1995	Faculty of Information Studies
University of Washington	1956	School of Librarianship
	1984	School of Library & Information Science
University of Western Ontario	1970	School of Library & Information Science
	1998	Graduate Programs in Library and Information Studies, Faculty of Communication & Open Learning
University of Wisconsin at Madison	1956	Library School
	1986	School of Library & Information Studies
University of Wisconsin at Milwaukee	1977	School of Library Science
	1983	School of Library & Information Science
Wayne State University	1968	Department of Library Science
	1976	Division of Library Science
	1989	Library Science Program
	1994	Library & Information Science Program

Number of Libraries in the United States, Canada, and Mexico

Statistics are from the 50th edition of the *American Library Directory* (*ALD*) 1997–1998 (R. R. Bowker, 1997). Data are exclusive of elementary and secondary school libraries.

Libraries in the United States

Public Libraries	16,099 *
Public libraries, excluding branches	9,767 †
Main public libraries that have branches	1,278
Public library branches	6,332
Academic Libraries	4,707 *
Junior college	1,265
Departmental	111
Medical	6
Religious	3
University and college	3,442
Departmental	1,466
Law	173
Medical	211
Religious	105
Armed Forces Libraries	378 *
Air Force	105
Medical	13
Army	158
Law	1
Medical	31
Navy	115
Law	1
Medical	15
Government Libraries	1,837 *
Law	419
Medical	218
Special Libraries (excluding public, academic, armed forces, and government)	9,983 *
Law	1,123
Medical	1,924
Religious	1,019
Total Special Libraries (including public, academic, armed forces, and government)	11,044
Total law	1,725
Total medical	2,423
Total religious	1,128
Total Libraries Counted(*)	33,004

Libraries in Regions Administered by the United States

Public Libraries	29	*
Public libraries, excluding branches	13	†
Main public libraries that have branches	3	
Public library branches	16	
Academic Libraries	54	*
Junior college	7	
University and college	47	
Departmental	21	
Law	2	
Medical	1	
Armed Forces Libraries	3	*
Air Force	1	
Army	1	
Navy	1	
Government Libraries	8	*
Law	1	
Medical	2	
Special Libraries (excluding public, academic, armed forces, and government)	17	*
Law	4	
Medical	5	
Religious	1	
Total Special Libraries (including public, academic, armed forces, and government)	19	
Total law	7	
Total medical	8	
Total religious	1	
Total Libraries Counted(*)	111	

Libraries in Canada

Public Libraries	1,723	*
Public libraries, excluding branches	781	†
Main public libraries that have branches	134	
Public library branches	942	
Academic Libraries	466	*
Junior college	129	
Departmental	36	
Medical	0	
Religious	3	
University and college	337	
Departmental	148	
Law	12	
Medical	15	
Religious	17	

Government Libraries	372 *
Law	21
Medical	8
Special Libraries (excluding public, academic, armed forces, and government)	1,358 *
Law	119
Medical	250
Religious	79
Total Special Libraries (including public, academic, and government)	1,457
Total law	159
Total medical	273
Total religious	127
Total Libraries Counted(*)	3,919

Libraries in Mexico

Public Libraries	24 *
Public libraries, excluding branches	24 †
Main public libraries that have branches	0
Public library branches	0
Academic Libraries	315 *
Junior college	0
Departmental	0
Medical	0
Religious	0
University and college	315
Departmental	244
Law	0
Medical	2
Religious	0
Government Libraries	9 *
Law	0
Medical	1
Special Libraries (excluding public, academic, armed forces, and government)	32 *
Law	0
Medical	10
Religious	0
Total Special Libraries (including public, academic, and government)	40
Total law	0
Total medical	14
Total religious	0
Total Libraries Counted(*)	380

Summary

Total U.S. Libraries	33,004
Total Libraries Administered by the United States	111
Total Canadian Libraries	3,919
Total Mexican Libraries	380
Grand Total of Libraries Listed	37,414

Note: Numbers followed by an asterisk are added to find "Total libraries counted" for each of the four geographic areas (United States, U.S.-administered regions, Canada, and Mexico). The sum of the four totals is the "Grand total of libraries listed" in *ALD*. For details on the count of libraries, see the preface to the 50th edition of *ALD—Ed.*

† Federal, state, and other statistical sources use this figure (libraries *excluding* branches) as the total for public libraries.

Highlights of NCES Surveys

Public Libraries

The following are highlights from *E.D. TABS Public Libraries in the United States: 1994* released in June 1997.

Number of Public Libraries and Their Service Outlets and Governance

- 8,921 public libraries (administrative entities) were reported in the 50 states and the District of Columbia in 1994.
- About 11 percent of the public libraries serve 70 percent of the population of legally served areas in the United States (derived from tables 1A and 1B). Each of these public libraries has a legal service area population of 50,000 or more.
- 1,455 public libraries (over 16 percent) reported one or more branch library outlets, with a total of 7,025. The total number of central library outlets reported was 8,879. The total number of stationary outlets reported (central library outlets and branch library outlets) was 15,904. About 9 percent of reporting public libraries had one or more bookmobile outlets, with a total of 997.
- About 55 percent of public libraries were part of a municipal government; nearly 12 percent were part of a county/parish; nearly 6 percent had multi-jurisdictional governance under an intergovernmental agreement; over 9 percent were nonprofit association or agency libraries; about 4 percent were part of a school district; and about 8 percent were separate government units known as library districts. Less than 1 percent were combinations of academic/public libraries or school/public libraries. Just over 5 percent did not report or reported a form of governance not mentioned here.
- 80.4 percent of public libraries had a single direct service outlet.

Income, Expenditure, and Staffing

- Public libraries reported that approximately 78 percent of their total operating income of about $5.3 billion came from local sources, about 12 percent from the state, 1 percent from federal sources, and over 8 percent from other sources, such as gifts and donations, service fees and fines.
- Per capita operating income from local sources was under $3 for 13 percent of public libraries, $3 to $14.99 for approximately 51 percent, and $15 to $29.99 for 25 percent of public libraries; 10.7 percent of libraries had a per capita income from local sources of $30 or more.
- Total operating expenditures for public libraries were over $4.9 billion in 1994. Of this, about 65 percent was expended for paid staff and nearly 15 percent for the library collection (table 12). the average U.S. per capita operating expenditure was $19.93. The highest average per capita operating expenditure in the 50 states was $35.40 and the lowest was $8.45.

- About 40 percent of public libraries reported operating expenditures of less than $50,000 in 1994, about 39 percent expended between $50,000 and $399,999, and about 22 percent exceeded $400,000.

Staffing and Collections

- Public libraries reported a total of nearly 112,823 paid full-time equivalent (FTE) staff.
- Nationwide, public libraries reported nearly 672 million books and serial volumes in their collections or 2.7 volumes per capita. By state, the number of volumes per capita ranged from 1.7 to 4.9.
- Nationwide, public libraries reported collections of nearly 24 million audio materials and nearly 9.3 million video materials.

Circulation and Interlibrary Loans

- Total nationwide circulation of library materials was nearly 1.6 billion or 6.4 per capita. Highest statewide circulation per capita in the 50 states was 11.8 and lowest was 3.1.
- Nationwide, nearly 7.9 million library materials were loaned by public libraries to other libraries.

Children's Services

- Nationwide circulation of children's materials was nearly 492 million or about 31 percent of total circulation. Attendance at children's programs was over 38 million.

The following are highlights from *Statistics in Brief: Use of Public Library Services by Households in the United States: 1996*, released in July 1997.

Public Library Use in the Past Month and Year

- About 44 percent of U.S. households included individuals who had used public library services in the month prior to the interview, and 65 percent of households had used public library services in the past year (including the past month). About one-third of households (35 percent) reported that no household members had used library services in the past year.
- When the entire past year is taken into account, households with children under 18 show substantially higher rates of use than households without children (82 percent versus 54 percent).

Ways of Using Public Library Services

- The most common way of using public library services in the past month was to go to a library to borrow or drop off books or tapes (36 percent).
- Eighteen percent of households reported visiting a library for other purposes, such as a lecture or story hour or to use library equipment (the second most common form of use).

- About 14 percent of households had called a library for information during the past month.
- Only very small percentages of households reported using a computer to link to a library (4 percent), having materials mailed or delivered to their homes (2 percent), or visiting a bookmobile (2 percent).

Purposes for Using Public Library Services

- The highest percentage of households reported library use for enjoyment or hobbies, including borrowing books and tapes or attending activities (32 percent).
- Two other purposes for using public libraries that were commonly acknowledged by household respondents were getting information for personal use (such as information on consumer or health issues, investments, and so on; 20 percent), and using library services or materials for a school or class assignment (19 percent).
- Fewer household respondents said that household members had used public library services for the purposes of keeping up to date at a job (8 percent), getting information to help find a job (5 percent), attending a program for children (4 percent), or working with a tutor or taking a class to learn to read (1 percent).

The following are highlights from *E.D. TABS Academic Libraries: 1994*, released in March 1998.

Services

- In 1993, 3,303 of the 3,639 institutions of higher education in the United States reported that they had their own academic library.
- In fiscal year 1994, general collection circulation transactions in the nation's academic libraries at institutions of high education totaled 183.1 million. Reserve collection circulation transactions totaled 48.4 million. For general and reference circulation transactions taken together, the median circulation was 16.6 per full-time equivalent (FTE) student. The median total circulation ranged from 9.5 per FTE in less than four-year institutions to 31.1 in doctorate-granting institutions.
- In 1994 academic libraries provided a total of about 8.8 million interlibrary loans to other libraries (both higher education and other types of libraries) and received about 6.3 million loans.
- Overall, the largest percentage of academic libraries (43 percent) reported having 60–70 hours of service per typical week. However, 41 percent provided 80 or more public service hours per typical week. The percent of institutions providing 80 or more public service hours ranged from 6.9 percent in less than four-year institutions to 77.8 percent in doctorate-granting institutions.
- Taken together, academic libraries reported a gate count of about 17.8 million visitors per typical week (about 1.8 visits per total FTE enrollment).

- About 21 million reference transactions were reported in a typical week. Over the fiscal year 1994, about 487,000 presentations to groups serving about 6.1 million were reported.

Collections

- Taken together, the nation's 3,033 academic libraries at institutions of higher education held a total of 776.4 million volumes (books, bound serials, and government documents), representing about 422.3 million unduplicated titles at the end of FY 1994.
- The median number of volumes held per FTE student was 56.9 volumes. Median volumes held ranged from 18.4 per FTE in less than four-year institutions to 111.2 in doctorate-granting institutions.
- Of the total volumes held at the end of the year, 43.3 percent (336.6 million) were held at the 125 institutions categorized under the 1994 Carnegie classification as Research I or Research II institutions. About 54.6 percent of the volumes were at those institutions classified as either Research or Doctoral in the Carnegie classification.
- In FY 1994, the median number of volumes added to collections per FTE student was 1.6. The median number added range from .6 per FTE in less than four-year institutions to 3.1 in doctorate-granting institutions.

Staff

- There was a total of 95,843 FTE staff working in academic libraries in 1994. Of these about 26,726 (27.9 percent) were librarians or other professional staff; 40,381 (42.1 percent) were other paid staff; 326 (.3 percent) were contributed services staff; and 28,411 (29.6 percent) were student assistants.
- Excluding student assistants, the institutional median number of academic library FTE staff per 1,000 FTE students was 5.9. The median ranged from 3.6 in less than four-year institutions to 9.8 in doctorate-granting institutions.

Expenditures

- In 1994, total operating expenditures for libraries at the 3,303 institutions of higher education totaled $4.01 billion. The three largest individual expenditure items for all academic libraries were salaries and wages, $2.02 billion (50.4 percent); current serial subscription expenditures, $690.4 million (17.2 percent); and books and bound serials, $442.5 million (11.0 percent).
- The libraries of the 514 doctorate-granting institutions (15.6 percent of the total institutions) accounted for $2.496 billion, or 62.2 percent of the total operating expenditure dollars at all college and university libraries.
- In 1994, the median total operating expenditure per FTE student was $290.81 and the median for information resource expenditures was $86.15.

- The median percentage of total institutional Education & General (E&G) expenditures for academic libraries was 2.8 percent in 1994. In 1990 the media was 3.0 percent (*Academic Library Survey: 1990*, unpublished tabulation).

State Library Agency Survey

The following are highlights from *E.D. TABS State Library Agencies, Fiscal Year 1995*, released in August 1997.

Governance

- Virtually all state library agencies (48 states and the District of Columbia) are located in the executive branch of government. Of these, over 60 percent are part of a larger agency, the most common being the state department of education. In two states, Arizona and Michigan, the agency reports to the legislature.

Allied and Other Special Operations

- A total of 19 state library agencies reported having one or more allied operations. Allied operations most frequently linked with a state library agency are the state archives (10 states), the state records management service (11 states), and the state legislative reference/research service (nine states).
- Fourteen state agencies contract with libraries in their states to serve as resource or reference/information service centers. Seventeen state agencies operate a State Center for the Book.

Electronic Network Development

- In all 50 states, the state library agency plans or monitors electronic network development, 42 states operate such networks, and 46 states develop network content.
- State agencies also provide significant support to library access to the Internet. Almost all of them (49 states and the District of Columbia) are involved in facilitating library access to the Internet in one or more of the following ways: training library staff or consulting in the use of the Internet; providing a subsidy for Internet participation; providing equipment needed to access the Internet; managing gophers, file servers, bulletin boards, or listservs; or mounting directors, data bases, or online catalogs.

Library Development Services

Services to Public Libraries

- Every state library agency provides these types of services to public libraries: administration of LSCA (Library Services and Construction Act) grants; collection of library statistics; continuing education; and library planning, evaluation, and research.

- Services to public libraries provided by at least three-quarters of state agencies include: administration of state aid, consulting services, interlibrary loan referral services, library legislation preparation or review, literacy program support, public relations or promotional campaigns, reference referral services, state standards or guidelines, summer reading program support, and union list development.

- Services to public libraries provided by at least half of state agencies include Online Computer Library Center (OCLC) Group Access Capability and certification of librarians.

- Less common services to public libraries include: accreditation of libraries, cooperative purchasing of library materials, preservation/conservation services, and retrospective conversion of bibliographic records.

Services to Academic Libraries

- Over two-thirds of state library agencies report the following services to the academic sector: administering LSCA Title III grants, referring interlibrary loans, offering reference referral services, and developing union lists. Three-fifths of state agencies serve academic libraries through continuing education.

- Less common services to academic libraries provided by state agencies include: literacy program support, preservation/conservation, retrospective conversion, and standards or guidelines. No state agency accredits academic libraries or certifies academic librarians.

Services to School Library Media Centers

- Over two-thirds of state library agencies provide interlibrary loan referral services to school library media centers (LMCs) (table 4c). Services to LMCs provided by over half of state agencies include: administration of LSCA Title III grants, continuing education, reference referral, and union list development.

- Less common services to LMCs include: administration of state aid and cooperative purchasing of library materials. No state agency accredits LMCs or certifies librarians.

Services to Special Libraries

- At least two-thirds of state agencies serve special libraries through administration of LSCA grants, continuing education, interlibrary loan referral, and reference referral. Over half provide union list development and consulting services.

- Less common services to special libraries include administration of state aid, cooperative purchase of library materials, or summer reading program support. No state agency accredits special libraries or certifies special librarians.

Services to Systems

- Three-fifths of state agencies serve library systems through administration of LSCA grants, consulting services, continuing education, interlibrary loan referral services, library legislation preparation or review, reference referral, and library planning, evaluation, and research.
- Accreditation of systems is provided by only six states and certification of system librarians by only seven states.

Service Outlets

- State library agencies reported a total of 159 service outlets. Main or central outlets accounted for 34 percent, other outlets (excluding bookmobiles) made up 58.5 percent (with Kentucky and Washington reporting the largest number, at 21 each) and bookmobiles represented 7.5 percent of the total.

Collections

- The number of books and serial volumes held by state library agencies totaled 20.3 million, with New York accounting for the largest collection (2.3 million). Five state agencies had book and serial volumes of over one million. In other states, these collections ranged from 500,000 to 1 million (11 states), 200,000 to 499,999 (8 states), 100,000 to 199,999 (12 states), 50,000 to 99,999 (5 states) and less than 50,000 (10 states). The state library agency in Maryland does not maintain a collection, and the District of Columbia does not maintain a collection in its function as a state library agency.
- The number of serial subscriptions held by state library agencies totaled almost 80,000, with New York holding the largest number (over 14,000). Seventeen state agencies reported serial subscriptions of over 1,000. In other states, these collections ranged from 500 to 999 (17 states), 100 to 499 (13 states), and under 100 (3 states).

Staff

- The total number of budgeted full-time equivalent (FTE) positions in state library agencies was 3,602.2. Librarians with ALA-MLS degrees accounted for 1,158.3 of these positions, or 32.2 percent of total FTE positions. Rhode Island reported the largest percentage (57.1) of ALA-MLS librarians, and West Virginia reported the lowest (16.1 percent).

Income

- State library agencies reported a total income of $752.9 million in FY 1995 (82.1 percent came from state sources, 16.3 percent from federal, and 1.6 percent from other sources).
- Of state library agency income received from state sources, nearly $420 million (67.9 percent) was designated for state aid to libraries. Massachusetts had the largest percentage of state library agency income

set aside for state aid (96.6 percent). Eight states targeted no state funds for aid to libraries. The District of Columbia, Hawaii, Iowa, Louisiana, Nevada, South Dakota, Vermont, and Washington reported state income only for operation of the state agency.

Expenditures

- State library agencies reported total expenditures of over $725.2 million. The largest percentage (81.6 percent) came from state funds, followed by federal funds (17.1 percent), and other funds (1.3 percent).
- Three states shared the highest percentage of expenditures from state sources (92 percent). These states were Georgia (92 percent), Illinois (91.7 percent), and New York (91.8 percent). Louisiana had the lowest percentage of expenditures from state sources (45 percent), with 54.7 percent of its expenditures coming from federal sources.
- Sixty-nine percent of total state library expenditures were for aid to libraries, with the largest percentages expended on individual public libraries (49.6 percent) and public library systems (21.1 percent).
- Sixteen state library agencies reported expenditures on allied operations totaling $18.8 million—just under 3 percent (2.6 percent) of total expenditures by state library agencies. Among the state agencies reporting such expenditures, the highest was reported by Texas ($3.2 million) and the lowest by Georgia ($6,000).
- Twenty-nine state library agencies reported a total of $20.6 million in grants and contracts expenditures to assist public libraries with state education reform initiatives or the National Education Goals. Almost three-quarters of the expenditures were used to promote adult literacy and lifelong learning, and over one-quarter to promote readiness for school. Of these state agencies, four (Minnesota, Nebraska, Pennsylvania, and Wisconsin) focused their grants and contracts expenditures exclusively on readiness-for-school projects, and five (Connecticut, Illinois, New Jersey, Oklahoma, and Texas) focused their expenditures exclusively on adult literacy and lifelong learning projects.

For further information about statistics collected by the National Center for Education Statistics, see the article in Part 1—*Ed.*

Library Acquisition Expenditures, 1996–1997: U.S. Public, Academic, Special, and Government Libraries

The information in these tables is taken from the 50th edition of the *American Library Directory* (*ALD*) (1997–1998), published by R. R. Bowker. The tables report acquisition expenditures by public, academic, special, and government libraries.

The total number of U.S. libraries listed in the 50th edition of *ALD* is 33,004, including 16,099 public libraries, 4,707 academic libraries, 9,983 special libraries, and 2,215 government libraries.

Understanding the Tables

Number of libraries includes only those U.S. libraries in *ALD* that reported annual acquisition expenditures (4,742 public libraries, 1,803 academic libraries, 1,564 special libraries, 381 government libraries). Libraries that reported annual income but not expenditures are not included in the count. Academic libraries include university, college, and junior college libraries. Special academic libraries, such as law and medical libraries, that reported acquisition expenditures separately from the institution's main library are counted as independent libraries.

The amount in the *total acquisition expenditures* column for a given state is generally greater than the sum of the categories of expenditures. This is because the total acquisition expenditures amount also includes the expenditures of libraries that did not itemize by category.

Figures in *categories of expenditure* columns represent only those libraries that itemized expenditures. Libraries that reported a total acquisition expenditure amount but did not itemize are only represented in the total acquisition expenditures column.

Unspecified includes monies reported as not specifically for books, periodicals, audiovisual materials and equipment, microform, preservation, other print materials, manuscripts and archives, machine-readable materials, or database fees (e.g., library materials). This column also includes monies reported for categories in combination—for example, audiovisual *and* microform. When libraries report only total acquisition expenditures without itemizing by category, the total amount is not reflected as unspecified.

Table 1 / Public Library Acquisition Expenditures

State	Number of Libraries	Total Acquisition Expenditures	Books	Other Print Materials	Periodicals	Manuscripts & Archives	AV Materials	AV Equipment	Microform	Machine Readable Materials	Preservation	Database Fees	Unspecified
Alabama	71	6,530,527	2,866,037	261,966	356,558	—	410,917	1,700	316,347	79,868	22,603	57,736	634,783
Alaska	31	1,653,114	536,698	47,724	466,485	—	32,623	26,515	1,000	8,003	1,515	32,605	754
Arizona	59	11,579,026	7,331,379	74,563	1,615,736	—	716,587	2,400	181,803	516,849	106,777	179,951	17,588
Arkansas	23	2,691,744	1,040,350	1,540	91,887	—	48,326	225	40,924	8,972	17,355	50,322	1,990
California	138	63,559,343	27,126,253	1,269,897	5,577,452	185,999	3,074,397	19,840	1,543,118	834,136	338,028	1,306,025	1,532,798
Colorado	70	10,231,475	4,680,697	829	744,475	11,000	533,496	19,879	100,163	269,447	17,303	251,299	326,847
Connecticut	125	12,632,994	6,083,721	624,289	817,459	400	569,150	25,202	185,745	176,220	44,060	292,259	204,926
Delaware	13	1,183,067	669,859	498	93,563	—	42,351	—	27,787	26,000	—	31,054	—
District of Columbia	3	8,506,345	32,125	—	5,537	—	5,683	—	—	—	—	—	5,000
Florida	102	36,249,276	17,268,787	124,959	4,759,729	26,000	2,075,215	159,495	733,324	1,041,035	148,373	383,606	440,523
Georgia	45	13,163,551	4,893,934	46,498	367,456	6,586	685,203	15,305	124,748	95,829	24,863	20,101	7,474
Hawaii	2	2,825,332	2,038,326	—	471,300	—	—	—	—	—	—	—	—
Idaho	46	2,113,737	1,185,383	—	146,467	—	123,087	10,718	9,505	23,242	3,973	108,417	8,889
Illinois	304	45,510,682	16,419,771	238,562	2,507,576	3,010	2,478,656	244,554	383,975	888,335	125,765	703,277	630,142
Indiana	159	29,723,189	14,286,014	30,900	1,904,723	5,500	3,237,640	86,529	415,689	438,750	161,582	275,745	901,272
Iowa	229	8,853,588	4,627,321	115,215	770,932	—	533,039	81,438	46,693	68,044	8,287	102,380	632,773
Kansas	98	6,715,864	3,885,611	49,336	522,308	—	507,485	12,853	101,003	262,255	14,790	131,670	162,364
Kentucky	60	7,228,653	2,242,063	45,611	305,735	911	306,124	169,290	28,425	146,858	6,560	242,145	146,914
Louisiana	42	9,875,899	5,414,138	57,811	986,512	—	435,647	11,360	116,567	40,919	41,821	117,531	9,238
Maine	103	2,217,378	1,153,281	2,220	180,876	798	103,681	7,080	7,264	10,900	12,045	36,273	3,285
Maryland	22	18,858,818	10,491,919	269,903	970,262	—	2,148,578	6,912	43,398	844,649	1,229	194,808	520,971
Massachusetts	209	13,654,175	7,613,112	23,344	1,241,453	1,000	675,228	37,476	275,544	283,422	17,040	392,563	180,732
Michigan	202	25,422,849	10,198,985	90,872	1,742,477	2,950	1,921,108	45,702	168,973	750,954	18,899	426,194	405,743
Minnesota	106	18,469,075	9,511,627	146,535	1,361,914	—	1,393,847	13,265	86,230	762,249	34,027	513,866	733,951
Mississippi	40	3,970,226	2,385,756	11,230	345,604	—	193,153	20,214	79,652	139,360	3,385	26,314	990

Missouri	87	17,711,477	83,773	1,626,489	319	1,546,017	46,365	662,505	540,420	23,741	139,514	292,425
Montana	47	1,783,487	665	140,288	—	29,680	700	2,754	11,084	6,620	98,255	33,594
Nebraska	68	1,589,976	13,068	168,136	200	233,407	2,000	20,391	16,672	10,020	66,260	1,000
Nevada	17	5,975,849	2,000	610,302	—	51,684	18,275	330,687	245,350	6,163	51,612	17,566
New Hampshire	119	2,784,295	22,873	169,138	—	111,758	9,000	70,668	18,994	10,902	17,326	10,062
New Jersey	184	32,836,041	31,411	3,090,526	3,750	1,488,717	162,622	411,703	703,531	65,054	587,251	572,602
New Mexico	27	3,653,802	15,000	95,398	—	38,946	10,500	4,000	28,122	10,378	10,150	15,672
New York	366	59,039,182	1,149,672	6,001,986	40,872	3,176,143	373,336	796,175	949,475	172,665	451,583	330,557
North Carolina	80	15,335,843	44,374	874,311	4,235	712,924	83,406	117,187	223,206	39,760	56,464	227,059
North Dakota	21	1,116,676	11,200	130,741	—	70,158	5,920	18,100	14,000	3,350	7,000	3,425
Ohio	160	56,256,264	918,576	5,513,229	3,895	5,985,819	93,151	1,057,380	1,062,126	879,559	1,424,707	503,824
Oklahoma	42	6,391,788	114,703	692,886	—	375,414	28,340	25,244	81,767	22,396	207,399	686,363
Oregon	75	27,128,345	23,692	1,082,376	—	683,293	36,653	30,151	190,116	68,044	46,466	29,426
Pennsylvania	237	20,079,500	56,571	1,236,758	4,491	731,323	40,900	411,208	202,825	55,227	202,973	342,763
Rhode Island	30	2,824,773	545	200,468	21,129	112,076	24,346	30,886	100,854	31,924	102,120	111,840
South Carolina	33	9,668,032	1,500	665,131	3,000	389,478	52,587	114,895	155,763	44,273	230,288	610,889
South Dakota	41	2,030,300	2,695	177,570	—	96,416	17,490	31,115	4,136	1,400	298,974	33,775
Tennessee	59	9,982,109	28,071	921,165	—	694,180	28,300	265,509	21,860	81,768	118,007	2,594,334
Texas	223	28,484,681	140,522	2,124,461	1,575	1,560,148	98,387	260,303	389,411	113,470	402,841	393,663
Utah	25	5,161,904	10,493	365,737	—	505,188	21,300	23,282	12,920	6,954	178,407	10,528
Vermont	73	1,079,023	42	61,801	—	27,398	1,697	1,717	2,500	—	6,750	5,862
Virginia	74	22,414,595	111,705	2,618,007	3,826	1,119,075	120,243	252,567	354,785	471,349	318,583	339,888
Washington	47	18,413,790	142,243	1,052,431	100	881,709	30,477	195,480	184,575	41,334	279,502	126,977
West Virginia	47	3,666,845	2,050	137,732	—	197,110	11,185	5,795	22,767	14,933	12,816	75,621
Wisconsin	235	16,713,930	78,996	1,807,734	—	1,084,581	53,036	122,882	189,263	33,195	583,987	355,695
Wyoming	21	2,503,652	—	85,412	—	95,386	2,950	35,500	26,066	7,280	76,076	16,850
Pacific Islands	1	57,102	—	5,839	—	6,372	—	—	—	—	—	—
Puerto Rico	1	8,000	—	—	—	—	—	—	—	—	—	8,000
Total	4,742	739,838,840	6,540,742	60,010,528	331,546	44,255,621	2,391,718	10,315,961	13,468,884	3,392,039	11,851,452	15,760,227
Estimated of Accusition Expenditure%		66.63	1.30	11.90	0.07	8.77	0.47	2.05	2.67	0.67	2.35	3.12

Table 2 / Academic Library Acquisition Expenditures

Categories of Expenditure (Amounts in U.S. Dollars)

State	Number of Libraries	Total Acquisition Expenditures	Books	Other Print Materials	Periodicals	Manuscripts & Archives	AV Materials	AV Equipment	Microform	Machine Readable Materials	Preservation	Database Fees	Unspecified
Alabama	20	5,076,789	1,671,320	48,710	2,134,486	3,500	52,757	36,901	147,087	148,853	103,862	24,024	135,423
Alaska	5	1,352,118	75,041	9,905	103,523	—	985	—	4,594	6,179	925	—	—
Arizona	16	12,124,397	4,161,920	—	5,173,333	—	125,170	12,800	472,032	79,770	277,191	296,305	1,324,570
Arkansas	14	5,703,409	1,097,013	—	1,358,800	—	63,935	20,134	177,259	136,683	59,852	31,124	14,074
California	124	61,208,346	16,006,172	889,010	25,755,755	2,323	516,486	331,653	1,169,460	1,430,799	1,620,022	1,213,822	1,344,414
Colorado	29	13,373,643	3,770,724	114,315	6,003,464	—	206,339	14,712	364,086	438,273	323,828	187,370	109,919
Connecticut	28	27,844,890	8,098,594	343,981	11,518,211	1,066,000	215,367	71,147	1,369,924	501,322	938,497	200,108	548,890
Delaware	5	5,050,475	2,192,596	32,000	2,632,944	—	4,049	5,403	16,352	20,346	1,100	14,750	130,315
District of Columbia	11	12,894,168	2,277,432	528	5,596,104	2,100	47,088	13,902	168,890	66,467	123,794	66,632	1,551,416
Florida	57	21,949,249	6,203,013	636,793	7,691,985	2,100	375,098	149,314	1,005,043	1,289,339	363,559	683,501	149,883
Georgia	40	20,730,240	6,015,241	76,715	10,769,830	32,500	242,376	128,436	1,057,036	601,829	182,849	373,784	656,495
Hawaii	9	4,330,575	499,231	25,514	274,912	—	58,974	18,320	182,509	22,943	274,341	91,250	2,431,536
Idaho	9	6,396,342	1,534,744	—	3,462,420	500	72,205	158,500	73,387	24,762	182,117	87,046	679,693
Illinois	72	45,893,825	13,086,353	472,583	18,638,599	3,900	505,755	618,110	713,595	841,126	540,398	722,531	649,390
Indiana	44	22,273,665	6,425,009	153,684	11,507,664	7,392	429,635	167,253	163,263	433,460	492,479	252,073	527,142
Iowa	35	18,692,385	3,428,626	151,570	4,933,745	200	162,094	131,906	194,382	126,468	320,198	131,839	258,625
Kansas	30	7,790,182	2,316,138	7,722	4,202,073	1,543	46,129	37,944	149,730	404,532	206,117	69,937	87,422
Kentucky	34	16,450,021	4,356,842	7,500	8,934,827	25,900	155,178	34,674	330,908	467,616	308,036	205,200	507,461
Louisiana	20	15,102,586	3,437,180	114,420	8,063,925	28,631	51,775	110,744	165,979	225,077	230,047	105,337	126,118
Maine	20	4,759,543	1,580,450	—	2,122,177	—	69,579	19,445	158,210	234,262	78,403	74,095	69,368
Maryland	29	13,129,931	3,784,766	37,502	6,288,613	—	175,377	98,552	487,672	556,296	325,978	180,642	646,717
Massachusetts	55	53,653,218	10,292,195	552,510	17,057,265	6,082	431,784	176,126	674,959	1,157,811	1,070,438	1,310,178	1,326,724
Michigan	56	40,741,067	8,442,921	374,388	15,168,438	11,250	303,045	80,107	801,851	717,621	630,207	672,433	1,084,190
Minnesota	33	18,885,663	5,718,318	416,885	9,495,104	8,000	178,884	78,847	155,552	314,633	206,415	190,680	153,449
Mississippi	26	10,298,425	1,443,367	—	5,296,229	3,547	263,554	66,601	302,613	274,721	201,167	104,022	307,170

State	No.												
Missouri	45	24,071,774	5,608,623	34,840	10,596,878	1,166	502,195	181,188	725,514	1,220,686	483,619	1,051,997	551,722
Montana	12	1,051,433	250,958	300	327,249	—	11,290	—	23,030	10,583	5,848	5,251	9,983
Nebraska	20	5,133,232	1,524,020	137,133	1,878,229	1,000	80,083	90,287	275,356	175,261	66,384	120,368	64,264
Nevada	7	6,901,437	1,265,969	1,359	1,517,814	20,000	96,787	9,270	337,532	365,261	133,349	54,169	22,217
New Hampshire	17	4,535,699	826,681	79,343	3,031,693	—	25,849	44,394	110,578	115,329	69,896	81,148	40,075
New Jersey	30	23,622,840	7,981,287	1,095,222	9,471,388	200,472	292,660	123,982	796,834	850,165	160,901	290,158	1,014,728
New Mexico	19	7,834,293	2,424,174	8,977	4,101,253	—	49,182	42,450	104,240	253,484	164,968	60,024	98,924
New York	139	93,193,852	20,128,102	1,394,620	36,217,427	15,024	886,516	208,365	2,386,264	3,107,039	1,827,892	1,916,997	6,080,817
North Carolina	77	39,522,841	9,294,348	99,089	12,889,013	10,150	811,280	559,266	977,003	971,890	347,573	647,066	592,700
North Dakota	8	1,899,503	451,356	17,200	1,158,802	—	38,792	25,600	68,244	15,260	—	39,658	10,425
Ohio	68	32,194,948	9,543,678	61,619	16,937,430	600	476,673	145,161	604,685	1,141,021	763,820	357,835	403,745
Oklahoma	33	12,647,204	2,172,443	37,964	5,076,130	2,400	65,541	126,232	314,193	235,326	204,332	351,554	214,737
Oregon	29	9,791,559	2,738,326	1,783	4,617,732	—	159,249	109,037	171,112	278,572	193,437	285,981	234,873
Pennsylvania	107	50,893,604	12,544,843	726,104	20,120,450	14,793	633,789	298,435	920,547	1,180,924	1,328,383	730,518	1,124,485
Rhode Island	11	4,491,174	1,271,801	76,625	2,219,125	4,494	78,874	25,072	146,698	192,303	79,203	109,855	66,882
South Carolina	27	11,498,526	3,385,967	30,004	6,464,139	700	89,846	22,972	132,805	310,619	361,292	118,933	73,323
South Dakota	13	4,639,998	1,070,337	4,113	2,005,506	—	35,672	133,219	72,568	231,830	76,430	73,907	460,892
Tennessee	43	22,751,152	5,026,155	361,292	12,619,139	2,050	239,260	139,639	504,920	581,184	278,456	332,617	1,588,116
Texas	90	49,285,533	11,537,837	718,040	18,129,226	39,550	1,195,576	563,415	1,681,846	2,114,732	901,043	1,689,819	1,457,988
Utah	7	4,028,181	923,116	500	2,049,313	1,502	67,978	95,055	65,326	172,306	136,109	149,414	93,997
Vermont	17	3,406,206	1,247,016	500	1,259,413	200	26,028	60,046	106,475	145,879	48,019	197,879	18,559
Virginia	41	31,369,181	9,624,316	671,696	13,306,673	68,609	456,511	156,601	881,290	1,728,990	367,296	357,813	1,121,678
Washington	34	23,304,617	6,598,431	82,407	13,152,681	2,500	276,350	150,974	217,452	216,377	210,555	382,214	117,646
West Virginia	20	4,449,139	1,143,495	35,465	1,448,458	—	54,521	175,608	181,390	139,816	30,314	88,568	886,139
Wisconsin	48	24,511,727	4,659,835	34,055	7,140,777	4,744	444,612	275,571	584,923	948,555	294,809	404,794	801,638
Wyoming	5	2,828,062	256,209	15,701	1,997,586	—	27,607	13,044	5,000	6,000	72,419	24,376	317,685
Pacific Islands	4	336,691	55,977	1,500	181,276	—	11,543	10,370	44,570	15,156	—	4,799	—
Puerto Rico	10	3,475,076	1,242,270	1,100	1,916,275	500	120,250	47,300	20,687	24,207	56,278	37,385	7,250
Virgin Islands	1	56,300	28,000	—	23,000	—	—	5,000	5,000	—	—	300	—
Total	1,803	969,430,934	242,740,776	10,194,756	406,038,901	1,593,822	12,008,132	6,414,244	22,972,455	27,269,943	17,724,445	17,254,080	32,295,892
Estimated % of Acquisition Expenditure			30.48	1.28	50.93	0.20	1.51	0.81	2.88	3.42	2.23	2.17	4.05

Table 3 / Special Library Acquisition Expenditures

Categories of Expenditure (Amounts in U.S. Dollars)

State	Number of Libraries	Total Acquisition Expenditures	Books	Other Print Materials	Periodicals	Manuscripts & Archives	AV Materials	AV Equipment	Microform	Machine Readable Materials	Preservation	Database Fees	Unspecified
Alabama	4	192,922	25,700	—	81,277	945	—	—	—	31,000	45,000	1,500	7,500	—
Alaska	4	20,271	12,535	—	5,550	300	86	—	—	—	1,600	200	—	—
Arizona	27	1,245,407	125,110	6,500	179,170	1,700	11,825	2,150	700	22,895	11,230	46,852	6,550
Arkansas	1	9,100	5,500	500	1,500	100	—	—	—	—	500	—	—
California	146	7,703,102	1,621,553	126,429	2,638,686	71,550	86,796	30,600	139,222	81,144	85,983	944,620	66,679
Colorado	31	2,354,921	536,302	39,000	700,320	33,420	18,850	1,600	25,000	44,900	7,840	272,500	17,827
Connecticut	32	3,122,837	565,570	131,299	897,554	56,669	34,325	16,500	29,575	60,175	173,480	235,113	24,846
Delaware	7	1,219,380	186,795	—	188,000	—	3,750	19,000	4,935	—	12,200	76,260	568,000
District of Columbia	41	10,660,612	1,824,015	286,250	1,576,680	—	2,400	700	21,500	62,700	68,550	144,235	2,800
Florida	45	1,565,511	246,151	3,800	278,326	3,050	23,802	18,286	27,007	58,015	17,901	246,200	14,850
Georgia	26	1,375,280	227,214	2,200	337,429	—	24,025	16,695	19,614	92,649	22,116	152,060	3,706
Hawaii	4	197,756	43,670	—	128,771	—	—	—	—	4,200	312	14,255	—
Idaho	8	284,713	47,200	60,000	81,035	—	—	—	—	10,000	178	11,000	—
Illinois	87	6,285,133	1,481,371	205,580	1,270,359	27,075	60,160	29,800	61,435	94,150	27,200	170,529	65,004
Indiana	40	1,939,424	151,001	4,100	315,139	—	22,160	11,550	38,700	81,321	1,475	245,925	—
Iowa	24	1,002,536	570,501	17,889	292,761	—	14,194	1,000	2,350	5,500	10,210	24,557	6,250
Kansas	11	161,721	42,413	4,500	94,153	—	—	4,750	5,700	—	2,850	5,855	—
Kentucky	16	641,107	137,075	—	172,807	—	12,200	5,000	18,500	—	2,400	2,525	—
Louisiana	6	170,626	31,000	2,425	70,000	2,000	9,751	—	—	8,000	3,000	3,450	—
Maine	19	397,198	51,132	2,418	64,874	200	5,725	4,680	40,000	1,300	54,040	27,450	984
Maryland	42	2,963,459	667,817	67,205	1,078,175	7,550	21,536	32,534	83,510	22,400	32,232	425,066	1,275
Massachusetts	59	3,529,220	727,046	8,810	1,399,287	1,875	35,054	3,857	14,679	237,423	47,089	188,463	128,820
Michigan	50	3,796,651	668,766	2,223	1,329,389	2,800	31,864	6,210	22,076	138,754	483	252,280	48,734
Minnesota	28	1,363,625	434,980	234,000	229,620	3,900	8,100	10,200	10,500	20,500	5,100	45,700	8,000
Mississippi	5	98,053	8,125	25	87,165	2,200	—	100	238	—	200	—	—

State	No.												
Missouri	31	3,909,736	470,861	53,139	2,122,507	300	3,355	300	8,300	50,200	156,359	53,651	30,012
Montana	9	68,168	15,076	1,030	30,565	—	973	—	39,102	300	1,250	716	308
Nebraska	17	341,636	28,804	450	52,295	2,000	2,012	—	210	—	2,600	3,395	10,071
Nevada	4	85,600	17,000	1,000	33,000	5,000	3,100	16,400	—	51,000	24,500	2,105	—
New Hampshire	19	1,064,005	234,608	4,000	453,020	3,450	26,658	13,866	210	125,150	97,025	33,379	22,320
New Jersey	53	3,897,262	1,000,193	8,739	1,635,556	—	4,550	100	53,397	—	200	388,433	225
New Mexico	17	211,582	87,795	1,300	81,109	—	—	—	750	—	—	2,000	—
New York	150	10,821,683	2,107,814	95,205	2,082,317	21,570	67,886	49,906	53,348	150,938	136,690	526,097	177,774
North Carolina	26	717,355	187,152	8,250	255,632	65	3,800	12,500	5,288	68,200	200	39,800	200
North Dakota	2	72,793	10,280	—	8,642	1,600	—	4,355	—	20,638	25,813	—	3,065
Ohio	71	5,869,703	686,843	32,193	1,265,657	—	40,612	8,559	24,185	88,595	34,554	369,902	28,023
Oklahoma	8	168,250	10,700	2,000	95,000	—	2,500	4,000	6,000	1,000	—	1,550	—
Oregon	17	518,541	88,481	4,065	183,999	219,315	9,178	—	4,000	9,360	885	26,611	—
Pennsylvania	95	5,119,760	518,269	58,607	1,363,185	—	40,002	9,270	32,018	26,618	78,403	287,016	45,273
Rhode Island	12	148,185	43,177	738	85,559	3,500	1,742	—	100	—	6,953	4,540	2,606
South Carolina	10	406,785	60,500	165	70,000	—	11,300	5,000	16,000	6,100	8,900	7,700	9,400
South Dakota	4	125,339	46,920	—	55,900	2,030	—	—	—	—	—	15,919	—
Tennessee	22	675,358	151,450	4,168	255,201	18,300	18,623	40	4,942	12,950	7,272	45,370	1,164
Texas	57	6,127,438	945,913	20,117	1,833,240	—	34,890	10,062	27,157	191,223	31,117	275,528	67,756
Utah	7	872,250	521,335	—	12,515	1,595	5,100	—	150,000	100,000	80,000	—	—
Vermont	12	178,352	14,269	371	10,406	56,665	280	4,875	—	—	5,071	4,400	—
Virginia	56	2,647,085	600,321	46,493	550,210	-7,750	21,036	7,775	108,279	71,566	20,526	37,929	9,065
Washington	29	1,719,561	170,747	3,887	661,862	4,200	5,813	3,175	1,100	9,700	10,496	150,250	—
West Virginia	9	573,068	93,450	1,900	423,230	100	7,150	15,000	10,500	4,185	2,642	11,954	—
Wisconsin	45	1,855,480	598,567	18,965	433,650	—	49,789	100	10,050	85,595	9,500	134,825	14,166
Wyoming	9	119,626	3,350	150	553	—	500	—	200	250	250	600	285
Pacific Islands	1	135,893	—	—	—	—	—	—	—	—	—	—	—
Puerto Rico	3	422,616	99,212	—	305,045	—	12,105	—	—	—	6,254	—	—
Total	1,564	473,558,882	130,124,849	201,373,085	89,851,129	570,074	803,507	383,495	1,149,812	2,161,194	1,334,729	5,989,065	1,386,648
Estimated % of Acquisition Expenditure		29.90	29.90	46.28	20.65	0.13	0.18	0.09	0.26	0.50	0.31	1.38	0.32

Table 4 / Government Library Acquisition Expenditures

State	Number of Libraries	Total Acquisition Expenditures	Books	Other Print Materials	Periodicals	Manuscripts & Archives	AV Materials	AV Equipment	Microform	Machine Readable Materials	Preservation	Database Fees	Unspecified
Alabama	6	485,004	211,396	3,000	122,345	—	11,200	—	5,672	11,096	—	97,675	5,450
Alaska	7	89,800	18,850	700	41,300	—	500	100	—	2,850	350	13,250	3,000
Arizona	8	397,459	215,062	—	10,618	500	—	—	—	8,274	1,938	3,987	33,908
Arkansas	2	386,200	5,000	—	235,200	—	—	—	2,000	—	—	144,000	—
California	33	6,548,414	1,158,681	311,139	2,650,325	—	22,884	30,778	158,296	128,927	165,358	88,377	40,537
Colorado	15	1,058,874	158,187	400	428,436	300	11,380	22,811	18,600	25,614	—	78,401	1,500
Connecticut	5	103,675	12,775	2,000	37,100	1,000	3,075	3,000	5,000	10,000	—	10,225	—
Delaware	2	172,623	170,673	—	1,000	—	—	—	—	—	950	—	—
District of Columbia	15	1,395,050	181,700	44,700	406,100	3,400	21,500	10,500	72,100	70,000	13,750	132,500	—
Florida	31	2,152,374	513,873	4,000	652,238	3,000	33,614	—	24,972	37,876	1,500	34,732	6,165
Georgia	3	124,000	20,400	—	16,100	—	—	—	5,000	7,500	—	—	—
Hawaii	3	779,416	227,305	515,582	12,900	—	—	—	3,470	—	2,000	—	18,159
Idaho	2	291,000	4,000	—	36,000	—	170	—	—	1,100	—	3,000	—
Illinois	13	4,629,913	1,201,385	—	448,965	—	4,900	—	28,000	700	3,000	51,000	—
Indiana	6	473,500	35,000	—	2,000	—	—	1,260	—	—	31,600	—	—
Iowa	2	219,500	5,000	—	9,000	—	400	400	—	4,000	—	700	—
Kansas	5	866,727	284,592	192,971	277,444	700	3,000	6,300	4,800	5,000	19,967	14,953	—
Kentucky	2	467,000	372,400	12,000	5,000	—	—	—	9,895	—	2,700	7,700	8,863
Louisiana	4	2,724,600	19,000	400	87,000	—	600	—	—	3,500	300	12,700	1,000
Maine	1	9,500	—	—	—	—	—	—	—	—	—	—	—
Maryland	9	5,349,650	213,450	2,000	49,400	—	5,800	2,500	—	—	4,000	67,500	—
Massachusetts	12	2,821,235	2,183,024	—	94,923	—	2,000	1,050	8,246	550	1,235	—	—
Michigan	9	675,108	119,336	6,350	221,670	—	20,603	100	7,100	14,100	120	21,929	20,500
Minnesota	6	592,601	43,463	212,650	207,632	—	5,467	3,400	13,319	23,894	10,500	66,451	5,675
Mississippi	3	306,090	19,500	—	85,000	—	3,892	—	—	23,894	—	1,168	—

State	No.											
Missouri	11	576,195	300	80,177	—	—	—	11,400	—	—	21,800	—
Montana	4	297,457	2,937	33,933	—	—	—	—	4,961	—	4,500	—
Nebraska	5	95,750	—	21,647	—	—	—	54,142	50	—	1,322	4,000
Nevada	3	616,653	2,000	24,248	—	1,000	—	3,914	4,816	4,088	63,214	—
New Hampshire	3	67,000	5,000	20,500	—	—	—	—	—	—	75,000	—
New Jersey	4	338,000	5,000	89,553	—	6,000	—	2,000	—	500	61,300	7,000
New Mexico	6	465,800	164,250	68,450	—	9,954	2,085	35,069	15,000	12,000	21,938	4,500
New York	30	2,630,701	4,350	556,423	—	4,500	300	53,029	16,748	18,100	6,240	15,275
North Carolina	9	1,122,146	3,050	481,439	—	—	—	—	5,741	16,612	—	—
North Dakota	—	—	—	—	—	—	—	—	—	—	—	—
Ohio	11	904,824	61,000	72,245	—	9,000	2,000	5,285	11,175	—	14,900	4,805
Oklahoma	7	189,872	132	100,010	—	267	1,000	—	424	1,539	1,295	1,021
Oregon	6	865,226	—	379,729	—	11,381	—	3,700	166,411	—	34,552	6,142
Pennsylvania	12	1,358,854	46,000	4,500	—	—	—	—	—	2,600	6,500	—
Rhode Island	2	72,587	—	46,749	—	2,040	—	1,895	12,417	—	—	—
South Carolina	3	106,273	—	100	—	500	—	14,333	—	—	54,355	—
South Dakota	3	71,044	—	46,137	—	1,700	342	2,425	—	—	600	2,900
Tennessee	3	33,791	—	2,845	—	—	—	6,000	—	—	2,900	—
Texas	9	119,333	150	44,561	117	1,000	4,000	3,000	4,000	4,478	448	7,290
Utah	3	276,665	—	124,902	—	12,740	10,000	60,000	6,339	9,000	30,372	—
Vermont	—	—	—	—	—	—	—	—	—	—	—	—
Virginia	11	867,945	24,000	198,320	22,000	1,800	—	7,000	88,600	3,500	139,700	130,300
Washington	12	1,567,791	—	198,117	—	15,347	—	3,000	22,245	12,000	12,150	5,860
West Virginia	4	516,760	400	68,500	400	3,000	4,000	10,000	1,200	1,000	35,900	802
Wisconsin	12	898,007	10,000	187,269	600	5,515	10,000	4,828	4,700	1,000	59,555	—
Wyoming	3	267,000	—	33,000	—	500	500	4,900	10,000	—	2,000	4,500
Puerto Rico	1	30,000	—	15,000	500	—	—	—	—	—	—	—
Total	381	47,474,987	1,636,461	9,036,050	32,017	302,771	116,426	591,809	724,847	344,685	1,500,789	339,152
Estimated % of Acquisition Expenditure		44.77	6.18	34.13	0.12	1.14	0.44	2.24	2.74	1.30	5.67	1.28

Price Indexes for Public and Academic Libraries

Research Associates of Washington, 1200 North Nash Street, No. 225, Arlington, VA 22209
703-243-3399

Kent Halstead

A rise in prices with the gradual loss of the dollar's value has been a continuing phenomenon in the U.S. economy. This article reports price indexes measuring this inflation for public libraries, college and university academic libraries, and school libraries. (Current data for these indexes are published annually by Research Associates of Washington. See *Inflation Measures for Schools, Colleges and Libraries, 1997 Update*.) Price indexes report the year-to-year price level of what is purchased. Dividing past expenditures per user unit by index values determines if purchasing power has been maintained. Future funding requirements to offset expected inflation may be estimated by projecting the indexes.

A price index compares the aggregate price level of a fixed market basket of goods and services in a given year with the price in the base year. To measure price change accurately, the *quality* and *quantity* of the items purchased must remain constant as defined in the base year. Weights attached to the importance of each item in the budget are changed infrequently—only when the relative *amount* of the various items purchased clearly shifts or when new items are introduced.

Public Library Price Index

The Public Library Price Index (PLPI) is designed for a hypothetical *average* public library. The index together with its various subcomponents are reported in Tables 2 through 6. The PLPI reflects the relative year-to-year price level of the goods and services purchased by public libraries for their current operations. The budget mix shown in Table 1 is based on national and state average expenditure patterns. Individual libraries may need to tailor the weighting scheme to match their own budget compositions.

The Public Library Price Index components are described below together with sources of the price series employed.

Personnel Compensation

PL1.0 Salaries and Wages

PL1.1 *Professional libraries*—Average salary of professional librarians at medium and large size libraries. Six positions are reported: director, deputy/associate/assistant director, department head/branch head, reference/information librarian, cataloger and/or classifier and children's and/or young adult services librarian. Source: Mary Jo Lynch, Margaret Myers, and Jeniece Guy, *ALA Survey of Librarian Salaries, 1994* Office for Research and Statistics, American Library Association, Chicago, IL, 1994.

(*text continues on page 445*)

Table 1 / Taxonomy of Public Library Current Operations Expenditures by Object Category, 1991–1992 estimate

Category	Mean	Percent	Distribution
Personnel Compensation			64.7
PL1.0 Salaries and Wages		81.8	
PL1.1 Professional librarians	44		
PL1.2 Other professional and managerial staff	6		
PL1.3 Technical staff (copy cataloging, circulation, binding, etc.)	43		
PL1.4 Support staff (clerical, custodial, guard, etc.)	7		
	100		
PL2.0 Fringe Benefits		18.2	
		100.0	
Acquisitions			15.2
PL3.0 Books and Serials		74.0	
PL3.1 Books printed	82		
PL3.1a Hardcover			
PL3.1b Trade paper			
PL3.1c Mass market paper			
PL3.2 Periodicals (U.S. and foreign titles)	16		
PL3.2a U.S. titles			
PL3.2b Foreign titles			
PL3.3 Other serials (newspapers, annuals, proceedings, etc.)	2		
	100		
PL4.0 Other Printed Materials		2.0	
PL5.0 Non-Print Media		22.0	
PL5.1 Microforms (microfiche and microfilm)	21		
PL5.2 Audio recordings (primarily instructional and children's content)	17		
PL5.2a Tape cassette			
PL5.2b Compact disk			
PL5.3 Video (TV) recordings (primarily books & children's content)	58		
PL5.3a VHS Cassette			
PL5.3b Laser disk			
PL5.4 Graphic image individual item use	2		
PL5.5 Computer files (CD-ROM, floppy disks, and tape)	2		
	100		
PL6.0 Electronic Services		2.0	
		100.0	
Operating Expenses			20.1
PL7.0 Office Operations		27.0	
PL7.1 Office expenses	20		
PL7.2 Supplies and materials	80		
	100		
PL8.0 Contracted Services		38.0	
PL9.0 Non-capital Equipment		1.0	
PL10.0 Utilities		34.0	
		100.0	100.0

Table 2 / Public Library Price Index and Major Component Subindexes, FY 1992 to 1996

1992=100 Fiscal year	Personnel Compensation		Acquisitions				Operating Expenses				Public Library Price Index^ PLPI
	Salaries and wages (PL1.0)	Fringe benefits (PL2.0)	Books and serials (PL3.0)	Other printed materials (PL4.0)	Non-print media (PL5.0)	Electronic services (PL6.0)	Office operations (PL7.0)	Contracted services (PL8.0)	Non-capital Equipment (PL9.0)	Utilities (PL10.0)	
1992	100	100	100	100	100	100	100	100	100	100	100
1993	102.5	104.8	101.6	102.9	75.3	101.9	99.2	102.6	101.8	101.5	101.5
1994	105.8	107.9	103.7	105.5	65.8	104.8	100.8	105.1	103.6	105.8	104.2
1995	110.5	110.6	104.9	107.7	64.8	108.5	102.6	107.7	105.7	103.8	107.2
1996	112.3	113.9	109.0	111.3	67.8	110.3	113.9	113.3	108.5	100.0	109.8
1993	2.50%	4.80%	1.60%	2.90%	-24.71%	1.90%	-.80%	2.60%	1.80%	1.50%	1.50%
1994	3.20%	3.00%	2.10%	2.50%	-12.61%	2.80%	1.60%	2.40%	1.70%	4.20%	2.60%
1995	4.40%	2.50%	1.20%	2.10%	-1.41%	3.50%	1.70%	2.50%	2.10%	-1.90%	2.90%
1996	1.60%	3.00%	3.90%	3.30%	4.70%	1.70%	11.1%	3.30%	2.60%	-3.60%	2.40%

^ PLPI weightings: See text.
Sources: See text.

Table 3 / Public Library Price Index, Personnel Compensation, FY 1992 to 1996

1992=100 Fiscal year	Salaries and wages						Salaries & wages index* (PL1.0)	Fringe benefits index (PL2.0)
	Professional librarians			Other professional & managerial (PL1.2)	Technical staff (PL1.3)	Support staff (PL1.4)		
	Medium size lib~	Large size lib~	Index^ (PL1.1)					
1992	100.0	100.0	100.0	100.0	100.0	100.0	100.0	100.0
1993	105.0	99.5	102.3	102.8	102.7	102.8	102.5	104.8
1994	109.2	102.7	106.0	105.7	105.7	106.0	105.8	107.9
1995	115.5	106.9	111.2	109.5	110.1	109.1	110.5	110.6
1996	113.7	108.9	111.3	112.9	113.2	112.1	112.3	113.9
1993	5.0	-0.5%	2.3%	2.8%	2.7%	2.8%	2.5%	4.8%
1994	4.0%	3.2%	3.6%	2.8%	2.9%	3.1%	3.2%	3.0%
1995	5.8%	4.1%	5.0%	3.6%	4.2%	2.9%	4.4%	2.5%
1996	-1.6%	1.9%	0.1%	3.1%	2.8%	2.7%	1.6%	3.0%

~ medium size libraries have service areas from 25,000 to 99,999 population; large libraries, 100,000 or more.
^ Professional librarian salary weights: 50% medium libraries + 50% large libraries.
* Salaries and wages index weights: 44% professional librarians + 6% other professional + 43% technical staff +7% support staff.
Sources: See text.

Table 4 / Public Library Price Index, Books and Serials, FY 1992 to 1996

1992=100	Books and Serials															
	Books printed							Periodicals						Other serials (newspapers)		
	Hardcover		Trade paper		Mass market		Books printed index* (PL3.1)	United States		Foreign				Other serials (newspapers)		Books & Serials index (PL3.0)	Other printed materials index (PL4.0)
Fiscal year	Price^	Index (PL3.1a)	Price^	Index (PL3.1b)	Price^	Index (PL3.1c)		Price^	Index (PL3.2a)	Price^	Index (PL3.2b)	Periodicals index~ (PL3.2)	Price	Index (PL3.3)		
1992	$12.85	100	$7.24	100	$2.71	100	100	$46.55	100.0	$119.55	100.0	100	$222.68	100	100	100
1993	12.98	101.0	7.40	102.2	2.79	103.0	101.2	48.12	103.4	125.70	105.7	103.6	229.92	103.3	101.6	102.9
1994	13.16	102.4	7.59	104.8	2.85	105.2	102.7	49.79	107.0	131.01	109.5	107.3	261.91	117.6	103.7	105.5
1995	13.19	102.6	7.75	107.0	2.98	110.0	103.2	51.76	111.2	140.87	117.8	112.0	270.22	121.3	104.9	107.7
1996	13.56	105.5	8.23	113.7	3.32	122.5	106.6	54.38	116.8	155.08	129.7	118.4	300.21	134.8	109.0	111.3
1997 (1997 data available from Research Associates of Washington)																
1993	1.00%		2.20%		3.00%		1.20%	3.40%			5.10%	3.60%		3.30%	1.60%	2.90%
1994	1.40%		2.60%		2.20%		1.50%	3.50%			4.20%	3.60%		13.90%	2.10%	2.50%
1995	0.20%		2.10%		4.60%		0.50%	4.00%			7.50%	4.40%		3.20%	1.20%	2.10%
1996	2.8%		6.20%		11.4%		3.3%	5.1%			10.1%	5.70%		11.1%	3.90%	3.30%

^ Eook and periodical prices are for calendar year. *Books prnted index weights: 89.5% hardcover + 8.2% trade paper + 2.3% mass market.
~ Feriodical index weights: 87.9% U.S.titles + 12.1% foreign titles. Shaded cell data estimated by Research Associates of Washingtor. Sources: See text.
^ Other serials prices are for calendar year. * Books & serials index weights: 82% books + 16% periodicals + 2% other serials. Sources: See text.

Table 5 / Public Library Price Index, Non-Print Media and On-Line Services, FY 1992 to 1996

1992=100 Fiscal year	Microforms (microfilm) Index (PL5.1)	Audio recordings					Video					Graphic image (PL5.4)	Computer files (CD-ROM)		Non-print media index* (PL5.0)	Electronic services index (PL6.0)
		Tape cassette		Compact disk		Audio recordings index* (PL5.2)	VHS cassette		Laser disk		Video index (PL5.3)					
		Price^	Index (PL5.2a)	Price^	Index (PL5.2b)		Price^	Index (PL5.3a)	Price^ (PL5.3b)	Index			Price^	Index (PL5.5)		
1992	100.0	$12.18	100	NA		100	$199.67	100	NA		100	100	$1,601	100	100	100
1993	104.3	11.73	96.3	NA		96.3	112.92	56.6	NA		56.6	97.3	1,793	112.0	75.3	101.9
1994	107.9	8.20	67.3	13.36	67.3	67.3	93.22	46.7	NA		46.7	108.4	1,945	121.5	65.8	104.8
1995	110.6	8.82	72.4	14.80	74.6	73.5	84.19	42.2	NA		42.2	111.3	1,913	119.5	64.8	108.5
1996	128.0	7.96	65.4	14.86	74.9	70.1	83.48	41.8	NA		41.8	114.5	1,988	124.2	67.8	110.3
1993	4.30%		-3.70%			-3.70%		-43.40%			-43.40%	-2.70%		12.0%	-24.70%	1.90%
1994	3.50%		-30.10%			-30.10%		-17.40%			-17.40%	11.40%		8.50%	-12.60%	2.80%
1995	2.50%		7.60%		10.80%	9.20%		-9.70%			-9.70%	2.70%		-1.60%	-1.50%	3.50%
1996	15.70%		-9.80%		0.04%	-4.60%		-0.80%			-0.08%	2.90%		3.90%	4.70%	1.70%

^ Prices are for immediate preceding calendar year, e.g., CY 1993 prices are reported for FY 1994.

* Audio recordings index weights: 50% tape cassette + 50% compact disk. Non-print media index weights: 21% microforms + 17% audio recordings +58% video + 2% graphic image + 2% computer files.

Sources: See text

Table 6 / Public Library Price Index, Operating Expenses, FY 1992 to 1996

1992=100	Office Operations		Office Operations index^ (PL7.0)	Contracted services index (PL8.0)	Noncapital equipment index (PL9.0)	Utilities index (PL10.0)
Fiscal year	Office expenses (PL7.1)	Supplies and materials (PL7.2)				
1992	100	100	100	100	100	100
1993	103.1	98.3	99.2	102.6	101.8	101.5
1994	107.3	99.2	100.8	105.1	103.6	105.8
1995	111.1	100.4	102.6	107.7	105.7	103.8
1996	117.8	117.9	113.9	111.3	108.5	100.0
1993	3.10%	-1.70%	-.80%	2.60%	1.80%	1.50%
1994	4.10%	1.0%	1.60%	2.40%	1.70%	4.20%
1995	3.50%	1.20%	1.70%	2.50%	2.10%	-1.90%
1996	6.1%	12.4%	11.1%	3.30%	2.60%	-3.60%

^ Office operations index weights: 20% office expenses + 80% supplies and materials.
Sources: See text.

(text continued from page 440)

PL1.2 *Other professional and managerial staff* (systems analyst, business manager, public relations, personnel, etc.)—Employment Cost Index (ECI) for wages and salaries for state and local government workers employed in "Executive, administrative, and managerial" occupations, *Employment Cost Index*, Bureau of Labor Statistics, U.S. Department of Labor, Washington, DC.

PL1.3 *Technical staff* (copy cataloging, circulation, binding, etc.)—ECI as above for government employees in "Service" occupations.

PL1.4 *Support staff* (clerical, custodial, guard, etc.)—ECI as above for government employees in "Administrative support, including clerical" occupations.

PL2.0 Fringe Benefits

ECI as above for state and local government worker "Benefits."

Acquisitions

PL3.0 Books and Serials

PL3.1 *Books printed*—Weighted average of sale prices (including jobber's discount) of hardcover (PL3.1a), trade paper (PL3.1b), and mass market paperback books (PL3.1c) sold to public libraries. Excludes university press publications and reference works. Source: Frank Daly, Baker & Taylor Books, Bridgewater, NJ.

PL3.2 *Periodicals*—Publisher's prices of sales of approximately 2,400 U.S. serial titles (PL3.2a) and 115 foreign serials (PL3.2b) sold to public libraries. Source: *Serials Prices 1991–1995*, EBSCO Subscription Services, Birmingham, AL.

PL3.3 *Other serials* (newspapers, annuals, proceedings, etc.)—Average prices of approximately 170 U.S. daily newspapers. Source: Genevieve S. Owens,

University of Missouri, St. Louis, and Wilba Swearingen, Louisiana State University Medical Center. Reported by Adrian W. Alexander, "Prices of U.S. and Foreign Published Materials," in *The Bowker Annual*, R. R. Bowker, New Providence, NJ.

PL4.0 Other Printed Materials (manuscripts, documents, pamphlets, sheet music, printed material for the handicapped, etc.)

No direct price series exists for this category. The proxy price series used is the Producer Price Index for publishing pamphlets and catalogs and directories, Bureau of Labor Statistics.

PL5.0 Non-Print Media

PL5.1 *Microforms*—Producer Price Index for micropublishing in microform, including original and republished material, Bureau of Labor Statistics.

PL5.2 *Audio recordings*

> PL5.2a *Tape cassette*—Cost per cassette of sound recording. Source: Dana Alessi, Baker & Taylor Books, Bridgewater, NJ. Reported by Alexander in *The Bowker Annual*, R. R. Bowker, New Providence, NJ.

> PL5.2b *Compact disk*—Cost per compact disk. Source: See Alessi above.

PL5.3 *Video (TV) recordings*

> PL5.3a. *VHS cassette*—Cost per video. Source: See Alessi above.

> PL5.3b. *Laser disk*—No price series currently available.

PL5.4 *Graphic image* (individual use of such items as maps, photos, art work, single slides, etc.). The following proxy is used. Average median weekly earnings for the following two occupational groups: painters, sculptors, craft artists, and artist printmakers; and photographers. Source: *Employment and Earnings Series*, U.S. Bureau of Labor Statistics

PL5.5 *Computer files* (CD-ROM, floppy disks, and tape). Average price of CD-ROM disks. Source: Martha Kellogg and Theodore Kellogg, University of Rhode Island. Reported by Alexander in *The Bowker Annual*, R. R. Bowker, New Providence, NJ.

PL6.0 Electronic Services

Average price for selected digital electronic computer and telecommunications networking available to libraries. Source: This source has requested anonymity.

Operating Expenses

PL7.0 Office Operations

PL7.1 *Office expenses* (telephone, postage and freight, publicity and printing, travel, professional fees, automobile operating cost, etc.)—The price series used for office expenses consists of the subindex for printed materials (PL4.0) described above; Consumer Price Index values for telephone and postage; CPI values for public transportation; the IRS allowance for individual business travel as reported by Runzheimer International; and CPI values for college tuition as a proxy for professional fees.

PL7.2 *Supplies and materials*—Producer Price Index price series for office supplies, writing papers, and pens and pencils. Source: U.S. Bureau of Labor Statistics.

PL8.0 Contracted Services (outside contracts for cleaning, building and grounds maintenance, equipment rental and repair, acquisition processing, binding, auditing, legal, payroll, etc.)

Prices used for contracted services include ECI wages paid material handlers, equipment cleaners, helpers, and laborers; average weekly earnings of production or non-supervisory workers in the printing and publishing industry, and the price of printing paper, as a proxy for binding costs; ECI salaries of attorneys, directors of personnel, and accountant, for contracted consulting fees; and ECI wages of precision production, craft, and repair occupations for the costs of equipment rental and repair.

PL9.0 Non-Capital Equipment

The type of equipment generally purchased as part of current library operations is usually small and easily movable. To be classified as "equipment" rather than as "expendable utensils" or "supplies," an item generally must cost $50 or more and have a useful life of at least three years. Examples may be hand calculators, small TVs, simple cameras, tape recorders, pagers, fans, desk lamps, books, etc. Equipment purchased as an operating expenditure is usually not depreciated. Items priced for this category include PPI commodity price series for machinery and equipment, office and store machines/equipment, hand tools, cutting tools and accessories, scales and balances, electrical measuring instruments, television receivers, musical instruments, photographic equipment, sporting and athletic goods, and books and periodicals.

PL10.0 Utilities

This subindex is a composite of the Producer Price Index series for natural gas, residual fuels, and commercial electric power, and the Consumer Price Index series for water and sewerage services. Source: U.S. Bureau of Labor Statistics.

Academic Library Price Indexes

The two academic library price indexes—the University Library Price Index (ULPI) and the College Library Price Index (CLPI)—together with their various subcomponents are reported for 1992–1995 in Tables 8–12A. The two indexes report the relative year-to-year price level of the staff salaries, acquisitions, and other goods and services purchased by university and college libraries respectively for their current operations. Universities are the 500 institutions with doctorate programs responding to the National Center for Education Statistics, U.S. Department of Education, *Academic Library Survey, 1992*. Colleges are the 1,472 responding institutions with master's and baccalaureate programs.

The composition of the library budgets involved, defined for pricing purposes, and the 1992 estimated national weighting structure are presented in Table 7.

The priced components are organized in three major divisions: personnel compensation; acquisitions; and contracted services, supplies, and equipment.

The various components of the University and College Library Price Indexes are described in this section. Different weightings for components are designated in the tables "UL" for university libraries, "CL" for college libraries, and "AL" common for both types. Source citations for the acquisitions price series are listed.

UL1.0 and CL1.0 Salaries and Wages

AL1.1 *Administrators* consists of the chief, deputy associate, and assistant librarian, e.g., important staff members having administrative responsibilities for management of the library. Administrators are priced by the head librarian salary series reported by the College and University Personnel Association (CUPA).

AL1.2 *Librarians* are all other professional library staff. Librarians are priced by the average of the median salaries for circulation/catalog, acquisition, technical service, and public service librarians reported by CUPA.

AL1.3 *Other professionals* are personnel who are not librarians in positions normally requiring at least a bachelor's degree. This group includes curators, archivists, computer specialists, budget officers, information and system specialists, subject bibliographers, and media specialists. Priced by the Higher Education Price Index (HEPI) faculty salary price series (H1.1) as a proxy.

AL1.4 *Nonprofessional staff* includes technical assistants, secretaries, and clerical, shipping, and storage personnel who are specifically assigned to the library and covered by the library budget. This category excludes general custodial and maintenance workers and student employees. This staff category is dominated by office-type workers and is priced by the HEPI clerical workers price series (H2.3) reported by the BLS Employment Cost Index.

AL1.5 *Students* are usually employed part-time for near minimum hourly wages. In some instances these wages are set by work-study program requirements of the institution's student financial aid office. The proxy price series used for student wages is the Employment Cost Index series for non-farm laborers, U.S. Bureau of Labor Statistics.

AL2.0 Fringe Benefits

The fringe benefits price series for faculty used in the HEPI is employed in pricing fringe benefits for library personnel.

UL3.0 and CL3.0 Books and Serials

UL3.1a *Books printed, universities.* Book acquisitions for university libraries are priced by the North American Academic Books price series reporting the average list price of approximately 60,000 titles sold to college and university libraries by four of the largest book vendors. Compiled by Stephen Bosch, University of Arizona.

CL3.1a *Books printed, colleges.* Book acquisitions for college libraries are priced by the price series for U.S. College Books representing approximately 6,300 titles compiled from book reviews appearing in *Choice* during the calendar year. Compiled by Donna Alsbury, Florida Center for Library Automation.

AL3.1b *Foreign Books.* Books with foreign titles *and* published in foreign countries are priced using U.S. book imports data. William S. Lofquist, U.S. Department of Commerce.

AL3.2a *Periodicals, U.S. titles.* U.S. periodicals are priced by the average subscription price of approximately 2,100 U.S. serial titles purchased by college and university libraries reported by EBSCO Subscription Services, Birmingham, AL.

AL3.2b *Periodicals, Foreign.* Foreign periodicals are priced by the average subscription price of approximately 600 foreign serial titles purchased by college and university libraries reported by EBSCO Subscription Services.

AL3.3 *Other Serials* (newspapers, annuals, proceedings, etc.). Average prices of approximately 170 U.S. daily newspapers. Source: Genevieve S. Owens, University of Missouri, St. Louis, and Wilba Swearingen, Louisiana State University Medical Center. Reported by Adrian W. Alexander, "Prices of U.S. and Foreign Published Materials," in *The Bowker Annual*, R. R. Bowker, New Providence, NJ.

Other Printed Materials

These acquisitions include manuscripts, documents, pamphlets, sheet music, printed material for the handicapped, and so forth. No direct price series exists for this category. The proxy price series used is the Producer Price Index (PPI) for publishing pamphlets (PC 2731-9) and catalogs and directories (PCU2741#B), Bureau of Labor Statistics, U.S. Department of Labor.

AL5.0 Non-Print Media

AL5.1 *Microforms.* Producer Price Index for micropublishing in microform, including original and republished material (PC 2741-597), Bureau of Labor Statistics.

AL5.2 *Audio recordings*
   AL5.2a *Tape cassette*—Cost per cassette of sound recording. Source: Dana Alessi, Baker & Taylor Books, Bridgewater, NJ. Reported by Alexander in *The Bowker Annual*, R. R. Bowker, New Providence, NJ.

   AL5.2b *Compact Disk*—Cost per compact disk. Source: See Alessi above.

AL5.3 *Video (TV) recordings*
   PL5.3a *VHS cassette*—cost per video. Source: See Alessi above.

AL5.4 *Graphic image* (individual use of such items as maps, photos, art work, single slides, etc.). No direct price series exists for graphic image materials. Average median weekly earnings for two related occupational groups (painters, sculptors, craft artists; artist printmakers; and photographers) is used as a proxy. these earnings series are reported in *Employment and Earnings Series*, U.S. bureau of Labor Statistics.

AL5.5 *Computer files* (CD-ROM floppy disks, and tape). Average price of CD-ROM disks; primarily bibliographic, abstracts, and other databases of interest to academic libraries. Source: Developed from *Faxon Guide to CD-ROM* by Martha Kellogg and Theodore Kellogg, University of Rhode Island. Reported by Alexander in *The Bowker Annual*, R. R. Bowker, New Providence, NJ.

AL6.0 Electronic Services

Average price for selected digital electronic computer and telecommunications networking available to libraries. The source of this price series has requested anonymity.

AL7.0 Binding/Preservation

In-house maintenance of the specialized skills required for binding is increasingly being replaced by contracting out this service at all but the largest libraries. No wage series exists exclusively for binding. As a proxy, the Producer Price Index (PPI) for bookbinding and related work (PC 2789) is used. Source: Bureau of Labor Statistics, U.S. Department of Labor.

AL8.0 Contracted Services

Services contracted by libraries include such generic categories as communications, postal service, data processing, and printing and duplication. The HEPI contracted services subcomponent (H4.0), which reports these items, is used as the price series. (In this instance the data processing component of H4.0 generally represents the library's payment for use of a central campus computer service.) However, libraries may also contract out certain specialized activities such as ongoing public access cataloging (OPAC) that are not distinctively priced in this AL8.0 component.

AL9.0 Supplies and Materials

Office supplies, writing papers, and pens and pencils constitute the bulk of library supplies and materials and are priced by these BLS categories for the Producer Price Index, Bureau of Labor Statistics, U.S. Department of Labor.

AL10.0 Equipment

This category is limited to small, easily movable, relatively inexpensive and short-lived items that are not carried on the books as depreciable capital equipment. Examples can include personal computers, hand calculators, projectors, fans, cameras, tape recorders, small TVs, etc. The HEPI equipment price series (H6.0) has been used for pricing.

Table 7 / Budget Composition of University Library and College Library Current Operations by Object Category, FY 1992 Estimate

Category	University Libraries Percent Distribution	College Libraries Percent Distribution
Personnel Compensation		
1.0 Salaries and wages.	43.4	47.2
1.1 Administrators (head librarian)	10	25
1.2 Librarians	20	15
1.3 Other professionals^	10	5
1.4 Nonprofessional staff	50	40
1.5 Students hourly employed	10	15
	100	100
2.0 Fringe benefits	10.6	11.5
Acquisitions		
3.0 Books and Serials	28.5	24.8
3.1 Books printed	35	47
3.1a U.S. titles	80	95
3.1b Foreign titles	20	5
3.2 Periodicals	60	48
3.2a U.S. titles	80	95
3.2b Foreign titles	20	5
3.3 Other serials (newspapers, annuals, proceedings, etc.)	5	5
	100	100
4.0 Other Printed Materials*	1.2	0.7
5.0 Non-Print Media	1.6	3.3
5.1 Microforms (microfiche and microfilm)	45	45
5.2 Audio recordings	5	5
5.2a Tape cassette		
5.2b Compact disc (CDs)		
5.3 Video (TV) VHS recordings	15	15
5.4 Graphic image individual item use~	5	5
5.5 Computer materials (CD-ROM, floppy disks, and tape)	30	30
	100	100
6.0. Electronic Services^^	4.0	3.5
Contracted Services, Supplies, Equipment		
7.0 Binding/preservation.	1.3	0.8
8.0 Services**	4.4	3.1
9.0 Supplies and materials	3.1	2.6
10.0 Equipment (non-capital)#	1.9	2.5
	100	100

^ Other professional and managerial staff includes systems analyst, business manager, public relations, personnel, etc.
* Other printed materials includes manuscripts, documents, pamphlets, sheet music, printed material for the handicapped, etc.
~ Graphic image individual item use includes maps, photos, art work, single slides, etc.
^^Electronic services includes software license fees, network intra-structure costs, terminal access to the Internet, desktop computer operating budget, and subscription services.
**Contracted services includes outside contracts for communications, postal service, data processing, printing and duplication, equipment rental and repair, acquisition processing, etc.
Relatively inexpensive items not carried on the books as depreciable capital equipment. Examples include microform and audiovisual equipment, personal computers, hand calculators, projectors, fans, cameras, tape recorders, and small TVs.
Source: Derived, in part, from data published in *Academic Libraries: 1992*, National Center for Education Statistics, USDE.

Table 8 / University Library Price Index and Major Component Subindexes, FY 1992 to 1996

1992=100 Fiscal year	Personnel Compensation		Acquisitions					Operating Expenses			University Library Price Index^
	Salaries and wages (UL1.0)	Fringe benefits (AL2.0)	Books and serials (UL3.0)	Other printed materials (AL4.0)	Non-print media (AL5.0)	Electronic services (AL6.0)	Binding/preservation (AL7.0)	Contracted services (AL8.0)	Supplies and material (AL9.0)	Equipment (AL10.0)	ULPI
1992	100.0	100.0	100.0	100.0	100.0	100.0	100.0	100.0	100.0	100.0	100.0
1993	103.2	105.4	105.4	102.9	98.7	101.9	100.5	102.6	98.3	101.8	103.7
1994	106.3	110.5	112.2	105.5	100.8	104.8	101.2	106.2	99.2	103.6	107.9
1995	110.0	114.2	120.3	107.7	102.1	108.5	102.9	108.4	100.4	105.7	112.6
1996	113.4	115.8	130.2	111.3	110.3	110.3	107.1	112.4	112.9	108.5	118.0

^ ULPI weights: See table 3-A.
Sources: See text.

Table 9 / College Library Price Index and Major Component Subindexes, FY 1992 to 1996

1992=100 Fiscal year	Personnel Compensation		Acquisitions					Operating Expenses			College Library Price Index^
	Salaries and wages (CL1.0)	Fringe benefits (AL2.0)	Books and serials (CL3.0)	Other printed materials (AL4.0)	Non-print media (AL5.0)	Electronic services (AL6.0)	Binding/preservation (AL7.0)	Contracted services (AL8.0)	Supplies and material (AL9.0)	Equipment (AL10.0)	CLPI
1992	100.0	100.0	100.0	100.0	100.0	100.0	100.0	100.0	100.0	100.0	100.0
1993	103.5	105.4	107.2	102.9	98.7	101.9	100.5	102.6	98.3	101.8	104.2
1994	106.5	110.5	113.1	105.5	100.8	104.8	101.2	106.2	99.2	103.6	108.2
1995	110.0	114.2	118.6	107.7	102.1	108.5	102.9	108.4	100.4	105.7	111.8
1996	113.8	115.8	126.0	111.3	110.3	110.3	107.1	112.4	112.9	108.5	116.6

^ CLPI weights: See table 3-A
Sources: See text.

Table 10 / Academic Library Price Indexes, Personnel Compensation, FY 1992 to 1996

1992=100 Fiscal year	Administrators (head librarian) (AL1.1)	Librarians (AL1.2)	Other professional (AL1.3)	Non-professional (AL1.4)	Students hourly employed (AL1.5)	Salaries and wages indexes Universities* (UL1.0)	Colleges^ (CL1.0)	Fringe benefits index (AL2.0)
1992	100.0	100.0	100.0	100.0	100.0	100.0	100.0	100.0
1993	105.0	102.6	102.5	103.2	102.7	103.2	103.5	105.4
1994	107.3	106.0	105.6	106.6	105.4	106.3	106.5	110.5
1995	110.6	110.2	109.3	110.1	108.5	110.0	110.0	114.2
1996	116.3	113.6	112.5	113.3	111.8	113.4	113.8	115.8

* University library salaries and wages index weights: 10 percent administrators, 20 percent librarians, 10 percent other professionals, 50 percent nonprofessional staff, and 10 percent students.

^ College library salaries and wages index weights: 25 percent administrators, 15 percent librarians, 5 percent other professionals, 40 percent nonprofessional staff, and 15 percent students.

Sources: See text.

Table 11 / Academic Library Price Indexes, Books and Serials, FY 1992 to 1996

1992=100 Fiscal year	Books printed North American Price~	Index (UL3.1a)	U.S. college Price~	Index (CL3.1a)	Foreign books Price	Index (AL3.1b)	Book indexes University* (UL3.1)	College^ (CL3.1)
1992	$45.84	100.0	$44.55	100.0	NA	100.0	100.0	100.0
1993	$45.91	100.2	$47.48	106.6		98.9	99.9	106.2
1994	$47.17	102.9	$48.92	109.8		96.7	101.7	109.2
1995	$48.16	105.1	$47.93	107.6		~05.0	105.0	107.5
1996	$48.11	105.0	$48.17	108.1		108.3	105.6	108.1

~ Prices are for previous calendar year, e.g., CY 1993 prices are reported for FY 1994.

* University library books printed index weights: 80 percent U.S. titles, 20 percent foreign titles.

^ College Library books printed index weights: 95 percent U.S. titles, 5 percent foreign titles.

Sources: See text.

NA Not Available

Table 11A / Academic Library Price Indexes, Books and Serials, FY 1992 to 1996

| 1992=100 | Periodicals | | | | | | Other serials (newspapers) | | Books and serials indexes | | Other printed materials index (AL4.0) |
| | US titles | | Foreign | | Periodical indexes | | | | | | |
Fiscal year	Price~	Index (AL3.2a)	Price~	Index (AL3.2b)	University* (UL3.2)	College^ (CL3.2)	Price~	Index (AL3.3)	University** (UL3.0)	College^^ (CL3.0)	
1992	$125.86	100.0	$341.02	100.0	100.0	100.0	$222.68	100.0	100.0	100.0	100.0
1993	$136.33	108.3	$377.48	110.7	108.8	108.4	$229.92	103.3	105.4	107.1	102.9
1994	$148.48	118.0	$400.82	117.5	117.9	118.0	$261.91	117.6	112.2	113.8	105.5
1995	$162.76	129.3	$437.96	128.4	129.1	129.3	$270.22	121.3	120.3	118.6	107.7
1996	$178.80	142.1	$518.78	152.1	144.1	142.6	$300.21	134.8	130.2	126.0	111.3

~ Prices are for previous calendar year, e.g., CY 1993 prices are reported for FY 1994.
* University library periodicals index weights: 80 percent U.S. titles, 20 percent foreign titles.
^ College library periodicals index weights: 95 percent U.S. titles, 5 percent foreign titles.
** University library books and serials index weights: 35 percent books, 60 percent periodicals, 5 percent other serials.
^^ College library books and serials index weights: 47 percent books, 48 percent periodicals, 5 percent other serials.
Sources: See text.

Table 12 / Academic Library Price Indexes, Non-Print Media and Electronic Services, FY 1992 to 1996

| 1992=100 | Microforms (microfilm) Index (AL5.1) | Audio recordings | | | | | Video | | |
| | | Tape cassette | | Compact disc | | Audio recordings index* (AL5.2) | VHS cassette | | Video index (AL5.3) |
Fiscal year		Price~	Index (AL5.2a)	Price~	Index (AL5.2b)		Price~	Index (AL5.3a)	
1992	100.0	$12.18	100.0	NA		100.0	$199.67	100.0	100.0
1993	104.3	$11.73	96.3	NA		96.3	$112.92	56.6	56.6
1994	107.9	$8.20	67.3	$13.36	67.3	67.3	$93.22	46.7	46.7
1995	110.6	$8.82	72.4	$14.80	74.6	73.5	$84.19	42.2	42.2
1996	128.0	$7.96	65.4	$14.86	74.9	70.1	$83.48	41.8	41.8

~ Prices are for previous calendar year, e.g., CY 1993 prices are reported for FY 1994.
* Audio recordings index weights: 50 percent tape cassette, 50 percent compact disc.
Sources: See text.
NA Not Available

Table 12A / Academic Library Price Indexes, Non-Print Media and Electronic Services, FY 1992 to 1996

1992=100 Fiscal year	Non-print Med			Non-print media index# (AL5.0)	Electronic services index (AL6.0)	Total Acquisitions Indexes		
	Graphic image (AL5.4)	Computer files (CD-ROM) Price~	Index (AL5.5)			Univ*	College^	All Institutions**
1992	100.0	$1,601	100.0	100.0	100.0	100.0	100.0	100.0
1993	97.3	$1,793	112.0	98.7	101.9	104.6	105.6	104.9
1994	108.4	$1,945	121.5	100.8	104.8	110.6	111.3	110.8
1995	111.3	$1,961	122.5	102.1	108.5	117.7	115.6	117.1
1996	114.5	$1,986	124.0	110.3	110.3	126.4	122.4	125.3

~ Prices are for immediate preceding calendar year, e.g., CY 1993 prices are reported for FY 1994.

Non-print media index weights: 45 percent microforms, 5 percent audio recordings, 15 percent video, 5 percent graphic image, 30 percent computer materials.

* University total acquisitions 1992 weights: 81 percent books, 3 percent other printed material, 5 percent non-print media, and 11 percent electronic services.

^ College total acquisitions 1992 weights: 77 percent books, 2 percent other printed material, 10 percent non-print media, and 11 percent electronic services.

** All institutions total acquisitions weights: 72 percent university acquisitions, 28 percent college acquisitions.

Sources: See text.

State Rankings of Selected Public Library Data, 1995

State	Circulation Transactions per capita*	Reference Transactions per capita	Book and Serials Vols. per capita	ALA-MLS Librarians per 25,000	Operating Expenditures per capita	Local Income per capita
Alabama	49	40	39	44	44	43
Alaska	33	30	23	18	8	7
Arizona	30	11	45	25	29	19
Arkansas	48	41	37	49	50	47
California	41	15	47	24	33	29
Colorado	12	8	33	17	11	9
Connecticut	13	12	10	4	5	6
Delaware	43	39	42	45	39	36
Dist. of Columbia †	51	1	8	2	3	1
Florida	36	2	49	23	30	27
Georgia	42	38	48	26	38	42
Hawaii	28	4	25	8	21	51
Idaho	17	26	22	43	34	31
Illinois	19	7	19	11	7	2
Indiana	2	18	13	10	6	8
Iowa	10	n.a.	14	30	31	30
Kansas	6	9	6	19	12	14
Kentucky	35	43	41	51	45	41
Louisiana	45	37	35	36	36	33
Maine	18	n.a.	1	27	26	32
Maryland	7	13	31	1	10	17
Massachusetts	24	n.a.	4	7	14	15
Michigan	37	24	28	14	23	24
Minnesota	5	5	26	20	13	13
Mississippi	50	42	46	46	51	49
Missouri	16	25	12	40	25	21
Montana	31	29	24	48	43	34
Nebraska	14	14	15	32	22	16
Nevada	38	31	40	39	32	7
New Hampshire	20	33	7	13	20	25
New Jersey	32	21	16	5	4	5
New Mexico	27	n.a.	20	22	27	28
New York	23	3	9	3	1	3
North Carolina	34	28	43	33	40	38
North Dakota	21	36	18	50	46	45
Ohio	1	6	17	9	2	48
Oklahoma	29	35	36	37	41	35
Oregon	4	32	34	21	18	11
Pennsylvania	40	34	38	28	37	44
Rhode Island	26	23	11	6	15	20
South Carolina	46	16	50	29	42	40
South Dakota	11	n.a.	5	41	28	18
Tennessee	47	19	51	42	49	46
Texas	44	20	44	31	47	39
Utah	8	n.a.	30	35	24	26
Vermont	25	n.a.	2	34	35	37
Virginia	22	17	32	16	19	22
Washington	3	n.a.	27	12	9	4
West Virginia	39	27	29	47	48	50
Wisconsin	9	10	21	15	17	12
Wyoming	15	22	3	38	16	10

Source: U.S. Department of Education, National Center for Education Statistics, Federal-State Cooperative System (FSCS) for Public Library Data, Public Libraries Survey, Fiscal Year 1995.

* Per capita and per 1,000 population calculations are based on population of legal service area.

† The District of Columbia, while not a state, is included in the state rankings. Special care should be used in making comparisons.

n.a.=not applicable.

Library Buildings, 1997:
The Renovation Role Model

Bette-Lee Fox

Managing Editor, *Library Journal*

Maya L. Kremen

Intern, *Library Journal*

Just when you thought you'd seen the last fashion metaphor, *Library Journal* jumps in with its own brand of style watching. This year, among the 225 public projects completed between July 1, 1996 and June 30, 1997, public library construction has taken on the challenge of the super remodel.

Step aside, Kate Moss. Our super remodels are weighty, costly affairs that, one hopes, will pay off in exposure and service appeal. Among the largest of the 128 addition/renovation projects are the Public Library of Cincinnati and Hamilton County ($49.4 million), the Louis Stokes Wing of the Cleveland Public Library ($67 million), and Multnomah County Central Library, Portland, Oregon ($25.7 million).

The 97 new building projects aren't exactly off the rack, with the new State Library of Virginia costing $51 million and the combined Sahara West Library and Fine Arts Museum in Las Vegas at $18.8 million.

Local funding for all public libraries remains strong (70 percent), but this year state funds, with the inclusion of two large projects, exceed 20 percent of total support.

Academic projects hold steady at the 1996 level of 40, with the newest stars including the Walsh Library of Fordham University ($54 million) and the Kansas State University addition/remodel ($30 million).

The total number of completed public projects is the third lowest in ten years, but expenditures are the second highest of all time. That old fashion adage holds true: the less material, the higher the price tag.

These were three public projects of note:

- Thomas Jefferson Building, Library of Congress, Washington, D.C. When it opened in 1897, the Jefferson building was called "the most beautiful public building in America." Now, after more than a decade of restoration and modernization, the Italian Renaissance building boasts a renovated 1925 Coolidge Auditorium (used for concerts), a new visitors center, new building systems, and a vastly refurbished Main Reading Room, which includes newly wired reader desks, additional seating, and (for the first time) carpeting. The project, which includes renovation of the nearby 1939 John Adams Building, has cost nearly $100 million.

- Multomah County Central Library, Portland, Oregon. To some Portlanders strolling by, the 1913 Multomah County Central Library may just seem spiffed up, but on the inside, a $26 million renovation and expansion

Adapted from the December 1997 issue of *Library Journal,* which also lists architects' addresses.

has wrought changes subtle and significant. New fourth and fifth floors centralize staff functions, thus increasing public space and making accessible 70 percent of the collection (up from 30 percent). Building system renovations (e.g., elevators, electrical, air conditioning) have been quietly centralized. Artwork, carpet, and light fixtures reflect the project's "Garden of Knowledge" theme.

- Cleveland Public Library. Like all good contemporary libraries, the new ten-story Louis Stokes Wing (named for a longtime Cleveland member of Congress) of the Cleveland Public Library serves as a bridge to both the past and the future. Its corner pavilions acknowledge the Beaux-Arts main library (and other nearby civic buildings), and its marble comes from the same source. But this $67 million addition, unlike the original 1925 library, orients the patron to points outside and beyond the building. Its painting scheme borrows colors from the main library and adds new accents. Providing 268,000 square feet of space, the new wing more than doubles the library's capacity, maintaining the library's open-stack tradition and expanding its access to electronic services.

Table 1 / New Public Library Buildings, 1997

Community	Pop. ('000)	Code	Project Cost	Const. Cost	Gross Sq. Ft.	Sq. Ft. Cost	Equip. Cost	Site Cost	Other Costs	Volumes	Federal Funds	State Funds	Local Funds	Gift Funds	Architect
Alabama															
Daphne	15	M	$2,895,371	$2,378,915	18,500	$128.59	$255,092	Owned	$261,364	67,000	0	0	$2,895,371	0	Gatlin Hudson
Eutaw	12	M	578,152	477,990	5,850	81.71	38,370	10,000	51,792	22,000	268,785	0	203,508	105,859	Ray Torode
Hazel Green	7	B	289,000	172,000	5,000	34.4	50,000	50,000	17,000	40,000	0	0	97,000	192,000	L. Hughes Assocs.
Luverne	3	M	502,675	408,047	5,290	77.14	44,484	15,605	34,539	12,120	213,450	0	10,300	284,737	Goodwyn, Mills...
Madison	28	B	2,140,000	1,400,000	15,000	93.33	300,000	320,000	120,000	120,000	0	22,000	1,498,000	620,000	L. Hughes Assocs.
Arizona															
Arivaca	2	B	409,705	272,767	2,600	104.91	56,029	22,506	58,403	12,500	50,000	0	359,705	0	CDG Architects
Phoenix	93	B	2,294,589	1,540,434	14,635	105.26	79,378	374,366	300,411	75,000	0	0	2,237,289	57,300	Randall Fonce
Scottsdale	27	B	1,538,256	661,836	8,400	78.79	594,360	261,360	20,700	25,000	0	0	792,346	745,910	Lescher & Mahoney
Arkansas															
Little Rock	23	B	1,390,419	1,118,419	8,500	131.57	100,000	75,000	97,000	30,000	0	0	1,390,419	0	Arch. Innovations
California															
Belvedere-Tiburon	11	M	3,490,600	2,360,000	10,500	224.76	418,000	Owned	712,600	60,000	0	0	1,600,000	1,900,000	Bull, Stockwell & Allen
Danville	62	B	7,155,784	4,832,686	17,000	284.28	286,380	1,473,000	563,418	70,000	0	0	6,955,784	200,000	Bull, Stockwell & Allen
Descanso	3	B	210,574	149,327	2,000	74.66	30,016	Owned	31,231	6,500	79,500	0	56,574	74,500	San Diego Cty.
Foster City	30	B	7,319,385	5,801,197	34,150	169.87	570,000	Leased	948,188	70,000	0	0	7,149,385	170,000	Arquitectonica
Jacumba	2	B	259,367	194,000	2,400	80.83	39,367	Owned	26,000	7,230	259,367	0	0	0	San Diego Cty.
Lancaster	123	B	13,457,762	6,388,573	48,721	131.13	1,049,235	3,944,411	2,075,543	320,000	0	0	13,418,162	39,600	Kudrave; Walton...
Los Angeles	44	B	3,311,345	2,943,047	9,035	325.74	162,333	Owned	205,965	40,000	0	0	3,311,345	0	Steven Ehrlich
Los Angeles	75	B	6,053,108	3,829,410	17,543	218.29	185,692	1,793,841	244,165	45,000	65,000	0	5,988,108	0	Lang/Lampert
Oakland	20	B	6,800,000	3,206,892	15,530	206.9	341,905	1,539,833	1,711,370	45,965	0	2,639,419	4,160,581	0	Marquis Assocs.
Redondo Beach	65	MS	15,354,332	10,391,240	143,037	72.65	369,301	3,530,203	1,063,588	200,000	0	9,980,315	5,374,017	0	Thirtieth St. Architects
San Diego	21	B	4,213,935	2,246,959	13,102	171.5	175,704	784,080	1,007,192	80,000	0	0	4,213,935	0	M.W. Steele Group
San Diego	50	B	6,774,637	2,332,784	12,484	186.86	128,563	3,346,750	966,540	80,000	0	0	2,931,637	3,843,000	Manuel Oncina
Colorado															
Avon	21	M	4,010,000	2,874,500	18,500	155.39	200,000	555,000	380,500	80,000	0	0	3,455,000	555,000	Snowden & Hopkins
Frisco	18	M	n/a	n/a	13,000	n/a	106,000	Owned	n/a	43,000	0	0	n/a	10,000	Caudill Gustafson

Symbol Code: B—Branch Library; BS—Branch & System Headquarters; M—Main Library; MS—Main & System Headquarters; S—System Headquarters; n/a—not available

Table 1 / New Public Library Buildings, 1997 *(cont.)*

Community	Pop. ('000)	Code	Project Cost	Const. Cost	Gross Sq. Ft.	Sq. Ft. Cost	Equip. Cost	Site Cost	Other Costs	Volumes	Federal Funds	State Funds	Local Funds	Gift Funds	Architect
La Junta	12	M	1,197,585	963,585	10,500	91.77	159,000	Owned	75,000	40,000	0	0	1,197,585	0	Barnes Architects
Windsor	7	M	1,842,089	1,343,979	14,102	95.3	210,805	100,000	187,305	50,000	0	0	1,990,150	111,350	Gifford Spurck
Connecticut															
New Hartford	6	M	2,285,815	1,341,228	9,200	145.79	350,000	395,284	199,303	40,000	100,000	350,000	0	1,835,815	Robert Orr & Assocs.
Florida															
Brandenton	60	B	1,408,331	1,067,000	15,000	71.13	120,000	Owned	221,331	75,000	400,000	0	908,331	100,000	Fawley Bryant
Fruit Cove	18	B	1,147,000	911,000	10,000	91.1	140,000	Owned	96,000	44,000	0	0	1,147,000	100,000	Hunter/McKellips
Tampa	20	B	4,375,000	2,600,000	25,000	104	347,180	Owned	1,427,820	100,000	0	0	4,375,000	0	Harvard Jolly Clees
Tampa	25	B	1,851,000	1,074,880	8,000	134.36	93,000	210,000	473,120	30,000	0	0	1,851,000	0	Robinson Green
Tarpon Springs	25	M	2,419,685	1,757,054	20,000	87.85	160,586	334,702	167,343	95,000	400,000	0	1,394,685	625,000	Gee & Jensen
Georgia															
Ball Ground	20	B	1,138,532	846,020	9,000	94.01	191,043	Owned	101,469	44,000	0	802,380	336,152	0	Walden, Ashworth
Fayetteville	88	B	4,593,728	2,821,610	28,000	100.78	580,500	500,000	691,618	100,000	0	1,999,044	2,539,574	55,110	Manley, Spangler, Smith
Folkston	n/a	B	599,068	448,940	5,000	89.79	94,330	Owned	55,798	30,500	0	505,277	87,555	6,236	John Tuten
Illinois															
Chicago	22	B	4,323,000	2,822,400	13,688	206.2	275,000	Owned	1,225,600	500,000	0	0	4,323,000	0	InterActive Design
Chicago	15	B	3,000,000	2,370,043	13,688	173.15	201,558	Owned	428,399	500,000	0	500,000	2,500,000	0	InterActive Design
Danville	34	M	4,676,236	3,471,211	39,800	87.22	341,731	319,000	544,294	167,970	0	400,000	2,873,000	1,403,236	Phillips Swager
Darien	44	M	5,892,326	4,116,276	43,394	94.86	797,858	491,400	486,792	140,000	0	250,000	5,632,468	9,858	LZT/Filliung
Indiana															
North Vernon	27	M	2,350,000	1,988,000	33,792	58.83	183,637	50,000	128,363	136,000	0	0	2,340,000	10,000	David Force
Portland	18	M	3,272,833	2,480,926	24,670	100.56	372,992	139,452	279,463	120,000	200,000	165,000	2,302,124	605,709	K.R. Montgomery
Rossville	3	B	422,626	332,626	5,000	66.52	20,000	45,000	25,000	29,252	0	10,000	259,824	152,802	Harry Mohler
Winslow	3	B	291,768	271,314	2,500	108.53	2,954	4,000	13,500	14,000	0	200,000	91,768	0	Wayne E. Seufert
Iowa															
North Liberty	4	M	640,000	120,000	6,400	18.75	89,500	250,000	180,500	60,000	0	0	600,000	40,000	Neumann Monson...

Symbol Code: B—Branch Library; BS—Branch & System Headquarters; M—Main Library; MS—Main & System Headquarters; S—System Headquarters; n/a—not available

Table 1 / New Public Library Buildings, 1997 *(cont.)*

Community	Pop. ('000)	Code	Project Cost	Const. Cost	Gross Sq. Ft.	Sq. Ft. Cost	Equip. Cost	Site Cost	Other Costs	Volumes	Federal Funds	State Funds	Local Funds	Gift Funds	Architect
Kansas															
Mt. Hope	1	M	287,000	227,000	3,200	70.93	45,000	10,000	5,000	20,000	30,000	30,000	200,000	30,000	Winter Architects
Wakeeney	3	M	318,855	286,000	5,250	54.48	16,045	Owned	16,810	25,000	60,000	11,094	179,361	68,400	Woods & Starr
Maryland															
Indian Head	33	B	1,254,071	1,024,046	10,900	93.95	146,500	Owned	83,525	25,000	0	0	1,254,071	0	FSI Design Group
Massachusetts															
Southampton	5	M	1,082,216	876,000	6,209	141.09	92,416	15,200	98,600	32,014	118,000	100,000	814,216	50,000	Galliher, Baier & Best
Michigan															
Grand Rapids	21	B	3,109,023	2,312,485	26,000	88.94	375,338	261,200	160,000	75,000	0	0	2,553,985	555,038	Van Wienen...
Grand Rapids	11	B	1,312,184	980,973	8,880	110.47	143,940	30,000	157,271	21,200	0	68,000	450,000	812,000	Fishbeck,Thompson...
Kalamazoo	120	B	1,358,510	1,020,800	11,000	92.8	205,865	Owned	131,825	23,000	0	0	1,358,510	0	David Milling
Nebraska															
Papillion	15	M	2,767,007	2,196,369	23,000	95.49	331,304	Owned	239,334	80,000	0	0	1,900,007	867,000	Sinclaire Hille
Wayne	5	M	819,829	640,000	6,700	95.52	14,329	89,500	76,000	30,000	0	0	468,829	351,500	Zenon Beringe`...
Nevada															
Las Vegas	50	B	18,768,651	14,608,215	122,000	119.74	1,171,281	1,103,208	1,885,947	250,000	0	0	18,768,651	0	Meyer, Scherer...
New Jersey															
Pompton Plains	14	M	1,545,000	1,150,000	12,000	100	345,000	Owned	50,000	100,000	0	0	1,200,000	345,000	James Cutillo
Woodbury	11	M	2,019,200	1,585,000	11,400	139.04	197,200	Owned	237,000	50,000	228,000	0	1,759,200	32,000	Phil Ruggieri
New Mexico															
Taos	24	M	2,200,000	1,860,000	14,400	129.17	250,000	Owned	90,000	65,000	116,000	250,000	1,684,000	150,000	Robert Sturtcman
New York															
Brooklyn	n/a	B	4,760,000	3,178,000	10,000	317.8	725,000	Owned	857,000	25,700	0	0	4,760,000	0	John Ciardullo
Mechanicville	8	M	596,923	411,410	5,400	76.19	129,023	Owned	56,490	24,000	0	20,399	576,524	0	Richard R. Butler
Montrose	15	M	3,059,950	2,429,562	15,990	151.94	226,430	225,000	178,958	75,000	0	0	3,059,950	0	Lothrop Assocs.
Staten Island	42	B	4,972,000	1,342,000	15,000	89.47	415,000	2,600,000	615,000	62,640	0	0	4,972,000	0	NYC Dept. of Design

Symbol Code: B—Branch Library; BS—Branch & System Headquarters; M—Main Library; MS—Main & System Headquarters; S—System Headquarters; n/a—not available

Table 1 / New Public Library Buildings, 1997 *(cont.)*

Community	Pop. ('000)	Code	Project Cost	Const. Cost	Gross Sq. Ft.	Sq. Ft. Cost	Equip. Cost	Site Cost	Other Costs	Volumes	Federal Funds	State Funds	Local Funds	Gift Funds	Architect
Valhalla	6	B	510,490	422,000	2,785	151.53	57,000	Leased	31,490	20,000	0	0	498,490	12,000	Lothrop Assocs.
Weedsport	5	M	432,940	357,000	4,400	81.14	30,000	9,000	36,940	20,000	40,648	61,419	0	330,873	Anne Hersh
North Carolina															
Charlotte	28	B	2,762,345	1,618,840	13,700	118.16	309,729	630,990	202,786	65,000	0	0	2,690,345	72,000	Gantt-Huberman
Raleigh	40	B	1,338,400	1,006,700	8,100	124.28	145,500	Owned	186,200	60,000	0	0	1,338,400	0	NBBJ Architects
Wake Forest	21	B	943,400	673,500	5,160	130.52	164,500	Owned	105,400	30,000	0	0	873,400	70,000	Boney Architects
Ohio															
Chillicothe	34	BS	1,803,968	1,288,493	10,500	122.71	276,645	135,000	103,830	32,372	0	0	1,803,968	0	Design Group...
Dillonvale	4	B	336,653	274,000	2,500	109.6	36,150	14,000	12,503	10,000	0	0	336,653	0	none
Geneva	19	B	1,909,843	1,494,000	17,720	84.31	141,300	130,000	144,543	40,000	0	0	1,894,843	15,000	Thomas Ziska
Lynchburg	7	B	360,067	234,456	4,000	58.61	43,973	46,424	35,214	30,000	0	0	350,067	10,000	McCarty Assocs.
McConnelsville	14	M	1,367,858	794,893	13,255	59.97	122,400	282,494	168,071	49,679	398,844	0	746,014	223,000	Beck & Tabeling
Oklahoma															
McLoud	3	M	$317,527	$256,338	3,200	$80.11	$27,168	$8,600	$25,421	12,000	$100,000	0	$75,000	$142,527	Olsen-Coffey Archs.
Oregon															
Portland	636	B	5,394,451	3,788,273	25,990	145.76	389,100	339,100	877,978	74,000	94,451	0	5,300,000	0	Thomas Hacker
Pennsylvania															
Carbondale	21	M	1,193,577	1,061,692	8,300	127.91	28,420	Owned	103,465	25,000	250,000	99,500	584,058	260,019	Palumbo & Baker
Clearfield	17	M	1,161,626	875,667	10,200	85.85	70,611	100,000	115,348	90,000	0	0	90,000	1,071,626	Image Assocs.
Erie	240	MS	13,518,820	10,796,054	91,275	118.28	1,578,765	Owned	1,144,001	350,000	500,304	2,560,000	8,879,751	1,578,765	Weber Murphy Fox
Hershey	19	M	5,728,769	4,173,919	29,038	143.73	545,606	319,200	690,044	100,000	0	0	5,068,769	660,000	Buchart Horn...
McDonald	9	M	466,660	418,859	4,000	104.71	0	18,000	29,801	45,000	87,430	171,151	20,500	187,579	Radelet McCarthy
Mechanicsburg	38	M	1,771,349	1,206,939	14,000	86.21	91,247	260,000	213,163	65,000	0	400,000	53,200	1,318,149	Harle Architectural
Stroudsburg	56	MS	2,702,000	820,000	15,000	54.67	130,000	1,700,000	52,000	90,000	0	0	130,000	2,572,000	Schoonover...
South Carolina															
Lyman	23	B	1,554,881	1,197,875	12,500	95.83	111,679	100,000	145,327	50,000	0	0	1,326,381	228,500	McGarity, Gilmore...
Simpsonville	69	B	1,774,827	1,217,890	11,159	109.14	188,316	238,500	130,121	65,000	0	0	1,431,758	343,069	Tarleton-Tankersley

Symbol Code: B—Branch Library; BS—Branch & System Headquarters; M—Main Library; MS—Main & System Headquarters; S—System Headquarters; n/a—not available

Table 1 / New Public Library Buildings, 1997 *(cont.)*

Community	Pop. ('000)	Code	Project Cost	Const. Cost	Gross Sq. Ft.	Sq. Ft. Cost	Equip. Cost	Site Cost	Other Costs	Volumes	Federal Funds	State Funds	Local Funds	Gift Funds	Architect
Spartanburg	227	M	14,910,100	10,124,490	105,000	96.42	1,710,000	1,091,129	1,984,481	440,000	0	0	11,321,875	3,588,225	McMillan Smith
Travelers Rest	37	B	1,714,962	1,203,440	11,159	107.84	236,475	135,000	140,047	65,000	0	0	1,333,234	381,728	Tarleton-Tankersley
Tennessee															
Memphis	50	B	6,245,373	4,566,388	31,000	147.3	484,879	750,594	443,512	125,000	0	0	6,245,373	0	Williamson, Haizlip...
Texas															
Arlington	45	B	2,537,994	1,123,213	10,000	112.32	202,051	261,230	951,500	55,000	0	0	2,444,292	93,702	Petrelli*assocs.
Austin	35	B	1,555,461	1,086,683	8,580	126.65	175,195	Owned	293,583	45,000	0	10,500	1,544,961	0	Architecture +
Austin	45	B	1,849,612	1,086,251	8,266	131.41	160,790	301,142	301,429	45,000	0	0	1,799,612	50,000	Austin Group
Forth Worth	90	B	3,633,340	2,403,411	24,000	100.14	424,124	474,059	331,746	100,000	0	0	3,513,340	120,000	Komatsu Rargel
Lubbock	30	B	1,400,000	696,000	10,426	66.75	191,300	Owned	512,700	50,000	0	0	1,385,000	15,000	MWM Architects
Utah															
Salt Lake City	12	B	2,072,080	1,537,225	13,000	118.25	291,610	81,137	162,138	70,977	255,425	0	1,470,099	345,556	Brixen & Christopher
Virginia															
Poquoson	12	M	1,705,800	1,050,800	14,200	74	187,000	345,600	122,400	65,500	0	0	1,565,900	139,900	Hanbury Evans...
Richmond	n/a	M	51,475,636	35,908,591	444,000	80.88	10,463,000	Owned	5,104,045	700,000	0	51,475,636	0	0	Skidmore Owings...
Williamsburg	25	M	5,850,000	2,900,000	35,000	82.86	1,014,152	280,000	1,655,848	150,000	0	0	5,850,000	0	Design Collaborative
Washington															
Burbank Heights	3	B	542,902	357,851	3,640	98.31	24,433	30,000	130,618	16,000	255,926	0	256,976	30,000	Lewis Architects
Spokane	43	B	3,382,164	2,583,895	17,850	144.76	449,924	Owned	348,345	82,188	0	0	3,382,164	0	Northwest Architecture
Wisconsin															
Spencer	6	B	231,991	187,533	2,072	90.5	33,151	Owned	11,307	14,000	0	0	231,991	0	Dale Langfoss
Sussex	16	M	2,444,654	1,690,372	23,418	72.18	305,317	283,000	168,965	76,000	0	0	2,149,654	295,000	HSR Assocs.

Symbol Code: B—Branch Library; BS—Branch & System Headquarters; M—Main Library; MS—Main & System Headquarters; S—System Headquarters; n/a—not available

Table 2 / Public Library Buildings, 1997: Additions and Renovations

Community	Pop. ('000)	Code	Project Cost	Const. Cost	Gross Sq. Ft.	Sq. Ft. Cost	Equip. Cost	Site Cost	Other Costs	Volumes	Federal Funds	State Funds	Local Funds	Gift Funds	Architect
Alabama															
Birmingham	29	B	$683,600	$549,000	6,000	$91.50	$36,500	Owned	$98,100	n/a	0	0	$683,600	0	Jerry A. Shadix
Huntsville	4	B	27,000	7,000	1,100	6.36	20,000	Leased	0	8,000	27,000	0	0	0	none
LaFayette	5	B	439,806	388,948	3,100	125.47	1,682	Owned	49,176	7,500	0	0	438,124	1,682	Jova, Daniels, Busby
Arizona															
Bullhead City	45	B	90,278	83,978	592	141.85	0	Owned	6,300	1,000	0	0	85,278	5,000	Paul Selberg
Douglas	14	M	933,308	816,820	8,000	102.1	90,632	Owned	25,856	32,000	248,500	0	684,808	0	Gresham & Beach
Yuma	168	M	60,000	59,450	300	33.16	0	Owned	550	n/a	49,500	0	10,500	0	Hunter & Company
California															
Arcadia	52	M	5,300,000	3,692,000	41,000	90.05	400,000	Owned	1,208,000	150,000	0	0	4,900,000	400,000	Charles Walton
Chino	60	B	763,000	512,000	10,647	48.08	201,000	Owned	50,000	56,000	0	0	763,000	0	WLC Architects
Corcoran	10	B	159,582	151,000	4,050	100	0	Owned	8,582	12,000	51,246	0	108,336	0	Marvin Armstrong
Del Mar	5	B	2,350,500	854,500	5,191	164.61	0	1,300,000	196,000	22,000	0	0	1,600,000	750,500	Cardwell/McGraw
Escondido	121	B	396,450	321,294	4,000	80.32	46,156	Owned	29,000	8,000	0	0	350,294	46,156	Robert McQuead
Los Angeles	53	B	1,596,123	1,373,862	6,258	219.54	76,077	Owned	146,184	35,000	1,056,600	0	539,523	0	Barton Choy Assocs.
Los Angeles	22	B	2,078,454	1,757,037	10,578	166.1	110,576	Owned	210,841	40,000	0	0	2,078,454	0	Miralles Assocs.
Pajaro	3	B	1,148,563	837,563	8,300	100.91	11,000	300,000	n/a	6,000	0	287,141	861,422	0	Synthesis Design
So. San Francisco	17	B	943,422	683,412	11,060	61.79	33,270	Owned	226,740	42,000	0	0	943,422	0	G. Wagner; Mock/...
Susanville	16	MS	980,000	578,500	11,100	52.12	41,100	287,900	72,500	80,000	480,500	0	400,000	99,500	Thomson & Hendricks
Van Nuys	69	B	369,426	280,756	10,393	27.01	88,670	Owned	0	75,000	0	0	369,426	0	Arch. Div., City of L.A.
Windsor	20	B	405,381	141,012	7,600	18.55	206,105	Owned	58,264	27,000	0	0	405,381	0	RMW
Connecticut															
Cheshire	28	M	3,305,000	2,600,000	33,000	78.79	320,000	Owned	385,000	135,000	0	350,000	2,955,000	0	Tuthill & Wells
Danbury	70	M	3,270,018	1,462,286	40,000	36.56	1,141,128	Owned	666,604	140,000	81,334	375,039	2,641,483	172,162	Galliher, Baier & Best
Niantic	15	M	12,000	5,000	350	14.29	7,000	Leased	0	400	0	0	7,000	5,000	Centerbrook Assocs.

Symbol Code: B—Branch Library; BS—Branch & System Headquarters; M—Main Library; MS—Main & System Headquarters; S—System Headquarters; n/a—not available

Table 2 / Public Library Buildings, 1997: Additions and Renovations *(cont.)*

Community	Pop. ('000)	Code	Project Cost	Const. Cost	Gross Sq. Ft.	Sq. Ft. Cost	Equip. Cost	Site Cost	Other Costs	Volumes	Federal Funds	State Funds	Local Funds	Gift Funds	Architect
Florida															
Cape Canaveral	10	B	1,052,820	888,531	15,000	59.24	70,000	Owned	94,289	70,000	0	0	1,052,820	0	Stottler, Starmer
Estero	395	B	6,101,543	2,500,000	32,600	76.69	1,230,776	2,057,500	313,267	141,920	0	0	6,101,543	0	Gora McGahey
Fort Lauderdale	1400	MS	1,500,000	922,301	7,900	116.75	185,000	Owned	392,699	20,000	0	500,000	0	1,000,000	Donald Singer
Fort Myers	46	B	1,333,224	1,050,000	10,000	105	203,224	Leased	80,000	33,623	0	25,678	1,307,546	0	Berger & Dean
Fort Myers	395	MS	1,462,825	800,000	25,770	31.04	489,529	Leased	173,296	120,470	0	93,161	1,369,664	0	Peter Wisniewski
Hastings	6	B	337,000	265,000	5,000	53	60,000	Leased	12,000	22,000	0	277,000	60,000	0	Les Thomas
Georgia															
Clarkesville	84	MS	$1,691,183	$991,000	15,000	$66.07	$552,953	Owned	$147,230	63,681	0	$1,180,000	$439,183	0	Bailey Assocs.
Statesboro	116	MS	2,385,000	1,332,610	31,528	42.27	439,458	Owned	612,932	147,000	0	1,688,609	633,086	63,305	Eckles, Martin & Rule
Illinois															
Cerro Gordo	4	M	264,692	232,665	1,600	146	9,757	Owned	22,270	9,450	0	84,000	166,123	15,000	BLDD Architects
Lincolnwood	11	M	2,609,150	1,950,000	17,535	111.21	466,150	Owned	193,000	75,000	0	93,150	2,500,000	16,000	InterActive Design
Loves Park	56	M	2,367,000	1,620,000	16,000	101.25	540,000	Owned	207,000	175,000	0	0	2,367,000	0	Pedriana Gustafson
Macomb	20	M	7,000	7,000	108	64.81	0	Owned	0	0	0	0	7,000	0	none
Mokena	13	M	3,103,150	2,650,000	27,200	97.28	301,150	Owned	152,000	94,350	17,055	250,000	2,828,595	7,500	Burnidge Cassell
Plainfield	16	M	608,404	453,183	5,000	90.64	144,767	Owned	10,454	45,000	0	0	608,404	0	Frye Gillan Molinaro
Roselle	25	M	1,497,820	972,466	25,000	38.39	292,679	Owned	232,675	110,000	0	250,000	1,247,820	0	LaRoi Architects
Sycamore	11	M	2,747,871	2,145,505	21,298	100.74	90,753	280,000	231,608	51,500	800,000	250,000	100,000	1,646,000	Frye Gillan Molinaro
Wauconda	22	M	5,000,000	3,700,000	27,000	137.04	180,000	Owned	1,120,000	120,000	0	250,000	4,750,000	0	O'Donnell, Wicklund...
Indiana															
Evansville	66	B	1,384,127	1,053,907	17,114	61.58	78,388	180,602	71,230	101,000	0	0	1,384,127	0	Jack R. Kinkel & Son
Ft. Wayne	45	B	859,547	677,047	7,761	87.24	130,000	Owned	52,500	92,565	0	0	859,547	0	Moake Park Group
Garrett	8	M	1,665,012	1,102,935	11,500	95.91	196,168	Owned	365,909	53,000	0	500,000	296,144	868,868	William D. Koster
Greencastle	29	M	3,178,887	2,513,872	24,000	104.74	100,500	48,625	515,890	90,000	151,000	0	2,992,387	35,500	Ratio Architects
North Judson	5	M	1,440,155	1,068,479	8,837	120.91	159,171	Owned	212,505	32,117	664,855	0	775,000	300	Halstead Thompson...

Symbol Code: B—Branch Library; BS—Branch & System Headquarters; M—Main Library; MS—Main & System Headquarters; S—System Headquarters; n/a—not available

Table 2 / Public Library Buildings, 1997: Additions and Renovations *(cont.)*

Community	Pop. ('000)	Code	Project Cost	Const. Cost	Gross Sq. Ft.	Sq. Ft. Cost	Equip. Cost	Site Cost	Other Costs	Volumes	Federal Funds	State Funds	Local Funds	Gift Funds	Architect
Iowa															
Bettendorf	32	M	6,100,000	4,310,282	53,000	81.33	1,030,740	Owned	758,978	155,000	0	0	5,300,000	800,000	Brown Healey Stone...
Keokuk	25	M	124,500	92,000	1,676	54.89	7,500	Owned	25,000	n/a	0	0	10,000	114,500	Brown Healey Stone...
Oskaloosa	22	M	3,711,000	2,737,000	25,822	105.99	623,000	71,000	280,000	57,000	0	0	3,650,000	61,000	OPN Architects
Kansas															
Centralia	1	M	54,208	34,901	2,590	13.47	3,785	15,000	522	n/a	0	0	0	54,208	none
Olathe	80	M	312,505	245,542	23,352	10.52	38,963	Owned	28,000	100,000	50,000	0	235,120	27,385	J. Kurt von Achen
Seneca	2	M	566,866	440,866	6,800	64.83	55,000	20,000	51,000	45,000	0	0	431,866	100,000	Dave Emig
Louisiana															
Innis	4	B	84,762	62,640	892	70.23	15,802	Owned	6,320	8,000	0	0	84,762	0	Glenn C. Morgan
Livonia	4	B	84,762	62,640	892	70.23	15,802	Owned	6,320	8,000	0	0	84,762	0	Glenn C. Morgan
Morganza	1	B	84,762	62,640	892	70.23	15,802	Owned	6,320	8,000	0	0	84,762	0	Glenn C. Morgan
New Roads	12	B	339,049	250,562	3,568	70.23	63,210	Owned	25,277	32,000	0	0	339,049	0	Glenn C. Morgan
Rougon	3	B	84,762	62,640	892	70.23	15,802	Owned	6,320	8,000	0	0	84,762	0	Glenn C. Morgan
Maine															
Camden	10	M	2,893,427	2,380,044	15,188	157	276,214	Owned	237,169	47,000	0	0	0	2,893,427	Scholz & Barclay
Lewiston	40	M	2,484,969	2,026,702	32,500	62.36	88,000	129,000	241,267	110,000	20,000	0	2,464,969	0	Providence Assocs.
Maryland															
Accident	1	B	147,000	135,000	3,600	37.5	7,000	Owned	5,000	20,000	0	0	140,000	7,000	Devlin, Inc.
Massachusetts															
Brewster	9	M	$3,275,401	$2,476,134	23,012	$107.60	$114,500	$149,192	$535,575	70,404	0	$1,255,133	$1,420,268	$600,000	Stephen Hale Assocs.
Malden	53	M	6,200,000	4,702,200	40,470	116.18	219,258	Owned	1,278,542	246,850	500,000	950,000	2,500,000	2,250,000	Stahl Assocs.
Natick	31	M	9,481,600	7,824,000	62,025	126.14	470,000	270,000	917,600	220,000	0	200,000	8,481,600	800,000	A. Anthony Tappé
Northampton	20	M	2,225,000	1,800,000	28,000	64.29	235,000	Owned	190,000	225,000	0	195,000	1,331,434	698,566	Arch. Resources...
Winchester	21	M	4,951,000	3,599,498	28,400	126.74	360,100	Owned	991,402	140,000	0	200,000	4,115,000	636,000	Thomson, French...
Michigan															
Auburn Hills	19	M	3,750,000	2,255,000	20,000	112.75	390,000	444,000	661,000	52,475	0	0	3,744,200	5,800	David W. Osler

Symbol Code: B—Branch Library; BS—Branch & System Headquarters; M—Main Library; MS—Main & System Headquarters; S—System Headquarters; n/a—not available

Community	Pop. ('000)	Code	Project Cost	Const. Cost	Gross Sq. Ft.	Sq. Ft. Cost	Equip. Cost	Site Cost	Other Costs	Volumes	Federal Funds	State Funds	Local Funds	Gift Funds	Architect
Comstock Park	12	B	1,553,851	515,701	10,687	48.25	114,489	867,330	56,331	20,000	0	0	1,548,460	5,391	Jeffrey Parker
Detroit	1028	M	488,946	192,500	2,610	73.75	110,281	Owned	186,165	n/a	100,000	0	388,946	0	none
Detroit	1028	B	239,467	157,100	9,950	15.79	37,880	Owned	44,487	100,000	0	0	239,467	0	Library Designs
Kalamazoo	120	B	939,500	678,700	7,600	89.3	91,280	Owned	169,520	14,500	0	0	939,500	0	David Milling
Menominee	11	M	1,675,096	1,449,474	16,161	89.69	70,399	Owned	155,223	55,000	1,600,000	0	45,096	30,000	Frye Gillan Molinaro
Vassar	9	M	312,000	238,000	6,496	36.64	45,000	Owned	29,000	40,000	118,000	0	18,000	176,000	Toshack Sobczak...
Minnesota															
Bird Island	1	M	133,000	101,000	2,800	36.07	8,000	20,000	4,000	10,000	0	0	116,000	17,000	none
Climax	1	B	40,602	30,000	2,079	14.43	602	10,000	0	n/a	0	0	27,802	12,800	none
Glenwood	10	M	622,878	531,350	6,472	75.18	19,128	Owned	72,400	6,370	0	199,000	372,197	51,681	Zuber, Baker...
Olivia	5	M	900,400	805,000	7,000	115	5,400	Owned	90,000	25,000	0	264,000	535,000	101,400	Vetter Johnson
Red Wing	20	M	586,900	366,300	14,245	25.71	161,300	Owned	59,300	90,000	0	13,500	442,400	131,000	Jeff Kelley Architects
Mississippi															
Biloxi	25	B	578,996	459,450	10,765	42.68	90,000	Owned	29,546	35,000	127,143	0	451,853	0	Loren D. Carlander
Canton	10	BS	1,059,112	859,500	17,896	48.03	158,196	Owned	41,416	55,000	0	105,576	923,536	30,000	Cooke, Douglass...
Hazlehurst	6	BS	2,100	2,100	144	14.58	0	Owned	0	500	0	0	0	2,100	Carl Nobles
Madison	14	B	844,106	703,846	9,681	72.7	107,920	Owned	32,340	40,000	0	219,800	615,756	8,550	Tompkins, Barron...
Oxford	33	MS	1,410,762	1,202,612	10,506	114.47	111,950	Owned	96,200	90,000	0	200,000	1,210,762	0	Thomas W. Faulkner
Missouri															
Gallatin	8	MS	417,990	285,385	10,600	26.93	24,408	86,500	21,697	50,000	118,581	0	100,039	199,370	Reed Architects
Springfield	44	B	432,220	387,000	14,330	27	22,000	Owned	23,220	80,000	0	0	410,220	22,000	Casey & Assocs.

Symbol Code: B—Branch Library; BS—Branch & System Headquarters; M—Main Library; MS—Main & System Headquarters; S—System Headquarters; n/a—not available

Table 2 / Public Library Buildings, 1997: Additions and Renovations (cont.)

Community	Pop. ('000)	Code	Project Cost	Const. Cost	Gross Sq. Ft.	Sq. Ft. Cost	Equip. Cost	Site Cost	Other Costs	Volumes	Federal Funds	State Funds	Local Funds	Gift Funds	Architect
New Hampshire															
Lincoln	1	M	273,510	238,503	3,100	76.94	20,625	Owned	14,382	20,000	40,000	0	203,675	29,835	Gary Snider Architects
Littleton	6	M	93,418	67,684	1,200	56.4	19,322	Owned	6,412	n/a	27,950	0	64,241	1,227	Stephen M. Crooker
Londonderry	22	M	2,300,000	1,683,965	19,800	85.05	174,700	Owned	441,335	78,180	0	0	2,300,000	0	Stahl Assocs.
New Jersey															
Trenton	140	B	1,802,371	1,538,828	23,895	64.4	0	Owned	263,543	916,000	0	1,802,371	0	0	LAN Assocs.
New York															
Bronx	4	B	495,000	0	5,000	0	495,000	Leased	0	22,150	0	95,000	400,000	0	Stephen Lepp Assocs.
North Carolina															
Asheville	20	B	482,774	287,000	4,800	59.79	101,000	Leased	94,774	25,000	0	0	482,774	0	John Fisher
Charlotte	60	B	3,683,654	1,567,147	18,670	83.94	449,464	Leased	178,743	125,000	0	0	3,683,654	0	TBA2 Architects
Raleigh	532	B	303,700	152,800	5,000	30.56	135,900	Owned	15,000	500	0	0	303,700	0	Shadoin Assocs.
North Dakota															
Valley City	15	M	501,000	453,000	4,138	109.47	6,724	Owned	41,276	55,000	125,300	0	160,000	215,700	Dan Smith & Assocs.
Ohio															
Cincinnati	868	MS	49,400,000	25,800,000	486,527	53.03	9,100,000	7,700,000	6,800,000	3,511,311	0	49,368,000	0	32,000	Shepley...; Gartner...
Cleveland	505	MS	67,515,954	50,419,619	267,981	188.15	4,627,440	Owned	12,468,895	1,300,000	0	0	67,515,954	0	URS Greiner; Hardy...
Clyde	6	M	1,600,812	1,261,599	12,200	103.4	145,843	Owned	193,370	35,000	0	0	1,551,000	49,812	David Holzheimer
Dayton	23	B	113,626	97,595	8,532	11.44	0	Leased	16,031	15,000	0	0	113,626	0	MATRIX Architects
Hamilton	65	MS	2,448,125	1,954,401	21,000	93.06	261,710	Owned	232,014	100,000	0	0	1,746,387	701,738	Steed Hammond Paul
Huber Heights	41	B	978,008	803,492	21,745	36.95	70,116	Leased	104,400	125,000	0	0	978,008	0	Woolpert Architects
Milford	37	B	337,827	310,304	14,280	21.73	6,840	Leased	20,683	50,000	0	0	337,827	0	KBA Architects
Paulding	20	M	123,000	112,000	n/a	n/a	0	Owned	11,000	n/a	0	0	123,000	0	Morrison, Kattman...
Wickliffe	15	M	2,074,000	1,494,082	19,090	78.27	271,650	Owned	308,268	115,000	0	0	2,074,000	0	David Holzheimer
Wilmington	35	M	1,500,000	1,411,000	10,446	135	0	Owned	89,000	n/a	400,000	0	1,100,000	0	Voorhis, Slone...

Symbol Code: B—Branch Library; BS—Branch & System Headquarters; M—Main Library; MS—Main & System Headquarters; S—System Headquarters; n/a—not available

Table 2 / Public Library Buildings, 1997: Additions and Renovations (cont.)

Community	Pop. ('000)	Code	Project Cost	Const. Cost	Gross Sq. Ft.	Sq. Ft. Cost	Equip. Cost	Site Cost	Other Costs	Volumes	Federal Funds	State Funds	Local Funds	Gift Funds	Architect
Oregon															
Portland	636	M	25,737,679	18,699,552	128,000	146.09	928,363	Owned	6,109,764	1,500,000	0	0	24,737,679	1,000,000	Fletcher Farr Ayotte
Pennsylvania															
Lewisburg	37	M	364,676	265,982	3,000	88.66	29,595	49,000	20,099	15,000	0		14,676	350,000	Robert A. Lack
Pittsburgh	34	M	4,404,000	3,334,000	29,300	113.78	515,000	176,000	379,000	160,000	250,000	25,000	3,093,000	1,036,000	Mark McCormick
Swarthmore	6	M	714,000	590,500	5,800	101.81	39,800	Leased	83,700	36,600	0	200,000	494,000	20,000	DMA Architec's
Wayne	29	M	170,725	115,531	5,000	23.11	29,419	Owned	25,775	45,000	0	0	25,681	145,044	A I Five Inc.
South Carolina															
Kershaw	6	B	306,764	233,696	4,924	47.46	55,042	Owned	18,026	18,000	100,000	0	151,722	55,042	W. Daniel Shelley
Tennessee															
Clarksville	121	M	3,919,828	2,968,653	74,000	40.12	750,198	Owned	200,977	150,000	0	0	3,919,828	0	Rufus Johnson Assocs.
Memphis	60	B	466,875	276,000	11,200	24.64	115,575	Owned	75,300	75,000	0	0	466,875	0	Mark Watson
Texas															
Austin	40	B	$323,262	$232,000	7,340	$431.60	$9,262	Owned	$82,000	40,000	0	0	$214,000	$109,262	O'Connell Robertson
Friendswood	29	M	115,638	92,637	2,253	41.12	14,984	Owned	8,017	12,000	50,000	0	62,915	2,723	Hall/Merriman
Hurst	35	M	1,417,267	1,164,306	11,000	105.85	133,996	Owned	118,965	55,000	0	0	1,417,267	0	William H. Hidell
Nacogdoches	54	M	2,965,000	1,950,000	45,000	43.33	125,000	625,000	265,000	95,000	0	0	2,915,000	50,000	Bucher, Willis...
San Antonio	120	B	761,016	657,159	13,074	50.26	27,898	Owned	75,959	58,520	0	0	761,016	0	Beaty Saunders
San Antonio	100	B	1,056,382	899,179	12,000	74.93	63,370	Owned	93,833	45,420	0	407,000	649,382	0	Overland Partners
San Antonio	99	BS	654,589	504,508	11,450	44.06	78,176	Owned	71,905	72,900	0	16,790	637,799	0	Reyna & Assocs.
Utah															
Draper	18	B	64,605	33,000	3,460	9.54	31,605	Leased	0	20,725	0	0	64,605	0	none
Springville	19	M	310,467	273,667	3,700	73.96	17,000	Owned	19,800	26,200	154,295	0	95,672	60,500	Kevin Scholz

Symbol Code: B—Branch Library; BS—Branch & System Headquarters; M—Main Library; MS—Main & System Headquarters; S—System Headquarters; n/a—not available

Table 2 / Public Library Buildings, 1997: Additions and Renovations *(cont.)*

Community	Pop. ('000)	Code	Project Cost	Const. Cost	Gross Sq. Ft.	Sq. Ft. Cost	Equip. Cost	Site Cost	Other Costs	Volumes	Federal Funds	State Funds	Local Funds	Gift Funds	Architect
Virginia															
Blacksburg	46	B	2,487,000	2,055,000	16,000	128.44	216,000	Owned	216,000	60,000	108,883	0	2,280,117	98,000	Design Collaborative
Washington															
Bainbridge Island	19	B	1,779,000	1,338,000	15,500	86.32	175,000	Owned	266,000	61,345	0	0	12,000	1,767,000	Lewis Architects
Bonney Lake	16	B	1,031,802	789,656	6,480	121.86	97,116	Owned	145,030	26,000	0	0	1,031,802	0	Boyle-Wagoner
Cheney	9	B	365,941	275,689	5,766	47.81	41,148	Owned	49,104	20,500	0	0	363,441	2,500	Integrus Architecture
Wisconsin															
Athens	5	B	224,592	176,341	2,750	64.12	31,195	Owned	17,056	14,000	0	0	224,592	0	Becher-Hoppe Assocs.
La Crosse	50	M	4,645,528	3,831,387	87,494	43.79	471,733	Owned	342,408	316,416	145,528	0	4,091,000	409,000	River Architects
Milwaukee	621	M	1,550,144	1,120,996	58,042	19.31	118,294	Owned	310,854	n/a	0	0	1,550,144	0	Uihlein Architects
Milwaukee	60	B	434,731	295,553	15,200	19.44	70,231	Owned	68,947	70,000	0	0	434,731	0	Uihlein Architects
Prairie du Sac	3	M	409,525	321,205	4,300	74.7	65,160	Owned	23,160	30,000	0	0	220,000	189,525	Potter Design Group
Sheboygan	51	M	4,900,000	3,951,713	71,890	54.97	278,708	Owned	669,579	465,000	0	0	4,900,000	0	Linde Jensen...
Wyoming															
Story	1	B	52,451	43,935	309	142.18	4,200	Owned	4,316	9,000	0	0	0	52,451	Robert Liebsack

Symbol Code: B—Branch Library; BS—Branch & System Headquarters; M—Main Library; MS—Main & System Headquarters; S—System Headquarters; n/a—not available

Table 3 / Public Library Buildings: Six-Year Cost Summary, 1992–1997

	Fiscal 1992	Fiscal 1993	Fiscal 1994	Fiscal 1995	Fiscal 1996	Fiscal 1997
Number of new buildings	118	113	108	99	100	97
Number of ARRs[1]	115	105	127	124	145	128
Sq. ft. new buildings	1,935,111	1,896,197	1,818,522	2,102,851	2,002,067	2,153,203
Sq. ft. ARRs	1,819,787	1,878,628	2,163,909	2,469,345	2,315,523	2,710,599
New Buildings						
Construction cost	$188,143,273	$183,978,065	$176,678,555	$232,050,462	$286,141,319	$227,740,506
Equipment cost	27,234,207	22,651,001	27,617,314	28,239,712	57,222,035	35,983,384
Site cost	21,011,768	28,353,201	34,696,765	31,406,749	16,391,748	33,630,070
Other cost	31,315,471	32,275,926	30,114,637	42,946,629	49,498,901	40,060,597
Total—Project cost	267,704,719	267,770,932	271,051,271	334,643,552	409,254,003	337,414,557
ARRs—Project cost	205,103,863	160,825,726	345,135,792	281,750,499	314,191,342	324,762,086
New and ARR Project Cost	$472,808,582	$428,596,658	$616,187,063	$616,394,051	$723,445,345	$662,176,643
Fund Sources						
Federal, new buildings	$9,851,065	$4,320,934	$4,483,792	$10,532,079	$17,719,253	$4,572,130
Federal, ARRs	7,413,576	3,646,307	6,188,756	3,292,272	13,771,483	7,698,270
Federal, total	$17,264,641	$7,967,241	$10,672,548	$13,824,351	$31,490,736	$12,270,400
State, new buildings	$10,753,499	$26,376,138	$45,559,588	$31,051,654	$32,089,611	$73,081,134
State, ARRs	43,002,552	10,841,063	10,361,213	28,482,199	21,212,540	62,169,948
State, total	$53,756,051	$37,217,201	$55,920,801	$59,533,853	$53,302,151	$135,251,082
Local, new buildings	$230,815,119	$208,363,930	$203,676,929	$268,609,523	$301,996,679	$228,793,054
Local, ARRs	139,135,045	141,961,411	302,050,882	227,108,845	182,163,428	233,525,418
Local, total	$369,950,164	$350,325,341	$505,727,811	$495,718,368	$484,160,107	$462,318,472
Gift, new buildings	$16,487,880	$28,878,559	$17,663,214	$25,433,205	$57,478,470	$31,168,178
Gift, ARRs	15,849,230	4,389,236	26,614,547	23,951,472	97,019,403	21,345,010
Gift, total	$32,337,110	$33,267,795	$44,277,761	$49,384,677	$154,497,873	$52,513,188
Total Funds Used	$473,307,966	$428,777,578	$616,598,921	$618,461,249	$723,450,867	$662,353,142

[1]Additions, remodelings, and renovations

Table 4 / New Academic Library Buildings, 1997

Institution	Project Cost	Gross Area	Sq. Ft. Cost	Construction Cost	Equipment Cost	Book Capacity	Seating Capacity	Architect
Walsh Lib., Fordham University, Bronx, N.Y.	$54,001,500	240,000	$181.25	$43,500,000	$10,501,500	1,200,000	1,500	Shepley, Bulfinch
Media Union Library, University of Michigan, Ann Arbor	45,000,000	250,000	132.00	33,000,000	8,000,000	500,000	1,500	Albert Khan Assocs.
Fairchild Lib. of Engineering & Applied Science, California Institute of Technology, Pasadena	9,630,000	36,619	220.02	8,057,000	1,573,000	168,000	218	Moore Ruble Yudell
Poynter Memorial Library, University of South Florida, St. Petersburg	9,020,000	81,000	94.27	7,635,870	1,100,000	300,000	650	Rowe Architects
Southwest Collection/Special Collections Lib., Texas Tech University, Lubbock	8,800,000	79,000	97.93	7,736,169	300,000	198,868	138	Komatsu/Rangel
Pardee Management Library, Boston University	8,200,000	25,000	263.00	6,575,000	940,000	80,000	320	Cannon
College of the Canyons, Santa Clarita, Cal.	7,124,000	35,689	186.05	6,640,000	714,000	73,000	400	Spencer/Hoskins Assocs.
Ohio State University at Marion/Marion Technical College	7,100,000	46,780	129.85	6,074,208	430,000	37,000	211	Moody/Nolan Ltd.
Wilder Library and LRC, Virginia Union University, Richmond	7,030,000	70,000	87.14	6,100,000	600,000	148,835	600	Livas Group Architects
Integrated Learning Resource Center, Burlington County College, Pemberton, N.J.	6,500,000	42,360	132.20	5,600,000	775,000	115,000	390	GBQC Architects
Lynn University, Boca Raton, Fla.	5,800,000	58,000	86.21	5,000,000	300,000	200,000	500	Herbert S. Newman & Partners
Johnson State College, Vt.	4,805,000	40,000	106.88	4,275,000	530,000	130,000	210	Gossens/Bachman Architects
Pierce College, Puyallup, Wash.	4,320,000	19,500	165.13	3,220,000	1,100,000	40,000	206	MSGS Architects
Athens State College Library, Ala.	3,836,910	32,000	113.81	3,641,910	195,000	140,000	279	PH & J Architects Inc.

Table 5 / Academic Library Buildings: Additions and Renovations, 1997

Institution	Status	Project Cost	Gross Area	Sq. Ft. Cost	Construction Cost	Equipment Cost	Book Capacity	Seating Capacity	Architect
Hale Library, Kansas State University, Manhattan	Total	$30,000,000	401,000	$72.82	$29,200,000	$800,000	2,000,000	2,000	Brent Bowman & Assocs.; Hammond Beeby & Babka
	New	n/a	153,000	n/a	n/a	n/a	n/a	n/a	
	Renovated	n/a	248,000	n/a	n/a	n/a	n/a	n/a	
Cook Library, University of Southern Mississippi, Hattiesburg	Total	13,040,065	226,696	44.28	10,037,662	2,212,086	1,500,000	1,632	Dean & Dean Assocs.
	New	n/a	125,557	63.54	7,977,875	n/a	n/a	n/a	
	Renovated	n/a	101,139	20.36	2,059,747	n/a	n/a	n/a	
Architecture Library, University of Notre Dame, South Bend, Ind.	Total	$12,000,000	62,000	$189.00	$11,718,000	n/a	35,000	60	Thomas Gordon Smith; Ellerbe Becket
	New	n/a	20,000	n/a	n/a	n/a	n/a	n/a	
	Renovated	n/a	42,000	n/a	n/a	n/a	n/a	n/a	
Sampson Library, Jackson State University, Miss.	Total	11,925,000	144,377	77.92	11,250,000	600,000	600,000	1,150	Foil-Wyatt Architects
	New	9,964,000	66,827	140.66	9,400,000	n/a	n/a	n/a	
	Renovated	1,961,000	77,550	23.85	1,850,000	n/a	n/a	n/a	
Rhys Carpenter Art & Archaeology Lib., Bryn Mawr College, Pa.	Total	11,500,000	43,000	197.67	8,500,000	500,000	100,000	250	Henry Myerberg Architects
	New	n/a	33,000	n/a	n/a	n/a	n/a	n/a	
	Renovated	n/a	10,000	n/a	n/a	n/a	n/a	n/a	
Chalmer Davee Library, University of Wisconsin–River Falls	Total	7,100,000	130,901	n/a	n/a	n/a	243,500	1,040	Miller Martin Architects
	New	n/a	19,084	n/a	n/a	n/a	0	66	
	Renovated	n/a	111,817	n/a	n/a	n/a	243,500	974	
Richard Stockton College of New Jersey, Pomona	Total	6,995,000	77,500	57.16	4,430,000	518,500	350,000	643	GBQC Architects
	New	n/a	29,500	94.92	2,800,000	n/a	n/a	n/a	
	Renovated	n/a	48,000	33.96	1,630,000	n/a	n/a	n/a	
Donnelly Library, New Mexico Highlands University, Las Vegas	Total	n/a	74,780	76.22	5,700,000	290,000	303,705	320	Van H. Gilbert Architects
	New	n/a	34,984	94.33	3,300,000	140,000	101,235	184	
	Renovated	n/a	39,796	60.31	2,400,000	150,000	202,470	136	

N/A—not available

473

Table 5 / Academic Library Buildings: Additions and Renovations, 1997 (cont.)

Institution	Status	Project Cost	Gross Area	Sq. Ft. Cost	Construction Cost	Equipment Cost	Book Capacity	Seating Capacity	Architect
Linscheid Library, East Central University, Ada, Okla.	Total	4,513,639	74,020	54.22	4,013,639	500,000	240,000	380	Ray James & Assocs.
	New	4,131,334	58,533	64.60	3,781,334	350,000	240,000	380	
	Renovated	382,305	15,487	15.00	232,305	150,000	0	0	
Mabee Learning Resources Ctr., Wayland Baptist University, Plainview, Texas	Total	4,300,000	60,000	60.60	3,635,844	664,156	125,000	n/a	BGR Architects-Engineers
	New	n/a	18,000	n/a	n/a	n/a	n/a	n/a	
	Renovated	n/a	42,000	43.71	1,835,844	n/a	n/a	n/a	
Puente Library, Capitol College, Laurel, Md.	Total	3,200,000	14,000	139.29	1,950,000	800,000	25,000	150	Geier Brown Renfrow
	New	2,350,000	10,000	165.00	1,650,000	600,000	20,000	110	
	Renovated	850,000	4,000	75.00	300,000	200,000	5,000	40	
Wilmot Library, Nazareth College of Rochester, N.Y.	Total	2,831,200	29,000	83.83	2,431,200	400,000	350,000	450	FJK Architects
	New	2,531,400	21,700	102.81	2,231,400	300,000	100,000	85	
	Renovated	299,800	7,300	27.37	199,800	100,000	250,000	365	
Richland College Library, Dallas	Total	2,007,200	61,697	30.80	1,900,000	107,200	90,000	243	SHW Group Inc.
	New	n/a	16,697	71.87	1,200,000	n/a	0	54	
	Renovated	n/a	45,000	15.56	700,000	n/a	90,000	189	
Community College of Philadelphia	Total	1,500,000	38,000	30.26	1,150,000	n/a	125,000	600	Hillier Group
	New	n/a	6,000	n/a	n/a	n/a	n/a	n/a	
	Renovated	n/a	32,000	n/a	n/a	n/a	n/a	n/a	
Fogler Library, University of Maine, Orono	Total	1,070,000	n/a	n/a	n/a	n/a	n/a	0	REA Design Assocs.
	New	1,000,000	13,000	53.85	700,000	100,000	200,000	0	
	Renovated	70,000	n/a	n/a	n/a	n/a	n/a	0	
Learning Resources Div., Univ. of the District of Columbia, Washington, D.C.	Total	982,000	58,300	16.33	952,000	30,000	460,000	520	Bryant & Bryant
	New	n/a	25,300	16.22	410,345	n/a	320,000	241	
	Renovated	n/a	33,000	16.41	541,655	n/a	140,000	279	

n/a—not available

474

Table 6 / Academic Library Buildings: Renovations Only, 1997

Institution	Project Cost	Gross Area	Sq. Ft. Cost	Construction Cost	Equipment Cost	Book Capacity	Seating Capacity	Architect
Southwestern University School of Law, Los Angeles	$9,600,000	92,000	$78.26	$7,200,000	$1,700,000	315,000	610	Altoon + Porter, Architects
Virginia Military Institute, Lexington	5,500,000	69,355	57.67	4,000,000	700,000	350,000	350	VMDO
Point Park College, Pittsburgh	n/a	65,000	70.77	4,600,000	n/a	n/a	350	Sylvester Damianos
Rosalind Denny Lewis Music Library, Mass. Inst. of Technology, Cambridge	1,250,000	7,000	109.71	768,000	150,000	10,000	49	Melanie R. Brothers
E.H. Butler Library, Buffalo State College, State University of New York	982,925	7,430	53.67	398,746	584,179	n/a	120	Wendel
Amelia Gayle Gorgas Library, University of Alabama, Tuscaloosa	265,341	12,940	11.32	146,500	118,841	n/a	n/a	Hugh W. Kilpatrick III
Penrose Memorial Library, Whitman College, Walla Walla, Wash.	250,000	3,723	65.27	243,000	7,000	n/a	n/a	Boyle-Wagoner Architects
Wheelock College Library, Boston	89,910	1,120	62.93	70,537	19,373	2,800	22	Architectural Resources

n/a—not available

Expenditures for Resources in School Library Media Centers, FY 1995–1996: Small Change

Marilyn L. Miller

Professor Emeritus and Former Chair, Department of Library and Information Studies,
University of North Carolina, Greensboro

Marilyn L. Shontz

Associate Professor, Department of Library and Information Studies,
University of North Carolina, Greensboro

Give a school library media specialist a materials budget and then two years later, after costs have risen, shrink it by $600.

That's the scenario facing school library media specialists nationally, according to our most recent survey of school library expenditures, the eighth in a biennial series of *School Library Journal (SLJ)* reports. These reports summarize developments during 1995–1996 in public and private school library media programs in the United States.

The title of the report is "Small Change." But it could just as easily be "No Change" when it comes to spending on books. Average book expenditures have not budged at all since our 1995 study, based on data from 1993–1994. Library media specialists (LMSs) spent an average of $4,000 then, and they spend an average of $4,000 now.

Dollars for most other resources—AV, periodicals, microforms, and CD-ROMs—have dropped slightly. Only software spending has managed to inch up.

Not surprisingly, the push for Internet access has attracted additional funding. In our 1995 study, 21.3 percent of library media centers (LMCs) had received additional funds needed to access the Internet. In this study, that number jumped to 34 percent. Local area networks (LANs) have also mushroomed: 66 percent of LMCs now have a LAN, compared to 38.8 percent in our 1995 report.

Our report also looks at professional practices, such as the extent of collaborative planning between LMSs and teachers. Despite promotion of the practice, the number of hours that LMSs meet with teachers has taken a dip at all grade levels.

We also closely examined a subset of media centers in which librarians are skillfully juggling the Internet, networks, cable TV, site-based management, and regular contact with their principals, among other things. For more on these high-service media centers, see Table 19.

What the Survey Offers

The purpose of this series, begun in 1983, has been to provide *SLJ* readers with an up-to-date account (as well as a longitudinal review) of national trends in expenditures. We offer this report so LMSs can compare local expenditures, services, and programs with a national norm.

Adapted from *School Library Journal*, October 1997.

Table 1 / Respondents
by Grade Level

Table 2 / Respondents
by Census Region

Table 3 / Respondents
by Enrollment

Table 1 / Respondents by Grade Level

Other 12%
High School 24%
Elementary 44%
Jr. High/Middle 20%

Table 2 / Respondents by Census Region

West 13%
Northeast 22%
North Central 24%
South 41%

Table 3 / Respondents by Enrollment

Over 2000 3%
Under 300 9%
1000-1999 14%
300-499 26%
700-999 19%
500-699 29%

All the *SLJ* reports have focused on the status of school library collections, expenditures, staffing, and instructional involvement. In addition, we have reported on the steady escalation in the use of computers and the emergence and expansion of telecommunications in LMCs. The report also includes data from schools serving large numbers of economically disadvantaged students.

We add new data to each report. This time, we:

- Report on the use of electronic reading programs and look at their impact on LMC expenditures (Tables 11–12)
- Examine LMC services in schools with site-based management (Tables 16–18)
- Look at what 141 high-service school library programs offer (Table 19)
- Describe the type and extent of communication between LMSs and principals (Table 21)

Table 4 / Mean and Median Expenditures All Resources, 1995–1996

Expenditures	Number Responding	Mean	Median
Total all local funds	575	$12,575	$9,080
Total all federal funds	208	3,588	1,979
Total all gift funds	347	3,398	1,200
Total all funds			
Books	556	6,415	5,165
Periodicals	536	1,308	900
Microforms	93	1,200	806
AV resources/equipment	450	2,834	1,700
Computer resources/equipment	410	7,429	3,090
Total expenditures	580	$15,707	$11,144

Note: Table 4 presents mean and median expenditures for all resources from most funding sources, including local school budgets, the federal government, gifts, and fund-raising. It does not include funds allocated through district media centers, regional consortiums, or other leasing or granting agencies. "Local" defines money allocated by local school boards, states, and/or counties that fund all or part of local school expenses and are administered through a local education agency (LEA).

Respondents (Tables 1–3, 13)

The response rate for this report is the smallest in the series. This may be due to a drop in high school respondents—from 31 percent of all respondents in the 1995 report to 24 percent in this report. At the same time, the number of elementary school respondents increased from 36 percent in the 1995 report to 44 percent in this report.

For information on respondents' certification status, education level, experience, and salary, see Table 13.

Spending (Tables 4–8)

Table 4 shows that median expenditures for all LMC resources dipped to $11,144 in the 1995–1996 school year, approximately $600 less than in 1993–1994. Obviously, spending for all types of resources did not keep pace with price increases or inflation.

Federal funds did not take up the slack. Slightly more than 50 percent of respondents turned to fund-raising, but to little avail: their efforts attracted nearly the same number of dollars as in the 1995 report.

Although a higher percentage of funding continues to go toward books than toward other resources, the median figure for book spending is unchanged from 1993–1994. In other words, average book expenditures are frozen.

Table 5 / Mean and Median Expenditures per School for LMC Resources, 1995–1996
(local funds only)

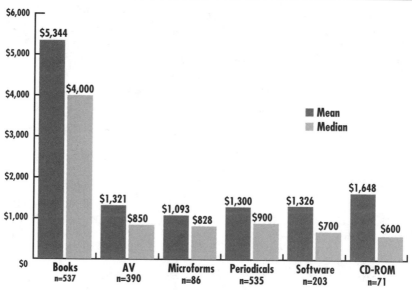

Tables 5 through 8 summarize expenditures of local funds for books (includes preprocessing costs); AV (now largely videotape purchases, rentals, and leasing); periodicals (includes magazines, journals, and newspapers for both student and professional use); software (includes online search fees and preprocessing costs, such as OCLC fees); CD-ROMs; and microforms.

Table 6 / Median Expenditures per School for LMC Resources, 1990–1996
(local funds only)

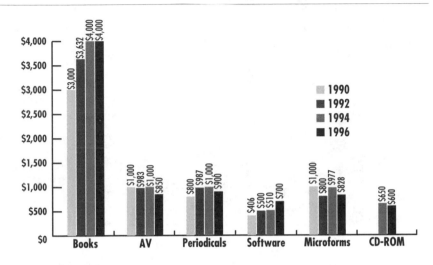

Table 7 / Mean and Median Expenditures per Pupil for LMC Resources, 1995–1996
(local funds only)

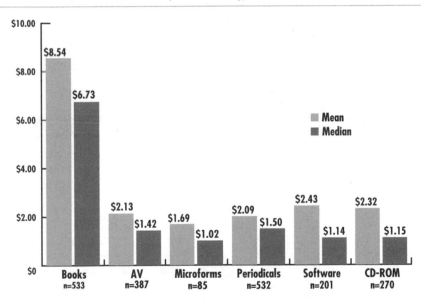

Average expenditures for resources, however, do not reflect the strong economy in which LMCs currently operate. Not shown in our charts is the fact that 38 percent saw an increase in their overall materials budget over the previous year, while 33 percent had larger book budgets. Forty-one percent worked with increased funds for computer software, 37 percent had more money for telecom-

Table 8 / Median Expenditures per Pupil for LMC Resources, 1990–1996
(local funds only)

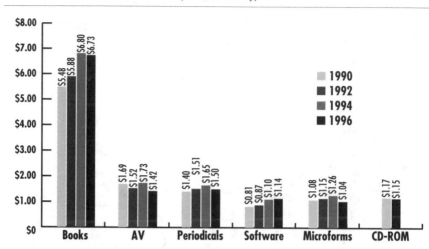

munications, and 34 percent had the funds to add more CD-ROMs to their collections.

Our report shows stagnant funding because there are other LMCs with budget problems that bring down average spending. Twenty-one percent saw cuts in overall materials budgets, while one-third were level-funded. A full 36 percent received less money for books.

By displaying both mean and median figures in Tables 5 and 7, the inequities between resource expenditures per school and per pupil are evident. Books still enjoy the largest allocation. We also see large differences between the mean and median figures for software and CD-ROM resources. These differences can possibly be attributed to higher investments in technology by those schools we define as high-tech—schools with library media centers that have both an online catalog and circulation system.

Tables 6 and 8 show trends over the past six years. Except for expenditures for computer software, which increased by $190 per school or four cents per pupil in the 1995–1996 school year over 1993–1994, expenditures for all resources except books have declined. Indeed, the best year for average per-pupil expenditures was the 1993–1994 school year.

This stagnation and decline are noteworthy during a healthy economy. Well into the vaunted "information age," schools are spending absolute minimums for the program that serves every student and teacher in the school.

Resources (Tables 9–13)

Book collections are deteriorating across the country. We've documented sobering evidence of the effects of frozen spending, the impact of inflation, and normal wear and tear on collections in this and all previous *SLJ* surveys.

Even more sobering are comparisons of book expenditures per pupil for books by grade level. We found that senior high school LMSs spend less money

Table 9 / LMC Collection Size and Local Expenditures by School Level, 1995–1996

	Elementary n=276		Jr. High/Middle n=128		Senior High n=154		Other n=72	
	median	mean	median	mean	median	mean	median	mean
Size of book collection	9,000	9,218	10,000	10,175	12,300	13,480	10,100	10,560
Volumes added, 1995–1996	377	535	300	418	350	473	400	548
Number of books per pupil	17	19	14	16	14	17	19	23
Volumes discarded, 1995–1996	100	246	148	263	128	413	100	180
Size of AV collection	250	501	175	391	150	360	200	534
Number of AV items added, 1995–1996	5	14	6	16	3	43	0	6
Number of AV items per pupil	0.53	0.95	0.24	0.59	0.24	0.46	0.35	1.04
AV items discarded, 1995–1996	3	65	10	54	0	61	0	11
Size of video collection	129	178	200	277	245	439	193	199
Videos added, 1995–1996	20	27	20	26	20	40	20	31
Videos per pupil	0.25	0.37	0.26	0.43	0.31	0.52	0.35	0.4
Videos discarded, 1995–1996	0	3	0	8	0	4	0	6
Size of software collection	30	117	25	90	14	49	20	94
Computer software added, 1995–1996	2	9	3	6	2	5	2	7
Computer software per pupil	0.07	0.22	0.04	0.12	0.02	0.07	0.05	0.18
Computer software discarded, 1995–1996	0	3.92	0	6.55	0	6.43	0	1.43
Size of CD-ROM collection	15	33	20	28	15	30	17	55
CD-ROMs added, 1995–1996	5	14	5	10	5	9	7	17
CD-ROMs per pupil	0.03	0.07	0.02	0.05	0.02	0.04	0.32	0.97
CD-ROMs discarded, 1995–1996	0	0.12	0	0.12	0	0.49	0	0.26

Table 9 / LMC Collection Size and Local Expenditures by School Level, 1995–1996 *(cont.)*

	Elementary n=276		Jr. High/Middle n=128		Senior High n=154		Other n=72	
	median	mean	median	mean	median	mean	median	mean
Expenditures								
Books	$3,446.00	$4,272.34	$5,000.00	$6,028.26	$6,000.00	$7,221.67	$3,000.00	$4,407.33
Books per pupil	6.73	8.49	7.30	9.13	6.27	8.51	6.33	7.66
Periodicals	600.00	659.29	1,100.00	1,280.88	2,000.00	2,466.45	1,150.00	1,346.71
Periodicals per pupil	1.17	1.35	1.67	2.06	2.32	3.32	1.97	2.43
Microforms	455.00	768.35	1,000.00	1,273.88	1,000.00	1,188.23	572.00	873.37
Microforms per pupil	0.79	1.27	1.02	1.82	1.07	1.82	0.95	1.55
AV materials	773.00	1,022.95	1,000.00	1,680.41	1,000.00	1,567.74	550.00	1,152.08
AV materials per pupil	1.43	2.06	1.48	2.39	1.25	2.04	1.11	2.04
Software	700.00	1,372.70	695.00	935.26	868.50	1,450.70	600.00	1,705.50
Software per pupil	1.32	2.88	0.93	1.52	1.13	2.52	0.63	2.57
CD-ROMs	300.00	612.04	619.50	981.73	2,650.00	3,130.55	650.00	1,679.33
CD-ROMs per pupil	0.68	1.21	1.00	1.67	2.91	3.90	1.16	2.28
*Total materials expenditures (TME)	$8,850.00	$12,610.98	$11,876.00	$15,358.84	$16,400.00	$21,908.28	$10,700.00	$15,127.15
TME per pupil	$17.05	$26.00	$17.18	$23.65	$18.20	$28.71	$22.70	$29.60

*Table 9 describes, quantitatively, the categories of media in LMCs by school level. Expenditures from all sources—local, federal, gifts, and fund-raising—are shown as Total Materials Expenditures (TME). TME is reported at the bottom of each column for purposes of comparison. TME excludes salaries, but reflects all expenditures for resources including AV equipment, computer hardware, online services, rentals, leasing, supplies, and maintenance.

Table 10 / LMCs and Technology, 1995–1996

	Number Responding	Percent
Additional funds provided for (n=565):		
Computer software	216	38
Telecommunications	190	34
CD-ROM	191	34
Videodiscs	66	12
Technical processing	80	14
Resource sharing	77	14
LMC Uses (n=600)		
Cable TV	430	72
Broadcast TV	233	39
Closed circuit TV	162	27
Distance education, 1-way audio-video	57	9
Distance education, 2-way audio-video	45	7
LMC Has (n=612)		
Local area network	401	66
Wide area network	255	42
Computers with modems	398	65
Access to telecommunications, Internet, e-mail	382	62
CD-ROM searching	513	84
Web access	303	49
Fax	115	19
Access to fax in school	390	64
LMC has telephone	523	85
LMC is member of resource-sharing network (n=600)	348	58
Network is linked electronically	185	31
LMC has online catalog (n=622)	372	60
LMC has online circulation system (n=622)	477	77
LMS presented teacher inservice on (n=485):		
Video production	61	13
CD-ROM use	323	67
Telecommunications	180	37
Web applications	159	33
Online searching	191	39
Internet use	186	38
LMC is "High Tech" (n=622) with both an online catalog and circulation system	365	59

Table 11 / Electronic Reading Programs in Schools and LMCs, 1995–1996

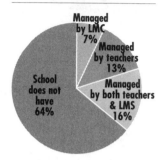

Managed by LMC 7%
Managed by teachers 13%
Managed by both teachers & LMS 16%
School does not have 64%

Table 12 / Percent of LMC Budget for Electronic Reading Program Materials, 1995–1996

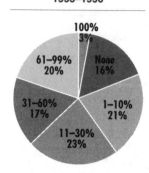

100% 3%
61–99% 20%
None 16%
31–60% 17%
1–10% 21%
11–30% 23%

per pupil on books than do those in lower grades. When comparing total materials expenditures, Table 9 shows that high school LMSs spend only $1 more per student than those in elementary and middle schools at a time when prices continue to escalate for adult trade books and reference titles.

Table 9 also illustrates the demise of the general AV collection, which includes filmstrips, films, and audiocassettes. When we compared general AV collections with video collections, we found that video collections had grown significantly in the average school. High school video collections, with a median number of 200 videos per school, are larger than high school AV collections, which now average 150 items.

Table 10 gives an overview of the types and extent of technology in LMCs. Sixty percent use at least eight technologies:

- Telephone in the LMC, 85 percent
- CD-ROM, 84 percent
- Online circulation system, 77 percent
- Cable television, 72 percent
- Computers with modems, 65 percent
- Access to a fax machine in the school, 64 percent
- Internet access, 62 percent
- Online catalog, 60 percent

Forty-nine percent of LMCs have web access. The table also shows that nearly one-third received extra funds to cover software, the Internet, and CD-ROMs.

New to the resource mix are the growing demands of electronic reading programs. In schools that use these programs, many LMSs find that they wreak havoc with both budgets and the freedom of LMSs to manage materials selection.

Table 11 shows how schools and LMCs use electronic reading programs. Sixty-four percent of the schools in the *SLJ* study have not yet succumbed to these programs. The next best piece of news is that only seven percent of LMCs have primary responsibility for the program. Classroom teachers and LMSs share

Table 13 / School Library Media Specialists: Experience, Salary, and Support Staff, 1995–1996

	Elementary (n=276)		Middle/Jr. High (n=128)		Senior High (n=154)		Other (n=72)		All Schools (n=630)	
	median	mean	median	mean	median	mean	median	mean	median	mean
Media specialists in school	1	0.92	1	1.02	1	1.24	1	1.05	1	1.03
Years experience/K–12 schools	19	18	21	19	22	21	13	14	20	18
Years library experience	11	13	14	14	14	15	11	12	13	14
Salary of head media specialist	$38,000	$38,868	$38,000	$38,806	$39,000	$39,377	$27,880	$27,927	$37,800	$37,773
Student assistants	0	3.44	3	5.26	3	5.29	0	2.53	0	4.17
Support staff/paid clerks	0.5	0.57	1	0.8	1	0.92	0.5	0.55	0.5	0.7
Adult volunteers	2	4.68	0	1.27	0	0.9	1	3.83	0	2.96

the responsibility in 16 percent of the schools. And 13 percent of classroom teachers manage the programs alone.

Table 12 shows the budgetary impact of these electronic reading programs, and by extension, the impact on collection development. Twenty-three percent of participating LMSs spend 61 to 100 percent of their budgets on books required by these programs. In many cases, the programs hold awesome power over expenditures as well as over building a collection designed to serve an entire curriculum. As LMSs study the argument raging on outsourcing professional services, they must consider themselves primary users of this strategy if they use electronic reading programs.

Human Resources (Table 13)

Human resources are largely unchanged. On average, LMCs are still staffed by one LMS. Only high schools enjoy full-time paid support staff. Both adult and student volunteers, found mostly in elementary and private schools, continue to fluctuate in number and are not a major source of assistance. As we expected, LMSs at all levels saw an average salary increase of $1,500 over the 1995 report.

Curriculum Planning (Tables 14–19)

In 1998 the American Association for School Librarians (AASL) and the Association for Educational Communications and Technology (AECT) will publish new joint standards for learning with a revision of *Information Power* (ALA, 1988). This document will focus on students as learners and will describe the successful LMS as one who collaborates with teachers and develops and manages a student-centered program.

In light of these new standards and guidelines, the information presented in Tables 14–19 becomes even more important.

Tables 14 and 15 describe collaborative planning in mean number of hours per week. High school LMSs do more planning with teachers, both formal and informal, than do LMSs at any other grade levels. Informal planning is twice as likely to take place as is formal planning at all levels. Collaborative planning of any kind is commendable, but the demands upon LMSs to become more productive partners in student learning will require more formal planning with teachers. Keep in mind that only means are used for Tables 14 and 15. Means skew data upward, making the figures look better.

Table 14 / Weekly LMS/Teacher Instructional Planning by Grade, 1995–1996

	Mean Hours Formal Instructional Planning	Mean Hours Informal Instructional Planning	Mean Hours Total Planning
Elementary (n=262)	0.91	2.18	3.08
Junior high/middle (n=124)	1.27	2.49	3.77
High school (n=145)	1.26	2.71	3.97
Other (n=70)	0.84	1.86	2.7
Total (n=601)	1.06	2.33	3.39

It is obvious from Table 15 that the type of LMC scheduling has an impact on the type of planning. The good news is that so few media specialists still use fixed schedules. On the other hand, it is puzzling that so many LMSs using flexible and/or combined schedules do not regularly plan with teachers. Regardless of the type of scheduling used, it is encouraging that the majority of LMSs work together with a substantial number of teachers.

What about site-based management? Does it benefit LMCs financially? Tables 16 and 17 indicate that LMS involvement on site-based management (SBM) teams may not lead to budget increases. Seventy percent of respondents are either members of SBM teams (44 percent) or serve as team consultants (26 percent). Ten percent saw their LMC budget decrease under SBM, and 24 saw it increase. But the majority—66 percent—saw no effect. This is worrisome. With so many media specialists involved in

Table 15 / Type of LMC Schedule Used, LMC Staffing, and LMS/Teacher Planning, 1995–1996

	Flexible Schedule n=238	Comb. Fixed/Flex n=257	Fixed Schedule n=122
LMS regularly plans with teachers			
Yes	81	74	56
No	19	26	44
Percent of teachers planning with LMS			
0–10%	16	17	33
11–30%	32	35	32
31–70%	34	26	26
More than 70%	17	22	9
Mean no. of hours of planning per week			
Formal	1.31	0.96	0.83
Informal	2.64	2.27	1.92
Total teacher/LMS planning hours	3.95	3.23	2.75
Mean no. LMS on staff—full & part-time	1.16	0.96	0.95
Mean no. support staff—full & part-time	0.96	0.56	0.5

Table 16 / LMSs and Site-Based Management, 1995–1996

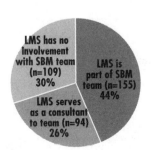

LMS has no involvement with SBM team (n=109) 30%

LMS is part of SBM team (n=155) 44%

LMS serves as a consultant to team (n=94) 26%

Table 17 / LMC Budget and Site-Based Management, 1995–1996

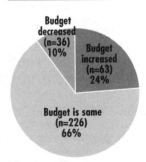

Budget decreased (n=36) 10%

Budget increased (n=63) 24%

Budget is same (n=226) 66%

SBM planning, we have to ask, "What are the barriers that keep them from successfully making the argument for budget increases?"

Services (Tables 18–20)

Still, site-based management may benefit library media centers in other ways. For this report, we identified 22 services and asked respondents which ones they provided. Table 18 compares services offered by site-based managed schools with those offered by non-SBM schools.

In most cases, LMSs in site-based managed schools provide a wider range of services than do their colleagues in non-SBM schools. For example, more LMSs in site-based managed schools:

- Help teachers develop, implement, and evaluate learning (68 percent vs. 56 percent)
- Offer an integrated skills curriculum (66 percent vs. 58 percent)
- Plan with teachers more than two hours a week (56 percent vs. 41 percent)
- Communicate proactively with the principal (47 percent vs. 33 percent)
- Conduct workshops for teachers (32 percent vs. 26 percent)

Table 18 / LMC Services and School Involvement in Site-Based Management, 1995–1996

		With SBM	Without SBM
LMC Service:			
1	Offers a program of curriculum-integrated skills instruction	66	58
2	Informally instructs students in the use of resources	96	92
3	Conducts workshops for teachers	32	26
4	Assists school curriculum committee with recommendations	57	38
5	Collaborates with teachers	86	81
6	Helps teachers develop, implement, and evaluate learning	68	56
7	Provides teachers with information about new resources	89	89
8	Provides reference assistance to students and teachers	99	99
9	Helps students and teachers use resources outside the school	80	76
10	Provides interlibrary loan service for students and teachers	60	60
11	Provides reading/listening/viewing guidance for students	95	88
12	Helps parents realize the importance of lifelong learning	55	49
13	Coordinates in-school production of materials	37	24
14	Coordinates video production	32	26
15	Coordinates cable TV and related activities	49	47
16	Coordinates computer networks	29	22
17	Provides online catalog and circulation systems	76	67
18	Provides access to CD-ROM searching	86	81
19	Provides Web access	49	49
20	Provides access to Internet and e-mail	64	59
21	Communicates proactively with the principal	47	33
22	Plans instruction with teachers more than two hours a week	56	41

To provide a profile of an active, progressive LMC program, we identified 141 high-service LMCs in our study—those that provide 17 or more of the 22 services listed in Table 18. We compared the high-service group to those LMCs that offered a smaller number of services, from 1 to 16 of those listed in Table 18.

Table 19 / LMC Characteristics by Level of Service, 1995–1996

	Hi-Service LMCs n=141		Non-Hi-Service LMCs n=487	
	count	percent	count	percent
*Use of library media advisory committee	49	36	90	19
*Availability of selection policy	128	94	368	79
*Book collection less than 30% out of date	120	86	374	78
*Planning with teachers for integrated instruction	127	91	320	66
*Total mean hours LMS/teacher planning more than 2	110	79	186	38
*More than 30% of teachers plan with LMS	83	65	144	30
*LMC member of network	105	78	243	52
*Added funds for resource sharing	30	26	47	10
*Telephone in LMC	127	93	396	81
*LMC uses cable TV	125	89	306	63
*LMC uses closed-circuit TV	67	47	96	20
*Online catalog	116	84	258	53
*Online circulation system	127	91	351	72
*LMC is high tech	114	82	250	51
*LMC has local area network	121	86	280	57
*LMC has wide area network	78	55	178	37
*LMC has computers with modems	116	82	283	58
*Telecommunications, Internet, e-mail	116	84	266	55
*CD-ROM searching	137	99	376	77
*Fax in LMC	44	31	71	15
*Web access	101	73	202	42
*LMC uses flexible or combined schedule	135	96	360	74
*LMC/principal communication is proactive	99	70	162	34
Electronic reading programs used	47	35	163	35
*Full-time/part-time district LM director	79	57	209	45
Less than 30% of students receive free lunch	89	63	279	58
*School uses site-based management	103	76	255	53
Head LMS has advanced degree in LIS	96	70	314	66

* Statistically significant <.05

Table 19 shows that 99 percent of high-service LMCs provide CD-ROM searching, compared to 77 percent of the non-high-service LMCs. High-service LMCs are also more likely to:

- Use flexible or combined scheduling (96 percent vs. 74 percent)
- Have a selection policy (94 percent vs. 79 percent)
- Have a telephone (93 percent vs. 81 percent)
- Use an online circulation system (91 percent vs. 72 percent)
- Plan with teachers for integrated instruction (91 percent vs. 66 percent)

LMSs in high-service LMCs are also twice as likely to use an advisory committee, plan with teachers more than two hours a week, plan with more than 30 percent of their teachers, and communicate directly with their principals.

Not surprisingly, having a district media coordinator also makes a significant difference in LMC services. This report reveals that slightly more LMSs have access to at least half-time district-level help than did their colleagues in the 1995 study.

Table 20 shows that LMSs with access to district library media leadership are more likely to plan with teachers for integrated instruction. They are also more likely to:

- Work in schools where fewer than 30 percent of students qualify for free lunch programs
- Be in a site-based-managed school
- Use flexible or combined scheduling
- Communicate directly with their principals
- Be high-service providers

On the other hand, LMSs with access to district media leadership are less likely to use electronic reading programs.

Principal Relations (Table 21)

In this survey, we introduced basic questions about the strategies used by LMSs to communicate with their principals. We asked them to describe how, and how often, they formally communicated with their principals.

Table 21 displays critical differences between LMSs who initiate communication with their principals and those who do not.

We found that LMSs who communicate well with their principals are also more likely to lead staff development activities. The staff development activities described here underscore the importance of educating teachers to use telecommunications. We compliment the 53 percent of LMSs who also assist with instructional design.

We want to note one interesting finding about video production. In our experience, both from reading research studies and personal observation, video production activities remain a low priority for many LMSs. Staff development in video production, often a potentially high profile and popular activity in many

Table 20 / LMC Characteristics with and without District-Level Media Coordinators, 1995–1996

	With Full-Time n=191		With Part-Time n=99		Without n=311	
	count	percent	count	percent	count	percent
*Use of library media advisory committee	64	34	24	24	49	16
Availability of selection policy	163	88	81	82	243	81
Book collection less than 30% out of date	153	81	77	78	240	79
*Planning with teachers for integrated instruction	154	84	66	67	210	69
*Total mean hours LMS/teacher planning > 2 per week	99	52	54	55	131	44
*More than 30% of teachers plan with LMS	85	45	37	37	95	30
*LMC is high-service	56	29	23	23	59	19
LMC member of network	115	63	54	55	163	53
Added funds for resource sharing	25	16	14	14	33	13
Telephone in LMC	157	82	85	86	256	82
LMC uses cable TV	144	75	77	78	200	64
LMC uses closed-circuit TV	73	38	20	20	69	22
*Online library catalog	123	65	64	65	166	54
*Automated circulation system	154	83	79	80	222	72

Table 20 / LMC Characteristics with and without District-Level Media Coordinators, 1995–1996 *(cont.)*

	With Full-Time n=191		With Part-Time n=99		Without n=311	
	count	percent	count	percent	count	percent
*LMC is high tech	117	61	61	62	166	54
LMC has local area network	122	64	64	65	197	63
LMC has wide area network	77	40	48	49	122	39
LMC has computers with modems	124	65	58	59	197	63
Telecommunications, Internet, e-mail	116	62	63	64	184	61
CD-ROM searching	150	81	85	86	252	83
Fax in LMC	36	19	14	14	59	19
Web access	90	48	49	50	145	48
LMC uses flexible or combined schedule	151	79	82	83	239	77
LMS/principal communication is proactive	83	44	38	39	128	42
Electronic reading programs used	73	38	37	37	96	50
*Less than 30% of students receive free lunch	99	52	63	64	193	62
*School uses site-based management	141	76	65	66	146	50
Head LMS has advanced degree in LIS	125	66	68	69	198	64

* Statistically significant at p=.05

Table 21 / LMS-Implemented Development and LMS-Initiated
Communication with Principal, 1995–1996

schools, still takes a back seat to telecommunications and its applications. That's true regardless of the level of LMS/principal communication.

Doing More with Less

As with all of our reports, we conclude with bittersweet reflections. We are amazed and almost awed by the explosion of services and programs in the telecommunications arena. On the flip side, we wish that we could sweeten the sour refrain of school library media specialists doing more with less, which, translated, means "providing more motivation and guidance in the art, joy, and necessity of reading while saddled with deteriorating print collections."

We know from many respondents' comments that the times are discouraging; the temptation to chuck it all is not uncommon. As always, however, we commend the majority who are learning new skills and expanding their vision of what school library media programs should be for today's students and teachers.

Methodology

In September 1996 we mailed a questionnaire to 1,440 school library media centers selected by systematic random sampling from the *SLJ* school-based subscription list covering 50 states. Questionnaires were mailed only to subscribers with a school name or some form of the title "library media specialist" in their address. Two subsequent mailings were sent to non-respondents.

By December, we received 659 responses—45.7 percent of the sample—and of those, 43.7 percent were usable. Of the total, 66, or 10.5 percent, came from private schools. The usable response rate for this report is the lowest received in the series, begun in 1983.

Each response was checked for accuracy, then coded and entered into the computer. Data analysis was done using the Statistical Package for the Social Sciences (SPSS). Measures of central tendency (means and medians) were produced for all of the budget items listed on the survey. Chi square and ANOVA tests were used in the statistical analysis of data presented in Tables 18 and 20.

Both means and medians are reported, wherever appropriate, to give a more accurate description of the data. The means allow for comparisons with earlier studies that have used this measure; the medians indicate accurately the expenditures reported by most LMCs.

Although the mean (or average) is the descriptive statistic most commonly used in studies of this type, analysis of the data showed that much of it was skewed upward because a few respondents reported spending extremely large amounts for various kinds of materials. With a wide data distribution like this, a few large scores make the mean a less desirable measure of central tendency because these inflate the mean.

To report only the mean in instances where data were skewed would be misleading. For example, one respondent reported adding 109 software titles, another added 150, while a third added 300. However, 29.7 percent of the respondents reported adding no software, and another 31 percent added 10 titles. If we used the mean, we would note that LMCs added 7.19 items. The median—a much more accurate picture—would indicate two items per LMC.

Book Trade Research and Statistics

Prices of U.S. and Foreign Published Materials

Stephen Bosch

Chair, ALA ALCTS Library Materials Price Index Committee

The Library Materials Price Index Committee (LMPIC) of the American Library Association's Association for Library Collections and Technical Services continues to monitor library prices for a variety of library materials and sources. As seen below, prices for library materials in general continued to increase in 1996 and 1997 at a rate much higher than the general U.S. Consumer Price Index (CPI). For 1997–1998 the CPI increased only 1.7 percent while journals increased by more than 10 percent. Information concerning the Consumer Price Index can be found at the Bureau of Labor Statistics CPI home page at http://stats.bls.gov/cpihome.htm.

		Percent Change		
Index	1994	1995	1996	1997/98
Consumer price index (1997)	2.7	2.9	3.3	1.7
Periodicals	5.5	10.8	9.9	10.3*
Serial services	5.0	6.6	3.9	4.5*
Hardcover books	22.7	5.6	6.0	n.a.
Academic books	2.1	-0.1	3.6	n.a.
College books	-2.0	4.7	1.8	n.a.
Mass market paperbacks	-1.4	15.4	12.3	n.a.
Trade paperbacks	-2.5	5.4	-1.3	n.a.

* Payments made in 1997 for 1998 receipt

U.S. Published Materials

Tables 1 through 10 consist of average prices and price indexes for library materials published primarily in the United States. These indexes include periodicals (Table 1), serial services (Table 2), U.S. hardcover books (Table 3), North American academic books (Table 4), college books (Table 5), mass market paperback books (Table 6), trade paperback books (Table 7), daily newspapers and international newspapers (Tables 8 and 8A), nonprint media (Table 9), and CD-ROMs (Table 10).

(text continues on page 506)

Table 1 / U.S. Periodicals: Average Prices and Price Indexes, 1996–1998
Index Base: 1984 = 100

Subject Area	1984 Average Price	1996 Average Price	1996 Index	1997 Average Price	1997 Index	1998 Average Price	1998 Index
U.S. periodicals excluding Russian translations*	$54.97	$165.61	301.3	$181.98	331.1	$200.74	365.2
U.S. periodicals including Russian translations	72.47	215.37	297.2	237.14	327.2	259.69	358.3
Agriculture	24.06	67.12	279.0	72.40	300.9	79.50	330.4
Business and economics	38.87	102.69	264.2	114.18	293.7	121.77	313.3
Chemistry and physics	228.90	867.00	378.8	957.36	418.2	1,062.49	464.2
Children's periodicals	12.21	21.65	177.3	23.08	189.0	24.15	197.8
Education	34.01	86.90	255.5	95.34	280.3	103.98	305.7
Engineering	78.70	247.72	314.8	273.31	347.3	306.60	389.6
Fine and applied arts	26.90	48.24	179.3	50.02	185.9	52.08	193.6
General interest periodicals	27.90	39.37	141.1	40.72	145.9	42.26	151.5
History	23.68	50.76	214.4	54.20	228.9	57.31	242.0
Home economics	37.15	92.44	248.8	98.88	266.2	100.39	270.2
Industrial arts	30.40	87.57	288.1	93.79	308.5	99.05	325.8

Journalism and communications	39.25	91.31	232.6	98.16	250.1	104.26	265.6
Labor and industrial relations	29.87	85.80	287.2	92.28	308.9	98.99	331.4
Law	31.31	82.48	263.4	85.57	273.3	89.81	286.8
Library and information sciences	38.85	72.50	186.6	78.00	200.8	86.12	221.7
Literature and language	23.02	44.16	191.8	46.72	203.0	49.98	217.1
Mathematics, botany, geology general science	106.56	342.07	321.0	379.84	356.5	420.36	394.5
Medicine	125.57	410.66	327.0	461.60	367.6	524.65	417.8
Philosophy and religion	21.94	45.71	208.3	48.84	222.6	51.71	235.7
Physical education and recreation	20.54	43.73	212.9	45.65	222.2	48.10	234.2
Political science	32.43	86.02	265.2	91.82	283.1	100.82	310.9
Psychology	69.74	211.72	303.6	233.90	335.4	258.91	371.3
Russian translations	381.86	1,099.42	287.9	1,216.51	318.6	1,311.50	343.5
Sociology and anthropology	43.87	125.77	286.7	137.54	313.5	151.01	344.2
Zoology	78.35	299.84	382.7	338.31	431.8	385.40	491.9
Total number of periodicals							
Excluding Russian translations	3,731		3,731		3,729		3,729
Including Russian translations	3,942		3,941		3,939		3,938

For further comments, see *American Libraries*, May 1995, May 1956, May 1997, and May 1998 issues.

Compiled by Adrian W. Alexander, the Faxon Company, and Brenda Dingley, University of Missouri, Kansas City.

*The category Russian translations was added in 1986.

Table 2 / U.S. Serial Services: Average Prices and Price Indexes, 1996–1998
(Index Base: 1977 = 100)

Subject Area	1977 Average Price	1996 Average Price	1996 Index	1997 Average Price	1997 Percent Increase	1997 Index	1998 Average Price	1998 Percent Increase	1998 Index
U.S. serial services*	$142.27	$556.58	391.2	$578.22	3.9	406.4	$604.31	4.5	204.8
Business	216.28	737.14	340.8	751.99	2.0	347.7	781.33	3.9	178.8
General and humanities	90.44	410.75	454.2	429.12	4.5	474.5	455.78	6.2	231.9
Law	126.74	593.81	468.5	592.84	-0.2	467.8	611.71	3.2	222.3
Science and technology	141.16	675.82	478.8	716.95	6.1	507.9	757.33	5.6	256.4
Social sciences	145.50	513.08	352.6	536.85	4.6	369.0	557.34	3.8	196.4
U.S. documents	62.88	129.37	205.7	151.38	17.0	240.7	162.32	7.2	166.7
Total number of services	1,432	1,280		1,281			1,282		

Compiled by Nancy J. Chaffin, Arizona State University (West) from data supplied by the Faxon Company, publishers list prices, and library acquisition records.

The definition of a serial service has been taken from *American National Standard for Library and Information Services and Related Publishing Practices—Library Materials—Criteria for Price Indexes* (ANSI 239.20—1983).

* Excludes Wilson Index; excludes Russian Translations as of 1988.

Table 3 / U.S. Hardcover Books Average Prices and Price Indexes, 1994–1997

Index Base 1977 = 100

Subject Area	1977 Average Price	1994 Average Price	1994 Volumes	1994 Index	1995 Volumes	1995 Average Price	1995 Index	1996 Final Volumes	1996 Final Average Price	1996 Final Index	1997 Preliminary Volumes	1997 Preliminary Average Price	1997 Preliminary Index
Agriculture	$16.24	$58.10	284	357.8	392	$49.00	301.7	399	$45.11	277.8	412	$48.73	300.1
Art	21.24	39.97	864	188.2	1,116	41.23	194.1	1,070	53.40	251.4	723	47.65	224.3
Biography	15.34	30.43	1,320	198.4	1,596	30.01	195.6	1,829	31.67	206.5	1,560	33.02	215.3
Business	18.00	42.72	854	237.3	972	46.90	260.6	1005	52.62	292.3	642	51.19	284.4
Education	12.95	47.98	536	370.5	610	43.00	332.0	652	47.10	363.7	407	44.81	346.0
Fiction	10.09	20.95	2,221	207.6	2,345	21.47	212.8	2,915	22.89	226.9	2,262	22.82	226.2
General works	30.99	60.41	952	194.9	1,209	54.11	174.6	1,181	68.36	220.6	1,005	60.36	194.8
History	17.12	40.20	1,457	234.8	1,691	42.19	246.4	2,028	45.62	266.5	1,771	43.97	256.8
Home economics	11.06	20.49	482	185.3	651	22.53	203.7	655	23.39	211.5	541	23.74	214.6
Juvenile	6.65	14.60	3,414	219.5	3,649	14.55	218.8	3,730	15.97	240.2	2,058	15.97	240.2
Language	14.96	52.09	293	348.2	320	54.89	366.9	399	58.81	393.1	328	55.87	373.5
Law	25.04	72.32	681	288.8	716	73.09	291.9	827	88.51	353.5	614	80.65	322.1
Literature	15.78	37.77	1,227	239.4	1,302	38.49	243.9	1,575	43.28	274.3	1,201	44.82	284.0
Medicine	24.00	76.30	1,761	317.9	2,035	75.80	315.8	2,480	81.48	339.5	1,852	86.58	360.8
Music	20.13	39.27	179	195.1	251	43.27	215.0	253	39.21	194.8	190	43.42	215.7
Philosophy and psychology	14.43	44.71	843	309.8	1,001	45.26	313.7	1,154	48.40	335.4	885	48.46	335.8
Poetry and drama	13.63	31.56	505	231.5	567	34.96	256.5	606	34.15	250.6	497	36.53	268.0
Religion	12.26	30.73	1,169	250.7	1,364	34.27	279.5	1,544	36.62	298.7	1,181	43.18	352.2
Science	24.88	90.12	1,712	362.2	2,095	93.52	375.9	2,372	90.63	364.3	1,982	77.38	311.0
Sociology and economics	29.88	50.24	4,303	168.1	5,145	55.51	185.8	5,973	53.82	180.1	4,702	54.56	182.6
Sports and recreation	12.28	33.39	435	271.9	517	32.14	261.7	591	34.71	282.7	531	32.20	262.2
Technology	23.61	81.03	1,041	343.2	1,454	88.28	373.9	1,599	91.60	388.0	1,281	84.77	359.0
Travel	18.44	32.13	181	174.2	199	38.30	207.7	179	33.92	183.9	184	32.07	173.9
Total	$19.22	$44.65	26,714	232.3	31,197	$47.15	245.3	35,016	$50.00	260.1	26,809	$49.86	259.4

Compiled by Stephen Bosch, University of Arizona, from data supplied by the R. R. Bowker Company. Price indexes on Tables 3 and 7 are based on books recorded in the R. R. Bowker Company's *Weekly Record* (cumulated in *American Book Publishing Record*). The 1997 preliminary figures include items listed during 1997 with an imprint date of 1997. Final data for previous years include items listed between January of that year and June of the following year with an imprint date of the specified year.

Table 4 / North American Academic Books: Average Prices and Price Indexes 1994–1996
(Index Base: 1989 = 100)

Subject Area	LC Class	1989		1994		1995		1996		
		No. of Titles	Average Price	No. of Titles	Average Price	No. of Titles	Average Price	No. of Titles	Average Price	% Change 1995–1996	Index
Agriculture	S	897	$45.13	985	$56.74	1,230	$67.41	1,173	$56.73	-15.8	125.7
Anthropology	GN	406	32.81	537	41.84	514	35.51	598	37.82	6.5	115.3
Botany	QK	251	69.02	207	97.80	204	82.05	212	100.21	22.1	145.2
Business and economics	H	5,979	41.67	6,576	48.91	6,294	48.65	6,823	51.07	5.0	122.6
Chemistry	QD	577	110.61	536	145.53	506	153.12	557	171.70	12.1	155.2
Education	L	1,685	29.61	2,083	37.77	2,200	35.10	2,506	38.18	8.8	128.9
Engineering and technology	T	4,569	64.94	4,864	77.81	5,076	74.82	5,630	78.68	5.2	121.2
Fine and applied arts	M-N	3,040	40.72	3,119	42.91	4,444	48.85	3,854	42.04	-13.9	103.2
General works	A	333	134.65	178	111.05	481	45.16	141	91.81	103.3	68.2
Geography	G	396	47.34	588	55.79	626	50.78	724	53.02	4.4	112.0
Geology	QE	303	63.49	193	71.90	207	86.69	205	80.95	-6.6	127.5
History	C-D-E-F	5,549	31.34	5,741	34.16	6,279	33.28	6,919	35.46	6.6	113.1
Home economics	TX	535	27.10	665	26.68	781	27.62	839	30.92	11.9	114.1
Industrial arts	TT	175	23.89	240	22.88	251	22.97	264	23.52	2.4	98.5
Law	K	1,252	51.10	1,494	58.83	1,455	59.49	1,609	62.92	5.8	123.1

Subject											
Library and information science	Z	857	44.51	641	48.53	764	49.95	820	56.11	12.3	126.1
Literature and language	P	10,812	24.99	11,316	27.95	12,235	29.58	13,369	30.71	3.8	122.9
Mathematics and computer science	QA	2,707	44.68	3,084	55.75	3,109	57.13	3,620	59.04	3.3	132.1
Medicine	R	5,028	58.38	5,350	66.22	5,707	66.14	6,665	67.58	2.2	115.8
Military and naval science	U-V	715	33.57	466	44.18	387	39.10	576	78.84	101.6	234.9
Physical education and recreation	GV	814	20.38	802	22.72	1,106	31.70	1,067	23.31	-26.5	114.4
Philosophy and religion	B	3,518	29.06	3,985	35.52	4,537	36.14	5,005	41.13	13.8	141.5
Physics and astronomy	QB	1,219	64.59	1,175	86.33	1,161	91.73	1,242	94.10	2.6	145.7
Political science	J	1,650	36.76	1,592	47.59	1,681	47.83	2,004	45.57	-4.7	124.0
Psychology	BF	890	31.97	968	37.38	1,046	38.71	1,245	37.00	-4.4	115.7
Science (general)	Q	433	56.10	427	70.02	360	73.06	446	81.12	11.0	144.6
Sociology	HM	2,742	29.36	3,402	38.40	3,692	37.36	4,186	37.13	-0.6	126.5
Zoology	QH,L,P,R	1,967	71.28	1,823	79.40	1,924	79.87	1,963	80.66	1.0	113.2
Average for all subjects		59,299	$41.69	63,037	$48.16	68,307	$48.11	74,262	$49.86	3.6	119.6

Compiled by Stephen Bosch, University of Arizona, from electronic data provided by Baker and Taylor, Blackwell North America, Coutts Library Services, and Yankee Book Peddler. This table covers titles published or distributed in the United States and Canada during the calendar years listed.

This index does include paperback editions. The overall average price of materials is lower than if the index consisted only of hardbound editions.

Table 5 / U.S. College Books: Average Prices and Price Indexes 1983, 1995, 1996, 1997
(Index Base for all years: 1983=100. 1996 also indexed to 1995; 1997 also indexed to 1996)

Subject Area	1983 No. of Titles	1983 Avg. Price Per Title	1995 No. of Titles	1995 Avg. Price Per Title	1995 Prices Indexed to 1983	1996 No. of Titles	1996 Avg. Price Per Title	1996 Prices Indexed to 1983	1996 Prices Indexed to 1995	1997 No. of Titles	1997 Avg. Price Per Title	1997 Prices Indexed to 1983	1997 Prices Indexed to 1996
General	11	$24.91	14	$46.90	188.3	32	$43.65	175.2	93.1	22	$46.10	185.1	105.6
Humanities	40	24.53	29	50.96	207.7	29	44.04	179.5	86.4	30	45.45	185.3	103.2
Art and architecture	372	40.31	278	54.61	135.5	269	58.36	144.8	106.9	253	59.34	147.2	101.7
Communication	51	22.22	76	43.15	194.2	77	42.06	189.3	97.5	64	45.92	206.7	109.2
Language and literature	109	23.39	117	41.45	177.2	128	45.56	194.8	109.9	90	44.12	188.6	96.8
African and Middle Eastern[5]	—	—	9	32.36	—	22	40.47	—	125.1	20	31.27	—	77.3
Asian and Oceanian[5]	—	—	12	36.03	—	31	38.66	—	107.3	25	41.30	—	106.8
Classical[2]	19	28.68	—	—	—	14	53.26	185.7	—	36	48.69	169.8	91.4
English and American	579	23.47	567	37.05	157.9	562	37.91	161.5	102.3	543	45.82	195.2	120.9
Germanic	53	20.45	37	42.87	209.6	36	47.64	233.0	111.1	42	48.78	238.5	102.4
Romance	93	20.47	103	35.48	173.3	126	37.66	184.0	106.1	111	44.04	220.0	119.6
Slavic	35	23.09	31	43.56	188.7	32	36.23	156.9	83.2	31	44.93	194.6	124.0
Non-European[4]	52	19.88	33	31.92	160.6	—	—	—	—	—	—	—	—
Performing arts	19	24.81	9	40.41	166.2	4	34.60	142.3	85.6	4	43.74	179.8	126.4
Film	67	24.32	74	41.61	167.7	83	42.51	171.3	102.2	82	43.50	175.3	102.3
Music	106	25.09	148	41.52	165.5	113	43.33	172.7	104.4	132	44.15	176.0	101.9
Theater and dance[6]	51	23.18	62	40.63	175.3	68	46.85	202.1	115.3	54	42.73	184.3	91.2
Philosophy	155	26.27	163	45.00	171.3	163	46.20	175.9	102.7	156	46.45	176.8	100.5
Religion	196	19.33	219	41.23	213.3	197	42.58	220.3	103.3	158	42.18	218.2	99.1
Total Humanities[7]	2,038	$26.26	1,967	$42.01	160.0	1,954	$43.74	166.6	104.1	1,831	$46.86	178.5	107.1
Science/Technology	159	$36.11	106	$41.00	113.5	81	$46.46	128.7	113.3	85	$39.89	110.5	85.9
History of science/technology	56	28.45	71	43.00	151.1	81	46.70	164.1	108.6	63	42.06	147.8	90.1
Astronautics/astronomy	18	27.78	42	56.23	202.4	51	48.42	174.3	86.1	53	47.94	172.6	99.0
Biology	145	39.28	128	49.53	126.1	130	50.66	129.0	102.3	104	50.34	128.2	99.4
Botany	23	31.78	66	57.96	182.4	78	53.07	167.0	91.6	81	65.08	204.8	122.6
Zoology	38	44.21	77	54.05	122.3	84	50.70	114.7	93.8	85	65.32	147.7	128.8
Chemistry	30	48.57	86	73.83	152.0	68	87.63	180.4	118.7	62	92.56	190.6	105.6
Earth science	42	35.43	53	65.00	183.7	57	58.81	166.0	90.4	55	68.04	192.0	115.7
Engineering	154	44.88	126	76.00	169.3	138	76.50	170.5	100.7	118	76.26	169.9	99.7
Health sciences	121	24.45	132	41.79	170.9	169	42.83	175.2	102.5	172	46.49	190.2	108.6
Information/computer science	63	29.48	69	51.05	173.2	62	43.87	148.8	85.9	82	48.30	163.8	110.1
Mathematics	44	32.82	97	48.54	147.9	88	52.83	161.0	108.8	103	55.03	167.7	104.2
Physics	38	34.13	54	46.83	137.2	69	58.46	171.3	124.8	59	53.59	157.0	91.7
Sports/physical education	61	18.67	46	39.08	209.3	41	39.04	209.1	99.9	58	37.08	198.6	95.0
Total Science/Technology	992	$34.77	1,153	$53.37	153.5	1,197	$54.39	156.4	101.9	1,180	$55.98	161.0	102.9
Social/Behavioral Sciences	173	$24.24	44	$42.18	174.0	48	$41.20	170.0	97.7	44	$40.98	169.1	99.5
Anthropology	98	26.68	118	45.55	170.7	143	46.47	174.2	102.0	125	49.20	184.4	105.9

Subject	No.	Avg. price	No.	Avg. price	Price index	No.	Avg. price	Price index	% change	No.	Avg. price	Price index	% change
Business management/labor	156	25.01	145	44.46	177.8	146	44.36	177.4	99.8	152	45.78	183.1	103.2
Economics	315	27.60	273	50.09	181.5	275	54.43	197.2	108.7	257	50.76	183.9	93.3
Education	120	20.23	122	40.88	202.1	124	43.38	214.4	106.1	138	44.36	219.3	102.3
History/geography/area studies	92	25.58	46	37.67	147.3	58	48.27	188.7	128.1	49	43.72	170.9	90.6
Africa	17	26.94	44	48.12	178.6	37	48.87	181.4	101.6	46	45.73	169.8	93.6
Ancient History[2]	46	31.80	—	—	—	9	67.94	213.6	—	44	56.09	176.4	82.6
Asia and Oceania	58	25.55	65	47.29	185.1	74	43.54	170.4	92.1	79	47.56	186.1	109.2
Central and Eastern Europe[1]	—	—	—	—	—	—	—	—	—	19	46.30	—	—
Europe	285	29.55	377	48.54	164.3	364	49.94	169.0	102.9	186	50.24	170.0	100.6
Latin America and Caribbean	25	24.72	48	45.63	184.6	56	46.85	189.5	102.7	63	46.53	188.2	99.3
Middle East and North Africa	33	28.42	52	50.74	178.5	26	52.56	184.9	103.6	38	55.31	194.6	105.2
North America	274	24.42	382	37.08	151.8	402	37.28	152.7	100.5	388	37.85	155.0	101.5
United Kingdom[1]	—	—	—	—	—	—	—	—	—	32	52.05	—	—
Western Europe[1]	—	—	—	—	—	—	—	—	—	54	51.14	—	—
Political science	439	25.00	8	39.93	159.7	52	44.23	176.9	110.8	55	47.45	189.8	107.3
Comparative politics[3]	—	—	229	43.42	—	183	50.64	—	116.6	175	52.24	—	103.2
International relations[3]	—	—	118	43.03	—	142	46.53	—	108.1	131	50.71	—	109.0
Political theory[3]	—	—	80	42.49	—	105	43.75	—	103.0	92	45.37	—	103.7
U.S. politics[3]	—	—	164	39.29	—	177	40.88	—	104.0	188	44.04	—	107.7
Psychology	162	26.57	159	39.25	147.7	172	42.22	158.9	107.6	180	45.10	169.7	106.8
Sociology	244	24.38	231	44.74	183.5	218	45.33	185.9	101.3	216	41.54	170.4	91.6
Total Social/Behavioral Sciences	2,537	$25.81	2,705	$43.74	169.5	2,811	$45.60	176.7	104.3	2,761	$46.13	178.7	101.2
Total General, Humanities, Social/ Science/Technology, Social/ behavioral sciences[7] (excluding Reference)	5,578	$27.57	5,839	$45.07	163.5	5,994	$46.74	169.5	103.7	5,794	$48.37	175.4	103.5
Reference	—	—	—	—	—	—	—	—	—	397	$78.31	—	—
General[1]	—	—	—	—	—	—	—	—	—	47	59.85	—	—
Humanities[1]	—	—	—	—	—	—	—	—	—	73	84.74	—	—
Science/Technology[1]	—	—	—	—	—	—	—	—	—	16	105.64	—	—
Social/Behavioral[1]	—	—	—	—	—	—	—	—	—	77	87.27	—	—
Total Reference	506	$44.75	668	$75.30	168.3	648	$84.60	168.3	112.4	610	$79.50	177.7	94.0
Grand Total (includes Reference)	6,084	$29.00	6,507	$48.17	166.1	6,642	$50.44	166.1	104.7	6,404	$51.33	177.0	101.8

Compiled by Donna Alsbury, Florida Center for Library Automation, from book reviews appearing in Choice during the calendar year indicated. The cooperation of the Choice editorial staff is gratefully acknowledged. Additional information about these data appears in the April issue of Choice.

1 Began appearing as separate sections in July 1997.

2 Reappeared as separate sections in September 1996.

3 Began appearing as separate sections in September 1996.

4 Replaced Other in 1994. Replaced by African & Middle Eastern and Asian & Oceanian in September 1995.

5 Began appearing as separate sections in September 1995.

6 Separate sections for Theater and Dance combined in September 1995.

7 1983 totals include Photography (incorporated into Art & Architecture in 1994) and Linguistics (incorporated into Language & Literature in 1985).

Table 6 / U.S. Mass Market Paperback Books: Average Prices and Price Indexes, 1994–1997
(Index Base: 1981 = 100)

Subject Area	1981 Average Price	1981 Volumes	1994 Volumes	1994 Average Price	1994 Index	1995 Volumes	1995 Average Price	1995 Index	1996 Final Volumes	1996 Final Average Price	1996 Final Index	1997 Preliminary Volumes	1997 Preliminary Average Price	1997 Preliminary Index
Agriculture	$2.54	7	7	$8.25	324.8	10	$9.13	359.4	13	$11.59	456.3	1	$12.95	509.8
Art	5.49	10	10	11.04	201.1	12	11.24	204.7	8	12.00	218.6	1	15.00	273.2
Biography	3.82	36	36	7.76	203.1	39	8.08	211.5	38	10.12	264.9	17	9.42	246.6
Business	4.63	17	17	11.76	253.9	18	10.81	233.5	19	13.25	286.2	6	13.48	291.1
Education	3.96	17	17	13.08	330.3	29	12.40	313.1	31	10.29	259.8	14	11.40	287.9
Fiction	2.47	1,944	1,944	4.75	192.3	3,680	5.51	223.1	3,569	6.25	253.0	3,030	8.16	330.4
General works	3.63	42	42	9.26	255.1	29	19.37	533.6	34	9.31	256.5	20	9.85	271.3
History	3.53	10	10	10.94	309.9	24	10.06	285.0	17	10.92	309.3	4	11.37	322.1
Home economics	4.35	57	57	8.02	184.4	43	8.70	200.0	35	8.67	199.3	24	21.03	483.4
Juvenile	1.79	230	230	3.71	207.3	396	3.99	222.9	288	4.25	237.4	53	5.15	287.7
Language	3.42	3	3	14.30	418.1	8	9.60	280.7	8	7.87	230.1	5	4.59	134.2
Law	3.09	3	3	6.66	215.5	5	9.79	316.8	5	10.39	336.2	5	13.17	426.2
Literature	3.42	16	16	6.42	187.7	47	8.73	255.3	72	9.42	275.4	30	11.81	345.3
Medicine	3.66	7	7	8.49	231.9	10	8.38	229.0	20	8.93	244.0	18	9.75	266.4
Music	5.68	2	2	17.50	308.1	3	24.98	439.8	5	20.57	362.1	1	5.99	105.5
Philosophy and psychology	2.84	37	37	9.17	322.9	103	4.83	170.1	108	7.58	266.9	22	9.87	347.5
Poetry and drama	3.22	8	8	8.80	273.3	32	9.70	301.2	28	10.88	337.9	7	13.68	424.8
Religion	2.70	11	11	8.31	307.7	16	9.39	347.8	16	8.93	330.7	11	12.21	452.2
Science	4.45	10	10	11.67	262.2	8	11.28	243.5	9	12.16	273.3	1	4.99	112.1
Sociology and economics	3.43	40	40	9.15	266.8	42	9.60	279.9	34	9.91	288.9	12	12.31	358.9
Sports and recreation	3.05	102	102	9.03	296.1	82	8.28	271.5	75	8.79	288.2	25	10.17	333.4
Technology	4.20	39	39	25.20	600.0	22	11.62	276.7	20	11.14	265.2	9	11.31	269.3
Travel	3.23	5	5	13.57	420.1	3	13.96	432.2	10	9.63	298.1	3	11.96	370.3
Total	$2.65	2,653	2,653	$5.70	215.1	4,661	$5.85	220.8	4,462	$6.57	247.9	3,319	$8.37	315.8

Compiled by Stephen Bosch, University of Arizona, from data supplied by the R. R. Bowker Company. Average prices of mass market paperbacks are based on listings of mass market titles in *Paperbound Books in Print*.

Table 7 / U.S. Trade (Higher Priced) Paperback Books: Average Prices and Price Indexes, 1994–1997
(Index Base: 1977 = 100)

Subject Area	1977 Average Price	1994 Volumes	1994 Average Price	1994 Index	1995 Volumes	1995 Average Price	1995 Index	1996 Final Volumes	1996 Final Average Price	1996 Final Index	1997 Preliminary Volumes	1997 Preliminary Average Price	1997 Preliminary Index
Agriculture	$5.01	173	$18.26	364.5	218	$26.96	538.1	248	$20.45	408.2	218	$21.33	425.7
Art	6.27	572	20.99	334.8	374	20.57	328.1	872	21.57	344.0	566	22.30	355.7
Biography	4.91	605	15.65	318.7	313	16.59	337.9	979	17.37	353.8	703	16.90	344.2
Business	7.09	471	23.94	337.7	709	24.23	341.5	687	26.08	367.8	587	25.70	362.5
Education	5.72	508	21.47	375.3	738	22.96	401.4	832	23.76	415.4	562	25.09	438.6
Fiction	4.20	953	14.94	355.7	1,275	12.71	302.6	1,852	12.35	294.0	1,315	13.54	322.4
General works	6.18	851	33.81	547.1	1,375	32.98	533.7	1,693	34.65	560.7	1,261	38.01	615.0
History	5.81	756	20.15	346.8	1,041	18.47	317.9	1,381	20.09	345.8	917	19.98	343.9
Home economics	4.77	376	14.72	308.6	629	14.87	311.7	727	15.35	321.8	634	15.37	322.2
Juvenile	2.68	1,030	6.83	254.8	990	15.74	587.3	1117	8.30	309.7	861	9.82	366.4
Language	7.79	269	23.82	305.8	304	21.58	277	427	21.17	271.8	296	21.64	277.8
Law	10.66	328	30.57	286.6	415	30.26	283.9	434	30.81	289.0	316	29.80	279.5
Literature	5.18	756	18.21	351.5	945	16.54	319.3	1278	17.69	341.5	861	18.99	366.6
Medicine	7.63	756	25.15	329.6	1,092	27.91	365.8	1,577	27.37	358.7	1,203	27.31	357.9
Music	6.36	127	19.48	306.3	174	19.81	311.5	183	20.14	316.7	126	21.06	331.1
Philosophy and psychology	5.57	621	18.19	326.6	800	19.91	557.5	989	18.83	338.1	855	19.28	346.1
Poetry and drama	4.71	444	13.25	280.3	712	15.69	333.1	862	12.92	274.3	576	14.41	305.9
Religion	3.68	1,303	14.69	399.2	1,723	14.59	396.5	2,100	14.93	405.7	1,673	15.89	431.8
Science	8.81	672	35.71	405.3	874	33.41	379.2	1134	32.95	374.0	779	33.31	378.1
Sociology and economics	6.03	2,615	23.19	384.6	3,321	23.68	392.7	3,983	23.47	389.2	2,836	24.91	413.1
Sports and recreation	4.87	513	16.39	336.6	900	16.53	339.4	1028	16.33	335.3	700	17.26	354.4
Technology	7.97	582	29.50	370.1	827	38.75	486.2	890	39.17	491.5	570	31.32	393.0
Travel	5.21	334	15.54	298.3	480	16.37	314.2	537	16.74	321.3	417	16.41	315.0
Total	$5.93	15,615	$20.56	346.7	21,229	$21.70	365.9	25,810	$21.42	361.2	18,832	$21.93	369.8

Compiled by Stephen Bosch, University of Arizona, from data supplied by the R. R. Bowker Company. Price Indexes on Tables 3 and 7 are based on books recorded in R. R. Bowker Company Weekly Record (cumulated in American Book Publishing Record). The 1997 preliminary figures include items listed during 1997 with an imprint date of 1997. Final data for previous years include items listed between January of that year and June of the following year with an imprint date of the specified year.

(text continued from page 495)

Periodical and Serial Prices

The LMPI Committee and the Faxon Company jointly produce the U.S. periodical price index (Table 1). The subscription prices shown are publishers' list prices, excluding publisher discount or vendor service charges. This report includes 1996, 1997, and 1998 data indexed to the base year of 1984. The base year has been updated this year from the previous base of 1977. A more extensive report, including subject breakdowns, Library of Congress (LC) class comparisons, and rankings by rate of increase and average price, was published annually in the April 15 issue of *Library Journal* through 1992, and is now published in the May issue of *American Libraries*.

Compiled by Adrian W. Alexander and Brenda Dingley, this table shows that U.S. periodical prices (excluding Russian translations) increased by 10.3 percent from 1997 to 1998. This figure represents a slight increase in the rate of inflation from the 9.9 percent figure posted in 1997. With the Russian translations category included, the single-year increase was only slightly lower, at 9.5 percent. This figure is 0.6 percent lower than the rate of 10.1 percent for the entire sample in 1997. While Zoology and Medicine led the various subject categories in rate of increase once again in 1998 with 13.9 percent and 13.7 percent, respectively, double-digit inflation was not limited to the sciences again this year. Psychology posted an increase of 10.7 percent in 1998 for its fourth consecutive year over 10 percent, while Library and Information Sciences jumped to 10.4 percent from a 1997 figure of 7.6 percent. Two other categories that posted double-digit increases in 1997 dropped sharply in 1998. Business & Economics fell from 11.2 percent last year to 6.6 percent, and Russian translations went from 10.7 percent in 1997 to 7.8 percent in 1998.

U.S. serial services (Table 2), compiled by Nancy Chaffin based on data from the Faxon Company, required the replacement of several titles as publications ceased. The replacements reflected the same subject areas, but prices were, overall, higher. Chaffin notes: "The few replacements that were made were harder to find. For these types of information sources (serial services) the logic of creating and publishing in electronic form seems to be taking hold and there is a growing number of new titles offered only in electronic form." A more detailed article on the topic of prices of serial services was to be published in the May 1998 issue of *American Libraries*.

The average subscription price for 1998 U.S. serial services, excluding "Wilson Index" titles and Russian translations, increased an overall 4.5 percent, reflecting a small increase over 1997. All subject areas exhibited increases. Surprisingly, U.S. government documents and general and humanities increased at a rate higher than the other subject areas.

The listing for Wilson Index was dropped from the serial services price index for 1998 at the request of Wilson Co.

Book Prices

U.S. hardcover books (Table 3) encompasses four years: 1994, 1995, final figures for 1996, and preliminary figures for 1997. American book title costs continued to rise in 1996 to an average price of $50.00, a modest increase of 6.0 percent and very similar to the 5.6 percent increase in 1995. This index is compiled from information published in Bowker's *Weekly Record*.

The average price of North American Academic Books in 1996 (Table 4) increased 3.6 percent in contrast to the preceding year, which showed a slight decrease in pricing. The data used for this index comprises titles treated by Baker and Taylor, Blackwell North America, Coutts, and Yankee Book Peddler in their approval plans during the calendar years listed. It does include paperback editions as provided by the vendors and the recent increase in the number of these editions as part of the approval plans has clearly influenced the prices reflected in the index figures. Thus the inflation variance (hardback versus paperback editions) is much less clear than it has been in previous years. Price changes vary, as always, among subject areas, with double-digit increases in botany, chemistry, home economics, library and information science, philosophy and religion, and general science.

U.S. college books (Table 5) is compiled by Donna Alsbury from reviews appearing in *Choice* during the calendar year. Hardcover prices were used when available. The table includes the past three years (1995, 1996, and 1997) and the base index year (1983). The 1.8 percent increase between 1996 and 1997 represents a continuing modest increase following the 4.7 percent increase in 1995. Note that a secondary index, based on the immediate preceding year, is now a feature of this index. The humanities showed the largest overall increases, while some subject areas in the sciences continue to experience large price increases.

U.S. mass market paperbacks (Table 6) and U.S. trade paperbacks (Table 7) are compiled from data supplied by Bowker's *Paperbound Books in Print*. Mass market paperback prices showed a sharp increase, rising from $5.85 in 1995 to $6.57 in 1996 for a 12.3 percent increase. U.S. trade paperbacks decreased slightly in price from $21.70 in 1995 to $21.42 in 1996 for a decrease of 1.3 percent.

One general trend in book price indexes that may be worth noting is the overall increase in the number of titles covered in most indexes. This is indicative of continued strength in U.S. book publishing.

Newspaper Prices

U.S. daily newspapers (Table 8A) includes two fewer titles than the previous year's index, reflecting the ongoing hard times of the newspaper industry as titles merge or cease altogether. Compilers Genevieve Owens and Wilba Swearingen observe that U.S. newspaper pricing continues to reflect a different dynamic than that of books or serials. Previously, pricing data suggested that increases occurred on an 18- or 24-month cycle rather than the more usual annual cycle that librarians see in other segments of the publishing industry. However, the increase in pricing for titles to be delivered in 1998 is 1.5 percent, breaking a consistent pattern of high/low price increases demonstrated since 1991. The shift from this pattern may be due to the stiff competition newspaper publishers face from other media sources, and may also be influenced by increased revenues newspapers may be receiving from electronic products that wouldn't be reflected in this price index.

Table 8A / U.S. Daily Newspapers, 1990–1998
(Index Base: 1990 = 100)

Year	No. Titles	Average Price	Percent Increase	Index
1990	165	$189.58	0.0	100.0
1991	166	198.13	4.5	104.5
1992	167	222.68	12.4	117.5
1993	171	229.92	3.3	121.3
1994	171	261.91	13.9	138.2
1995	172	270.22	3.2	142.5
1996	166	300.21	11.1	158.4
1997	165	311.77	3.9	164.5
1998	163	316.60	1.5	167.0

Compiled by Genevieve S. Owens, Williamsburg Regional Library, and Wilba Swearingen, Louisiana State University Medical Center Library, New Orleans, from data supplied by EBSCO Subscription Services. We thank EBSCO's Kathleen Born for her assistance with this project.

Table 8B / International Newspapers: Average Prices and Price Indexes 1993–1998
(Index Base: 1993 = 100)

Year	No. Titles	Average Price	Percent Increase	Index
1993	46	$806.91	0.0	100.0
1994	46	842.01	4.3	104.3
1995	49	942.13	11.9	116.3
1996	50	992.78	5.4	123.0
1997	53	1,029.49	3.7	127.6
1998	55	1,049.11	1.9	130.0

Compiled by Genevieve S. Owens, Williamsburg Regional Library, and Wilba Swearingen, Louisiana State University Medical Center Library, New Orleans, from data supplied by EBSCO Subscription Services. We thank EBSCO's Kathleen Born for her assistance with this project.

Table 9 / U.S. Nonprint Media: Average Prices and Price Indexes, 1986–1996
Index Base: 1980 = 100

Category	1980 Average Price	1996 Average Price	1996 Index	1997 Average Price	1997 Index
Videocassettes					
Rental cost per minute	$1.41*	$1.97	140.00	$1.63	116.00
Purchase cost per minute	7.59	2.03	26.80	1.72	22.70
Cost per video	217.93	82.10	30.20	72.31	26.60
Length per video (min.)		40.40		41.84	
Sound recordings					
Average cost per cassette	9.34	8.13	87.00	8.31	89.00
Average cost per CD	13.36	16.43	123.00	14.35	107.40

Compiled by Dana Alessi, Baker & Taylor, from data in Booklist, Library Journal, and School Library Journal.
* Rental cost per minute for 16 mm films.
** Base year for compact discs = 1993
Note: The 16 mm film and filmstrip categories were discontinued due to the small number of reviews of these products.

A price index for international newspapers (Table 8B) appears for the first time this year. This price index is based on price information supplied by EBSCO. The increase in pricing for titles to be delivered in 1998 is a modest 1.9 percent. No consistent pattern of high/low price increases has been demonstrated in this index since 1993 and other factors than those impacting U.S. news publishing may be driving price changes in international newspapers. These factors may include shipping costs, currency fluctuations, or the local cost of newsprint.

Prices of Other Media

Data for the U.S. nonprint media index (Table 9) including videocassettes and sound recordings are compiled by Dana Alessi. The index for 1997 continues the methodology used to prepare the 1994 index, utilizing a database of titles reviewed in *Booklist*, *Library Journal*, and *School Library Journal*. However, beginning in 1997, *Video Librarian*, which has developed into a standard reviewing tool for the video market, has been added to the list of titles used for the compilation of the database. This has led, in general, to an increased number of videos counted in the index.

While there is significant overlap among the review sources, about 15 percent of the videos were unique to *Video Librarian*. The database was created to insure that each title is counted only once in the index. Since the review media frequently differ in price and length assigned to the reviewed media, the index assumes the higher price and the longer length.

Once again, videos have taken a significant downturn in price. Clearly, many videos are directed at a mass market, especially in the consumer interest, self-help, travel, and instructional areas. Many of these videos are equally pertinent in the library or classroom setting, although the video is targeted—and priced—for the sell-through market. Additionally, those producers and distributors who were formerly in the 16mm market, or who sell exclusively to the library/education market, have found that they must compete with the lower-cost mass market distributors. Although library/educational videos still carry a higher price, it is notable especially in the high-end video that prices have generally declined. With the increase in the consumer market, pricing has, like audio, become more standardized, both within producer as well as within genre. Sound recordings again increased in average cost per cassette. This may be attributable to the increased numbers of cassettes reviewed, especially children's music cassettes, and a slight reduction in the number of recorded books reviewed, both abridged and unabridged. However, CDs declined in price, attributable to both an increasing number of CDs reviewed and competitive pricing.

Data for the CD-ROM price inventory (Table 10) was compiled by Martha Kellogg and Theodore Kellogg from the *Faxon Guide to CD-ROMs* and *CD-ROMs in Print*, supplemented by selected publishers' catalogs. All prices used are for single-user (non-networked) workstations at the most complete level of service, including all archival discs. Only those titles with current year price information are included in the index. Prices remain steady with a very meager 0.2 percent decrease. Subject areas reflect wide fluctuations. These tend to be the result of the small number of titles within some categories, or the way in which supplementary discs are included one year, but not the next, or the inclusion of new and more expensive titles in the title mix. The index includes both monograph and serial titles.

Foreign Prices

U.S. Purchasing Power Abroad

The U.S. dollar made consistent gains against the major currencies during 1997. The strength of the dollar is expected to continue in 1998, although volatility in East Asian financial markets may inject unknown factors into the previous assumption. The following chart reports rates in currency per U.S. dollar based on quotations in the *Wall Street Journal*. Readers interested in quotations for earlier years should refer to previous volumes of the *Bowker Annual* or directly to the *Wall Street Journal*. Historical data concerning rates of exchange are also maintained at a U.S. Federal Reserve Board Web site, http://www.bog.frb.fed.us/releases/H10/hist.

	12/30/94	6/30/95	12/31/95	12/31/96	12/31/97
Canada	1.4088	1.3724	1.3644	1.3705	1.3657
France	5.3640	4.8405	4.9050	5.1900	6.0190
U.K.	0.6412	0.6272	0.6439	0.5839	0.6058
Germany	1.5525	1.3820	1.4365	1.5400	1.7991
Japan	99.65	84.71	103.43	115.85	130.45
Netherlands	1.7391	1.5477	1.6080	1.7410	2.0265

Price indexes are included for British academic books (Table 11), German academic books (Table 12), German academic periodicals (Table 13), Dutch English-language periodicals (Table 14), and Latin American Periodicals (Table 15).

British Prices

The price index for British books is compiled by Curt Holleman from information supplied by B. H. Blackwell. The average price (in British pounds) was 39.77 in 1997, which reflects an increase of 6.1 percent over the 1996 average price of 37.50. During 1996, prices increased 4.2 percent over the 1995 average of £36.00. Compiler Curt Holleman notes that the pound experienced an increase of 4.9 percent in 1997 in its average daily value compared to the dollar but that the output of British academic books declined by 7.8 percent. When we combine these two factors with the inflation of 6.1 percent in the cost of each British book in 1997, we find that the cost for U. S. academic libraries of maintaining a proportional collection of British books rose 2.6 percent in 1997 over 1996. Note that the total number of titles exceeds the sum of the subject areas, since some titles, included in the data, are not classified by subject.

(text continues on page 518)

Table 10 / CD-ROM Price Inventory 1995–1997: Average Costs By Subject Classification

Classification	LC Class	Number of Titles			Average Price per Title			Percent Change	
		1995	1996	1997	1995	1996	1997	1995–1996	1996–1997
General works	A	134	128	127	$1,603	$1,805	$1,735	13	-4
Philosophy, psychology, and religion	B	24	22	22	1,170	1,153	1,059	-1	-8
History: general & Old World	D	7	7	7	783	786	777	0	-1
History: America	E-F	20	20	20	632	641	645	1	1
Geography, anthropology, and recreation	G	37	35	36	1,767	1,884	1,876	7	0
Social sciences	H	91	101	108	2,317	2,196	2,667	-5	21
Business	HB-HJ	109	118	122	3,855	3,700	3,298	-4	-11
Political science	J	18	19	20	1,272	1,297	1,467	2	13
Law	K	27	27	28	2,095	2,074	2,016	-1	-3
Education	L	23	30	30	936	921	958	-2	4
Music	M	14	12	12	822	974	961	18	-1
Fine arts	N	36	36	36	1,227	1,278	1,344	4	5
Language & literature	P	45	44	46	2,956	2,983	2,860	1	-4
Science	Q	171	172	175	1,931	2,045	2,173	6	6
Medicine	R	177	188	198	1,458	1,404	1,382	-4	-2
Agriculture	S	34	32	31	3,836	4,139	3,754	8	-9
Technology	T	67	72	79	2,248	2,208	2,119	-2	-4
Military science	U-V	24	25	28	1,252	1,094	1,061	-13	-3
Bibliography, library science	Z	73	72	73	1,388	1,430	1,525	3	7
Totals		1,131	1,160	1,198	$1,938	$2,012	$2,007	1	0

Compiled by Martha Kellogg and Theodore Kellogg, University of Rhode Island

Note: In 1996, 103 titles were added and 74 removed. In 1997, 72 titles were added and 34 removed.

Table 11 / British Academic Books: Average Prices and Price Indexes, 1995–1997

(Index Base: 1985 = 100; prices listed are pounds sterling)

Subject Area	1985		1995			1996			1997		
	No. of Titles	Average Price	No. of Titles	Average Price	Index	No. of Titles	Average Price	Index	No. of Titles	Average Price	Index
General works	29	£30.54	29	£40.72	133.3	38	£66.88	219.0	35	£34.62	113.4
Fine arts	329	21.70	407	35.82	165.1	472	32.16	148.2	423	32.95	151.8
Architecture	97	20.68	159	31.81	153.8	203	32.17	155.6	150	37.66	182.1
Music	136	17.01	164	29.79	175.1	132	28.89	169.8	136	31.01	182.3
Performing arts except music	110	13.30	130	24.98	187.8	178	26.43	198.7	175	32.38	243.5
Archaeology	146	18.80	159	33.86	180.1	192	33.57	178.6	173	36.98	196.7
Geography	60	22.74	60	35.68	156.9	63	40.65	178.8	57	41.19	181.1
History	1,123	16.92	1,352	32.80	193.9	1,505	34.51	204.0	1373	38.63	228.3
Philosophy	127	18.41	180	35.70	193.9	233	42.07	228.5	221	42.70	231.9
Religion	328	10.40	452	24.08	231.5	486	25.68	246.9	421	24.47	235.2
Language	135	19.37	157	36.64	189.2	218	41.06	212.0	193	42.41	218.9
Miscellaneous humanities	59	21.71	61	28.73	132.3	64	30.39	140.0	49	34.98	161.1
Literary texts (excluding fiction)	570	9.31	522	16.15	173.5	581	18.64	200.2	500	15.09	162.1
Literary criticism	438	14.82	492	37.02	249.8	579	36.22	244.4	491	36.01	243.0
Law	188	24.64	317	47.38	192.3	364	46.26	187.7	379	49.10	199.3
Library science and book trade	78	18.69	67	37.46	200.4	78	54.39	291.0	76	42.54	227.6
Mass communications	38	14.20	96	29.94	210.8	109	30.78	216.8	116	34.80	245.1
Anthropology and ethnology	42	20.71	80	37.05	178.9	90	39.77	192.0	62	41.10	198.5
Sociology	136	15.24	174	38.60	253.3	229	45.55	298.9	199	50.89	333.9
Psychology	107	19.25	157	32.72	170.0	146	36.60	190.1	148	39.12	203.2
Economics	334	20.48	540	51.06	249.3	525	49.67	242.5	585	59.99	292.9
Political science, international relations	314	15.54	423	34.58	222.5	549	37.06	238.5	541	40.31	259.4
Miscellaneous social sciences	20	26.84	14	33.84	126.1	23	42.75	159.3	19	38.55	143.6
Military science	83	17.69	38	36.57	206.7	59	32.92	186.1	46	49.14	277.8
Sports and recreation	44	11.23	61	20.06	178.6	82	19.97	177.8	75	20.03	178.4
Social service	56	12.17	90	28.76	236.3	106	28.45	233.8	75	27.20	223.5
Education	295	12.22	333	28.46	232.9	423	28.51	233.3	372	29.42	240.8
Management and business administration	427	19.55	504	36.10	184.7	594	44.11	225.6	599	38.74	198.2
Miscellaneous applied social sciences	13	9.58	17	23.04	240.5	28	31.58	329.6	30	42.20	440.5

Subject											
Criminology	45	11.45	66	31.51	275.2	69	36.29	316.9	76	34.78	303.8
Applied interdisciplinary social sciences	254	14.17	515	33.02	233.0	601	33.50	236.4	509	35.96	253.8
General science	43	13.73	36	59.32	432.0	40	37.11	270.3	37	40.60	295.7
Botany	55	30.54	37	43.99	144.0	57	46.58	152.5	35	50.64	165.8
Zoology	85	25.67	67	44.70	174.1	80	41.48	161.6	56	53.14	207.0
Human biology	35	28.91	28	55.60	192.3	32	46.57	161.1	19	58.46	202.2
Biochemistry	26	33.57	35	44.76	133.3	43	54.39	162.0	28	86.84	258.7
Miscellaneous biological sciences	152	26.64	131	43.44	163.1	158	43.20	162.2	148	49.69	186.5
Chemistry	109	48.84	93	76.30	156.2	100	75.81	155.2	99	89.07	182.4
Earth sciences	87	28.94	91	55.59	192.1	117	59.55	205.8	95	56.63	195.7
Astronomy	43	20.36	37	42.79	210.2	50	35.33	173.5	50	48.61	238.8
Physics	76	26.58	103	65.67	247.1	97	65.99	248.3	110	60.58	227.9
Mathematics	123	20.20	167	35.70	176.7	170	37.21	184.2	177	39.11	193.6
Computer sciences	150	20.14	213	36.64	181.9	227	38.12	189.3	174	39.51	196.2
Interdisciplinary technical fields	38	26.14	63	43.36	165.9	68	42.45	162.4	49	39.55	151.3
Civil engineering	134	28.68	120	52.77	184.0	155	58.66	204.5	129	61.74	215.3
Mechanical engineering	27	31.73	32	59.19	186.5	45	57.42	181.0	36	77.36	243.8
Electrical and electronic engineering	100	33.12	86	46.06	139.1	112	52.56	159.0	104	54.84	165.6
Materials science	54	37.93	69	77.45	204.2	99	95.89	252.8	87	83.38	219.8
Chemical engineering	24	40.43	34	73.53	181.6	37	69.22	171.0	45	83.95	207.4
Miscellaneous technology	217	36.33	210	52.57	144.7	248	52.58	144.7	215	59.11	162.7
Food and domestic science	38	23.75	41	45.08	189.8	40	54.27	228.5	43	60.03	252.8
Non-clinical medicine	97	18.19	137	31.55	173.4	177	29.02	159.5	159	34.54	189.9
General medicine	73	21.03	67	39.70	188.8	68	44.43	211.3	73	38.85	184.7
Internal medicine	163	27.30	168	46.99	172.1	179	45.29	165.9	171	57.14	209.3
Psychiatry and mental disorders	71	17.97	130	33.52	186.5	132	32.00	178.1	138	31.98	178.0
Surgery	50	29.37	55	62.94	214.3	62	64.60	220.0	63	65.88	224.3
Miscellaneous medicine	292	22.08	278	41.39	187.5	301	39.16	177.4	342	42.34	191.8
Dentistry	20	19.39	21	44.65	230.3	22	50.22	259.0	16	34.89	179.9
Nursing	71	8.00	86	17.46	218.2	99	17.96	224.5	92	20.14	251.8
Agriculture and forestry	78	23.69	69	41.94	177.0	69	45.65	192.7	58	49.72	209.9
Animal husbandry and veterinary medicine	34	20.92	46	45.08	215.5	46	37.69	180.2	47	35.43	169.4
Natural resources and conservation	58	22.88	39	34.73	151.8	42	40.82	178.4	35	38.58	168.6
Total, all books	9,049	£19.07	10,605	£36.00	188.8	12,622	£37.50	196.6	11,710	£39.77	208.5

Compiled by Curt Holleman, Southern Methodist University, from data supplied by B.·H. Blackwell and the Library and Information Statistics Unit at Loughborough University.

Table 12 / German Academic Books: Average Prices and Price Index, 1995–1997

(Index Base: 1989=100; prices listed are Deutsche marks.)

Subject	LC Class	1989 Average Price	1995 No. of Titles	1995 Average Price	1995 Index	1996 No. of Titles	1996 Average Price	1996 Index	1997 No. of Titles	1997 Average Price	1997 Index
Agriculture	S	DM74.99	376	DM69.53	92.7	335	DM72.62	96.8	306	DM76.83	102.5
Anthropology	GN-GT	70.88	164	68.03	96.0	187	75.81	107.0	156	81.54	115.0
Botany	QK	109.94	108	106.87	97.2	94	115.01	104.6	74	108.26	98.5
Business and economics	H-HJ	86.82	2,240	70.12	80.8	2,560	74.54	85.9	2,432	78.72	90.7
Chemistry	QD	116.50	231	136.09	116.8	214	125.86	108.0	147	155.73	133.7
Education	L	41.64	490	46.06	110.6	679	49.83	119.7	572	50.66	121.7
Engineering and technology	T	79.49	1,221	90.10	113.4	994	91.60	115.2	823	127.14	160.0
Fine and applied arts	M-N	55.57	1,963	77.07	138.7	2,515	70.08	126.1	1,937	88.18	158.7
General works	A	59.63	47	301.69	505.9	58	166.11	278.5	42	296.50	497.2
Geography	G-GF	48.96	126	97.76	199.7	150	76.68	156.6	158	93.03	190.0
Geology	QE	77.10	83	121.90	158.1	76	79.18	102.7	60	535.79	694.9
History	C,D,E,F	62.93	2,332	60.60	96.3	2,194	67.92	107.9	1,837	74.99	119.1
Law	K	100.52	1,771	90.85	90.4	1,889	87.72	87.3	1,935	106.35	105.8
Library and information science	Z	94.71	183	333.33	352.0	165	151.38	159.8	145	221.55	233.9
Literature and language	P	52.10	3,797	56.41	108.3	3,689	62.59	120.1	3,750	67.69	129.9
Mathematics and computer science	QA	68.16	717	85.39	125.3	779	80.89	118.7	689	84.89	124.5
Medicine	R	82.67	1,628	96.34	116.5	1,849	93.01	112.5	1,643	88.02	106.5
Military and naval science	U-V	70.43	49	78.39	111.3	52	90.15	128.0	44	63.07	89.6
Natural history	QH	85.23	230	97.24	114.1	185	102.95	120.8	142	93.77	110.0
Philosophy and religion	B	56.91	1,510	73.58	129.3	1,638	73.46	129.1	1,398	90.38	158.8
Physical education and recreation	GV	35.65	134	43.52	122.1	149	39.82	111.7	142	46.68	131.0
Physics and astronomy	QB-QC	85.12	317	86.84	102.0	347	91.61	107.6	239	97.12	114.1
Physiology	QM-QR	124.67	210	113.55	91.1	168	128.73	103.3	153	114.28	91.7
Political science	J	50.38	651	56.46	112.1	615	59.63	118.4	571	62.79	124.6
Psychology	BF	54.95	205	55.88	101.7	220	58.85	107.1	204	58.97	107.3
Science (general)	Q	115.90	94	79.36	68.5	86	80.19	69.2	90	95.62	82.5
Sociology	HM-HX	41.52	1,013	45.62	109.9	1,034	49.75	119.8	1,069	47.85	115.3
Zoology	QL	82.74	98	85.03	102.8	91	100.07	120.9	100	133.58	161.4
Total		DM67.84	21,988	DM75.41	111.2	23,012	DM74.81	110.3	20,858	DM84.65	124.8

Compiled by John Haar, Vanderbilt University, from approval plan data supplied by Otto Harrassowitz. Data represent a selection of materials relevant to research and documentation published in Germany (see text for more information regarding the nature of the data). Unclassified material as well as titles in home economics and industrial arts have been excluded. The index is not adjusted for high-priced titles.

Table 13 / German Academic Periodical Price Index, 1996–1998
(Index Base: 1990 = 100)

Subject Area	LC Class	1990 Average Price	1996 No. of Titles	1996 Average Price	1996 Percent Increase	1996 Index	1997 No. of Titles	1997 Average Price	1997 Percent Increase	1997 Index	1998 Prelim. No. of Titles	1998 Prelim. Average Price	1998 Prelim. Percent Increase	1998 Prelim. Index
Agriculture	S	DM235.11	162	DM362.52	22.2	154.2	164	DM379.09	14.3	161.2	173	DM362.89	-4.3	154.3
Anthropology	GN	112.88	15	152.75	-58.4	135.3	13	171.71	12.4	152.1	13	154.28	-10.2	136.7
Botany	QK	498.79	16	821.19	12.9	164.6	17	847.27	3.2	169.9	18	824.18	-2.7	165.2
Business and economics	H-HJ	153.48	278	218.06	5.7	142.1	256	225.16	3.3	146.7	268	229.82	2.1	149.7
Chemistry	QD	553.06	46	1,448.40	39.1	261.9	47	2,007.13	38.6	362.9	51	2,014.91	0.4	364.3
Education	L	70.86	54	85.65	4.4	120.9	58	91.30	6.6	128.8	62	92.26	1.0	130.2
Engineering & technology	T-TT	239.40	359	319.29	19.6	133.4	362	343.03	7.4	143.3	379	370.32	8.0	154.7
Fire and applied arts	M-N	84.15	172	101.50	0.4	120.6	170	104.75	3.2	124.5	174	106.61	1.8	126.7
General works	A	349.37	84	457.56	8.1	131.0	72	385.87	-15.7	110.4	73	412.74	7.0	118.8
Geography	G	90.42	19	136.87	6.7	151.4	24	150.36	9.9	166.3	24	151.38	0.7	167.4
Geology	QE	261.30	39	454.72	23.3	174.0	35	513.18	12.9	196.4	36	519.08	1.1	198.7
History	C,D,E,F	66.09	151	92.73	3.2	140.3	158	98.42	6.1	148.9	159	99.07	0.7	149.9
Law	K	193.88	156	301.15	12.6	155.3	152	314.98	4.6	162.5	158	322.18	2.3	166.2
Library and information science	Z	317.50	59	609.72	5.0	192.0	46	369.97	-39.3	116.5	47	374.35	1.2	117.9
Literature & language	P	102.69	176	137.93	9.3	134.3	188	143.70	4.2	139.9	188	143.49	-0.1	139.7
Mathematics and computer science	QA	1,064.62	40	1,663.11	38.3	156.2	47	1,404.42	-15.6	131.9	52	1,356.31	-3.4	127.4
Medicine	R	320.62	368	630.78	22.9	196.7	367	595.81	-5.5	185.8	384	596.88	0.2	186.2
Military and naval science	U-V	86.38	20	100.65	24.6	116.5	23	96.14	-4.5	111.3	23	96.74	0.6	112.0
Natural history	QH	728.36	52	1,361.30	34.1	186.9	55	1,476.30	8.4	202.7	57	1,523.64	3.2	209.2
Philosophy and religion	B	65.00	197	104.53	3.4	160.8	205	108.18	3.5	166.4	206	110.77	2.4	170.4
Physical education and recreation	GV	81.96	46	96.77	-2.0	118.1	46	98.61	1.9	120.3	47	100.44	1.9	122.5
Physics and astronomy	QB-QC	684.40	48	1,378.60	32.0	201.4	40	1,470.19	6.6	214.8	50	2,028.90	38.0	296.4
Physiology	QM-QR	962.83	11	2,763.69	38.1	287.0	10	3,257.10	17.9	338.3	10	3,287.68	0.9	341.5
Politica science	J	80.67	137	104.03	3.2	129.0	142	103.69	-0.3	128.5	143	103.93	0.2	128.8
Psychology	BF	94.10	36	144.41	10.0	153.5	35	157.58	9.1	167.5	35	159.83	1.2	169.5
Science (general)	Q	310.54	33	429.52	22.2	138.3	30	490.22	14.1	157.9	31	503.83	2.8	162.2
Sociology	HM-HX	109.61	59	143.32	16.0	130.8	69	140.18	-2.2	127.9	71	142.44	1.6	130.0
Zoology	QL	161.02	29	264.53	2.3	164.3	26	302.63	14.4	187.9	27	293.32	-3.1	182.2
Total		DM228.40	2,862	DM370.71	19.6	162.3	2,857	DM373.88	0.9	163.7	2,959	DM397.78	6.4	174.2

Data, supplied by Otto Harrassowitz, represent periodical and newspaper titles published in Germany; prices listed in marks. Price information for 1998 is preliminary, price data are 87 percent complete. Index is compiled by Steven E. Thompson, Brown University Library.

Table 14 / Dutch (English-Language) Periodicals Price Index 1995–1998
(Index Base 1995=100, Currency Unit: DFL.)

Subject Area	LC Class	1995		1996			1997			1998		
		No. of Titles	Average Price	No. of Titles	Average Price	Index	No. of Titles	Average Price	Index	No. of Titles	Average Price	Index
Agriculture	S	35	1,109.06	36	1,215.10	109.6	37	1,335.84	120.45	36	1,559.27	140.59
Botany	QK	10	1,470.30	10	1,654.90	112.6	10	1,899.60	129.20	11	1,948.09	132.50
Business and economics	H-HJ	82	678.94	86	721.95	106.3	92	766.85	112.95	94	846.98	124.75
Chemistry	QD	35	3,836.81	32	4,258.83	111.0	32	4,886.74	127.36	39	5,319.49	138.64
Education	L	6	386.00	6	411.67	106.6	6	483.83	125.35	8	518.88	134.42
Engineering and technology	T-TS	71	1,458.27	77	1,526.30	104.7	78	1,725.26	118.31	79	2,084.85	142.97
Fine and applied arts	M-N	4	249.34	3	326.67	131.0	2	444.50	178.27	1	539.00	216.17
Geography	G	7	1,429.57	8	1,425.88	99.7	8	1,563.38	109.36	9	1,668.28	116.70
Geology	QE	24	1,433.07	25	1,587.60	110.8	26	1,764.78	123.15	26	1,956.62	136.53
History	C,D,E,F	9	236.25	9	257.00	108.8	9	290.06	122.77	12	312.33	132.20
Law	K	13	452.46	14	494.21	109.2	14	531.50	117.47	29	525.45	116.13
Library and information science	Z	6	254.33	6	262.67	103.3	6	281.83	110.81	6	302.83	119.07
Literature and language	P	33	336.55	35	348.26	103.5	34	380.32	113.01	41	396.34	117.77
Mathematics and computer science	QA	55	1,367.23	56	1,473.25	107.8	56	1,664.64	121.75	63	1,791.70	131.05
Medicine	R	60	1,214.67	62	1,357.47	111.8	63	1,577.76	129.89	72	1,705.82	140.43
Military and naval science	U-V	2	200.00	1	295.00	147.5	1	278.00	139.00	2	181.50	90.75
Natural history	QH	30	2,070.96	33	2,225.92	107.5	39	2,196.41	106.06	40	2,430.53	117.36
Philosophy and religion	B,BL,BP	31	384.29	33	407.21	106.0	34	436.97	113.71	34	487.62	126.89
Physics and astronomy	QB-QC	44	3,847.54	43	4,329.47	112.5	44	4,694.05	122.00	47	5,007.64	130.15
Physiology	QM-QR	16	3,149.88	16	3,568.00	113.3	16	4,071.56	129.26	17	4,260.00	135.24
Political science	J	3	467.67	4	428.25	91.6	4	508.25	108.68	5	474.20	101.40
Psychology	BF	4	810.25	4	925.50	114.2	5	977.00	120.58	9	931.11	114.92
Science (general)	Q	11	921.30	12	1,071.98	116.4	12	1,203.92	130.68	10	1,244.70	135.10
Sociology	HM-HX	6	365.67	6	377.33	103.2	5	448.60	122.68	3	457.33	125.07
Zoology	QL	10	712.80	11	776.21	108.9	10	992.60	139.25	10	1,100.00	154.32
Total		607	1,452.52	628	1,560.44	107.4	643	1,734.69	119.43	703	1,892.15	130.27

No data exist for Anthropology, General works, Physical education

Source: Martinus Nijhoff International. Compiled by Bas Guijt and Frederick C. Lynden

Table 15 / Latin American Periodicals, 1996–1997
(Index Base: 1992 = 100)

	Number of Titles	Average Price*	Index	Weighted Average Price*	Index
Argentina	135	$91.51	91.0	$35.79	43.0
Bolivia	6	81.97	254.0	142.98	438.0
Brazil	182	70.30	114.0	65.13	119.0
Caribbean	36	150.96	368.0	38.21	93.0
Chile	81	93.14	134.0	79.98	149.0
Colombia	63	70.33	138.0	80.73	149.0
Costa Rica	26	62.52	191.0	62.41	158.0
Cuba	19	53.67	192.0	54.99	190.0
Ecuador	11	39.86	109.0	40.00	113.0
El Salvador	11	46.17	205.0	40.60	195.0
Guatemala	10	128.25	144.0	166.92	175.0
Honduras	n.a.	n.a.	n.a.	n.a.	n.a.
Jamaica	14	85.88	239.0	61.51	172.0
Mexico	202	77.59	115.0	61.51	99.0
Nicaragua	7	29.39	73.0	26.73	111.0
Panama	5	39.10	138.0	34.15	142.0
Paraguay	7	28.07	151.0	33.43	117.0
Peru	50	129.80	133.0	119.51	112.0
Uruguay	22	67.63	134.0	79.06	188.0
Venezuela	18	205.50	182.0	103.63	173.0
Region					
Caribbean	69	54.65	141.0	48.72	128.0
Central America	33	65.33	146.0	71.96	143.0
South America	601	82.91	111.0	78.12	121.0
Mexico	202	77.59	115.0	61.51	99.0
Latin America	905	79.07	115.0	72.29	123.0
Subjects					
Social sciences		86.41	121.0	73.46	136.0
Humanities		50.27	125.0	43.76	120.0
Science/technology		68.44	116.0	73.65	131.0
General		96.50	110.0	88.73	96.0
Law		63.14	61.0	72.55	84.0
Newspapers		440.59	109.0	337.49	83.0
Totals w/o newspapers		$79.07	115.0	$72.29	123.0
Totals with newspapers		$99.18	113.0	$77.95	121.0

Compiled by Scott Van Jacob, Notre Dame University, from data supplied by the Library of Congress field office in Rio de Janeiro, the Faxon Company, and the University of Texas at Austin. Index based on 1992 LAPPI mean prices. Totals based on all subscription titles for Latin America. In compliance with ANSI standards, 1995–96 subscription prices were included in this year's index if a new subscription price was not given.

* = Without newspapers

n.a. = fewer than five subscriptions were found

(text continued from page 510)

German Prices

The price index for German academic books (Table 12) is based on data supplied by Otto Harrassowitz. The index includes all German publications made available for purchase to U.S. libraries during the calendar year. It also includes some CD-ROMs and other audiovisual materials. Both mixed media and stand-alone CD prices are included in the data. Compiler John Haar notes that "these media form only a very small portion of the index" and because mixed media are implicitly reflected in book indexes he does not see the inclusion of such data as invalidating the index.

The index indicates the total average price increase this year is 13.2 percent. Last year the index reported a slight decrease 0.8 percent. It is thought this was a statistical quirk due to a number of multi-volume sets being counted as one title. Thus, what the index may really be indicating is an "adjustment" for under-reporting price inflation during 1996. Among individual subjects, the As and Zs saw large percentage increases, but these two areas are often volatile. Geology is the only subject where the increase seems out of line. John Haar notes, "this is probably caused by one or more large, expensive sets appearing in geology." Harrassowitz's database counts each set as one title, so in a field where a relatively small number of books is published one or two sets could have a disproportionate influence.

The index for German academic periodicals (Table 13) is compiled by Steven Thompson and is based on data from Otto Harrassowitz. The preliminary data for 1998 shows 22 disciplines with increases, but only one is extraordinary (Physics/Astronomy at 38 percent); the rest are all single-digit increases. Overall inflation for serial titles is a modest 6.4 percent in contrast to 1997's sharply lower increase of 0.9 percent and 1996's increase of 19.6 percent. Steve Thompson notes, "The final 1997 figures (0.9 percent) are lower than the preliminary data reported last year (3.1 percent overall). It is difficult to discern exactly why this occurs, but the preliminary data is usually 86 percent to 87 percent complete and thus some adjustment in the final figures is inevitable."

Dutch Prices

Dutch (English-language) periodicals (Table 14) is compiled by Fred Lynden based on data supplied by Martinus Nijhoff International. In past years, the data provided have varied in the number of titles included. Nijhoff continues to add titles to the data supplied; consequently, the sample shifts from year to year. This causes some unusual results in specific subject areas due to changes in the number of titles in the data. The index is reported in Dutch guilders in order to avoid the impact of currency conversion in price changes. A further potential complication for all European Community member countries is the adoption of a single Euro currency. This is not yet a settled issue and the LMPI Committee will monitor the situation as it pertains to library materials pricing. The 1998 overall price increase of 9.08 percent shows a slight decrease over 1997's rise of 11.17 percent. Due to the small number of titles in some subjects, the price changes from year to year in some specific areas may be suspect, but overall it appears that science, technology, fine arts, and philosophy all experienced double-digit inflation for 1998.

Latin American Prices

The price survey of Latin American books that was included as Table 15 in last year's report has been discontinued with 1997. A formal book price index is being developed and should be completed later in 1998. This new index is based on title lists supplied by Latin American book vendors.

Latin American periodicals (Table 15), compiled by Scott Van Jacob, provides an analysis of prices quoted by the Faxon Company, the Library of Congress's Rio field office, and the University of Texas at Austin. Weighted mean prices by subject grouping continue to follow a consistent trend. Humanities journals remain the least expensive, while science journals are slightly more expensive than social science titles. The prices, indexed to 1992, provide data both including and excluding newspapers, recognizing that foreign newspapers have a significant influence on average price figures. From 1995–1996 to 1996–1997 the average price for all Latin American periodicals increased 1.6 percent from $71.10 to $72.29 with social sciences and science/technology showing the greatest increases.

Using the Price Indexes

Librarians are encouraged to monitor both trends in the publishing industry and changes in economic conditions when preparing budget projections. The ALA ALCTS Library Materials Price Index Committee endeavors to make information on publishing trends readily available by sponsoring the annual compilation and publication of the price data contained in Tables 1–15. The indexes cover newly published library materials and document prices and rates of price changes at the national/international level. They are useful benchmarks against which local costs may be compared, but because they reflect retail prices in the aggregate, they are not a substitute for cost data that reflect the collecting patterns of individual libraries and they are not a substitute for specific cost studies.

In part, differences arise because the national indexes exclude discounts, service charges, shipping and handling fees, or other costs that the library may bear. Discrepancies may also be related to subject focus, mix of current and retrospective materials, and the portion of total library acquisitions composed of foreign imprints. Such variables can affect the average price paid by a particular library although the library's rate of price increase may not significantly differ from national price indexes. LMPIC is interested in pursuing studies correlating a particular library's costs with national prices and would appreciate being informed of any planned or ongoing studies. The committee welcomes interested parties to its meetings at the ALA annual and midwinter conferences.

In addition to the tables included, you may wish to consult a new publication on the costs of law materials: *Price Index for Legal Publications, 1997*, prepared by Margaret Mae Axtmann and published by the American Association of Law

Libraries. In addition, Yale University Libraries has established a very useful Web page, "Price and Title Output Reports for Collection Management," at http://www.library.yale.edu/colldev/.

Current members of the Library Materials Price Index Committee are Stephen Bosch (chair), Margaret Axtmann, Penny Schroeder, Nancy Slight-Gibney, Beverly Harris, Wanda Dole, Gay N. Dannelly, Martha L. Brogan, Marifran Bustion, and Brenda Dingley. They are joined by consultants Dana Alessi, Adrian W. Alexander, Donna D. Alsbury, Catherine Barr, Dave Bogart, Nancy Chaffin, John Haar, Curt Holleman, Martha Kellogg, Fred Lynden, Genevieve Owens, Wilba Swearingen, Steve Thompson, and Scott Van Jacob.

Book Title Output and Average Prices: 1996 Final and 1997 Preliminary Figures

Gary Ink

Research Librarian, *Publishers Weekly*

American book title production continued to soar in 1996, according to figures compiled by R. R. Bowker, reaching a total of 68,175 titles published. This figure represents an increase of 6,136 titles over the 1995 final figure of 62,039 titles. Although less dramatic than the astounding 10,176-title increase recorded in 1995, this figure represents a continued escalation of the stunning increase in book title output that began in 1995. American book title output had reached a post-World War II high of 56,027 in 1987, but began to experience a decline in 1988 and the years following, reaching its lowest point in 1990, when only 46,743 titles were issued, according to Bowker's figures.

Since 1991, book title output has increased noticeably each year, culminating in dramatic highs experienced in 1995 and 1996. Title output for the years 1995 and 1996 represent, respectively, the largest and the second-largest year-to-year increases recorded in the post-World War II era. Preliminary figures for 1997 show 2,443 fewer books than comparable figures in 1996, so this trend may be slowing.

Output by Format and by Category

Title output in 1996 increased for hardcover books and for trade paperbacks, but showed a small decline for mass market paperbacks. Hardcover output increased by 3,819 titles; trade paperback output increased by 4,581 titles, making it once again the format with the largest increase in new title output; and mass market output decreased by 199 titles. A larger decline in mass market output was recorded in 1994, but appeared to reverse itself in 1995. The 1996 decline may indicate the beginning of publisher reaction to the turbulent conditions currently existing in mass market book sales. Overall category totals (Table 1) indicate that most categories experienced growth in 1996. Categories showing significant growth include sociology and economics with an increase of 1,166 titles; fiction with an increase of 968 titles; and history with an increase of 577 titles. Categories showing a decline in growth include children's books (Juveniles) with a decrease of 225 titles, and business with a decrease of 55 titles. Children's books (Juveniles) saw a decline in title output in 1993 and 1994, which was reversed with a noticeable increase in new titles in 1995. This 1995 increase may have been an anomaly, however, since the decline in children,s title output has resumed once again.

Mass market output (Table 3), which recorded a large decline in 1994 but appeared to make a healthy recovery in 1995, has once again registered a small decline of 199 titles. Mass market sales have been experiencing difficulties during the past two years, which could indicate the beginning of a declining trend in

(text continues on page 523)

Table 1 / American Book Title Production, 1995–1997

Category	1995 All Hard and Paper*	1996 Final Hard and Trade Paper Books	Editions	Total	All Hard and Paper*	1997 Preliminary Hard and Trade Paper Books	Editions	Total	All Hard and Paper*
Agriculture	673	575	87	662	675	564	114	678	679
Art	2,168	1,858	167	2,025	2,033	1,359	145	1,504	1,505
Biography	2,658	2,636	333	2,969	3,007	2,250	288	2,538	2,555
Business	1,843	1,380	389	1,769	1,788	1,144	280	1,424	1,431
Education	1,526	1,324	240	1,564	1,595	1,098	194	1,292	1,306
Fiction	7,605	4,704	283	4,987	8,573	3,683	198	3,881	7,010
General Works	2,751	2,552	439	2,991	3,027	2,108	450	2,558	2,579
History	2,999	3,068	491	3,559	3,576	2,663	400	3,063	3,067
Home Economics	1,395	1,231	181	1,412	1,447	1,101	150	1,251	1,275
Juveniles	5,678	4,881	180	5,061	5,353	3,227	103	3,330	3,383
Language	732	703	187	890	898	606	194	800	805
Law	1,230	952	400	1,352	1,357	831	295	1,126	1,131
Literature	2,525	2,689	321	3,010	3,082	2,067	302	2,369	2,400
Medicine	3,510	3,280	923	4,203	4,223	2,744	760	3,504	3,522
Music	479	381	75	456	461	293	59	352	354
Philosophy, Psychology	2,068	1,903	322	2,225	2,333	1,724	324	2,048	2,071
Poetry, Drama	1,407	1,443	95	1,538	1,566	1,159	38	1,197	1,204
Religion	3,324	3,298	489	3,787	3,803	2,791	447	3,238	3,249
Science	3,323	3,105	611	3,716	3,725	2,803	546	3,349	3,350
Sociology, Economics	9,362	9,247	1,247	10,494	10,528	7,835	1,153	8,988	9,000
Sports, Recreation	1,591	1,470	205	1,675	1,751	1,193	199	1,392	1,417
Technology	2,470	2,116	493	2,609	2,629	1,728	347	2,075	2,084
Travel	722	505	230	735	745	460	182	642	645
Totals	62,039	55,301	8,388	63,689	68,175	45,431	7,168	52,599	56,022

* Includes mass market paperbacks (see Table 3).

Note: Figures for mass market paperbound book production are based on entries in R. R. Bowker's *Paperbound Books in Print*. Other figures are from the *Weekly Record* (*American Book Publishing Record*) database. Figures under Books and Editions designate new books and new editions.

Table 2 / Paperbacks (Excluding Mass Market), 1995–1997

Category	1995 Totals	1996 Final			1997 Preliminary		
		Books	Editions	Totals	Books	Editions	Totals
Fiction	748	582	170	752	559	184	743
Nonfiction	21,921	22,272	4,596	26,868	19,145	4,141	23,286
Total	22,669	22,854	4,766	27,620	19,704	4,325	24,029

Table 3 / Mass Market Paperbacks, 1995–1997

Category	1994	1995	1996 Final	1997 Preliminary
Agriculture	7	10	13	1
Art	10	12	8	1
Biography	40	39	38	17
Business	17	18	19	7
Education	17	29	31	14
Fiction	1,944	3701	3,586	3,129
General Works	42	31	36	21
History	10	24	17	4
Home Economics	58	43	35	24
Juveniles	230	398	292	53
Language	3	8	8	5
Law	3	5	5	5
Literature	16	47	72	31
Medicine	7	10	20	18
Music	2	3	5	2
Philosophy, Psychology	37	103	108	23
Poetry, Drama	8	32	28	7
Religion	11	16	16	11
Science	10	8	9	1
Sociology, Economics	40	42	34	12
Sports, Recreation	102	82	76	25
Technology	39	22	20	9
Travel	5	3	10	3
Total	2,658	4686	4,486	3,423

title output as publishers attempt to come to terms with the reality of the market. While ten categories showed declines in title output, the largest declines were registered by fiction with a decrease of 111 titles, and by children's books (Juveniles) with a decrease of 108 titles. Thirteen categories showed at least a small increase in title output for 1996, with the largest increases recorded by literature with 25 titles, and by medicine with 10 titles.

(text continues on page 525)

Table 4 / Imported Titles, 1995–1997
(Hard and Trade Paper Only)

Category	1995 Totals	1996 Final			1997 Preliminary		
		Books	Editions	Totals	Books	Editions	Totals
Agriculture	97	61	11	72	71	12	83
Art	273	193	10	203	122	10	132
Biography	142	190	31	221	105	9	114
Business	268	197	41	238	128	15	143
Education	285	261	19	280	133	3	136
Fiction	251	244	36	280	171	9	180
General works	367	384	40	424	251	43	294
History	462	466	70	536	311	34	345
Home economics	41	20	2	22	8	1	9
Juveniles	63	47	0	47	26	1	27
Language	263	268	45	313	209	33	242
Law	215	231	33	264	181	29	210
Literature	308	391	37	428	201	17	218
Medicine	611	597	123	720	423	113	536
Music	73	56	11	67	27	3	30
Philosophy, psychology	346	364	29	393	262	41	303
Poetry, drama	206	213	18	231	91	5	96
Religion	235	282	28	310	183	30	213
Science	1068	916	142	1058	670	96	766
Sociology, economics	2,198	2,181	211	2,392	1,329	139	1,468
Sports, recreation	118	126	10	136	80	7	87
Technology	487	436	84	520	303	42	345
Travel	162	71	45	116	28	17	45
Total		8,195	1076	9,271	5,313	709	6,022

Table 5 / Translations into English, 1992–1997

	1992	1993	1994	1995	1996 Final	1997 Prelim.
Arabic	26	23	17	36	25	8
Chinese	49	50	55	63	40	39
Danish	25	14	21	15	13	20
Dutch	30	35	39	50	55	48
Finnish	42	4	4	4	2	2
French	383	339	374	438	444	373
German	337	353	362	477	517	403
Hebrew	47	40	35	54	61	42
Italian	91	87	132	118	125	122
Japanese	70	59	50	58	78	51
Latin	10	55	46	72	78	63
Norwegian	62	2	5	9	15	12
Russian	146	133	137	100	141	105
Spanish	122	135	120	119	193	163
Swedish	25	27	13	20	26	15
Turkish	0	1	2	0	2	1
Yiddish	4	3	6	6	14	6
Total	1,469	1,360	1,418	1,639	1829	1,473

Note: Total covers only the languages listed here

Table A / Hardcover Average Per-Volume Prices, 1994–1997

Category	1994 Prices	1995 Prices	1996 Final Vols.	1996 Final $ Total	1996 Final Prices	1997 Preliminary Vols.	1997 Preliminary $ Total	1997 Preliminary Prices
Agriculture	$58.10	$49.00	399	$17,997.48	$45.11	412	$20,076.98	$48.73
Art	39.97	41.23	1,070	57,138.74	53.40	723	34,448.11	47.65
Biography	30.43	30.01	1,829	57,933.32	31.67	1,560	51,509.14	33.02
Business	42.72	46.90	1005	52,884.81	52.62	642	32,866.49	51.19
Education	47.98	43.00	652	30,706.73	47.10	407	18,238.67	44.81
Fiction	20.95	21.47	2,915	66,728.90	22.89	2,262	51,613.03	22.82
General Works	60.41	54.11	1,181	80,738.15	68.36	1,005	60,663.21	60.36
History	40.20	42.19	2,028	92,512.08	45.62	1,771	77,872.04	43.97
Home Economics	20.49	22.53	655	15,317.95	23.39	541	12,840.82	23.74
Juveniles	14.60	14.55	3,730	59,582.22	15.97	2,058	32,861.44	15.97
Language	52.09	54.89	399	23,466.37	58.81	328	18,325.62	55.87
Law	72.32	73.09	827	73,195.20	88.51	614	49,518.12	80.65
Literature	37.77	38.49	1,575	68,162.29	43.28	1,201	53,830.73	44.82
Medicine	76.30	75.80	2,480	202,069.60	81.48	1,852	160,348.94	86.58
Music	39.27	43.27	253	9,919.74	39.21	190	8,249.61	43.42
Philosophy, Psychology	44.71	45.26	1,154	55,856.69	48.40	885	42,889.28	48.46
Poetry, Drama	31.56	34.96	606	20,695.74	34.15	497	18,155.19	36.53
Religion	30.73	34.27	1,544	56,547.18	36.62	1,181	51,000.35	43.18
Science	90.12	93.52	2,372	214,981.53	90.63	1,982	153,367.38	77.38
Sociology, Economics	50.24	55.51	5,973	321,454.02	53.82	4,702	256,540.57	54.56
Sports, Recreation	33.39	32.14	591	20,512.80	34.71	531	17,096.15	32.20
Technology	81.03	88.28	1,599	146,461.02	91.60	1,281	108,588.65	84.77
Travel	32.13	38.30	179	6,070.88	33.92	184	5,901.61	32.07
Total	$44.65	$47.15	35,016	$1,750,933.44	$50.00	26,809	$1,336,802.03	$49.86

Price Data Shows Mixed Results

Average book prices for 1996, as a whole, showed curiously mixed results. The overall average price for hardcover books (Table A) increased by $2.85 between 1995 and 1996, registering an even larger increase than the hefty $2.50 registered in 1995. The overall average price for trade paperbacks (Table B) actually decreased by 29 cents between 1995 and 1996, after registering an increase of $1.13 in 1995. The overall average price for mass market paperbacks (Table C) increased by 72 cents between 1995 and 1996, after registering an increase of only 15 cents in 1995. The relatively large average price increase for mass market paperbacks is surprising given the already difficult sales environment being experienced within this format.

Hardcover books recorded price increases in most categories for 1996. Fiction was once more above the $20 mark, with an increase of $1.42 to $22.89. Children books (Juveniles), which recorded a slight decrease of 5 cents in 1995, also recorded an increase of $1.42 to $15.97. The largest category increases were recorded in law with an increase of $15.42, general works with an increase of $14.25, and art with an increase of $12.17. Mass market paperbacks also saw a

Table A1 / Hardcover Average Per-Volume Prices—Less Than $81, 1994–1997

Category	1994 Prices	1995 Prices	Vols.	1996 Final $ Total	Prices	Vols.	1997 Preliminary $ Total	Prices
Agriculture	$30.67	$30.75	340	$10,003.83	$29.42	346	$10,431.53	$30.15
Art	36.20	36.10	979	37,543.44	38.35	675	26,789.11	39.69
Biography	27.53	27.46	1,759	49,572.37	28.18	1,482	42,127.49	28.43
Business	37.74	38.30	910	37,443.55	41.15	570	24,033.85	42.16
Education	38.76	38.98	609	25,992.67	42.68	388	16,548.02	42.65
Fiction	20.35	20.98	2,896	61,556.05	21.26	2,254	50,309.18	22.32
General works	41.02	41.63	963	42,642.96	44.28	834	35,662.96	42.76
History	37.18	37.26	1,909	72,103.13	37.77	1,664	60,957.64	36.63
Home economics	20.35	22.00	653	15,102.95	23.13	539	12,570.82	23.32
Juveniles	13.91	14.33	3,718	54,892.42	14.76	2,050	30,534.54	14.89
Language	38.57	41.01	323	13,587.54	42.07	265	11,059.42	41.73
Law	44.20	45.08	566	26,483.15	46.79	417	19,827.02	47.55
Literature	35.07	36.24	1,482	56,850.14	38.36	1,113	44,150.38	39.67
Medicine	40.66	40.91	1,490	62,352.10	41.85	1,082	45,768.96	42.30
Music	38.26	40.24	233	8,508.84	36.52	179	7,233.91	40.41
Philosophy, psychology	37.89	38.89	1054	42,748.84	40.56	810	32764.43	40.45
Poetry, drama	29.49	30.36	585	18,583.14	31.77	469	15,083.79	32.16
Religion	28.68	28.92	1413	42,853.46	30.33	1086	34,644.10	31.90
Science	46.79	47.85	1,475	69,218.17	46.93	1,354	58,403.89	43.13
Sociology, economics	41.90	41.33	5,478	237,903.61	43.43	4,275	188,193.82	44.02
Sports, recreation	31.67	31.19	573	18,703.60	32.64	518	15,278.90	29.50
Technology	48.16	49.31	933	44,703.31	47.91	801	37,111.72	46.33
Travel	28.60	28.96	171	5,053.87	29.55	179	5,372.16	30.01
Total	$32.65	$33.29	30,512	$1,054,403.14	$34.56	23,350	$824,857.64	$35.33

price increase for fiction of 74 cents, and a price increase for children's books of 25 cents. Figures shown here are derived from R. R. Bowker databases— *American Book Publishing Record* for hardcovers and trade paperbacks, and from *Paperbound Books in Print* for mass market paperbacks (Tables A–C).

Subject Groups

Each of the 23 standard subject groups used here represents one or more specific Dewey Decimal Classification numbers, as follows: Agriculture, 630–639, 712–719; Art, 700–711, 720–779; Biography, 920–929; Business, 650–659; Education, 370–379; Fiction; General Works, 000–099; History, 900–909, 930–999; Home Economics, 640–649; Juveniles; Language, 400–499; Law, 340–349; Literature, 800–810, 813–820, 823–899; Medicine, 610–619; Music, 780–789; Philosophy, Psychology, 100–199; Poetry, Drama, 811, 812, 821, 822; Religion, 200–299; Science, 500–599; Sociology, Economics, 300–339, 350–369, 380–389; Sports, Recreation, 790–799; Technology, 600–609, 620–629, 660–699; Travel, 910–919.

Table B / Mass Market Paperbacks Average Per-Volume Prices, 1995–1997

Category	1995 Prices	1996 Final			1997 Preliminary		
		Vols.	$ Total	Prices	Vols.	$ Total	Prices
Agriculture	$9.13	13	$150.63	$11.59	1	$12.95	$12.95
Art	11.24	8	95.99	12.00	1	15.00	15.00
Biography	8.09	38	384.41	10.12	17	160.19	9.42
Business	10.81	19	251.66	13.25	6	80.85	13.48
Education	12.40	31	318.97	10.29	14	159.66	11.40
Fiction	5.51	3,569	22,317.73	6.25	3,030	24,728.92	8.16
General Works	19.38	34	316.66	9.31	20	197.05	9.85
History	10.06	17	185.63	10.92	4	45.49	11.37
Home Economics	8.71	35	303.55	8.67	24	504.78	21.03
Juveniles	4.00	288	1,224.20	4.25	53	273.05	5.15
Language	9.61	8	62.94	7.87	5	22.95	4.59
Law	9.79	5	51.97	10.39	5	65.84	13.17
Literature	8.73	72	678.14	9.42	30	354.25	11.81
Medicine	8.39	20	178.69	8.93	18	175.55	9.75
Music	24.98	5	102.85	20.57	1	5.99	5.99
Philosophy, Psychology	4.84	108	818.65	7.58	22	217.09	9.87
Poetry, Drama	9.71	28	304.75	10.88	7	95.78	13.68
Religion	9.39	16	142.90	8.93	11	134.29	12.21
Science	11.29	9	109.40	12.16	1	4.99	4.99
Sociology, Economics	9.60	34	337.01	9.91	12	147.67	12.31
Sports, Recreation	8.28	75	659.47	8.79	25	254.37	10.17
Technology	11.62	20	222.74	11.14	9	101.80	11.31
Travel	13.97	10	96.34	9.63	3	35.89	11.96
Total	$5.85	4,462	$29,315.28	$6.57	3,319	$27,794.40	$8.37

Table C / Trade Paperbacks Average Per-Volume Prices, 1994–1997

Category	1994 Prices	1995 Prices	1996 Final			1997 Preliminary		
			Vols.	$ Total	Prices	Vols.	$ Total	Prices
Agriculture	$18.26	$26.97	248	$5,070.81	$20.45	218	$4,649.06	$21.33
Art	20.99	20.58	872	18,807.38	21.57	566	12,624.03	22.30
Biography	15.65	16.59	979	17,009.36	17.37	703	11,879.63	16.90
Business	23.94	24.24	687	17,920.08	26.08	587	15,086.27	25.70
Education	21.47	22.96	832	19,765.59	23.76	562	14,101.82	25.09
Fiction	14.94	12.71	1,852	22,877.56	12.35	1,315	17,805.53	13.54
General Works	33.81	32.99	1,693	58,654.91	34.65	1,261	47,933.01	38.01
History	20.15	18.48	1,381	27,742.92	20.09	917	18,324.62	19.98
Home Economics	14.72	14.87	727	11,161.79	15.35	634	9,747.05	15.37
Juveniles	6.83	15.75	1117	9,274.56	8.30	861	8,451.46	9.82
Language	23.82	21.58	427	9,040.92	21.17	296	6,406.52	21.64
Law	30.57	30.26	434	13,372.93	30.81	316	9,417.85	29.80
Literature	18.21	16.54	1278	22,604.76	17.69	861	16,354.63	18.99
Medicine	25.15	27.91	1,577	43,169.86	27.37	1,203	32,848.39	27.31
Music	19.48	19.81	183	3,686.31	20.14	126	2,653.20	21.06
Philosophy, Psychology	18.19	19.92	989	18,622.36	18.83	855	16,488.24	19.28
Poetry, Drama	13.25	15.69	862	11,139.24	12.92	576	8,300.01	14.41
Religion	14.69	14.60	2,100	31,356.98	14.93	1,673	26,581.89	15.89
Science	35.71	33.42	1134	37,365.16	32.95	779	25,947.63	33.31
Sociology, Economics	23.19	23.69	3,983	93,480.92	23.47	2,836	70,647.93	24.91
Sports, Recreation	16.39	16.53	1,028	16,782.34	16.33	700	12,082.29	17.26
Technology	29.50	38.75	890	34,861.24	39.17	570	17,855.20	31.32
Travel	15.54	16.38	537	8,988.33	16.74	417	6,843.11	16.41
Total	$20.56	$21.71	25,810	$552,756.31	$21.42	18,832	$413,029.37	$21.93

Book Sales Statistics, 1997:
AAP Preliminary Estimates

Association of American Publishers

The industry estimates shown in the following table are based on the U.S. Census of Manufactures. This Census is conducted every fifth year.

Between censuses, the Association of American Publishers (AAP) estimates are "pushed forward" by the percentage changes that are reported to the AAP statistics program, and by other industry data that are available. Some AAP data are collected in a monthly statistics program, and it is largely this material that is shown in this preliminary estimate table. More detailed data are available from, and additional publishers report to, the AAP annual statistics program, and this additional data will be incorporated into Table S1 that will be published in the AAP 1997 Industry Statistics.

Readers comparing the estimated data with census reports should be aware that the U.S. Census of Manufactures does not include data on many university presses or on other institutionally sponsored and not-for-profit publishing activities, or (under SIC 2731: Book Publishing) for the audiovisual and other media materials that are included in this table. On the other hand, AAP estimates have traditionally excluded "Sunday School" materials and certain pamphlets that are incorporated in the census data. These and other adjustments have been built into AAP's industry estimates.

As in prior reports, the estimates reflect the impact of industry expansion created by new establishments entering the field, as well as nontraditional forms of book publishing, in addition to incorporating the sales increases and decreases of established firms.

It should also be noted that the "Other Sales" category includes only incidental book sales, such as music, sheet sales (both domestic and export, except those to prebinders), and miscellaneous merchandise sales.

The estimates include domestic sales and export sales of U.S. product, but they do not cover indigenous activities of publishers' foreign subsidiaries.

Non-rack-size Mass Market Publishing is included in Trade—Paperbound. Prior to the 1988 AAP Industry Statistics, this was indicated as Adult Trade Paperbound. It is recognized that part of this is Juvenile (1987 estimate: 20 percent), and adjustments have been made in this respect. AAP also notes that this area includes sales through traditional "mass market paperback channels" by publishers not generally recognized as being "mass market paperback."

Table 1 / **Estimated Book Publishing Industry Sales, 1987, 1992, 1995–1997**
(Millions of Dollars)

	1987 $	1992 $	1995 $	1996 $	1996 % Change from 1995	1997 $	1997 % Change from 1996	Compound growth rate (%) 1987–1997	Compound growth rate (%) 1992–1997
Trade (total)	2,712.8	4,661.6	5,560.8	5,643.0	1.5	5,453.2	-3.4	7.2	3.2
Adult hardbound	1,350.6	2,222.5	2,646.9	2,586.0	-2.3	2,410.2	-6.8	6.0	1.6
Adult paperbound	727.1	1,261.7	1,587.2	1,609.4	1.4	1,685.0	4.7	8.8	6.0
Juvenile hardbound	478.5	850.8	836.6	867.7	3.7	887.7	2.3	6.4	0.9
Juvenile paperbound	156.6	326.6	490.1	579.9	18.3	470.3	-18.9	11.6	7.6
Religious (total)	638.8	907.1	1,036.9	1,093.4	5.4	1,132.7	3.6	5.9	4.5
Bibles, testaments, hymnals, etc.	177.6	260.1	293.0	294.8	0.6	285.4	3.2	4.9	1.9
Other religious	461.2	647.0	743.9	798.6	7.4	847.3	6.1	6.3	5.5
Professional (total)	2,207.3	3,106.7	3,869.3	3,985.0	3.0	4,156.4	4.3	6.5	6.0
Business	388.8	490.3	617.6	721.4	16.8	—	—	—	—
Law	780.0	1,128.1	1,400.4	1,429.8	2.1	—	—	—	—
Medical	406.5	622.7	809.3	815.8	0.8	—	—	—	—
Technical, scientific, other prof'l	632.0	865.6	1,042.0	1,018.0	-2.3	—	—	—	—
Book clubs	678.7	742.3	976.1	1,091.8	11.9	1,145.3	4.9	5.4	9.1
Mail order publications	657.6	630.2	559.5	579.5	3.6	521.0	-10.1	-2.3	-3.7
Mass market paperback, rack-sized	913.7	1,263.8	1,499.6	1,555.1	3.7	1,433.8	-7.8	4.6	2.6
University presses	170.9	280.1	339.7	349.3	2.8	367.8	5.3	8.0	5.6
Elementary and secondary text	1,695.6	2,080.9	2,466.2	2,619.1	6.2	2,959.6	13.0	5.7	7.3
College text	1,549.5	2,084.1	2,324.8	2,485.8	6.9	2,669.7	7.4	5.6	5.1
Standardized tests	104.0	140.4	167.3	178.7	6.8	191.4	7.1	6.3	6.4
Subscription reference	437.6	572.3	670.8	706.1	5.3	736.5	4.3	5.3	5.2
Other sales (incl. AV)	423.8	449.0	476.0	493.2	3.6	510.0	3.4	1.9	2.6
Total	12,190.3	16,918.5	19,947.0	20,780.0	4.2	21,277.4	2.4	5.7	4.7

Source: Association of American Publishers

United States Trade in Books: 1997

William S. Lofquist

Senior Analyst, U.S. Department of Commerce

While domestic sales of U.S. books proved disappointing in 1997, publishers were able to recoup a measure of success through their international efforts. Accurate data on revenues obtained from the licensing of foreign rights and permissions are not available, but statistics on U.S. book exports provide clues to the fortunes of publishers' overseas activities.

Despite a strong U.S. dollar and a downturn in book demand from several Asian economies, U.S. book exports surged to $1.9 billion in 1997, a gain of 7 percent over 1996. In contrast, U.S. book imports grew by 5 percent in 1997 over 1996, totaling $1.3 billion. Growth in the level of U.S. book exports in 1997 halted, at least temporarily, two trends: (1) the heretofore declining shares of publisher's exports compared to domestic revenues, and (2) a progressive narrowing of the gap between U.S. book exports over imports. Part of this gap-narrowing was the inadvertent result of changes in the statistical allocation of products classified as books.

Changes in Book Classification

The U.S. government's classification of what constitutes products of the U.S. book industry was revised in 1997. Removed from the book classification were children's toy and picture books; these were products more clearly identified as

Table 1 / U.S. Exports of Books: 1997

Category	Value (millions of current $)	Percent change, 1997–96	Units (millions of copies)	Percent change, 1997–96
Dictionaries and thesauruses	$19.0	253.2%	2.7	87.2%
Encyclopedias	25.6	-33.2	4.0	-28.6
Textbooks	370.5	16.9	58.4	16.9
Religious books	53.5	3.3	37.8	-8.1
Technical, scientific and professional books	549.4	8.5	80.9	1.6
Art and pictorial books	19.6	61.4	20.8	40.7
Hardcover books, n.e.s	146.5	-20.6	49.1	-12.1
Mass market paperbound books	233.1	12.0	118.5	15.0
Books: flyers/circulars, 1–4 pages	8.8	117.2	14.6	122.0
Books: pamphlets/brochures, 5–48 pages	31.4	-5.0	56.8	-10.4
Books: 49 or more pages	419.5	6.0	476.7	5.5
Music books	16.6	4.2	3.1	25.2
Atlases	2.9	1.1	0.5	5.7
Total, all books	$1,896.6	6.8%	923.8	5.4%

Notes: n.e.s.=Not elsewhere specified. Individual shipments are excluded from the foreign trade data if valued under $2,500. Data for individual categories may not add to totals due to statistical rounding.

Source: U.S. Department of Commerce, Bureau of the Census.

manufactured by the toys and games industry. Added to the imported book classifications were crossword puzzle books (formerly associated with periodical publishing) and book blocks (signatures, gathered but not bound). Also added to both the export and import book classification were flyers/circulars and pamphlets/brochures; these items are more clearly identified with the book printing and publishing industry than they were with general commercial printing. The net economic effect of these changes in the foreign trade data was minimal for book exports (a net gain of $19.1 million or 1.0 percent) but reasonably significant for book imports (a net loss of $74.2 million or 6.1 percent).

Table 2 / U.S. Book Exports to Principal Countries: 1997

Country	Value (millions of current $)	Percent change, 1997–96	Units (millions of copies)	Percent change, 1997–96
Canada	$823.6	11.2%	464.6	9.3%
United Kingdom	254.4	12.4	96.5	9.8
Australia	138.1	16.9	64.4	14.1
Japan	120.3	-7.1	30.8	-25.5
Mexico	58.2	-6.1	52.4	-11.4
Germany	48.8	15.3	17.4	8.1
Singapore	36.9	2.3	19.8	0.5
Netherlands	31.4	14.7	14.5	85.9
Korea, Republic of	29.2	-14.1	16.2	15.0
Taiwan	28.7	4.6	8.8	-22.4
Brazil	26.4	-8.7	10.5	-18.4
Hong Kong	23.9	9.0	5.8	-8.5
Philippines	19.7	-26.0	9.2	-13.9
New Zealand	18.6	27.1	7.2	-14.0
South Africa, Republic of	18.2	3.1	9.8	22.1
France	18.1	3.3	4.7	-25.9
India	17.8	22.2	7.8	12.2
Argentina	10.8	39.0	6.6	100.3
Denmark	10.0	-38.7	2.5	-35.1
Italy	9.9	-10.3	3.0	13.0
Switzerland	8.8	-27.9	4.6	6.9
Israel	8.7	-12.4	2.8	63.8
Belgium	8.4	1.0	2.2	-6.1
Colombia	8.2	-12.3	4.4	4.1
Saudi Arabia	7.0	-6.5	4.0	97.6
China	6.6	22.9	2.8	-17.1
Spain	6.5	-18.1	1.8	-30.5
Thailand	5.4	-31.0	1.9	-36.0
Venezuela	5.4	63.1	4.2	57.7
Malaysia	5.3	-7.4	2.3	9.5
Total, all countries	$1,896.6	6.8%	923.8	5.4%

Notes: Individual shipments are excluded from the foreign trade data if valued under $2,500.

Source: U.S. Department of Commerce, Bureau of the Census.

U.S. Book Exports

United States book exports, which declined fractionally in 1996 compared to 1995, experienced strong growth in 1997. As shown in Table 1, the dollar value of U.S. book exports reached $1.897 billion, an increase of 6.8 percent over 1996. Four of the five largest export categories showed growth of at least 6 percent in 1997 versus 1996, with only hardcover books, n.e.s. (i.e. adult and juvenile trade books) recording a decline.

This growth in dollar value can partially but not wholly be attributed to higher prices. The number of books exported increased by 5.4 percent in 1997 vs. 1996, reaching 924 million units. Four major book categories showed gains in copies exported in 1997: textbooks, technical/scientific/professional books, mass market paperbound books, and the category "books: 49 or more pages" (i.e. trade paperbound books). A 12 percent downturn was recorded in unit exports of trade hardcover books (hardcover books, n.e.s.).

Foreign demand for U.S. books in 1997 was not broadly based. The strong U.S. dollar, coupled with financial difficulties in several economies, reduced markets for U.S. books in significant parts of Asia and Latin America. But double-digit demand by four of the six United States' major trading partners—Canada, the United Kingdom, Australia, and Germany—spurred 1997 growth in U.S. book exports. A listing of the 30 largest foreign markets for U.S. books appears in Table 2.

Table 3 / U.S. Imports of Books: 1997

Category	Value (millions of current $)	Percent change, 1997–96	Units (millions of copies)	Percent change, 1997–96
Dictionaries and thesauruses	$7.4	5.5%	2.2	8.2
Encyclopedias	5.4	-18.2	0.8	-32.5
Textbooks	111.6	-6.0	22.0	-17.7
Religious books	50.6	-3.0	27.9	-28.1
Technical, scientific and professional books	182.6	10.2	34.2	5.3
Art and pictorial books, valued under $5	14.8	-3.0	8.9	0.8
Art and pictorial books, valued at $5 or more	17.4	-16.6	1.6	-16.2
Hardcover books, n.e.s	411.7	-8.7	131.1	-1.0
Mass market paperbound books	75.2	82.6	41.6	52.9
Books: flyers/circulars, 1–4 pages	5.5	0.2	49.8	-2.9
Books: pamphlets/brochures, 5–48 pages	68.6	10.4	262.3	13.2
Books: 49 or more pages	326.2	24.5	200.4	32.0
Music books	5.9	76.7	0.9	-4.3
Atlases	4.0	-6.7	1.5	15.0
Books: signatures	3.9	145.3	0.1**	302.8
Crossword puzzle books	6.5	-23.3	31.2	15.3
Total, all books	$1,297.5	4.6%	816.5*	11.0

Notes: * Excludes quantities measured in kilograms.

** kilograms.

n.e.s.=Not elsewhere specified. Individual shipments are excluded from the foreign trade data if valued under $1,250. Data for individual categories may not add to totals due to statistical rounding.

Source: U.S. Department of Commerce, Bureau of the Census.

Asian economies showing weak demand for U.S. book exports in 1997 included Thailand (-31 percent), the Philippines (-26 percent), Korea (-14 percent), Malaysia (-7 percent) and Japan (- 7 percent). Asian countries with strong economies (Taiwan) or not linked to foreign currency fluctuations (China and Hong Kong) recorded increased demand for U.S. books in 1997. Latin America showed vivid contrasts in demand for U.S. books, with robust markets in Argentina (+39 percent) and Venezuela (+63 percent), but considerably softer markets in Brazil (-9 percent), Colombia (-12 percent) and Mexico (-6 percent).

U.S. Book Imports

United States demand for imported books totaled 1.3 billion in 1997, reflecting a growth rate over 1996 (+4.6 percent) that was almost identical to the rate of growth (+4.7 percent) achieved in 1996 compared to 1995. A strong U.S. dollar discourages exports but invites imports, and this phenomenon is effectively illustrated by data at the aggregate level as shown in Table 3. While the dollar value of U.S. book imports rose 4.6 percent in 1997 vs. 1996, the purchasing power of the strong dollar provided a yield in units (number of imported books) in 1997 that was 11 percent higher than units imported in 1996.

The U.S. imported book market exhibited few pronounced trends in 1997. Of the four largest book categories, two showed an expansion in market demand (technical/scientific/professional books and "books: 49 or more pages"[trade paperbound books]) while two found a weakening in demand (textbooks and "hardcover books, n.e.s."[trade books]).

Although the purchasing power of the strong U.S. dollar is evident at the aggregate level in Table 3, its display is far less pronounced from an examination of the data in Table 4. Not even a high valued U.S. dollar could overcome weakness in U.S. demand for trade books in 1997, and this weakness brought down U.S. publisher's demand for foreign printing. Countries supplying the bulk of such U.S. contract printing—including Hong Kong, Singapore, Italy, Korea, Taiwan, and Colombia—all recorded declines in U.S. demand for their products in 1997. Exceptions to this trend were Canada, China, Spain, and Mexico—countries whose sizable printing operations found favor with the printing and binding needs of U.S. publishers and book packagers.

Foreign/Domestic Book Trade

Weakness in U.S. demand for trade books depressed the level of U.S. book imports in 1997, with U.S. publishers reducing their needs for foreign printing and binding. But, as shown in Table 5, the overall trend in ratios between U.S. book exports and book imports remains relatively unchanged. Over the period 1970–1997, U.S. book exports rose at an annual average of 9.2 percent—compared to a rate of 10.3 percent for U.S. book imports. The gap between U.S. book exports and imports is gradually closing, the result of global changes in technology and communication.

Digital printing, also known as desktop publishing, is providing the world's publishers with opportunities for their globally marketed products to be locally manufactured. With advanced technology available in virtually every economy,

Table 4 / U.S. Book Imports from Principal Countries: 1997

Country	Value (millions of current $)	Percent change, 1997–96	Units (millions of copies)	Percent change, 1997–96
United Kingdom	$283.4	1.4%	61.6	-5.2
Hong Kong	203.2	-8.4	115.1	-8.9
Canada	189.4	29.7	376.0	35.1
Singapore	92.1	-4.2	38.1	1.0
Italy	85.5	-6.3	38.4	-7.2
China	73.3	27.7	45.3	49.7
Japan	66.3	0.4	20.7	2.4
Germany	57.5	6.3	12.8	19.8
France	41.0	23.1	5.7	-20.9
Spain	36.7	16.9	11.8	9.1
Mexico	19.0	21.7	23.2	-46.0
Korea, Republic of	17.5	-17.4	8.6	-11.7
Belgium	15.0	4.3	5.5	-16.4
Netherlands	14.0	0.2	1.8	13.2
Taiwan	11.8	-3.3	10.9	27.7
New Zealand	11.4	57.8	4.0	24.1
Australia	8.5	-11.1	3.2	-0.2
Israel	8.3	-2.6	1.9	-6.0
Switzerland	7.9	-2.0	1.6	27.2
Colombia	7.0	-8.9	5.9	-10.4
Thailand	5.6	-4.1	5.6	36.5
Sweden	4.8	-24.3	2.7	-23.6
Malaysia	4.1	10.0	2.2	46.8
Ecuador	4.0	114.5	1.4	76.4
Russia	3.7	377.5	0.7	-1.5
Ireland	3.4	30.5	0.8	-35.7
Portugal	2.6	1.2	0.9	8.5
India	2.5	7.4	1.5	14.3
United Arab Emirates	2.4	12.9	1.3	101.6
Argentina	1.7	17.5	0.4	-1.1
Total, all countries	$1,297.5	4.6%	816.5*	11.0

Notes: * Excludes quantities measured in kilograms. Individual shipments are excluded from the foreign trade data if valued under $1,250.

Source: U.S. Department of Commerce, Bureau of the Census.

publishers will increasingly favor the speed and convenience of local production of their books. As international copyright protection becomes a global reality, linkages among the world's publishers to translate, manufacture, and distribute each others' products will increase. Within major publishing houses, foreign licensing and permissions operations are growing in size and profitability equal to that of their export brethren.

Table 6 explores the importance of U.S. book exports relative to the book industry's total shipments. The high water mark of U.S. exports-to-shipments was reached in 1990: 9.2 percent. For reasons given above, it is unlikely that this ratio will be exceeded.

Table 5 / U.S. Trade in Books: 1970–1997
(in millions of current dollars)

Year	U.S. Book Exports	U.S. Book Imports	Ratio, U.S. Book Exports/Imports
1997	$1,896.6	$1,297.5	1.46
1996	1,775.6	1,240.1	1.43
1995	1,779.5	1,184.5	1.50
1990	1,415.1	855.1	1.65
1985	591.2	564.2	1.05
1980	518.9	306.5	1.69
1975	269.3	147.6	1.82
1970	174.9	92.0	1.90

Source: U.S. Department of Commerce, Bureau of the Census. Due to (1) changes in the classification of U.S. traded products, and (2) changes in what constitutes products classified as books, data prior to 1990 are not strictly comparable to data beginning in 1990.

Table 6 / U.S. Book Industry Shipments Compared to U.S. Book Exports: 1970–1997
(in millions of current dollars)

Year	Total Shipments, U.S. Book Industry	U.S. Book Exports	Exports as a Percent of Total Shipments
1997	$23,151.0[1]	$1,896.6	8.2
1996	21,799.0	1,775.6	8.1
1995	20,603.6	1,779.5	8.6
1990	15,317.9	1,415.1	9.2
1985	10,196.2	591.2	5.8
1980	6,114.4	518.9	8.5
1975	3,536.5	269.3	7.6
1970	2,434.2	174.9	7.2

1 Estimated by International Trade Administration, U.S. Department of Commerce.

Source: U.S. Department of Commerce, Bureau of the Census. Due to (1) changes in the classification of U.S. traded products, and (2) changes in what constitutes products classified as books, data prior to 1990 are not strictly comparable to data beginning in 1990.

International Book Title Output: 1990–1995

William S. Lofquist
Senior Analyst, U.S. Department of Commerce

Title output by the world's leading publishing economies set new records in 1995, a tribute both to the viability of books and global expansion of the reading habit. Most notable was the number of new titles and/or new editions issued by firms in the United Kingdom: 101,764. This marked the first time ever that the United Kingdom, the world's largest publisher of works in the English language, surpassed the six-digit level in title output. Other countries with impressive gains in book title output in 1995 were Germany, Spain, Italy, and the United States. After a decade of annual title output concentrated in the 45,000–55,000 range, U.S. publishers witnessed an extraordinary 20 percent rise in new titles/new editions in 1995 over 1994, reaching 62,039.

Gathering information on the world's production of books falls to the Paris-based statistical offices of UNESCO. Insight into the difficulties faced by UNESCO in accomplishing this task may be gleaned by a review of the accompanying table.

UNESCO's problems are twofold:

1 Failure/inability to report. Of the 35 countries shown in this table, 10—or 29 percent—did not report their economies' book title output in the most recent year (1995). One global publisher—Taiwan—is unable to make known its publishing output in United Nations documents since it is not a U.N. member.

2 Discrepancies in reporting. Several major publishing economies—Japan, Belgium, and Australia—show marked gaps in reporting their annual title output. Other countries—Canada and the Netherlands—report on a reasonably regular basis but exhibit vast year-to-year discrepancies in the values reported. Accounting for these discrepancies poses a challenge. The difference, for example, in Canada's title output in the years since 1993 may be attributable to the addition of public sector publications in Canada's title count.

The table *International Book Title Output: 1990–1995* lists book production by the world's 35 largest publishing economies (minus Taiwan). The countries are listed in order of magnitude, based on title output for the highest year in the period 1990–1995. The minimum cut-off point was 6,000 titles.

With 25 countries reporting title output in both 1994 and 1995, the average increase in title production by this group over the 1994–1995 period was 4.3 percent. This compares unfavorably with the 8.0 percent increase in the number of titles produced over the period 1993–1994. Nineteen countries showed gains in title output in 1995, led by the 10,176 increase in titles published in the United States. Six countries recorded a decline in 1995 title output compared to 1994, with France's drop of 10,545 titles (-23 percent) the most significant.

The world's demand for books is influenced by levels of economic develop-ment and incomes, educational attainment, and market access. Changes in book title output, as illustrated by this table, is a reflection of trends both cultural and economic. Tracking the advancement of knowledge within the world's economies invites subjectivity, but one objective measure in this field must sure-ly be found in a country's book title output.

International Book Title Output: 1990–1995

Country	1990	1991	1992	1993	1994	1995
United Kingdom	n.a.	n.a.	86,573	n.a.	95,015	101,764
China	73,923	90,156	n.a.	92,972	100,951	n.a
Germany	61,015	67,890	67,277	67,206	70,643	74,174
United States	46,743	48,146	49,276	49,757	51,863	62,039
Spain	36,239	39,082	41,816	40,758	44,261	48,467
France	41,720	43,682	45,379	41,234	45,311	34,766
Korea, Republic of	39,330	29,432	27,889	30,861	34,204	35,864
Japan	n.a.	n.a.	35,496	n.a.	n.a.	n.a.
Italy	25,068	27,751	29,351	30,110	32,673	34,470
Netherlands	13,691	11,613	15,997	34,067	n.a.	n.a.
Russia	n.a.	34,050	28,716	29,017	30,390	33,623
Brazil	n.a.	n.a.	27,557	20,141	21,574	n.a.
Canada	8,291	8,722	9,056	22,208	21,701	17,931
India	13,937	14,438	15,778	12,768	11,460	11,643
Switzerland	13,839	14,886	14,663	14,870	15,378	15,771
Belgium	12,157	13,913	n.a.	n.a.	n.a.	n.a.
Sweden	12,034	11,866	12,813	12,895	13,822	12,700
Finland	10,153	11,208	11,033	11,785	12,539	13,494
Denmark	11,082	10,198	11,761	11,492	11,973	12,478
Poland	10,242	10,688	10,727	9,788	10,874	11,925
Australia	n.a.	n.a.	n.a.	n.a.	10,835	n.a.
Iran	n.a.	5,018	6,822	n.a.	10,753	9,716
Hungary	8,322	8,133	8,536	9,170	10,108	9,314
Serbia	9,797	4,049	2,618	n.a.	n.a.	n.a.
Czech Republic	8,585	9,362	6,743	8,203	9,309	8,994
Argentina	4,915	6,092	5,628	n.a.	9,065	9,113
Austria	3,740	6,505	4,986	5,628	7,987	8,222
Thailand	7,783	7,676	7,626	n.a.	n.a.	n.a.
Norway	3,712	3,884	4,881	4,943	6,946	7,265
Ukraine	7,046	5,857	4,410	5,002	4,882	6,225
Portugal	6,150	6,430	6,462	6,089	6,667	n.a.
Turkey	6,291	6,365	6,549	5,978	4,473	6,275
Malaysia	n.a.	3,748	n.a.	3,799	4,050	6,465
Indonesia	1,518	1,774	6,303	n.a.	n.a.	n.a.
Romania	2,178	2,914	3,662	6,130	4,074	5,517

Notes: n.a.=Not available.

Source: UNESCO Statistical Yearbook, 1997.

Book Review Media Statistics

Compiled by the staff of *The Bowker Annual*

Number of Books Reviewed by Major Book-Reviewing Publications, 1996–1997

	Adult		Juvenile		Young Adult		Total	
	1996	1997	1996	1997	1996	1997	1996	1997
Booklist [1]	4,080	4,308	2,397	2,429	712	832	7,189	7,569
Bulletin of the Center for Children's Books [2]	—	—	800	800	—	—	800	800
Chicago Tribune	650	884	—	29	—	—	650	913
Choice [3]	6,728	6,788	—	—	—	—	6,728	6,788
Horn Book Magazine	8	9	410	274	71	78	489	361
Horn Book Guide [4]	—	—	3,000	3,312	—	—	3,000	3,312
Kirkus Reviews [4]	3,085	n/a	1,225	n/a	—	—	4,310	n/a
Library Journal [5]	5,553	5,955	—	—	—	—	5,553	5,955
Los Angeles Times	1,760	1,760	110	110	—	—	1,870	1,870
New York Review of Books	408	410	—	—	—	—	408	410
New York Times Sunday Book Review [4]	1,800	1,900	285	300	—	—	2,085	2,200
Publishers Weekly	6,300	4,800	1,600	1,800	—	—	7,900	6,600
Rapport (formerly *West Coast Review of Books*	520	714	—	—	—	—	520	714
School Library Journal [6]	305	289	2,454	1,653	662	1,353	3,421	3,662
Washington Post Book World	1,941	1,362	58	40	59	23	2,058	1,425

n/a=not available

1 All figures are for a 12 month period from September 1 to August 31; 1997 figures are for September 1, 1996–August 31, 1997 (vol. 93). Some YA books are included in the juvenile total, and the YA total includes reviews of adult books that are appropriate for young adults.

2 All figures are for 12 month period beginning September and ending July/August.

3 All books reviewed in *Choice* are scholarly publications intended for undergraduate libraries.

4 Juvenile figures include young adult titles.

5 This includes 153 reviews in roundups. In addition, *LJ* reviewed 64 magazines, 354 audio books, 370 videos, 750 books in "Prepub Alert," 357 books in "Collection Development," 161 Web sites, and 200 CD-ROMs.

6 Total includes 146 "Curriculum Connectors," 63 December holiday books, 44 books in Spanish, 95 reference books, and 19 books in "At-a-Glance."

Number of Book Outlets in the United States and Canada

The *American Book Trade Directory* has been published by R. R. Bowker since 1915. Revised annually, it features lists of booksellers, wholesalers, periodicals, reference tools, and other information about the U.S. and Canadian book markets. The data shown in Table 1, the most current available, are from the 1997–1998 edition of the directory.

The 29,925 stores of various types shown are located throughout the United States, Canada, and regions administered by the United States. "General" bookstores stock trade books and children's books in a general variety of subjects. "College" stores carry college-level textbooks. "Educational" outlets handle school textbooks up to and including the high school level. "Mail order" outlets sell general trade books by mail and are not book clubs; all others operating by mail are classified according to the kinds of books carried. "Antiquarian" dealers sell old and rare books. Stores handling secondhand books are classified as "used." "Paperback" stores have more than 80 percent of their stock in paperbound books. Stores with paperback departments are listed under the appropriate major classification ("general," "department store," "stationer," etc.). Bookstores with at least 50 percent of their stock on a particular subject are classified by subject.

Table 1 / Bookstores in the United States and Canada, 1997

Category	United States	Canada
Antiquarian General	1,497	89
Antiquarian Mail Order	606	12
Antiquarian Specialized	283	6
Art Supply Store	69	1
College General	3,479	182
College Specialized	145	11
Comics	302	30
Computer Software	270	0
Cooking	183	7
Department Store	2,206	85
Educational*	281	72
Federal Sites†	289	1
Foreign Language*	134	33
General	6,861	911
Gift Shop	375	20
Juvenile*	382	41
Mail Order General	405	21
Mail Order Specialized	860	23
Metaphysics, New Age, and Occult	304	22
Museum Store and Art Gallery	591	36
Nature and Natural History	162	6
Newsdealer	134	7
Office Supply	54	16
Other§	2,362	210
Paperback‡	379	15
Religious*	4,050	238
Self Help/Development	63	13
Stationer	23	28
Toy Store	115	9
Used*	827	89
Totals	27,691	2,234

* Includes Mail Order Shops for this topic, which are not counted elsewhere in this survey.

† National Historic Sites, National Monuments, and National Parks.

‡ Includes Mail Order. Excludes used paperback bookstores, stationers, drugstores, or wholesalers handling paperbacks.

§ Stores specializing in subjects or services other than those covered in this survey.

Part 5
Reference Information

Bibliographies

The Librarian's Bookshelf

Cathleen Bourdon, MLS

Executive Director, Reference and User Services Association,
American Library Association

New books on providing Internet services, searching the Internet, designing Web pages, and Internet filtering were prevalent this year and are well represented in this bibliography. Outsourcing was another topic that captured the profession's attention and resulted in the new books listed here. Most of the books in this selective bibliography have been published since 1990; a few earlier titles are retained because of their continuing importance.

General Works

Alternative Library Literature, 1994/1995: A Biennial Anthology. Ed. by Sanford Berman and James P. Danky. McFarland, 1996. Paper $35.

American Library Directory, 1997–98. 2v. Bowker, 1997. $259.95. Also available online as file number 460 on Knight-Ridder's DIALOG and on CD-ROM as *Publishing Market Place Reference PLUS* (see below).

The Bowker Annual Library and Book Trade Almanac, 1998. Bowker, 1998. $175.

CALL: Current Awareness-Library Literature. Goldstein Associates. Monthly. $25.

Concise Dictionary of Library and Information Science. By Stella Keenan. Bowker Saur, 1996. $50.

Directory of Library and Information Science Professionals. 2v. Gale, 1991. $380.

Encyclopedia of Library and Information Science. 61v. to date. Marcel Dekker, 1968–. $117/v.

The International Encyclopedia of Information and Library Science. Ed. by John Feather and Paul Sturges. Routledge, 1997. $130.

The Librarian's Companion: A Handbook of Thousands of Facts on Libraries/Librarians, Books/Newspapers, Publishers/Booksellers. 2d ed. By Vladimir F. Wertsman. Greenwood Press, 1996. $65.

Librarians' Thesaurus: A Concise Guide to Library and Information Terms. By Mary Ellen Soper and others. American Library Association, 1990. Paper $25.

Library and Information Science Annual. Vol 6. Ed. by Bohdan S. Wynar. Libraries Unlimited, 1998. $65.

Library Literature. H. W. Wilson, 1921. Also available online (http://www.epnet.com) and on CD-ROM, 1984–. Library Reference Center. Indexes 30 periodicals in librarianship for the past five years.

Library Technology Reports. American Library Association, 1965–. Bi-monthly. $215.

Publishing Market Place Reference PLUS. CD-ROM. Bowker, annual. $895. Formerly titled *Library Reference PLUS.* Contains several Bowker titles, such as the *American Library Directory* and *Literary Market Place.*

The Whole Library Handbook: Current Data, Professional Advice, and Curiosa about

Libraries and Library Services. 2d ed. Comp. by George Eberhart. American Library Association, 1995. Paper $30.

Academic Libraries

ACRL University Library Statistics, 1996–1997. Association of College and Research Libraries/American Library Association, 1998. $79.95.

ARL Statistics. Association of Research Libraries. Annual. 1964–. $65.

The Academic Library Director: Reflections on a Position in Transition. Ed. by Frank D'Andraia. Haworth, 1997. Paper $39.95.

The Academic Library: Its Context, Its Purposes, and Its Operation. By John M. Budd. Libraries Unlimited, 1998. Paper $35.

Administering the Community College Learning Resources Program. By Wanda K. Johnston. G. K. Hall, 1994. $40.

The Challenge and Practice of Academic Accreditation: A Sourcebook for Library Administrators. Ed. by Edward G. Garten. Greenwood Press, 1995. $65.

CLIP (College Library Information Packet) *Notes.* Association of College and Research Libraries/American Library Association, 1980–. Most recent volume is No. 26, 1997. $28.50.

Electronic Services in Academic Libraries. Ed. by Mary Jo Lynch. American Library Association, 1996. Paper $6. A statistical survey.

The Gateway Library: Reinventing Academic Libraries. By Caroline M. Kent and Laura Farwell. American Library Association, 1997. Paper $35.

Measuring Academic Library Performance: A Practical Approach. By Nancy Van House, Beth Weil, and Charles McClure. American Library Association, 1990. Paper $36. Accompanying diskette with data collection and analysis forms. $60.

Preparing for Accreditation: A Handbook for Academic Librarians. By Patricia Ann Sacks and Sara Lou Whildin. American Library Association, 1993. Paper $18.

Restructuring Academic Libraries: Organizational Development in the Wake of Technological Change. Ed. by Charles Schwartz.

Association of College and Research Libraries/American Library Association, 1997. Paper $28.

SPEC Kits. Association of Research Libraries. 1973–. 10/yr. $280.

Tenure and Promotion for Academic Librarians: A Guidebook with Advice and Vignettes. By Carol W. Cubberly. McFarland, 1996. $32.50.

Administration and Personnel

The ABCs of Collaborative Change: The Manager's Guide to Library Renewal. By Kerry David Carson, Paula Phillips Carson and Joyce Schouest Phillips. American Library Association, 1997. Paper $35.

The ALA Library Personnel Companion: New Strategies in Human Resources. Ed. by Jeniece Guy. American Library Association, 1997. Paper $25.

Avoiding Liability Risk: An Attorney's Advice to Library Trustees and Others. By Renee Rubin. American Library Association, 1994. Paper $17.

Budgeting for Information Access: Resource Management for Connected Libraries. By Murray Martin and Milton Wolf. American Library Association, 1997. Paper $35.

Complete Guide to Performance Standards for Library Personnel. By Carole E. Goodson. Neal-Schuman, 1997. Paper $49.95.

Costing and Pricing in the Digital Age: A Practical Guide for Information Services. By Herbert Snyder and Elisabeth Davenport. Neal-Schuman, 1997. Paper $45.

Getting Political: An Action Guide for Librarians and Library Supporters. By Anne M. Turner. Neal-Schuman, 1997. Paper $39.95.

Keeping the Books: Public Library Financial Practices. Ed. by Jane B. Robbins and Douglas L. Zweizig. Highsmith Press, 1992. $39.

Library Personnel Administration. By Lowell Martin. Scarecrow Press, 1995. $29.50.

Library Public Relations, Promotions and Communications: A How-to-Do-It Manual. By Lisa Wolfe. Neal-Schuman, 1997. Paper $39.95.

Library Security and Safety Handbook: Prevention, Policies and Procedures. Bruce A.

Shuman. American Library Association, 1997. Paper $38.

Managing Student Library Employees PLUS: A Workshop for Supervisors. By Michael and Jane Kathman. Library Solutions Press, 1995. Paper $45. An accompanying diskette contains presentation slides.

Multiculturalism in Libraries. By Rosemary Ruhig DuMont, Lois Buttlar, and William Caynon. Greenwood Press, 1994. $55. Discusses the recruitment of a diverse staff and education for multicultural librarianship.

Organizational Structure of Libraries Rev. ed. By Lowell A. Martin. Scarecrow Press, 1996. $39.50.

Practical Help for New Supervisors. 3d ed. Ed. by Joan Giesecke. American Library Association, 1997. Paper $22.

Successful Staff Development: A How-to-Do-It Manual. By Marcia Trotta. Neal-Schuman, 1995. Paper $39.95.

Technology and Management in Library and Information Services. By F. W. Lancaster and Beth Sandore. University of Illinois, Urbana-Champaign, 1997. $39.95.

Total Quality Management in Information Services. By Guy St. Clair. Bowker-Saur, 1996. $45.

Using Consultants in Libraries and Information Centers: A Management Handbook. Ed. by Edward D. Garten. Greenwood, 1992. $55.

Bibliographic Instruction

Evaluating Library Instruction: Sample Questions, Forms, and Strategies for Practical Use. Ed. by Diana Shonrock. American Library Association, 1995. Paper $34.

Information for a New Age: Redefining the Librarian. Libraries Unlimited, 1995. Paper $26.50. Papers from a program in honor of ALA's Library Instruction Round Table.

Teaching Electronic Literacy: A Concepts-based Approach for School Library Media Specialists. By Kathleen Craver. Greenwood, 1997. $39.95.

Teaching Library Skills in Grades K through 6: A How-to-Do-It Manual. By Catharyn Roach and JoAnne Moore. Neal-Schuman, 1993. Paper $35.

Teaching Library Skills in Middle and High School: A How-to-Do-It Manual. By Linda J. Garrett and JoAnne Moore. Neal-Schuman, 1993. Paper $35.

Teaching the New Library: A How-to-Do-It Manual. By Michael Blake and others from the Electronic Teaching Center for the Harvard College Libraries. Neal-Schuman, 1996. Paper $45.

Cataloging and Classification

A Beginner's Guide to Copy Cataloging on OCLC/PRISM. By Lois Massengale Schultz. Libraries Unlimited, 1995. $35.

The Bibliographic Record and Information Technology. 3rd ed. By Ronald Hagler. American Library Association, 1997. Paper $45.

Cataloging and Classification: Trends, Transformations, Teaching and Training. Ed. by James Sheearer and Alan Thomas. Haworth, 1997. Paper $19.95.

Cataloging Correctly for Kids: An Introduction to the Tools. 3rd ed. Ed. by Sharon Zuiderveld. American Library Association, 1997. Paper $20.

Cataloging with AACR2 and MARC. By Debra A. Fritz. American Library Association, 1997. Paper $60.

Immroth's Guide to the Library of Congress Classification. 4th ed. By Lois Mai Chan. Libraries Unlimited, 1990. $42.50.

Introduction to Cataloging and Classification. 8th ed. By Arlene G. Taylor and Bohdan S. Wynar. Libraries Unlimited, 1991. Cloth $47.50; Paper $37.50.

Library of Congress Subject Headings: Principles and Application. 3d ed. By Lois Mai Chan. Libraries Unlimited, 1995. $46.

Standard Cataloging for School and Public Libraries. 2d ed. By Sheila S. Intner and Jean Weihs. Libraries Unlimited, 1996. $32.50.

SUPERLCSS on CD-ROM. Gale, 1998. $3,400. The text of the Library of Congress classification schedules integrated with all changes through June 1998.

CD-ROM

CD-ROM for Library Users: A Guide to Managing and Maintaining User Access. Ed. by Pat Ensor and Paul Nicholls. Information Today, 1995. $37.50.

The CD-ROM Primer: The ABCs of CD-ROM. By Cheryl LaGuardia. Neal-Schuman, 1994. Paper $45.

Networking CD-ROMs: The Decision Maker's Guide to Local Area Network Solutions. By Ahmed M. Elshami. American Library Association, 1996. Paper $50.

Children's and Young Adult Services and Materials

African-American Voices in Young Adult Literature: Tradition, Transition, Transformation. By Karen Patricia Smith. Scarecrow, 1994. $45.

Against Borders: Promoting Books for a Multicultural World. By Hazel Rochman. Booklist/American Library Association, 1993. Paper $25.

Bibliotherapy with Young People: Librarians and Mental Health Professionals Working Together. By Beth and Carol Doll. Libraries Unlimited, 1997. Paper $23.

Building a Special Collection of Children's Literature in Your Library. Ed. by Dolores Blythe Jones. American Library Association, 1997. Paper $40.

The Center for the Study of Books in Spanish for Children and Adolescents at California State University, San Marcos Web site (http://www.csusm.edu/campus_centers/csb). Lists recommended books published worldwide in Spanish for youth.

Connecting Young Adults and Libraries: A How-to-Do-It Manual. 2nd ed. By Patrick Jones. Neal-Schuman, 1997. Paper $45.

Excellence in Library Services to Young Adults: The Nation's Top Programs. 2nd ed. By Mary K. Chelton. American Library Association, 1997. Paper $22.

The Frugal Youth Cybrarian: Bargain Computing for Kids. By Calvin Ross. American Library Association, 1997. Paper $28.

Inviting Children's Authors and Illustrators: A How-to-Do-It Manual for School and Public Librarians. By Kathy East. Neal-Schuman, 1995. Paper $32.50.

Managing Children's Services in the Public Library. 2nd ed. By Adele M. Fasick. Libraries Unlimited, 1998. $34.50.

Output Measures and More: Planning and Evaluating Public Library Services for Young Adults. By Virginia A. Walter. American Library Association, 1995. Paper $25.

Output Measures for Public Library Service to Children: A Manual of Standardized Procedures. By Virginia A. Walter. American Library Association, 1992. Paper $25.

School Library Journal's Best: A Reader for Children's, Young Adult and School Librarians. Ed. by Lillian N. Gerhardt, Marilyn L. Miller, and Thomas W. Downen. Neal-Schuman, 1997. Paper $35.

Collection Development

Collection Development & Finance: A Guide to Strategic Library-Materials Budgeting. By Murray S. Martin. American Library Association, 1995. Paper $30.

Collection Management for the 21st Century: A Handbook for Librarians. Ed. by G. E. Gorman and Ruth H. Miller. Greenwood, 1997. $75.

Cooperative Collection Management: The Conspectus Approach. Ed. by Georgine N. Olson and Barbara Allen. Neal-Schuman, 1994. Paper $29.95.

Guide for Training Collection Development Librarians. Ed. by Susan Fales. American Library Association, 1996. Paper $15.

Guide to Cooperative Collection Development. Ed. by Bart Harloe. American Library Association, 1994. Paper $10.

Guide for Written Collection Policy Statements. 2d ed. Ed. by Joanne S. Anderson. American Library Association, 1996. Paper $15.

Recruiting, Educating, and Training Librarians for Collection Development. Ed. by Peggy Johnson and Sheila S. Intner. Greenwood Press, 1994. $55.

Weeding Library Collections: Library Weeding Methods. 4th ed. By Stanley J. Slote. Libraries Unlimited, 1997. $55.

Copyright

The Copyright Primer for Librarians and Educators. 2d ed. By Janis H. Bruwelheide. American Library Association, 1995. Paper $25.

Does Your Project Have a Copyright Problem? A Decision-Making Guide for Librarians. By Mary Brandt-Jensen. McFarland, 1996. Paper $25.

Libraries and Copyright: A Guide to Copyright Law in the Nineties. By Laura N. Gasaway and Sarah K. Wiant. Special Libraries Association, 1994. Paper $50.

Technology and Copyright Law: A Guidebook for the Library, Research and Teaching Professions. By Arlene Bielefield and Lawrence Cheesemen. Neal-Schuman, 1997. Paper $49.95.

Customer Service

Customer Service: A How-to-Do-It Manual for Librarians. By Suzanne Walters. Neal-Schuman, 1994. Paper $39.95.

Customer Service and Innovation in Libraries. By Glenn Miller. Highsmith Press, 1996. Paper $12.

Customer Service Excellence: A Concise Guide for Librarians. By Darlene E. Weingand. American Library Association, 1997. Paper $27.

Patron Behavior in Libraries: A Handbook of Positive Approaches to Negative Situations. Ed. by Beth McNeil and Denise J. Johnson. American Library Association, 1995. Paper $25.

Serving the Difficult Customer: A How-to-Do-It Manual for Library Staff. By Kitty Smith. Neal-Schuman, 1994. Paper $45.

Education for Librarianship

The Closing of American Library Schools: Problems and Opportunities. By Larry J. Ostler, Therrin C. Dahlin, and J. D. Willardson. Greenwood Press, 1995. $55.

Education for the Library/Information Profession: Strategies for the Mid-1990s. Ed. by Patricia Reeling. McFarland, 1993. Paper $19.95.

The Electronic Library

"Books, Bricks and Bytes." *Daedalus,* vol. 125, no. 4, Fall, 1996. $10.95. Prominent librarians write about the future of the library in this issue of *Daedalus* totally devoted to the topic.

Buildings, Books, and Bytes: Libraries and Communities in the Digital Age. The Benton Foundation, 1996. http://www.benton. org/library/kellogg/buildings.html. Interviews with the public about their views of libraries show that they have trouble figuring out where libraries fit in the new digital world.

Future Libraries: Dreams, Madness, and Reality. By Walt Crawford and Michael Gorman. American Library Association, 1995. Paper $28. Deflates the overblown "virtual" library concept.

A Nation of Opportunity: Realizing the Promise of the Information Superhighway. By the National Information Infrastructure Advisory Council. The Benton Foundation, 1996. http://www.bcnton.org/library/KickStart/nation.home.html.

The National Electronic Library: A Guide to the Future for Library Managers. Ed. by Gary M. Pitkin. Greenwood Press, 1996. $55.

Scholarly Journals at the Crossroads: A Subversive Proposal for Electronic Publishing. Ed. by Ann Okerson and James J. O'Donnell. Association of Research Libraries, 1995. Paper $20.

"State of the State Reports: Statewide Library Automation, Connectivity, and Resource Access Initiatives." *Library Hi-Tech,* vol. 14, numbers 2–3, 1996. $44. Reports from 46 states.

Evaluation of Library Services

Brief Tests of Collection Strength: A Methodology for All Types of Libraries. By Howard D. White. Greenwood Press, 1995. $55.

The TELL IT! Manual: The Complete Program for Evaluating Library Performance. By Douglas Zweizig, Debra Wilcox Johnson, and Jane Robbins. American Library Association, 1996. Paper $30.

Fund-Raising

Becoming a Fundraiser: The Principles and Practice of Library Development. By Victoria Steele and Stephen D. Elder. American Library Association, 1992. Paper $27.

The Big Book of Library Grant Money 1996–1997: Profiles of Private and Corporate Foundations and Direct Corporate Givers Receptive to Library Grant Proposals. By the Taft Group. American Library Association, 1996. Paper $225. Also available on CD-ROM as *The Searchable Big Book of Library Grant Money.* American Library Association, 1997. DOS $450.

Friends of Libraries Sourcebook. 3rd ed. Ed. by Sandy Dolnick. American Library Association, 1996. Paper $32.

Getting Your Grant: A How-to-Do-It Manual for Librarians. By Peggy Barber and Linda Crowe. Neal-Schuman, 1993. Paper $45.

Library Fundraising: Models for Success. Ed. by Dwight Burlingame. American Library Association, 1995. Paper $25.

Organizing Friends Groups: A How-to-Do-It Manual for Librarians. By Mark Y. Herring. Neal-Schuman, 1993. Paper $39.95.

Government Documents

Introduction to United States Government Information Sources. 5th ed. By Joe Morehead. Libraries Unlimited, 1996. Cloth $55; paper $40.

Management of Government Information Resources in Libraries. Ed. by Diane H. Smith. Libraries Unlimited, 1993. $40.

Subject Guide to U.S. Government Reference Sources. 2d ed. By Gayle J. Hardy and Judith Schiek Robinson. Libraries Unlimited, 1996. $45.

Intellectual Freedom

Banned Books Resource Guide. Office for Intellectual Freedom/American Library Association, 1998. Paper $20.

Banned in the U.S.A.: A Reference Guide to Book Censorship in Schools and Public Libraries. By Herbert N. Foerstel. Greenwood Press, 1994. $45.

Hit List: Frequently Challenged Books for Young Adults. By Donna R. Pistolis. American Library Association, 1996. $22.

Hit List: Frequently Challenged Books for Children. By Merri M. Monks and Donna Reidy Pistolis. American Library Association, 1996. $22.

Intellectual Freedom Manual. 5th ed. ALA Office for Intellectual Freedom. American Library Association, 1996. Paper $35.

Protecting the Right to Read: A How-to-Do-It Manual for School and Public Librarians. By Ann K. Symons and Charles Harmon. Neal-Schuman, 1995. Paper $39.95.

Interlibrary Loan, Document Delivery, and Resource Sharing

The Economics of Access versus Ownership. Ed. by Bruce R. Kingma. Haworth Press, 1996. $29.95.

The Future of Resource Sharing. Ed. by Shirley K. Baker and Mary E. Jackson. Haworth Press, 1995. $34.95.

Interlibrary Loan/Document Delivery and Customer Satisfaction. Ed. by Pat Weaver-Meyers, Wilbur Stolt, and Yem Fong. Haworth, 1996. $19.95.

Interlibrary Loan: Theory and Management. By Lois C. Gilmer. Libraries Unlimited, 1994. $37.50.

Interlibrary Loan Policies Directory. 5th ed. Ed. by Leslie R. Morris. Neal-Schuman, 1995. Paper $135.

Interlibrary Loan Practices Handbook. 2d ed. By Virginia Boucher. American Library Association, 1996. Paper $45.

The Internet

All-Out Internet Access: The Cambridge Public Library Model. By Miles R. Fidelman. American Library Association, 1997. Paper $28.

Authoritative Guide to Web Search Engines. By Susan Maze, David Moxley, and Donna J. Smith. Neal-Schuman, 1997. Paper $49.95.

Basic Internet for Busy Librarians: A Quick Course for Catching Up. By Laura K. Murray. American Library Association, 1997. Paper $26.

Building the Service-Based Web Site: A Step-by-Step Guide to Design and Options. By Kristen L. Garlock and Sherry Piontek. American Library Association, 1996. Paper $25.

Coyle's Information Highway Handbook: A Practical File on the New Information Order. By Karen Coyle. American Library Association, 1997. Paper $30.

The Cybrarian's Manual. Ed. by Pat Ensor. American Library Association, 1997. Paper $42. Excerpts from this book are on the Web at http://www.ala.org/editions/cyberlib.net.

Internet Access and Use: Metropolitan Public Libraries, Sample Internet Policies. 2v. Urban Libraries Council, 1997. Paper $50.

Internet Issues and Applications, 1997–98. Ed. by Bert J. Dempsey and Paul Jones. Scarecrow Press, 1998. $22.50

The Internet Resource Directory for K–12 Teachers and Librarians, 96/97 Edition. By Elizabeth B. Miller. Libraries Unlimited, 1996. $25.

More Internet Troubleshooter: New Help for the Logged-On and Lost. By Nancy R. John and Edward J. Valauskas. American Library Association, 1997. Paper $36.

The 1997 National Survey of Public Libraries and the Internet. By John Carlo Bertot, Charles R. McClure, and Patricia Diamond Fletcher. National Commission on Libraries and Information Science/American Library Association, 1997. http://www.ala.org/oitp/research/plcon97sum.

A Practical Guide to Internet Filters. By Karen Schneider. Neal-Schuman, 1997. Paper $49.95.

Using the World Wide Web and Creating Home Pages: A How-to-Do-It Manual for Librarians. By Ray E. Metz and Gail Junion-Metz. Neal-Schuman, 1996. Paper $49.95.

World Wide Web Troubleshooter: Help for the Ensnared and Entangled. By Nancy R. John and Edward J. Valauskas. American Library Association, 1997. Paper $36.

Librarians and Librarianship

The Age Demographics of Academic Libraries: A Profession Apart. By Stanley J. Wilder. Association of Research Libraries, 1995. Paper $30. Shows that 32 percent of librarians in large university libraries will retire by 2005.

The ALA Survey of Librarian Salaries 1997. Ed. by Mary Jo Lynch. American Library Association, 1997. Paper $55.

ARL Annual Salary Survey, 1996–97. Association of Research Libraries, 1996. Paper $65.

Discovering Librarians: Profiles of a Profession. Ed. by Mary Jane Scherdin. Association of College & Research Libraries/American Library Association, 1994. Paper $35.95.

Information Ethics for Librarians. By Mark Alfino and Linda Pierce. McFarland, 1997. $34.50.

The Manley Art of Librarianship. By Will Manley. McFarland, 1993. $23.95. Other humorous books by Manley include *The Truth About Reference Librarians* and *The Truth About Catalogers.*

Our Singular Strengths: Meditations for Librarians. By Michael Gorman. American Library Association, 1997. Paper $20.

What Else You Can Do With a Library Degree: Career Options for the '90s and Beyond. Ed. by Betty-Carol Sellen. Neal-Schuman, 1997. Paper $29.95.

Library Automation

Advances in Library Automation and Networking. Annual. JAI Press. $73.25.

Automating Media Centers and Small Libraries: A Microcomputer-Based Approach. By Dania Meghabghab. Libraries Unlimited, 1997. Paper $30.

Automating Small Libraries. By James Swan. Highsmith Press, 1996. Paper $15.

Automation for School Libraries: How to Do It from Those Who Have Done It. By Teresa Thurman Day, Bruce Flanders, and Gregory Zuck. American Library Association, 1994. Paper $22.

Directory of Library Automation Software, Systems, and Services. Ed. by Pamela Cibbarelli. Information Today, 1998. Paper $89. Published biannually.

Integrated Library Systems for PCs & PC Networks. By Marshall Breeding. Information Today, 1996. $42.50.

Introducing and Managing Library Automation Projects. Ed. by John W. Head and Gerald B. McCabe. Greenwood Press, 1996. $59.95.

Local Area Networking for the Small Library: A How-to-Do-It Manual. 2nd. ed. By Norman Howden. Neal-Schuman, 1997. Paper $35.

Planning for Automation. 2nd. ed. By John Cohn, Ann Kelsey, and Keith Fiels. Neal-Schuman, 1997. Paper $49.95.

Library Buildings and Space Planning

Administrators' Guide to Library Building Maintenance. By Dianne Lueder and Sally Webb. American Library Association, 1992. Paper $45.

Checklist of Building Design Considerations. 3rd ed. By William W. Sannwald. American Library Association, 1996. Paper $30.

Designing and Renovating School Library Media Centers. By Jane P. Klasing. American Library Association, 1991. Paper $25.

Determining Your Public Library's Future Size: A Needs Assessment and Planning Model. By Lee B. Brawner and Donald K. Beck, Jr. American Library Association, 1996. $30.

The Evolution of the American Academic Library Building. By David Kaser. Scarecrow Press, 1996. $36.

Financing Public Library Buildings. By Richard B. Hall. Neal-Schuman, 1994. Paper $55.

Library Building Projects: Tips for Survival. By Susan B. Hagloch. Libraries Unlimited, 1994. $27.50.

Library Buildings, Equipment, and the ADA: Compliance Issues and Solutions. By Susan E. Cirilolo and Robert E. Danford. American Library Association, 1996. Paper $25.

Planning Library Interiors: The Selection of Furnishings for the 21st Century. 2nd. ed.

By Carol Brown. Oryx Press, 1994. Paper $29.95.

Library History

Carnegie Libraries Across America: A Public Legacy. By Theodore Jones. Wiley, 1997. $29.95.

Censorship and the American Library: The American Library Association's Response to Threats to Intellectual Freedom, 1939–1969. By Louise Robbins. Greenwood Press, 1996. $59.95.

Enrichment: A History of the Public Library in the United States in the Twentieth Century. By Lowell A. Martin. Scarecrow Press, 1998. $35.

History of Libraries in the Western World. 4th ed. By Michael H. Harris. Scarecrow Press, 1995. $39.50.

Irrepressible Reformer: A Biography of Melvil Dewey. By Wayne A. Wiegand. American Library Association, 1996. Paper $35.

Libraries and Philanthropy. By Donald G. Davis, Jr. Graduate School of Library and Information Science, University of Texas at Austin, 1996. $25.

Louis Shores: Defining Educational Librarianship. By Lee Shiflett. Scarecrow Press, 1996. $36.

The Nation's Great Library: Herbert Putnam and the Library of Congress, 1899–1939. By Jane A. Rosenberg. University of Illinois Press, 1993. $39.95.

Zoia! Memoirs of Zoia Horn, Battler for the People's Right to Know. By Zoia Horn. McFarland, 1995. $25.

Nonprint Materials

Audio Book Breakthrough: A Guide to Selection and Use in Public Libraries and Education. By Preston Hoffman and Carol H. Osteyee. Greenwood Press, 1993. $39.95.

Developing and Managing Video Collections in Libraries: A How-to-Do-It Manual for Public Libraries. By Sally Mason-Robinson. Neal-Schuman, 1996. Paper $39.95.

A Library Manager's Guide to the Physical Processing of Nonprint Materials. By

Karen C. Driessen and Sheila A. Smyth. Greenwood Press, 1995. $65.

Video Acquisitions and Cataloging: A Handbook. By James C. Scholtz. Greenwood Press, 1995. $55.

Online Searching

Cases in Online Search Strategy. By Bruce A. Shuman. Libraries Unlimited, 1993. Paper $30.

The Online Deskbook: Online Magazine's Essential Desk Reference for Online and Internet Searches. By Mary Ellen Bates. Pemberton Press, 1996. Paper $29.95.

Online Retrieval: A Dialogue of Theory and Practice. By Geraldene Walker and Joseph Janes. Libraries Unlimited, 1993. $35.

Secrets of the Super Net Searchers. By Reva Basch. Pemberton Press, 1996. Paper $29.95.

Preservation

Advances in Preservation and Access. v.2. Ed. by Barbra Buckner Higginbotham. Information Today, 1995. $49.50.

Book Repair: A How-to-Do-It Manual for Librarians. By Kenneth Lavender and Scott Stockton. Neal Schuman, 1992. Paper $39.95.

Digital Imaging Technology for Preservation. Ed. by Nancy E. Elkington. Research Libraries Group, 1995. Paper $20.

Disaster Response and Planning for Libraries. By Miriam B. Kahn. American Library Association, 1997. Paper $38.

Emergency Response and Salvage Wheel. National Task Force on Emergency Response, 1997. $5.95. A two-sided cardboard wheel with tips for quick action in an emergency.

New Tools for Preservation: Assessing Long-Term Environmental Effects on Library and Archives Conditions. By James M. Reilly, Douglas W. Nishimura, and Edward Zinn. Commission on Preservation and Access, 1996. Paper $10.

Preservation Microfilming: A Guide for Librarians and Archivists. 2d ed. By Lisa L. Fox. American Library Association, 1996. $70.

Preserving Digital Information. By Donald Waters and John Garrett. Commission on Preservation and Access. 1996. Paper $15.

Public Libraries

Achieving School Readiness: Public Libraries and National Education Goal 1. Ed. by Barbara Froling Immroth and Viki Ash-Geisler. American Library Association, 1995. $30.

Administration of the Small Public Library. 3d ed. By Darlene E. Weingand. American Library Association, 1992. Paper $30.

Collecting and Using Public Library Statistics. By Mark L. Smith. Neal-Schuman, 1996. Paper $45.

Innovation and the Library: The Adoption of New Ideas in Public Libraries. By Verna L. Pungitore. Greenwood Press, 1995. $52.95.

The Library Trustee: A Practical Guidebook. 5th ed. By Virginia G. Young. American Library Association, 1995. $37.

Long Range Planning: A How-to-Do-It Manual for Public Libraries. By Suzanne W. Bremer. Neal-Schuman, 1994. Paper $39.95.

Managing Today's Public Library: Blueprint for Change. By Darlene E. Weingand. Libraries Unlimited, 1994. $30.

Output Measures for Public Libraries: A Manual of Standardized Procedures. 2d ed. By Nancy A. Van House and others. American Library Association, 1987. Paper $25

Public Library Data Service Statistical Report. Public Library Association/ALA, 1997. Paper $75.

The Public Library Effectiveness Study: The Complete Report. By Nancy A. Van House and Thomas A. Childers. American Library Association, 1993. Paper $25.

Public Library Planning: Case Studies for Management. By Brett Sutton. Greenwood Press, 1995. $69.95.

The Responsive Public Library: How to Develop and Market It. By Sharon L. Baker. Libraries Unlimited, 1993. $45.

Sample Evaluations of Public Library Directors. Ed. by Sharon Saulman. American

Library Trustee Association/American Library Association, 1997. Paper $23.

Strategic Management for Public Libraries: A Handbook. By Robert M. Hayes and Virginia A. Walter. Greenwood Press, 1996. $59.95.

What's Good? Describing Your Public Library's Effectiveness. By Thomas A. Childers and Nancy A. Van House. American Library Association, 1993. Paper $25.

Why Adults Use the Public Library: A Research Perspective. By Maurice P. Marchant. Libraries Unlimited, 1994. Paper $24.

Winning Library Referenda Campaigns: A How-to-Do-It Manual. By Richard B. Hall. Neal-Schuman, 1995. Paper $39.95.

Reference and Readers' Advisory

Developing Readers' Advisory Services: Concepts and Commitments. Ed. by Kathleen de la Peña and others. Neal-Schuman, 1993. Paper $35.

Introduction to Reference Work. 7th ed. 2v. By William A. Katz. McGraw-Hill, 1997. $57.75.

Readers' Advisory Service in the Public Library. 2nd ed. By Joyce G. Saricks and Nancy Brown. American Library Association, 1997. Paper $22.

Reference and Information Services: An Introduction. 2d ed. Ed. by Richard E. Bopp and Linda C. Smith. Libraries Unlimited, 1995. $47.50.

The Reference Assessment Manual. Comp. by the Evaluation of Reference & Adult Services Committee of RASD/ALA. Pierian Press, 1995. Paper $35. A disk with copies of assessment instruments is also available for $15.

Reference and Collection Development on the Internet: A How-to-Do-It Manual. By Elizabeth Thomsen. Neal-Schuman, 1996. Paper $45.

The Reference Interview as a Creative Art. By Elaine and Edward Jennerich. Libraries Unlimited, 1997. $26.50

Reference Services Planning in the 90s. Ed. by Gail Z. Eckwright and Lori M. Keenan. Haworth Press, 1995. $29.95.

Rethinking Reference in Academic Libraries. Ed. by Anne G. Lipow. Library Solutions Press, 1993. Paper $32.

Where to Find What: A Handbook to Reference Service. 4th ed. By James M. Hillard. Scarecrow Press, 1998. $45.

School Libraries/Media Centers

Achieving a Curriculum-Based Library Media Center: The Middle School Model for Change. By Jane Bandy Smith. American Library Association, 1995. Paper $25.

Best Kept Secrets: Ideas for Promoting Your School Library Media Center. Comp. by Ann Wasman. American Library Association, 1996. Looseleaf $30.

The Collection Program in Schools: Concepts, Practices, and Information Sources. 2d ed. By Phyllis J. Van Orden. Libraries Unlimited, 1995. Cloth $42.50; paper $32.50.

Developing a Vision: Strategic Planning and the Library Media Specialist. By John D. Crowley. Greenwood Press, 1994. $35.

Helpful Hints for the School Library: Ideas for Organization, Time Management and Bulletin Boards. By Carol Smallwood. McFarland, 1993. Paper $22.95.

Helping Teachers Teach: A School Library Media Specialist's Role. 2d ed. By Philip M. Turner. Libraries Unlimited, 1993. Paper $26.50.

Information Power: Guidelines for School Library Media Programs. American Library Association, 1988. Paper $20.

The Impact of School Library Media Centers on Academic Achievement. By Keith Lance and others. Hi Willow, 1993. Paper $25.

School Library Media Centers in the 21st Century. By Kathleen W. Craver. Greenwood Press, 1995. $35.

The School Library Media Manager. By Blanche Woolls. Libraries Unlimited, 1994. Cloth $38.50; paper $31.50.

School Library Reference Services in the '90s: Where We Are, Where We're Heading. Ed. by Carol Truett. Haworth, 1994. $49.95.

Serving Linguistically and Culturally Diverse Students: Strategies for the School Library

Media Specialist. By Melvina A. Dame. Neal-Schuman, 1993. Paper $29.95.

Special Events Programs in School Library Media Centers. By Marcia Trotta. Greenwood, 1997. $35.

The Virtual School Library: Gateways to the Information Superhighway. Ed. by Carol Collier Kuhlthau. Libraries Unlimited, 1996. Paper $24.

Serials

Guide to Performance Evaluation of Serials Vendors. Association for Library Collections and Technical Services/American Library Association, 1997. Paper $15.

International Subscription Agents. 6th ed. By Lenore Rae Wilkas. American Library Association, 1993. Paper $35.

Management of Serials in Libraries. By Thomas E. Nisonger. Libraries Unlimited, 1998. $55.

Services for Special Groups

Choosing and Using Books with Adult New Readers. By Marguerite Crowley Weibel. Neal-Schuman, 1996. Paper $39.95.

Disabilities, Children, and Libraries: Mainstreaming Services in Public Libraries and School Library Media Centers. By Linda Lucas Walling and Marilyn H. Karrenbrock. Libraries Unlimited, 1993. $35.

A Guide to Homeschooling for Librarians. By David C. Brostrom. Highsmith Press, 1995. Paper $15.

Information Services for People with Developmental Disabilities: The Library Manager's Handbook. Ed. by Linda Lucas Walling and Marilyn M. Irwin. Greenwood Press, 1995. $69.95.

Libraries Inside: A Practical Guide for Prison Librarians. Ed. by Rhea Joyce Rubin and Daniel Suvak. McFarland, 1995. $41.50.

Preparing Staff to Serve Patrons with Disabilities: A How-to-Do-It Manual for Librarians. By Courtney Deines-Jones and Connie Van Fleet. Neal-Schuman, 1995. Paper $39.95.

Serving Print Disabled Library Patrons: A Textbook. Ed. by Bruce Edward Massis. McFarland, 1996. $42.50.

Special Libraries

The Best of OPL II. Ed. by Andrew Berner and Guy St. Clair. Special Libraries Association, 1996. $36. An anthology of articles published 1989–1994 in *The One-Person Library.*

Internet Tools of the Profession: A Guide for Information Professional. 2nd ed. Ed. by Hope N. Tillman. Special Libraries Association, 1997. Paper $40.

Special Libraries: A Guide for Management. 4th ed. By Cathy Porter, Mary Beall, Janice Chindlund, Rebecca Corliss, Christina Krawczyk, Sara Tompson, and Lorri Zipperer. Special Libraries Association, 1997. Paper $42.

Technical Services

Directory of Library Technical Services Homepages. By Barbara Stewart. Neal-Shuman, 1997. Paper $55.

Guide to Technical Services Resources. Ed. by Peggy Johnson. American Library Association, 1994. $65.

Introduction to Technical Services. 6th ed. By G. Edward Evans and Sandra M. Heft. Libraries Unlimited, 1993. Paper $30.

New Directions in Technical Services: Trends and Sources (1993–1995). Ed. by Peggy Johnson. American Library Association, 1997. Paper $35. Continues "Year's Work in Technical Services" which used to appear in *Library Resources and Technical Services.*

Outsourcing Library Technical Services: A How-to-Do-It Manual for Librarians. By Arnold Hirshon and Barbara Winters. Neal-Schuman, 1996. $49.95. (Sample RFPs are available on diskette for $20 via *Outsourcing Technical Services: Ready-to-Import RFP Specifications Disk.*)

Outsourcing Library Technical Services Operations: Practices in Public, Academic and Special Libraries. Ed. by Karen A.

Wilson and Marylou Colver. American Library Association, 1997. Paper $38.

Planning and Implementing Technical Services Workstations. Ed. by Michael Kaplan. American Library Association, 1996. Paper $30.

Technical Services in the Medium-Sized Library. By Sheila S. Intner and Josephine R. Fang. Shoe String, 1991. $35.

Volunteers

Library Volunteers—Worth the Effort! A Program Manager's Guide. By Sally Gardner Reed. McFarland, 1994. Paper $27.50.

Recruiting and Managing Volunteers in Libraries: A How-to-Do-It Manual for Librarians. By Bonnie F. McCune and Charleszine "Terry" Nelson. Neal-Schuman, 1995. Paper $39.95.

Periodicals and Periodical Indexes

Acquisitions Librarian
Advanced Technology Libraries
Against the Grain
American Libraries
American Society for Information Science Journal
Behavioral and Social Sciences Librarian
Book Links
Book Report: Journal for Junior and Senior High School Librarians
Booklist
The Bottom Line
Cataloging and Classification Quarterly
CHOICE
College and Research Libraries
Collection Management
Community and Junior College Libraries
Computers in Libraries
The Electronic Library
Government Information Quarterly
Internet Reference Services Quarterly
Journal of Academic Librarianship
Journal of Information Ethics
Journal of Interlibrary Loan, Document Delivery and Information Supply
Journal of Library Administration

Journal of Youth Services in Libraries
Knowledge Quest
Law Library Journal
Legal Reference Services Quarterly
Libraries & Culture
Library Administration and Management
Library and Information Science Research (LIBRES)
Library Issues: Briefings for Faculty and Academic Administrators (also on the Web by subscription at http://www.netpubsintl.com/LI.html)
Library Hi-Tech
Library Journal
The Library Quarterly
Library Resources and Technical Services
Library Talk: The Magazine for Elementary School Librarians
Library Trends
MLS: Marketing Library Services
Medical Reference Services Quarterly
MultiCultural Review
MultiMedia Schools
Music Library Association Notes
Music Reference Services Quarterly
The One-Person Library
Online & CD-ROM Review
Online–Offline: Themes and Resources
Public and Access Services Quarterly
Public Libraries
Public Library Quarterly
Rare Books and Manuscripts Librarianship
Reference and User Services Quarterly (formerly *RQ*)
Reference Librarian
Reference Services Review
Resource Sharing & Information Networks
Rural Libraries
School Library Journal
Science & Technology Libraries
Serials Librarian
Serials Review
Searcher: The Magazine for Database Professionals
Special Libraries
Technical Services Quarterly
Technicalities
Video Librarian
Voice of Youth Advocates (VOYA)

Ready Reference

Publishers' Toll-Free Telephone Numbers

Publishers' toll-free numbers continue to play an important role in ordering, verification, and customer service. This year's list comes from *Literary Market Place* (R. R. Bowker) and includes distributors and regional toll-free numbers, where applicable. The list is not comprehensive, and toll-free numbers are subject to change. Readers may want to call for toll-free directory assistance (800-555-1212).

Publisher/Distributor	Toll-Free No.
A D D Warehouse, Plantation, FL	800-233-9273
A-R Editions Inc., Madison, WI	800-736-0070
Abacus, Grand Rapids, MI	800-451-4319
Abbeville Publishing Group, New York, NY	800-ART-BOOK
ABC-CLIO, Santa Barbara, CA	800-368-6868
	800-422-2546
Abdo & Daughters Publishing, Minneapolis, MN	800-458-8399
ABELexpress, Carnegie, PA	800-542-9001
Aberdeen Group, Addison, IL	800-837-0870
ABI Professional Publications, Arlington, VA	800-551-7776
Abingdon Press, Nashville, TN	800-251-3320
Harry N Abrams Inc., New York, NY	800-345-1359
Academic Press, San Diego, CA	(cust serv) 800-321-5068
Academic Therapy Publications, Novato, CA	800-422-7249
Academy Chicago Publishers, Chicago, IL	800-248-READ
ACCESS Publishers Network, Grawn, MI	800-345-0096
ACS Publications, San Diego, CA	(orders only) 800-888-9983
ACTA Publications, Chicago, IL	800-397-2282
Action Direct, Miami, FL	800-472-2388
ACU Press, Abilene, TX	800-444-4228
Adams-Blake Publishing, Fair Oaks, CA	800-368-ADAM
Adams Media Corp., Holbrook, MA	800-872-5627
ADAPT Publishing Co. .Inc., Austin, TX	800-333-8429
Addison Wesley Longman Publishing Co., Reading, MA (orders only)	
	(school serv team) 800-552-2259
	(college serv team) 800-322-1377
	(college sales) 800-552-2499
	(trade & agency) 800-358-4566

Publisher/Distributor	Toll-Free No.
(corporate & professional)	800-822-6339
Addison Wesley Longman, San Francisco, CA	800-387-8028
Adi, Gaia, Esalen Publications Inc., Los Angeles, CA	800-652-8574
(order fulfillment)	800-263-1991
(fax order fulfillment)	800-458-0025
(fax)	800-931-1778
Aegean Park Press, Laguna Hills, CA	800-736-3587
Aegis Publishing Group Ltd., Newport, RI	800-828-6961
The AEI Press, Washington, DC	800-223-2336
African American Images, Chicago, IL	800-552-1991
Afton Publishing, Andover, NJ	888-238-6665
Agora Inc., Baltimore, MD	800-433-1528
Ahsahta Press, Boise, ID	800-992-TEXT
AIHA Publications of America (ALPHA Publications of America Inc.), Tucson, AZ	800-528-3494
AIMS Education Foundation, Fresno, CA	888-733-2467
Alba House, Staten Island, NY	800-343-ALBA
The Alban Institute Inc., Bethesda, MD	800-486-1318
Alexander Books, Alexander, NC	800-472-0438
Alfred Publishing Co. Inc., Van Nuys, CA	800-292-6122
ALI-ABA Committee on Continuing Professional Education, Philadelphia, PA	800-CLE-NEWS
Allied Health Publications, National City, CA	800-221-7374
Allworth Press, New York, NY	800-491-2808
Allyn & Bacon, Needham Heights, MA	800-223-1360
AlphaBooks Inc., Topanga, CA	800-957-3529
Alpine Publications Inc., Loveland, CO (orders only)	800-777-7257
Alyson Publications Inc., Los Angeles, CA	800-525-9766
AMACOM Books, New York, NY (orders)	800-538-4761
Frank Amato Publications Inc., Portland, OR	800-541-9498
Amboy Associates, San Diego, CA	800-448-4023
America West Pubs, Carson City, NV	800-729-4130
American Academy of Orthopaedic Surgeons, Rosemont, IL	800-626-6726
American Academy of Pediatrics, Elk Grove Village, IL	800-433-9016
American Alliance for Health, Physical Education, Recreation & Dance, Reston, VA	800-213-7193
American Association for Vocational Instructional Materials (AAVIM), Winterville, GA	800-228-4689
American Association of Cereal Chemists, St. Paul, MN	800-328-7560
American Association of Community Colleges (AACC), Washington, DC	800-250-6557
American Association of Engineering Societies, Washington, DC	888-400-2237
American Bible Society, New York, NY (orders only)	800-322-4253
American Business Directories, Omaha, NE	800-555-6124
American Chemical Society, Washington, DC	800-227-9919
American College of Physician Executives, Tampa, FL	800-562-8088

Publisher/Distributor	Toll-Free No.
American Correctional Association, Lanham, MD	800-222-5646
American Council on Education, Washington, DC	800-279-6799, ext 642
American Counseling Association, Alexandria, VA	800-422-2648
American Diabetes Association, Alexandria, VA	800-232-6733
American Eagle Publications Inc., Show Low, AZ	800-719-4957
The American Federation of Arts, New York, NY	800-AFA-0270
American Foundation for the Blind (AFB Press), New York, NY	800-232-3044
American Geophysical Union, Washington, DC	800-966-2481
American Guidance Service Inc., Circle Pines, MN	800-328-2560
American Health Publishing Co., Dallas, TX	800-736-7323
American Institute of Aeronautics & Astronautics, Reston, VA	800-639-2422
The American Institute of Architects Press, Washington, DC (orders)	800-365-ARCH
American Institute of Certified Public Accountants, Jersey City, NJ	800-862-4272
American Institute of Chemical Engineers (AIChE), New York, NY	800-242-4363
American Law Institute, Philadelphia, PA	800-CLE-NEWS
American Library Association (ALA), Chicago, IL	800-545-2433
American Map Corp., Maspeth, NY	800-432-MAPS
American Marketing Association, Chicago, IL	800-262-1150
American Mathematical Society, Providence, RI	800-321-4267
American Nurses Publishing, Washington, DC	800-637-0323
American Occupational Therapy Association Inc., Bethesda, MD	800-877-1383
American Phytopathological Society, St. Paul, MN	800-328-7560
American Printing House for the Blind Inc., Louisville, KY (cust serv)	800-223-1839
(sales & marketing)	800-572-0844
American Psychiatric Press Inc., Washington, DC	800-368-5777
American Showcase Inc., New York, NY	800-894-7469
American Society for Nondestructive Testing, Columbus, OH	800-222-2768
American Society of Civil Engineers, New York, NY	800-548-2723
American Society of Mechanical Engineers (ASME), New York, NY (cust serv)	800-843-2763
American & World Geographic Publishing, Helena, MT	800-654-1105
Amsco School Publications Inc., New York, NY	800-969-8398
The Analytic Press, Hillsdale, NJ (orders only)	800-926-6579
Ancestry Inc., Salt Lake City, UT	800-531-1790
Anderson Publishing Co., Cincinnati, OH	800-582-7295
Andrews McMeel Publishing, Kansas City, MO	800-826-4216
Andrews University Press, Berrien Springs, MI (Visa & Mastercard)	800-467-6369
Angelus Press, Kansas City, MO	800-966-7337
Ann Arbor Press Inc., Chelsea, MI	800-858-5299
Annabooks, San Diego, CA	800-462-1042
Annual Reviews Inc., Palo Alto, CA	800-523-8635
ANR Publications University of California, Oakland, CA	800-994-8849
Antique Collectors Club Ltd., Wappingers Falls, NY	800-252-5231
Antique Publications, Marietta, OH	800-533-3433
Antique Trader Books, Dubuque, IA	800-480-5168
AOCS Press, Champaign, IL	800-336-AOCS

Publisher/Distributor	Toll-Free No.
Aperture, New York, NY	800-929-2323
The Apex Press, New York, NY	800-316-2739
Applause Theatre Book Publishers, New York, NY	800-798-7787
Aqua Quest Publications Inc., Locust Valley, NY	800-933-8989
Archival Services Inc., Shreveport, LA	800-484-8274, ext 8900
Ardis Publishers, Dana Point, CA	(orders) 800-877-7133
ARE Press, Virginia Beach, VA	800-723-1112
Ariel Press, Alpharetta, GA	800-336-7769
The Arion Press, San Francisco, CA	800-550-7737
Jason Aronson Inc., Northvale, NJ	(orders) 800-782-0015
Arrow Map Inc., Bridgewater, MA	800-343-7500
Artabras Inc., New York, NY	800-ART-BOOK
Arte Publico Press, Houston, TX	800-633-ARTE
Artech House Inc., Norwood, MA	800-225-9977
ASCP Press, Chicago, IL	800-621-4142
Ashgate Publishing Co., Brookfield, VT	800-535-9544
ASM International, Materials Park, OH	800-336-5152
Aspen Publishers Inc., Gaithersburg, MD	(orders) 800-638-8437
Association for Supervision & Curriculum Development, Alexandria, VA	800-933-2723
Association for the Advancement of Medical Instrumentation, Arlington, VA	800-332-2264
Association of College & Research Libraries, Chicago, IL	800-545-2433
Astronomical Society of the Pacific, San Francisco, CA	(orders only) 800-335-2624
ATL Press, Shrewsbury, MA	800-835-7543
Augsburg Fortress Publishers, Publishing House of the Evangelical Lutheran Church in America, Minneapolis, MN	800-328-4648
	(orders) 800-426-0115
August House Publishers Inc., Little Rock, AR	800-284-8784
Augustinian Press, Villanova, PA	800-871-9404
Austin & Winfield Publishers Inc., Bethesda, MD	800-99-AUSTIN
Ave Maria Press, Notre Dame, IN	800-282-1865
Avery Publishing Group Inc., Wayne, NJ	800-548-5757
Avon Books, New York, NY	800-238-0658
Back to the Bible, Lincoln, NE	800-759-2425
Baha'i Publishing Trust, Wilmette, IL	800-999-9019
Baker Books, Grand Rapids, MI	800-877-2665
The Ballantine Publishing Group Ballantine/Del Rey/Fawcett/House of Collectibles/Ivy/One World, New York, NY	800-638-6460
The Banner of Truth, Carlisle, PA	800-263-8085
Bantam Books, New York, NY	800-223-6834
Bantam Doubleday Dell Books for Young Readers, New York, NY	800-223-6834
Bantam Doubleday Dell Publishing Group Inc., New York, NY	800-223-6834
Baptist Spanish Publishing House, El Paso, TX	(cust serv & orders) 800-755-5958
Barcelona Publishers/Pathway Book Service, Gilsum, NH	800-345-6665

Publisher/Distributor	Toll-Free No.
Barnes & Noble Books (Imports & Reprints), Lanham, MD	800-462-6420
Barron's Educational Series Inc., Hauppauge, NY	800-645-3476
Battelle Press, Columbus, OH	800-451-3543
Baywood Publishing Co. Inc., Amityville, NY	800-638-7819
Beacham Publishing Corp., Osprey, FL	800-466-9644
Beacon Hill Press of Kansas City, Kansas City, MO	800-877-0700
Bear & Co. Inc., Santa Fe, NM	800-932-3277
Peter Bedrick Books Inc., New York, NY	800-788-3123
Thomas T Beeler Publisher, Hampton Falls, NH	800-251-8726
Beginning Press, Seattle, WA	800-831-4088
Frederic C Beil Publisher Inc., Savannah, GA	800-829-8406
Bell Springs Publishing, Willits, CA	800-515-8050
Bellerophon Books, Santa Barbara, CA	800-253-9943
R Bemis Publishing Ltd., Marietta, GA	800-497-6663
Matthew Bender & Co. Inc., New York, NY	(outside NY) 800-227-5158
	800-722-3288
The Benefactory, Fairfield, CT	800-729-7251
John Benjamins Publishing Co., Erdenheim, PA	800-562-5666
Robert Bentley Publishers, Cambridge, MA	800-423-4595
R J Berg & Co., Publishers, Indianapolis, IN	800-638-3909
Berkeley Hills Books, Berkeley, CA	888-848-7303
Berkley Publishing Group, New York, NY	800-223-0510
Berkshire House Publishers, Lee, MA	800-321-8526
Berlitz Publishing Co. Inc., Princeton, NJ	800-923-7548
Bernan Associates, Lanham, MD	800-274-4888
Bess Press, Honolulu, HI	800-910-2377
Bethany House Publishers, Minneapolis, MN	800-328-6109
Bethlehem Books, Minto, ND	800-757-6831
Betterway Books	800-289-0963
Beverage Marketing Corp., Mingo Junction, OH	800-332-6222
Beyond Words Publishing Inc., Hillsboro, OR	800-284-9673
Bhaktivedanta Book Publishing Inc., Los Angeles, CA	800-927-4152
Biblical Archaeology Society, Washington, DC	800-221-4644
Biblo & Tannen Booksellers & Publishers Inc., Cheshire, CT	
	(voice & fax) 800-272-8778
Bicycle Books Inc., San Francisco, CA	800-468-8233
Binford & Mort, Portland, OR	888-221-4514
Birkhauser Boston, Cambridge, MA	800-777-4643
George T Bisel Co., Philadelphia, PA	800-247-3526
Bisk Publishing Co., Tampa, FL	800-874-7877
Black Belt Press, Montgomery, AL	800-959-3245
Black Diamond Book Publishing, Los Angeles, CA	800-444-2524
Blackbirch Press Inc., Woodbridge, CT	800-831-9183
John F Blair, Publisher, Winston-Salem, NC	800-222-9796
Bloomberg Press, Princeton, NJ	800-388-2749
Blue Dolphin Publishing Inc., Nevada City, CA	800-643-0765

Publisher/Distributor	Toll-Free No.
Blue Dove Press, San Diego, CA	800-691-1008
Blue Moon Books Inc., New York, NY	800-535-0007
Blue Mountain Press Inc., Boulder, CO	800-525-0642
Blue Note Publications, Cape Canaveral, FL	800-624-0401
Blue Poppy Press Inc., Boulder, CO	800-487-9296
Bluestar Communication Corp., Woodside, CA	800-625-8378
Bluestocking Press, Placerville, CA	800-959-8586
Blushing Rose Publishing, San Anselmo, CA	800-898-2263
BNA Books, Washington, DC	800-960-1220
Bob Jones University Press, Greenville, SC	800-845-5731
Bold Strummer Ltd., Westport, CT	800-375-3786
Bonus Books Inc., Chicago, IL	800-225-3775
Book Peddlers, Minnetonka, MN	800-255-3379
Book Publishing Co., Summertown, TN	800-695-2241
Book Sales Inc., Edison, NJ	800-526-7257
Book World Inc./Blue Star Productions, Sun Lakes, AZ	888-472-2665
BookPartners Inc., Wilsonville, OR	800-895-7323
BookWorld Press Inc., Sarasota, FL	800-444-2524
Thomas Bouregy & Co. Inc., New York, NY	800-223-5251
R R Bowker, New Providence, NJ	800-521-8110
	(sales) 888-269-5372
Boyds Mills Press, Honesdale, PA	800-949-7777
Boynton/Cook Publishers Inc., Portsmouth, NH	(orders) 800-793-2154
Boys Town Press, Boys Town, NE	800-282-6657
Brain Sync, Santa Fe, NM	800-984-7962
Branden Publishing Co. Inc., Brookline Village, MA	
	(Mastercard & Visa only) 800-537-7335
Brassey's Inc., Dulles, VA	800-775-2518
Breakthrough Publications, Ossining, NY	800-824-5000
Brethren Press, Elgin, IL	800-323-8039
Brick House Publishing Co., Amherst, NH	(orders only) 800-446-8642
Bridge Learning Systems Inc., American Canyon, CA	800-487-9868
Bridge Publications Inc., Los Angeles, CA	800-722-1733
	(CA) 800-843-7389
Bridge-Logos Publishers, North Brunswick, NJ	800-631-5802
Brill Academic Publishers Inc., Kinderhook, NY	800-962-4406
Bristol Publishing Enterprises Inc., San Leandro, CA	800-346-4889
Broadman & Holman Publishers, Nashville, TN	800-251-3225
Broadway Books, New York, NY	800-290-2929
Paul H Brookes Publishing Co., Baltimore, MD	800-638-3775
The Brookings Institution, Washington, DC	800-275-1447
Brookline Books Inc., Cambridge, MA	800-666-2665
Brooks/Cole Publishing Co., Pacific Grove, CA	800-354-9706
Brunner/Mazel Publishing, Bristol, PA	800-821-8312
Building News, Needham, MA	800-873-6397
Bull Publishing Co., Palo Alto, CA	800-676-2855

Publisher/Distributor	Toll-Free No.
Burrelle's Information Services, Livingston, NJ	800-876-3342
Business & Legal Reports Inc., Madison, CT	800-727-5257
Business & Professional: Appleton & Lange, Stamford, CT	800-423-1359
Business Research Services Inc., Washington, DC	800-845-8420
Butte Publications Inc., Hillsboro, OR	800-330-9791
Butterworth-Heinemann, Newton, MA	(orders & cust serv) 800-366-2665
C & T Publishing, Lafayette, CA	800-284-1114
Cambridge Educational, Charleston, WV	800-468-4227
Cambridge University Press, New York, NY	800-221-4512
Camden House Inc., Columbia, SC	(orders only) 800-723-9455
Cameron & Co., San Francisco, CA	800-779-5582
Cardoza Publishing, Brooklyn, NY	800-777-WING
The Career Press Inc., Franklin Lakes, NJ	800-CAREER-1
Career Publishing Inc., Orange, CA	800-854-4014
William Carey Library, Pasadena, CA	800-647-7466; 777-6371
Editorial Caribe, Nashville, TN	800-322-7423
Carolina Biological Supply Co., Scientific Publications Dept., Burlington, NC	800-334-5551
Carolrhoda Books Inc.	800-328-4929
The Carroll Press, New York, NY	800-366-7086
CarTech Inc., North Branch, MN	800-551-4754
CAS, Columbus, OH	800-848-6538
Castle Books Inc., Edison, NJ	(orders) 800-526-7257
Catbird Press, North Haven, CT	800-360-2391
Catholic News PublishingCo. Inc., New Rochelle, NY	800-433-7771
The Caxton Printers Ltd., Caldwell, ID	800-657-6465
Cedar Fort Inc./C F I Distribution, Springville, UT	800-759-2665
Cedco Publishing Co., San Rafael, CA	800-227-6162
CEF Press, Warrenton, MO	800-748-7710
Celestial Arts, Berkeley, CA	800-841-BOOK
Center for Futures Education Inc., Grove City, PA	800-966-2554
Center for International Training & Education (CITE), New York, NY	800-316-2739
Central Conference of American Rabbis/CCAR Press, New York, NY	800-935-CCAR
Chalice Press, St. Louis, MO	800-366-3383
Richard Chang Associates Inc., Irvine, CA	800-756-8096
Chapman & Hall Inc., New York, NY	(cust serv) 800-842-3636
Chariot Victor Publishing, Colorado Springs, CO	800-437-4337
CharismaLife Publishers, Lake Mary, FL	800-451-4598
Chartwell Books Inc., Edison, NJ	(orders) 800-526-7257
Chatelaine Press, Burke, VA	800-249-9527
Chelsea Green Publishing Co., White River Junction, VT	800-639-4099
Chelsea House Publishers, Broomall, PA	800-848-BOOK
Chemical Publishing Co. Inc., New York, NY	800-786-3659
Cherokee Publishing Co., Marietta, GA	800-653-3952
Chess Combination Inc., Bridgeport, CT	800-354-4083
Chicago Spectrum Press, Evanston, IL	800-594-5190

Publisher/Distributor	Toll-Free No.
Chitra Publications, Montrose, PA	800-628-8244
Chivers North America Inc., Hampton, NH	800-621-0182
Chockstone Press Inc., Evergreen, CO	800-337-5012
Chosen Books, Grand Rapids, MI	800-877-2665
Christendom Press, Front Royal, VA	800-877-5456
Christian Literature Crusade Inc., Fort Washington, PA	(orders) 800-659-1240
Christian Publications Inc., Camp Hill, PA	800-233-4443
Christian Schools International, Grand Rapids, MI	800-635-8288
The Christian Science Publishing Society, Boston, MA	800-288-7090
Christopher Gordon Publishers Inc., Norwood, MA	800-934-8322
Chronicle Books, San Francisco, CA	(orders) 800-722-6657
Chronicle Guidance Publications Inc., Moravia, NY	800-622-7284
Chronimed Publishing, Minnetonka, MN	800-444-5951
Churchill Livingstone, New York, NY	800-553-5426
Cinco Puntos Press, El Paso, TX	800-566-9072
Citadel Press, Secaucus, NJ	(cust serv) 800-866-1966
Clarity Press Inc., Atlanta, GA (COD or credit card orders only)	800-533-0301
Classics International Entertainment Inc., Chicago, IL	800-569-2434
Clear Light Publishers, Santa Fe, NM	800-253-2747
Cleis Press, San Francisco, CA	800-780-2279
Cliffs Notes Inc., Lincoln, NE	800-228-4078
Close Up Publishing, Alexandria, VA	800-765-3131
Clymer Publications, Overland Park, KS	800-262-1954
The Cobb Group Inc., Louisville, KY	800-223-8720
Cold Spring Harbor Laboratory Press, Cold Spring Harbor, NY	800-843-4388
Cole Group Inc., Santa Rosa, CA	800-959-2717
Collector Books, Paducah, KY	800-626-5420
Collectors Press Inc., Portland, OR	800-423-1848
College Press Publishing Co., Joplin, MO	800-289-3300
Colorado Railroad Museum, Golden, CO	800-365-6263
Columbia Books Inc., Washington, DC	888-265-0600
Columbia University Press, New York, NY	800-944-8648
Comex Systems Inc., Mendham, NJ	800-543-6959
Communication Publications & Resources, Alexandria, VA	800-888-4402
Communication Skill Builders, San Antonio, TX	800-211-8378
	800-228-0752
Commuters Library, Falls Church, VA	800-643-0295
Compact Books, Hollywood, FL	800-771-3355
Compact Clinicals, Kansas City, MO	800-408-8830
Comprehensive Health Education Foundation (CHEF), Seattle, WA	800-323-2433
Conari Press, Berkeley, CA	800-685-9595
Conciliar Press, Ben Lomond, CA	800-967-7377
Concordia Publishing House, St. Louis, MO	800-325-3040
Congressional Information Service Inc., Bethesda, MD	800-638-8380
Congressional Quarterly Books, Washington, DC	800-638-1710
The Continuum Publishing Group, New York, NY	800-937-5557

Publisher/Distributor	Toll-Free No.
Conway Greene Publishing Co., South Euclid, OH	800-977-2665
Copley Publishing Group, Acton, MA	800-562-2147
Cornell Maritime Press Inc., Centreville, MD	800-638-7641
CorpTech (Corporate Technology Information Services Inc.), Woburn, MA	800-333-8036
Cortina Learning International Inc., Wilton, CT	800-245-2145
Cottonwood Press Inc., Fort Collins, CO	800-864-4297
Council for Exceptional Children, Reston, VA	800-232-7323
Council Oak Books LLC, Tulsa, OK	800-247-8850
Council of State Governments, Lexington, KY	800-800-1910
Country Roads Press Inc., Oaks, PA	800-462-6420
The Countryman Press, Woodstock, VT	800-245-4151
Countrysport Press, Traverse City, MI	800-367-4114
Course Technology Inc., Cambridge, MA	800-648-7450
Covered Bridge Press, North Attleboro, MA (New England only)	800-752-3769
Cowles Creative Publishing Inc., Minnetonka, MN	800-328-0590
Cowley Publications, Boston, MA	800-225-1534
CQ Staff Directories Ltd., Alexandria, VA	800-252-1722
Crabtree Publishing Co., New York, NY	800-387-7650
Craftsman Book Co., Carlsbad, CA	800-829-8123
Crane Hill Publishers, Birmingham, AL	800-841-2682
CRC Publications, Grand Rapids, MI	800-333-8300
Creative Arts Book Co., Berkeley, CA	800-848-7789
The Creative Co., Mankato, MN	800-445-6209
Creative Homeowner Press, Upper Saddle River, NJ	800-631-7795
Creative Teaching Press/Youngheart Music, Cypress, CA	800-444-4287
CRICKET: The Magazine For Children (orders)	800-BUG PALS
Crisp Publications Inc., Menlo Park, CA	800-442-7477
Cross Cultural Publications Inc., South Bend, IN	800-273-6526
The Crossing Press, Freedom, CA	800-777-1048
The Crossroad Publishing Co. Inc., New York, NY	800-395-0690
Crossway Books, Wheaton, IL	800-323-3890
Crystal Clarity Publishers, Nevada City, CA	800-424-1055
Crystal Productions, Glenview, IL	800-255-8629
CT Publishing, LLC, Redding, CA	800-767-0511
Cumberland House Publishing Inc., Nashville, TN	800-439-2665
Current Clinical Strategies Publishing, Laguna Hills, CA	800-331-8227
Current Medicine, Philadelphia, PA	800-427-1796
Da Capo Press Inc., New York, NY	800-221-9369
Dandy Lion Publications, San Luis Obispo, CA	800-776-8032
John Daniel & Co., Publishers, Santa Barbara, CA	800-662-8351
Dark Horse Comics, Milwaukie, OR	800-862-0052
Dartnell Books, Chicago, IL	800-621-5463
DATA Business Publishing, Englewood, CO	800-447-4666
Data Research Inc., Eagan, MN	800-365-4900
Data Trace Publishing Co., Towson, MD (orders only)	800-342-0454

Publisher/Distributor	Toll-Free No.
Databooks, Worcester, MA	800-642-6657
Davies-Black Publishing, Palo Alto, CA	800-624-1765
F A Davis Co., Philadelphia, PA	800-523-4049
Davis Publications Inc. (MA), Worcester, MA	800-533-2847
Dawbert Press, Duxbury, MA	800-93-DAWBERT
The Dawn Horse Press, Middletown, CA	800-524-4941
Dawn Publications, Nevada City, CA	800-545-7475
Dawn Sign Press, San Diego, CA	800-549-5350
DBI Books, Vernon Hills, IL	800-767-6310
DDC Publishing, New York, NY	800-528-3897
De Vorss & Co. Inc., Marina del Rey, CA	(CA) 800-331-4719
	(outside CA) 800-843-5743
Ivan R Dee Inc., Chicago, IL	(orders) 800-634-0226
Marcel Dekker Inc., New York, NY	(outside NY) 800-228-1160
Dell Publishing, New York, NY	800-223-6834
Delmar Publishers, Albany, NY	(NY) 800-347-7707
Delta Books	(outside NY state only) 800-223-6834
Delta Systems Co. Inc., McHenry, IL	800-323-8270
Demibach Editions, Stockton, CA	800-366-8577
Demos Vermande, New York, NY	800-532-8663
T S Denison & Co. Inc., Minneapolis, MN	800-328-3831
Derrydale Press Inc., Lyon, MS	800-443-6753
Deseret Book Co., Salt Lake City, UT	800-453-3876
Destiny Image, Shippensburg, PA	(orders only) 800-722-6774
Developmental Studies Center, Oakland, CA	800-666-7270
Dharma Publishing, Berkeley, CA	800-873-4276
Diablo Press Inc., Emeryville, CA	800-488-2665
Diamond Communications Inc., South Bend, IN	800-480-3717
Diamond Farm Book Publishers, Alexandria Bay, NY	800-481-1353
Dimensions for Living, Nashville, TN	800-281-3320
Discipleship Publications International (DPI), Woburn, MA	888-DPI-Book
Discipleship Resources, Nashville, TN	800-814-7833
	(orders) 800-685-4370
Discovery Enterprises Ltd., Carlisle, MA	800-729-1720
Discovery House Publishers, Grand Rapids, MI	800-653-8333
Distributed Art Publishers (DAP), New York, NY	800-338-2665
Diversity Press, Idabel, OK	800-642-0779
F W Dodge Analyses & Forecasts, Lexington, MA	800-591-4462
Dog-Eared Publications, Middleton, WI	888-364-3277
Doheny Publications Inc., Edmonds, WA	888-436-4369
Dominie Press Inc., Carlsbad, CA	800-232-4570
The Donning Co./Publishers, Virginia Beach, VA	800-296-8572
Doral Publishing, Wilsonville, OR	(orders) 800-633-5385
Dorset House Publishing Co. Inc., New York, NY	800-DHBOOKS
Doubleday, New York, NY	800-223-6834
Dover Publications Inc., Mineola, NY	(orders) 800-223-3130

Publisher/Distributor	Toll-Free No.
Down East Books, Camden, ME	800-766-1670
The Dramatic Publishing Co., Woodstock, IL	800-448-7469
The Dryden Press, Fort Worth, TX	800-447-9479
Dual Dolphin Publishing Inc., Winter Springs, FL	800-336-5746
Dufour Editions, Chester Springs, PA	800-869-5677
Duke Communications International, Loveland, CO	800-621-1544
Dun & Bradstreet, Murray Hill, NJ	800-526-0651
Duquesne University Press, Pittsburgh, PA	800-666-2211
Dushkin/McGraw-Hill, Guilford, CT	(cust serv) 800-338-3987
Dustbooks, Paradise, CA	800-477-6110
E M C Corp., St. Paul, MN	800-328-1452
E M Press Inc., Manassas, VA	800-727-4630
Eagle's View Publishing, Liberty, UT	(orders over $100) 800-547-3364
Eakin Press, Austin, TX	800-880-8642
East View Publications, Minneapolis, MN	800-477-1005
Eastland Press, Vista, CA	(fax) 800-453-3278
	(US & Canada only) 800-241-3329
Eckankar Inc., Minneapolis, MN	800-509-5556
EDC Publishing, Tulsa, OK	800-475-4522
Nellie Edge Resources Inc., Salem, OR	800-523-4594
Editorial Bautista Independiente, Sebring, FL	800-398-7187
Editorial Unilit, Miami, FL	800-767-7726
Educational Impressions Inc., Hawthorne, NJ	800-451-7450
Educational Insights Inc., Carson, CA	800-933-3277
Educational Ministries Inc., Prescott, AZ	800-221-0910
Educational Press, Baltimore, MD	800-645-6564
Educational Technology Publications, Englewood Cliffs, NJ	
	(US & Canada, orders only) 800-952-BOOK
Educators Publishing Service Inc., Cambridge, MA	800-225-5750
Edupress, San Juan Capistrano, CA	800-835-7978
Wm B Eerdmans Publishing Co., Grand Rapids, MI	800-253-7521
Edward Elgar Publishing Inc., Lyme, NH	(orders) 800-390-3149
Elysium Growth Press, Los Angeles, CA	800-350-2020
Emanuel Publishing Corp., Larchmont, NY	800-362-6835
Emerald Books, Lynnwood, WA	800-922-2143
Emerald City Publications, Granger, IN	888-778-7226
EMIS Inc., Durant, OK	800-225-0694
Encore Performance Publishing, Orem, UT	800-927-1605
Encyclopaedia Britannica Educational Corp	800-554-9862
Encyclopaedia Britannica Inc., Chicago, IL	800-323-1229
Energeia Publishing Inc., Salem, OR	800-639-6048
Engineering Information Inc. (Ei), Hoboken, NJ	800-221-1044
Engineering & Management Press, Norcross, GA	800-494-0460
Engineering Press, Austin, TX	800-800-1651
EPM Publications Inc., McLean, VA	800-289-2339
Eric Clearinghouse on Higher Education, Washington, DC	800-773-ERIC

Publisher/Distributor	Toll-Free No.
ERIC Clearinghouse on Reading, English & Communication, Bloomington, IN	800-759-4723
Lawrence Erlbaum Associates Inc., Mahwah, NJ	(orders only) 800-9-BOOKS-9
ETC Publications, Palm Springs, CA	800-382-7869
ETR Associates, Santa Cruz, CA	800-321-4407
Eurotique Press Inc., West Palm Beach, FL	800-547-4326
Evan-Moor Educational Publishers, Monterey, CA	800-777-4362
Evangel Publishing House, Nappanee, IN	800-253-9315
Evanston Publishing Inc., Evanston, IL	800-594-5190
Everyday Learning Corp., Chicago, IL	800-382-7670
Exley Giftbooks, New York, NY	800-423-9539
Explorers Guide Publishing, Rhinelander, WI	800-497-6029
F C & A Publishing, Peachtree City, GA	800-226-8024
Faber & Faber Inc., Winchester, MA	(outside NY) 800-666-2211
	(NY, CUP services orders) 607-666-2211
Factor Press, Mobile, AL	(orders only) 800-304-0077
Facts & Comparisons, St. Louis, MO	800-223-0554
Facts On File Inc., New York, NY	800-322-8755
Fairchild Books & Visuals, New York, NY	800-247-6622
Fairview Press, Minneapolis, MN	800-544-8207
Faith & Life Press, Newton, KS	800-743-2484
Faith Publishing Co., Milford, OH	800-576-6477
Falcon Press Publishing Co. Inc., Helena, MT	800-582-2665
Fantagraphics Books, Seattle, WA	800-657-1100
W D Farmer Residence Designer Inc., Atlanta, GA	800-225-7526
	(GA) 800-221-7526
Favorite Recipes Press, Nashville, TN	800-358-0560
The Faxon Co. (A Dawson Co), Westwood, MA	800-999-3594
Federal Publications Inc., Washington, DC	800-922-4330
Philipp Feldheim Inc., Nanuet, NY	800-237-7149
Fell Publishers, Hollywood, FL	800-771-FELL
Ferguson Publishing Co., Chicago, IL	800-306-9941
Finley-Greene Publications Inc., Island Park, NY	800-431-1131
Fire Engineering Books & Videos, Saddle Brook, NJ	800-752-9768
Firebird Publications Inc., Rockville, MD	800-854-9595
Firefly Books Ltd., Buffalo, NY	800-387-5085
Fisher Books, Tucson, AZ	800-255-1514
The Fisherman Library, Point Pleasant, NJ	800-553-4745
Fitzroy Dearborn Publishers, Chicago, IL	800-850-8102
Flatiron Publishing Inc., New York, NY	800-LIBRARY
Flower Valley Press Inc., Gaithersburg, MD	800-735-5197
Focus Publishing, Bemidji, MN	800-913-6287
Focus Publishing/R Pullins Co. Inc., Newburyport, MA	(orders) 800-848-7236
Fodor's Travel Publications Inc., New York, NY	800-733-3000
	800-533-6478
Foghorn Press, Petaluma, CA	800-FOGHORN

Publisher/Distributor	Toll-Free No.
Fondo de Cultura Economica USA Inc., San Diego, CA	800-532-3872
Fordham University Press, Bronx, NY	800-247-6553
Forest House Publishing Co. Inc., Lake Forest, IL	800-394-READ
Forward Movement Publications, Cincinnati, OH	800-543-1813
The Foundation Center, New York, NY	800-424-9836
The Foundation for Economic Education Inc., Irvington-on-Hudson, NY	800-452-3518
Franciscan University Press, Steubenville, OH	800-783-6357
Fraser Publishing Co., Burlington, VT	800-253-0900
Free Spirit Publishing Inc., Minneapolis, MN	800-735-7323
Friends United Press, Richmond, IN	800-537-8839
Frog Ltd., Berkeley, CA	(book orders only) 800-337-2665
Front Row Experience, Byron, CA	(voice & fax) 800-524-9091
Fulcrum Publishing Inc., Golden, CO	800-992-2908
Futura Publishing Co. Inc., Armonk, NY	800-877-8761
Future Horizons Inc., Arlington, TX	800-489-0727
G W Medical Publishing Inc., St. Louis, MO	800-600-0330
P Gaines Co., Oak Park, IL	800-578-3853
Gale, Detroit, MI	(cust serv) 800-877-GALE
	(edit) 800-347-GALE
Gallopade Publishing Group, Atlanta, GA	800-536-2GET
Gareth Stevens Inc., Milwaukee, WI	800-341-3569
Garrett Educational Corp., Ada, OK	800-654-9366
Garrett Publishing Inc., Deerfield Beach, FL	(book orders) 800-333-2069
Gateway Books, Oakland, CA	(credit card orders only) 800-669-0773
Gateways Books & Tapes, Nevada City, CA	800-869-0658
Gaunt Inc., Holmes Beach, FL	800-942-8683
Gayot/Gault Millau Inc., Los Angeles, CA	800-LE BEST 1
Gefen Books, Hewlett, NY	800-477-5257
GemStone Press, Woodstock, VT	800-962-4544
Genealogical Publishing Co. Inc., Baltimore, MD	800-296-6687
General Publications Group, Boston, MA	800-288-7090
Genesis Press Inc., Columbus, MS	888-463-4461
Geological Society of America (GSA), Boulder, CO	800-472-1988
Georgetown University Press, Washington, DC	800-246-9606
Gessler Publishing Co. Inc., Roanoke, VA	800-456-5825
The C R Gibson Co., Norwalk, CT	800-243-6004
Giga Information Group, Norwell, MA	800-874-9980
Gleim Publications Inc., Gainesville, FL	800-87-GLEIM
Glenbridge Publishing Ltd., Lakewood, CO	800-986-4135
Glencoe/McGraw-Hill, Westerville, OH	800-848-1567
The Glenlake Publishing Co. Ltd., Chicago, IL	800-537-5920
Peter Glenn Publications Ltd., New York, NY	888-332-6400
The Globe Pequot Press, Old Saybrook, CT	800-243-0495
David R Godine Publisher Inc., Lincoln, MA	800-344-4771
The Gold Book, Atlanta, GA	800-842-6848

Publisher/Distributor	Toll-Free No.
Gold Horse Publishing Inc., Annapolis, MD	800-966-DOLL
Golden Aura Publishing, Philadelphia, PA	800-979-8642
Golden Books Family Entertainment, New York, NY	(cust serv) 800-558-5972
Golden West Publishers, Phoenix, AZ	800-658-5830
Golf Gifts & Gallery Inc., Powers Lake, IL	800-552-4430
Goodheart-Willcox Publisher, Tinley Park, IL	800-323-0440
Goosefoot Acres Press, Cleveland Heights, OH	800-697-4858
Gospel Publishing House, Springfield, MO	800-641-4310
Gould Publications Inc., Longwood, FL	800-847-6502
Government Research Service, Topeka, KS	800-346-6898
Grafco Productions Inc., Marietta, GA	888-656-1500
Grail Foundation Press, Gambier, OH	800-427-9217
Donald M Grant Publisher Inc., Hampton Falls, NH	800-476-0510
Grapevine Publications Inc., Corvallis, OR	800-338-4331
Graphic Arts Center Publishing Co., Portland, OR	800-452-3032
Graphic Arts Publishing Inc., Livonia, NY	800-724-9476
Graphic Arts Technical Foundation, Sewickley, PA	800-910-GATF
Graphic Learning, Waterbury, CT	800-874-0029
Grayson Bernard Publishers, Bloomington, IN	800-925-7853
Great Quotations Inc., Glendale Heights, IL	800-354-4889
Warren H Green Inc., St. Louis, MO	800-537-0655
Greenhaven Press Inc., San Diego, CA	800-231-5163
Greenwillow Books, New York, NY	800-631-1199
Greenwood Publishing Group Inc., Westport, CT	(orders) 800-225-5800
Grey House Publishing Inc., Lakeville, CT	800-562-2139
Griffin Publishing, Glendale, CA	800-826-4849
Grolier Educational, Danbury, CT	800-243-7256
Group Publishing Inc., Loveland, CO	800-447-1070
Grove's Dictionaries Inc., New York, NY	800-221-2123
Grove/Atlantic Inc., New York, NY	800-521-0178
Gryphon Editions, New York, NY	800-633-8911
Gryphon House Inc., Beltsville, MD	800-638-0928
The Guild, Madison, WI	800-969-1556
The Guilford Press, New York, NY	(orders) 800-365-7006
Gulf Publishing Co., Book Division, Houston, TX	(TX) 800-392-4390
	(all other except AK & HI) 800-231-6275
H C I A Inc., Baltimore, MD	800-568-3282
H D I Publishers, Houston, TX	800-321-7037
Hachai Publications Inc., Brooklyn, NY	800-50-HACHAI
Hagstrom Map Co. Inc., Maspeth, NY	800-432-MAPS
Hal Leonard Corp., Milwaukee, WI	800-524-4425
Half Halt Press Inc., Boonsboro, MD	800-822-9635
Hambleton Hill Publishing Inc., Nashville, TN	800-327-5113
Alexander Hamilton Institute, Ramsey, NJ	800-879-2441
Hammond Inc., Maplewood, NJ	800-526-4953
Hampton Press Inc., Cresskill, NJ	800-894-8955

Publisher/Distributor	Toll-Free No.
Hampton Roads Publishing Co. Inc., Charlottesville, VA	800-766-8009
Hampton-Brown Co. Inc., Carmel, CA	800-933-3510
Hanley & Belfus Inc., Philadelphia, PA	800-962-1892
Hanser Gardner Publications, Cincinnati, OH	800-950-8977
Harcourt Brace & Co., Orlando, FL	(cust serv) 800-225-5425
Harcourt Brace College Publishers, Fort Worth, TX	(cust serv) 800-782-4479
Harcourt Brace Legal & Professional Publications, Chicago, IL	(orders) 800-787-8717
Harcourt Brace Professional Publishing, San Diego, CA	800-831-7799
Harcourt Brace School Publishers, Orlando, FL	(cust serv) 800-225-5425
Harmonie Park Press, Warren, MI	800-886-3080
HarperCollins Publishers, New York, NY	800-242-7737
	(PA) 800-982-4377
Harris InfoSource, Twinsburg, OH	800-888-5900
Harris Media/Newspower, Northfield, MA	800-346-8330
Harrison House Publishers, Tulsa, OK	800-888-4126
Hartley & Marks Publishers Inc., Point Roberts, WA	800-277-5887
Harvard Business School Press, Boston, MA	800-988-0886
Harvard University Press, Cambridge, MA	(orders, US & Canada) 800-448-2242
Harvest House Publishers Inc., Eugene, OR	800-547-8979
Hasbro Inc., Pawtucket, RI	800-242-7276
Hatherleigh Press, New York, NY	800-367-2550
The Haworth Press Inc., Binghamton, NY	800-342-9678
Hay House Inc., Carlsbad, CA	(orders) 800-654-5126
Haynes Publications Inc., Newbury Park, CA	800-442-9637
Hazelden Publishing & Education, Center City, MN	800-328-9000
HB Trade Division San Diego Office, San Diego, CA	(cust serv) 800-543-1918
Health Communications Inc., Deerfield Beach, FL	(cust serv) 800-851-9100
	(orders) 800-441-5569
Health for Life, Marina del Rey, CA	800-874-5339
Health Information Network Inc., San Ramon, CA	800-446-1947
Health Leadership Associates Inc., Potomac, MD	800-435-4775
Health Press, Santa Fe, NM	800-643-BOOK
Health Science, Santa Barbara, CA	800-446-1990
Healthy Healing Publications, Sonora, CA	800-736-6015
Heartland Samplers Inc., Minneapolis, MN	800-999-2233
Hearts & Tummies Cookbook Co., Wever, IA	800-571-BOOK
Heartsfire Books, Sante Fe, NM	800-988-5170
William S Hein & Co. Inc., Buffalo, NY	800-828-7571
Heinemann, Westport, CT	800-541-2086
Heinle & Heinle Publishers, Boston, MA	800-237-0053
Hemingway Western Studies Series, Boise, ID	800-992 TEXT
Hendrickson Publishers Inc., Peabody, MA	800-358-3111
Virgil Hensley Publishing, Tulsa, OK	800-288-8520
Herald House, Independence, MO	800-767-8181
Herald Press, Scottdale, PA	800-245-7894

Publisher/Distributor	Toll-Free No.
Heritage Books Inc., Bowie, MD	800-398-7709
Heritage House, Indianapolis, IN	800-419-0200
Hewitt Homeschooling Resources, Washougal, WA	800-348-1750
Hi Willow Research & Publishing, Castle Rock, CO	800-873-3043
Hi-Time Publishing Corp., Milwaukee, WI	800-558-2292
High Mountain Press, Santa Fe, NM	800-4-ONWORD
Highsmith Press LLC, Fort Atkinson, WI	800-558-2110
Hill & Wang, New York, NY	(orders, cust serv) 800-631-8571
Hillsdale College Press, Hillsdale, MI	800-437-2268
Hogrefe & Huber Publishers, Kirkland, WA	800-228-3749
Hohm Press, Prescott, AZ	800-381-2700
Holbrook & Kellogg, Vienna, VA	800-506-4450
Hollywood Creative Directory, Santa Monica, CA	(outside Los Angeles) 800-815-0503
Holmes & Meier Publishers Inc., New York, NY	(orders only) 800-698-7781
Henry Holt & Co. Inc., New York, NY	800-488-5233
Holt, Rinehart & Winston, Fort Worth, TX	800-447-9479
Holt, Rinehart & Winston, Austin, TX	(cust serv) 800-782-4479
Home Builder Press, Washington, DC	800-223-2665
Home Planners Inc., Tucson, AZ	800-322-6797
Homestyles Publishing & Marketing Inc., St. Paul, MN	888-626-2026
HomeTech Information Systems, Bethesda, MD	800-638-8292
Hoover's Inc., Austin, TX	(orders only) 800-486-8666
Hope Publishing Co., Carol Stream, IL	800-323-1049
Horizon Books, Camp Hill, PA	800-233-4443
Horizon Publishers & Distributors Inc., Bountiful, UT	800-453-0812
Houghton Mifflin Co., Boston, MA	(trade books) 800-225-3362
	(textbooks) 800-257-9107
	(college texts) 800-225-1464
Howard Publishing, West Monroe, LA	800-858-4109
Howell Press Inc., Charlottesville, VA	800-868-4512
Human Kinetics Inc., Champaign, IL	800-747-4457
Human Resource Development Press, Amherst, MA	800-822-2801
Humanics Publishing Group, Atlanta, GA	800-874-8844
Hunter House Inc., Publishers, Alameda, CA	800-266-5592
Huntington House Publishers, Lafayette, LA	800-749-4009
Huntington Press Publishing, Las Vegas, NV	800-244-2224
Hyperion, New York, NY	(orders) 800-343-9204
I O P Publishing Inc., Philadelphia, PA	800-358-4677
IBC USA (Publications) Inc., Ashland, MA	800-343-5413
IBFD Publications USA Inc. (International Bureau of Fiscal Documentation), Valatie, NY	800-299-6330
Iconografix Inc., Osceola, WI	(orders only) 800-289-3504
ICS BOOKS Inc., Merrillville, IN	800-541-7323
ICS Press, San Francisco, CA	800-326-0263
IDG Books Worldwide Inc., Foster City, CA	800-762-2974
IEEE Computer Society Press, Los Alamitos, CA	800-272-6657

Publisher/Distributor	Toll-Free No.
Ignatius Press, San Francisco, CA	(orders only) 800-651-1531
IllumiNet Press, Lilburn, GA	800-236-INET
Imaginart Press, Bisbee, AZ	800-828-1376
Incentive Publications Inc., Nashville, TN	800-421-2830
Index Publishing Group Inc., San Diego, CA	800-546-6707
Indiana Historical Society, Indianapolis, IN	(orders only) 800-447-1830
Indiana University Press, Bloomington, IN	(orders only) 800-842-6796
InfoBooks, Santa Monica, CA	800-669-0409
Information Guides, Hermosa Beach, CA	800-347-3257
Information Plus, Wylie, TX	800-463-6757
Inner Traditions International Ltd., Rochester, VT	800-246-8648
Innisfree Press Inc., Philadelphia, PA	(nontrade orders) 800-367-5872
	(trade orders) 800-283-3572
Innovanna Publishing Co. Inc., Sugar Land, TX	800-577-9810
Insiders' Publishing Inc., Manteo, NC	800-765-2665
Institute for International Economics, Washington, DC	800-229-3266
Institute for Language Study, Wilton, CT	800-245-2145
Institute for Research & Education, Minneapolis, MN	800-372-7775
Inter Trade Corp., Norcross, GA	800-653-7363
Interarts/Geo Systems, Cambridge, MA	800-626-4655
Interchange Inc., St. Louis Park, MN	800-669-6208
International Chess Enterprises (I C E), Seattle, WA	800-26-CHESS
International Foundation of Employee Benefit Plans, Brookfield, WI	888-33-IFEBP
International Law Library Book Publishers Inc., Arlington, VA	800-876-0226
International Linguistics Corp., Kansas City, MO	800-237-1830
International Risk Management Institute Inc., Dallas, TX	800-827-4242
International Scholars Publications, Bethesda, MD	800-55-PUBLISH
International Society for Technology in Education, Eugene, OR	(orders only) 800-336-5191
International Wealth Success, Merrick, NY	800-323-0548
Interstate Publishers Inc., Danville, IL	800-843-4774
InterVarsity Press, Downers Grove, IL	800-843-7225
Interweave Press, Loveland, CO	800-272-2193
Iowa State University Press, Ames, IA	(orders only) 800-862-6657
IRI/Skylight Training & Publishing Inc., Arlington Heights, IL	800-348-4474
Irwin/McGraw-Hill, Burr Ridge, IL	(cust serv) 800-338-3987
Ishiyaku EuroAmerica Inc., St. Louis, MO	800-633-1921
Island Press, Washington, DC	800-828-1302
J & B Editions Inc., Richmond, VA	800-266-5480
Jalmar Press, Carson, CA	800-662-9662
Jameson Books Inc., Ottawa, IL	800-426-1357
Jane's Information Group, Alexandria, VA	800-243-3852
January Productions Inc., Hawthorne, NJ	800-451-7450
Jewish Lights Publishing, Woodstock, VT	800-962-4544
Jewish Publication Society, Philadelphia, PA	800-234-3151

Publisher/Distributor	Toll-Free No.
JIST Works Inc., Indianapolis, IN	800-648-5478
	(fax) 800-547-8329
The Johns Hopkins University Press, Baltimore, MD	800-537-5487
Johnson Institute, Minneapolis, MN	800-231-5165
Jones & Bartlett Publishers Inc., Sudbury, MA	800-832-0034
Jones Publishing Inc., Iola, WI	800-331-0038
Joy Publishing, Fountain Valley, CA	800-783-6265
Judaica Press Inc., Brooklyn, NY	800-972-6701
Judson Press, Valley Forge, PA	800-331-1053
Kaeden Corp., Rocky River, OH	800-890-7323
Kaleidoscope Press, Edgewood, WA	800-977-7323
Kalmbach Publishing Co., Waukesha, WI	800-558-1544
Kar-Ben Copies Inc., Rockville, MD	800-4-KARBEN
KC Publications Inc., Las Vegas, NV	800-626-9673
Keats Publishing Inc., New Canaan, CT	800-858-7014
Kendall/Hunt Publishing Co., Dubuque, IA	(orders only) 800-228-0810
Kennedy Publications, Fitzwilliam, NH	800-531-0007
Kensington Publishing Corp., New York, NY	800-221-2647
Kent State University Press, Kent, OH	(orders) 800-247-6553
Key Curriculum Press, Berkeley, CA	800-338-7638
Kids Can Press Ltd., Buffalo, NY	800-265-0884
Kidsbooks Inc., Chicago, IL	800-515-KIDS
Kirkbride Bible Co. Inc., Indianapolis, IN	800-428-4385
Kitchen Sink Press, Northampton, MA	800-365-SINK
Neil A Kjos Music Co., San Diego, CA	800-854-1592
Kluwer Law International (KLI), Cambridge, MA	800-577-8118
Alfred A Knopf Inc., New York, NY	800-638-6460
Knopf Publishing Group	800-638-6460
Kodansha America Inc., New York, NY	800-788-6262
Krause Publications, Iola, WI	800-258-0929
Kregel Publications, Grand Rapids, MI	(order line) 800-733-2607
Kumarian Press Inc., West Hartford, CT	(orders only) 800-289-2664
LADYBUG: The Magazine for Children	(orders) 800-BUG PALS
Lakewood Publications, Minneapolis, MN	800-328-4329
Langenscheidt Publishers Inc., Maspeth, NY	800-432-MAPS
LangMarc Publishing, San Antonio, TX	800-864-1648
Laredo Publishing Co. Inc., Beverly Hills, CA	800-547-5113
Larousse Kingfisher Chambers Inc., New York, NY	800-497-1657
Larson Publications, Burdett, NY	800-828-2197
Laureate Press, Bangor, ME	800-946-2727
Lawyers Cooperative Publishing, Rochester, NY	800-527-0430
Leadership Publishers Inc., Des Moines, IA	800-814-3757
Leading Edge Reports, Commack, NY	800-866-4648
The Learning Connection, Frostproof, FL	800-338-2282
Learning Links Inc., New Hyde Park, NY	800-724-2616
Learning Publications Inc., Holmes Beach, FL	(orders) 800-222-1525

Publisher/Distributor	Toll-Free No.
Learning Resources Network (LERN), Manhattan, KS	(orders only) 800-678-5376
Lectorum Publications Inc., New York, NY	800-345-5946
Legacy Publishing Group, Clinton, MA	800-322-3866
Leisure Arts Inc., Little Rock, AR	800-643-8030
Leisure Books, New York, NY	(orders) 800-481-9191
Lerner Publications Co., Minneapolis, MN	800-328-4929
Liberty Fund Inc., Indianapolis, IN	800-955-8335
Libraries Unlimited Inc., Englewood, CO	800-237-6124
Lickle Publishing Inc., West Palm Beach, FL	888-454-2553
Mary Ann Liebert Inc., Larchmont, NY	800-654-3237
Lifetime Books Inc., Hollywood, FL	800-771-3355
Liguori Publications, Liguori, MO	800-464-2555
Lincoln Institute of Land Policy, Cambridge, MA	800-LAND-USE
LinguiSystems Inc., East Moline, IL	800-PRO-IDEA
Linton Day Publishing Co., Stone Mountain, GA	800-549-6757
Lippincott-Raven Publishers, Philadelphia, PA	(MD) 800-638-3030
Little, Brown and Company Inc., Boston, MA	800-759-0190
Little Tiger Press, Pewaukee, WI	800-541-2205
Littlefield, Adams Quality Paperbacks, Lanham, MD	800-462-6420
The Liturgical Press, Collegeville, MN	800-858-5450
Liturgy Training Publications, Chicago, IL	(US & Canada only) 800-933-1800
Llewellyn Publications, St. Paul, MN	800-843-6666
Loizeaux Brothers Inc., Neptune, NJ	800-526-2796
London Bridge, Buffalo, NY	800-805-1083
Lone Eagle Publishing Co., Los Angeles, CA	800-345-6257
Lonely Planet Publications, Oakland, CA	(orders) 800-275-8555
Longstreet Press, Marietta, GA	800-927-1488
Loompanics Unlimited, Port Townsend, WA	800-380-2230
Looseleaf Law Publications Inc., Flushing, NY	800-647-5547
Lost Classics Book Co., Lake Wales, FL	888-611-2665
Lothrop, Lee & Shepard Books, New York, NY	800-843-9389
Lotus Light Publications, Twin Lakes, WI	(orders only) 800-824-6396
Loyola Press, Chicago, IL	800-621-1008
Lucent Books Inc., San Diego, CA	800-231-5163
Lyle Stuart, Secaucus, NJ	(cust serv) 800-866-1966
Lyrick Publishing, Allen, TX	800-418-2371
Macalester Park Publishing Co., Minneapolis, MN	800-407-9078
The McDonald & Woodward Publishing Co., Fort Pierce, FL	800-233-8787
Macmillan Computer Publishing USA, Indianapolis, IN	800-545-5914
Macmillan Digital Publishing USA, Indianapolis, IN	800-545-5914
Macmillan Online USA, Indianapolis, IN	800-545-5914
Madison Books Inc., Lanham, MD	800-462-6420
Madison House Publishers, Madison, WI	800-604-1776
Mage Publishers Inc., Washington, DC	800-962-0922
Maharishi International University Press, Fairfield, IA	800-831-6523
Mancorp Publishing Inc., Tampa, FL	800-853-3888

Publisher/Distributor	Toll-Free No.
Mangajin Inc., Atlanta, GA	800-552-3206
Many Cultures Publishing, San Francisco, CA	800-484-4173, ext 1073
MAR CO Products Inc., Warminster, PA	800-448-2197
MARC Publications, Monrovia, CA	(US only) 800-777-7752
Market Data Retrieval Inc., Shelton, CT	800-333-8802
Marketing Directions Inc., Avon, CT	800-562-4357
Markowski International Publishers, Hummelstown, PA	800-566-0534
Marlor Press Inc., St. Paul, MN	800-669-4908
MarshMedia, Kansas City, MO	800-821-3303
Marsilio Publishers Corp., New York, NY	800-992-9685
Massachusetts Continuing Legal Education Inc., Boston, MA	800-966-6253
Masters Press, Indianapolis, IN	800-9-SPORTS
The Mathematical Association of America, Washington, DC	(orders) 800-331-1622
Maval Publishing Inc., Denver, CO	800-746-3088
Maverick Publications Inc., Bend, OR	800-800-4831
Mayfield Publishing Co., Mountain View, CA	800-433-1279
McBooks Press, Ithaca, NY	888-266-5711
McClanahan Publishing House Inc., Kuttawa, KY	800-544-6959
McCormack's Guides, Martinez, CA	800-222-3602
McFarland & Co. Inc., Publishers, Jefferson, NC	(orders only) 800-253-2187
McGraw-Hill College, Boston, MA	(cust serv) 800-338-3987
McGraw-Hill Higher Education, Burr Ridge, IL	(cust serv) 800-338-3987
McGraw-Hill School Systems, Monterey, CA	(orders) 800-663-0544
McPherson & Co., Kingston, NY	800-613-8219
MDRT Center for Productivity, Park Ridge, IL	800-879-6378
Meadowbrook Press Inc., Minnetonka, MN	800-338-2232
R S Means Co. Inc., Kingston, MA	800-448-8182
Medbooks, Richardson, TX	800-443-7397
Media Associates, Wilton, CA	(orders) 800-373-1897
Media & Methods, Philadelphia, PA	800-555-5657
Medical Economics, Montvale, NJ	800-442-6657
Medical Physics Publishing Corp., Madison, WI	800-442-5778
Medicode, Salt Lake City, UT	800-999-4600
The Russell Meerdink Co. Ltd., Neenah, WI	800-635-6499
Mel Bay Publications Inc., Pacific, MO	800-863-5229
Menasha Ridge Press Inc., Birmingham, AL	800-247-9437
Mercer University Press, Macon, GA	(outside GA) 800-637-2378, ext 2880
	(GA) 800-342-0841, ext 2880
Meriwether Publishing Ltd/Contemporary Drama Service, Colorado Springs, CO	800-937-5297
Merlyn's Pen: Stories by American Students, East Greenwich, RI	800-247-2027
Merriam-Webster Inc., Springfield, MA	(orders & cust serv) 800-828-1880
Merritt Publishing, Santa Monica, CA	800-638-7597
Merryant Publishers Inc., Vashon, WA	800-228-8958
Mesorah Publications Ltd., Brooklyn, NY	800-637-6724
Metal Bulletin Inc., New York, NY	800-METAL-25

Publisher/Distributor	Toll-Free No.
Metamorphous Press, Portland, OR	800-937-7771
MGI Management Institute Inc., White Plains, NY	800-932-0191
Michelin Travel Publications, Greenville, SC	800-423-0485
	800-223-0987
Michie, Charlottesville, VA	800-446-3410
MicroMash, Englewood, CO	800-272-7277
Microsoft Press, Redmond, WA	800-MSPRESS
MidWest Plan Service, Ames, IA	800-562-3618
Midwest Traditions Inc., Mount Horeb, WI	800-736-9189
Milady Publishing, Albany, NY	800-998-7498
Milkweed Editions, Minneapolis, MN	800-520-6455
The Millbrook Press Inc., Brookfield, CT	800-462-4703
Millennium Publishing Group, Monterey, CA	800-524-6826
Miller Freeman Inc., San Francisco, CA (orders only)	800-848-5594
Milliken Publishing Co., St. Louis, MO	800-325-4136
The Minerals, Metals & Materials Society (TMS), Warrendale, PA	800-759-4867
Ministry Publications, Scottsdale, AZ	800-573-4105
Minnesota Historical Society Press, St. Paul, MN	800-647-7827
The MIT Press, Cambridge, MA (orders only)	800-356-0343
Mitchell Lane Publishers, Elkton, MD	800-814-5484
MMB Music Inc., St. Louis, MO	800-543-3771
Momentum Books Ltd., Troy, MI	800-758-1870
Monday Morning Books Inc., Palo Alto, CA	800-255-6048
Mondo Publishing, Greenvale, NY	800-242-3650
Money Market Directories Inc., Charlottesville, VA	800-446-2810
Monthly Review Press, New York, NY	800-670-9499
Moody Press, Chicago, IL	800-678-8812
Moon Travel Handbooks, Chico, CA	800-345-5473
Moonbeam Publications Inc., Traverse City, MI	800-445-2391
Morehouse Publishing Co., Harrisburg, PA (orders only)	800-877-0012
Morgan Kaufmann Publishers Inc., San Francisco, CA	800-745-7323
Morgan Quitno Corp., Lawrence, KS	800-457-0742
Morgan-Rand Inc., Huntingdon Valley, PA	800-677-3839
Morningside Bookshop, Dayton, OH	800-648-9710
Morrow Junior Books, New York, NY	800-843-9389
Morton Publishing Co., Englewood, CO	800-384-3777
Mosaic Press, Buffalo, NY	800-387-8992
Mosby, St. Louis, MO	800-325-4177
Motorbooks International Publishers & Wholesalers Inc., Osceola, WI	800-458-0454
Mountain Press Publishing Co., Missoula, MT	800-234-5308
The Mountaineers Books, Seattle, WA	800-553-4453
Andrew Mowbray Inc. Publishers, Lincoln, RI	800-999-4697
Moznaim Publishing Corp., Brooklyn, NY	800-364-5118
Mulberry Paperback Books, New York, NY	800-843-9389
Multnomah Publishers Inc., Sisters, OR	800-929-0910
Municipal Analysis Services Inc., Austin, TX	800-488-3932

Publisher/Distributor	Toll-Free No.
Mike Murach & Associates Inc., Fresno, CA	800-221-5528
MUSA Video Publishing, Carrolton, TX	800-933-6872
Music Sales Corp., New York, NY	800-431-7187
Mustang Publishing Co. Inc., Memphis, TN	800-250-8713
NAFSA: Association of International Educators, Washington, DC	800-836-4994
The Naiad Press Inc., Tallahassee, FL	(orders only) 800-533-1973
NAPSAC Reproductions, Marble Hill, MO	800-758-8629
Narwhal Press Inc., Charleston, SC	800-981-1943
National Academy Press, Washington, DC	800-624-6242
National Archives & Records Administration, Washington, DC	(orders) 800-234-8861
National Association of Broadcasters, Washington, DC	800-368-5644
National Association of Secondary School Principals, Reston, VA	800-253-7746
National Association of Social Workers (NASW), Washington, DC	800-638-8799
National Braille Press, Boston, MA	800-548-7323
National Center for Non-profit Boards, Washington, DC	800-883-6262
National Council of Teachers of English (NCTE), Urbana, IL	800-369-6283
National Geographic Society, Washington, DC	800-638-4077
National Golf Foundation, Jupiter, FL	800-733-6006
National Institute for Trial Advocacy, Notre Dame, IN	800-225-6482
National Learning Corp., Syosset, NY	800-645-6337
The National Museum of Women in the Arts, Washington, DC	800-222-7270
National Notary Association, Chatsworth, CA	800-876-6827
National Science Teachers Association (NSTA), Arlington, VA	(sales) 800-722-NSTA
National Textbook Co. (NTC), Lincolnwood, IL	(orders only) 800-323-4900
National Underwriter Co., Cincinnati, OH	800-543-0874
Naturegraph Publishers Inc., Happy Camp, CA	800-390-5353
Naval Institute Press, Annapolis, MD	800-233-8764
NavPress Publishing Group, Colorado Springs, CO	800-366-7788
NBM Publishing Inc., New York, NY	800-886-1223
National Council on Radiation Protection & Measurements (NCRP), Bethesda, MD	800-229-2652
Neibauer Press, Warminster, PA	800-322-6203
Nelson Information, Port Chester, NY	800-333-6357
Thomas Nelson Inc., Nashville, TN	800-251-4000
NelsonWord Childrens Publication Group, Nashville, TN	800-251-4000
New City Press, Hyde Park, NY	(orders only) 800-462-5980
New Dimensions in Education, Waterbury, CT	800-227-9120
New Directions Publishing Corp., New York, NY	(PA) 800-233-4830
New Editions International Ltd., Sedona, AZ	800-777-4751
New Harbinger Publications Inc., Oakland, CA	(orders only) 800-748-6273
New Horizon Press, Far Hills, NJ	(orders only) 800-533-7978
New Leaf Press Inc., Green Forest, AR	800-643-9535
The New Press, New York, NY	(orders) 800-233-4830
New Readers Press, Syracuse, NY	800-448-8878

Publisher/Distributor	Toll-Free No.
New Rivers Press, Minneapolis, MN	800-339-2011
New Victoria Publishers, Norwich, VT	800-326-5297
New World Library, Novato, CA	(retail orders) 800-227-3900
New York Academy of Sciences, New York, NY	800-843-6927
New York University Press, New York, NY	(orders) 800-996-6987
Newcastle Publishing Co. Inc., North Hollywood, CA	800-932-4809
NewLife Publications, Orlando, FL	800-235-7255
Newmarket Press, New York, NY	800-669-3903
Nightingale-Conant, Niles, IL	800-572-2770
Nightshade Press, Troy, ME	(orders only) 800-497-9258
Nolo Press, Berkeley, CA	800-992-6656
Norman Publishing, San Francisco, CA	800-544-9359
North Country Press, Unity, ME	800-722-2169
North Light Books	800-289-0963
North River Press Inc., Great Barrington, MA	800-486-2665
North South Books, New York, NY	800-282-8257
Northland Publishing Co., Flagstaff, AZ	800-346-3257
Northmont Publishing Co., West Bloomfield, MI	800-472-3485
Jeffrey Norton Publishers Inc., Guilford, CT	800-243-1234
W W Norton & Company Inc., New York, NY	(orders & cust serv) 800-233-4830
Nova Press, Los Angeles, CA	800-949-6175
NTC Contemporary Publishing Co., Lincolnwood, IL	800-323-4900
Nystrom, Chicago, IL	800-621-8086
Oasis Press/Hellgate Press, Grants Pass, OR	800-228-2275
Ocean View Books, Denver, CO	800-848-6222
Official Airline Guides, Oak Brook, IL	800-323-3537
Ohara Publications Inc., Valencia, CA	800-423-2874
Ohio University Press, Athens, OH	800-621-2736
The Oliver Press Inc., Minneapolis, MN	800-8-OLIVER
Omnibus Press, New York, NY	800-431-7187
Omnigraphics Inc., Detroit, MI	800-234-1340
The One-Off CD Shop Washington Inc., White Plains, MD	800-678-8760
OneOnOne Computer Training, Addison, IL	800-424-8668
Online Press Inc./Quick Course Books, Bellevue, WA	800-854-3344
Open Court Publishing Co., Peru, IL	800-435-6850
Open Horizons Publishing Co., Fairfield, IA	800-796-6130
Optical Society of America (OSA), Washington, DC	800-582-0416
Orbis Books, Maryknoll, NY	(orders) 800-258-5838
Orca Book Publishers, Custer, WA	800-210-5277
Orchard Books, New York, NY	800-433-3411
Oregon Catholic Press, Portland, OR	800-548-8749
O'Reilly & Associates Inc., Sebastopol, CA	800-998-9938
Organization for Economic Cooperation & Development (OECD), Washington, DC	800-456-6323
Orion Research Corp., Scottsdale, AZ	800-844-0759
The Oryx Press, Phoenix, AZ	800-279-6799

Publisher/Distributor	Toll-Free No.
Osborne/McGraw-Hill, Berkeley, CA	800-227-0900
Oughten House Publications, Livermore, CA	888-ORDER-IT
Our Sunday Visitor Publishing, Huntington, IN	(orders) 800-348-2440
The Overmountain Press, Johnson City, TN	800-992-2691
Richard C Owen Publishers Inc., Katonah, NY	800-336-5588
Oxbridge Communications Inc., New York, NY	800-955-0231
Oxford University Press, Inc., New York, NY	(orders) 800-451-7556
Oxmoor House Inc., Birmingham, AL	800-633-4910
Ozark Publishing Inc., Prairie Grove, AR	800-321-5671
P P I Publishing, Kettering, OH	800-668-7325
P R B Productions, Albany, CA	800-772-0780
P & R Publishing Co., Phillipsburg, NJ	800-631-0094
P S M J Resources Inc., Newton, MA	800-537-7765
Pacific Press Publishing Association, Nampa, ID	800-447-7377
Paladin Press, Boulder, CO	800-392-2400
Palm Island Press, Key West, FL	800-763-4345
Panoptic Enterprises, Burke, VA	800-594-4766
Pantheon Books/Schocken Books, New York, NY	800-638-6460
Papier-Mache Press, Watsonville, CA	800-776-1956
Paraclete Press, Orleans, MA	800-451-5006
Paradigm Publications, Brookline, MA	800-873-3946
Paradigm Publishing Inc., St. Paul, MN	800-328-1452
Paradise Cay Publications, Arcata, CA	800-736-4509
Parenting Press Inc., Seattle, WA	800-99-BOOKS
Parker Publications Division, Carlsbad, CA	800-452-9873
Parlay International, Emeryville, CA	800-457-2752
Parthenon Publishing Group Inc., Pearl River, NY	800-735-4744
Passage Press, Sandy, UT	800-873-0075
Passport Books, Lincolnwood, IL	(orders only) 800-323-4900
Pathfinder Publishing of California, Ventura, CA	800-977-2282
Path Press Inc., Chicago, IL	800-548-2600
Pathways Publishing, Maynard, MA	888-333-7284
Patrice Press, Tucson, AZ	800-367-9242
Patrick's Press Inc., Columbus, GA	800-654-1052
Pauline Books & Media, Boston, MA	800-876-4463
Paulist Press, Mahwah, NJ	(fax orders only) 800-836-3161
PBC International Inc., Glen Cove, NY	800-527-2826
Peachtree Publishers Ltd., Atlanta, GA	800-241-0113
T H Peek Publisher, Palo Alto, CA	800-962-9245
Peer-to-Peer Communications, San Jose, CA	800-420-2677
Pelican Publishing Co. Inc., Gretna, LA	800-843-1724
	888-5PELICAN
Penbrooke Publishing, Tulsa, OK	888-493-2665
Pencil Point Press Inc., Fairfield, NJ	800-356-1299
Penfield Press, Iowa City, IA	800-728-9998
DAW Books Inc., New York, NY	800-526-0275

Publisher/Distributor	Toll-Free No.
The Pennsylvania State University Press, University Park, PA	800-326-9180
PennWell Books, Tulsa, OK	800-752-9764
Pentrex Pub, Pasadena, CA	(continental US only) 800-950-9333
Per Annum Inc., New York, NY	800-548-1108
Peradam Press, Santa Barbara, CA	800-241-8689
The Perfection Learning Corp., Des Moines, IA	800-762-2999
Peter Pauper Press Inc., White Plains, NY	800-833-2311
Peterson's, Princeton, NJ	800-338-3282
Petroleum Extension Service Petex, Austin, TX	800-687-4132
Pfeifer-Hamilton Publishers, Duluth, MN	800-247-6789
Phi Delta Kappa Educational Foundation, Bloomington, IN	800-766-1156
Philosophy Documentation Center, Bowling Green, OH	800-444-2419
Phoenix Learning Resources, New York, NY	800-221-1274
Phoenix Publishing, Lansing, MI	800-345-0325
Phoenix Society for Burn Survivors, Levittown, PA	800-888-BURN
Picture Me Books, Akron, OH	800-762-6775
Pieces of Learning, Dayton, OH	800-729-5137
The Pierian Press, Ann Arbor, MI	800-678-2435
The Pilgrim Press/United Church Press, Cleveland, OH	800-537-3394
Pineapple Press Inc., Sarasota, FL	(orders) 800-746-3275
Pinon Press, Colorado Springs, CO	800-746-0744
Pitspopany Press, New York, NY	800-232-2931
PJS Publications Inc., Peoria, IL	800-521-2885
Planning/Communications, River Forest, IL	888-366-5200
Pleasant Co. Publications, Middleton, WI	800-845-0005
Plenum Publishing Corp., New York, NY	800-221-9369
The Plough Publishing House, Farmington, PA	800-521-8011
Police Executive Research Forum, Washington, DC	(orders only) 888-202-4563
Pomegranate Artbooks Inc., Rohnert Park, CA	800-227-1428
Popular Culture Ink, Ann Arbor, MI	800-678-8828
The Popular Press, Bowling Green, OH	800-515-5118
Clarkson Potter Publishers, New York, NY	800-526-4264
Practising Law Institute, New York, NY	800-260-4754
Prakken Publications Inc., Ann Arbor, MI	(orders only) 800-530-9673
Precept Press, Chicago, IL	800-225-3775
Prentice Hall Canada, Scarborough, ON	800-263-7733
PREP Publishing, Fayetteville, NC	800-533-2814
Preservation Press, Washington, DC	800-766-6847
Preservation Press Inc., Swedesboro, NJ	888-233-0911
Presidio Press, Novato, CA	800-966-5179
Pride Publications, Radnor, OH	888-902-5983
Princeton Architectural Press, New York, NY	800-722-6657
Princeton Book Co. Publishers, Pennington, NJ	800-220-7149
Princeton University Press, Princeton, NJ	800-777-4726
The Printers Shopper, Chula Vista, CA	800-854-2911
Pro Lingua Associates, Brattleboro, VT	800-366-4775

Publisher/Distributor	Toll-Free No.
PRO-ED, Austin, TX	800-897-3202
Productivity Press Inc., Portland, OR	800-394-6868
The Professional Education Group Inc., Minnetonka, MN	800-229-2531
Professional Publications Inc., Belmont, CA	800-426-1178
Professional Publishing, Burr Ridge, IL	800-2McGraw
Professional Resource Exchange Inc., Sarasota, FL	800-443-3364
Professional Tax & Business Publications, Columbia, SC	800-829-8087
Prometheus Books, Amherst, NY	800-421-0351
Pruett Publishing Co., Boulder, CO	800-247-8224
Prufrock Press, Waco, TX	800-998-2208
PST Inc., Redmond, WA	800-284-7043
Psychological Assessment Resources Inc. (PAR), Lutz, FL	800-331-8378
The Psychological Corp., San Antonio, TX	(cust serv) 800-228-0752
PT Publications, West Palm Beach, FL	800-547-4326
Purdue University Press, West Lafayette, IN	800-933-9637
Purple Mountain Press Ltd., Fleischmanns, NY	800-325-2665
The Putnam Berkley Group Inc., New York, NY	800-631-8571
QED Press, Fort Bragg, CA	800-773-7782
Quail Ridge Press, Brandon, MS	800-343-1583
Quality Education Data, Denver, CO	800-525-5811
Quality Medical Publishing Inc., St. Louis, MO	800-423-6865
Quality Press, Milwaukee, WI	800-248-1946
Quality Resources, New York, NY	800-247-8519
Queenship Publishing Co., Santa Barbara, CA	800-647-9882
Quintessence Publishing Co. Inc., Carol Stream, IL	800-621-0387
Quixote Press, Wever, IA	800-571-BOOK
Ragged Edge Press, Shippensburg, PA	888-WHT-MANE
Rainbow Books Inc., Highland City, FL	(book orders) 800-356-9315
Rainbow Publishers, La Jolla, CA	800-323-7337
Rainbow Studies International, El Reno, OK	800-242-5348
Raintree/Steck-Vaughn Publishers, Austin, TX	800-531-5015
Rand McNally, Skokie, IL	800-333-0136
Random House Inc., New York, NY	800-726-0600
RandomSoft, New York, NY	800-788-8815
Ransom Hill Press, Ramona, CA	800-423-0620
Rayve Productions Inc., Windsor, CA	800-852-4890
RCL (Resources for Christian Living), Allen, TX	800-527-5030
Reader's Digest Association Inc., Pleasantville, NY	800-431-1726
Reader's Digest USA, Pleasantville, NY	800-431-1726
Reader's Digest USA Condensed Books, Pleasantville, NY	800-431-1726
Record Research Inc., Menomonee Falls, WI	800-827-9810
Red Crane Books Inc., Santa Fe, NM	800-922-3392
Redleaf Press, St. Paul, MN	800-423-8309
Thomas Reed Publications Inc., Boston, MA	800-995-4995
Regal Books, Ventura, CA	800-235-3415
Regnery Publishing Inc., Washington, DC	800-462-6420

Publisher/Distributor	Toll-Free No.
Regular Baptist Press, Schaumburg, IL	(orders only) 800-727-4440
	888-588-1600
Rei America Inc., Miami, FL	800-726-5337
Renaissance Media, Los Angeles, CA	800-266-2834
Research Press, Champaign, IL	800-519-2707
Resurrection Press Ltd., Williston Park, NY	800-892-6657
Retail Reporting Corp., New York, NY	800-251-4545
Fleming H Revell, Grand Rapids, MI	800-877-2665
Review & Herald Publishing Association, Hagerstown, MD	800-234-7630
Rip Off Press Inc., Auburn, CA	800-468-2669
Rising Sun Publishing, Marietta, GA	800-524-2813
The Riverside Publishing Co., Itasca, IL	800-656-8420
	(orders) 800-767-3378
Rizzoli International Publications Inc., New York, NY	
	(orders & cust serv) 800-221-7945
Roberts Rinehart Publishing Co., Boulder, CO	800-352-1985
Rockbridge Publishing Co., Berryville, VA	800-473-3943
Rock Hill Press, Bala Cynwyd, PA	888-ROCKHILL
Rockwell Publishing, Bellvue, WA	800-221-9347
Rocky River Publishers, Shepherdstown, WV	800-343-0686
Rodale Press Inc., Emmaus, PA	800-848-4735
The Rosen Publishing Group Inc., New York, NY	800-237-9932
Ross Books, Berkeley, CA	800-367-0930
Norman Ross Publishing Inc., New York, NY	800-648-8850
Fred B Rothman & Co., Littleton, CO	800-457-1986
The Rough Notes Co. Inc., Carmel, IN	800-428-4384
Rowman & Littlefield Publishers Inc., Lanham, MD	800-462-6420
Royal House Publishing Co. Inc., Beverly Hills, CA	800-277-5535
Rubenseque Romances, Tarrytown, NY	888-RubensR
Rudi Publishing, San Francisco, CA	(orders only) 800-999-6901
Rudra Press, Portland, OR	800-876-7798
Runestone Press, Minneapolis, MN	800-328-4929
Running Press Book Publishers, Philadelphia, PA	(orders) 800-345-5359
Russell Sage Foundation, New York, NY	800-666-2211
Rutgers University Press, New Brunswick, NJ	(orders only) 800-446-9323
Rutledge Books Inc., Bethel, CT	800-278-8533
Rutledge Hill Press, Nashville, TN	800-234-4234
William H Sadlier Inc., New York, NY	800-221-5175
Sagamore Publishing Inc., Champaign, IL	(orders) 800-327-5557
St. Anthony Messenger Press, Cincinnati, OH	800-488-0488
Saint Anthony Publishing Inc., Reston, VA	800-632-0123
St. Bede's Publications, Petersham, MA	(orders) 800-247-6553
St. Martin's Press Inc., New York, NY	800-221-7945
	(College Division) 800-470-4767
Saint Mary's Press, Winona, MN	800-533-8095
Saint Nectarios Press, Seattle, WA	800-643-4233

Publisher/Distributor	Toll-Free No.
Salem Press Inc., Englewood Cliffs, NJ	800-221-1592
Howard W Sams & Co., Indianapolis, IN	800-428-7267
J S Sanders & Co. Inc., Nashville, TN	800-350-1101
Sandlapper Publishing Inc., Orangeburg, SC	800-849-7263
Santa Monica Press, Santa Monica, CA	800-784-9553
Santillana USA Publishing Co. Inc., Miami, FL	800-245-8584
Sarpedon, New York, NY	800-207-8045
Sasquatch Books, Seattle, WA	800-775-0817
W B Saunders Company, Philadelphia, PA	(cust serv) 800-545-2522
Savage Press, Superior, WI	800-732-3867
Scarborough House, Lanham, MD	800-462-6420
Scepter Publishers, Princeton, NJ	800-322-8773
Schaffer Frank Publications Inc., Torrance, CA	(cust serv) 800-421-5565
Scholarly Resources Inc., Wilmington, DE	800-772-8937
Scholastic Professional Books:, New York, NY	800-325-6149
Schonfeld & Associates Inc., Lincolnshire, IL	800-205-0030
School Zone Publishing Co., Grand Haven, MI	800-253-0564
Arthur Schwartz & Co. Inc., Woodstock, NY	800-669-9080
Scott & Daughters Publishing Inc., Los Angeles, CA	800-547-2688
Scott Publications, Livonia, MI	800-458-8237
Scott Publishing Co., Sidney, OH	800-572-6885
Seal Press, Seattle, WA	(orders) 800-754-0271
Search Resources, Houston, TX	800-460-4673
SelectiveHouse Publishers Inc., Gaithersburg, MD	(orders only) 888-256-6399
Self-Counsel Press Inc., Bellingham, WA	800-663-3007
Seven Locks Press Inc., Santa Ana, CA	800-354-5348
Seven Worlds Corp., Knoxville, TN	800-848-5547
Severn House Publishers Inc., New York, NY	800-830-3044
M E Sharpe Inc., Armonk, NY	800-541-6563
Harold Shaw Publishers, Wheaton, IL	800-SHAW-PUB
Sheed & Ward, Kansas City, MO	(cust serv) 800-333-7373
	800-444-8910
Sheep Meadow Press, Bronx, NY	800-972-4491
Signature Books Inc., Salt Lake City, UT	(ordering) 800-356-5687
Sigo Press, Gloucester, MA	800-338-0446
SIGS Books & Multimedia, New York, NY	(orders only) 800-871-7447
Silver Moon Press, New York, NY	800-874-3320
Silver Pixel Press, Rochester, NY	800-394-3686
Simon & Schuster, New York, NY	(cust serv) 800-223-2348
	(orders) 800-223-2336
Simon & Schuster Education Group, Adult Education Division:	
Invest Learning, San Diego, CA	800-927-9997
Simon & Schuster Trade Division, New York, NY	(orders) 800-223-2336
	(cust serv) 800-223-2348
Macmillan Publishing USA, Indianapolis, IN	800-545-5914
Singular Publishing Group Inc., San Diego, CA	800-521-8545

Publisher/Distributor	Toll-Free No.
Skidmore-Roth Publishing Inc., Aurora, CO	800-825-3150
SkillPath Publications, Mission, KS	800-873-7545
Sky Publishing Corp., Cambridge, MA	800-253-0245
Slack Incorporated, Thorofare, NJ	800-257-8290
Gibbs Smith Publisher, Layton, UT	800-748-5439
Smith & Kraus Inc. Publishers, North Stratford, NH	800-895-4331
M Lee Smith Publishers & Printers LLC, Brentwood, TN	800-274-6774
Smithmark Publishers, New York, NY	800-645-9990
Smithsonian Press/Smithsonian Productions, Washington, DC	800-782-4612
Smyth & Helwys Publishing Inc., Macon, GA	800-747-3016
	800-568-1248
Snow Lion Publications Inc., Ithaca, NY	800-950-0313
Society for Industrial & Applied Mathematics, Philadelphia, PA	800-447-SIAM
Society for Mining, Metallurgy & Exploration Inc., Littleton, CO	800-763-3132
Society of Manufacturing Engineers, Dearborn, MI	800-733-4SME
Solitaire Publishing, Tampa, FL	800-226-0286
Sophia Institute Press, Manchester, NH	800-888-9344
Sopris West, Longmont, CO	800-547-6747
Soundprints, Norwalk, CT	800-228-7839
South Carolina Bar, Columbia, SC	(SC only) 800-768-7787
South-Western Educational Publishing, Cincinnati, OH	800-543-0487
Southern Illinois University Press, Carbondale, IL	800-346-2680
Southern Institute Press, Indian Rocks Beach, FL	800-633-4891
Space Link Books, New York, NY	800-444-2524
Specialty Press Publishers & Wholesalers, North Branch, MN	800-895-4585
Spider	(orders) 800-BUGPALS
Spinsters Ink, Duluth, MN	800-301-6860
SPIRAL Books, Bedford, NH	800-SPIRALL
Spizzirri Publishing Inc., Rapid City, SD	800-325-9819
Spoken Arts Inc., New Rochelle, NY	800-326-4090
Springer-Verlag New York Inc., New York, NY	800-SPRINGER
Springhouse Corp., Springhouse, PA	800-346-7844
Squarebooks Inc., Santa Rosa, CA	800-345-6699
ST Publications Book Division, Cincinnati, OH	800-925-1110
STA-Kris Inc., Marshalltown, IA	800-369-5676
Stackpole Books, Mechanicsburg, PA	800-732-3669
Stalsby-Wilson Press, Rockville, MD	800-642-3228
Standard Publishing Co., Cincinnati, OH	800-543-1301
Standard Publishing Corp., Boston, MA	800-682-5759
Starburst Publishers, Lancaster, PA	(orders only) 800-441-1456
Starlite Inc., St. Petersburg, FL	800-577-2929
State House Press, Austin, TX	800-421-3378
State University of New York Press, Albany, NY	800-666-2211
Steck-Vaughn Co., Austin, TX	800-531-5015
Stenhouse Publishers, York, ME	(sales) 800-988-9812
Sterling House Publisher, Pittsburgh, PA	800-898-7886

Publisher/Distributor	Toll-Free No.
Sterling Publishing Co. Inc., New York, NY	800-367-9692
Stillpoint Publishing, Walpole, NH	800-847-4014
Stockton Press, New York, NY	800-221-2123
Stoeger Publishing Co., Wayne, NJ	800-631-0722
Stone Bridge Press, Berkeley, CA	800-947-7271
Storey Publishing, Pownal, VT	800-359-7436
Story Press	800-289-0963
Strang Communications Co/Creation House, Lake Mary, FL	800-451-4598
Studio Press, Soulsbyville, CA	800-445-7160
Sulzburger & Graham Publishing Co. Ltd., New York, NY	800-366-7086
Summers Press Inc., Austin, TX	800-743-6491
Summit Publications, Indianapolis, IN	800-419-0200
The Summit Publishing Group, Arlington, TX	800-875-3346
Summit University Press, Corwin Springs, MT	800-245-5445
Summy-Birchard Inc., Miami, FL	800-327-7643
Sunbelt Books, El Cajon, CA	800-626-6579
Sundance Publishing LP, Littleton, MA	800-245-3388
SunRise Publishing, Orem, UT	888-732-2470
Sunset Books, Menlo Park, CA	800-227-7346
	(CA) 800-321-0372
Surrey Books Inc., Chicago, IL	800-326-4430
Swedenborg Foundation Inc., West Chester, PA	(cust serv) 800-355-3222
SYBEX Inc., Alameda, CA	800-227-2346
Syracuse University Press, Syracuse, NY	(orders only) 800-365-8929
The Taft Group, Detroit, MI	800-877-8238
Tapestry Press Ltd., Acton, MA	800-535-2007
The Taunton Press Inc., Newtown, CT	(orders) 800-283-7252
	800-888-8286
Taylor & Francis Publishers Inc., Bristol, PA	800-821-8312
Taylor Publishing Co., Dallas, TX	(voice & fax) 800-677-2800
te Neues Publishing Co., New York, NY	800-352-0305
TEACH Services, Brushton, NY	800-367-1844
Teacher Created Materials Inc., Westminster, CA	800-662-4321
Teacher Ideas Press, Englewood, CO	800-237-6124
Teachers Friend Publications Inc., Riverside, CA	800-343-9680
Teaching Strategies, Washington, DC	800-637-3652
Technical Association of the Pulp & Paper Industry (TAPPI), Atlanta, GA	800-332-8686
Technology Training Systems Inc., Aurora, CO	800-676-8871
Technomic Publishing Co. Inc., Lancaster, PA	800-233-9936
Telecom Library Inc., New York, NY	800-542-7279
Tellurian Press, Mariposa, CA	800-745-2631
Temple University Press, Phiiadelphia, PA	800-447-1656
Templegate Publishers, Springfield, IL	800-367-4844
Ten Speed Press, Berkeley, CA	800-841-BOOK
Tesla Book Co., Chula Vista, CA	800-398-2056

Publisher/Distributor	Toll-Free No.
Tetra Press, Blacksburg, VA	800-526-0650
Texas A & M University Press, College Station, TX	(orders) 800-826-8911
Texas Instruments Data Book Marketing, Dallas, TX	800-336-5236
Texas Tech University Press, Lubbock, TX	800-832-4042
Texas Western Press, El Paso, TX	800-488-3789 (4UTEP-TWP)
TFH Publications Inc., Neptune, NJ	800-631-2188
Thames and Hudson Inc., New York, NY	800-233-4830
That Patchwork Place Inc., Bothell, WA	800-426-3126
Theosophical Publishing House, Wheaton, IL	800-669-9425
Theta Reports, Rocky Hill, CT	800-995-1550
Thieme Medical Publishers Inc., New York, NY	800-782-3488
Thinkers Press, Davenport, IA	800-397-7117
Thinking Publications, Eau Claire, WI	800-225-4769
Third Story Books, Wichita, KS	800-334-6018
Charles C Thomas Publisher Ltd., Springfield, IL	800-258-8980
Thomas Geale Publications Inc., Montara, CA	800-554-5457
Thomas Publications, Gettysburg, PA	800-840-6782
Thomson Financial Publishing, Skokie, IL	800-321-3373
Thorndike Press, Thorndike, ME	800-223-6121
Tiare Publications, Lake Geneva, WI	800-420-0579
Tidewater Publishers, Centreville, MD	800-638-7641
Timber Press Inc., Portland, OR	800-327-5680
Time Being Books—Poetry in Sight & Sound, St. Louis, MO	800-331-6605
Time Life Inc., Alexandria, VA	800-621-7026
Timeless Books, Spokane, WA	800-251-9273
Times Books, New York, NY	800-733-3000
T L C Genealogy, Miami Beach, FL	800-858-8558
Todd Publications, Nyack, NY	800-747-1056
TODTRI Productions Ltd., New York, NY	800-241-4477
Tor Books, New York, NY	(cust serv) 800-221-7945
Torah Aura Productions, Los Angeles, CA	800-238-6724
Toucan Books, Pacific Palisades, CA	800-484-4783, ext 2484
Tower Publishing Co., Standish, ME	800-969-8693
J N Townsend Publishing, Exeter, NH	800-333-9883
Traders Press Inc., Greenville, SC	800-927-8222
Tradery House, Memphis, TN	800-727-1034
Trafalgar Square Publishing, North Pomfret, VT	800-423-4525
Trafton Publishing, Cary, NC	800-356-9315
Trails Illustrated/National Geographic Maps, Evergreen, CO	800-962-1643
Trakker Maps Inc., Miami, FL	(FL) 800-432-1730
	800-327-3108
Transaction Publishers, New Brunswick, NJ	888-999-6778
Transnational Publishers Inc., Irvington-on-Hudson, NY	(orders) 800-914-8186
Transportation Technical Service Inc., Fredericksburg, VA	888-ONLY-TTS
Travelers' Tales Inc., Sebastopol, CA	800-998-9938
Treehaus Communications Inc., Loveland, OH	(orders) 800-638-4287

Publisher/Distributor	Toll-Free No.
Tricycle Press, Berkeley, CA	800-841-2665
Trinity Press International, Harrisburg, PA	800-877-0012
TripBuilder Inc., New York, NY	800-525-9745
TriQuarterly Books, Evanston, IL	(orders only) 800-621-2736
Troll Communications LLC, Mahwah, NJ	800-526-5289
Turtle Point Press, Chappaqua, NY	800-453-2992
Charles E Tuttle Co. Inc., Boston, MA	(cust serv) 800-526-2778
Twenty-Third Publications Inc., Mystic, CT	800-321-0411
Twin Sisters Productions Inc., Akron, OH	800-248-8946
Two Roads Publishing, Santa Barbara, CA	800-438-7444
2 13 61 Publications Inc., Los Angeles, CA	800-992-1361
Tyndale House Publishers Inc., Wheaton, IL	800-323-9400
Type & Temperament Inc., Gladwyne, PA	800-IHS-TYPE
UAHC Press, New York, NY	888-489-VAHC
ULI—The Urban Land Institute, Washington, DC	800-462-1254
Ulysses Press, Berkeley, CA	800-377-2542
UMI, Ann Arbor, MI	800-521-0600
Unarius Academy of Science Publications, El Cajon, CA	800-475-7062
Unicor Medical Inc., Montgomery, AL	800-825-7421
Unique Publications Books & Videos, Burbank, CA	800-332-3330
The United Methodist Publishing House, Nashville, TN	800-251-3320
United Nations Publications, New York, NY	800-253-9646
United Seabears Corp., Culver City, CA	800-421-3388
United States Holocaust Memorial Museum, Washington, DC	(orders) 800-259-9998
United States Institute of Peace Press, Washington, DC	(cust serv) 800-868-8064
United States Pharmacopoeial Convention Inc., Rockville, MD	800-227-8772
United States Tennis Association, White Plains, NY	800-223-0456
Universal Reference Publications, Boca Raton, FL	800-377-7551
The University Museum of Archaeology & Anthropology, Philadelphia, PA	800-306-1941
University of Alabama Press, Tuscaloosa, AL	(orders only) 800-825-9980
University of Alaska Press, Fairbanks, AK	(US only) 888-252-6657
The University of Arizona Press, Tucson, AZ	(orders) 800-426-3797
The University of Arkansas Press, Fayetteville, AR	800-626-0090
University of California Press, Berkeley, CA	800-822-6657
University of Chicago Press, Chicago, IL	(orders) 800-621-2736
University of Denver Center for Teaching International Relations Publications, Denver, CO	800-967-2847
University of Georgia Press, Athens, GA	(orders only) 800-266-5842
University of Hawaii Press, Honolulu, HI	800-956-2840
University of Idaho Press, Moscow, ID	800-847-7377
University of Illinois Press, Champaign, IL	(orders) 800-545-4703
University of Iowa Press, Iowa City, IA	(orders only) 800-235-2665
University of Missouri Press, Columbia, MO	800-828-1894
University of Nebraska Press, Lincoln, NE	(orders) 800-755-1105
University of New Mexico Press, Albuquerque, NM	(orders only) 800-249-7737

Publisher/Distributor	Toll-Free No.
The University of North Carolina Press, Chapel Hill, NC	(orders only) 800-848-6224
University of Notre Dame Press, Notre Dame, IN	(orders) 800-621-2736
University of Oklahoma Press, Norman, OK	(orders) 800-627-7377
University of Oregon ERIC Clearinghouse on Educational Management, Eugene, OR	800-438-8841
University of Pennsylvania Press, Philadelphia, PA	(orders & cust serv) 800-445-9880
University of Pittsburgh Press, Pittsburgh, PA	800-666-2211
University of the South Press, Sewanee, TN	800-367-1179
University of the South Press, Sewanee, TN	800-367-1179
University of Tennessee Press, Knoxville, TN	(warehouse, continental US except IL) 800-621-2736
University of Texas at Austin Bureau of Economic Geology, Austin, TX	888-839-4365
University of Utah Press, Salt Lake City, UT	800-773-6672
University of Washington Press, Seattle, WA	800-441-4115
University of Wisconsin Press, Madison, WI	800-829-9559
University Press of America Inc., Lanham, MD	800-462-6420
University Press of Florida, Gainesville, FL	(sales calls only) 800-226-3822
The University Press of Kentucky, Lexington, KY	800-666-2211
University Press of Mississippi, Jackson, MS	800-737-7788
University Press of New England, Hanover, NH	(orders only) 800-421-1561
University Publications of America, Bethesda, MD	800-692-6300
University Publishing Group, Frederick, MD	800-654-8188
Upper Room Books, Nashville, TN	800-972-0433
US Catholic Conference, Washington, DC	800 235-8722
US Games Systems Inc., Stamford, CT	800-544-2637 (800-54GAMES)
USA Gymnastics, Indianapolis, IN	800-4-USAGYM
Utah State University Press, Logan, UT	800-239-9974
VanDam Inc., New York, NY	800-UNFOLDS
Vandamere Press, Arlington, VA	800-551-7776
Vanderbilt University Press, Nashville, TN	(orders only) 800-937-5557
Vernon Publications Inc., Bellevue, WA	800-726-4707
The Vestal Press Ltd., Lanham, MD	800-462-6420
VGM Career Horizons, Lincolnwood, IL	(orders only) 800-323-4900
Visible Ink Press, Detroit, MI	800-776-6265
Vista Publishing Inc., Long Branch, NJ	800-634-2498
Visual Education Association, Springfield, OH	(US only) 800-243-7070
Volcano Press Inc., Volcano, CA	800-879-9636
Voyageur Press, Stillwater, MN	800-888-9653
Wadsworth Publishing Co., Belmont, CA	800-354-9706
George Wahr Publishing Co., Ann Arbor, MI	800-805-2497
Waite Group Press, Corte Madera, CA	800-368-9369
J Weston Walch Publisher, Portland, ME	800-341-6094
Walker & Co., New York, NY	800-AT-WALKER
Wallace Homestead Book Co., Iola, WI	888-457-2873
Walnut Creek CDROM, Concord, CA	800-786-9907

Publisher/Distributor	Toll-Free No.
Walter Foster Publishing Inc., Laguna Hills, CA	800-426-0099
Warner Brothers Publications Inc., Miami, FL	800-468-5010
Warren, Gorham & Lamont, New York, NY	800-922-0066
Warren Publishing House, Everett, WA	800-421-5565
Washington State University Press, Pullman, WA	800-354-7360
Waterfront Books, Burlington, VT	(orders) 800-639-6063
Watson-Guptill Publications, New York, NY	800-451-1741
WCB/McGraw-Hill, Burr Ridge, IL	(cust serv) 800-338-3987
Weatherhill Inc., New York, NY	800-788-7323
Weil Publishing Co. Inc., Augusta, ME	800-877-WEIL
Samuel Weiser Inc., York Beach, ME	800-423-7087
Weka Publishing Inc., Shelton, CT	800-222-9352
Wellspring, York, PA	800-533-3561
Wesleyan University Press, Middletown, CT	800-421-1561
West Group, Cleveland, OH	800-362-4500
Westcliffe Publishers Inc., Englewood, CO	800-523-3692
Western Psychological Services, Los Angeles, CA	(US & Canada) 800-648-8857
The Westminster John Knox Press, Louisville, KY	800-227-2872
WH&O International, Wellesley, MA	800-553-6678
Wheatherstone Press, Portland, OR	800-980-0077
Whispering Coyote Press, Dallas, TX	800-929-6104
Whitaker Distributors, New Kensington, PA	800-444-4484
White Cloud Press, Ashland, OR	800-380-8286
White Mane Publishing Co. Inc., Shippensburg, PA	888-WHT-MANE
White Wolf Publishing, Clarkston, GA	800-454-WOLF
Whitehorse Press, North Conway, NH	800-531-1133
Albert Whitman & Co., Morton Grove, IL	800-255-7675
Whitman Distribution Center, Lebanon, NH	800-353-3730
Whittier Publications Inc., Long Beach, NY	800-897-TEXT
Whole Person Associates Inc., Duluth, MN	800-247-6789
Wide World of Maps Inc., Phoenix, AZ	800-279-7654
Wilderness Adventures Press, Gallatin Gateway, MT	800-925-3339
Wilderness Press, Berkeley, CA	800-443-7227
John Wiley & Sons Inc., New York, NY	(orders only) 800-CALL WILEY
William K Bradford Publishing Co. Inc., Acton, MA	800-421-2009
Williams & Wilkins, Baltimore, MD	800-638-0672
Williamson Publishing Co., Charlotte, VT	800-234-8791
Willow Creek Press, Minocqua, WI	800-850-9453
H W Wilson Co., Bronx, NY	800-367-6770
The Wimmer Companies/CookBook Distribution, Memphis, TN	800-727-1034
Win Publications!, Tulsa, OK	800-749-4597
Windsor Books, Babylon, NY	800-321-5934
Windward Publishing Inc., Miami, FL	800-330-6232
The Wine Appreciation Guild Ltd., South San Francisco, CA	800-231-9463

Publisher/Distributor	Toll-Free No.
Winston-Derek Publishers Group Inc., Nashville, TN	800-826-1888
Wintergreen/Orchard House Inc., New Orleans, LA	800-321-9479
Wisconsin Dept. of Public Instruction, Madison, WI	800-243-8782
WJ Fantasy Inc., Bridgeport, CT	800-ABC-PLAY
Woodbine House, Bethesda, MD	800-843-7323
Woodbridge Press Publishing Co., Santa Barbara, CA	800-237-6053
Woodholme House Publishers, Baltimore, MD	800-488-0051
Woodland Books, Pleasant Grove, UT	800-777-2665
Wordware Publishing Inc., Plano, TX	800-229-4949
Workman Publishing Company Inc., New York, NY	800-722-7202
World Bible Publishers Inc., Iowa Falls, IA	800-247-5111
World Book Educational Products, Chicago, IL	(cust serv) 800-621-8202
World Book Inc., Chicago, IL	800-255-1750
World Citizens, Mill Valley, CA	(orders only) 800-247-6553
World Eagle, Littleton, MA	800-854-8273
World Information Technologies Inc., Northport, NY	800-WORLD-INFO
World Music Press, Danbury, CT	800-810-2040
World Resources Institute, Washington, DC	800-822-0504
World Scientific Publishing Co. Inc., River Edge, NJ	800-227-7562
Worldtariff, San Francisco, CA	800-556-9334
The Wright Group, Bothell, WA	(training dept.) 800-523-2371
	800-345-6073
Write Way Publishing, Aurora, CO	800-680-1493
Writer's Digest Books, Cincinnati, OH	800-289-0963
Wrox Press Inc., Chicago, IL	800-814-4527
Wyndham Hall Press, Bristol, IN	888-947-2665
Wyrick & Co., Charleston, SC	800-227-5898
Yardbird Books, Airville, PA	(sales) 800-622-6044
YMAA Publication Center, Jamaica Plain, MA	800-669-8892
York Press Inc., Timonium, MD	800-962-2763
Young Discovery Library, Ossining, NY	800-343-7854
Young People's Press Inc. (YPPI), San Diego, CA	800-231-9774
Yucca Tree Press, Las Cruces, NM	800-383-6183
YWAM Publishing, Seattle, WA	800-922-2147
Zagat Survey, New York, NY	800-333-3421
Zaner-Bloser Inc., Columbus, OH	800-421-3018
Ziff-Davis Press, Emeryville, CA	800-428-5331
Zondervan Publishing House, Grand Rapids, MI	(cust serv) 800-727-1309

How to Obtain an ISBN

Emery Koltay

Director Emeritus
United States ISBN Agency

The International Standard Book Numbering (ISBN) system was introduced into the United Kingdom by J. Whitaker & Sons Ltd., in 1967 and into the United States in 1968 by the R. R. Bowker Company. The Technical Committee on Documentation of the International Organization for Standardization (ISO TC 46) defines the scope of the standard as follows:

> . . . the purpose of this standard is to coordinate and standardize the use of identifying numbers so that each ISBN is unique to a title, edition of a book, or monographic publication published, or produced, by a specific publisher, or producer. Also, the standard specifies the construction of the ISBN and the location of the printing on the publication.
>
> Books and other monographic publications may include printed books and pamphlets (in various bindings), mixed media publications, other similar media including educational films/videos and transparencies, books on cassettes, microcomputer software, electronic publications, microform publications, braille publications and maps. Serial publications and music sound recordings are specifically excluded, as they are covered by other identification systems. [ISO Standard 2108]

The ISBN is used by publishers, distributors, wholesalers, bookstores, and libraries, among others, in 116 countries to expedite such operations as order fulfillment, electronic point-of-sale checkout, inventory control, returns processing, circulation/location control, file maintenance and update, library union lists, and royalty payments.

Construction of an ISBN

An ISBN consists of 10 digits separated into the following parts:

1 Group identifier: national, geographic, language, or other convenient group
2 Publisher or producer identifier
3 Title identifier
4 Check digit

When an ISBN is written or printed, it should be preceded by the letters *ISBN,* and each part should be separated by a space or hyphen. In the United States, the hyphen is used for separation, as in the following example: ISBN 1-879500-01-9. In this example, 1 is the group identifier, 879500 is the publisher identifier, 01 is the title identifier, and 9 is the check digit. The group of English-speaking countries, which includes the United States, Australia, Canada, New Zealand, and the United Kingdom, uses the group identifiers 0 and 1.

The ISBN Organization

The administration of the ISBN system is carried out at three levels— through the International ISBN Agency in Berlin, Germany; the national agencies; and the publishing houses themselves. Responsible for assigning country prefixes and for coordinating the worldwide implementation of the system, the International ISBN Agency in Berlin has an advisory panel that represents the International Organization for Standardization (ISO), publishers, and libraries. The International ISBN Agency publishes the *Publishers International ISBN Directory,* which is distributed in the United States by R. R. Bowker. As the publisher of *Books in Print,* with its extensive and varied database of publishers' addresses, R. R. Bowker was the obvious place to initiate the ISBN system and to provide the service to the U.S. publishing industry. To date, the U.S. ISBN Agency has entered more than 95,630 publishers into the system.

ISBN Assignment Procedure

Assignment of ISBNs is a shared endeavor between the U.S. ISBN Agency and the publisher. The publisher is provided with an application form, an Advance Book Information (ABI) form, and an instruction sheet. After an application is received and verified by the agency, an ISBN publisher prefix is assigned, along with a computer-generated block of ISBNs. The publisher then has the responsibility to assign an ISBN to each title, to keep an accurate record of the numbers assigned by entering each title in the ISBN Log Book, and to report each title to the *Books in Print* database. One of the responsibilities of the ISBN Agency is to validate assigned ISBNs and to retain a record of all ISBNs in circulation.

ISBN implementation is very much market-driven. Wholesalers and distributors, such as Baker & Taylor, Brodart, and Ingram, as well as such large retail chains as Waldenbooks and B. Dalton recognize and enforce the ISBN system by requiring all new publishers to register with the ISBN Agency before accepting their books for sale. Also, the ISBN is a mandatory bibliographic element in the International Standard Bibliographical Description (ISBD). The Library of Congress Cataloging in Publication (CIP) Division directs publishers to the agency to obtain their ISBN prefixes.

Location and Display of the ISBN

On books, pamphlets, and other printed material, the ISBN shall be on the verso of the title leaf or, if this is not possible, at the foot of the title leaf itself. It should also appear at the foot of the outside back cover if practicable and at the foot of the back of the jacket if the book has one (the lower right-hand corner is recommended). If neither of these alternatives is possible, then the number shall be printed in some other prominent position on the outside. The ISBN shall also appear on any accompanying promotional materials following the provisions for location according to the format of the material.

On other monographic publications, the ISBN shall appear on the title or credit frames and any labels permanently affixed to the publication. If the publication is issued in a container that is an integral part of the publication, the ISBN shall be displayed on the label. If it is not possible to place the ISBN on the item or its label, then the number should be displayed on the bottom or the back of the container, box, sleeve, or frame. It should also appear on any accompanying material, including each component of a multitype publication.

Printing of ISBN in Machine-Readable Coding

In the last few years, much work has been done on machine-readable representations of the ISBN, and now all books should carry ISBNs in bar code. The rapid worldwide extension of bar code scanning has brought into prominence the 1980 agreement between the International Article Numbering, formerly the European Article Numbering (EAN), Association and the International ISBN Agency that translates the ISBN into an ISBN Bookland EAN bar code.

All ISBN Bookland EAN bar codes start with a national identifier (00–09 representing the United States), *except* those on books and periodicals. The agreement replaces the usual national identifier with a special "ISBN Bookland" identifier represented by the digits 978 for books (see Figure 1) and 977 for periodicals. The 978 ISBN Bookland/EAN prefix is followed by the first nine digits of the ISBN. The check digit of the ISBN is dropped and replaced by a check digit calculated according to the EAN rules.

Figure 1 /   Printing the ISBN in Bookland/EAN Symbology

ISBN 1 - 879500 - 01 - 9

9 781879 500013

The following is an example of the conversion of the ISBN to ISBN Bookland/EAN:

ISBN	1-879500-01-9
ISBN without check digit	1-879500-01
Adding EAN flag	978187950001
EAN with EAN check digit	9781879500013

Five-Digit Add-On Code

In the United States, a five-digit add-on code is used for additional information. In the publishing industry, this code can be used for price information or some other specific coding. The lead digit of the five-digit add-on has been designated a currency identifier, when the add-on is used for price. Number 5 is the code for the U.S. dollar; 6 denotes the Canadian dollar; 1 the British pound; 3 the Australian dollar; and 4 the New Zealand dollar. Publishers that do not want to indicate price in the add-on should print the code 90000 (see Figure 2).

Figure 2 / Printing the ISBN Bookland/EAN Number in Bar Code with the Five-Digit Add-On Code

978 = ISBN Bookland/EAN prefix
5 + Code for U.S. $
0995 = $9.95

90000 means no information
in the add-on code

Reporting the Title and the ISBN

After the publisher reports a title to the ISBN Agency, the number is validated and the title is listed in the many R. R. Bowker hard-copy and electronic publications, including *Books in Print, Forthcoming Books, Paperbound Books in Print, Books in Print Supplement, Books Out of Print, Books in Print Online, Books in Print Plus-CD ROM, Children's Books in Print, Subject Guide to Children's Books in Print, On Cassette: A Comprehensive Bibliography of Spoken Word Audiocassettes, Variety's Complete Home Video Directory, Software Encyclopedia, Software for Schools,* and other specialized publications.

For an ISBN application form and additional information, write to United States ISBN Agency, R. R. Bowker Company, 121 Chanlon Rd., New Providence, NJ 07974, or call 908-665-6770. The e-mail address is ISBN-SAN@ bowker.com. The ISBN Web site is at http://www.bowker.com/standards/.

How to Obtain an ISSN

National Serials Data Program
Library of Congress

Two decades ago, the rapid increase in the production and dissemination of information and an intensified desire to exchange information about serials in computerized form among different systems and organizations made it increasingly clear that a means to identify serial publications at an international level was needed. The International Standard Serial Number (ISSN) was developed and has become the internationally accepted code for identifying serial publications. The number itself has no significance other than as a brief, unique, and unambiguous identifier. It is an international standard, ISO 3297, as well as a U.S. standard, ANSI/NISO Z39.9. The ISSN consists of eight digits in arabic numerals 0 to 9, except for the last, or check, digit, which can be an X. The numbers appear as two groups of four digits separated by a hyphen and preceded by the letters ISSN—for example, ISSN 1234-5679.

The ISSN is not self-assigned by publishers. Administration of the ISSN is coordinated through the ISSN Network, an intergovernmental organization within the UNESCO/UNISIST program. The network consists of national and regional centers, coordinated by the ISSN International Centre, located in Paris. Centers have the responsibility to register serials published in their respective countries.

Because serials are generally known and cited by title, assignment of the ISSN is inseparably linked to the key title, a standardized form of the title derived from information in the serial issue. Only one ISSN can be assigned to a title; if the title changes, a new ISSN must be assigned. Centers responsible for assigning ISSNs also construct the key title and create an associated bibliographic record.

The ISSN International Centre handles ISSN assignments for international organizations and for countries that do not have a national center. It also maintains and distributes the collective ISSN database that contains bibliographic records corresponding to each ISSN assignment as reported by the rest of the network. The database contains more than 850,000 ISSNs.

In the United States, the National Serials Data Program at the Library of Congress is responsible for assigning and maintaining the ISSNs for all U.S. serial titles. Publishers wishing to have an ISSN assigned can either request an application form from or send a current issue of the publication to the program and ask for an assignment. Assignment of the ISSN is free, and there is no charge for its use.

The ISSN is used all over the world by serial publishers to distinguish similar titles from each other. It is used by subscription services and libraries to manage files for orders, claims, and back issues. It is used in automated check-in systems by libraries that wish to process receipts more quickly. Copyright centers use the ISSN as a means to collect and disseminate royalties. It is also used as an identification code by postal services and legal deposit services. The ISSN is included as a verification element in interlibrary lending activities and for union catalogs as a collocating device. In recent years, the ISSN has been incorporated into bar codes for optical recognition of serial publications and into the standards for the identification of issues and articles in serial publications.

For further information about the ISSN or the ISSN Network, U.S. libraries and publishers should contact the National Serials Data Program, Library of Congress, Washington, DC 20540-4160 (202-707-6452; fax 202-707-6333; e-mail issn@loc.gov). Non-U.S. parties should contact the ISSN International Centre, 20 rue Bachaumont, 75002 Paris, France (telephone: (33 1) 44-88-22-20; fax (33 1) 40-26-32-43; e-mail issnic@issn.org).

ISSN application forms and instructions for obtaining an ISSN are also available via the Library of Congress World Wide Web Site, http://lcweb.loc. gov/issn, and from the Library of Congress Internet gopher site, LC MARVEL; point your gopher client to marvel.loc.gov (use port 70), or telnet to marvel.loc. gov and log in as marvel).

How to Obtain an SAN

Emery Koltay

Director Emeritus
United States ISBN/SAN Agency

SAN stands for Standard Address Number. It is a unique identification code for addresses of organizations that are involved in or served by the book industry, and that engage in repeated transactions with other members within this group. For purposes of this standard, the book industry includes book publishers, book wholesalers, book distributors, book retailers, college bookstores, libraries, library binders, and serial vendors. Schools, school systems, technical institutes, colleges, and universities are not members of this industry, but are served by it and therefore included in the SAN system.

The purpose of SAN is to facilitate communications among these organizations, of which there are several hundreds of thousands, that engage in a large volume of separate transactions with one another. These transactions include purchases of books by book dealers, wholesalers, schools, colleges, and libraries from publishers and wholesalers; payments for all such purchases; and other communications between participants. The objective of this standard is to establish an identification code system by assigning each address within the industry a discrete code to be used for positive identification for all book and serial buying and selling transactions.

Many organizations have similar names and multiple addresses, making identification of the correct contact point difficult and subject to error. In many cases, the physical movement of materials takes place between addresses that differ from the addresses to be used for the financial transactions. In such instances, there is ample opportunity for confusion and errors. Without identification by SAN, a complex record-keeping system would have to be instituted to avoid introducing errors. In addition, it is expected that problems with the current numbering system such as errors in billing, shipping, payments, and returns, will be significantly reduced by using the SAN system. SAN will also eliminate one step in the order fulfillment process: the "look-up procedure" used to assign account numbers. Previously a store or library dealing with 50 different publishers was assigned a different account number by each of the suppliers. SAN solved this problem. If a publisher indicates its SAN on its stationery and ordering documents, vendors to whom it sends transactions do not have to look up the account number, but can proceed immediately to process orders by SAN.

Libraries are involved in many of the same transactions as are book dealers, such as ordering and paying for books, charging and paying for various services to other libraries. Keeping records of transactions, whether these involve buying, selling, lending, or donations, entails similar operations that require a SAN. Having the SAN on all stationery will speed up order fulfillment and eliminate errors in shipping, billing, and crediting; this, in turn, means savings in both time and money.

History

Development of the Standard Address Number began in 1968 when Russell Reynolds, general manager of the National Association of College Stores (NACS), approached the R. R. Bowker Company and suggested that a "Standard Account Number" system be implemented in the book industry. The first draft of a standard was prepared by an American National Standards Institute (ANSI) Committee Z39 subcommittee, which was co-chaired by Russell Reynolds and Emery Koltay. After Z39 members proposed changes, the current version of the standard was approved by NACS on December 17, 1979.

The chairperson of the ANSI Z39 Subcommittee 30, which developed the approved standard, was Herbert W. Bell, former senior vice president of McGraw-Hill Book Company. The subcommittee comprised the following representatives from publishing companies, distributors, wholesalers, libraries, national cooperative online systems, schools, and school systems: Herbert W. Bell (chair), McGraw-Hill Book Company; Richard E. Bates, Holt, Rinehart and Winston; Thomas G. Brady, The Baker & Taylor Companies, Paul J. Fasana, New York Public Library; Emery I. Koltay, R. R. Bowker Company; Joan McGreevey, New York University Book Centers; Pauline F. Micciche, OCLC, Inc.; Sandra K. Paul, SKP Associates; David Gray Remington, Library of Congress; Frank Sanders, Hammond Public School System; and Peter P. Chirimbes (alternate), Stamford Board of Education.

Format

SAN consists of six digits plus a seventh *Modulus 11* check digit; a hyphen follows the third digit (XXX-XXXX) to facilitate transcription. The hyphen is to be used in print form, but need not be entered or retained in computer systems. Printed on documents, the Standard Address Number should be preceded by the identifier "SAN" to avoid confusion with other numerical codes (SAN XXX-XXXX).

Check Digit Calculation

The check digit is based on *Modulus 11*, and can be derived as follows:

1. Write the digits of the basic number.   2 3 4 5 6 7
2. Write the constant weighting factors associated
   with each position by the basic number.   7 6 5 4 3 2
3. Multiply each digit by its associated weighting factor.   14 18 20 20 18 14
4. Add the products of the multiplications. $14 + 18 + 20 + 20 + 18 + 14 = 104$
5. Divide the sum by *Modulus 11*
   to find the remainder. $104 \div 11 = 9$ plus a remainder of 5
6. Subtract the remainder from the *Modulus 11* to generate
   the required check digit. If there is no remainder,

generate a check digit of zero. If the check digit is 10,
generate a check digit of X to represent 10,
since the use of 10 would require an extra digit. $11 - 5 = 6$

7. Append the check digit to create the standard
seven-digit Standard Address Number. SAN 234-5676

SAN Assignment

The R. R. Bowker Company accepted responsibility for being the central admin-istrative agency for SAN, and in that capacity assigns SANs to identify uniquely the addresses of organizations. No SANs can be reassigned; in the event that an organization should cease to exist, for example, its SAN would cease to be in cir-culation entirely. If an organization using SAN should move or change its name with no change in ownership, its SAN would remain the same, and only the name or address would be updated to reflect the change.

SAN should be used in all transactions; it is recommended that the SAN be imprinted on stationery, letterheads, order and invoice forms, checks, and all other documents used in executing various book transactions. The SAN should always be printed on a separate line above the name and address of the organiza-tion, preferably in the upper left-hand corner of the stationery to avoid confusion with other numerical codes pertaining to the organization, such as telephone number, zip code, and the like.

SAN Functions and Suffixes

The SAN is strictly a Standard Address Number, becoming functional only in applications determined by the user; these may include activities such as pur-chasing, billing, shipping, receiving, paying, crediting, and refunding. Every department that has an independent function within an organization could have a SAN for its own identification. Users may choose to assign a suffix (a separate field) to its own SAN strictly for internal use. Faculty members ordering books through a library acquisitions department, for example, may not have their own separate SAN, but may be assigned a suffix by the library. There is no standard-ized provision for placement of suffixes. Existing numbering systems do not have suffixes to take care of the "subset" type addresses. The SAN does not stan-dardize this part of the address. For the implementation of SAN, it is suggested that wherever applicable the four-position suffix be used. This four-position suf-fix makes available 10,000 numbers, ranging from 0000 to 9999, and will accom-modate all existing subset numbering presently in use.

For example, there are various ways to incorporate SAN in an order fulfill-ment system. Firms just beginning to assign account numbers to their customers will have no conversion problems and will simply use SAN as the numbering system. Firms that already have an existing number system can convert either on a step-by-step basis by adopting SANs whenever orders or payments are processed on the account, or by converting the whole file by using the SAN list-ing provided by the SAN Agency. Using the step-by-step conversion, firms may adopt SANs as customers provide them on their forms, orders, payments, and returns.

For additional information or suggestions, please write to Diana Fumando, SAN Coordinator, ISBN/SAN Agency, R. R. Bowker Company, 121 Chanlon Rd., New Providence, NJ 07974, call 908-771-7755, or fax 908-665-2895. The e-mail address is ISBN-SAN@bowker.com. The SAN Web site is at http://www.bowker.com/standards/.

Distinguished Books

Best Books of 1997

This list for the general reader has been compiled by the Notable Books Council of the American Library Association's Reference and User Services Association (RUSA). Titles have been selected for their contribution to the expansion of knowledge and for the pleasure they can provide to adult readers.

Fiction

Alvarez, Julia. *Yo!* Algonquin (320 pp.) $18.95. ISBN 1-56512-157-0.

Atwood, Margaret. *Alias Grace*. Doubleday (484 pp.) $24.95. ISBN 0-385-47571-3.

Choy, Wayson. *The Jade Peony*. Picador USA (238 pp.) ISBN 0-312-15556-5.

Deane, Seamus. *Reading in the Dark.* Knopf (272 pp.) $23. ISBN 0-394-57440-0.

Frazier, Charles. *Cold Mountain*. Atlantic Monthly (368 pp.) $23. ISBN 0-87113-679-1.

Garcia, Cristina. *Aguero Sisters*. Knopf (288 pp.) $24. ISBN 0-679-45090-4.

Murakami, Haruki. *The Wind-Up Bird Chronicle*. Knopf (640 pp.) $25.95. ISBN 0-679-44669-9.

Perota, Tom. *The Wishbones*. Putnam (304 pp.) $21.95. ISBN 0-399-14267-3.

Smith, Lee. *News of the Spirit*. Putnam (256 pp.) $23.95. ISBN 0-399-14281-9.

Stollman, Aryeh Lev. *The Far Euphrates*. Riverhead/Putnam (224 pp.) $21.95. ISBN 1-57322-075-2.

Yamanaka, Lois-Ann. *Blu's Hanging*. Farrar, Straus & Giroux (288 pp.) $22. ISBN 0-374-11499-4.

Nonfiction

Alvarez, Walter. *T. Rex and the Crater of Doom*. Princeton Univ. (152 pp.) $24.95. ISBN 0-691-01630-5.

Bragg, Rick. *All Over But the Shoutin'*. Pantheon (352 pp.) $25. ISBN 0-679-44258-8.

Ehrenreich, Barbara. *Blood Rites: Origins & History of the Passions of War*. Metropolitan/Henry Holt (280 pp.) $25. ISBN 0-8050-5077-9.

Figes, Orlando. *A People's Tragedy: A History of the Russian Revolution*. Viking (894 pp.) $34.95. ISBN 0-670-85916-8.

Fouts, Roger, and Stephen Tukel Mills. *Next of Kin: What Chimpanzees Have Taught Me about Who We Are*. Morrow (432 pp.) $25. ISBN 0-688-14862-X.

Fraser, Kennedy. *Ornament and Silence: Essays on Women's Lives*. Knopf (288 pp.) $25. ISBN 0-394-58539-9.

Junger, Sebastian. *The Perfect Storm: A True Story of Men Against the Sea*. Norton (256 pp.) $25. ISBN 0-393-04016-X.

Krakauer, Jon. *Into Thin Air: A Personal Account of the Mt. Everest Disaster*. Villard (256 pp.) $24. ISBN 0-679-45752-6.

Maier, Pauline. *American Scripture: Making the Declaration of Independence*. Knopf (352 pp.) $27.50. ISBN 0-679-45492-6.

Raban, Jonathan. *Bad Land: An American Romance*. Pantheon (352 pp.) $25. ISBN 0-679-44254-5.

Solomon, Deborah. *Utopia Parkway: The Life and Work of Joseph Cornell*. Farrar (380 pp.) $30. ISBN 0-374-18012-1.

Winchester, Simon. *The River at the Center of the World: A Journey Up the Yangtze and Back in Chinese Time*. Holt (448 pp.) $27.50. ISBN 0-8050-3888-4.

Poetry

Lindsay, Sarah. *Primate Behavior.* Grove Atlantic $20. ISBN 0-8021-1619-1.

Piercy, Marge. *What Are Big Girls Made Of?* Knopf (160 pp.) $25. ISBN 0-679-45065-3; paper, $15 ISBN 0-679-76594-8.

Walcott, Derek. *The Bounty.* Farrar, Straus & Giroux (80 pp.) $18. ISBN 0-374-11556-7.

Best Young Adult Books

Each January a committee of the Young Adult Library Services Association (YALSA), a division of the American Library Association, compiles a list of best books published for young adults in the preceding 16 months, selected for their proven or potential appeal to the personal reading taste of the young adult.

Alexander, Lloyd. *Iron Ring.* Dutton.

Appelt, Kathi. *Just People & Paper/Pen/Poem.* Absey & Co.

Bartoletti, Susan Campbell. *Growing Up in Coal Country.* Houghton Mifflin.

Berg, Elizabeth. *Joy School.* Random.

Bernstein, Sara Tuvel. *Seamstress.* Putnam.

Bitton-Jackson, Livia. *I Have Lived a Thousand Years.* Simon & Schuster.

Bloor, Edward. *Tangerine.* Harcourt Brace.

Brooks, Martha. *Bone Dance.* Orchard.

Buck, Rinker. *Flight of Passage.* Hyperion.

Carroll, Joyce Armstrong, and Wilson, Edward E. *Poetry After Lunch: Poems to Read Aloud.* Absey & Co.

Carter, Alden R. *Bull Catcher.* Scholastic.

Chadwick, Douglas, and Sartore, Joel. *Company We Keep: America's Endangered Species.* National Geographic.

Chang, Pang-Mei Natasha. *Bound Feet and Western Dress.* Doubleday.

Cook, Karen. *What Girls Learn.* Pantheon.

Cooney, Caroline B. *What Child Is This? A Christmas Story.* Delacorte.

Corbett, Sara. *Venus to the Hoop.* Doubleday.

Cormier, Robert. *Tenderness.* Delacorte.

Creech, Sharon. *Chasing Redbird.* HarperCollins.

De Lint, Charles. *Trader.* Tor.

Del Cazo, Nick. *Triumphant Spirit.* Triumphant Spirit Publishing.

Deuker, Carl. *Painting the Black.* Houghton Mifflin.

Dorris, Michael. *Window.* Hyperion.

Draper, Sharon. *Forged by Fire.* Atheneum.

Dyer, Daniel. *Jack London: A Biography.* Scholastic.

Elders, Joycelyn, and Chanoff, David. *Joycelyn Elders, M.D.* Morrow.

Fleischman, Paul. *Seedfolks.* HarperCollins.

Fogle, Bruce. *Encyclopedia of the Cat.* DK Publishing.

Fradin, Dennis B. *Planet Hunters.* Simon & Schuster.

Gallo, Donald R., ed. *No Easy Answers: Short Stories about Teenagers Making Tough Choices.* Delacorte.

Giblin, James Cross. *Charles A. Lindbergh, A Human Hero.* Clarion.

Glenn, Mel. *Jump Ball: A Basketball Season in Poems.* Lodestar.

Glenn, Mel. *The Taking of Room 114.* Dutton.

Greenfield, Susan, ed. *Human Mind Explained.* Holt.

Griffin, Adele. *Sons of Liberty.* Hyperion.

Haddix, Margaret Peterson. *Leaving Fishers.* Simon & Schuster.

Hayes, Daniel. *Flyers.* Simon & Schuster.

Hesse, Karen. *Out of the Dust.* Scholastic.

Hogan, James P. *Bug Park.* Baen.

Howe, James. *Watcher.* Atheneum.

Jiang, Ji Li. *Red Scarf Girl: A Memoir of the Cultural Revolution.* HarperCollins.

Kelton, Elmer. *Cloudy in the West.* Tor/Forge.

Kerner, Elizabeth. *Song in the Silence.* Tor.

Kindl, Patrice. *The Woman in the Wall.* Houghton Mifflin.

Krisher, Trudy. *Kinship.* Delacorte.

Klause, Annette Curtis. *Blood and Chocolate.* Delacorte.

Krakauer, Jon. *Into Thin Air.* Villard.

Lantz, Frances. *Someone to Love.* Avon.

Lee, Marie G. *Necessary Roughness.* Harper-Collins.

Levenkron, Steven. *The Luckiest Girl in the World.* Scribner.

Levine, Gail. *Ella Enchanted.* HarperCollins.

McDonald, Joyce. *Swallowing Stones.* Delacorte.

McKinley, Robin. *Rose Daughter.* Greenwillow.

McLaren, Clemence. *Inside the Walls of Troy.* Atheneum.

Maxwell, Robin. *Secret Diary of Anne Boleyn.* Arcade.

Mazer, Anne, ed. *Working Days: Short Stories about Teenagers at Work.* Persea.

Mazer, Norma Fox. *When She Was Good.* Scholastic.

Meyer, Carolyn. *Jubilee Journey.* Harcourt Brace.

Myers, Walter Dean. *Harlem.* Scholastic.

Napoli, Donna Jo. *Stones in Water.* Dutton.

Nix, Garth. *Shade's Children.* HarperCollins.

Nolan, Han. *Dancing on the Edge.* Harcourt Brace.

Nye, Naomi Shihab. *Habibi.* Simon & Schuster.

Orr, Wendy. *Peeling the Onion.* Holiday.

Oughton, Jerrie. *War in Georgia.* Houghton Mifflin.

Paulsen, Gary. *Schernoff Discoveries.* Delacorte.

Penman, Sharon. *The Queen's Man.* Holt.

Philip, Neil. *In a Sacred Manner I Live: Native American Wisdom.* Clarion.

Pullman, Philip. *Subtle Knife.* Knopf.

Reynolds, Marjorie. *The Starlite Drive-In.* Morrow.

Naylor, Phyllis Reynolds. *Outrageously Alice.* Atheneum.

Rinaldi, Ann. *Acquaintance With Darkness.* Gulliver.

Rochman, Hazel, ed. *Leaving Home.* Harper-Collins.

Shoup, Barbara. *Stranded in Harmony.* Hyperion.

Shusterman, Neal. *The Dark Side of Nowhere.* Little, Brown.

Skurzynski, Gloria. *Virtual War.* Simon & Schuster.

Soto, Gary. *Buried Onions.* Harcourt Brace.

Steger, Will. *Over the Top of the World: Explorer Will Steger's Trek Across the Arctic.* Scholastic.

Sullivan, Charles, ed. *Imaginary Animals.* Harry N. Abrams.

Tate, Sonsyrea. *Little X.* Harper.

Thomas, Rob. *Doing Time: Notes from the Undergrad.* Simon & Schuster.

Tillage, Leon Walter. *Leon's Story.* Farrar, Straus & Giroux.

Wersba, Barbara. *Whistle Me Home.* Holt.

Williams, Carol Lynch. *True Colors of Caitlynne Jackson.* Delacorte.

Yee, Paul. *Breakaway.* Groundwood Books.

Notable Children's Films and Videos

This list of notable children's films and videos has been released by the Association of Library Service to Children (ALSC), a division of the American Library Association. Recommended titles are selected by children's librarians and educators on the basis of their originality, creativity, and suitability.

Get to Know Gerald McDermott. 21 min. Produced and distributed by Harcourt Brace Trade Division. $40.

Officer Buckle and Gloria. 11 min. Produced by Weston Woods, distributed by Scholastic. $60.

Take Joy! The Magical World of Tasha Tudor. 47 min. Produced by Weston Woods, distributed by Scholastic. $30.

A Visit With Tomie dePaola. 25 min. Produced by Red Eft Productions, distributed by Putnam & Grosset Group. $39.95.

Willa: An American Snow White. 88 min. Produced by Tom Davenport, distributed by Davenport Films. $39.95.

Best Children's Books

A list of notable children's books is selected each year by the Notable Children's Books Committee of the Association for Library Service to Children (ALSC), a division of the American Library Association. Recommended titles are selected by children's librarians and educators based on originality, creativity, and suitability for children. [See "Literary Prizes, 1997" later in Part 5 for Caldecott, Newbery, and other award winners—*Ed.*]

Picture Books

Cowan, Catherine, translator and adaptor. *My Life with the Wave*. Based on the story by Octavio Paz. Illus. by Mark Buehner. Lothrop, Lee & Shepard.

Davol, Marguerite W. *The Paper Dragon*. Illus. by Robert Sabuda. Atheneum.

Diakit. *The Hunterman and the Crocodile: A West African Folktale*. Scholastic.

Fleming, Candace. *Gabriella's Song*. Illus. by Giselle Potter. Atheneum/Anne Schwartz.

Lasky, Kathryn. *Marven of the Great North Woods*. Illus. by Kevin Hawkes. Harcourt Brace.

Lee, Milly. *Nim and the War Effort*. Illus. by Yangsook Choi. Farrar, Straus & Giroux/Frances Foster.

Melmed, Laura Krauss. *Little Oh*. Illus. by Jim LaMarche. Lothrop, Lee & Shepard Books.

Miranda, Anne. *To Market, To Market*. Illus. by Janet Stevens. Harcourt Brace.

Raschka, Chris. *Mysterious Thelonious*. Orchard Books.

Stanley, Diane. *Rumpelstiltskin's Daughter*. Morrow Junior Books.

Stewart, Sarah. *The Gardener*. Illus. by David Small. Farrar, Straus & Giroux.

Taback, Simms. *There Was an Old Lady Who Swallowed a Fly*. Viking.

Tunnell, Michael O. *Mailing May*. Illus. by Ted Rand. Greenwillow/Tambourine.

Voake, Charlotte. *Ginger*. Candlewick Press.

Fiction

Alexander, Lloyd. *The Iron Ring*. Dutton.

Fine, Anne. *The Tulip Touch*. Little, Brown.

Giff, Patricia Reilly. *Lily's Crossing*. Delacorte Press.

Henkes, Kevin. *Sun & Spoon*. Greenwillow.

Hesse, Karen. *Out of the Dust*. Scholastic Press.

Holub, Josef. *The Robber and Me*. Trans. by Elizabeth D. Crawford. Henry Holt.

Levine, Gail Carson. *Ella Enchanted*. HarperCollins.

Napoli, Donna Jo. *Stones in Water*. Dutton.

Nye, Naomi Shihab. *Habibi*. Simon & Schuster.

Spinelli, Jerry. *Wringer*. HarperCollins/Joanna Cotler Books.

Nonfiction

Adler, David A. *Lou Gehrig: The Luckiest Man*. Illus. by Terry Widener. Harcourt Brace/Gulliver Books.

Burleigh, Robert. *Hoops*. Illus. by Stephen T. Johnson. Harcourt Brace/Silver Whistle.

Giblin, James Cross. *Charles A. Lindbergh: A Human Hero*. Clarion.

Janisch, Heinz, adaptor. *Noah's Ark*. Illus. by Lisbeth Zwerger. North-South Books.

Jiang, Ji-Li. *Red Scarf Girl: A Memoir of the Cultural Revolution*. HarperCollins.

Lelooska, Chief. *Echoes of the Elders*. DK Ink.

Manna, Anthony L. and Mitakidou, Christodoula, retellers. *Mr. Semolina-Semolinus: A Greek Folktale*. Illus. by Giselle Potter. Atheneum.

Mochizuki, Ken. *Passage to Freedom: The Sugihara Story*. Illus. by Dom Lee. Lee & Low.

Myers, Walter Dean. *Harlem*. Illus. by Christopher Myers. Scholastic Press.

Prelutsky, Jack, selector. *The Beauty of the Beast: Poems from the Animal Kingdom*. Illus. by Mielo So. Knopf.

Pringle, Laurence. *An Extraordinary Life: The Story of a Monarch Butterfly*. Illus. by Bob Marstall. Orchard Books.

Shepard, Aaron, reteller. *The Sea King's Daughter: A Russian Legend.* Illus. by Gennady Spirin. Atheneum.

Simms, Laura. *The Bone Man: A Native American Modoc Tale.* Illus. by Michael McCurdy. Hyperion.

Steptoe, Javaka, illustrator. *In Daddy's Arms I Am Tall: African Americans Celebrating Fathers.* Lee & Low.

Szabo, Corinne. *Sky Pioneer: A Photobiography of Ameila Earhart.* National Geographic Society.

Tillage, Leon Walter. *Leon's Story.* Illus. by Susan L. Roth. Farrar, Straus & Giroux.

Wick, Walter. *A Drop of Water: A Book of Science and Wonder.* Scholastic Press.

Zelinsky, Paul O. *Rapunzel.* Dutton.

Notable Recordings for Children

This list of notable recordings for children has been released by the Association for Library Service to Children (ALSC), a division of the American Library Association. Recommended titles, many of which are recorded books, are chosen by children's librarians and educators on the basis of their originality, creativity, and suitability. Selections are cassettes unless otherwise indicated.

"All Aboard." Sony Wonder. 40 min. $9.98. CD, $13.98.

"Are You There, God? It's Me, Margaret." Listening Library. 3 hr. 9 min. $16.98.

"Ballad of Lucy Whipple." Recorded Books. 4 hr. 45 min. $34.

"Battle for the Castle." Listening Library. 4 hr. 33 min. $23.98.

"Boggart and the Monster." Listening Library. 4 hr. 43 min. $23.98.

"Charlie Daniels: By the Light of the Moon—Campfire Songs and Cowboy Tunes." Sony Wonder. 40 min. $9.98. CD, $13.98.

"Chuck and Danielle." Listening Library. 1 hr. 56 min. $16.98.

"Coconut Moon." Performed by the Green Chili Jam Band. Squeaky Wheel Productions. 44 min. $14.98.

"Crash." Recorded Books. 4 hr. $26.

"Giving Thanks." Weston Woods. Book/cassette, $24.95.

"The Great Gilly Hopkins." Recorded Books. 4 hr. 45 min. $34.

"Harlem." Spoken Arts. 8 min. Book/cassette, $27.90.

"Harriet and the Promised Land." Spoken Arts. 7 min. Book/cassette, $16.95.

"The House at Pooh Corner." Performed by Charles Kuralt. Penguin Audiobooks. 3 hours. $16.95.

"Lily's Crossing." Recorded Books. 4 hr. 25 min. $26.

"Mick Harte Was Here." Listening Library. 1 hr. 42 min. $16.98.

"Now I Lay Me Down to Sleep: Lullabies for All Ages." Performed by Kevin Roth. Star Gazer Productions. 42 minutes. $11.98, CD $15.98.

"Officer Buckle and Gloria." Performed by John Lithgow. Weston Woods. Book/cassette, $24.95.

"Rainbow Tales, Too." Various performers. Rounder Records. 74 min. $9.98, CD $14.98.

"Redwall." Performed by Brian Jacques. Listening Library, Inc. $64.98.

"Shadow of a Bull." Performed by Francisco Rivela. Listening Library, Inc. 3 hr. 34 min. $16.98.

"Shakin' a Tailfeather." Performed by Taj Mahal, Linda Tillery and the Cultural Heritage Choir, and Eric Bibb. Music for Little People. 42 min. $9.98, CD $15.98.

"Skull of Truth." Performed by Bruce Coville and the Words Take Wing Repertory Company. Listening Library, Inc. 3 hr. 50 min. $23.98.

"Sun Upon the Lake Is Low." Performed by Mae Robertson and Don Jackson. Lyric Partners. 58 minutes. $10, CD $15.

"This Land Is Your Land." Performed by Woody Guthrie and Arlo Guthrie. Rounder Records. 38 min. $9.98, CD $14.98.

"The View from Saturday." Listening Library, Inc. 4 hr. 47 min. $23.98.

"We Can Do." Performed by Jim Newton and Noel Paul Stookey. Celebration Shop, Inc. 42 minutes. $10, CD $14.

"Winnie-the-Pooh." Performed by Charles Kuralt. Penguin Audiobooks. 3 hours. $16.95.

"Zeely." Performed by Lynne Thigpen. Recorded Books, Inc. 3 hours. $26.

Notable Children's Software and Web Sites

These lists of children's computer software and Web sites are chosen by committees of the Association for Library Service to Children (ALSC), a division of the American Library Association.

Software

The American Girls Premiere. The Learning Company. Windows/Mac. $34.99.

Cat in the Hat. Broderbund. Windows/Mac. $34.95.

The Digital Field Trip to the Rainforest. Digital Frog International. Windows/Mac. $49; educational version $99.

My Amazing Human Body. DK Multimedia. Windows/Mac. $29.95.

Piano Discovery for Kids. Jump! Music. Windows/Mac. $49.95.

Web Sites

Amazing Travel Bureau (National Geographic), http://www.nationalgeographic.com/features/97/bureau/.

Arthur Page, http://www.pbs.org/wgbh/pages/arthur/

CyberJacques, http://www.cyberjacques.com/.

Dav Pilkey's Web Site o' Fun, http://www.pilkey.com/.

Jan Brett's Home Page, http://www.janbrett.com.

KIDLINK, http://www.kidlink.org.

Kids' Space, http://www.ks-connection.com.

Learner Online Exhibits Collection, http://www.learner.org/exhibits/.

Little Explorers, http://www.EnchantedLearning.com/Dictionary.html.

Nine Planets: an Interactive Tour of the Solar System, http://seds.lpl.arizona.edu/nineplanets/nineplanets/nineplanets.html.

Sesame Street Central, http://www.ctw.org/sscentral/.

Theodore Tugboat, http://www.cochran.com/theodore/.

Virtual Renaissance: A Journey Through Time, http://www.twingroves.district96.k12.il.us/Renaissance/VirtualRen.html.

Quick Picks for Reluctant Young Adult Readers

The Young Adult Library Service Association (YALSA), a division of the American Library Association, selects these titles as suitable for reluctant young adult readers.

Nonfiction

Aaseng, Nathan. *Poisonous Creatures* (Scientific American Sourcebooks). Illus. Twenty-First Century. $18.98. ISBN 0-8050-4690-9.

Adoff, Arnold, ed. *I Am the Darker Brother: An Anthology of Modern Poems by African Americans*. Rev. ed. Simon & Schuster. $16. ISBN 0-689-81241-8.

Blum, Mark. *Beneath the Sea in 3-D*. Illus. Chronicle. $18.95. ISBN 0-8118-1412-2.

Branzei, Sylvia. *Grossology Begins at Home: The Science of Really Gross Things in Your Everyday Life*. Illus. Addison Wesley Longman/Planet Dexter. $12.99 ISBN 0-201-95993 3.

Canfield, Jack, Hansen, Mark, and Kirberger, Kimberly. *Chicken Soup for the Teenage Soul: 101 Stories of Life, Love and Learning*. Health Communications. $24. ISBN 1-5587-44681.

Coville, Bruce. *William Shakespeare's Macbeth*. Illus. Penguin/Dial. $16.99. ISBN 0-8037-1899-3.

Fletcher, Ralph. *Ordinary Things: Poems From a Walk in Early Spring*. Illus. Atheneum. $15. ISBN 0-689 81035-0.

Fogle, Bruce. *Dachshund* (Dog breed handbooks). Illus. Dorling Kindersley. $14.95. ISBN 0-7894-1613-1.

Fogle, Bruce. *Poodle* (Dog breed handbooks). Illus. Dorling Kindersley. $14.95. ISBN 0-7894-1612-3.

Fogle, Bruce. *The Encyclopedia of the Cat*. Illus. Dorling Kindersley. $34.95. ISBN 0-7894-1970-X.

Gates, Phil. *Medicine*. Illus. Candlewick. $15.99. ISBN 0-7636-0316-3.

Glenn, Mel. *Jump Ball: A Basketball Season in Poems*. Dutton/Lodestar. $15.99. ISBN 0-525-67554-X.

Glenn, Mel. *The Taking of Room 114: A Hostage Drama in Poems*. Dutton/Lodestar. $16.99. ISBN 0-525-67548-5.

Greenfield, Lauren. *Fast Forward: Growing Up in the Shadow of Hollywood*. Illus. Knopf. $35. ISBN 0-679-45453-5.

Hampton, Wilborn. *Kennedy Assassinated! The World Mourns: A Reporter's Story*. Illus. Candlewick. $17.99. ISBN 1-56402-811-9.

Hirsch, Karen D. *Mind Riot: Coming of Age in Comix*. Illus. Simon & Schuster/Aladdin. $9.99. ISBN 0-689-80622-1.

Janulewicz, Mike. *Yikes! Your Body up Close!* Illus. Simon & Schuster. $15. ISBN 0-689-81520-4.

King, Martin Luther. *I Have a Dream*. Illus. Scholastic. $16.95. ISBN 0-590-20516-1.

Kleinbaum, Nancy H. *The Magnificent Seven: The Authorized Story of American Gold*. 1996. Illus. Bantam. $19.95. ISBN 0-553-09774-1.

Kramer, Stephen. *Eye of the Storm: Chasing Storms with Warren Faidley*. Illus. Putnam. $18.95. ISBN 0-399-23029-7.

Kwan, Michelle (told to Laura James). *Michelle Kwan: Heart of a Champion*. Illus. Scholastic. $14.95. ISBN 0-590-76340-7.

Marschall, Ken. *Inside the Titanic*. Illus. Little, Brown. $18.95. ISBN 0-316-5716-1.

Morgan, Rowland. *In the Next Three Seconds*. Illus. Dutton/Lodestar. $13.99. ISBN 0-525-67551-5.

Myers, Walter Dean. *Harlem*. Illus. Scholastic. $16.95. ISBN 0-590-54340-7.

O'Grady, Scott. *Basher Five-Two: The True Story of F-16 Fighter Pilot Captain Scott O'Grady*. Illus. Doubleday. $16.95. ISBN 0-385-32300-X.

Peters, Mike. *Grimmy: King of the Heap!* Illus. Tor. $10.95. ISBN 0-312-86069-3.

Platt, Richard. *Stephen Biesty's Incredible Everything*. Illus. Dorling Kindersley. $19.95. ISBN 0-7894-2049-X.

Polk, Milbry. *Egyptian Mummies: A Pop-Up Book*. Illus. Penguin/Dutton. $16.99. ISBN 0-525-45839-5.

Rees, Dafydd. *Encyclopedia of Rock Stars.* Dorling Kindersley. $29.95. ISBN 0-7894-1263-2.

Richards, Joy. *The Fantastic Cutaway Book of Speed.* Illus. Millbrook/Copper Beech. $23.90. ISBN 0-7613-0554-8.

Schroeder, Russell. *Mickey Mouse: My Life in Pictures.* Illus. Disney. $14.95. ISBN 0-7868-3150-2.

Stine, R. L. *It Came From Ohio: My Life as a Writer.* Illus. Scholastic. $9.95. ISBN 0-590-36674-2.

Tanaka, Shelley. *Discovering the Iceman.* Illus. Disney/Hyperion. $16.95. ISBN 0-7868-0284-7.

Thomas, Velma Maia. *Lest We Forget: The Passage From Africa to Slavery and Emancipation.* Illus. Crown. $29.95. ISBN 0-609-60030-3.

Willson, Quentin. *Classic American Cars.* Illus. Dorling Kindersley. $29.95. ISBN 0-7894-2083-X.

Fiction

Alten, Steve. *Meg: A Novel of Deep Terror.* Doubleday. $22.95. ISBN 0-385-48905-6.

Anderson, M. T. *Thirsty.* Candlewick. $17.99. ISBN 0-7636-0048-2.

Carter, Alden. *Bull Catcher.* Scholastic. $15.95. ISBN 0-590-50958-6.

Cole, Brock. *The Facts Speak for Themselves.* Front Street. $15.95. ISBN 1-886910-14-6.

Cooney, Caroline. *The Terrorist.* Scholastic. $15. ISBN 0-590-22853-6.

Cooney, Caroline. *Wanted!* Scholastic. $4.50. ISBN 0-590-88849-2.

Cusick, Richie Tankersley. *The Harvest* (Buffy the Teenage Vampire Slayer). Archway/Pocket. $3.99. ISBN 0-671-01712-8.

Draper, Sharon M. *Forged by Fire.* Atheneum. $16. ISBN 0-689-80699-X.

Duncan, Lois. *Gallows Hill.* Delacorte. $15.95. ISBN 0-385-32331-X.

Fleischman, Paul. *Seed Folks.* HarperCollins. $13.95. ISBN 0-06-027471-9.

Gallo, Donald, ed. *No Easy Answers: Short Stories About Teenagers Making Tough Choices.* Delacorte. $16.95. ISBN 0-385-32290-9.

Giberga, Jane Sughrue. *Friends to Die For.* Dial. $15.99. ISBN 0-8037-2094-7.

Hogan, James P. *Bug Park.* Baen. $22. ISBN 0-671-87773-9.

Jenkins, A. M. *Breaking Boxes.* Delacorte. $14.95. ISBN 0-385-32513-4.

Klause, Annette Curtis. *Blood and Chocolate.* Delacorte. $16.95. ISBN 0-385-32305-0.

Levine, Gail Carson. *Ella Enchanted.* HarperCollins. $14.95. ISBN 0-06-027510-3.

Mazer, Harry, ed. *Twelve Shots: Outstanding Stories About Guns.* Delacorte. $15.95. ISBN 0-385-32238-0.

Morris, Winifred. *Liar.* Walker. $15.95. ISBN 0-8234-1289-X.

Paulsen, Gary. *Sarny: A Life Remembered.* Delacorte. $15.95. ISBN 0-385-32195-3.

Paulsen, Gary. *The Schernoff Discoveries.* Delacorte. $15.95. ISBN 0-385-32194-5.

Petersen, P. J. *White Water.* Simon & Schuster. $15. ISBN 0-689-80644-7.

Qualey, Marsha. *Thin Ice.* Delacorte. $14.95. ISBN 0-385-32298-4.

Rochman, Hazel and McCampbell, Darlene Z. *Leaving Home.* HarperCollins. $16.95. ISBN 0-06-024873-4.

Shusterman, Neal. *The Dark Side of Nowhere.* Little, Brown. $15.95. ISBN 0-316-78907-0.

Skurzynski, Gloria. *Virtual War.* Simon & Schuster. $16. ISBN 0-689-81374-0.

Sleator, William. *The Beasties.* Penguin/Dutton. $15.99. ISBN 0-525-45598-1).

Soto, Gary. *Buried Onions.* Harcourt Brace. $17. ISBN 0-15-201333-4.

Stoker, Bram. *Dracula* (Eyewitness classics). Illus. Dorling Kindersley. $14.95. ISBN 0-7894-1489-9.

Thomas, Rob. *Doing Time: Notes from the Undergrad.* Simon & Schuster. $16. ISBN 0-689-80958-1.

Vande Velde, Vivian. *Curses, Inc. and Other Stories.* Harcourt Brace. $16. ISBN 0-15-201452-7.

Wersba, Barbara. *Whistle Me Home.* Henry Holt. $14.95. ISBN 0-8050-4850-2.

Williams, Carol Lynch. *The True Colors of Caitlynne Jackson.* Delacorte. $14.95. ISBN 0-385-32249-6.

Bestsellers of 1997

Hardcover Bestsellers: Jockeying for Position

Daisy Maryles
Executive Editor, *Publishers Weekly*

After 25 years of writing this annual feature, it's getting harder and harder to find a fresh lead. For the past 15 years, and especially throughout the 1990s, the best-seller news has always been the same: more books selling over the 100,000 mark and most of those (particularly those in the higher slots) by veteran novelists or, in the case of nonfiction, by well-known names or *about* well-known names.

Last year was the first time that the number of novels that sold more than 100,000 copies hit three figures—there were 100, to be exact. The previous record, in both 1995 and 1996, was 93 fiction titles. A new record was also set for nonfiction, with 128 books exceeding the 100,000 mark, handily breaking the record of 109, set in 1996.

And an author had to have appeared on these annual lists over and over again to score among the top 15 fiction. John Grisham was at the top *again*; three books by Danielle Steel sold over the million mark; there were two high rollers by Patricia Cornwell; and more by some of the other familiar names—Sidney Sheldon, Mary Higgins Clark, Robert Ludlum, Nelson DeMille, etc. One especially bright note last year was a stellar first novel, *Cold Mountain*, that garnered rave reviews and some impressive literary awards. Charles Frazier's work began with a modest first printing of 25,000 copies and by end of the year had shipped and billed more than 1.4 million copies. It's still high on the charts (38 weeks at this writing) and is one of the titles that was embraced by both independent booksellers and major chains early on. And even more notable, considering the hold the major publishers have on national bestsellers, was the fact that it came from Grove/Atlantic and was distributed by PGW, a company that began its successful life dedicated to getting books by independent presses into retail outlets of all sizes.

In nonfiction, too, the subjects of the top sellers rang familiar notes. Six of 1997's top 15 sellers had been on our lists before. It was John Gray's fourth appearance; total sales for *Men Are from Mars, Women Are from Venus* are close to the 6.7-million mark. Sarah Ban Breathnach's *Simple Abundance* marks its third appearance on these year-end charts; Warner sold the three-millionth copy last month. *Midnight in the Garden of Good and Evil* had its highest annual sale in its third year in the marketplace. The first major overhaul of one of the best-selling classic cookbooks, *Joy of Cooking*, also attained a high ranking on the 1997 annual chart. Scribner spent more than $5 million on all the revisions, but with about $1 million in sales in 1997 alone the expenditure seems to have been well worth it. With books like these regularly occupying the top spots on the weekly charts, it's easy to see why having a longer run was harder for some new-comers.

Adapted from *Publishers Weekly*, March 23, 1998

Publishers Weekly 1997 Bestsellers

FICTION

1. **The Partner** by John Grisham. Doubleday (3/97) **2,625,000
2. **Cold Mountain** by Charles Frazier. Atlantic Monthly (6/97) 1,458,280
3. **The Ghost** by Danielle Steel. Delacorte (12/97) 1,161,121
4. **The Ranch** by Danielle Steel. Delacorte (5/97) 1,158,631
5. **Special Delivery** by Danielle Steel. Delacorte (7/97) 1,152,937
6. **Unnatural Exposure** by Patricia Cornwell. Putnam (7/97) 869,682
7. **The Best Laid Plans** by Sidney Sheldon. Morrow (9/97) 730,755
8. **Pretend You Don't See Her** by Mary Higgins Clark. Simon & Schuster (4/97) **725,000
9. **Cat & Mouse** by James Patterson. Little, Brown (11/97) 701,237
10. **Hornet's Nest** by Patricia Cornwell. Putnam (1/97) 636,400
11. **The Letter** by Richard Paul Evans. Simon & Schuster (10/97) **575,000
12. **Flood Tide** by Clive Cussler. Simon & Schuster (9/97) **550,000
13. **Violin** by Anne Rice. Knopf (10/97) 501,702
14. **The Matarese Countdown** by Robert Ludlum. Bantam (11/97) **500,000
15. **Plum Island** by Nelson DeMille. Warner (5/97) 474,848

NONFICTION

1. **Angela's Ashes** by Frank McCourt. Scribner (9/96) *1,650,000
2. **Simple Abundance** by Sarah Ban Breathnach. Warner (11/95) *1,462,663
3. **Midnight in the Garden of Good and Evil** by John Berendt. Random House (1/94) *1,300,799
4. **The Royals** by Kitty Kelley. Warner (9/97) 1,120,943
5. **Joy of Cooking** by Irma S. Rombauer, Marion Rombauer Becker, and Ethan Becker. Scribner (11/97) 1,000,000
6. **Diana: Her True Story** by Andrew Morton. Simon & Schuster (10/97) **825,000
7. **Into Thin Air** by Jon Krakauer. Villard (5/97) 784,969
8. **Conversations with God, Book I** by Neale Donald Walsch. Putnam (10/96) *749,001
9. **Men Are from Mars. . .** by John Gray. HarperCollins (4/93) *687,267
10. **Eight Weeks to Optimum Health** by Andrew Weil. Knopf (3/97) 674,117
11. **Just As I Am** by Billy Graham. Harper San Francisco/Zondervan (4/97) 647,008
12. **The Man Who Listens to Horses** by Monty Roberts. Random House (8/97) 593,165
13. **The Millionaire Next Door** by Thomas J. Stanley and William D. Danko. Longstreet (10/96) *585,924
14. **The Perfect Storm** by Sebastian Junger. Norton (5/97) **550,000
15. **Kids Are Punny** by Rosie O'Donnell. Warner (4/97) 558,880

Note: Rankings are determined by sales figures provided by publishers; the numbers generally reflect reports of copies "shipped and billed" in calendar year 1997 and publishers were instructed to adjust sales figures to include returns through Feb. 10, 1998. Publishers did not at that time know what their total returns would be—indeed, the majority of returns occur after that cut-off date—so none of these figures should be regarded as final net sales. (Dates in parentheses indicate month and year of publication.)

*Sales figures reflect books sold only in calendar year 1997.

**Sales figures were submitted to PW in confidence, for use in placing titles on the lists. Numbers shown are rounded down to the nearest 25,000 to indicate relationship to sales figures of other titles.

Most of the other books on the year-end list also have a familiar feel. The untimely death of Princess Diana at the end of the summer proved to be a boon for many titles, especially for two biographies that made it onto the top 15—Kitty Kelley and Andrew Morton's warts-and-all books on the Royal Family and on Diana, respectively. And the increasing influence of matters both spiritual and religious was evident in the success of *Conversations with God, Book 1*, with a total of 57 weeks on the weekly charts so far, and Billy Graham's biography, *Just As I Am*, a strong bestseller in both the general and Christian markets.

There was one unlikely bestseller among the top 15: *The Man Who Listens to Horses* by Monty Roberts, a real-life "horse whisperer" who performed dozens and dozens of live demonstrations of his special techniques for gentling horses as he toured the country.

So, What's News?

But while the "big numbers" picture seems to remain the same and the kinds of books don't change much, there are some subtle changes in the 1997 figures that point to the beginning of shifts in these year-end wrap-ups. A few of these shifts are more obvious in fiction, where those seven additional titles that sold more than 100,000 copies were among the lower rankings—titles in the 100,000–150,000 range. In the top 15 fiction books for 1997, No. 15 sold well under 500,000 copies—the lowest sales figure since 1992 for that position. In nonfiction, the bestseller growth seems to be in the 200,000–350,000 range. Also, there seems to be a reversal of a trend that began in this decade, when fiction sales outpaced nonfiction. The 1997 nonfiction bestsellers wound up at a higher level than fiction for the first time in five years; 40 titles had sales of 300,000 or more, compared with 27 on the fiction side. And there is another trend that is appearing more often in nonfiction than in fiction, and that is the number of books with reported sales of 100,000+ that didn't land even once on *Publishers Weekly*'s weekly charts. In 1997, the nonfiction figure was 60, compared with 39 for 1996 and 30 for 1995; last year's fiction tally was 25, compared with 18 for 1996 and 13 for 1995.

Despite the fact that none of the figures offered here are final net sales and that, in many cases, the bulk of returns are still to come, there are still a few harbingers of change:

- A trend toward keeping a tighter rein on printings is beginning to emerge, especially in hardcover fiction. Evidently, this is a response to the huge returns of recent years. And yes, the blockbuster books by the likes of Grisham, Steel, Cornwell, Sheldon, and Clark (there were no hardcover Kings or Clancys last year) continue to sell in significant numbers, with only a few exhibiting a slight fall-off. The fact that the top 30 bestselling novels of 1997 bottomed out at around 275,000, the lowest in three years, also points to publishers' more careful watch over bestselling inventory.

- Trying to get a fiction title on the weekly bestseller lists continues to be a very difficult business, and the number of wannabes that don't make it continues to increase. Of the 100 top-selling fiction titles, only four of the first 50 did not land on our weekly charts; 21 of the bottom half are still waiting for a turn on the list. Eleven of the 21 novels with sales of less than 125,000 were no-shows. Clearly, returns on those titles will be heavier than for the 10 that made it to the weekly charts for one to 15 weeks.

- The high number of nonfiction books with nary a week on the weekly charts may reflect a serious level of returns. In fact, the majority of these books were those with reported sales of 225,000 or less—a hefty 55 of the total 60 that haven't yet made it onto a *PW* bestseller list. But this figure may also be a strong indicator of the increasing numbers of books selling in nontraditional outlets, e.g., specialty stores and discount chains like Kmart and Target, and perhaps even cyberstore sales.

The Usual Disclaimer

As in previous years, all our calculations are based on shipped-and-billed figures supplied by publishers for new books issued in 1997 and 1996 (a few books published earlier that continued their tenure on this year's bestseller charts are also included). These figures reflect only 1997 domestic trade sales; publishers were specifically instructed not to include book-club and overseas transactions. And this year we asked publishers to take into account returns through February 10. All sales figures in these pages should not be considered final net sales. For many of the books, especially those published in the latter half of 1997, returns are still to be calculated.

The Fiction Runners-Up

The fiction runners-up, too, are a familiar batch, with lots of repeat performers who often land in the 16–30 range. Most of the books enjoyed at least a one- to two-month tenure on *PW*'s weekly charts, with Caleb Carr, Sandra Brown, and Don DeLillo making it to three months. The longest run—54 weeks over two years—was Nicholas Sparks's *The Notebook*; combined 1996 and 1997 sales totaled more than 800,000. LaVyrle Spencer has two books, although the majority of sales for *Then Came Heaven* were in the first month of this year. Spencer's fans will have to switch their allegiance to another author, for, after writing 23 successful books, she announced her retirement and plans to spend her free time with family. It's also the swan song for Jonathan Kellerman at Bantam; his 13th novel, *Survival of the Fittest*, had the highest shipped-and-billed figures of any previous Kellerman title. (It will be interesting to see if Random House, which paid him between $20 and $24 million for a five-book deal, will be able to land him among the top 15 on these annual lists.) As for David Baldacci, his latest book, *The Winner*, was his strongest in terms of sales; for Dean Koontz, his almost-300,000-copy sale for *Sole Survivor* fell well short of his 1994 high—more than 600,000 copies for *Dark Rivers of the Heart*.

16. *The Winner* by David Baldacci (Warner, 433,648)
17. *Then Came Heaven* by LaVyrle Spencer (Putnam, 349,671)

18. *The Angel of Darkness* by Caleb Carr (Random House, 348,335)
19. *Fat Tuesday* by Sandra Brown (Warner, 339,089)
20. *Small Town Girl* by LaVyrle Spencer (Putnam, 331,550)
21. *Survival of the Fittest* by Jonathan Kellerman (Bantam)
22. *This Year It Will Be Different* by Maeve Binchy (Delacorte, 324,708)
23. *Another City, Not My Own* by Dominick Dunne (Crown, 313,367)
24. *Come the Spring* by Julie Garwood (Pocket)
25. *Chromosome 6* by Robin Cook (Putnam, 311,281)
26. *Comanche Moon* by Larry McMurtry (Simon & Schuster)
27. *The Notebook* by Nicholas Sparks (Warner, 300,597 in 1997; 512,254 in 1996)
28. *Sole Survivor* by Dean Koontz (Knopf, 299,615)
29. *Underworld* by Don DeLillo (Scribner, 290,000)
30. *10 Lb. Penalty* by Dick Francis (Putnam, 275,794)

21 More 200,000+ Titles

The first eight books in this group shipped and billed more than 225,000 copies last year, an impressive number. While most of the books enjoyed a bestseller run of at least a month, a handful—*3001*, *Evening Class* and *The God of Small Things*—stayed on for considerably longer. The last-named title, one of the more successful fiction debuts of the year, is still on *PW*'s charts and has amassed a total of 32 weeks. On the other hand, three books in this group—*All I Need Is You*, *Tidings of Great Joy* and *Homecoming*—have never made it to *PW*'s lists.

In ranked order, the 21 novels with sales of more than 200,000 copies are: *Sanctuary* by Nora Roberts (Putnam), *Night Crew* by John Sandford (Putnam), *The List* by Steve Martini (Putnam), *3001: The Final Odyssey* by Arthur C. Clarke (Del Rey), *Wobegon Boy* by Garrison Keillor (Viking), *All I Need Is You* by Johanna Lindsey (Avon), *Silent Witness* by Richard North Patterson (Knopf), *Evening Class* by Maeve Binchy (Delacorte), *The God of Small Things* by Arundhati Roy (Random), *Tidings of Great Joy* by Sandra Brown (Bantam), *The President's Daughter* by Jack Higgins (Putnam), *McNally's Gamble* by Lawrence Sanders (Putnam), *Deja Dead* by Kathy Reichs (Scribner), *The Clinic* by Jonathan Kellerman (Bantam), *Drums of Autumn* by Diana Gabaldon (Delacorte), *The Maze* by Catherine Coulter (Putnam), *Homecoming* by Belva Plain (Delacorte), *The Cobra Event* by Richard Preston (Random), *Lucky You* by Carl Hiaasen (Knopf), *Timequake* by Kurt Vonnegut (Putnam), and *The Cat Who Tailed a Thief* by Lilian Jackson Braun (Putnam).

At the 150,000+ Level

There were 13 works of fiction with sales of 150,000+ that did not make it onto the year's top 30, two fewer than on the 1996 year-end list. In this group, the longest-running bestseller was *London*, with 19 weeks on our weekly charts, followed by *The Tenth Justice*, with 10 weeks. Books by Griffin, Travolta, Kleier, Plain, Zahn, and the Pocket romance collection did not hit our lists.

In ranked order, books with sales of 150,000+ copies are: *London* by Edward Rutherfurd (Crown), *The Last Heroes* by W. E. B. Griffin (Putnam), *A Certain Justice* by P. D. James (Knopf), *The Tenth Justice* by Brad Meltzer (Morrow/Rob Weisbach), *If This World Were Mine* by E. Lynn Harris (Doubleday), *Propeller One-Way Night Coach* by John Travolta (Warner), *The Last Day* by Glenn Kleier (Warner), *Serpent's Tooth* by Faye Kellerman (Morrow), *Secrecy* by Belva Plain (Delacorte), *Apaches* by Lorenzo Carcaterra (Ballantine), *Upon a Midnight Clear* by Stef Ann Holm, Jude Deveraux, Linda Howard, Margaret Allison, and Mariah Stewart (Pocket), *A Thin Dark Line* by Tami Hoag (Bantam), and *Star Wars: Specter of the Past* by Timothy Zahn (Bantam).

The 125,000+ Group

There were 15 books with reported sales of 125,000 copies or more that did not make our top-30 chart, four more than in 1996. All but three had a brief run on the weekly lists or the monthly religion list. Robert Parker landed two books in this group.

Out of the 12 that made the charts, two titles tied for the longest-runner, seven weeks each—*Small Vices* by Robert Parker (Putnam) and *Deception on His Mind* by Elizabeth George (Bantam). Other titles with appearances on weekly charts are: *Out to Canaan* by Jan Karon (Viking), *Night Passage* by Robert Parker (Putnam), *End of the Drive* by Louis L'Amour (Bantam), *Polgara the Sorceress* by David and Leigh Eddings (Del Rey), *Touched by an Angel: A Christmas Miracle* by Martha Williamson (Thomas Nelson), *Temple of the Winds* by Terry Goodkind (Tor), *Star Trek: Avenger* by William Shatner (Pocket), *Cosmic Christmas* by Max Lucado (Word), *Deep Waters* by Jayne Ann Krentz (Pocket), and *Affair* by Amanda Quick (Bantam).

The three that did not make an appearance on the weekly lists are: *Fatal Terrain* by Dale Brown (Putnam), *Amber Beach* by Elizabeth Lowell (Avon), and *The Presence* by John Saul (Fawcett).

Fiction's 100,000+ Group

Last year, 21 novels sold more than 100,000 copies, five more than in 1996. A little over half of these books never made it onto our weekly charts. Of the 10 that made a showing, Peter Mayle, Pete Hamill, and Thomas Pynchon were the three longest-running authors, at 15, 10, and nine weeks, respectively. However, Arthur Golden's first novel, *Memoirs of a Geisha*, with six weeks in 1997, is still active on the weekly charts—it's among the top five—and at this writing had racked up 17 weeks.

In ranked order, the 100,000+ titles that did make it onto the weekly charts are: *Acts of Love* by Judith Michael (Crown), *Reign in Hell* by William Diehl (Ballantine), *Mason & Dixon* by Thomas Pynchon (Holt), *Running with the Demon* by Terry Brooks (Del Rey), *Memoirs of a Geisha* by Arthur Golden (Knopf), *Snow in August* by Pete Hamill (Little, Brown), *Chasing Cezanne* by

Peter Mayle (Knopf), *Dragonseye* by Anne McCaffrey (Del Rey), *American Pastoral* by Philip Roth (Houghton Mifflin), and *The Unlikely Spy* by Daniel Silva (Villard).

The 11 no-shows on *PW*'s lists are: *Three Wishes* by Barbara Delinsky (Simon & Schuster), *Life Support* by Tess Gerritsen (Pocket), *A Return to Christmas* by Chris Heimerdinger (Ballantine), *The Cat Who Could Read Backwards* by Lilian Jackson Braun (Putnam), *The Genesis Code* by John Case (Ballantine), *Only Love* by Erich Segal (Putnam), *Meg* by Steve Alten (Doubleday), *The World of Robert Jordan's The Wheel of Time* by Robert Jordan and Teresa Peterson (Tor), *Hawk O'Toole's Hostage* by Sandra Brown (Bantam), *Star Wars: Planet of Twilight* by Barbara Hambly (Bantam), and *Public Secrets* by Nora Roberts (Bantam).

Nonfiction Runners-Up

In this group, only Steven Covey's book did not make it onto *PW*'s weekly charts last year. Either Golden is going to take a huge hit on this book or it's one of those titles that makes a stronger run in nontraditional outlets; perhaps a bit of both. Considering the hefty sales in this second tier of the year's top-selling non-fiction—in fact, the numbers are the highest ever achieved by this group on these year-end lists—even brief runs of less than two months seem insufficient for a respectable sell-through. Last year saw the debut of Rob Weisbach Books, and two of his three national bestsellers are in this group. That's the good news; the bad is that both Reiser's and Goldberg's books are reported to be slated for heavier returns.

Celebrity bestsellers also figure high in this group, with books about Princess Diana and JFK; another O. J. book by one of the prosecuting stars; a title by Rosie O'Donnell (doing what Art Linkletter used to do, recording how funny kids can be); and one by Drew Carey, perhaps one of the better-performing books by a comedian on last year's charts. A controversial book on foretelling the future by deciphering codes in the Bible and another offering help with arthritis for aging boomers enjoyed close to four months each on the charts. The best performance in this group was by Sebastian Junger: 26 weeks on the 1997 charts and, so far, an additional 12 (as of March) on this year's lists.

16. *The Celestine Vision* by James Redfield (Warner, 551,656 in 1997)

17. *Diana: A Tribute to the People's Princess* by Peter Donnelly (Courage, 539,000)

18. *Into the Storm* by Tom Clancy and General Fred Franks (Putnam, 527,017)

19. *The 7 Habits of Highly Effective Families* by Stephen R. Covey (Golden Books, 505,000)

20. *Without a Doubt* by Marcia Clark with Teresa Carpenter (Viking, 502,605)

21. *Don't Worry, Make Money* by Richard Carlson (Hyperion 495,401)

22. *The Arthritis Cure* by Jason Theodosakis, Brenda Adderly, and Barry Fox (St. Martin's, 441,117)

23. *The Bible Code* by Michael Drosnin (Simon & Schuster)

24. *The Dark Side of Camelot* by Seymour Hersh (Little, Brown, 408,526)
25. *Babyhood* by Paul Reiser (Morrow/Rob Weisbach, 404,781)
26. *Dirty Jokes and Beer* by Drew Carey (Hyperion, 396,292)
27. *Better Homes and Gardens New Cook Book* by Better Homes and Gardens editors (Meredith, 392,120)
28. *Book* by Whoopi Goldberg (Morrow/Rob Weisbach, 367,156)
29. *The Dilbert Future* by Scott Adams (HarperBusiness, 362,000)
30. *Underboss* by Peter Maas (HarperCollins, 351,373)

Lower Ranks for Higher Numbers

In assessing the 1996 sales, the big news was that for the first time three nonfiction books with sales over the 300,000 point did not make the top-30 rankings. In 1997, the news is that there were 10 such titles. They are: *Conversations with God, Book 2* by Neale Donald Walsch (Hampton Roads), *Brain Droppings* by George Carlin (Hyperion), *Citizen Soldiers* by Stephen Ambrose (Simon & Schuster), *The Gift of Peace* by Joseph Cardinal Bernardin (Loyola Univ. Press), *Tuesdays with Morrie* by Mitch Albom (Doubleday), *Nestle Toll House Best-Loved Cookies* by Better Homes and Gardens editors (Meredith), *The Zone* by Barry Sears (ReganBooks), *Eat Right 4 Your Type* by Peter D'Adamo (Putnam), *Suzanne Somers' Eat Great, Lose Weight* by Suzanne Somers (Crown), and *The Merck Manual of Medical Information, Home Edition* (Merck Research Laboratories).

The 200,000+ Nonfiction Players

This level, once again, reached a new high, with 26 titles over 1996's 19-book record. All but five made it onto *PW*'s weekly charts or our monthly religion charts. The best performers were *Mastering the Zone, Personal History,* and *The Gift of Fear*, with 18, 15, and 13 weeks, respectively. Three of the five that did not have a weekly showing were cookbooks or business titles that often do well in nonbook and/or specialty markets.

In ranked order, the books with sales of 200,000 copies or more are: *Mastering the Zone* by Barry Sears (ReganBooks), *Mars and Venus on a Date* by John Gray (HarperCollins), *Illuminated Prayers* by Marianne Williamson (Simon & Schuster), *Sources of Strength* by Jimmy Carter (Times Books), *Success Is a Choice* by Rick Pitino (Broadway), *The Gift of Fear* by Gavin deBecker (Little, Brown), *10 Stupid Things Men Do to Mess Up Their Lives* by Laura Schlessinger (HarperCollins), *Diana: A Tribute in Photographs* by Michael O'Mara (St. Martin's), *Training a Tiger* by Earl Woods (HarperCollins), *His Name Is Ron* by the family of Ron Goldman with William and Marilyn Hoffer (Morrow), *Murder in Brentwood* by Mark Fuhrman (Regnery), *Mothers and Daughters* by Carol Saline and Sharon Wolmuth (Doubleday), *Tears of Rage* by John Walsh with Susan Schindehette (Pocket), *Even the Stars Look Lonesome* by Maya Angelou (Random House), *Personal History* by Katherine Graham (Knopf), *Martha*

Stewart's Healthy Quick Cook by Martha Stewart (Clarkson Potter), *The Nine Steps to Financial Freedom* by Suze Orman (Crown), *Miracle Cures* by Jean Carper (HarperCollins), *The Weigh Down Diet* by Gwen Shamblin (Doubleday), *The Secret Language of Relationships* by Gary Goldschneider and Joost Elffers (Penguin Studio), *Daughters & Mothers* by Lauren Cowen, photographs by Jayne Wexler (Courage), *Holiday in Your Heart* by LeAnn Rimes and Tom Carter (Doubleday), *The Great House of God* by Max Lucado (Word), *Evidence Dismissed* by Tom Lange and Philip Vannatter as told to Dan E. Moldea (Pocket), *Butterfly Kisses* by J. Countryman and Bob Carlisle (Word), and *Better Homes and Gardens 75 Years of All-Time Favorites* by Better Homes and Gardens editors (Meredith).

150,000+ Group in Nonfiction

The number of books in this group bounced back this year, to 21 titles with sales over 150,000 that did not make the top-30 list, from only eight in 1996 and breaking the record of 20 in 1994.

However, the downside of this record is that only four of the 21 titles occupied slots on *PW*'s bestseller lists in 1997. The longest-running was Kevin Aucoin's *Making Faces* (Little, Brown) with six weeks on the charts; the remaining three books each descend by a week: *Dogs Never Lie About Love* by Jeffrey Moussaieff Masson (Crown), three weeks; *Wait Till Next Year* by Doris Kearns Goodwin (Simon & Schuster), two weeks; and *Rock This!* by Chris Rock (Hyperion) checking in with just a one-week showing.

The books that didn't make the charts are: *Walk on the Wild Side* by Dennis Rodman (Delacorte), *Sweetie Pie* by Richard Simmons (GT Publishing), *The Healing of America* by Marianne Williamson (Simon & Schuster), *Seven Years in Tibet* by Heinrich Harrer (Putnam/Tarcher), *Letters from a Nut* by Ted L. Nancy (Avon), *Angels Along the Way* by Della Reese (Putnam), *Zone-Perfect Meals in Minutes* by Barry Sears (ReganBooks), *The Only Way I Know* by Cal Ripken, Jr. and Mike Bryan (Viking), *Financial Peace* by Dave Ramsey (Viking), *The Road Less Traveled and Beyond* by Richard Peck (Simon & Schuster), *Our Sacred Honor*, edited by William J. Bennett (Simon & Schuster), *Forever Yours, Faithfully* by Lorrie Morgan (Ballantine), *Better Homes and Gardens The New Decorating Book* by Better Homes and Gardens editors (Meredith), *The Seven Spiritual Laws for Parents* by Deepak Chopra (Harmony), *Emeril's Creole Christmas* by Emeril Lagasse and Marcelle Bienvenu (Morrow), *Naomi's Home Companion* by Naomi Judd (GT Publishing), and *The Messengers* by Julia Ingram and G. W. Hardin (Pocket).

Nonfiction's 125,000 Group

This group includes 15 titles that did not make *PW*'s annual top-30 list, matching the 1995 number and three less than the 1996 record of 18.

Only three titles showed up on our bestseller charts, with Jerry Oppenheimer's *Martha Stewart: Just Desserts* (Morrow) the longest running at six weeks. *Joy for the Journey* by J. Countryman (Word) enjoyed three appearances on *PW*'s monthly religion list, and *Strong Women Stay Young* by Miriam Nelson and Sara Wernick (Bantam) had a one-week visit.

The 12 that did not make a weekly *PW* slot are: *Trump: The Art of the Comeback* by Donald Trump (Times Books), *Simplify Your Life with Kids* by Elaine St. James (Andrews McMeel), *James Herriot's Animal Stories* by James Herriot (St. Martin's), *Better Homes and Gardens Home Landscaping* by Better Homes and Gardens editors (Meredith), *The Day After Roswell* by Col. Philip Corso (Ret.) with William Birnes (Pocket), *Between Each Line of Pain and Glory* by Gladys Knight (Hyperion), *Any Given Day* by Jessie Lee Brown Fouveaux (Warner), *We Should Be So Lucky* by Kathy Levine with Jane Scovell (Pocket), *Rogue Warrior: Designation Gold* by Richard Marcinko and John Weisman (Pocket), *Tupac Shakur* by Vibe editors (Crown), *Diana: The Last Year* by Donald Spoto (Harmony), and *Better Homes and Gardens New Dieter's Cookbook* by Better Homes and Gardens editors (Meredith).

Nonfiction's 100,000+ List

This group comprised 25 books that did not make *PW*'s top-30 annual list, compared with 31 last year.

Once again only a few of these titles—six of the 25—saw any *PW* chart activity. Both *Joan Lunden's Healthy Living* by Joan Lunden and Laura Morton (Crown) and *Die Broke* by Stephen Pollan (HarperBusiness) were on for three weeks. *Dr. Susan Love's Hormone Book* by Susan M. Love with Karen Lindsay (Random House) had a two-week run, and *Naked* by David Sedaris (Little, Brown) was on for one week. On *PW*'s monthly religion charts were *In the Grip of Grace* by Max Lucado (Word), for eight months, and *God's Inspirational Promise Book* by J. Countryman and Max Lucado (Word), for four.

The 19 that did not show on the weekly charts are: *Rules II* by Ellen Fein and Sherrie Schneider (Warner), *The Way You Wear Your Hat* by Bill Zehme (HarperCollins), *Nickel Dreams* by Tanya Tucker with Patsi Bale Cox (Hyperion), *Pour Your Heart into It* by Howard Schultz with Dori Jones Yang (Hyperion), *Streams in the Desert* by L. B. Cowman, edited by James Reimann (Zondervan), *Giving the Love That Heals* by Harville Hendrix and Helen Hunt (Pocket), *Selling the Invisible* by Harry Beckwith (Warner), *David: A Man of Passion & Destiny* by Charles R. Swindoll (Word), *Favre: Born on the Bayou, Bred for Green Bay* by Brett Favre and Chris Havel (Doubleday), *Walk This Way: The Autobiography of Aerosmith* by Aerosmith with Stephen Davis (Avon), *I Make My Own Rules* by LL Cool J with Karen Hunter (St. Martin's), *Dave Barry's Book of Bad Songs* by Dave Barry (Andrews McMeel), *The Joy in Loving*, compiled by Jaya Chaliha and Edward Le Joly (Viking), *Billions and Billions* by Carl Sagan (Random House), *The Kingdom of Shivas Irons* by Michael Murphy (Broadway), *No Greater Love* by Mother Teresa (New World Library), *Just a Rangeball in a Box of Titleists* by Gary McCord (Putnam), *Rediscovering American Values* by Dick DeVos (Dutton), and *Counterfeit Revival* by Hank Hanegraaff (Word).

Paperback Bestsellers:
Oprah's Tender Takeover of Trade Paperbacks

The familiar balance of spiritual solace, health, comics, and computer instruction that has dominated trade paperbacks for several years has been altered by Oprah Winfrey. In the past, a literary title might be represented near the top (think *Snow Falling on Cedars, Shipping News,* or movie tie-ins, such as *Schindler's List).* But this is the first year in decades to see so much fiction so high on the list.

The reason, of course, is Oprah's Book Club. Wally Lamb's *She's Come Undone,* Ursula Hegi's *Stones from the River,* Mary McGarry Morris's *Songs in Ordinary Time,* and Sheri Reynolds's *Rapture of Canaan* (not to mention Maya Angelou's autobiographical *Heart of a Woman)* are all in the top dozen slots, and all are Oprah picks. And these are just paperbacks printed in 1996 or 1997.

Outside of Oprah, the trade paperback list looks very familiar, particularly in the endless ladles of chicken soup for sundry souls or absolutely anything for dummies books (suggested bestsellers for next year: *Chicken Soup for Dummies, The Soul for Dummies, Windows95 for the Soul).* Other mainstays are here (say, Calvin and Hobbes) but further down the list.

Oprah's influence also extends into mass market: Jacquelyn Mitchard's *The Deep End of the Ocean* sold nearly two million this year. And, as it was last year, certain series have done well—John Saul's Blackstone Chronicles and Julie Garwood's Rose books. Still the top of the list remains the province of a handful of writers—Grisham, Steel, Clancy, King, Clark, Crichton, and Cornwell.

Both trade paperback and mass market figures reflect originals, reprints, or dual editions published in 1996 or 1997 for which publishers have billed and shipped at least 50,000 copies (for trade paperbacks) or one million copies (for mass markets) in 1997. They do not always reflect net sales. Titles released in 1996 are marked by an asterisk.

Trade Paperbacks

100,000+

Don't Sweat the Small Stuff and It's All Small Stuff. Richard Carlson. Orig. Hyperion (4,506,683)

*Chicken Soup for the Woman's Soul. Jack Canfield, Mark Victor Hansen et al. Orig. Health Communications (2,228,000)

*She's Come Undone. Wally Lamb. Rep. Pocket/Washington Square (1,520,566)

Chicken Soup for the Mother's Soul. Jack Canfield, Mark Victor Hansen et al. Orig. Health Communications (1,406,739)

Wizard and Glass. Stephen King. Orig. Plume (1,298,664)

Stones from the River. Ursula Hegi. Rep. Scribner (1,285,000)

*Prescription for Nutritional Healing. James F. & Phyllis A. Balch. Orig. Avery (1,275,000)

Windows 95 for Dummies, 2nd ed. Andy Rathbone. Orig. IDG (1,148,107)

Chicken Soup for the Christian Soul. Jack Canfield, Mark Victor Hansen et al. Orig. Health Communications (1,263,328)

*Songs in Ordinary Time. Mary McGarry Morris. Rep. Penguin (1,120,000)

A 4th Course of Chicken Soup for the Soul. Jack Canfield, Mark Victor Hansen et al. Orig. Health Communications (1,088,952)

Rapture of Canaan. Sheri Reynolds. Rep. Berkley (1,000,000)

Listings compiled by Ingrid Chevannes, Dermot McEvoy and Maria Simson

Heart of a Woman. Maya Angelou. Rep. Bantam

Petals on the River. Kathleen E. Woodiwiss. Orig. Avon (621,529)

Undaunted Courage. Stephen E. Ambrose. Rep. Touchstone (589,000)

Casual Day Has Gone Too Far. Scott Adams. Orig. Andrews and McMeel (575,000)

Spontaneous Healing. Andrew Weil, M.D. Rep. Fawcett (557,779)

The Internet for Dummies, 4th ed. John Levine. Orig. IDG (537,391)

Color of Water. James McBride. Rep. Riverhead (500,000)

Seven Years of Highly Defective People. Scott Adams. Orig. Andrews and McMeel (495,000)

Into the Wild. Jon Krakauer. Rep. Anchor (458,667)

Prescription for Nutritional Healing, 2nd ed. James F. and Phyllis A. Balch. Orig. Avery (454,037)

A Civil Action. Jonathan Harr. Rep. Vintage (423,044)

Chicken Soup for the Soul at Work. Jack Canfield, Mark Victor Hansen et al. Orig. Health Communications (358,075)

Stories for the Heart. Compiled by Alice Gray. Orig. Multnomah (357,111)

The Dilbert Principle. Scott Adams. Rep. HarperBusiness (300,000)

Emotional Intelligence. Daniel Goleman. Rep. Bantam

MS Office 97 for Windows for Dummies. Wally Wang. Orig. IDG (295,559)

Windows 95 for Dummies Quick Reference, 3rd ed. Gregory A. Harvey. Orig. IDG (285,673)

Before Women Had Wings. Connie May Fowler. Rep. Fawcett (276,646)

Under the Tuscan Sun: At Home in Italy. France Mayes. Rep. Broadway (274,919)

Left Behind. Jerry Jenkins & Tim LaHaye. Orig. Tyndale (274,023)

The Fat Free Living Super Cookbook. Jyl Steinbeck. Rep. Warner (273,339)

The Celestine Prophecy. James Redfield. Rep. Warner (273,188)

How Could You Do That? Laura Schlessinger. Rep. HarperPaperbacks (254,605)

These High Green Hills. Jan Karon. Rep. Penguin (250,000)

Hey, Mom, I'm Hungry. Susan Powter. Orig. Fireside (233,000)

Teach Yourself Windows 95 Visually. Marangraphics. Orig. IDG (227,263)

Tribulation Force. Jerry Jenkins & Tim LaHaye. Orig. Tyndale (225,626)

USA Cookbook. Sheila Lukins. Orig. Workman (221,506)

Airborne. Tom Clancy. Rep. Berkley (221,285)

Chocolate for a Woman's Soul. Kay Allenbaugh. Orig. Fireside (203,000)

Seven Years in Tibet. Heinrich Harrer. Rep. Tarcher (200,000)

Living Somewhere Between Estrogen and Death. Barbara Johnson. Rep. Word (196,471)

Photomosaics. Robert Silvers. Orig. Holt (186,182)

Motley Fool Investment Guide. David & Tom Gardner. Rep. Fireside (186,000)

Day of Deception. John Hagee. Orig. Thomas Nelson (185,198)

Another Homecoming. Janette Oke and T. Davis Bunn. Rep. Bethany House (179,869)

Dogbert's Top Secret Management Handbook. Scott Adams. Rep. HarperBusiness (175,00)

Dr. Atkins Quick & Easy New Diet. Robert C. Atkins, M.D. & Veronica Atkins. Orig. Fireside (175,000)

A Reporter's Life. Walter Cronkite. Rep. Ballantine (174,466)

The Illustrated Dream Dictionary. Orig. Sterling (172,394)

The Simpsons: A Guide to Our Favorite Family. Matt Groening. Orig. HarperPaperbacks (171, 276)

The Demon-Haunted World. Carl Sagan. Rep. Ballantine (169,647)

PCs for Dummies, 4th ed. Dan Gookin. Orig. IDG (165,319)

Martin Dressler. Steven Millhauser. Rep. Vintage (164,828)

Cloister Walk. Kathleen Norris. Rep. Riverhead (164,112)

Servant of the Bones. Anne Rice. Rep. Ballantine (162,003)

America Online for Dummies, 3rd ed. John Kaufeld. Orig. IDG (159,152)

The Internet for Dummies Quick Reference, 3rd ed. John Levine. Orig. IDG (158,286)

The Oath. Frank Peretti. Rep. Word (156,934)

The World's Best-Kept Beauty Secrets. Diane Irons. Orig. Sourcebooks (155,791)

An Unquiet Mind. Kay Jamison. Rep. Vintage (154,848)

How Good Do We Have to Be. Harold Kushner. Rep. Little, Brown (154,381)

*Investing for Dummies. Eric Tyson. Orig. IDG (152,944)

*A Cup of Chicken Soup for the Soul. Jack Canfield, Mark Victor Hansen et al. Orig. Health Communications (151,075)

Hitler's Willing Executioners. Daniel Goldhagen. Rep. Vintage (152,211)

*Golf for Dummies. Gary McCord. Orig. IDG (150,944)

*Word 97 for Windows for Dummies. Dan Gookin. Orig. IDG (150,055)

First Things First Everyday. Stephen R. Covey. Orig. Fireside (150,000)

Meditations on Conversations with God. Walsh. Rep. Berkley (150,000)

Kitchen Table Wisdom. Rachel Remen. Rep. Riverhead (149,817)

Forever, Erma. Erma Bombeck. Rep. Andrews and McMeel (147,000)

*Better Homes and Gardens New Cook Book. Editors of Better Homes and Gardens Books. Rep. Meredith (145,538)

*Chicken Soup for the Surviving Soul. Jack Canfield, Mark Victor Hansen et al. Orig. Health Communications (142,865)

Succulent Wild Woman. Sark. Orig. Fireside (142,000)

*Personal Finance for Dummies, 2nd ed. Eric Tyson. Orig. IDG (140,250)

*The Pleasure Prescription. Paul Pearsall. Orig. Hunter House (139,146)

*40-30-30 Fat Burning Nutrition. Joyce and Gene Daouost. Rep. Wharton (138,840)

Divine Secrets of the Ya-Ya Sisterhood. Rebecca Wells. Rep. HarperPaper (136,816)

Good Things. Editors of *Martha Stewart Living.* Orig. Clarkson Potter (135,527)

*Moosewood Restaurant Low-Fat Favorites. Moosewood Collective. Rep. Clarkson Potter (134,746)

Western Landscaping Books. Sunset Editors. Orig. Sunset (134,959)

MTV's The Real World. James Solomon. Orig. Pocket/MTV 130,641

Accordion Crimes. E. Annie Proulx. Rep. Scribner (130,000)

The Shelter of Each Other. Mary Pipher. Rep. Ballantine (128,448)

All the Birds of North America. Jack Griggs. Orig. HarperPaperbacks (127,974)

*Shoes. Linda O'Keeffe. Orig. Workman (126,435)

Christmas with Martha Stewart Living. Editors of *Martha Stewart Living.* Orig. Clarkson Potter (105,201)

Built to Last: Successful Habits of Visionary Companies. James C. Collins and Jerry I. Porras. Rep. HarperBusiness (125,000)

Java in a Nutshell. David Flanagan. Orig. O'Reilly (124,268)

*Dr. Atkins New Carbohydrate Gram Counter. Robert C. Atkins. M.D. Orig. M. Evans (124,000)

Birdsong. Sebastian Faulks. Rep. Vintage (123,361)

Drinking: A Love Story. Caroline Knapp. Rep. Dell/Delta (121,757)

Stand in the Gap: The Prayer Journal. Bill McCartney. Rep. Word (121,730)

The Soul's Code. James Hillman. Rep. Warner (121,703)

Garfield Hams It Up (#31). Jim Davis. Orig. Ballantine (116,405)

*Girl Friend's Guide to Pregnancy. Vicki Iovine. Orig. Pocket (116,140)

Top Secret Restaurant Recipes. Todd Wilbur. Orig. Plume (115,541)

Gods and Generals. Jeff Shaara. Rep. Ballantine (114,111)

1001 Ways to Energize Employees. Bob Nelson. Orig. Workman (113,600)

*Mars & Venus Together Forever. John Gray. Rep. HarperPaperbacks (112,980)

How to Say It. Rosalie Maggio. Rep. Prentice Hall (112,600)

The Magnetic Poetry Book of Poetry. Dave Kapell & Sally Steenland. Orig. Workman (112,000)

*It's a Magical World: A Calvin & Hobbes Collection. Bill Watterson. Orig. Andrews and McMeel (110,000)

You Can Be Happy No Matter What, rev. ed. Richard Carlson. Orig. New World Library (109,886)

When Angels Speak. Martha Williamson. Orig. Fireside (109,000)

Love Coupons. Gregory J. P. Godek. Orig. Sourcebooks (103,608)

*Condensed Chicken Soup for the Soul. Jack Canfield, Mark Victor Hansen et al. Orig. Health Communications (100,840)

The Shunning. Beverly Lewis. Rep. Bethany House (100,566)

75,000+

Cooking for Dummies. Marie Rama & John Mariani. Orig. IDG (99,917)

Beginning of the End. John Hagee. Orig. Thomas Nelson (99,519)

Girlfriends Guide to Surviving the First Year of Motherhood. Vicki Iovine. Rep. Perigee (98,672)

Alias Grace. Margaret Atwood. Rep. Doubleday/Anchor (98,467)

Tax Saver's Strategy Guide. Ernst & Young. Orig. Wiley (98,000)

DHEA: A Practical Guide. Ray Sahelian, M.D. Orig. Avery (98,000)

Ship Fever: Stories. Andrea Barrett. Rep. Norton (96,026)

MTV's Road Rules. Alison Pollet and Leif Ueland. Orig. Pocket/MTV (95,687)

Anatomy of the Spirit. Caroline Myss, Ph.D. Rep. Three Rivers (95,012)

Anything Considered. Peter Mayle. Rep. Vintage (95,241)

Last Chapter & Worse. Gary Larson. Orig. Andrews & McMeel. (95,000)

There's Treasure Everywhere: A Calvin & Hobbes Collection. Bill Watterson. Orig. Andrews and McMeel (95,000)

The Beardstown Ladies' Stitch-in-Time Guide to Growing Your Nest Egg. Beardstown Ladies Investment Club with Robin Dellabough. Orig. Hyperion (94,500)

In the Beauty of the Lilies. John Updike. Rep. Fawcett (94,050)

Last Orders. Graham Swift. Rep. Vintage (90,139)

El Secreto De Selena. Maria Celeste Arrarás. Dual. Libros en español (89,000)

Quilts! Quilts!! Quilts!!! 2nd ed. Diana McClun & Laura Nownes. Orig. NTC Contemporary (88,350)

MTV's Beavis and Butt-Head Travel Log. Created by Mike Judge; written by Kristofor Brown. Orig. Pocket/MTV (87,000)

Star Wars: The Essential Guide to Vehicles and Vessels. Bill Smith. Orig. Del Rey (86,818)

I Love You Mom Coupons. Orig. Sourcebooks (86,754)

Gardening for Dummies. National Gardening Assoc. Orig. IDG (86,598)

Everyone Is Entitled to My Opinion. David Brinkley. Rep. Ballantine (85,518)

Come Closer, Roger, There's a Mosquito on Your Nose. Bill Amend. Orig. Andrews and McMeel (85,000)

Harley Hahn's Internet & Web Yellow Pages, 5th Anniversary Ed. Harley Hahn. Orig. Osborne/McGraw-Hill (84,653)

Simple Gifts. Judith McNaught and Jude Deveraux. Rep. Pocket (82,826)

MTV's Beavis & Butt-Head's: The Butt-Files. Mike Judge, Aimee Keillor, and Greg Grabianski. Orig. Pocket/MTV 82,188

Great Parties. Editors of *Martha Stewart Living.* Orig. Clarkson Potter (79,694)

97 Ways to Make Baby Laugh. Jack Moore. Orig. Workman (81,195)

Little Red Buckets. Nelson. Rep. Perigee (81,098)

I Love You Dad Coupons. Orig. Sourcebooks (80,968)

I Kissed Dating Goodbye. Joshua Harris. Rep. Multnomah (80,166)

Secrets of Fat-Free Italian Cooking. Sandra Woodruff, R.D. Orig. Avery (80,000)

The World's Dumbest Criminals. Daniel Butler and Alan Ray. Orig. Rutledge Hill (80,000)

Touched by an Angel. Martha Williamson with Robin Sheets. Orig. Zondervan (79,764)

L.A. Confidential. James Ellroy. Rep. Warner (78,944)

Bury Me Standing. Isabel Fonseca. Rep. Vintage (78,665)

Ain't Gonna Be the Same Fool Twice. April Sinclair. Rep. Avon (78,241)

Garfield Thinks Big (#32). Jim Davis. Orig. Ballantine (78,228)

The Five Love Languages of Children. Gary Chapman. Orig. Moody (78,000)

FoxTrot Beyond a Doubt. Bill Amend. Orig. Andrews and McMeel(77,000)

The Matchmakers. Janette Oke. Rep. Bethany House (75,374)

The Confession. Beverly Lewis. Rep. Bethany House (75,278)

365 TV-Free Activities You Can Do with Your Child. Steve & Ruth Bennett. Rep. Adams (75,100)

Darling Jasmine. Bertrice Small. Orig. Kensington (75,000)

Hanson: The Official Book. Jarrod Gollihare. Orig. Watson-Guptill (75,000)

I Know Why the Caged Bird Sings. Maya Angelou. Rep. Bantam

50,000+

A Good Walk Spoiled. John Feinstein. Rep. Little, Brown (74,890)

Blood Sport. James B. Stewart. Rep. Touchstone (74,000)

Italian So Fat, Low Fat, No Fat. Betty Rohde. Orig. Fireside (74,000)

Peterson's Four-Year Colleges. Rep. Peterson's (73,990)

Living Buddha, Living Christ. Thich Nhat Hanh. Rep. Riverhead (73,720)

Don't Know Much About the Civil War. Kenneth C. Davis. Rep. Avon (73,241)

*Home Buying for Dummies. Eric Tyson and Ray Brown. Orig. IDG (72,722)

1,003 Great Things About Getting Older. Lisa Birnbach et al. Orig. Andrews and McMeel (72,500)

Tiger Woods. Sports Illustrated. Rep. Fireside (72,000)

Jolly Old Santa Claus. Sparkie. Rep. Ideals Publications (71,487)

The Family Manager's Guide for Working Moms. Kathy Peel. Rep. Ballantine (70,877)

*Creatine: Nature's Muscle Builder. Ray Sahelian, M.D., and Dave Tuttle. Orig. Avery (69,900)

Rose. Martin Cruz Smith. Rep. Ballantine (69,750)

*Diabetic Healthy Exchanges. Lund. Rep. Perigee (69,384)

Hit the Spot. Denise Austin. Orig. Fireside (69,000)

The Tightwad Gazette III. Amy Dacyczyn. Orig. Villard (68,624)

The Moor's Last Sigh. Salman Rushdie. Rep. Vintage (67,862)

Cracking the SAT & PSAT. Adam Robinson and John Katzman. Orig. Princeton Review/ Random (67,707)

Moosewood Restaurant Book of Desserts. Moosewood Collective. Orig. Clarkson Potter (66,208)

Gourmet Cooking for Dummies. Charles Trotter. Orig. IDG (66,742)

Passion and Purity: Learning to Bring Your Love Life Under Christ's Control. Elisa-

beth Elliott. Rep. Baker Book House (66,455)

The Making of the Lost World. Jody Duncan. Orig. Ballantine (66,403)

*The Western Guide to Feng Shui. Terah Kathryn Collins. Orig. Hay House (66,236)

More Stories for the Heart. Compiled by Alice Gray. Orig. Multnomah (65,767)

Bad Land. Jonathan Raban. Rep. Vintage (65,627)

Resumes That Knock 'em Dead. Martin Yate. Rep. Adams. (65,600)

How to Get the Most from God's Word. John MacArthur. Rep. Word (65,203)

The Real Vitamin & Mineral Book, 2nd ed. Shari Lieberman & Nancy Bruning. Orig. Avery (65,000)

Living Lean. Larry North. Rep. Fireside (65,000)

*From Fatigued to Fantastic! Jacob Teitelbaum, M.D. Avery (64,500)

Practical Intuition: How to Harness the Power of Your Instinct and Make It Work for You. Laura Day. Rep. Broadway (64,465)

Book of Outdoor Gardening. Smith & Hawken. Orig. Workman (64,346)

Lowfat Cooking for Dummies. Lynn Fischer. Orig. IDG (64,291)

Write Your Own Pleasure Prescription. Paul Pearsall. Orig. Hunter House (64,224)

Wall Street Journal Guide to Understanding Person Finance. Kenneth M. Morris. Orig. Fireside (64,000)

Stokes Guide to Birds: Eastern Region. David and Lillian Stokes. Orig. Little, Brown (63,872)

Tiptionary. Mary Hunt. Orig. Broadman & Holman (63,422)

I Was Amelia Earhart. Jane Mendelsohn. Rep. Vintage (63,287)

Big Girls Don't Cry. Connie Briscoe. Rep. Ballantine (62,255)

Desperation Dinners. Beverly Mills & Alicia Ross. Orig. Workman (62,000)

On My Own at 107. Sarah Delany. Rep. Harper San Francisco (62,000)

Tender Years. Janette Oke. Rep. Bethany House (61,637)

Star Wars: The Essential Guide to Weapons and Technology. Bill Smith. Orig. Del Rey (61,549)

*Fibromyalgia and Chronic Myofascial Pain Syndrome: A Survival Manual. Devin Star-

lanyl & Mary Ellen Copeland. Orig. New Harbinger (61,488)

150 Ways to Tell if You're Ghetto. Shawn Wayans, Suli McCullough and Chris Spencer. Orig. Dell/DTP (61,343)

*Intercessory Prayer. Dutch Sheets. Rep. Regal (61,128)

The Ninth Garfield Treasury. Jim Davis. Orig. Ballantine (60,900)

Ramses, Vol. I. Christian Jacq. Rep. Warner (60,750)

The Verbally Abusive Relationship. Patricia Evans. Rep. Adams. (60,300)

Girlfriends Talk About Men. Carmen Renee Berry and Tamara Traeder. Orig. Wildcat Canyon (59,814)

Penn & Teller's How to Play in Traffic. Jillette & Teller. Rep. Berkley (59,683)

Brain Lock. Jeffrey Schwartz. Rep. Regan/Harper (59,182)

The Practical Guide to Practically Everything. Peter Bernstein and Christopher Ma. Orig. Random (58,473)

Photoshop 4 for Macintosh: Visual QuickStar Guide. Elaine Weinman & Peter Lourekas. Orig. Peachpit (58,462)

Cover Letters that Knock 'em Dead. Martin Yate. Rep. Adams. (58,400)

HTML for the WWW: Visual QuickStar Guide, 2nd ed. Elizabeth Castro. Orig. Peachpit (58,134)

Tumbling. Diane McKinney-Whetstone. Rep. Scribner (58,000)

The Odyssey. Trans. by Roger Fagles. Rep. Penguin (58,000)

*1-2-3 Magic: Effective Discipline for Children 2–12. Thomas W. Phelan. Orig. Child Management Inc. (57,384)

*101 Nights of Great Romance. Laura Corn. Orig. Park Avenue/LPC (56,681)

Only Love Is Real. Brian Weiss. Rep. Warner (56,045)

One Minute After You Die. Erwin W. Lutzer. Orig. Moody (56,000)

Redeeming Love. Francine Rivers. Orig. Multnomah (55,392)

Live and Learn and Pass it On, Vol. III. H. Jackson Brown Jr. Rep. Rutledge Hill (55,000)

Great Books. David Denby. Rep. Touchstone (55,000)

*Hidden Meaning of Birthdays. Orig. Andrews & McMeel. (55,000)

Vein of Gold: A Journey to Your Creative Heart. Julia Cameron. Rep. Tarcher (55,000)

The Scorecard. Greg Gutfield. Orig. Holt (54,815)

Real Moments for Lovers. Barbara De Angelis. Rep. Dell/DTP (54,387)

Joan Lunden's Healthy Healthy Cooking. Rep. Little, Brown (54,207)

Chicken Poop for the Soul. Davis Fisher. Orig. Pocket 54,157

Dave Barry in Cyberspace. Dave Barry. Rep. Fawcett (54,150)

Unbelievably Good Deals and Great Adventures That You Absolutely Can't Get Unless You're over 50, 9th ed. Jean Rattner Heilman. NTC Contemporary (54,140)

Heart Steps: Prayers and Declarations for a Creative Life. Julia Cameron. Orig. Tarcher (54,000)

*The End of Work. Jeremy Rifkin. Rep. Tarcher (54,000)

Steak Lover's Cookbook. William Rice. Orig. Workman (53,906)

Diana: An Intimate Portrait, Special Ed. Ingrid Seward. NTC Contemporary (53,251)

St. John's Wort: Nature's Blues Buster. Hyla Cass, M.D. Orig. Avery (53,000)

Vegetarian Planet. Didi Emmons. Orig. Harvard Common (52,995)

Personality Plus, 2nd Ed.: How to Understand Others by Understanding Yourself. Florence Littaver. Rep. Baker Book House (52,748)

Essential Guide to Prescription Drugs. Long & Rybacki. HarperPaper (52,686)

The Debt to Pleasure. John Lanchester. Rep. Holt (52,650)

Like Judgment Day: The Ruin and Redemption of a Town Called Rosewood. Michael D'Orso. Rep. Berkley (52,206)

Christmas Stories for the Heart. Compiled by Alice Gray. Orig. Multnomah (52,137)

Don't Go to the Cosmetics Counter Without Me, 3rd ed. Paula Begoun. Orig. Beginning Press (52,008)

When a Man Loves a Walnut. Gavin Edwards. Orig. Fireside (52,000)

Corel WordPerfect Suite 8: The Official Guide. Alan Neibauer. Orig. Osborne/McGraw-Hill (51,788)

Jen-X: Jenny McCarthy's Open Book. Jenny McCarthy with Neal Karlen. Orig. Harper/Regan (51,417)

Stokes Beginner's Guide to Birds. Donald and Lillian Stokes. Orig. Little, Brown (51,377)

Downsize This. Michael Moore. Rep. Harper-Paper (51,136)

HTML Definitive Guide. Orig. O'Reilly (51,074)

Slouching Towards Gomorrah. Robert Bork. Rep. HarperPaper (51,048)

Joy of Cooking, Rev. Ed. Irma S. Rombauer and Marion Rombauer Becker. Rep. Plume (51,018)

Selena's Secret. Maria Celeste Arrarás. Dual. Fireside (51,000)

The Highly Sensitive Person: How to Thrive When the World Overwhelms You. Elaine Aron. Rep. Broadway (50,699)

Biggest Riddle Book in the World. Orig. Sterling (50,546)

*2001: The Edge of Eternity. Jack Van Impe. Rep. Word (50,543)

Infinite Jest. David Foster Wallace. Rep. Little, Brown (50,313)

*Mrs. Fields Best Cookie Book Ever! Debbie Fields. Orig. Time-Life (50,255)

Star Trek: Phase II. Judith and Garfield Reeves-Stevens. Orig. Pocket (50,010)

Dynamic Nutrition for Maximum Performance. Daniel Gastelu and Fred Hatfield. Orig. Avery (50,000)

Ginkgo: A Practical Guide. Georges Halpern, M.D. Orig. Avery (50,000)

Love You to Bits and Pieces. Gillian Helfgott. Orig. Penguin (50,000)

The Wonder of Boys. Michael Gurian. Rep. Tarcher (50,000)

Good Luck Book. Stefan Bechtel and Laurence Stains. Orig. Workman (50,000)

Run of His Life. Jeffrey Toobin. Rep. Touchstone (50,000)

Salt Dancers. Ursula Hegi. Rep. Scribner (50,000)

The Godfather Legacy. Harlan Lebo. Orig. Fireside (50,000)

Almanacs, Atlases & Annuals

The World Almanac and Book of Facts 1998. Robert Famighetti. Orig. World Almanac (1,747,386)

Ernst and Young Tax Guide 1997. Orig. Wiley (390,000)

The World Almanac and Book of Facts 1997. Robert Famighetti. Orig. World Almanac (283,221)

The Old Farmer's Almanac, 1998 ed. Edited by Judson D. Hale. Villard (185,403)

Birnbaum's Walt Disney World 1998. Birnbaum Travel Guides. Orig. Hyperion (160,028)

The Wall Street Journal Almanac 1998. Wall Street Journal editors. Orig. Ballantine (152,200)

Taxes for Dummies, 98 Edition. Eric Tyson and David Silverman. Orig. IDG (129,101)

Christmas Ideals 97. Ideals Editors. Orig. Ideals Publications (103,378)

Sports Illustrated Almanac '98. Sports Illustrated. Orig. Little, Brown (102,648)

The New York Times Almanac 1998. Edited by John W. Wright with Editors and Reporters of the Times. Orig. Penguin (91,000)

1998 ESPN Information Please Sports Almanac. Orig. Hyperion (84,579)

Kovels Antiques and Collectibles Price List, 30th Ed. Ralph and Terry Kovel. Orig. Three Rivers (76,756)

Video Hound's Golden Movie Retrievers 1997. Edited by Jim Croldock and Martin Connors. Orig. Visible Ink (72,208)

H&R Block 1998 Income Tax Guide. H&R Block. Orig. Fireside (70,000)

The Witches' Almanac. Edited by Elizabeth Pepper and John Wilcock. Orig. Witches' Almanac (60,819)

Hugh Johnson's Pocket Encyclopedia of Wine 1998. Hugh Johnson. Orig. Fireside (60,000)

Mass Market

2 Million+

The Runaway Jury. John Grisham. Rep. Dell/Island (4,995,438)

Five Days in Paris. Danielle Steel. Rep. Dell (2,932,226)

Malice. Danielle Steel. Rep. Dell (2,930,012)

Silent Honor. Danielle Steel. Rep. Dell (2,821,930)

Executive Orders. Tom Clancy. Rep. Berkley (2,400,000)

Moonlight Becomes You. Mary Higgins Clark. Rep. Pocket (2,164,192)

Desperation. Stephen King. Rep. Signet (2,088,269)

My Gal Sunday. Mary Higgins Clark. Rep. Pocket (2,087, 426)

Airframe. Michael Crichton. Ballantine. Rep. (2,002,049)

Cause of Death. Patricia Cornwell. Rep. Berkley (2,000,000)

1 Million+

The Deep End of the Ocean. Jacquelyn Mitchard. Rep. Signet (1,904,414)

Ticktock. Dean Koontz. Orig. Ballantine. (1,817,299)

The Regulators. Richard Bachman. Rep. Signet (1,813,788)

The Lost World. Michael Crichton. Movie tie-in. Ballantine (1,689,113)

The Hornet's Nest. Patricia Cornwell. Rep. Berkley (1,600,000)

Neanderthal. John Darnton. Rep. St. Martin's (1,575,000)

Sole Survivor. Dean Koontz. Rep. Ballantine (1,548,355)

Demon Seed. Dean Koontz. Reissue. Berkley (1,535,134)

An Eye for an Eye: The Doll. John Saul. Orig. Fawcett (1,515,147)

Invasion. Robin Cook. Rep. Berkley (1,500,956)

The Last Don. Mario Puzo. Rep. Ballantine (1,471,241)

Heart Song. V.C. Andrews. Orig. Pocket (1,462,646)

Unfinished Symphony. V.C. Andrews. Orig. Pocket (1,449,085)

Promises. Belva Plain. Rep. Dell (1,420,544)

The Third Twin. Ken Follett. Rep. Fawcett (1,412,187)

How Stella Got Her Groove Back. Terry McMillan. Rep. Signet (1,404,732)

Jack and Jill. James Patterson. Rep. Warner (1,359,414)

Silent Witness. Richard North Patterson. Rep. Ballantine (1,357,779)

Twist of Fate: The Locket. John Saul. Orig. Fawcett (1,345,684)

One Pink Rose. Julie Garwood. Orig. Pocket (1,335,256)

One White Rose. Julie Garwood. Orig. Pocket (1,308,977)

Montana Sky. Nora Roberts. Rep. Jove (1,300,000)

Sudden Prey. John Sanford. Rep. Berkley (1,300,000)

Dr. Atkins New Diet Revolution. Robert C. Atkins, MD. Rep. Avon (1,294,450)

The Laws of Our Fathers. Scott Turow. Rep. Warner (1,286,283)

One Red Rose. Julie Garwood. Orig. Pocket (1,270,153)

Ashes to Ashes: The Dragon's Flame. John Saul. Orig. Fawcett (1,244,364)

Remember When. Judith McNaught. Rep. Pocket (1,235,743)

Say You Love Me. Johanna Lindsey. Avon (1,233,225)

Total Control. David Baldacci. Rep. Warner (1,226,768)

Wild Baron. Catherine Coulter. Rep. Jove (1,200,000)

Finding the Dream. Nora Roberts. Rep. Jove (1,177,727)

Guilty As Sin. Tami Hoag. Rep. Bantam (1,150,000)

Dark Paradise. Tami Hoag. Reissue. Bantam (1,150,000)

The Wedding. Julie Garwood. Rep. Pocket (1,148,651)

Diana: Her True Story. Andrew Morton. Pocket (1,138,920)

In the Shadow of Evil: The Handkerchief. John Saul. Orig. Fawcett (1,137,233)

This Year It Will Be Different. Maeve Binchy. Rep. Dell (1,114,767)

Power Plays: Politika. Tom Clancy. Rep. Berkley (1,100,000)

Rosehaven. Catherine Coulter. Rep. Jove (1,100,000)

The List. Steve Martini. Rep. Jove (1,100,000)

The Clinic. Jonathan Kellerman. Rep. Bantam 1,100,000

Exclusive. Sandra Brown. Rep. Warner (1,079,246)

Legend. Jude Deveraux. Rep. Pocket.

Day of Reckoning: The Stereoscope. John Saul. Orig. Fawcett (1,050,541)

The Rainmaker. John Grisham. Movie Tie-in. Dell/Island (1,025,000)

Asylum. John Saul. Orig. Fawcett. (1,003,900)

The MacGregor Brides. Nora Roberts. Orig. Silhouette/Harlequin (1,000,000)

The Ugly Duckling. Iris Johansen. Rep. Bantam (1,000,000)

Long After Midnight. Iris Johansen. Rep. Bantam (1,000,000)

Children's Bestsellers:
Movie and TV Tie-ins Lead the Kids' Pack

The picture from the children's end of the business is mixed. Hardcover frontlist continues to gain ground; in 1997, 39 titles sold more than 200,000 copies, compared to 24 titles in 1996 and 15 in 1995. And 150 titles sold more than 75,000 copies last year, compared to 1996's total of 80. This is a boon to hardcover publishers, especially for any company with Disney-related titles; sales of Disney tie-ins claimed seven of the top 10 spaces on the list, as well as many others all the way down the line. Other standouts included *The Children's Book of Heroes*, which sold more than 300,000 copies; many Rugrats, Arthur and Pooh titles, showing the strong influence of TV on the list; board book editions of Dr. Seuss and Eric Carle classics; *William Wegman's Puppies*; and Janell Cannon's *Verdi*.

There were gains in hardcover backlist as well: 17 titles sold more than 300,000 copies in 1997, compared to 13 in 1996, and 42 titles sold more than 200,000 copies (32 in 1996). The hardcover backlist also features many tie-in titles (Disney, Pooh, Barney) that show no sign of waning in popularity.

News was not so good on the paperbacks side. There were roughly the same number of frontlist titles selling more than 125,000 last year as in 1996, but there were only six that sold above 500,000 copies, compared to 21 in 1996 (20 of those were Goosebumps titles, indicating the falloff in sales that series has experienced). Seven of the top 10 paperback frontlist titles last year were Goosebumps titles, but at greatly reduced sales levels (for example, 1996's No. 1 paperback title, Goosebumps #44, sold 2,140,000 copies, compared to 1997's No. 1 title, Goosebumps #53, which sold 886,000 copies).

And in terms of paperback backlist, the picture was even worse. In 1996, 122 titles sold more than 125,000 copies and made our list; in 1997 there were only 77. In 1996 there were 10 titles (nine Goosebumps titles and *Love You Forever*) that sold more than 500,000 copies, compared to only one title (*Love You Forever*) in 1997. In fact, only two Goosebumps titles made 1997's paperback backlist list: *Welcome to Dead House*, with 143,000 copies sold, and *Say Cheese and Die!*, with 128,000 copies sold, while there were 39 Goosebumps titles on the 1996 list.

Many paperback backlist staples were down in sales either slightly or noticeably, including *The Giver* (302,000 in 1997; 346,700 in 1996), *The Outsiders* (154,300 in 1997; 248,100 in 1996) and *Where the Wild Things Are* (201,800 in 1997; 269,300 in 1996). Others held their own (*Charlotte's Web, Tuck Everlasting, The Boxcar Children*) or even increased somewhat in sales (*Shiloh, My Side of the Mountain, The Pigman*).

For this roundup, publishers were asked to supply trade figures only, reflecting returns as of February 1, 1998. Since figures do not include total returns, they consequently do not necessarily represent net sales. Some books appear on our lists without sales figures; these figures were supplied in confidence, for use in ranking the titles only.

Hardcover Frontlist

200,000+

1. *Hercules (Classic).* Disney/Mouse Works (558,992)
2. *Anastasia (Little Golden Book).* Golden (396,360)
3. *Disney: Pooh's Grand Adventure.* Golden (376,950)
4. *Disney: Pooh and the Dragon.* Golden (364,610)
5. *Sesame Street: Tickle Me: My Name Is Elmo.* Golden (349,400)
6. *Disney's Hercules.* Golden (314,800)
7. *The Children's Book of Heroes.* Edited by William J. Bennett, illus. by Michael Hague. S&S (311,888)
8. *Disney's Pooh: Eeyore, Be Happy!* Golden (307,070)
9. *Disney's Pooh: Happy Easter.* Golden (301,810)
10. *Disney's 101 Dalmatians.* Golden (295,260)
11. *Dr. Seuss' ABC (board book).* Dr. Seuss. Random House (264,047)
12. *Mr. Brown Can Moo: Can You? (board book).* Dr. Seuss. Random House (258,504)
13. *Seussisms.* Dr. Seuss. Random House (256,693)
14. *Disney's Bambi.* Golden (255,860)
15. *Sesame Street: Shake a Leg!* Golden (254,550)
16. *Disney's Beauty and the Beast: The Enchanted Christmas.* Golden (254,200)
17. *The Little Mermaid (Classic).* Disney/Mouse Works (250,520)
18. *Anastasia.* Maggie Blackwell, illus. by Eddie Young. HarperActive (249,375)
19. *Disney's Sleeping Beauty.* Golden (245,340)
20. *The Many Adventures of Winnie the Pooh: A Classic Disney Treasury.* Disney (236,246)
21. *Say the Magic Word.* Marc Brown. Random House (233,342)
22. *The Twelve Days of Christmas (mini).* Anne Geddes. Cedco (231,382)
23. *Disney's Hercules.* Golden (231,350)
24. *Pooh Friendly Tales.* Disney/Mouse Works (228,618)
25. *Miss Spider's Tea Party: The Counting Book (board book).* David Kirk. Scholastic/Callaway (226,000)
26. *Kiss Hello, Kiss Good-Bye.* Marc Brown. Random House (221,053)
27. *My First Word Board Book.* DK (220,000)
28. *Barney's Silly Alphabet Soup.* Mary Ann Dudko, photos by Dennis Full. Lyrick/Barney (219,824)
29. *Arthur's Neighborhood.* Marc Brown. Random House (219,255)
30. *Disney's Bambi and the Butterfly.* Golden (218,820)
31. *The Hat.* Jan Brett. Putnam (218,463)
32. *Barney: The Best Christmas Ever!* Golden (216,190)

33. *Barney: Catch That Hat!* Golden (214, 360)
34. *Pooh: Who Hid in the Honey Tree?* Disney/Mouse Works (208,686)
35. *Pooh: A Walk in the Woods.* Disney/Mouse Works (206,351)
36. *Verdi.* Janell Cannon. Harcourt Brace (205,000)
37. *Pooh: Good Friends.* Disney/Mouse Works (202,145)
38. *Disney's The Little Mermaid: The Whole Story.* Golden (202,070)

100,000+

39. *Sesame Street: The Bunny Hop.* Golden (195,480)
40. *The Very Quiet Cricket (board book).* Eric Carle. Philomel (185,242)
41. *Pooh: The Perfect Picnic Spot.* Disney/Mouse Works (184,319)
42. *Arthur's Really Helpful Word Book.* Marc Brown. Random House (176,103)
43. *Arthur's New Puppy (board book).* Marc Brown. Little, Brown (175,532)
44. *I Spy Super Challenger.* Jean Marzollo, photos by Walter Wick. Scholastic (172,000)
45. *Rugrats: Tommy and Chuckie on the Go!* Sarah Willson, illus. by Peter Panas. Simon Spotlight (171,601)
46. *Polar Bear, Polar Bear, What Do You Hear? (board book).* Bill Martin Jr., illus. by Eric Carle. Holt (170,298)
47. *Rugrats: It's a Circus.* Sarah Willson, illus. by Peter Panas. Simon Spotlight (164,793)
48. *William Wegman's Puppies.* William Wegman. Hyperion (164,226)
49. *The Never-Forgotten Doll (Chicken Soup for Little Souls).* Jack Canfield. Health Communications (163,000)
50. *Annabelle's Wish.* Golden (162,110)
51. *The Best Night Out with Dad (Chicken Soup for Little Souls).* Jack Canfield. Health Communications (162,000)
52. *Hush Little Baby.* Sylvia Long. Chronicle (160,751)
53. *Precious Moments: Easter.* Golden (156,900)
54. *Go, Dog, Go!* P. D. Eastman. Random House (155,830)
55. *Where's Waldo? The Wonder Book.* Martin Handford. Candlewick (154,629)
56. *The Velveteen Rabbit.* Golden (152,060)
57. *Barbie: The Special Sleepover.* Golden (151,580)
58. *The Goodness Gorillas (Chicken Soup for Little Souls).* Jack Canfield. Health Communications (151,000)
59. *Disney's Treasury of Children's Classics.* Gina Ingoglia. Disney (150,000)
60. *Miss Spider's New Car.* David Kirk. Scholastic/Callaway (149,000)
61. *Diana, Queen of Hearts.* Random House (146,259)
62. *Disney's Snow White & the Seven Dwarfs.* Golden (145,650)
63. *Squeeze Me: Thank Heavens for Pegasus.* Disney/Mouse Works (141,129)

64. *Barney's Clothes.* Mary Ann Dudko, photos by Dennis Full. Lyrick/Barney (137,344)
65. *Butterfly Kisses.* Bob and Brooke Carlisle, illus. by Carolyn Ewing. Golden (134,240)
66. *I Spy Little Book.* Jean Marzollo, photos by Walter Wick. Scholastic (134,000)
67. *Pooh and Friends (box set).* Disney/Mouse Works (131,380)
68. *Piglet Friendly Tales.* Disney/Mouse Works (131,267)
69. *Arthur's Baby (board book).* Marc Brown. Little, Brown (130,134)
70. *Disney's The Jungle Book.* Golden (129,930)
71. *Tigger Friendly Tales.* Disney/Mouse Works (129,385)
72. *Pooh: Merry Christmas to You.* Disney/Mouse Works (128,794)
73. *There's a Wocket in My Pocket! (board book).* Dr. Seuss. Random House (125,598)
74. *The Shape of Me and Other Stuff (board book).* Dr. Seuss. Random House (125,190)
75. *My Little People School Bus.* Doris Tomaselli, illus. by Carolyn Bracken. Reader's Digest (122,207)
76. *Big Bird Meets Santa Claus.* Golden (119,900)
77. *Tomie's Little Mother Goose (board book).* Tomie dePaola. Putnam (119,697)
78. *Big Bird's Ticklish Christmas.* Golden (117,420)
79. *My Little People Farm.* Doris Tomaselli, illus. by the Thompson Brothers. Reader's Digest (117,125)
80. *Oh Brother! It's the Easter Bunny.* Disney/Mouse Works (116,148)
81. *Across the Wide and Lonesome Prairie (Dear America).* Kristiana Gregory. Scholastic (116,000)
82. *Oh, Baby, The Places You'll Go!* Adapted by Tish Rabe. Random House (115,522)
83. *Time for Bed (board book).* Mem Fox, illus. by Jane Dyer. Harcourt Brace (115,000)
84. *The Foot Book (board book).* Dr. Seuss. Random House (114,457)
85. *Disney's Mickey and Friends: Let's Go to the Firestation.* Golden (114,450)
86. *Disney's Lady and the Tramp.* Golden (113,330)
87. *Barney's Treasure Hunt.* Guy Davis, illus. by Darren McKee. Lyrick/Barney (112,858)
88. *From Head to Toe.* Eric Carle. HarperCollins (112,233)
89. *Pocket Full of Pooh-isms.* Disney/Mouse Works (108,450)
90. *Muppet Babies: I Can Go Potty.* Golden (107,680)
91. *The Little Mermaid's Sea Sayings.* Disney/Mouse Works (105,989)
92. *Elmo's Furry Face Book.* Random House (104,139)

93. *Disney's Pooh: Trick or Treat!* Golden (103,780)
94. *Disney's Pooh: Happy Easter.* Golden (102,700)
95. *Noah's Ark (board book).* Retold by Lucy Cousins. Candlewick (102,516)
96. *Disney's Beauty and the Beast.* Golden (102,400)
97. *Disney's Hercules: Zero to Hero (Extra Smart Pages).* Golden (101,390)
98. *The DK Illustrated Family Bible.* DK (101,000)
99. *Disney's Fantasia: The Sorcerer's Apprentice.* Golden (100,520)
100. *Barney's This Little Piggy (Squeak Book).* Adapted by Margie Larsen, illus. by Jay Johnson. Lyrick/Barney (100,323)
101. *Barney: Through the Seasons.* Golden (99,950)

75,000+

102. *Disney's Lady and the Tramp: The Lost Tag.* Golden (99,940)
103. *The Little Mermaid: Ariel's Glittering Sea Sparkle.* Disney/Mouse Works (98,968)
104. *Eeyore Friendly Tales.* Disney/Mouse Works (98,884)
105. *The Legend of the Candy Cane: The Inspirational Story of Our Favorite Christmas Candy.* Lori Walburg. Zondervan (98,883)
106. *Pooh's Storybook Treasury.* Disney/Mouse Works (98,080)
107. *Disney's Knock-Knock Jokes.* Disney/Mouse Works (97,314)
108. *Where's Waldo? (revised ed.).* Martin Handford. Candlewick (96,814)
109. *The Small One (board book).* Alex Walsh, illus. by Jesse Clay. Disney (96,565)
110. *Disney's Totally Cool Trivia.* Disney/Mouse Works (96,491)
111. *Macmillan Dictionary for Children.* S&S (96,073)
112. *Arthur's Computer Disaster.* Marc Brown. Little, Brown (95,981)
113. *The Nutcracker.* Adapted by Daniel Walden, illus. by Don Daily. Running Press/Courage (95,299)
114. *Milo and the Magical Stones.* Marcus Pfister. North-South (91,633)
115. *The Little Mermaid's Little Library.* Disney/Mouse Works (89,870)
116. *Tickle Me, Elmo!* Stephanie St. Pierre, illus. by David Prebenna. Random House (89,857)
117. *Cookie Count.* Robert Sabuda. Little Simon (89,566)
118. *The Inheritance.* Louisa May Alcott. Dutton (89,493)
119. *Barney: A Very Musical Day.* Golden (89,220)
120. *A Picture of Freedom (Dear America).* Patricia C. McKissack. Scholastic (87,000)
121. *My Anastasia Storybook and Necklace.* Diane Molleson, illus. by Brad McMahon. Harper Active (85,908)
122. *Disney's Hercules: My Favorite Sound Story.* Golden (85,750)
123. *Precious Moments: The Gifts of Christmas.* Golden (85,450)

124. *The Little Mermaid's Missing Music.* Disney/Mouse Works (85,235

125. *Robbie's Reindeer's Present.* Gaby Goldsack, illus. by Teresa Foster. Reader's Digest (84,787)

126. *What's That Noise? All About Farm Animals.* Susan Hood, illus. by Rosa and Marta Serrat. Reader's Digest (82,828)

127. *Sleeping Beauty (Classic).* Disney/Mouse Works (82,130)

128. *Anastasia: A Princess in Paris (Extra Smart Pages).* Golden (81,950)

129. *Dinosaur World.* Christopher Santoro. Random House (80,712)

130. *Inside, Outside.* Stan and Jan Berenstain. Random House (80,641)

131. *Bananas in Pajamas: Rain, Rain, Go Away!* Golden (80,250)

132. *Fuzzytail Friends.* Lisa McCue. Random House (80,248)

133. *Hercules (Little Library).* Disney/Mouse Works (80,046)

134. *Arthur Writes a Story.* Marc Brown. Little, Brown (80,001)

135. *Old Hat, New Hat.* Stan and Jan Berenstain. Random House (79,904)

136. *Pooka Visits Paris.* Illus. by Josie Yee. Harper Active (78,258)

137. *My Symphony.* Mary Engelbreit. Andrews & McMeel (78,000)

138. *Christmas with Kathie Lee: A Treasury of Holiday Stories, Songs, Poems, and Activities for Little Ones.* Kathie Lee Gifford. Disney (77,641)

139. *Snoozers.* Sandra Boynton. Little Simon (77,073)

140. *All Aboard Thidwick.* Louise Gikow and R&B Barto. Random House (77,057)

141. *The Poky Little Puppy Comes to Sesame Street.* Golden (76,650)

142. *Better Homes and Gardens New Junior Cookbook.* Meredith (76,323)

143. *If I Went on Safari! All About Numbers.* Susan Hood, illus. by Francese Rigol. Reader's Digest (76,208)

144. *The Grinch's Song.* Louise Gikow and R&B Barto. Random House (76,085)

145. *Disney's Pooh: Peekaboo, Eeyore!* Golden (75,630)

146. *Anastasia Mini Library.* Illus. by Greg Huber. Harper Active (75,787)

147. *The Whispering Rabbit.* Margaret Wise Brown, illus. by Cyndy Szekeres. Golden (75,480)

148. *Pumpkin Ted (Halloween Fluffy Tales).* Gaby Goldsack, illus. by Caroline Jayne Church. Reader's Digest (75,392)

149. *Barney & Me at the Circus.* Kimberly Kearns, illus. by Bill Alger. Lyrick/Barney (75,377)

150. *Little Cottontail.* Golden (75,250)

Hardcover Backlist

300,000+

1. *Disney's Pooh: Thank You, Pooh!* Golden, 1996 (598,820)

2. *Disney's Pooh: A Grand and Wonderful Day.* Golden, 1996 (494,300)

3. *Guess How Much I Love You (board book).* Sam McBratney, illus. by Anita Jeram. Candlewick, 1995 (481,488)
4. *Goodnight Moon (board book).* Margaret Wise Brown, illus. by Clement Hurd. HarperFestival, 1991 (468,240)
5. *Disney's 101 Dalmatians.* Golden, 1996 (448,930)
6. *Brown Bear, Brown Bear, What Do You See? (board book).* Bill Martin Jr., illus. by Eric Carle. Holt, 1996 (441,709)
7. *Disney's Pooh: The Sweetest Christmas.* Golden, 1996 (433,130)
8. *Oh, the Places You'll Go!* Dr. Seuss. Random House, 1990 (408,779)
9. *Arthur Goes to School.* Marc Brown. Random House, 1995 (394,880)
10. *The Scholastic Children's Dictionary.* Scholastic, 1996 (368,000)
11. *Disney's Pooh: Winnie the Pooh and the Honey Tree.* Golden, 1994 (351,960)
12. *Barney: Sharing Is Caring.* Golden, 1996 (348,060)
13. *Green Eggs and Ham.* Dr. Seuss. Random House, 1966 (333,318)
14. *Disney's The Lion King: Way to Go Simba.* Golden, 1996 (332,300)
15. *Sesame Street: Count to Ten.* Golden, 1993 (328,980)
16. *Disney's Pooh: Eeyore, You're the Best.* Golden, 1996 (312,850)

200,000+

17. *The Complete Adventures of Curious George.* Margret and H.A. Rey. Houghton Mifflin, 1995 (292,723)
18. *Disney's Pooh Has Ears.* Golden, 1995 (292,130)
19. *Where the Sidewalk Ends.* Shel Silverstein. HarperCollins, 1974 (288,647)
20. *Barney Goes to the Zoo.* Linda Cress Dowdy, illus. by Karen Malzeke-McDonald. Lyrick/Barney, 1993 (284,374)
21. *My First Little Mother Goose.* Golden, 1996 (283,700)
22. *Sesame Street: Another Monster at the End of This Book.* Jon Stone, illus. by Mike Smollin. Golden, 1996 (280,100)
23. *The Three Bears.* Golden, 1993 (268,260)
24. *Peter Pan Illustrated Classic.* Todd Strasser. Disney, 1994 (262,738)
25. *Baby Mickey's Book of Shapes.* Golden, 1996 (261,280)
26. *The Very Hungry Caterpillar (board book).* Eric Carle. Philomel, 1994 (259,923)
27. *Falling Up.* Shel Silverstein. HarperCollins. 1996 (258,407)
28. *Zip! Pop! Hop! and Other Fun Words to Say.* Golden, 1996 (256,500)
29. *A Day with Barney.* Mary Ann Dudko and Margie Larsen, illus. by Larry Daste. Lyrick/Barney, 1994 (248,689)
30. *Guess How Much I Love You.* Sam McBratney, illus. by Anita Jeram. Candlewick, 1995 (245,048)
31. *Barney's Number Friends.* Adapted by Mark S. Bernthal, illus. by Darren McKee. Lyrick/Barney, 1996 (235,997)

32. *The Wheels on the Bus.* Golden, 1993 (235,640)
33. *The Cat in the Hat.* Dr. Seuss. Random House, 1957 (226,411)
34. *The Littlest Angel.* Charles Tazewell, illus. by Paul Micich. Ideals/Hambleton-Hill, 1995 (225,957)
35. *Barbie: Scavenger Hunt.* Golden, 1996 (222,830)
36. *The Giving Tree.* Shel Silverstein. HarperCollins, 1964 (221,815)
37. *Disney's Cinderella.* Golden, 1996 (207,350)
38. *One Fish, Two Fish, Red Fish, Blue Fish.* Dr. Seuss. Random House, 1966 (205,413)
39. *The Light in the Attic.* Shel Silverstein. HarperCollins, 1981 (204,177)

100,000+

40. *Baby Animals on the Farm.* Golden, 1993 (194,620)
41. *Children's Letters to God.* Stuart Hample and Eric Marshall. Workman, 1991 (193,359)
42. *The Rainbow Fish.* Marcus Pfister. North-South, 1992 (191,253)
43. *Stellaluna.* Janell Cannon. Harcourt Brace, 1993 (190,000)
44. *My First Book of Sounds.* Golden, 1995 (184,990)
45. *Disney's 101 Dalmatians: Snow Puppies.* Golden, 1996 (180,360)
46. *Barney Plays Nose to Toes.* Mary Ann Dudko and Margie Larsen, photos by Dennis Full. Lyrick/Barney, 1996 (180,295)
47. *I Spy School Days.* Jean Marzollo, photos by Walter Wick. Scholastic, 1995 (177,000)
48. *Snuggle Up with Pooh.* Disney/Mouse Works, 1996 (174,477)
49. *The Rainbow Fish (board book).* Marcus Pfister. North-South, 1996 (173,549)
50. *Disney's the Lion King: The Cave Monster.* Golden, 1996 (170,740)
51. *Bedtime for Baby Bop.* Donna Cooner, illus. by Bill Alger. Lyrick/Barney, 1996 (170,666)
52. *Disney's Peter Pan.* Golden, 1996 (168,970)
53. *Pat the Bunny.* Dorothy Kunhardt. Golden, 1994 (167,940)
54. *Barney's Color Surprise.* Mary Ann Dudko and Margie Larsen, photos by Dennis Full. Lyrick/Barney, 1993 (167,250)
55. *I Spy Spooky Night.* Jean Marzollo, photos by Walter Wick. Scholastic, 1996 (167,000)
56. *Rudolph the Red-Nosed Reindeer.* Richard Scarry. Golden, 1996 (166,160)
57. *Winnie the Pooh* (Classic). Disney/Mouse Works, 1993 (165,546)
58. *The Three Little Pigs.* Golden, 1996 (165,150)
59. *Disney's Pooh: Tigger's Counting Book.* Golden, 1996 (163,750)
60. *My First Counting Book.* Golden, 1996 (161,500)
61. *Barney's Farm Animals.* Kimberly Kearns and Marie O'Brien, illus. by Karen Malzeke-McDonald. Lyrick/Barney, 1993 (161,219)

62. *Are You My Mother?* P. D. Eastman. Random House, 1960 (157,294)
63. *I Spy Christmas.* Jean Marzollo, photos by Walter Wick. Scholastic, 1992 (155,000)
64. *Disney's Mickey's Christmas Carol.* Golden, 1996 (153,270)
65. *Sesame Street: Elmo's Twelve Days of Christmas.* Golden, 1996 (152,250)
66. *My Little Golden Book About God.* Golden, 1994 (152,140)
67. *Disney's Pooh: All Year Long.* Golden, 1990 (150,870)
68. *Lilly's Purple Plastic Purse.* Kevin Henkes. Greenwillow, 1996 (150,000)
69. *Good Night Gorilla (board book).* Peggy Rathmann. Putnam, 1996 (148,857)
70. *Barney's Friends.* Mary Ann Dudko, illus. by June Valentine-Ruppe. Lyrick/Barney, 1995 (147,490)
71. *The Complete Tales of Winnie the Pooh.* A. A. Milne. Dutton, 1996 (146,659)
72. *Toy Story* (Classic). Disney/Mouse Works, 1996 (143,182)
73. *Dr. Seuss's ABC Book.* Dr. Seuss. Random House, 1966 (142,994)
74. *Go, Dog Go!* P. D. Eastman. Random House, 1966 (142,205)
75. *Muppet Babies: Be Nice!* Golden, 1993 (140,740)
76. *I Spy Fantasy.* Jean Marzollo, photos by Walter Wick. Scholastic, 1994 (136,000)
77. *Bambi* (Classic). Disney/Mouse Works, 1996 (133,775)
78. *Prayers for Children.* Golden, 1994 (130,810)
79. *Barbie: Very Busy Barbie.* Golden, 1993 (130,200)
80. *Elmo's Big Lift and Look Book.* Anna Ross. Random House, 1994 (129,770)
81. *Hop on Pop.* Dr. Seuss. Random House, 1966 (127,887)
82. *Put Me In the Zoo.* Robert Lopshire. Random House, 1960 (127,050)
83. *Love You Forever.* Robert Munsch, illus. by Sheila McGraw. Firefly, 1986 (126,234)
84. *The Very Busy Spider (board book).* Eric Carle. Philomel, 1995 (126,213)
85. *I Spy Mystery.* Jean Marzollo, photos by Walter Wick. Scholastic, 1993 (125,000)
86. *Sesame Street: The Monster at the End of This Book.* Jon Stone, illus. by Mike Smollin. Golden, 1993 (118,760)
87. *The Jungle Book* (Classic). Disney/Mouse Works, 1995 (118,495)
88. *The Polar Express.* Chris Van Allsburg. Houghton Mifflin, 1985 (117,959)
89. *If You Give a Mouse a Cookie.* Laura Numeroff, illus. by Felicia Bond. HarperCollins, 1985 (116,122)
90. *The Little Engine That Could (board book).* Watty Piper. Grosset & Dunlap, 1978 (112,232)
91. *Goodnight Moon.* Margaret Wise Brown, illus. by Clement Hurd. HarperCollins, 1947 (111,788)

92. *Disney's Pooh: I Am Winnie the Pooh.* Golden, 1994 (111,270)
93. *The Mitten (board book).* Jan Brett. Putnam, 1996 (109,400)
94. *The Cat in the Hat Comes Back.* Dr. Seuss. Random House, 1966 (105,596)
95. *Disney's Pooh Can, Can You?* Golden, 1994 (105,130)
96. *The View from Saturday.* E. L. Konigsburg. Atheneum, 1996 (104,714)
97. *The Poky Little Puppy.* Janette Sebring Lowrey, illus. by Gustaf Tenggren. Golden, 1996 (103,660)
98. *Pooh: I See the Sun.* Disney/Mouse Works, 1995 (103,080)
99. *Miss Spider's Tea Party.* David Kirk. Scholastic/Callaway, 1994 (103,000)
100. *Sesame Street: Elmo's Guessing Game.* Golden, 1994 (102,970)
101. *The Little Bunny.* Stewart Cowley, illus. by Susi Adams. Reader's Digest, 1996 (102,478)
102. *Baby's First Bible.* Colin and Moira MacLean. Reader's Digest, 1996 (102,211)
103. *Peter Pan* (Classic). Disney/Mouse Works, 1994 (101,955)
104. *A Fly Went By.* Mike McClintock and Fritz Siebel. Random House, 1958 (101,407)
105. *Pooh: Where's Piglet?* Disney/Mouse Works, 1995 (100,657)
106. *On the Day You Were Born.* Debra Frasier. Harcourt Brace, 1991 (100,000)

Paperback Frontlist

500,000+

1. *Chicken Soup for the Teenage Soul.* Jack Canfield. Health Communications (2,290,200)
2. *Chicken, Chicken (Goosebumps #53).* R. L. Stine. Scholastic (886,000)
3. *Don't Go to Sleep (GB #54).* R. L. Stine. Scholastic (797,000)
4. *The Curse of Camp Cold Lake (GB #56).* R. L. Stine. Scholastic (757,000)
5. *The Blob That Ate Everyone (GB #55).* R. L. Stine. Scholastic (753,000)
6. *How I Learned to Fly (GB #52).* R. L. Stine. Scholastic (674,000)
7. *My Best Friend Is Invisible (GB #57).* R. L. Stine. Scholastic (591,000)
8. *Deep Trouble II (GB #58).* R. L. Stine. Scholastic (499,000)
9. *The Meanest Thing to Say (Little Bill #1).* Bill Cosby. Scholastic (428,000)
10. *The Best Way to Play (Little Bill #2).* Bill Cosby. Scholastic (419,000)
11. *Treasure Hunt (Little Bill #3).* Bill Cosby. Scholastic (417,000)
12. *Barney Goes to the Dentist.* Linda Dowdy, photos by Dennis Full. Lyrick/Barney (405,770)
13. *The Haunted School (GB #59).* R. L. Stine. Scholastic (400,000)
14. *Werewolf Skin (GB #60).* R. L. Stine. Scholastic (367,000)
15. *Hanson: MMMBop to the Top.* Jill Matthews. Pocket/Archway (361,987)

16. *The World Almanac for Kids 1998.* Judith Levey. World Almanac (346,740)
17. *Meet Josefina (American Girls).* Valerie Tripp, illus. by Jean Paul Tibbles. Pleasant Co. (345,383)
18. *Barney and Baby Bop Go to the Grocery Store.* Donna Cooner, photos by Dennis Full. Lyrick/Barney (344,978)
19. *The Alien (Animorphs #8).* K. A. Applegate. Scholastic (343,000)
20. *Please Don't Feed the Vampire (Give Yourself Goosebumps #15).* R. L. Stine. Scholastic (319,000)
21. *I Live In Your Basement (GB #61).* R. L. Stine. Scholastic (311,000)
22. *Monster Blood IV (GB #62).* R. L. Stine. Scholastic (305,000)

200,000+

23. *Batman and Robin.* Alan Grant, adapted by Akiva Goldsman. Little, Brown (297,881)
24. *The Andalite's Gift (Animorphs Megamorphs #1).* K. A. Applegate. Scholastic (291,000)
25. *The Capture (Animorphs #6).* K. A. Applegate. Scholastic (288,000)
26. *The Stranger (Animorphs #7).* Scholastic (287,000)
27. *Secret Agenda Grandma (GYGB #16).* R. L. Stine. Scholastic (286,000)
28. *Disney's Hercules: Friends and Foes.* Golden (283,580)
29. *Josefina Learns a Lesson (American Girls).* Valerie Tripp, illus. by Jean Paul Tibbles. Pleasant Co. (279,628)
30. *The Secret (Animorphs #9).* K. A. Applegate. Scholastic (279,000)
31. *Attack of the Beastly Babysitter (GYGB #18).* R. L. Stine. Scholastic (273,000)
32. *The Change (Animorphs #13).* K. A. Applegate. Scholastic (271,000)
33. *Cry of the Cat (Goosebumps Series 2000 #1).* R. L. Stine. Scholastic (265,000)
34. *The Little Comic Shop of Horrors (GYGB #17).* R. L. Stine. Scholastic (264,000)
35. *Disney's Hercules.* Golden (260,160)
36. *Josefina's Surprise (American Girls).* Valerie Tripp, illus. by Jean Paul Tibbles. Pleasant Co. (260,068)
37. *The Forgotten (Animorphs #11).* K. A. Applegate. Scholastic (259,000)
38. *The Creepy Creations of Professor Shock (GYGB #14).* R. L. Stine. Scholastic (258,000)
39. *The Reaction (Animorphs #12).* K. A. Applegate. Scholastic (254,000)
40. *Batman and Robin: Movie Storybook.* Golden (252,740)
41. *The Android (Animorphs #10).* K. A. Applegate. Scholastic (251,000)
42. *The Unknown (Animorphs #14).* K. A. Applegate. Scholastic (242,000)

43. *Escape from Camp Run-for-Your-Life (GYGB #19).* R. L. Stine. Scholastic (235,000)

44. *The Andalite Chronicles: A Trilogy.* K. A. Applegate. Scholastic (231,000)

45. *The Golden One (Lucasfilms Alien Chronicles).* Deborah Chester. Ace (225,000)

46. *Batman and Robin: Heroes and Villains.* Golden (216,900)

47. *Barney's Trick or Treat.* Mark S. Bernthal, illus. by Bill Alger. Lyrick/Barney (214,778)

48. *Barney's Book of Hugs.* Sheryl and Patrick Leach, illus. by June Valentine-Ruppe. Lyrick/Barney (214,390)

49. *Barney's Christmas Wishes.* Steven White, illus. by Darren McKee. Lyrick/Barney (211,358)

50. *Rugrats: Stormy Weather.* Molly Wigand, illus. by Barry Goldberg. Simon Spotlight (210,884)

51. *Rugrats Blast Off!* Stephanie St. Pierre, illus. by George Ulrich. Simon Spotlight (205,408)

52. *Leonardo DiCaprio: Modern Day Romeo.* Grace Catalano. Dell/Laurel-Leaf (204,687)

53. *Diversity Alliance (Star Wars: Young Jedi Knights).* Kevin J. Anderson and Rebecca Moesta. Boulevard (200,000)

125,000+

54. *Junk, Sweet Junk (Rugrats).* Molly Wigand, illus. by Barry Goldberg. Simon Spotlight (199,562)

55. *Rugrats: Reptar to the Rescue.* Stephanie St. Pierre, illus. by George Ulrich. Simon Spotlight (194,584)

56. *Eaten Alive (Star Wars: Galaxy of Fear).* John Whitman. Bantam (193,852)

57. *Anastasia (Look Look Book).* Golden (191,860)

58. *The Adventures of Wishbone: Be a Wolf.* Brad Strickland. Lyrick/Big Red Chair (188,323)

59. *Arthur's First Sleepover.* Marc Brown. Little, Brown (187,755)

60. *Three Evil Wishes (Ghosts of Fear Street #19).* R. L. Stine. Pocket/Minstrel (186,116)

61. *The Nightmare Machine (Star Wars: Galaxy of Fear).* John Whitman. Bantam (182,059)

62. *Toy Terror (GYGB #20).* R. L. Stine. Scholastic (181,000)

63. *The Adventures of Wishbone: The Prince and the Pooch.* Caroline Leavitt. Lyrick/Big Red Chair (180,526)

64. *The Adventures of Wishbone: Robin Crusoe.* Caroline Leavitt. Lyrick/Big Red Chair (178,937)

65. *Disney's Beauty and the Beast: The Enchanted Christmas.* Golden (177,690)

66. *Prince William: The Boy Who Will Be King.* Randi Reisfeld. Pocket/Archway (176,686)

67. *Delusions of Grandeur (Star Wars: Young Jedi Knights).* Kevin J. Anderson and Rebecca Moesta. Boulevard (175,000)

68. *City of the Dead (Star Wars Galaxy of Fear).* John Whitman. Bantam (171,513)

69. *Barney's Easter Egg Hunt.* Steven White, illus. by June Valentine-Ruppe. Lyrick/Barney (165,744)

70. *Hanson: An Unauthorized Biography.* Michael-Anne Johns. Scholastic (158,000)

71. *I Know What You Did Last Summer.* Lois Duncan. Pocket/Archway (155,002)

72. *The Cat (Fear Street #45).* R. L. Stine Pocket/Archway (154,317)

73. *Silent Night (Fear Street Collector's Edition).* R. L. Stine. Pocket/Archway (153,876)

74. *The Hidden Evil (Fear Street Sagas #5).* R. L. Stine. Pocket/Archway (153,243)

75. *The Killer's Kiss (Fear Street #42).* R. L. Stine. Pocket/Archway (152,387)

76. *Taylor Hanson: Totally Taylor!* Nancy Krulik. Pocket/Archway (151,947)

77. *The Emperor's Plague (Star Wars: Young Jedi Knights).* Kevin J. Anderson and Rebecca Moesta. Boulevard (150,000)

78. *Jedi Beauty (Star Wars: Young Jedi Knights).* Kevin J. Anderson and Rebecca Moesta. Boulevard (150,000)

79. *The Beginning (Fear Street: Fear Hall).* R. L. Stine. Pocket/Archway(148,830)

80. *Elmo Saves Christmas.* Tony Geiss and Christine Ferrare, illus. by Ellen Appleby. Random House (148,576)

81. *All Night Party (Fear Street #43).* R. L. Stine. Pocket/Archway (147,499)

82. *The Rich Girl (Fear Street #44).* R. L. Stine. Pocket/Archway (145,626)

83. *Execution of Innocence.* Christopher Pike. Pocket/Archway (144,912)

84. *The Twisted Tale of Tiki Island (GYGB #21).* R. L. Stine. Scholastic (143,000)

85. *The Complete Star Wars Trilogy Scrapbook.* Scholastic (142,000)

86. *Goodnight Kiss (Fear Street Collector's Edition).* R. L. Stine. Pocket/Archway (140,672)

87. *Pearls of Lutra.* Brian Jacques. Ace (140,000)

88. *High Tide (Fear Street Super Chiller).* R. L. Stine. Pocket/Archway(139,316)

89. *Turtle Time.* Sandol Stoddard, illus. by Lynn Munsinger. Houghton Mifflin/Lorraine (136,238)

90. *The Star Wars Movie Storybook.* Scholastic (134,000)

91. *Daughters of Silence (Fear Street Saga #6).* R. L. Stine. Pocket/Archway (133,916)

92. *Ghost of the Jedi (Star Wars Galaxy of Fear).* John Whitman. Bantam (131,101)

93. *House of a Thousand Screams (Ghosts of Fear Street #17).* R. L. Stine. Pocket/Minstrel (128,839)

94. *Who Killed the Homecoming Queen? (Fear Street #48).* R. L. Stine. Pocket/Archway (128,434)

95. *Children of Fear (Fear Street Sagas #7).* R. L. Stine. Pocket/Archway(128,097)

96. *Knots on a Counting Rope.* Bill Martin, Jr., and John Archambault, illus. by Ted Rand. Holt/Owl (127,423)

97. *Sabrina, the Teenage Witch (#1).* David Cody Weiss and Bobbi J G Weiss. Pocket/Archway (126,911)

98. *Batman and Mr. Freeze.* Golden (126,020)

99. *Showdown at the Mall (Sabrina, the Teenage Witch #2).* Diana Gallagher. Pocket/Archway (125,817)

100. *The Outcast of Redwall.* Brian Jacques. Ace (125,000)

Paperback Backlist

200,000+

1. *Love You Forever.* Robert Munsch, illus. by Sheila McGraw. Firefly, 1986 (626,489)

2. *Arthur's Birthday.* Marc Brown. Little, Brown, 1991 (369,871)

3. *Barney's Christmas Surprise.* Mark S. Bernthal, illus. by Bill Alger. Lyrick/Barney, 1996 (331,545)

4. *Barney and Baby Bop Go to the Doctor.* Margie Larsen, photos by Dennis Full. Lyrick/Barney, 1996 (320,158)

5. *Barney and Baby Bop Go to School.* Mark S. Bernthal, photos by Dennis Full. Lyrick/Barney, 1996 (312,235)

6. *The Giver.* Lois Lowry. Dell, 1994 (302,059)

7. *Disney's Pooh: Just Be Nice to Your Little Friends.* Golden, 1996 (301,170)

8. *Barney and BJ Go to the Fire Station.* Mark S. Bernthal, photos by Dennis Full. Lyrick/Barney, 1996 (277,654)

9. *Shiloh.* Phyllis Reynolds Naylor. Dell, 1992 (262,344)

10. *Charlotte's Web.* E.B. White, illus. by Garth Williams. HarperTrophy, 1974 (259,330)

11. *The Invasion (Animorphs #1).* K. A. Applegate. Scholastic, 1996 (249,000)

12. *The Message (Animorphs #4).* K. A. Applegate. Scholastic, 1996 (231,000)

13. *The Encounter (Animorphs #3).* K. A. Applegate. Scholastic, 1996 (225,000)

14. *Where the Red Fern Grows.* Wilson Rawls. Bantam, 1984 (221,680)

15. *The Visitor (Animorphs #2).* K. A. Applegate. Scholastic, 1996 (218,000)

16. *Hatchet.* Gary Paulsen. Aladdin, 1996 (210,094)
17. *Arthur's Christmas.* Marc Brown. Little, Brown, 1985 (209,584)
18. *The Lion, the Witch and the Wardrobe.* C. S. Lewis, illus. by Pauline Baynes. HarperTrophy, 1994 (209,053)
19. *Stone Fox.* John Reynolds Gardiner, illus. by Bruce Minney. HarperTrophy, 1983 (203,396)
20. *Barney's Big Balloon.* Mark S. Bernthal, illus. by Chris Sharp and David McGlothlin. Lyrick/Barney, 1995 (203,180)
21. *Kids' U.S. Road Atlas.* Rand McNally, 1992 (198,285)
22. *Where the Wild Things Are.* Maurice Sendak. HarperTrophy, 1988 (201,843)

125,000+

23. *The Predator (Animorphs #5).* K. A. Applegate. Scholastic, 1996 (198,000)
24. *Little Critter: Just Me and My Dad.* Mercer Mayer. Golden, 1994 (197,790)
25. *Arthur's Baby.* Marc Brown. Little, Brown, 1990 (196,576)
26. *Arthur's New Puppy.* Marc Brown. Little Brown, 1995 (192,486)
27. *Disney's Pooh: The Merry Christmas Mystery.* Golden, 1995 (188,720)
28. *Arthur's Tooth.* Marc Brown. Little, Brown, 1986 (188,682)
29. *Arthur's Family Vacation.* Marc Brown. Little, Brown, 1995 (187,517)
30. *Arthur's Chicken Pox.* Marc Brown. Little, Brown, 1996 (184,651)
31. *Roll of Thunder, Hear My Cry.* Mildred Taylor. Puffin, 1991 (180,666)
32. *Arthur's Pet Business.* Marc Brown. Little, 1993 (179,729)
33. *Sarah, Plain and Tall.* Patricia MacLachlan. HarperTrophy, 1987 (177,536)
34. *Curious George.* H. A. Rey. Houghton Mifflin, 1941 (176,859)
35. *Are We There Yet?* Rand McNally, 1996 (175,914)
36. *Barnyard Dance!* Sandra Boynton. Workman, 1993 (175,909)
37. *Disney's Pooh: Just Be Nice and Not Too Rough.* Golden, 1996 (174,500)
38. *Bridge to Terabithia.* Katherine Paterson. HarperTrophy, 1987 (170,902)
39. *The Sign of the Beaver.* Elizabeth Speare. Dell, 1993 (169,620)
40. *Barney's Halloween Party.* Mary Ann Dudko and Margie Larsen, illus. by Darren McKee. Lyrick/Barney, 1996 (167,101)
41. *Arthur's Teacher Trouble.* Marc Brown. Little, Brown, 1989 (164,681)
42. *My Name Is Elmo.* Golden, 1993 (163,220)
43. *Little Critter: The New Potty.* Mercer Mayer. Golden, 1992 (162,490)
44. *Little House in the Big Woods.* Laura Ingalls Wilder, illus. by Garth Williams. HarperTrophy, 1971 (160,019)
45. *Lyle at the Office.* Bernard Waber. Houghton Mifflin, 1994 (157,323)
46. *Arthur's Halloween.* Marc Brown. Little, Brown, 1983 (155,287)
47. *Little Critter: The New Baby.* Mercer Mayer. Golden, 1996 (155,010)
48. *Number the Stars.* Lois Lowry. Dell, 1990 (154,579)

49. *The Outsiders.* S. E. Hinton. Puffin, 1991 (154,318)
50. *Best Travel Activity Book Ever!* Rand McNally, 1993 (154,099)
51. *Goodnight Moon.* Margaret Wise Brown, illus. by Clement Hurd. HarperTrophy, 1977 (153,541)
52. *The Pigman.* Paul Zindel. Bantam, 1978 (152,966)
53. *The Chocolate Touch.* Patrick Catling. Dell, 1996 (149,925)
54. *The M&M's Brand Chocolate Candies Counting Book.* Barbara McGrath. Charlesbridge, 1994 (149,088)
55. *Walk Two Moons.* Sharon Creech, illus. by Steven Rydberg. HarperTrophy, 1996 (148,629)
56. *Sesame Street: Rise and Shine.* Golden, 1996 (147,950)
57. *Meet Samantha (American Girls).* Susan Adler, illus. by Nancy Niles. Pleasant Co., 1986 (146,508)
58. *Barney Says, "Please and Thank You."* Stephen White, illus. by Rick Grayson. Lyrick/Barney, 1994 (145,760)
59. *Welcome to Dead House (Goosebumps #1).* R. L. Stine. Scholastic, 1992 (143,000)
60. *Little Critter: I Just Forgot!* Mercer Mayer. Golden, 1990 (141,680)
61. *My Side of the Mountain.* Jean Craighead George. Puffin, 1991 (138,484)
62. *Arthur Meets the President.* Marc Brown. Little, Brown. 1992 (138,181)
63. *Little Critter: Just Go to Bed.* Mercer Mayer. Golden, 1994 (138,070)
64. *Tuck Everlasting.* Natalie Babbitt. FSG/Sunburst, 1985 (137,439)
65. *Little House on the Prairie.* Laura Ingalls Wilder, illus. by Garth Williams. HarperTrophy, 1971 (137,204)
66. *Arthur Goes to Camp.* Marc Brown. Little, Brown, 1984 (135,844)
67. *Clifford's Happy Easter.* Norman Bridwell. Scholastic, 1994 (135,000)
68. *Oh My Oh My Oh Dinosaurs!* Sandra Boynton. Workman, 1993 (134,578)
69. *Maniac Magee.* Jerry Spinelli. HarperTrophy, 1992 (132,728)
70. *Tales of a Fourth Grade Nothing.* Judy Blume. Dell, 1976 (131,079)
71. *Games and Giggles.* Illus. by Paul Meisel. Pleasant Co., 1995 (129,192)
72. *Johnny Tremain.* Esther Forbes. Dell, 1996 (128,666)
73. *The Boxcar Children.* Gertrude Chandler Warner. Albert Whitman, 1989 (128,649)
74. *Say Cheese and Die! (GB #4).* R. L. Stine. Scholastic, 1992 (128,000)
75. *The Magician's Nephew.* C. S. Lewis, illus. by Pauline Baynes. HarperTrophy, 1994 (127,192)
76. *A Wrinkle in Time.* Madeleine L'Engle. Dell, 1973 (126,534)
77. *Little Critter: Just Me in the Tub.* Mercer Mayer. Golden, 1994 (125,750)

Literary Prizes, 1997

Gary Ink
Research Librarian, *Publishers Weekly*

ABBY Awards. To honor titles that members have most enjoyed handselling in the past year. *Offered by:* American Booksellers Association. *Winners:* (adult) Frank McCourt for *Angela's Ashes* (Scribner); (children's) Kevin Henkes for *Lilly's Purple Plastic Purse* (Greenwillow).

J. R. Ackerley Award (United Kingdom). For autobiography. *Offered by:* PEN (UK). *Winner:* Tim Lott for *The Scent of Dried Roses* (Viking).

Jane Addams Children's Book Award. For a book promoting the cause of peace, social justice, and world community. *Offered by:* Women's International League for Peace and Freedom and the Jane Addams Peace Association. *Winner:* Susan Campbell for *Growing Up in Coal Country* (Houghton Mifflin); (picture book) Katherine Krull for *Wilma Unlimited* (Harcourt Brace).

Ambassador Book Awards. To recognize books that have made an exceptional contribution to the interpretation of life and culture in the United States. *Offered by:* English-Speaking Union. *Winners:* (poetry) Robert Pinsky; (biography) Robert Merry; (fiction) John Updike; (American studies) Stephen E. Ambrose.

American Academy of Arts and Letters Award of Merit Medal for the Novel. *Offered by:* American Academy of Arts and Letters. *Winner:* Richard Ford.

American Academy of Arts and Letters Awards in Literature. *Offered by:* American Academy of Arts and Letters. *Winners:* Charles Baxter, Lane Dunlop, Allen Grossman, Maureen Howard, Jayne Anne Phillips, Luc Sante, Wallace Shawn, Jane Smiley.

Bancroft Prizes. For books of exceptional merit and distinction in American history, American diplomacy, and the international relations of the United States. *Offered by:* Columbia University. *Winners:* David E. Kyvig for *Explicit and Authentic Acts: Amending the U.S. Constitution, 1776–1995* (University of Kansas); James T. Patterson for *Grand Expectations: the United States, 1945–1974* (Oxford).

Mildred L. Batchelder Award. For an American publisher of a children's book originally published in a foreign language in a foreign country, and subsequently published in English in the United States. *Offered by:* American Library Association, Association for Library Service to Children. *Winner:* Farrar, Straus & Giroux for *The Friends* by Kazumi Yumoto.

Before Columbus Foundation American Book Awards. For literary achievement by people of various ethnic backgrounds. *Offered by:* Before Columbus Foundation. *Winners:* Alurista for *Raza* (Bilingual Press); Dorothy Baressi for *The Post-Rapture Diner* (University of Pittsburgh); Martin Espada for *Imagine the Angels of Bread* (Norton); Guillermo Gomez-Pena for *The New World Border* (City Lights); Derrick Bell for *Gospel Choirs* (Basic Books); Thulani Davis for *Maker of Saints* (Scribner); Tom DeHaven for *Derby Dugan's Depression Funnies* (Metropolitan Books); Montserrat Fontes for *Dreams of the Centaur* (Norton); Louis Owens for *Nightland* (Dutton); (creative nonfiction award) Shirley Geok-lin Lim for *Among the White Moon Faces* (Feminist Press); (editor/publisher award) Allan Kornblum.

Curtis Benjamin Award for Creative Publishing. *Offered by:* Association of American Publishers. *Winner:* Thomas McCormack.

Helen B. Bernstein Award for Excellence in Journalism. *Offered by:* New York Public Library. *Winner:* David Quammen for *The Song of the Dodo* (Scribner).

James Tait Black Memorial Prizes (United Kingdom). For the best biography and the best novel of the year. *Offered by:* University of Edinburgh. *Winners:* (biography) Diarmaid MacCulloch for *Thomas Cranmer: A Life* (Yale University); (fiction)

Graham Swift for *Last Orders* (Picador); Alice Thompson for *Justine* (Canongate).

Bollingen Prize in Poetry. For the best collection of poetry published in the United States during the previous two years, or for lifetime achievement in poetry. *Offered by:* Yale University. *Winner:* Gary Snyder.

Booker Prize for Fiction (United Kingdom). *Offered by:* Book Trust and Booker PLC. *Winner:* Arundhati Roy for *The God of Small Things* (Flamingo).

Booker Russian Novel Prize (Russia). *Offered by:* British Council in Moscow and Booker PLC. *Winner:* Anatoly Azolsky for *The Cell* (Novy Mir).

Boston Globe/Horn Book Awards. For excellence in text and illustration. *Winners:* (fiction) Kazumi Yumoto for *The Friends* (Farrar, Straus & Giroux); (nonfiction) Walter Wick for *A Drop of Water* (Scholastic); (picture book) Brian Pinkney for *The Adventures of Sparrowboy* (Simon & Schuster).

Witter Bynner Prize for Poetry. To support the work of young poets. *Offered by:* American Academy of Arts and Letters. *Winner:* Mark Doty.

Caldecott Medal. For the artist of the most distinguished picture book. *Offered by:* R. R. Bowker Company. *Winner:* David Wisniewski for *Golem* (Clarion Books).

John W. Campbell Memorial Award. For outstanding science fiction writing. *Offered by:* Center for the Study of Science Fiction. *Winner:* Michael A. Burstein.

Carnegie Medal (United Kingdom). For the outstanding children's book of the year. *Offered by:* The Library Association. *Winner:* Melvin Burgess for *Junk* (Andersen Press/ Penguin).

Children's Book Award (United Kingdom). To recognize the achievement of authors and illustrators. *Offered by:* Federation of Children's Book Groups. *Winner:* Jeremy Strong for *The Hundred-Mile-an-Hour Dog* (Viking).

Cholmondeley Awards (United Kingdom). For contributions to poetry. *Offered by:* Society of Authors. *Winners:* Alison Brackenbury, Gillian Clarke, Tony Curtis, Anne Stevenson.

Arthur C. Clarke Award (United Kingdom). For the best science fiction novel of the year. *Offered by:* British Science Fiction Association. *Winner:* Amitav Ghosh for *The Calcutta Chromosome* (Picador).

Commonwealth Writers Prize (United Kingdom). *Offered by:* Commonwealth Institute. *Winners:* Earl Lovelace for *Salt* (Faber); (first work) Ann-Marie MacDonald for *Fall on Your Knees* (Cape).

Thomas Cook Travel Book Award (United Kingdom). *Offered by:* Book Trust. *Winner:* Nicholas Crane for *Clear Waters Rising* (Penguin).

Crime Writers' Association Awards (United Kingdom). (Gold Dagger) Ian Rankin for *Black and Blue* (Orion); (Silver Dagger) Janet Evanovich for *Three to Get Deadly* (Penguin); (Gold Dagger for nonfiction) Paul Britton for *The Jigsaw Man* (Bantam Press).

Alice Fay Di Castagnola Award. For a work in progress to recognize a poet at a critical stage of his or her work. *Offered by:* Poetry Society of America. *Winner:* Chase Twichell for *The Snow Watcher* (work-in-progress).

Philip K. Dick Award. For a distinguished paperback original published in the United States. *Offered by:* Norwescon. *Winner:* Stephen Baxter for *The Time Ships* (HarperPrism).

T. S. Eliot Prize (United Kingdom). For poetry. *Offered by:* Poetry Book Society. *Winner:* Les Murray for *Subhuman Redneck Poems* (Carcanet Press).

Encore Award (United Kingdom). For a second novel. *Offered by:* Society of Authors. *Winner:* David Flusfeder for *Like Plastic* (Cape).

Norma Farber First Book Award. For a first book of poetry. *Offered by:* Poetry Society of America. *Winner:* Susan Yuzna for *Her Slender Dress* (University of Akron).

Faulkner Award for Fiction. To honor the best work of fiction published by an American. *Offered by:* PEN American Center. *Winner:* Gina Berriault for *Women in Their Beds* (Counterpoint).

E. M. Forster Award in Literature. To a young writer from England, Ireland, Scotland, or Wales for a stay in the United

States. *Offered by:* American Academy of Arts and Letters. *Winner:* Glyn Maxwell.

Forward Poetry Prize (United Kingdom). For best poetry published in the United Kingdom or the Republic of Ireland. *Offered by:* The *Forward*. *Winners:* (best collection) Jamie McKendrick for *The Marble Fly* (Oxford); (best first collection) Robin Robertson for *A Painted Field* (Chatto); (best individual poem) Tolman Cunard for *A World Where News Travelled Slowly*.

Frost Medal for Distinguished Achievement. To recognize achievement in poetry over a lifetime. *Offered by:* Poetry Society of America. *Winner:* Josephine Jacobsen.

Guardian Fiction Prize (United Kingdom). For recognition of a novel by a British or Commonwealth writer. *Offered by:* The *Guardian*. *Winner:* Anne Michaels for *Fugitive Pieces* (Bloomsbury).

Golden Kite Awards. For outstanding children's books. *Offered by:* Society of Children's Book Writers and Illustrators. *Winners:* (fiction) Eloise McGraw for *The Moorchild* (Margaret McElderry); (nonfiction) Peg Kehret for *Small Steps* (Whitman); (Illustration) Holly Berry for *Market Day* by Eve Bunting (HarperCollins); (picture book) Diane Stanley for *Saving Sweetness* (Putnam).

Governor General's Literary awards (Canada). For the best English-language and French-language books by Canadian authors. *Offered by:* Canada Council for the Arts. *Winners:* (fiction) Jane Urquart for *The Underpainter* (McClelland & Stewart); Aude for *Cet Imperceptible Mouvement* (XYZ Editeur); (poetry) Dionne Brand for *Land to Light On* (McClelland & Stewart); Pierre Nepveu for *Romans-Fleuves* (Editions du Noroit); (nonfiction) Rachel Manley for *Drumblair* (Knopf); Roland Viau for *Enfants du Néant et Mangeurs d'Ames* (Editions du Boréal; (children's literature/text) Kit Pearson for *Awake and Dreaming* (Viking); Michel Noel for *Pien* (Editions Michel Quintin); (children's literature/illustration) Barbara Reid for *The Party* (North Winds); Stéphane Poulin for *Poil de Serpent, Dent d'Araignée*, text by Danielle Marcotte (Editions Les 400 Coups); (translation) Howard Scott for *The Eugue-lion* (*L'Euguelionne*) by Louky Bersianik (Alter Ego Press); Marie José Thériault for *Arracher les Montagnes* (*Digging Up the Mountains*) by Neil Bissoondath (Macmillan Canada).

Kate Greenaway Medal (United Kingdom). For children's book illustration. *Offered by:* The Library Association. *Winner:* Helen Cooper for *The Baby Who Wouldn't Go to Bed* (Doubleday).

Eric Gregory Trust Awards (United Kingdom). For poets under the age of 30. *Offered by:* Society of Authors. *Winners:* Matthew Clegg, Polly Clark, Sarah Corbett, Tim Kendal, Graham Nelson, Matthew Welton.

Drue Heinz Literature Prize. To recognize and encourage writing of short fiction. *Offered by:* Drue Heinz Foundation and University of Pittsburgh. *Winner:* Katherine Vaz for *Fado and Other Stories* (University of Pittsburgh).

Ernest Hemingway Foundation Award. For a work of first fiction by an American. *Offered by:* PEN American Center. *Winner:* Ha Jin for *Ocean of Words* (Zoland).

IMPAC Dublin Literary Award (Ireland). For a book of high literary merit written in English, or translated into English. *Offered by:* IMPAC Corp. and the City of Dublin. *Winner:* Javier Maras for *A Heart So White*, translated by Margaret Jull Costa (Harvill).

Irish Fiction Prize (Ireland). *Offered by:* Irish Times. *Winner:* Seamus Deane for *Reading in the Dark* (Vintage).

Irish Prize for Nonfiction (Ireland). *Offered by:* Irish Times. *Winner:* Declan Kiberd for *Inventing Ireland* (Vintage).

Irish Prize for Poetry (Ireland). *Offered by:* Irish Times. *Winner:* Paul Muldoon for *New Selected Poems* (Faber).

Irish Times International Fiction Prize (Ireland). *Offered by:* Irish Times. *Winner:* Seamus Deane for *Reading in the Dark* (Vintage).

Jewish Book Awards. For contributions to Jewish literature. *Offered by:* Jewish Book Council. *Winners:* (fiction) Saul Bellow for *The Actual* (Viking); (nonfiction) Ruth Gay for *Unfinished People: Eastern European Jews Encounter America* (Norton); (children's) Barbara Rogasky for *The*

Golem, illus. by Trina Schart Hyman (Holiday House).

Sue Kaufman Prize for First Fiction. *Offered by:* American Academy of Arts and Letters. *Winner:* Brad Watson for *The Last Days of the Dog Men* (Norton).

Coretta Scott King Awards. For works that promote the cause of peace and brotherhood. *Offered by:* American Library Association Social Responsibilities Round Table. *Winner:* (author award) Walter Dean Myers for *Slam!* (Scholastic); (illustrator award) Jerry Pinkney for *Minty: A Story of Young Harriet Tubman* by Alan Schroeder (Dial).

Kiriyama Pacific Rim Book Prize. To promote books that contribute to greater understanding and increased cooperation among the peoples of the nations of the Pacific Rim. *Offered by:* Kiriyama Pacific Rim Foundation and the University of San Francisco. *Winner:* Patrick Smith for *Japan: A Reinterpretation* (Pantheon).

Robert Kirsch Award. To a living author whose residence or focus has been in the West, or whose career contributions to American letters merit recognition. *Offered by:* Los Angeles Times. *Winner:* Gary Snyder.

Harold Morton Landon Translation Award. For a book of verse translated into English by a single translator. *Offered by:* Academy of American Poets. *Winner:* David Hinton for *The Selected Poems of Li Po* (New Directions) and *The Late Poems of Meng Chiao* (Princeton University).

Lannan Literary Awards. *Offered by:* Lannan Foundation. *Winners:* (fiction) John Banville, Anne Michaels, Grace Paley; (nonfiction) David Quammen; (poetry) Ken Smith; (Lifetime Achievement Award) William H. Gass.

James Laughlin Award. To support the publication of a second book of poetry. *Offered by:* Academy of American Poets. *Winner:* Tony Hoagland for *Donkey Gospel* (Graywolf).

Ruth Lilly Poetry Prize. To a United States poet whose accomplishments warrant extraordinary recognition. *Offered by:* Modern Poetry Association. *Winner:* William Matthews.

Anne Spencer Lindbergh Prize. For the best children's fantasy novel in English. *Offered by:* Lindbergh Foundation. *Winner:* Joan Aiken for *Cold Shoulder Road* (Red Fox).

Locus Awards. For science fiction writing. *Offered by:* Locus Publications. *Winners:* (science fiction novel) Kim Stanley Robinson for *Blue Mars* (Bantam); (fantasy novel) George R. R. Martin for *A Game of Thrones* (Bantam); (dark fantasy/horror novel) Stephen King for *Desperation* (Viking); (first novel) Sage Walker for *Whiteout* (Tor); Sarah Zettel for *Reclamation* (Warner); (nonfiction) John Clute for *Look at the Evidence* (Serconia Press); (art book) Cathy Burnett et al., eds. for *Spectrum III: The Best in Contemporary Fantasy Art* (Underwood Books); (collection) Joe Haldeman for *None So Blind* (Morrow/AvoNova); (anthology) Gardner Dozois, ed. for *The Year's Best Science Fiction: Thirteenth Annual Collection* (St. Martin's).

Los Angeles Times Book Prizes. To honor literary excellence. *Winners:* (fiction) Rohinton Mistry for *A Fine Balance* (Random House); (poetry) Alan Shapiro for *Mixed Company* (University of Chicago); (history) Neal Ascherson for *Black Sea* (Hill & Wang); (biography) Frank McCourt for *Angela's Ashes* (Scribner); (science and technology) Carl Sagan for *The Demon-Haunted World* (Random House); (current interest) Peter Maas for *Love Thy Neighbor* (Random House); (Art Seidenbaum Award for First Fiction) Mark Behr for *The Smell of Apples* (St. Martin's).

McKitterick Prize (United Kingdom). For a first novel by a writer over the age of 40. *Offered by:* Society of Authors. *Winner:* Patricia Dunker for *Hallucinating Foucault* (Serpent's Tail).

Kurt Maschler Award (United Kingdom). For a children's book in which text and illustrations are both excellent and perfectly harmonious. *Offered by:* Book Trust. *Winner:* William Mayne for *Lady Muck*, illus. by Jonathan Heale (Heinemann).

Somerset Maugham Awards (United Kingdom). For young British writers to gain experience in foreign countries. *Offered by:* Society of Authors. *Winners:* Rhidian Brook for *The Testimony of Taliesin Jones*

(Flamingo); Kate Clanchey for *Slattern* (Chatto); Philip Hensher for *Kitchen Venom* (Hamish Hamilton); Francis Spufford for *I May Be Some Time* (Faber).

National Arts Club Medal of Honor for Literature. *Offered by:* National Arts Club. *Winner:* Margaret Atwood.

National Book Awards. *Offered by:* National Book Foundation. *Winners:* (fiction) Charles Frazier for *Cold Mountain* (Atlantic Monthly); (nonfiction) Joseph Ellis for *American Sphinx* (Knopf); (poetry) William Meredith for *Effort at Speech* (Northwestern University); (children's) Han Nolan for *Dancing on the Edge* (Harcourt).

National Book Critics Circle Awards. *Offered by:* National Book Critics Circle. *Winners:* (fiction) Gina Berriault for *Women in Their Beds* (Counterpoint); (general nonfiction) Jonathan Raban for *Bad Land: An American Romance* (Pantheon); (biography/autobiography) Frank McCourt for *Angela's Ashes* (Scribner); (poetry) Robert Hass for *Sun Under Wood* (Ecco Press); (criticism) William Glass for *Finding a Form* (Knopf).

National Book Foundation Medal for Distinguished Contribution to American Letters. *Offered by:* National Book Foundation. *Winner:* Studs Terkel.

NCR Book Award (United Kingdom). For the best nonfiction book of the year. *Offered by:* NCR Corp. *Winner:* Orlando Figes for *A People's Tragedy* (Cape).

Nebula Awards. For the best science fiction writing. *Offered by:* Science Fiction Writers of America. *Winners:* (best novel) Nicola Griffin for *Slow River* (Del Rey); (Grand Master) Jack Vance.

John Newbery Medal. For the most distinguished contribution to literature for children. *Donor:* American Library Association, Association for Library Service to Children. *Medal Contributed by:* Daniel Melcher. *Winner:* E. L. Konigsburg for *The View from Saturday* (Atheneum).

Nobel Prize in Literature. For the total literary output of a distinguished writer. *Offered by:* Swedish Academy. *Winner:* Dario Fo.

Flannery O'Connor Awards for Short Fiction. *Offered by:* PEN American Center.

Winners: Ha Jin for *Under the Red Flag* (University of Georgia); Andy Plattner for *Winter Money* (University of Georgia).

Scott O'Dell Award for Historical Fiction. *Offered by: Bulletin of the Center for Children's Books*, University of Chicago. *Winner:* Katherine Paterson for *Jip: His Story* (Lodestar).

Orange Prize for Fiction (United Kingdom). For the best novel written by a woman and published in the United Kingdom. *Offered by:* Orange PLC. *Winner:* Anne Michaels for *Fugitive Pieces* (Bloomsbury).

PEN Award for Poetry in Translation. *Offered by:* PEN American Center. *Winner:* Edward Snow for *Uncollected Poems* by Rainer Maria Rilke (Farrar, Straus & Giroux).

PEN Book-of-the-Month Club Translation Award. *Offered by:* PEN American Center. *Winner:* Arnold Pomerans for *The Letters of Vincent van Gogh* (Viking).

PEN Center USA West Annual Literary Awards. For outstanding literary achievement by writers living west of the Mississippi. *Winners:* (fiction) William T. Vollmann for *The Atlas* (Viking); (creative nonfiction) Jonathan Raban for *Bad Land* (Pantheon); (research nonfiction) Edward Humes for *No Matter How Loud I Shout* (Simon & Schuster); (poetry) Bob Kaufman for *Cranial Guitar* (Coffee House); (translation) Maryellen Toman Mori for *Kangaroo Notebook* (Knopf); (children's Literature) Peg Kehret for *Small Steps* (Albert Whitman).

PEN/Barbara Goldsmith Freedom-to-Write Awards. For writers outside the United States who have defended freedom of speech in their countries. *Offered by:* PEN American Center. *Winners:* Aysenur Zarakolu (Turkey); Godwin Agbroko (Nigeria).

PEN/Ralph Manheim Medal for Translation. For lifetime achievement in the field of translation. *Offered by:* PEN American Center. *Winner:* Robert Fagles.

PEN/Newman's Own First Amendment Award. To recognize extraordinary actions in defense of freedom of expression. *Offered by:* PEN American Center and Newman's Own. *Winner:* Nancy Hsu Fleming.

Edgar Allan Poe Awards. For outstanding mystery, crime, and suspense writing. *Offered by:* Mystery Writers of America.

Winners: (novel) Thomas A. Cook for *The Chatham School Affair* (Bantam); (first novel) John Morgan Wilson for *Simple Justice* (Doubleday); (original paperback) Harlan Coben for *Fade Away* (Dell); (fact crime) Darcy O'Brien for *Power to Hurt* (HarperCollins); (critical/biographical) Michael Atkinson for *The Secret Marriage of Sherlock Holmes* (University of Michigan); (young adult) Willa Davis Roberts for *Twisted Summer* (Atheneum); (juvenile) Dorothy Reynolds Miller for *The Clearing* (Simon & Schuster); (Grand Master) Ruth Rendell.

Poets' Prize. For the best book of poetry published in the United States in the previous year. *Offered by:* Nicholas Roerich Museum. *Winner:* Josephine Jacobsen.

Renato Poggioli Translation Award. To assist a translator of Italian whose work in progress is especially outstanding. *Offered by:* PEN American Center. *Winner:* Ann McGarrell for *The Face of Isis* by Vittoria Ronchey (work in progress).

Premio Aztlan. To a Chicano or Chicana fiction writer who has published no more than two books. *Offered by:* Rudolfo and Patricia Anaya and University of New Mexico. *Winner:* Wendell Mayo.

Pulitzer Prizes in Letters. To honor distinguished work by American writers, dealing preferably with American themes. *Offered by:* Columbia University, Graduate School of Journalism. *Winners:* (fiction) Steven Millhauser for *Martin Dressler* (Crown); (history) Jack N. Rakove for *Original Meanings* (Knopf); (biography) Frank McCourt for *Angela's Ashes* (Scribner); (general nonfiction) Richard Kluger for *Ashes to Ashes* (Knopf); (poetry) Lisel Mueller for *Alive Together* (Louisiana State University).

QPB New Visions Award. For the most distinctive and promising work of nonfiction offered by the Quality Paperback Book Club. *Offered by:* Quality Paperback Book Club. *Winner:* Bia Lowe for *Wild Ride* (HarperPerennial).

QPB New Voices Award. For the most distinctive and promising work of fiction offered by the Quality Paperback Book Club. *Offered by:* Quality Paperback Book Club. *Winner:* Bruce Olds for *Raising Holy Hell* (Holt).

Rea Award for the Short Story. To honor a living writer who has made a significant contribution to the short story as an art form. *Offered by:* Dungannon Foundation. *Winner:* Gina Berriault.

Rhone-Poulenc Science Book Award (United Kingdom). *Offered by:* Rhone-Poulenc. *Winners:* Alan Walker and Pat Shipman for *The Wisdom of the Bones* (Weidenfeld); (juvenile) Nick Arnold and Tony de Saulles for *Blood, Bones and Body Bits* (Hippo).

John Llewellyn Rhys Memorial Award (United Kingdom). *Offered by:* The *Mail on Sunday*. *Winner:* Nicola Barker for *Heading Inland* (Faber).

Rainier Maria Rilke International Prize for Poetry (Germany). To honor the lifetime work of a poet who has published poetry in more than one European language. *Offered by:* International Academy of Poetry and Poetics. *Winner:* Oswald LeWinter.

Romance Writers of America RITA Awards. For excellence in the romance genre. *Offered by:* Romance Writers of America. *Winners:* (traditional) Lauryn Chandler for *Her Very Own Husband* (Silhouette); (inspirational) Francine Rivers for *The Scarlet Thread* (Tyndale House); (short contemporary) Anne McAllister for *Cowboy Pride* (Silhouette); (long contemporary) Naomi Horton for *Wild Blood* (Silhouette); (romantic suspense) Bethany Campbell for *See How They Run* (Bantam); (contemporary single) Barbara Freethy for *Daniel's Gift* (Avon); (paranormal) Lynn Kurland for *Stardust of Yesterday* (Berkley); (Regency) Carla Sue Kelly for *The Lady's Companion* (Penguin); (short historical) Lorraine Heath for *Always to Remember* (Berkley/Jove); (long historical) Laura Lee Guhrke for *Conor's Way* (HarperCollins); (best first book) Lynn Kurland for *Stardust of Yesterday* (Berkley).

Rome Fellowship in Literature. For a one-year residence at the American Academy in Rome. *Offered by:* American Academy of Arts and Letters and Philip Morris Companies. *Winner:* Fae Myenne Ng.

Richard and Hinda Rosenthal Foundation Award. For a work of fiction that is a considerable literary achievement though not necessarily a commercial success. *Offered by:* American Academy of Arts and Letters. *Winner:* Mary Kay Zuravleff.

Sagittarius Prize (United Kingdom). For a first novel by a writer over the age of 40. *Offered by:* Society of Authors. *Winner:* Barbara Hardy for *London Lovers* (Peter Owen).

Shamus Awards. For the best private eye fiction. *Offered by:* Private Eye Writers of America. *Winners:* (best novel) Robert Crais for *Sunset Express* (Hyperion); (best paperback original) Harlan Coben for *Fade Away* (Dell); (best first novel) Carole Lea Benjamin for *This Dog for Hire* (Walker).

Shelley Memorial Award. To a poet living in the United States who is chosen on the basis of genius and need. *Offered by:* Poetry Society of America. *Winner:* Frank Bidart.

Smarties Book Prizes (United Kingdom). To encourage high standards and to stimulate interest in books for children. *Offered by:* Book Trust and Nestle Rowntree. *Winners:* (ages 9–11) J. K. Rowling for *Harry Potter and the Philosopher's Stone* (Bloomsbury); (ages 6–8) Jenny Nimmo for *The Owl Tree*, illus. by Anthony Lewis (Walker); (ages 0–5) Charlotte Voake for *Ginger* (Walker).

W. H. Smith Literary Award (United Kingdom). For a significant contribution to literature. *Offered by:* W. H. Smith. *Winner:* Orlando Figes for *A People's Tragedy* (Cape).

Templeton Prize for Progress in Religion. *Offered by:* Templeton Foundation. *Winner:* Pandurang Shautri Athavale.

Betty Trask Awards (United Kingdom). For works of a romantic or traditional nature by writers under the age of 35. *Offered by:* Society of Authors. *Winners:* Alex Garland for *The Beach* (Penguin); Josie Barnard for *Poker Face* (Virago); Ardashir Vakil for *Beach Boy* (Hamish Hamilton); Diran Adebayo for *Some Kind of Black* (Virago); Sanjida O'Connell for *Theory of Mind* (Black Swan).

Kate Frost Tufts Discovery Award. For a first or very early book of poetry by an emerging poet. *Offered by:* Claremont Graduate School. *Winner:* Lucia Perillo for *The Body Mutinies* (Purdue University).

Kingsley Tufts Poetry Award. *Offered by:* Claremont Graduate School. *Winner:* Campbell McGrath for *Spring Comes to Chicago* (Ecco Press).

Harold D. Vursell Memorial Award in Literature. *Offered by:* American Academy of Arts and Letters. *Winner:* Elizabeth McCracken.

Lila Wallace–Reader's Digest Fund Writer's Awards. *Offered by:* Lila Wallace Foundation. *Winners:* Edwidge Danicat, Thulani Davis, Ron Hansen, Askold Melnyczuk, Fae Myenne Ng, Simon Ortiz, Luis Rodriguez, Mac Wellman.

Whitbread Book of the Year (United Kingdom). *Offered by:* Booksellers Association of Great Britain. *Winner:* Seamus Heaney for *The Spirit Level* (Farrar, Straus & Giroux).

Whitbread Children's Book of the Year (United Kingdom). *Offered by:* Booksellers Association of Great Britain. *Winner:* Anne Fine for *The Tulip Touch* (Little, Brown).

William Allen White Children's Book Award. *Offered by:* Emporia State University. *Winner:* Mary Downing Hahn for *Time for Andrew* (Clarion).

Whiting Writers Awards. For outstanding talent and promise. *Offered by:* Mrs. Giles Whiting Foundation. *Winners:* JoAnn Beard, Connie Deanovich, Erik Ehn, Forrest Gander, Jody Gladding, Suketu Mehta, Ellen Meloy, Josip Novakovich, Melanie Rae Thon, Mark Turpin.

Walt Whitman Award. For poetry. *Offered by:* Academy of American Poets. *Winner:* Barbara Ras for *Bite Every Sorrow* (Louisiana State University).

William Carlos Williams Award. For the best book of poetry published by a small, nonprofit, or university press. *Offered by:* Poetry Society of America. *Winner:* David Ignatow for *I Have a Name* (Wesleyan University).

Robert H. Winner Memorial Award. For a poem or sequence of poems characterized by a delight in language and the possibilities of ordinary life. *Offered by:* Poetry Society of America. *Winner:* P. H. Liotta.

World Fantasy Convention Awards. For outstanding fantasy writing. *Offered by:* World Fantasy Convention. *Winners:*

(novel) Rachel Pollack for *Godmother Night* (St. Martin's); (anthology) Patrick Nielsen Hayden, ed., *Starlight 1* (Tor); (collection) Jonathan Lethem for *The Wall of the Sky, The Wall of the Eye* (Harcourt Brace); (lifetime achievement) Madeleine L'Engle.

World Science Fiction Convention Hugo Awards. For outstanding science fiction writing. *Offered by:* World Science Fiction Convention. Winners: (best novel) Kim Stanley Robinson for *Blue Mars* (Harper-Collins); (best nonfiction book) L. Sprague de Camp for *Time & Chance* (Donald Grant).

Morton Dauwen Zabel Award in Poetry. *Offered by:* American Academy of Arts and Letters. *Winner:* Wendy Lesser.

Part 6
Directory of Organizations

Directory of Library and Related Organizations

Networks, Consortia, and Other Cooperative Library Organizations

This list is taken from the 1997–1998 edition of *American Library Directory* (R. R. Bowker), which includes additional information on member libraries and primary functions of each organization.

United States

Alabama

Alabama Health Libraries Association, Inc. (ALHeLa), Univ. of Alabama, Lester Hill Lib., 1700 University Blvd., Birmingham 35294-0013. SAN 372-8218. Tel. 205-934-2230, fax 205-975-8313. *Pres.* Kay Hogan.

American Gas Association–Library Services (AGA–LSC), c/o Alabama Gas Corp., 2101 Sixth Ave. N., Birmingham 35203. SAN 371-0890. Tel. 205-326-8436, fax 205-326-2617, e-mail cbaker@go1. energen.com. *Chair* Calvin Baker.

Jefferson County Hospital Librarians Association, Brookwood Medical Center, 2010 Brookwood Medical Center Dr., Birmingham 35209. SAN 371-2168. Tel. 205-877-1131, fax 205-877-1189. *Coord.* Lucy Moor.

Library Management Network, Inc., 915 Monroe St., Box 443, Huntsville 35804. SAN 322-3906. Tel. 205-532-5963, fax 205-536-1772, e-mail charlotte@lmn.lib. al.us. *System Coord.* Charlotte Moncrief.

Marine Environmental Sciences Consortium, Dauphin Island Sea Lab, Box 369-370, Dauphin Island 36528. SAN 322-0001. Tel. 334-861-2141, fax 334-861-4646. *Dir.* George Crozier; *Libn.* Connie Mallon.

Network of Alabama Academic Libraries, c/o Alabama Commission on Higher Educa-

tion, Box 302000, Montgomery 36130-2000. SAN 322-4570. Tel. 334-242-2211, fax 334-242-0270. *Dir.* Sue O. Medina.

Alaska

Alaska Library Network (ALN), 344 W. Third Ave., Suite 125, Anchorage 99501. SAN 371-0688. Tel. 907-269-6570, fax 907-269-6580, e-mail slanc@muskox. alaska.edu.

Arizona

Central Arizona Biomedical Librarians (CABL), c/o Scientific Information Center, Steris Laboratories, 6200 N. 51 St., Phoenix 85043. SAN 370-7598. Tel. 602-447-3476, fax 602-447-3498. *Pres.* Dawn Murray Humay; *Program Chair* Donna Gerometta.

Maricopa County Community College District, 2411 W. 14 St., Tempe 85281-6941. SAN 322-0060. Tel. 602-731-8776, fax 602-731-8787, e-mail lynch@maricopa. *Coord. Acquisitions* Randi Sher; *Coord. Catalog* Vince Jenkins.

Arkansas

Arkansas Area Health Education Center Consortium (AHEC), Sparks Regional Medical

Center, 1311 South I St., Box 17006, Fort Smith 72917-7006. SAN 329-3734. Tel. 501-441-5337, fax 501-441-5339, e-mail grace@sparks.org. *Regional Health Science Libn.* Grace Anderson.

Independent College Fund of Arkansas, 1 Riverfront Pl., Suite 610, North Little Rock 72114. SAN 322-0079. Tel. 501-378-0843, fax 501-374-1523, e-mail kdietz@icfa.fihe.org. *Pres.* E. Kearney Dietz.

Northeast Arkansas Hospital Library Consortium, 223 E. Jackson, Jonesboro 72401. SAN 329-529X. Tel. 501-972-1290, fax 501-931-0839. *Dir.* Karen Crosser.

South Arkansas Film Coop, 202 E. Third St., Malvern 72104. SAN 321-5938. Tel. 501-332-5442, fax 501-332-6679. *Coord.* Tammy Lackey; *Project Dir.* Mary Cheatham.

California

Area Wide Library Network (AWLNET), 2420 Mariposa St., Fresno 93721. SAN 322-0087. Tel. 209-488-3229. *Dir. Info. Services* Sharon Vandercook.

Bay Area Library and Information Network (BAYNET), 405 14th St., Suite 211, Oakland 94612. SAN 371-0610. Tel. 415-353-0421, fax 415-561-0307, e-mail rosef@exploritorium.edu. *Pres.* Rose Falanga; *Treas.* Sara O'Keefe.

Central Association of Libraries (CAL), 605 N. El Dorado St., Stockton 95202. SAN 322-0125. Tel. 209-937-8698, fax 209-937-8292. *Supervising Libn.* Deborah Westler.

Consortium for Distance Learning, 2595 Capitol Oaks Dr., Sacramento 95833. SAN 329-4412. Tel. 916-565-0188, fax 916-565-0189. *Exec. Dir.* Jerome Thompson; *Operations Mgr.* Sandra Scott-Smith.

Consumer Health Information Program and Services (CHIPS), County of Los Angeles Public Lib., 151 E. Carson St., Carson 90745. SAN 372-8110. Tel. 310-830-0909, fax 310-834-4097. *Libn.* Scott A. Willis; *Aide* Mona Porotesano.

Cooperating Libraries in Claremont (CLIC), c/o Honnold Lib., 800 Dartmouth Ave., Claremont Colleges, Claremont 91711. SAN 322-3949. Tel. 909-621-8045, fax 909-621-8681. *Dir.* Bonnie J. Clemens; *Assoc. Dir.* Alberta Walker.

Hewlett-Packard Library Information Network, 1501 Page Mill Rd., Palo Alto 94304. SAN 375-0019. Tel. 650-857-3091, 857-6620, fax 650-852-8146, e-mail eugenie_prime@hp.com. *Chair* Eugenie Prime.

Inland Empire Academic Libraries Cooperative, Azusa Pacific Univ., 901 E. Alosta Ave., Azusa 90712-7000. SAN 322-015X. Tel. 626-815-6000, ext. 3282, fax 626-969-6611. *Coord.* Debra Quast.

Inland Empire Medical Library Cooperative (IEMLC), c/o Kaiser Permanente Medical Center, 10800 Magnolia Ave., Riverside 92505. SAN 371-8980. Tel. 909-353-3658, fax 909-353-3262. *Chair* Shirley Younce.

Kaiser Permanente Library System–Southern California Region (KPLS), Health Sciences Lib., 4647 Zion Ave., San Diego 92120. SAN 372-8153. Tel. 619-528-7323, fax 619-528-3444. *Dir.* Sheila Latus.

Knight-Ridder Information, Inc., 2440 El Camino Real, Mountain View 94040. SAN 322-0176. Tel. 650-254-7000, fax 650-254-8093. *Pres.* Jeffery S. Galt.

Learning Resources Cooperative, 5201 Linda Vista Rd., Suite 105, San Diego 92111. SAN 371-0785. Tel. 619-292-3608, fax 619-467-1549.

Learning Resources Cooperative, Southwestern College, 900 Otay Lakes Rd., Chula Vista 91910. SAN 375-006X. Tel. 619-421-6700, fax 619-482-6413, e-mail jconte@swc.cc.ca.us. *Pres.* Joseph Conte.

Metropolitan Cooperative Library System (MCLS), 3675 E. Huntington Dr., Suite 100, Pasadena 91107. SAN 371-3865. Tel. 626-683-8244, fax 626-683-8097. *Exec. Dir.* Linda Katsouleas.

National Network of Libraries of Medicine–Pacific Southwest Region (PSRML), Louise Darling Biomedical Lib., 12-077 Center for Health Sciences, Box 951798, Los Angeles 90095-1798. SAN 372-8234. Tel. 310-825-1200, fax 310-825-5389. *Dir.* Alison Bunting; *Assoc. Dir.* Beryl Glitz.

Northern California and Nevada Medical Library Group, 2140 Shattuck Ave., Box 2105, Berkeley 94704. SAN 329-4617.

Tel. 916-734-3529. *Pres.* Rochelle Perrine Schmalz.

Northern California Association of Law Libraries (NOCALL), 1800 Market St., Box 109, San Francisco 94102. SAN 323-5777. Tel. 415-393-2560, fax 415-576-3099. *Pres.* Jo Caporaso.

Northern California Consortium of Psychology Libraries (NCCPL), California School of Professional Psychology, 1005 Atlantic, Alameda 94501. SAN 371-9006. Tel. 510-523-2300, ext. 185, fax 510-523-5943, e-mail pgsp@itsa.ucsf.edu. *Chair* Deanna Gaige.

OCLC Pacific, 9227 Haven Ave., Suite 260, Rancho Cucamonga 91730. SAN 370-0747. Tel. 909-941-4220, fax 909-948-9803. *Dir.* Mary Ann Nash.

Peninsula Libraries Automated Network (PLAN), 25 Tower Rd., San Mateo 94402-4000. SAN 371-5035. Tel. 650-358-6704, fax 650-358-6706. *Data Base Mgr.* Susan Yasar.

Performing Arts Libraries Network of Southern California (PALNET), Univ. of Southern California Cinema-Television Lib., University Park, Los Angeles 90089. SAN 371-3997. Tel. 213-740-3994, fax 213-747-3301. *Chair* Steve Hanson.

Research Libraries Group, Inc. (RLG), 1200 Villa St., Mountain View 94041-1100. SAN 322-0206. Tel. 800-537-7546, fax 415-964-0943, e-mail Internet: bl.ric@rlg.stanford.edu. *Pres.* James Michalko.

Sacramento Area Health Sciences Librarians, Mercy Health Care Sacramento Lib., 6501 Coyle Ave., Carmichael 95608. SAN 322-4007. Tel. 916-537-5218. *Pres.* Catherine Hanson-Tracy.

San Bernardino, Inyo, Riverside Counties United Library Services (SIRCULS), 3581 Mission Inn Ave., Box 468, Riverside 92502. SAN 322-0222. Tel. 909-369-7995, fax 909-784-1158. *Exec. Dir.* Kathleen F. Aaron; *Reference Libn.* Linda Taylor.

San Francisco Biomedical Library Network (SFBLN), c/o California College of Podiatric Medicine, 1210 Scott St., San Francisco 94115. SAN 371-2125. Tel. 415-292-0409, fax 415-292-0467. *Pres.* Douglas Varner.

Santa Clarita Interlibrary Network (SCIL-NET), 24700 McBean Pkwy., Santa Clarita 91355. SAN 371-8964. Tel. 805-253-7885, fax 805-254-4561. *Pres.* Judith Hist; *Recorder* Judy Trapenberg.

Serra Cooperative Library System, 5555 Overland Ave., Bldg. 15, San Diego 92123. SAN 372-8129. Tel. 619-694-3600, fax 619-495-5905. *System Coord.* Susan Swisher.

The SMERC Library, 101 Twin Dolphin Dr., Redwood City 94065-1064. SAN 322-0265. Tel. 650-802-5655, fax 650-802-5665. *Educ. Svcs. Mgr.* Karol Thomas; *Electronic Reference Svcs. Coord.* Carol Quigley.

SOUTHNET, c/o South Bay Cooperative Lib. System, 180 W. San Carlos St., San Jose 95113. SAN 322-4260. Tel. 408-294-2345, fax 408-295-7388. *Asst. Systems Dir.* Susan Holmer.

Substance Abuse Librarians and Information Specialists (SALIS), Box 9513, Berkeley 94709-0513. SAN 372-4042. Tel. 510-642-5208, fax 510-642-7175. *Chair* Sharon Crockett.

Total Interlibrary Exchange (TIE), 4882 McGrath St., Suite 230, Ventura 93003-7721. SAN 322-0311. Tel. 805-650-7732, fax 805-642-9095, e-mail jsegel@eis.calstate.edu. *Pres.* Ed Tennen.

Colorado

Arkansas Valley Regional Library Service System (AVRLSS), 635 W. Corona, Suite 113, Pueblo 81004. SAN 371-5094. Tel. 719-542-2156, fax 719-542-3155, e-mail dmorris@uscolo.edu. *Dir.* Donna Jones Morris; *Chair* Charles Bates.

Bibliographical Center for Research, Rocky Mountain Region, Inc., 14394 E. Evans Ave., Aurora 80014-1478. SAN 322-0338. Tel. 303-751-6277, fax 303-751-9787. *Exec. Dir.* David H. Brunell.

Central Colorado Library System (CCLS), 4350 Wadsworth, Suite 340, Wheat Ridge 80033-4638. SAN 371-3970. Tel. 303-422-1150, fax 303-431-9752. *Dir.* Gordon C. Barhydt; *Asst. Dir.* Judy Zelenski.

Colorado Alliance of Research Libraries, 3801 E. Florida Ave., Suite 515, Denver 80210. SAN 322-3760. Tel. 303-759-

3399, fax 303-759-3363. *Exec. Dir.* Alan Charnes.

Colorado Association of Law Libraries, Box 13363, Denver 80201. SAN 322-4325. Tel. 303-825-8400, fax 303-871-6999. *Pres.* Tom Duggan.

Colorado Council of Medical Librarians (CCML), Denison Memorial Lib., Univ. Colorado Health Science Center, 4200 E. Ninth Ave., Campus Box A-003, Denver 80262-0003. SAN 370-0755. Tel. 303-315-6444, fax 303-315-6255, e-mail catherine. reiter@uchsc.edu. *Pres.* Catherine M. Reiter.

Colorado Library Resource Sharing and Information Access Board, c/o Colorado State Lib., 201 E. Colfax, Denver 80203-1799. SAN 322-3868. Tel. 303-866-6900, fax 303-866-6940. *Coord.* Ann Schwab.

High Plains Regional Library Service System, 800 Eighth Ave., Suite 341, Greeley 80631. SAN 371-0505. Tel. 970-356-4357, fax 970-353-4355, e-mail nknepel@csn. org. *Dir.* Nancy Knepel; *Chair* Verl Manwarren.

Irving Library Network, c/o Jefferson County Public Lib., 10200 W. 20th Ave., Lakewood 80215. SAN 325-321X. Tel. 303-232-7114, 275-2250, fax 303-467-6978. *Network Mgr.* John Zacrep.

Peaks and Valleys Library Consortium, c/o Arkansas Valley Regional Lib. Service System, 635 W. Corona Ave., Suite 113, Pueblo 81004. SAN 328-8684. Tel. 719-542-2156, fax 719-546-4484. *Secy.* Carol Ann Smith.

Southwest Regional Library Service System (SWRLSS), Drawer B, Durango 81302-1090. SAN 371-0815. Tel. 970-247-4782, fax 970-247-5087. *Dir.* S. Jane Ulrich; *Tech. Svcs. Sharing Mgr.* Judith M. Griffiths.

Connecticut

Capitol Area Health Consortium, 270 Farmington Ave., Suite 252, Farmington 06032-1909. SAN 322-0370. Tel. 860-676-1110, fax 860-676-1303. *Pres.* Robert Boardman.

Capitol Region Library Council, 599 Matianuck Ave., Windsor 06095-3567. SAN 322-0389. Tel. 860-298-5319, fax 860-298-5328, e-mail office@crlc.org. *Exec. Dir.* Dency Sargent.

Connecticut Association of Health Sciences Libraries (CAHSL), 74 Terrace Ave., Hamden 06517. SAN 322-0397. Tel. 203-288-7701. *Pres.* Janice Swiatek.

Council of State Library Agencies in the Northeast (COSLINE), Connecticut State Lib., 231 Capitol Ave., Hartford 06106. SAN 322-0451. Tel. 860-566-4301, 207-287-5600 (Maine), fax 860-566-8940. *Pres.* Gary Nichols.

CTW Library Consortium, Olin Memorial Lib., Wesleyan Univ., Middletown 06457-6065. SAN 329-4587. Tel. 860-685-3889, fax 860-685-2661, e-mail ahagyard@ wesleyan. *Dir.* Alan E. Hagyard; *Applications Programmer* Mary Wilson.

Eastern Connecticut Libraries (ECL), Franklin Commons, 106 Rte. 32, Franklin 06254. SAN 322-0478. Tel. 860-885-2760, fax 860-885-2757, e-mail pholloway@ecl.org. *Dir.* Patricia Holloway; *Asst. Dir.* Sandra Brooks.

Hartford Consortium for Higher Education, 260 Girard Ave., Hartford 06105. SAN 322-0443. Tel. 860-236-1203, fax 860-233-9723. *Exec. Dir.* Marilyn Meyerson-Wood.

LEAP (Library Exchange Aids Patrons), 110 Washington Ave., North Haven 06473. SAN 322-4082. Tel. 203-239-1411, fax 203-234-6398. *Chair* Lois Baldini.

Libraries Online, Inc. (LION), 123 Broad St., Middletown 06457. SAN 322-3922. Tel. 860-347-1704, fax 860-346-3707. *Pres.* Anne G. Calvert; *Exec. Dir.* William F. Edge, Jr.

National Network of Libraries of Medicine, New England Region (NN-LM NE Region), Univ. of Connecticut Health Center, 263 Farmington Ave., Farmington 06030-5370. SAN 372-5448. Tel. 860-679-4500, fax 860-679-1305. *Dir.* Ralph D. Arcari; *Assoc. Dir.* John Stey.

Northwestern Connecticut Health Science Libraries, Charlotte Hungerford Hospital, Torrington 06790. SAN 329-5257. Tel. 860-496-6689, fax 860-496-6631. *Coord.* Jackie Rorke.

Southern Connecticut Library Council, 2405 Whitney Ave., Suite 3, Hamden 06518. SAN 322-0486. Tel. 203-288-5757, fax 203-287-0757, e-mail office@sclc.org.

Dir. Michael Golrick; *Project Dir.* Sue Eisner.

Western Connecticut Library Council, Inc., 530 Middlebury Rd., Suite 210B, Box 1284, Middlebury 06762. SAN 322-0494. Tel. 203-577-4010, fax 203-577-4015, e-mail abarney@wclc.org. *Exec. Dir.* Anita R. Barney.

Delaware

Central Delaware Library Consortium, Dover Public Lib., 45 S. State St., Dover 19901. SAN 329-3696. Tel. 302-736-7030, fax 302-736-5087. *Pres.* Robert S. Wetherall.

Delaware Library Consortium (DLC), Delaware Academy of Medicine, 1925 Lovering Ave., Wilmington 19806. SAN 329-3718. Tel. 302-656-6398, fax 302-656-0470. *Pres.* Gail P. Gill.

Kent Library Network, Robert W. O'Brien Bldg., Rm. 209, 414 Federal St., Dover 19901. SAN 371-2214. Tel. 302-736-2265, fax 302-736-2262. *Pres.* Richard Krueger.

Libraries in the New Castle County System (LINCS), Hockessin Public Lib., Hockessin 19707. SAN 329-4889. Tel. 302-239-5160, fax 302-239-1519. *Pres.* Louise Tabasso.

Sussex Help Organization for Resources Exchange (SHORE), Box 589, Georgetown 19947. SAN 322-4333. Tel. 302-855-7890, fax 302-855-7895.

Wilmington Area Biomedical Library Consortium (WABLC), Delaware Academy of Medicine, 1925 Lovering Ave., Wilmington 19806. SAN 322-0508. Tel. 302-656 6398, fax 302-656-0470. *Pres.* Gail P. Gill.

District of Columbia

American Zoo and Aquarium Association (AZA-LSIG), National Zoological Park, Washington 20008. SAN 373-0891. Tel. 202-673-4771, fax 202-673-4900. *Chair* Kay Kenyon; *Ed.* Suzanne Braun.

CAPCON Library Network, 1990 M St. N.W., Suite 200, Washington 20036. SAN 321-5954. Tel. 202-331-5771, fax 202-331-5788, e-mail capcon@capcon.net. *Pres.* Dennis Reynolds.

Coalition for Christian Colleges and Universities, 329 Eighth St. N.E., Washington 20002.

SAN 322-0524. Tel. 202-546-8713, fax 202-546-8913. *Pres.* Robert C. Andringa.

District of Columbia Health Sciences Information Network (DOCHSIN), Providence Hospital Health Sciences Lib., 1150 Varnum St. N.E., Washington 20017. SAN 323-9918. Tel. 202-269-7144, fax 202-269-7142. *Pres.* Rosemarie Leone.

Educational Resources Information Center (ERIC), U.S. Dept. of Education, Office of Educational Resources and Improvement, 555 New Jersey Ave. N.W., Washington 20208-5721. SAN 322-0567. Tel. 202-219-1692, fax 202-219-1696, e-mail Internet: eric@inet.ed.gov. *Dir.* Keith Stubbs.

EDUCOM, c/o 1112 16th St. N.W., Suite 600, Washington 20036. SAN 371-487X. Tel. 202-872-4200, fax 202-872-4318. *Pres.* Robert Heterick, Jr; *Publications Mgr.* John Gehl.

FEDLINK (Federal Library and Information Network), c/o Federal Lib. and Info. Center Committee, Lib. of Congress, Washington 20540-5110. SAN 322-0761. Tel. 202-707-4800, fax 202-707-4818, e-mail fliccfno@loc.gov. *Dir.* Susan M. Tarr; *Network Coord.* Milton Megee.

NASA Library Network ARIN (Aerospace Research Information Network), NASA Headquarters, Code JT, Washington 20546-0001. SAN 322-0788. Tel. 202-358-4485, fax 202-358-3062, e-mail rridgeway@sti.nasa.gov. *Project Dir.* Roland Ridgeway.

National Library Service for the Blind and Physically Handicapped, Lib. of Congress (NLS), 1291 Taylor St. N.W., Washington 20542. SAN 370-5870. Tel. 202-707-5100, fax 202-707-0712, e-mail nls@loc. gov. *Dir.* Frank Kurt Cylke; *Asst. to the Dir.* Marvine R. Wanamaker.

Transportation Research Information Services (TRIS), 2101 Constitution Ave. N.W., Washington 20418. SAN 370-582X. Tel. 202-334-3250, fax 202-334-3495. *Dir.* Jerome T. Maddock.

Veterans Affairs Library Network (VAL-NET), Lib. Div. Programs Office, 810 Vermont Ave. N.W., Washington 20420. SAN 322-0834. Tel. 202-273-8696, fax 202-273-9386. *Dir. Lib. Programs* Wendy N. Carter.

Washington Theological Consortium, 487 Michigan Ave. N.E., Washington 20017-1585. SAN 322-0842. Tel. 202-832-2675, fax 202-526-0818. *Exec. Dir.* Richard Abbott.

Florida

Central Florida Library Cooperative (CFLC), 431 E. Horatio Ave., Suite 230, Maitland 32751. SAN 371-9014. Tel. 407-644-9050, fax 407-644-7023. *Exec. Dir.* Marta Westall.

Florida Library Information Network, c/o Bureau of Lib. and Network Svcs., State Lib. of Florida, R. A. Gray Bldg., Tallahassee 32399-0250. SAN 322-0869. Tel. 904-487-2651, fax 904-488-2746. *Chief, Bureau Lib. and Network Svcs.* Debbie Sears.

Miami Health Sciences Library Consortium (MHSLC), c/o VA Hospital, 1201 N.W. 16 St., Miami 33125. SAN 371-0734. Tel. 305-324-3187. *Chair* Susan Harker.

Palm Beach Health Sciences Library Consortium (PBHSLC), c/o Good Samaritan Medical Center Medical Lib., Box 3166, West Palm Beach 33402. SAN 370-0380. Tel. 407-650-6315, fax 407-650-6417. *Chair* Linda Kressal.

Panhandle Library Access Network (PLAN), 5 Miracle Strip Loop, Suite 2, Panama City Beach 32407. SAN 370-047X. Tel. 904-233-9051, fax 904-235-2286, e-mail Internet: jaskows@firnvx.firn.edu; Bitnet: jaskows@firnvx. *Exec. Dir.* William P. Conniff; *Lib. Resources Specialist* Carol A. DeMent.

Southeast Florida Library Information Network, Inc. (SEFLIN), 100 S. Andrews Ave., Fort Lauderdale 33301. SAN 370-0666. Tel. 954-357-7318, fax 954-357-6998, e-mail currye@mail.seflin.org. *Exec. Dir.* Elizabeth Curry; *Pres.* Jerry W. Brownlee.

Tampa Bay Library Consortium, Inc., 10002 Princess Palm Ave., Suite 124, Tampa 33619. SAN 322-371X. Tel. 813-622-8252, fax 813-628-4425. *Exec. Dir.* Diane Solomon; *Pres.* Derrie Roark.

Tampa Bay Medical Library Network (TABAMLN), Suncoast Hospital Medical Lib., 2025 Indian Rocks Rd., Largo 33774.

SAN 322-0885. Tel. 813-586-7103, fax 813-585-7205. *Pres.* Dorothy Kelly.

Georgia

Association of Southeastern Research Libraries, Univ. of Georgia Libs., Athens 30602-1641. SAN 322-1555. Tel. 706-542-0621, fax 706-542-4144, e-mail channing@lib.wfu.edu. *Chair* William Gray Potter.

Atlanta Health Science Libraries Consortium, Piedmont Hospital, Sauls Memorial Lib., 1968 Peachtree Rd. N.W., Atlanta 30309. SAN 322-0893. Tel. 404-605-3641, fax 404-609-6641. *Pres.* Edie Lacy.

Biomedical Media (formerly Emory Medical Television Network), 1440 Clifton Rd. N.E., Rm. 113, Atlanta 30322. SAN 322-0931. Tel. 404-727-9797, fax 404-727-9798. *Dir.* Fred Westbrook; *Business Mgr.* Marilane Bond.

Georgia Health Sciences Library Association (GHSLA), Univ. Hospital, 1350 Walton Way, Augusta 30901. SAN 372-8307. Tel. 706-774-5078, fax 706-774-8672. *Pres.* Darra Combs.

Georgia Interactive Network for Medical Information (GaIN), c/o Medical Lib., School of Medicine, Mercer Univ., 1550 College St., Macon 31207. SAN 370-0577. Tel. 912-752-2515, fax 912-752-2051. *Dir.* Jocelyn A. Rankin.

Georgia Online Database (GOLD), c/o Public Lib. Svcs., 156 Trinity Ave. S.W., 1st flr., Atlanta 30303-3692. SAN 322-094X. Tel. 404-657-6220, fax 404-656-7297. *Dir.* Tom Ploeg; *Coord.* Jo Ellen Ostendorf.

Health Science Libraries of Central Georgia (HSLCG), c/o J. Rankin Medical Lib., School of Medicine, Mercer Univ., 1550 College St., Macon 31207. SAN 371-5051. Tel. 912-752-2515, fax 912-752-2051. *In Charge* Michael Shadix.

Southeastern Library Network (SOLINET), 1438 W. Peachtree St. N.W., Suite 200, Atlanta 30309-2955. SAN 322-0974. Tel. 404-892-0943, fax 404-892-7879, e-mail mrichard@mail.solinet.net. *Exec. Dir.* Kate Nevins.

South Georgia Associated Libraries, 208 Gloucester St., Brunswick 31520-7007. SAN 322-0966. Tel. 912-267-1212, fax

912-267-9597. *Pres.* Tena Roberts; *Secy.-Treas.* Jim Darby.

Southwest Georgia Health Science Library Consortium (SWGHSLC), Colquitt Regional Medical Center, Health Sciences Lib., Moultrie 31776. SAN 372-8072. Tel. 912-890-3460, fax 912-891-9345. *Medical Libn.* Susan Statom.

University Center in Georgia, Inc., 50 Hurt Plaza, Suite 465, Atlanta 30303-2923. SAN 322-0990. Tel. 404-651-2668, fax 404-651-1797. *Exec. Dir.* Charles B. Bedford.

Hawaii

Hawaii-Pacific Chapter of the Medical Library Association (HIPAC-MLA), 1221 Punchbowl St., Honolulu 96813. SAN 371-3946. Tel. 808-536-9302, fax 808-524-6956. *Chair* Sharon Berglund.

Idaho

Boise Valley Health Sciences Library Consortium (BVHSLC), Health Sciences Lib., St. Alphonsus Regional Medical Center, Boise 83706. SAN 371-0807. Tel. 208-367-2271, fax 208-367-2702. *Contact* Judy Balcerzak.

Canyon Owyhee Library Group, c/o Homedale Junior-Senior High School, 203 E. Idaho, Homedale 83628. SAN 375-006X. Tel. 208-337-4613, fax 208-337-4933. *Contact* Ned Stokes.

Catalyst, c/o Boise State Univ. Lib., Box 46, Boise 83707-0046. SAN 375-0078. Tel. 208-385-4024, fax 208-385-1394. *Contact* Timothy A. Brown.

Cooperative Information Network (CIN), 8385 N. Government Way, Hayden Lake 83835-9280. SAN 323-7656. Tel. 208-772-5612, fax 208-772-2498. *Contact* John Hartung.

Eastern Idaho Library System, 457 Broadway, Idaho Falls 83402. SAN 323-7699. Tel. 208-529-1450, fax 208-529-1467. *Contact* Paul Holland.

Gooding County Library Consortium, c/o Gooding High School, 1050 Seventh Ave. W., Gooding 83330. SAN 375-0094. Tel. 208-934-4831, fax 208-934-4403, e-mail senators@northrim.com. *Contact* Cora Caldwell.

Grangeville Cooperative Network, c/o Grangeville Centennial Lib., 215 W. North St., Grangeville 83530-1729. SAN 375-0108. Tel. 208-983-0951, fax 208-983-2336. *Contact* Linda Ruthruff.

Idaho Health Information Association (IHIA), c/o Idaho Health Sciences Lib., Idaho State Univ., Campus Box 8089, Pocatello 83209. SAN 371-5078. Tel. 208-236-4686, fax 208-236-4687. *Pres.* Nancy Griffin.

Lynx, c/o Boise Public Lib., 715 Capitol Blvd., Boise 83702-7122. SAN 375-0086. Tel. 208-384-4237, fax 208-384-4025. *Contact* Lynn Melton.

Palouse Area Library Information Services (PALIS), c/o Latah County Free Lib. District, 110 S. Jefferson, Moscow 83843-2833. SAN 375-0132. Tel. 208-882-3925, fax 208-882-5098, e-mail lkeenan@norby. latah.lib.id.us. *Contact* Lori Keenan.

Southeast Idaho Document Delivery Network, c/o American Falls District Lib., 308 Roosevelt St., American Falls 83211-1219. SAN 375-0140. Tel. 208-226-2335, fax 208-226-2303. *Contact* Margaret McNamara.

VALNET, Lewis Clark State College Lib., 500 Eighth Ave., Lewiston 83501. SAN 323-7672. Tel. 208-799-2227, fax 208-799-2831. *Contact* Paul Krause.

Illinois

Alliance Library System, 845 Brenkman Dr., Pekin 61554. SAN 371-0637. Tel. 309-353-4110, fax 309-353-8281. *Exec. Dir.* Valerie J. Wilford.

American Theological Library Association (ATLA), 820 Church St., Suite 400, Evanston 60201-5613. SAN 371-9022. Tel. 847-869-7788, fax 847-869-8513. *Dir. Member Svcs.* Melody S. Chartier.

Areawide Hospital Library Consortium of Southwestern Illinois (AHLC), c/o St. Elizabeth Hospital Health Sciences Lib., 211 S. Third St., Belleville 62222. SAN 322-1016. Tel. 618-234-2120, ext. 1181, fax 618-234-0408, e-mail campese@apci. net, campese@exl.com. *Coord.* Michael Campese.

Association of Chicago Theological Schools (ACTS), c/o Garrett-Evangelical Theological Seminary, 2121 Sheridan Rd., Evanston 60201. SAN 370-0658. Tel. 847-866-3900, fax 847-866-3884, e-mail nfisher@nwv.edu *Pres.* Neal Fisher.

Capital Area Consortium, Prevention First Inc., 2800 Montvale Dr., Springfield 62704. SAN 322-1024. Tel. 217-793-7353, fax 217-793-7354. *Coord.* Pat Ruestman.

Catholic Library Association, Dominican Univ. Graduate School of Lib. and Info. Science, 7900 W. Division St., River Forest 60305. SAN 329-1030. Tel. 708-524-6641, fax 708-524-6657. *Exec. Dir.* Jean R. Bostley, SSJ.

Center for Research Libraries, 6050 S. Kenwood, Chicago 60637-2804. SAN 322-1032. Tel. 773-955-4545, fax 773-955-4339, e-mail simpson@uhuru.uchicago.edu. *Pres.* Donald B. Simpson.

Chicago and South Consortium, St. Joseph Medical Center, Health Science Lib., 333 N. Madison Ave., Joliet 60435. SAN 322-1067. Tel. 815-725-7133, ext. 3530, fax 815-725-9459. *Coord.* Virginia Gale.

Chicago Library System (CLS), 224 S. Michigan, Suite 400, Chicago 60604. SAN 372-8188. Tel. 312-341-8500, fax 312-341-1985. *Exec. Dir.* Alice Calabrese.

Consortium of Museum Libraries in the Chicago Area, c/o John G. Shedd Aquarium, Info. Svcs. and Technology, 1200 S. Lake Shore Dr., Chicago 60605. SAN 371-392X. Tel. 312-986-2289, fax 312-939-2216. *Chair* Michael T. Stieber; *Secy.* Laura Jenkins.

Council of Directors of State University Libraries of Illinois (CODSULI), Eastern Illinois Univ., Booth Lib., Charleston 61920. SAN 322-1083. Tel. 217-581-6061, fax 217-581-6066, e-mail snyderca@siucvmb.siu.edu. *Chair* Allen Lanham.

East Central Illinois Consortium, Carle Foundation Hospital Lib., 611 W. Park St., Urbana 61801. SAN 322-1040. Tel. 217-383-3011, fax 217-383-3452. *Coord.* Anita Johnson.

Fox Valley Health Science Library Consortium, Mercy Center for Healthcare Svcs., 1325 N. Highland Ave., Aurora 60506. SAN 329-3831. Tel. 630-801-2686, fax 630-801-2687. *Coord.* Mary Howrey.

Heart of Illinois Library Consortium, Bromenn Healthcare, Health Science Lib., Bloomington 61701. SAN 322-1113. Tel. 309-827-4321, fax 309-829-0707. *Coord.* Toni Tucker.

Illinois Health Libraries Consortium, c/o Meat Industry Info. Center, National Cattleman's Beef Assn., 444 N. Michigan Ave., Chicago 60611. SAN 322-113X. Tel. 312-670-9272, fax 312-494-2572. *Coord.* William D. Siarny, Jr.

Illinois Library and Information Network (ILLINET), c/o Illinois State Lib., 300 S. Second St., Springfield 62701-1796. SAN 322-1148. Tel. 217-782-2994, fax 217-785-4326. *Dir.* Bridget L. Lamont; *Asst. Dir. for Lib. Development, Grants, and Programs* Patricia Norris.

Illinois Library Computer Systems Office (ILCSO), Univ. of Illinois, 205 Johnstowne Centre, 502 E. John St., Champaign 61820. SAN 322-3736. Tel. 217-244-7593, fax 217-244-7596, e-mail khammer@uiuc.edu. *Dir.* Kristine Hammerstrand; *Lib. Systems Coord.* Mary Ellen Farrell.

Illinois State Curriculum Center (ISCC), Univ. of Illinois at Springfield, K-80, Springfield 62794-9423. SAN 371-5108. Tel. 217-786-6375, fax 217-786-6036, e-mail iscc@uis.edu. *Dir.* Rebecca Woodhull; *Libn.* Susie Shackleton.

Judaica Library Network of Metropolitan Chicago (JLNMC), 145 Laurel Ave., Highland Park 60035. SAN 370-0615. Tel. 847-433-2006, fax 847-433-2106, e-mail wolfecg@interaccess.com. *Pres.* Nira Wolfe.

Libras, Inc., Judson College, Elgin 60123. SAN 322-1172. Tel. 847-695-2500, ext. 3040, fax 847-695-0407. *Pres.* Cathleen Zange.

Lincoln Trail Libraries System, 1704 W. Interstate Dr., Champaign 61821-1068. SAN 303-7932. Tel. 217-352-0047, fax 217-352-7153. *Dir.* Jan Ison; *Assoc. Dir.* Brenda Pacey.

Metropolitan Consortium of Chicago, Northwest Community Healthcare, Health Resource Lib., 800 W. Central Rd., Arlington Heights 60005. SAN 322-1180. Tel.

847-618-5180, fax 847-618-5189. *Coord.* Joy Kennedy.

National Network of Libraries of Medicine, c/o Lib. of the Health Sciences, Univ. of Illinois at Chicago, 1750 W. Polk St., Chicago 60612-7223. SAN 322-1202. Tel. 312-996-2464, fax 312-996-2226. *Dir.* Elaine Martin; *Assoc. Dir.* Jean Sayre.

Northern Illinois Learning Resources Cooperative (NILRC), 1011 Lake St., Suite 434, Oak Park 60301. SAN 329-5583. Tel. 630-466-4848, fax 630-466-4895, e-mail jberry@aakton.edu. *Exec. Dir.* John W. Berry.

Private Academic Libraries of Illinois (PALI), c/o North Park College Lib., 3225 W. Foster Ave., Chicago 60625. SAN 370-050X. Tel. 773-244-5582, fax 773-244-4891. *Dir.* Sonia Bodi.

Quad Cities Libraries in Cooperation (QUAD-LINC), Box 125, Coal Valley 61240. SAN 373-093X. Tel. 309-799-3155, fax 309-799-5103, e-mail rbls@libby.rbls.lib.il.us. *Dir.* Robert McKay; *Asst. Dir.* Mary Anne Stewart.

Quad City Area Biomedical Consortium, Perlmutter Lib., 855 Hospital Rd., Silvis 61282. SAN 322-435X. Tel. 309-792-4360, fax 309-792-4362. *Coord.* Barbara Tharp.

River Bend Library System (RBLS), Box 125, Coal Valley 61240. SAN 371-0653. Tel. 309-799-3155, fax 309-799-7916. *Coord.* Nancy Buikema.

Sangamon Valley Academic Library Consortium, c/o Illinois College, Schewe Lib., 1101 W. College Ave., Jacksonville 62650. SAN 322-4406. Tel. 217-245-3020, fax 217-243-2520. *Chair* Martin Gallas; *Secy.-Treas.* W. Michael Westbrook.

Shabbona Consortium, c/o Illinois Valley Community Hospital, 925 West St., Peru 61354. SAN 329-5133. Tel. 815-223-3300, ext. 502, fax 815-223-3394.

Upstate Consortium, c/o KSB Hospital, 403 E. First St., Dixon 61021. SAN 329-3793. Tel. 815-288-5530, fax 815-285-5871. *Coord.* Terry Harden.

USA Toy Library Association, 2530 Crawford Ave., Suite 111, Evanston 60201. SAN 371-215X. Tel. 847-864-3330, fax 847-864-3331, e-mail soliog@aol.com. *Exec. Dir.* Judith Q. Iacuzzi.

Indiana

Association of Vision Science Librarians (AVSL), Indiana Univ., Optometry Lib., Bloomington 47405. SAN 370-0569. Tel. 812-855-8629, fax 812-855-6616. *Chair* Douglas Freeman.

Central Indiana Health Science Libraries Consortium, St. Vincent Hospital and Health Care Center, Garceau Lib., 2001 W. 86 St., Indianapolis 46260. SAN 322-1245. Tel. 317-338-2095, fax 317-338-6516, e-mail lshass@stvincent.org or lhass@iquest.net. *Pres.* Louise Hass.

Collegiate Consortium Western Indiana, c/o Cunningham Memorial Lib., Indiana State Univ., Terre Haute 47809. SAN 329-4439. Tel. 812-237-3700, fax 812-237-2567. *Dean* Ellen Watson.

Evansville Area Library Consortium, 3700 Washington Ave., Evansville 47750. SAN 322-1261. Tel. 812-485-4151, fax 812-485-7564. *Coord.* E. Jane Saltzman.

Indiana Cooperative Library Services Authority (INCOLSA), 6202 Morenci Trail, Indianapolis 46268-2536. SAN 322-1296. Tel. 317-298-6570, fax 317-328-2380. *Exec. Dir.* Millard Johnson; *Asst. Exec. Dir.* Jan Cox.

Indiana State Data Center, Indiana State Lib., 140 N. Senate Ave., Indianapolis 46204-2296. SAN 322-1318. Tel. 317-232-3733, fax 317-232-3728. *Libns.* Cynthia St. Martin, Ronald Sharpe.

Northeast Indiana Health Science Libraries Consortium (NEIHSL), Lutheran Center for Health Services, Health Sciences Lib., 3024 Fairfield Ave., Fort Wayne 46807. SAN 373-1383. Tel. 219-458-2277, fax 219-458-3077. *Provisional Coord.* Lauralee Aven.

Northwest Indiana Health Science Library Consortium, c/o N.W. Center for Medical Education, Indiana Univ. School of Medicine, 3400 Broadway, Gary 46408-1197. SAN 322-1350. Tel. 219-980-6852, fax 219-980-6566, e-mail fyoung@iunhaw1.iun.indiana.edu. *Coord.* Felicia Young.

Society of Indiana Archivists, c/o Conner Prairie Museum, Rudell Lib., 13400 Alisonville Rd., Fishers 46038. SAN 329-5508. Tel. 317-776-6000, fax 317-776-6014. *Pres.* Tim Crumrin; *Secy.-Treas.* Joan Cunningham.

Wabash Valley Health Science Library Consortium, Indiana State Univ., Cunningham Memorial Lib., Terre Haute 47809. SAN 371-3903. Tel. 812-237-2540, fax 812-237-8028, e-mail libbirk@cml.indstate.edu. *Medical Libn. and Consortium Coord.* Evelyn J. Birkey.

Iowa

Consortium of College and University Media Centers, Iowa State Univ., 121 Pearson Hall, Ames 50011-2203. SAN 322-1091. Tel. 515-294-1811, fax 515-294-8089, e-mail e1dar@isuvax.bitnet. *Exec. Dir.* Don A. Rieck.

Dubuque Area Library Information Consortium, c/o Finley Hospital Lib., 350 N. Grandview Ave., Dubuque 52001. SAN 322-1407. Tel. 319-557-2897, fax 319-557-2813. *Pres.* Debra Pfab.

Iowa Private Academic Library Consortium (IPAL), c/o Clarke College, Schrup Lib., 1550 Clarke Dr., Dubuque 52001. SAN 329-5311. Tel. 319-588-6320, fax 319-588-8160, e-mail proberts@keller.clarke.edu. *Chair* Paul Roberts.

Linn County Library Consortium, Stewart Memorial Lib., Coe College, Cedar Rapids 52406. SAN 322-4597. Tel. 319-399-8023, fax 319-399-8019. *Pres.* Richard Doyle; *V. Pres.* Margaret White.

Polk County Biomedical Consortium, c/o State Lib. of Iowa, E. 12 and Grand, Des Moines 50319. SAN 322-1431. Tel. 515-281-5772, fax 515-281-3384. *Coord.* Pam Rees.

Sioux City Library Cooperative (SCLC), c/o Sioux City Public Lib., 529 Pierce St., Sioux City 51101-1203. SAN 329-4722. Tel. 712-255-2933, ext. 251, fax 712-279-6432. *Agent* Betsy J. Thompson.

State of Iowa Libraries Online Interlibrary Loan (SILO-ILL), (formerly Iowa Resource and Information Sharing), State Lib. of Iowa, E. 12 and Grand, Des Moines 50319. SAN 322-1415. Tel. 515-281-4105, fax 515-281-6191. *State Libn.* Sharman B. Smith.

Tri-College Cooperative Effort, Loras College, c/o Wahlert Memorial Lib., 1450 Alta Vista, Dubuque 52004-0178. SAN 322-1466. Tel. 319-588-7164, fax 319-588-7292, e-mail klein@loras.edu. *Dir.* Robert Klein.

Kansas

Associated Colleges of Central Kansas, 210 S. Main St., McPherson 67460. SAN 322-1474. Tel. 316-241-5150, fax 316-241-5153. *Dir.* Donna Zerger.

Dodge City Library Consortium, c/o Northwest Elementary School, 2100 Sixth St., Dodge City 67801. SAN 322-4368. Tel. 316-227-1604. *Pres.* Linda Zupancic.

Kansas Library Network Board, State Capital, Rm. 343N, 300 S.W. 10, Topeka 66612-1593. SAN 329-5621. Tel. 913-296-3875, fax 913-296-6650, e-mail ksstl2lb@ink.org. *Exec. Dir.* Michael Piper.

Kentucky

Association of Independent Kentucky Colleges and Universities, Box 46, Danville 40423-0046. SAN 322-1490. Tel. 606-236-3533, fax 606-236-3534, e-mail aikcu@mis.net. *Pres.* M. Fred Mullinax.

Bluegrass Medical Librarians (BML), Health Dimensions at Fayette Mall Lib., 3559 Nicholasville Rd., Suite F616, Lexington 40503. SAN 371-3881. Tel. 606-272-6099, fax 606-245-1057. *Pres.* Emily Sanderholm; *Secy.-Treas.* Elliot Appelbaum.

Eastern Kentucky Health Science Information Network (EKHSIN), c/o Camden-Carroll Library, Morehead State Univ., Morehead 40351. SAN 370-0631. Tel. 606-783-2610, fax 606-783-5311. *Coord.* William J. DeBord.

Kentuckiana Metroversity, Inc., 3113 Lexington Rd., Louisville 40206. SAN 322-1504. Tel. 502-897-3374, fax 502-895-1647. *Exec. Dir.* Jack Will.

Kentucky Health Science Libraries Consortium, VA Medical Center, Lib. Services 142D, 800 Zorn Ave., Louisville 40206-1499. SAN 370-0623. Tel. 502-894-6240, fax 502-894-6134. *Pres.* Jim Kastner.

Kentucky Library Information Center (KLIC), Kentucky Dept. for Libs. and Archives, 300 Coffee Tree Rd., Box 537, Frankfort 40602. SAN 322-1512. Tel. 502-564-8300, fax 502-564-5773. *Branch Mgr. Network Development* Linda Sherrow.

Kentucky Library Network, Inc., 300 Coffee Tree Rd., Box 537, Frankfort 40602. SAN 371-2184. Tel. 502-564-8300, fax 502-564-5773. *Pres.* Cathy Reilender.

State Assisted Academic Library Council of Kentucky (SAALCK), c/o Steely Lib., Northern Kentucky Univ., Highland Heights 41099. SAN 371-2222. Tel. 606-572-5483, fax 606-572-6181, e-mail winner@nku.edu. *Chair and Pres.* Marian C. Winner.

Theological Education Association of Mid America (TEAM-A), c/o Southern Baptist Theological Seminary, 2825 Lexington Rd., Louisville 40280-0294. SAN 322-1547. Tel. 502-897-4807, fax 502-897-4600. *Dir.* Ronald F. Deering.

Louisiana

Baton Rouge Hospital Library Consortium, Earl K. Long Hospital, 5825 Airline Hwy., Baton Rouge 70805. SAN 329-4714. Tel. 504-358-1089, fax 504-342-5983, e-mail estanl@mail.ekl.lsvmc.edu. *Pres.* Eileen Stanley.

Health Sciences Library Association of Louisiana Medical Library, Earl K. Long Medical Lib., 5825 Airline Hwy., Baton Rouge 70805. SAN 375-0035. Tel. 504-358-1089, fax 504-342-5983, e-mail estanley@chmcat.cem.lsu.edu. *Chair* Eileen Stanley.

Lasernet, State Lib. of Louisiana, Box 131, Baton Rouge 70821. SAN 371-6880. Tel. 504-342-4923, 342-4922, fax 504-342-3547. *Dep. Asst. Libn.* Michael R. McKann; *Automation Consultant* Sara Taffae.

Louisiana Government Information Network (LaGIN), c/o State Lib. of Louisiana, Box 131, Baton Rouge 70821. SAN 329-5036. Tel. 504-342-4914, fax 504-342-3547. *Coord.* Judith D. Smith.

New Orleans Educational Telecommunications Consortium, 2929 S. Carrollton Ave., New Orleans 70118. SAN 329-5214. Tel. 504-861-3028, fax 504-861-3021. *Chair* Gregory O'Brien; *Exec. Dir.* Robert J. Lucas.

Maine

Health Science Library Information Consortium (HSLIC), USVAM ROC, Box 3395, Togus 04330. SAN 322-1601. Tel. 207-743-5933, ext. 323, fax 207-743-1566, e-mail brunjes@saturn.caps.maine.edu. *Chair* Kathy Brunjes.

Maryland

American Library Association VideoLibrary Video Network (ALA Video-LVN), 320 York Rd., Towson 21204. SAN 375-5320. Tel. 410-887-2082, fax 410-887-2091, e-mail inlib@mail.bcpl.lib.md.us. *Production Mgr.* Jeff Lifton; *Program Mgr.* Kathy Coster.

ERIC Processing and Reference Facility, 1100 West St., Laurel 20707-3598. SAN 322-161X. Tel. 301-497-4080, fax 301-953-0263, e-mail Internet: ericfac@inet.ed.gov. *Dir.* Ted Brandhorst.

Maryland Interlibrary Organization (MILO), c/o Enoch Pratt Free Lib., 400 Cathedral St., Baltimore 21201-4484. SAN 343-8600. Tel. 410-396-5498, fax 410-396-5837, e-mail pwallace@mail.pratt.lib.md.us. *Admin.* Patricia E. Wallace.

National Clearinghouse for Alcohol and Drug Information (NCADI), Box 2345, Rockville 20847-2345. SAN 371-9162. Tel. 301-468-2600, fax 301-468-6433, e-mail info@health.org. *Project Dir.* John Noble; *Deputy Dir.* Shari Tavel.

National Library of Medicine, Medical Literature Analysis and Retrieval System (MEDLARS), 8600 Rockville Pike, Bethesda 20894. SAN 322-1652. Fax 301-496-0822, e-mail mms@nlm.nih.gov. *MEDLARS Management Section* Carolyn Tilley.

National Network of Libraries of Medicine (NN-LM), National Lib. of Medicine, 8600 Rockville Pike, Rm. B1E03, Bethesda 20894. SAN 373-0905. Tel. 301-496-4777, fax 301-480-1467, e-mail blyon@nlm.nih.gov. *Head* Becky Lyon.

National Network of Libraries of Medicine, Univ. of Maryland Health Sciences Lib., 111 S. Greene St., Baltimore 21201-1583. SAN 322-1644. Tel. 410-706-2855, fax 410-706-0099, e-mail Internet: fmeakin@umab.umd.edu. *Exec. Dir.* Janice Kelly; *RML Dir.* Frieda Weise.

Washington Research Library Consortium (WRLC), 901 Commerce Dr., Upper Marlboro 20772. SAN 373-0883. Tel. 301-390-2000, fax 301-390-2020. *Exec. Dir.* Lizanne Payne; *Dir. Computing and Telecommunications* Carl Whitman.

Massachusetts

Boston Area Music Libraries (BAML), Music Lib., Wellesley College, Wellesley 02140. SAN 322-4392. Tel. 617-283-2076, fax 617-283-3687, e-mail dgilbert@wellesley.edu. *Coord.* David Gilbert.

Boston Biomedical Library Consortium (BBLC), Alexander Joslin Diabetes Center, Marble Lib., 1 Joslin Pl., Boston 02215. SAN 322-1725. Tel. 617-732-2641, fax 617-732-2542, e-mail bambos@joslin.harvard.edu. *Chair* Barbara Ambos.

Boston Library Consortium, 666 Boylston St., Rm. 317, Boston 02117. SAN 322-1733. Tel. 617-262-0380, fax 617-262-0163, e-mail hstevens@bpl.org. *Exec. Dir.* Hannah M. Stevens.

Boston Theological Institute Library Program, 45 Francis Ave., Cambridge 02138. SAN 322-1741. Tel. 617-495-5780, 527-4880, fax 617-495-9489, e-mail putney@harvarda.harvard.edu. *Lib. Coord.* Clifford Putney.

Cape Libraries Automated Materials Sharing (CLAMS), 270 Communication Way, Unit 4E-4F, Hyannis 02601. SAN 370-579X. Tel. 508-790-4399, fax 508-771-4533, e-mail clams.lib.ma.us. *Pres.* Ann Tyra; *Exec. Dir.* Monica Grace.

Central Massachusetts Consortium of Health Related Libraries (CMCHRL), c/o Lamar Soutter Lib., Univ. Massachusetts Medical Center, 55 Lake Ave. N, Worcester 01655-0121. SAN 371-2133. Tel. 508-856-2399, fax 508-856-5899. *Pres.* Annanaomi Sams.

Consortium for Information Resources, Emerson Hospital, Old Rd. to Nine Acre Corner, Concord 01742. SAN 322-4503. Tel. 508-287-3090, fax 508-287-3651. *Pres.* Nancy Callander.

Cooperating Libraries of Greater Springfield (CLGS), c/o Westfield State College Lib., 577 Western Ave., Westfield 01086. SAN 322-1768. Tel. 413-572-5233, fax 413-572-5520. *Dir.* Hal Gibson.

Corporate Library Group (CLG), 50 Nagog Park, AK02-3/E10, Acton 01720. SAN 370-0534. Tel. 508-264-6500. *Mgr.* Mary Lee Kennedy.

C W Mars (Central/Western Massachusetts Automated Resource Sharing), 1 Sunset Lane, Paxton 01612-1197. SAN 322-3973. Tel. 508-755-3323, fax 508-755-3721. *Exec. Dir.* Joan Kuklinski; *Supv. User Svcs.* Gale E. Eckerson.

Essex County Cooperating Libraries, Essex Agricultural Institute Lib., 562 Maple St., Hathorne 01937. SAN 322-1776. Tel. 508-774-0050, ext. 37, fax 508-774-6530. *Pres.* Paula Byrne.

Fenway Libraries Online (FLO), Wentworth Institute of Technology, 550 Huntington Ave., Boston 02115. SAN 373-9112. Tel. 617-442-2384, fax 617-442-1519. *Network Dir.* Jamie Ingram; *Technician and User Support* Stephanie Norris.

Fenway Library Consortium, Emerson College, 150 Beacon St., Boston 02116. SAN 327-9766. Tel. 617-824-8670, fax 617-824-8717, e-mail ecl_maz@flo.org. *Coord.* Mickey Zemon.

Merrimac Interlibrary Cooperative, c/o J. V. Fletcher Lib., 50 Main, Westford 01886. SAN 329-4234. Tel. 508-692-5555, fax 508-692-4418, e-mail jefferso@mvlc.lib.ma.us. *Co-Chairs* Sue Jefferson, Nanette Eichell.

Merrimack Valley Library Consortium, c/o Memorial Hall Lib., Elm Sq., Andover 01810. SAN 322-4384. Tel. 508-475-7632, fax 508-475-8158. *Pres.* Sue Ellen Holmes; *Network Admin.* Evelyn Kuo.

Minuteman Library Network, 4 California Ave., 5th flr., Framingham 01701. SAN 322-4252. Tel. 508-879-8575, fax 508-879-5470, e-mail ccaro.@mln.lib.ma.us. *Exec. Dir.* Carol B. Caro.

NELINET, Inc., 2 Newton Executive Park, Newton 02162. SAN 322-1822. Tel. 617-969-0400, fax 617-332-9634, e-mail admin@nelinet.org nelinet@bcvms.bitnet. *Exec. Dir.* Marshall Keys.

New England Law Library Consortium, Inc., Harvard Law School Lib., Langdell Hall, Cambridge 02138. SAN 322-4244. Tel. 252-9636, 508-428-5342, fax 508-428-7623, e-mail klaiber@law.harvard.edu. *Exec. Dir.* Diane Klaiber.

Northeast Consortium of Colleges and Universities In Massachusetts (NECCUM), c/o Gordon College, 255 Grapevine Rd.,

Wenham 01984. SAN 371-0602. Tel. 508-927-2300, ext. 4068, fax 508-524-3708. *Coord.* Stephen MacLeod.

Northeastern Consortium for Health Information (NECHI), c/o Salem State College Lib., 352 Lafayette St., Salem 01970. SAN 322-1857. Tel. 508-741-6762, fax 508-744-6596, e-mail glynn@noblenet.org. *Chair* Camilla Glynn.

North Atlantic Health Sciences Libraries, Inc (NAHSL), c/o Baystate Medical Center, 759 Chestnut, Springfield 01199. SAN 371-0599. Tel. 413-784-4294, fax 413-784-4197, e-mail lfornes@library.bhs.org. *Chair* Laurie Fornes; *Chair-Elect* Bob Sekerak.

North of Boston Library Exchange, Inc. (NOBLE), 26 Cherry Hill Dr., Danvers 01923. SAN 322-4023. Tel. 508-777-8844, fax 508-750-8472. *Exec. Dir.* Ronald A. Gagnon; *Member Svcs. Mgr.* Elizabeth B. Thomsen.

Southeastern Automated Libraries, Inc (SEAL), 547 W. Grove St., Box 4, Middleboro 02346. SAN 371-5000. Tel. 508-946-8600, fax 508-946-8605. *Exec. Dir.* Deborah K. Conrad; *Coord. User Svcs.* Barbara Bonville.

Southeastern Massachusetts Consortium of Health Science Libraries (SEMCO), c/o Saint Luke's Hospital, Health Science Lib., 101 Page St., New Bedford 02741. SAN 322-1873. Tel. 508-961-5267, fax 508-999-0219, e-mail ubh0341@slh.org. *Chair* Bonnie Hsu.

Southeastern Massachusetts Cooperating Libraries (SMCL), c/o Wheaton College, Madeleine Clark Wallace Lib., Norton 02766-0849. SAN 322-1865. Tel. 508-285-8225, fax 508-285-8275, e-mail pdeekle@wheatonma.edu. *Chair* Peter Deekle.

Western Massachusetts Health Information Consortium, c/o Holyoke Hospital Medical Lib., 575 Beech St., Holyoke 01040. SAN 329-4579. Tel. 413-534-2500, ext. 5282, fax 413-534-2664, e-mail mcaraker@mail.map.com. *Pres.* Mary Caraker.

West of Boston Network (WEBNET), Horn Library, Babson College, Babson Park 02157. SAN 371-5019. Tel. 617-239-4308, fax 617-239-5226, e-mail cohenjo@hcc01.babson.edu. *Systems Admin.* Joshua Cohen; *Network Pres.* Hope Tillman.

Worcester Area Cooperating Libraries, c/o Worcester State College Learning Resources Center, Rm. 221, 486 Chandler, Worcester 01602-2597. SAN 322-1881. Tel. 508-754-3964, 793-8000, ext. 8544, fax 508-793-8198, e-mail gwood@mecn.mass.edu. *Coord.* Gladys Wood.

Michigan

Berrien Library Consortium, c/o Saint Joseph Public Lib., 500 Market St., Saint Joseph 49085. SAN 322-4678. Tel. 616-983-7167, fax 616-983-5804. *Pres.* Bob Nichols; *Treas.* Harvey Brenneise.

Capital Area Library Network, Inc. (CALNET), 706 Curtis St., Mason 48854. SAN 370-5927. Tel. 517-676-8445, fax 517-676-9646. *Chair* Cliff Taylor; *Contact* Kathleen M. Vera.

Cloverland Processing Center, c/o Bay de Noc Community College LRC, 2001 N. Lincoln Rd., Escanaba 49829-2511. SAN 322-189X. Tel. 906-786-5802, ext. 122, fax 906-786-5802, ext. 244, e-mail holmesc@bayone.baydenoc.cc.mi.us. *Dean* Christian Holmes.

Council on Resource Development (CORD), Nissan Research and Development, Inc., Box 9200, Farmington Hills 48331. SAN 374-6119. Tel. 248-488-4025. *Chair* Sara Bowker; *V. Chair* Michele Whalen.

Detroit Area Consortium of Catholic Colleges, c/o Sacred Heart Seminary, 2701 Chicago Blvd., Detroit 48206. SAN 329-482X. Tel. 313-883-8500, fax 313-868-6440. *Rector and Pres.* Allen H. Vigneron.

Detroit Associated Libraries Region of Cooperation (DALROC), Detroit Public Lib., 5201 Woodward Ave., Detroit 48202. SAN 371-0831. Tel. 313-833-4036, fax 313-832-0877. *Chair* Patrice Merritt; *Regional Contact* James Lawrence.

Eastern Regional Health Science Libraries Association, c/o Mercy Hospital Medical Lib., 2601 Electric Ave., Port Huron 48060. SAN 329-4757. Tel. 810-985-1378, fax 810-985-1508. *Pres.* Bonnie Swegles.

Kalamazoo Consortium for Higher Education (KCHE), Kalamazoo College, 1200 Academy St., Kalamazoo 49006. SAN 329-4994. Tel. 616-337-7220, fax 616-337-

7305. *Pres.* James F. Jones, Jr.; *Admin. Coord.* Margie Flynn.

Lakeland Area Library Network (LAKE-NET), 60 Library Plaza N.E., Grand Rapids 49503. SAN 371-0696. Tel. 616-454-0272, fax 616-454-4517. *Coord.* Harriet Field.

Library Cooperative of Macomb (LCM), 16480 Hall Rd., Clinton Township 48038. SAN 373-9082. Tel. 810-286-5750, fax 810-286-8951. *Dir.* Susan Hill.

The Library Network, 33030 Van Born Rd., Wayne 48184. SAN 370-596X. Tel. 313-326-8910, fax 313-326-3035, 326-5140, e-mail hrc@tlnlib.mi.us. *Dir.* Harry Courtright; *Dep. Dir.* Kerry Sanders.

Michigan Association of Consumer Health Information Specialists (MACHIS), c/o Amberg Health Sciences Lib., 100 Michigan N.E., Grand Rapids 49503-2560. SAN 375-0043. Tel. 616-391-3145, fax 616-391-3527, e-mail dhummel@bw.brhn.org. *Chair* Diane Hummel.

Michigan Health Sciences Libraries Association (MHSLA), c/o Butterworth Hospital, 100 Michigan Ave. N.E., Grand Rapids 49503. SAN 323-987X. Tel. 616-774-1655, fax 616-732-3527. *Pres.* Deborah Adams.

Michigan Library Consortium (MLC), 6810 S. Cedar St., Suite 8, Lansing 48911. SAN 322-192X. Tel. 517-694-4242, fax 517-694-9303. *Exec. Dir.* Randy Dykhuis.

Northland Interlibrary System (NILS), 316 E. Chisholm St., Alpena 49707. SAN 329-4773. Tel. 517-356-1622, fax 517-354-3939, e-mail cawleyr@northland.lib.mi.us. *Dir.* Rebecca E. Cawley.

Southeastern Michigan League of Libraries (SEMLOL), c/o Detroit Public Lib., 5201 Woodward Ave., Detroit 48202. SAN 322-4481. Tel. 313-833-4038, fax 313-832-0877. *Chair* Nancy Skowronski.

Southern Michigan Region of Cooperation (SMROC), 415 S. Superior, Suite A, Albion 49224-2135. SAN 371-3857. Tel. 517-629-9469, fax 517-628-3812. *Fiscal Agent* James C. Seidl.

Southwest Michigan Library Cooperative (SMLC), 305 Oak St., Paw Paw 49079. SAN 371-5027. Tel. 616-657-4698, fax 616-657-4494. *Dir.* Alida L. Geppert.

UMI Information Store, Inc., 300 N. Zeeb Rd., Box 1346, Ann Arbor 48106-1346. SAN 374-7913. Tel. 415-433-5500, fax 415-433-0100. *Dir. Operations* Cheri Marken.

Upper Peninsula of Michigan Health Science Library Consortium, c/o Marquette General Hospital, 420 W. Magnetic, Marquette 49855. SAN 329-4803. Tel. 906-225-3429, fax 906-225-3524. *Chair* Kenneth Nelson.

Upper Peninsula Region of Library Cooperation, Inc., 1615 Presque Isle Ave., Marquette 49855. SAN 329-5540. Tel. 906-228-7697, fax 906-228-5627; *Pres.* Carol Hiney. *Treas.* Suzanne Dees.

Minnesota

Capital Area Library Consortium (CALCO), c/o Minnesota Dept. of Health, R. N. Barr Lib., 717 S.E. Delaware St., Box 9441, Minneapolis 55440. SAN 374-6127. Tel. 612-623-5090, fax 612-623-5385. *Chair* Diane Jordan.

Central Minnesota Libraries Exchange (CMLE), c/o Learning Resources, Rm. 61, Saint Cloud State Univ., Saint Cloud 56301-4498. SAN 322-3779. Tel. 612-255-2950, fax 612-654-5131, e-mail ppeterson@tigger.stcloud.msus.edu. *Dir.* Patricia E. Peterson.

Chiropractic Library Consortium (CLIB-CON), North Western College of Chiropractic, 2501 W. 84 St., Bloomington 55431-1599. SAN 328-8218. Tel. 612-885-5419. *Chair* Cheryl Duggan.

Community Health Science Library, c/o Saint Francis Medical Center, 415 Oak St., Breckenridge 56520. SAN 370-0585. Tel. 218-643-7516, fax 218-643-7487. *Dir.* Terry Tschakert.

Cooperating Libraries in Consortium (CLIC), 1619 Dayton Ave., Suite 204A, Saint Paul 55104. SAN 322-1970. Tel. 612-644-3878, fax 612-644-6258, e-mail olsonc@macalester.edu. *Exec. Dir.* Chris Olson; *Computer Systems Specialist* Steve Waage.

Metronet, 2324 University Ave. W., Suite 116, Saint Paul 55114. SAN 322-1989. Tel. 612-646-0475, fax 612-646-0657. *Dir.* Mary Treacy.

Metropolitan Library Service Agency (MELSA), 570 Asbury St., Suite 201, Saint Paul 55104-1849. SAN 371-5124.

Tel. 612-645-5731, fax 612-649-3169, e-mail melsa@gopher.melsa.lib.mn.us. *Acting Dir.* Tzvee Morris.

Minitex Library Information Network, c/o S-33 Wilson Lib., Univ. of Minnesota, 309 19th Ave. S., Minneapolis 55455-0414. SAN 322-1997. Tel. 612-624-4002, fax 612-624-4508. *Dir.* William DeJohn; *Admin. Dir.* Anne Stagg.

Minnesota Department of Human Services Library DHS Library and Resource Center, 444 Lafayette, Saint Paul 55155-3821. SAN 371-0750. Tel. 612-297-8708, fax 612-282-5340, e-mail kate.o.nelson@state.mn.us. *Dir. and Coord.* Kate Nelson.

Minnesota Theological Library Association (MTLA), c/o Luther Seminary Lib., 2375 Como Ave., Saint Paul 55108. SAN 322-1962. Tel. 612-641-3202, fax 612-641-3280, e-mail twalker@luthersem.edu. *Pres.* Mary Martin.

North Country Library Cooperative, Olcott Plaza, Suite 110, 820 Ninth St. N., Virginia 55792-2298. SAN 322-3795. Tel. 218-741-1907, fax 218-741-1907. *Dir.* Jennifer Semon.

Northern Lights Library Network, 318 17th Ave. E., Box 845, Alexandria 56308 0845. SAN 322-2004. Tel. 320-762-1032, fax 320-762-1032. *Dir.* Joan B. Larson.

SMILE (Southcentral Minnesota Inter-Library Exchange), Box 3031, Mankato 56002-3031. SAN 321-3358. Tel. 507-625-7555, fax 507-625-4049. *Dir.* Lucy Lowry.

Southeast Library System (SELS), 107 W. Frontage Rd., Hwy. 52 N., Rochester 55901. SAN 322-3981. Tel. 507-288-5513, fax 507-288-8697. *Admin.* Ann Hutton.

Southwest Area Multi-county Multi-Type Interlibrary Exchange (SAMMIE), Southwest State Univ. Lib., Marshall 56258. SAN 322-2039. Tel. 507-532-9013, fax 507-532-2039. *Coord.* Robin Chaney.

Twin Cities Biomedical Consortium, c/o Health East Midway Health Services Lib., 1700 University Ave., Saint Paul 55104. SAN 322-2055. Tel. 612-232-5193. *Chair* Karen Brudvig.

Valley Medical Network, Lake Region Hospital Lib., 712 S. Cascade St., Fergus Falls 56537. SAN 329-4730. Tel. 218-736-8158, fax 218-736-8723. *Pres.* Connie Schulz.

Waseca Interlibrary Resource Exchange (WIRE), c/o Waseca High School, 1717 Second St. N.W., Waseca 56093. SAN 370-0593. Tel. 507-835-5470, ext. 218, fax 507-835-1724, e-mail tlouganl@platec.net. *Dir.* Les Tlougan.

Westlaw, 620 Opperman Dr., Box 64779, Saint Paul 55164-0779. SAN 322-4031. Tel. 612-687-7000, fax 612-687-5614. *V. Pres.* Joy Lindsay.

Mississippi

Central Mississippi Consortium of Medical Libraries (CMCML), Medical Center, U.S. Dept. of Veterans Affairs, 1500 E. Woodrow Wilson Dr., Jackson 39216. SAN 372-8099. Tel. 601-362-4471, 362-5378, 362-1680. *Chair* Rose Anne Tucker; *V. Chair* Wanda King.

Central Mississippi Library Council (CMLC), c/o Mississippi College Law Lib., 151 E. Griffith St., Jackson 39201. SAN 372-8250. Tel. 601-925-7120, fax 601-925-7112, e-mail eggert@mc.edu. *Chair* Maureen Eggert; *Secy.* Charles Brenner.

Mississippi Biomedical Library Consortium, c/o College of Veterinary Medicine, Mississippi State Univ., Box 9825, Mississippi State 39762. SAN 371-070X. Tel. 601-325-1240, fax 601-325-1141, e-mail kinkus@cvm.msstate.edu. *Pres.* Jane Kinkus.

Missouri

Kansas City Library Network, Inc., Univ. of Missouri Dental Lib., 650 E. 25 St., Kansas City 64108. SAN 322-2098. Tel. 816-235-2030, fax 816-235-2157.

Kansas City Metropolitan Library Network, 15624 E. 24 Hwy., Independence 64050. SAN 322-2101. Tel. 816-521-7257, fax 816-521-7253. *Office Mgr.* Susan Burton.

Kansas City Regional Council for Higher Education, Park College, Box 40, 8700 N.W. River Park Dr., Parkville 64152-3795. SAN 322-211X. Tel. 816-741-2000, ext. 6435, fax 816-741-1296, e-mail kcrche@aol.com, or rondoering@aol.com, or michmangus@aol.com. *Pres.* Ron Doering.

Missouri Library Network Corporation, 10332 Old Olive St. Rd., Saint Louis 63141. SAN

322-466X. Tel. 314-567-3799, fax 314-567-3798. *Dir.* Susan Singleton.

Municipal Library Cooperative, 140 E. Jefferson, Kirkwood 63122. SAN 322-2152. Tel. 314-966-5568, fax 314-822-3755.

PHILSOM-PHILNET-BACS Network, c/o Washington Univ., Bernard Becker Medical Lib., 660 S. Euclid Ave., Saint Louis 63110. SAN 322-2187. Tel. 314-362-2778, fax 314-362-0190, e-mail libsys@medicine.wustl.edu. *Mgr.* Russ Monika.

Saint Louis Regional Library Network, 9425 Big Bend, Saint Louis 63119. SAN 322-2209. Tel. 314-965-1305, fax 314-965-4443. *Admin.* Bernyce Christiansen.

Montana

Helena Area Health Science Libraries Consortium (HAHSLC), Corette Lib., Carroll College, Helena 59625. SAN 371-2192. Tel. 406-447-4341, fax 406-447-4525. *Chair* Lois Fitzpatrick.

Nebraska

Eastern Library System (ELS), 11929 Elm St., Suite 12, Omaha 68144. SAN 371-506X. Tel. 402-330-7884, fax 402-330-1859, e-mail ktooker@nde.unl.edu. *Admin.* Kathleen Tooker; *Board Pres.* Nina Little.

Information Consortium (ICON) (formerly Metro Omaha Health Information Consortium), c/o McGoogan Lib. of Medicine, 600 S. 42 St., Omaha 68198-6705. SAN 372-8102. Tel. 402-398-6092, fax 402-398-6923.

Lincoln Health Sciences Library Group (LHSLG), Univ. of Nebraska–Lincoln, 427 Hamilton Hall, Lincoln 68588-0305. SAN 329-5001. Tel. 402-472-2739, fax 402-472-0225. *Chair* Richard E. Voeltz.

Meridian Library System, 3423 Second Ave., Suite 301, Kearney 68847. SAN 325-3554. Tel. 308-234-2087, fax 308-234-4040, e-mail sosenga@nol.org. *Pres.* Carol Reed; *Admin.* Sharon Osenga.

Mid-America Law School Library Consortium (MALSLC), c/o Klutznick Law Lib., Creighton Univ. School of Law, Lincoln 68178-0001. SAN 371-6813. Tel. 402-280-2251, fax 402-280-2244, e-mail andrus@culaw.creighton.edu. *Chair* Kay L. Andrus.

National Network of Libraries of Medicine–Midcontinental Region (NN-LM-MR), c/o McGoogan Lib. of Medicine, Univ. of Nebraska Medical Center, 600 S. 42 St., Box 686706, Omaha 68198-6706. SAN 322-225X. Tel. 402-559-4326, fax 402-559-5482, e-mail pmullaly@unmcvm.unmc.edu. *Dir.* Nancy N. Woelfl; *Assoc. Dir.* Peggy Mullaly-Quijas.

NEBASE, c/o Nebraska Lib. Commission, 1200 N St., Suite 120, Lincoln 68508-2023. SAN 322-2268. Tel. 402-471-4031, fax 402-471-2083; *Dir.* Jo Budler; *Network Svcs. Staff Asst.* Jeanette Powell.

Northeast Library System, 2813 13th St., Columbus 68601. SAN 329-5524. Tel. 402-564-1586; *Admin.* Carol Speicher.

Southeast Nebraska Library System, Union College Lib., 3800 S. 48 St., Lincoln 68506. SAN 322-4732. Tel. 402-486-2555, fax 402-486-2557. *Admin.* Richard Miller; *Admin. Asst.* Sara Schott.

Nevada

Information Nevada, Interlibrary Loan Dept., Nevada State Lib. and Archives, Capitol Complex, Carson City 89710-0001. SAN 322-2276. Tel. 702-687-8325, fax 702-687-8330, e-mail akelley@lahontan.clan.lib.nv.us. *Dir.* Joan Kerschner; *ILL Mgr.* Annie Kelley.

Nevada Cooperative Medical Library, 2040 W. Charleston Blvd., Suite 500, Las Vegas 89102. SAN 321-5962. Tel. 702-383-2368, fax 702-383-2369. *Dir. Lib. Svcs.* Aldona Jonynas.

Nevada Medical Library Group (NMLG), Barton Memorial Hospital Lib., 2170 S Ave., Box 9578, South Lake Tahoe 89520. SAN 370-0445. Tel. 916-542-3000, ext. 2903, fax 916-543-0239, e-mail kanton@oakweb.com. *Chair* Laurie Anton.

Western Council of State Libraries, Inc., Nevada State Lib., Capitol Complex, Carson City 89710. SAN 322-2314. Tel. 702-687-8315, fax 702-687-8311. *Pres.* Amy Owen.

New Hampshire

Carroll County Library Cooperative, Box 240, Madison 03849. SAN 371-8999. Tel. 603-367-8545. *Secy.* Carolyn Busell.

Hillstown Cooperative, 3 Meetinghouse Rd., Bedford 03110. SAN 371-3873. Tel. 603-472-2300, fax 603-472-2978. *Chair* Frances M. Wiggin; *Secy.* Sarah Chapman.

Librarians of the Upper Valley Coop. (LUV), Enfield Public Lib., Main St., Box 1030, Enfield 03748-1030. SAN 371-6856. Tel. 603-632-7145; *Secy.* Marjorie Carr. *Treas.* Patricia Hand.

Merri-Hill-Rock Library Cooperative, c/o Kimball Public Lib., 3 Academy Ave., Atkinson 03811. SAN 329-5338. Tel. 603-362-5234, fax 603-362-5305, e-mail htjk@lilac.nhsl.lib.nh.us. *Chair* Joe Rodio.

New Hampshire College and University Council, Libraries Committee, 116S River Rd., D4, Bedford 03110. SAN 322-2322. Tel. 603-669-3432, fax 603-623-8182. *Exec. Dir.* Thomas R. Horgan.

North Country Consortium (NCC), Gale Medical Library, Littleton Regional Hospital, 262 Cottage St., Littleton 03561. SAN 370-0410. Tel. 603-444-7731, ext. 164, fax 603-444-0443. *Coord.* Linda L. Ford.

Nubanusit Library Cooperative, c/o Peterborough Town Lib., 2 Concord, Peterborough 03458. SAN 322-4600. Tel. 603-924-8040, fax 603-924-8041. *Contact* Ann Geisel.

Scrooge and Marley Cooperative, 310 Central, Franklin 03235. SAN 329-515X. Tel. 603-934-2911. *Chair* Randy Brough.

Seacoast Coop. Libraries, North Hampton Public Lib., 235 Atlantic Ave., North Hampton 03862. SAN 322-4619. Tel. 603-964-6326, fax 603-964-1107. *Contact* Pam Schwatzer.

New Jersey

Bergen County Cooperative Library System, 810 Main St., Hackensack 07601. SAN 322-4546. Tel. 201-489-1904, fax 201-489-4215. *Exec. Dir.* Robert W. White; *Mgr. Computer Svcs.* Brian DeSantis.

Bergen Passaic Health Sciences Library Consortium, c/o Englewood Hospital and Medical Center, 350 Engle St., Englewood 07631. SAN 371-0904. Tel. 201-894-3069, fax 201-894-9049, e-mail yoga@csnet.net. *ILL Coord. and Board Rep.* Lia Sabbagh.

Central Jersey Health Science Libraries Association, Saint Francis Medical Center Medical Lib., 601 Hamilton Ave., Trenton 08629. SAN 370-0712. Tel. 609-599-5068, fax 609-599-5773. *Dir.* Donna Barlow; *Technical Info. Specialist* Joan O'Donnell.

Central Jersey Regional Library Cooperative–Region V, 4400 Rte. 9 S., Freehold 07728-1383. SAN 370-5102. Tel. 908-409-6484, fax 908-409-6492. *Dir.* Leslie Burger.

Cosmopolitan Biomedical Library Consortium, Medical Lib., East Orange General Hospital, 300 Central Ave., East Orange 07018. SAN 322-4414. Tel. 201-266-8519. *Pres.* Peggy Dreker.

Dow Jones News Retrieval, Box 300, Princeton 08543-0300. SAN 322-404X. Tel. 609-452-1511, fax 609-520-4775. *Customer Svcs.* Maggie Landis.

Health Sciences Library Association of New Jersey (HSLANJ), UMDNJ Health Sciences Lib., 1 Medical Center Dr., Stratford 08084. SAN 370-0488. Tel. 609-566-6800, fax 609-435-8246, e-mail skica@umdnj.edu. *Pres.* Janice Skica.

Highlands Regional Library Cooperative, 31 Fairmount Ave., Box 486, Chester 07930. SAN 329-4609. Tel. 908-879-2442, fax 908-879-8812, e-mail ckeller@hrlc.org. *Exec. Dir.* Cecy Keller; *Acting Program Coord.* Barbara A. Carroll.

Infolink Eastern New Jersey Regional Library Cooperative, Inc., 44 Stelton Rd., Suite 330, Piscataway 08854. SAN 371-5116. Tel. 908-752-7720, 201-673-2343, fax 908-752-7785, 201-673-2710, e-mail glr@infolink.org. *Exec. Dir.* Gail L. Rosenberg; *Program and Svcs. Coord.* Cheryl O'Connor.

LMX Automation Consortium, 1030 Saint George, Suite 203, Avenel 07001. SAN 329-448X. Tel. 908-750-2525, fax 908-750-9392. *Exec. Dir.* Ellen Parravano.

Lucent Technologies Library Network (formerly AT&T Information Services Network), 600 Mountain Ave., Rm. 3A-426, Murray Hill 07974. SAN 329-5400. Tel. 908-582-6880, fax 908-582-3146, e-mail njm@library.mt.lucent.com. *Managing Dir.* Nancy J. Miller.

Monmouth-Ocean Biomedical Information Consortium (MOBIC), Community Medical Center, 99 Hwy. 37 W., Toms River 08755. SAN 329-5389. Tel. 908-240-8117, fax 908-240-8354. *Dir.* Reina Reisler.

Morris Automated Information Network (MAIN), Box 900, Morristown 07963-0900. SAN 322-4058. Tel. 201-989-6112, fax 201-989-6109, e-mail mainhelp@main. morris.org. *Network Admin. and Div. Head* Ellen Sleeter.

Morris-Union Federation, 214 Main St., Chatham 07928. SAN 310-2629. Tel. 201-635-0603, fax 201-635-7827. *Treas.* Diane O'Brien.

New Jersey Academic Library Network, c/o The College of New Jersey, Roscoe L. West Lib., Hillwood Lakes CN-4700, Trenton 08650-4700. SAN 329-4927. Tel. 609-771-2332, fax 609-771-3458, e-mail mbiggs@tcnj.edu. *Chair* Mary Biggs.

New Jersey Health Sciences Library Network (NJHSN), Mountainside Hospital, Health Sciences Lib., Montclair 07042. SAN 371-4829. Tel. 201-429-6240, fax 201-680-7850. *Chair* Patricia Regenberg.

New Jersey Library Network, Lib. Development Bureau, 185 W. State St., CN-520, Trenton 08625-0520. SAN 372-8161. Tel. 609-984-3293, fax 609-984-7898. *Svcs. Coord.* Marilyn R. Veldof.

Pinelands Consortium for Health Information, c/o Kennedy Memorial Hospital/Washington Township Division Medical Lib., 435 Huffville-Cross Keys Rd., Turnersville 08012. SAN 370-4874. Tel. 609-582-2675, fax 609-582-3190. *Coord.* William Dobkowski.

Society for Cooperative Healthcare and Related Education (SCHARE), 1776 Raritan Rd., Scotch Plains 07076. SAN 371-0718. Tel. 908-889-6410, fax 908-889-2487. *Chair* Eden Trinidad; *Coord.* Anne Calhoun.

South Jersey Regional Library Cooperative, Paint Works Corporate Center, 10 Foster Ave., Suite F-3, Gibbsboro 08026. SAN 329-4625. Tel. 609-346-1222, fax 609-346-2839. *Exec. Dir.* Karen Hyman; *Program Development Coord.* Katherine Schalk-Greene.

New Mexico

New Mexico Consortium of Academic Libraries, c/o Panell Lib., New Mexico Junior College, 5317 Lovington Hwy., Hobbs 88240. SAN 371-6872. Tel. 505-392-5473, fax 505-392-2527, e-mail ctownley@lib.nmsu.edu. *Pres.* Randall Gaylor.

New Mexico Consortium of Biomedical and Hospital Libraries, c/o Lovelace Medical Lib., 5400 Gibson Blvd. S.E., Albuquerque 87108. SAN 322-449X. Tel. 505-262-7158, fax 505-262-7897. *Contact* Sandy Spurlock.

New York

Academic Libraries of Brooklyn, Saint Francis College Lib., 180 Remsen St., Brooklyn 11201. SAN 322-2411. Tel. 718-522-2300, ext. 306, fax 718-522-1274, e-mail Bitnet: chick@pratt. *Dir.* Wendell Guy.

Associated Colleges of the Saint Lawrence Valley, Merritt Hall, State Univ. of New York at Potsdam, Potsdam 13676-2299. SAN 322-242X. Tel. 315-267-3331, fax 315-267-2389, e-mail larranaj@potsdam. edu. *Exec. Dir.* Anneke J. Larrance.

Brooklyn-Queens-Staten Island Health Sciences Librarians (BQSI), Saint John's Episcopal Hospital, South Shore Div. Medical Lib., Rockaway Pkwy. and Linden Blvd., Far Rockaway 11691. SAN 370-0828. Tel. 718-869-7699. *Pres.* Kalpana Desai.

Capital District Library Council for Reference and Research Resources, 28 Essex St., Albany 12206. SAN 322-2446. Tel. 518-438-2500, fax 518-438-2872. *Exec. Dir.* Charles D. Custer; *Admin. Secy.* Carol Houlihan.

Central New York Library Resources Council (CLRC), 3049 E. Genesee St., Syracuse 13224-1690. SAN 322-2454. Tel. 315-446-5446, fax 315-446-5590, e-mail washburn@clrc.org. *Exec. Dir.* Keith E. Washburn; *Asst. Dir.* Jeannette Smithee.

Consortium of Foundation Libraries, c/o Council on Foreign Relations, 58 E. 68 St., New York 10021. SAN 322-2462. Tel. 212-434-9400, fax 212-861-3524, e-mail lgusts@email.cfr.org. *Chair* Lilita Gusts.

Council of Archives and Research Libraries In Jewish Studies (CARLJS), 330 Seventh Ave., 21st flr., New York 10001. SAN 371-

053X. Tel. 212-629-0500, ext. 205, fax 212-629-0508, e-mail nsjc@jewishculture. org. *Pres.* Michael Grunberger; *Dir. Cultural Svcs.* Jerome Chanes.

Educational Film Library Association, c/o AV Resource Center, Cornell Univ., Business and Technology Park, Ithaca 14850. SAN 371-0874. Tel. 607-255-2090, fax 607-255-9946. *AV Sales* Rich Gray; *AV Technician* Gerry KIalk.

Health Information Libraries of Westchester (HILOW), New York Medical College, Medical Science Lib., Basic Sciences Bldg., Valhalla 10595. SAN 371-0823. Tel. 914-993-4205, fax 914-993-4191. *Pres.* Christine Hunter.

Library Consortium of Health Institutions in Buffalo, Roswell Park Cancer Institute, Elm and Carlton, Buffalo 14263. SAN 329-367X. Tel. 716-845-5966. *Pres.* Gay Ablove.

Long Island Library Resources Council, Melville Lib. Bldg., Suite E5310, Stony Brook 11794-3399. SAN 322-2489. Tel. 516-632-6650, fax 516-632-6662, e-mail hbiblo@ccmail.sunysb.edu. *Dir.* Herbert Biblo; *Asst. Dir.* Judith Neufeld.

Manhattan-Bronx Health Sciences Libraries Group, c/o KPR Medical Lib., 333 E. 38 St., New York 10016. SAN 322-4465. Tel. 212-856-8721, fax 212-856-8884. *Pres.* Penny Klein.

Medical and Scientific Libraries of Long Island (MEDLI), c/o Palmer School of Lib. and Info. Science, C. W. Post Campus, Long Island Univ., Brookville 11548. SAN 322-4309. Tel. 516-299-2866, fax 516-299-4168, e-mail westerma@titan. lfuref.edu. *Pres.* Barbara Odani.

Medical Library Center of New York, 5 E. 102 St., 7th flr., New York 10029. SAN 322-3957. Tel. 212-427-1630, fax 212-860-3496, 876-6697, e-mail mlcny@ metgate.metro.org. *Dir.* Lois Weinstein.

Middle Atlantic Region National Network of Libraries of Medicine, New York Academy of Medicine, 1216 Fifth Ave., New York 10029-5293. SAN 322-2497. Tel. 212-822-7396, fax 212-534-7042, e-mail rml@nyam.org. *Dir.* Arthur Downing; *Assoc. Dir.* Mary Mylenki.

New York Metropolitan Reference and Research Library Agency (METRO), 57 E. 11 St.,

New York 10003. SAN 322-2500. Tel. 212-228-2320, fax 212-228-2598. *Exec. Dir.* Dottie Hiebing.

New York State Interlibrary Loan Network (NYSILL), c/o New York State Lib., Albany 12230. SAN 322-2519. Tel. 518-474-5129, fax 518-474-5786, e-mail ill@unixII. nysed.gov. *Interim Dir.* GladysAnn Wells; *Principal Libn.* J. Van der veer Judd.

North Country Reference and Research Resources Council, 7 Commerce Lane, Canton 13617. SAN 322-2527. Tel. 315-386-4569, fax 315-379-9553, e-mail john@ northnet.org, or doyle@northnet.org, or blauvelt@northnet.org. *Exec. Dir.* John J. Hammond; *Head of Bibliographical Svcs.* Tom Blauvelt.

Northeast Foreign Law Cooperative Group, Fordham Univ., 14 W. 62 St., New York 10023. SAN 375-0000. Tel. 212-636-6913, fax 212-977-2662, e-mail vessien@ law.fordham.edu. *Libn.* Victor Essien.

Research Library Association of South Manhattan, New York Univ., Bobst Lib., 70 Washington Sq. S., New York 10012. SAN 372-8080. Tel. 212-998-2566, fax 212-995-4583, e-mail grant@is.nyu.edu. *Coord.* Joan Grant.

Rochester Regional Library Council (RRLC), 390 Packetts Landing, Box 66160, Fairport 14450. SAN 322-2535. Tel. 716-223-7570, fax 716-223-7712, e-mail rrlcwml@ ritvax.isc.rit.edu. *Dir.* Janet M. Welch.

South Central Research Library Council, 215 N. Cayuga St., Ithaca 14850. SAN 322-2543. Tel. 607-273-9106, fax 607-272-0740, e-mail scrlc@lakenet.org. *Exec. Dir.* Jean Currie.

Southeastern New York Library Resources Council, 220 Rte. 299, Box 879, Highland 12528. SAN 322-2551. Tel. 914-691-2734, fax 914-691-6987, e-mail senylrc@ sebridge.org. *Exec. Dir.* John L. Shaloiko; *Asst. Dir.* Ron Covisier.

State University of New York–OCLC Library Network (SUNY-OCLC), System Admin., State University Plaza, Albany 12246. SAN 322-256X. Tel. 518-443-5444, fax 518-432-4346, e-mail sunyoclc@slscva.sysadm. suny.edu. *Dir.* Mary-Alice Lynch.

Western New York Library Resources Council, 4455 Genesee St., Box 400, Buffalo

14225-0400. SAN 322-2578. Tel. 716-633-0705, fax 716-633-1736. *Exec. Dir.* Betsy Sywetz.

North Carolina

Cape Fear Health Sciences Information Consortium, c/o Robeson Community College, Box 1420, Lumberton 28359. SAN 322-3930. Tel. 910-738-7101, ext. 228, fax 910-671-4143. *Dir.* Marilyn Locklear-Hunt.

Consortium of South Eastern Law Libraries (COSELL), North Carolina Central Univ., School of Law Lib., 1512 S. Alston Ave., Durham 27707. SAN 372-8277. Tel. 919-560-5241, fax 919-560-5321. *Pres.* Deborah Jefferies.

Microcomputer Users Group for Libraries in North Carolina (MUGLNC), Perkins Library, Duke Univ., Durham 27708-0177. SAN 322-4449. Tel. 919-660-5932, fax 919-684-2855, e-mail jrl@duke.edu. *Pres.* John Little; *Treas.* Barbara Thompson.

Mid-Carolina Academic Library Network (MID-CAL), Campbell Univ., Carrie Rich Lib., Box 98, Bules Creek 27506. SAN 371-3989. Tel. 910-893-1460, fax 910-893-1470, e-mail gregory@ecsvax.uncecs.edu. *Chair* Ronnie Faulkner.

North Carolina Area Health Education Centers, Health Sciences Lib., CB 7585, Univ. of North Carolina, Chapel Hill 27599-7585. SAN 323-9950. Tel. 919-962-0700, fax 919-966-5592. *Network Coord.* Diana C. McDuffee.

North Carolina Community College System (NCCCS), 200 W. Jones St., Raleigh 27603-1379. SAN 322-2594. Tel. 919-733-7051, fax 919-733-0680. *Pres.* Lloyd V. Hackley.

North Carolina Library Information Network, 109 E. Jones St., Raleigh 27601-2807. SAN 329-3092. Tel. 919-733-2570, fax 919-733-8748. *Dir.* Open.

Northwest AHEC Library at Salisbury, c/o Rowan Regional Medical Center, 612 Mocksville Ave., Salisbury 28144. SAN 322-4589. Tel. 704-638-1069, fax 704-636-5050. *Lib. Dir.* Donna Bancroft.

Northwest AHEC Library Information Network, Northwest Area Health Education Center, Bowman Gray School of Medi-cine, Medical Center Blvd., Winston-Salem 27157-1060. SAN 322-4716. Tel. 910-713-7015, fax 910-713-7028, e-mail bladner@bgsm.edu. *Network Coord.* Betty Ladner.

Resources for Health Information Consortium (REHI), c/o Wake Medical Center Medical Lib., 3024 Newbern Ave., Suite 601, Raleigh 27610. SAN 329-3777. Tel. 919-250-8529, fax 919-250-8836. *Assoc. Dir.* Beverly Richardson.

Triangle Research Libraries Network, Wilson Lib., CB No. 3940, Chapel Hill 27514-8880. SAN 329-5362. Tel. 919-962-8022, fax 919-962-4452, e-mail david-carlson@unc.edu. *Exec. Dir.* Jordan M. Scepanski.

Unifour Consortium of Health Care and Educational Institutions, c/o Northwest AHEC Library at Hickory, Catawba Memorial Hospital, 810 Fair Grove Church Rd., Hickory 28602. SAN 322-4708. Tel. 704-326-3662, fax 704-326-7164. *Dir.* Karen Lee Martines; *Assoc. Dir.* Donna Bancroft.

Western North Carolina Library Network (WNCLN), D. Hiden Ramsey Lib., 1 University Heights, Univ. of North Carolina at Asheville, Asheville 28804-3299. SAN 376-7205. Tel. 704-232-5095, e-mail reichelml@appstate.edu or moulrh@appstate.edu. *Chair* Mary Reichel; *Exec. Dir.* Richard Moul.

North Dakota

Dakota West Cooperating Libraries (DWCL), 3315 University Dr., Bismarck 58504. SAN 373-1391. Tel. 701-255-3285, fax 701-221-6854. *Chair* Charlene Weis; *Secy.-Treas.* Kelly Steckler.

North Dakota Network for Knowledge, c/o North Dakota State Lib., Liberty Memorial Bldg., Capitol Grounds, 604 E. Blvd. Ave., Bismarck 58505-0800. SAN 322-2616. Tel. 701-328-2492, fax 701-328-2040. *State Libn.* Mike Jaugstetter.

Tri-College University Libraries Consortium, 209 Engineering Technology, North Dakota State Univ., Fargo 58105. SAN 322-2047. Tel. 701-231-8170, fax 701-231-7205. *Coord.* John W. Beecher; *Provost, Tri-College Univ.* Jean Strandness.

Ohio

Central Ohio Hospital Library Consortium, Medical Lib., Riverside Methodist Hospital, 3535 Olentangy River Rd., Columbus 43214. SAN 371-084X. Tel. 614-566-5230, fax 614-265-2437. *Archivist* Jo Yeoh.

Cleveland Area Metropolitan Library System (CAMLS), 20600 Chagrin Blvd., Suite 500, Shaker Heights 44122-5334. SAN 322-2632. Tel. 216-921-3900, fax 216-921-7220.

Columbus Area Library and Information Council of Ohio (CALICO), c/o Westerville Public Lib., 126 S. State St., Westerville 43081. SAN 371-683X. Tel. 614-882-7277, fax 614-882-5369. *Treas.* Norma Ekleberry.

Consortium of Popular Culture Collections in the Midwest (CPCCM), c/o Popular Culture Lib., Bowling Green State Univ., Bowling Green 43403-0600. SAN 370-5811. Tel. 419-372-2450, fax 419-372-7996, e-mail bmccall@epic.bgsu.edu. *Chair* Jeanne Somers.

Greater Cincinnati Library Consortium, 3333 Vine St., Suite 605, Cincinnati 45220-2214. SAN 322-2675. Tel. 513-751-4422, fax 513-751-0463, e-mail gclc@uc.edu. *Exec. Dir.* Martha J. McDonald.

Miami Valley Libraries (MVL), c/o Greenville Public Lib., 520 Sycamore St., Greenville 45331. SAN 322-2691. Tel. 937-548-3915, fax 937-548-3837, e-mail gplibrary@wesnet.com. *Exec. Dir.* John L. Vehre, Jr.

MOLO Regional Library System, 1260 Monroe Ave., New Philadelphia 44663-4147. SAN 322-2705. Tel. 330-364-8535, fax 330-364-8537, e-mail molo@tusco.net. *Exec. Dir.* Dave Simmons.

NEOUCOM Council of Associated Hospital Librarians, Ocasek Regional Medical Info. Center, Box 95, Rootstown 44272-0095. SAN 370-0526. Tel. 330-325-2511, ext. 542, fax 330-325-0522, e-mail lse@neoucom.edu. *Dir. and Chief Medical Libn.* Larry Ellis.

NOLA Regional Library System, 4445 Mahoning Ave. N.W., Warren 44483. SAN 322-2713. Tel. 330-847-7744, fax 330-847-7704. *Dir.* Gary Silver.

Northeastern Ohio Major Academic and Research Libraries (NEOMARL), Oberlin College Lib., Oberlin 44074. SAN 322-

4236. Tel. 216-775-8285, ext. 231, fax 216-775-8739. *Contact* Ray English.

Northwest Library District (NORWELD), c/o Wood County Public Lib., 251 N. Main St., Bowling Green 43402. SAN 322-273X. Tel. 419-354-2903, fax 419-354-0405. *Dir.* Allan Gray; *Consultant* Susan Hill.

OCLC (Online Computer Library Center, Inc.), 6565 Frantz Rd., Dublin 43017-3395. SAN 322-2748. Tel. 614-764-6000, fax 614-764-6096, e-mail oclc@oclc.org. *Pres.* K. Wayne Smith.

Ohio-Kentucky Cooperative Libraries, Box 647, Cedarville 45314. SAN 325-3570. Tel. 513-766-7842, 766-2955, fax 513-766-2337; *Ed.* Janice Bosma. *Asst. Ed.* Kelly Hellwig.

Ohio Library and Information Network (Ohio-LINK), 2455 N. Star Rd., Columbus 43221. SAN 374-8014. Tel. 614-728-3600, fax 614-728-3610. *Exec. Dir.* Thomas J. Sanville; *Dir. Lib. Systems* Anita I. Cook.

OHIONET, 1500 W. Lane Ave., Columbus 43221-3975. SAN 322-2764. Tel. 614-486-2966, fax 614-486-1527. *Exec. Dir.* Michael P. Butler; *Mgr. Computer Svcs;* Robert Busick.

Ohio Network of American History Research Centers, Ohio Historical Society Archives/Lib., 1982 Velma Ave., Columbus 43211-2497. SAN 323-9624. Tel. 614-297-2501, fax 614-297-2546, e-mail gparkins@winslo.ohio.gov. *Archivist* George Parkinson.

Ohio Regional Consortium of Law Libraries (ORCLL), Univ. of Akron School of Law Lib., 150 University Blvd., Akron 44325-2902. SAN 371-3954. Tel. 330-972-7330, fax 330-972-4948. *Dir.* Paul Richert.

Ohio Valley Area Libraries (OVAL), 252 W. 13 St., Wellston 45692-2299. SAN 322-2756. Tel. 614-384-2103, fax 614-384-2106, e-mail ovaorls@winslo.ohio.gov. *Dir.* Eric S. Anderson; *Consultant* Gail Zachariah.

Southwestern Ohio Council for Higher Education, 3171 Research Blvd., Suite 141, Dayton 45420-4014. SAN 322-2659. Tel. 937-259-1370, fax 937-259-1380, e-mail soche@soche.org. *Dir.* Tamara Yeager; *Chair Lib. Div.* Jean Mulhern.

The Sworl Group, 505 Kathryn Dr., Wilmington 45177-2274. SAN 322-2780. Tel.

513-382-2503, fax 513-382-2504, e-mail swr0jsn@winslo.ohio.gov. *Dir.* Corinne Johnson.

Oklahoma

Greater Oklahoma Area Health Sciences Library Consortium, Hillcrest Health Center Lib., 2129 S.W. 59, Oklahoma City 73119. SAN 329-3858. Tel. 405-680-2190, e-mail walee-chotikavanic@vokhsc.edu. *Pres.* Walee Chotikavanic.

Metropolitan Libraries Network of Central Oklahoma, Inc. (MetroNetwork), Box 250, Oklahoma City 73101-0250. SAN 372-8137. Tel. 405-231-8602, fax 405-236-5219. *Chair* Cheryl Suttles.

Midwest Curriculum Coordination Center, 1500 W. Seventh Ave., Stillwater 74074-4364. SAN 329-3874. Tel. 405-377-2000, fax 405-743-5142, e-mail jugawill@genesis.odvte.state.ok.us. *Dir.* Julie G. Willcut.

Oklahoma Health Sciences Library Association (OHSLA), Univ. of Oklahoma, HSC Bird Health Science Lib., Box 26901, Oklahoma City 73190. SAN 375-0051. Tel. 271-2672, fax 405-271-3297, e-mail jwilkers@rex.vokhsc.edu. *Pres.* Judy Wilkerson.

Oregon

Chemeketa Cooperative Regional Library Service, c/o Chemeketa Community College, 4000 Lancaster Dr. N.E., Salem 97309-7070. SAN 322-2837. Tel. 503-399-5105, fax 503-399-5214, e-mail cocl@chemek.cc.or.us. *Coord.* Linda Cochrane.

Coos County Library Service District, Extended Service Office, Tioga 107, 1988 Newmark, Coos Bay 97420. SAN 322-4279. Tel. 541-888-7260, fax 541-888-7285. *Extension Svcs. Coord.* Mary Jane Fisher.

Library Information Network of Clackamas County, 16239 S.E. McLoughlin Blvd., Suite 208, Oak Grove 97267. SAN 322-2845. Tel. 503-655-8550, fax 503-655-8555. *Network Admin.* Joanna Rood; *Systems Libn.* Wayne Hay.

Northwest Association of Private Colleges and Universities (NAPCU), c/o Shoen Lib., Marylhurst College, Marylhurst 97036. SAN 375-5312. Tel. 503-699-

6261, ext. 3374, fax 503-636-1957. *Pres.* John Popko.

Oregon Health Sciences Libraries Association (OHSLA), Willamette Falls Hospital, 1500 Division St., Oregon City 97045. SAN 371-2176. Tel. 503-650-6757, fax 503-650-6836. *Pres.* Kathy Martin.

Portland Area Health Sciences Librarians, c/o Legacy Emanuel Lib., 2801 N. Gantenbein, Portland 97227. SAN 371-0912. Tel. 503-413-2558, fax 503-413-2544, e-mail wittend@ohsu.edu. *Coord.* Dana Witten.

Southern Oregon Library Federation, c/o Jackson County Lib. System, Medford Lib. Branch, 413 W. Main St., Medford 97501. SAN 322-2861. Tel. 541-776-7281, fax 541-776-7295; *Pres.* Gary Sharp.

Washington County Cooperative Library Services, 17880 S.W. Blanton St., Box 5129, Aloha 97006. SAN 322-287X. Tel. 503-642-1544, fax 503-591-0445. *Mgr.* Peggy Forcier; *Automation Specialist* Eva Calcagno.

Pennsylvania

Associated College Libraries of Central Pennsylvania, c/o Blough-Weis Lib., Susquehanna Univ., Selinsgrove 17870. SAN 322-2888. Tel. 717-372-4321, fax 717-372-4310. *Pres.* Rebecca Wilson; *Treas.* Scott Anderson.

Basic Health Sciences Library Network, Latrobe Area Hospital Health Sciences Lib., 121 W. Second Ave., Latrobe 15650-1096. SAN 371-4888. Tel. 412-537-1275, fax 412-537-1890. *Chair* Marilyn Daniels.

Berks County Library Association (BCLA), RD 1, Box 1343, Hamburg 19526. SAN 371-0866. Tel. 610-655-6355. *Treas.* Pamela Hehr.

Berks County Public Libraries (BCPLS), Agricultural Center, Box 520, Leesport 19533. SAN 371-8972. Tel. 610-378-5260, fax 610-378-1525, e-mail bcpl@epix.net. *Admin.* Julie Rinehart; *Extension Svcs. Libn.* Susan Harvard.

Central Pennsylvania Consortium, c/o Franklin and Marshall College, Box 3003, Lancaster 17604-3003. SAN 322-2896. Tel. 717-291-3919, fax 717-399-4455. *Exec. Asst.* Molly Seidel.

Central Pennsylvania Health Science Library Association (CPHSLA), c/o Geisinger

Medical Center, Health Science Lib., 100 N. Academy Ave., Danville 17822-2101. SAN 375-5290. Tel. 717-271-8198, fax 717-271-5738, e-mail srobishaw@smpp. geisinger.edu. *Pres.* Susan Robishaw; *Pres.-Elect* Martha Ruff.

Consortium for Health Information and Library Services, 1 Medical Center Blvd., Upland 19013-3995. SAN 322-290X. Tel. 610-447-6163, fax 610-447-6164, e-mail ch1@hslc.org. *Exec. Dir.* Stephanie Schneider.

Cooperating Hospital Libraries of the Lehigh Valley Area, Easton Hospital Medical Lib., 250 S. 21st St., Easton 18042. SAN 371-0858. Tel. 610-250-4130, fax 610-250-4905. *Libn.* Kristine Petre.

Delaware Valley Information Consortium, c/o The Wistar Institute, 3601 Spruce St., Philadelphia 19104. SAN 329-3912. Tel. 215-898-3826, fax 215-898-3856, e-mail nlong@wista.wistar.upenn.edu. *Coord.* Nina P. Long.

Eastern Mennonite Associated Libraries and Archives (EMALA), 2215 Millstream Rd., Lancaster 17602. SAN 372-8226. Tel. 717-393-9745. *Chair* Ray K. Hacker; *Secy.* Lloyd Zeager.

Erie Area Health Information Library Cooperative (EAHILC), DuBois Regional Medical Center, Box 447, DuBois 15801. SAN 371-0564. Tel. 814-375-3575, fax 814-375-3576, e-mail scott@hslc.org. *Chair* Kathy Scott.

Greater Philadelphia Law Library Association (GPLLA), Box 335, Philadelphia 19105. SAN 373-1375. Tel. 215-979-1000, fax 215-979-1020, e-mail dwfalk@duanemorris. com. *Pres.* Don Arndt.

Health Information Library Network of Northeastern Pennsylvania, c/o Wyoming Valley Health Care System, Inc., Lib. Svcs., Wilkes-Barre 18764. SAN 322-2934. Tel. 717-552-1175, fax 717-552-1183. *Chair* Rosemarie Taylor.

Health Sciences Libraries Consortium, 3600 Market St., Suite 550, Philadelphia 19104-2646. SAN 323-9780. Tel. 215-222-1532, fax 215-222-0416, e-mail info@hslc.org. *Exec. Dir.* Joseph C. Scorza; *Assoc. Dir.* Alan C. Simon.

Interlibrary Delivery Service of Pennsylvania, 471 Park Lane, State College 16803-3208. SAN 322-2942. Tel. 814-238-0254, fax 814-238-9686. *Admin. Dir.* Janet C. Phillips.

Laurel Highlands Health Sciences Library Consortium, Owen Lib., Rm. 209, Univ. of Pittsburgh, Johnstown 15904. SAN 322-2950. Tel. 814-269-7280, fax 814-266-8230. *Dir.* Heather W. Brice.

Lehigh Valley Association of Independent Colleges, Inc., 119 W. Greenwich St., Bethlehem 18018-2307. SAN 322-2969. Tel. 610-882-5275, fax 610-882-5515. *Dir.* Galen C. Godbey.

Mid-Atlantic Law Library Cooperative (MALLCO), c/o Allegheny County Law Lib., 921 City/County Bldg., Pittsburgh 15219. SAN 371-0645. Tel. 412-350-5353, fax 412-350-5889. *Dir.* Joel Fishman; *Coord.* Frank Liu.

NEIU Consortium, 1200 Line St., Archbald 18403. SAN 372-817X. Tel. 717-876-9268, fax 717-876-8663. *IMS Dir.* Robert Carpenter; *Program Coord.* Rose Bennett.

Northeastern Pennsylvania Bibliographic Center, c/o Learning Resources Center, Marywood College, Scranton 18509-1598. SAN 322-2993. Tel. 717-348-6260, fax 717-961-4769, e-mail chs@ac.marywood. edu. *Dir.* Catherine H. Schappert.

Northwest Interlibrary Cooperative of Pennsylvania (NICOP), Erie County Public Lib., 160 E. Front St., Erie 16507-1554. SAN 370-5862. Tel. 814-451-6920, fax 814-451-6907. *Chair* Tony Keck.

Oakland Library Consortium (OLC), Univ. of Pittsburgh Lib., 271 Hillman Lib., Pittsburgh 15260. SAN 370-5803. Tel. 412-648-7753, fax 412-648-7887, e-mail sf0v@andrew. cmu.edu. *Board Pres.* Rush Miller; *Secy.* Staci Quackenbush.

PALINET and Union Library Catalogue of Pennsylvania, 3401 Market St., Suite 262, Philadelphia 19104. SAN 322-3000. Tel. 215-382-7031, fax 215-382-0022, e-mail palinet@palinet.org. *Exec. Dir.* James E. Rush; *Mgr. OCLC and Info. Svcs.* Meryl Cinnamon.

Pennsylvania Citizens for Better Libraries (PCBL), 806 West St., Homestead 15120. SAN 372-8285. Tel. 412-461-1322, fax

412-461-1250. *Chief Exec. Officer* Sharon A. Alberts.

Pennsylvania Community College Library Consortium, c/o Harrisburg Area Community College, 1 Hacc Dr., Harrisburg 17110-2999. SAN 329-3939. Tel. 717-780-2468, fax 717-780-2462.

Pennsylvania Library Association, 1919 N. Front St., Harrisburg 17102. SAN 372-8145. Tel. 717-233-3113, fax 717-233-3121. *Exec. Dir.* Glenn R. Miller; *Pres.* Karl Helicher.

Philadelphia Area Consortium of Special Collections Libraries (PACSCL), Dept. of Special Collections, Univ. of Pennsylvania Lib., 3420 Walnut St., Philadelphia 19104-6206. SAN 370-7504. Tel. 215-898-7552, fax 215-573-9079. *Pres.* Michael Ryan.

Pittsburgh Council on Higher Education (PCHE), 3814 Forbes Ave., Pittsburgh 15213-3506. SAN 322-3019. Tel. 412-683-7905, fax 412-648-1492, e-mail hunterb@pitt.edu. *Exec. Dir.* Betty K. Hunter.

Pittsburgh-East Hospital Library Cooperative, Harmarville Rehabilitation Center, Guys Run Rd., Box 11460, Pittsburgh 15238. SAN 322-3027. Tel. 412-826-2741.

Southeastern Pennsylvania Theological Library Association (SEPTLA), c/o St. Charles Borromeo Seminary, Ryan Memorial Lib., 1000 E. Wynnewood Rd., Wynnewood 19096-3012. SAN 371-0793. Tel. 610-645-9319, fax 610-645-5707, e-mail ebasemlib@ebts.edu or stcthelib@hslc.org. *Pres.* Melody Mazuk.

State System of Higher Education Libraries Council (SSHELCO), c/o Louis L. Manderino Lib., California Univ. of Pennsylvania, California 15419-1394. SAN 322-2918. Tel. 412-938-4096, fax 412-938-5901. *Chair* William L. Beck.

Susquehanna Library Cooperative, c/o Geisinger Medical Lib., 100 N. Academy Ave., Danville 17822-0403. SAN 322-3051. Tel. 717-271-8198, fax 717-271-5738, e-mail srobishaw@smpp.geisinger.edu. *Pres.* Susan Robishaw; *Treas.* Brian Bunnett.

Tri-State College Library Cooperative (TCLC), c/o Rosemont College Lib., 1400 Montgomery Ave., Rosemont 19010-1699. SAN 322-3078. Tel. 610-525-0796, fax 610-525-1939, e-mail tclc@shrsys.hslc.org. *Coord.* Ellen Gasiewski.

Rhode Island

Association of Rhode Island Health Sciences Libraries (ARIHSL), c/o Providence College, River Ave. at Eaton, Providence 02918. SAN 371-0742. Tel. 401-865-2631, fax 401-865-2823, e-mail jschustr@providence.edu. *Pres.* Janice Schuster.

Consortium of Rhode Island Academic and Research Libraries (CRIARL), Box 40041, Providence 02940-0041. SAN 322-3086. Tel. 401-865-2244, fax 401-865-2823, e-mail amaxwell@acad.bryant.edu. *Pres.* Edgar C. Bailey, Jr.

Cooperating Libraries Automated Network (CLAN), c/o Providence Public Lib., 225 Washington St., Providence 02903. SAN 329-4560. Tel. 401-455-8044, 455-8085, 732-7687 (Exec. Dir), fax 401-455-8080. *Chair* Carol Brouwer; *V. Chair* Mary Ellen Hardiman.

Rhode Island Library Network (RHILINET), c/o Office of Lib. and Info. Services, 1 Capitol Hill, 4th flr., Providence 02908-5870. SAN 371-6821. Tel. 401-277-1220, ext. 128, fax 401-277-4260. *Dir.* Barbara Weaver; *Deputy Dir.* Dorothy Frechette.

South Carolina

Catawba-Wateree Area Health Education Consortium, 1228 Colonial Commons, Box 2049, Lancaster 29721. SAN 329-3971. Tel. 803-286-4121, fax 803-286-4165. *Libn.* Martha Williams.

Columbia Area Medical Librarians' Association (CAMLA), Professional Lib., 1800 Colonial Dr., Box 202, Columbia 29202. SAN 372-9400. Tel. 803-734-7136, fax 803-734-7087. *Coord.* Neeta N. Shah.

South Carolina AHEC, c/o Medical Univ. of South Carolina, 171 Ashley Ave., Charleston 29425. SAN 329-3998. Tel. 803-792-4431, fax 803-792-4430. *Exec. Dir.* Sabra C. Slaughter; *Allied Health-Pharmacy Program Dir.* Beth Kennedy.

South Carolina Library Network, South Carolina State Lib., 1500 Senate St., Box 11469, Columbia 29211-1469. SAN 322-4198. Tel. 803-734-8666, fax 803-734-

8676, e-mail lea@leo.scsl.state.sc.us. *State Libn.* James B. Johnson, Jr; *Dir. Network Svcs.* Lea Walsh.

Upper Savannah AHEC Medical Library, Self Memorial Hospital, 1325 Spring St., Greenwood 29646. SAN 329-4110. Tel. 864-227-4851, fax 864-227-4838, e-mail hilltw@ais.ais-gwd.com. *Libn.* Thomas Hill.

South Dakota

South Dakota Library Network (SDLN), University Station, Box 9672, Spearfish 57799-9672. SAN 371-2117. Tel. 605-642-6835, fax 605-642-6298. *Dir.* Gary Johnson.

Tennessee

Association of Memphis Area Health Science Libraries (AMAHSL), c/o Health Sciences Lib., Le Bonheur Children's Medical Center, 50 N. Dunlap Ave., Memphis 38103. SAN 323-9802. Tel. 901-572-3167, fax 901-572-5203, e-mail palmertreek@delphi.com. *Pres.* Kerry Palmertree.

Consortium of Southern Biomedical Libraries (CONBLS), Meharry Medical College, 1005 Dr. D. B. Todd Blvd., Nashville 37208. SAN 370-7717. Tel. 615-327-6728, fax 615-321-2932. *Treas.* Cheryl Hamburg.

Knoxville Area Health Sciences Library Consortium (KAHSLC), Fort Sanders Medical-Nursing Lib., 1915 White Ave., Knoxville 37916. SAN 371-0556. Tel. 423-541-1293, fax 423-541-1762, e-mail njcook@usit.net. *Pres.* Nedra J. Cook.

Mid-Tennessee Health Science Librarians Association, Saint Thomas Hospital, Box 380, Nashville 37202. SAN 329-5028. Tel. 615-222-6658, fax 615-222-6765, e-mail alovvorn@stthomas.org. *Pres.* Alice Lovvorn.

Tennessee Health Science Library Association (THeSLA), Holston Valley Medical Center Health Sciences Lib., Box 238, Kinsport 37662. SAN 371-0726. Tel. 423-224-6870, fax 423-224-6014, e-mail forbeseh@Ctrvax.vanderbilt.edu. *Pres.* Patsy Ellis.

Tri-Cities Area Health Sciences Libraries Consortium, East Tennessee State Univ., James H. Quillen College of Medicine, Medical Lib., Box 70693, Johnson City 37614-0693. SAN 329-4099. Tel. 423-439-6252, fax 423-439-7025, e-mail fisherj@medserv.etsu-tn.edu. *Pres.* Andrea Batson.

West Tennessee Academic Library Consortium, c/o Lane College Lib., Lane Ave., Jackson 38301. SAN 322-3175. Tel. 901-426-7654, fax 901-423-4931. *Chair* Darlene Brooks.

Texas

Abilene Library Consortium, ACU Sta., Box 29208, Abilene 79699-9208. SAN 322-4694. Tel. 915-674-6525, fax 915-674-2202, e-mail gillette@alcon.acu.edu. *System Mgr.* Robert Gillette.

Alliance for Higher Education Alliance, Suite 250, LB 107, 17103 Preston Rd., Dallas 75248-1373. SAN 322-3337. Tel. 972-713-8170, fax 972-713-8209. *Pres.* Allan Watson.

AMIGOS Bibliographic Council, Inc., 12200 Park Central Dr., Suite 500, Dallas 75251. SAN 322-3191. Tel. 972-851-8000, fax 972-991-6061, e-mail amigos@amigos.org; *Exec. Dir.* Bonnie Juergens. *Dir. Business Svcs.* Barry Breen.

APLIC International Census Network, c/o Population Research Center (PRC), 1800 Main Bldg., Univ. of Texas, Austin 78712. SAN 370-0690. Tel. 512-471-8335, fax 512-471-4886. *Dir.* Gera Draaijer; *Libn.* Diane Fisher.

Council of Research and Academic Libraries (CORAL), AL/HR-SDKL Technical Lib., 7909 Lindbergh Dr., Brooks AFB 78235-5352. SAN 322-3213. Tel. 210-536-2651, fax 210-536-2902, e-mail goff@alhr.brooks.af.mil. *Pres.* Marilyn Goff.

Del Norte Biosciences Library Consortium, c/o Reference Dept. Lib., Univ. of Texas at El Paso, 500 W. University, El Paso 79968. SAN 322-3302. Tel. 915-747-6714, fax 915-747-5327, e-mail emoreno@mail.uted.edu. *Pres.* Esperanza A. Moreno.

Forest Trail Library Consortium, Inc. (FTLC), 222 W. Cotton St., Longview 75601. SAN 374-6283. Tel. 903-237-1340, fax 903-237-1327. *Pres.* Dennis Read; *V. Pres./Pres.-Elect* Jerry McCulley.

Harrington Library Consortium, Box 447, Amarillo 79178. SAN 329-546X. Tel. 806-371-5135, fax 806-345-5678, e-mail roseann@hlc.actx.edu. *Exec. Dir.* Roseann Perez.

Health Library Information Network, John Peter Smith Hospital Lib., 1500 S. Main St., Fort Worth 76104. SAN 322-3299. Tel. 817-921-3431, ext. 5088, fax 817-923-0718. *Chair* Leslie Herman.

Health Oriented Libraries of San Antonio (HOLSA), Briscoe Lib., Univ. of Texas Health Sciences Center, 7703 Floyd Curl Dr., San Antonio 78284. SAN 373-5907. Tel. 210-567-2425, fax 210-567-2490. *Pres.* Dorothy Jobe.

Houston Area Research Library Consortium (HARLiC), Prairieview A&M Univ., John B. Coleman Lib., Third St., Prairieview 77446. SAN 322-3329. Tel. 409-857-2012, fax 409-857-2755, e-mail dudley-yates@tamu.edu. *Pres.* Dudley Yates.

National Network of Libraries of Medicine–South Central Region, c/o HAM-TMC Lib., 1133 M. D. Anderson Blvd., Houston 77030-2809. SAN 322-3353. Tel. 713-799-7880, fax 281-790-7030, e-mail maryr@library.tmc.edu. *Contact* Mary Ryan.

Northeast Texas Library System (NETLS), 625 Austin, Garland 75040-6365. SAN 370-5943. Tel. 972-205-2566, fax 972-205-2523. *Dir.* Claire Bausch; *Coord.* Dale Fleeger.

Piasano Consortium, Victoria College, Univ. of Houston at Victoria, 2602 N. Ben Jordan, Victoria 77901-5699. SAN 329-4943. Tel. 512-573-3291, 576-3151, fax 512-788-6227, e-mail dahlstromj@jadc.vic.uh. edu. *Coord.* Joe F. Dahlstrom.

South Central Academic Medical Libraries Consortium (SCAMeL), 3500 Camp Bowie Blvd., Fort Worth 76107. SAN 372-8269. Tel. 817-735-2380, fax 817-735-5158. *Chair* Richard C. Wood.

Texas Council of State University Librarians, Univ. of Texas Health Science Center, 7703 Floyd Curl Dr., San Antonio 78284-7940. SAN 322-337X. Tel. 210-567-2400, fax 210-567-2490, e-mail bowden@uthscsa. edu. *Chair* Virginia M. Bowden.

TEXNET, Box 12927, Austin 78711. SAN 322-3396. Tel. 512-463-5465, fax 512-463-5436. *Mgr.* Rebecca Linton.

Utah

FS-INFO, Intermountain Research Sta., 324 25th St., Ogden 84401. SAN 322-032X. Tel. 801-625-5445, fax 801-625-5129. *Coord.* Carol A. Ayer.

Utah Academic Library Consortium (UALC), Utah Valley State College Lib., 800 W. 1200 S., Orem 84058. SAN 322-3418. Tel. 801-222-8000, fax 801-764-7065. *Chair* Michael J. Freeman.

Utah Health Sciences Library Consortium, c/o Eccles Health Science Lib., Univ. of Utah, Salt Lake City 84112. SAN 376-2246. Tel. 801-581-8771, fax 801-581-3632. *V. Chair* Kathleen McCloskey.

Vermont

Vermont Resource Sharing Network, c/o Vermont Dept. of Libs., 109 State, Montpelier 05609-0601. SAN 322-3426. Tel. 802-828-3261, fax 802-828-2199. *Contact* Marjorie Zunder.

Virginia

American Indian Higher Education Consortium (AIHEC), 121 Oronoco St., Alexandria 22314. SAN 329-4056. Tel. 703-838-0400, fax 703-838-0388, e-mail aihec@aol. com. *Pres.* Carty Monette.

Defense Technical Information Center, 8725 John J. Kingman Rd., Suite 0944, Fort Belvoir 22060-6218. SAN 322-3442. Tel. 703-767-9100, fax 703-767-9183. *Admin.* Kurt N. Molholm.

Huntington Health Science Library Consortium, Marshall Univ. Health Science Libs., Huntington 25755-9210. SAN 322-4295. Tel. 304-696-6426, fax 304-696-6740. *Chair* Edward Dzierzak.

Interlibrary Users Association (IUA), c/o PRC Inc., 1500 PRC Dr., McLean 22102. SAN 322-1628. Tel. 703-556-1166, fax 703-556-1174, e-mail kopp_barbara@prc.com. *Pres.* Barbara Kopp; *V. Pres.* Nancy Minter.

Lynchburg Area Library Cooperative, Knight-Capron Lib., Lynchburg College, 1501 Lakeside Dr., Lynchburg 24501. SAN 322-3450. Tel. 804-544-8441, fax 804-544-8499, e-mail dunn@lynchburg.edu. *Chair* Virginia Dunn; *V. Chair* Steve Preston.

Lynchburg Information Online Network, Knight-Capron Lib., Lynchburg College, Lynchburg 24501. SAN 374-6097. Tel. 804-544-8398, fax 804-544-8499, e-mail Telnet: leo.lion.ed. *Project Dir.* John G. Jaffe; *System Admin.* Marjorie Freeman.

Metropolitan Area Collection Development Consortium (MCDAC), c/o Arlington County Dept. of Libs., 1015 N. Quincy St., Arlington 22201. SAN 323-9748. Tel. 703-358-5981, fax 703-358-5998. *Chief, Materials Mgt. Div.* Eleanor K. Pourron.

Questel Orbit, Inc., 8000 Westpark Dr., McLean 22102. SAN 322-2438. Tel. 703-442-0900, fax 703-893-4632. *Pres.* Osmon Sultan.

Richmond Academic Library Consortium (RALC), Virginia State Univ., Box 9406, Petersburg 23806. SAN 371-3938. Tel. 804-524-5040, fax 804-524-5482, e-mail estephens@vsu.edu. *Pres.* Elsie Weatherington.

Richmond Area Film-Video Cooperative, Virginia Commonwealth Univ., Cabell Media Resource Svcs., Box 842033, Richmond 23284-2033. SAN 322-3469. Tel. 804-828-1088, fax 804-828-7473, e-mail nchenaul@vcu.edu. *Chair* Nell Chenault.

Southside Virginia Library Network (SVLN), Longwood College, 201 High St., Farmville 23909-1897. SAN 372-8242. Tel. 804-395-2433, fax 804-395-2453. *Dir.* Calvin J. Boyer; *Head, Technical Svcs.* Rebecca R. Laine.

Southwestern Virginia Health Information Librarians (SWVAHILI), Danville Regional Medical Center, 142 S. Main St., Danville 24541. SAN 323-9527. Tel. 804-799-4418, fax 804-799-2255. *Chair* Ann Sasser; *Secy. and Treas.* Kathy Mohler.

Virginia Independent College and University Library Association, c/o Mary Helen Cochran Lib., Sweet Briar College, Sweet Briar 24595. SAN 374-6089. Tel. 804-381-6139, fax 804-381-6173. *Chair* John G. Jaffe.

Virginia Library and Information Network (VLIN), c/o The Lib. of Virginia, 800 E. Broad St., Richmond 23219-1905. SAN 373-0921. Tel. 804-692-3993, fax 804-692-3771. *State Libn.* Nolan T. Yelich.

Virginia Tidewater Consortium for Higher Education, 5215 Hampton Blvd., William Spong Hall, Rm. 129, Norfolk 23529-0293. SAN 329-5486. Tel. 757-683-3183, fax 757-683-4515, e-mail lgdotolo@aol.com. *Pres.* Lawrence G. Dotolo.

United States Army Training and Doctrine Command (TRADOC), ATBO-FL, Bldg. 5A, Rm. 102, Fort Monroe 23651-5000. SAN 322-418X. Tel. 757-727-4096, fax 757-728-5300. *Dir.* Janet Scheitle; *Systems Analyst* James Bradley.

Washington

Consortium for Automated Library Services (CALS), Evergreen State College Lib. L2300, Olympia 98505. SAN 329-4528. Tel. 360-866-6000, ext. 6260, fax 360-866-6790, e-mail metcalfs@elwha.evergreen.edu. *System Mgr.* Steven A. Metcalf.

Council on Botanical Horticultural Libraries, Lawrence Pierce Lib., Rhododendron Species Federation, 2525 S. 336 St., Box 3798, Federal Way 98063-3798. SAN 371-0521. Tel. 206-927-6960, fax 206-838-4686. *Chair* Mrs. George Harrison.

Inland Northwest Health Sciences Libraries (INWHSL), Box 10283, Spokane 99209-0283. SAN 370-5099. Tel. 509-324-7344, fax 509-324-7349, e-mail Ontyme: icfne or pringle@wsuvmi.csc.wsu.edu. *Chair* Mary Curtis-Kellett.

Inland Northwest Library Automation Network (INLAN), Foley Center, Gonzaga Univ., Spokane 99258. SAN 375-0124. Tel. 509-328-4220, ext. 3132, fax 509-324-5855. *Contact* Robert Burr.

National Network of Libraries of Medicine–Pacific Northwest Region (NN-LM PNR), Univ. of Washington, Box 357155, Seattle 98195-7155. SAN 322-3485. Tel. 206-543-8262, fax 206-543-2469, e-mail nnlm@u.washington.edu. *Dir.* Sherrilynne S. Fuller.

Spokane Cooperative Library Information System (SCOLIS), E12004 Main, Spokane 99206-5193. SAN 322-3892. Tel. 509-922-1371, fax 509-926-7139. *Mgr.* Linda Dunham.

WLN, Box 3888, Lacey 98509-3888. SAN 322-3507. Tel. 360-923-4000, fax 360-923-4009, e-mail info@wln.com. *Pres.*

and Chief Exec. Officer Paul McCarthy; *Dir. Lib. Svcs.* Sharon West.

West Virginia

East Central Colleges, Box AJ, Bethany 26032-1434. SAN 322-2667. Tel. 304-829-7812, fax 304-829-7546. *Exec. Dir.* Dennis Landon.

Mountain States Consortium, c/o Alderson Broaddus College, Philippi 26416. SAN 329-4765. Tel. 304-457-1700, fax 304-457-6239. *Treas.* Leonard Lobello.

Southern West Virginia Library Automation Corporation, 221 N. Kanawha St., Box 1876, Beckley 25802. SAN 322-421X. Tel. 304-255-0511, fax 304-255-9161. *Pres.* Judy Gunsaulis; *Systems Mgr.* Margaret Thompson.

Wisconsin

Arrowhead Health Sciences Library Network, WITC-Superior/District LRC, 600 N 21 St., Superior 54880. SAN 322-1954. Tel. 715-394-6677, fax 715-394-3771; *Coord.* Judy Lyons.

Bi-State Academic Libraries (BI-SAL), c/o Marycrest International Univ., Davenport 52804. SAN 322-1393. Tel. 319-326-9255.

Council of Wisconsin Libraries, Inc. (COWL), 728 State St., Rm. 464, Madison 53706-1494. SAN 322-3523. Tel. 608-263-4962, fax 608-263-3684, e-mail schneid@doit. wisc.edu. *Dir.* Kathryn Schneider Michaelis.

Fox River Valley Area Library Consortium, Holy Family Memorial Medical Center, Box 1450, Manitowoc 54221-1450. SAN 322-3531. Tel. 920-684-2011, ext. 260, fax 920-684-2522. *Coord.* Dan Eckert.

Fox Valley Library Council (FVLC), c/o Appleton Medical Center Lib., 1818 N. Meade St., Appleton 54911. SAN 323-9640. Tel. 920-831-5089, fax 920-738-6389. *Pres.* Nancy Greene.

Library Council of Metropolitan Milwaukee, Inc., 814 W. Wisconsin Ave., Milwaukee 53233-2309. SAN 322-354X. Tel. 414-271-8470, fax 414-286-2794, e-mail ricec@ vms.csd.mu.edu. *Exec. Dir.* Corliss Rice.

North East Wisconsin Intertype Libraries, Inc. (NEWIL), c/o Nicolet Federated Lib. System, 515 Pine St., Green Bay 54301.

SAN 322-3574. Tel. 920-448-4412, fax 920-448-4420, e-mail tdhowe@mail.wiscnet.net. *Coord.* Terrie Howe.

South Central Wisconsin Health Science Library Cooperative, c/o FAMHS Medical Lib., 611 Sherman Ave. E., Fort Atkinson 53538. SAN 322-4686. Tel. 920-568-5194, fax 920-568-5059, e-mail carrie. garity@famhs.org. *Representative* Carrie Garity.

Southeastern Wisconsin Health Science Library Consortium, c/o All Saints Healthcare, St. Mary's Medical Center Lib., 3801 Spring St., Racine 53405. SAN 322-3582. Tel. 414-636-8914, fax 414-636-4175. *Contact* Vicki Budzisz.

Southeastern Wisconsin Information Technology Exchange, Inc. (SWITCH), 6801 N. Yates Rd., Milwaukee 53217-3985. SAN 371-3962. Tel. 414-351-2423, fax 414-352-6062, e-mail cagould@acs.stritch.edu.

Wisconsin Area Research Center Network ARC Network, 816 State St., Madison 53706. SAN 373-0875. Tel. 608-264-6480, fax 608-264-6486, e-mail archives. reference@ccmail.adp.wisc.edu. *State Archivist* Peter Gottlieb.

Wisconsin Interlibrary Services (WILS), 728 State St., Rm. 464, Madison 53706-1494. SAN 322-3612. Tel. 608-263-4962, fax 608-263-3684, e-mail schneid@doit.wisc. edu. *Dir.* Kathryn Schneider Michaelis; *Asst. Dir.* Mary Williamson.

Wisconsin Valley Library Service (WVLS), 300 N. First St., Wausau 54403. SAN 371-3911. Tel. 715-847-5549, fax 715-845-4270, e-mail wvlsgen@mail.wiscnet.net; *Dir.* Heather Ann Eldred. *Business Admin.* Marla Sepnafski.

Wyoming

Health Sciences Information Network (HSIN), Univ. of Wyoming, 205 Coe Lib., Box 3334, Laramie 82071-3334. SAN 371-4861. Tel. 307-766-6537, fax 307-766-3062, e-mail jgahagan@uwyo.edu. *Coord.* Janice Gahagan.

WYLD Network, c/o Wyoming State Lib., Supreme Court and State Lib. Bldg., Cheyenne 82002. SAN 371-0661. Tel. 307-777-7281, fax 307-777-6289. *State*

Libn. Helen Meadors Maul; *WYLD Program Mgr.* Corky Walters.

Virgin Islands

VILINET (Virgin Islands Library and Information Network), c/o Division of Libs., Museums and Archives, 23 Dronningens Gade, Saint Thomas 00802. SAN 322-3639. Tel. 809-774-3407 (DLMAS), 774-3407, fax 809-775-1887. *Chair* Jeanette Allis Bastian.

Canada

Alberta

Alberta Association of College Librarians (AACL), Grant MacEwan Community College, Box 1796, Edmonton T5J 2P2. SAN 370-0763. Tel. 403-497-5894, fax 403-497-5895, e-mail lloydp@admin.gmcc.ab.ca. *Chair* Patricia Lloyd.

Alberta Government Libraries Council (AGLC), c/o Alberta Education Lib., 1160 Jasper Ave., Edmonton T5K 0L5. SAN 370-0372. Tel. 403-427-2985, fax 403-427-5927, e-mail candrews@edc.gov.ab.ca. *Chair* Christina Andrews.

Northern Alberta Health Libraries Association (NAHLA), Longview Crescent, No. 6, 10025 Jasper Ave., Box 2222, Saint Albert T8N 2W2. SAN 370-5951. Tel. 403-459-4084, fax 403-492-6960, e-mail nahla@freenet.edmonton.alberta.ca. *Pres.* Georgia Makowski.

British Columbia

British Columbia College and Institute Library Services, Langara College Lib., 100 W. 49 Ave., Vancouver V5Y 2Z6. SAN 329-6970. Tel. 604-323-5237, fax 604-323-5544. *Contact* Phyllis Mason.

Media Exchange Cooperative (MEC), Trinity Western Univ. Lib., 7600 Glover Rd., Langley V2Y 1Y1. SAN 329-6954. Tel. 604-888-7511, fax 604-888-3786, e-mail tgosh@twu.ca. *Pres.* Ted Goshulak.

Manitoba

Manitoba Government Libraries Council (MGLC), 360-1395 Ellice Ave., Winnipeg R3G 3P2. SAN 371-6848. Tel. 204-945-6569, fax 204-945-8427, e-mail mlavergne@em.gov.mb.ca. *Chair* Monique Lavergne.

Manitoba Library Consortium, Inc (MLCI), c/o Aikins, MacAulay and Thorvaldson, Commodity Exchange Tower, 360 Main St., Winnipeg R3C 4G1. SAN 372-820X. Tel. 204-822-5529, fax 204-822-3798. *Chair* Iris Loewen.

Nova Scotia

Maritimes Health Libraries Association (MHLA/ABSM), c/o IWK Grace Health Center, 5980 University Ave., Halifax B3H 4N1. SAN 370-0836. Tel. 902-420-6729, fax 902-420-3122. *Pres.* Darlene Chapman.

Novanet, 6080 Young St., Suite 601, Halifax B3K 5L2. SAN 372-4050. Tel. 902-453-2451, ext. 2461, fax 902-453-2369, e-mail novanet@ac.dal.ca. *Mgr. Info. Systems* Scott W. Nickerson.

Ontario

Bibliocentre, 80 Cowdray Court, Scarborough M1S 4N1. SAN 322-3663. Tel. 416-289-5151, fax 416-299-4841, e-mail falt@cencol.on.ca. *Dir.* Annetta Protain.

Canadian Association of Research Libraries/ Association des Bibliothèques de Recherche du Canada (CARL ABRC), Univ. of Ottawa, Morisset Hall, Rm. 602, 65 University St., Ottawa K1N 9A5. SAN 323-9721. Tel. 613-562-5800, ext. 3652, fax 613-562-5195, e-mail carl-acadvm1.uottawa.ca. *Interim Exec. Dir.* Timothy Mark.

Canadian Health Libraries Association (CHLA-ABSC), Office of Secretariat, 3332 Yonge St., Box 94038, Toronto M4N 3R1. SAN 370-0720. Tel. 416-485-0377, fax 416-485-0377. *Pres.* Susan Murray.

County and Regional Municipal Library (CARML), Frontenac County Lib., Frontenac County Courthouse, Court St., Kingston K7L 2N4. SAN 323-9705. *Chair* Marion Watkins; *V. Chair* Mary Anne Evans.

Disability Resource Library Network (DRLN), c/o North York Public Lib., 5120 Yonge St., North York M2N 5N9. SAN 323-9837. Tel. 416-395-5581, fax 416-395-5594. *Contact* Joanne Bar.

Education Libraries Sharing of Resources—A Network (ELSOR), 45 York Mills Rd., North York M2P 1B6. SAN 370-0399. Tel. 416-397-2523, fax 416-397-2640. *Chair* Catherine Spiridanov.

Hamilton and District Health Library Network, c/o Health Sciences Lib., McMaster Univ., Hamilton L8N 3Z5. SAN 370-5846. Tel. 905-525-9140, ext. 22322, fax 905-528-3733. *Network Coord.* Linda Panton.

Health Science Information Consortium of Toronto, Univ. of Toronto, 7 King's College Circle, Toronto M5S 1A5. SAN 370-5080. Tel. 416-978-6359, fax 416-971-2637, e-mail leishman@vax.library.utoronto.ca.

Hi-tech Libraries Network, c/o Cal Corp., 1050 Morrison Dr., Ottawa K2H 8K7. SAN 323-9586. Tel. 613-820-8280, fax 613-820-8314. *Contact* Sandra Spence.

Information Network for Ontario Ministry of Citizenship, Culture and Recreation: Cultural Partnerships Branch, 77 Bloor St. W, 3rd flr., Toronto M7A 2R9. SAN 329-5605. Fax 416-314-7635. *Dir.* Michael Langford.

Kingston Area Health Libraries Association (KAHLA), c/o Staff Lib., Kingston Psychiatric Hospital, Bag 603, Kingston K7L 4X3. SAN 370-0674. Tel. 613-546-1101, ext. 5745, fax 613-548-5588. *Pres.* Karen Gagnon.

Ontario Council of University Libraries (OCUL), Laurentian Univ., Ramsey Lake Rd., Sudbury P3E 2C6. SAN 371-9413. Tel. 705-675-1151, fax 705-675-4877, e-mail jgarnett@library.laurentian.ca. *Chair* Joyce Garnett.

Ontario Hospital Libraries Association (OHLA), Toronto Hospital Lib. and Info. Svcs., 585 University Ave., Toronto M5G 2C4. SAN 370-0739. Tel. 416-340-3094, fax 416-340-4384, e-mail reid@vax.library.utoronto.ca. *Pres.* Elizabeth Reid.

QL Systems Limited, 1 Gore St., Box 2080, Kingston K7L 5J8. SAN 322-368X. Tel. 613-549-4611, fax 613-548-4260, e-mail hlawford@glsys.ca. *Pres.* Hugh Lawford.

Shared Library Services (SLS), South Huron Hospital, 24 Huron St. W., Exeter N0M 1S2. SAN 323-9500. Tel. 519-235-2700, ext. 249, fax 519-235-3405. *Dir.* Linda Wilcox.

Sheridan Park Association, Lib. and Info. Science Committee (SPA-LISC), 2275 Speakman Dr., Mississauga L5K 1B1. SAN 370-0437. Tel. 905-823-6160, fax 905-823-6160.

Toronto Health Libraries Association (THLA), Box 94056, Toronto M4N 3R1. SAN 323-9853. Tel. 416-485-0377. *Pres.* Colleen Mulloy.

Toronto School of Theology, c/o Wycliffe College, 5 Hoskin Ave., Toronto M5S 1H7. SAN 322-452X. Tel. 416-979-2870, fax 416-979-0471, e-mail derrenbacker@vax.lib.utoronto.ca. *Secy. Lib. Committee* Cindy Derrenbacker.

Wellington Waterloo Dufferin (WWD) Health Library Network, c/o William Howitt Memorial Health Sciences Lib., Guelph General Hospital, 115 Delhi St., Guelph N1E 4J4. SAN 370-0496. Tel. 519-837-6440, ext. 215, fax 519-837-6467. *Coord.* Brenda Vegso.

Quebec

Association des Bibliothèques de la Santé Affiliées a l'Université De Montréal (ABSAUM), c/o Health Lib., Box 6128, Sta. Downtown, Univ. of Montreal, Montreal H3C 3J7. SAN 370-5838. Tel. 514-343-6826, fax 514-343-2350. *Secy.* Danielle Tardif.

Canadian Heritage Information Network (CHIN), 15 Eddy St., 4th flr., Hull K1A 0C8. SAN 329-3076. Tel. 819-994-1200, fax 819-994-9555, e-mail service@chin.gc.ca. *Dir. Gen.* Lyn Elliot Sherwood; *Dir. Info. Svcs.* Bruce Williams.

Center for Information Technology Innovation (CITI), 1575 Blvd. Chomedy, Laval H7V 2X2. SAN 327-9111. Tel. 514-973-5700, fax 514-973-5757. *Acting Dir. Gen.* Marcel Drouin.

McGill Medical and Health Libraries Association (MMAHLA), c/o Royal Victoria Hospital, Women's Pavillion Lib., 3830 Lacombe Ave., Rm. F4-24, Montreal H3A 1A1. SAN 374-6100. Tel. 514-842-1231, ext. 4738, fax 514-843-1678. *Co-Chairs* Lynda Dickson, Irene Shanefield.

Montreal Health Libraries Association (MHLA), 2365 Côte de Liesse, Montreal H4N 2M7. SAN 323-9608. Tel. 514-333-2057, fax 514-331-6387. *Pres.* Donna Gibson.

Montreal Medical Online Users Group (MMOUG), McGill Health Sciences Lib., 3655 Drummond St., Montreal H3G 1Y6. SAN 370-0771. Tel. 514-398-4475, ext. 09184, fax 514-398-3890. *Coord.* Angella Lambrou.

Saskatchewan

Saskatchewan Government Libraries Council (SGLC), c/o Saskatchewan Agriculture and Food Lib., 3085 Albert St., Regina S4S 0B1. SAN 323-956X. Tel. 306-787-5151, fax 306-787-0216, e-mail Envoy 100 sk.ag.lib. *Chair* Helene Stewart.

National Library and Information-Industry Associations, United States and Canada

American Association of Law Libraries

Executive Director, Roger Parent
53 W. Jackson Blvd., Suite 940, Chicago, IL 60604
312-939-4764, fax 312-431-1097
World Wide Web http://www.aallnet.org

Object

The American Association of Law Libraries (AALL) is established for educational and scientific purposes. It shall be conducted as a nonprofit corporation to promote and enhance the value of law libraries to the public, the legal community, and the world; to foster the profession of law librarianship; to provide leadership in the field of legal information; and to foster a spirit of cooperation among the members of the profession. Established 1906.

Membership

Memb. 5,000. Persons officially connected with a law library or with a law section of a state or general library, separately maintained. Associate membership available for others. Dues (Indiv., Indiv. Assoc., and Inst.) $126; (Inst. Assoc.) $242 times the number of members; (Retired) $32.50; (Student) $28; (SIS Memb.) $12 each per year. Year. July 1 to June 30.

Officers

Pres. Judith Meadows, State Law Lib. of Montana, Justice Bldg., 215 N. Sanders, Helena, MT 59620-3004. Tel. 406-444-3660, fax 406-444-3603, e-mail jmeadows@mt. gov; *V.P./Pres.-Elect* James S. Heller, College of William & Mary, Marshall-Whythe Law Lib., S. Henry St., Williamsburg, VA 23187-8795. Tel. 757-221-3252, fax 757-221-3051, e-mail jshell@facstaff.wm.edu; *Past Pres.* Frank G. Houdek, School of Law

Lib., Southern Illinois Univ., Mail Code 6803, Lesar Law Bldg., Carbondale, IL 62901-6803. Tel. 618-453-8788, fax 618-453-8728, e-mail houdek@siu.edu; *Secy.* Susan P. Siebers, Katten Muchin and Zavis, 525 W. Monroe St., Suite 1600, Chicago, IL 60661-3693. Tel. 312-902-5675, fax 312-902-1626, e-mail ssiebers@kmz.com; *Treas.* Anne W. Grande, Hennepin County Law Lib., C-2451 Government Center, Minneapolis, MN 55487. Tel. 612-348-7977, fax 612-348-4230, e-mail anne.grande@co.hennepin. mn.us.

Executive Board

Shelley L. Dowling (1998), e-mail annex@ capcon.net; Mark Folmsbee (2000), Washburn Univ. of Topeka School of Law Lib., 1700 College, Topeka, KS 66621. Tel. 913-231-1010, ext. 1041, fax 903-232-8087, e-mail zzfolm@acc.wuacc.edu; Nancy P. Johnson (1999), e-mail lawnpj@gsusgi2.gsu. edu; Kathleen S. Martin (1999), e-mail mart7131@mlb.com; Carol Avery Nicholson (1998), e-mail carol_nicholson@unc.edu; Heather Braithwaite Simmons (2000), General Motors Corp., Law Lib., Box 33121, Detroit, MI 48232. Tel. 313-974-1901, fax 313-974-0806, e-mail Inusgmb.qz31dc@ gmeds.com.

Committee Chairpersons

Annual Meeting Program Selection. Michael Saint-Onge.
Awards. Victoria Trotta.

Bylaws. Carla Evans.
Call for Papers. Barbara Golden.
Chapter Relations (Ad Hoc Advisory Group). Sarah Holterhoff.
Citation Format. Marcia J. Koslov.
Copyright. Jonathan A. Franklin.
Diversity. Joyce McCrea Pearson.
Government Relations. Jacqueline Wright.
Grants. Grace Mills.
Index to Foreign Legal Periodicals (Advisory). Leonette Williams.
Indexing Periodical Literature (Advisory). Gordon Russell.
Information Technology and Implementation (Ad Hoc Working Group). Timothy L. Coggins.
Law Library Journal and AALL Spectrum (Advisory). Patrick Kehoe.
Local Arrangements (Advisory). Aleta Benjamin.
Mentoring and Retention. Georgianna Wellford.
Nominations. Pauline M. Aranas.
Placement. Joann Dugan.
Preservation. Gail Warren.
Professional Development. Jean Holcombe.
Public Relations. Sarah Holterhoff.
Publications Policy. Barbara Bintiff.
Recruitment. Karen Brunner.

Relations with Information Vendors. Judy Laver.
Research. Elizabeth McKenzie.
Scholarships. Rhea Ballard-Thrower.
Statistics. Susanne Zumbio.

Special-Interest Section Chairpersons

Academic Law Libraries. Scott Pagel.
Computing Services. Judith Kaul.
Foreign, Comparative, and International Law. William McCloy.
Government Documents. Paul Arrigo.
Legal History and Rare Books. Gretchen Feltes.
Legal Information Services to the Public. Elizabeth McKenzie.
Micrographics and Audiovisual. John Pedini.
Online Bibliographic Services. Jacqueline Paul.
Private Law Libraries. Anne Ellis.
Research Instruction and Patron Services. Kori Staheli.
SIS Council. James Milles.
Social Responsibility. Bruce Kleinschmidt.
State Court and County Law Libraries. Gail Warren.
Technical Services. Joseph Thomas.

American Library Association

Executive Director, William R. Gordon
50 E. Huron St., Chicago, IL 60611
800-545-2433, 312-280-3215, fax 312-944-3897
World Wide Web http://www.ala.org

Object

The mission of the American Library Association (ALA) is to provide leadership for the development, promotion, and improvement of library and information services and the profession of librarianship in order to enhance learning and ensure access to information for all. Founded 1876.

Membership

Memb. (Indiv.) 53,165; (Inst.) 2,754; (Total) 55,919. Any person, library, or other organization interested in library service and librarians. Dues (Indiv.) 1st year, $50; 2nd year, $75, 3rd year and later, $100; (Trustee and Assoc. Memb.) $45; (Student) $25; (Foreign Indiv.) $60; (Other) $35; (Inst.) $70 and up, depending on operating expenses of institution.

Officers (1997–1998)

Pres. Barbara J. Ford, Exec. Dir., Univ. Lib. Services, Virginia Commonwealth Univ., 901 Park Ave., Box 842033, Richmond, VA 23284-2033. Tel. 804-828-1107, fax 804-828-0151, e-mail bjford@vcu.edu; *Pres.-Elect* Ann K. Symons, Librarian, Juneau-Douglas H.S., 10014 Crazy Horse Dr., Juneau, AK 99801. Tel. 907-463-1947, fax 907-463-1932, e-mail symonsa@jsd.k12.ak.us; *Immediate Past Pres.* Mary R. Somerville, Dir., Miami-Dade Public Lib. System, 101 W. Flagler St., Miami, FL 33130-1523. Tel. 305-375-5026, fax 305-375-5545, e-mail mspres@dcfreenet.seflin.lib.fl.us; *Treas.* Bruce E. Daniels, Onondaga County Public Lib., 447 S. Salina St., Syracuse, NY 13202-2494. Tel. 315-435-1800, fax 315-435-8533, e-mail ocplbed@transit.appliedtheory.com; *Exec. Dir.* William R. Gordon, ALA Headquarters, 50 E. Huron St., Chicago, IL 60611. Tel. 312-280-3215, fax 312-944-3897.

Executive Board

Charles M. Brown (1999); Martin J. Gomez (2001); Nancy C. Kranich (1998); James G. Neal (2000); Robert R. Newlen (2000); Sally G. Reed (2001); Patricia H. Smith (1999); Evie Wilson-Lingbloom (1998).

Endowment Trustees

Bernard A. Margolis (1998); one member to be elected; *Exec. Board Liaison* Bruce E. Daniels; *Staff Liaison* Gregory L. Calloway.

Divisions

See the separate entries that follow: American Assn. of School Libns.; American Lib. Trustee Assn.; Assn. for Lib. Collections and Technical Services; Assn. for Lib. Service to Children; Assn. of College and Research Libs.; Assn. of Specialized and Cooperative Lib. Agencies; Lib. Admin. and Management Assn.; Lib. and Info. Technology Assn.; Public Lib. Assn.; Reference and User Services Assn.; Young Adult Lib. Services Assn.

Publications

ALA Handbook of Organization and Membership Directory 1997–1998 (ann.).
American Libraries (11 per year; membs.; organizations $60; foreign $70; single copy $6).
Book Links (6 per year; U.S. $24.95; foreign $29.95; single copy $5).
Booklist (22 per year; U.S. and possessions $69.50; foreign $85; single copy $4.50).
Choice (11 per year; U.S. $185; foreign $210; single copy $24).

Round Table Chairpersons

(ALA staff liaison is given in parentheses.)
Armed Forces Libraries. Lucille M. Rosa (Patricia A. Muir).
Continuing Library Education Network and Exchange. Darlene E. Weingand (Mark Knoblauch).
Ethnic Materials and Information Exchange. Joshua Cohen (Satia Orange).
Exhibits. J. Bo Macreery (Diedre Ross).
Federal Librarians. Jewell Armstrong Player (Patricia A. Muir).
Government Documents. Daniel C. Barkley (Patricia A. Muir).
Independent Librarians Exchange. Linda Cooper (Mark Knoblauch).
Intellectual Freedom. Fay A. Golden (Cynthia Robinson).
International Relations. Nancy R. John (Carol Erickson).
Library History. Louise S. Robbins (Mary Jo Lynch).
Library Instruction. Lynn Ossolinski (Mary Jo Lynch).
Library Research. Ronald Powell (Mary Jo Lynch).
Map and Geography. Karl Longstreth (Danielle Alderson).
New Members. Ann Snoeyenbos (Gerald Hodges).
Social Responsibilities. Wendy Thomas (Satia Orange).
Staff Organizations. Leon Bey (Mark Knoblauch).
Support Staff Interests. Patricia Clingman (Mark Knoblauch).
Video. James Massey (Irene Wood).

Committee Chairpersons

Accreditation (Standing). Carla D. Hayden (Mary C. Taylor).

American Libraries Advisory (Standing). Ilene Rockman (Leonard Kniffel).

Appointments (Standing). To be appointed (Emily Melton).

Awards (Standing). Sarah Ann Long (Daphne Whitehead).

Budget Analysis and Review (Standing). Lizbeth Bishoff (Gregory Calloway).

Chapter Relations (Standing). Susan M. Anderson (Gerald Hodges).

Committee on Committees (Elected Council Committee). Ann Symons (Emily Melton).

Conference Comittee. Bettie Estes-Rickner (Mary W. Ghikas; Diedre Ross).

Conference Program (Special). Fred E. Goodman (Mary W. Ghikas; Diedre Ross).

Constitution and Bylaws (Standing). Pamela Klipsch (Sylvia Kraft-Walker).

Council Orientation. Antoinette Negro (Lois Ann Gregory-Wood).

Education. Carolyn Anthony (Mark Knoblauch).

Election. Judith M. Baker (Ernest Martin).

Information Technology. Nancy Roderer (Andrew Magpantay).

Intellectual Freedom. Joseph Boisse (Judith F. Krug).

International Relations. Robert Seal (Carol Erickson).

Legislation. Patricia A. Wand (Carol C. Henderson).

Library of Congress (Special, advisory). Ann E. Prentice (Carol C. Henderson).

Library Records Retention (ad hoc). Deanna B. Marcum (To be appointed).

Literacy and Outreach. Carla Stoffle (Satia Orange).

Membership. Terri Tomchyshyn (Gerald Hodges).

Minority Concerns and Cultural Diversity. Gloria J. Leonard (Satia Orange).

Nominating—1998 Election. Barbara Imroth (Emily I. Melton).

Organization. Jennifer Stone Abramson (Lois Ann Gregory-Wood).

Pay Equity. Tami Echavarria (Mark Knoblauch).

Policy Monitoring. Donald J. Sager (Lois Ann Gregory-Wood).

Professional Ethics. Johannah Sherrer (Judith F. Krug).

Public Awareness. Wayne Coco (Linda K. Wallace).

Publishing. James Rettig (Donald Chatham).

Research and Statistics. Peggy Rudd (Mary Jo Lynch).

Resolutions. Mark Goniwiecha (Filippa A. Genovese).

Standards. Irene M. Padilla (Mary Jo Lynch).

Structure Revision (Special). Sarah M. Pritchard (Emily I. Melton).

Status of Women in Librarianship. Theresa Tobin (Mark Knoblauch).

Joint Committee Chairpersons

American Association of Law Libraries/American Correctional Association–ASCLA Committee on Institution Libraries (joint). Thea B. Chesley (ACA); To be appointed (ASCLA).

American Federation of Labor/Congress of Industrial Organizations–ALA, Library Service to Labor Groups, RASD. Mary F. Hicks (ALA); Anthony Sarmiento (AFL/CIO).

Anglo-American Cataloguing Rules Fund. Donald Chatham (ALA); To be appointed (Canadian Lib. Assn.); Ross Shimmon (Library Assn.).

Anglo-American Cataloguing Rules, Joint Steering Committee for Revision of. Brian Schottlaender (ALA), Ralph W. Manning (Canadian Commission on Cataloguing), Margaret Stewart (National Lib. of Canada), Ann Huthwaite (Australian Commission on Cataloguing), Sally Strutt (British Lib.), Barbara B. Tillett (Lib. of Congress).

Association for Educational Communications and Technology–AASL. Daniel D. Barron (AASL), Annette C. Lamb (AECT).

Association of American Publishers–ALA. Barbara J. Ford (ALA); To be appointed (AAP).

Association of American Publishers–ALCTS. Jana L. Longberger (ALCTS); Linda Parise (AAP).

Children's Book Council–ALA. Mary Rinato Berman (ALA); Lauren Wohl (CBC).

Society of American Archivists–ALA (Joint Committee on Library-Archives Relation-ships). Samuel Boldrick (ALA); William E. Brown, Jr. (SAA).

American Library Association
American Association of School Librarians

Executive Director, Julie A. Walker
50 E. Huron St., Chicago, IL 60611
312-280-4381, 800-545-2433 Ext. 4386, fax 312-664-7459

Object

The American Association of School Librarians (AASL) is interested in the general improvement and extension of library media services for children and young people. AASL has specific responsibility for planning a program of study and service for the improvement and extension of library media services in elementary and secondary schools as a means of strengthening the educational program; evaluation, selection, interpretation, and utilization of media as they are used in the context of the school program; stimulation of continuous study and research in the library field and establishing criteria of evaluation; synthesis of the activities of all units of the American Library Association in areas of mutual concern; representation and interpretation of the need for the function of school libraries to other educational and lay groups; stimulation of professional growth, improvement of the status of school librarians, and encouragement of participation by members in appropriate type-of-activity divisions; conducting activities and projects for improvement and extension of service in the school library when such projects are beyond the scope of type-of-activity divisions, after specific approval by the ALA Council. Established in 1951 as a separate division of ALA.

Membership

Memb. 8,098. Open to all libraries, school library media specialists, interested individuals, and business firms with requisite membership in ALA.

Officers (1997–1998)

Pres. Ken Haycock, 5118 Meadfield Rd., West Vancouver, BC V7W 3G2, Canada. Tel. 604-822-4991, fax 604-822-6006, e-mail haycock@unixg.ubc.ca; *Pres.-Elect* Sharon Coatney, Oak Hill School, 10200 N. 124 St., Overland Park, KS 66216. Tel. 913-681-4325, fax 913-681-4329, e-mail sacoatney@cctr.umkc.edu; *Treas./Financial Officer* Nancy Zimmerman, School of Lib. and Info. Science, SUNY at Buffalo, 381 Baldy Hall, Buffalo, NY 14051. Tel. 716-645-6474, fax 716-645-3775, e-mail liszimme@ubvms.cc.buffalo.edu; *Past Pres.* Barbara Stripling, Public Education Foundation, 100 E. Tenth St., Suite 500, Chattanooga, TN 37402. Tel. 423-265-9403, fax 423-265-9832, e-mail bstripli@cecasun.utc.edu.

Board of Directors

Officers; Christine A. Allen; Judy Arteaga; Augie Beasley; Susan Bryan; Jody Charter; Su Eckhardt; Phyllis Heroy; Judith King; Carol Kroll; Vivian Melton; Drucilla Raines; Jean van Duesen; Barbara Weathers; Julie A. Walker.

Publications

Knowledge Quest (5/yr.; memb.; nonmemb. $40). *Eds.* Nancy L. Teger, e-mail tegern@gate.net; Debbie Abilock, e-mail debbie@neuva.pvt.k12.ca.us.
School Library Media Quarterly (nonsubscription electronic publication available to memb. and nonmemb. at http://www.

ala.org/assl/SLMQ; memb.; nonmemb. $40). *Ed*. Daniel Callison, School of Lib. and Info. Sciences, 10th and Jordan, Indiana Univ., Bloomington, IN 47405. E-mail callison@indiana.edu.

Committee Chairpersons

AASL/Highsmith Research Grant. Susan M. Easun.
ABC-CLIO Leadership Grant. Joane Proctor.
Access Through Technology. Drucie Raines.
Advocacy Task Force. Pam Chesky.
American Univ. Press. Antoinette Negro.
Bylaws and Organization. Judy King.
Distinguished Service Award. Karen Whitney.
Education for School Library Media Specialists Task Force. Paulette Bracy; Selvin Royal.
Frances Henne Award. Diane C. Pozar.
General Conference—Birmingham, 1999. Carolyn Hayes; Connie Mitchell.
ICONnect Task Force. Pam Berger.
Intellectual Freedom Award. Susan Choi.

Information Technology Pathfinder Award (formerly Microcomputer in the Media Center Award). Clara Hoover.
Knowledge Quest Editorial Board. Nancy Teger; Debbie Abilock.
Learning Through the Library Task Force. Vi Harada.
Legislation. Blanche Woolls.
Membership/Mentoring Task Force. Joseph Mattie; Catherine Miller.
National Guidelines—Vision. Betty Marcoux.
National School Library Media Program of the Year. David Loertscher.
National Guidelines: Implementation. Barbara Jeffus.
National Guidelines: Vision. Betty Marcoux.
Nominating Committee, 1998. Charles White.
Presidential Task Force for Coordinating the Implementation of the New National Guidelines and Standards. Ken Haycock.
Publications. Frances Bradburn.
Research/Statistics. June Kahler Berry.
SLMQ Electronic Editorial Board. Daniel Callison.

American Library Association
American Library Trustee Association

Executive Director, Susan Roman
50 E. Huron St., Chicago, IL 60611-2795
312-280-2161, 800-545-2433 Ext. 2161, fax 312-280-3257

Object

The American Library Trustee Association (ALTA) is interested in the development of effective library service for all people in all types of communities and in all types of libraries; it follows that its members are concerned, as policymakers, with organizational patterns of service, with the development of competent personnel, the provision of adequate financing, the passage of suitable legislation, and the encouragement of citizen support for libraries. ALTA recognizes that responsibility for professional action in these fields has been assigned to other divisions of ALA; its specific responsibilities as a division, therefore, are

1. A continuing and comprehensive educational program to enable library trustees to discharge their grave responsibilities in a manner best fitted to benefit the public and the libraries they represent.

2. Continuous study and review of the activities of library trustees.

3. Cooperation with other units within ALA concerning their activities relating to trustees.

4. Encouraging participation of trustees in other appropriate divisions of ALA.

5. Representation and interpretation of the activities of library trustees in contacts outside the library profession,

particularly with national organizations and governmental agencies.

6. Promotion of strong state and regional trustee organizations.

7. Efforts to secure and support adequate library funding.

8. Promulgation and dissemination of recommended library policy.

9. Assuring equal access of information to all segments of the population.

10. Encouraging participation of trustees in trustee/library activities, at local, state, regional, and national levels.

Organized 1890. Became an ALA division in 1961.

Membership

Memb. 1,566. Open to all interested persons and organizations. For dues and membership year, see ALA entry.

Officers (1997–1998)

Pres. Clifford Dittrich; *1st V.P./Pres.-Elect* Ruth Newell-Minor; *Past Pres.* Virginia M. McCurdy; *Councilor* Judith Baker.

Board of Directors

Officers; *Trustee Voice Ed.* Tari Marshall Sliz (1999); *Regional V.P.s* To be appointed; *Ex officio* Susan Roman.

Staff

Exec. Dir. Susan Roman; *Deputy Exec. Dir.* To be appointed; *Admin. Secy.* Dollester Thorp-Hawkins.

Publication

Trustee Voice (q.; memb.). *Ed.* Tari Marshall Sliz.

American Library Association
Association for Library Collections and Technical Services

Executive Director, Karen Muller
50 E. Huron St., Chicago, IL 60611
800-545-2433 ext. 5031, fax 312-280-3257
E-mail kmuller@ala.org

Object

The Association for Library Collections and Technical Services (ALCTS) is responsible for the following activities: acquisition, identification, cataloging, classification, and preservation of library materials; the development and coordination of the country's library resources; and those areas of selection and evaluation involved in the acquisition of library materials and pertinent to the development of library resources. ALCTS has specific responsibility for:

1. Continuous study and review of the activities assigned to the division

2. Conduct of activities and projects within its area of responsibility

3. Syntheses of activities of all units within ALA that have a bearing on the type of activity represented

4. Representation and interpretation of its type of activity in contacts outside the profession

5. Stimulation of the development of librarians engaged in its type of activity, and stimulation of participation by members in appropriate type-of-library divisions

6. Planning and development of programs of study and research for the type of activity for the total profession

ALCTS will provide its members, other ALA divisions and members, and the library and information community with leadership and a program for action on the access to, and identification, acquisition, description, organization, preservation, and dissemination of information resources in a dynamic collaborative environment. In addition, ALCTS provides forums for discussion, research, and development and opportunities for learning in all of these areas. To achieve this mission, ALCTS has the following organizational goals:

1. To promote the role of the library and information science in an information society
2. To provide its members with opportunities for information exchange
3. To promote innovative and effective library education and training, to foster the recruitment of individuals with diverse qualities to library work, and to provide continuing education for librarians and library practitioners
4. To develop, support, review, and promote standards to meet library and information needs
5. To provide opportunities for members to participate through research and publications and professional growth
6. To manage the association effectively and efficiently

Established 1957; renamed 1988.

Membership

Memb. 5,072. Any member of the American Library Association may elect membership in this division according to the provisions of the bylaws.

Officers (July 1997–July 1998)

Pres. Janet Swan Hill, Assoc. Dir., Norlin Lib., Univ. of Colorado, Boulder, CO 80309-0184. Tel. 303-492-3797, fax 303-492-0494, e-mail hilljs@colorado.edu; *Pres.-Elect* Sheila S. Intner, Professor, Simmons College, 300 The Fenway, Boston, MA 02115. Tel. 617-521-2790, fax 617-521-3192, e-mail sintner@simmons.edu; *Past Pres.* Carol E.

Chamberlain, Northeastern Univ., Boston, MA 02115. Tel. 617-373-4960, fax 617-373-5409, e-mail cchamber@neu.edu.

Address correspondence to the executive director.

Directors

Officers; exec. dir.; *Div. Councilor* Alexander Bloss; *CRG Rep.* Dorothy H. Hope; *Dirs.* Alice J. Allen, Patricia L. Bril, Shirley F. Coleman, Cindy Hepfer, Peggy Johnson, Dorothy McGarry, John J. Reimer, Mark S. Roosa, Brian Schottlaender, Sally W. Somers, Dale S. Swensen.

Publications

ALCTS Network News (irreg.; free). *Ed.* Karen Whittlesey. Subscribe via listproc@ala.org "subscribe an2 [yourname]."
ALCTS Newsletter (6 per year; memb.; nonmemb. $25). *Ed.* Dale S. Swensen, Lee Lib., Brigham Young Univ., Provo, UT 84602.
Library Resources and Technical Services (q.; memb.; nonmemb. $55). *Ed.* Jennifer A. Younger, Univ. of Notre Dame Libs., Notre Dame, IN 46556. Tel. 219-631-7792.

Section Chairpersons

Acquisitions. Sally W. Somers.
Cataloging and Classification. Dorothy McGarry.
Collection Management and Development. Patricia L. Bril.
Preservation and Reformatting. Mark S. Roosa.
Serials. Cindy Hepfer.

Committee Chairpersons

Association of American Publishers/ALCTS Joint Committee. Jana L. Lonberger, Linda Parise.
Audiovisual. Mary Beth Fecko.
Best of *LRTS*. Paula A. De Stefano.

Blackwell's Scholarship Award. Ann Okerson.

Budget and Finance. Brian E. Schottlaender.

Catalog Form and Function. Arlene G. Taylor.

Commercial Technical Services. Karen H. Wilhoit.

Digital Resources. Ann Sandberg-Fox.

Duplicates Exchange Union. Rebecca House Stankowski.

Education. Margaret Maes Axtmann.

International Relations. Marjorie Bloss.

Legislation. Basil W. Sozansky.

Library Materials Price Index. Stephen J. Bosch.

LRTS Editorial Board. Jennifer A. Younger.

MARBI. Jacquelene W. Riley.

Membership. Beverley Geer.

Nominating. Edward Swanson.

Organization and Bylaws. Carol E. Chamberlain.

Esther J. Piercy Award Jury. Christian M. Boissonnas.

Planning. Shirley F. Coleman.

Publications. Bonita Bryant.

Publisher/Vendor Library Relations. James R. Mouw.

Research and Statistics. Thomas J. Dorst.

Discussion Groups

Authority Control in the Online Environment. Mary Lasater.

Automated Acquisitions/In-Process Control Systems. Christa Easton.

Cataloging Norms. Karen Davis.

Chief Collection Development Officers of Large Research Libraries. Gay Dannelly.

CMDS/PARS. Richard Ring.

Collection Development Librarians of Academic Lilbraries. Marlene Manoff.

Collection Management in Public Libraries. Marsha L. Rogers, Diane E. Brodsen.

Cooperative Preservation Programs. Sharla D. Richards, Christine S. Wiseman.

Creative Ideas in Technical Services. Cheryl C.Kugler, Pamela Moffett Padley.

Gifts and Exchange. Howard C. Bybee.

Library Binding. Brian G. Baird.

MARC Formats, LITA/ALCTS. Rebecca S. Guenther.

Microcomputer Support of Technical Services, LITA/ALCTS. John B. Ross.

Micropublishers. Nicholas L. Chiarkas.

Newspaper. Andrea Vanek.

Out of Print. Narda Tafuri.

PARS. Whitney D. Pape, Hilary T. Seo.

Physical Quality and Treatment of Library Materials. Harry H. Campbell.

Pre-Order and Pre-Catalog Searching. Robin Crumrin.

Preservation Administration. John Dean, Winston Atkins.

Preservation Course and Workshop Instructors. Christine S. Wiseman.

Preservation Education and Outreach. Peter D. Verheyen.

Preservation Issues in Small to Mid-Sized Libraries. Cathy Mook.

Research Libraries. Anne E. McKee.

Retrospective Conversion, LITA/ALCTS. Kathy Allen.

Role of the Professional in Academic Research Technical Services Departments. Regina C. McBride.

Serials Automation Interest Group, LITA/ALCTS. Mahnaz K. Moshfegh, Taemin K. Park.

Technical Services Administrators of Medium-Sized Research Libraries. Cynthia D. Clark.

Technical Services Directors of Large Research Libraries. John Lubans, Jr.

Technical Services in Public Libraries. To be appointed.

Scholarly Communication. Diane K. Harvey.

American Library Association
Association for Library Service to Children

Executive Director, Susan Roman
50 E. Huron St., Chicago, IL 60611
312-280-2163, 800-545-2433
E-mail sroman@ala.org

Object

Interested in the improvement and extension of library services to children in all types of libraries. Responsible for the evaluation and selection of book and nonbook materials for, and the improvement of techniques of, library services to children from preschool through the eighth grade or junior high school age, when such materials or techniques are intended for use in more than one type of library. Founded 1901.

Membership

Memb. 3,609. Open to anyone interested in library services to children. For information on dues, see ALA entry.

Officers

Pres. Elizabeth Watson. E-mail ewatson@cwmarsmail.cwmars.org; *Pres.-Elect* Leslie Edmonds Holt. E-mail lholt@slpl.lib.mo.us; *Past Pres.* Steven Herb. E-mail slh@psulias.psu.edu.

Address correspondence to the executive director.

Directors

Clara Nalli Bohrer, Margery Cuyler, Eliza Dresang, Barbara Genco, Sylvia Mavrogenes, Sue McCleaf Nespeca, Cynthia K. Richey, Anitra Steele, Kathy Toon; *Councilor* Eliza Dresang; *Staff Liaison* Susan Roman.

Publications

ALSC Newsletter (q.; memb.). *Ed.* Anitra T. Steele.

Journal of Youth Services in Libraries (q.; memb.; nonmemb. $40; foreign $50). *Eds.* Donald J. Kenney, Virginia Polytechnic Institute, Box 90001, Blacksburg, VA 24062-9001; Linda J. Wilson, Dept. of Educational Studies, 206A Russell Hall, Radford Univ., Radford, VA 24142.

Committee Chairpersons

Priority Group I: Child Advocacy

Consultant. Cynthia K. Richey.
Legislation.
Liaison with Mass Media.
Liaison with National Organizations Serving Children and Youth.
National Children and Youth Membership Organizations Outreach.

Priority Group II: Evaluation of Media

Consultant. Judith Davie.
Computer Software Evaluation.
Film and Video Evaluation.
Notable Children's Books.
Recording Evaluation.
Selection of Children's Books from Various Cultures.

Priority Group III: Professional Development

Consultant. Leslie Edmonds Holt.
Arbuthnot Honor Lecture.
Louise Seaman Bechtel Fellowship.
Distinguished Service Award.
Econo-Clad Literature Program Award.
Education.
Managing Children's Services (Committee and Discussion Group).
Putnam and Grosset Group Awards.

Scholarships: Melcher and Bound to Stay Bound.

Teachers of Children's Literature (Discussion Group).

Priority Group IV: Social Responsibilities

Consultant. Carole D. Fiore.
Intellectual Freedom.
International Relations.
Library Service to Children with Special Needs.
Preschool Services (Discussion Group).
Preschool Services and Parent Education.
Social Issues (Discussion Group).
Social Issues in Relation to Materials and Services for Children.

Priority Group V: Planning and Research

Consultant. Kate McClelland.
Caldecott Medal Calendar.

Collections of Children's Books for Adult Research (Discussion Group).
Local Arrangements.
Membership.
National Planning of Special Collections.
National Reading Program.
Nominating.
Oral Record Project (Advisory Committee).
Organization and Bylaws.
Planning and Budget.
Preconference Planning.
Publications.
Research and Development.
Storytelling (Discussion Group).

Priority Group VI: Award Committees

Consultant. Jan Moltzan.
Mildred L. Batchelder Award Selection.
Pura Belpré Award.
Caldecott Award.
Carnegie Award.
Newbery Award.
Wilder Award.

American Library Association
Association of College and Research Libraries

Executive Director, Althea H. Jenkins
50 E. Huron St., Chicago, IL 60611-2795
312-280-3248, 800-545-2433 Ext. 2521, fax 312-280-2520
E-mail ajenkins@ala.org

Object

The Association of College and Research Libraries (ACRL) provides leadership for development, promotion, and improvement of academic and research library resources and services to facilitate learning, research, and the scholarly communication process. ACRL promotes the highest level of professional excellence for librarians and library personnel in order to serve the users of academic and research libraries. Founded 1938.

Membership

Memb. 10,779. For information on dues, see ALA entry.

Officers

Pres. W. Lee Hisle, Assoc. V.P. for Learning Resource Services, Austin Community College, 1212 Rio Grande Ave., Austin, TX 78701. Tel. 512-223-3069, fax 512-495-7431; *Pres.-Elect* Maureen Sullivan, Organizational Development Consultant, 3696 Thomas Point Rd., Annapolis, MD 21403-5026. Tel. 410-268-3539, fax 410-268-3810, e-mail maureen@arl.org; *Past Pres.* William Miller, Dir. of Libs., S. E. Wimberly Lib., Florida Atlantic Univ., Box 3092, Boca Raton, FL 33431-0992. Tel. 561-367-3717, fax 561-338-3863; *Budget and Finance Chair* Ray English, Dir. of Libs., Oberlin College Lib., 148 W. College St., Oberlin, OH 44074. Tel. 216-775-8285 Ext. 231, fax

216-775-8739, e-mail ray.english@oberlin. edu; *ACRL Councilor* Helen H. Spalding, Associate Director of Libs., Univ. of Missouri–Kansas City (postal address: 600 Roman Rd., Kansas City, MO 65113-2037). Tel. 816-235-1558, fax 816-333-5584, e-mail spaldinh@smtpgate.umkc.edu. Tel. 408-656-2341, fax 408-656-2842.

Board of Directors

Officers; Jill B. Fatzer, Bernard Fradkin, Victoria A. Montavon, Linda S. Muroi, Carol Pfeiffer, Mary Reichel, John Sheridan.

Publications

ACRL Publications in Librarianship (formerly ACRL Monograph Series) (irreg.). *Ed.* Stephen E. Wiberly, Jr., Univ. of Illinois at Chicago, Chicago, IL 60680.
Choice (11 per year; $185; foreign $210).
College and Research Libraries (6 per year; memb.; nonmemb. $55). *Ed.* Donald E. Riggs, Univ. of Michigan, 818 Hatcher Grad. Lib., Ann Arbor, MI 48109.
College and Research Libraries News (11 per year; memb.; nonmemb. $35). *Ed.* Mary Ellen Kyger Davis.
Rare Books and Manuscripts Librarianship (2 per year; $30). *Ed.* Sidney E. Berger, Special Collections, Univ. of California, Riverside, CA 92517-5900.
List of other publications available through the ACRL office, ALA, 50 E. Huron St., Chicago, IL 60611-2795; or call 312-280-2517.

Committee and Task Force Chairpersons

Academic Library Outcomes Assessment (Task Force). Jill B. Fatzer.
Academic or Research Librarian of the Year Award. Vicki Gregory.
Appointments (1998). Mary Jane Scherdin.
Hugh C. Atkinson Memorial Award. Jennifer Cargill.
Budget and Finance. Ray English.
Chapters and Affiliates Task Force. John Collins, Ray English.
Choice Editorial Board. Victoria L. Hanawalt.
Colleagues. William Miller, Betsy Wilson.
College and Research Libraries Editorial Board. Donald E. Riggs.
College and Research Libraries News Editorial Board. Gary B. Thompson.
Community Information Organizations Advisory. John A. Shuler.
Conference Program Planning, Washington, D.C. (1998). W. Lee Hisle.
Constitution and Bylaws. Nancy L. Magnuson.
Copyright. Julia C. Blixrud.
Council of Liaisons. Althea H. Jenkins.
Doctoral Dissertation Fellowship. William Gray Potter.
Equal Access to Software Information Advisory Committee. Tom McNulty.
Government Relations. Carolyn Gray.
Institutional Priorities and Faculty Rewards. W. Bede Mitchell.
Intellectual Freedom. Susana Hinojosa.
International Relations. Patricia Wand.
Samuel Lazerow Fellowship. Cynthia Gozzi.
Leadership Center (Advisory Committee). Elaine Didier.
Media Resources. Kristine R. Brancolini.
Membership. Ray Metz.
National Conference Executive Committee, Detroit, 1999. Charles E. Beard.
New Publications Advisory. Cynthia S. Faries.
Nominations (1999). Anne K. Beaubien.
Orientation. William Miller.
President's Program Planning (1998). Katherine Anne Branch.
Professional Development. Laurene E. Zaporozhetz.
Professional Enhancement. Sandra J. Phaler.
Publications. Ann C. Schaffner.
Publications in Librarianship Editorial Board. Stephen E. Wiberley, Jr.
Racial and Ethnic Diversity. Clarence Toomer.
Rare Books and Manuscripts Librarianship Editorial Board. Sidney E. Berger.
Research. Fred Olive, III.
K. G. Saur Award for Best *College and Research Libraries* Article. William Jones.
Standards and Accreditation. Virginia O'Herron.
Statistics. Jean Major.

Discussion Group Chairpersons

Alliances for New Directions in Teaching/ Learning. Mari Miller.

Australian Studies. Faye Christenberry.

Canadian Studies. Margaret S. Brill.

Electronic Library Development. Steven Bischof.

Electronic Reserves. Ann M. Sprunger.

Electronic Text Centers. Steven Ellis.

Exhibits and Displays. Michael M. Miller.

Fee-Based Information Service Centers in Academic Libraries. Dottie Smith.

Fund-Raising and Development. Eva Sartori.

Heads of Public/Readers Services. Karen N. Nagy.

Home Economics/Human Ecology Librarians. Linda Lawrence Stein.

Library Science Librarians. Cathy Rentschler.

Medium-Sized Libraries. Jeanne G. Sohn.

MLA International Bibliography. Reinhart Sonnenburg.

Personnel Administrators and Staff Development Officers. Detrice Bankhead, Denise Weintraub.

Philosophical, Religious, and Theological Studies. Barbara L. Berman.

Popular Culture and Libraries. Steven R. Ellis.

Public Relations in Academic Libraries. Chandler C. Jackson.

Research. Darrell L. Jenkins.

Undergraduate Librarians. David C. Taylor.

Section Chairpersons

Afro-American Studies Librarians. Itibari M. Zulu.

Anthropology and Sociology. Joyce L. Ogburn.

Arts. Stephen Bloom.

Asian, African and Middle Eastern. Robert B. Marks Ridinger.

College Libraries. Larry R. Oberg.

Community and Junior College Libraries. Wanda K. Johnston.

Educational and Behavioral Sciences. Nancy Becker.

English and American Literature. Betty H. Day.

Extended Campus Library Services. Nancy J. Burich.

Instruction. Randy Burke Hensley.

Law and Political Science. Stephen J. Stillwell.

Rare Books and Manuscripts. Laura Stalker.

Science and Technology. Allison V. Level.

Slavic and East European. Bradley L. Schaffner.

University Libraries. Lori A. Goetsch.

Western European Specialists. Heleni Marques Pedersoli.

Women's Studies. Jessica Grim.

American Library Association
Association of Specialized and Cooperative Library Agencies

Executive Director, Cathleen Bourdon
50 E. Huron St., Chicago, IL 60611
312-280-4395, 800-545-2433 ext. 4396, fax 312-944-8085

Object

To represent state library agencies, specialized library agencies, and multitype library cooperatives. Within the interest of these types of library organizations, the Association of Specialized and Cooperative Library Agencies (ASCLA) has specific responsibility for

1. Development and evaluation of goals and plans for state library agencies, specialized library agencies, and multitype library cooperatives to facilitate the implementation, improvement, and extension of library activities designed to foster improved user services, coordinating such activities with other appropriate ALA units.
2. Representation and interpretation of the role, functions, and services of state library agencies, specialized library agencies, and multitype library cooperatives within and outside the profession, including contact with national organizations and government agencies.
3. Development of policies, studies, and activities in matters affecting state library agencies, specialized library agencies, and multitype library cooperatives relating to (a) state and local library legislation, (b) state grants-in-aid and appropriations, and (c) relationships among state, federal, regional, and local governments, coordinating such activities with other appropriate ALA units.
4. Establishment, evaluation, and promotion of standards and service guidelines relating to the concerns of this association.
5. Identifying the interests and needs of all persons, encouraging the creation of services to meet these needs within the areas of concern of the association, and promoting the use of these services provided by state library agencies, specialized library agencies, and multitype library cooperatives.
6. Stimulating the professional growth and promoting the specialized training and continuing education of library personnel at all levels of concern of this association and encouraging membership participation in appropriate type-of-activity divisions within ALA.
7. Assisting in the coordination of activities of other units within ALA that have a bearing on the concerns of this association.
8. Granting recognition for outstanding library service within the areas of concern of this association.
9. Acting as a clearinghouse for the exchange of information and encouraging the development of materials, publications, and research within the areas of concern of this association.

Membership

Memb. 1,420.

Board of Directors (1997–1998)

Pres. Nancy M. Bolt, Deputy State Libn., Colorado State Lib., Dept. of Educ., 201 E. Colfax Ave., Denver, CO 80203-1704. Tel. 303-866-6732, fax 303-866-6940, e-mail nbolt@csn.org; *1st V.P.* John M. Day, Dir., Gallaudet Univ. Lib., 800 Florida Ave. N.E., Washington, DC 20002-3660. Tel. 202-651-5231, fax 202-651-5213, e-mail JMDAY@ gallau.gallaudet.edu; *Past Pres.* Kate Nevins,

Exec. Dir., SOLINET, 1438 W. Peachtree St. N.W., Suite 200, Atlanta, GA 30309-2955. Tel. 404-892-0943, 800-999-8558, fax 404-892-7879, e-mail kate_nevins@solinet.net; *Dirs.-at-Large* John D. Christenson, Keith Michael Fiels, Michael G. Gunde, Sarah E. Hamrick, Amy L. Kellerstrass, Patricia L. Owens, Rhea J. Rubin; *Div. Councilor* Kendall F. Wiggin; *Ex officio* Frederick Duda, Janice Beck Ison, Donna Z. Pontau.

Executive Staff

Exec. Dir. Cathleen Bourdon; *Deputy Exec. Dir.* Lillian Lewis.

Publications

Interface (q.; memb.; nonmemb. $20). *Ed.* Frederick Duda, Talking Book Service, 4884 Kestral Park Circle, Sarasota, FL 34231-3369. Tel. 941-742-5914, fax 941-751-7098.

Committee Chairpersons

American Correctional Association/ASCLA Joint Committee on Institution Libraries. Thea Chesley, Tim Brown.

Awards. H. Neil Kelley.

Budget and Finance. John Day.

Conference Program Coordination. Diane Solomon.

Guidelines for Library Service for People with Developmental Disabilities. Marilyn Irwin.

Legislation. Barbara Will.

Library Personnel and Education. Amy Kellerstrass.

Membership Promotion. Marjorie MacKenzie.

Organization and Bylaws. Donna Pontau.

Planning. Nancy Bolt.

Publications. Tina Roose.

Research. Ruth Kowal.

Standards Review. Ethel Himmell.

American Library Association
Library Administration and Management Association

Executive Director, Karen Muller
50 E. Huron St., Chicago, IL 60611
312-280-5031, 800-545-2433 ext. 5031, fax 312-280-3257
E-mail kmuller@ala.org

Object

The Library Administration and Management Association (LAMA) provides an organizational framework for encouraging the study of administrative theory, for improving the practice of administration in libraries, and for identifying and fostering administrative skill. Toward these ends, the division is responsible for all elements of general administration that are common to more than one type of library. These may include organizational structure, financial administration, personnel management and training, buildings and equipment, and public relations. LAMA meets this responsibility in the following ways:

1. Study and review of activities assigned to the division with due regard for changing developments in these activities.

2. Initiating and overseeing activities and projects appropriate to the division, including activities involving bibliography compilation, publication, study, and review of professional literature within the scope of the division.

3. Synthesizing the activities of other ALA units which have a bearing upon the responsibilities or work of the division.

4. Representing and interpreting library administrative activities in contacts outside the library profession.

5. Aiding the professional development of librarians engaged in administration and encouraging their participation in appropriate type-of-library divisions.

6. Planning and developing programs of study and research in library administrative problems which are most needed by the profession.

Established 1957.

Membership

Memb. 5,064.

Officers (July 1997–July 1998)

Pres. Charles E. Kratz, Jr., Dir., Harry and Jeanette Weinberg Memorial Lib., Univ. of Scranton, Scranton, PA 18510-4700. Tel. 717-941-4008, fax 717-941-7817, e-mail kratzc1@lion.uofs.edu; *Pres.-Elect* Thomas L. Wilding, Dir. of Libs., Univ. of Texas at Arlington, Arlington, TX 76019-0497. Tel. 817-272-3390, fax 817-272-5797, e-mail wilding@uta.edu; *Past Pres.* William Sannwald, Dir., San Diego Public Lib., 820 E St., San Diego, CA 92101-6416. Tel 619-236-5871, fax 619-236-5878, e-mail wws@citymgr.sannet.gov; *Div. Councilor* Judith A. Adams, Dir., Lockwood Lib., State Univ. of New York–Buffalo, Buffalo, NY 14260-1625. Tel. 716-645-2816, fax 716-645-3859, e-mail adamsj@acsu.buffalo.edu.

Address correspondence to the executive director.

Board of Directors

Dirs. Charles E. Kratz, Jr., William Sannwald, Thomas L. Wilding; *Div. Councilor* Judith A. Adams; *Dirs.-at-Large* Susan F. Gregory, Rebecca R. Martin; *Section Chairs* Jack F. Bulow, Melissa Carr, Eddy Hogan, Patricia M. Larsen, Louise S. McAulay, Caroline M. Oyama, Marion T. Reid; *Ex officio* Charles A. Hansen, Mary M. Harrison,

Susanne Henderson, Rod Henshaw, Sarah C. Michalak, Rita A. Scherrei, Virginia Steel, Joyce G. Taylor; *Ed.* Barbara G. Preece; *Assoc. Ed.* Barbara G. Preece; *Exec. Dir.* Karen Muller.

Publications

Library Administration and Management (q.; memb.; nonmemb. $55; foreign $65). *Ed.* Barbara G. Preece.
LEADS from LAMA (approx. weekly; free through Internet. *Ed.* Elizabeth Dreazen. To subscribe, send to listproc@ala.org the message SUBSCRIBE LAMALEADS (first name last name).

Committee Chairpersons

Budget and Finance. Rodney M. Hersberger.
Certified Public Library Administrator Certification, LAMA/PLA/ASCLA. Robert H. Rohlf.
Council of LAMA Affiliates. Barbara Simpson.
Cultural Diversity. Joyce K. Thornton.
Editorial Advisory Board. Nancy A. Davenport.
Education. Philip Tramdack.
Governmental Affairs. Doria Beachell Grimes.
Membership. Robert A. Daugherty.
Nominating, 1998 Elections. Diane J. Graves.
Organization. Susanne Henderson.
Orientation. Kate W. Ragsdale.
Partners. Pamela Gay Bonnell.
Program. J. Linda Williams.
Publications. John Lubans, Jr.
Recognition of Achievement. Carol L. Anderson.
Small Libraries Publications Series. Anders C. Dahlgren.
Special Conferences and Programs. Paul M. Anderson.

Section Chairpersons

Buildings and Equipment. Marion T. Reid.
Fund-Raising and Financial Development. Jack F. Bulow.
Library Organization and Management. Louise S. McAulay.
Personnel Administration. Melissa Carr.

Public Relations. Caroline M. Oyama.

Statistics. Patricia M. Larsen.

Systems and Services. Eddy Hogan.

Discussion Groups

Assistants-to-the-Director. Eileen Theodore-Shusta.

Diversity Officers. Joseph R. Diaz.

Library Storage. June DeWeese, Catherine L. Murry-Rust.

Middle Management. Felice E. Maciehjewski, Marie A. Morgan.

Networked Information. Robert F. Moran.

Total Quality Management. Larry Nash White.

Women Administrators. Cheryl C. Kugler.

American Library Association
Library and Information Technology Association

Executive Director, Jacqueline Mundell
50 E. Huron St., Chicago, IL 60611
312-280-4270, 800-545-2433

Object

The Library and Information Technology Association (LITA) envisions a world in which the complete spectrum of information technology is available to everyone. People in all their diversity will have access to a wealth of information technology in libraries, at work, and at home. In this world, everybody can realize their full potential with the help of information technology. The very boundaries of human relations will expand beyond the limitations of time and space we experience today. The outer limits are still unknown; what is known is that the exploration will be challenging.

LITA provides its members, other ALA divisions and members, and the library and information science field as a whole with a forum for discussion, an environment for learning, and a program for action on the design, development, and implementation of automated and technological systems in the library and information science field.

LITA is concerned with the planning, development, design, application, and integration of technologies within the library and information environment, with the impact of emerging technologies on library service, and with the effect of automated technologies on people. Its major focus is on the interdisciplinary issues and emerging technologies. LITA disseminates information, provides educational opportunities for learning about information technologies and forums for the discussion of common concerns, monitors new technologies with potential applications in information science, encourages and fosters research, promotes the development of technical standards, and examines the effects of library systems and networks.

LITA's strategic planning goals are to provide opportunities for professional growth and performance in areas of information technology; to influence national- and international-level initiatives relating to information and access; to promote, participate in, and influence the development of technical standards related to the storage, dissemination, and delivery of information; and to strengthen the association and assure its continued success.

Membership

Memb. 5,310.

Officers (1997–1998)

Pres. Linda D. Miller; *V.P./Pres.-Elect* Barbra B. Higginbotham; *Past Pres.* Thomas W. Leonhardt.

Directors

Officers; Pat Ensor (2000); Pamela R. Mason (1998); Edward J. Valauskas (1998); Kathleen A. Wakefield (1999); Florence Wilson (1999); *Councilor* Tamara Miller; *Bylaws and Organization* Sara L. Randall (1998); *Exec. Dir.* Jacqueline Mundell.

Publications

Information Technology and Libraries (q.; memb.; nonmemb. $50; single copy $15). *Ed.* James J. Kopp. For information or to send manuscripts, contact the editor.

LITA Newsletter (q.; electronic only at http://www.lita.org). *Ed.* Martin Kalfatovic.

Committee Chairpersons

Committee Chair Coordinator. Linda J. Robinson, e-mail robinsol@oclc.org.

Hugh C. Atkinson Memorial Award. Jennifer Cargill, e-mail notjsc@lsuvm.sncc.lsu.edu.

Budget Review. Thomas W. Leonhardt, e-mail leonhart@oit.edu.

Bylaws and Organization. Sara L. Randall, e-mail slr5@lehigh.edu.

Education. Xiao-Yan Shen, e-mail xshen@scuacc.scu.edu.

Executive. Linda D. Miller, e-mail lmil@loc.gov.

Information Technology and Libraries (ITAL) Editorial Board. James J. Kopp, e-mail kopp@porrtals.org.

International Relations. John R. James, e-mail John.R.James@Dartmouth.edu.

Leadership Development. Mary Ann Sheble, e-mail sheblema@udmercy.edu.

Legislation and Regulation. Marilyn Lutz, e-mail lutz@maine.maine.edu.

LITA/Gaylord Award. Carol A. Parkhurst, e-mail carolp@unr.edu.

LITA/Geac Scholarship. John Popko, e-mail jpopko@seattleu.edu.

LITA/*Library Hi Tech* Award. Walt Crawford, e-mail br.wcc@rlg.stanford.edu.

LITA National Forum, 1998. Karen Coyle, e-mail kec@dla.ucop.edu.

LITA Newsletter (Subcommittee). Martin A. Kalfatovic, e-mail mkalfato@sil.si.edu.

LITA/OCLC Kilgour Award. Michael Gorman, e-mail michael_gorman@csufresno.edu.

LITA/OCLC and LITA/LSSI Minority Scholarships. Anita Coleman, e-mail coleman_anita@cc.rancho.cc.ca.us.

Machine-Readable Form of Bibliographic Information (MARBI). Jacquelene W. Riley, e-mail jacquelene.riley@uc.edu.

Membership. Sue Kopp, e-mail koppcs@pacificu.edu.

Nominating. Gail M. Persky, e-mail persky@newschool.edu.

Program Planning. Lynne D. Lysiak, e-mail lysiakld@appstate.edu.

Publications. George S. Machovec, e-mail gmachove@coalliance.org.

Regional Institutes. Mark A. Beatty, e-mail mbeatty@wils.wisc.edu.

Research. Don L. Bosseau, e-mail bosseau@exchange.ir.miami.edu.

Technical Standards for Library Automation (TESLA). Jennie L. McKee, e-mail jennie@reed.com.

Technology and Access. Charles W. Husbands, e-mail charles_husbands@harvard.edu.

Telecommunications Electronic Reviews (TER) Board. Thomas C. Wilson, e-mail twilson@uh.edu.

Web Editorial Board. Mary M. Deane, e-mail fclmmd@nersp.nerdc.ufl.edu.

Interest Group Chairpersons

Interest Group Coordinator. Mary Ann Van Cura, e-mail vancuram@mlc.lib.mi.us.

Adaptive Technologies. Jeffrey Trzeciak, e-mail jtrzeciak@wright.edu.

Artificial Intelligence/Expert Systems (AI/ES). John W. Forys, Jr., e-mail johnforys@uiowa.edu.

Authority Control in the Online Environment (LITA/ALCTS). Mary Charles Lasater, e-maillaster@library.vanderbilt.edu.

Customized Applications for Library Microcomputers (CALM). Andy D. Boze, e-mail Boze.1@nd.edu.

Distance Learning. Susan Logue, e-mail slogue@lib.isu.edu.

Distributed Systems and Networks. Mark H. Needleman, e-mail mark.needleman@ucop.edu.

Electronic Publishing/Electronic Journals. Lloyd Davidson, e-mail ldavids@nwu.edu.

Emerging Technologies. Martin Halbert, e-mail mhalber@emory.edu.

Geographic Information Systems (GIS). Dean K. Jue, e-mail djue@opus.freac.fsu.edu.

Human/Machine Interface. Dorothy Day, e-mail day@indiana.edu.

Imagineering. Sandra Ballasch, e-mail sandra-ballasch@uiowa.edu.

Internet Resources. Deleyne Wentz, e-mail delwen@cc.usu.edu.

Library Consortia/Automated Systems. Gregory Zuck, e-mail gzuck1@jinx.sckans.edu.

MARC Formats (LITA/ALCTS). Rebecca Guenther, e-mail rgue@loc.gov.

Microcomputer Users. John B. Ross, e-mail john.ross@sdsu.edu.

Online Catalogs. Ellen Crosby, e-mail ecrosby@statelib.lib.in.us.

Optical Information Systems. Debra Shapiro, e-mail dshapiro@binc.net.

Programmer/Analyst. Roberta Y. Rand, e-mail rrand@nal.usda.gov.

Retrospective Conversion. Kathy Allen, e-mail kallen@talx.com.

Secure Systems and Services. Mack A. Lundy, III, e-mail mack@mail.swem.wm.edu.

Serials Automation (LITA/ALCTS). Taemin K. Park, e-mail park@indiana.edu.

Technical Services Workstations (formerly Microcomputer Support of Technical Services). Steven J. Oberg, e-mail so67@midway.uchicago.edu.

Technology and the Arts. Brad Eden, e-mail beden@nhmccd.edu.

Telecommunications. Peter Burslem, e-mail pburslem@umabnet.ab.umd.edu.

Vendor/User. Faye Chartoff, e-mail faye@iii.com.

American Library Association
Public Library Association

Executive Director, Greta K. Southard
50 E. Huron St., Chicago, IL 60611
312-280-5752, 800-545-2433 ext. 5752, fax 312-280-5029
E-mail pla@ala.org

Object

The Public Library Association (PLA) has specific responsibility for

1. Conducting and sponsoring research about how the public library can respond to changing social needs and technical developments.

2. Developing and disseminating materials useful to public libraries in interpreting public library services and needs.

3. Conducting continuing education for public librarians by programming at national and regional conferences, by publications such as the newsletter, and by other delivery means.

4. Establishing, evaluating, and promoting goals, guidelines, and standards for public libraries.

5. Maintaining liaison with relevant national agencies and organizations engaged in public administration and human services, such as the National Association of Counties, the Municipal League, and the Commission on Post-Secondary Education.

6. Maintaining liaison with other divisions and units of ALA and other

library organizations, such as the Association of American Library Schools and the Urban Libraries Council.

7. Defining the role of the public library in service to a wide range of user and potential user groups.

8. Promoting and interpreting the public library to a changing society through legislative programs and other appropriate means.

9. Identifying legislation to improve and to equalize support of public libraries.

PLA enhances the development and effectiveness of public librarians and public library services. This mission positions PLA to

- Focus its efforts on serving the needs of its members
- Address issues that affect public libraries
- Promote and protect the profession
- Commit to quality public library services that benefit the general public

To carry out its mission, PLA will identify and pursue specific goals. These goals will drive PLA's structure, governance, staffing, and budgeting, and will serve as the basis for all evaluations of achievement and performance. The following broad goals and strategies were established for PLA in 1997 for accomplishment by the year 2000:

1. PLA will provide market-driven, mission-focused programs and services delivered in a variety of formats.

2. PLA will have increased its members and diversified its leadership.

3. PLA will have maximized its fiscal resources to enable the full implementation of its goals and to take full advantage of strategic opportunities.

4. PLA will be recognized as a positive, contemporary champion of public librarians and public libraries.

5. PLA will have demonstrated its leadership in developing and promoting

sound public policies affecting public libraries.

6. PLA will have implemented, evaluated, and refined its structure and governance.

7. PLA will have the facilities, technology, staff, and systems required to achieve its mission.

Membership

Memb. 7,500+. Open to all ALA members interested in the improvement and expansion of public library services to all ages in various types of communities.

Officers (1997–1998)

Pres. Ginnie Cooper, Multnomah County Lib., Lib. Assn. of Portland, 205 N.E. Russell St., Portland, OR 97212. Tel. 503-248-5403, fax 503-248-5441, e-mail ginniec@nethost. multnomah.lib.or.us; *Past Pres.* Linda Mielke, Carroll County Public Lib., 115 Airport Dr., Westminster, MD 21157. Tel. 410-876-6008, fax 410-876-3002, e-mail lmielke@ccpl.carr. lib.md.us; *V.P./Pres.-Elect* Christine L. Hage, Rochester Hills Public Lib., 500 Olde Towne Rd., Rochester, MI 58307. Tel. 248-650-7122, fax 248-650-7121, e-mail hagec@ metronet.lib.mi.us.

Board of Directors

Officers; *Dirs.-at-Large* Luis Herrera, Christine McDonald, Catherine O'Connell, Margaret P. Stillman, Nancy H. Tessman, Jerry A. Thrasher; *Div. Councilor* Jo Ann Pinder (1998); *Ex officio/Nonvoting Members:* Exec. Dir. *Greta K. Southard.*

Publication

Public Libraries (bi-m.; memb.; nonmemb. $50; foreign $60; single copy $10). *Managing Ed.* Kathleen Hughes, PLA, 50 E. Huron St., Chicago, IL 60611.

Section Presidents

Adult Lifelong Learning (ALLS). June E. Eiselstein.
Community Information (CIS). Angie Stuckey.
Marketing of Public Library Services (MPLSS). Susan Marshall.
Metropolitan Libraries (MLS). Joan L. Clark.
Planning, Measurement, and Evaluation (PLMES). Toni A. Garvey.
Public Library Systems (PLSS). Martha E. Knott.
Public Policy for Public Libraries (PPPLS). Kay K. Runge.
Small and Medium-Sized Libraries (SMLS). Nann Blaine Hilyard.

Committee Chairpersons

Audiovisual. James E. Massey.
Awards. John Brooks-Barr.
Budget and Finance. Victor Frank Kralisz.
Bylaws and Organization. Harriet Henderson.
Cataloging Needs of Public Libraries. Margaret Shen.
Conference Program Coordinating (1998). Annette M. Milliron, Kelley Glancy-Grabowski.
Conference Program Coordinating (1999). Sandra K. Norlin.
Electronic Communications Advisory (subcommittee). Donald Napoli.
Intellectual Freedom. John Moorman.

Leadership Development (1998). Sandra Nelson.
Leadership Development (1999). Gretchen Wronka.
Legislation. Roberta A. E. Cairns.
LSCA Ad Hoc (Special). Sarah Ann Long.
Membership. Christine L. Hage.
National Conference (1998). Sarah A. Long.
National Conference (1998) Exhibitors Advisory. Joe K. Weed.
National Conference (1998) Local Arrangements. Daniel J. Bradbury.
National Conference (1998) Program. Clara N. Bohrer.
Nominating (1998). Judith A. Drescher.
PLA Monographs. Susan K. Schmidt.
PLA Partners. Kay K. Runge.
President's Events (1998). Kay K. Runge.
President's Events (1999). Clara N. Bohrer.
Publications. Barbara Webb.
Public Libraries Advisory (subcommittee). Jane S. Eickhoff.
Research and Statistics. Barbara G. Smith.
Services to Business. Don W. Barlow.
Services to Children. Gretchen Wronka.
Statistical Report Advisory (subcommittee)/ Publications. Janice Feye-Stukas.
Technology in Public Libraries. William H. Ptacek.
2000 National Conference. Fran C. Freimarck.
2000 National Conference (Local Arrangements). Lois Kilkka.
2000 National Conference (Program). Claudia B. Sumler.

American Library Association
Reference and User Services Association

Executive Director, Cathleen Bourdon
50 E. Huron St., Chicago, IL 60611
312-944-6780, 800-545-2433 Ext. 4398, fax 312-944-8085

Object

The Reference and User Services Association (RUSA) is responsible for stimulating and supporting in every type of library the delivery of reference/information services to all groups, regardless of age, and of general library services and materials to adults. This involves facilitating the development and conduct of direct service to library users, the development of programs and guidelines for service to meet the needs of these users, and assisting libraries in reaching potential users.

The specific responsibilities of RUSA are

1. Conduct of activities and projects within the division's areas of responsibility.

2. Encouragement of the development of librarians engaged in these activities and stimulation of participation by members of appropriate type-of-library divisions.

3. Synthesis of the activities of all units within the American Library Association that have a bearing on the type of activities represented by the division.

4. Representation and interpretation of the division's activities in contacts outside the profession.

5. Planning and development of programs of study and research in these areas for the total profession.

6. Continuous study and review of the division's activities.

Membership

Memb. 5,382. For information on dues, see ALA entry.

Officers (June 1997–June 1998)

Pres. Caroline Long; *Pres.-Elect* Jo Bell Whitlarch; *Secy.* Ruth A. Carr.

Directors and Other Members

Nancy B. Crane, Karen Liston Newsome, Bernard F. Pasqualini; *Councilor* Pam Sieving; *Past Pres.* Kathleen Kluegel; *Ed., RUSA Update* Beth Woodard; *Eds., RUSQ* Gail Schlachter; *Exec. Dir.* Cathleen Bourdon.

Address correspondence to the executive director.

Publications

RUSA Update (q.; memb.; nonmemb. $20).
RUSQ (q.; memb; nonmemb. $50).

Section Chairpersons

Business Reference and Services. Carol Z. Womack.
Collection Development and Evaluation. John M. Budd.
History. David L. Langenberg.
Machine-Assisted Reference. Amy Tracy Wells.
Management and Operation of Public Services. Louise S. Sherby.

Committee Chairpersons

Access to Information. James P. Niessen.
AFL/CIO Joint Committee on Library Services to Labor Groups. Mary Hicks.
Awards Coordinating. Candace R. Benefiel.
Conference Program. Kathleen A. Sullivan.
Conference Program Coordinating. Janice Simons-Welburn.
Dartmouth Medal. Richard Bleiler.
Denali Press Award. Deborah Hollis.
Facts on File Grant. Christine Bulson.
Gale Research Award for Excellence in Reference and Adult Services. Joanne Harrar.
Membership. Joyce C. Wright.
Margaret E. Monroe Library Adult Services Award. Linda Friend.
Isadore Gilbert Mudge/R. R. Bowker Award. Louise S. Sherby.
Nominating. Carol M. Kelley.
Organization. Laryne J. Dallas.
Planning and Finance. Kathleen Kluegel.
Publications. Geralding Biking.
Reference Services Press Award. David Null.
John Sessions Memorial Award. Carol H. Krismann.
Louis Shores/Oryx Press Award. Hope H. Yelich.
Standards and Guidelines. Rebecca J. Whitaker.

American Library Association
Young Adult Library Services Association

Executive Director, Julie A. Walker
50 E. Huron St., Chicago, IL 60611
312-280-4390, 800-545-2433 ext. 4390, fax 312-664-7459
E-mail yalsa@ala.org

Object

In every library in the nation, quality library service to young adults is provided by a staff that understands and respects the unique informational, educational, and recreational needs of teenagers. Equal access to information, services, and materials is recognized as a right, not a privilege. Young adults are actively involved in the library decision-making process. The library staff collaborates and cooperates with other youth-serving agencies to provide a holistic, community-wide network of activities and services that support healthy youth development. To ensure that this vision becomes a reality, the Young Adult Library Services Association (YALSA), a division of the American Library Association (ALA)

1. Advocates extensive and developmentally appropriate library and information services for young adults, ages 12 to 18

2. Promotes reading and supports the literacy movement

3. Advocates the use of information and communications technologies to provide effective library service

4. Supports equality of access to the full range of library materials and services, including existing and emerging information and communications technologies, for young adults

5. Provides education and professional development to enable its members to serve as effective advocates for young people

6. Fosters collaboration and partnerships among its individual members with the library community and other groups involved in providing library and information services to young adults

7. Influences public policy by demonstrating the importance of providing library and information services that meet the unique needs and interests of young adults

8. Encourages research and is in the vanguard of new thinking concerning the provision of library and information services for youth

Membership

Memb. 2,200. Open to anyone interested in library services and materials for young adults. For information on dues, see ALA entry.

Officers (July 1997–July 1998)

Pres. Michael Cart, 4220 Arch Dr., Apt. 10, Studio City, CA 91604. Tel. 818-769-1278, fax 818-769-0729, e-mail mrmcart@aol.com; *V.P./Pres.-Elect* Joel Shoemaker, 3101 Raven St., Iowa City, IA 52245. Tel. 319-339-6823, fax 319-339-5735, e-mail shoemaker@Iowa-city.k12.Ia.us; *Past Pres.* Deborah Taylor, Enoch Pratt Free Lib., 400 Cathedral St., Baltimore, MD 21201. Tel. 410-396-5356, fax 410-396-1095, e-mail dtaylor@mail.pratt.lib.md.us; *Councilor* Pamela Spencer, 9101 Patton Blvd., Alexandria, VA 22309. Tel. 703-503-7414, fax 703-978-3001, e-mail pspencer@pen.k12.va.us.

Directors

Officers; Mary Arnold (1999), Audra Caplan (2000), Rosemary Chance (2000), Susan Farber (1998), Phyllis Fisher (1999), Judy Sasges (1998); *Ex officio Chair, Budget and Finance* Jennifer Gallant; *Ex officio Chair, Organization and Bylaws* Daphne Daly; *Ex officio Chair, Strategic Planning* Patricia Muller.

Publications

Journal of Youth Services in Libraries (q.; memb.; nonmemb. $40; foreign $50). *Eds.* Donald J. Kenney, Director's Office, Virginia Polytechnic Institute, Box 90001, Blacksburg, VA 24062-9001. Tel. 703-231-5595, fax 703-231-9263; Linda J. Wilson, Dept. of Educational Studies, Radford Univ., 206A Russell Hall, Radford, VA 24142. Tel. 703-831-5344, fax 703-831-5302.

Voices: Newsletter of the Young Adult Services Association (s. ann.; memb.). *Ed.* Jana Fine, Clearwater Public Lib., 100 N. Osceola Ave., Clearwater, FL 34615. Tel. 813-462-6800 ext. 252, fax 813-462-6420, e-mail finej@mail.firn.edu.

Committee Chairpersons

ALSC/YALSA JOYS Editorial (Advisory). Betty Carter, Keith Swigger.

Best Books for Young Adults (1998). Karlan Sick.

Best Books for Young Adults (1999). Carol Fox.

Budget and Finance. Jennifer Gallant.

Cybercafe Task Force. Linda Braun.

Division Promotion. Ellen Duffy.

Education. Elizabeth Rosen.

Margaret A. Edwards Adult Books for Young Adults Task Force. Deborah Taylor.

Margaret A. Edwards Award (1998). Jeri Baker.

Margaret A. Edwards Award (1999). Jana Fine.

Intellectual Freedom. Christine Allen.

Legislation. Bill Stack.

Media Selection and Usage. Stephen Crowley.

Membership. Susan Raboy.

National Organizations Serving the Young Adult (liaison). Dale McNeill.

Nominating (1998). Jennifer Gallant.

Nominating (1999). Charles Harmon.

Organization and Bylaws. Daphne Daly.

Outreach to Young Adults with Special Needs. Beryl Eber.

Outstanding Books for the College Bound. Donald Kenney.

Oversight. Patricia Muller.

Popular Paperbacks for Young Adults. Mary Huebscher, Nancy Reich.

Program Planning Clearinghouse and Evaluation. Connie Bush.

Publications. Kathy Latrobe.

Publishers' Liaison. David Mowery.

Quick Picks for Reluctant Young Adult Readers (1998). Judy Nelson.

Quick Picks for Reluctant Young Adult Readers (1999). Diana Herald.

Research. Pat Feehan.

Selected Films and Videos for Young Adults (1998). Mary Flournoy.

Selected Films and Videos for Young Adults (1999). Ranae Pierce.

Strategic Planning. Patricia Muller.

Teaching Young Adult Literature Discussion Group. Joan Atkinson.

Technology for Young Adults. Keith Swigger.

Youth Participation. Sarah Flowers.

American Merchant Marine Library Association

(An affiliate of United Seamen's Service)
Executive Director, Roger T. Korner
One World Trade Center, Suite 2161, New York, NY 10048
212-775-1038

Object

Provides ship and shore library service for American-flag merchant vessels, the Military Sealift Command, the U.S. Coast Guard, and other waterborne operations of the U.S. government. Established 1921.

Officers (1997–1998)

Pres. Talmage E. Simpkins; *Chair, Exec. Committee* Arthur W. Friedberg; *V.P.s* John M. Bowers, Capt. Timothy E. Brown, James Capo, Ernest Corrado, Remo DiFiore, John Halas, René Lioeanjie, George E. Murphy, S. Nakanishi, Capt. Gregorio Oca, Michael Sacco, John J. Sweeney; *Secy.* Lillian Rabins; *Treas.* William D. Potts; *Exec. Dir.* Roger T. Korner.

American Society for Information Science

Executive Director, Richard B. Hill
8720 Georgia Ave., Suite 501, Silver Spring, MD 20910
301-495-0900, fax 301-495-0810, e-mail ASIS@asis.org

Object

The American Society for Information Science (ASIS) provides a forum for the discussion, publication, and critical analysis of work dealing with the design, management, and use of information, information systems, and information technology.

Membership

Memb. (Indiv.) 3,700; (Student) 600; (Inst.) 200. Dues (Indiv.) $115; (Student) $30; (Inst.) $425 and $650.

Officers

Pres. Michael K. Buckland, Univ. of California; *Pres.-Elect* Candy Schwartz, Simmons College; *Treas.* Ernest DiMattia, Ferguson Lib.; *Past Pres.* Debora Shaw, Indiana Univ.

Address correspondence to the executive director.

Board of Directors

Dirs.-at-Large Steve Hardin, Samantha Kelly Hastings, Julie M. Hurd, Ray R. Larson, Merri Beth Lavagnino, Bonnie Lawlor, Pat Molholt, Ellen L. Sleeter; *Deputy Dirs.* Janet M. Arth, Michael Stallings; *Exec. Dir.* Richard B. Hill.

Publications

Advances in Classification Research, Vols. 1–7. *Eds.* Barbara Kwasnik and Raya Fidel. Available from Information Today, 143 Old Marlton Pike, Medford, NJ 08055.

Annual Review of Information Science and Technology. Available from Information Today, 143 Old Marlton Pike, Medford, NJ 08055.

ASIS Thesaurus of Information Science and Librarianship. Available from Information Today, 143 Old Marlton Pike, Medford, NJ 08055.

Bulletin of the American Society for Information Science. Available from ASIS.

Challenges in Indexing Electronic Texts and Images. Eds. Raya Fidel, Trudi Bellardo (Hahn), Edie M. Rasmussen, and Philip J. Smith. Available from Information Today, 143 Old Marlton Pike, Medford, NJ 08055.

Electronic Publishing: Applications and Implications. Eds. Elisabeth Logan and Myke Gluck. Available from Information Today, 143 Old Marlton Pike, Medford, NJ 08055.

Entertainment Technology and the Information Business. Thomas E. Kinney. Available from ASIS.

From Print to Electronic: The Transformation of Scientific Communication. Susan Y. Crawford, Julie M. Hurd, and Ann C. Weller. Available from Information Today, 143 Old Marlton Pike, Medford, NJ 08055.

Information Management for the Intelligent Organization: The Art of Environmental Scanning. Chun Wei Choo. Available from ASIS.

Interfaces for Information Retrieval and Online Systems: The State of the Art. Ed. Martin Dillon. Available from Greenwood Press, 88 Post Rd. W., Westport, CT 06881.

Journal of the American Society for Information Science. Available from John Wiley and Sons, 605 Third Ave., New York, NY 10016.

Proceedings of the ASIS Annual Meetings. Available from Information Today, 143 Old Marlton Pike, Medford, NJ 08055.

Scholarly Publishing: The Electronic Frontier. Eds. Robin P. Peek and Gregory B. Newby. Available from MIT Press, Cambridge, Massachusetts.

Studies in Multimedia. Eds. Susan Stone and Michael Buckland. Based on the Proceedings of the 1991 ASIS Mid-Year Meeting. Available from Information Today, 143 Old Marlton Pike, Medford, NJ 08055.

Committee Chairpersons

Awards and Honors. Paula Galbraith, Carol Tenopir.

Budget and Finance. Ernest DiMattia.

Constitution and Bylaws. Shirley Lincicum.

Education. Beth Logan.

Membership. Robert Gresehover.

Standards. Kurt Kopp.

American Theological Library Association

820 Church St., Suite 400, Evanston, IL 60201-5613
847-869-7788, fax 847-869-8513

Object

To bring its members into close working relationships with each other, to support theological and religious librarianship, to improve theological libraries, and to interpret the role of such libraries in theological education, developing and implementing standards of library service, promoting research and experimental projects, encouraging cooperative programs that make resources more available, publishing and disseminating literature and research tools and aids, cooperating with organizations having similar aims, and otherwise supporting and aiding theological education. Founded 1946.

Membership

Memb. (Inst.) 220; (Indiv.) 575. Membership is open to persons engaged in professional library or bibliographical work in theological or religious fields and others who are interested in the work of theological librarianship. Dues (Inst.) $75 to $500, based on total library expenditure; (Indiv.) $15 to $100, based on salary scale. Year. Sept. 1–Aug. 31.

Officers (July 1997–June 1998)

Pres. M. Patrick Graham, Pitts Theology Lib., Emory Univ., Atlanta, GA 30322. Tel. 404-727-4165, fax 404-727-2915, e-mail libmpg@emory.edu; *V.P.* Sharon Taylor, Franklin Trask Lib., Andover Newton Theological School, 169 Herrick Rd., Newton Centre, MA 02159. Tel. 617-964-1100; *Secy.* Christopher Brennan, Ambrose Swasey Lib., Colgate Rochester Divinity School, 1100 S. Goodman St., Rochester, NY 14620. Tel. 716-271-1320, fax 716-271-2166, e-mail crbn@uhura.cc.rochester.edu.

Board of Directors

Officers; Richard R. Berg, David Bundy, Linda Corman, William Hook, Alan D. Krieger, Roger L. Loyd, Paul Stuehrenberg, Sharon A. Taylor, Dorothy G. Thomason; *Exec. Dir.* Dennis A. Norlin; *Dir. of Finance* Patricia Adamek; *Dir. of Development* John Bollier; *Dir. of Member Services* Melody S. Chartier.

Publications

ATLA Indexes in MARC Format (semi-ann.).
ATLA Religion database on CD-ROM, 1949– (Mar./Sept.).
Biblical Studies on CD-ROM (ann.).
Catholic Periodical and Literature Index on CD-ROM (ann.).
Index to Book Reviews in Religion (ann.).

Newsletter (q.; memb.; nonmemb. $10). *Ed.* Melody Chartier.
Old Testment Abstracts on CD-ROM (ann.).
Proceedings (ann.; memb.; nonmemb. $20). *Ed.* Melody Chartier.
Religion Index One: Periodicals (semi-ann.).
Religion Index Two: Multi-Author Works (ann.).
Religion Indexes: RIO/RIT/IBRR 1975–on CD-ROM.
Research in Ministry: An Index to Doctor of Ministry Project Reports (ann.).
South African Theological Bibliography on CD-ROM (ann.).

Committee Chairpersons and Other Officials

Annual Conference. Christine Wenderoth.
Archivist. Boyd Reese.
Collection Evaluation and Development. Martha Smalley.
College and University. Elizabeth Leahy.
Education. Roberta Schaafsma.
NISO Representative. Myron Chace.
Nominating. David Bundy.
OCLC Theological User Group. Linda Umoh.
Online Reference Resource. Charles Willard.
Oral History. Alice Kendrick.
Preservation. Myron Chace.
Public Services. Alva Caldwell.
Publication. William Miller.
Special Collections. Steve Crocco.
Technical Services. Christine Schone.
Technology. William Hook.

Archivists and Librarians in the History of the Health Sciences

(formerly the Association of Librarians in the History of the Health Sciences)
President, Elizabeth Borst White
Houston Academy of Medicine–Texas Medical Center Library
1133 M. D. Anderson Blvd., Houston, TX 77030
713-799-7139

Object

This association is established exclusively for educational purposes to serve the professional interests of librarians, archivists, and other specialists actively engaged in the librarianship of the history of the health sciences by promoting the exchange of information and by improving the standards of service.

Membership

Memb. (Voting) 200. Dues $10, membs.; outside U.S. and Canada $16.

Officers (May 1996–May 1998)

Pres. Elizabeth Borst White, HAM-TMC Lib., 1133 M. D. Anderson Blvd., Houston, TX 77030. Tel. 713-795-4200, e-mail ewhite@library.tmc.edu; *Secy.-Treas.* Elizabeth Ihrig, Bakken Lib. of Electricity, 3537 Zenith Ave. S., Minneapolis, MN 55416. Tel. 612-927-6508, e-mail eihrig@aol.com; *Eds.* Jodi Koste, Special Collections and Archives, Medical College of Virginia, MCV Box 582, Richmond, VA 23113-0582. E-mail jkoste@gems.vcu.edu; Joan Echtenkamp Klein, Historical Collections, Univ. of Virginia Health Sciences Center, Box 234, Charlottesville, VA 22908. E-mail jre@virginia.edu.

Steering Committee

Officers; Billie Broaddus, Historical, Archival and Museum Services, Univ. of Cincinnati, 231 Bethesda Ave., Cincinnati, OH 45267-0574; Suzanne Porter, Medical Center Lib., Duke Univ., DUMC 3702, Durham, NC 27710.

Committees

Archives. Thomas A. Horrocks, College of Physicians of Philadelphia, 19 S. 22 St., Philadelphia, PA 19103.
Awards. Philip Tiegen, Historical Medical Div., National Lib. of Medicine, 8600 Rockville Pike, Bethesda, MD 20894.
Nominating. Elaine Challacombe, Wangensteen Historical Lib., Bio-Medical Lib., Diehl Hall, 505 Essex St. S.E., Minneapolis, MN 55455.
Membership. Jonathon Erlen, 123 Northview Dr., Pittsburgh, PA 15261.

Publication

Watermark (q.; memb.; nonmemb. $16). *Eds.* Jodi Koste, Special Collections and Archives, Medical College of Virginia, MCV Box 582, Richmond, VA 23113-0582. E-mail jkoste@gems.vcu.edu; Joan Echtenkamp Klein, Historical Collections, Univ. of Virginia, Health Sciences Center, Box 234, Charlottesville, VA 22908. E-mail jre@virginia.edu.

ARMA International
(Association of Records Managers and Administrators)

Executive Director/CEO, Peter R. Hermann, CAE
4200 Somerset Dr., Suite 215, Prairie Village, KS 66208
800-422-2762, 913-341-3808, fax 913-341-3742
E-mail phermann@arma.org, World Wide Web http://www.arma.org/hq

Object

To advance the practice of records and information management as a discipline and a profession; to organize and promote programs of research, education, training, and networking within that profession; to support the enhancement of professionalism of the membership; and to promote cooperative endeavors with related professional groups.

Membership

Membership application is available through ARMA headquarters. Annual dues are $100 for international affiliation. Chapter dues vary from city to city. Membership categories are chapter member ($100 plus chapter dues), student member ($15), and unaffiliated member.

Officers (1997–1998)

Pres. Robert Nawrucki, 10287 Cedar Ridge Dr., Manassas, VA 22110. Tel. 703-361-3879, fax 703-257-5459; *Immediate Past Pres. and Chair of the Board* Kenneth L. Hopkins, Team Works Personnel, 4915 W. Cypress St., Suite 130, Tampa, FL 33607. Tel. 813-286-2830, fax 813-286-2737; *Pres.-Elect* Christine M. Ardern, Canadian Imperial Bank of Commerce, Commerce Ct. N., Seventh flr., Toronto, ON M5L 1A2, Canada. Tel. 416-980-7966, fax 416-861-3666. *Treas.* Kristi K. Woods, Document Bank, 20815 N.E. 16 Ave., B-23, North Miami, FL 33179. Tel. 305-770-9933, fax 305-770-4375; *Region Directors: Region I* H. Larry Eiring; *Region II* Timothy W. Hughes; *Region III* Jack R. Ingle; *Region IV* Wayne Duncan; *Region V* Tad Howington; *Region VI* Linda L. Masquefa; *Region VII* Anne Taylor-Butler; *Region VIII* Susan A. Dalati; *Region IX* Rosalie C. Stremple; *Region X* Carole Guy Blowers; *Region XI* Phyllis W. Parker; *Region XII* Hella Jean Bartolo.

Publication

Records Management Quarterly. Ed. Ira Penn, 310 Appomattox Dr., Brentwood, TN 37027. Tel. 615-376-2732, e-mail rmqeditor@aol.com.

Committee Chairpersons

Awards. Robert F. Nawrocki, 10287 Cedar Ridge Dr., Manassas, VA 20110. Tel. 703-361-3879, fax 703-257-5459.

Canadian Legislative and Regulatory Affairs (CLARA). Raphael Thierrin, 4515 45 St. S.W., Calgary, AB T3E 6K7. Tel. 403-686-3310, fax 403-686-0075.

Education Development. Deborah J. Marshall, Wilkes Artis Hedrick and Lane, 1666 K St. N.W., Suite 1100, Washington, DC 20000-2866. Tel. 202-457-7869, fax 202-457-7814.

Financial Planning/Management Audit. Kristi K. Woods, Document Bank, 20815 N.E. 16 Ave., Suite B-23, North Miami, FL 33179. Tel. 305-770-9933, fax 305-770-4375.

Industry Action. Timothy W. Hughes, Madison Gas and Electric Co., Box 1231, Madison, WI 53701-1231. Tel. 608-252-4799, fax 608-252-7098.

Industry Specific Program. Lee G. Webster, School Dist. of Philadelphia, 734 Schuylkill Ave., Rm. 234, Philadelphia, PA 19146-2397. Tel. 215-875-3938, fax 215-875-5780.

Industry Specific Program Assistants. Nyoakee B. Salway, Occidental Petroleum

Corp., 10889 Wilshire Blvd., Suite 920, Los Angeles, CA 90024. Tel. 310-443-6219, fax 310-443 6340; Kate Brass, Phone Poulenc Rorer Pharmaceuticals, 500 Arcola Rd. H-11, Collegeville, PA 19426. Tel. 610-454-3028, fax 610-454-5299; Joyce W. Ellis, Whitehall-Robins, Box 9113, Richmond, VA 23227. Tel. 804-257-2794, fax 804-329-6721; Donald J. Prososki, Hallmark Cards, Box 419580, Kansas City, MO 64141-6580. Tel. 816-274-4559, fax 816-274-4323.

Information Technology. John T. Phillips, 1803 Nantasket Rd., Knoxville, TN 37922. Tel./fax 615-966-9413.

Marketing (Advisory). Brian Moriki, First Hawaiian Bank, Records and Security Dept., Box 1959, Honolulu, NI 96805-1959. Tel. 808-844-3056, fax 808-844-3839.

Nominating. Ken Hopkins, Team Works Personnel, 4915 W. Cypress St., Suite 130, Tampa, FL 33607. Tel. 813-286-2830, fax 813-286-2737.

Professional Issues. David O. Stephens, Zasio, Box 2674, Smithfield, NC 27577. Tel. 919-989-1106, fax 919-989-6453.

Publications Coordination. Jean K. Brown, Univ. Archives, Univ. of Delaware, Pearson Hall, Newark, DE 19716. Tel. 302-831-2750, fax 302-831-6903.

Standards Advisory and Development (Subcommittee). Marti Fischer, First American Records Management, 559 Charcot Ave., San Jose, CA 95131. Tel. 408-435-8141, fax 408-435-0701.

U.S. Government Relations. Andrea D. Lentz, Info. Mgt. Section, Ohio Dept. of Human Services, 2098 Integrity Dr. N., Columbus, OH 43209. Tel. 614-443-5800, fax 614-443-2822.

Art Libraries Society of North America

Executive Director, Penney De Pas, CAE
4101 Lake Boone Trail, Suite 201
Raleigh, NC 27607
919-787-5181, fax 919-787-4916
E-mail arlisna@compuserve.com, World Wide Web http://afalib.uflib.ufl.edu/arlis

Object

To foster excellence in art librarianship and visual resources curatorship for the advancement of the visual arts. Established 1972.

Membership

Memb. 1,325. Dues (Inst.) $80; (Indiv.) $65; (Business Affiliate) $100; (Student/Retired/Unemployed) $40; (Sustaining) $200; (Sponsor) $500; (Overseas) $80. Year. Jan. 1–Dec. 31. Membership is open and encouraged for all those interested in visual librarianship, whether they be professional librarians, students, library assistants, art book publishers, art book dealers, art historians, archivists, architects, slide and photograph curators, or retired associates in these fields.

Officers (1997–1998)

Pres. Roger Lawson, National Gallery of Art Lib., Sixth St. and Constitution Ave. N.W., Washington, DC 20565. Tel. 202-842-6529, fax 202-408-8530, e-mail r-lawson@nga.gov; *V.P./Pres.-Elect* Mary E. Graham, Arizona State Museum Lib., Univ. of Arizona, Tucson, AZ 85721-0026. Tel. 520-621-4695, fax 520-621-2976, e-mail megraham@u.arizona.edu; *Past Pres.* Jack Robertson, Fiske Kimball Fine Arts Lib., Univ. of Virginia, Bayly Dr., Charlottesville, VA 22903. Tel. 804-924-6601, fax 804-982-2678, e-mail jsr8s@virginia.edu; *Secy.* Jeanne Brown, Lib., Univ. of Nevada–Las Vegas, Box 45-7001, Las Vegas, NV 89154-7001. Tel. 702-895-4369, fax 702-895-1975, e-mail jeanneb@nevada.edu; *Treas.* Ross Day, Robert Goldwater Lib., Metropolitan Museum of Art,

1000 Fifth Ave., New York, NY 10028-0198. Tel. 212-570-3707, fax 212-570-3879, e-mail rglib2@metgate.metro.org.

Address correspondence to the executive director.

Executive Board

Officers; *Regional Reps.* (Northeast) Margaret N. Webster, (South) Lee R. Sorenson, (Midwest) Jane A. Carlin, (West) Deborah Barlow Smedstad, (Canada) Cheryl Siegel.

Publications

ARLIS/NA Update (bi-m.; memb.).
Art Documentation (semi-ann.; memb., subsc.).
Handbook and List of Members (ann.; memb.).
Occasional Papers (price varies).
Miscellaneous others (request current list from headquarters).

Committees

Awards.
Cataloging (Advisory).
Collection Development.
Conference.
Development.
Diversity.
Finance.
International Relations.
Membership.
Gerd Muehsam Award.
Nominating.
North American Relations.
Professional Development.
Public Policy.
Publications.
Research.
Standards.
Technology Education.
Technology Relations.
Travel Awards.
George Wittenborn Award.

Chapters

Arizona; Canada (National); Central Plains; D.C.-Maryland-Virginia; Delaware Valley; Michigan; Midstates; Montreal-Ottawa-Quebec; Mountain West; New England; New Jersey; New York; Northern California; Northwest; Ohio Valley; Ontario; Southeast; Southern California; Texas; Twin Cities; Western New York.

Asian/Pacific American Librarians Association

President, Abdulfazal M. Fazle Kabir
Associate Professor, School of Library and Information Studies,
Clark Atlanta University,
223 James P. Brawley Dr. S.W., Atlanta, GA 30314-4391
404-880-8701, fax 404-880-8977, e-mail akabir@cau.edu

Object

To provide a forum for discussing problems and concerns of Asian/Pacific American librarians; to provide a forum for the exchange of ideas by Asian/Pacific American librarians and other librarians; to support and encourage library services to Asian/Pacific American communities; to recruit and support Asian/Pacific American librarians in the library/information science professions; to seek funding for scholarships in library/information science schools for Asian/Pacific Americans; and to provide a vehicle whereby Asian/Pacific American librarians can cooperate with other associations and organizations having similar or allied interests. Founded 1980; incorporated 1981; affiliated with the American Library Association 1982.

Membership

Open to all librarians and information specialists of Asian/Pacific descent working in U.S. libraries and information centers and other related organizations and to others who support the goals and purposes of APALA. Asian/Pacific Americans are defined as those who consider themselves Asian/Pacific Americans. They may be Americans of Asian/Pacific descent, Asian/Pacific people with the status of permanent residency, or Asian/Pacific people living in the United States. Dues (Inst.) $25; (Indiv.) $10; (Students/Unemployed Librarians) $5.

Officers (July 1997–June 1998)

Pres. Abulfazal M. Fazle Kabir, School of Lib. and Info. Studies, Clark Atlanta Univ., 223 James P. Brawley Dr. S.W., Atlanta, GA 30314. Tel. 404-880-8701, fax 404-880-8977; *V.P./Pres.-Elect* Soon J. Jung, Head of Cataloging, Newport Beach Public Lib., 1000 Avocado Ave., Newport Beach, CA 92660. Tel. 714-717-3824, fax 714-640-5681, e-mail sjung@city.newport-beach.ca.us. *Past Pres.* Kenneth A. Yamashita, Lib. Div. Mgr., Central Lib. and Technical Services, Stockton–San Joaquin County Public Lib., 605 N. El Dorado St., Stockton, CA 95202. Tel. 209-937-8467, fax 209-937-8683, e-mail yamask04@stockton.lib.ca.us; *Secy.* Fenghua Wang, Libn., SUNY College at Purchase

Lib., 735 Anderson Hill Rd., Purchase, NY 10577. Tel. 914-251-6435, fax 914-251-6437, e-mail fwang@brick.purchase.edu; *Treas.* Rama Vishwanatham, Libn., Lib. of Health Sciences M/C 763, 1750 Polk St., Chicago, IL 60612. Tel. 312-996-8993, fax 312-996-1899, e-mail rama@uic.edu.

Advisory Committee

Officers; immediate past president; Sharad Karkhanis; Suzine Har-Nicolescu.

Publication

APALA Newsletter. Ed. Sandra Yamate, Polychrome Publishing Corp., 4509 N. Francisco Ave., Chicago, IL 60625. Tel. 773-478-4455, fax 773-478-0786.

Committee Chairpersons

Awards. Suzine Har-Nicolescu.
Constitution and Bylaws. Lourdes Collantes.
Finance. To be appointed.
Membership. Rosario P. Galura.
Newsletter and Publications. Sandra Yamate.
Nominations. Kenneth A. Yamashita.
Program. To be appointed.
Publicity. To be appointed.
Recruitment and Scholarship. Rochelle Amores.

Association for Information and Image Management

President, John F. Mancini
1100 Wayne Ave., Suite 1100, Silver Spring, MD 20910
301-587-8202, fax 301-587-2711
E-mail aiim@aiim.org, World Wide Web http://www.aiim.org

Object

The mission of the Association for Information and Image Management is to be the leading global association bringing together the users of document technologies with the providers of that technology. Our focus is on helping corporate and institutional users understand these technologies and how they can be applied to improve critical business processes.

Officers

Chair Barry N. Lurie, Unisys Corp., Box 500, MS B230, Blue Bell, PA 19424; *V. Chair* David S. Silver, Kofax Image Products, 3 Jenner St., Irvine, CA 92618. *Treas.* John A. O'Connell, Staffware PLC, Staffware House, 3 The Switchback, Gardener Rd., Maidenhead, Berkshire SL6 7RJ, United Kingdom.

Publication

INFORM (10 per year; memb.). *Ed.* Robert Head.

Association for Library and Information Science Education

Executive Director, Sharon J. Rogers
Box 7640, Arlington, VA 22207
703-243-8040, e-mail sroger7@ibm.net
World Wide Web http://www.alise.org

Object

The Association for Library and Information Science Education (ALISE) is an association devoted to the advancement of knowledge and learning in the interdisciplinary field of information studies. Established 1915.

Membership

Memb. 725. Dues (Inst.) for ALA-accredited programs, sliding scale; (International Affiliate Inst.) $75; (Indiv.) $90 or $50. Year. Sept.–Aug. Any library/information science school with a program accredited by the ALA Committee on Accreditation may become an institutional member. Any school that offers a graduate degree in librarianship or a cognate field but whose program is not accredited by the ALA Committee on Accreditation may become an institutional member at the lower rate. Any school outside the United States and Canada offering a program comparable to that of institutional membership may become an international affiliate institutional member. Any faculty member, administrator, librarian, researcher, or other individual employed full time may become a personal member. Any retired or part-time faculty member, student, or other individual employed less than full time may become a personal member at the lower rate.

Officers (1997–1998)

Pres. Toni Carbo, Univ. of Pittsburgh. E-mail carbo@sis.pitt.edu; *V.P./Pres.-Elect* Shirley Fitzgibbons, Indiana Univ. E-mail Fitzgibbons@indiana.edu. *Past Pres.* Joan C. Durrance, Univ. of Michigan. E-mail durrance@umich.edu; *Secy.-Treas.* Lynne C. Howarth, Univ. of Toronto. E-mail howarth@fis.toronto.edu.

Directors

Officers; Elfreda Chatman, Univ. of North Carolina (1998). E-mail Chatman@ils.unc.edu; Carol Kuhlthau, Rutgers Univ. (2000). E-mail kuhlthau@scils.rutgers.edu; Dan O'Connor, Rutgers Univ. (1999). E-mail oconnor@scils.rutgers.edu; *Co-Eds.* Joseph Mika (1999), Wayne State Univ. E-mail jmika@cms.cc.wayne.edu; Ronald W. Powell (1999), Wayne State Univ. E-mail rpowell@cms.cc.wayne.edu; *Exec. Dir.* Sharon J. Rogers. E-mail Sroger7@ibm.net; *Parliamentarians* Charles A. Bunge, Norman Horrocks.

Publications

ALISE Library and Information Science Education Statistical Report (ann.; $64, foreign $65).

Journal of Education for Library and Information Science (4 per year; $78; foreign $88).

Membership Directory (ann.; $55).

Committee Chairpersons

Awards and Honors. Margaret Kimmel, Univ. of Pittsburgh.

Conference Planning. Toni Carbo, Univ. of Pittsburgh.

Editorial Board. Danny Wallace, Kent State Univ.

Government Relations. Elizabeth Aversa, Catholic Univ.

International Relations. Kelly Rodriguez, Texas Woman's Univ.

LIS Education Statistical Report Project. Evelyn Daniel and Jerry Saye, Univ. of North Carolina.

Membership. Jose-Marie Griffiths, Univ. of Michigan.

Nominating. Ken Haycock, Univ. of British Columbia.

Organization and Bylaws. Ken Shearer, North Carolina Central Univ.

Recruitment. Kathleen McCook, Univ. of South Florida.

Research. Bob Williams, Univ. of South Carolina.

Resolutions. Marianne Cooper, Queens College.

Tellers. Margaret Taylor, Univ. of Michigan.

Association of Academic Health Sciences Libraries

2033 Sixth Ave., Suite 804, Seattle, WA 98121
206-441-6020, fax 206-441-8262
E-mail sbinc@halcyon.com

Object

To promote—in cooperation with educational institutions, other educational associations, government agencies, and other nonprofit organizations—the common interests of academic health sciences libraries located in the United States and elsewhere, through publications, research, and discussion of problems of mutual interest and concern, and to advance the efficient and effective operation of academic health sciences libraries for the benefit of faculty, students, administrators, and practitioners.

Membership

Memb. 142. $200. Regular membership is available to nonprofit educational institutions operating a school of health sciences that has full or provisional accreditation by the Association of American Medical Colleges. Regular members shall be represented by the chief administrative officer of the member institution's health sciences library. Associate membership (and nonvoting representation) is available to organizations having an interest in the purposes and activities of the association.

Association of Jewish Libraries

15 E. 26 St., Rm. 1034, New York, NY 10010
212-678-8093, fax 212-678-8998

Object

To promote the improvement of library services and professional standards in all Jewish libraries and collections of Judaica; to serve as a center of dissemination of Jewish library information and guidance; to encourage the establishment of Jewish libraries and collections of Judaica; to promote publication of literature that will be of assistance to Jewish librarianship; and to encourage people to enter the field of librarianship. Organized in 1965 from the merger of the Jewish Librarians Association and the Jewish Library Association.

Membership

Memb. 1,100. Dues $35; (Student/Retired) $21. Year. July 1–June 30.

Officers (June 1996–June 1998)

Pres. Esther Nussbaum, Ramaz Upper School Lib., 60 E. 78 St., New York, NY 10021; *V.P./Pres.-Elect* David Gilner, Hebrew Union College–J.I.R., Lib., 3101 Clifton Ave., Cincinnati, OH 45220; *Past Pres.* Zachary Baker, Lib., YIVO Inst. for Jewish Research, 555 W. 57 St., New York, NY 10019; *V.P., Memb.* Shoshanah Seidman, Univ. of Chicago, 1100 E. 57 St., Chicago, IL 60637; *Treas.* Nira Wolfe, Hebrew Theological College, 7135 Carpenter Rd., Skokie, IL 60077; *Rec. Secy.* Frances Wolf, Congregation Beth Shalom, 9400 Wornall Rd., Kansas City, MO 64114; *Corresponding Secy.* Sarah Spiegel, Lib., Jewish Theological Seminary of America, 3080 Broadway, New York, NY 10027; *Publications V.P.* Beverly Newman, 11808 High Dr., Leawood, KS 66211.

Address correspondence to the association.

Publications

AJL Newsletter (q.). *Eds.* Irene Levin-Wixman, 5494 Palm Springs Lane, Boynton Beach, FL 33437; Hazel Karp, 880 Somerset Dr. N.W., Atlanta, GA 30327.

Judaica Librarianship (irreg.). *Ed.* Bella Hass Weinberg, Div. of Lib. and Info. Science, Saint John's Univ., 8000 Utopia Pkwy., Jamaica, NY 11439.

Division Presidents

Research and Special Library. Rick Burke.
Synagogue, School, and Center Libraries. Fred Isaac.

Association of Research Libraries

Executive Director, Duane E. Webster
21 Dupont Circle N.W., Suite 800, Washington, DC 20036
202-296-2296, fax 202-872-0884
E-mail arlhq@arl.org, World Wide Web http://www.arl.org

Object

The mission of the Association of Research Libraries (ARL) is to shape and influence forces affecting the future of research libraries in the process of scholarly communication. ARL's programs and services promote equitable access to and effective use of recorded knowledge in support of teaching, research, scholarship, and community service. The association articulates the concerns of research libraries and their institutions, forges coalitions, influences information policy development, and supports innovation and improvement in research library operations. ARL is a not-for-profit membership organization comprising the libraries of North American research institutions and operates as a forum for the exchange of ideas and as an agent for collective action.

Membership

Memb. 121. Membership is institutional. Dues $15,100. Year. Jan.–Dec.

Officers (Oct. 1997–Oct. 1998)

Pres. James Neal, Dir. of Libs., Johns Hopkins Univ.; *Pres.-Elect* Betty Bengtson, Univ. of Washington; *Past Pres.* Gloria Werner, Univ. Libn., UCLA.

Board of Directors

Shirley K. Baker, Washington Univ. (Saint Louis); Betty L. Bengtson, Univ. of Washington; Scott Bennett, Yale Univ.; William J. Crowe, Univ. of Kansas; Kenneth Frazier, Univ. of Wisconsin; Paula Kaufmann, Univ. of Tennessee; Carole Moore, Univ. of Toronto; James G. Neal, Johns Hopkins Univ.; William G. Potter, Univ. of Georgia; Carla Stoffle, Univ. of Arizona; Gloria Werner, UCLA.

Publications

ARL: A Bimonthly Newsletter of Research Libraries Issues and Actions (bi-m.; memb. $25; nonmemb. $50).
ARL Academic Law and Medical Library Statistics (ann.; memb. $35; nonmemb. $65).
ARL Annual Salary Survey (ann.; memb. $35; nonmemb. $65).
ARL Preservation Statistics (ann.; memb. $35; nonmemb. $65).
ARL Statistics (ann.; memb. $35; nonmemb. $65).
Developing Indicators for Academic Library Performance: Ratios from the ARL Statistics 1993–94 and 1994–95 (ann.; memb. $25; nonmemb. $50).
Directory of Electronic Journals, Newsletters, and Academic Discussion Lists. (ann.; memb. $65; nonmemb. $95).
Proceedings of the ARL Membership Meetings (2 per yr.; memb. $45; nonmemb. $70).
Systems and Procedures Exchange Center (SPEC): Kits and Flyers (10 per year; kits: memb. $185, nonmemb. $280; flyers $50).

Committee and Work Group Chairpersons

Access to Information Resources. Shirley Baker, Washington Univ., Saint Louis.
Copyright Issues (Working Group). James G. Neal, Johns Hopkins Univ.
Diversity. Nancy Baker, Washington State Univ.
Information Policies. Fred Heath, Texas A&M Univ.

Leadership and Management of Research Library Resources. Paul Kobulnicky, Univ. of Connecticut.

Preservation of Research Library Materials. Meredith Butler, SUNY Albany.

Research Collections. Joe A. Hewitt, Univ. of North Carolina at Chapel Hill.

Scholarly Communication. Elaine F. Sloan, Columbia Univ.

Scientific and Technical Information (Working Group). Marilyn Sharrow. Univ. of California at Davis.

SPARC (Working Group). Kenneth Frazier, Univ. of Wisconsin.

Statistics and Measurement. William J. Studer, Ohio State Univ.

Units

Coalition for Networked Information. Formed by ARL, CAUSE, and EDUCOM in March 1990 to advance scholarship and intellectual productivity by promoting the provision of information resources on existing and future telecommunications networks, and the linkage of research libraries to these networks and to their respective constituencies.

Office of Management Services. Provides consulting, training, and publishing services on the management of human and material resources in libraries.

Office of Research and Development. Pursues the ARL research agenda through the identification and development of projects in support of the research library community's mission.

Office of Scholarly Communication. Established in 1990 to identify and influence the forces affecting the production, dissemination, and use of scholarly and scientific information.

ARL Membership

Nonuniversity Libraries

Boston Public Lib., Canada Inst. for Scientific and Technical Info., Center for Research Libs., Linda Hall Lib., Lib. of Congress, National Agricultural Lib., National Lib. of Canada, National Lib. of Medicine, New York Public Lib., New York State Lib., Smithsonian Institution Libs.

University Libraries

Alabama, Alberta, Arizona, Arizona State, Auburn, Boston, Brigham Young, British Columbia, Brown, California (Berkeley), California (Davis), California (Irvine), California (Los Angeles), California (Riverside), California (San Diego), California (Santa Barbara), Case Western Reserve, Chicago, Cincinnati, Colorado, Colorado State, Columbia, Connecticut, Cornell, Dartmouth, Delaware, Duke, Emory, Florida, Florida State, Georgetown, Georgia, Georgia Inst. of Technology, Guelph, Harvard, Hawaii, Houston, Howard, Illinois (Chicago), Illinois (Urbana), Indiana, Iowa, Iowa State, Johns Hopkins, Kansas, Kent State, Kentucky, Laval, Louisiana State, McGill, McMaster, Manitoba, Maryland, Massachusetts, Massachusetts Inst. of Technology, Miami (Fla.), Michigan, Michigan State, Minnesota, Missouri, Nebraska (Lincoln), New Mexico, New York, North Carolina, North Carolina State, Northwestern, Notre Dame, Ohio, Ohio State, Oklahoma, Oklahoma State, Oregon, Pennsylvania, Pennsylvania State, Pittsburgh, Princeton, Purdue, Queen's (Kingston, Canada), Rice, Rochester, Rutgers, Saskatchewan, South Carolina, Southern California, Southern Illinois, Stanford, SUNY (Albany), SUNY (Buffalo), SUNY (Stony Brook), Syracuse, Temple, Tennessee, Texas, Texas A&M, Texas Tech, Toronto, Tulane, Utah, Vanderbilt, Virginia, Virginia Polytechnic, Washington, Washington (Saint Louis, Mo.), Washington State, Waterloo, Wayne State, Western Ontario, Wisconsin, Yale, York.

Association of Vision Science Librarians

Chair, Judith Schaeffer Young, Wills Eye Hospital, Medical Lib., 900 Walnut St.,
Philadelphia, PA 19107
215-928-3288, e-mail young@hslc.org

Object

To foster collective and individual acquisition and dissemination of vision science information, to improve services for all persons seeking such information, and to develop standards for libraries to which members are attached. Founded 1968.

Membership

Memb. (U.S.) 60; (Foreign) 15.

Publications

Guidelines for Vision Science Libraries.
Opening Day Book Collection—Visual Science.
PhD Theses in Physiological Optics (irreg.).
Standards for Vision Science Libraries.
Union List of Vision-Related Serials (irreg.).

Meetings

Annual meeting held in December in connection with the American Academy of Optometry; midyear mini-meeting with the Medical Library Association.

Beta Phi Mu
(International Library and Information Studies Honor Society)

Executive Director, F. William Summers
School of Information Studies, Florida State University,
Tallahassee, FL 32306-2100
850-644-3907, fax 850-644-6253
E-mail beta_phi_mu@lis.fsu.edu

Object

To recognize high scholarship in the study of librarianship and to sponsor appropriate professional and scholarly projects. Founded at the University of Illinois in 1948.

Membership

Memb. 23,000. Open to graduates of library school programs accredited by the American Library Association who fulfill the following requirements: complete the course requirements leading to a fifth year or other advanced degree in librarianship with a scholastic average of 3.75 where A equals 4 points (this provision shall also apply to planned programs of advanced study beyond the fifth year that do not culminate in a degree but that require full-time study for one or more academic years) and in the top 25 percent of their class; receive a letter of recommendation from their respective library schools attesting to their demonstrated fitness for successful professional careers.

Officers

Pres. Marion T. Reid, Dean of Lib. Services, California State Univ. at San Marcos, 820 Los Vallecitos Blvd., San Marcos, CA 92096-0001. Tel. 619-750-4330, fax 619-750-3287, e-mail mreid@mailhost1.csusm.edu; *V.P./ Pres.-Elect* Barbara Immroth, Graduate

School of Lib. and Info. Science, Univ. of Texas at Austin, Austin, TX 78712-1276. Tel. 512-471-3875, fax 512-471-3971, e-mail immroth@uts.cc.utexas.edu; *Past Pres.* Mary Biggs, West Lib., Trenton State College, Hillwood Lakes, CN 4700, Trenton, NJ 08650-4700; *Treas.* Sondra Taylor-Furbee, State Lib. of Florida, 500 S. Bronough St., Tallahassee, FL 32399; *Exec. Dir.* F. William Summers, School of Info. Studies, Florida State Univ., Tallahassee, FL 32306-2100. Tel. 850-644-8111, fax 850-644-6253, e-mail Beta_Phi_Mu@lis.fsu.edu.

Directors

Darlene E. Weingand (1998); *Dirs.-at-Large* Susan Webreck Alman, Nancy P. Zimmerman.

Publications

Beta Phi Mu Monograph Series. Book-length scholarly works based on original research in subjects of interest to library and information professionals. Available from Greenwood Press, 88 Post Rd. W., Box 5007, Westport, CT 06881-9990.

Chapbook Series. Limited editions on topics of interest to information professionals. Call Beta Phi Mu for availability.

Newsletter. Ed. William Scheeren.

Chapters

Alpha. Univ. of Illinois, Grad. School of Lib. and Info. Science, Urbana, IL 61801; *Beta.* (Inactive). Univ. of Southern California, School of Lib. Science, Univ. Park, Los Angeles, CA 90007; *Gamma.* Florida State Univ., School of Lib. and Info. Studies, Tallahassee, FL 32306; *Delta* (Inactive). Loughborough College of Further Education, School of Libnshp., Loughborough, England; *Epsilon.* Univ. of North Carolina, School of Lib. Science, Chapel Hill, NC 27599; *Zeta.* Atlanta Univ., School of Lib. and Info. Studies, Atlanta, GA 30314; *Theta.* Pratt Inst., Grad. School of Lib. and Info. Science, Brooklyn, NY 11205; *Iota.* Catholic Univ. of America,

School of Lib. and Info. Science, Washington, DC 20064; Univ. of Maryland, College of Lib. and Info. Services, College Park, MD 20742; *Kappa.* (Inactive). Western Michigan Univ., School of Libnshp., Kalamazoo, MI 49008; *Lambda.* Univ. of Oklahoma, School of Lib. Science, Norman, OK 73019; *Mu.* Univ. of Michigan, School of Lib. Science, Ann Arbor, MI 48109; *Nu.* (Inactive); *Xi.* Univ. of Hawaii, Grad. School of Lib. Studies, Honolulu, HI 96822; *Omicron.* Rutgers Univ., Grad. School of Lib. and Info. Studies, New Brunswick, NJ 08903; *Pi.* Univ. of Pittsburgh, School of Lib. and Info. Science, Pittsburgh, PA 15260; *Rho.* Kent State Univ., School of Lib. Science, Kent, OH 44242; *Sigma.* Drexel Univ., School of Lib. and Info. Science, Philadelphia, PA 19104; *Tau..* (Inactive). State Univ. of New York at Geneseo, School of Lib. and Info. Science, Geneseo, NY 14454; *Upsilon.* (Inactive). Univ. of Kentucky, College of Lib. Science, Lexington, KY 40506; *Phi.* Univ. of Denver, Grad. School of Libnshp. and Info. Mgt., Denver, CO 80208; *Chi.* Indiana Univ., School of Lib. and Info. Science, Bloomington, IN 47401; *Psi.* Univ. of Missouri at Columbia, School of Lib. and Info. Sciences, Columbia, MO 65211; *Omega.* (Inactive). San Jose State Univ., Div. of Lib. Science, San Jose, CA 95192; *Beta Alpha.* Queens College, City College of New York, Grad. School of Lib. and Info. Studies, Flushing, NY 11367; *Beta Beta.* Simmons College, Grad. School of Lib. and Info. Science, Boston, MA 02115; *Beta Delta.* State Univ. of New York at Buffalo, School of Info. and Lib. Studies, Buffalo, NY 14260; *Beta Epsilon.* Emporia State Univ., School of Lib. Science, Emporia, KS 66801; *Beta Zeta.* Louisiana State Univ., Grad. School of Lib. Science, Baton Rouge, LA 70803; *Beta Eta.* Univ. of Texas at Austin, Grad. School of Lib. and Info. Science, Austin, TX 78712; *Beta Theta.* (Inactive). Brigham Young Univ., School of Lib. and Info. Science, Provo, UT 84602; *Beta Iota.* Univ. of Rhode Island, Grad. Lib. School, Kingston, RI 02881; *Beta Kappa.* Univ. of Alabama, Grad. School of Lib. Service, University, AL 35486; *Beta Lambda.* North Texas State Univ., School of Lib. and Info. Science, Denton, TX 76203; Texas Woman's Univ., School of Lib. Science, Denton, TX

76204; *Beta Mu*. Long Island Univ., Palmer Grad. Lib. School, C. W. Post Center, Greenvale, NY 11548; *Beta Nu*. Saint John's Univ., Div. of Lib. and Info. Science, Jamaica, NY 11439. *Beta Xi*. North Carolina Central Univ., School of Lib. Science, Durham, NC 27707; *Beta Omicron*. (Inactive). Univ. of Tennessee at Knoxville, Grad. School of Lib. and Info. Science, Knoxville, TN 37916; *Beta Pi*. Univ. of Arizona, Grad. Lib. School, Tucson, AZ 85721; *Beta Rho*. Univ. of Wisconsin at Milwaukee, School of Lib. Science, Milwaukee, WI 53201; *Beta Sigma*. (Inactive). Clarion State College, School of Lib. Science, Clarion, PA 16214; *Beta Tau*. Wayne State Univ., Div. of Lib. Science, Detroit, MI 48202; *Beta Upsilon*. (Inactive). Alabama A & M Univ., School of Lib. Media, Normal, AL 35762; *Beta Phi*. Univ. of South Florida, Grad. Dept. of Lib., Media, and Info. Studies, Tampa, FL 33647; *Beta Psi*. Univ. of Southern Mississippi, School of Lib. Service, Hattiesburg, MS 39406; *Beta Omega*. Univ. of South Carolina, College of Libnshp., Columbia, SC 29208; *Beta Beta Alpha*. Univ. of California at Los Angeles, Grad. School of Lib. and Info. Science, Los Angeles, CA 90024; *Beta Beta Gamma*. Rosary College, Grad. School of Lib. and Info. Science, River Forest, IL 60305; *Beta Beta Delta*. Univ. of Cologne, Germany; *Beta Beta Epsilon*. Univ. of Wisconsin at Madison, Lib. School, Madison, WI 53706; *Beta Beta Zeta*. Univ. of North Carolina at Greensboro, Dept. of Lib. Science and Educational Technology, Greensboro, NC 27412; *Beta Beta Theta*. Univ. of Iowa, School of Lib. and Info. Science, Iowa City, IA 52242; *Beta Beta Iota*. State Univ. of New York, Univ. at Albany, School of Info. Science and Policy, Albany, NY 12222; *Pi Lambda Sigma*. Syracuse Univ., School of Info. Studies, Syracuse, NY 13210.

Bibliographical Society of America

Executive Secretary, Michèle E. Randall
Box 1537, Lenox Hill Station, New York, NY 10021
212-452-2710 (voice/fax), e-mail bibsocamer@aol.com

Object

To promote bibliographical research and to issue bibliographical publications. Organized 1904.

Membership

Memb. 1,200. Dues $50. Year. Jan.–Dec.

Officers (Jan. 1997–Jan. 1998)

Pres. Roger E. Stoddard; *V.P.* Hope Mayo; *Treas.* R. Dyke Benjamin; *Secy.* Nancy Burkett.

Council

T. Kimball Brooker (2000), Peter S. Graham (1998), James N. Green (1999), Robert H. Hirst (2000), T. H. Howard-Hill (2000), Leslie Morris (1999), Fred Schreiber (1998), Alice Schreyer (1998), William P. Stoneman (1998), Michael Winship (1999), Elizabeth Witherell (2000), David S. Zeidberg (1999).

Publication

Papers (q.; memb.). *Ed.* T. H. Howard-Hill, Dept. of English, Univ. of South Carolina, Columbia, SC 29208.

Committee Chairpersons

Bibliographical Projects. Michael Winship.
Delegate to American Council of Learned Societies. Marcus McCorison.
Fellowship Program. Richard Landon.
Finance. Paul Gourary.
Publications. Katharine Kyes Leab.

Canadian Association for Information Science
(Association Canadienne des Sciences de l'Information)

140 Saint George St., Toronto, ON M5S 1A1, Canada
416-978-8876

Object

To bring together individuals and organizations concerned with the production, manipulation, storage, retrieval, and dissemination of information, with emphasis on the application of modern technologies in these areas. The Canadian Association for Information Science (CAIS) is dedicated to enhancing the activity of the information transfer process; utilizing the vehicles of research, development, application, and education; and serving as a forum for dialogue and exchange of ideas concerned with the theory and practice of all factors involved in the communication of information.

Membership

Institutions and individuals interested in information science and involved in the gathering, organization, and dissemination of information (computer scientists, documentalists, information scientists, librarians, journalists, sociologists, psychologists, linguists, administrators, etc.) can become members of CAIS. Dues (Inst.) $165; (Personal) $75; (Student) $40.

Publication

Canadian Journal of Information and Library Science (q.; $95; outside Canada $110).

Canadian Library Association

Acting Executive Director, Lacey O'Brian
200 Elgin St., Ottawa, ON K2P 1L5, Canada
613-232-9625, ext. 307; fax 613-563-9895
E-mail ai077@freenet.carleton.ca

Object

To provide leadership in the promotion, development, and support of library and information services in Canada for the benefit of association members, the profession, and Canadian society. Offers library school scholarship and book awards; carries on international liaison with other library associations; makes representation to government and official commissions; offers professional development programs; and supports intellectual freedom. Founded in 1946, CLA is a nonprofit voluntary organization governed by an elected executive council.

Membership

Memb. (Indiv.) 4,000; (Inst.) 1,000. Open to individuals, institutions, and groups interested in librarianship and in library and information services. Dues (Indiv.) $175; (Inst.) $300. Year. Anniversary date renewal.

Officers (1997–1998)

Pres. Paul Whitney, Chief Libn., Burnaby Public Lib., 6100 Willingdon Ave., Burnaby, BC V5H 4N5. Tel 604-436-5431, fax 604-436-2961, e-mail pwhitnea@sfu.ca; *V.P./Pres.-Elect* Sydney Jones, Dir., Lib. Operations, Metro Toronto Reference Lib., 789

Yonge St., Toronto, ON M4W 2G8. Tel. 416-393-7214, fax 416-393-7229, e-mail syd@mtrl.toronto.on.ca; *Treas.* Ruth Reedman, Libn., Canadian Wheat Board, Box 816, 423 Main St., Winnipeg, MB R3C 2P5. Tel. 204-983-3437, fax 204-983-4031, e-mail ruth_reedman@cwb.ca; *Past Pres.* Karen Harrison, Edward D. Jones and Co., 331 Parkridge Way S.E., Calgary, AB T2J 4Z5. Tel. 403-271-0805, fax 403-271-3421, e-mail karenh@cadvision.com.

Publication

Feliciter (10 per year; newsletter).

Division Representatives

Canadian Association of College and University Libraries (CACUL). Melody C. Burton, Head of Access Services, Queen's Univ., Stauffer Lib., Kingston, ON K7L 5C4.

Canadian Association of Public Libraries (CAPL). Beth Hovius, Marketing Mgr., Hamilton Public Lib., Box 2700, Sta. LCD 1, Hamilton, ON L8N 4E4.

Canadian Association of Special Libraries and Information Services (CASLIS). Mary-Lu Brennan, 3 Greystone Walk Dr., PH 29, Scarborough, ON M1K 5J4.

Canadian Library Trustees' Association (CLTA). Gary Archibald, Box 2680, R.R. 2, Yarmouth, NS B5A 4A6.

Canadian School Library Association (CSLA). Mary V. Latham, Waterloo County Board of Educ., 1034 Vine St., Cambridge, ON N3H 2Z9.

Catholic Library Association

Executive Director, Jean R. Bostley, SSJ
100 North St., Suite 224, Pittsfield, MA 01201-5109

Object

The promotion and encouragement of Catholic literature and library work through cooperation, publications, education, and information. Founded 1921.

Membership

Memb. 1,300. Dues $45–$500. Year. July–June.

Officers (1997–1999)

Pres. Julanne M. Good, St. Louis Public Lib., 5005 Jamieson Ave., St. Louis, MO 63109-3027. Tel. 314-832-2319, e-mail bopeep@inlink.com; *V.P./Pres.-Elect* Rev. Bonaventure Hayes, OFM, Christ the King Seminary, 711 Knox Rd., East Aurora, NY 1452-0607. Tel. 716-652-8940, fax 716-652-8903.

Address correspondence to the executive director.

Executive Board

Officers; Nicholas Falco, 1256 Pelham Pkwy., Bronx, NY 10461; Mary E. Gallagher, SSJ, College of Our Lady of the Elms, 291 Springfield St., Chicopee, MA 01013; Barbara Anne Kilpatrick, RSM, Saint Bernard Academy, 2020 24th Ave. S., Nashville, TN 37212-4202; Mary Agnes Casey, SSJ, Marist High School 1241 Kennedy Blvd., Bayonne, NJ 07002-9807; Linda B. Gonzales, Sacred Heart School of Theology, Box 429, Hales Corners, WI 53130-0429; Sally Anne Thompson, Orangedale School Lib., 7015 E. San Miguel, Paradise Valley, AZ 85253; H. Warren Willis, 5209 Rayland Dr., Bethesda, MD 20814-1427.

Publications

Catholic Library World (q.; memb.; nonmemb. $60). *Ed.* Anthony Prete.

Catholic Periodical and Literature Index (q.; $92 for first calendar year; for subsequent years, $4 for each periodical received in the library and indexed in *CPLI*, with an annual $92 minimum). *Ed.* Dana Cernaianu.

Section Chairpersons

Academic Libraries/Library Education. Anthony Amodeo.
Archives. Bonaventure Hayes, OFM.
Children's Libraries. Sandra Duplessis.
High School Libraries. Mary Agnes Casey, SSJ.
Parish/Community Libraries. Sue Rosebraugh.

Round Table Chairpersons

Bibliographic Instruction. Sister Margaret Ruddy.
Cataloging and Classification. Tina-Karen Forman.

Committee Chairpersons

Catholic Library World Editorial. Arnold Rzepecki.
Catholic Periodical and Literature Index. Rev. Bonaventure Hayes, OFM.
Constitution and Bylaws. Mary A. Grant.
Elections. Sister Celine Kelly.
Finance. Rev. Paul J. DeAntoniis.
Grant Development. Sister Jean R. Bostley.
Membership Development. Carolyn W. Field.
Nominations. Irma Godfrey.
Public Relations. Sister Mary Elizabeth Gallagher.
Publications. Sister Marie Melton.
Scholarship. Peggy Sullivan.

Special Appointments

American Friends of the Vatican Library Board. Emmett Corry.
Convention Program Coordinator. Jean R. Bostley, SSJ.
Parliamentarian. Rev. Joseph P. Browne, CSC.

Chief Officers of State Library Agencies

167 W. Main Street, Suite 600, Lexington, KY 40507
606-231-1885, fax 606-231-1928

Object

To provide a means of cooperative action among its state and territorial members to strengthen the work of the respective state and territorial agencies, and to provide a continuing mechanism for dealing with the problems faced by the heads of these agencies, which are responsible for state and territorial library development.

Membership

The Chief Officers of State Library Agencies (COSLA) is an independent organization of the men and women who head the state and territorial agencies responsible for library development. Its membership consists solely of the top library officers of the 50 states, the District of Columbia, and the territories, variously designated as state librarian, director, commissioner, or executive secretary.

Officers (1996–1998)

Pres. Sara Parker, State Libn., Missouri State Lib., 600 W. Main, Box 387, Jefferson City, MO 65102-0387. Tel. 573-751-2751, fax 573-751-3612, e-mail sparker@mail.sos. state.mo.us; *V.P./Pres.-Elect* C. Ray Ewick, Dir., State Lib., 140 N. Senate Ave., Indianapolis, IN 46204. Tel. 317-232-3692, fax 317-232-0002, e-mail ewick@statelib.lib.in. us; *Secy.* Kendall F. Wiggin, State Libn., 20

Park St., Concord, NH 03301-6314. Tel. 603-271-2397, fax 603-271-6826, e-mail wiggin@lilac.nhsl.lib.nh.us; *Treas.* Nancy Bolt, Deputy State Libn. and Assistant Commissioner, Dept. of Educ., 201 E. Colfax Ave., Denver, CO 80203. Tel. 303-866-6733, fax 303-866-6940, e-mail nbolt@csn.net.

Directors

Officers; *Immediate Past Pres.* J. Maurice Travillian, Asst. State Superintendent for Libs., Div. of Lib. Development and Services, Dept. of Educ., 200 W. Baltimore St., Baltimore, MD 21201-2595. Tel. 410-767-0435, fax 410-333-2507, e-mail maurice@charm.net; *Dirs.* Keith Fiels, Dir., Bd. of Lib. Commissioners, 648 Beacon St., Boston, MA 02215. Tel. 617-267-9400, fax 617-421-9833, e-mail Keith.Fiels@state.ma.us; Edwin S. Gleaves, State Libn. and Archivist, 403 Seventh Ave. N., Nashville, TN 37243-0312. Tel. 615-741-7996, fax 615-741-6471, e-mail egleaves@mail.state.tn.us.

Chinese-American Librarians Association

Executive Director, Sheila S. Lai
California State University, Sacramento
University Library, Room 2053, 2000 University Dr. E., Sacramento, CA 95819-6039
916-278-6201, fax 916-363-0868
E-mail sheilalai@csus.edu

Object

To enhance communications among Chinese-American librarians as well as between Chinese-American librarians and other librarians; to serve as a forum for discussion of mutual problems and professional concerns among Chinese-American librarians; to promote Sino-American librarianship and library services; and to provide a vehicle whereby Chinese-American librarians may cooperate with other associations and organizations having similar or allied interest.

Membership

Memb. 770. Open to everyone who is interested in the association's goals and activities. Dues (Regular) $15; (Student/Nonsalaried) $7.50; (Inst.) $45; (Permanent) $200.

Officers (July 1997–June 1998)

Pres. Harriet Ying; *V.P./Pres.-Elect* Linna Yu; *Exec. Dir.* Sheila S. Lai; *Treas.* Ming Li.

Publications

Journal of Library and Information Science (2 per year; memb.; nonmemb. $15).
Membership Directory (memb.).
Newsletter (3 per year; memb.; nonmemb. $10).

Committee Chairpersons

Awards. Sally C. Tseng.
Constitution and Bylaws. Amy D. Seetoo.
Finance. Susan L. Tsui.
International Relations. Sha Li Zhang.
Membership. Margaret S. Feng.
Public Relations/Fund-Raising. Nora Yeh.
Publications. Liana Zhou.

Chapter Presidents

California. Carl Chan.
Greater Mid-Atlantic. Nora Yeh.
Midwest. Weng-ling Liu.
Northeast. Diana Shih.
Southwest. George Teoh.

Journal Officers

Newsletter Eds. Philip Ng, Center for Research Libs., 6050 S. Kenwood Ave., Chicago, IL 60637. Tel. 312-955-4545 ext. 327, fax 312-955-4339, e-mail ng@cr/mail.uchicago.edu; Lan Yang, Sterling C. Evans Lib., Texas A&M Univ., College Station, TX 77843-5000. Tel. 409-862-1904, fax 409-862-4575, e-mail qyang@tamu.edu.

Church and Synagogue Library Association

Box 19357, Portland, OR 97280-0357
503-244-6919, e-mail CSLA@worldaccessnet.com
World Wide Web http://www.worldaccessnet.com/~CSLA

Object

To act as a unifying core for the many existing church and synagogue libraries; to provide the opportunity for a mutual sharing of practices and problems; to inspire and encourage a sense of purpose and mission among church and synagogue librarians; to study and guide the development of church and synagogue librarianship toward recognition as a formal branch of the library profession. Founded 1967.

Membership

Memb. 1,900. Dues (Inst.) $125; (Affiliated) $60; (Church/Synagogue) $35; (Indiv.) $20. Year. July–June.

Officers (July 1997–June 1998)

Pres. Lois Ward, 502 North St., Box 368, Prospect, OH 43302; *1st V.P.* Barbara Mall, 5137 Oven Bird Green, Columbia, MD 21004; *2nd V.P.* Russell Newburn, 9493 Moulin Ave., Alliance, OH 44601; *Treas.* Marilyn Demeter, 3145 Corydon Rd., Cleveland Heights, OH 44118; *Administrator* Judith Janzen; *Financial Asst.* J. Robert Waggoner, 413 Robindale Ave., Dearborn, MI 48128; *Publications Ed.* Karen Bota; *Book Review Ed.* Charles Snyder.

Executive Board

Officers; committee chairpersons.

Publications

Bibliographies (1–5; price varies).
Church and Synagogue Libraries (bi-mo.; memb.; nonmemb. $25; Canada $35). *Ed.* Karen Bota.
CSLA Guides (1–17; price varies).

Committee Chairpersons

Awards. Alrene Hall.
Chapters. Gail Waggoner.
Conference. Barbara Messner.
Finance and Fund-raising. J. Robert Waggoner.
Library Services. Dianne Oswald.
Nominations and Elections. Beverley Manning.
Personnel. Joyce Allen.
Publications. Carol Campbell.

Council of Planning Librarians

101 N. Wacker Dr., Suite CM 190, Chicago, IL 60606
312-409-3349

Object

To provide a special interest group in the field of city and regional planning for libraries and librarians, faculty, professional planners, university, government, and private planning organizations; to provide an opportunity for exchange among those interested in problems of library organization and research and in the dissemination of information about city and regional planning; to sponsor programs of service to the planning profession and librarianship; to advise on library organization for new planning programs; and to aid and support administrators, faculty, and librarians in their efforts to educate the public and their appointed or elected representatives to the necessity for strong library programs in support of planning. Founded 1960.

Membership

Memb. 142. Open to any individual or institution that supports the purpose of the council, upon written application and payment of dues to the treasurer. Dues (Inst.) $45; (Indiv.) $35; Year. July 1–June 30.

Officers and Board (1997–1998)

Pres. Julia M. Gelfand, Univ. Lib., Univ. of California at Irvine, Box 19557, Irvine, CA 92713. Tel. 714-824-4971; *V.P./Pres.-Elect* Jan Horah, Jack Brause Lib., Real Estate Inst., New York Univ., 11 W. 42 St., Suite 510, New York, NY 10036-8002. Tel. 212-790-1325; *Past Pres.* Linda S. Drake, Chapin Planning Lib., CB 3140, Univ. of North Carolina, Chapel Hill, NC 27599-3140. Tel. 919-962-4770; *Member-at-Large* Priscilla Yu, Library, 203 Mumford Hall, Univ. of Illinois, 1301 W. Gregory Dr., Urbana, IL 61801-3608. Tel. 317-333-0424; *Secy./Treas.* Deborah Sommer, Environmental Design Lib., 210 Wurster Hall, Univ. of California, Berkeley, CA 94720. Tel. 510-642-4819.

Publications

CPLFYI-L. Electronic Discussion List. Contact Marilyn Myers at iadmxm@asuvm. inre.asu.edu.

Council on Library and Information Resources

1755 Massachusetts Ave. N.W., Suite 500, Washington, DC 20036-2188
202-939-4750, fax 202-939-4765
World Wide Web http://clir.stanford.edu

Object

In 1997 the Council on Library Resources (CLR) and the Commission on Preservation and Access (CPA) merged and became the Council on Library and Information Resources (CLIR). The mission of the council is to identify and define the key emerging issues related to the welfare of libraries and the constituencies they serve, convene the leaders who can influence change, and promote collaboration among the institutions and organizations that can achieve change. The council's interests embrace the entire range of information resources and services from traditional library and archival materials to emerging digital formats. It assumes a particular interest in helping institutions cope with the accelerating pace of change associated with the transition into the digital environment. The council pursues this mission out of the conviction that information is a public good and has great social utility.

The term *library* is construed to embrace its traditional meanings and purposes and to encompass any and all information agencies and organizations that are involved in gathering, cataloging, storing, preserving, and distributing information and in helping users meet their information requirements.

While maintaining appropriate collaboration and liaison with other institutions and organizations, the council operates independently of any particular institutional or vested interests.

Through the composition of its board, it brings the broadest possible perspective to bear upon defining and establishing the priority of the issues with which it is concerned.

Membership of Board

The council's membership and board of directors are limited to 18 members.

Officers

Chair Stanley Chodorow; *V. Chair* Marilyn Gell Mason; *Pres.* Deanna B. Marcum. E-mail dmarcum@CLIR.org; *V.P.* James Morris; *Secy.* David B. Gracy, II; *Treas.* Dan Tonkery.

Address correspondence to headquarters.

Publications

Annual Report.
Various program publications.

Federal Library and Information Center Committee

Executive Director, Susan M. Tarr
Library of Congress, Washington, DC 20540-4930
202-707-4800
World Wide Web http://lcweb.loc.gov/flicc

Object

The committee makes recommendations on federal library and information policies, programs, and procedures to federal agencies and to others concerned with libraries and information centers. The committee coordinates cooperative activities and services among federal libraries and information centers and serves as a forum to consider issues and policies that affect federal libraries and information centers, needs and priorities in providing information services to the government and to the nation at large, and efficient and cost-effective use of federal library and information resources and services. Furthermore, the committee promotes improved access to information, continued development and use of the Federal Library and Information Network (FEDLINK), research and development in the application of new technologies to federal libraries and informa-

tion centers, improvements in the management of federal libraries and information centers, and relevant education opportunities. Founded 1965.

Membership

Libn. of Congress, Dir. of the National Agricultural Lib., Dir. of the National Lib. of Medicine, Dir. of the National Lib. of Education, representatives from each of the other executive departments, and representatives from each of the following agencies: National Aeronautics and Space Admin., National Science Foundation, Smithsonian Institution, U.S. Supreme Court, U.S. Info. Agency, National Archives and Records Admin., Admin. Offices of the U.S. Courts, Defense Technical Info. Center, Government Printing Office, National Technical Info. Service (Dept. of Commerce), and Office of Scientific and Technical Info. (Dept. of Energy), Exec. Office of the President, Dept. of the Army, Dept. of the Navy, Dept. of the Air Force, and chairperson of the FEDLINK Advisory Council. Fifteen additional voting member agencies shall be selected on a rotating basis by the voting members of FEDLINK. These rotating members will serve a three-year term. One representative from each of the following agencies is invited as an observer to committee meetings: General Accounting Office, General Services Admin., Joint Committee on Printing, National Commission on Libs. and Info. Science, Office of Mgt. and Budget, Office of Personnel Mgt., and Lib. of Congress U.S. Copyright Office.

Officers

Chair James H. Billington, Libn. of Congress; *Chair Designate* Winston Tabb, Assoc. Libn. for Lib. Services, Lib. of Congress; *Exec. Dir.* Susan M. Tarr, Federal Lib. and Info. Center Committee, Lib. of Congress, Washington, DC 20540-4930.

Address correspondence to the executive director.

Publications

Annual FLICC Forum on Federal Information Policies (summary and papers).
FEDLINK Technical Notes (m.).
FLICC Newsletter (q.).

Federal Publishers Committee

Chairperson, Glenn W. King
Bureau of the Census, Washington, DC 20233
301-457-1171, fax 301-457-4707
E-mail glenn.w.king.@ccmail.census.gov

Object

To foster and promote effective management of data development and dissemination in the federal government through exchange of information, and to act as a focal point for federal agency publishing.

Membership

Memb. 700. Membership is available to persons involved in publishing and dissemination in federal government departments, agencies, and corporations, as well as independent organizations concerned with federal government publishing and dissemination. Some key federal government organizations represented are the Joint Committee on Printing, Government Printing Office, National Technical Info. Service, National Commission on Libs. and Info. Science, and the Lib. of Congress. Meetings are held monthly during business hours.

Officers

Chair Glenn W. King; *V.-Chair, Programs* Sandra Smith; *V.-Chair, Roundtables* June Malina; *Secy.* Marilyn Marbrook.

Roundtable Leaders

Marketing and Promotion. John Ward.
Subscriptions and Periodicals. Nancy Nicoletti.

Information Industry Association

1625 Massachusetts Ave. N.W., Suite 700, Washington, DC 20036
202-986-0280, fax 202-638-4403
E-mail info@infoindustry.org

Membership

Memb. 500+ companies. Open to companies involved in the creation, distribution, and use of information products, services, and technologies. For details on membership and dues, write to the association headquarters.

Staff

Pres. Ronald G. Dunn; *V.P.* Emily Pilk; *V.P., Government Relations* Dan Duncan; *Dir., Finance* John Dragovich; *Staff Advisor, Divisions and Councils* Irene Hughes; *Acting Dir., Membership* Sheri R. Robey; *Exec. Asst.* Virginia Nelson; *Ed./Publisher* Serge I. Obolensky.

Board of Directors

Chair Robert Aber; *Past Chair* Patrick J. Tierney, Thomson Business Information; *Chair Elect* James E. Coane, Telebase Systems; *Treas.* Patrick J. Marshall, GTE Directories Corp.; *Secy.* Steven L. Schneider, Disclosure, Inc.; *V. Chairs* Herbert R. Brinberg, Parnassus Associates International; Marjorie M. K. Hlava, Access Innovations; Oakleigh Thorne, TBG Information Investors.

Publication

Information Sources (ann.; memb. $45; nonmemb. $125).

Lutheran Church Library Association

Executive Director, Leanna D. Kloempken
122 W. Franklin Ave., No. 604, Minneapolis, MN 55404
612-870-3623, fax 612-870-0170
E-mail lclahq@aol.com

Object

To promote the growth of church libraries by publishing a quarterly journal, *Lutheran Libraries*; furnishing booklists; assisting member libraries with technical problems; and providing workshops and meetings for mutual encouragement, guidance, and exchange of ideas among members. Founded 1958.

Membership

Memb. 1,800 churches, 250 personal. Dues $25, $37.50, $50, $75, $100, $500, $1,000. Year. Jan.–Jan.

Officers (1997–1998)

Pres. Vernita Kennen; *V.P.* Willis Erickson; *Secy.* Dorothy Anderson; *Treas.* Diane Erickson.
Address correspondence to the executive director.

Directors

Doris Engstrom, Jeannette Johnson, Jan Koski, Betsy Papp, Henrietta Pruissen, Karen Trageser.

Publication

Lutheran Libraries (q.; memb.; nonmemb. $25).

Board Chairpersons

Advisory. Rolf Aaseng.
Finance. L. Edwin Wang.

Library Services. Betty Le Dell.
Publications. Rod Olson.
Telecommunications. Chuck Mann

Medical Library Association

Executive Director, Carla Funk
6 N. Michigan Ave., Suite 300, Chicago, IL 60602
312-419-9094, fax 312-419-8950
E-mail info@mlahq.org; World Wide Web http://mlanet.org

Object

The major purposes of the Medical Library Association (MLA) are to foster medical and allied scientific libraries, to promote the educational and professional growth of health science librarians, and to exchange medical literature among the members. Through its programs and publications, MLA encourages professional development of its membership, whose foremost concern is dissemination of health sciences information for those in research, education, and patient care. Founded 1898; incorporated 1934.

Membership

Memb. (Inst.) 1,300; (Indiv.) 3,700. Institutional members are medical and allied scientific libraries. Individual members are people who are (or were at the time membership was established) engaged in professional library or bibliographic work in medical and allied scientific libraries or people who are interested in medical or allied scientific libraries. Dues (Student) $25; (Emeritus) $40; (Intro.) $75; (Indiv.) $110; (Sustaining) $345; and (Inst.) $175–$410, based on the number of the library's periodical subscriptions. Members may be affiliated with one or more of MLA's 23 special-interest sections and 14 regional chapters.

Officers

Pres. Rachael K. Anderson, Arizona Health Sciences Lib., 1501 N. Campbell Ave., Tuc-son, AZ 85724; *Pres.-Elect* Jacqueline Donaldson Doyle, Samaritan Health System, 1111 E. McDowell Rd., Box 2989, Phoenix AZ 85062-2989; *Past Pres.* Naomi C. Broering, Houston Academyh of Medicine, Texas Medical Center Lib., 1133 M. D. Anderson Blvd., Houston, TX 77030.

Directors

Shelley A. Bader (1998), Cynthia H. Goldstein (1998), Elaine Russo Martin (1999), James Shedlock (1999), Diane Schwartz (2000), Bernie Todd Smith (2000), Patricia L. Thibodeau (1999), Linda A. Watson (1999), Kay E. Wellik (1998).

Publications

Bulletin of the Medical Library Association (q.; $136).
Directory of the Medical Library Association, 1992/93 ($150).
MLA News (10 per year; $48.50).
Miscellaneous (request current list from association headquarters).

Committee Chairpersons

Awards. Thomas Williams.
Books (Panel). Elizabeth H. Wood.
Bulletin Editorial Board. J. Michael Homan.
Bylaws. Mary Mylenki.
Continuing Education. Judith Robinson.
Credentialing. Billie Jean Schorre.
Exchange (Advisory). Deborah H. Sibley.

Governmental Relations. Roger Guard.

Grants and Scholarships. Brenda Faye Green.

Health Sciences Library Technicians. Marcia I. Batchelor.

Joseph Leiter NLM/MLA Lectureship. Frances E. Johnson.

Membership. Theresa L. Knott.

National Program (1998). Frieda O. Weise

National Program (1999). Mark E. Funk.

National Program (2000). Brett A. Kirkpatrick.

Oral History. Tom Flemming.

Professional Recognition (Review Panel). Alan Carr.

Publications. Kelly Hensley.

Publishing and Information Industries Relations. Ruth H. Maniken.

Status and Economic Interests. Kathleen Cimpl Wagner.

Ad Hoc Committee and Task Force Charges

Centennial Coordinating. June H. Fulton.

Executive. Naomi C. Broering.

Joint MLA/AAHSLD Legislative (Task Force). Marianne Puckett.

Research Policy Implementation. Joanne G. Marshall.

Professional Development. Carol G. Jenkins.

Role of Information Professionals in the 21st Century. Wayne P. Peay.

Music Library Association

Box 487, Canton, MA 02021
617-828-8450, fax 617-828-8915
E-mail adadsvc@aol.com

Object

To promote the establishment, growth, and use of music libraries; to encourage the collection of music and musical literature in libraries; to further studies in musical bibliography; to increase efficiency in music library service and administration; and to promote the profession of music librarianship. Founded 1931.

Membership

Memb. 2,000. Dues (Inst.) $90; (Indiv.) $75; (Retired) $45; (Student) $35. Year. Sept. 1–Aug. 31.

Officers

Pres. Diane Parr Walker, Office of the Libn., Alderman Lib., Univ. of Virginia, Charlottesville, VA 22903-2498. Tel. 804-924-4606, fax 804-924-1431, e-mail dpw@poe. acc.virginia.edu; *V.P./Pres.-Elect* Paula D.

Matthews George and Helen Ladd Lib., Bates College, Lewiston, ME 04240. Tel. 207-786-6266, fax 207-786-6055, e-mail pmatthew@abacus.bates.edu. *Rec. Secy.* Roberta Chodacki, Music Lib., East Carolina Univ., Greenville, NC 27858-4353. Tel. 252-328-1239, fax 252-328-1243, e-mail chodackir@mail.ecu.edu; *Treas.* James P. Cassaro, 550 Warren Rd., Ithaca, NY 14850-1853. Tel. 607-255-7046, fax 607-254-2877, e-mail jpc3@cornell.edu; *Exec. Secy.* Bonna J. Boettcher, Music Lib. and Sound Recording Archives, Jerome Lib., 3rd fl., Bowling Green State Univ., Bowling Green, OH 43403-0179. Tel. 419-372-2307, fax 419-372-7996, e-mail bboettc@bgnet.bgsu.edu.

Members-at-Large

Deborah Campana, Northwestern Univ.; Michael Colby, Univ. of California–Davis; Robert Curtis, Tulane Univ.; Bonnie Jo Dopp, Univ. of Maryland; Edwin A. (Ned) Quist, Peabody Conservatory of Music; Daniel Zager, Concordia Univ.

Special Officers

Advertising Mgr. Susan Dearborn, 1572 Massachusetts Ave., No. 57, Cambridge, MA 02138. Tel. 617-876-0934; *Business Mgr.* Academic Services, c/o Music Library Assn., Box 487, Canton, MA 02021. Tel. 781-828-8450, fax 781-828-8915, e-mail acadsvc@aol.com; *Convention Mgr.* Susan H. Hitchens, 225 N. Oakhurst Dr., No. 17, Aurora, IL 60504. Tel. 630-585-6115, e-mail susadorm@ameritech.net; *Placement* Elizabeth Rebman, Music Lib., Morrison Hall, Univ. of California, Berkeley, CA 94720. Tel. 510-643-5198, e-mail arcbman@library.berkeley.edu; *Publicity* Leslie Bennett, Knight Lib., Music Services, Univ. of Oregon, Eugene, OR 97103. Tel. 503-346-1930, e-mail lbennett@oregon.uoregon.edu.

Publications

MLA Index and Bibliography Series (irreg.; price varies).
MLA Newsletter (q.; memb.).
MLA Technical Reports (irreg.; price varies).
Music Cataloging Bulletin (mo.; $25).
Notes (q.; indiv. $70; inst. $80).

Committee and Roundtable Chairpersons

Administration. Deborah Pierce, Univ. of Washington.

Bibliographic Control. Linda Barnhart, Univ. of California–San Diego.

Development. Laura Dankner, Loyola Univ.

Education. Lois Kuyper-Rushing, Louisiana State Univ.

Finance. Michael Colby, Univ. of California at Davis.

Legislation. Lenore Coral, Cornell Univ.

Membership. Geraldine Ostrove, Lib. of Congress.

Nominating, November 1998 ballot. Marjorie Hassen, Univ. of Pennsylvania.

Preservation. Brenda Nelson-Strauss, Chicago Symphony Orchestra.

Public Libraries. Jeannette Casey, Chicago Public Lib.

Publications. Susan T. Sommer, New York Public Lib.

Reference and Public Service. Ruthann McTyre, Baylor Univ.

Resource Sharing and Collection Development. William Coscarelli, Univ. of Georgia.

National Association of Government Archives and Records Administrators

Executive Director, Bruce W. Dearstyne
48 Howard St., Albany, NY 12207
518-463-8644, fax 518-463-8656
E-mail nagara@caphill.com

Object

Founded in 1984, the association is successor to the National Association of State Archives and Records Administrators, which had been established in 1974. NAGARA is a growing nationwide association of local, state, and federal archivists and records administrators, and others interested in improved care and management of government records. NAGARA promotes public awareness of government records and archives management programs, encourages interchange of information among government archives and records management agencies, develops and implements professional standards of government records and archival administration, and encourages study and research into records management problems and issues.

Membership

Most NAGARA members are federal, state, and local archival and records management agencies.

Officers

Pres. Kathryn Hammond Baker, Pres., Archives of the Commonwealth of Massachusetts; *V.P.* Pete Schinkel, Georgia Dept. of Archives and History; *Secy.* Gerald G. Newborg, State Historical Society of North Dakota; *Treas.* Jim Berberich, Florida Bureau of Archives and Records Management.

Directors

David H. Hoober, Arizona Dept. of Lib., Archives and Public Records; Laura McGee, City of Dallas, Texas; Michael Miller, U.S. Environmental Protection Agency; Robert Martin, Texas State Lib.; Roy Turnbaugh, Oregon State Archives; Terry Ellis, Salt Lake County (UT) Records Managment and Archives.

Publications

Clearinghouse (q.; memb.).
Crosswords.
Government Records Issues (series).
Preservation Needs in State Archives (report).
Program Reporting Guidelines for Government Records Programs.

National Federation of Abstracting and Information Services

Executive Director, Richard T. Kaser
1518 Walnut St., Philadelphia, PA 19102
215-893-1561, fax 215-893-1564
E-mail nfais@nfais.org

Object

NFAIS is an international, not-for-profit membership organization comprising leading information producers, distributors, and corporate users of secondary information. Its purpose is to serve the information community through education, research, and publication. Founded 1958.

Membership

Memb. 60+. Full membership (regular and government) is open to organizations that, as a substantial part of their activity, produce secondary information services for external use. Secondary information products are compilations containing printed or electronic summaries of, or references to, multiple sources of publicly available information. For example, organizations that assemble biblio-graphic citations, abstracts, indexes, and data are all secondary information services.

Associate membership is available to organizations that operate or manage online information services, networks, in-house information centers, and libraries; conduct research or development work in information science or systems; are otherwise involved in the generation, promotion, or distribution of secondary information products under contract; or publish primary information sources. Members pay dues annually based on the fiscal year of July 1–June 30. Dues are assessed based on the member's revenue derived from information-related activities.

Officers (1997–1998)

Pres. John Anderson; *Past Pres.* Taissa Kusma; *Pres.-Elect* James E. Lohr; *Secy.* Gladys Cotter; *Treas.* George Lewicky.

Directors

Dennis Auld, Brian Earle, Sheldon Kotzin, Jim Mcginty, Brian Sweet, Michael Tansey.

Staff

Exec. Dir. Richard T. Kaser; *Asst. Dir.* Marian H. Gloninger; *Office Mgr.* Wendy Carter; *Customer Service* Margaret Manson.

Publications

Automated Support to Indexing (1992; memb. $50; nonmemb. $75).
Beyond Boolean (1996; memb. $50; nonmemb. $75).
Careers in Electronic Information (1997; memb. $29; nonmemb. $39).
Changing Roles in Information Distribution (1994; memb. $50; nonmemb. $75).
Developing New Markets for Information Products (1993; memb. $50; nonmemb. $75).
Document Delivery in an Electronic Age (1995; memb. $50, nonmemb. $75).
Flexible Workstyles in the Information Industry (1993; memb. $50; nonmemb. $75).
Government Information and Policy: Changing Roles in a New Administration (1994; memb. $50; nonmemb. $75).
Guide to Careers in Abstracting and Indexing (1992; memb. $25; nonmemb. $35).
Guide to Database Distribution, 2nd ed., (1994; memb. $100; nonmemb. $175).
Impacts of Changing Production Technologies (1995; memb. $50, nonmemb. $75).
NFAIS Member Directory and Guide to Leading Information Companies (1996; memb. $25, nonmemb. $35).
NFAIS Newsletter (mo.; North America $120; elsewhere $135).
Partnering in the Information Industry (1996; memb. $50, nonmemb. $75).

National Information Standards Organization

Executive Director, Patricia R. Harris
4733 Bethesda Ave., Suite 300, Bethesda, MD 20814
301-654-2512, fax 301-654-1721
E-mail nisohq@cni.org, World Wide Web http://www.niso.org

Object

To develop technical standards used in libraries, publishing, and information services. Experts from the information field volunteer to lend their expertise in the development and writing of NISO standards. The standards are approved by the consensus of NISO's voting membership, which consists of 70 voting members representing libraries, government, associations, and private businesses and organizations. NISO is supported by its membership and corporate grants. Formerly a committee of the American National Standards Institute (ANSI), NISO, formed in 1939, was incorporated in 1983 as a nonprofit educational organization. NISO is accredited by ANSI and serves as the U.S. Technical Advisory Group to ISO/TC 46.

Membership

Memb. 70. Open to any organization, association, government agency, or company willing to participate in and having substantial concern for the development of NISO standards.

Officers

Chair Joel H. Baron, Publisher, The *New England Journal of Medicine*, 1440 Main St., Waltham, MA 02154; *Past Chair* Michael J. McGill, Chief Info. Officer, Univ. of Michigan Medical Center, 4251 Plymouth Rd., Suite 3300, Ann Arbor, MI 48105; *V. Chair/ Chair-Elect* Donald J. Muccino, Exec. V.P./ COO, Online Computer Library Center, 6565

Frantz Rd., Dublin, OH 43017-0702; *Exec. Dir./Secy.* Patricia R. Harris, NISO, 4733 Bethesda Ave., Suite 300, Bethesda, MD 20814; *Dirs.* Robert C. Badger, Springer Verlag, New York, NY; Vinod Chachra, VTLS, Blacksburg, VA; Elizabeth Bole Eddison, Inmagic, Woburn, MA; Brian Green, BIC/EDitEUR, London, UK; Marjorie Hlava, Access Innovations, Albuquerque, NM; Beverly P. Lynch, UCLA; Clifford Lynch, Univ. of California, Oakland, CA; Donald J. Muccino, OCLC, Dublin, OH; Nolan F. Pope, Univ. of Wisconsin–Madison; Albert Simmonds, R. R. Bowker, New Providence, NJ; Lennie Stovel, Research Lib. Group, Mountain View, CA; Howard Turtle, West Publishing, Eagan, MN 55123.

Publications

Information Standards Quarterly (q.; $78; foreign $120).

NISO published standards are available from NISO Press Fulfillment, Box 338, Oxon Hill, MD 20750-0338. Tel. 301-567-9522, 800-282-6476, fax 301-567-9553, e-mail nisohq@cni.org.

NISO Press catalogs and the *NISO Annual Report* are available on request.

REFORMA
(National Association to Promote Library Services to the Spanish Speaking)

President, Sandra Balderrama, American Library Association
50 E. Huron St., Chicago, IL 60611
E-mail sbalderr@ala.org

Object

Promoting library services to the Spanish-speaking for more than 25 years, REFORMA, an ALA affiliate, works in a number of areas: to promote the development of library collections to include Spanish-language and Hispanic-oriented materials; the recruitment of more bilingual and bicultural professionals and support staff; the development of library services and programs that meet the needs of the Hispanic community; the establishment of a national network among individuals who share our goals; the education of the U.S. Hispanic population in regard to the availability and types of library services; and lobbying efforts to preserve existing library resource centers serving the interest of Hispanics.

Officers

Pres. Sandra Balderrama, American Lib. Assn., 50 E. Huron St., Chicago, IL 60611. E-mail sbalderr@ala.org; *V.P./Pres.-Elect* Jacqueline Ayala, Box 88756, Los Angeles, CA 90009-8756. Tel. 310-282-6279, fax 310-827-9187, e-mail jayala@earthlink.net; *Past Pres.* Edward Erazo, New Mexico State Univ., Box 30006, Dept. 3475, Las Cruces, NM 88003-8006. Tel. 505-646-6930, fax 505-646-6940, e-mail ederazo@lib.nmsu.edu; *Treas.* Rene Amaya, East Los Angeles Public Lib., 4801 E. Third St., Los Angeles, CA 90033. Tel. 213-264-0155, fax 213-264-5465; *Secy.* Vivian Pisano, Oakland Public Lib., 125 14th St., Oakland, CA 94612. Tel. 510-238-6719; *Newsletter Ed.* Denice Adkins; *Archivist* Salvador Guerena; *Membership Coordinator* Al Milo.

Membership

Memb. 900. Any person who is supportive of the goals and objectives of REFORMA.

Publications

REFORMA Membership Directory. Eds. Al Milo, Dir., Fullerton Public Lib., 353 W.

Commonwealth Ave., Fullerton, CA 92632; Edward Erazo, REFORMA, New Mexico State Univ., Box 30006, Dept. 3475, Las Cruces, NM 88003-8006. Tel. 505-646-6930, fax 505-646-6940, e-mail ederazo@lib.nmsu.edu.

REFORMA Newsletter (q.; memb.). *Ed.* Ramiro Gonzalez, San Diego Public Lib., James P. Beckworth Branch, 721 Pasqual, San Diego, CA 92113. Tel. 619-527-3408, fax 619-236-5878, e-mail r4g@library.sannet.gov.

Committees

Children's and Young Adult Service. Oralia Garza de Cortez.

Information Technology. Carlos Rodriguez.

Librarian-of-the-Year Award. Lillian Castillo-Speed.

Nominations. Ben Ocon.

Organizational Development. Linda Chavez Doyle.

Public Relations. Edward Erazo.

Scholarship. Luis Chaparro.

Meetings

General membership and board meetings take place at the American Library Association's Midwinter meeting and annual conference.

Research Libraries Group, Inc.

Manager of Corporate Communications, Jennifer Hartzell
1200 Villa St., Mountain View, CA 94041-1100
650-691-2207, fax 650-964-0943
E-mail bl.jlh@rlg.org, World Wide Web http://www.rlg.org

Object

The Research Libraries Group, Inc. (RLG) is a not-for-profit membership corporation of over 150 universities, archives, historical societies, national libraries, and other institutions devoted to improving access to information that supports research and learning. RLG exists to support its members in containing costs, improving local services, and contributing to the nation's collective access to scholarly materials. For its members, RLG develops and operates cooperative programs to manage, preserve, and extend access to research library, museum, and archival holdings. For both its members and for nonmember institutions and individuals worldwide, RLG develops and operates databases and software to serve an array of information access and management needs. Ariel, CitaDel, Eureka, Marcadia, RLIN, and Zephyr are trademarks of the Research Libraries Group, Inc.

Membership

Memb. 150+. Membership is open to any nonprofit institution with an educational, cultural, or scientific mission. There are two membership categories: general and special. General members are institutions that serve a clientele of more than 5,000 faculty, academic staff, research staff, professional staff, students, fellows, or members. Special members serve a similar clientele of 5,000 or fewer.

Directors

RLG has a 19-member board of directors, comprising 12 directors elected from and by RLG's member institutions, up to six at-large directors elected by the board itself, and the president. Theirs is the overall responsibility for the organization's governance and for ensuring that it faithfully fulfills its purpose and goals. Annual board elections are held in the spring. In 1998 the board's chair is Martin Runkle, Director, University of Chicago Library. For a current list of directors, contact RLG.

Staff

Pres. James Michalko; *V.P.* John W. Haeger; *Dir., Member Programs and Initiatives* Linda West; *Dir., Customer and Operations Support* Jack Grantham; *Dir., Computer Development* David Richards; *Dir., Finance and Administration* Molly Singer.

Publications

Digital Imaging Technology for Preservation (symposium proceedings).
Electronic Access to Information: A New Service Paradigm (symposium proceedings).

Research Libraries Group News (3 per year; 16-page news magazine).
RLG Archives Microfilming Manual (RLG-developed guidelines and practice).
RLG DigiNews (bi-m.; Web-based newsletter to help keep pace with preservation uses of digitization.)
RLG Digital Image Access Project *(final workshop proceedings).*
RLG Preservation Microfilming Handbook *(RLG-developed guidelines and practice).*
RLIN Focus *(bi-m.; eight-page user services newsletter).*
Scholarship in the New Information Environment *(symposium proceedings).*
Selecting Library and Archive Collections for Digital Reformatting *(symposium proceedings).*
Contact RLG for other informational and user publications available.

Society for Scholarly Publishing

Executive Directors, Francine Butler, Jerry Bowman
10200 W. 44 Ave., Suite 304, Wheat Ridge, CO 80033
303-422-3914, fax 303-422-8894
E-mail 5686814@mcimail.com

Object

To draw together individuals involved in the process of scholarly publishing. This process requires successful interaction of the many functions performed within the scholarly community. The Society for Scholarly Publishing (SSP) provides the leadership for such interaction by creating opportunities for the exchange of information and opinions among scholars, editors, publishers, librarians, printers, booksellers, and all others engaged in scholarly publishing.

Membership

Memb. 950. Open to all with an interest in the scholarly publishing process and dissemination of information. There are four cate-

gories of membership: individual ($65), contributing ($500), sustaining ($1,000), and sponsoring ($1,500). Year. Jan. 1–Dec. 31.

Executive Committee (July 1997–June 1998)

Pres. Jan Fleming, Cadmus Journal Services, 940 Elkridge Landing Rd., Linthicum, MD 21090-2908; *Pres.-Elect* Frederick Bowes, III, Bowes & Assoc., Box 1637, Buxbury, MA 02331-1637; *Secy.-Treas.* Patricia Sabosik, Elsevier Science, 655 Ave. of the Americas, New York, NY 10010-5107; *Past Pres.* Margaret Foti, American Assn. for Cancer Research, Public Ledger Bldg., Suite 816, 150 S. Independence Mall W., Philadelphia, PA 19106-3485.

Meetings

An annual meeting is conducted in June. The location changes each year. Additionally, SSP conducts several seminars throughout the year.

Publications

Scholarly Publishing Today (q.; memb., non-memb. $70)

Society of American Archivists

Executive Director, Susan E. Fox
527 S. Wales St., Fifth flr., Chicago, IL 60607
312-922-0140, fax 312-347-1452

Object

To promote sound principles of archival economy and to facilitate cooperation among archivists and archival agencies. Founded 1936.

Membership

Memb. 3,800. Dues (Indiv.) $65–$170, graduated according to salary; (Assoc.) $65, domestic; (Student) $40, with a two-year maximum on membership; (Inst.) $210; (Sustaining) $410.

Officers (1997–1998)

Pres. William J. Maher; *V.P.* Loretta Duranti; *Treas.* Robert Sink.

Council

Valerie Browne, Bruce Bruemmer, Fynnette Eaton, Anne Gilliland-Swetland, Lori Hefner, Peter Hirtle, Karen Jefferson, Sharon Thibodeau, Sharron Uhler.

Staff

Exec. Dir. Susan E. Fox; *Meetings/Memb. Coord.* Bernice E. Brack; *Publications Dir.* Teresa Brinati; *Publications Asst.* Troy Sturdivant; *Bookkeeper* Carroll Dendler; *Educ. Dir.* Joan Sander.

Publications

American Archivist (q.; $75; foreign $90). *Ed.* Philip Eppard; *Managing Ed.* Teresa Brinati. Books for review and related correspondence should be addressed to the managing editor.
Archival Outlook (bi-m.; memb.). *Ed.* Teresa Brinati.

Special Libraries Association

Executive Director, David R. Bender
1700 18 St. N.W., Washington, DC 20009-2508
202-234-4700, fax 202-265-9317
E-mail slal@sla.org, World Wide Web http://www.sla.org

Object

To advance the leadership role of special librarians in putting knowledge to work in the information and knowledge-based society. The association offers myriad programs and services designed to help its members serve their customers more effectively and succeed in an increasingly challenging environment of information management and technology.

Membership

Memb. 14,500. Dues (Sustaining) $400; (Indiv.) $105; (Student) $25. Year. July–June.

Officers (July 1997–June 1998)

Pres. Judith J. Field. *Pres.-Elect* L. Susan Hayes; *Past Pres.* Sylvia E. A. Piggott; *Treas.* Richard Wallace; *Chapter Cabinet Chair* Peter S. Moon; *Chapter Cabinet Chair-Elect* Anne K. Abate; *Div. Cabinet Chair* Rebecca Vargha; *Div. Chapter Chair-Elect* Richard P. Hulser.

Directors

Officers; Stephen Abram (1999), Monica M. Ertel (2000), Cynthia V. Hill (2000), Bruce Hubbard (1998), Sharyn Ladner (1999), Julia C. Peterson (1998).

Publications

Information Outlook (mo.) (memb., non-memb. $65/yr. *Ed.* Douglas Newcomb.

Committee Chairpersons

Affirmative Action. Rosalind Lett.
Association Office Operations. Sylvia E. A. Piggott.
Awards and Honors. Jane Dysart.
Bylaws. Eleanor MacLean.
Cataloging. Dorothy McGarry.
Committees. James B. Tchobanoff.
Conference Program (1998). Gloria Zamora.
Conference Program (1999). Susan Klopper.
Consultation Service. Janice Suter.
Copyright. Lawrence Guthrie.
Finance. Richard Wallace.
Government Relations. Joan Gervino.
Innovations in Technology Award. Hope Tillman.
International Relations. Barbara Hutchinson.
Networking. Sandra Spurlock.
Nominating, Spring 1999 Election. Ethel Salonen.
Professional Development. Carol Ginsberg.
Public Relations. Mary E. Marshall.
Research. Laura N. Gasaway.
SLA Scholarship. Bill Fisher.
Strategic Planning. Stephen Abram.
Student and Academic Relations. Barbara Semonche.
Technical Standards. Marjorie Hlava.
Tellers. Marilyn Bromley.
H. W. Wilson Award. Anne Galler.

Theatre Library Association

c/o The Shubert Archive, 149 W. 45th St., New York, NY 10036
212-944-3895, fax 212-944-4139

Object

To further the interests of collecting, preserving, and using theater, cinema, and performing-arts materials in libraries, museums, and private collections. Founded 1937.

Membership

Memb. 500. Dues (Indiv./Inst.) $30. Year. Jan. 1–Dec. 31.

Officers

Pres. Geraldine Duclow, Free Lib. of Philadelphia; *V.P.* Susan Brady, Yale Univ.; *Exec. Secy.* Maryann Chach, Shubert Archive; *Treas.* Jane Suda, New York Public Lib. for the Performing Arts.

Executive Board

Susan Peters, Nena Couch, Rosemary Cullen, Annette Fern, B. Donald Grose, Mary Ann Jensen, Martha S. LoMonaco, Lois Erickson McDonald, Paul Newman, Louis A. Rachow, Anne G. Schlosser, Kevin Winkler; *Ex officio* Madeleine Nichols; *Honorary* Paul Myers; *Historian* Louis A. Rachow.

Publications

Broadside (q.; memb.). *Ed.* Maryann Chach. *Performing Arts Resources* (ann.; memb.). *Ed.* Publications Committee.

Committee Chairpersons

Awards. Richard Wall.
Membership. Geraldine Duclow.
Nominations. Martha S. LoMonaco.
Program and Special Events. Kevin Winkler.
Publications. Maryann Chach, Catherine Johnson.

Urban Libraries Council

President, Eleanor Jo (Joey) Rodger
1603 Orrington Ave., Suite 1080, Evanston, IL 60201
847-866-9999, fax 847-866-9989
E-mail ulc@gpl.glenview.lib.il.us; World Wide Web http://www.clpgh.org/ulc/

Object

To identify and make known the problems relating to urban libraries serving cities of 50,000 or more individuals, located in a Standard Metropolitan Statistical Area; to provide information on state and federal legislation affecting urban library programs and systems; to facilitate the exchange of ideas and programs of member libraries and other libraries; to develop programs that enable libraries to act as a focus of community development and to supply the informational needs of the new urban populations; to conduct research and educational programs that will benefit urban libraries and to solicit and accept grants, contributions, and donations essential to their implementation.

ULC currently receives most of its funding from membership dues. Future projects will involve the solicitation of grant funding.

ULC is a 501(c)(3) not-for-profit corporation based in the state of Illinois.

Membership

Membership is open to public libraries serving populations of 50,000 or more located in a Standard Metropolitan Statistical Area and to corporations specializing in library-related materials and services. Dues are based on the size of the organization's operating budget, according to the following schedule: under $2 million, $1,000; $2 million to $5 million, $1,250; $5 million to $10 million, $1,500; $10 million to $15 million, $2,000; over $15 million, $2,500. In addition, ULC member libraries may choose Sustaining or Contributing status (Sustaining, $10,000; Contributing, $5,000).

Officers (1997–1998)

Chair Robert B. Croneberger, Carnegie Lib. of Pittsburgh, 4400 Forbes Ave., Pittsburgh, PA 15213. Tel. 412-622-3100, fax 412-622-6278, e-mail croneberger@clpgh.org; *V. Chair/Chair Elect* Andrew Blau, Communications Policy Project, Benton Foundation, 1634 Eye Street, 12th flr., Washington, DC 20006. Tel. 202-638-5770, fax 202-638-5771, e-mail blau@benton.org; *Secy./Treas.* Susan Kent, Los Angeles Public Lib., 630 W. Fifth St., Los Angeles, CA 90071. Tel. 213-228-7516, fax 213-228-7519, e-mail skent@lapl.org.

Officers serve one-year terms, members of the executive board two-year terms. New officers are elected and take office at the summer annual meeting of the council.

Executive Board

Steven A. Coulter. E-mail coult@pacbell.net; Mary Doty. Tel. 612-332-7853; Toni Garvey. E-mail tgarvey@ci.phoenix.az.us; Harriet Henderson. E-mail Hendeh@co.mo.md.us; Frances Hunter. E-mail fran@cua3.csuohio.edu; Marilyn Jackson. E-mail marilyn.jackson@state.mn.us; G. Victor Johnson. E-mail Vic-Johnson@Checkers-LLP.COM; Roslyn Kurland. E-mail rkurland@mailer.fsu.edu; Betty Jane Narver. E-mail bjnarver@u.washington.edu; Elliot L. Shelkrot. E-mail shelkrot@hslc.org; Edward M. Szynaka. E-mail eds@imcpl.lib.in.us.

Key Staff

Pres. Eleanor Jo Rodger; *V.P., Admin. and Program* Bridget A. Bradley; *Project Dir.* Marybeth Schroeder; *Admin. Assistant* Sheila Kessler.

Publications

Frequent Fast Facts Surveys: *Fund Raising and Financial Development Survey Results* (1993); *Staffing Survey Results* (1993); *Collection Development Survey Results* (1994); *Library Security Survey Results* (1994); *Public Libraries and Private Fund Raising: Opportunities and Issues* (1994); *Off Site Survey Results* (1995); *Governance and Funding of Urban Public Libraries Survey Results* (1997); *Internet Access and Use Survey Results* (1997).
Urban Libraries Exchange (mo.; memb.).

State, Provincial, and Regional Library Associations

The associations in this section are organized under three headings: United States, Canada, and Regional. Both the United States and Canada are represented under Regional associations.

United States

Alabama

Memb. 1,200. Term of Office. Apr. 1997–Apr. 1998. Publication. *The Alabama Librarian* (q.).

Pres. Nancy Simms Donahoo, North Shelby County Lib.; *Secy.* Jane Garrett, 3533 Honeysuckle Rd., Montgomery 36109; *Treas.* Donna Fitch, 2917 Dublin Dr., Helena 35080; *Exec. Dir.* Barbara Black, 400 S. Union St., Suite 255, Montgomery 36104. Tel. 334-262-5210, fax 334-834-6398.

Address correspondence to the executive director.

Alaska

Memb. 359. Publication. *Newspoke* (bi-mo.).

Pres. Barbara Berg. E-mail barbarab@muskox.alaska.edu; *V.P.* Charlotte Glover. E-mail charg@muskox.alaska.edu; *Secy.* Judy Green. E-mail afjfg@uaa.alaska.edu; *Treas.* Peg Thompson. E-mail pegt@muskox.alaska.edu; *Exec. Secy.* Bob Anderl. E-mail boba@muskox.alaska.edu. Association e-mail akla@alaska.net, fax 907-479-4784.

Address correspondence to the secretary, Alaska Library Association, Box 81084, Fairbanks 99708.

Arizona

Memb. 1,200. Term of Office. Nov. 1997–Dec. 1998. Publication. *AzLA Newsletter* (mo.). Articles for the newsletter should be sent to the attention of the newsletter editor.

Pres. Louise Stephens, Glendale Public Lib., 5959 W. Brown St., Glendale 85302. Tel. 602-930-3567, fax 602-842-4209, e-mail lstephe@glenpub.lib.az.us; *Treas.* Sharon Laser, Scottsdale Public Lib., 3839 Civic Center Blvd., Scottsdale 85251. Tel. 602-994-2692, fax 602-994-7993; *Exec. Secy.* Jean Johnson, 14449 N. 73 St., Scottsdale 85260-3133. Tel. 602-998-1954, fax 602-998-7838, e-mail meetmore@aol.com.

Address correspondence to the executive secretary.

Arkansas

Memb. 603. Term of Office. Jan.–Dec. 1998. Publication. *Arkansas Libraries* (bi-mo.).

Pres. Mary Farris, Dir., Lib., Garland County Community College, 101 College Dr., Hot Springs 71913; *Exec. Dir.* Jennifer Coleman, Arkansas Lib. Assn., 9 Shackleford Plaza, Little Rock 72211. Tel. 501-661-1127, fax 501-228-5535.

Address correspondence to the executive director.

California

Memb. 2,500. Term of Office. Nov. 1997–Nov. 1998. Publication. *California Libraries* (mo., except July/Aug., Nov./Dec.).

Pres. Anne Marie Gold, Contra Costa County Lib.; *V.P./Pres.-Elect* Anne Campbell, National City Public Lib.; *Exec. Dir.* Mary Sue Ferrell, California Lib. Assn., 717 K St., Suite 300, Sacramento 95814. Tel. 916-447-8541, fax 916-447-8394, e-mail info@cal-net.org. Organization World Wide Web site http://www.cla-net.org.

Address correspondence to the executive director.

Colorado

Memb. 863. Term of Office. Oct. 1997–Oct. 1998. Publication. *Colorado Libraries* (q.). *Ed.* Nancy Carter, Univ. of Colorado, Campus Box 184, Boulder 80309.

Pres. William Knott, Jefferson County Public Lib., 10200 W. 20th Ave., Lakewood 80215. Tel. 303-275-2200, fax 303-275-2202, e-mail wknott@csn.net; *V.P./Pres.-Elect* James LaRue, Douglas Public Lib. District, 961 S. Plum Creek Blvd., Castle

Rock 80104. Tel. 303-688-8752, fax 303-688-1942, e-mail jlarue@csn.net; *Treas.* George Jaramillo, Univ. of Northern Colorado, Greeley 80634; *Exec. Dir.* Ruth Jarles.

Address correspondence to the executive director at the association, Box 140355, Edgewater 80214. Tel. 303-205-9284, fax 303-205-9285.

Connecticut

Memb. 1,100. Term of Office. July 1997–June 1998. Publication *Connecticut Libraries* (11 per year). *Ed.* David Kapp, 4 Llynwood Dr., Bolton 06040. Tel. 203-647-0697.

Pres. Robert Gallucci, Brookfield Lib., Brookfield 06804. Tel. 203-775-0235; *V.P./ Pres.-Elect* Michael Moran, Asnuntuck Community Technical College, Enfield 06082. Tel. 860-253-3171; *Treas.* Jeanne Sohn, Burnett Lib., Central Connecticut State Univ., New Britain 06050. Tel. 860-832-2097; *Administrator* Karen Zoller, Connecticut Lib. Assn., Franklin Commons, 106 Rte. 32, Franklin 06254. Tel. 860-885-2758.

Address correspondence to the administrator.

Delaware

Memb. 300. Term of Office. Apr. 1997–Apr. 1998. Publication *DLA Bulletin* (3 per year).

Pres. David Burdash, Wilmington Institute Lib., Wilmington. Tel. 302-571-7400; *V.P./ Pres.-Elect* Robert Dugan, Wesley College Lib., Dover. Tel. 302-736-2413; *Secy.* Charles Longfellow, Delaware State Univ., Dover. Tel. 302-739-5111; *Treas.* Paula Davino, Dover Public Lib. Tel. 302-736-7030.

Address correspondence to the association, Box 816, Dover 19903-0816.

District of Columbia

Memb. 600. Term of Office. Aug. 1997–Aug. 1998. Publication *INTERCOM* (mo.).

Pres. Dennis Reynolds, Exec. Dir., CAPCON, 1320 19th St. N.W., Suite 400, Washington 20036-1679. Tel. 202-331-5771, fax 202-797-7719, e-mail dreynold@capcon.net. *Secy.* Blanche Anderson, Arlington County Public Lib., 1015 N. Quincy St., Arlington, VA 22201. Tel. 703-358-6334, fax 703-358-

7720, e-mail banderso@leo.vsla.edu; *Treas.* Mary A. Martin, Sugar Assn., 1101 15 St. N.W., Suite 600, Washington 20005. Tel. 202-785-1122, fax 202-785-5019.

Address correspondence to the association, Box 14177, Benjamin Franklin Sta., Washington 20044.

Florida

Memb. (Indiv.) 1,506; (In-state Inst.) 93. Term of Office. July 1997–June 1998. Publication. *Florida Libraries* (bi-mo.).

Pres. Patricia De Salvo Young, Seminole Community College Lib., 100 Weldon Blvd., Sanford 32773. Tel. 407-328-4722, fax 407-328-2233, e-mail youngpscl@lincc.ccla.lib.fl.us; *Secy.* Laurie Linsley, Seminole Community College Lib., 100 Weldon Blvd., Sanford 32773. Tel. 407-328-4722 ext. 3335, fax 407-328-2233, e-mail llinsley@ipo.seminole.cc.fl.us; *Treas.* Kathleen de la Peña McCook, Univ. of South Florida, Box 1027, Ruskin 33570. Tel. 813-974-3520, fax 813-974-6840, e-mail kmccook@cis01.cis.usf.edu; *Exec. Secy.* Marjorie Stealey, Florida Lib. Assn., 1133 W. Morse Blvd., Suite 201, Winter Park 32789. Tel. 407-647-8839, fax 407-629-2502.

Address correspondence to the executive secretary.

Georgia

Memb. 1,100. Term of Office. Oct. 1997–Oct. 1998. Publication *Georgia Librarian.* *Ed.* Susan Cooley, Sara Hightower Regional Lib., 203 Riverside Pkwy., Rome 30161. Tel. 706-236-4621.

Pres. Alan Kaye, Dir., Roddenbery Memorial Lib., 320 N. Broad St., Cairo 31728. Tel. 912-377-3632, fax 912-377-7204, e-mail akaye@mail.grady.public.lib.ga.us; *1st V.P./ Pres.-Elect* Ann Hamilton, Assoc. Univ. Libn., Zach S. Henderson Lib., Georgia Southern Univ., Box 8074, Statesboro 30460-8074. Tel. 912-681-5115, fax 912-681-0093, e-mail ahamilton@gasou.edu; *2nd V.P.* Susan Kendall, Mgr., Sibley Branch, Cobb County Public Lib., 1539 S. Cobb Dr., Marietta 30060. Tel. 770-528-2520, fax 770-528-2594, e-mail mri@writeme.com; *Secy.* Susan White, Mgr., Pickens County Lib., 100

Library La., Jasper 30143. Tel. 706-692-5411, fax 706-692-9518, e-mail whites@mail.cherokee.public.lib.ga.us; *Treas.* Tom Budlong, Mgr., Buckhead Branch, Atlanta-Fulton Public Lib., 269 Buckhead Ave., Atlanta 30305. Tel. 404-814-3502, fax 404-814-3503, e-mail tbudlong@af.public.lib.ga.us; *Past Pres.* Richard Leach, East Central Regional Lib., 902 Greene St., Augusta 30901. Tel. 706-821-2600, fax 706-724-6762, e-mail leachr@mail.richmond.public.lib.ga.us; *ALA Councillor* Ralph E. Russell, 8160 Willow Tree Way, Alpharetta 30202. E-mail r1933@mindspring.com.

Address correspondence to the president.

Hawaii

Memb. 450. Publications. *HLA Newsletter* (q.); *HLA Journal* (ann.); *HLA Membership Directory* (ann.).

Address correspondence to the association, Box 4441, Honolulu 96812-4441.

Idaho

Memb. 500. Term of Office. Oct. 1997–Oct. 1998. Publication *Idaho Librarian* (q.). *Ed.* Mary Bolin, Univ. of Idaho Lib., Moscow 83844-2363. Tel. 208-885-7737, e-mail mbolin@uidaho.edu.

Pres. Dawn Wittman, Rte. 1, Box 47, Cul de Sac, Idaho 83524. Tel. 208-843-2960; *1st V.P.* Ron Force, Univ. of Idaho Lib., Moscow, Idaho 83844. Tel. 208-885-6534. *Treas.* Sandi Shropshire, F. M. Oboler Lib., Idaho State Univ., Box 8089, Pocatello 83209. Tel. 208-236-2671.

Address correspondence to the president.

Illinois

Memb. 3,000. Term of Office. July 1997–1998. Publication *ILA Reporter* (bi-mo.).

Pres. Kathleen M. Balcom, Arlington Heights Memorial Lib., 500 N. Dunton Ave., Arlington Heights 60004-5966. Tel. 847-506-2612, fax 847-506-2650, e-mail kbalcom@nslsilus.org; *V.P./Pres.-Elect* Pamela Gaitskill, Prairie State College, 202 S. Halsted st., Chicago Heights 60411-8226. Tel. 708-709-3551, fax 708-709-3940, e-mail pgaitskill@prairie.cc.il.us; *Treas.* Susan K. Herring, Peoria Public Lib., 107 N.E. Monroe St., Peoria 61602-1070. Tel. 309-672-8835, fax 309-674-0116, e-mail sherring@darkstar.rsa.lib.il.us; *Exec. Dir.* Robert P. Doyle, 33 W. Grand Ave., Suite 301, Chicago 60610. Tel. 312-644-1896, fax 312-644-1899, e-mail doyle@ila.org. Organization World Wide Web site http://www.ila.org.

Address correspondence to the executive director.

Indiana

Memb. (Indiv.) 3,000; (Inst.) 300. Term of Office. May 1997–May 1998. Publications. *Focus on Indiana Libraries* (11 per year), *Indiana Libraries* (s. ann.). *Ed.* Patricia Tallman.

Pres. Steven Schmidt, 50 S. Butler Ave., Indianapolis 46219. Tel. 317-274-0470, fax 317-274-0492, e-mail schmidt@library.iupui.edu; *1st V.P.* Charr Skirvin, Plainfield Public Lib., 1120 Stafford Rd., Plainfield 46168. Tel 317-839-6602, fax 317-839-4044, e-mail cskirvin.plpl@incolsa.palni.edu; *Secy.* Cheryl Blevens, Vigo County Public Lib., 1800 E. Fort Harrison, No. 5, Terre Haute 47804-1492. Tel. 812-232-1113; *Treas.* Connie Patsiner, IVAN, 6201 LaPaz Trail, Suite 280, Indianapolis 46268. Tel./fax 317-329-9163; *Past Pres.* Sally Otte, 5251 N. Delaware St., Indianapolis 46220. Tel. 317-257-5800; *Exec. Dir.* Linda D. Kolb.

Address correspondence to the Indiana Lib. Federation, 6408 Carrollton Ave., Indianapolis 46220. Tel. 317-257-2040, fax 317-257-1393.

Iowa

Memb. 1,700. Term of Office. Jan.–Dec. 1997. Publication *The Catalyst* (bi-mo.). *Ed.* Naomi Stovall.

Pres. Susan Kling, Marion Public Lib., 1095 Sixth Ave., Marion 52302; *V.P.* Mary Wegner, Central Iowa Health Systems, Des Moines 50300.

Address correspondence to the association, 505 Fifth Ave., Suite 823, Des Moines 50309. Tel. 515-243-2172, fax 515-243-0614, e-mail ialib@acad.drake.edu.

Kansas

Memb. 1,100. Term of Office. July 1997–
June 1998. Publications. *KLA Newsletter* (q.);
KLA Membership Directory (ann.).

Exec. Secy. Leroy Gattin, South Central
Kansas Lib. System, 901 N. Main St., Hutchinson 67501. Tel. 316-663-5441 ext. 110, fax
316-663-9506, e-mail lgatt@hplsck.org;
Secy. Marianne Eichelberger, Newton Public
Lib., 720 N. Oak, Newton 67114. Tel. 316-
283-2890, fax 316-283-2916; *Treas.* Marcel-
la Ratzlaff, Hutchinson Public Lib., 901 N.
Main St., Hutchinson 67501. Tel. 316-663-
5441.

Address correspondence to the executive
secretary.

Kentucky

Memb. 1,900. Term of Office. Oct. 1997–
Oct. 1998. Publication *Kentucky Libraries* (q.).

Pres. Sally Livingston. Tel. 502-485-3091;
V.P./Pres.-Elect Carol Brinkman. Tel. 502-
852-1008; *Secy.* Judith Gibbons. Tel. 606-
873-5191; *Exec. Secy.* Tom Underwood,
1501 Twilight Trail, Frankfort 40601. Tel.
502-223-5322.

Address correspondence to the executive
secretary.

Louisiana

Memb. (Indiv.) 1,500; (Inst.) 60. Term of
Office. July 1997–June 1998. Publication.
LLA Bulletin (q.). *Ed.* Mary Cosper Le
Boeuf, 424 Roussell St., Houma 70360. Tel.
504-876-5861, fax 504-876-5864, e-mail
ter@pelican.state.lib.la.us.

Pres. Carol Billings, 12 Swallow St., New
Orleans 70124. Tel. 504-568-5706, fax 504-
568-5069; *1st V.P./Pres.-Elect* Gloria Spooner,
312 Margaret St., Baton Rouge 70802-7038.
Tel. 504-342-4931, fax 504-342-3547, e-mail
gspooner@pelican.state.lib.la.us; *Exec. Secy.*
Christa Chandler. Tel. 504-342-4928.

Address correspondence to the association,
Box 3058, Baton Rouge 70821. Tel. 504-
342-4928, fax 504-342-3547, e-mail lla
@pelican.state.lib.la.us.

Maine

Memb. 900. Term of Office. (Pres., V.P.)
Spring 1996–Spring 1998. Publications.
Maine Entry (q.); *Maine Memo* (mo.).

Pres. Karen Reilly, Lib., Eastern Maine
Technical College, Bangor 04401. Tel. 207-
941-4606; *V.P.* Elizabeth Moran, Camden
Public Lib., Camden 04843. Tel. 207-236-
3440; *Secy.* Leanne Pander, Hawthorne-Long-
fellow Lib., Bowdoin College, Brunswick
04011. Tel. 207-725-3260; *Treas.* Robert Fil-
gate, McArthur Public Lib., Biddeford 04005.
Tel. 207-284-4181.

Address correspondence to the association,
60 Community Dr., Augusta 04330. Tel. 207-
623-8428, fax 207-626-5947.

Maryland

Memb. 1,300. Term of Office. July 1997–
1998. Publication *The Crab.*

Pres. Sharan Marshall, Southern Maryland
Regional Lib. Assn., Box 459, Charlotte Hall
20622-0459. Tel. 301-934-9442, fax 301-
884-0438; *V.P.* Sandra E. Owen, Harford
County Lib., 1221-A Brass Mill Road, Bel-
camp 21017. Tel. 410-273-5600 ext. 249, fax
410-273-5606, e-mail owen@vax1.harf.lib.
md.us.

Address correspondence to the association,
400 Cathedral St., Baltimore 21201-4401.
Tel. 410-727-7422, fax 410-625-9594, e-mail
mla@epfl1.epflbalto.org.

Massachusetts

Memb. (Indiv.) 950; (Inst.) 100. Term of
Office. July 1997–June 1998. Publication.
Bay State Librarian (10 per year).

Pres. Dierdre Hanley, Reading Public
Lib., 64 Middlesex Ave., Reading 01867.
Tel. 781-942-9110; *Treas.* Cynthia Roach,
Ostelville Free Lib., 43 Wianno Ave., Ostel-
ville 02655. Tel. 508-428-5757; *Exec. Secy.*
Barry Blaisdell, Massachusetts Lib. Assn.,
Countryside Offices, 707 Turnpike St., North
Andover 01845. Tel. 508-686-8543, e-mail
masslib@world.std.com.

Address correspondence to the executive
secretary.

Michigan

Memb. (Indiv.) 2,200; (Inst.) 375. Term of Office. July 1997–June 1998. Publication. *Michigan Librarian Newsletter* (10 per year).
Pres. Pamela Grudzien, Park Lib., Central Michigan Univ., Mount Pleasant, 48000; *Treas.* Tom Genson, Grand Rapids Public Lib., 60 Library Plaza N.E., Grand Rapids 49503; *Exec. Dir.* Marianne Hartzell, Michigan Lib. Assn., 6810 S. Cedar St., Suite 6, Lansing 48911. Tel. 517-694-6615.
Address correspondence to the executive director.

Minnesota

Memb. 1,079. Term of Office. (Pres., Pres.-Elect) Jan.–Dec. 1998; (Treas.) Jan. 1998–Dec. 1999; (Secy.) Jan. 1997–Dec. 1998. Publication. *MLA Newsletter* (6 per year).
Pres. Mary Martin, Univ. of Saint Thomas, 2115 Summit Ave., Saint Paul 55105; *Pres.-Elect* Beth Kelley, Duluth Public Lib., 520 Superior St., Duluth 55802; *ALA Chapter Councillor* Gretchen Marie Wronka, Hennepin County Lib., 12601 Ridgedale Dr., Minnetonka 55343; *Secy.* Janet Urbanowicz, Minneapolis Public Lib., 300 Nicollet Mall, Minneapolis 55401; *Treas.* Donald Kelsey, Univ. of Minnesota, Twin Cities; *Exec. Dir.* William R. Brady, 2324 University Ave. W., Suite 103, Saint Paul 55114-1843. Tel. 612-641-0982, fax 612-641-1035.
Address correspondence to the executive director.

Mississippi

Memb. 1,100. Term of Office. Jan.–Dec. 1998. Publication *Mississippi Libraries* (q.).
Pres. Susanna Turner, 305 Edgewood Dr., Starkville 39759. Tel. 601-325-8391; *Exec. Secy.* Mary Julia Anderson, Box 20448, Jackson 39289-1448. Tel. 601-352-3917.
Address correspondence to the executive secretary, Box 20448, Jackson 39289-1448.

Missouri

Memb. 1,000. Term of Office. Oct. 1997–Oct. 1998. Publication *MO INFO* (bi-mo.). *Ed.* Jean Ann McCartney.

Pres. Elizabeth Ader, Univ. of Missouri Kansas City Lib., 5100 Rockhill Rd. Kansas City 64110-2499. tel. 816-235-1530; *V.P./Pres.-Elect* Elinor Barrett, Daniel Boone Regional Lib., 100 W. Broadway, Columbia 65203-1267. Tel. 573-443-3161; *Secy.* Molly Lawson, Central Missouri State Univ., Warrensburg 64093-5020. Tel. 660-543-8780; *Treas.* Fred Moore, Ferguson Public Lib., 35 N. Florissant Rd., Ferguson 63135-2473. Tel. 314-524-7840; *ALA Councillor* June De Weese, Head of Access Services, Ellis Lib., Univ. of Missouri, Columbia 65201-5149. Tel. 573-882-7315, fax 573-882-8044, e-mail elsjune@mizzou1.missouri.edu; *Exec. Dir.* Jean Ann McCartney, Missouri Lib. Assn., 1306 Business 63 S., Suite B, Columbia 65201. Tel. 573-449-4627, fax 573-449-4655, e-mail jmccartn@mail.more.net.
Address correspondence to the executive director.

Montana

Memb. 700. Term of Office. July 1997–June 1998. Publication *Montana Library Focus* (bi-mo.). *Ed.* Dee Ann Redman, Box 505 Helena 59624.
Pres. Darlene Staffeldt, Montana State Lib., Box 201800, Helena 59620-1800. Tel. 406-444-5381, fax 406-444-5612, e-mail dmstaff@wln.com; *V.P./Pres.-Elect* Bill cochran, Parmly Billings Lib., 510 N. Broadway, Billings 59101. Tel. 406-657-8292, fax 406-657-8293, e-mail cochran@billings.lib.mt.us; *Secy./Treas.* Bonnie Williamson, Havre-Hill County Lib., 402 Third St., Havre 59501. Tel. 406-265-2123, e-mail bwilliam@mtlib.org; *Admin. Asst.* John Thomas, Box 505, Helena 59624-0505. Tel. 406-442-9446.
Address correspondence to the administrative assistant.

Nebraska

Memb. 1,000. Term of Office. Oct. 1997–Oct. 1998. Publication *NLA Quarterly* (q.).
Pres. Donna Peterson, Lincoln Public Schools, Lincoln; *Exec. Dir.* Margaret Harding, Box 98, Crete 68333. Tel. 402-826-2636, e-mail ghl2521@mail.ltec.net.
Address correspondence to the executive director.

Nevada

Memb. 400. Term of Office. Jan.–Dec. 1998. Publication *Nevada Libraries* (q.).

Pres. Frankie Lukasko, Washoe County School District. Tel. 702-333-5585; *V.P./Pres.-Elect* Bonnie Buckley, Nevada State Lib. and Archives. Tel. 702-687-8324; *Treas.* Duncan McCoy, Boulder City Lib. Tel. 702-293-0239; *Exec. Secy.* Keri Putnam, Nevada State Lib. and Archives, 100 N. Shivart St., Carson City 89701-4285. Tel. 702-687-5154, fax 702-687-8311, e-mail putnam@equinox.unr.edu.

Address correspondence to the executive secretary.

New Hampshire

Memb. 700. Publication. *NHLA Newsletter* (bi-mo.).

Pres. John Brisbin, Manchester City Lib., 405 Pine St., Manchester 03104-6199. Tel. 603-624-6550; *Secy.* Lindalee Lambert, Ossipee Public Lib., 74 Main St., Box 638, Center Ossipee 03814-0638. Tel. 603-539-6390.

Address correspondence to the association, Box 2332, Concord 03302-2332.

New Jersey

Memb. 1,700. Term of Office. July 1997–June 1998. Publications. *New Jersey Libraries* (q.); *New Jersey Libraries Newsletter* (mo.).

Pres. Alex Boyd, Newark Public Lib., Box 630, Newark 07101; *V.P./Pres.-Elect* Cynthia Czesak, Clifton Lib., 292 Piaget Ave., Clifton 07011; *Treas.* James Hecht, Somerset County Lib., Box 6700, Bridgewater 08807; *Exec. Dir.* Patricia Tumulty, New Jersey Lib. Assn., 4 W. Lafayette St., Trenton 08608. Tel. 609-394-8032.

Address correspondence to the executive director, Box 1534, Trenton 08607.

New Mexico

Memb. 550. Term of Office. Apr. 1997–Apr. 1998. Publication *New Mexico Library Association Newsletter* (q.). *Ed.* Jackie Shane. Tel. 505-277-5410, e-mail jshane@unm.edu.

Pres. Betty Long, Roswell Public Lib., 301 N. Pennsylvania, Roswell 88201. Tel. 505-622-3400, fax 505-622-7107; *1st V.P.* Ellanie Sampson, 918 Kopra, Torc 878901. Tel. 505-894-3027, fax 505-894-2068, e-mail torcpl@nm-us.campus.mci.net.

Address correspondence to the association, Box 26074, Albuquerque 87125.

New York

Memb. 3,000. Term of Office. Oct. 1997–Nov. 1998. Publication *NYLA Bulletin* (10 per year). *Ed.* Paul Girsdansky.

Pres. Paul Crumlish, Warren/Hunting/Smith Lib., Hobart and William Smith College, Geneva 14456-3398. E-mail crumlish@hws.edu. *Exec. Dir.* Susan Lehman Keitel, New York Lib. Assn., 252 Hudson Ave., Albany 12210. Tel. 518-432-6952.

Address correspondence to the executive director.

North Carolina

Memb. 2,200. Term of Office. Oct. 1997–Oct. 1999. Publication *North Carolina Libraries* (q.). *Ed.* Frances Bradburn, Media and Technology, N.C. Dept. of Public Instruction, 301 N. Wilmington St., Raleigh 27601-2825.

Pres. Beverley Gass, Guilford Technical Community College, Box 309, Jamestown 27282-0309. Tel. 910-334-4822 ext. 2434, fax 910-841-4350; *V.P./Pres.-Elect* Al Jones, Dir. of Lib. Service, Catawba College, 2300 W. Innes St., Salisbury, NC 28144. Tel. 704-6t37-4449; *Secy.* Elizabeth Jackson, West Lake Elementary School, 207 Glen Bonnie La., Cary, NC 27511. Tel. 919-380-8232; *Treas.* Diane Kester, Dept. of Lib. Services Education and Technology, East Carolina Univ., 105 Longview Dr., Goldsboro, NC 27534. Tel. 919-328-6621.

Address correspondence to the secretary.

North Dakota

Memb. (Indiv.) 367; (Inst.) 18. Term of Office. Oct. 1997–Sept. 1998. Publication. *The Good Stuff* (q.). *Ed.* Kelly Steckler, Mandan Public Lib., 108 First St. N.W., Mandan 58554.

Pres. Ellen Kotrba, ODIN Box 7085, Grand Forks 58202-7085. Tel. 701-777-6346; *V.P./Pres.-Elect* Barb Knight, UND Medical Lib., Box 9002, Grand Forks 58202-9002. Tel. 701-777-2166; *Secy.* Phyllis Bratton, Raugust Lib., 6070 College La., Jamestown 58405-0002. Tel. 701-252-3467; *Treas.* Donna Maston, Bismarck Public Lib., 515 N. Fifth St., Bismarck 58501. Tel. 701-222-6414.

Address correspondence to the president.

Ohio

Memb. 3,090. Term of Office. Jan.–Dec. 1997. Publications. *Access* (mo.); *Ohio Libraries* (q.).

Chair Terry Casey, 249 Overbrook Dr., Columbus 43214; *Secy.* Jack Carlson, 2904 Green Vista Dr., Fairborn 45324.

Address correspondence to the association, 35 E. Gay St., Suite 305, Columbus 43215. Tel. 614-221-9057.

Oklahoma

Memb. (Indiv.) 1,050; (Inst.) 60. Term of Office. July 1997–June 1998. Publication. *Oklahoma Librarian* (bi-mo.).

Pres. Deborah Engel, Pioneer Lib. System, 225 N. Webster, Norman 73069. Tel. 405-321-1481; *Secy.* Gary Phillips, Oklahoma Dept. of Libs., 200 N.E. 18th St., Oklahoma City 73105. Tel. 405-521-2502; *Treas.* John Augelli, Stillwater Public Lib., 1107 S. Duck, Stillwater 74074. Tel. 405-372-3633; *Exec. Dir.* Kay Boies, 300 Hardy Dr., Edmond 73013. Tel./fax 405-348-0506, e-mail kboies@ionet.net.

Address correspondence to the executive director.

Oregon

Memb. (Indiv.) 1,000. Publications. *OLA Hotline* (bi-w.), *OLA Quarterly.*

Pres. Ed House, Albany Public Lib., 1390 Waverly Dr. S.E., Albany 97321. Tel. 503-967-4307; *Secy.* Anne Van Sickle, McMinnville Public Lib., 225 N. Adams St., McMinnville 97128. Tel. 503-434-7433.

Address correspondence to the secretary.

Pennsylvania

Memb. 1,500. Term of Office. Jan.–Dec. 1998. Publication *PaLA Bulletin* (mo.).

Pres. Sally Felix, Lackawanna County Lib. System, 520 Vine St., Scranton 18509. Tel. 717-348-3003, e-mail sfelix19@soho.ios.com; *1st V.P.* Barbara Casini, Albert Einstein Medical Center, Luria Medical Lib., 5501 Old York Rd., Philadelphia 19141. Tel. 215-456-5882, e-mail casini@hslc.org; *Exec. Dir.* Glenn R. Miller, Pennsylvania Lib. Assn., 1919 N. Front St., Harrisburg 17102. Tel. 717-233-3113, e-mail plassn@hslc.org.

Address correspondence to the executive director.

Rhode Island

Memb. (Indiv.) 341; (Inst.) 59. Term of Office. Nov. 1997–Nov. 1998. Publication. *Rhode Island Library Association Bulletin. Ed.* To be appointed.

Pres. Kathy Ellen Bullard, Woonsocket Harris Public Lib., 303 Clinton St., Woonsocket 02895. Tel. 401-769-9044, fax 401-767-4140, e-mail kathybd@dsl.rhilinet.gov; *Secy.* James A. Barrett, Univ. Lib., Univ. of Rhode Island, 15 Lippitt Rd., Kingston 02881. Tel. 401-874-2662, fax 401-874-4608, e-mail barrett@uriacc.uri.edu.

Address correspondence to the secretary.

South Carolina

Memb. 700. Term of Office. Jan.–Dec. 1997. Publication *News and Views.*

Pres. Faith Line, Sumter County Lib., Sumter. Tel. 803-773-7273, fax 803-773-4875 e-mail fline@ftc-i-net; *V.P.* Betsey Carter, The Citadel, Charleston. Tel. 803-953-6844, fax 803-953-5190, e-mail cartere@citadel.edu; *Secy.* Terry Barksdale, Greenville County Lib., Greenville. Tel. 864-242-5000 ext. 222, fax 864-235-8375, e-mail tbarksdale@infoave.net; *Exec. Secy.* Drucie Raines, South Carolina Lib. Assn., Box 219, Goose Creek 29445. Tel. 803-764-3668, fax 803-824-2690, e-mail Rainesd@citadel.edu.

Address correspondence to the executive secretary.

South Dakota

Memb. (Indiv.) 432; (Inst.) 55. Term of Office. Oct. 1997–Oct. 1998. Publication. *Book Marks* (bi-mo.).
Pres. Risë Smith, Karl E. Mundt Lib., Dakota State Univ., Madison 57042. Tel. 605-256-7128, fax 605-256-5208, e-mail smithr@columbia.dsu.edu; *V.P./Pres.-Elect* Mike Mullin, Watertown Regional Lib., Watertown 57201. Tel. 605-882-6226, fax 605-882-6221, e-mail mmullin@sdln.net; *Secy.* Jane Goettsch, Siouxland Libs., Ronning Branch, 3100 E. 49 St., Sioux Falls 57103. Tel. 605-367-4607; *Treas.* Ann Eichinger, South Dakota State Lib., 800 Governors Dr., Pierre 57501; *ALA Councillor* Ethelle Bean, Karl E. Mundt Lib., Dakota State Univ., Madison 57042; *MPLA Rep.* Colleen Kirby, E. Y. Berry Lib., Black Hills State Univ., Spearfish 57783. Tel. 605-642-6361.

Address correspondence to Ann Smith, Exec. Secy., SDLA, c/o Mikkelsen Lib., Augustana College, Sioux Falls 57197. Tel. 605-336-4921, fax 605-336-5442, e-mail asmith@inst.augie.edu.

Tennessee

Memb. 934. Term of Office. July 1997–July 1998. Publications. *Tennessee Librarian* (q.), *TLA Newsletter* (bi-mo.).
Pres. Lynette Sloan, Fort Loudoun Regional Lib., Athens 37303. Tel. 800-624-1982, fax 423-745-8086; *V.P./Pres.-Elect* Evealyn Clowers, Trustee, Cleveland Public Lib., 2205 Brentwood Dr., Cleveland 37311. Tel. 423-745-5194, fax 423-339-9791; *Treas.* Dolores Nichols, Upper Cumberland Regional Lib., Cookeville 38501. Tel. 615-526-4016, fax 615-528-3311; *Past Pres./Exec. Secy.* John Evans, Univ. of Memphis Libs., Memphis 38152. Tel. 901-678-4485, fax 901-678-8218, e-mail evansje@cc.memphis.edu.

Address correspondence to the executive secretary.

Texas

Memb. 6,500. Term of Office. Apr. 1997–Apr. 1998. Publications. *Texas Library Journal* (q.); *TLACast* (9 per year).
Pres. JoAnne Moore; *Exec. Dir.* Patricia Smith, TLA, 3355 Bee Cave Rd., Suite 401, Austin 78746-6763. Tel. 512-328-1518, fax 512-328-8852, e-mail pats@txla.org.

Address correspondence to the executive director.

Utah

Memb. 650. Term of Office. May 1997–May 1998. Publication *UTAH Libraries News* (bi-mo.).
Pres. Warren Babcock; *Treas./Exec. Secy.* Chris Anderson. Tel. 801-581-8771.

Address correspondence to the executive secretary, Box 711789, Salt Lake City 84171-8789.

Vermont

Memb. 450. Publication *VLA News* (10 per year).
Pres. Hilari Farrington, Stowe Free Lib., Box 1029, Stowe 05672. Tel. 802-253-6145; *Secy.* Kathy Naftaly, Rutland Free Lib., 10 Court St., Rutland 05701. Tel. 802-773-1860; *ALA Councillor* Melissa Malcolm, Mount Abraham Union H.S., 7 Airport Dr., Bristol 05443. Tel. 802-453-2333; *NELA Rep.* Pamela Murphy, Hartness Lib., Vermont Technical College, Randolph Center 05060. Tel. 802-728-1236.

Address correspondence to the president.

Virginia

Memb. 1,500+. Term of Office. Jan.–Dec. 1998. Publications. *Virginia Libraries* (q.), *Ed.* Cy Dillon; *VLA Newsletter* (10 per year), *Ed.* Mary Hansbrough, 2505 Gloucester Dr., Blacksburg 24060.
Pres. Thomas Hehman, Bedford Public Lib. Tel. 540-586-8744; *V.P./Pres.-Elect* Sandra Heinemann, Hampden-Sydney College Lib., Box 122, Hamden-Sydney 23943. Tel. 804-223-6196; *2nd V.P.* Stella Pool, Gordan Ave. Lib., Charlottesville 23903-1991. Tel. 804-296-5544; *Secy.* Patricia Howe, Longwood College HC-02, Box 213, Buckingham, VA 23291. Tel. 804-395-2443; *Past Pres.* Lisabeth Chabot, Grafton Lib., Mary Baldwin College, Staunton, VA 24401. Tel. 540-887-7085; *Treas.* Terry Sumey, Box 770, Stuarts Draft, VA 24477. Tel. 540-337-2630; *Exec. Dir.* Linda Hahne, Box 8277,

Norfolk 23503-0277. Tel. 757-583-0041, fax 757-583-5041, e-mail lhahne@leo.vsla.edu. Organization World Wide Web site http://www.vla.edu.

Address correspondence to the executive director.

Washington

Memb. 1,200. Term of Office. Apr. 1997–Apr. 1999. Publications. *ALKI* (3 per year); *WLA Link* (5 per year).

Pres. Judy Carlson. Tel. 253-566-5710, fax 253-566-5626, e-mail jcarlson@halcyon.com; *V.P.* Paul M. Christensen. Tel. 360-598-8423, fax 360-598-8406, e-mail nkviking@esd224.wednet.edu; *Treas.* Barbara J. Baker. Tel. 425-823-0836, fax 425-821-5254, e-mail denmother@worldnet.att.net; *Secy.* Jennifer G. Larson. Tel. 425-888-1921, fax 425-888-1934, e-mail jennifer_larson@snogvalerie.wednet.edu.

Address correspondence to the association, 4016 First Ave. N.E., Seattle 98105-6502. Tel. 206-545-1529, fax 206-545-1543, e-mail washla@wln.org.

West Virginia

Memb. 700. Term of Office. Dec. 1997 Nov. 1998. Publication *West Virginia Libraries* (6/yr.). *Eds.* Karen Goff, West Virginia Lib. Commission, and Marjorie Price, West Virginia Supreme Court of Appeals Law Lib.

Pres. Judy Duncan, Saint Albans Public Lib., 602 Fourth St., Saint Albans 25177-2820. Tel. 304-722-4244, fax 304-722-4276, e-mail duncanj@wvlc.wvnet.edu; *Past Pres.* Marjorie Price, West Virginia Supreme Court of Appeals Law Lib., Bldg. 1-E404, 1900 Kanawha Blvd. E., Charleston 25305. Tel. 304-558-2607, fax 304-558-3815, e-mail mprice@wvlv.wvnet.edu. Tel. 304-558-2607, fax 304-558-3673, e-mail pricem@wvnvm.wvnet.edu; *1st V.P./Pres.-Elect* Betty Gunnoe, Martinsburg Public Lib., 101 W. King St., Martinsburg 25401. Tel. 304-267-8933, fax 304-267-9720; *2nd V.P.* Rebecca Van Der Meer, Andrew S. Thomas Memorial Lib., Univ. of Charleston, 2300 MacCorkle Ave. S.E., Charleston 25304-1099. Tel. 304-357-4779, fax 304-357-4715, e-mail vandermr@wvlc.wvnet.edu; *Treas.* R. David Childers, West Virginia Lib. Commission,

Cultural Center, 1900 Kanawha Blvd. E., Charleston 25305. Tel. 304-558-2041, fax 304-558-2044; *Secy.* Linda Lindsey, Richwood Public Lib., 8 White Ave., Richwood 26261-1338. Tel./fax 304-846-6222; *ALA Councillor* Joseph W. Barnes, Scarborough Lib., Shepherd College, Shepherdstown 25443. Tel. 304-876-5312, fax 304-876-0731, e-mail jbarnes@scvax.wvnet.edu.

Address correspondence to the president.

Wisconsin

Memb. 2,100. Term of Office. Jan.–Dec. 1998. Publication *WLA Newsletter* (bi-mo.).

Pres. Paul E. Nelson. Tel. 608-835-5131; *Exec. Dir.* Lisa Strand. Tel. 608-245-3640, fax 608-245-3646.

Address correspondence to the executive director.

Wyoming

Memb. (Indiv.) 450; (Inst.) 21; (Subscribers) 24. Term of Office. Oct. 1997–Oct. 1998.

Pres. Mary Jayne Jordan, Sundace Jr. High, Box 850, Sundance 82729. Tel. 307-283-1007; *Past Pres.* Crystal Havely-Stratton; *V.P./Pres.-Elect* Keith Cottan; *Exec. Secy.* Laura Grott, Box 1387, Cheyenne 82003. Tel. 307-632-7622, fax 307-638-3469.

Address correspondence to the executive secretary.

Guam

Memb. 75. Publication. *Guam Library Association News* (mo. during school year).

Address correspondence to the association, Box 20981 GMF, Guam 96921.

Canada

Alberta

Memb. 500. Term of Office. May 1997–Apr. 1998. Publication *Letter of the LAA* (5 per year).

Pres. Pilar Martinez, Yellowhead Regional Lib. Box 400, 433 King St., Spruce Grove T7X 2Y1. Tel. 403-962-2003, fax 403-962-2770; *Exec. Dir.* Christine Sheppard, 80 Baker Crescent N.W., Calgary T2L 1R4. Tel. 403-284-5832, fax 403-282-6646.

Address correspondence to the executive director.

British Columbia

Memb. 750. Term of Office. Apr. 1997–May 1998. Publication *BCLA Reporter. Ed.* Ted Benson.

Pres. Frieda Wiebe; *V.P./Pres.-Elect* Greg Buss.

Address correspondence to the association, 110-6545 Bonsor Ave., Burnaby V5H 1H3. Tel. 604-430-9633, fax 604-430-8595, e-mail bcla@unixg.ubc.ca.

Manitoba

Memb. 494. Term of Office. May 1997–May 1998. Publication *Newsline* (mo.).

Pres. Karen Hunt; *Office Mgr.* Jeannette Dankewych.

Address correspondence to the association, 208-100 Arthur St., Winnipeg R3B 1H3. Tel. 204-943-4567, fax 204-942-1555.

Ontario

Memb. 3,800+. Term of Office. Jan. 1998–Jan. 1999. Publications. *Access* (q.); *Teacher-Librarian* (q.); *Inside OLA* (mo.).

Pres. Brian Bell, Oakville Public Lib.; *Treas.* June Wilson, Ministry of Transportation Lib. Tel. 905-477-5733.

Address correspondence to the association, 100 Lombard St., Suite 303, Toronto M5C 1M3. Tel. 416-363-3388, fax 416-941-9581, e-mail info@accessola.com.

Quebec

Memb. (Indiv.) 140; (Inst.) 26; (Commercial) 3. Term of Office. June 1997–May 1998. Publication. *ABQ/QLA Bulletin* (3 per year).

Pres. Anne Howard, Pierrefonds Comprehensive H.S., 13800 Pierrefonds Blvd., Pierrefonds H9A 1A7; *Exec. Secy.* Pat Fortin, Quebec Lib. Assn., Box 1095, Pointe Claire H9S 4H9. Tel. 514-630-4875, e-mail abqla@johnabbott.qc.ca.

Address correspondence to the executive secretary.

Saskatchewan

Memb. 350. Term of Office. July 1997–June 1998. Publication *Forum* (5 per year).

Pres. Asa Kachan; *Exec. Dir.* Andrea Wagner, Box 3388, Regina S4P 3H1. Tel. 306-780-9413, fax 306-780-9447, e-mail sla@pleis.lib.sk.ca.

Address correspondence to the executive director.

Regional

Atlantic Provinces: N.B., Nfld., N.S., P.E.I.

Memb. (Indiv.) 252; (Inst.) 25. Term of Office. May 1997–May 1998. Publications. *APLA Bulletin* (bi-mo.), *Ed.* John Neilson; *Membership Directory and Handbook* (ann.).

Pres. John Teskey; *V.P./Pres.-Elect* Dan Savage; *V.P., Nova Scotia* Faye Hopkins; *V.P., Prince Edward Island* Norine Hanus; *V.P., New Brunswick* Charlotte Dionne; *V.P., Newfoundland* Beverley Neable; *V.P., Memb.* Elizabeth Browne; *Secy.* Jocelyne Thompson. Tel. 506-453-2354; *Treas.* Elaine MacLean.

Address correspondence to Atlantic Provinces Lib. Assn., c/o School of Lib. and Info. Studies, Dalhousie Univ., Halifax, NS B3H 4H8.

Midwest: Ill., Ind., Minn., Ohio

Pres. Kathy East. Tel. 419-352-5104; *Secys.* Diane Bever. Tel. 317-455-9265; Linda Kolb. Tel. 317-257-2040.

Mountain Plains: Ariz., Colo., Kans., Mont., Neb., Nev., N.Dak., Okla., S.Dak., Utah, Wyo.

Memb. 920. Term of Office. One year. Publications. *MPLA Newsletter* (bi-mo.), *Ed. and Adv. Mgr.* Heidi M. Nickisch, I. D. Weeks Lib., Univ. of South Dakota, Vermillion, SD 57069. Tel. 605-677-6088, e-mail nickisch@sunbird.usd.edu; *Membership Directory* (ann.).

Pres. Carol J. Connor, Lincoln City Libs., 136 S. 14 St., Lincoln, NE 68502. Tel. 402-441-8510, e-mail cjc@rand.lcl.lib.ne.us; *V.P./Pres.-Elect* Roann Masterson, Univ. of Mary, 7500 University Dr., Bismarck, ND

58504-9652. Tel. 701-255-7500, ext. 447, fax 701-255-7690, e-mail r.masterson@mail.cdln.lib.nd.us; *Exec. Secy.* Joe Edelen, I. D. Weeks Lib., Univ. of South Dakota, Vermillion, SD 57069. Tel. 605-677-6082, e-mail jedelen@sunbird.usd.edu.

Address correspondence to the executive secretary, Mountain Plains Lib. Assn.

New England: Conn., Maine, Mass., N.H., R.I., Vt.

Memb. (Indiv.) 1,200; (Inst.) 100. Term of Office. One year (Treas., Dirs., two years). Publication. *New England Libraries* (bi-mo.). *Ed.* Cara Barlow, Massachusetts Board of Libs. Commission, 648 Beacon St., Boston, MA 02115. Tel. 617-267-9400.

Exec. Secy. Barry Blaisdell, New England Lib. Assn., 707 Turnpike St., North Andover, MA 01845. Tel. 508-685-5966, e-mail nela@world.std.com.

Address correspondence to the executive secretary.

Pacific Northwest: Alaska, Idaho, Mont., Oreg., Wash., Alberta, B.C.

Memb. (Active) 550; (Subscribers) 100. Term of Office. Oct. 1997–Sept. 1999. Publication. *PNLA Quarterly. Ed.* Sue Samson, Mansfield Lib., Univ. of Montana, Missoula, MT 59812-1195. Tel. 406-243-4335, fax 406-243-2060, e-mail ss@selway.umt.edu.

Pres. Gordon Ray, 2392 Woodstock Dr., Abbotsford, BC V3G 2E5. Tel. 604-852-6731, e-mail Gordon_Ray@bc.cympatico.ca; *1st V.P./Pres.-Elect* Andrew Johnson, Government Publications Div., Univ. of Washington Lib., Box 352900, Seattle WA 98195-2900. Tel. 206-543-9156; fax 206-685-8049, e-mail afj@u.washington.edu; *2nd V.P./Memb.* Barry Brown, Mansfield Lib., Univ. of Montana, Missoula, MT 59812. Tel. 406-243-6811, fax 406-243-2060, e-mail barry@selway.umt.edu; *Secy.* Marg Anderson, Lib. and Info. Technology Program, SAIT, 1301 16th Ave. N.W., Calgary, AB T3H 1K2. Tel. 403-284-7016, fax 403-284-7121, e-mail marg.anderson@sait.ab.ca; *Treas.* Monica Weyhe, State Dept. of Administration, 118 Troy Ave., Juneau, AK 99801. Tel. 907-465-6989, fax 907-465-2665, e-mail mweyhe@ptialaska.net.

Address correspondence to the president, Pacific Northwest Lib. Assn.

Southeastern: Ala., Ark., Fla., Ga., Ky., La., Miss., N.C., S.C., Tenn., Va., W. Va.

Memb. 1,350. Term of Office. Oct. 1996–Oct. 1998. Publication *The Southeastern Librarian* (q.).

Pres. Lorraine D. Summers, State Lib. of Florida, R. A. Gray Bldg., Tallahassee, FL 32399-0250; *V.P./Pres.-Elect* Frances N. Coleman, 2403 Maple Dr., Starkville, MS 39759; *Secy.* Carolyn T. Wilson, Crisman Memorial Lib., David Lipscomb Univ., Nashville, TN 37204; *Treas.* Billy Pennington, 397 Cambo Lane, Birmingham, AL 35226.

Address correspondence to the president or executive secretary, SELA Administrative Services, SOLINET, 1438 W. Peachtree St. N.W., Atlanta, GA 30309-2955. Tel. 404-892-0943.

State and Provincial Library Agencies

The state library administrative agency in each of the U.S. states will have the latest information on its state plan for the use of federal funds under the Library Services and Technology Act. The directors and addresses of these state agencies are listed below.

Alabama

Patricia L. Harris, Dir., Alabama Public Lib. Service, 6030 Monticello Dr., Montgomery 36130-2001. Tel. 334-213-3900, fax 334-213-3993, e-mail pharris@apls. state.al.us.

Alaska

Karen Crane, Dir., Div. of Libs., Archives, and Museums, Alaska Dept. of Educ., Box 110571, Juneau 99811-0571. Tel. 907-465-2910, fax 907-465-2151, e-mail karenc@ muskox.alaska.edu.

Arizona

Gladysann Wells, Dept. of Lib., Archives, and Public Records, State Capitol, 1700 W. Washington, Suite 200, Phoenix 85007-2896. Tel. 602-542-4035, fax 602-542-4972, e-mail gawells@dlapr.lib.az.us.

Arkansas

John A. (Pat) Murphey, Jr., State Libn., Arkansas State Lib., One Capitol Mall, Little Rock 72201-1081. Tel. 501-682-1526, fax 501-682-1529, e-mail jmurphey@ comp.uark.edu.

California

Kevin Starr, State Libn., California State Lib., Box 942837, Sacramento 94237-0001. Tel. 916-654-0174, fax 916-654-0064, e-mail kstarr@library.ca.gov.

Colorado

Nancy M. Bolt, Asst. Commissioner, Colorado State Lib., 201 E. Colfax Ave., Rm. 309, Denver 80203. Tel. 303-866-6900, fax 303-866-6940, e-mail nbolt@csn.org.

Connecticut

Richard G. Akeroyd, Jr., State Libn., Connecticut State Lib., 231 Capitol Ave., Hartford 06106. Tel. 806-566-4301, fax 806-566-8940, e-mail rakeroyd@csl.ctstateu. edu.

Delaware

Tom Sloan, State Libn. and Div. Dir., Div. of Libs., 43 S. DuPont Hwy., Dover 19901. Tel. 302-739-4748, fax 302-739-6787, e-mail tsloan@kentnet.dtcc.edu.

District of Columbia

Mary E. Raphael, Acting Dir., Dist. of Columbia Public Lib., 901 G St. N.W., Suite 400, Washington 20001. Tel. 202-727-1101, fax 202-727-1129.

Florida

Barratt Wilkins, State Libn., State Lib. of Florida, R. A. Gray Bldg., Tallahassee 32399-0250. Tel. 904-487-2651, fax 904-488-2746, e-mail bwilkins@dlis.state.fl.us.

Georgia

Thomas A. Ploeg, Acting Dir., Div. of Public Lib. Services, Atlanta 30345-3692. Tel. 404-982-3565, fax 404-656-7297, e-mail tploeg@mail.gpls.public.lib.ga.us.

Hawaii

Bartholomew A. Kane, State Libn., Hawaii State Public Lib. System, 465 S. King St., Rm. B1, Honolulu 96813. Tel. 808-586-3704, fax 808-586-3715.

Idaho

Charles A. Bolles, State Libn., Idaho State Lib., 325 W. State St., Boise 83702-6072. Tel. 208-334-2150, fax 208-334-4016, e-mail cbolles@isl.state.id.us.

Illinois

Bridget L. Lamont, Dir., Illinois State Lib., 300 S. Second St., Springfield 62701-1796. Tel. 217-782-2994, fax 217-785-4326, e-mail blamont@library.sos.state.il.us.

Indiana

C. Ray Ewick, Dir., Indiana State Lib., 140 N. Senate Ave., Indianapolis 46204-2296. Tel. 317-232-3692, fax 317-232-0002, e-mail ewick@statelib.lib.in.us.

Iowa

Sharman Smith, State Libn., State Lib. of Iowa, E. 12 and Grand, Des Moines 50319. Tel. 515-281-4105, fax 515-281-6191, e-mail ssmith@mail.lib.state.ia.us.

Kansas

Duane F. Johnson, State Libn., Kansas State Lib., 300 S.W. Tenth Ave., Rm. 343, Topeka 66612-1593. Tel. 913-296-3296, fax 913-296-6650, e-mail duanej@ink.org.

Kentucky

James A. Nelson, State Libn./Commissioner, Kentucky Dept. for Libs. and Archives, 300 Coffee Tree Rd., Box 537, Frankfort 40602-0537. Tel. 502-564-8300, fax 502-564-5773, e-mail jnelson@ctr.kdla.state.ky.us.

Louisiana

Thomas F. Jaques, State Libn., State Lib. of Louisiana, Box 131, Baton Rouge 70821-0131. Tel. 504-342-4923, fax 504-342-3547, e-mail tjaques@pelican.state.lib.la.us.

Maine

J. Gary Nichols, State Libn., Maine State Lib., LMA Bldg., 64 State House Sta., Augusta 04333-0064. Tel. 207-287-5600, fax 207-287-5615, e-mail gary.nichols@state.me.us.

Maryland

J. Maurice Travillian, Asst. State Superintendent for Libs., Div. of Lib. Development and Services, Maryland State Dept. of Educ., 200 W. Baltimore St., Baltimore 21201-2595. Tel. 410-767-0435, fax 410-333-2507, e-mail mj54@umail.umd.ed.

Massachusetts

Keith M. Fiels, Dir., Massachusetts Board of Lib. Commissioners, 648 Beacon St., Boston 02215. Tel. 617-267-9400, fax 617-421-9833, e-mail kfiels@mecn.mass.edu.

Michigan

George M. Needham, State Libn., Lib. of Michigan, 717 Allegan St., Box 30007, Lansing 48909-9945. Tel. 517-373-1580, fax 517-373-4480, e-mail gneedham@libomich.lib.mi.us.

Minnesota

Joyce C. Swanger, Dir., Office of Lib. Development and Service, Minnesota Dept. of Educ., 440 Capitol Sq. Bldg., 550 Cedar St., Saint Paul 55101. Tel. 612-296-2821, fax 612-296-5418, e-mail joyce.swanger@state.mn.us.

Mississippi

Jane Smith, Acting Exec. Dir., Mississippi Lib. Commission, 1221 Ellis Ave., Box 10700, Jackson 39289-0700. Tel. 601-359-1036, fax 601-354-4181.

Missouri

Sara Parker, State Libn., Missouri State Lib., 600 W. Main, Box 387, Jefferson City 65102-0387. Tel. 573-751-2751, fax 573-

751-3612, e-mail sparker@mail.sos.state. mo.us.

Montana

Karen Strege, State Libn., Montana State Lib., 1515 E. Sixth Ave., Helena 59620-1800. Tel. 406-444-3116, fax 406-444-5612, e-mail kstrege@msl.mt.gov.

Nebraska

Rod Wagner, Dir., Nebraska Lib. Commission, The Atrium, 1200 N St., Suite 120, Lincoln 68508-2023. Tel. 402-471-2045, fax 402-471-2083, e-mail rwagner@neon. nlc.state.ne.us.

Nevada

Joan Kerschner, Dir., Museums, Lib. and Arts, Nevada State Lib. and Archives, Capitol Complex, Carson City 89710. Tel. 702-687-8315, fax 702-687-8311, e-mail jgkersch@clan.lib.nv.us.

New Hampshire

Kendall F. Wiggin, State Libn., New Hampshire State Lib., 20 Park St., Concord 03301-6314. Tel. 603-271-2397, fax 603-271-6826, e-mail wiggin@lilac.nhsl.lib. nh.us.

New Jersey

John H. Livingstone, Jr., Acting State Libn., New Jersey State Lib., 185 W. State St., CN520, Trenton 08625-0520. Tel. 609-292-6200, fax 609-292-2746, e-mail jaliving@pilot.njin.net.

New Mexico

Karen Watkins, State Libn., New Mexico State Lib., 325 Don Gaspar Ave., Santa Fe 87501-2777. Tel. 505-827-3804, fax 505-827-3888, e-mail kwatkins@stlib.state. nm.us.

New York

State Libn./Asst. Commissioner for Libs., New York State Lib., C.E.C., Rm. 10C34, Empire State Plaza, Albany 12230. Tel. 518-474-5930, fax 518-474-2718.

North Carolina

Sandra M. Cooper, Dir./State Libn., State Lib. of North Carolina, Dept. of Cultural Resources, 109 E. Jones St., Raleigh 27601-2807. Tel. 919-733-2570, fax 919-733-8784, e-mail scooper@hal.dcr.state. nc.us.

North Dakota

Mike Jaugstetter, Dir., North Dakota State Lib., Capitol Grounds, 604 E. Boulevard Ave., Bismarck 58505-0800. Tel. 701-328-4654, fax 701-328-2040, e-mail mjaugstetter@ranch.state.nd.us.

Ohio

Michael Lucas, State Libn., State Lib. of Ohio, 65 S. Front St., Columbus 43215-4163. Tel. 614-644-6845, fax 614-466-3584, e-mail mlucas@mail.slonet.ohio. gov.

Oklahoma

Robert L. Clark, Jr., State Libn., Oklahoma Dept. of Libs., 200 N.E. 18 St., Oklahoma City 73105-3298. Tel. 405-521-2502, fax 405-525-7804, e-mail rclark@oltn.odl. state.ok.us.

Oregon

Jim Scheppke, State Libn., Oregon State Lib., State Lib. Bldg., Salem 97310-0640. Tel. 503-378-4367, fax 503-588-7119, e-mail jim.b.scheppke@state.or.us.

Pennsylvania

Gary D. Wolfe, Deputy Secy. of Educ. for Commonwealth Libs., Box 1601, Harrisburg 17105. Tel. 717-787-2646, fax 717-772-3265, e-mail wolfe@hslc.org.

Rhode Island

Barbara Weaver, Chief Information Officer, Rhode Island Dept. of Administration, 1

Capitol Hill, Providence 02903-4222. Tel. 401-277-1220, fax 401-831-1131, e-mail barbarawr@dsl.rhilinet.gov.

South Carolina

James B. Johnson, Dir., South Carolina State Lib., 1500 Senate St., Box 11469, Columbia 29211. Tel. 803-734-8666, fax 803-734-8676, e-mail jim@leo.scsl.state.sc.us.

South Dakota

Jane Kolbe, State Libn., South Dakota State Lib., 800 Governors Dr., Pierre 57501-2294. Tel. 605-773-3131, fax 605-773-4950, e-mail janeK@stlib.state.sd.us.

Tennessee

Edwin Gleaves, State Libn./Archivist Tennessee State Lib. and Archives, 403 Seventh Ave. N., Nashville 37243-0312. Tel. 615-741-7996, fax 615-741-6471, e-mail egleaves@mail.state.tn.us.

Texas

Robert S. Martin, Dir./State Libn., Texas State Lib., 1201 Brazos St., Box 12927, Austin 78711-2927. Tel. 512-463-5460, fax 512-463-5436, e-mail rmartin@tsl.state.tx.us.

Utah

Amy Owen, Dir., State Lib. Div., 2150 S. 300 W., Suite 16, Salt Lake City 84115-2579. Tel. 801-468-6770, fax 801-533-4657, e-mail aowen@inter.state.lib.ut.us.

Vermont

Patricia E. Klinck, State Libn., Vermont Dept. of Libs., 109 State St., Montpelier 05609-0601. Tel. 802-828-3265, fax 802-828-2199, e-mail pklinck@dol.state.vt.us.

Virginia

Nolan T. Yelich, State Libn., Lib. of Virginia, 11 St. at Capitol Sq., Richmond 23219-3491. Tel. 804-692-3535, fax 804-692-3771, e-mail nyelich@leo.vsla.edu.

Washington

Nancy L. Zussy, State Libn., Washington State Lib., Box 42460, Olympia 98504-2460. Tel. 360-753-2915, fax 360-586-7575, e-mail nzussy@wln.com.

West Virginia

R. David Childers, Acting Sec., West Virginia Lib. Commission, Cultural Center, Charleston 25305. Tel. 304-558-2041, fax 304-558-2044, e-mail childers@wvlc.wvnet.edu.

Wisconsin

Larry Nix, Asst. Superintendent, Div. for Libs. and Community Learning, 125 S. Webster St., Box 7841, Madison 53707-7841. Tel. 608-266-2205, fax 608-267-1052.

Wyoming

Helen Meadors Maul, State Libn., Wyoming State Lib., Supreme Court and State Lib. Bldg., Cheyenne 82002-0060. Tel. 307-777-7281, fax 307-777-6289, e-mail hmeado@windy.state.wy.us.

American Samoa

Emma C. Penn, Program Dir., Office of Lib. Services, Box 1329, Pago Pago 96799. Tel. LD Operator 633-1181 or 1182.

Guam

Christine K. Scott-Smith, Dir./Territorial Libn., Guam Public Lib., 254 Martyr St., Agana 96910-0254. Tel. 671-477-6913, 472-1389, fax 671-477-9777, e-mail csctsmth@kuentos.guam.net.

Northern Mariana Islands

Paul Steere, Dir., Joeten-Kiyu Public Lib., Box 1092, Commonwealth of the Northern Mariana Islands, Saipan 96950. Tel. 670-235-7322, fax 670-235-7550, e-mail psteere@saipan.com; William Matson, Federal Programs Coordinator, Dept. of Educ., Commonwealth of the Northern

Mariana Islands, Saipan 96950. Tel. 670-322-6405, fax 670-322-4056.

Palau (Republic of)

Masa-Aki N. Emeschiol, Federal Grants Coord., Ministry of Educ., Box 189, Koror 96940. Tel. 680-488-2570, ext. 1003, fax 680-488-2830, e-mail emesiocm@prel. hawaii.edu.; Fermina Salvador, Libn., Palau Public Lib., Box 189, Koror 96940. Tel. 680-488-2973, fax 680-488-3310.

Puerto Rico

Victor Fajardo, Secy., Dept. of Educ., Apartado 190759, San Juan 00919-0759. Tel. 809-754-5972, fax 809-754-0843.

Virgin Islands

Jeannette Allis Bastian, Dir. and Territorial Libn., Div. of Libs., Archives and Museums, 23 Dronningens Gade, Saint Thomas 00802. Tel. 809-774-3407, fax 809-775-1887, e-mail jbastia@icarus.lis.pitt.edu.

Canada

Alberta

Punch Jackson, Mgr. Libs. Section, Arts & Libs. Branch, 901 Standard Life Center, 10405 Jasper Ave., Edmonton T5J 4R7. Tel. 403-427-6315, fax 403-422-9132.

British Columbia

Barbara Greeniaus, Dir., Lib. Services Branch, Ministry of Municipal Affairs and Housing, Box 9490 Stn. Prov. Govt., Victoria V8W 9N7. Tel. 250-356-1791, fax 250-953-3225, e-mail bgreeniaus@hq.marh. gov.bc.ca.

Manitoba

Sylvia Nicholson, Dir., Manitoba Culture, Heritage, and Citizenship, Public Lib. Services, Unit 200, 1525 First St., Brandon R7A 7A1. Tel. 204-726-6864, fax 204-726-6868.

New Brunswick

Jocelyne LeBel, Dir., New Brunswick Lib. Service, Box 6000, Fredericton E3B 5H1. Tel. 506-453-2354, fax 506-453-2416, e-mail jlebel@gov.nb.ca.

Newfoundland

David Gale, Provincial Dir., Provincial Information and Library Resources Board, Arts and Culture Centre, Allandale Rd., St. John's A1B 3A3. Tel. 709-737-3964, fax 709-737-3009, World Wide Web http://www.publib.nf.ca/.

Northwest Territories

Suliang Feng, Territorial Libn., Northwest Territories Lib. Services, Rm. 207, 2nd fl., Wright Centre, 62 Woodland Dr., Hay River X0E 1G1. Tel. 867-874-6531, fax 867-874-3321, e-mail suliang@gov.nt.ca.

Nova Scotia

Marion L. Pape, Provincial Libn., Nova Scotia Provincial Lib., 3770 Kempt Rd., Halifax B3K 4X8. Tel. 902-424-2457, fax 902-424-0633, e-mail mpape@nshpl. library.ns.ca.

Ontario

Michael Langford, Dir., Cultural Partnerships Branch, Ontario Government Ministry of Citizenship, Culture, and Recreation, 77 Bloor St. W., 3rd fl., Toronto M7A 2R9. Tel. 416-314-7342, fax 416-314-7635.

Prince Edward Island

Harry Holman, Dir., P.E.I. Provincial Lib., Red Head Rd., Box 7500, Morell C0A 1S0. Tel. 902-961-7320, fax 902-961-7322, e-mail plshq@gov.pe.ca.ca.

Quebec

Denis Delangie, Dir., Direction des politiques et de la coordination des programmes, 225 Grande Allée Est, Bloc C, 2e étage, Quebec G1R 5G5. Tel. 418-644-0485, fax 418-643-4080, e-mail patrimoi@mail. mccq.gouv.gc.ca.

Saskatchewan

Maureen Woods, Provincial Libn., Saskatchewan Provincial Lib., 1352 Winnipeg St., Regina S4P 3V7. Tel. 306-787-2976, fax 306-787-2029, e-mail srp.adm@provlib.lib.sk.ca.

Yukon Territory

Linda R. Johnson, Dir., Dept. of Educ., Libs., and Archives, Box 2703, Whitehorse Y1A 2C6. Tel. 867-667-5309, fax 867-393-6253, e-mail Linda.Johnson@gov.yk.ca.

State School Library Media Associations

Alabama

Children's and School Libns. Div., Alabama Lib. Assn. Memb. 650. Publication. *The Alabama Librarian* (q.).

Exec. Dir. Missy Mathis, 400 S. Union St., Suite 255, Montgomery 36104. Tel. 334-262-5210, fax 334-262-5255, e-mail alala@mindspring.com. World Wide Web site http://davisref.samford.edu/alala/alala.htm.

Address correspondence to the executive director.

Alaska

Alaska Assn. of School Libns.

Pres. Janet Hadley. E-mail hadleyj@ves. ssd.k12.ak.us; *Secy.* Linda Thibodeau. E-mail thibodel@jsd.k12.ak.us; *Treas.* Jane Meacham. E-mail janem@muskox.alaska.edu; *Alaska School Lib. Media Coord.* Della Matthis, 344 W. Third Ave., Suite 125, Anchorage 99501-2337. E-mail dellam@muskox.alaska.edu.

Arizona

School Lib. Media Div., Arizona Lib. Assn. Memb. 500. Term of Office. Nov. 1997–Dec. 1998. Publication. *AZLA Newsletter*.

Pres. Gail Scheck, Curtis O. Greenfield School, 7009 S. 10th St., Phoenix 85040. Tel. 602-232-4240, fax 602-243-4973. *Pres.-Elect* Paul Kreamer. Tel. 520-733-8027.

Address correspondence to the president.

Arkansas

Arkansas Assn. of School Libns. and Media Educators. Term of Office. Jan.–Dec. 1997.

Chair Barbie James, Forrest City H.S., 467 Victoria St., Forrest City 72335. Tel. 870-633-1464, ext. 12, e-mail jamesb.FORREST_csd@pcsd.grsc.k12.ar.us; *Secy.-Treas.* Carol Ann Hart, Forrest City H.S., 467 Victoria St., Forrest City 72335. Tel. 870-633-1464.

Address correspondence to the chairperson.

California

California School Lib. Assn. Memb. 1,500. Term of Office. June 1997–May 1998. Publi-

cation. *Journal of the CSLA*. (mo.) *Ed.* John Archer. Job Hotline 415-697-8832; *Good Ideas!* (ann.); *TLC's (Together: Libraries + Classrooms)*.

Pres. Janet Minami, Los Angeles Unified School Dist., 1320 W. Third St., Rm. 140, Los Angeles 90017. Tel. 213-625-6971; *Pres.-Elect* Betty Silva, Fairfield H.S. Lib., 205 E. Atlantic, Fairfield 94533. Tel. 707-422-8672; *Secy.* Cynthia Wong, Pacoima Middle School, 9919 Laurel Canyon Blvd., Pacoima 91331. Tel. 818-899-5291; *Treas.* George Skyles, El Rancho H.S., 6501 S. Passons Blvd., Pico Rivera 90660. Tel. 562-801-5335; *Business Office Secy.* Nancy D. Kohn, CSLA, 1499 Old Bayshore Hwy., Suite 142, Burlingame 94010. Tel. 650-692-2350, fax 650-692-4956.

Address correspondence to the business office secretary.

Colorado

Colorado Educational Media Assn. Memb. 400. Term of Office. Feb. 1997–Feb. 1998. Publication. *The Medium*. (6/yr.)

Pres. Beth Hager; *Pres.-Elect* Sandy Martinez; *Secy.* Jean Parry; *Exec. Secy.* Heidi Baker.

Address correspondence to the executive secretary, Box 22814, Wellshire Sta., Denver 80222. Tel. 303-292-5434.

Connecticut

Connecticut Educational Media Assn. Memb. 550. Term of Office. May 1997–May 1998. Publications. *CEMA Update Quarterly*; *CEMA Gram Monthly*.

Pres. Judy Savage, 15 Evergreen Rd., Northford 06472. Tel. 860-346-7735; *V.P.* Frances Nadeau, 440 Matthews St., Bristol 06010. Tel. 203-589-0813; *Secy.* Joan Schneider, 20 Lantern La., Niantic 06357. Tel. 860-739-0775; *Treas.* Wendell Rector, 4 Woodbury Pl., Woodbury 06798. Tel. 203-263-2707; *Admin. Secy.* Anne Weimann, 25 Elmwood Ave., Trumbull 06611. Tel. 203-372-2260.

Address correspondence to the administrative secretary.

Delaware

Delaware School Lib. Media Assn., Div. of Delaware Lib. Assn. Memb. 115. Term of Office. Apr. 1997–Apr. 1998. Publications. *DSLMA Newsletter* (irreg.); column in *DLA Bulletin* (3 per year).

Pres. Susan Cushwa, Middletown H.S. Appoquinimink, 504 S. Broad St., Middletown. Tel. 302-378-5290, e-mail scushwa@dpi1.k12.state.de.us.

Address correspondence to the president.

District of Columbia

District of Columbia Assn. of School Libns. Memb. 93. Term of Office. Jan. 98–Jan. 99. Publication. *Newsletter* (4 per year).

Pres. Lydia Jenkins; *Rec. Secy.* Olivia Hardison; *Treas.* Mary Minnis; *Financial Secy.* Connie Lawson; *Corres. Secy.* Sharon Sorrels, Banneker H.S., 800 Euclid St. N.W., Washington 20001.

Florida

Florida Assn. for Media in Education. Memb. 1,450. Term of Office. Jan. 1998–Jan. 1999. Publication. *Florida Media Quarterly. Ed.* Nancy Teger, 2560 Bass Way, Cooper City 33026. Tel. 954-431-5322, e-mail tegern@gate.net.

Pres. Sandra Nelson, 1816 Southeast First St., Cape Coral 33990. Tel. 941-337-8553, fax 941-337-8543, e-mail sandyn@lee.k12.fl; *V.P.* Chuck St. Louis, 16808 Waterline Rd., Bradenton 34202. Tel. 941-741-3470 ext. 204, fax 941-741-3480, e-mail stlouisc@gate.net; *Assn. Exec.* Louise Costello, Box 70577, Fort Lauderdale 33307. Tel./fax 954-566-1312, e-mail costell@mail.firn.edu.

Address correspondence to the the association executive.

Georgia

School Lib. Media Div., Georgia Lib. Assn. Memb. 217. Term of Office. Oct. 1997–Oct. 1998.

Chair Anne Maish, Hephzibah Elementary School, Box 130, Hephzibah 30815. Tel./fax 706-592-3703; *Chair-Elec.* Lydia Piper, Wilkinson Gardens Elementary School, 1918 Tubman Home Rd., Augusta 30906. Tel.

706-481-1621; *Secy.* Diane Barton, Lincoln County Elementary School, Lincolnton 30817. Tel. 706-359-3449.

Hawaii

Hawaii Assn. of School Libns. Memb. 299. Term of Office. June 1997–May 1998. Publications. *HASL Newsletter* (1 per semester); *Golden Key Journal* (1 every 5 years).

Pres. Myles Furubayashi; *1st V.P.* Derri-Lynn Slavensi.

Address correspondence to the association, Box 235019, Honolulu 96823.

Idaho

Educational Media Div., Idaho Lib. Assn. Memb. 125. Term of Office. Oct. 1997–Oct. 1998. Publication. Column in *The Idaho Librarian* (q.).

Chair Barbara Barrett, Hillside Jr. H.S., 6806 Fernwood, Boise 83709. Tel. 208-376-7180; *Secy.* Sue Crafts, 33 Purdue Ave., Pocatello 83204.

Address correspondence to the chairperson.

Illinois

Illinois School Lib. Media Assn. Memb. 1,000. Term of Office. June 1997–July 1998. Publications. *ISLMA News* (5 per year), *ISLMA Membership Directory* (ann.).

Pres. Joan Herron, 505 S. Henry, Eureka 61530. Tel. 309-467-6004, e-mail jherron@mtco.com; *Pres.-Elect* Donna Lutkehaus, R.R. 21, Box 29, Bloomington 61704. Tel. 309-828-0958, e-mail lutkehaus?tch@as400.unit5.mclean.k12.il.us; *Exec. Secy.* Kay Maynard, Box 598, Canton 61520. Tel. 309-649-0911, fax 309-647-0140, e-mail ISLMA@aol.com.

Address correspondence to the executive secretary.

Indiana

Assn. for Indiana Media Educators. Memb. 1,013. Term of Office. May 1997–Apr. 1998. Publications. *AIME News* (10/yr.); *Indiana Media Journal* (2/yr.).

Pres. Nancy McGriff, South Central Schools, 9808 S. 600 W., Union Mills 46382.

Tel. 219-767-2263, fax 219-767-2260; *Pres.-Elect* Jackie Carrigan, Plainfield Schools, 709 Stafford Rd., Plainfield 46168. Tel. 317-838-3556, fax 317-838-3671, e-mail jcarrigan@plainfield.k12.in.us; *Past Pres.* Anne M. Mallett, Gary Community School/Corp., 620 E. Tenth Place, Gary 46402. Tel. 219-881-5462, fax 219-886-6432; *Assn. Mgt. Consultant* Karen G. Burch, 1908 E. 64 St., South Dr., Indianapolis 46220. Tel. 317-257-8558, fax 317-259-4191, e-mail aime@doe.state.in.us. World Wide Web site http://ideanet.doe.state.in.us/aime.

Address correspondence to the association management consultant.

Iowa

Iowa Educational Media Assn. Memb. 500. Term of Office. Mar. 1997–Mar. 1998. Publication. *Iowa Media Message* (4 per year). *Ed.* Linda Macrae, 1206 Second Ave. N., Northwood 50459.

Pres. MaryJo Langhorne; *Pres.-Elect* Laura Pratt; *Secy.* Loretta Moon; *Treas.* Rick Valley; *Exec. Secy.* Paula Behrendt, 2306 Sixth, Harlan 51537. Tel./fax 712-755-5918, e-mail paulab@harlannet.com.

Address correspondence to the executive secretary.

Kansas

Kansas Assn. of School Libns. Memb. 700. Term of Office. Aug. 1998–July 1999. Publication. *KASL Newsletter* (s. ann.).

Pres. Sue Buhler, 620 Illinois, Pratt 67124. Tel. 316-672-7752; *Exec. Secy.* Judith Eller, 5201 N. St. Clair, Wichita 67204. Tel. 316-838-6395.

Address correspondence to the executive secretary.

Kentucky

Kentucky School Media Assn. Memb. 695. Term of Office. Oct. 1997–Oct. 1998. Publication. *KSMA Newsletter* (q.).

Pres. Emmalee Hill, 11800 Taylor Mills Rd., Independence 41051. Tel. 606-356-0183, e-mail ehill@kenton.k12.ky.us; *Secy.* Shirley Wathen, Bend Gate Elementary School, 920 Bend Gate Rd., Henderson 42420. Tel. 502-831-5040, fax 502-831-5043, e-mail swathen@henderson.k12.ky.us; *Treas.* Lisa Hughes, Ballard Memorial H.S., 3561 Paducah Rd., Barlow 42024. Tel. 502-665-5151, fax 502-665-5312, e-maillhughes@msmail.bmhs.ballard.k12.ky.us.

Address correspondence to the president.

Louisiana

Louisiana Assn. of School Libns. Memb. 500. Term of Office. July 1997–June 1998.

Pres. Penny Lee Johnson, 6531 Burke, Shreveport 71108. Tel. 318-635-9633; *1st V.P./Pres.-Elect* Catherine Brooks, 6123 Hagerstown Dr., Baton Rouge 70817. Tel. 504-775-5924; *Secy.* Debra Rollins, 107 Rock Pointe E., Pineville 71360. Tel. 318-776-9371.

Address correspondence to the association, c/o Louisiana Lib. Assn., Box 3058, Baton Rouge 70821.

Maine

Maine Educational Media Assn. Memb. 350. Term of Office. May 1997–May 1999. Publication. *Maine Entry* (with the Maine Lib. Assn.; q.).

Pres. Sylvia K. Norton, Freeport H.S. Lib., 30 Holbrook St., Freeport 04032. Tel. 207-865-4706, e-mail sylvian@saturn.caps.maine.edu; *1st V.P.* Susan J. Nelson, Portland H.S., 284 Cumberland Ave., Portland 04101. Tel. 207-874-8250, e-mail sjnelson@saturn.caps.maine.edu; *Secy.* Nancy B. Grant, Penquis Valley H.S., 35 W. Main St., Milo 04463. Tel. 207-943-7346.

Address correspondence to the president.

Maryland

Maryland Educational Media Organization. Term of Office. July 1997–June 1998. Publication. *MEMORANDOM.*

Pres. Linda Williams; *Secy.* Jayne Moore, 25943 Fox Grape Rd., Greensboro 21639.

Address correspondence to the association, Box 21127, Baltimore 21228.

Massachusetts

Massachusetts School Lib. Media Assn. Memb. 800. Term of Office. June 1997–May 1998. Publication. *Media Forum* (q.).

Pres. Joe Angelo. Tel. 781-383-6100, ext. 33, e-mail angeloj10@aol.com; *Pres.-Elect* Doris Smith. Tel. 781-275-1700, e-mail dorsmith@hac.net; *Secy.* Carolann Costello. Tel. 508-841-8821, e-mail costello@miol.mass. edu; *Admin. Asst.* Sue Rebello, MSLMA, 18 Sasur St., Three Rivers 01080-1031. Tel./fax 413-283-6675.

Address correspondence to the administrative assistant.

Michigan

Michigan Assn. for Media in Education. Memb. 1,400. Term of Office. Jan.–Dec. 1998. Publications. *Media Spectrum* (4 per year); *MAME Newsletter* (5 per year).

Pres. Ruth Lumpkins, Grand Rapids Public Schools, 1440 Davis N.W., Grand Rapids 49504. Tel. 616-771-2595; *Pres.-Elect* Dee Gwattney, South Redford Public Schools, 26255 Schoolcraft, Redford 48239. Tel. 313-535-4000; *V.P. for Regions/Special Interest Groups* Diane Nye, Saint Joseph Public Schools, 2214 S. State St., Saint Joseph 49085. Tel. 616-982-4626; *Secy.* Kathleen Nist, Algonac Community Schools, 5200 Taft Rd., Algonac 48001. Tel. 810-794-4911; *Treas.* Susan Luse Thornton, Napoleon Community Schools, Box 308, Napoleon 49261. Tel. 517-536-8637; *Past Pres.* Elaine Woods, Livonia Public Schools, 32401 Pembroke, Livonia 48152; *Exec. Dir.* Burton H. Brooks, 6810 S. Cedar St., Suite 8, Lansing 48911. Tel. 517-699-1717, fax 616-842-9195, e-mail bhbrooks@aol.com.

Address correspondence to the executive director.

Minnesota

Minnesota Educational Media Organization. Memb. 750. Term of Office. (Pres.) Aug. 1998–Aug. 1999. Publications. *Minnesota Media* (3 per year); *ImMEDIAte*; *MEMOrandom* (mo.).

Co-Pres. Judy Arnold, 13301 Maple Knoll Way, Maple Grove 55369; Lars Steltzner, 15998 Putnam Blvd. S., Afton 55001; *Co-Pres.-Elect* Al Edwards, 2824 The Narrows Dr. S.W., Alexandria 56308; Leslie Erickson, 1396 Summit Ave., Saint Paul 55105-2218; *Secy.* Virjean Griensewic, 304 Stoltzman Rd.,

Mankato 56001; *Treas.* Sybil Solting, 502 Second Ave. S.E., Box 154, Mapleton 56065. Tel. 507-524-3917, e-mail 2135mrhs@ informns.k12.mn.us; *Admin. Asst.* Evie Funk, 331 Wedgewood La. N., Plymouth 56467.

Mississippi

School Section, Mississippi Lib. Assn. Memb. 1,300.

Chair Florence Box; *Secy.* Robert McKay.

Address correspondence to the association, c/o Mississippi Lib. Assn., Box 20448, Jackson 39289-1448.

Missouri

Missouri Assn. of School Libns. Memb. 985. Term of Office. June 1997–May 1998. *Media Horizons* (ann.).

Pres. Sara Stubbins, Greenwood Lab School, Springfield 63600. Tel. 417-836-5958; *1st V.P./Pres.-Elect* Kay Rebstock; *2nd V.P.* Brenda Steffens; *Secy.* Patricia Bibler; *Treas.* Donna Livengood.

Address correspondence to the association, 1552 Rue Riviera, Bonne Terre 63628-9349. Tel./fax 573-358-1053, e-mail masloffice@ aol.com.

Montana

Montana School Lib. Media Div., Montana Lib. Assn. Memb. 215. Term of Office. July 1997–June 1998. Publication. *FOCUS* (published by Montana Lib. Assn.) (q.).

Chair Suzanne Goodman, Park H.S., 102 View Vista Dr., Livingston 59047. Tel. 406-222-0448; *Chair-Elect* Arlene Garvey, 1030 W. Gold, Butte 59701. Tel. 406-782-5995; *Admin. Asst.* John Thomas, Box 505, Helena 59624-0505.

Address correspondence to the chairperson.

Nebraska

Nebraska Educational Media. Assn. Memb. 350. Term of Office. July 1997–June 1998. Publication. *NEMA News* (q.).

Pres. Joie Taylor, 2301 31st St., Columbus 68601. Tel. 402-564-1781, fax 402-563-7003, e-mail jtaylor@gilligan.esu7.k12.ne.us; *Past Pres.* Roger Adkins, ESU 16, 314 W. First St., Ogallah 69153. Tel. 308-284-8481, e-mail radkins@esu16.k12.ne.us; *Pres.-Elect* Sue Divan, West Kearney High School, Youth Rehabilitation & Treatment Center, 2802 30th St., Kearney 68847. Tel. 308-865-5313, e-mail sdivan@genie.esu10.k12.ne.us; *Secy.* Terry Zimmers, Syracuse Public Schools, Box 94, 388 Eighth St., Syracuse 68446. Tel 402-269-2994, fax 402-269-3028, e-mail tzimmers@esu6.k12.ne.us; *Treas.* Deborah Smith, Pleasanton Public School, 303 W. Church St., Pleasanton 68866. Tel. 308-388-2041, fax 308-388-5502, e-mail dsmith@genie.esu10.k12.ne.us; *Exec. Secy.* Phyllis Brunken, ESU 7, 2657 44th Ave., Columbus 68601. Tel. 402-564-5753, fax 402-563-1121, e-mail pbrunke@gilligan. esu7.k12.ne.us.

Address correspondence to the executive secretary.

Nevada

Nevada School and Children's Lib. Section, Nevada Lib. Assn. Memb. 120. Term of Office. One year.

Chair Jennifer Fakolt, Youth Services Libn., Carson City Lib., 900 Roop St., Carson City 89701. Tel. 702-887-2244, fax 702-887-2273; *Exec. Secy.* Keri Putnam, Nevada State Lib. and Archives, 100 N. Stewart St., Carson City 89701. Tel. 702-687-5154, fax 702-687-8311.

New Hampshire

New Hampshire Educational Media Assn., Box 418, Concord 03302-0418. Memb. 265. Term of Office. June 1997–June 1998. Publications. *Online* (5 per year). *Ed.* Nancy J. Keane, Rundlett Jr. H.S., 144 South St., Concord 03301. Tel. 603-225-0862, fax 603-226-3288; *Taproot* (s. ann.).

Pres. Kay Klein, Peter Woodbury Elementary School, 180 Country Rd., Bedford 03110. E-mail kay@kleins.mv.com; *Pres.-Elect* Jeannette Lizotte, Bow H.S., 32 White Rock Hill Rd., Bow 03304. Tel. 603-228-2210, fax 603-228-2212, e-mail jlizotte@bow.k12.nh.us; *Treas.* Jeffrey Kent, Broken Ground School, Portsmouth St., Concord 03301. Tel. 603-225-0825, fax 603-225-0869, e-mail jeff.kent@bg.concord.k12.nh.us.

Address correspondence to the president.

New Jersey

Educational Media Assn. of New Jersey. Memb. 1,100. Term of Office. June 1997–June 1998. Publications. *Bookmark* (mo.); *Emanations* (s. ann.).

Pres. Lois Wilkins, Sussex County Technical School, 105 N. Church Rd., Sparta 07871. Tel. 201-383-6700 ext. 257, e-mail lwilkins@tapnet.net; *Pres.-Elect* Nina Kemps, Horace Mann Elementary School, 150 Walt Whitman Blvd., Cherry Hill 08003. E-mail nkeps@recom.com; *V.P.* Villy Gandhi, Lakeside Middle School, 316 Lakeside Ave., Pompton Lakes 07442. Tel. 973-835-6221, e-mail villy@cybertnex.net.

Address correspondence to the president, president-elect, or vice president.

New Mexico

[See "New Mexico" under "State, Provincial, and Regional Library Associations" earlier in Part 6—*Ed.*].

New York

School Lib. Media Section, New York Lib. Assn., 252 Hudson St., Albany 12210. Tel. 518-432-6952, 800-252-6952. Memb. 950. Term of Office. Oct. 1997–Oct. 1998. Publications. *SLMSGram* (q.); participates in *NYLA Bulletin* (mo. except July and Aug.).

Pres. Paul W. Crumlish, Warren Hunting Smith Lib., Hobart Eva Effron, Box 336, West Islip 11795-0336; *V.P./Pres.-Elect* Sue Norkeliunas, Box 98, Hyde Park 12538. Tel. 914-486-4880; *Past Pres.* Carolyn Giambra, Williamsville North H.S. Lib., 1595 Hopkins Rd., Williamsville 14221. Tel. 716-626-8025; *Secy.* Robert Brewster, 10-6 Loudon Dr., Fishkill 12524. Tel. 914-279-5051; *Treas.* Carol Brown, R.D. 1, Box 337, Fillmore 14735.

Address correspondence to the president or secretary.

North Carolina

North Carolina Assn. of School Libns. Memb. 800. Term of Office. Oct. 1997–Oct. 1999.

Chair Melinda Ratchford, Gaston County Schools, 366 W. Garrison Blvd., Gastonia 28054. Tel. 704-866-6251, e-mail meleis@aol.

com; *Chair-Elect* Karen Gavigan, Burlington Day School, 1615 Greenwood Terrace, Burlington 27215. Tel. 336-228-0296, e-mail kpwg@aol.com.

Address correspondence to the chairperson.

North Dakota

School Lib. and Youth Services Section, North Dakota Lib. Assn. Memb. 108. Term of Office. Sept. 1997–Sept. 1998. Publication. *The Good Stuff* (q).

Pres. Marvia Boettcher, Bismarck Public Lib., 515 Fifth St. N., Bismarck 58501. Tel. 701-222-6412, fax 701-221-6854, e-mail m.boettcher@mail.cdln.lib.nd.us; *V.P./Pres.-Elect* Paulette Nelson, Minot Public Lib., 516 Second Ave. S.W., Minot 58701-3792. Fax 701-852-2595, e-mail pnelson@minotpl.ndak.net; *Secy.* Darlene Schwarz, Simle Middle School, 1215 N. 19 St., Bismarck 58501. Tel. 701-221-3579, e-mail SM_library@mail.lmo.bismarck.k12.nd.us.

Address correspondence to the president.

Ohio

Ohio Educational Lib. Media Assn. Memb. 1,300. Publication. *Ohio Media Spectrum*

Exec. Dir. Ann Hanning, 1631 N.W. Professional Plaza, Columbus 43220. Tel. 614-326-1460, fax 614-459-2087, e-mail oelma@mec.ohio.gov.

Address correspondence to the executive director.

Oklahoma

Oklahoma Assn. of School Lib. Media Specialists. Memb. 3005. Term of Office. July 1997–June 1998. Publication. *Information Powerline.*

Chair Buffy Edwards, Lakeview Elementary School, 3310 108th Ave. N.E., Norman 73071. Tel. 405-366-5899, e-mail beverlys@norman.k12.ok.us; *Chair-Elect* Carol Fox, State Dept. of Educ., 2500 N. Lincoln Blvd., Oklahoma City 73105. E-mail cfox@oltn.odl.state.ok.us; *Secy.* Lori Bradley, Yukon Public Schools, 2800 Mustang Rd., Yukon 73099. Tel. 405-354-4852, e-mail gmbdog@aol.com; *Treas.* Vicki Stewart, Bartlesville Public Schools, 801 S.E. 13th,

Bartlesville 74003. Tel. 918-337-6204, e-mail vickis4476@aol.com; *AASL Delegate* Bettie Estes Rickner, 12400 S. Mustang Rd., Mustang 73064. E-mail ber@ionet.net.

Address correspondence to the chairperson.

Oregon

Oregon Educational Media Assn. Memb. 600. Term of Office. Aug. 1997–July 1998. Publication. *INTERCHANGE.*

Pres. Tom Sprott; *Pres.-Elect* Patty Sorensen; *Treas.* Jeri Petzel; *Exec. Dir.* Jim Hayden, Box 277, Terrebonne 97760. Tel./fax 541-923-0675.

Address correspondence to the executive director.

Pennsylvania

Pennsylvania School Libns. Assn. Term of Office. July 1996–June 1998. Publication. *Learning and Media* (4 per year).

Pres. Peggy Benjamin, R.R. 6, Box 6362, Moscow 18444. Tel. 717-842-7201, fax 717-842-7026.

Address correspondence to the president.

Rhode Island

Rhode Island Educational Media Assn. Memb. 368. Term of Office. June 1997–May 1998. Publication. *RIEMA Newsletter* (8 per year). *Ed.* Dwight D. Barrett, 32 Glen Ave., Cranston 02905. Tel. 401-941-0094.

Pres. Marykay Schnare, 11 Nelson St., Providence 02908. Tel. 401-331-2050; *V.P.* Richard Dressler, 284 Allens Ave., Providence 02905. Tel. 401-467-5050; *Secy.* Patricia Menoche, Tiverton Middle School, 10 Quintal Dr., Tiverton 02878. Tel. 401-624-6668.

Address correspondence to the association, Box 762, Portsmouth 02871.

South Carolina

South Carolina Assn. of School Libns. Memb. 1,100. Term of Office. June 1997–May 1998. Publication. *Media Center Messenger* (5 per year).

Pres. Olivia Padgett, Bells Elementary School, 12088 Bells Highway, Ruffin 29475.

Tel. 843-866-2417, fax 843-866-7361, e-mail opadgett@lowcountry.com; *Secy.* Kwamine Simpson, Media Specialist, Lower Richland H.S., 7717 Burdell Dr., Columbia 29709. Tel. 803-783-9172; *Treas.* Sue Waddell, Lakeview Middle School, 3801 Old Buncombe Rd., Greenville 29609. Tel. 864-294-4361, fax 864-294-4236, e-mail lakeview@greenville.k12.sc.

Address correspondence to the secretary.

South Dakota

South Dakota School Lib. Media Assn., Section of the South Dakota Lib. Assn. and South Dakota Education Assn. Memb. 146. Term of Office. Oct. 1997–Oct. 1998.

Pres. Janet Winkelman, Estelline H.S., Estelline 57234; *Pres.-Elect* Peggy Morris, Redfield Public School, Redfield 57469; *Secy.-Treas.* Linda Demery, Faulkton School, Box 161, Faulkton 57438.

Address correspondence to the secretary-treasurer.

Tennessee

Tennessee Assn. of School Libns. (affiliated with the Tennessee Education Assn.). Memb. 450. Term of Office. Jan. 1998–Dec. 1998. Publication. *Footnotes* (q.).

Pres. D. S. Thompson, 1555 Eastlawn, Memphis 38111. Tel. 901-320-6100 or 901-744-0361 fax 901-320-6133, e-mail ThompsonD01@Ten-Nash.ten.k12.tn.us; *V.P./Pres.-Elect* Mary J. Smith, 8707 Bradley Creek Rd., Lascassas 37085; *Secy.* Margaret Moore, 1403 N. Tennessee Blvd., Murfreesboro 37130; *Treas.* Carol Burr, 2523 Stinson Rd., Nashville 37214.

Address correspondence to the president.

Texas

Texas Assn. of School Libns (Div. of Texas Lib. Assn.). Memb. 3,315. Term of Office. Apr. 1998–Apr. 1999. Publication. *Media Matters* (3 per year).

Chair Pat Jefferson, 796 Windemere Way, Keller 76248-5210. Tel. 817-481-1425.

Address correspondence to the association, 3355 Bee Cave Rd., Suite 401, Austin 78746.

Tel. 512-328-1518, fax 512-328-8852, e-mail tla@txla.org.

Utah

Utah Educational Lib. Media Assn. Memb. 327. Term of Office. Mar. 1997–Feb. 1998. Publication. *UELMA Newsletter* (4 per year).

Pres. Julie Bentley, Hawthorne Elementary School, 1675 S. 600 E., Salt Lake City 84105. Tel. 801-481-4824, fax 801-481-4927, e-mail julie.bentley@slc.k12.ut.us; *Secy.* Gary Berensen, Mont Harmon Jr. H.S., 60 W. 400 N., Price 84501. Tel. 801-637-0510, fax 801-637-6074, e-mail berensen@mhjh.carbon.k12.ut.us; *Exec. Dir.* Larry Jeppesen, Cedar Ridge Middle School, 65 N. 200 W., Hyde Park 84318. Tel. 801-563-6229, fax 801-563-3915, e-mail larry.jeppesen@m.k12.ut.us.

Address correspondence to the executive director.

Vermont

Vermont Educational Media Assn. Memb. 203. Term of Office. May 1997–May 1998. Publication. *VEMA News* (q.).

Pres. Harriette Phillips-Hamblett, Lake Region H.S., R.R. 1, Box 76, Orleans 05860. Tel. 802-754-6521; *Pres.-Elect* Merlyn Miller, Burr & Burton Seminary, Seminary Ave., Manchester 05254; *Secy.* Dianne Wyllie, Teacher Learning Center, 7 Cherry St., Saint Johnsbury 05819. Tel 802-748-4569.

Address correspondence to the president.

Virginia

Virginia Educational Media Assn. Memb. 1,230. Term of Office. (Pres. and Pres.-Elect) Oct. 1997–Oct. 1998 (other offices 2 years in alternating years). Publications. *Mediagram* (q.).

Pres. Melinda Younger, 152 Bon Ton Rd., Lynchburg 24503. Tel. 804-582-1120; *Pres.-Elect* Ann Martin, 5039 Bonnie Brae Rd., Richmond 23234. Tel. 804-378-2420; *Exec. Mgr.* Jean Remler. Tel./fax 703-764-0719, e-mail jremler@pen.k12.va.us.

Address correspondence to the association, Box 2744, Fairfax 22031-2744.

Washington

Washington Lib. Media Assn. Memb. 1,200. Term of Office. Oct. 1997–Oct. 1998. Publications. *The Medium* (3 per year); *The Message* (s.ann.). *Ed.* Mary Lou Gregory, 711 Spruce St., Hoquiam 98550. Tel. 206-533-4897.

Pres. Barbara L. Baker, 320 Baker Rd., Selah 98942. Tel. 509-697-4234, e-mail barbbk@aol.com; *V.P.* Paul Christensen, Box 50, Indianaola 98342. Tel. 360-297-2965; *Secy.* Jan Weber, 6622 W. Victoria Ave., Kennewick 99336. Tel. 509-783-3789, e-mail jweber@anchor.doit.k12.wa.us.

Address correspondence to the president.

West Virginia

West Virginia Educational Media Assn. Memb. 150. Term of Office. Apr. 1997–Apr. 1998. Publication. *WVEMA Focus* (q.).

Pres. Theresa Bruner, Follett Software, 309 Mackin St., Grafton 26354. Tel. 800-323-3397, fax 304-265-4731, e-mail tbruner@fsc.follett.com; *Secy.* June Geiger, John Marshall H.S., 1444 Sunset Lane, Glendale 26038. Tel. 304-843-4444, fax 304-843-4419, e-mail jgeiger@access.k12.wv.us.

Address correspondence to the president.

Wisconsin

Wisconsin Educational Media Assn. Memb. 1,122. Term of Office. Apr. 1998–Apr. 1999. Publications. *Dispatch* (7 per year); *Wisconsin Ideas in Media* (ann.).

Pres. Sherry Freiberg, Fond du Lac School Dist., 72 S. Portland St., Fond du Lac 54935. Tel. 920-929-2780, e-mail freibergs@fonddulac.k12.wi.us; *Past Pres.* Helen Adams, Rosholt H.S., 346 W. Randolph St., Rosholt 54473. Tel. 715-677-4541, e-mail hadams@coredcs.com.

Address correspondence to the president.

Wyoming

Section of School Library Media Personnel, Wyoming Lib. Assn. Memb. 80. Term of Office. Oct. 1997–Oct. 1998. Publication. *WLA Newsletter.*

Chair Vickie Hoff, Rawlins H.S., 1401 Colorado, Rawlins 82301. Tel. 307-328-9280 ext. 41, fax 307-328-9286; *Chair-Elect* Jan Segerstrom, Jackson Hole Middle School, Box 568, Jackson, Wyoming 83001. Tel. 307-733-4234, fax 307-733-4254.

Address correspondence to the chairperson.

International Library Associations

International Association of Agricultural Information Specialists

c/o J. van der Burg, President
Boeslaan 55, 6703 ER Wageningen, Netherlands
Tel./fax 31-317-422820

Object

The association shall, internationally and nationally, promote agricultural library science and documentation as well as the professional interest of agricultural librarians and documentalists. Founded 1955.

Membership

Memb. 600+. Dues (Inst.) $90; (Indiv.) $35.

Officers

Pres. J. van der Burg, Boeslaan 55, 6703 ER Wageningen, Netherlands; *Secy.-Treas.* Margot Bellamy, c/o CAB International, Wallingford, Oxon, OX10 8DE, United Kingdom. Tel./fax 44-1491-833508.

Publications

Quarterly Bulletin of the IAALD (memb.).
World Directory of Agricultural Information Resource Centres.

International Association of Law Libraries

Box 5709, Washington, DC 20016-1309
804-924-3384, fax 804-924-7239

Object

IALL is a worldwide organization of librarians, libraries, and other persons or institutions concerned with the acquisition and use of legal information emanating from sources other than their jurisdictions, and from multinational and international organizations.

IALL's basic purpose is to facilitate the work of librarians who must acquire, process, organize, and provide access to foreign legal materials. IALL has no local chapters but maintains liaison with national law library associations in many countries and regions of the world.

Membership

Over 500 members in more than 50 countries on five continents.

Officers

Pres. Larry Wenger (USA); *1st V.P.* Roberta Shaffer (USA) *2nd V.P.* Fred Chapman (Switzerland); *Secy.* Britt S. M. Kjolstad (Switzerland); *Treas.* Gloria F. Chao (USA).

Board Members

Marie-Louise Bernal (USA); Jacqueline Elliott (Australia); Claire M. Germain (USA); Holger Knudsen (Germany); Ann Morrison (Canada); Harald Mueller (Germany); Josep Sort i Ticó (Spain); Jules Winterton (England).

Publications

International Journal of Legal Information (3 per year; US$55 for individuals; $80 for institutions).

Committee Chairpersons

Publications. Richard A. Danner (USA)

International Association of Music Libraries, Archives and Documentation Centres (IAML)

c/o Alison Hall, Secretary-General
Cataloging Dept., Carleton University Library
1125 Colonel By Drive, Ottawa, ON K15 5B6, Canada
Fax 613-520-3583

Object

To promote the activities of music libraries, archives, and documentation centers and to strengthen the cooperation among them; to promote the availability of all publications and documents relating to music and further their bibliographical control; to encourage the development of standards in all areas that concern the association; and to support the protection and preservation of musical documents of the past and the present.

Membership

Memb. 1,900.

Board Members (1995–1998)

Pres. Veslemöy Heintz, Svenskt Musikhistoriskt Arkiv, Box 16326, S-103 26 Stockholm, Sweden; *Past Pres.* Don Roberts, Music Lib., Northwestern Univ., Evanston, IL 60208-2300; *V.P.s* Hugh Cobbe, Music Lib., British Lib., Great Russell St., London WC1B 3DG, England; John Roberts, Music Lib., 240 Morrison Hall, Univ. of California, Berkeley, Berkeley, CA 94720; Joachim Jaenecke, Staatsbibliothek zu Berlin, Preussischer Kulturbesitz, Musikabteilung, D 1902 Berlin; Massimo Gentili-Tedeschi, Ufficio Ricerca Fondi Musicali, Via Conservatorio 12, I-20122 Milan; *Secy.-Gen.* Alison Hall,

Cataloging Dept., Carleton Univ. Lib., 1125 Colonel By Dr., Ottawa ON K1S 5B6; *Treas.* Pam Thompson, Royal College of Music Lib., Prince Consort Rd., London SW7 2BS, England.

Publication

Fontes Artis Musicae (4 per year; memb.). *Ed.* Susan T. Sommer, New York Public Lib. for the Performing Arts, 111 Amsterdam Ave., New York, NY 10023-7498.

Professional Branches

Archives and Documentation Centres. Inger Enquist, Statens musikbibliotek, Box 16326, S-10326 Stockholm, Sweden.
Broadcasting and Orchestra Libraries. Kauko Karjalainen, Yleisradio Oy, P.O. Box 76, FIN-00024 Yleisradio, Finland.
Libraries in Music Teaching Institutions. Federica Riva, Conservatorio di Musica G. Verdi, Via del Conservatorio 12, I-20122 Milano, Italy.
Public Libraries. Kirsten Voss-Eliassen, Herlev Bibliotek, Musikafdeling, Bygaden 70, DK-2730, Denmark.
Research Libraries. Ann Kersting, Music- und Theaterabteilung, Stadt- und Universitätsbibliothek, Bockenheimer Landstr. 134-138, D-60325 Frankfurt, Germany.

International Association of School Librarianship

Ken Haycock, Executive Director
Box 34069, Dept. 300, Seattle, WA 98124-1069
604-925-0266, fax 604-925-0566, e-mail iasl@rockland.com

Object

To encourage the development of school libraries and library programs throughout all countries; to promote the professional preparation of school librarians; to bring about close collaboration among school libraries in all countries, including the loan and exchange of literature; to initiate and coordinate activities, conferences, and other projects in the field of school librarianship. Founded 1971.

Membership

Memb. 800.

Officers and Executive Board

Pres. Sigrún Klara Hannesdottir, Iceland; *V.P.s* Peter Genco, USA; Dianne Oberg, Canada; Ross Todd, Australia; Blanche Woolls, USA; *Dirs.* Marvene Dearman, North America; Mary Jamil Fasheh, North Africa/Middle East; Isabel Gomez, Latin America; James Henri, Australasia; Mieko Nagakura, Japan/Asia; Monica Milsson, Europe; Sandra Olën, Africa; Cherrell Shelley-Robinson, Caribbean; Diljit Singh, Pacific Region.

Publications

Books and Borrowers.
Connections: School Library Associations and Contact People Worldwide.
IASL Conference Proceedings (ann.).
IASL Monograph Series.
School Libraries Worldwide (s-ann.).

U.S. Association Members

American Assn. of School Libns.; Illinois School Lib. Media Assn.; International Reading Assn.; Louisiana Assn. of School Libns.; Maryland Educational Media Organization; Michigan Assn. for Media in Education; Washington Lib. Media Assn.

International Association of Technological University Libraries

c/o President, Nancy Fjällbrant, Chalmers University of Technology Library,
412 96 Gothenburg, Sweden
46 31 7723754, fax 46 31 168494, e-mail nancyf@lib.chalmers.se

Object

To provide a forum where library directors can meet to exchange views on matters of current significance in the libraries of universities of science and technology. Research projects identified as being of sufficient interest may be followed through by working parties or study groups.

Membership

Ordinary, official observer, sustaining, and nonvoting associate. Membership fee is 550 Danish kroner per year (1,450 kroner for three years, 2,300 kroner for five years). Memb. 198 (in 43 countries).

Officers and Executives

Pres. Nancy Fjällbrant, Chalmers University of Technology Library, 412 96 Gothenburg, Sweden. Tel. 46 31 7723754, fax 46 31 168494, e-mail nancyf@lib.chalmers.se. *Secy.* Sinikka Koskiala, Helsinki Univ. of Technology Lib., Box 7000, FIN-02015 HUT, Finland. Tel. 358-9-4514112, fax 358-9-4514132, e-mail Sinikka.Koskiala@hut.fi; *Treas.* Leo Waaijers, Delft Univ. of Technology Lib., Postbus 98, 2600 MG Delft, Netherlands. Tel. 3115-785-656, fax 3115-158-759, e-mail Waaijers@library.tudelft.nl; *Membs.* Gaynor Austen, Australia; Michael L. Breaks, Scotland; Egbert D. Gerryts, South Africa; *North American Regional Group Chair* Richard P. Widdicombe, USA; *Ed.* Nancy Fjällbrant, Sweden.

Publications

IATUL News (irreg.).
IATUL Proceedings (ann.).

International Council on Archives

Charles Kecskeméti, Secretary General
60 Rue des Francs-Bourgeois, F-75003
Paris, France
33-1-4027-6306, fax 33-1-4272-2065, e-mail 100640.54@compuserve.com

Object

To establish, maintain, and strengthen relations among archivists of all lands, and among all professional and other agencies or institutions concerned with the custody, organization, or administration of archives, public or private, wherever located. Established 1948.

Membership

Memb. 1,528 (representing 160 countries and territories). Dues (Indiv.) $80 or $125; (Inst.) $125; (Archives Assns.) $125 or $275; (Central Archives Directorates) $275 or $150 minimum, computed on the basis of GNP and GNP per capita.

Officers

Secy.-Gen. Charles Kecskeméti. *Deputy Secy.-Gen.* George P. MacKenzie.

Publications

Archivum (ann.; memb. or subscription to K. G. Saur Verlag, Ortlerstr. 8, Postfach 70 16 20, 81-316 Munich, Germany).
Guide to the Sources of the History of Nations (Latin American Series, 12 vols. pub.; African Series, 17 vols. pub.; Asian Series, 21 vols. pub.), North Africa, Asia, and Oceania: 15 vols. pub.; other guides, 3 vols. pub.; *ICA Bulletin* (s. ann.; memb.).
Janus (s. ann.; memb.)
List of other publications available from the secretariat.

International Federation for Information and Documentation (FID)

Box 90402, 2509 LK The Hague, Netherlands
3140671, fax 3140667, e-mail fid@python.konbib.nl

Object

To promote, through international cooperation, research in and development of information science, information management, and documentation, which includes inter alia the organization, storage, retrieval, repackaging, dissemination, value adding, and evaluation of information, however recorded, in the fields of science, technology, industry, social sciences, arts, and humanities.

Program

FID devotes much of its attention to corporate information; industrial, business, and finance information; information policy research; the application of information technology; information service management; the marketing of information systems and services; content analysis, for example, in the design of database systems; linking information and human resources; and the repackaging of information for specific user audiences. The following commissions, committees, and groups have been established to execute FID's program of activities: *Regional Commissions:* Commission for Western, Eastern and Southern Africa (FID/CAF), Commission for Asia and Oceania (FID/CAO), Commission for Latin America (FID/CLA), Commission for the Caribbean and North America (FID/CNA), Commission for Northern Africa and the Near East (FID/NANE), Regional Organization for Europe (FID/ROE); *Committees:* Classification Research for Knowledge Organization, Education and Training, Fundamental Theory of Information, Information for Industry, Information Policies and Programmes, Intellectual Property Issues, Social Sciences Documentation and Information; *Special Interest Groups:* Archives and Records Management; Banking, Finance, and Insurance Information; Environmental Information; Business Information; Organizational Excellence; Roles, Careers, and Development of the Modern Information Professional; Safety Control and Risk Management.

Publications

FID Annual Report (ann.).
FID Directory (bienn.).
FID News Bulletin (bi.-mo.) with quarterly inserts
Document Delivery Survey and *ET Newsletter*.
FID Publications List (irreg.).
International Forum on Information and Documentation (q.).
Proceedings of congresses; directories; bibliographies on information science, documentation, education and training, and classification research.

International Federation of Film Archives (FIAF)

Secretariat, Rue Defacqz 1, 1000 Brussels, Belgium
(32-2) 538-3065, fax (32-2) 534-4774, e-mail fiaf@mail.interpac.be
World Wide Web http://www.cinema.ucla.edu/FIAF/fiaf.html

Object

To facilitate communication and cooperation between its members, and to promote the exchange of films and information; to maintain a code of archive practice calculated to satisfy all national film industries, and to encourage industries to assist in the work of the federation's members; to advise its members on all matters of interest to them, especially the preservation and study of films; to give every possible assistance and encouragement to new film archives and to those interested in creating them. Founded in Paris, 1938. Affiliates: 120 (in more than 60 countries).

Officers

Pres. Michelle Aubert, France; *V.P.s* Ivan Trujillo Bolio, Mexico; *Secy.-Gen.* Roger Smither, UK; *Treas.* Mary Lea Bandy, USA.

Address correspondence to Christian Dimitriu, Senior Administrator, c/o the Secretariat.

Executive Committee

Officers; Vittorio Boarini, Italy; Steven Ricci, USA; Nelly Cruz Rodríguez, Puerto Rico; Gabrielle Claes, Belgium; Clyde Jeav-ons, UK; José Maria Prado, Spain; Ivan Trujillo Bolio, Mexico; Peter Konlechner, Austria; Hervé Dumont, Switzerland.

Publications

Annual Bibliography of FIAF Members Publications.

Bibliography of National Filmographies.

Evaluating Computer Cataloguing Systems (a guide for film archivists).

FIAF Cataloguing Rules for Film Archives.

FIAF Journal of Film Preservation. Glossary of Filmographic Terms in English, French, German, Spanish, and Russian (a second version in 12 languages).

Handbook for Film Archives (available in English or French).

International Directory to Film & TV Documentation Sources.

International Index to Film Periodicals (cumulative volumes).

International Index to Film and Television Periodicals (available on CD-ROM).

International Index to Television Periodicals (cumulative volumes).

Study on the Usage of Computers for Film Cataloguing.

Technical Manual of the FIAF Preservation Commission.

International Federation of Library Associations and Institutions (IFLA)

Box 95312, 2509 CH The Hague, Netherlands
31-70-3140884, fax 31-70-3834027
e-mail IFLA.HQ@IFLA.NL, World Wide Web http://www.nlc-bnc.ca/ifla/

Object

To promote international understanding, cooperation, discussion, research, and development in all fields of library activity, including bibliography, information services, and the education of library personnel, and to provide a body through which librarianship can be represented in matters of international interest. Founded 1927.

Membership

Memb. (Lib. Assns.) 153; (Inst.) 1,070; (Aff.) 291; Sponsors: 32.

Officers and Executive Board

Pres. Christine Deschamps, Bibliothèque de l'Université Paris V–René Descartes, Paris, France; *1st V.P.* Ekaterina U. Genieva, M. I. Rudomino All-Russia State Lib. of Foreign Literature, Moscow, Russia; *Treas.* Derek Law, King's College London Lib., London, United Kingdom; *Exec. Board* Nancy John, Univ. of Illinois at Chicago; Klaus-Dieter Lehmann, Die Deutsche Bibliothek, Frankfurt am Main, Germany; Beixin Sun, National Lib. of China, Beijing, China; Børge Sørensen, Copenhagen Public Libs., Copenhagen, Denmark; *Ex officio memb.* Sissel Nilsen, Baerum Public Lib., Oslo, Norway; *Secy.-Gen.* Leo Voogt; *Coord. Professional Activities* Winston Roberts; *IFLA Office for Universal Bibliographic Control and International MARC Program Dir.* Kurt Nowak; *Program Officer* Marie-France Plassard, c/o Deutsche Bibliothek, Frankfurt am Main, Germany; *IFLA International Program for UAP Program Dir.* Graham Cornish, c/o British Lib. Document Supply Centre, Boston

Spa, Wetherby, West Yorkshire, England; *IFLA Office for Preservation and Conservation Program Dir.* M. T. Varlamoff, c/o Bibliothèque Nationale de France, Paris; *IFLA Office for University Dataflow and Telecommunications Program Dir.* Leigh Swain, c/o National Lib. of Canada, Ottawa, Canada; *IFLA Office for the Advancement of Librarianship in the Third World Program Dir.* Birgitta Bergdahl, c/o Uppsala Univ. Lib., Uppsala, Sweden; *IFLA Office for International Lending Dir.* Graham Cornish.

Publications

IFLA Directory (bienn.).
IFLA Council Report 1995–1997
IFLA Journal (q.).
IFLA Professional Reports.
IFLA Publications Series.
International Cataloguing and Bibliographic Control (q.).
PAC Newsletter.
UAP Newsletter (s. ann.).
UDT Digest (electronic).

American Membership

American Assn. of Law Libs.; American Lib. Assn.; Art Libs. Society of North America; Assn. for Lib. and Info. Science Education; Assn. of Research Libs.; International Assn. of Law Libs.; International Assn. of School Libns.; Medical Lib. Assn.; Special Libs. Assn. *Institutional Membs.* There are 125 libraries and related institutions that are institutional members or consultative bodies and sponsors of IFLA in the United States (out of a total of 1,070), and 80 personal affiliates (out of a total of 291).

International Organization for Standardization (ISO)

ISO Central Secretariat, 1 ruc dc Varembé, Case Postale 56, CH-1211 Geneva 20,
Switzerland
41-22-749-0111, fax 41-22-733-3430, e-mail central@iso.ch

Object

Worldwide federation of national standards bodies, founded in 1947, at present comprising 124 members, one in each country. The object of ISO is to promote the development of standardization and related activities in the world with a view to facilitating international exchange of goods and services, and to developing cooperation in the spheres of intellectual, scientific, technological, and economic activity. The scope of ISO covers international standardization in all fields except electrical and electronic engineering standardization, which is the responsibility of the International Electrotechnical Commission (IEC). The results of ISO technical work are published as *International Standards*.

Officers

Pres. Licw Mun Leong, Singapore; *V.P. (Policy)* H. Reihlen, Germany; *V.P. (Technical Management)* J. Kean, Canada; *Secy.-Gen.* L. D. Eicher.

Technical Work

The technical work of ISO is carried out by some 180 technical committees. These include:

ISO/TC 46—Information and documentation (Secretariat, Deutsches Institut für Normung, 10772 Berlin, Germany. Scope: Standardization of practices relating to libraries, documentation and information centers, indexing and abstracting services, archives, information science, and publishing.

ISO/TC 37—Terminology (principles and coordination) (Secretariat, Österreiches Normungsinstitut, Heinestr. 38, Postfach 130, A-1021 Vienna, Austria). Scope: Standardization of methods for creating, compiling, and coordinating terminologies.

ISO/IEC JTC 1—Information technology (Secretariat, American National Standards Institute, 11 W. 42 St., 13th fl., New York, NY 10036). Scope: Standardization in the field of information technology.

Publications

ISO Annual Report.
ISO Bulletin (mo.).
ISO Catalogue (ann.).
ISO International Standards.
ISO 9000 News (bi-mo.).
ISO Memento (ann.).
ISO Online information service on World Wide Web (http://www.iso.ch/).

Foreign Library Associations

The following list of regional and national library associations around the world is a selective one. A more complete list can be found in *International Literary Market Place* (R. R. Bowker).

Regional

Africa

Standing Conference of African Univ. Libs., c/o E. Bejide Bankole, Editor, African Journal of Academic Librarianship, Box 46, Univ. of Lagos, Akoka, Yaba, Lagos, Nigeria. Tel. 1-524968.

The Americas

Asociación de Bibliotecas Universitarias, de Investigación e Institucionales del Caribe (Assn. of Caribbean Univ., Research and Institutional Libs.), Box S, University Station, Rio Piedras 00931, Puerto Rico. Tel. 809-790-8054, fax 809-763-5685. *Exec. Secy.* Oneida R. Ortiz.

Seminar on the Acquisition of Latin American Lib. Materials, c/o *Exec. Secy.* Sharon A. Moynahan, General Lib., Univ. of New Mexico, Albuquerque, NM 87131-1466. Tel. 505-277-5102.

Asia

Congress of Southeast Asian Libns. IV (CONSAL IV), c/o Serafin D. Quiason, National Historic Institute of the Philippines, T. M. Kalaw St., 100 Ermita, Box 2926, Manila, Philippines. Tel./fax 2-590646.

The Commonwealth

Commonwealth Lib. Assn., c/o *Exec. Secy.* Norma Amenu-Kpodo, Box 144, Mona, Kingston 7, Jamaica. Tel. 809-927-2123, fax 809-927-1926. *Pres.* Elizabeth Watson; *Exec. Secy.* Norma Amenu-Kpodo.

Standing Conference on Lib. Materials on Africa, Univ. of London, Institute of Commonwealth Studies, Thornhaugh St., Russell Square, London WC1H 0XG, England. Tel. 171-637-2388, fax 171-636-2834, e-mail rt4@soas.ac.uk. *Chair* J. Pinfold.

Europe

Ligue des Bibliothèques Européennes de Recherche (LIBER) (Assn. of European Research Libs.), c/o H.-A. Koch, Staats- und Universitätsbibliothek, Postfach 330440, 28334 Bremen, Germany. Tel. 421-218-3361.

National

Argentina

Asociación de Bibliotecarios Graduados de la República Argentina (Assn. of Graduate Libns. of Argentina), Corrientes 1642, 1° piso, Of. 22-2° cuerpo, 1042 Buenos Aires. Tel./fax 1-384-4821, 384-8095. *Pres.* Ana María Peruchena Zimmermann; *Exec. Secy.* Rosa Emma Monfasani.

Australia

Australian Council of Libs. and Info. Services, Box E 202, Queen Victoria Terrace, Canberra, ACT 2600. Tel. 6-262-1244, fax 6-273-4493. *Pres.* Helen Hayes; *Exec. Officer* Gordon Bower.

Australian Lib. and Info. Assn., Box E 441, Queen Victoria Terrace, Canberra, ACT 2600. Tel. 6-285-1877, fax 6-282-2249.

Australian Society of Archivists, Box 83, O'Connor, ACT 2602. Tel. 7-3875-8705, fax 7-3875-8764, e-mail shicks@gil.com.au. *Pres.* Kathryn Dan; *Secy.* Fiona Burn.

Council of Australian State Libs., c/o State Lib. of Queensland, Queensland Cultural Centre, South Brisbane, Qld. Tel. 7-840-7666, fax 7-846-2421. *Chair* D. H. Stephens.

Austria

Österreichische Gesellschaft für Dokumentation und Information (Austrian Society for Documentation and Info.), c/o TermNet, Simmeringer Hauptstr. 24, A-1110 Vienna. Tel. 1-74040280, fax 1-74040281. *Pres.* Gerhard Richter.
Vereinigung Österreichischer Bibliothekarinnen und Bibliothekare (Assn. of Austrian Libns.), A-1082, Vienna. Tel. 1-4000-84936, 1-4000-7219, e-mail post@ m09magwieu.gv.at. *Pres.* Mag Eva Ramminger; *Secy.* Ruth Lotter.

Bangladesh

Lib. Assn. of Bangladesh, c/o Bangladesh Central Public Institute of Library & Information Sciences, Library Bldg., Shahbagh, Ramna, Dacca 1000. Tel. 2-504-269, e-mail msik@bangla.net. *Pres.* M. Shamsul Islam Khan; *Gen. Secy.* Kh Fazlur Rahman.

Barbados

Lib. Assn. of Barbados, Box 827E, Bridgetown. *Pres.* Shirley Yearwood; *Secy.* Hazelyn Devonish.

Belgium

Archives et Bibliothèques de Belgique/ Archief-en Bibliotheekwezen in België (Archives and Libs. of Belgium), 4 Blvd. de l'Empereur, B-1000 Brussels. Tel. 2-519-5351, fax 2-519-5533. *Gen. Secy.* Wim De Vos.
Association Belge de Documentation/Belgische Vereniging voor Documentatie (Belgian Assn. for Documentation), Chausee de Wavre 1683, Waversesteenweg, B-1160 Brussels. Tel. 2-675-5862, fax 2-672-7446. *Pres.* Jean-Louis Janssens; *Secy.* Philippe Laurent.
Association Professionnelle des Bibliothécaires et Documentalistes, B.P. 31, B-1070 Brussels. *Pres.* Michel Gilles; *Secy.* Georges Lecocq.
Vlaamse Vereniging voor Bibliotheek-, Archief-, en Documentatiewezen (Flemish Assn. of Libns., Archivists, and Documentalists), Waterloostraat 11, 2600 Berchem,

Antwerp. Tel. 3-281-4457, fax 3-218-8077, e-mail ms.vvbad@innet.be. *Pres.* Erwin Pairon; *Exec. Dir.* Marc Storms.

Belize

Belize Lib. Assn., c/o Central Lib., Bliss Inst., Box 287, Belize City. Tel. 2-7267. *Pres.* H. W. Young; *Secy.* Robert Hulse.

Bolivia

Asociación Boliviana de Bibliotecarios (Bolivian Lib. Assn.), c/o Biblioteca y Archivo Nacional, Calle Bolivar, Sucre.

Bosnia and Herzegovina

Drustvo bibliotekara Bosne i Hercegovine (Libns. Society of Bosnia and Herzegovina), Obala v Stepe 42, 71000 Sarajevo. Tel. 71-283245. *Pres.* Neda Cukac.

Botswana

Botswana Lib. Assn., Box 1310, Gaborone. Tel. 31-351151, ext. 2297, fax 0267-356591. *Chair* Amos P. Thapisa; *Secy.* Edwin Qabose.

Brazil

Associação dos Arquivistas Brasileiros (Assn. of Brazilian Archivists), Rua da Candelária, 9-sala 1004, Centro, Rio de Janeiro RJ 20091-020. Tel./fax 21-233-7142. *Pres.* Lia Temporal Malcher; *Secy.* Laura Regina Xavier.

Brunei

Persatuan Perpustakaan Kebangsaan Negara Brunei (National Lib. Assn. of Brunei), c/o Language and Literature Bureau Lib., Jalan Elizabeth II, Bandar Seri Begawan. Tel. 2-43511.

Bulgaria

Sajuz na Bibliotechnite i Informazionnite Rabotnitzi (Union of Libns. and Info. Officers), Pl. Slavejkov 4, Rm. 609, Box 269, 1000 Sofia. Tel. 2-864264. *Pres.* Maria Kapitanova-Iordandva.

Cameroon

Association des Bibliothècaires, Archivistes, Documentalistes et Muséographes du Cameroon (Assn. of Libns., Archivists, Documentalists and Museum Curators of Cameroon), Université de Yaounde, Bibliothèque Universitaire, B.P. 337, Yaounde. Tel. 220744.

Canada

Bibliographical Society of Canada/La Société Bibliographique du Canada, Box 575, Postal Sta. P, Toronto, ON M5S 2T1. World Wide Web: http://www.library.utoronto.ca/~bsc.

Canadian Assn. for Info. Science/Association Canadienne de Science de l'Information, c/o CAIS Secretariat, Univ. of Toronto, 140 Saint George St., Toronto, ON M5S 3G6. Tel. 416-978-8876, fax 416-971-1399, e-mail caisasst@fis.utoronto.ca.

Canadian Council of Lib. Schools/Conseil Canadien des Ecoles de Bibliothéconomie, Univ. of Toronto, 140 Saint George St., Toronto M5S 1A1. Tel. 416-978-3202, fax 416-978-5762.

Canadian Lib. Assn., c/o Exec. Dir. Karen Adams, 200 Elgin St., Suite 602, Ottawa, ON K2P 1L5. Tel. 613-232-9625, fax 613-563-9895. (For detailed information on the Canadian Lib. Assn. and its divisions, see "National Library and Information-Industry Associations, United States and Canada"; for information on the library associations of the provinces of Canada, see "State, Provincial, and Regional Library Associations.")

Chile

Colegio de Bibliotecarios de Chile AG (Chilean Lib. Assn.), Diagonal Paraguay 383, Depto 122 Torre 11, Santiago 3741. Tel. 2-222-5652, e-mail cdb@interaccesses.cl. Pres. Elfriede Herbstaedt Yañez; Secy. Sergio Rodriguez Quezada.

China

China Society for Lib. Science, 39 Bai Shi Qiao Rd., Beijing 100081. Tel. 10-684-15566 ext. 5563, fax 10-684-19271. Secy.-Gen. Liu Xiangsheng.

Colombia

Asociación Colombiana de Bibliotecarios (Colombian Lib. Assn.), Calle 10, No. 3-16, Apdo. Aéreo 30883, Bogotá.

Costa Rica

Asociación Costarricense de Bibliotecarios (Costa Rican Assn. of Libns.), Apdo. 3308, San José. Secy.-Gen. Nelly Kopper.

Croatia

Hrvatsko Bibliotekarsko Drustvo (Croation Lib. Assn.), Ulica Hrvatske bratske zajednice b b, 10000 Zagreb. Tel. 616-4111, fax 611-64186. Pres. Dubravka Kunstek; Secy. Dunja Gabriel.

Cuba

Lib. Assn. of Cuba, Biblioteca Nacional José Martí, Apdo 6881, Ave. de Independencia e/20 de Mayo y Aranguren, Plaza de la Revolución, Havana. Tel. 708-277. Dir. Marta Terry González.

Cyprus

Kypriakos Synthesmos Vivliothicarion (Lib. Assn. of Cyprus), Box 1039, Nicosia. Pres. Costas D. Stephanov; Secy. Paris G. Rossos.

Czech Republic

Svaz Knihovníkua Informačních Pracovníků Ceské Republiky (Assn. of Lib. and Info. Professionals of the Czech Republic), Klementinum 190, c/o Národní Knihovna, 110 01 Prague 1. Tel./fax 2-2166-3295, e-mail burget@mondia.cz. Pres. Jarmila Burgetová.

Ústřední knihovnícká rada CR (Central Lib. Council of the Czech Republic), Valdštejnské nám. 4, 11811 Prague 1. Tel. 2-531-225, fax 2-532-185. Pres. Jaroslav Vyčichlo; Secy. Adolf Knoll.

Denmark

Arkivforeningen (Archives Society), c/o Landsarkivet for Sjaelland, jagtvej 10, 2200 Copenhagen K. Tel. 3139-3520, fax

3315-3239. *Pres.* Tyge Krogh; *Secy.* Charlotte Steinmark.

Bibliotekarforbundet (Union of Libns.), Lindevangs Allé 2, DK-2000 Frederiksberg. Tel. 3888-2233, fax 3888-3201. *Pres.* Anja Rasmussen; *V.P.* Flemming Faarup.

Danmarks Biblioteksforening (Danish Lib. Assn.), Telegrafvej 5, DK-2750 Ballerup. Tel. 4468-1466, fax 4468-1103. *Dir.* Jens Thorhauge.

Danmarks Forskningsbiblioteksforening (Danish Research Lib. Assn.), Danmarks Tekniske Bibliotek, Anker Engelundsvej 1, DK-2800 Lyngby. Tel. 4593-9979, fax 4288-3040. *Pres.* Lars Bjørnshauge; *Secy.* D. Skovgaard.

Danmarks Skolebiblioteksforening (Assn. of Danish School Libns.), Mariavej 1, Sdr Bjert, 6091 Bjert. Tel. 755-7101, fax 4239-4349. *Chair* Gert Larsen.

Dominican Republic

Asociación Dominicana de Bibliotecarios (Dominican Assn. of Libns.), c/o Biblioteca Nacional, Plaza de la Cultura, Cesar Nicolás Penson 91, Santo Domingo. Tel. 809-688-4086. *Pres.* Prospero J. Mella-Chavier; *Secy.-Gen.* V. Regús.

Ecuador

Asociación Ecuatoriana de Bibliotecarios (Ecuadoran Lib. Assn.), c/o Casa de la Cultura Ecuatoriana Benjamín Carrión, Apdo 67, Ave. 6 de Diciembre 794, Quito. Tel. 2-528-840, 02-263-474. *Pres.* Eulalia Galarza.

Egypt

Egyptian Assn. for Lib. and Info. Science, c/o Dept. of Archives, Librarianship and Info. Science, Faculty of Arts, Univ. of Cairo, Cairo. Tel. 2-728-211. *Pres.* M. El-Shenity; *Secy.* Hamed Diab.

El Salvador

Asociación de Bibliotecarios de El Salvador (El Salvador Lib. Assn.), c/o Biblioteca Nacional, 8A Avda. Norte y Calle Delgado, San Salvador. Tel. 216-312.

Asociación General de Archivistas de El Salvador (Assn. of Archivists of El Salvador), Archivo General de la Nación, Palacio Nacional, San Salvador. Tel. 229-418.

Ethiopia

Ye Ethiopia Betemetshaft Serategnoch Mahber (Ethiopian Lib. Assn.), Box 30530, Addis Ababa. Tel. 1-121-363, fax 1-552-544. *Pres.* Mulugeta Hunde; *Secy.* Girma Makonnen.

Fiji

Fiji Lib. Assn., Govt. Bldgs., Box 2292, Suva. *Secy.* E. Qica.

Finland

Suomen Kirjastoseura (Finnish Lib. Assn.), Kansakouluk 10 A 19, FIN-00100 Helsinki. Tel. 0-694-1858, fax 0-694-1859, e-mail fla@fla.fi. *Pres.* Kaarina Dromberg; *Secy.-Gen.* Tuula Haavisto.

Tietopalveluseura ry (Finnish Society for Info. Services), Harakantie 2, SF-02600 Espoo. Tel. 90-518-138, fax 90-518-167. *Secy.* H. Heikkinen.

France

Association des Archivistes Français (Assn. of French Archivists), 60 Rue des Francs-Bourgeois, F-75141 Paris cedex 3. Tel. 1-4027-6000. *Pres.* Jean-Luc Eichenlaub; *Secy.* Jean LePottier.

Association des Bibliothècaires Français (Assn. of French Libns.), 7 Rue des Lions-Saint-Paul, F-75004 Paris. Tel. 1-4887-9787, fax 4887-9713. *Pres.* F. Danset; *Gen. Secy.* Catherine Schmitt.

Association des Professionnels de l'Information et de la Documentation (French Assn. of Info. and Documentation Professionals), 25 Rue Claude Tillier, F-75012 Paris. Tel. 1-4372-2525, fax 1-4372-3041, e-mail adbs@adbs.fr. *Pres.* Jean Michel.

Germany

Arbeitsgemeinschaft der Spezialbibliotheken (Assn. of Special Libs.), c/o M. Schwarzer, Kekulé-Bibliothek, Bayer AG, 51368

Leverkusen-Bayerwerk. Tel. 214-307-819. *Chair* Wolfrudolf Laux; *Secretariat Dir.* Marianne Schwarzer.

Deutsche Gesellschaft für Dokumentation (German Society for Documentation), Ostbahnhofstr. 13, 60314 Frankfurt-am-Main 1. Tel. 69-430-313, fax 69-490-9096. *Pres.* Arnoud de Kemp.

Deutscher Biblioteksverband eV (German Lib. Assn.), Alt-Moabit 101A, 10559 Berlin. Tel. 30-3907-7274, fax 30-393-8011. *Pres.* Christof Eichert.

Verein der Bibliothekare an Öffentlichen Bibliotheken (Assn. of Libns. at Public Libs.), Postfach 1324, 72703 Reutlingen. Tel. 7121-346-999, fax 7121-300-433. *Pres.* Konrad Umlauf; *Secy.* Katharina Boulanger.

Verein der Diplom-Bibliothekare an Wissenschaftlichen Bibliotheken (Assn. of Certified Libns. at Academic Libs.), c/o *Chair* Marianne Saule, Universitätsbibliothek, Universitätsstr. 31, 93053 Regensburg. Tel. 941-943-3952, fax 941-943-3285.

Verein Deutscher Archivare (Assn. of German Archivists), Westphälisches Archivamt, 48133 Münster. Tel. 251-591-3886, fax 251-591-269. *Chair* Norbert Reimann.

Verein Deutscher Bibliothekare (Assn. of German Libns.), Krummer Timpen 3-5, 48143 Munsten. Tel. 251-832-4032, fax 251-832-8398. *Pres.* Klaus Hilgemann; *Secy.* Lydia Jungnickel.

Ghana

Ghana Lib. Assn., Box 4105, Accra. Tel. 2-668-731. *Pres.* E. S. Asiedo; *Secy.* A. W. K. Insaidoo.

Great Britain

See United Kingdom.

Greece

Enosis Hellinon Bibliothekarion (Greek Lib. Assn.), Skouleniou 4, 10561 Athens. Tel. 1-322-6625. *Pres.* K. Xatzopoulou; *Gen. Secy.* A. Solomou.

Guatemala

Asociación Bibliotecológica de Guatemala (Lib. Assn. of Guatemala), Apartdao Postal 2086, Guatemala City 01901. Tel. 711525. *Pres.* María Teresa Cuyún.

Guyana

Guyana Lib. Assn., c/o National Lib., Church St. & Ave. of the Republic, Georgetown. Tel. 2-62690, 2-62699. *Pres.* Hetty London; *Secy.* Dianand Indra.

Honduras

Asociación de Bibliotecarios y Archiveros de Honduras (Assn. of Libns. and Archivists of Honduras), 11a Calle, 1a y 2a Avdas. No. 105, Comayagüela DC, Tegucigalpa. *Pres.* Fransisca de Escoto Espinoza; *Secy.-Gen.* Juan Angel R. Ayes.

Hong Kong

Hong Kong Lib. Assn., GPO 10095, Hong Kong. E-mail sechkla@hk.super.nct. *Pres.* Grace Cheng; *Hon. Secy.* Louisa Lam.

Hungary

Magyar Könyvtárosok Egyesülete (Assn. of Hungarian Libns.), Szabó Ervin tér 1, H-1088 Budapest. Tel./fax 1-118-2050. *Pres.* Tibor Horváth; *Secy.* István Papp.

Iceland

Bókavardafélag Islands (Icelandic Lib. Assn.), Box 1497, 121 Reykjavik. *Pres.* A. E. Bjarkadóttir; *Secy.* E. R. Gudmundsdóttir.

India

Indian Assn. of Special Libs. and Info. Centres, P-291, CIT Scheme 6M, Kankurgachi, Calcutta 700054. Tel. 33-349651.

Indian Lib. Assn., c/o Dr. Mukerjee Nagar, A/40-41, Flat 201, Ansal Bldg., Delhi 110009. Tel. 11-711-7743. *Pres.* P. S. G. Kumar.

Indonesia

Ikatan Pustakawan Indonesia (Indonesian Lib. Assn.), Jalan Merdeka Selatan No. 11, Box 274, Jakarta, Pusat. Tel. 21-375-718, fax 21-310-3554. *Pres.* S. Kartosdono.

Iraq

Iraqi Lib. Assn., c/o National Lib., Bab-el-Muaddum, Box 594, Baghdad. Tel. 1-416-4190. *Dir.* Abdul Hameed Al-Alawchi.

Ireland

Cumann Leabharlann Na h-Eireann (Lib. Assn. of Ireland), 53 Upper Mount St., Dublin. Tel. 1-661-9000, fax 1-676-1628, e-mail laisec@iol.ie. *Pres.* L. Ronayne; *Hon. Secy.* Brendan Teeling.

Israel

Israel Lib. Assn., Box 303, Tel Aviv 61002. *Chair* Avraham Vilner; *Secy.* R. Eidelstein.

Israel Society of Special Libs. and Info. Centers, Atidim Scientific Park, 2 Dvora Haneviah St., Tel Aviv 61430. Tel. 3-492-064. *Chair* Liliane Frenkiel.

Italy

Associazione Italiana Biblioteche (Italian Lib. Assn.), C.P. 2461, I-00100 Rome A-D. Tel. 6-446-3532, fax 6-444-1139, e-mail aib.italia@agora.stm.it. *Pres.* Rossella Caffo; *Secy.* Luca Bellingeri.

Ivory Coast (Côte d'Ivoire)

Association pour le Développement de la Documentation des Bibliothèques et Archives de la Côte d'Ivoire (Assn. for the Development of Documentation Libs. and Archives of the Ivory Coast), c/o Bibliothèque Nationale, B.P. V 180, Abidjan. *Dir.* Ambroise Agnero; *Secy.-Gen.* Cangah Guy.

Jamaica

Jamaica Lib. Assn., Box 58, Kingston 5. *Pres.* A. Jefferson; *Secy.* G. Greene.

Japan

Joho Kagaku Gijutsu Ky kai (Info. Science and Technology Assn.), Sasaki Bldg., 5-7 Koisikawa 2, Bunkyo-ku, Tokyo. *Pres.* T. Gondoh; *Gen. Mgr.* Yukio Ichikawa.

Nihon Toshokan Kykai (Japan Lib. Assn.), c/o *Secy.-Gen.* Reiko Sakagawa, 1-10 Taishido, 1-chome, Setagaya-ku, Tokyo 154. Tel. 3-3410-6411, fax 3-3421-7588.

Senmon Toshokan Kyogikai (Japan Special Libs. Assn.), c/o National Diet Lib., 10-1 Nagata-cho, 1-chome, Chiyoda-ku, Tokyo 100. Tel. 3-3581-1364, fax 3-5532-8831. *Pres.* Kousaku Inaba; *Exec. Dir.* Fumihisa Nakagawa.

Jordan

Jordan Lib. Assn., Box 6289, Amman. Tel. 6-629-412. *Pres.* Anwar Akroush; *Secy.* Yousra Abu Ajamieh.

Kenya

Kenya Lib. Assn., Box 46031, Nairobi. *Chair* Jacinta Were; *Secy.* Alice Bulogosi.

Korea (Democratic People's Republic of)

Lib. Assn. of the Democratic People's Republic of Korea, Grand People's Study House of the Democratic People's Republic of Korea, Pyongyang. Tel. 3-4066. *Exec. Secy.* Li Geng.

Korea (Republic of)

Korean Lib. Assn., c/o *Exec. Dir.* Dae Kwon Park, 60-1 Panpo Dong, Box 2041, Seocho-ku, Seoul. Tel. 2-535-4868, fax 2-535-5616, e-mail klanet@kol.co.kr. *Pres.* Chal Sakong; *Exec. Dir.* Ho Jo Won.

Laos

Association des Bibliothècaires Laotiens (Assn. of Laotian Libns.), c/o Direction de la Bibliothèque Nationale, Ministry of Education, B.P. 704, Vientiane. *Dir.* Somthong.

Latvia

Lib. Assn. of Latvia, Latvian National Lib., Kr. Barona iela 14, 1423 Riga. Tel./fax 132-289-874. *Pres.* Aldis Abele.

Lebanon

Lebanese Lib. Assn., c/o American Univ. of Beirut, Univ. Lib./Gifts and Exchange, Box 113/5367, Beirut. Tel. 1-340740 ext. 2603. *Pres.* Rafi' Ma'rouf; *Exec. Secy.* Linda Sadaka.

Lesotho

Lesotho Lib. Assn., Private Bag A26, Maseru. *Chair* E. M. Nthunya; *Secy.* M. M. Moshoe-shoe-Chadzingwa.

Malawi

Malawi Lib. Assn., Box 429, Zomba. Tel. 50-522-222, fax 50-523-225. *Chair* Joseph J. Uta; *Secy.* Vote D. Somba.

Malaysia

Persatuan Perpustakaan Malaysia (Lib. Assn. of Malaysia), Box 12545, 50782 Kuala Lumpur. Tel. 3-756-6516. *Pres.* Chew Wing Foong; *Secy.* Leni Abdul Latif.

Mali

Association Malienne des Bibliothècaires, Archivistes et Documentalistes (Mali Assn. of Libns., Archivists, and Documentalists), c/o Bibliothèque Nationale du Mali, Ave.
Kasse Keita, B.P. 159, Bamako. Tel. 224963. *Dir.* Mamadou Konoba Keita.

Malta

Ghaqda Bibljotekarji/Lib. Assn. (Malta), c/o Univ. Lib., Msida MSD 06. Tel. 243473. *Secy.* Marion Borg.

Mauritania

Association Mauritanienne des Bibliothè-caires, Archivistes et Documentalistes (Mauritanian Assn. of Libns., Archivists, and Documentalists), c/o Bibliothèque Nationale, B.P. 20, Nouakchott. *Pres.* O. Diouwara; *Secy.* Sid'Ahmed Fall dit Dah.

Mauritius

Mauritius Lib. Assn., c/o The British Council, Royal Rd., Box 11, Rose Hill. Tel. 541-602, fax 549-553. *Pres.* K. Appadoo; *Secy.* S. Rughoo.

Mexico

Asociación Mexicana de Bibliotecarios (Mexican Assn. of Libns.), Apdo. 27-102, Admin. de Correos 27, México D.F. Tel. 5-550-1398, fax 5-550-7461. *Pres.* S. Peniche; *Secy.* Elías Cid Ramírez.

Myanmar

Myanmar Lib. Assn., c/o National Lib., Strand Rd., Yangon. *Chief Libn.* Ukhin Maung Tin.

Nepal

Nepal Lib. Assn., c/o National Lib., Harihar Bhawan, Pulchowk Lib., Box 2773, Kathmandu. Tel. 521-132. *Libn.* Shusila Dwivedi.

The Netherlands

Nederlandse Vereniging van Bibliothecaris-sen, Documentalisten en Literatuur Onderzoekers (Netherlands Libns. Society), NVB-Verenigingsbureau, Plompetorengracht 11, NL-3512 CA Utrecht. Tel. 231-1263, fax 231-1830, e-mail nvbinfo@worldaccess.nl. *Pres.* H. C. Kooyman-Tibbles; *Secy.* R. Tichelaar.

UKB (Universiteitsbibliotheek Vriji Universiteit) (Assn. of the Univ. Libs., the Royal Lib., and the Lib. of the Royal Netherlands Academy of Arts and Sciences), De Boelelaan 1103, NL-1081 HV Amsterdam. Tel. 44-45140, fax 44-45259. *Pres.* A. C. Klugkist; *Libn.* J. H. de Swart.

New Zealand

New Zealand Lib. and Info. Assn., 86 Lambton Quay, Level 8, Wellington Mall, Box 12-212, Wellington. Tel. 4-473-5834, fax 4-

499-1480, e-mail nzlia@netlink.co.nz.
Exec. Dir. Lydia Klimovitch.

Nicaragua

Asociación Nicaraguense de Bibliotecarios y
Profesionales a Fines (Nicaraguan Assn. of
Libns.), Apdo. Postal 3257, Managua.
Exec. Secy. Susana Morales Hernández.

Nigeria

Nigerian Lib. Assn., c/o National Lib. of
Nigeria, 4 Wesley St., PMB 12626, Lagos.
Tel. 1-634704, fax 1-616404. *Pres.* A. O.
Banjo; *Secy.* L. I. Ehigiator.

Norway

Arkivarforeningen (Assn. of Archivists), c/o
Riksarkivet, Folke Bernadottes Vei 21,
Postboks 10, N-0807 Oslo. Tel. 22-022-
600, fax 22-237-489.

Norsk Bibliotekforening (Norwegian Lib.
Assn.), Malerhaugveien 20, N-0661 Oslo.
Tel. 2-268-8550, fax 2-267-2368. *Dir.*
Berit Aaker.

Norsk Fagbibliotekforening (Norwegian
Assn. of Special Libs.), c/o Technical
Univ. Lib. of Norway, Chemistry Branch
Lib., N-7034 Trondheim 6. Tel. 7-359-
4188, fax 7-359-5103. *Chair* Else-Mar-
grethe Bredland.

Pakistan

Pakistan Lib. Assn., c/o Pakistan Inst. of
Development Economics, Univ. Campus,
Box 1091, Islamabad. Tel. 921-4041, fax
92-51-921-0886, e-mail arshad%pide@
sdnpk.undp.org. *Pres.* Azmat Ullah Bhatti;
Secy.-Gen. Hafiz Khubaib Ahmed.

Panama

Asociación Panameña de Bibliotecarios
(Panama Lib. Assn.), c/o Biblioteca Inter-
americana Simón Bolívar, Estafeta Uni-
versitaría, Panama City. *Pres.* Bexie
Rodríguez de León.

Paraguay

Asociación de Bibliotecarios del Paraguay
(Assn. of Paraguayan Libns.), Casilla de
Correo 1505, Asunción. *Secy.* Mafalda
Cabrerar.

Peru

Asociación de Archiveros del Perú (Peruvian
Assn. of Archivists), Archivo Central
Slaverry 2020 Jesús Mario, Universidad
del Pacifico, Lima 11. *Pres.* José Luis
Abanto Arrelucea.

Asociación Peruana de Bibliotecarios (Peruvian Assn of Libns.), Bellavista 561 Mira-
flores, Apdo. 995, Lima 18. Tel. 14-474869.
Pres. Martha Fernandez de Lopez; *Secy.*
Luzmila Tello de Medina.

Philippines

Assn. of Special Libs. of the Philippines, Rm.
301, National Lib. Bldg., T. M. Kalaw St.,
Manila. Tel. 2-590177. *Pres.* Filamena C.
Mercado; *Secy.* Edna P. Ortiz.

Bibliographical Society of the Philippines,
National Lib. of the Philippines, T. M.
Kalaw St., 1000 Ermita, Box 2926, Mani-
la. Tel. 2-583252, fax 2-502329. *Secy.-*
Treas. Leticia R. Maloles.

Philippine Libns. Assn., c/o National Lib. of
the Philippines, Rm. 301, T. M. Kalaw St.,
Manila. Tel. 2-590177. *Pres.* Belen M.
Vibar; *Secy.* Lisa LeGuiab.

Poland

Stowarzyszenie Bibliotekarzy Polskich (Polish
Libns. Assn.), Ul. Konopczyńskiego 5/7,
00950 Warsaw. Tel. 22-275296. *Chair*
Stanislaw Czajka; *Secy.-Gen.* Dariusz
Kuzminski.

Portugal

Associação Portuguesa de Bibliotecários,
Arquivistas e Documentalistas (Portuguese
Assn. of Libns., Archivists, and Documentalists), R Morais Soares, 43C-1 DTD,
1900 Lisbon. Tel. 1-815-4479, fax 1-815-
4508, e-mail badbn@telepac.pt. *Pres.*
António Pina Falcão.

Puerto Rico

Sociedad de Bibliotecarios de Puerto Rico (Society of Libns. of Puerto Rico), Apdo. 22898, Universidad de Puerto Rico Sta., Rio Piedras 00931. Tel. 809-758-1125. *Pres.* Aura Jiménez de Panepinto; *Secy.* Olga L. Hernández.

Romania

Asociaţia Bibliotecarilor din Bibliotecile Publice-România (Assn. of Public Libns. of Romania), Strada Ion Ghica 4, Sector 3, 79708 Bucharest. Tel. 1-614-2434, fax 1-312-3381, e-mail bnr@ul.ici.ro. *Pres.* Gheorghe-Iosif Bercan; *Secy.* Georgeta Clinca.

Russia

Lib. Council, State V. I. Lenin Lib., Prospect Kalinina 3, Moscow 101000. Tel. 95-202-4656. *Exec. Secy.* G. A. Semenova.

Senegal

Association Sénégalaise des Bibliothècaires, Archivistes et Documentalistes (Senegalese Assn. of Libns., Archivists and Documentalists), BP 3252, Dakar. Tel. 246-981, fax 242-379. *Pres.* Mariétou Diongue Diop; *Secy.* Emmanuel Kabou.

Sierra Leone

Sierra Leone Assn. of Archivists, Libns., and Info. Scientists, c/o Sierra Leone Lib. Board, Box 326, Freetown. *Pres.* Deanna Thomas.

Singapore

Lib. Assn. of Singapore, c/o Bukit Merah Central, Box 0693, 150162 Singapore. *Hon. Secy.* Siti Hanifah Mustapha.

Slovenia

Zveza Bibliotekarskih Drustev Slovenije (Lib. Assn. of Slovenia), Turjaska 1, 61000 Ljubljana. Tel. 61-150131, fax 61-213052. *Pres.* Ivan Kanic; *Secy.* Liljana Hubej.

South Africa

African Lib. Assn. of South Africa, c/o Lib., Univ. of the North, Private Bag X1106, Sovenga 0727. Tel. 1521-689111. *Secy. and Treas.* A. N. Kambule.

Spain

Asociación Española de Archiveros, Bibliotecarios, Museólogos y Documentalistas (Spanish Assn. of Archivists, Libns., Curators and Documentalists), Recoletos 5, 28001 Madrid. Tel. 575-1727. *Pres.* Alonso Vicenta Cortés.

Sri Lanka

Sri Lanka Lib. Assn., Professional Center, 275/75 Bauddhaloka Mawatha, Colombo 7. Tel. 94-1-589103, e-mail postmast@slla.ac.lk. *Pres.* Harrison Perera; *Secy.* Wilfred Ranasinghe.

Swaziland

Swaziland Lib. Assn., Box 2309, Mbabane. Tel. 84011. *Chair* M. R. Mavuso; *Secy.* F. K. Tawete.

Sweden

Svenska Arkivsamfundet (Swedish Assn. of Archivists), c/o Riksarkivet, Fyrverkarbacken 13-17, Box 12541, S-102 29 Stockholm. Tel. 8-737-6350, fax 8-737-6474, e-mail anna-christina.ulfsparre@riksarkivet.ra.se. *Pres.* Anna Christina Ulfsparre.

Sveriges Allmänna Biblioteksförening (Swedish Lib. Assn.), Box 3127, S-103 62 Stockholm. Tel. 8-241020/723-0082, fax 8-723-0083, e-mail christina.stenberg@scib.se. *Secy.-Gen.* Christina Stenberg.

Swedish School of Library and Information Science Library, Box 874, S-50115 Borås. Tel. 33-164-000, fax 33-111-053. Exec. *Secy.* Staffan Lööf.

Switzerland

Association des Bibliothèques et Bibliothècaires Suisses/Vereinigung Schweizerischer Bibliothekare/Associazione dei Bibliotecari Svizzeri (Assn. of Swiss Libns.), Effingerstr.

35, CH-3008 Berne. Tel. 31-382-4240, fax 31-382-4648, e-mail bbss@bbs.ch, World Wide Web http://www.bbs.ch. *Secy.* Myriam Boussina Mercille.

Schweizerische Vereinigung für Dokumentation/Association Suisse de Documentation (Swiss Assn. of Documentation), Schmidgasse 4, Postfach 601, CH-6301, Zug. Tel. 41-726-4505, fax 41-726-4509. *Pres.* S. Holláander; *Secy.* H. Schweuk.

Vereinigung Schweizerischer Archivare (Assn. of Swiss Archivists), Archivstr. 24, CH-3003 Berne. Tel. 31-618989. *Secy.* Bernard Truffer.

Taiwan

Lib. Assn. of China, c/o National Central Lib., 20 Chungshan S. Rd., Taipei. Tel. 2-331-2475, fax 2-382-0747. *Pres.* James S. C. Hu; *Secy.-Gen.* Teresa Wang Chang.

Tanzania

Tanzania Lib. Assn., Box 33433, Dar es Salaam. Tel. 51-402-6121. *Chair* T. E. Mlaki; *Secy.* A. Nkebukwa.

Thailand

Thai Lib. Assn., 273 Vibhavadee Rangsit Rd., Phayathai, Bangkok 10400. Tel. 2-271-2084. *Pres.* K. Gesmankit; *Secy.* Karnmanee Suckcharoen.

Trinidad and Tobago

Lib. Assn. of Trinidad and Tobago, Box 1275, Port of Spain. Tel. 868-624-5075, e-mail latt@fm1.wow.net. *Pres.* Esahack Mohammed; *Secy.* Shamin Renwick.

Tunisia

Association Tunisienne des Documentalistes, Bibliothècaires et Archivistes (Tunisian Assn. of Documentalists, Libns., and Archivists), B.P. 380, 1015 Tunis. *Pres.* Ahmed Ksibi.

Turkey

Türk Küüphaneciler Dernegi (Turkish Libns. Assn.), Elgün Sok-8/8, 06440 Yenisehir, Ankara. Tel./fax 4-230-1325. *Pres.* S. Aslan; *Secy.* A. Kaygusuz.

Uganda

Uganda Lib. Assn., Box 5894, Kampala. Tel. 141-285001 ext. 4. *Chair* P. Birungi; *Secy.* L. M. Ssengero.

Ukraine

Ukrainian Library Assn., 14 Chyhorin St., Kyiv 252042, Ukraine. Tel. 380-44-268-2263, fax 380-44-295-8296. *Pres.* Valentyna S. Pashkova.

United Kingdom

ASLIB (The Assn. for Info. Management), Information House, 20-24 Old St., London EC1V 9AP, England. Tel. 171-253-4488, fax 171-430-0514. *Dir.* R. B. Bowes.

Bibliographical Society, c/o The Welcome Institute, 183 Euston Rd., London NW1 2BE, England. Tel. 171-611-7244, fax 171-611-8703, e-mail d.pearson@welcome.ac.uk. *Hon. Secy.* David Pearson.

The Lib. Assn., 7 Ridgmount St., London WC1E 7AE, England. Tel. 171-636-7543, fax 171-436-7218, e-mail info@la-hq.org.uk. *Chief Exec.* Ross Shimmon.

School Lib. Assn., Liden Lib., Barrington Close, Liden, Swindon, Wiltshire SN3 6HF, England. Tel. 1793-617-838. *Pres.* Frank N. Hogg; *Exec. Secy.* Kathy Lemaire.

Scottish Lib. Assn., 1 John St., Hamilton ML3 7EU, Scotland. Tel. 1698-458-888, fax 1698-458-899, e-mail sctlb@leapfrog.almac.co.uk. *Dir.* Robert Craig.

Society of Archivists, Information House, 20-24 Old St., London, EC1V 9AP, England. Tel. 171-253-5087, fax 171-253-3942. *Exec. Secy.* P. S. Cleary.

Standing Conference of National and Univ. Libs., 102 Euston St., London NW1 2HA, England. Tel. 171-387-0317, fax 171-383-3197. *Exec. Secy.* G. M. Pentelow.

Welsh Lib. Assn., c/o Publications Office, The Lib., Univ. of Wales, Swansea, West Glamorgan SA2 8PP, Wales. Tel. 1792-295-174, fax 1792-295-851, e-mail a.m.w.green@swansea.ac.uk. *Exec. Officer* Glyn Collins.

Uruguay

Agrupación Bibliotecológica del Uruguay (Uruguayan Lib. and Archive Science Assn.), Cerro Largo 1666, 11200 Montevideo. Tel. 2-405-740. *Pres.* Luis Alberto Musso.

Asociación de Bibliocólogos del Uruguay, Eduardo V Haedo 2255, CC 1315, 11200 Montevideo. Tel. 2-499-989.

Vatican City

Biblioteca Apostolica Vaticana, 00120 Vatican City, Rome. Tel. 6-698-83302, fax 6-698-84795, e-mail Libr@librsbk.vatlib.it. *Prefect* Leonard E. Boyle.

Venezuela

Colegio de Bibliotecólogos y Archivólogos de Venezuela (Assn. of Venezuelan Libns. and Archivists), Apdo. 6283, Caracas. Tel. 2-781-3245. *Pres.* O. Ruiz LaScalea.

Vietnam

Hôi Thu-Vién Viet Nam (Vietnamese Lib. Assn.), National Lib. of Viet Nam, 31 Trang Thi, 10000 Hanoi. Tel. 4-52643.

Zaire

Association Zairoise des Archivistes, Bibliothècaires et Documentalistes (Zaire Assn. of Archivists, Librarians, and Documentalists), B.P. 805, Kinshasa X1. Tel. 12-30123/4. *Exec. Secy.* E. Kabeba-Bangasa.

Zambia

Zambia Lib. Assn., Box 32339, Lusaka. *Chair* C. Zulu; *Hon. Secy.* W. C. Mulalami.

Zimbabwe

Zimbabwe Lib. Assn., Box 3133, Harare. *Chair* A. L. Ngwenya; *Hon. Secy.* Driden Kunaka.

Directory of Book Trade and Related Organizations

Book Trade Associations, United States and Canada

For more extensive information on the associations listed in this section, see the annual edition of *Literary Market Place* (R. R. Bowker).

American Booksellers Assn. Inc., 828 S. Broadway, Tarrytown, NY 10591. Tel. 800-637-0037, 914-591-2665, fax 914-591-2720; *Pres.* Barbara Bonds Thomas, Toad Hall, Austin, TX 78705; *V.P.* Richard Howorth, Square Books, Oxford, MS 38665; *Secy.* Norman Laurila, A Different Light Bookstore, New York, NY 10011; *Treas.* Ned Densmore, Village Book Store Littleton, NH 03561; *Exec. Dir.* Avin Mark Domnitz.

American Institute of Graphic Arts, 164 Fifth Ave., New York, NY 10010. Tel. 212-807-1990, fax 212-807-1799, e-mail aiganatl@aol.com. *Exec. Dir.* Richard Grefé.

American Medical Publishers Assn., 14 Fort Hill Rd., Huntington, NY 11734. Tel./fax 516-423 0075. *Pres.* Jack Farrell; *Exec. Dir.* Jill Rudansky, e-mail jillrudanskyampa@msn.com.

American Printing History Assn., Box 4922, Grand Central Sta., New York, NY 10163-1005. *Pres.* Martin W. Hutner; *Exec. Secy.* Stephen Crook.

American Society of Indexers, Inc., Box 48267 Seattle WA 98148-0627. Tel. 206-241-9196, fax 206-727-6430, e-mail asi@well.com, World Wide Web http://www.well.com/user/asi. *Pres.* Carolyn McGovern; *Administrator* Linda K. Fetters.

American Society of Journalists and Authors, 1501 Broadway, Suite 302, New York, NY 10036. Tel. 212-997-0947, fax 212-768-7414, e-mail ASJA@compuserve.com. *Exec. Dir.* Alexandra Cantor Owens.

American Society of Media Photographers, 14 Washington Rd., Suite 502, Princeton Junction, NJ 08550-1033. Tel. 609-799-8300, fax 609-799-2233. *Pres.* Les Riess; *Exec. Dir.* Richard Weisgrau.

American Society of Picture Professionals, Inc., 2025 Pennsylvania Ave. N.W., Suite 226, Washington, D.C. 20006. Tel. 202-955-5578. *Exec. Dir.* Cathy Sachs; *National Pres.* Susan Soroko, Folio, Washington, D.C. Tel. 202-965-2410.

American Translators Assn., 1800 Diagonal Rd., Suite 220, Alexandria, VA 22314-2840. Tel. 703-683-6100, fax 703-683-6122. *Pres.* Muriel Jerome-O'Keeffe; *Pres.-Elect* Ann MacFarlane; *Secy.* Eric McMillan; *Treas.* Monique-Paule Tubb; *Exec. Dir.* Walter W. Bacak, Jr.

Antiquarian Booksellers Assn. of America, 20 W. 44 St., Fourth flr., New York, NY 10036-6604. Tel. 212-944-8291, fax 212-944-8293, e-mail abaa@panix.com, World Wide Web http://www.abaa-booknet.com; *Exec. Dir.* Liane Wade.

Assn. of American Publishers, 71 Fifth Ave., New York, NY 10003. Tel. 212-255-0200. *Pres./CEO* Patricia S. Schroeder; *Exec. V.P.* Thomas D. McKee; *V.P.* Richard F. Blake; *Dir.* Barbara Meredith; *Washington Office* 1718 Connecticut Ave. N.W., Washington, DC 20009. Tel. 202-232-3335;

V.P.s Allan Adler, Carol Risher; *Dir.* Judith Platt; *Chair* Richard Robinson, Scholastic; *V. Chair* Peter Jovanovich, Addison Wesley Longman; *Treas.* Thomas A. Paul, International Thomson Publishing; *Secy.* Brian J. Knez, Harcourt Brace & Co.

Assn. of American Univ. Presses, 584 Broadway, Suite 410, New York, NY 10012. Tel. 212-941-6610. *Pres.* Joanna Hitchcock, Univ. of Texas Press; *Exec. Dir.* Peter Givler; *Assoc. Exec. Dir.* Hollis Holmes. Address correspondence to the executive director.

Assn. of Authors' Representatives, Inc., 10 Astor Place, Third fl., New York, NY 10003. Tel. 212-353-3709. *Pres.* Ginger Barber; *Admin. Secy.* Ginger Knowlton.

Assn. of Book Travelers, 100 Fifth Ave., New York, NY 10011. Tel. 212-206-7102, fax 212-645-8437. *Pres.* Paul Gottlieb; *Treas.* Eileen O'Neil. Address correspondence to the president.

Assn. of Canadian Publishers, 110 Eglinton Ave. W., Suite 401, Toronto, ON M4R 1A3, Canada. Tel. 416-487-6116, fax 416-487-8815. *Exec. Dir.* Paul Davidson. Address correspondence to the executive director.

Assn. of Jewish Book Publishers, c/o Jewish Lights Publishing, Box 237, Woodstock, VT 05091. Tel. 802-457-4000, fax 802-457-4004. *Pres.* Stuart M. Matlins. Address correspondence to the president.

Assn. of Graphic Communications, 330 Seventh Ave., New York, NY 10001. Tel. 212-279-2100, fax 212-279-5381, e-mail BDage@JUNO.com, World Wide Web http://www.agcomm.org. *Pres.* William A. Dirzulaitis; *Dir. Ed.* Pam Suett; *Dir. Exhibits* Carl Gessman.

Book Industry Study Group, Inc., 160 Fifth Ave., New York, NY 10010. Tel. 212-929-1393, fax 212-989-7542, World Wide Web http://www.bisg.org. *Chair* Kent Freeman; *V.Chair* Robert Severud; *Treas.* Seymour Turk; *Secy.* Richard W. Hunt; *Managing Agent* SKP Assocs. Address correspondence to William Raggio.

Book Manufacturers Institute, 65 William St., Suite 300, Wellesley, MA 02181-4007. Tel. 617-239-0103. *Pres.* Charles

Nason, Worzalla Publishing Co.; *Exec. V.P.* Stephen P. Snyder. Address correspondence to the executive vice president.

Book Publicists of Southern California, 6464 Sunset Blvd., Suite 580, Hollywood, CA 90028. Tel. 213-461-3921, fax 213-461-0917. *Pres.* Barbara Gaughen-Muller; *V.P.* Ernest Weckbaugh; *Secy.* Jeanne Baird; *Treas.* Lynn Walford.

Bookbinders Guild of New York, c/o *Secy.* Thomas P. Roche, 1527 Ninth St., Fort Lee, NJ 07024. Tel. 201-461-6491; *Pres.* Linda Palladino, William Morrow & Co., 1350 Ave. of the Americas, New York, NY 10019. Tel. 212-261-6675; *V.P.* Jim Arch, E. B. Eddy, 1085 Morris Ave., Union, NJ 07083; *Treas.* Irwin Wolf, Graphic Design Studio, 108 John St., North Massapequa, NY 11758; *Financial Secy.* Michelle Rothfarb, World Color, 43 Springbrook Rd., Livingston, NJ 07039.

Bookbuilders of Boston, Inc., 1660 Soldiers Field Rd., Boston, MA 02135. Tel. 617-746-2902, fax 617-783-2835, e-mail bbboston@romnet.com. *Pres.* James Rigney, Addison Wesley Longman; *1st V.P.* Nan Fritz, Editorial Services of New England; *2nd V.P.* Leanne Prevo Rodd, Maple-Vail Book Manufacturing; *Treas.* John Walsh, Harvard Univ. Press; *Auditor* Sarah Ambrose, Houghton Mifflin Company; *Secy.* Elizabeth M. McMullen, Crossen Consulting, Ltd.

Bookbuilders West, Box 7046, San Francisco, CA 94120-9727. Tel. 415-273-5790, jobs bank 415-643-8600, World Wide Web http://www.bookbuilders.org; *Pres.* Arlene Cowan; *Pres.-Elect* Leslie Austin.

Canadian Booksellers Assn., 301 Donlands Ave., Toronto, ON M4J 3R8, Canada. Tel. 416-467-7883, fax 416-467-7886, e-mail enquiries@cbabook.org, World Wide Web http://www.cbabook.org. *Exec. Dir.* Sheryl M. McKean, ext. 225; *Ed., Canadian Bookseller* Kim Laudrum, ext. 230.

Catholic Book Publishers Assn. Inc., 2 Park Ave., Manhasset, NY 11030. Tel. 516-869-0122, fax 516-627-1381; *Pres.* John Thomas; *V.P.* Bernadette Price; *Exec. Dir.* Charles A. Roth.

Chicago Book Clinic, 104 S. Michigan Ave., Suite 1500, Chicago, IL 60603. Tel. 312-

553-2200. *Exec. Dir.* Gene Johannes; *Pres.* Dan Bach.

Children's Book Council, Inc., 568 Broadway, New York, NY 10012. Tel. 212-966-1990, e-mail staff@CBCbooks.org, World Wide Web http://www.cbcbooks.org. *Dir., Marketing and Publicity* JoAnn Sabatino.

Christian Booksellers Assn., Box 200, Colorado Springs, CO 80901. Tel. 719-576-7880. *Pres.* William Anderson.

Educational Paperback Assn., *Pres.* Robert J. Laronga; *V.P.* Fred Johnson; *Treas.* Bill Hanlon; *Exec. Secy.* Marilyn Abel, Box 1399, East Hampton, NY 11937. Tel. 212-879-6850.

Evangelical Christian Publishers Assn., 1969 E. Broadway Rd., Suite 2, Tempe, AZ 85282. Tel. 602-966-3998, fax 602-966-1944. *Pres.* Doug Ross.

Graphic Artists Guild Inc., 90 John St., Suite 403, New York, NY 10038. Tel. 212-791-3400, fax 212-792-0333, e-mail paulatgag@aol.com. *Exec. Dir.* Paul Basista. Address correspondence to the executive director.

Great Lakes Booksellers Assn., c/o *Exec. Dir.* Jim Dana, Box 901, 509 Lafayette, Grand Haven, MI 49417. Tel. 616-847-2460, fax 616-842-0051, e-mail glba@aol.com, World Wide Web http://www.books-glba.com. *Pres.* Brad Eft, MicroCenter, 4119 Leap Road, Hilliard, OH 43026.

Guild of Book Workers, 521 Fifth Ave., New York, NY 10175. Tel. 212-292-4444. *Pres.* Karen Crisalli. Tel. 908-264-0306, e-mail karenc5071@aol.com.

International Copyright Information Center, c/o Assn. of American Publishers, 1718 Connecticut Ave. N.W., Seventh fl., Suite 700, Washington, DC 20009-1148. Tel. 202-232-3335 ext. 228, fax 202-745-0694, e-mail crisher@publishers.org. *Dir.* Carol Risher.

International Standard Book Numbering U.S. Agency, 121 Chanlon Rd., New Providence, NJ 07974. Tel. 908-665-6700, fax 908-665-2895. *Chair* Neal Goff; *Dir.* Albert Simmonds; *Dir. Emeritus* Emery I. Koltay; *Industrial Relations Mgr.* Don Riseborough; *ISBN Mgr.* Lynn Ann Sahner; *SAN Mgr.* Diana Fumando.

Jewish Book Council, 15 E. 26 St., New York, NY 10010. Tel. 212-532-4949, ext. 297, fax 212-481-4174. *Pres.* Arthur Kurzweil; *Exec. Dir.* Carolyn Starman Hessel.

Library Binding Institute, 7401 Metro Blvd., Suite 325, Edina, MN 55439. Tel. 612-835-4707, fax 612-835-4780, e-mail 71035.3504@compuserve.com. *Exec. Dir.* Sally Grauer.

Metropolitan Lithographers Assn., 950 Third Ave., Suite 1500, New York, NY 10022. Tel. 212-838-8480, fax 212-644-1936. *Pres.* Frank Stillo; *Secy.* Cynthia Luzon.

Midwest Independent Publishers Assn., Box 581432, Minneapolis, MN 55458-1432. Tel. 612-646-0475, fax 612-646-0657; e-mail 733243.2012@compuserve.com, World Wide Web http://www. mipa.org; *Pres.* Paul Druckman.

Miniature Book Society Inc., c/o *Pres.* Arthur Keir, 506 Buell Ave., Joliet, IL 60435. Tel. 815-726-1286; *V.P.* Donn Sanford, 210 Swarthmore Court, Woodstock, IL 60098-7879. Tel. 815-337-2323; *Secy.* Evron Collins, 1008 Boone Ct., Bowling Green, OH 43402; *Treas.* Loretta Gentile, 10 Albert St., Waltham, MA 02154.

Minnesota Book Publishers Roundtable. *Pres.* Lisa Bullard, Graywolf Press, 2402 University Ave. S., Suite 203, Saint Paul 55114. Tel. 612-641-0077, fax 612-641-0036, e-mail bullard@graywolfpress.org; *V.P.* Kathy Raskob, Capstone Press, 151 Good Counsel Dr., Mankato 56002; *Secy.-Treas.* Brad Vogt, Bradley & Assoc., 40214 Wallaby Rd., Rice 56367. Address correspondence to the secretary-treasurer.

Mountains and Plains Booksellers Assn., 19 Old Town Sq., Suite 238, Fort Collins, CO 80524. Tel. 970-484-5856, fax 970-407-1479, e-mail lknumpba@rmi.com, World Wide Web http://www.mountainsplains.org. *Exec. Dir.* Lisa Knudsen; *Pres.* Patricia Nelson; *V.P.* Gayle Shanks; *Secy.* Eric Boss; *Treas.* Tracey Ballast.

National Assn. of College Stores, 500 E. Lorain St., Oberlin, OH 44074-1294. Tel. 440-775-7777, fax 440-775-4769, e-mail jbuchs@nacs.org, World Wide Web http://www.nacs.org. *Pres./Treas.* George Herbert, Jr.; *Exec. Dir.* Garis Distelhorst; *Pub-*

lic Relations Dir. Jerry L. Buchs. Address correspondence to the public relations director.

New Atlantic Independent Booksellers Assn., 108 S. 13 St., Philadelphia, PA 19107. Tel. 215-732-5207, fax 215-735-2670, e-mail naiba@ix.netcom.com. *Exec. Dir.* Larry Robin.

New England Booksellers Assn., 847 Massachusetts Ave., Cambridge, MA 02139. Tel. 617-576-3070, fax 617-576-3091. *Pres.* Fran Keilty; *V.P.* Susan Avery; *Treas.* Sarah Zacks; *Exec. Dir.* Wayne A. Drugan.

New Mexico Book League, 8632 Horacio Place N.E., Albuquerque, NM 87111. Tel. 505-299-8940, fax 505-294-8032. *Editor, Book Talk* Carol A. Myers.

Northern California Independent Booksellers Assn., 5643 Paradise Dr., Suite 12, Corte Madera, CA 94925. Tel. 415-927-3937, fax 415-927-3971, e-mail office@nciba. com, World Wide Web http://www.nciba. com; *Exec. Dir.* Hut Landon.

Pacific Northwest Booksellers Assn., 1510 Mill St., Eugene, OR 97401-4258. Tel. 541-683-4363, fax 541-683-3910. *Pres.* Patrick Moody, Snow Goose Bookstore, Box 939, Stanwood, WA 98292; *Exec. Dir.* Thom Chambliss.

Periodical and Book Assn. of America, Inc., 475 Park Ave. S., Eighth flr., New York, NY 10016. Tel. 212-689-4952, fax 212-545-8328. *Pres.* Will Michalopoulos, Consumer Reports; *V.P.s* Bob Bruno, Disney Magazine Publishing; Gerald Cohen, Total Publisher Services; Kathi Robold, Scientific American; *Treas.* Edward Handi, LFP; *Secy.* Gary Michelson, Consumer Reports; *Exec. Dir.* Richard T. Browne; *Asst. Exec. Dir.* Keith E. Furman; *Legal Counsel* Lee Feltman; *Advisers to the Pres.* Marcia Orovitz, Times Mirror Magazines; Mary C. McEvoy, McEvoy Associates.

Periodical Marketers of Canada, 1007-175 Bloor St. E., South Tower, Toronto, ON M4W 3R8, Canada. Tel. 416-968-7218, fax 416-968-6182. *Pres.* Ray Argyle; *Secy.-Treas.* Steve Shepherd, Ottawa Valley News Co., Box 157, Arnprior, ON K7S

3H4, Canada. Tel. 613-623-3197; *Asst. Exec. Dir.* Janette Hatcher. Tel. 416-968-7218.

Philadelphia Book Clinic, c/o *Secy.-Treas.* Thomas Colaiezzi, 136 Chester Ave., Yeadon, PA 19050-3831. Tel. 610-259-7022, fax 610-394-9886.

Publishers Advertising and Marketing Assn., c/o Pocket Books, 1230 Ave. of the Americas, New York, NY 10020. Tel. 212-698-7383, fax 212-698-2891; *Pres.* Ronni Stolzengerg; *V.P.* Michael Kazan; *Secy.* Pam Sabin; *Treas.* Rochelle Stolzenberg.

Publishers Marketing Assn., 627 Aviation Way, Manhattan Beach, CA 90266. Tel. 310-372-2732, fax 310-374-3342, e-mail pmaonline@aol.com, World Wide Web http://www.pma-online.org.

Research and Engineering Council of the Graphic Arts Industry, Inc., Box 639, Chadds Ford, PA 19317. Tel. 610-388-7394, fax 610-388-2708. *Pres.* James Henderson; *Exec. V.P./Secy.* Ted Ringman; *Exec. V.P./Treas.* Edmund Funk; *Managing Dir.* Ronald Mihills.

Small Publishers Assn. of North America (SPAN), Box 1306, Buena Vista, CO 81211-1306. Tel. 719-395-4790, fax 719-395-8374, e-mail SPAN@span-assn.org. World Wide Web http://www.SPANnet. org; *Exec. Dir.* Marilyn Ross.

Technical Assn. of the Pulp and Paper Industry, Technology Pk./Atlanta, Box 105113, Atlanta, GA 30348-5113. Tel. 770-446-1400, fax 770-446-6947. *Exec. Dir.* W. H. Gross.

West Coast Book People Assn., 27 McNear Dr., San Rafael, CA 94901. *Secy.* Frank G. Goodall. Tel. 415-459-1227, fax 415-459-1227.

Women's National Book Assn., 160 Fifth Ave., New York, NY 10010. Tel. 212-675-7805, fax 212-989-7542, e-mail skpassoc@internetmci.com; *Pres.* Donna Paz; *V.P.* Diane Ullius; *Secy.* Dorothy S. O'Connor; *Treas.* Margaret Auer; *Chapters in*: Atlanta, Binghamton, Boston, Dallas, Detroit, Los Angeles, Nashville, New York, San Francisco, Washington, D.C.

International and Foreign Book Trade Associations

For Canadian book trade associations, see the preceding section, "Book Trade Associations, United States and Canada." For a more extensive list of book trade organizations outside the United States and Canada, with more detailed information, consult *International Literary Market Place* (R. R. Bowker), which also provides extensive lists of major bookstores and publishers in each country.

International

Afro-Asian Book Council, 4835/24 Ansari Rd., Daryaganj, New Delhi 110-002, India. Tel. 11-326-1487, fax 11-326-7437. *Chair* Dato Jaji Jumaat; *Secy.-Gen.* Asang Machwe; *Dir.* Abul Hasan.

Centre Régional pour la Promotion du Livre en Afrique (Regional Center for Book Promotion in Africa), Box 1646, Yaoundé, Cameroon. Tel. 22-4782/2936. *Secy.* William Moutchia.

Centro Régional para el Fomento del Libro en América Latina y el Caribe (CERLALC) (Regional Center for Book Promotion in Latin America and the Caribbean), Calle 70, No. 9-52, Apdo. Aeréo 57348, Santafé de Bogotá 2, Colombia. Tel. 1-212-6056/321-7501, fax 1-321-7503. *Dir.* Carmen Barvo.

Federation of European Publishers, 92 Ave. de Tervuren, 1040 Brussels, Belgium. Tel. 2-736-3616, fax 2-736-1987. *Pres.* Volker Schwarz; *Secy. Gen.* Mechtild Von Alemann.

International Board on Books for Young People (IBBY), Nonnenweg 12, Postfach, CH-4003 Basel, Switzerland. Tel. 61-272-29-17, fax 61-272-27-57. *Dir.* Leena Maissen.

International Booksellers Federation, Boulevard Lambermont 140/1, B1030 Brussels, Belgium. Tel./fax 2-242-0957. *Pres.* Yvonne Steinberger; *Gen. Secy.* Christiane Vuidar.

International Group of Scientific, Technical and Medical Publishers (STM), Keizersgracht 462, 1016 GE Amsterdam, Netherlands. Tel. 20-225214, fax 20-381566. *Secy.* Lex Lefebvre.

International League of Antiquarian Booksellers, Box 323, Victoria Sta., Montreal, PQ H3Z 2V8, Canada. Tel. 514-844-5344, fax 514-499-9274 *Pres.* Anton Gerits; *Secy.* Helen Kahn.

International Publishers Assn. (Union Internationale des Editeurs), Ave. Miremont 3, CH-1206 Geneva, Switzerland. Tel. 22-346-3018, fax 22-347-5717. *Pres.* Alain Gründ; *Secy.-Gen.* J. Alexis Koutchoumow.

National

Argentina

Cámara Argentina de Publicaciones (Argentine Publications Assn.), Reconquista 1011, piso 6° D, 1074 Buenos Aires. Tel. 01-311-6855. *Contact* Augustin dos Santos.

Cámara Argentina del Libro (Argentine Book Assn.), Avda. Belgrano 1580, 6° piso, 1093 Buenos Aires. Tel. 541-381-9277, fax 541-381-9253. *Dir.* Norberto J. Pou.

Fundación El Libro (Book Foundation), Avda. Cordoba 744 PB Dto. 1, 1054 Buenos Aires. Tel. 322-2225, fax 325-5681, e-mail fund@libro.satlink.net. *Pres.* Jorge Navelro; *Dir.* Marta V. Diaz.

Australia

Australian and New Zealand Assn. of Antiquarian Booksellers, 161 Commercial Rd., South Yarra, Vic. 3141. Tel. 3-826-1779, fax 3-521-3412. *Secy.* Nicholas Dawes.

Australian Booksellers Assn., Box 1088, Carlton, Vic. 3053. Tel. 3-966-37-888, fax 3-966-37-557. *Pres.* Tim Peach; *Exec. Dir.* Celia Pollock.

Australian Publishers Assn., Suite 60, 89 Jones St., Ultimo, Sydney, N.S.W. 2007. Tel. 2-9281-9788, fax 2-9281-1073, e-mail ape@magna.com.au. *Dir.* Susan Blackwell.

National Book Council, Suite 3, 21 Drummond Pl., Carlton, Vic. 3053. Tel. 3-663-

8655, fax 3-663-8658. *Pres.* Michael G. Zifcak; *Exec. Dir.* Thomas Shapcott.

Austria

Hauptverband des Österreichischen Buchhandels (Austrian Publishers and Booksellers Assn.), Grünangergasse 4, A-1010 Vienna. Tel. 1-512-1535, fax 1-512-8482. *Pres. and Secy.* Anton C. Hilscher.

Österreichischer Buchhändlerverband (Austrian Booksellers Assn.), Grünangergasse 4, A-1010 Vienna. Tel. 1-512-1535, fax 1-512-8482. *Pres.* Michael Kernstock.

Österreichischer Verlegerverband (Assn. of Austrian Publishers), Grünangergasse 4, A-1010 Vienna. Tel. 1-512-1535, fax 1-512-8482. *Pres.* Gustav Glöckler.

Verband der Antiquare Österreichs (Austrian Antiquarian Booksellers Assn.), Grünangergasse 4, A-1010 Vienna. Tel. 1-512-1535, fax 1-512-8482. *Pres.* Hansjörg Krug.

Belarus

National Book Chamber of Belarus, 31a Very Khoruzhey St., 220002 Minsk. Tel./fax 172-769-396, e-mail palata@palata.minsk.by. *Contact* Anatolij Voronko.

Belgium

Vereniging ter Bevordering van het Vlaamse Boekwezen (Assn. for the Promotion of Dutch Language Books/Books from Flanders), Hof ter Schrieclaan 17, 2600 Berchem/Antwerp. Tel. 3-230-8923, fax 3-281-2240. *Pres.* Luc Demeester; *Gen. Secy.* Wim de Mont.

Vlaamse Boekverkopersbond (Flemish Booksellers Assn.), Hof ter Schrieclaan 17, 2600 Berchem/Antwerp. Tel. 3-230-8923, fax 3-281-2240. *Pres.* Luc Vander Velpen; *Gen. Secy.* Carlo Van Baelen.

Bolivia

Cámara Boliviana del Libro (Bolivian Booksellers Assn.), Casilla 682, Avda. 20 de Octubre 2005, Edificio Las Palmas, Planta Baja, La Paz. Tel. 2-327-039, fax 2-391-817. *Pres.* Rolando S. Condori; *Secy.* Teresa G. de Alvarez.

Brazil

Associação Brasileira do Livro (Brazilian Booksellers Assn.), Ave. 13 de Maio, 16°, 20031 Rio de Janeiro. Tel. 21-240-9115. *Pres.* Ernesto Zahar.

Associação Nacional de Livrarias (National Assn. of Bookstores), Ave. Ipiranga 1267, 10° andar, 01039-907 Sao Paulo SP. Tel. 11-225-8277, fax 11-229-7463. *Pres.* Eduardo Yasuda.

Câmara Brasileira do Livro (Brazilian Book Assn.), Av. Ipiranga 1267, 10° andar, 01039-907 Sao Paulo. Tel. 11-225-8277, fax 11-229-7463. *Gen. Mgr.* Aloysio T. Costa.

Sindicato Nacional dos Editores de Livros (Brazilian Book Publishers Assn.), Av. Rio Branco 37, 15° andar, Salas 1503/6e, 1510/12, 20090-003 Rio de Janeiro. Tel. 21-233-6481, fax 21-253-8502. *Pres.* Sérgio Abreu da Cruz Machado; *Exec. Secy.* Henrique Maltese.

Chile

Câmara Chilena del Libro AG (Chilean Assn. of Publishers, Distributors and Booksellers), Avda. Libertador Bernardo O'Higgins 1370, Of. 501, 13526 Santiago. Tel. 2-698-9519, fax 2-698-9226, e-mail camlibro@reuna.cl. *Exec. Secy.* Carlos Franz.

Colombia

Câmara Colombiana del Libro (Colombian Book Assn.), Carrera 17A, No. 37-27, Apdo. Aereo 8998, Santafé de Bogotá. Tel. 1-245-1940, 232-7550, 288-6188, fax 1-287-3320.

Cuba

Câmara Cubano del Libro (Cuban Book Assn.), Calle 15 N 604 entre B y C, Vedado, La Habana CP 10400. Tel. 573-3-6034, fax 537-338212, e-mail cclfilh@ceniai.cu. *Pres.* José A. Robert Gasset.

Cyprus

Cyprus Booksellers Assn., Box 1455, Nicosia 1509. Tel. 2-449500, fax 2-367433. *Secy.* Socrates Heracleous.

Czech Republic

Svaz ceskych knihkupcu a nakladetelu (Czech Publishers and Booksellers Assn.), Jana Masaryka 56, 120 00 Prague 2. Tel./fax 2-2423-5302, e-mail book@login.cz.

Denmark

Danske Antikvarboghandlerforening (Danish Antiquarian Booksellers Assn.), Postboks 2028, DK-1012 Copenhagen K. Fax 33-125-494. *Chair* P. J. Poulsen.

Den Danske Boghandlerforening (Danish Booksellers Assn.), Siljangade 6, DK-2300 Copenhagen S. Tel. 3154-2255, fax 3157-2422, e-mail ddb@gognost.dk. *Pres.* Hanne Madsen.

Danske Forlaeggerforening (Danish Publishers Assn.), Købmagergade 11/13, DK-1150 Copenhagen K. Tel. 3-315-6688, fax 3-315-6588, e-mail publassn@webpartner. dk. *Dir.* Erik V. Krustrup.

Ecuador

Cámara Ecuatoriana del Libro, Guayaquil 1629, 4° piso, Casilla 17-01-3329, Quito. Tel. 2-322-1226, fax 2-325-66340. *Pres.* Fausto A. Coba.

Egypt

General Egyptian Book Organization, Box 1660, Corniche El-Nile, Boulac, Cairo. Tel. 2-77-549, 77-500, fax 2-93-932. *Pres.* Ezz El Dine Ismail.

Estonia

Estonian Publishers Assn., Box 3366, EE-0090 Tallinn. Tel. 2-650-5592, fax 2-650-5596. *Dir.* A. Tarvis.

Finland

Kirja-ja Paperikauppojen Liitto ry (Finnish Booksellers and Stationers Assn.), Eerikinkatu 15-17 D 43-44, 00100 Helsinki. Tel. -694-4899, fax -694-4900. *Chief Exec.* Olli Eräkivi.

Suomen Kustannusyhdistys ry (Finnish Book Publishers Assn.), Box 177, FIN-00121 Helsinki. Tel. 9-2287-7250, fax 9-612-1226, e-mail finnpubl@skyry.pp.fi. *Dir.* Veikko Sonninen.

France

Cercle de la Librairie (Circle of Professionals of the Book Trade), 35 Rue Grégoire-de-Tours, F-75006 Paris. Tel. 1-44-41-28-00, fax 1-44-41-28-65. *Pres.* Marc Friedel.

Fédération Française des Syndicats de Libraires—FFSL (French Booksellers Assn.), 43 Rue de Châteaudun, F-75009 Paris. Tel. 1-42-82-00-03, fax 1-42-82-10-51. *Pres.* Jean-Luc Dewas.

France Edition, 35 Rue Grégoire-de-Tours, F-75006 Paris. Tel. 1-44-41-13-13, fax 1-46-34-63-83. *Chair* Bernard Foulon. *New York Branch* French Publishers Agency, 853 Broadway, New York, NY 10003-4703. Tel. 212-254-4520, fax 212-979-6229.

Syndicat National de la Librairie Ancienne et Moderne (National Assn. of Antiquarians and Modern Booksellers), 4 Rue Git-le-Coeur, F-75006 Paris. Tel. 1-43-29-46-38, fax 1-43-25-41-63. *Pres.* Jean-Etienne Huret.

Syndicat National de l'Edition (National Union of Publishers), 115 Blvd. Saint-Germain, F-75006 Paris. Tel. 1-441-4050, fax 1-441-4077. *Pres.* Serge Eyrolles; *Secy.* Jean Sarzana.

Union des Libraires de France, 40 Rue Grégoire-de-Tours, F-75006 Paris. Tel. 1-43-29-88-79, fax 1-46-33-65-27. *Pres.* Eric Hardin; *Gen. Delegate* Marie-Dominique Doumenc.

Germany

Börsenverein des Deutschen Buchhandels e.V. (Stock Exchange of German Booksellers), Postfach 100442, 60004 Frankfurt-am-Main. Tel. 69-130-6311, fax 69-130-6300. *Gen. Mgr.* Hans-Karl von Kupsch.

Bundesverband der Deutschen Versandbuchhändler e.V. (National Federation of German Mail-Order Booksellers), An der Ringkirche 6, 65197 Wiesbaden. Tel. 611-44-9091, fax 611-48451. *Mgrs.* Stefan Rutkowsky, Kornelia Wahl.

Verband Deutscher Antiquare e.V. (German Antiquarian Booksellers Assn.), Kreuzgasse 2-4, Postfach 10-10-20, 50450 Cologne. Tel./fax 221-92-54-82-82; *Pres.* Jochen Granier; *V.P.* Inge Utzt.

Ghana

Ghana Book Development Council, Box M430, Accra. Tel. 21-22-9178, fax 21-22-0271. *Deputy Exec. Dir.* Annor Nimako.

Great Britain

See United Kingdom

Greece

Book Publishers Assn., Themistocleous 73, 10683 Athens. Tel./fax 1-330-1956. *Pres.* Magda Kotzia.
Hellenic Federation of Publishers and Booksellers, Themistocleous 73, 10683 Athens. Tel. 1-330-0924, fax 1-330-1617. *Pres.* Dimitris Pandeleskos.

Hungary

Magyar Könyvkiadók és Könyvterjesztök Egyesülése (Assn. of Hungarian Publishers and Booksellers), Vörösmarty tér 1, 1051 Budapest (mail: PB 130, 1367 Budapest). Tel. 1-117-6222. *Pres.* István Bart; *Secy.-Gen.* Péter Zcntai.

Iceland

Félag Islenskra Bókaútgefenda (Icelandic Publishers Assn.), Sudurlandsbraut 4A, 108 Reykjavik. Tel. 5538020, fax 5888668. *Chair* Olafur Ragnarsson; *Gen. Mgr.* Vilborg Hardardóttir.

India

Federation of Indian Publishers, Federation House, 18/1-C Institutional Area, JNU Rd., Aruna Asaf Ali Marg, New Delhi 110067. Tel. 11-696-4847, 685-2263, fax 11-686-4054. *Pres.* Shri R. C. Govil; *Exec. Secy.* S. K. Ghai.

Indonesia

Ikatan Penerbit Indonesia (Assn. of Indonesian Book Publishers), Jl. Kalipasir 32, Jakarta 10330. Tel. 21-314-1907, fax 21-314-1433. *Pres.* Rozali Usman; *Secy. Gen.* Setia Dharma Majidd.

Ireland

Booksellers Assn. of Great Britain and Ireland (Irish Branch), 54 Middle Abbey St., Dublin 1. *Admin.* Cecily Golden.
CLÉ: The Irish Book Publishers Assn., The Writers Centre, 19 Parnell Sq., Dublin 1. Tel. 1-872-9090, fax 1-872-2035. *Contact* Orla Martin.

Israel

Book and Printing Center, Israel Export Institute, 29 Hamered St., Box 50084, Tel Aviv 68125. Tel. 3-514-2910, fax 3-514-2815. *Dir.* Corine Knafo.
Book Publishers Assn. of Israel, Box 20123, Tel Aviv 61201. Tel. 3-561-4121, fax 3-561-1996. *Managing Dir.* Amnon Ben-Shmuel.

Italy

Associazione Italiana Editori (Italian Publishers Assn.), Via delle Erbe 2, 20121 Milan. Tel. 2-86-46-3091, fax 2-89-01-0863.
Associazione Librai Antiquari d'Italia (Antiquarian Booksellers Assn. of Italy), Via Jacopo Nardi 6, I-50132 Florence. Tel./fax (55) 24-3253. *Pres.* Vittorio Soave; *Secy.* Francesco Scala.
Associazione Librai Italiani (Italian Booksellers Assn.), Corso Venezia 49, 20121 Milan. Tel. 2-775-0216, fax 2-775-0248. *Pres.* Susanna Schwarz Bellotti.

Jamaica

Booksellers Assn. of Jamaica, c/o Novelty Training Co. Ltd., Box 80, Kingston. Tel. 809-922-5883, fax 809-922-4743. *Pres.* Keith Shervington.

Japan

Japan Book Importers Assn., Chiyoda Kaikan 21-4, Nihonbashi 1-chome, Chuo-ku, Tokyo 103. Tel. 3-32-71-6901, fax 3-32-71-6920. *Secy.* Shunji Kanda.
Japan Book Publishers Assn., 6 Fukuromachi, Shinjuku-ku, Tokyo 162. Tel. 3-32-68-1301, fax 3-32-68-1196. *Pres.* Takao Watanabe; *Exec. Dir.* Toshikazu Gomi.

Kenya

Kenya Publishers Assn., c/o Phoenix Publishers Ltd., Box 18650, Nairobi. Tel. 2-22-2309, 22-3262, fax 2-33-9875. *Secy.* Stanley Irura.

Korea (Republic of)

Korean Publishers Assn., 105-2 Sagan-dong, Jongro-gu, Seoul 110-190. Tel. 2-735-2701, fax 2-738-5414, e-mail kpasibf@soback.kornet.nm.kr. *Pres.* Na Choon Ho; *Secy.-Gen.* Jong-Jin Jung.

Latvia

Latvian Book Publishers Assn., Aspazijas Bulvaris 24, 1050 Riga. Tel. 371-722-5843, fax 371-783-0518.

Lithuania

Lithuanian Publishers Assn., K. Sirvydo 6, 2600 Vilnius. Tel. 3702-628-945, fax 3702-619-696. *Pres.* Vincas Akelis.

Mexico

Cámara Nacional de la Industria Editorial Mexicana, Holanda No. 13, CP 04120 Mexico 21. Tel. 5-688-2221, fax 5-604-3147. *Secy.-Gen.* R. Servin.

The Netherlands

Koninklijke Nederlandse Uitgeversbond (Royal Dutch Publishers Assn.), Postbus 12040, 1100 AA Amsterdam. Tel. 20-626-7736, fax 20-620-3859. *Pres.* Karel Leeflang; *Secy.* R. M. Vrij.

Koninklijke Vereeniging ter Bevordering van de Belangen des Boekhandels (Royal Dutch Book Trade Assn.), Postbus 15007, 1001 MA Amsterdam. Tel. 20-624-0212, fax 20-620-8871. *Secy.* M. van Vollenhoven-Nagel.

Nederlandsche Vereeniging van Antiquaren (Netherlands Assn. of Antiquarian Booksellers), Postbus 664, 1000 AR Amsterdam. Tel. 20-627-2285, fax 20-625-8970. *Pres.* F. W. Kuyper; *Secy.* A. Gerits.

Nederlandse Boekverkopersbond (Dutch Booksellers Assn.), Postbus 32, 3720 AA Bilthoven. Tel. 30-228-7956, fax 30-228-4566. *Pres.* W. Karssen; *Exec. Secy.* A. C. Doeser.

New Zealand

Book Publishers Assn. of New Zealand, Box 101 271 North Shore Mail, Auckland. Tel. 9-480-2711, fax 9-480-1130.

Booksellers New Zealand, Box 11-377, Wellington. Tel. 4-472-8678, fax 4-472-8628. *Chair* Joan MacKenzie; *Pres.* Tony Harkins; *Chief Exec.* Jo Breese.

Nigeria

Nigerian Publishers Assn., GPO Box 3541, Dugbe, Ibadan. Tel. 22-411-557. *Pres.* A. O. Echebiri.

Norway

Norske Bokhandlerforening (Norwegian Booksellers Assn.), Ovre Vollgate 15, 0158 Oslo. Tel. 22-396800, fax 22-356810. *Dir.* Einar J. Einarsson.

Norske Forleggerforening (Norwegian Publishers Assn.), Ovre Vollgate 15, 0158 Oslo 1. Tel. 22-007580, fax 22-333830, e-mail dnf@forleggerforeningen.no. *Dir.* Paul Martens Røthe.

Pakistan

National Book Council of Pakistan, Block 14D, 1st fl., Al-Markaz F/8,, Box 1610, Islamabad. Tel. 51-853-581. *Dir. Gen.* Rafiq Ahmad.

Paraguay

Cámara Paraguaya de Editores, Libreros y Asociados (Paraguayan Publishers Assn.), Caballero 270, Asunción. Tel. 21-496-991, fax 21-448-721. *Dir.* Alejandro Gatti.

Peru

Cámara Peruana del Libro (Peruvian Publishers Assn.), Apdo Postal 102533, Lima 1. Tel. 14-715152. *Pres.* Julio César Flores Rodriguez; *Exec. Dir.* Loyda Moran Bustamente.

Philippines

Philippine Educational Publishers Assn., 84 P Florentino St., 3008 Quezon City. Tel. 2-968-316, fax 2-921-3788. *Pres.* D. D. Buhain.

Poland

Polskie Towarzystwo Wydawców Ksiazek (Polish Society of Book Editors), ul. Mazowiecka 2/4, 00-048 Warsaw. Tel./fax 22-8260735. *Pres.* Janusz Fogler; *Gen. Secy.* Donat Chruscicki.

Stowarzyszenie Ksiegarzy Polskich (Assn. of Polish Booksellers), ul. Mokotowska 4/6, 00-641 Warsaw. Tel. 22-252-874. *Pres.* Tadeusz Hussak.

Portugal

Associação Portuguesa de Editores e Livreiros (Portuguese Assn. of Publishers and Booksellers), Largo de Andaluz, 16-7 Esq., 1000 Lisbon. Tel. 1-556241, fax 1-3153553. *Pres.* Francisco Espadinha; *Secy. Gen.* Jorge de Carvalho Sa Borges.

Russia

All-Union Book Chamber, Kremlevskaja nab 1/9, 121019 Moscow. Tel. 95-202-7172, fax 95-202-3992. *Dir.-Gen.* Yuri Torsuev.

Publishers Assn., 44B Hertsen Str., 121069 Moscow. Tel. 95-202-1174, fax 95-202-3989. *Contact* M. Shishigin.

Singapore

Singapore Book Publishers Assn., Block 86, Marine Parade Central, No. 03-213, Singapore 440086. Tel. 344-7801, fax 447-0897. *Pres.* K. P. Sivan; *Honorary Secy.* Wu Cheng Tan.

Slovenia

Zdruzenje Zaloznikov in Knjigotrzcev Slovenije Gospodarska Zbornica Slovenije (Assn. of Publishers and Booksellers of Slovenia), Dimiòeva 9, 1504 Ljubljana. Tel./fax 61-342-398. *Contact* Joze Korinsek.

South Africa

Associated Booksellers of Southern Africa, Box 870, Bellville 7530. Tel. 21-951-6611, fax 21-951-4903. *Pres.* M. Hargraves; *Secy.* R. Stoltenkamp.

Publishers Assn. of South Africa, Box 116, 46 St. James. Tel. 21-788-6470, fax 21-788-6469. *Chair* Basil Van Rooyen.

Spain

Federación de Gremios de Editores de España (Federation of Spanish Publishers Assns.), Juan Ramón Jiménez, 45-9° Izda, 28036 Madrid. Tel. 1-350-9105, fax 1-345-4351. *Pres.* Pere Vincens; *Secy.* Ana Molto.

Gremio de Libreros de Barcelona (Booksellers Assn. of Barcelona and Catalonia), Mallorca 274, 08037 Barcelona. Tel. 3-215-4254.

Sri Lanka

Sri Lanka Assn. of Publishers, 112 S. Mahinda Mawatha, Colombo 10. Tel. 1-695-773, fax 1-696-653. *Pres.* Dayawansa Jayakody.

Sudan

Sudanese Publishers Assn., H. Q. Al Ikhwa Bldg., Flat 7, 7th fl., Box 2771, Khartoum. Tel. 249-11-75051, 79180.

Suriname

Publishers Assn. Suriname, Domineestr. 26, Box 1841, Paramaribo. Tel. 472-545, fax 410-563. *Mgr.* E. Hogenboom.

Sweden

Svenska Förläggareföreningen (Swedish Publishers Assn.), Drottninggatan 97, S-11360 Stockholm. Tel. 8-736-1940, fax 8-736-1944. *Dir.* Kristina Ahlinder.

Switzerland

Schweizerischer Buchhändler- und Verleger-Verband (Swiss German-Language Booksellers and Publishers Assn.), Baumackerstr. 42, Postfach 9045, 8050 Zurich.

Tel. 1-3186400, fax 1-3186462, e-mail sbvv@dm.krinfo.ch. *Secy.* Egon Räz.

Societa Editori della Svizzera Italiana (Publishers Assn. for Italian-Speaking Switzerland), Via San Gottardo 50, 6900 Lugano. Tel. 91-232-271, fax 91-232-805. *Pres.* Alfonso Pezzati.

Société des Libraires et Editeurs de la Suisse Romande (Assn. of Swiss French-Language Booksellers and Publishers), 2 Ave. Agassiz, 1001 Lausanne. Tel. 21-319-7111, fax 21-319-7910. *Contact* Philippe Schibli.

Tanzania

Publishers Assn. of Tanzania, Box 1408, Dar es Salaam. Tel. 51-512-7608. *Dir.* A. Saiwaad.

Thailand

Publishers and Booksellers Assn. of Thailand, 320 Lat Phrao 94-aphat Pracha-u-thit Rd., Bangkok 10310. Tel. 2-662-559-3348, fax 2-662-538-1499.

Uganda

Uganda Publishers and Booksellers Assn., Box 7732, Plot 2C Kampala Rd., Kampala. Tel. 41-259163, fax 41-251160. *Contact* Martin Okia.

United Kingdom

Antiquarian Booksellers Assn., Sackville House, 40 Piccadilly, London W1V 9PA, England. Tel. 171-439-3118, fax 171-439-3119. *Administrators* Philippa Gibson; Deborah Stratford.

Assn. of Learned and Professional Society Publishers, 48 Kelsey Lane, Beckenham, Kent BR3 3NE, England. Tel. 181-658-0459, fax 181-663-3583, e-mail donovan@alpsp.demon.co.uk. *Secy.-Gen.* B. T. Donovan.

Book Trust, 45 E. Hill, Wandsworth, London SW18 2QZ. Tel. 181-870-9055, fax 181-874-4790.

Book Trust Scotland, Scottish Book Centre, 137 Dundee St., Edinburgh EH11 1BG, Scotland. Tel. 131-229-3663, fax 131-228-4293. *Exec. Dir.* Lindsey Fraser.

Booksellers Assn. of Great Britain and Ireland, Minster House, 272 Vauxhall Bridge Rd., London SW1V 1BA, England. Tel. 171-834-5477, fax 171-834-8812, e-mail 100437.2261@compuserve.com. *Chief Exec.* Tim Godfray.

Educational Publishers Council, 19 Bedford Sq., London WC1B 3HJ, England. Tel. 171-580-6321, fax 171-636-5375. *Dir.* John R. M. Davies.

Publishers Assn., 1 Kingsway, London WC2B 6XF, England. Tel. 171-580-6321, fax 171-636-5375. *Pres.* Trevor Glover; *Chief Exec.* Clive Bradley; *Secy.* Mandy Knight.

Scottish Publishers Assn., Scottish Book Centre, 137 Dundee St., 1st fl., Edinburgh EH11 1BG, Scotland. Tel. 131-228-6866, fax 131-228-3220. *Dir.* Lorraine Fannin; *Chair* Mike Miller.

Welsh Books Council (Cyngor Llyfrau Cymraeg), Castell Brychan, Aberystwyth, Dyfed SY23 2JB, Wales. Tel. 1970-624151, fax 1970-625385. *Dir.* Gwerfyl Pierce Jones.

Uruguay

Cámara Uruguaya del Libro (Uruguayan Publishers Assn.), Juan D. Jackson 1118, 11200 Montevideo. Tel. 2-241-5732, fax 2-241-1860.

Venezuela

Cámara Venezolana del Libro (Venezuelan Publishers Assn.), Ave. Andrés Bello, Torre Oeste, 11° piso, Of. 112-0, Apdo. 51858, Caracas 1050-A. Tel. 2-793-1347, fax 2-793-1368. *Secy.* M. P. Vargas.

Zambia

Booksellers and Publishers Assn. of Zambia, Box 31838, Lusaka. Tel. 1-222-647, fax 1-225-195; *Exec. Dir.* Basil Mbewe.

National Information Standards Organization (NISO) Standards

Book Production and Publishing

Z39.14-1997	Guidelines for Abstracts
Z39.22-1989	Proof Corrections
Z39.41-1997	Printed Information on Spines
Z39.43-1993	Standard Address Number (SAN) for the Publishing Industry
Z39.48-1992 (R 1997)	Permanence of Paper for Publications and Documents in Libraries and Archives
Z39.66-1992	Durable Hard-Cover Binding for Books

Codes and Numbering Systems

Z39.9-1992	International Standard Serial Numbering (ISSN)
Z39.23-1997	Standard Technical Report Number
Z39.43-1993	Standard Address Number (SAN) for the Publishing Industry
Z39.47-1993	Extended Latin Alphabet Coded Character Set for Bibliographic Use (ANSEL)
Z39.53-1994	Codes for the Representation of Languages for Information Interchange
Z39.56-1996	Serial Item and Contribution Identifier
Z39.64-1989 (R 1995)	East Asian Character Code for Bibliographic Use
Z39.76-1996	Data Elements for Binding Library Materials
NISO/ANSI/ISO 3166	Codes for the Representation of Names of Countries
NISO/ANSI/ISO 2108	International Standard Book Numbering (ISBN)

Indexes, Thesauri, and Database Development

Z39.19-1993	Guidelines for the Construction, Format, and Management of Monolingual Thesauri

Microforms

Z39.62-1993	Eye-Legible Information on Microfilm Leaders And Trailers and on Containers of Processed Microfilm on Open Reels

| Z39.74-1996 | Guides to Accompany Microform Sets |
| Z39.32-1996 | Information on Microform Headers |

Technical Writing

Z39.18-1995	Scientific and Technical Reports—Elements, Organization, and Design
Z39.23-1997	Standard Technical Report Number
Z39.19-1993	Guidelines for the Construction, Format, and Management of Monolingual Thesauri
Z39/14-1997	Guidelines for Abstracts

Serial Publications

Z39.5-1985*	Abbreviation of Titles of Publications
Z39.9-1992	International Standard Serial Numbering (ISSN)
Z39.48-1992 (R 1997)	Permanence of Paper for Printed Publications
Z39.56-1996	Serial Item and Contribution Identifier

Library Automation and Electronic Publishing

Z39.2-1994	Information Interchange Format
Z39.47-1993	Extended Latin Alphabet Coded Character Set for Bibliographic Use (ANSEL)
Z39.50-1995	Information Retrieval (Z39.50) Application Service Definition and Protocol Specification
Z39.57-1989 (R 1995)	Holding Statements for Non-Serial Items
Z39.58-1992*	Common Command Language for Interactive Information Retrieval
Z39.63-1989*	Interlibrary Loan Data Elements
Z39.67-1993	Computer Software Description
NISO/ANSI/ISO 3166	Codes for the Representation of Names of Countries
NISO/ANSI/ISO 12083	Electronic Manuscript Preparation and Markup
Z39.26-1997	Micro Publishing Product Information

Library Management and Administration

| Z39.7-1995 | Library Statistics |
| Z39.73-1994 | Single-Tier Steel Bracket Library Shelving |

In Development

Environmental Conditions for the Exhibition of Library and Archival Materials
Preservation Product Information
Library Binding
Revision of Z39.29-1977 Bibliographic References
Standard Format for Downloading Records from Bibliographic and Abstracting Indexing Databases

Holding Statements for Bibliographic Items
Title Page Information for Conference Proceedings
Book Item and Contribution Identifier (BICI)
The Digital Talking Book: A System for Audio Access to Printed Material
Criteria for Price Indexes for Print Library Materials

NISO Technical Reports

TR-01-1995	Environmental Guidelines for the Storage of Paper Records
TR-02-1997	Guidelines for Indexes and Related Information Retrieval Devices

*This standard is being reviewed by NISO's Standards Development Committee or is under revision. For further information, please contact NISO, 4733 Bethesda Ave., Suite 300, Bethesda, MD 20814. Tel. 301-654-2512, fax 301-654-1721, e-mail nisohq@cni.org , World Wide Web http:\\ www.niso.org.

Calendar, 1998–2002

The list below contains information on association meetings or promotional events that are, for the most part, national or international in scope. State and regional library association meetings are also included. To confirm the starting or ending date of a meeting, which may change after the *Bowker Annual* has gone to press, contact the association directly. Addresses of library and book trade associations are listed in Part 6 of this volume. For information on additional book trade and promotional events, see the *Exhibits Directory*, published annually by the Association of American Publishers; *Chase's Annual Events*, published by Contemporary Books, 180 N. Michigan Ave., Chicago, IL 60601; *Literary Market Place* and *International Literary Market Place*, published by R. R. Bowker; and the "Calendar" section in each issue of *Publishers Weekly* and *Library Journal*.

1998

May

2–3	American Society of Journalists and Authors	New York, NY
3	Chief Officers of State Library Agencies	Washington, D.C.
6–7	Archivists and Librarians in the History of the Health Sciences	Toronto, ON
7–9	North Dakota/Manitoba Library Assns.	Regina, SK
8	Delaware Library Assn.	Dover, DE
11–14	Assn. for Information and Image Management	Anaheim, CA
14–17	Antiquarian Booksellers Assn./ILAB	Paris, France
20	American Merchant Marine Library Assn.	New York, NY
22–25	Atlantic Provinces Library Assn.	Wolfville, NS
22–27	Medical Libraries Assn.	Philadelphia, PA
27–29	Religious Booksellers Trade Exhibit	St. Charles, IL
28–6/1	Mountain Plains Library Assn.	Salt Lake City, UT
28–6/1	Utah Library Assn.	Salt Lake City, UT

June

1–7	International Assn. of Technological Univ. Libraries	Pretoria, South Africa

June 1998 *(cont.)*

2–5	International Assn. of Agricultural Information Specialists	Freising, Germany
3–5	Society for Scholarly Publishing	San Diego, CA
4–7	Antiquarian Booksellers Assn./ILAB	London, UK
6–11	Special Libraries Assn.	Indianapolis, IN
17–20	American Theological Library Assn.	Philadelphia, PA
17–21	Canadian Booksellers Assn.	Toronto, ON
18–21	Canadian Library Assn.	Victoria, BC
21–24	Association of Jewish Libraries	Philadelphia, PA
21–26	International Assn. of Music Libraries, Archives, and Documentation Centres (IAML)	San Sebastian, Spain
25–7/2	American Library Assn.	Washington, DC
26–29	Assn. of American University Presses	Washington, DC
*	Colorado Educational Media Assn.	Greeley, CO

July

5–9	International Assn. of School Librarianship	Ramat-Gan, Israel
10–12	Texas Library Assn.	Austin, TX
11–16	American Assn. of Law Libraries	Anaheim, CA
11–16	Christian Booksellers Assn.	Dallas, TX
26–28	Church and Synagogue Library Assn.	Cleveland, OH

August

12–15	Pacific Northwest Library Assn.	Sun Valley, ID
16–27	International Federation of Library Assns. and Institutions (IFLA)	Amsterdam, Netherlands
31–9/6	Society of American Archivists	Orlando, FL

September

4–7	Miniature Book Society Conclave	Charleston, SC
2–5	International Assn. of Agricultural Information Specialists	Beijing, China
6–13	International Conference of the Round Table on Archives (CITRA)	Stockholm, Sweden
16–18	North Carolina Assn. of School Librarians	Raleigh, NC
17–18	Oklahoma Library Assn.	Oklahoma City, OK
18–20	Pacific Northwest Booksellers Assn.	Eugene, OR
21–25	International Assn. of Law Libraries	Rome, Italy
23–25	Manitoba Library Assn.	Brandon, MN
23–26	North Dakota Library Assn.	Grand Forks, ND
25–27	Mountain Plains Booselleres Assn.	Denver, CO
29–10/3	Arkansas Library Assn.	Little Rock, AK

* To be determined

29–10/3	Southeastern Library Assn.	Little Rock, AK
30–10/3	South Dakota Library Assn.	Pierre, SD

October

1	National Information Standards Organization (NISO)	New Orleans, LA
1–4	Nevada Library Assn.	Las Vegas, NV
2–4	Great Lakes Booksellers Assn.	Cleveland, OH
2–4	New England Booksellers Assn.	Boston, MA
3–4	New Atlantic Independent Booksellers Assn.	Philadelphia, PA
3–5	Chief Officers of State Library Agencies	Portsmouth, NH
3–5	New England Library Assn.	Providence, RI
7–9	Council of Media Organizations	Macon, GA
7–9	Minnesota Library Assn.	Rochester, MN
9–11	American Printing History Assn.	Chicago, IL
9–11	ILAB Book Fair	Vienna, Austria
13–15	Idaho Library Assn.	Sun Valley, ID
13–15	Pacific Northwest Library Assn.	Sun Valley, ID
14–16	Iowa Library Assn.	Waterloo, IA
15–16	Montana Education Assn.	Great Falls, MT
15–17	Virginia Library Assn./Virginia Educational Media Assn.	Virginia Beach, VA
18–21	ARMA International	Cincinnati, OH
21–23	Michigan Library Assn.	Grand Rapids, MI
21–23	Nebraska Library Assn.	Grand Island, NE
21–24	Kentucky Library Assn.	Louisville, KY
22–24	Educational Media Assn. of New Jersey	Parsippany, NJ
22–26	Colorado Library Assn.	Colorado Springs, CO
24–28	Evangelical Christian Publishers Assn.	New Orleans, LA
29–31	Assn. for Library Service to Children/ American Library Trustee Assn.	Indianapolis, IN
29–31	Tennessee Assn. of School Librarians	Memphis, TN
*	ISBN International Agency Advisory Board	Berlin, Germany
*	Wyoming Library Assn.	Jackson, WY

November

1–2	Massachusetts School Library Media Assn.	Worcester, MA
4–6	Ohio Educational Library Media Assn.	Columbus, OH
4–7	Michigan Assn. for Media in Education	Acme, MI
4–8	American Translators Assn.	Hilton Head, SC
5–7	Illinois School Library Media Assn.	Arlington Heights, IL
6–8	Oregon Educational Media Assn.	Sunriver, OR
8–11	Pennsylvania Library Assn.	Hershey, PA
14–17	California Library Assn.	Oakland, CA

* To be determined

November 1998 *(cont.)*

16–17	Library Information and Technology Assn.	Oakland, CA
*	Connecticut Library Assn.	Cromwell, CT

December

2–5	Arizona Library Assn.	Phoenix, AZ
7–9	West Virginia Library Assn.	White Sulphur Springs, WV

1999

January

29–2/3	American Library Assn.	Philadelphia, PA

February

*	Colorado Educational Media Assn.	Colorado Springs, CO

March

4–6	Association for Indiana Media Educators	Indianapolis, IN
4–6	Great Lakes Booksellers Assn.	Chicago, IL
25–31	Art Libraries Society of North America	Vancouver, BC

April

6–9	Catholic Library Assn.	New Orleans, LA
7–9	Kansas Library Assn.	Salina, KS
7–11	Alabama Library Assn.	Perdido, AL
9–12	Assn. of College and Research Libraries	Detroit, MI
28–30	Washington Library Assn.	Pasco, WA
*	FIAF–International Federation of Film Archives	Madrid, Spain

May

17–22	International Assn. of Technological Univ. Libraries	Chania, Crete

June

5–10	Special Libraries Assn.	Minneapolis, MN
13–16	Montana Library Assn.	Big Sky, MT
13–16	Mountain Plains Library Assn.	Big Sky, MT
24–7/1	American Library Assn.	New Orleans, LA
*	Society for Scholarly Publishing	Boston, MA

* To be determined

July

19–24	International Assn. of Music Libraries, Archives, and Documentation Centres (IAML)	Wellington, New Zealand

August

20–28	International Federation of Library Assns. and Institutions (IFLA)	Bangkok, Thailand
23–29	Society of American Archivists	Pittsburgh, PA

September

26–28	New England Library Assn.	Manchester, NH
29–10/1	Minnesota Library Assn.	Duluth, MN

October

6–9	Idaho Library Assn.	Boise, ID
6–9	South Dakota Library Assn.	Watertown, SD
8–10	Great Lakes Booksellers Assn. Fall Trade Show	Lansing, MI
13–15	Iowa Library Assn.	Dubuque, IA
28–30	Illinois School Library Media Assn.	Decatur, IL

November

3–5	Ohio Educational Library Media Assn.	Columbus, OH

2000

January

14–19	American Library Assn.	San Antonio, TX

March

9–11	Association for Indiana Media Educators	Indianapolis, IN
16–23	Art Libraries Society of North America	Pittsburgh, PA

April

5–7	Kansas Library Assn.	Wichita, KS
25–28	Catholic Library Assn.	Baltimore, MD
26–29	Montana Library Assn.	Billings, MT
*	FIAF–International Federation of Film Archives	London, England

June

10–15	Special Libraries Assn.	Philadelphia, PA

* To be determined

August

5–12	International Assn. of Music Libraries, Archives, and Documentation Centres (IAML)	Edinburgh, Scotland
28–9/3	Society of American Archivists	Denver, CO

October

4–7	Idaho Library Assn.	Lewiston, ID
7–10	Arkansas Library Assn.	Springdale, AR
11–13	Minnesota Library Assn.	Minneapolis/Saint Paul, MN
18–20	Iowa Library Assn.	Ames, IA
24–28	Alabama Library Assn.	Mobile, AL
24–28	Southeastern Library Assn.	Mobile, AL

November

2–4	Illinois School Library Media Assn.	Lincolnshire, IL

2001

March

*	Assn. for Indiana Media Educators	Indianapolis, IN

April

4–6	Kansas Library Assn.	Topeka, KS
17–20	Catholic Library Assn.	Milwaukee, WI
25–28	Montana Library Assn.	Kalispell, MT

October

10–12	Iowa Library Assn.	Davenport, IA

2002

March

*	Assn. for Indiana Media Educators	Indianapolis, IN

April

24–27	Montana Library Assn.	Great Falls, MT

* To be determined

Acronyms

A

AALL. American Association of Law Libraries

AAP. Association of American Publishers

AASL. American Association of School Librarians

ABA. American Booksellers Association

ABFFE. American Booksellers Foundation for Free Expression

ACRL. Association of College and Research Libraries

AGRIS. Agricultural Science and Technology Database

AHRI. American Heritage Rivers Initiative

AJL. Association of Jewish Libraries

ALA. American Library Association

ALCTS. Association for Library Collections and Technical Services

ALISE. Association for Library and Information Science Education

ALS. Academic Libraries Survey

ALSC. Association for Library Service to Children

ALTA. American Library Trustee Association

APALA. Asian/Pacific American Librarians Association

ARL. Association of Research Libraries

ARLIS/NA. Art Libraries Society of North America

ARMA. ARMA International (Association of Records Managers and Administrators)

ASCLA. Association of Specialized and Cooperative Library Agencies

ASIS. American Society for Information Science

ATLA. American Theological Library Association

ATPA. American Technology Preeminence Act

AWIC. National Agricultural Library, Animal Welfare Information Center

B

BAM. Books-A-Million

BCR. Bibliographic Center for Research

BEA. BookExpo America

BOS. American Booksellers Association, Booksellers Order Service

BPI. Booksellers Publishing, Inc.

C

CACUL. Canadian Association of College and University Libraries

CAIS. Canadian Association for Information Science

CALA. Chinese-American Librarians Association

CAPL. Canadian Association of Public Libraries

CASLIS. Canadian Association of Special Libraries and Information Services

CBD. Commerce Business Daily

CD-ROM. Compact Disc Read-Only Memory

CDA. Communications Decency Act

CIEC. Citizens Internet Empowerment Coalition

CIPS. National Archives and Records Administration, Centers Information Processing System

CISTI. Canadian Institute for Scientific and Technical Information

CLA. Canadian Library Association; Catholic Library Association

CLTA. Canadian Library Trustees Association

CONFU. United States Conference on Fair Use

CORDS. Library of Congress, Copyright Office Electronic Registration, Recordation and Deposit System

COSLA. Chief Officers of State Library Agencies

CPL. Council of Planning Librarians

CRS. Library of Congress, Congressional Research Service

CSLA. Canadian School Library Association; Church and Synagogue Library Association

D

DFC. Digital Future Coalition

DLF. Digital Library Foundation

DOE. Education, U.S. Department of

DOI. Digital Object Identifier system

E

ECIP. Library of Congress, Electronic Cataloging in Publication

EDRS. Educational Resources Information Center, ERIC Document Reproduction Service

EMIERT. American Library Association, Ethnic Material and Information Exchange Round Table

ENAL. Egyptial National Agricultural Library

ERIC. Educational Resources Information Center

F

FBB. GPO Access, Federal Bulletin Board

FDLP. Government Printing Office, Federal Depository Library Program

FEDRIP. National Technical Information Service, Federal Research in Progress Database

FIAF. International Federation of Film Archives

FID. International Federation for Information and Documentation

FLICC. Federal Library and Information Center Committee

FLRT. American Library Association, Federal Librarians Round Table

FPC. Federal Publishers Committee

G

GALILEO. Georgia Libraries Learning Online

GILS. Government Printing Office, Government Information Locator Service

GIS. Geographic Information Systems

GLIN. Global Legal Information Network

GPO. Government Printing Office

H

HEA. Higher Education Act

HPCC. High Performance Computing and Communications Program

HSMRS. National Agricultural Library, Healthy School Meals Resource System

I

IALL. International Association of Law Libraries

IAML. International Association of Music Libraries, Archives and Documentation Centres

IASL. International Association of School Librarianship

IATUL. International Association of Technological University Libraries

ICLC. International Coalition of Library Consortia

ICSECA. International Contributions for Scientific, Educational and Cultural Activities

IDLHs. Immediately Dangerous to Life or Health Concentrations Database

IFLA. International Federation of Library Associations and Institutions

IFRT. American Library Association, Intellectual Freedom Round Table

IIA. Information Industry Association

ILL. Interlibrary loan

ILS. Integrated Library System

IMLS. Institute of Museum and Library Services

IPEDS. Integrated Postsecondary Data System

IRC. Special Libraries Association, Information Resources Center

ISBN. International Standard Book Number

ISLD. International Special Librarians Day

ISO. International Organization for Standardization

ISP. Internet service provider

ISSN. International Standard Serial Number

J

JWGT. National Agricultural Library, Joint Working Group on Telemedicine

L

LAMA. Library Administration and Management Association

LHRT. American Library Association, Library History Round Table

LILAA. Literacy in Libraries Across America

LIS. Library of Congress, Legislative Information System; Library/information science

LITA. Library and Information Technology Association

LJ. Library Journal

LPS. Government Printing Office, Library Programs Service

LRRT. American Library Association, Library Research Round Table

LSCA. Library Services and Construction Act

LSP. National Center for Education Statistics, Library Statistics Program

LSTA. Library Services and Technology Act

M

MAGERT. American Library Association, Map and Geography Round Table

MDC. Special Libraries Association, Management Document Collection

MLA. Medical Library Association; Music Library Association

N

NAGARA. National Association of Government Archives and Records Administrators

NAILDD. North American Interlibrary Loan and Document Delivery Project

NAL. National Agricultural Library

NARA. National Archives and Records Administration

NBBW. National Black Bookstore Week

NCBI. National Center for Biotechnology Information

NCES. National Center for Education Statistics

NCLIS. National Commission on Libraries and Information Science

NDLF. National Digital Library Federation

NEA. National Endowment for the Arts

NEH. National Endowment for the Humanities

NET. No Electronic Theft Act

NFAIS. National Federation of Abstracting and Information Services

NGI. Next Generation Internet

NIBW. National Independent Bookstore Week

NII. National information instructure

NIOSH. National Institute for Occupational Safety and Health

NISO. National Information Standards Organization

NLC. National Library of Canada

NLE. National Library of Education

NLM. National Library of Medicine

NLS. National Library Service for the Blind and Physically Handicapped

NMAM. National Institute for Occupational Safety and Health, Manual of Analytical Methods

NMRT. American Library Association, New Members Round Table

NPG. National Institute for Occupational Safety and Health, NIOSH Pocket Guide to Chemical Hazards

NPIN. National Parent Information Network

NRMM. National Register of Microform Masters

NTIS. National Technical Information Service

O

OCLC. Online Computer Library Center
OERI. Education, U.S. Department of, Office of Educational Research and Improvement

P

PALCI. Pennsylvania Academic Library Connection Initiative
PDQ. United States Information Agency, library programs, Public Diplomacy Query database
PGDIC. National Agricultural Library, Plant Genome Data and Information Center
PICS. Platform for Internet Content Selection
PLA. Public Library Association
PW. Publishers Weekly

R

RASD. American Library Association, Reference and Adult Services Division. *See new name* Reference and User Services Association
RLG. Research Libraries Group
RTECS. Registry of Toxic Effects of Chemical Substances
RUSA. Reference and User Services Association

S

SAA. Society of American Archivists
SAN. Standard Address Number
SLA. Special Libraries Association
SLJ. School Library Journal

SPARC. Scholarly Publishing & Academic Resources Coalition
SRRT. American Library Association, Social Responsibilities Round Table
SSP. Society for Scholarly Publishing

T

TIIAP. Telecommunications and Information Infrastructure Assistance Program
TLA. Theatre Library Association

U

UCAID. University Consortium for Advanced Internet Development
ULC. Urban Libraries Council
USDA. Agriculture, U.S. Department of
USEIN. United States Education Information Network
USIA. United States Information Agency
USIS. United States Information Service, overseas name for United States Information Agency
USPS. Postal Service, U.S.

W

WIPO. World Intellectual Property Organization
WWW. World Wide Web

Y

YALSA. Young Adult Library Services Association

Index Of Organizations

Please note that this index includes cross-references to the Subject Index. Many additional organizations can be found in Part 6 under the following headings: Networks, Consortia, and Cooperative Library Organizations; National Library and Information-Industry Associations, United States and Canada; State, Provincial, and Regional Library Associations; State and Provincial Library Agencies; State School Library Media Associations; International Library Associations; Foreign Library Associations; Book Trade Associations, United States and Canada; International and Foreign Book Trade Associations

A

AGRICOLA (Agricultural OnLine Access), 39, 103

Agricultural Network Information Center (AgNIC), 104

Agriculture, U.S. Department of (USDA) *see* National Agricultural Library

AGRIS (Agricultural Science and Technology Database, 39

American Association of Law Libraries (AALL), 686–687
  awards, 377
  grants, 409–410

American Association of School Librarians (AASL), 690–691
  awards, 379
  grants, 408–409
  KidsConnect, 150
  public relations, 11

American Booksellers Association (ABA), 171–183
  awards, 175–176
  Book Buying Study, 181
  Booksellers Order Service (BOS), 183
  bookstore promotions, 181–183
  BookWeb, 173–174
  convention and trade exhibit, 173, 174–176
  education and professional development, 177–178
  membership, 173–174
  publications, 178
  research, 180–181

strategic plan, 173

American Booksellers Foundation for Free Expression (ABFFE), 176–177

American Geophysical Union, 245

American Heritage Rivers Initiative (AHRI), 106–107

American Library Association (ALA), 147–154, 687–709
  accredited graduate programs, title changes, 415–418
  Armed Forces Libraries Round Table awards, 379–380
  awards, 149–150, 153, 377–387
  Banned Books Week, 149
  Born to Read, 152
  conferences, 153–154, 266, 411
  Ethnic Material and Information Exchange Round Table (EMIERT) awards, 382
  Exhibits Round Table awards, 382–383
  Federal Librarians Round Table award, 383
  filtering software, statement on, 9
  Goal 2000, 147, 150
  grants, 407–408
  Intellectual Freedom, Office for (OIF), 149
  Intellectual Freedom Round Table award, 383
  Library History Round Table (LHRT) awards, 384
  Library Research Round Table (LRRT) awards, 384
  Literacy in Libraries Across America (LILAA), 151

Subject Index

Please note that many cross-references refer to entries listed in the Index of Organizations

A

ABACUS, 181

Academic books, prices and price indexes, 448–449, 452(table), 453(table)
British averages, 512–513(table)
German averages, 514(table), 518
North American averages, 500–501(table)
U.S. college books, averages, 502–503(table)
See also Association of American Publishers, Professional and Scholarly Publishing Division; Society for Scholarly Publishing

Academic libraries, *see* Academic Libraries Survey; College and research libraries

Academic Libraries Survey (ALS), 59–62, 405–406
collections, 60
expenditures, 61–62
services, 60
staff, 61

ACLU; Reno v., 278–279

Acquisitions
expenditures, 431–439
academic libraries, 434–435(table), 452(table)
government libraries, 438–439(table)
public libraries, 432–433(table), 441(table), 445–446
special libraries, 436–437(table)
prices and price indexes for major components, 452(table)
See also specific types of libraries, i.e., Public libraries

Adults, services for
cultural programming, 405
See also Literacy programs; Reference and User Services Association

African Americans
National Black Bookstore Week (NBBW), 182
students, scholarships for, 152
writers, 25, 149, 175–176

Agencies, library, *see* Library associations and agencies

Agricultural libraries, *see* International Association of Agricultural Information Specialists; National Agricultural Library

AIDS/HIV information services; NAC collection, 35

ALA v. *Pataki*, 161

Alabama
networks and cooperative library organizations, 655
school library media associations, 764

Alaska
networks and cooperative library organizations, 655
school library media associations, 764

Almanacs, bestselling, 627

America Reads Challenge, 165, 182, 315

American Booksellers Book of the Year (ABBY), 645

American Geophysical Union v. *Texaco*, 245

American Memory Fellows Program, 77–78

American Technology Preeminence Act (ATPA), 34

Angela's Ashes (McCourt), 175

Animal care, on CD-ROM, 106

Archives
acquisition expenditures
academic libraries, 434–435(table)
government libraries, 438–439(table)
public libraries, 432–433(table)
special libraries, 436–437(table)
digital, 203

B